# Oxford
# School
# Dictionary

Chief Editor: Andrew Delahunty

**OXFORD**
UNIVERSITY PRESS

# OXFORD
## UNIVERSITY PRESS

Great Clarendon Street, Oxford OX2 6DP

Oxford University Press is a department of the University of Oxford.
It furthers the University's objective of excellence in research,
scholarship, and education by publishing worldwide in

Oxford   New York

Auckland   Cape Town   Dar es Salaam   Hong Kong   Karachi
Kuala Lumpur   Madrid   Melbourne   Mexico City   Nairobi
New Delhi   Shanghai   Taipei   Toronto

With offices in

Argentina   Austria   Brazil   Chile   Czech Republic   France   Greece
Guatemala   Hungary   Italy   Japan   Poland   Portugal   Singapore
South Korea   Switzerland   Thailand   Turkey   Ukraine   Vietnam
Oxford is a registered trade mark of Oxford University Press
in the UK and in certain other countries

• First published as *Oxford Pocket School Dictionary* 1990 • Second edition 1996
• Third edition 2003 • Fourth edition with supplement 2005 • Fifth edition 2007
• First published as *Oxford School Dictionary* in pocket-sized paperback 2012
• This edition 2016

British Library Cataloguing in Publication Data

Data available

ISBN-13: 978-0-19-274710-5

10 9 8

Printed in Poland by Opolgraf SA

Paper used in the production of this book is a natural,
recyclable product made from wood grown in sustainable forests.
The manufacturing process conforms to the environmental
regulations of the country of origin.

**Oxford OWL**

**For school**
Discover eBooks, inspirational
resources, advice and support

**For home**
Helping your child's learning
with free eBooks, essential
tips and fun activities

**www.oxfordowl.co.uk**

# Contents

# Preface

The *Oxford School Dictionary* has been specially written for students aged 10 and above. It is particularly useful for students who are about to start secondary school and who need an up-to-date, student-friendly dictionary that they can use at home or at school. The dictionary is specially designed for students and includes a range of curriculum vocabulary, covering subjects such as Science, Information and Communication Technology, and Geography.

The *Oxford School Dictionary* can also be used very effectively in conjunction with the *Oxford School Thesaurus* which offers further support in creative writing and vocabulary building.

The *Oxford School Dictionary* gives all the information students need for exams in an accessible and easy-to-use format. Use of the dictionary will help students to develop their English language skills and equip them with the best reading, writing and speaking skills for years to come.

The publishers and editors are indebted to all the advisors, consultants and teachers who were involved in the planning of this dictionary. Special thanks go to Andrew Delahunty, Chief Editor.

# Introduction

➤ **How does a word get into a dictionary?**
The simple answer to this question is that people use it. If enough people use a word, it will eventually appear in print and online, and dictionary compilers (lexicographers) will spot it. Thousands of new words are invented every year but only a few become generally known and make their way into the permanent record of a dictionary. Thousands of slang or informal terms are coined and discarded every year but if everybody learns them, then the dictionary will record them.

➤ **What do you use a dictionary for?**
If your answer to this is 'To look up spellings' or even 'To check the meaning of a word', then you are missing out on a great deal that a dictionary has to offer.

Dictionaries tell you how to pronounce a word, what word class it is, what its plural is, where in the world it has come from, and what other words are associated with the word you are looking up.

In addition to these, the *Oxford School Dictionary* gives you even more language support to help you at home and at school. The **Vocabulary Toolkit** section offers guidance on such topics as prefixes and suffixes, confusable words and phrases, phrases from different languages, and idioms and proverbs. There are **spelling**, **punctuation**, **grammar** and **usage** panels throughout which provide useful tips, help and guidance that will make a difference to your vocabulary, your writing and your spelling.

# Panels in this dictionary

## Punctuation
You will find a panel at each of these words.

- apostrophe
- bracket
- colon
- comma
- dash
- exclamation mark
- full stop
- hyphen
- inverted commas
- question mark
- quotation marks
- semicolon

## Grammar
There is a panel giving grammar support at each of these words.

- a
- active and passive
- adjective
- adverb
- adverbial
- be
- clause
- command
- comparative
- conjunction
- contraction
- determiner
- direct speech
- do
- exclamation
- have
- noun
- number
- phrase
- plural
- possessive
- prefix
- preposition
- pronoun
- punctuation
- question
- quotation
- relative pronoun
- sentence
- shall
- statement
- suffix
- superlative
- synonym
- tense
- the
- verb
- which
- word class

## Spelling
You will find notes at tricky **words** to help you improve your spelling.

**symmetry** *NOUN*
the quality of being symmetrical or well-proportioned

> **SPELLING**
> The 'i' sound is spelt with a y in symmetry.
> Do not forget to double the m.

## Usage
Usage notes give extra information and context.

**inflammable** *ADJECTIVE*
able to be set on fire

> **USAGE**
> This word means the same as flammable.
> If you want to say that something is
> not able to be set on fire, use non-
> flammable.

# How to use this dictionary

**word origins are given to increase language knowledge**

**up-to-date examples help to make meaning clear**

**word forms are given in full**

**includes common phrases**

**headwords are in blue to find words easily**

**plumb** ADVERB (*informal*) exactly or precisely
• *It fell plumb in the middle.*

**plumber** NOUN plumbers
a person who fits and mends plumbing

**plumbing** NOUN
❶ the water pipes, water tanks and drainage pipes in a building ❷ the work of a plumber
WORD ORIGIN from Latin *plumbum* = lead (because water pipes used to be made of lead)

**plumb line** NOUN plumb lines
a cord with a weight on the end, used to find how deep something is or whether a wall etc. is vertical

**plume** NOUN plumes
❶ a large feather ❷ a thin column of something that rises in the air • *a plume of smoke*

**plumed** ADJECTIVE
decorated with plumes • *a plumed helmet*

**plummet** VERB plummets, plummeting, plummeted
❶ to drop downwards quickly • *The plane plummeted towards the ground.* ❷ to decrease rapidly in value • *Prices have plummeted.*

**plump** ADJECTIVE
having a full, rounded shape; slightly fat
• *plump cheeks*
➤ **plumpness** NOUN

**plump** VERB plumps, plumping, plumped
to plump up a cushion or pillow is to shake it to give it a rounded shape
➤ **plump for something** (*informal*) to choose something

**plunder** VERB plunders, plundering, plundered
to rob a person or place using force, especially during a war • *The invading army plundered many of the churches and monasteries.*
➤ **plunderer** NOUN

**plunder** NOUN
❶ plundering a person or place ❷ goods that have been plundered

**plunge** VERB plunges, plunging, plunged
❶ to jump or dive into water with force ❷ to push something forcefully into something
• *She plunged the knife into his chest.* ❸ to fall or go downwards suddenly • *The car plunged off the cliff.* ❹ to force someone or something into an unpleasant situation • *They plunged the world into war.* • *The room was suddenly plunged into darkness.*

**plunge** NOUN plunges
a sudden fall or dive
➤ **take the plunge** to start a bold course of action

**plunger** NOUN plungers
a rubber cup on a handle used for clearing blocked pipes

**plural** NOUN plurals
the form of a noun or verb used when it stands for more than one person or thing
• *The plural of 'child' is 'children'.* Compare with **singular**.

**plural** ADJECTIVE
in the plural; meaning more than one
• *'Mice' is a plural noun.*

**GRAMMAR**

Most words in English form their plurals by adding -s or –es (ants, branches). However, some types of words have more unusual plurals:

words which are the same in the singular and plural, e.g. *aircraft, deer, fish, sheep, series* and *species*.

words which have irregular plurals: *child, children; goose, geese; louse, lice; mouse, mice; ox, oxen; tooth, teeth.*

words of Greek and Latin origin which keep a Greek or Latin plural form:

*–a, –ae,* e.g. *antenna, antennae; formula, formulae*

*–ex, –ices,* e.g. *index, indices; vortex, vortices*

*–is, –es,* e.g. *axis, axes; basis, bases; thesis, theses*

*–ix, –ices,* e.g. *appendix, appendices*

*–on, –a,* e.g. *phenomenon, phenomena*

*–um, –a,* e.g. *medium, media*

*–us, –i,* e.g. *radius, radii; sarcophagus, sarcophagi*

Sometimes the use of a Latin or Greek plural is optional, e.g. *plectrums* or *plectra, radiuses* or *radii;* it can also depend on meaning, e.g. the form *appendixes* is used for parts of the body, but *appendices* for sections of a book.

Words from other languages which keep their original plurals, e.g. *gateau, gateaux.*

518

**grammar and punctuation panels give useful extra information**

the 'try also' tips guide you to other possible spellings if you cannot find the word you are looking for

scherzo        try also ce-, ci-, cy-, ps- or sc-        scoop

**scherzo** (say **skairts**-oh) NOUN scherzos
a lively piece of music WORD ORIGIN Italian, = joke

**schism** (say skizm or sizm) NOUN schisms
the splitting of a group into two opposing sections because they disagree about something important

**schizophrenia** (say skid-zo-free-nee-a) NOUN
a kind of mental illness in which people cannot relate their thoughts and feelings to reality
➤ schizophrenic ADJECTIVE & NOUN

**scholar** NOUN scholars
❶ a person who has studied a subject thoroughly ❷ a person who has been awarded a scholarship WORD ORIGIN from Latin scholaris = to do with a school

**scholarly** ADJECTIVE
showing knowledge and learning

**scholarship** NOUN scholarships
❶ a grant of money given to someone to help to pay for their education ❷ serious study of an academic subject and the knowledge you get

**scholastic** ADJECTIVE
to do with schools or education; academic

**school** NOUN schools
❶ a place where teaching is done, especially of pupils aged 5–18 ❷ the pupils in a school ❸ the time when teaching takes place in a school • School ends at 4.30 p.m. ❹ a group of people who have the same beliefs or style of work ❺ a large group of fish, whales or dolphins

**school** VERB schools, schooling, schooled
to teach or train a person or animal • She was schooling her horse for the competition.

**schoolchild** NOUN schoolchildren
a child who goes to school
➤ schoolboy NOUN
➤ schoolgirl NOUN

**schooling** NOUN
education at a school

**schoolteacher** NOUN schoolteachers
a person who teaches in a school
➤ schoolmaster NOUN
➤ schoolmistress NOUN

**schooner** (say skoon-er) NOUN schooners
❶ a sailing ship with two or more masts ❷ a tall glass for serving sherry

**science** NOUN sciences
❶ the study of the physical world by means of observation and experiment ❷ a branch of this, such as chemistry, physics or biology WORD ORIGIN from Latin scientia = knowledge

**science fiction** NOUN
stories about imaginary scientific discoveries or space travel and life on other planets, often set in the future

**science park** NOUN science parks
an area set up for industries using science or for organizations doing scientific research

**scientific** ADJECTIVE
❶ to do with science or scientists • scientific instruments ❷ studying things in an organized, logical way and testing ideas carefully • a scientific study of the way we use language
➤ scientifically ADVERB

**scientist** NOUN scientists
❶ an expert in science ❷ someone who uses scientific methods

**scimitar** (say sim-it-ar) NOUN scimitars
a curved oriental sword

**scintillating** ADJECTIVE
❶ sparkling ❷ lively and witty • The conversation was scintillating. WORD ORIGIN from Latin scintilla = spark

**scion** (say sy-on) NOUN scions
a descendant, especially of a noble family

**scissors** PLURAL NOUN
a cutting instrument used with one hand, with two blades joined so that they can close against each other

> SPELLING
> There is a tricky bit in scissors—it begins with sc.

**scoff** VERB scoffs, scoffing, scoffed
❶ to laugh or speak in a mocking way about something you think is silly • She scoffed at my superstitions. ❷ (informal) to eat something greedily or to eat it all up
➤ scoffer NOUN

**scold** VERB scolds, scolding, scolded
to speak angrily to someone because they have done wrong; to tell someone off
➤ scolding NOUN

**scone** (say skon or skohn) NOUN scones
a soft flat cake, usually eaten with butter

**scoop** NOUN scoops
❶ a kind of deep spoon for serving ice cream

a b c d e f g h i j k l m n o p q r s t u v w x y z

definitions are clear and accurate

word classes are given to build grammatical skills

pronunciations are given for difficult words

spelling and usage notes help to improve spelling and show how words are used in English

611

related words show how groups of words are connected with one another

# Aa

**a** *DETERMINER* (called the indefinite article and changing to an before most vowel sounds)
❶ one (but not any special one) • *Can you lend me a book?* ❷ each; per • *I go there twice a month.*

**GRAMMAR**

The word *a* (or *an*) is known as the **indefinite article.** You use it before a singular noun or noun phrase when the person or thing you are talking about has not yet been mentioned or you want to refer to them in a general way:

*I saw a cave and a dragon in my dream.*

*Jupiter is a gas planet.*

*A* is used before words which begin with a consonant (*a beetle, a text*), and *an* before those which begin with a vowel (*an ant, an email*). Abbreviations take either *a* or *an* depending on whether they begin with the *sound* of a consonant or a vowel: *a DVD,* but *an MP; an IQ test,* but *a UFO.*

See also the panels on **the** and on **determiners.**

**aback** *ADVERB*
➤ taken aback surprised and slightly shocked • *Rose was taken aback by this request.*

**abacus** (say **ab**-a-kus) *NOUN* abacuses
a frame with rows of beads that slide on wires, used for counting and adding

**abandon** *VERB* abandons, abandoning, abandoned
❶ to stop doing something when it becomes impossible • *The search for the missing climbers was abandoned after two days.*
❷ to leave someone or something without intending to return • *He abandoned his family and went off to Australia.*
➤ **abandonment** *NOUN*

**abandon** *NOUN*
a careless and uncontrolled manner • *She danced with wild abandon.*

**abandoned** *ADJECTIVE*
left and no longer wanted or used • *an abandoned car*

**abashed** *ADJECTIVE*
feeling guilty and embarrassed

**abate** *VERB* abates, abating, abated
to become less or die down • *The storm showed no sign of abating.*
➤ **abatement** *NOUN*

**abattoir** (say **ab**-at-wahr) *NOUN* abattoirs
(*British*) a place where animals are killed for food; a slaughterhouse

**abbess** *NOUN* abbesses
the head of a convent

**abbey** *NOUN* abbeys
❶ a monastery or convent ❷ a church that was once part of a monastery • *Westminster Abbey*

**abbot** *NOUN* abbots
the head of an abbey of monks

**abbreviate** *VERB* abbreviates, abbreviating, abbreviated
to shorten a word or phrase • *abbreviated text messages*

**abbreviation** *NOUN* abbreviations
a shortened form of a word or words, especially one using the initial letters, such as St. or USA • *She uses lots of abbreviations when she texts.*

**abdicate** *VERB* abdicates, abdicating, abdicated
a queen or king abdicates if they give up the throne
➤ **abdication** *NOUN*

**abdomen** (say **ab**-dom-en) *NOUN* abdomens
❶ the lower front part of a person's or animal's body, containing the stomach, intestines and other digestive organs ❷ the rear section of an insect's body
➤ **abdominal** (say ab-**dom**-in-al) *ADJECTIVE*

**abduct** *VERB* abducts, abducting, abducted
to take a person away by force and against their will; to kidnap someone
➤ **abduction** *NOUN*
➤ **abductor** *NOUN*

**abet** *VERB* abets, abetting, abetted
to help or encourage someone to commit a crime

**abeyance** (say ab-**ay**-ans) *NOUN*
➤ in abeyance not being used at the moment • *More serious punishments are being held in abeyance.*

**abhor** *VERB* abhors, abhorring, abhorred
(*formal*) to hate or dislike something very

a b c d e f g h i j k l m n o p q r s t u v w x y z

much **WORD ORIGIN** from Latin *abhorrere* = shrink away in horror

**abhorrence** *NOUN*
hatred or strong dislike • *She could not disguise her abhorrence of the man.*
➤ **abhorrent** *ADJECTIVE*

**abide** *VERB* abides, abiding, abided
❶ you can't abide something when you detest it or can't bear it • *I really can't abide garlic.* ❷ to abide by a promise or agreement is to keep it and do what you said you would • *He promised to abide by the rules.*

**abiding** *ADJECTIVE*
lasting or permanent • *The idea soon became an abiding passion.*

**ability** *NOUN* abilities
❶ ability is being able to do something • *Tiredness affects your ability to concentrate.* ❷ an ability is a special skill or talent • *students of mixed abilities*

**abject** (say ab-jekt) *ADJECTIVE*
❶ hopeless or pitiful • *They were living in abject poverty.* ❷ grovelling or humiliating • *an abject apology*

**ablaze** *ADJECTIVE*
❶ on fire and burning fiercely • *The whole building was soon ablaze.* ❷ full of bright light or colours • *The hall was ablaze with candlelight.*

**able** *ADJECTIVE*
❶ having the power or skill or opportunity to do something • *I was not able to move.* ❷ skilful or clever • *John is a very able musician.*
➤ **ably** *ADVERB*

**able-bodied** *ADJECTIVE*
fit and healthy; not disabled

**abnormal** *ADJECTIVE*
not normal; unusual • *abnormal weather conditions*
➤ **abnormally** *ADVERB*
➤ **abnormality** *NOUN*

**aboard** *ADVERB & PREPOSITION*
on or into a ship or aircraft or train

**abode** *NOUN* abodes (*formal*)
the place where someone lives • *Welcome to my humble abode.*

**abolish** *VERB* abolishes, abolishing, abolished
to put an end to a law or custom • *Slavery was abolished in Britain in 1807.*

**abolition** (say ab-ol-ish-on) *NOUN*
getting rid of a law or custom • *the abolition of slavery*

**abominable** *ADJECTIVE*
very bad or unpleasant • *an abominable crime*
➤ **abominably** *ADVERB*

**abomination** *NOUN* abominations
something that disgusts you

**aborigine** (say ab-er-ij-in-ee) *NOUN* aborigines
one of the original inhabitants of a country
➤ **aboriginal** *ADJECTIVE & NOUN*
➤ **Aborigine** a member of the people who were living in Australia before European settlers arrived
**WORD ORIGIN** from Latin *ab origine* = from the beginning

**abort** *VERB* aborts, aborting, aborted
to put an end to something before it has been completed • *They had to abort the space flight because of technical problems.*

**abortion** *NOUN* abortions
an operation to remove an unborn child from the womb before it has developed enough to survive

**abortive** *ADJECTIVE*
unsuccessful • *an abortive attempt*

**abound** *VERB* abounds, abounding, abounded
❶ things abound when there are a lot of them • *Fish abound in the river.* ❷ a place abounds in things when there are a lot of them there • *The river abounds in fish.*

**about** *PREPOSITION*
❶ near in amount or size or time; approximately • *She's about five feet tall.* • *Come about two o'clock.* ❷ on the subject of; in connection with • *I don't want to talk about it.* ❸ all round; in various parts of • *A dog was running about the yard.*

**about** *ADVERB*
❶ in various directions • *They were running about.* ❷ not far away • *There were wild animals about.*
➤ **be about to** to be going to do something • *We were just about to leave.*

**above** *PREPOSITION*
❶ higher than • *There was a window above the door.* ❷ more than • *The temperature was just above freezing.*

**above** *ADVERB*
at or to a higher place or point • *Look at the stars above.*

**above board** ADJECTIVE & ADVERB
honest; without deception
**WORD ORIGIN** from card-players cheating by
changing their cards under the table

**abrasion** NOUN abrasions
an area of skin that has been scraped

**abrasive** ADJECTIVE
❶ something abrasive rubs or scrapes things
• *an abrasive wheel* ❷ a person is abrasive
when they are harsh or hurtful in what they
say • *an abrasive manner*

**abreast** ADVERB
❶ side by side • *They walked three abreast.*
❷ to keep abreast of a situation is to have all
the most recent information about it

**abridged** ADJECTIVE
using fewer words than the original and
therefore shorter • *an abridged paperback
edition*

**abroad** ADVERB
(*British*) in or to another country

**abrupt** ADJECTIVE
❶ sudden and unexpected • *his abrupt
departure* ❷ rather rude and unfriendly
• *She has quite an abrupt manner.*
➤ **abruptly** ADVERB
➤ **abruptness** NOUN

**abscess** (say **ab**-sis) NOUN abscesses
an inflamed place where pus has formed in
the body

**abscond** VERB absconds, absconding,
absconded
to go away secretly, especially after doing
something wrong • *The cashier had
absconded with the money.*

**abseil** VERB abseils, abseiling, abseiled
(*British*) to lower yourself down a steep cliff
or rock by sliding down a rope

**absence** NOUN absences
not being in the place where you are
expected • *No one noticed his absence.*

**absent** (say **ab**-sent) ADJECTIVE
not in the place you should be; not present
• *absent from school*

**absent** (say ab-**sent**) VERB absents, absenting,
absented
➤ **absent yourself** to stay away from
somewhere you should be

**absentee** NOUN absentees
a person who is not present when they are
expected to be

**absent-minded** ADJECTIVE
having your mind on other things; forgetful
➤ **absent-mindedly** ADVERB

**absolute** ADJECTIVE
complete; not restricted • *absolute power*

**absolutely** ADVERB
❶ completely ❷ (*informal*) yes, I agree
**SPELLING**
Absolutely = absolute + ly. Don't forget
to keep the e after the t.

**absolute zero** NOUN
the lowest possible temperature, calculated
as -273.15°C

**absolution** NOUN
in Christianity, a priest's formal statement
that someone's sins are forgiven

**absolve** VERB absolves, absolving, absolved
❶ to clear a person of blame or guilt • *The
train driver was absolved of any blame for
the crash.* ❷ to release a person from a
promise or obligation

**absorb** VERB absorbs, absorbing, absorbed
❶ to soak up a liquid or gas ❷ to receive
something and reduce its effects • *The
buffers absorbed most of the shock.* ❸ to
take up a person's attention or time • *They
were completely absorbed in what they were
doing.*
➤ **absorption** NOUN

**absorbent** ADJECTIVE
able to soak up liquids easily • *absorbent
paper*

**abstain** VERB abstains, abstaining, abstained
❶ to keep yourself from doing something you
enjoy ❷ to choose not to use your vote

**abstinence** NOUN
going without something, especially from
alcohol

**abstract** (say **ab**-strakt) ADJECTIVE
❶ to do with ideas and not with physical
things • *Truth, hope and danger are all
abstract.* ❷ an abstract painting or sculpture
shows the artist's ideas or feelings rather than
showing a recognizable person or thing

**abstract** (say **ab**-strakt) NOUN abstracts
❶ a summary of a longer piece of writing
❷ an abstract painting or sculpture

**abstract** (say ab-**strakt**) VERB abstracts,
abstracting, abstracted (*formal*) to take
something out or remove it • *He abstracted
some cards from the pack.*

a b c d e f g h i j k l m n o p q r s t u v w x y z

**abstracted** ADJECTIVE
with your mind on other things; not paying attention

**abstraction** NOUN
thinking deeply about something and not paying attention • *He gazed with an air of abstraction through the window.*

**absurd** ADJECTIVE
ridiculous or foolish • *I've never heard anything so absurd.*
➤ **absurdly** ADVERB

**absurdity** NOUN absurdities
something that is ridiculous or foolish • *She laughed at the absurdity of the question.*

**abundance** NOUN
a large amount of something, often more than you need • *There was an abundance of food and drink.*

**abundant** ADJECTIVE
things are abundant when there are plenty of them • *Fish are abundant in the lake.*
➤ **abundantly** ADVERB

**abuse** (say ab-**yooz**) VERB abuses, abusing, abused
❶ to use something badly or wrongly; to misuse something ❷ to hurt someone or treat them cruelly ❸ to say unpleasant things about a person or thing

**abuse** (say ab-**yooss**) NOUN abuses
❶ a misuse of something • *the abuse of power* ❷ physical harm or cruelty done to someone ❸ words that offend or insult a person • *a torrent of abuse*

**abusive** ADJECTIVE
rude and insulting • *abusive remarks*

**abysmal** (say ab-**iz**-mal) ADJECTIVE
extremely bad • *The weather was abysmal.*

**abyss** (say ab-**iss**) NOUN abysses
a deep dark hole or pit that seems to go on for ever WORD ORIGIN from Greek *abyssos* = bottomless

**AC** ABBREVIATION
alternating current

**academic** ADJECTIVE
❶ to do with education or studying, especially at a school or college or university ❷ theoretical; having no practical use • *an academic point*
➤ **academically** ADVERB

**academic** NOUN academics
a university or college teacher

**academy** NOUN academies
❶ a school or college, especially one for specialized training ❷ a society of scholars or artists • *The French Academy of Sciences* WORD ORIGIN from *Akademeia*, the name of the garden where the Greek philosopher Plato taught his pupils

**accede** (say ak-**seed**) VERB accedes, acceding, acceded
❶ to accede to a request or suggestion is to agree to it ❷ to accede to the throne is to become queen or king

**accelerate** VERB accelerates, accelerating, accelerated
to become quicker; to increase speed
• *The plane was accelerating for take-off.*

**acceleration** NOUN accelerations
❶ the rate at which the speed of something increases ❷ the rate of change of velocity

**accelerator** NOUN accelerators
the pedal that a driver presses to make a motor vehicle go faster

**accent** (say **ak**-sent) NOUN accents
❶ the way a person pronounces the words of a language • *She has a French accent.* ❷ the emphasis or stress used in pronouncing a word • *In 'cuckoo', the accent is on the first syllable.* ❸ a mark placed over a letter to show how it is pronounced, e.g. in *résumé*

**accented** ADJECTIVE
spoken with a foreign accent • *He spoke in heavily accented English.*

**accentuate** (say ak-**sent**-yoo-ayt) VERB
accentuates, accentuating, accentuated
to make something more obvious • *His pale complexion was accentuated by his black moustache.*

**accept** VERB accepts, accepting, accepted
❶ to take a thing that is offered or presented to you ❷ to say yes to an invitation or offer

SPELLING
Take care not to confuse with **except**.

**acceptable** ADJECTIVE
good enough to accept; satisfactory • *We think it is an acceptable offer.*

**acceptance** NOUN
❶ accepting something, such as an invitation or offer ❷ agreeing with something and approving of it

**access** (say **ak**-sess) NOUN
❶ a way to enter or reach something
❷ the right to use or look at something

**access** VERB accesses, accessing, accessed
to read and use the information that has been stored in a computer

**accessible** ADJECTIVE
able to be reached or understood easily
• The style is accessible and easy to read.
➤ accessibility NOUN

**accession** NOUN accessions
reaching a rank or position; becoming king or queen • The monarchy was restored with the accession of Charles II.

**accessory** (say ak-**sess**-er-ee) NOUN
accessories
❶ an extra thing that goes with something
❷ a person who helps someone else to commit a crime

**accident** NOUN accidents
something unexpected that happens, especially when something is broken or someone is hurt or killed
➤ by accident by chance; without meaning to

SPELLING

Accidentally – accident + ally. Don't forget the a and the double l before the y.

**accidental** ADJECTIVE
happening or done by accident • accidental damage

**accidentally** ADVERB
to do something accidentally is to do it by mistake or without meaning to • Hal had accidentally pressed the wrong button.

**acclaim** VERB acclaims, acclaiming, acclaimed
to praise someone or something enthusiastically • Her plays are highly acclaimed.

**acclaim** NOUN
enthusiastic praise • The book was published to huge acclaim.

**acclamation** NOUN
loud and enthusiastic approval

**acclimatize** (also **acclimatise**) VERB
acclimatizes, acclimatizing, acclimatized
to become used to a new climate or new surroundings

**accolade** (say ak-ol-**ayd**) NOUN accolades
praise or a prize given to someone for something they have done

WORD ORIGIN from Latin collum = neck (because in the past, when a man was knighted, the king put his arms round the man's shoulders)

**accommodate** VERB accommodates, accommodating, accommodated
❶ to provide someone with a place to live, work or sleep overnight ❷ to help someone by providing what they need • We were able to accommodate everyone with skis.

**accommodating** ADJECTIVE
willing to help or cooperate • Thank you for being so accommodating.

**accommodation** NOUN
somewhere to live, work or sleep overnight

SPELLING

There is a double c and double m in accommodation.

**accompanist** NOUN accompanists
a pianist or other musician who plays to support a singer or another musician

**accompany** VERB accompanies, accompanying, accompanied
❶ to go somewhere with somebody
❷ to happen or appear with something else
• The cheers were accompanied by a few boos. ❸ to play music, especially on a piano, that supports a singer or another musician
➤ accompaniment NOUN

**accomplice** (say a-**kum**-pliss) NOUN
accomplices
a person who helps another in a crime or bad act

**accomplish** VERB accomplishes, accomplishing, accomplished
to do something successfully • He hoped to accomplish the journey in six days.

**accomplished** ADJECTIVE
skilled or talented • She was an accomplished painter.

**accomplishment** NOUN accomplishments
something you have achieved or are good at

**accord** NOUN
agreement or consent
➤ of your own accord without being asked or told to do it
➤ with one accord (formal) doing the same thing at the same time • With one accord they sprang to their feet.

**accord** VERB accords, according, accorded
❶ to be consistent with something • This theory does not accord with the facts.

**A**

❷ (formal) to give or grant something • He was not accorded the respect he deserved.

**accordance** NOUN
➤ **in accordance with** in agreement with • This is done in accordance with the rules.

**accordingly** ADVERB
❶ in the way that is suitable • I've given you your instructions and I expect you to act accordingly. ❷ because of what has just been said; therefore • Accordingly, the name was changed.

**according to** PREPOSITION
❶ used to show where a piece of information comes from • According to Josie, he's really clever. ❷ used to show how one thing relates to another • Apples are priced according to their size.

**accordion** NOUN accordions
a portable musical instrument like a large concertina with a set of piano-type keys at one end, played by squeezing it in and out and pressing the keys

**accost** VERB accosts, accosting, accosted
to go up to a person and speak to them, especially in an annoying way

**account** NOUN accounts
❶ a description or story about something that has happened ❷ a statement of the money someone owes or has received; a bill ❸ an arrangement to keep money in a bank or building society ❹ an arrangement to use a computing or social media service • an email account
➤ **on account of** because of
➤ **on no account** under no circumstances; certainly not
➤ **take something into account** to consider or include it when making a decision or calculation

**account** VERB accounts, accounting, accounted
➤ **account for** to explain why something happens • I can't account for this defeat.

**accountable** ADJECTIVE
responsible for something and having to explain why you have done it • The company should be held accountable for the pollution it has caused.
➤ **accountability** NOUN

**accountant** NOUN accountants
a person whose job is to record and organize the money a person or organization spends and receives
➤ **accountancy** NOUN

**accounting** NOUN
the business of keeping financial accounts

**accredited** ADJECTIVE
officially recognized • an accredited health inspector

**accumulate** VERB accumulates, accumulating, accumulated
❶ to collect things or pile them up ❷ to increase in quantity • Snow accumulates throughout the long winters.
➤ **accumulation** NOUN

**accumulator** NOUN accumulators
a large battery that can be recharged

**accuracy** NOUN
being exactly right or correct • I was impressed with the accuracy of his guesses.

**accurate** ADJECTIVE
correct or exact • an accurate map

**accurately** ADVERB
correctly or exactly • Solar eclipses can be accurately predicted.

**accusation** NOUN accusations
a statement accusing a person of a crime or doing something wrong

**accuse** VERB accuses, accusing, accused
to say that a person has committed a crime or done something wrong • He accused her of lying about it.
➤ **accuser** NOUN

**accustom** VERB accustoms, accustoming, accustomed
to be accustomed to something is to be used to it • She was accustomed to getting her own way.

**ace** NOUN aces
❶ a playing card with one spot ❷ (in tennis) a serve that is too good for the other player to reach ❸ a very skilful person • a flying ace

**acetylene** (say a-**set**-il-een) NOUN
a gas that burns with a bright flame, used in cutting and welding metal

**ache** NOUN aches
a dull continuous pain

**ache** VERB aches, aching, ached
to have an ache • He was tired and his feet ached.

**achieve** VERB achieves, achieving, achieved
to succeed in doing or producing something • Modern go-karts can achieve speeds of more than 150 km per hour.
➤ **achievable** ADJECTIVE

**achievement** NOUN achievements
something good or worthwhile that you
have succeeded in doing • *These paintings
are among the greatest achievements in the
history of art.*

SPELLING

There is an ie in achievement.

**acid** NOUN acids
a chemical substance that contains hydrogen
and neutralizes alkalis. The hydrogen can be
replaced by a metal to form a salt.
➤ **acidity** NOUN

**acid** ADJECTIVE
❶ sharp-tasting; sour ❷ looking or sounding
bitter • *an acid reply*
➤ **acidly** ADVERB

**acidic** ADJECTIVE
❶ very sour ❷ containing acid

**acid rain** NOUN
rain made acid by mixing with waste gases
from factories etc.

**acknowledge** VERB acknowledges,
acknowledging, acknowledged
❶ to admit that something is true ❷ to let
someone know that you have received or
noticed something • *They wrote back to
acknowledge my application.* ❸ to express
thanks or appreciation for something • *He
raised his hand to acknowledge the applause.*
➤ **acknowledgement** NOUN

**acme** (say **ak**-mee) NOUN
the highest degree of something • *the acme
of perfection*

**acne** (say **ak**-nee) NOUN
inflamed red pimples on the face and neck

**acorn** NOUN acorns
the seed of the oak tree

**acoustic** (say a-**koo**-stik) ADJECTIVE
❶ to do with sound or hearing ❷ an acoustic
guitar or other musical instrument does not
use an electric amplifier

**acoustics** (say a-**koo**-stiks) PLURAL NOUN
❶ the qualities of a hall or room that make
it good or bad for carrying sound ❷ the
properties of sound

**acquaint** VERB acquaints, acquainting,
acquainted
to tell somebody about something • *Please
acquaint me with the facts of the case.*
➤ **be acquainted with someone** to know
someone slightly

**acquaintance** NOUN acquaintances
❶ a person you know slightly ❷ getting to
know someone • *I am delighted to make your
acquaintance.*

**acquiesce** (say ak-wee-**ess**) VERB acquiesces,
acquiescing, acquiesced
to agree to something, even though you
might not like it completely
➤ **acquiescence** NOUN

**acquire** VERB acquires, acquiring, acquired
to get or be given something • *She has
acquired a good knowledge of astronomy.*

**acquisition** NOUN acquisitions
❶ something you have got or been
given recently • *My latest acquisition is
a surfboard.* ❷ the process of acquiring
something • *a child's acquisition of language*

**acquit** VERB acquits, acquitting, acquitted
to decide that somebody is not guilty of a
crime • *The jury acquitted her.*
➤ **acquittal** NOUN
➤ **acquit yourself well** to perform or do
something well

**acre** (say **ay**-ker) NOUN acres
an area of land measuring 4,840 square yards
or 0.405 hectares
➤ **acreage** NOUN

**acrid** ADJECTIVE
having a strong bitter smell or taste • *acrid
smoke*

**acrobat** NOUN acrobats
a person who performs spectacular gymnastic
feats for entertainment
➤ **acrobatic** ADJECTIVE
➤ **acrobatics** PLURAL NOUN
WORD ORIGIN from Greek *akrobatos* = walking
on tiptoe

**acronym** (say **ak**-ron-im) NOUN acronyms
a word or name that is formed from the initial
letters of other words and pronounced as a
word in its own right • *Nato is an acronym of
North Atlantic Treaty Organization.*

**across** PREPOSITION & ADVERB
❶ from one side to the other • *Swim across
the river.* • *Are you across yet?* ❷ on the
opposite side • *the house across the street*

**acrostic** NOUN acrostics
a word puzzle or poem in which the first or
last letters of each line form a word or words

**acrylic** (say a-**kril**-ik) NOUN
a kind of fibre, plastic or resin made from an
organic acid

a b c d e f g h i j k l m n o p q r s t u v w x y z

7

**acrylics** PLURAL NOUN
a type of paint used by artists

**act** NOUN acts
❶ something someone does ❷ a pretence
• *She is only putting on an act.* ❸ one of the main divisions of a play or opera ❹ each of a series of short performances in a programme of entertainment • *a juggling act* ❺ a law passed by a parliament

**act** VERB acts, acting, acted
❶ to do something; to behave in a certain way • *Try to act normally.* ❷ to perform a part in a play or film etc. ❸ to function or have an effect • *He stuck out his feet to act as brakes.*

**action** NOUN actions
❶ doing something • *Now is the time for action.* ❷ something you do • *Can you explain your actions that night?* ❸ a battle; fighting • *He was killed in action.* ❹ a lawsuit
➤ **out of action** not working or functioning
➤ **take action** to decide to do something

**action replay** NOUN action replays
(*British*) playing back a piece of sports action on television, especially in slow motion

**activate** VERB activates, activating, activated
to activate a machine or process is to start it working • *The alarm is activated by movement.*
➤ **activation** NOUN

**active** ADJECTIVE
❶ taking part in many activities; energetic ❷ functioning or working; in operation • *an active volcano* ❸ (*in grammar*) describing the form of a verb when the subject of the verb is performing the action. In 'The shop *sells* DVDs' the verb is active; in 'DVDs *are sold* by the shop' the verb is passive.
➤ **actively** ADVERB

GRAMMAR

Verbs can be either **active** or **passive**; these two choices are sometimes called **active voice** and **passive voice**.

A verb is active when the subject of the verb performs the action: *The sun rises in the East*; *My father wrote these words.* In these sentences, the verbs (*rises* and *wrote*) are active because their subjects (*the sun* and *my father*) are performing the actions. But when the verb takes an object (*these words* in the second sentence), you can turn the sentence round and say *These words were written*

*by my father.* Now, the verb (*were written*) is passive, because the subject of the sentence is *these words*, and the subject and object are the other way round. You use the passive voice when you want the object to be the main topic of the sentence (i.e. in the previous example, when you want to focus on *the words*, and not *your father*).

If a verb does not take an object (like *rises* in the first example), it can only be active; you cannot turn *The sun rises in the East* into a passive sentence because there is no object to make into the subject.

In passive sentences, the performer of the action often comes after the word *by*: *The mystery was solved by our neighbour*; *The penalty will be taken by the Welsh captain.* But sometimes the performer is unknown, or is not identified: *All the tickets have been sold*; *That file has been deleted.*

**activist** NOUN activists
a person who takes action to try to bring about change, especially in politics

**activity** NOUN activities
❶ an activity is an action or occupation • *outdoor activities* ❷ activity is doing things or being busy • *The streets were full of activity.*

**actor** NOUN actors
a person who acts a part in a play or film etc.

**actress** NOUN actresses
a woman who acts a part in a play or film etc.

**actual** ADJECTIVE
really happening or existing

**actually** ADVERB
really; in fact • *Actually, I think you are wrong.*

**acumen** (say **ak**-yoo-men) NOUN
the ability to make good judgements and take quick decisions

**acupuncture** (say **ak**-yoo-punk-cher) NOUN
pricking parts of the body with needles to relieve pain or cure disease
➤ **acupuncturist** NOUN

**acute** ADJECTIVE
❶ sharp or strong • *acute pain* ❷ having a sharp mind
➤ **acuteness** NOUN

**acute accent** NOUN acute accents
a mark over a vowel, as over é in *résumé*

**acute angle** NOUN acute angles
an angle of less than 90°

**acutely** ADVERB
very or very strongly • *He was acutely embarrassed.*

**AD** ABBREVIATION
Anno Domini (Latin = in the year of Our Lord), used in dates counted from the birth of Jesus Christ

**adamant** (say **ad-am-ant**) ADJECTIVE
determined not to change your mind

**Adam's apple** NOUN Adam's apples
the lump at the front of a man's neck
**WORD ORIGIN** from the story that when Adam (the first man, according to the Bible) ate an apple, which God had forbidden him to do, a piece of it stuck in his throat

**adapt** VERB adapts, adapting, adapted
❶ to change something so that it is suitable for a new purpose ❷ to become used to a new situation • *She gradually adapted to her new life.*

**adaptable** ADJECTIVE
able to adapt to or become suitable for different situations • *The red fox is one of the most adaptable animals.*

**adaptation** NOUN adaptations
❶ a play or film that is based on a novel etc. ❷ changing to suit a new situation • *New species come about because of adaptation.*

**adaptor** NOUN adaptors
a device that connects pieces of electrical or other equipment

**add** VERB adds, adding, added
❶ to put one thing with another ❷ to make another remark • *'And get back soon,' he added.*
➤ **add up** ❶ to make or work out a total ❷ (*informal*) to make sense; to seem reasonable • *The things they said just don't add up.*

**addenda** PLURAL NOUN
things added at the end of a book

**adder** NOUN adders
a small poisonous snake **WORD ORIGIN** from Old English; originally called *a nadder*, which later became *an adder*

**addict** NOUN addicts
a person who does or uses something that

they cannot give up
➤ **addiction** NOUN

**addicted** ADJECTIVE
not able to give up a habit or drug • *He is addicted to computer games.*

**addictive** ADJECTIVE
causing a habit that people cannot give up
• *an addictive drug*

**addition** NOUN additions
❶ the process of adding ❷ something added
• *You are a welcome addition to our team.*
➤ **in addition** also; as an extra thing

**additional** ADJECTIVE
extra; as an extra thing • *There is a small additional charge for using of the swimming pool.*
➤ **additionally** ADVERB

**additive** NOUN additives
a substance added to another in small amounts for a special purpose, e.g. as a flavouring

**addled** ADJECTIVE
muddled or confused • *His brain was addled with all the questions.*

**address** NOUN addresses
❶ the details of the place where someone lives or of where letters or parcels should be delivered to a person or firm ❷ (*in computing*) a string of characters which shows a destination for email messages or the location of a website • *What's your email address?* ❸ a speech to an audience

**address** VERB addresses, addressing, addressed
❶ to write an address on a letter or parcel ❷ to make a remark or speech to somebody
• *He stood up to address the crowd.*

**SPELLING**

There is a double d and double s in **address**.

**adenoids** PLURAL NOUN
thick spongy flesh at the back of the nose and throat, which can make breathing difficult

**adept** (say a-**dept**) ADJECTIVE
very good or skilful at something • *He was adept at sign language.*

**adequate** ADJECTIVE
enough or good enough
➤ **adequately** ADVERB
➤ **adequacy** NOUN

**adhere** VERB adheres, adhering, adhered
❶ to stick to something ❷ to adhere to a belief or rule is to keep to it

**adherence** (say ad-**heer**-ens) NOUN
keeping to a particular belief or rule

**adherent** (say ad-**heer**-ent) NOUN adherents
a person who supports a certain group or theory etc.

**adhesive** ADJECTIVE
sticky; causing things to stick together

**adhesive** NOUN adhesives
a substance used to stick things together; glue

**ad hoc** ADJECTIVE & ADVERB
done or arranged only when necessary and not planned in advance • We had to make a number of ad hoc decisions.

**Adi Granth** (say ah-di-**grunt**) NOUN
the holy book of the Sikhs

**ad infinitum** (say in-fin-y-tum) ADVERB
without limit; for ever WORD ORIGIN Latin, = to infinity

**adjacent** ADJECTIVE
near or next to • I waited in an adjacent room.

SPELLING
There is a d before the j, and the 's' sound is spelt with a c in adjacent.

**adjective** NOUN adjectives
a word that describes a noun or adds to its meaning, e.g. big, honest, strange

GRAMMAR
Adjectives are words that describe a person, place or thing, e.g. tall, pale, delicious, jagged, unique, untrue. They can come before a noun (e.g. a tall giraffe, a jagged cliff), or they can come after a verb like be, become or grow (e.g. The soup was delicious; My companion became pale; The weather grew cold). Some adjectives can only be used in one position: e.g. afraid can only be used after a verb, and utter can only be used before a noun. You can say The crew were afraid but not an afraid crew; and you can say It was an utter disaster but not The disaster was utter.

Non-gradable adjectives classify people and things, e.g. Australian (an Australian actor) or square (a square envelope). These are 'all-or-nothing' adjectives

because actors are either Australian or not Australian, and things are either square or not.

Gradable adjectives describe a quality that people or things may have, e.g. tall (a tall teenager) or smelly (a smelly cheese). These adjectives are called gradable because the amount to which people or things have a particular quality may vary; e.g. some teenagers are taller than others, and some cheeses are smellier than others.

See also the panels on comparative forms and superlative forms.

**adjoin** VERB adjoins, adjoining, adjoined
to be next or nearest to something • a little room adjoining the stage

**adjourn** (say a-**jern**) VERB adjourns, adjourning, adjourned
❶ to break off a meeting until a later time
❷ to break off and go somewhere else • They adjourned to the library.
➤ adjournment NOUN

**adjunct** (say **aj**-unkt) NOUN adjuncts
something added that is useful but not essential

**adjust** VERB adjusts, adjusting, adjusted
❶ to change something slightly, especially because it is not in the right position • He adjusted his tie in the mirror. ❷ to adjust to something new is to get used to it • It took a moment for her eyes to adjust to the dark.
➤ adjustable ADJECTIVE

**adjustment** NOUN adjustments
a small change that you make to something

**ad lib** ADVERB
done or spoken without any rehearsal or preparation WORD ORIGIN from Latin ad libitum = according to pleasure

**ad-lib** VERB ad-libs, ad-libbing, ad-libbed
to say or do something without any rehearsal or preparation

**administer** VERB administers, administering, administered
❶ to give or provide something • The doctor administered the antidote. ❷ to make sure that something is carried out properly • He was known for administering justice fairly. ❸ to control or manage the affairs of a business, organization or country

**administration** NOUN administrations
❶ the work of running a business or

governing a country ❷ the group of people who run an organization; the government of a country ❸ administering something • *the administration of justice*

**administrative** *ADJECTIVE*
to do with running a business or country

**administrator** *NOUN* administrator
a person who helps to run a business or organization

**admirable** *ADJECTIVE*
worth admiring; excellent
➤ **admirably** *ADVERB*

**admiral** *NOUN* admirals
a naval officer of high rank
**WORD ORIGIN** from Arabic *amir* = commander

**admiration** *NOUN*
a feeling of thinking that someone or something is very good • *I am full of admiration for what she's done.*

**admire** *VERB* admires, admiring, admired
❶ to think that someone or something is very good ❷ to look at something and enjoy it • *He paused to admire the view.*

**admirer** *NOUN* admirers
a person who likes someone or something very much • *My sister has many admirers.*

**admissible** *ADJECTIVE*
able to be allowed or accepted as being valid
• *admissible evidence*

**admission** *NOUN* admissions
❶ permission to go in • *Admission to the show is by ticket only.* ❷ the charge for being allowed to go in ❸ a statement admitting something; a confession • *He is guilty by his own admission.*

**admit** *VERB* admits, admitting, admitted
❶ to allow someone or something to come in ❷ to say reluctantly that something is true; to confess something • *We admit that the task is difficult.* • *He admitted his crime.*

**admittance** *NOUN*
permission to go in, especially to a private place

**admittedly** *ADVERB*
as an agreed fact; without denying it
• *Admittedly the place is a bit expensive, but the food's great.*

**admonish** *VERB* admonishes, admonishing, admonished
to tell someone that you do not approve of

what they have done or to warn them
➤ **admonition** *NOUN*

**ado** *NOUN*
➤ **without more** or **further ado** without wasting any more time

**adolescence** (say ad-ol-**ess**-ens) *NOUN*
the time between being a child and being an adult

**adolescent** *NOUN* adolescents
a young person at the age between being a child and being an adult

**adolescent** *ADJECTIVE*
at the age between being a child and being an adult

**adopt** *VERB* adopts, adopting, adopted
❶ to take a child into your family as your own child ❷ to accept something; to take something and use it • *They adopted new methods of working.*
➤ **adoption** *NOUN*

**adorable** *ADJECTIVE*
lovely; sweet and attractive • *adorable kittens*

**adore** *VERB* adores, adoring, adored
to love a person or thing very much
➤ **adoration** *NOUN*

**adorn** *VERB* adorns, adorning, adorned
to decorate something or make it pretty
• *Photos adorned the mantelpiece.*
➤ **adornment** *NOUN*

**adrenalin** (say a-**dren**-al-in) *NOUN*
a hormone produced when you are afraid or excited. It stimulates the nervous system, making your heart beat faster and increasing your energy and your ability to move quickly.

**adrift** *ADJECTIVE & ADVERB*
a boat is adrift when it is drifting and out of control • *He was set adrift in a small boat.*

**adroit** (say a-**droit**) *ADJECTIVE*
clever and skilful **WORD ORIGIN** from French
*à droit* = according to right

**adulation** *NOUN*
a lot of admiration or flattery

**adult** (say **ad**-ult) *NOUN* adults
a fully grown person or animal

**adultery** *NOUN*
a sexual relationship between a married person and someone who is not their husband or wife
➤ **adulterous** *ADJECTIVE*

**advance** NOUN advances
❶ a forward movement ❷ a development or improvement • *the latest advances in medicine* ❸ a loan of money or a payment made before it is due
➤ **in advance** beforehand; ahead

**advance** ADJECTIVE
given or arranged beforehand • *advance warning*

**advance** VERB advances, advancing, advanced
❶ to move forward • *The army advanced towards the city.* ❷ to make progress • *Technology has advanced at great pace over the decades.*
➤ **advancement** NOUN

**advanced** ADJECTIVE
at a high level; highly developed • *an advanced maths course*

**advantage** NOUN advantages
❶ something useful or helpful ❷ (in tennis) the next point won after deuce
➤ **take advantage of someone** to treat someone unfairly when they are not likely to complain
➤ **take advantage of something** to make good use of something or benefit from it
➤ **to advantage** making a good effect • *The painting can be seen to its best advantage here.*
➤ **to your advantage** that helps or benefits you

**advantageous** (say ad-van-**tay**-jus) ADJECTIVE
giving an advantage; beneficial

**Advent** NOUN
the period just before Christmas, when Christians celebrate the coming of Christ

**advent** NOUN
the arrival of a new person or thing • *the advent of computers*

**adventure** NOUN adventures
❶ an exciting or dangerous experience ❷ doing exciting and daring things • *She had a love of adventure.*
➤ **adventurer** NOUN

**adventurous** ADJECTIVE
liking to do exciting and daring things

**adverb** NOUN adverbs
a word that adds to the meaning of a verb or adjective or another adverb and tells how, when or where something happens, e.g. *gently, soon* and *upstairs*
➤ **adverbial** ADJECTIVE

GRAMMAR

Adverbs answer questions such as *when?, where?, why?, how?,* and *how much?* Some adverbs go with adjectives: for example, *The map is <u>very</u> old* tells you how old the map is, and *a <u>fairly</u> expensive car* describes a car that is quite (but not very) expensive. Other adverbs go with verbs: for example, *The dog ate <u>ravenously</u>* tells you how the dog was eating, *It rains here <u>frequently</u>* tells you how often it rains, and *Hammering was heard <u>downstairs</u>* tells you where hammering was heard. Adverbs like these are often formed by adding *-ly* to an adjective, e.g. *ravenously, frequently.* Notice that adverbs can also go with other adverbs: *Sam smiled <u>rather</u> <u>sheepishly</u>.*

If an adverb refers to a whole sentence, it usually comes at the beginning: *<u>Honestly</u>, I didn't know where to look; <u>Clearly</u>, we had a long wait ahead.*

See also the panels on **comparative forms** and **superlative forms**.

**adverbial** NOUN adverbials
a group of words that functions as an adverb. Examples of adverbials are *last night* in the sentence *We saw him last night* and *more or less* in the sentence *She had more or less finished.*

GRAMMAR

A group of words that functions as an adverb is called an **adverbial**: for example, in the sentence *We email each other <u>whenever we can</u>,* the underlined phrase answers the question *when?* and is an adverbial (equivalent to *often* or *regularly*).

**adversary** (say **ad**-ver-ser-ee) NOUN adversaries
an opponent or enemy

**adverse** (say **ad**-vers) ADJECTIVE
bad or harmful • *adverse weather conditions*
➤ **adversely** ADVERB

**adversity** NOUN adversities
trouble or misfortune

**advert** NOUN adverts
(*British*) (*informal*) an advertisement

**advertise** VERB advertises, advertising, advertised
❶ to give out information about the good features of a product or service in order

to get people to buy it or use it ❷ to make something publicly known • *The meeting which was advertised for the evening of November 7th.* ❸ to give information about someone you need for a job • *A local firm was advertising for a secretary.*
➤ **advertiser** *NOUN*

**advertisement** *NOUN* advertisements
a public notice or announcement, especially one advertising goods or services in newspapers, on posters or in broadcasts

**advice** *NOUN*
❶ telling someone what you think they should do ❷ a piece of information • *We received advice that the goods had been sent.*

**SPELLING**

Advice is a noun, e.g. • *a word of advice,* and advise is a verb, e.g. • *I advise you to forget the whole thing.*

**advisable** *ADJECTIVE*
that is the wise or sensible thing to do • *It may be advisable to drink bottled water when you are abroad.*
➤ **advisability** *NOUN*

**advise** *VERB* advises, advising, advised
❶ to tell someone what you think they should do ❷ to inform someone about something
➤ **adviser** *NOUN*
➤ **advisory** *ADJECTIVE*

**advocate** (say **ad**-vok-ayt) *VERB* advocates, advocating, advocated
to speak in favour of something; to recommend something • *We advocate changing the law.*

**advocate** (say **ad**-vok-at) *NOUN* advocates
❶ a person who recommends or publicly supports something • *She was a strong advocate of women's rights.* ❷ a lawyer presenting someone's case in a law court

**aerial** *NOUN* aerials
a wire or rod for receiving or transmitting radio or television signals

**aerial** *ADJECTIVE*
from or in the air or from an aircraft • *an aerial photograph*

**aerobatics** *PLURAL NOUN*
a spectacular display by flying aircraft
➤ **aerobatic** *ADJECTIVE*

**aerobics** *PLURAL NOUN*
exercises to improve your breathing and strengthen the heart and lungs
➤ **aerobic** *ADJECTIVE*

**aerodrome** *NOUN* aerodromes
(*British*) an old word for an airfield or small airport

**aerodynamic** *ADJECTIVE*
designed to move through the air quickly and easily

**aeronautics** *NOUN*
the study of aircraft and flying
➤ **aeronautic** *ADJECTIVE*
➤ **aeronautical** *ADJECTIVE*

**aeroplane** *NOUN* aeroplanes
(*British*) a flying vehicle with wings and at least one engine

**aerosol** *NOUN* aerosols
a container that holds a liquid under pressure and can let it out in a fine spray

**aerospace** *NOUN*
the industry of building aircraft, vehicles and equipment to be sent into space

**aesthetic** (say iss-**thet**-ik) *ADJECTIVE*
to do with beauty or art

**afar** *ADVERB*
far away • *The din was heard from afar.*

**affable** *ADJECTIVE*
polite and friendly
➤ **affably** *ADVERB*
➤ **affability** *NOUN*

**affair** *NOUN* affairs
❶ an event or matter • *Dinner time was a gloomy affair.* ❷ a brief romantic relationship between two people who are not married to each other

**affairs** *PLURAL NOUN*
the business and activities that are part of private or public life • *Keep out of my affairs.*
• *current affairs*

**affect** *VERB* affects, affecting, affected
❶ to have an effect on someone or something; to influence them • *What we eat can affect our health.* ❷ to pretend to have or feel something • *She affected ignorance.*

**SPELLING**

Affect is a verb and is different from effect, which is a noun, e.g. • *the effects of climate change.*

**affectation** *NOUN* affectations
unnatural behaviour that is intended to impress other people

**affected** *ADJECTIVE*
unnatural and meant to impress other people

• *She was talking in a loud and affected voice.*

**affection** NOUN affections
a strong liking for a person

**affectionate** ADJECTIVE
showing affection; loving
➤ **affectionately** ADVERB

**affidavit** (say af-id-**ay**-vit) NOUN affidavits
a statement that someone has written down and sworn to be true, for use as legal evidence

**affiliated** ADJECTIVE
officially connected with a larger organization

**affinity** NOUN affinities
a close similarity, relationship or understanding between two things or people
• *Italian has an affinity with Spanish.*

**affirm** VERB affirms, affirming, affirmed
to state something definitely or firmly
➤ **affirmation** NOUN

**affirmative** ADJECTIVE
that says 'yes' • *an affirmative reply*
Compare with **negative**.

**affix** (say a-**fiks**) VERB affixes, affixing, affixed
to affix something is to stick it on to something else • *A wax seal was affixed to the bottom of the document.*

**affix** (say **aff**-iks) NOUN affixes
a prefix or suffix

**afflict** VERB afflicts, afflicting, afflicted
to be afflicted with something unpleasant, such as a disease or problem, is to suffer from it • *He is afflicted with shyness.*
➤ **affliction** NOUN

**affluent** (say **af**-loo-ent) ADJECTIVE
having a lot of money; wealthy
➤ **affluence** NOUN

**afford** VERB affords, affording, afforded
❶ to have enough money to pay for something ❷ to be able to do something without suffering bad consequences • *We can't afford to make any more mistakes.* ❸ to have enough time to do something

**afforestation** NOUN
the planting of trees to form a forest

**affray** NOUN affrays
(*formal*) a fight or riot that takes place in public

**affront** VERB affronts, affronting, affronted
to insult or offend someone • *She looked affronted by this suggestion.*

**affront** NOUN affronts
an insult

**afield** ADVERB
at or to a distance; away from home • *Her travels took her as far afield as India.*

**aflame** ADJECTIVE & ADVERB
in flames; glowing • *His cheeks were aflame with embarrassment.*

**afloat** ADJECTIVE & ADVERB
floating; on the sea • *Somehow we kept the boat afloat.*

**afoot** ADJECTIVE
happening or likely to happen • *Great changes are afoot.*

**aforesaid** ADJECTIVE
mentioned previously

**afraid** ADJECTIVE
frightened or alarmed
➤ **I'm afraid** I am sorry; I regret • *I'm afraid I won't be able to come.*

**afresh** ADVERB
again; in a new way • *We must start afresh.*

**African** ADJECTIVE
to do with Africa or its people

**African** NOUN Africans
an African person

**African Caribbean** NOUN African Caribbeans
a person of African descent living in or coming from the Caribbean
➤ **African–Caribbean** ADJECTIVE

**Afrikaans** (say af-rik-**ahns**) NOUN
a language developed from Dutch, used in South Africa

**Afrikaner** (say af-rik-**ah**-ner) NOUN Afrikaners
a white person in South Africa whose language is Afrikaans

**Afro-Caribbean** NOUN & ADJECTIVE
African Caribbean

**aft** ADVERB
at or towards the back of a ship or aircraft

**after** PREPOSITION
❶ later than • *Come after dinner.* ❷ next in position or order • *Which letter comes after H?* ❸ trying to catch; following • *Run after him.* ❹ as a result of • *After the way he behaved, I won't invite him again.* ❺ in

imitation or honour of • *She is named after her aunt.* ⑥ about or concerning • *He asked after you.*

**after** *ADVERB*
later • *They met again the summer after.*
➤ **after all** even though you thought something different would happen • *They've decided to stay at home after all.*

**afterbirth** *NOUN*
the placenta and other membranes that come out of the mother's womb after she has given birth

**aftermath** *NOUN*
events or circumstances that come after something bad or unpleasant • *Hundreds of families needed help in the aftermath of the earthquake.* **WORD ORIGIN** from *after* + *math*, which is a mowing of new grass. An *aftermath* was originally the new grass that grew up after the old grass had been mowed.

**afternoon** *NOUN* afternoons
the time from noon or lunchtime to evening

**aftershave** *NOUN*
a pleasant-smelling lotion that men put on their skin after shaving

**afterthought** *NOUN* afterthoughts
something you think of or add later

**afterwards** *ADVERB*
after that; at a later time

**again** *ADVERB*
① another time; once more • *Let's try again.*
② as before • *You will soon be well again.*
**SPELLING**
The end of **again** is spelt ain.

**against** *PREPOSITION*
① touching or hitting • *He was leaning against the wall.* ② opposed to; not in favour of • *It is against the law. They voted against the proposal.* ③ in order to protect from • *Vitamin C helps to protect us against infection.*

**age** *NOUN* ages
① how old you are; the length of time a person has lived or a thing has existed ② a special period of history or geology • *the Bronze Age • the ice age*
➤ **ages** *PLURAL NOUN*
(informal) a very long time • *We've been waiting for ages.*
➤ **come of age** to reach the age when you have an adult's legal rights and obligations (normally 18 years)

**age** *VERB* ages, ageing, aged
to become old or to make someone old

**aged** *ADJECTIVE*
① (say ayjd) having the age of • *a girl aged 9*
② (say **ay**-jid) very old • *an aged man*

**age group** *NOUN* age groups
people who are all about the same age
• *Anyone in the 10-12 age group would enjoy this book.*

**agency** *NOUN* agencies
an office or business that provides a special service • *a travel agency*

**agenda** (say a-**jen**-da) *NOUN* agendas
a list of things that people have to do or talk about at a meeting • *What is the next item on the agenda?* **WORD ORIGIN** Latin, = things that have to be done

**agent** *NOUN* agents
① a person or business that organizes things for other people • *a travel agent* ② a spy
• *a secret agent*

**agglomeration** *NOUN* agglomerations
a mass of things collected together

**aggravate** *VERB* aggravates, aggravating, aggravated
① to make a thing worse or more serious
• *Pollution can aggravate asthma.*
② (informal) to annoy someone
➤ **aggravation** *NOUN*
**WORD ORIGIN** from Latin *gravare* = make something heavy

**aggregate** (say **ag**-rig-at) *ADJECTIVE*
combined or total • *the aggregate amount*

**aggregate** *NOUN* aggregates
a total amount or score

**aggression** *NOUN*
starting an attack or war; aggressive behaviour

**aggressive** *ADJECTIVE*
likely to attack people; forceful • *an aggressive dog*
➤ **aggressively** *ADVERB*

**aggressor** *NOUN* aggressors
the person or nation that started an attack or war

**aggrieved** (say a-**greevd**) *ADJECTIVE*
resentful because you think you have been treated unfairly • *There was an aggrieved tone in her voice.*

**aghast** ADJECTIVE
shocked and horrified • *She stared at him aghast.*

**agile** ADJECTIVE
moving quickly or easily
➤ **agilely** ADVERB

**agility** NOUN
the ability to move quickly or easily • *She scrambled up the rocks with great agility.*

**agitate** VERB agitates, agitating, agitated
❶ to make someone feel upset or anxious
❷ to shake something about
➤ **agitation** NOUN

**agitated** ADJECTIVE
showing that you are anxious or nervous • *He was getting increasingly agitated.*

**aglow** ADJECTIVE
glowing • *His face was aglow with enthusiasm.*

**agnostic** (say ag-**nost**-ik) NOUN agnostics
a person who believes that it is impossible to know whether God exists
➤ **agnosticism** NOUN

**ago** ADVERB
in the past • *She died three years ago.*

**agog** ADJECTIVE
eager and excited **WORD ORIGIN** from French *en gogues* = in a happy mood, ready for fun

**agonizing** (also **agonising**) ADJECTIVE
❶ causing great pain or suffering • *an agonizing death* ❷ an agonizing choice or decision is one that you find very difficult to make

**agony** NOUN agonies
very great pain or suffering

**agoraphobia** (say ag-er-a-**foh**-bee-a) NOUN
**WORD ORIGIN** from Greek *agora* = market place, + **phobia**

**agree** VERB agrees, agreeing, agreed
❶ to agree with someone is to think or say the same as they do • *I agree that we need to act quickly.* ❷ to agree to do something is to say that you are willing to • *She agreed to come.* ❸ to suit a person's health or digestion • *Spicy food doesn't agree with me.* ❹ to correspond in grammatical number, gender or person. In 'They were good teachers' *they* agrees with *teachers* (both are plural forms) and *were* agrees with *they*; *was* would be incorrect because it is singular.

**agreeable** ADJECTIVE
❶ willing to agree to something • *We shall go if you are agreeable.* ❷ pleasant or enjoyable • *a most agreeable surprise*
➤ **agreeably** ADVERB

**agreement** NOUN agreements
❶ having the same opinion • *Are we in agreement?* ❷ an arrangement that people have agreed on

**agriculture** NOUN
cultivating land on a large scale and rearing livestock; farming
➤ **agricultural** ADJECTIVE

**aground** ADVERB & ADJECTIVE
stuck on the bottom in shallow water • *The ship had run aground.*

**ah** EXCLAMATION
a cry of surprise, pity, admiration, etc.

**ahead** ADVERB
❶ further forward; in front • *The road ahead was blocked.* ❷ before; more advanced • *They arrived a few minutes ahead of us.* ❸ winning • *Our team was ahead by five points.*

**ahoy** EXCLAMATION
a shout used by sailors to attract attention

**aid** NOUN aids
❶ help • *She walks with the aid of a stick.* • *His friends rushed to his aid.* ❷ something that helps someone to do something more easily • *a hearing aid* ❸ money, food, etc. sent to another country to help it • *overseas aid*
➤ **in aid of** for the purpose of; to help something

**aid** VERB aids, aiding, aided
to help someone

**aide** NOUN aides
an assistant

**Aids** NOUN
a disease caused by the HIV virus, which greatly weakens a person's ability to resist infections **WORD ORIGIN** from the initial letters of 'acquired immune deficiency syndrome'

**ail** VERB ails, ailing, ailed (old use)
to make a person ill or troubled • *What ails you?*

**ailing** ADJECTIVE
❶ ill; in poor health • *her ailing grandfather* ❷ in difficulties; not successful • *the ailing ship industry*

**ailment** NOUN ailments
a slight illness

**aim** VERB aims, aiming, aimed
❶ to point a gun or other weapon at a target ❷ to throw or kick a ball etc. in a particular direction ❸ to try or intend to do something • *We aim to leave after breakfast.*

**aim** NOUN aims
❶ aiming a gun or other weapon • *She took careful aim.* ❷ a purpose or intention • *The aim of the expedition was to reach the South Pole.*

**aimless** ADJECTIVE
without a definite aim or purpose • *They wandered around in an aimless manner.*
➤ **aimlessly** ADVERB

**air** NOUN airs
❶ the mixture of gases that surrounds the earth and which everyone breathes ❷ the space around and above things • *She through a ball into the air.* ❸ an appearance or impression of something • *an air of mystery* ❹ a grand or haughty manner • *He puts on airs.*
➤ **by air** in or by aircraft
➤ **in the air** probably going to happen soon • *A feeling of change was in the air.*
➤ **on the air** on radio or television

**air** VERB airs, airing, aired
❶ to put clothes etc. in a warm place to finish drying ❷ to allow air to circulate round a room ❸ to express an opinion or complaint • *People will have a chance to air their views.*

**airborne** ADJECTIVE
❶ an aircraft is airborne when it has taken off and is in flight ❷ carried by the air • *an airborne virus*

**air-conditioning** NOUN
a system for controlling the temperature, purity, etc. of the air in a room or building
➤ **air-conditioned** ADJECTIVE

**aircraft** NOUN aircraft
an aeroplane, glider or helicopter etc.

**aircraft carrier** NOUN aircraft carriers
a large ship with a long deck where aircraft can take off and land

**airfield** NOUN airfields
an area equipped with runways etc. where aircraft can take off and land

**air force** NOUN air forces
the part of a country's armed forces that is equipped with aircraft

**airgun** NOUN airguns
a gun in which compressed air shoots a pellet or dart

**airily** ADVERB
in a casual way that shows you are not treating something as serious • *'Oh, nothing,' she replied airily.*

**airline** NOUN airlines
a company that provides a regular service of transport by aircraft

**airliner** NOUN airliners
a large aircraft for carrying passengers

**airlock** NOUN airlocks
❶ a compartment with an airtight door at each end, through which people can go in and out of a pressurized chamber ❷ a bubble of air that stops liquid flowing through a pipe

**airmail** NOUN
letters and parcels carried by air

**airman** NOUN airmen
a man who is a member of an air force or of the crew of an aircraft

**airport** NOUN airports
a place where aircraft land and take off, with passenger terminals and other buildings

**air raid** NOUN air raids
an attack by aircraft, in which bombs are dropped

**airship** NOUN airships
a large balloon with engines, designed to carry passengers or goods

**airstrip** NOUN airstrips
a strip of ground prepared for aircraft to land and take off

**airtight** ADJECTIVE
not letting air in or out • *an airtight container*

**airy** ADJECTIVE
❶ with plenty of fresh air • *The room was cool and airy.* ❷ casual and not treating something as serious • *He dismissed her with an airy wave of the hand.*

**aisle** (rhymes with mile) NOUN aisles
❶ a passage between rows of seats, pews in a church or shelves in a supermarket ❷ a side part of a church

**ajar** ADVERB & ADJECTIVE
slightly open • *Please leave the door ajar.*

**akimbo** ADVERB
➤ **arms akimbo** with hands on hips and elbows out

17

**akin** ADJECTIVE
related or similar to • *a feeling akin to regret*

**alabaster** (say al-a-bast-er) NOUN
a kind of hard white stone

**à la carte** ADJECTIVE & ADVERB
ordered and paid for as separate items from a
menu WORD ORIGIN French, = from the menu

**alacrity** NOUN
speed and willingness • *She accepted the
invitation with alacrity.*

**alarm** NOUN alarms
❶ a warning sound or signal; a piece of
equipment for giving this ❷ a feeling of fear
or worry • *He cried out in alarm.* ❸ an alarm
clock

**alarm** VERB alarms, alarming, alarmed
to make someone frightened or anxious • *I'm
sorry, I didn't mean to alarm you.*
➤ **alarming** ADJECTIVE
WORD ORIGIN from Italian *all' arme!* = to
arms! (a call to go and fight)

**alarm clock** NOUN alarm clocks
a clock that can be set to ring or bleep at a
fixed time to wake someone who is asleep

**alas** EXCLAMATION
a cry of sorrow

**albatross** NOUN albatrosses
a large seabird with very long wings

**albino** (say al-**been**-oh) NOUN albinos
a person or animal with no colouring pigment
in the skin and hair (which are white)

**album** NOUN albums
❶ a book with blank pages in which
you keep a collection of photographs,
stamps, autographs, etc. ❷ a collection
of songs on a CD, record or other medium
WORD ORIGIN Latin, = white piece of stone etc.
on which to write things

**albumen** (say **al**-bew-min) NOUN
the white of an egg

**alchemy** (say **al**-kim-ee) NOUN
an early form of chemistry, the chief aim of
which was to turn ordinary metals into gold
➤ **alchemist** NOUN
WORD ORIGIN from Arabic *al-kimiya* = the art
of changing metals

**alcohol** NOUN
❶ a colourless liquid made by fermenting
sugar or starch ❷ drinks containing this liquid
(e.g. wine, beer, whisky), that can make people
drunk

**alcoholic** ADJECTIVE
containing alcohol

**alcoholic** NOUN alcoholics
a person who is seriously addicted to alcohol
➤ **alcoholism** NOUN

**alcove** NOUN alcoves
a section of a room that is set back from the
main part

**alder** NOUN alders
a kind of tree, often growing in marshy places

**alderman** (say **awl**-der-man) NOUN aldermen
a senior member of an English county or
borough council

**ale** NOUN ales
a type of beer

**alert** ADJECTIVE
watching for something; ready to act
• *Security guards need to be alert at all
times.*
➤ **alertness** NOUN

**alert** NOUN alerts
a warning or alarm
➤ **on the alert** on the lookout for danger or
attack; watchful • *Be on the alert for any sign
of trouble.*

**alert** VERB alerts, alerting, alerted
to warn someone of danger etc.; to make
someone aware of something • *A knock
on the door alerted her to their arrival.*
WORD ORIGIN from Italian *all' erta!* = to the
watchtower!

**A level** NOUN A levels
(in the UK except Scotland) an exam in a
subject taken by school students aged 16-
18, or the course leading up to it; short for
Advanced Level

**alfresco** ADJECTIVE & ADVERB
in the open air • *an alfresco meal*

**algae** (say **al**-jee) PLURAL NOUN
plants that grow in water, with no true stems
or leaves

**algebra** (say **al**-jib-ra) NOUN
mathematics in which letters and symbols are
used to represent quantities
➤ **algebraic** (say al-jib-**ray**-ik) ADJECTIVE
WORD ORIGIN from Arabic *al-jabr* = putting
together broken parts

**algorithm** NOUN algorithms
a process or set of rules a computer uses to
make calculations or to solve a problem

**alias** (say ay-lee-as) NOUN aliases
a false or different name • *He was travelling under the alias 'John Brown'.*

**alias** ADVERB
also named • *Clark Kent, alias Superman*

**alibi** (say al-i-by) NOUN alibis
evidence that a person accused of a crime was somewhere else when it was committed

**alien** (say ay-lee-en) NOUN aliens
❶ in stories, a being from another world ❷ a person who is not a citizen of the country where he or she is living; a foreigner

**alien** ADJECTIVE
❶ foreign ❷ not natural or familiar • *Cruelty is alien to her nature.*

**alienate** (say ay-lee-en-ayt) VERB alienates, alienating, alienated
to make someone less friendly or sympathetic towards you • *His comments have alienated a lot of local people.*

**alight** ADJECTIVE
❶ on fire • *The roof was soon alight.* ❷ bright or shining • *Her face was alight with joy.*

**alight** VERB alights, alighting, alighted
❶ to get out of a vehicle or down from a horse etc. • *The lady alighted from her carriage.* ❷ to fly down and settle • *The bird alighted on a nearby branch.*

**align** (say a-lyn) VERB aligns, aligning, aligned
to arrange things so they are in the correct position or form a straight line • *Make sure the wheels are aligned properly.*
➤ **alignment** NOUN

**alike** ADJECTIVE
like one another • *The twins are very alike.*

**alike** ADVERB
in the same way • *He treats everybody alike.*

**alimentary canal** NOUN alimentary canals
the tube along which food passes through the body

**alive** ADJECTIVE
❶ living ❷ you are alive to something when you are well aware of it • *She is alive to all the possible dangers.*

**alkali** (say alk-al-y) NOUN alkalis
a chemical substance that neutralizes an acid to form a salt
➤ **alkaline** ADJECTIVE

**all** DETERMINER
the whole number or amount of • *All my friends came.* • *No one had seen her all day.*

**all** PRONOUN
❶ everything • *That is all I know.*
❷ everybody • *So, are we all agreed?*

**all** ADVERB
❶ completely • *She was dressed all in white.*
❷ to each team or competitor • *The score is fifteen all.*
➤ **all there** (*informal*) having an alert mind
➤ **all the same** in spite of this; making no difference • *I like him, all the same.*

**Allah** NOUN
the Muslim name of God

**allay** (say a-lay) VERB allays, allaying, allayed
to calm or relieve an unpleasant feeling
• *Even these assurances did not allay her fears.*

**all-clear** NOUN
a signal that a danger has passed

**allegation** (say al-ig-ay-shon) NOUN allegations
a statement accusing someone of doing something wrong, made without proof

**allege** (say a-lej) VERB alleges, alleging, alleged
to accuse someone of doing something wrong without being able to prove it • *He alleged that I had cheated.*
➤ **alleged** ADJECTIVE
➤ **allegedly** (say a-lej-id-lee) ADVERB

**allegiance** (say a-lee-jans) NOUN allegiances
loyal support • *an oath of allegiance*

**allegory** (say al-ig-er-ee) NOUN allegories
a story in which the characters and events represent or symbolize a deeper meaning, e.g. to teach a moral lesson
➤ **allegorical** (say al-ig-o-rik-al) ADJECTIVE

**alleluia** EXCLAMATION
praise to God

**allergic** ADJECTIVE
you are allergic to something that is normally safe when it makes you feel ill or unwell • *He is allergic to pollen, which gives him hay fever.*

**allergy** (say al-er-jee) NOUN allergies
a condition of the body that makes you react badly to something that is normally safe

**alleviate** (say a-lee-vee-ayt) VERB alleviates, alleviating, alleviated
to alleviate a pain or difficulty is to make it less severe
➤ **alleviation** NOUN

**alley** NOUN alleys
❶ a narrow street or passage ❷ a place where you can play skittles or tenpin bowling

**alliance** (say a-**leye**-ans) NOUN alliances
an agreement between countries or groups who wish to support each other and work together

**allied** ADJECTIVE
❶ joined as allies; on the same side • *allied forces* ❷ of the same kind; closely connected • *stories of allied interest*

**alligator** NOUN alligators
a large reptile of the crocodile family
**WORD ORIGIN** from Spanish *el lagarto* = the lizard

**alliteration** NOUN
the repetition of the same letter or sound at the beginning of several words, e.g. in *whisper words of wisdom*

**SPELLING**
There is a double l in alliteration, and only one t before the er.

**allocate** VERB allocates, allocating, allocated
to give things to a number of people
• *Everyone has been allocated a locker.*
➤ **allocation** NOUN

**allot** VERB allots, allotting, allotted
to give a number of things to different people
• *You have all been allotted tasks.*

**allotment** NOUN allotments
a small rented piece of public land used for growing vegetables, fruit or flowers

**allow** VERB allows, allowing, allowed
❶ to let someone do something • *Smoking is not allowed.* ❷ to decide on a certain amount for a particular purpose • *She was allowed £20 for travel expenses.*
➤ **allowable** ADJECTIVE

**SPELLING**
Allowed means to be permitted to do something, e.g. *Running in the corridors is not allowed.* Aloud means in a voice that can be heard, e.g. *He read the letter aloud.*

**allowance** NOUN allowances
an amount of money that is given regularly for a particular purpose
➤ make allowances to take something into consideration and excuse it • *We must make allowances for his age.*

**alloy** NOUN alloys
a metal formed by mixing two or more metals etc.

**all right** ADJECTIVE & ADVERB
❶ satisfactory ❷ in good condition ❸ yes, I agree

**SPELLING**
All right is two words, not one.

**all-round** ADJECTIVE
(*British*) able to do many different things well; general • *an all-round athlete*
➤ **all-rounder** NOUN

**allude** VERB alludes, alluding, alluded
to mention something briefly or indirectly
• *He alluded to an incident the previous day.*

**allure** VERB allures, alluring, allured
to attract or fascinate someone
➤ **allure** NOUN

**alluring** ADJECTIVE
attractive or fascinating • *The offer was an alluring one.*

**allusion** NOUN allusions
a reference made to something without actually naming it

**ally** (say **al**-eye) NOUN allies
❶ a country that has agreed to support another country ❷ a person who cooperates with another person

**ally** VERB allies, allying, allied
to form an alliance • *Saruman the wizard allied himself with Sauron.*

**almanac** NOUN almanacs
an annual publication containing a calendar and other information

**almighty** ADJECTIVE
❶ having complete power ❷ (*informal*) very great • *an almighty row*
➤ the Almighty a name for God

**almond** (say **ah**-mond) NOUN almonds
an oval edible nut

**almost** ADVERB
near to being something but not quite • *I am almost ready.*

**alms** (say ahmz) PLURAL NOUN (*old use*)
money and gifts given to the poor

**almshouse** NOUN almshouses
a house founded by charity for poor people

**aloft** ADVERB
high up; up in the air • *He held the lamp aloft.*

**alone** ADJECTIVE & ADVERB
without any other people or things; without help

**along** PREPOSITION
following the length of something • *Walk along the path.*

**along** ADVERB
❶ on or onwards • *Push it along.*
❷ accompanying somebody • *I've brought my brother along.*

**alongside** PREPOSITION & ADVERB
next to something; beside • *The boat drew alongside.*

**aloof** ADVERB
apart; not taking part • *We kept aloof from their quarrels.*

**aloof** ADJECTIVE
distant and not friendly in manner • *She seemed aloof.*

**aloud** ADVERB
in a voice that can be heard

> **SPELLING**
> Aloud is different from allowed • *He read the letter aloud.* • *Running in the corridors is not allowed.*

**alpha** NOUN
the first letter of the Greek alphabet, equivalent to Roman *A, a*

**alphabet** NOUN alphabets
the letters used in a language, arranged in a set order **WORD ORIGIN** from alpha, beta, the first two letters of the Greek alphabet

**alphabetical** ADJECTIVE
to do with the alphabet • *The names are listed in alphabetical order.*
➤ **alphabetically** ADVERB

**alpine** ADJECTIVE
to do with high mountains • *alpine plants*
**WORD ORIGIN** from the Alps, mountains in Switzerland

**already** ADVERB
by now; before now

**Alsatian** (say al-**say**-shan) NOUN Alsatians
a German shepherd dog

**also** ADVERB
in addition; besides

**altar** NOUN altars
a table or similar structure used in religious ceremonies

> **SPELLING**
> Take care not to confuse with the verb alter.

**alter** VERB alters, altering, altered
to make something different in some way; to become different • *We've altered our plans.*

> **SPELLING**
> Take care not to confuse with the noun altar.

**alteration** NOUN alterations
a change you make to something • *The jacket needed a few alterations.*

**altercation** (say ol-ter-**kay**-shon) NOUN altercations
a noisy argument or quarrel

**alter ego** (say ol-ter **ee**-go) NOUN alter egos
another, very different, side of someone's personality • *Superman's alter ego, Clark Kent* **WORD ORIGIN** Latin, = other self

**alternate** (say ol-**tern**-at) ADJECTIVE
❶ coming in turns, one after the other • *The snake had alternate rings of red and black.* ❷ one in every two • *We meet up on alternate Fridays.*

> **USAGE**
> The words alternate and alternative have different meanings. See the note at alternative.

**alternate** (say ol-tern-ayt) VERB alternates, alternating, alternated
to use or come in turns, one after the other • *She alternated between excitement and nerves.* • *Blue stripes alternate with red ones.*
➤ **alternation** NOUN

**alternately** ADVERB
in turns, one after the other • *The sky looked alternately bright, then cloudy.*

**alternating current** NOUN alternating currents
electric current that keeps reversing its direction at regular intervals

a b c d e f g h i j k l m n o p q r s t u v w x y z

**alternative** ADJECTIVE
for you to choose instead of something else
• *Is there an alternative route?*
➤ **alternatively** ADVERB

USAGE
Do not confuse alternative with
alternate. If there are *alternative colours*
it means that there is a choice of two or
more colours, but *alternate colours* means
that there is first one colour and then the
other.

**alternative** NOUN alternatives
one of two or more things that you can
choose between • *Technology has given us
alternatives to fossil fuels.*
➤ **no alternative** no choice

**alternative medicine** NOUN
types of medical treatment that are not
part of ordinary medicine. Acupuncture,
homeopathy and osteopathy are all forms of
alternative medicine.

**although** CONJUNCTION
though; in spite of the fact that

SPELLING
There is only one l in although.

**altimeter** NOUN altimeters
an instrument used in aircraft etc. for
showing the height above sea level

**altitude** NOUN altitudes
the height of something, especially above sea
level • *an altitude of 10,000 metres*

**alto** NOUN altos
❶ an adult male singer with a very high voice
❷ a female singer with a low voice

**altogether** ADVERB
❶ with all included; in total • *There were six
of us altogether.* ❷ completely • *The stream
dries up altogether in summer.* ❸ on the
whole • *Altogether, it was a good concert.*

SPELLING
Altogether is different from all together,
which means together in a group
• *They wanted to be all together for the
photographs.*

**altruistic** (say al-troo-**ist**-ik) ADJECTIVE
unselfish; thinking of other people's welfare
➤ **altruism** NOUN

**aluminium** NOUN
a lightweight silver-coloured metal

**always** ADVERB
❶ at all times • *He has always been very
strict.* ❷ often or constantly • *You are always
crying.* ❸ whatever happens • *You can always
sleep on the floor.*

**Alzheimer's disease** NOUN
a serious disease of the brain which affects
mainly older people and makes them
confused and forgetful WORD ORIGIN named
after a German scientist, A. *Alzheimer*

**a.m.** ABBREVIATION
before 12 o'clock midday WORD ORIGIN short
for Latin *ante meridiem* = before noon

**amalgam** NOUN amalgams
❶ an alloy of mercury ❷ a mixture or
combination

**amalgamate** VERB amalgamates,
amalgamating, amalgamated
to mix or combine things

**amass** VERB amasses, amassing, amassed
to heap up or collect something • *By the time
he died, he had amassed a fortune.*

**amateur** (say **am**-at-er) NOUN amateurs
a person who does something for pleasure,
not for money as a job • *an amateur painter*
WORD ORIGIN from Latin *amator* = lover

**amateurish** ADJECTIVE
not done or made very well; not skilful

**amaze** VERB amazes, amazing, amazed
to surprise somebody greatly; to be difficult
for somebody to believe • *It amazes me that
anyone could be so stupid.*

**amazed** ADJECTIVE
very surprised • *He was amazed to discover
the truth.*

**amazement** NOUN
a feeling of great surprise • *She stared at him
in amazement.*

**amazing** ADJECTIVE
very surprising or remarkable; difficult to
believe

**ambassador** NOUN ambassadors
a person sent to a foreign country to
represent his or her own government

**amber** NOUN
❶ a hard clear yellowish substance used for
making jewellery and ornaments ❷ a yellow
traffic light shown as a signal for caution,
placed between red for 'stop' and green for
'go'

**ambidextrous** ADJECTIVE
able to use either your left hand or your right
hand equally well WORD ORIGIN from Latin

*ambo* = both + *dextrous* = skilful (related to **dexterity**)

**ambiguous** *ADJECTIVE*
having more than one possible meaning; unclear • *His reply was ambiguous.*
➤ **ambiguity** *NOUN*

> **SPELLING**
>
> Do not forget the **u** before the **ous** in **ambiguous**.

**ambition** *NOUN* ambitions
❶ a strong desire to do well and be successful ❷ something you want to do very much • *Her ambition is to be world champion.*

**ambitious** *ADJECTIVE*
❶ wanting very much to do well and be successful ❷ difficult or challenging • *an ambitious plan*

**amble** *VERB* ambles, ambling, ambled
to walk at a slow easy pace • *We ambled down to the beach.*

**ambrosia** (say am-**broh**-zee-a) *NOUN*
something delicious **WORD ORIGIN** in Greek mythology, ambrosia was the food of the gods

**ambulance** *NOUN* ambulances
a vehicle equipped to take sick or injured people to hospital **WORD ORIGIN** from French *hôpital ambulant*, a mobile military hospital; from Latin *ambulare* = walk

**ambush** *NOUN* ambushes
a surprise attack from a hidden place
**ambush** *VERB* ambushes, ambushing, ambushed
to attack someone after lying in wait for them

**amen** *EXCLAMATION*
a word used at the end of a prayer or hymn, meaning 'may it be so'

**amenable** (say a-**meen**-a-bul) *ADJECTIVE*
willing to accept or try out a suggestion or idea

**amend** *VERB* amends, amending, amended
to change something slightly in order to improve it
**amend** *NOUN*
➤ **make amends** to make up for having done something wrong

**amendment** *NOUN* amendments
a change that is made to a piece of writing, especially to a law

**amenity** (say a-**men**-it-ee or a-**meen**-it-ee) *NOUN* amenities

a pleasant or useful feature of a place • *The town has many amenities, such as a sports centre and a multiplex cinema.*

**American** *ADJECTIVE*
❶ to do with the continent of America ❷ to do with the United States of America
➤ **American** *NOUN*

**amethyst** *NOUN* amethysts
a purple precious stone **WORD ORIGIN** from Greek *lithos amethystos* = stone against drunkenness (because people believed that they would not get drunk if there was an amethyst in their drink)

**amiable** *ADJECTIVE*
friendly and good-tempered
➤ **amiably** *ADVERB*

**amicable** *ADJECTIVE*
done in a friendly way, without argument
➤ **amicably** *ADVERB*

**amid, amidst** *PREPOSITION*
in the middle of; among

**amino acid** (say a-**meen**-oh) *NOUN* amino acids
an acid found in proteins

**amiss** *ADJECTIVE*
wrong or faulty • *She knew something was amiss.*
➤ **not go amiss** to be useful or pleasant
• *Another piece of cake wouldn't go amiss.*
➤ **take something amiss** to be offended or upset by something • *Don't take what I'm about to say amiss.*

**ammonia** *NOUN*
a colourless gas or liquid with a strong smell

**ammunition** *NOUN*
a supply of bullets, shells, grenades, etc. for use in fighting

**amnesia** (say am-**nee**-zee-a) *NOUN*
loss of memory

**amnesty** *NOUN* amnesties
a general pardon for people who have committed a crime **WORD ORIGIN** from Greek *amnestia* = forgetfulness (because the crimes are legally 'forgotten')

**amoeba** (say a-**mee**-ba) *NOUN* amoebas
a microscopic creature consisting of a single cell which constantly changes shape and can split itself in two

**amok** *ADVERB*
➤ **run amok** to rush about wildly in a violent rage
WORD ORIGIN from Malay (a language spoken in Malaysia), = fighting mad

**among, amongst** *PREPOSITION*
❶ surrounded by; in the middle of • *There were weeds among the flowers.* ❷ between • *Divide the sweets among the children.*

**amoral** (say ay-**mo**ral) *ADJECTIVE*
not based on moral standards; neither moral nor immoral

**amorous** *ADJECTIVE*
showing or feeling love or passion • *amorous glances*

**amorphous** (say a-**mor**-fus) *ADJECTIVE*
shapeless • *an amorphous mass*

**amount** *NOUN* amounts
❶ a quantity ❷ a total

**amount** *VERB* amounts, amounting, amounted
➤ **amount to** ❶ to add up to • *The damage amounted to $3 million.* ❷ to be equivalent to • *Their reply amounts to a refusal.*
WORD ORIGIN from Latin *ad montem* = to the mountain, upwards

**amp** *NOUN* amps
❶ an ampere ❷ (*informal*) an amplifier

**ampere** (say **am**-pair) *NOUN* amperes
a unit for measuring electric current
WORD ORIGIN named after the French scientist A. M. *Ampère*

**ampersand** *NOUN* ampersands
the symbol &, which means 'and'
WORD ORIGIN from the phrase *and per se and* = '& by itself means and' (Latin *per se* = by itself). The symbol '&' was added to the end of the alphabet in children's school books, and when they came to it, pupils reciting the alphabet would say the phrase; they thought it was the name of the symbol

**amphetamine** *NOUN* amphetamines
a drug used as a stimulant

**amphibian** *NOUN* amphibians
❶ an animal able to live both on land and in water, such as a frog, toad, newt and salamander ❷ a vehicle that can move on both land and water WORD ORIGIN from Greek *amphi* = around + *bios* = life

**amphibious** *ADJECTIVE*
able to live or move both on land and in water

**amphitheatre** *NOUN* amphitheatres
an oval or circular building without a roof and with rows of seats round a central arena
WORD ORIGIN from Greek *amphi* = all round, + *theatre*

**ample** *ADJECTIVE*
❶ quite enough • *We've got ample time.*
❷ large • *This car has an ample boot.*

**amplifier** *NOUN* amplifiers
a piece of equipment for making a sound or electrical signal louder or stronger

**amplify** *VERB* amplifies, amplifying, amplified
❶ to make a sound or electrical signal louder or stronger ❷ to give more details about something • *Could you amplify that point?*
➤ **amplification** *NOUN*

**amplitude** *NOUN*
(*in science*) the greatest distance that a wave, especially a sound wave, vibrates

**amply** *ADVERB*
generously; with as much as you need or even more • *You will be amply rewarded.*

**amputate** *VERB* amputates, amputating, amputated
to cut off an arm or leg by a surgical operation
➤ **amputation** *NOUN*

**amuse** *VERB* amuses, amusing, amused
❶ to make a person laugh or smile ❷ to amuse yourself is to find pleasant things to do

**amusement** *NOUN* amusements
❶ a game or activity that makes time pass pleasantly ❷ being amused

**amusement arcade** *NOUN* amusement arcades
(*British*) an indoor area where people can play on automatic game machines

**amusement park** *NOUN* amusement parks
a large outdoor area with fairground rides and other amusements

**amusing** *ADJECTIVE*
making you laugh or smile

**an** *DETERMINER*
see a

**anachronism** (say an-**ak**-ron-izm) *NOUN* anachronisms
something wrongly placed in a particular historical period or regarded as out of date • *Bows and arrows would be an anachronism in modern warfare.* WORD ORIGIN from Greek *ana* = backwards + *khronos* = time

**anaemia** (say a-**nee**-mee-a) NOUN
a lack of red cells or iron in the blood, that makes a person pale and tired
➤ **anaemic** ADJECTIVE

**anaesthesia** NOUN
❶ the use of anaesthetic during medical operations ❷ the state of being unable to feel pain

**anaesthetic** (say an-iss-**thet**-ik) NOUN anaesthetics
a substance or gas that makes you unable to feel pain

**anaesthetist** (say an-**ees**-thet-ist) NOUN anaesthetists
a person trained to give anaesthetics
➤ **anaesthetize** VERB

**anagram** NOUN anagrams
a word or phrase made by rearranging the letters of another • '*Strap' is an anagram of 'parts'.*

**anal** (say **ay**-nal) ADJECTIVE
to do with the anus

**analgesic** (say an-al-**jee**-sik) NOUN analgesics
a substance that relieves pain

**analogous** (say a-**nal**-o-gus) ADJECTIVE
similar in some ways to something else and so able to be compared with it • *In the poem sleep is thought to be analogous to death.*

**analogy** (say a-**nal**-oj-ee) NOUN analogies
a comparison or similarity between two things that are alike in some ways • *the analogy between the human heart and a pump*

**analyse** VERB analyses, analysing, analysed
❶ to examine and interpret something • *This book analyses the causes of the war.* ❷ to separate something into its parts

**analysis** NOUN analyses
❶ a detailed examination of something ❷ a separation of something into its parts
➤ **analytical** ADJECTIVE

**analyst** NOUN analysts
a person who analyses things

**anarchist** (say **an**-er-kist) NOUN anarchists
a person who believes that all forms of government are bad and should be abolished

**anarchy** (say **an**-er-kee) NOUN
❶ lack of government or control, leading to a breakdown in law and order ❷ complete disorder

**anathema** (say an-**ath**-em-a) NOUN
something that you detest • *All blood sports are anathema to me.*

**anatomy** (say an-**at**-om-ee) NOUN
❶ the study of the structure of the bodies of humans or animals ❷ the structure of an animal's body
➤ **anatomical** ADJECTIVE
➤ **anatomist** NOUN

**ancestor** NOUN ancestors
anyone from whom a person is descended
➤ **ancestral** ADJECTIVE

**ancestry** NOUN ancestries
your ancestry is the people from whom you are descended • *She was proud of her ancestry.*

**anchor** NOUN anchors
a heavy object joined to a ship by a chain or rope and dropped to the bottom of the sea to stop the ship from moving

**anchor** VERB anchors, anchoring, anchored
❶ to fix or be fixed by an anchor ❷ to fix something firmly • *Make sure the table is securely anchored.*

**anchorage** NOUN anchorages
a place where a ship can be anchored

**anchovy** NOUN anchovies
a small fish with a strong flavour

**ancient** ADJECTIVE
❶ very old ❷ belonging to the distant past • *ancient history*

**ancillary** (say an-**sil**-er-ee) ADJECTIVE
helping or supporting the people who do the main work • *doctors, nurses and ancillary staff*

**and** CONJUNCTION
❶ together with; in addition to • *We had cakes and ice cream.* ❷ so that; with this result • *Ask there and they may be able to help.* ❸ to • *Go and bring another chair.*

**android** NOUN androids
(in science fiction) a robot that looks like a human being **WORD ORIGIN** from Greek *andros* = man

**anecdote** NOUN anecdotes
a short amusing or interesting story about a real person or thing

**anemone** (say a-**nem**-on-ee) NOUN anemones
a plant with cup-shaped red, purple or white flowers **WORD ORIGIN** from Greek, = windflower (from the belief that the flower opens when it is windy)

**anew** ADVERB
again; in a new or different way • *We must begin anew.*

**angel** NOUN angels
❶ an attendant or messenger of God
❷ a very kind or beautiful person
**WORD ORIGIN** from Greek *angelos* = messenger

**angelic** (say an-jel-ik) ADJECTIVE
kind or beautiful; like an angel • *an angelic smile*

**angelica** NOUN
a sweet-smelling plant whose crystallized stalks are used in cookery as a decoration

**anger** NOUN
a strong feeling that you want to quarrel or fight with someone

**anger** VERB angers, angering, angered
to make a person angry

**angle** NOUN angles
❶ the space between two lines or surfaces that meet; the amount by which a line or surface must be turned to make it lie along another ❷ a point of view • *She considered the problem from all angles.*

**angle** VERB angles, angling, angled
❶ to put something in a slanting position • *Ben angled his phone so Kate could see the screen.* ❷ to present news or a story from one point of view

**angler** NOUN anglers
a person who fishes with a fishing rod and line
➤ **angling** NOUN

**Anglican** ADJECTIVE
to do with the Church of England
➤ **Anglican** NOUN

**Anglo-Saxon** NOUN Anglo-Saxons
❶ an English person, especially of the time before the Norman conquest in 1066 ❷ the form of English spoken from about 700 to 1150; Old English **WORD ORIGIN** from Old English *Angulseaxe* = an English Saxon (contrasted with the Old Saxons on the Continent)

**angry** ADJECTIVE angrier, angriest
feeling that you want to quarrel or fight with someone
➤ **angrily** ADVERB

**anguish** NOUN
severe suffering or misery • *a cry of anguish*
➤ **anguished** ADJECTIVE

**angular** ADJECTIVE
❶ an angular person is bony and not plump • *his thin, angular face* ❷ having angles or sharp corners • *a design of angular shapes*

**animal** NOUN animals
❶ a living thing that can feel and usually move about • *Horses, birds, fish, bees and people are all animals.* ❷ a cruel or uncivilized person

**animate** VERB animates, animating, animated
❶ to make a thing lively ❷ to produce something as an animated film
➤ **animator** NOUN

**animated** ADJECTIVE
❶ lively and excited ❷ an animated film is one made by photographing a series of still pictures and showing them rapidly one after another, so they appear to move

**animation** NOUN
❶ being lively or excited ❷ the technique of making a film by photographing a series of still pictures

**animosity** (say an-im-oss-it-ee) NOUN animosities
a feeling of strong dislike and anger towards someone • *There was a lot of animosity in his voice.*

**aniseed** NOUN
a sweet-smelling seed used for flavouring things

**ankle** NOUN ankles
the part of the leg where it joins the foot

**annals** PLURAL NOUN
a history of events, especially when written year by year

**annex** VERB annexes, annexing, annexed
❶ to take control of another country or region by force • *Rome first annexed Cyprus in 58 BC.* ❷ to add or join a thing to something else

**annexe** NOUN annexes
a building added to a larger or more important building

**annihilate** (say an-y-il-ayt) VERB annihilates, annihilating, annihilated
to destroy something completely
➤ **annihilation** NOUN
**WORD ORIGIN** from Latin *nihil* = nothing

**anniversary** NOUN anniversaries
a day when you remember something special that happened on the same day in a previous year

**annotate** (say **an**-oh-tayt) *VERB* annotates, annotating, annotated
to add notes of explanation to something written or printed
➤ **annotation** *NOUN*

**announce** *VERB* announces, announcing, announced
to make something known, especially by saying it publicly or to an audience

**announcement** announcements *NOUN*
a statement that tells people about something publicly or officially • *Ladies and gentlemen, I'd like to make an announcement.*

**announcer** *NOUN* announcers
a person who announces items in a radio or television broadcast

**annoy** *VERB* annoys, annoying, annoyed
❶ to make a person slightly angry ❷ to be troublesome to someone

**annoyance** *NOUN* annoyances
❶ the feeling of being annoyed • *He bit his lip in annoyance.* ❷ something that annoys you • *Wasps are a great annoyance at a picnic.*

**annual** *ADJECTIVE*
❶ happening or done once a year • *her annual visit* ❷ calculated over one year • *our annual income* ❸ living for one year or one season • *an annual plant*
➤ **annually** *ADVERB*

**annual** *NOUN* annuals
❶ a book that comes out once a year ❷ a plant that lives for one year or one season

**annuity** (say a-**new**-it-ee) *NOUN* annuities
a fixed annual allowance of money, especially from a kind of investment

**annul** *VERB* annuls, annulling, annulled
to cancel a law or contract; to end something legally • *Their marriage was annulled.*
➤ **annulment** *NOUN*

**anode** *NOUN* anodes
the electrode by which electric current enters a device. Compare with **cathode**.

**anoint** *VERB* anoints, anointing, anointed
to put oil or ointment on someone or something, especially in a religious ceremony

**anomaly** (say an-**om**-al-ee) *NOUN* anomalies
something that does not follow the general rule or that is unlike the usual or normal kind

**anon** *ADVERB* (old use)
soon • *I will say more about this anon.*

**anon.** *ABBREVIATION*
anonymous

**anonymous** (say an-**on**-im-us) *ADJECTIVE*
without the name of the person responsible being known or made public • *an anonymous donation*
➤ **anonymously** *ADVERB*
➤ **anonymity** (say an-on-**im**-it-ee) *NOUN*

**anorak** *NOUN* anoraks
a thick warm jacket with a hood
**WORD ORIGIN** from an Inuit word

**anorexia** (say an-er-**eks**-ee-a) *NOUN*
an illness that makes a person so anxious to lose weight that he or she refuses to eat

**anorexic** *ADJECTIVE*
suffering from anorexia

**another** *DETERMINER & PRONOUN*
a different or extra person or thing • *another day* • *choose another*

**answer** *NOUN* answers
❶ a reply ❷ the solution to a problem

**answer** *VERB* answers, answering, answered
❶ to give or find an answer to a question or for a person asking it ❷ to respond to a signal • *Holly went to answer the phone.*
➤ **answer back** to be rude or cheeky in replying to someone
➤ **answer for something** to be punished for something or have to explain it
➤ **answer to the name of** to be called • *His dog answers to the name of Roxy.*

**SPELLING**
There is a silent **w** in **answer**.

**answerable** *ADJECTIVE*
having to explain your actions to someone; responsible for something

**answering machine** *NOUN* answering machines
a machine that records messages from people who telephone while you are out

**answerphone** *NOUN* answerphones
(*British*) a telephone answering machine

**ant** *NOUN* ants
a very small insect that lives as one of an organized group

**antagonism** (say an-**tag**-on-izm) *NOUN*
an unfriendly feeling; hostility • *She could not understand his antagonism towards her.*
➤ **antagonistic** *ADJECTIVE*

**antagonist** *NOUN* antagonists
your opponent in a fight or contest

**antagonize** (also **antagonise**) *VERB*
antagonizes, antagonizing, antagonized
to do something to make someone angry with
you • *He didn't want to antagonize her any
further, so he kept quiet.*

**anteater** *NOUN* anteaters
an animal that feeds on ants and termites

**antelope** *NOUN* antelope or antelopes
a fast-running animal like a deer, found in
Africa and parts of Asia

**antenatal** (say an-tee-**nay**-tal) *ADJECTIVE*
(*British*) to do with the period during
pregnancy before childbirth

**antenna** *NOUN*
❶ antennae a feeler on the head of an insect
or crustacean ❷ antennas an aerial

**ante-room** *NOUN* ante-rooms
a room leading to a more important room

**anthem** *NOUN* anthems
a religious or patriotic song, usually sung by a
choir or group of people

**anther** *NOUN* anthers
the part of a flower's stamen that contains
pollen

**anthill** *NOUN* anthills
a mound of earth over an ants' nest

**anthology** *NOUN* anthologies
a collection of poems, stories, songs, etc. in
one book • *an anthology of ghost stories*
**WORD ORIGIN** from Greek *anthos* = flower +
-*logia* = collection

**anthrax** *NOUN*
a a very serious disease of sheep and cattle
that can also infect people

**anthropoid** *ADJECTIVE*
looking like a human being • *Gorillas are
anthropoid apes.*

**anthropology** *NOUN*
the study of human beings and their customs
➤ **anthropological** *ADJECTIVE*
➤ **anthropologist** *NOUN*

**anti–** *PREFIX*
against or preventing something (as in
*antifreeze*)

**anti-aircraft** *ADJECTIVE*
used against enemy aircraft

**antibiotic** *NOUN* antibiotics
a substance (e.g. penicillin) that destroys
bacteria or prevents them from growing

**antibody** *NOUN* antibodies
a protein that forms in the blood as a defence
against certain substances which it then
attacks and destroys

**anticipate** *VERB* anticipates, anticipating,
anticipated
❶ to expect something to happen and
be ready for it • *As he had anticipated, it
rained all afternoon.* ❷ to look forward to
something • *We are eagerly anticipating their
arrival.*

**anticipation** *NOUN*
looking forward to something • *A ripple of
anticipation swept through the stadium.*
➤ **in anticipation of** expecting something to
happen and being ready for it • *The table had
been set in anticipation of their visit.*

**anticlimax** *NOUN* anticlimaxes
a disappointing ending or result where
something exciting had been expected

**anticlockwise** *ADVERB & ADJECTIVE*
(*British*) moving in the opposite direction to
the hands of a clock

**antics** *PLURAL NOUN*
funny or foolish actions • *She couldn't help
laughing at his antics.*

**anticyclone** *NOUN* anticyclones
an area where air pressure is high, usually
producing fine settled weather

**antidote** *NOUN* antidotes
something that takes away the bad effects of
a poison or disease

**antifreeze** *NOUN*
a liquid added to water to make it less likely
to freeze

**antihistamine** *NOUN* antihistamines
a drug that protects people against
unpleasant effects when they are allergic to
something

**antimony** *NOUN*
a brittle silvery metal

**antipathy** (say an-**tip**-ath-ee) *NOUN*
a strong dislike • *He has always had an
antipathy to dogs.*

**antipodes** (say an-**tip**-od-eez) *PLURAL NOUN*
➤ **the Antipodes** Australia, New Zealand and
the areas near them, in relation to Europe
➤ **Antipodean** *ADJECTIVE*
**WORD ORIGIN** from Greek, = having the feet
opposite (*podes* = feet), because you have your
feet on the opposite side of the world from
Europe

A B C D E F G H I J K L M N O P Q R S T U V W X Y Z

**antiquarian** (say anti-**kwair**-ee-an) ADJECTIVE
to do with the study of antiques

**antiquated** ADJECTIVE
old-fashioned or out of date

**antique** (say an-**teek**) NOUN antiques
something that is valuable because it is very
old

**antique** ADJECTIVE
very old; belonging to the distant past

**antiquities** PLURAL NOUN
objects that were made in ancient times • *a
collection of Egyptian antiquities*

**antiquity** (say an-**tik**-wit-ee) NOUN
ancient times • *The statue was brought to
Rome in antiquity.*

**anti-Semitic** (say anti-sim-**it**-ik) ADJECTIVE
hostile or prejudiced towards Jews
➤ **anti-Semitism** (say anti-**sem**-it-izm) NOUN

**antiseptic** ADJECTIVE
❶ able to destroy bacteria, especially those
that cause things to become septic or to
decay ❷ thoroughly clean and free from
germs

**antiseptic** NOUN antiseptics
a substance with an antiseptic effect

**antisocial** ADJECTIVE
unfriendly or inconsiderate towards other
people • *antisocial behaviour*

**antithesis** (say an-**tith**-iss-iss) NOUN
antitheses
the antithesis of something is the exact
opposite • *His brother's personality was the
antithesis of his own.*

**antivirus** ADJECTIVE
designed to find and destroy computer
viruses • *antivirus software*

**antivivisectionist** NOUN antivivisectionists
a person who is opposed to carrying out
experiments on live animals

**antler** NOUN antlers
the horn of a deer, which divides into several
branches

**antonym** (say **ant**-on-im) NOUN antonyms
a word that is opposite in meaning to another
• *'Soft' is an antonym of 'hard'.*

> GRAMMAR
> See also the panel on synonyms and
> antonyms.

**anus** (say **ay**-nus) NOUN anuses
the opening at the lower end of the

alimentary canal, through which solid waste
matter leaves the body

**anvil** NOUN anvils
a large block of iron on which a blacksmith
hammers metal into shape

**anxiety** NOUN anxieties
❶ anxiety is a feeling of being worried ❷ an
anxiety is something that you are worried
about

**anxious** ADJECTIVE
❶ worried and slightly afraid ❷ wanting to
do something very much • *She is anxious to
please us.*
➤ **anxiously** ADVERB

**any** DETERMINER & PRONOUN
❶ one or some • *Have you any wool?* • *There
isn't any.* ❷ no matter which • *Come any day
you like.* ❸ every • *Any fool knows that!*

**any** ADVERB
at all; in some degree • *Is it any good?*

**anybody** PRONOUN
any person

**anyhow** ADVERB
❶ anyway; in any case • *Anyhow, it doesn't
matter.* ❷ (*informal*) carelessly; in no special
way • *Things had been put on the floor
anyhow.*

**anyone** PRONOUN
anybody

**anything** PRONOUN
any thing

**anyway** ADVERB
whatever happens; whatever the situation
may be • *If it rains, we'll go anyway.*

**anywhere** ADVERB
in or to any place

**anywhere** PRONOUN
any place • *Anywhere will do.*

**aorta** (say ay-**or**-ta) NOUN aortas
the main artery that carries blood away from
the left side of the heart

**apace** ADVERB
quickly • *The darkness grew apace.*

**apart** ADVERB
❶ away from each other; separately • *The
trees were planted far apart.* ❷ into pieces
• *It fell apart.* ❸ excluded • *Joking apart,
what do you think of it?*
➤ **apart from** excluding, other than • *Apart
from a banana, he'd eaten nothing all day.*

**apartheid** (say a-**part**-hayt) *NOUN*
the political policy that used to be practised in South Africa, of keeping people of different races apart

**apartment** *NOUN* **apartments**
❶ a set of rooms ❷ (*North American*) a flat

**apathy** (say **ap**-ath-ee) *NOUN*
not having much interest in or caring about something • *There is widespread apathy among the voters.*

**ape** *NOUN* **apes**
any of the four kinds of monkey (gorillas, chimpanzees, orangutans, gibbons) that do not have a tail

**ape** *VERB* **apes, aping, aped**
to copy or imitate something, often in a ridiculous way • *She aped his expression of horror.*

**aperture** *NOUN* **apertures**
an opening

**apex** (say **ay**-peks) *NOUN* **apexes**
the tip or highest point • *the apex of a triangle*

**aphid** (say **ay**-fid) *NOUN* **aphids**
a tiny insect (e.g. a greenfly) that sucks the juices from plants

**aphis** (say **ay**-fiss) *NOUN* **aphides** (say **ay**-fid-eez)
an aphid

**apiece** *ADVERB*
to, for or by each • *They cost fifty cents apiece.*

**aplomb** (say a-**plom**) *NOUN*
dignity and confidence • *She handled the crisis with great aplomb.*

**apocryphal** (say a-**pok**-rif-al) *ADJECTIVE*
not likely to be true; invented • *This account of his travels is apocryphal.*

**apologetic** *ADJECTIVE*
showing or saying that you are sorry • *She gave him an apologetic smile.*
➤ **apologetically** *ADVERB*

**apologize** (also **apologise**) *VERB* **apologizes, apologizing, apologized**
to tell someone that you are sorry for something you have done • *I apologize for my behaviour yesterday.*

**apology** *NOUN* **apologies**
❶ a statement saying that you are sorry for doing something wrong or badly

❷ something very poor • *this feeble apology for a meal*

**apoplectic** (say ap-o-**plek**-tik) *ADJECTIVE*
violently or fiercely angry

**apoplexy** (say **ap**-op-lek-see) *NOUN*
❶ sudden loss of the ability to feel and move, caused by the blocking or breaking of a blood vessel in the brain ❷ (*informal*) rage or anger

**Apostle** *NOUN* **Apostles**
in Christianity, any of the twelve men sent out by Christ to preach the Gospel

**apostrophe** (say a-**poss**-trof-ee) *NOUN* **apostrophes**
the punctuation mark (') used to show that letters have been missed out (as in *I can't* = I cannot) or to show that something belongs to someone (as in *the boy's book*; *the boys' books*)

**PUNCTUATION**

Apostrophes have two main uses:

to show that letters are missed out of a shortened word, e.g. *didn't* (for *did not*) or *we'd* (for *we would*), or in a time, e.g. *six o'clock* (originally 'of the clock').

to show what someone or something owns or possesses, e.g. *the bat's ears* (= the ears of the bat), or what something is associated with, e.g. *the day's news* (= the news of the day).

Where does the apostrophe for possession go?

For most nouns you add an apostrophe followed by an s: *the dragon's claw* (= the claw of the dragon), *the children's shoes* (= the shoes of the children), *the city's cathedral* (= the cathedral in the city), *the boss's desk* (= the desk belonging to the boss), *in a week's time* (= after a week).

When the noun is plural and already ends in s, you add an apostrophe by itself: *the dragons' claws* (= the claws of the dragons), *the cities' cathedrals* (= the cathedrals in the cities), *the bosses' desks* (= the desks belonging to the bosses), *in three weeks' time* (= after three weeks).

When a person's name ends in s, you add an apostrophe followed by s if you normally say an extra s in speaking: *Venus's orbit; St Thomas's Hospital.* But you just add an apostrophe when you don't say an extra s in speaking: *Achilles' armour.*

There is no apostrophe in ordinary plurals like *bicycles*, *videos* and *Mondays* or in possessive pronouns like *hers* and *its*.

You don't need an apostrophe for plurals of abbreviations, e.g. *CDs* and *DVDs*, or for plurals of decades, e.g. *in the 1990s.*

**apothecary** (say a-**poth**-ik-er-ee) NOUN
apothecaries (*old use*)
a chemist who prepares medicines

**app** NOUN apps
a computer program designed to do a particular job, especially one you use on a smartphone

**appal** VERB appals, appalling, appalled
to shock somebody very much • *She stared at him, appalled.* **WORD ORIGIN** from Old French *apalir* = become pale

**appalling** ADJECTIVE
shocking; very unpleasant • *Some of the children live in appalling conditions.*

**apparatus** NOUN
the equipment for a particular experiment or task

**apparel** NOUN
(*formal*) a person's clothes

**apparent** ADJECTIVE
❶ clear or obvious • *For no apparent reason, everyone was whispering.* ❷ seeming; appearing to be true but not really so • *I could not understand her apparent indifference.*

**apparently** ADVERB
as it seems; so it appears • *The door had apparently been locked.*

**apparition** NOUN apparitions
something that you imagine you can see, especially a ghost • *a ghostly apparition at the window*

**appeal** VERB appeals, appealing, appealed
❶ to ask for something that you badly need • *Police are appealing for information.* ❷ to ask for a decision to be changed • *He appealed against the prison sentence.* ❸ to seem attractive or interesting • *Golf doesn't appeal to me.*

**appeal** NOUN appeals
❶ asking for something you badly need
❷ asking for a decision to be changed

❸ attraction or interest • *I don't understand the appeal of the countryside.*

**appear** VERB appears, appearing, appeared
❶ to come into sight; to begin to exist
❷ to seem • *They appeared very anxious.*
❸ to take part in a play, film or show etc.

**SPELLING**
There is a double p in **appear**.

**appearance** NOUN appearances
❶ coming into sight ❷ taking part in a play, film or show etc. ❸ what somebody looks like; what something appears to be

**appease** VERB appeases, appeasing, appeased
to calm someone down, often by giving them what they want • *Nothing would appease the goddess.*
➤ **appeasement** NOUN

**appendage** NOUN appendages
something added or attached; a thing that forms a natural part of something larger

**appendicitis** NOUN
inflammation of the appendix

**appendix** NOUN
❶ appendixes a small tube leading off from the intestine ❷ appendices a section added at the end of a book

**appetite** NOUN appetites
❶ desire for food ❷ an enthusiasm for something • *These stories had given her an appetite for adventure.*

**appetizer** (also **appetiser**) NOUN appetizers
a small amount of food eaten before the main meal

**appetizing** (also **appetising**) ADJECTIVE
appetizing food looks and smells good to eat

**applaud** VERB applauds, applauding, applauded
to show that you like something, especially by clapping your hands

**applause** NOUN
clapping by the audience at the end of a performance • *He was given a huge round of applause.*

**apple** NOUN apples
a round fruit with a red, yellow or green skin
➤ **the apple of your eye** a person or thing that you love and are proud of

**appliance** NOUN appliances
a device or piece of equipment • *electrical appliances*

a
b
c
d
e
f
g
h
i
j
k
l
m
n
o
p
q
r
s
t
u
v
w
x
y
z

**applicable** (say ap-lik-a-bul) *ADJECTIVE*
suitable or relevant • *Ignore any questions which are not applicable.*

**applicant** *NOUN* applicants
a person who applies for a job or position

**application** *NOUN* applications
❶ a formal written request for something, such as a job ❷ a computer program or piece of software designed for a particular purpose ❸ the practical use of something • *One of the important applications of virtual reality is in medical education.* ❹ hard work or effort

**applied** *ADJECTIVE*
put to practical use • *applied maths*

**apply** *VERB* applies, applying, applied
❶ to put or spread one thing on another • *She applied lipstick to her mouth.* ❷ to start using something • *He applied the brakes.* ❸ to ask for something in writing • *Mina applied for a place on the course.* ❹ something applies to a person or thing when it concerns them and they are affected by it • *This rule does not apply to you.*
➤ **apply yourself** to give all your attention to a task or piece of work

**appoint** *VERB* appoints, appointing, appointed
❶ to choose a person for a job ❷ an appointed time is one officially decided on for a meeting or deadline • *Everyone was assembled at the appointed time.*

**appointment** *NOUN* appointments
❶ an arrangement to meet or visit somebody at a particular time ❷ choosing somebody for a job ❸ a job or position

**apportion** *VERB* apportions, apportioning, apportioned
to divide something among people; to give someone a share of something • *Great care was taken in apportioning the parts.*

**appraise** *VERB* appraises, appraising, appraised
to judge the value or quality of a person or thing • *She stepped back to appraise her workmanship.*
➤ **appraisal** *NOUN*

**appreciable** *ADJECTIVE*
large enough to be noticed or felt • *The engine showed no appreciable signs of wear.*

**appreciate** *VERB* appreciates, appreciating, appreciated
❶ to enjoy or value something • *It's nice to be appreciated.* ❷ to be grateful for something • *Thank you, I really appreciate*

your help ❸ to understand something • *I do appreciate the seriousness of the situation.* ❹ to increase in value

**appreciation** *NOUN*
❶ showing that you enjoy or value something • *She had a keen appreciation of poetry.* ❷ the feeling of being grateful for something • *Please accept this small token of my appreciation.* ❸ understanding of a situation or problem

**appreciative** *ADJECTIVE*
❶ showing pleasure or admiration • *an appreciative audience* ❷ grateful for something • *He was very appreciative of our efforts to help.*

**apprehend** *VERB* apprehends, apprehending, apprehended
❶ to seize or arrest someone ❷ to understand something

**apprehension** *NOUN*
❶ fear or worry • *His mouth was dry with apprehension.* ❷ the arrest of a person

**apprehensive** *ADJECTIVE*
anxious or worried

**apprentice** *NOUN* apprentices
a person who is learning a trade or craft by a legal agreement with an employer

**apprentice** *VERB* apprentices, apprenticing, apprenticed
to give someone a position as an apprentice • *At 13 he was apprenticed to a printer.*

**apprenticeship** *NOUN* apprenticeships
the time when someone is an apprentice • *He began his apprenticeship as a butcher.*

**approach** *VERB* approaches, approaching, approached
❶ to come near • *Robin approached the door on tiptoe.* ❷ to go to someone with a request or offer • *They approached me for help.* ❸ to set about doing something or tackling a problem • *What is the best way to approach this problem?*

**approach** *NOUN* approaches
❶ a way of dealing with something • *He brought a fresh approach to filmmaking.* ❷ coming near • *She did not notice the approach of the two girls.* ❸ a way or road leading up to something • *Two soldiers guarded the approach to the bridge.*

**approachable** *ADJECTIVE*
friendly and easy to talk to

**approbation** *NOUN*
formal or official approval

**appropriate** (say a-**proh**-pree-at) *ADJECTIVE*
suitable or right for a particular situation
➤ **appropriately** *ADVERB*

**appropriate** (say a-**proh**-pree-ayt) *VERB*
appropriates, appropriating, appropriated
to take something, usually without permission
and use it as your own • *Someone had
appropriated my locker.*

**approval** *NOUN*
❶ thinking well of someone or something
• *Bob was always seeking his father's
approval.* ❷ agreeing to a plan or request
• *The king nodded his approval.*
➤ **on approval** received by a customer to
examine before deciding to buy

**approve** *VERB* approves, approving, approved
❶ to say or think that a person or thing
is good or suitable ❷ to agree formally to
something • *The committee has approved the
expenditure.*

**approximate** (say a-**proks**-im-at) *ADJECTIVE*
almost exact or correct but not completely so
• *All the dates in brackets are approximate.*

**approximate** (say a-**proks**-im-ayt)
*VERB* approximates, approximating,
approximated
to be almost the same as something • *I
tried on several jackets before finding one
approximating my size.*

**approximately** *ADVERB*
roughly; almost exactly • *It's approximately
fifty miles from here.*

**approximation** *NOUN* approximations
a number or amount that is a rough estimate
and not exact

**apricot** *NOUN* apricots
a juicy orange-coloured fruit with a stone
in it

**April** *NOUN*
the fourth month of the year

**apron** *NOUN* aprons
❶ a piece of clothing worn over the front
of the body, especially to protect other
clothes ❷ a hard-surfaced area on an airfield
where aircraft are loaded and unloaded
**WORD ORIGIN** originally *a naperon*, from
French *nappe* = tablecloth

**apse** *NOUN* apses
a domed semicircular part at the east end of
a church

**apt** *ADJECTIVE*
❶ to be apt to do something is to be likely
to do it or to do it a lot • *He is apt to be
careless.* ❷ appropriate or suitable • *an apt
quotation*
➤ **aptly** *ADVERB*
➤ **aptness** *NOUN*

**aptitude** *NOUN*
to have an aptitude for something is to be
naturally good at it • *She had a natural
aptitude for drama.*

**aqualung** *NOUN* aqualungs
a diver's portable breathing apparatus, with
cylinders of compressed air connected to a
face mask

**aquamarine** *NOUN* aquamarines
a bluish-green precious stone
**WORD ORIGIN** from Latin *aqua marina* – sea
water

**aquarium** *NOUN* aquariums
a tank or building in which live fish and other
water animals are displayed

**aquatic** *ADJECTIVE*
to do with water or living in water • *the
Olympics aquatic centre* • *aquatic plants*

**aquatint** *NOUN* aquatints
an etching made on copper by using nitric
acid

**aqueduct** *NOUN* aqueducts
a bridge carrying a water channel across low
ground or a valley

**aquiline** (say **ak**-wi-lyn) *ADJECTIVE*
an aquiline nose is hooked like an eagle's beak

**Arab** *NOUN* Arabs
a member of a Semitic people living in parts
of the Middle East and North Africa
➤ **Arabian** *ADJECTIVE*

**Arabic** *ADJECTIVE*
to do with the Arabs or their language

**Arabic** *NOUN*
the language of the Arabs

**Arabic numerals** *PLURAL NOUN*
the figures 1, 2, 3, 4, etc. Compare with
Roman numerals.

**arable** *ADJECTIVE*
arable land is suitable for ploughing or
growing crops on

**arachnid** (say a-**rak**-nid) *NOUN* arachnids
a member of the group of animals that
includes spiders and scorpions

a
b
c
d
e
f
g
h
i
j
k
l
m
n
o
p
q
r
s
t
u
v
w
x
y
z

**arbitrary** (say **ar**-bit-rer-ee) ADJECTIVE
chosen or done on an impulse, not according
to a rule or law • *an arbitrary decision*

**arbour** (say **ar**-ber) NOUN **arbours**
a shady place among trees

**arc** NOUN **arcs**
❶ a curve; part of the circumference of a
circle ❷ a luminous electric current passing
between two electrodes

**arcade** NOUN **arcades**
a covered passage or area, especially for
shopping (WORD ORIGIN) French or Italian, from
Latin *arcus* = curve (because early arcades had
curved roofs)

**arcane** ADJECTIVE
secret or mysterious (WORD ORIGIN) from Latin
*arcere* = to shut up, from *arca* = box

**arch** NOUN **arches**
❶ a curved structure that helps to support
a bridge or other building etc. ❷ something
shaped like this

**arch** VERB **arches, arching, arched**
to form something in an arch; to curve
• *The cat arched its back and hissed.*

**arch** ADJECTIVE
pretending to be playful; mischievous • *an
arch smile*
➤ **archly** ADVERB

**archaeology** (say ar-kee-**ol**-oj-ee) NOUN
the study of ancient civilizations by digging
for the remains of their buildings, tools, etc.
and examining them
➤ **archaeological** ADJECTIVE
➤ **archaeologist** NOUN

**archaic** (say ar-**kay**-ik) ADJECTIVE
belonging to former or ancient times

**archangel** NOUN **archangels**
an angel of the highest rank

**archbishop** NOUN **archbishops**
the chief bishop of a region

**arch-enemy** NOUN **arch-enemies**
a person's chief enemy

**archer** NOUN **archers**
a person who shoots with a bow and arrows

**archery** NOUN
the sport of shooting at a target with a bow
and arrows

**archipelago** (say ark-i-**pel**-ag-oh) NOUN
**archipelagos**
a large group of islands or the sea containing
these

**architect** (say **ark**-i-tekt) NOUN **architects**
a person who designs buildings

**architecture** NOUN
❶ the work of designing buildings
❷ a particular style of building • *Elizabethan
architecture*
➤ **architectural** ADJECTIVE

**archive** (say **ark**-yv) NOUN
❶ (also **archives**) a collection of old
documents and records that show the history
of an organization or community
❷ (*in computing*) a set of computer files that
are stored and no longer in active use
SPELLING
The 'k' sound is spelt **ch** in archive.

**archivist** (say **ar**-kiv-ist) NOUN **archivists**
a person trained to deal with archives

**archway** NOUN **archways**
an arched passage or entrance

**arc lamp, arc light** NOUN **arc lamps, arc
lights**
a light using an electric arc

**arctic** ADJECTIVE
very cold • *The weather was arctic.*

**ardent** ADJECTIVE
enthusiastic or passionate • *an ardent
admirer*
➤ **ardently** ADVERB

**ardour** (say **ar**-der) NOUN
enthusiasm or passion

**arduous** ADJECTIVE
needing much effort; difficult and tiring • *an
arduous voyage*

**area** NOUN **areas**
❶ the extent or measurement of a surface;
the amount of space a surface covers • *The
area of the room is 20 square metres.* ❷ a
particular region or piece of land ❸ a subject
or activity • *an interesting area of biology*

**arena** (say a-**reen**-a) NOUN **arenas**
an area with seats around it where
sports events or concerts are held
(WORD ORIGIN) Latin, = sand (because the floors
of Roman arenas were covered with sand)

**aren't** (*mainly spoken*)
are not

> **aren't I?** (*informal*) am I not?

SPELLING

Aren't = are + not. Add an apostrophe
between the **n** and the **t**.

**arguable** *ADJECTIVE*
❶ able to be stated as a possibility ❷ open to
doubt; not certain

**arguably** *ADVERB*
used to give your opinion about something,
especially when you think others might not
agree • *This is arguably his best book.*

**argue** *VERB* argues, arguing, argued
❶ to say that you disagree; to exchange
angry comments ❷ to state that something
is true and give reasons • *Some people argue
that we are using too many fossil fuels too
quickly.*

**argument** *NOUN* arguments
❶ a disagreement or quarrel ❷ a reason or
series of reasons someone puts forward

SPELLING

There is no e after the **u** in **argument**.

**argumentative** *ADJECTIVE*
fond of arguing

**aria** (say **ar-ee-a**) *NOUN* arias
a solo in an opera or oratorio

**arid** *ADJECTIVE*
having little or no rain; dry and barren

**arise** *VERB* arises, arising, arose, arisen
❶ to come into existence; to come to people's
notice • *Now a serious problem arose.* ❷ (*old
use*) to rise; to stand up • *Arise, Sir Francis.*

**aristocracy** (say a-ris-**tok**-ra-see) *NOUN*
people of the highest social rank; members of
the nobility

**aristocrat** (say **a**-ris-tok-rat) *NOUN* aristocrats
a member of the aristocracy
> **aristocratic** *ADJECTIVE*

**arithmetic** *NOUN*
the science or study of numbers; calculating
with numbers
> **arithmetical** *ADJECTIVE*

**ark** *NOUN* arks
❶ (in the Bible) the ship in which Noah and
his family escaped the Flood ❷ a wooden box
in which the writings of the Jewish Law were
kept

**arm** *NOUN* arms
❶ either of the two upper limbs of the body,

between the shoulder and the hand
❷ a sleeve ❸ something shaped like an arm
or jutting out from a main part ❹ the raised
side part of a chair, on which you can rest
your arm

**arm** *VERB* arms, arming, armed
to prepare someone to fight by supplying
them with weapons • *We armed ourselves
with heavy sticks and waited.*

**armada** (say ar-**mah**-da) *NOUN* armadas
a fleet of warships
> **the Armada** or **Spanish Armada** the
warships sent by Spain to invade England in
1588

**armadillo** *NOUN* armadillos
a small burrowing South American animal
whose body is covered with a shell of bony
plates **WORD ORIGIN** Spanish, = little armed
man

**armaments** *PLURAL NOUN*
the weapons of an army etc.

**armature** *NOUN* armatures
the part of a dynamo or electric motor that
carries the current

**armchair** *NOUN* armchairs
a large comfortable chair with arms

**armed** *ADJECTIVE*
❶ carrying a weapon, especially a gun • *an
armed gang* ❷ involving weapons • *armed
robbery*

**armed forces, armed services** *PLURAL NOUN*
a country's army, navy and air force

**armful** *NOUN* armfuls
the amount you can carry in your arms

**armistice** *NOUN* armistices
an agreement to stop fighting in a war or
battle

**armour** *NOUN*
❶ metal clothing worn in the past to protect
soldiers in battle ❷ a metal covering on a
warship, tank or car to protect it from missiles
> **armoured** *ADJECTIVE*

**armoury** *NOUN* armouries
a place where weapons and ammunition are
stored

**armpit** *NOUN* armpits
the hollow underneath the top of the arm,
below the shoulder

**arms** *PLURAL NOUN*
❶ weapons • *The two armies laid down their
arms and made peace.* ❷ a coat of arms • *In*

a b c d e f g h i j k l m n o p q r s t u v w x y z

the centre of the shield are the royal arms.
➤ **up in arms** protesting angrily about something

**arms race** NOUN
competition between nations in building up supplies of weapons, especially nuclear weapons

**army** NOUN armies
❶ a large number of people trained to fight on land ❷ a large group of people doing something together • *There was an army of servants working in the kitchen.*

**aroma** (say a-**roh**-ma) NOUN aromas
a smell, especially a pleasant one

**aromatic** (say a-ro-**mat**-ik) ADJECTIVE
having a pleasant smell • *aromatic herbs*

**around** ADVERB & PREPOSITION
all round; about • *They stood around the pond.* • *Stop running around.*

**arouse** VERB arouses, arousing, aroused
❶ to stir up a feeling in someone • *You've definitely aroused my curiosity.* ❷ to wake someone up

**arpeggio** (say ar-**pej**-ee-oh) NOUN arpeggios
(*in music*) the notes of a chord played one after the other instead of together

**arrange** VERB arranges, arranging, arranged
❶ to make plans and preparations for something • *We're arranging a surprise party for Johnny.* ❷ to put things into a certain order • *Arrange the chairs in a circle.* ❸ to prepare music for a particular purpose

**arrangement** NOUN arrangements
❶ arrangement is how you arrange or display something • *a flower arrangement* ❷ an arrangement is something you agree with someone else • *We made an arrangement to meet at the clock tower.*

**array** NOUN arrays
a large display or choice of things • *a huge array of books*

**array** VERB arrays, arraying, arrayed
❶ to be arrayed in fine or special clothes is to be wearing them noticeably • *She was arrayed in purple and gold robes.* ❷ to arrange things in a special order • *His pots of paint were arrayed around his feet.*

**arrears** PLURAL NOUN
❶ money that is owing and ought to have been paid earlier ❷ a backlog of work etc.
➤ **in arrears** behind with payments

**arrest** VERB arrests, arresting, arrested
to seize a person by authority of the law

**arrest** NOUN arrests
arresting somebody • *The police made several arrests.*

**arrival** NOUN arrivals
❶ reaching the place to which you were travelling • *On our arrival we were met by the mayor.* ❷ a person or thing that has just arrived • *Have you met the new arrivals?*

**arrive** VERB arrives, arriving, arrived
❶ to reach the end of a journey or a point on it ❷ to come to a decision or agreement ❸ to come or happen • *The great day arrived.*
**WORD ORIGIN** from Latin *ad-* = to + *ripa* = shore; the basic meaning is 'come to shore'

**SPELLING**

> There is a double r in arrive.

**arrogant** ADJECTIVE
behaving in an unpleasantly proud way because you think you are better than other people
➤ **arrogantly** ADVERB
➤ **arrogance** NOUN

**arrow** NOUN arrows
❶ a pointed stick to be shot from a bow ❷ a sign with an outward-pointing V at the end, used to show direction or position
➤ **arrowhead** NOUN

**arsenal** NOUN arsenals
a place where weapons and ammunition are stored or manufactured

**arsenic** NOUN
a strong poison made from a metallic element
**WORD ORIGIN** originally the name of arsenic sulphide, which is yellow; from Persian *zar* = gold

**arson** NOUN
the crime of deliberately setting fire to a house or building
➤ **arsonist** NOUN

**art** NOUN arts
❶ producing something beautiful, especially by painting, drawing or sculpture; things produced in this way ❷ a skill • *the art of sailing*

**artefact** NOUN artefacts
an object made by humans, especially one from the past that is studied by archaeologists

**artery** NOUN arteries
❶ one of the tubes that carry blood away

**artesian well** NOUN artesian wells
a well that is dug straight down into a place where water will rise easily to the surface

**artful** ADJECTIVE
crafty or cunning
➤ **artfully** ADVERB

**arthritis** (say arth-**ry**-tiss) NOUN
a disease that makes joints in the body stiff and painful
➤ **arthritic** (say arth-**rit**-ik) ADJECTIVE

**arthropod** NOUN arthropods
an animal of the group that includes insects, spiders, crabs and centipedes
**WORD ORIGIN** from Greek *arthron* = joint + *podes* = feet (because arthropods have jointed limbs)

**artichoke** NOUN artichokes
a kind of plant with a flower head used as a vegetable

**article** NOUN articles
❶ a piece of writing published in a newspaper or magazine ❷ an object or item • *articles of clothing*
➤ **definite article** the word 'the'
➤ **indefinite article** the word 'a' or 'an'

**articulate** (say ar-**tik**-yoo-lat) ADJECTIVE
able to express things clearly and fluently

**articulate** (say ar-**tik**-yoo-layt) VERB
articulates, articulating, articulated
to say or speak clearly • *She articulated the words very carefully.*
➤ **articulation** NOUN

**articulated** ADJECTIVE
(British) an articulated vehicle is one in two sections that are connected by a flexible joint
• *an articulated lorry*

**artifice** NOUN artifices
a piece of clever trickery • *The clown fell flat on his face, with magnificent artifice.*

**artificial** ADJECTIVE
not natural; made by human beings in imitation of a natural thing
➤ **artificially** ADVERB

**artificial intelligence** NOUN
the use of computers to perform tasks normally requiring human intelligence, e.g. decision-making

**artificial respiration** NOUN
helping someone to start breathing again after their breathing has stopped

**artillery** NOUN
❶ large guns ❷ the part of the army that uses large guns

**artisan** (say art-iz-**an**) NOUN artisans
a skilled worker

**artist** NOUN artists
❶ a person who produces works of art, especially a painter ❷ an entertainer

**artistic** ADJECTIVE
❶ to do with art or artists • *Michelangelo's artistic career began at the age of twelve.*
❷ having or showing a talent for art • *She's always been artistic.*
➤ **artistically** ADVERB

**artistry** NOUN
the skill of an artist

**artless** ADJECTIVE
simple and natural • *the little girl's artless prattle*
➤ **artlessly** ADVERB

**arts** PLURAL NOUN
subjects (e.g. languages, literature, history) in which opinion and interpretation are very important, as opposed to sciences where measurements and calculations are used
➤ **the arts** painting, music and writing etc., considered together

**as** ADVERB
used in making a comparison • *I got dressed as quickly as I could.*

**as** PREPOSITION
in the function or role of • *Use it as a handle.*

**as** CONJUNCTION
❶ when or while • *She slipped as she got off the bus.* ❷ because • *As he was late, we missed the train.* ❸ in a way that • *Leave it as it is.*
➤ **as for** with regard to • *As for you, I despise you.*
➤ **as it were** in a way • *She became, as it were, her own enemy.*
➤ **as well** also

**asbestos** NOUN
a fireproof material made up of fine soft fibres

**Asbo** (say **az**-boh) ABBREVIATION
anti-social behaviour order

**ascend** VERB ascends, ascending, ascended
to go up to a higher point • *He slowly*

37

ascended a steep staircase. • The eagle
ascended higher and higher.
➤ **ascend the throne** to become king or
queen

**ascendancy** NOUN
being in control over other people • They
gained ascendancy over others.

**ascending** ADJECTIVE
going up from the lowest to the highest
• Here are the scores for each team, in
ascending order.

**ascension** NOUN
the process of going up

**ascent** NOUN ascents
❶ the process of going up; a climb • Nobody
spoke as the lift began its ascent. ❷ a way
up; an upward path or slope • The ascent is
very steep.

**ascertain** (say as-er-**tayn**) VERB ascertains,
ascertaining, ascertained
to find something out • We are trying to
ascertain the extent of the damage.

**ascetic** (say a-**set**-ik) ADJECTIVE
not allowing yourself pleasure and luxuries
• an ascetic life
➤ **asceticism** NOUN

**ascetic** NOUN ascetics
a person who leads an ascetic life, often for
religious reasons

**ascribe** VERB ascribes, ascribing, ascribed
to ascribe an event or situation to something
is to regard that thing as the cause or source
• She ascribes her success to good luck.

**asexual** ADJECTIVE (in biology)
by other than sexual methods • asexual
reproduction

**ash** NOUN ashes
❶ the powder that is left after something has
been burned ❷ a tree with silver-grey bark
➤ **ashy** ADJECTIVE

**ashamed** ADJECTIVE
feeling shame • You ought to be ashamed of
yourself.

**ashen** ADJECTIVE
grey or pale • Her face was ashen.

**ashore** ADVERB
to or on the shore • The girls jumped ashore.

**ashtray** NOUN ashtrays
a small bowl for putting cigarette ash in

**Asian** ADJECTIVE
to do with Asia or its people

**Asian** NOUN Asians
an Asian person

**Asiatic** ADJECTIVE
to do with Asia

**aside** ADVERB
❶ to or at one side • He moved aside to let
her pass. ❷ to put something aside is to keep
it in case you need it later

**aside** NOUN asides
words spoken so that only certain people will
hear

**ask** VERB asks, asking, asked
❶ to speak so as to find out or get something
❷ to ask for something is to say that you
want it ❸ to ask someone to something is to
invite them • Ask her to the party.

**askance** (say a-**skanss**) ADVERB
➤ **look askance at** to regard a person or
situation with distrust or disapproval

**askew** ADVERB & ADJECTIVE
crooked; not straight or level • His wig
seemed to be slightly askew.

**asleep** ADVERB & ADJECTIVE
sleeping

**AS level** NOUN AS levels
(in the UK except Scotland) an exam in a
subject that represents the first part of an
A level qualification; short for Advanced
Subsidiary Level

**asp** NOUN asps
a small poisonous snake

**asparagus** NOUN
a plant whose young shoots are eaten as a
vegetable

**aspect** NOUN aspects
❶ one part of a problem or situation
• The writer covers most aspects of life
on a submarine. ❷ a person's or thing's
appearance • The chief was an elderly man of
noble aspect.

**aspen** NOUN aspens
a tree with leaves that move in the slightest
wind

**asperity** NOUN
harshness or severity

**aspersions** PLURAL NOUN
➤ **cast aspersions on somebody** to attack
his or her reputation or integrity

**WORD ORIGIN** from *asperse* = spatter (with water or mud), from Latin *spergere* = sprinkle

**asphalt** (say ass-falt) *NOUN*
a sticky black substance like tar, often mixed with gravel to make a surface for roads, etc.

**asphyxia** (say ass-fiks-ee-a) *NOUN*
a condition in which the body does not take in enough oxygen, causing unconsciousness or death

**asphyxiate** (say ass-fiks-ee-ayt) *VERB* asphyxiates, asphyxiating, asphyxiated
to suffocate someone

**aspic** *NOUN*
a savoury jelly used for coating meats, eggs, etc.

**aspidistra** *NOUN* aspidistras
a house plant with broad leaves

**aspirant** (say asp-er-ant) *NOUN* aspirants
a person who tries to achieve something
• *young aspirants for glory*

**aspirate** (say asp-er-at) *NOUN* aspirates
the sound of 'h'

**aspiration** *NOUN* aspirations
ambition; strong desire • *She had aspirations to become an actress.*

**aspire** *VERB* aspires, aspiring, aspired
to have an ambition to achieve something
• *He aspired to be a writer.*

**aspirin** *NOUN* aspirins
a medicinal drug used to relieve pain or reduce fever

**ass** *NOUN* asses
❶ a donkey ❷ (*informal*) a stupid person

**assailant** *NOUN* assailants
a person who attacks someone

**assassin** *NOUN* assassins
a person who assassinates someone
**WORD ORIGIN** from Arabic *hashishi* = hashish-takers, used as a name for a group of Muslims at the time of the Crusades, who were popularly believed to take hashish (= the drug cannabis) before going out on killing missions

**assassinate** *VERB* assassinates, assassinating, assassinated
to kill an important person deliberately and violently, especially for political reasons
➤ **assassination** *NOUN*

**assault** *NOUN* assaults
a violent or illegal attack

**assault** *VERB* assaults, assaulting, assaulted
to assault someone is to attack them violently

**assegai** (say ass-ig-y) *NOUN* assegais
an iron-tipped spear used by South African peoples

**assemble** *VERB* assembles, assembling, assembled
❶ to assemble something is to fit the separate parts of it together • *The machine is now ready to be assembled.* ❷ to assemble is to come together in one place • *The whole school assembled in the gym.* ❸ to assemble people or things is to bring them together in one place • *The gallery has assembled more than 200 of the painter's finest works.*

**assembly** *NOUN* assemblies
❶ an assembly is a regular meeting, such as when everyone in a school meets together
• *At the end of assembly, the children streamed out of the hall.* ❷ an assembly is also a group of people who regularly meet for a special purpose; a parliament • *Parliaments are law-making assemblies.* ❸ assembly is putting the parts of something together to make it • *The bookcase is now ready for assembly.*

**assembly line** *NOUN* assembly lines
a series of workers and machines along which a product passes to be assembled part by part

**assent** *NOUN*
assent is agreement or permission to do something • *There were murmurs of assent.*

**assent** *VERB* assents, assenting, assented
If you assent to something, you say you agree or give your permission. • *'All right', he assented*

**SPELLING**
Do not forget the double s in assent.

**assert** *VERB* asserts, asserting, asserted
to state something firmly • *He asserted he was attacked by three men.*
➤ **assert yourself** to behave in a confident and forceful way

**assertion** *NOUN* assertions
a statement that you make confidently

**assertive** *ADJECTIVE*
acting forcefully and with confidence

**assess** *VERB* assesses, assessing, assessed
to decide or estimate the value or quality of a person or thing • *People came out of their houses to assess the damage.*
➤ **assessor** *NOUN*

**assessment** NOUN assessments
an opinion about the value or quality of a person or thing • *We have swimming assessment in the evening.*

**asset** NOUN assets
something useful or valuable to someone • *He's a great asset to the team.*

**assets** PLURAL NOUN
a person's or company's property that they could sell to pay debts or raise money

**assign** VERB assigns, assigning, assigned
❶ to give a task or duty to someone • *She assigned each of us a job to do.* ❷ to appoint a person to perform a task • *A guard had been assigned to watch her.*

**assignment** NOUN assignments
a piece of work or task given to someone • *This was his most dangerous assignment yet.*

**assimilate** VERB assimilates, assimilating, assimilated
to take in and absorb something, e.g. nourishment into the body or knowledge into the mind • *Maggie had a gift for assimilating knowledge.*

**assist** VERB assists, assisting, assisted
to help someone, usually in a practical way • *The chefs were assisted by four waitresses.*

**assistance** NOUN
help someone gets when they need information or support • *Fortunately, a passer-by came to her assistance.*

**assistant** NOUN assistants
❶ a person whose job is to help another person in their work ❷ a person who serves customers in a shop

**assistant** ADJECTIVE
helping a person and ranking next below him or her • *the assistant manager*

**associate** (say a-**soh**-si-ayt) VERB associates, associating, associated
❶ to associate one thing with another is to connect them in your mind • *In some countries, black is often associated with bad luck and death.* ❷ to associate with a group of people is to spend time or have dealings with them • *I'm not sure we ought to associate with them.*

**associate** (say a-**soh**-si-at) NOUN associates
a colleague or companion

**association** NOUN associations
❶ an organization for people sharing an interest or doing the same work
❷ a connection or link in your mind • *This place has strange associations for me.*
❸ being friendly with or working with someone • *Depp has had a long association with the film director Tim Burton.*

**Association football** NOUN
(*British*) the game usually known as football, which uses a round ball that may not be handled during play except by the goalkeeper

**assonance** (say **ass**-on-ans) NOUN
a close similarity of the vowel sounds in two or more words, e.g. in **sonnet** and **porridge**

**assorted** ADJECTIVE
of various kinds put together; mixed and different • *assorted sweets*

**assortment** NOUN assortments
a mixed collection of things

**assuage** (say a-**swayj**) VERB assuages, assuaging, assuaged
to assuage a strong or uncomfortable feeling is to reduce it • *She ate some berries to assuage the pangs of hunger.*

**assume** VERB assumes, assuming, assumed
❶ to accept without proof that something is true or sure to happen • *Let's assume you are right.* ❷ to assume a particular manner or expression is to show it or put it on • *Rick assumed an air of wide-eyed innocence.* ❸ to assume a burden or responsibility is to agree to take it on • *This is my fault and I assume full responsibility for it.*
➤ **assumed name** a false name that someone uses for a special purpose

**assumption** NOUN assumptions
something that you accept without proof that it is true or sure to happen

**assurance** NOUN assurances
❶ a promise or guarantee that something is true or will happen • *We gave him our assurances that we would be on time.*
❷ confidence in yourself • *Tom spoke with such assurance that Mr Swift believed him.*

**assure** VERB assures, assuring, assured
❶ to tell someone something confidently • *I haven't mentioned it to anyone, I assure you.* ❷ to make something certain to happen • *Their future was assured.*

**aster** NOUN asters
a garden plant with daisy-like flowers in various colours

**asterisk** NOUN asterisks
a star-shaped sign * used to draw attention
to something (WORD ORIGIN) from Greek
*asteriskos* = little star

**astern** ADVERB
❶ at the back of a ship or aircraft • *The boat
was now directly astern.*

**asteroid** NOUN asteroids
one of the small planets found mainly
between the orbits of Mars and Jupiter

**asthma** (say **ass**-ma) NOUN
a disease that makes breathing difficult

**asthmatic** ADJECTIVE
suffering from asthma

**asthmatic** NOUN asthmatics
a person who suffers from asthma

**astonish** VERB astonishes, astonishing,
astonished
to surprise somebody greatly • *They were
astonished to see him at the door.*

**astonishment** NOUN
a feeling of great surprise • *She looked at him
in astonishment.*

**astound** VERB astounds, astounding,
astounded
to astonish or shock someone greatly • *What
she saw astounded her.*

**astray** ADVERB & ADJECTIVE
➤ **go astray** to be lost or mislaid
➤ **lead someone astray** to make someone do
something wrong

**astride** ADVERB & PREPOSITION
with one leg on each side of something • *The
knight sat astride a black stallion.*

**astrology** NOUN
the study of the position and movements
of stars and planets in the belief that they
influence people's lives
➤ **astrologer** NOUN
➤ **astrological** ADJECTIVE

**astronaut** NOUN astronauts
a person who travels in a spacecraft
(WORD ORIGIN) from Greek *astron* = star +
*nautes* = sailor

**astronomical** ADJECTIVE
❶ to do with astronomy • *astronomical
observations* ❷ extremely large • *an
astronomical phone bill*

**astronomy** NOUN
the study of the stars and planets and their

movements
➤ **astronomer** NOUN

**astute** ADJECTIVE
clever and good at understanding situations
quickly; shrewd
➤ **astutely** ADVERB
➤ **astuteness** NOUN

**asunder** ADVERB (literary)
apart; into pieces • *He felt his heart had been
torn asunder.*

**asylum** NOUN asylums
❶ refuge and safety offered by one country
to political refugees from another • *The main
character is a young woman who is seeking
asylum in the UK.* ❷ (old use) an institution
for the care of mentally ill people

**asymmetrical** (say ay-sim-**et**-rik-al) ADJECTIVE
not symmetrical • *The vase has an
asymmetrical shape.*

**at** PREPOSITION
This word is used to show
❶ position or location (*I was at the hospital.*),
❷ time (*at midnight*), ❸ direction towards
something (*Aim at the target.*), ❹ cost or
level (*Water boils at 100°C.*), ❺ cause (*We
were annoyed at the delay.*)
➤ **at all** in any way
➤ **at it** doing or working at something
➤ **at once** ❶ immediately ❷ at the same
time • *It all came out at once.*

**atheist** (say **ayth**-ee-ist) NOUN atheists
a person who believes that there is no God
➤ **atheism** NOUN

**athlete** NOUN athletes
a person who is good at sport, especially
athletics

**athletic** ADJECTIVE
❶ physically fit and active; good at sports
❷ to do with athletics
➤ **athletically** ADVERB

**athletics** PLURAL NOUN
physical exercises and sports, e.g. running,
jumping and throwing

**atlas** NOUN atlases
a book of maps (WORD ORIGIN) named after
Atlas, a giant in Greek mythology, who was
made to support the universe on his shoulders.
His picture was put in the front of early atlases.

**atmosphere** NOUN atmospheres
❶ the air around the earth ❷ a feeling or
mood given by surroundings • *Suddenly the
atmosphere in the room changed.* ❸ a unit

of pressure, equal to the pressure of the
atmosphere at sea level

**atmospheric** ADJECTIVE
❶ to do with the earth's atmosphere
❷ having a strong atmosphere • *an
atmospheric building*

**atoll** NOUN atolls
a ring-shaped coral reef

**atom** NOUN atoms
the smallest particle of a chemical element
**WORD ORIGIN** from Greek *atomos* = unable to
be divided

**atom bomb, atomic bomb** NOUN atom
bombs, atomic bombs
a bomb using atomic energy

**atomic** ADJECTIVE
❶ to do with an atom or atoms ❷ to do with
atomic energy or atom bombs

**atomic energy** NOUN
energy created by splitting the nuclei of
certain atoms

**atomic number** NOUN atomic numbers
(*in science*) the number of protons in the
nucleus of the atom of a chemical element

**atomizer** (also **atomiser**) NOUN atomizers
a device for making a liquid into a fine spray

**atone** VERB atones, atoning, atoned
to make amends; to make up for having done
something wrong • *He promised to atone for
his stupidity.*
➤ **atonement** NOUN
**WORD ORIGIN** from *at one*, because people
who make amends are 'at one' (= on good terms
again) with those they have wronged

**atrocious** (say a-**troh**-shus) ADJECTIVE
extremely bad or wicked • *atrocious weather*
➤ **atrociously** ADVERB

**atrocity** (say a-**tross**-it-ee) NOUN atrocities
an extremely bad or wicked thing that
someone does, such as killing a large number
of people

**attach** VERB attaches, attaching, attached
❶ to fix or join one thing to something else
❷ to attach importance or significance to
something is to believe that it is important
or worth thinking about • *The newspapers
attached great importance to these rumours.*
➤ **attached** to be attached to someone or
something is to be very fond of them

SPELLING

There is no t before the ch in attach. Do
not forget the double t at the beginning.

**attaché** (say a-**tash**-ay) NOUN attachés
a special assistant to an ambassador • *our
military attaché*

**attaché case** NOUN attaché cases
a small case in which documents etc. may be
carried

**attachment** NOUN attachments
❶ an extra part to add to a piece if
equipment for a special purpose • *The garden
hose has an attachment for washing cars.*
❷ a file or piece of software sent with an
email ❸ fondness or friendship • *She formed
a strong attachment to my sisters.*

**attack** NOUN attacks
❶ a violent attempt to hurt or overcome
someone ❷ a piece of strong criticism ❸ a
sudden illness or pain ❹ the players in a team
whose job is to score goals; an attempt to
score a goal

**attack** VERB attacks, attacking, attacked
to act violently against someone or to start a
fight with them
➤ **attacker** NOUN

**attain** VERB attains, attaining, attained
to succeed in doing or getting something
• *This is the highest speed ever attained on
the sea.*

**attainment** NOUN attainments
something you have achieved

**attempt** VERB attempts, attempting,
attempted
to make an effort to do something

**attempt** NOUN attempts
an effort to do something; a try

**attend** VERB attends, attending, attended
❶ to attend something like a meeting or a
wedding is to be there ❷ to attend school or
college is to be a pupil or student there ❸ to
attend to someone is to look after them ❹ to
attend to something is to spend time dealing
with it • *Excuse me, I have some business to
attend to.*

**attendance** NOUN attendances
❶ attendance is being present at a place
• *Attendance at these classes is not
compulsory.* ❷ the number of people present
at an event • *It was the club's highest
attendance of the season.*

**attendant** NOUN attendants
a person who helps or goes with someone
else

**attention** NOUN
❶ watching, listening to or thinking about someone or something carefully • *Pay attention to what I'm saying.* • *She grabbed his arm to get his attention.* ❷ a position in which a soldier stands with feet together and arms straight downwards

**attentive** ADJECTIVE
giving your attention to something • *She smiled at the circle of attentive faces.*
➤ **attentively** ADVERB
➤ **attentiveness** NOUN

**attest** VERB attests, attesting, attested
to declare or prove that something is true or genuine • *His skill and bravery during the battle are well attested.*

**attic** NOUN attics
a room in the roof of a house

**attire** NOUN (formal)
a person's clothes • *She cast a doubtful look at my attire.*

**attire** VERB attires, attiring, attired (formal)
to be attired in particular clothes is to be wearing them • *He was attired in an elegant blue suit.*

**attitude** NOUN attitudes
❶ the way you think or feel about something and the way you behave ❷ the position of the body or its parts; posture

**attorney** NOUN attorneys
❶ a person who is appointed to act on behalf of another in business matters ❷ (North American) a lawyer

**attract** VERB attracts, attracting, attracted
❶ to get someone's attention or interest; to seem pleasant to someone • *A slight noise attracted my attention.* ❷ to make something come • *Moths are attracted to light.* ❸ to pull something by means of a physical force • *A magnet attracts many metal objects.*

**attraction** NOUN attractions
❶ the process of attracting or the ability to attract • *I can't see the attraction of living in the countryside.* ❷ something that attracts visitors • *The Eiffel Tower is one of Paris's main tourist attractions.*

**attractive** ADJECTIVE
❶ pleasant or good-looking ❷ interesting or appealing • *It was an attractive idea.*
➤ **attractively** ADVERB
➤ **attractiveness** NOUN

**attribute** (say a-**trib**-yoot) VERB attributes, attributing, attributed
to believe that something belongs to or is caused by a particular person or thing • *She attributes her perfect health to her diet.*

**attribute** (say **at**-rib-yoot) NOUN attributes
a quality or characteristic • *A sense of compassion is one of his finest attributes.*

**attrition** (say a-**trish**-on) NOUN
gradually wearing down an enemy by repeatedly attacking them • *a war of attrition*

**attuned** ADJECTIVE
familiar with and used to something • *My eyes were now attuned to the darkness.*

**aubergine** (say **oh**-ber-zheen) NOUN aubergines
(British) a deep-purple vegetable with thick flesh

**auburn** ADJECTIVE
auburn hair is reddish-brown

**auction** NOUN auctions
a public sale where things are sold to the person who offers the most money for them

**auction** VERB auctions, auctioning, auctioned
to sell something in an auction • *The fan who grabbed the ball auctioned it on a website.*

**auctioneer** NOUN auctioneers
an official in charge of an auction

**audacious** (say aw-**day**-shus) ADJECTIVE
bold or daring • *It was an audacious plan.*
➤ **audaciously** ADVERB

**audacity** NOUN
the confidence to do something daring or shocking • *The sheer audacity of the idea took my breath away.*

**audible** ADJECTIVE
loud enough to be heard • *Her voice was barely audible now.*
➤ **audibly** ADVERB

**audience** NOUN audiences
❶ the people who have come to hear or watch a performance ❷ a formal interview with an important person

**audio** NOUN
reproduced sounds • *You can listen to audio clips on the website.*

**audio–visual** ADJECTIVE
using both sound and pictures to give information

**audit** NOUN audits
an official examination of a company's
financial accounts to see that they are correct

**audit** VERB audits, auditing, audited
to make an audit of accounts
➤ **auditor** NOUN

**audition** NOUN auditions
a test to see if an actor or musician is suitable
for a job

**audition** VERB audition, auditioning,
auditioned
to have or give someone an audition • *I had
to audition to get the part.*

**auditorium** NOUN auditoriums
the part of a theatre or hall where the
audience sits

**augment** VERB augments, augmenting,
augmented
to increase or add to something • *Kathy got
a job in a shop to augment the family
income.*

**augur** (say **awg**-er) VERB augurs, auguring,
augured
to augur well or augur badly is to be a good
sign or a bad sign • *He glared at me in a way
that did not augur well.*

**August** NOUN
the eighth month of the year
**WORD ORIGIN** named after *Augustus* Caesar,
the first Roman emperor

**august** (say aw-**gust**) ADJECTIVE
majestic or impressive

**auk** NOUN auks
a kind of seabird

**aunt** NOUN aunts
the sister of your father or mother or your
uncle's wife

**auntie, aunty** NOUN aunties
(*informal*) aunt

**au pair** (say oh **pair**) NOUN au pairs
a person from abroad, usually a young
woman, who works for a time in a family's
home, helping to look after the children
**WORD ORIGIN** from a French phrase
meaning 'on equal terms'

**aura** (say **or**-a) NOUN auras
a general feeling surrounding a person
or thing • *An aura of mystery surrounds
her.*

**aural** (say **or**-al) ADJECTIVE
to do with the ear or hearing
**WORD ORIGIN** from Latin *auris* = ear

**SPELLING**

> Take care not to confuse with oral, which
> means to do with or using your mouth.

**au revoir** (say oh rev-**wahr**) EXCLAMATION
goodbye for the moment
**WORD ORIGIN** French, literally = to the seeing
again

**aurora** (say aw-**raw**-ra) NOUN auroras
bands of coloured light appearing in the sky
at night, the **aurora borealis** (say bor-ee-**ay**-
liss)
in the northern hemisphere and the **aurora
australis** (say aw-**stray**-liss)
in the southern hemisphere

**auspices** (say **aw**-spiss-eez) PLURAL NOUN
➤ **under the auspices of** someone with the
help, support or protection of an organization
• *The clinic was set up under the auspices of
the Red Cross.*
**WORD ORIGIN** originally = omens; later =
influence, protection; same origin as **auspicious**

**auspicious** (say aw-**spish**-us) ADJECTIVE
showing signs that something is likely
to be successful in the future • *It was
an auspicious start to her acting career.*
**WORD ORIGIN** from Latin *auspicium* = telling
the future from the behaviour of birds, from
*avis* = bird

**austere** (say aw-**steer**) ADJECTIVE
❶ very simple and plain; without luxuries
❷ an austere person is very strict and serious

**austerity** NOUN
❶ a plain or simple way of living, without
much comfort or luxury ❷ a time when
people do not have much money to spend
because there are bad economic conditions

**authentic** ADJECTIVE
genuine or true • *an authentic signature*

**authenticate** VERB authenticates,
authenticating, authenticated
to confirm something as being authentic
➤ **authentication** NOUN

**authenticity** NOUN
authenticity is being genuine or true • *There's
no doubt about the authenticity of the letter.*

**author** NOUN authors
the writer of a book, play, poem, etc.
➤ **authorship** NOUN

**authoritarian** ADJECTIVE
believing that people should be completely

obedient to those in authority

**authoritative** *ADJECTIVE*
having proper authority or expert knowledge
• *He sounded quietly authoritative.*

**authority** *NOUN* authorities
❶ authority is the right or power to give orders to other people ❷ an authority is a person or organization with the right to give orders ❸ an authority on a subject is a person or book that gives reliable information about it • *an authority on spiders*

**authorize** (also **authorise**) *VERB* authorizes, authorizing, authorized
to give official permission for something
➤ authorization *NOUN*

**autistic** (say aw-**tist**-ik) *ADJECTIVE*
having a mental condition that makes it difficult for someone to communicate with other people
➤ autism *NOUN*

**auto** *NOUN* autos (*informal esp. North American*)
a car • *the auto industry*

**autobiography** *NOUN* autobiographies
the story of a person's life written by himself or herself
➤ autobiographical *ADJECTIVE*

**autocracy** (say aw-**tok**-ra-see) *NOUN*
autocracies
rule by one person who has total and unlimited power

**autocrat** *NOUN* autocrats
a ruler with total and unlimited power
➤ autocratic *ADJECTIVE*

**autocue** *NOUN* autocues (*trade mark*)
(*British*) a device that displays the script for a television presenter or public speaker to read

**autograph** *NOUN* autographs
the signature of a famous person

**automate** *VERB* automates, automating, automated
to make something work by an automatic process • *The assembly system is now fully automated.*

**automatic** *ADJECTIVE*
❶ working on its own without continuous attention or control by people • *automatic doors* ❷ done without thinking • *After all their rehearsing, their actions were automatic.*

**automatically** *ADVERB*
❶ by automatic means; without having to use controls all the time • *The door opened automatically.* ❷ without thinking
• *He automatically reached for his sword.*

**automation** *NOUN*
making processes automatic; using machines instead of people to do jobs

**automaton** (say aw-**tom**-at-on) *NOUN*
automatons
❶ a robot ❷ a person who seems to act mechanically without thinking

**automobile** *NOUN* automobiles
(*North American*) a car

**autonomy** (say aw-**ton**-om-ee) *NOUN*
❶ self-government ❷ the right to act independently without being told what to do
➤ autonomous *ADJECTIVE*

**autopsy** (say **aw**-top-see) *NOUN* autopsies
an examination of a dead body to find out the cause of death; a post-mortem
**WORD ORIGIN** from Greek *autopsia* = seeing with your own eyes

**autumn** *NOUN* autumns
the season between summer and winter
**SPELLING**
There is a silent n in autumn.

**autumnal** *ADJECTIVE*
in autumn; to do with autumn • *autumnal colours*

**auxiliary** *ADJECTIVE*
giving help and support • *auxiliary services*

**auxiliary** *NOUN* auxiliaries
a person who gives help and support

**auxiliary verb** *NOUN* auxiliary verbs
a verb such as *do*, *have* and *will*, which is used to form parts of other verbs, e.g. *have* in *I have finished.*
**GRAMMAR**
See also the panels on **be**, **do**, and **have**.

**avail** *NOUN*
➤ to or of no avail of no use; without success • *Their pleas for mercy were all to no avail.*

**avail** *VERB* avails, availing, availed
➤ avail yourself of to make use of something • *He gladly availed himself of their hospitality.*

**available** *ADJECTIVE*
able to be found or used • *These sweatshirts are available in a range of colours.*
➤ availability *NOUN*

**avalanche** NOUN avalanches
a mass of snow or rock falling down the side of a mountain

**avant-garde** (say av-ahn-**gard**) NOUN
people who use a very modern style in art or literature etc.
➤ **avant-garde** ADJECTIVE

**avarice** (say av-er-iss) NOUN
greed for money or possessions
➤ **avaricious** ADJECTIVE

**avenge** VERB avenges, avenging, avenged
to punish someone for something they have done to harm you or your family • *He vowed to avenge the death of his father.*
➤ **avenger** NOUN

**avenue** NOUN avenues
❶ a wide street ❷ a road with trees along both sides

**average** NOUN averages
❶ the value obtained by adding several quantities together and dividing by the number of quantities ❷ the usual or ordinary standard

**average** ADJECTIVE
❶ worked out as an average • *Their average age is ten.* ❷ of the usual or ordinary standard

**average** VERB averages, averaging, averaged
to work out, produce or amount to as an average • *The rainfall averages more than 2500mm a year.*

**averse** (say a-**vers**) ADJECTIVE
unwilling to do something or opposed to something • *I'm not averse to a bit of hard work.*

**aversion** NOUN
a strong dislike • *She had an aversion to water and soap.*

**avert** VERB averts, averting, averted
❶ to turn something away • *As he answered, he blushed and averted his eyes.* ❷ to prevent something • *We realized we had only seconds to avert a disaster.*

**aviary** NOUN aviaries
a large cage or building for keeping birds

**aviation** NOUN
the flying of aircraft (WORD ORIGIN) from Latin *avis* = bird

**aviator** NOUN aviators (*old use*)
a person who flies an aircraft

**avid** (say av-id) ADJECTIVE
keen or eager • *an avid reader*
➤ **avidly** ADVERB

**avocado** (say av-ok-ah-doh) NOUN avocados
a pear-shaped tropical fruit

**avoid** VERB avoids, avoiding, avoided
❶ to avoid a person or place is to stay away from them ❷ to avoid doing something is to make sure you do not do it • *Emily tried to avoid getting involved in the argument.*
➤ **avoidance** NOUN

**avuncular** ADJECTIVE
kind and friendly towards someone younger, like an uncle

**await** VERB awaits, awaiting, awaited
to wait for someone to come or something to happen • *His friends were anxiously awaiting his return.*

**awake** ADJECTIVE
not asleep • *She lay awake for a long time.*

**awake** VERB awakes, awaking, awoke, awoken
to wake up • *Jack awoke to the sound of birdsong.*

**awaken** VERB awakens, awakening, awakened
❶ to wake up or to make someone wake up • *He was awakened by someone shouting.* ❷ to produce a feeling in someone • *The letter awakened her curiosity.*
➤ **awakening** NOUN

**award** VERB awards, awarding, awarded
to give something officially as a prize, payment or penalty • *De Klerk and Mandela were awarded the Nobel Peace Prize in 1993.*

**award** NOUN awards
something awarded, such as a prize or a sum of money

**aware** ADJECTIVE
knowing or realizing something • *Were you aware of the danger?*
➤ **awareness** NOUN

**awash** ADJECTIVE
with waves or water flooding over it • *Her face was awash with tears.*

**away** ADVERB
❶ to or at a distance; not at the usual place • *Go away and leave me alone.* ❷ until disappearing completely • *The noise gradually died away.* ❸ continuously or persistently • *We worked away at it for days.*

**away** ADJECTIVE
played on an opponent's ground • *an away match*

**awe** NOUN
1 a feeling of great wonder and perhaps slight fear • *I looked up at the starry sky with awe.* 2 to be in awe of someone is to respect and admire them a lot
➤ **awed** ADJECTIVE
➤ **awestricken** ADJECTIVE
➤ **awestruck** ADJECTIVE

**awe-inspiring** ADJECTIVE
causing a feeling of great wonder and admiration

**awesome** ADJECTIVE
1 very impressive and perhaps slightly frightening • *The mountains were an awesome sight.* 2 (*informal*) excellent

**awful** ADJECTIVE
1 very bad • *an awful accident* 2 (*informal*) very great • *That's an awful lot of money.*

**awfully** ADVERB
(*informal*) very, extremely • *I'm awfully sorry.*

**awhile** ADVERB
for a short time

**awkward** ADJECTIVE
1 difficult to use or deal with; not convenient • *The box isn't heavy, but it's awkward to carry.* 2 embarrassed and not at ease • *I often feel awkward in a group of people.* 3 clumsy or uncomfortable • *She has been sleeping in an awkward position.*
➤ **awkwardly** ADVERB
➤ **awkwardness** NOUN

**awl** NOUN awls
a small pointed tool for making holes in leather, wood, etc.

**awning** NOUN awnings
a roof-like shelter made of canvas etc.

**awry** ADVERB & ADJECTIVE
1 twisted to one side; crooked 2 wrong; not according to plan. • *Our plans have gone awry.*

**axe** NOUN axes
1 a tool for chopping things 2 (*informal*) a person or organization faces the axe when they are about to be made redundant or closed • *A number of workers face the axe.*
➤ **have an axe to grind** to have a personal reason for being involved in something

**axe** VERB axes, axing, axed
to cancel or abolish something

**axiom** NOUN axioms
an established general truth or principle

**axis** NOUN axes
1 a line through the centre of a spinning object 2 a line dividing a thing in half 3 the horizontal or vertical line on a graph

**axle** NOUN axles
the rod through the centre of a wheel, on which the wheel turns

**ayatollah** (say eye-a-**tol**-a) NOUN ayatollahs
a Muslim religious leader in Iran

**aye** (rhymes with by) ADVERB
(*dialect or old use*) yes

**azalea** (say a-**zay**-lee-a) NOUN azaleas
a kind of flowering shrub

**azure** ADJECTIVE
sky-blue

**baa** NOUN baas
the cry of a sheep or lamb

**babble** VERB babbles, babbling, babbled
1 to talk very quickly without making sense • *What are you babbling on about?* 2 to make a gentle bubbling sound • *a babbling stream*
➤ **babble** NOUN

**babe** NOUN babes
(*old use*) a baby

**baboon** NOUN baboons
a kind of large monkey from Africa and Asia, with a long muzzle and short tail

**baby** NOUN babies
a very young child or animal
**WORD ORIGIN** probably from the sounds a baby makes when it first tries to speak

**babyish** ADJECTIVE
like a baby or suitable for a baby • *She is too old for such babyish toys.*

**babysit** VERB babysits, babysitting, babysat
to look after a child while its parents are out

**babysitter** NOUN babysitters
someone who looks after a child while its parents are out

**bachelor** NOUN bachelors
a man who has not married

a
b
c
d
e
f
g
h
i
j
k
l
m
n
o
p
q
r
s
t
u
v
w
x
y
z

➤ **Bachelor of Arts or Science** a person who has taken a first degree in arts or science

**bacillus** (say ba-**sil**-us) NOUN bacilli
a rod-shaped bacterium

**back** NOUN backs
❶ the part that is furthest from the front
❷ the back part of a person's or animal's body, from the shoulders to the base of the spine ❸ the back part of a chair etc. that your back rests against ❹ a defending player near the goal in football, hockey, etc.

**back** ADJECTIVE
❶ placed at or near the back • *Let's sit in the back row.* ❷ to do with the back • *back pain*

**back** ADVERB
❶ to or towards the back ❷ to the place you have come from • *Go back home.* ❸ to an earlier time or position • *Think back to when you were little.*

**back** VERB backs, backing, backed
❶ to move backwards or drive a vehicle backwards ❷ to give someone support or help ❸ to bet on something ❹ to cover the back of something • *Back the rug with canvas.*
➤ **back down** to admit that you were wrong about something
➤ **back out** to refuse to do what you agreed to do
➤ **back someone up** to give someone support or help
➤ **back something up** (*in computing*) to make a spare copy of a file, disk, etc. to be stored in safety separately from the original

**backbencher** NOUN backbenchers
a Member of Parliament who does not hold an important position

**backbiting** NOUN
unkind or nasty things said about someone who is not there

**backbone** NOUN backbones
❶ the column of small bones down the centre of the back; the spine ❷ strength of character; courage • *Show some backbone, girl.*

**backdrop** NOUN backdrops
a large painted cloth that is hung across the back of a stage

**backer** NOUN backers
someone who supports a project or plan by providing money

**backfire** VERB backfires, backfiring, backfired
❶ if a car backfires, it makes a loud noise,

caused by an explosion in the exhaust pipe
❷ if a plan backfires, it goes wrong

**backgammon** NOUN
a game played on a board with draughts and dice

**background** NOUN backgrounds
❶ the back part of a picture, scene or view
❷ all the things that help to explain why an event or situation happened • *I am reading about the background to the American Civil War.* ❸ a person's family, upbringing and education
➤ **in the background** not noticeable or obvious • *I could hear voices in the background.*

**backhand** NOUN backhands
a stroke made in tennis etc. with the back of the hand turned outwards
➤ **backhanded** ADJECTIVE

**backing** NOUN
❶ support or help ❷ material that is used to line the back of something ❸ music that is played or sung to support the main singer or tune

**backlash** NOUN backlashes
a strong and angry reaction to an event

**backlog** NOUN backlogs
an amount of work that should have been finished but is still waiting to be done

**backpack** NOUN backpacks
a bag with straps for carrying on your back; a rucksack

**backpacking** NOUN
travelling or hiking with your belongings in a rucksack
➤ **backpacker** NOUN

**backside** NOUN backsides (*informal*)
your backside is your bottom

**backstage** ADVERB
in or towards the parts of a theatre behind the stage • *We went backstage to meet the cast.*

**backstroke** NOUN
a way of swimming lying on your back

**back-up** NOUN back-ups
(*in computing*) a spare copy of a file, disk, etc. stored in safety separately from the original

**backward** ADJECTIVE
❶ facing or moving towards the back • *She walked off without a backward glance.*

❷ having not developed at the expected rate
➤ **backwardness** NOUN

**backward** ADVERB
backwards

> USAGE
>
> The adverb **backward** is mainly used in American English.

**backwards** ADVERB
❶ to or towards the back ❷ with the back end going first ❸ in reverse order • *Count backwards from 10.*
➤ **backwards and forwards** in each direction alternately; to and fro

**backwater** NOUN backwaters
❶ a branch of a river that comes to a dead end with stagnant water ❷ a quiet place that is not affected by progress or new ideas

**backyard** NOUN backyards
❶ an open area with a hard surface behind a house ❷ (*North American*) a back garden

**bacon** NOUN
smoked or salted meat from the back or sides of a pig

**bacterium** NOUN bacteria
a microscopic organism that can cause disease
➤ **bacterial** ADJECTIVE

> USAGE
>
> Take care not to use the plural form **bacteria** as if it were the singular. It is incorrect to say 'a bacteria' or 'this bacteria'; correct usage is *this bacterium* or *these bacteria*.

**bad** ADJECTIVE worse, worst
❶ of poor quality; not good ❷ not able to do something very well • *I've always been bad at sport.* ❸ serious or unpleasant • *a bad accident* • *I've got some bad news.* ❹ ill or unhealthy • *Sweets are bad for your teeth.* ❺ decayed or rotten • *This meat has gone bad.* ❻ wicked or evil
➤ **not bad** quite good
➤ **badness** NOUN

**baddy** NOUN baddies (*informal*)
an evil or wicked character in a story

**bade**
old past tense of **bid**

**badge** NOUN badges
a button or sign that you wear to show people who you are, what school or club you belong to or what kind of thing you like

**badger** NOUN badgers
a grey animal with a black and white head, which lives underground and is active at night

**badger** VERB badgers, badgering, badgered
to keep asking someone to do something; to pester someone about something • *She's been badgering me to get tickets for the concert.* WORD ORIGIN perhaps from **badge** (because of the markings on a badger's head)

**badly** ADVERB worse, worst
❶ in a bad way; not well • *I did badly in my exams.* ❷ severely; causing serious injury • *He was badly wounded.* ❸ very much • *She badly wanted to win.*

**badminton** NOUN
a game in which players use rackets to hit a light object called a shuttlecock across a high net

**bad-tempered** ADJECTIVE
always angry and in a bad mood

**baffle** VERB baffles, baffling, baffled
to puzzle or confuse someone • *The instructions baffled me completely.*
➤ **baffled** ADJECTIVE
➤ **baffling** ADJECTIVE

**bag** NOUN bags
a container made of a soft material, for holding or carrying things
➤ **bags of** (*informal*) plenty of • *There's no hurry, we've got bags of time.*

**bag** VERB bags, bagging, bagged
❶ (*informal*) to catch or claim something • *I bagged the best seat.* ❷ to put something into bags

**bagatelle** NOUN
a game played on a board in which small balls are struck into holes

**bagel** NOUN bagels
a ring-shaped bread roll

**baggage** NOUN
luggage

**baggy** ADJECTIVE
baggy clothes hang loosely from your body

**bagpipes** PLURAL NOUN
a musical instrument in which air is squeezed out of a bag into pipes. Bagpipes are played especially in Scotland.

**bail** NOUN bails
❶ money that is paid or promised as a guarantee that a person who is accused of a crime will return for trial if he or she is released in the meantime ❷ one of the two

small pieces of wood placed on top of the stumps in cricket

**bail** *VERB* bails, bailing, bailed
❶ to provide bail for a person ❷ to scoop out water that has got into a boat
➤ **bail someone out** to help someone get out of trouble

**bailey** *NOUN* baileys
the courtyard of a castle; the wall round this courtyard

**bailiff** *NOUN* bailiffs
❶ an official who takes people's property when they owe money ❷ a law officer who helps a sheriff by serving writs and carrying out arrests

**Bairam** (say by-**rahm**) *NOUN*
either of two Muslim festivals, one in the tenth month and one in the twelfth month of the Islamic year

**bairn** *NOUN* bairns
(*Scottish*) a child

**Baisakhi** *NOUN*
a Sikh festival held in April to commemorate the founding of the Khalsa

**bait** *NOUN*
❶ food that is put on a hook or in a trap to catch fish or animals ❷ something that is meant to tempt someone

**bait** *VERB* baits, baiting, baited
❶ to put bait on a hook or in a trap ❷ to try to make someone angry by teasing them

**baize** *NOUN*
the thick green cloth that is used for covering snooker tables

**bake** *VERB* bakes, baking, baked
❶ to cook food in an oven with dry heat; to make bread or cakes ❷ to become very hot, especially in the sun ❸ to make clay hard by heating it

**baked beans** *PLURAL NOUN*
cooked white beans, usually tinned with tomato sauce

**baker** *NOUN* bakers
a person who bakes or sells bread or cakes

**bakery** *NOUN* bakeries
a place where bread and cakes are baked or a shop where they are sold

**baking powder** *NOUN*
a powder used to make bread and cakes rise when they are baked

**baking soda** *NOUN*
sodium bicarbonate

**bakkie** *NOUN* bakkies (*S. African*)
❶ a small pick-up truck with an open back ❷ a small bowl or basin

**balaclava, balaclava helmet** *NOUN*
balaclavas, balaclava helmets
(*chiefly British*) a hood covering the head and neck and part of the face
**WORD ORIGIN** named after *Balaclava*, a village in the Crimea (because the helmets were worn by soldiers fighting near there during the Crimean War)

**balance** *NOUN* balances
❶ a steady position, with the weight or amount evenly distributed ❷ a person's feeling of being steady • *She lost her balance and fell to the ground.* ❸ a device for weighing things, with two containers hanging from a bar ❹ the difference between money paid into an account and money taken out of it ❺ the amount of money that someone owes

**balance** *VERB* balances, balancing, balanced
❶ to balance on something is to make yourself steady on it ❷ something is balanced when it is steady with its weight evenly distributed

**balcony** *NOUN* balconies
❶ a platform that sticks out from an outside wall of a building ❷ the upstairs part of a theatre or cinema

**bald** *ADJECTIVE*
❶ without hair on the top of the head ❷ a bald statement or description is one without any details or explanation
➤ **baldly** *ADVERB*
➤ **baldness** *NOUN*

**bale** *NOUN* bales
a large bundle of hay, straw or cotton, usually tied up tightly

**bale** *VERB* bales, baling, baled
➤ **bale out** (*British*)
to jump out of an aircraft with a parachute in an emergency

**baleful** *ADJECTIVE*
menacing or harmful • *He gave her a baleful stare.*
➤ **balefully** *ADVERB*

**ball** *NOUN* balls
❶ a round object used in many games ❷ anything that has a round shape • *a ball of string* ❸ a formal party where people dance

➤ **ball of the foot** the rounded part of the foot at the base of the big toe

**ballad** *NOUN* ballads
❶ a traditional song or poem that tells a story ❷ a slow romantic pop song

**ballast** (say **bal**-ast) *NOUN*
heavy material that is carried in a ship or hot-air balloon to keep it steady

**ball bearings** *PLURAL NOUN*
small steel balls rolling in a groove on which machine parts can move easily

**ballcock** *NOUN* ballcocks
a floating ball that controls the water level in a cistern

**ballerina** (say bal-er-**een**-a) *NOUN* ballerinas
a female ballet dancer

**ballet** (say **bal**-ay) *NOUN* ballets
a style of dancing in which a group of dancers perform precise steps and movements to tell a story to music

**ballistic** (say bal-**ist**-ik) *ADJECTIVE*
to do with objects that are fired through the air, especially bullets and missiles
➤ **go ballistic** (*informal*) to become very angry

**ballistic missile** *NOUN* ballistic missiles
a missile that is powered and guided when it is launched and then falls under gravity on its target

**balloon** *NOUN* balloons
❶ a bag made of thin rubber that can be inflated and used as a toy or decoration ❷ a large round bag inflated with hot air or light gases to make it rise in the air, often carrying a basket in which passengers may ride ❸ an outline round spoken words in a cartoon

**SPELLING**

There is a double l and double o in **balloon**.

**ballot** *NOUN* ballots
❶ a secret method of voting, usually by making a mark on a piece of paper and putting it in a box ❷ a piece of paper on which a vote is made **WORD ORIGIN** from Italian *ballotta* = small ball (because one way of voting is by placing a ball in a box; the colour of the ball shows whether you are voting for something or against it)

**ballpoint pen** *NOUN* ballpoint pens
a pen with a tiny ball round which the ink flows

**ballroom** *NOUN* ballrooms
a large room where dances are held

**balm** *NOUN*
❶ a sweet-scented ointment ❷ something that soothes you

**balmy** *ADJECTIVE*
❶ balmy weather is gentle and warm • *a balmy breeze* ❷ sweet-scented like balm

**balsa** *NOUN*
a kind of very lightweight wood

**balsam** *NOUN* balsams
❶ a kind of sweet-smelling oily resin produced by certain trees, used to make perfumes and medicines ❷ a tree producing balsam

**balti** *NOUN* baltis
a type of Pakistani curry, cooked in a bowl-shaped pan

**balustrade** *NOUN* balustrades
a row of short posts or pillars that supports a rail or strip of stonework round a balcony or staircase **WORD ORIGIN** from Italian *balustra* = pomegranate flower (because the pillars of a balustrade were the same shape as the flower)

**bamboo** *NOUN* bamboos
❶ a tall plant with hard hollow stems ❷ a stem of the bamboo plant

**bamboozle** *VERB* bamboozles, bamboozling, bamboozled (*informal*)
to puzzle or trick someone • *Lucy looked completely bamboozled.*

**ban** *VERB* bans, banning, banned
to officially forbid someone from doing something • *He has been banned from driving for six months.*

**ban** *NOUN* bans
an order that bans something

**banal** (say ban-**ahl**) *ADJECTIVE*
ordinary and uninteresting
➤ **banality** *NOUN*

**banana** *NOUN* bananas
a long curved fruit with a yellow or green skin

**band** *NOUN* bands
❶ an organized group of people doing something together • *a band of robbers* ❷ a group of people playing music together ❸ a strip or loop of something ❹ a range of values, wavelengths, etc.

**band** *VERB* bands, banding, banded
to band together is to form an organized group

**A**

**B**

**C**

**bandage** *NOUN* bandages
a strip of material for tying round a wound

**bandage** *VERB* bandages, bandaging, bandaged
to tie a bandage round a wound

**bandit** *NOUN* bandits
a member of a gang of robbers who attack travellers

**D**

**E**

**F**

**bandstand** *NOUN* bandstands
a platform for a band playing music outdoors, usually in a park

**bandwagon** *NOUN*
➤ jump on the bandwagon to join other people in something that has become successful or popular

**G**

**H**

**I**

**bandy** *ADJECTIVE*
bandy legs curve outwards at the knees

**bandy** *VERB* bandies, bandying, bandied
if a name, word or story is bandied about, it is mentioned or told by a lot of different people

**J**

**K**

**L**

**bane** *NOUN*
if something is the bane of your life, it causes you a lot of trouble or worry

**bang** *NOUN* bangs
❶ a sudden loud noise like that of an explosion ❷ a sharp blow or knock

**M**

**N**

**O**

**bang** *VERB* bangs, banging, banged
❶ to hit or shut something noisily • *Don't bang the door when you go out.* ❷ to make a sudden loud noise ❸ to bump part of your body against something • *She banged her knee on the desk.*

**P**

**Q**

**bang** *ADVERB*
(*informal*) exactly • *bang in the middle* • *bang on time*

**R**

**S**

**T**

**banger** *NOUN* bangers (*British*)
❶ a firework that explodes noisily ❷ (*informal*) a sausage ❸ (*informal*) a noisy old car

**U**

**bangle** *NOUN* bangles
a stiff bracelet

**V**

**W**

**banish** *VERB* banishes, banishing, banished
❶ to punish a person by ordering them to leave a place • *He was banished from the kingdom forever.* ❷ to drive away a thought or feeling from your mind • *She struggled to banish these fears.*
➤ **banishment** *NOUN*

**X**

**Y**

**banisters** *PLURAL NOUN*
a handrail with upright supports beside a staircase

**Z**

**banjo** *NOUN* banjos
a musical instrument like a small guitar with a round body

**bank** *NOUN* banks
❶ a business that looks after people's money ❷ a reserve supply • *a blood bank* ❸ a sloping piece of ground at either side of a river ❹ a long piled-up mass of earth, sand or snow ❺ a long thick mass of cloud or fog ❻ a row of lights or switches

**bank** *VERB* banks, banking, banked
❶ to put money in a bank ❷ to pile up to form a bank ❸ to tilt sideways while changing direction • *The plane banked as it prepared to land.*
➤ **bank on** to rely or depend on something

**banker** *NOUN* bankers
a person who runs a bank

**bank holiday** *NOUN* bank holidays
(*British*) a public holiday, when banks are officially closed

**banknote** *NOUN* banknotes
a piece of paper money issued by a bank

**bankrupt** *ADJECTIVE*
not able to pay your debts • *The company must cut its costs or it will go bankrupt.*
➤ **bankruptcy** *NOUN*

**banner** *NOUN* banners
❶ a strip of cloth with a design or slogan on it, carried on a pole or two poles in a procession or demonstration ❷ a flag

**banns** *PLURAL NOUN*
an announcement in a church that the two people named are going to marry each other

**banquet** *NOUN* banquets
a large formal dinner for invited guests which includes several courses
➤ **banqueting** *NOUN*

**bantam** *NOUN* bantams
a kind of small hen

**banter** *NOUN*
playful teasing or joking
➤ **banter** *VERB*

**Bantu** *NOUN* Bantu or Bantus
❶ a member of a group of central and southern African peoples ❷ the group of languages spoken by these peoples

**bap** *NOUN* baps
(*British*) a soft flat bread roll

**baptism** *NOUN* baptisms
the ceremony in which a person is formally baptized

**Baptist** *NOUN* Baptists
a member of a group of Christians who believe that a person should not be baptized until he or she is old enough to understand what baptism means

**baptize** (also **baptise**) *VERB* baptizes, baptizing, baptized
to receive someone into the Christian Church in a ceremony in which they are sprinkled with or dipped in water and usually given a name or names

**bar** *NOUN* bars
❶ a long straight piece of metal • *the bars of a prison cell* ❷ a block of something solid • *a bar of soap* ❸ a band of colour or light ❹ a counter or room where refreshments, especially alcoholic drinks, are served ❺ one of the small equal sections into which music is divided • *Can you sing the first few bars?*
➤ **behind bars** in prison

**bar** *VERB* bars, barring, barred
❶ to fasten something with a bar or bars • *All the windows were barred.* ❷ to bar someone's way or path is to stop them getting past ❸ to forbid or ban someone from doing something

**barb** *NOUN* barbs
the backward-pointing spike of a spear, arrow or fish hook, which makes it difficult to pull out

**barbarian** *NOUN* barbarians
an uncivilized or brutal person
**WORD ORIGIN** from Greek *barbaros* = babbling, not speaking Greek

**barbaric, barbarous** *ADJECTIVE*
savage and cruel
➤ **barbarity** *NOUN*
➤ **barbarism** *NOUN*

**barbecue** *NOUN* barbecues
❶ a metal frame for grilling food over an open fire outdoors ❷ a party where food is cooked in this way

**barbecue** *VERB* barbecues, barbecuing, barbecued
to cook food on a barbecue

**barbed** *ADJECTIVE*
❶ having a barb or barbs ❷ a barbed comment or remark is deliberately hurtful

**barbed wire** *NOUN*
wire with small spikes in it, used to make fences

**barber** *NOUN* barbers
a men's hairdresser **WORD ORIGIN** from Latin *barba* = beard

**bar chart** *NOUN* bar charts
a diagram that shows amounts as bars of equal width but varying height

**bar code** *NOUN* bar codes
a set of black lines that are printed on goods, library books, etc. and can be read by a computer to give information about the goods, books, etc.

**bard** *NOUN* bards (*literary*)
a poet or minstrel

**bare** *ADJECTIVE*
❶ without clothing or covering • *bare feet* • *a patch of bare ground* ❷ empty • *The cupboard was bare.* ❸ plain and simple, without details • *the bare facts* ❹ only just enough • *the bare necessities of life*
➤ **bareness** *NOUN*
➤ **with your bare hands** without weapons or tools

**bare** *VERB* bares, baring, bared
to uncover or reveal something • *The dog bared its teeth in a snarl.*

**bareback** *ADJECTIVE & ADVERB*
riding on a horse without a saddle

**barefaced** *ADJECTIVE*
a barefaced lie is one that is told boldly without any shame or guilt

**barely** *ADVERB*
only just; with difficulty • *I was so tired I was barely able to stand.*

**bargain** *NOUN* bargains
❶ an agreement about doing something in return for something else • *Come on, we've kept our side of the bargain.* ❷ something that you buy cheaply

**bargain** *VERB* bargains, bargaining, bargained
to argue over the price to be paid or what you will do in return for something
➤ **bargain for** to expect something to happen and be ready for it • *He got more than he bargained for.*

**barge** *NOUN* barges
a long flat-bottomed boat used on canals

**barge** *VERB* barges, barging, barged
to barge into someone is to bump clumsily into them or push them out of the way
➤ **barge in** to rush into a room rudely • *My brother suddenly came barging in.*

a
b
c
d
e
f
g
h
i
j
k
l
m
n
o
p
q
r
s
t
u
v
w
x
y
z

**baritone** *NOUN* baritones
a male singer with a voice between a tenor and a bass

**barium** (say **bair**-ee-um) *NOUN*
a soft silvery-white metal

**bark** *NOUN* barks
❶ the short harsh sound made by a dog or fox ❷ the outer covering of a tree's branches or trunk

**bark** *VERB* barks, barking, barked
❶ to make the sound of a bark ❷ to speak loudly and harshly

**barley** *NOUN*
a cereal plant from which malt is made

**barley sugar** *NOUN* barley sugars
a sweet made from boiled sugar

**bar mitzvah** *NOUN* bar mitzvahs
a religious ceremony for Jewish boys aged 13, when they take on the responsibilities of an adult under Jewish law **WORD ORIGIN** Hebrew, = son of the commandment

**barmy** *ADJECTIVE* (*informal*)
(*British*) crazy or mad **WORD ORIGIN** literally full of froth, from *barm* = yeast, froth

**barn** *NOUN* barns
a farm building for storing hay or grain

**barnacle** *NOUN* barnacles
a shellfish that attaches itself to rocks and the bottoms of ships

**barn dance** *NOUN* barn dances
a kind of country dance; an informal gathering for dancing

**barnyard** *NOUN* barnyards
a farmyard next to a barn

**barometer** (say ba-**rom**-it-er) *NOUN* barometers
an instrument that measures air pressure, used in forecasting the weather

**baron** *NOUN* barons
❶ a member of the lowest rank of noblemen ❷ a powerful owner of an industry or business • *a newspaper baron*
➤ **baronial** (say ba-**roh**-nee-al) *ADJECTIVE*

**baroness** *NOUN* baronesses
a female baron or a baron's wife

**baronet** *NOUN* baronets
a nobleman with a knighthood inherited from his father

**baroque** (say ba-**rok**) *NOUN*
an elaborately decorated style of architecture used in the 17th and 18th centuries

**barracks** *NOUN*
a large building or group of buildings for soldiers to live in

**barrage** (say ba-rahzh) *NOUN* barrages
❶ a dam built across a river ❷ heavy gunfire ❸ a large number of questions or comments that come quickly • *He faced a barrage of questions from reporters.*

**barrel** *NOUN* barrels
❶ a large rounded container with flat ends ❷ the metal tube of a gun, through which the shot is fired

**barrel organ** *NOUN* barrel organs
a musical instrument which you play by turning a handle

**barren** *ADJECTIVE*
❶ barren land is not able to produce crops or has no vegetation ❷ a barren woman is not able to have children ❸ a barren plant or tree is one that cannot bear fruit

**barricade** *NOUN* barricades
a barrier, especially one put up hastily across a street or door

**barricade** *VERB* barricades, barricading, barricaded
to block a street or door with a barricade • *They had barricaded themselves inside the house.* **WORD ORIGIN** French, from Spanish *barrica* = barrel (because barrels were sometimes used to build barricades)

**barrier** *NOUN* barriers
❶ a fence or wall that prevents people from getting past ❷ something that stops you doing something • *Lack of confidence can be a barrier to success.*

**barrier reef** *NOUN* barrier reefs
a coral reef close to the shore but separated from it by a channel of deep water

**barrister** *NOUN* barristers
a lawyer in England or Wales who represents people in the higher law courts

**barrow** *NOUN* barrows
❶ (*British*) a wheelbarrow ❷ (*British*) a small cart that is pushed or pulled by hand ❸ a mound of earth over a prehistoric grave

**barter** *VERB* barters, bartering, bartered
to exchange goods for other goods, without using money • *She bartered her jacket for some food.*

**barter** *NOUN*
the system of bartering

**basalt** (say **bas**-awlt) *NOUN*
a kind of dark volcanic rock

**base** *NOUN* bases
❶ the lowest part of something; the part on which a thing stands ❷ a starting point or foundation; a basis ❸ a headquarters ❹ each of the four corners that must be reached by a runner in baseball ❺ a substance that can combine with an acid to form a salt ❻ (*in mathematics*) the number in terms of which other numbers can be expressed in a number system. 10 is the base of the decimal system and 2 is the base of the binary system.

**base** *VERB* bases, basing, based
❶ to base one thing on another thing is to use the second thing as the starting point for the first • *She based the story on an event in her own childhood.* ❷ to be based somewhere is to live there or work from there

**base** *ADJECTIVE*
❶ showing no honour or moral principles • *base motives* ❷ a base metal is one that has no great value
➤ **basely** *ADVERB*

**baseball** *NOUN* baseballs
❶ a game in which runs are scored by hitting a ball and running round a series of four bases, played mainly in North America ❷ the ball used in this game

**basement** *NOUN* basements
a room or part of a building below ground level

**bash** *VERB* bashes, bashing, bashed
to hit something or someone hard

**bash** *NOUN* bashes
❶ a hard hit ❷ (*informal*) a try • *Have a bash at it.*

**bashful** *ADJECTIVE*
shy and self-conscious
➤ **bashfully** *ADVERB*

**basic** *ADJECTIVE*
forming an essential part or starting point • *He has a basic knowledge of French.* • *Food is a basic human need.*

**basically** *ADVERB*
at the simplest or most fundamental level • *She is basically lazy.*

**basil** *NOUN*
a Mediterranean herb used in cooking

**basilica** (say ba-**zil**-ik-a) *NOUN* basilicas
a large oblong church with two rows of columns and an apse at one end

**basilisk** (say **baz**-il-isk) *NOUN* basilisks
a mythical reptile that was said to be able to kill people just by looking at them
**WORD ORIGIN** from Greek *basilikos* = little king

**basin** *NOUN* basins
❶ a deep bowl for mixing food in ❷ a washbasin ❸ a sheltered area of water for mooring boats ❹ the area from which water drains into a river • *the Amazon basin*

**basis** *NOUN* bases
❶ something to start from or add to; the main principle or ingredient • *She used her diaries as the basis for her book.* ❷ the way in which something is done or organized • *They meet on a regular basis.*

**bask** *VERB* basks, basking, basked
to sit or lie comfortably warming yourself in the sun

**basket** *NOUN* baskets
a container for holding or carrying things, made of strips of flexible material or wire woven together

**basketball** *NOUN* basketballs
❶ a game in which goals are scored by putting a ball through high nets ❷ the ball used in this game

**bass** (say bayss) *ADJECTIVE*
deep-sounding; the bass part of a piece of music is the lowest part

**bass** (say bayss) *NOUN* basses
❶ a male singer with a very deep voice ❷ a bass instrument or part

**bass** (say bas) *NOUN* bass
a fish of the perch family

**basset** *NOUN* bassets
a short-legged dog with drooping ears

**bassoon** *NOUN* bassoons
a bass woodwind instrument

**bastard** *NOUN* bastards
❶ (*old use*) an illegitimate child ❷ (*offensive*) an unpleasant or difficult person or thing

**baste** *VERB* bastes, basting, basted
❶ to moisten meat with fat while it is cooking ❷ to sew fabric together loosely with long stitches

**bastion** *NOUN* bastions
❶ a part of a fortified building that sticks out

a
b
c
d
e
f
g
h
i
j
k
l
m
n
o
p
q
r
s
t
u
v
w
x
y
z

from the rest ❷ something that protects a belief or way of life

**bat** NOUN bats
❶ a shaped piece of wood used to hit the ball in sports like cricket, baseball and table tennis ❷ a flying mammal that looks like a mouse with wings
➤ **off your own bat** without help from other people

**bat** VERB bats, batting, batted
to have a turn at using a bat in cricket or baseball
➤ **not bat an eyelid** to show no surprise or embarrassment when something unusual happens

**batch** NOUN batches
a set of things or people dealt with together

**bated** ADJECTIVE
➤ **with bated breath** waiting anxiously

**bath** NOUN baths
❶ washing your whole body while sitting in water • *I'm going to have a bath.* ❷ a large container for water in which to wash your whole body; the water in a bath • *Your bath is getting cold.* ❸ a liquid in which something is placed • *an acid bath*

**bath** VERB baths, bathing, bathed (*British*) to give someone a bath • *to bath the baby*

**bathe** VERB bathes, bathing, bathed
❶ (*British*) to go swimming in the sea or a river ❷ to wash something gently ❸ to be bathed in light is to have light shining all over you

**bathe** NOUN bathes (*British*) a swim
➤ **bather** NOUN
➤ **bathing suit** NOUN

> **SPELLING**
>
> Bathe with an e sounds like b-ay-the.

**bathos** NOUN
a sudden change from a serious subject or tone to a ridiculous or trivial one

**bathroom** NOUN bathrooms
a room containing a bath or shower, a washbasin and often a toilet

**baths** PLURAL NOUN
❶ (*British*) a public swimming pool ❷ a place where people went in the past to wash or have a bath • *Roman baths*

**bat mitzvah** NOUN bat mitzvahs
a religious ceremony for Jewish girls aged 13, when they take on the responsibilities of an

adult under Jewish law **WORD ORIGIN** Hebrew, = daughter of the commandment

**baton** NOUN batons
a short stick, e.g. one used to conduct an orchestra or in a relay race

**batsman** NOUN batsmen
a player who uses a bat in cricket

**battalion** NOUN battalions
an army unit containing two or more companies

**batten** NOUN battens
a strip of wood or metal that holds something in place

**batten** VERB battens, battening, battened
to fasten something down firmly

**batter** VERB batters, battering, battered
to hit something hard and often • *Huge waves battered the rocks.*

**batter** NOUN batters
❶ a beaten mixture of flour, eggs and milk, used for making pancakes or coating food to be fried ❷ a player who is batting in baseball

**battered** ADJECTIVE
no longer looking new; damaged or out of shape • *a battered leather briefcase*

**battering ram** NOUN battering rams
a heavy pole that is used to break down walls or gates

**battery** NOUN batteries
❶ a device for storing and supplying electricity ❷ a set of pieces of equipment that are used together, especially a group of large guns ❸ a series of cages in which poultry or animals are kept close together • *battery farming*

**battle** NOUN battles
❶ a fight between two armies ❷ a struggle

**battle** VERB battles, battling, battled
to fight or struggle • *She battled to stay afloat.*

**battlefield** NOUN battlefields
a piece of ground on which a battle is or was fought

**battlements** PLURAL NOUN
the top of a castle wall, often with gaps from which the defenders could fire at the enemy

**battleship** NOUN battleships
a heavily armed warship

**batty** ADJECTIVE (*informal*)
(*British*) crazy or eccentric **WORD ORIGIN** from

the phrase *to have bats in the belfry* = to be crazy

**bauble** *NOUN* baubles
❶ a bright and showy ornament that has little value ❷ a decorative ball hung on a Christmas tree

**bauxite** *NOUN*
the clay-like substance from which aluminium is obtained

**bawl** *VERB* bawls, bawling, bawled
❶ to shout loudly ❷ to cry noisily

**bay** *NOUN* bays
❶ an area of the sea and coast where the shore curves inwards ❷ an area that is marked out to be used for parking vehicles, storing things, etc • *a loading bay*
➤ **at bay** cornered but defiantly facing your attackers • *a stag at bay*
➤ **keep something at bay** to prevent something from coming near or threatening you • *He struggled to keep his fears at bay.*

**bay** *ADJECTIVE*
a bay horse is reddish-brown in colour

**bay** *VERB* bays, baying, bayed
to howl or cry, like a hunting dog chasing its prey • *a pack of baying hounds*

**bayonet** *NOUN* bayonets
a blade that can be fixed to the end of a rifle and used for stabbing

**bay window** *NOUN* bay windows
a window that sticks out from the main wall of a house

**bazaar** *NOUN* bazaars
❶ a sale held to raise money for charity ❷ a market place in a Middle Eastern country
**WORD ORIGIN** from Persian *bazar* = market

**bazooka** *NOUN* bazookas
a tube-shaped portable weapon for firing anti-tank rockets **WORD ORIGIN** the word originally meant a musical instrument rather like a trombone

**BC** *ABBREVIATION*
before Christ (used with dates counting back from the birth of Jesus Christ)

**be** *VERB* am, are, is; was, were; being, been
❶ to exist; to occupy a position • *The shop is on the corner.* ❷ to happen; to take place • *When is your birthday?*
**be** This verb is also used
❶ to describe a person or thing or give more information about them (*He is my teacher.*),
❷ to form parts of other verbs (*It is raining.*)

➤ **have been somewhere** to have gone to a place as a visitor • *We have been to Rome.*

**GRAMMAR**

Be is a common verb. Its inflections are very different from the infinitive *be* form:

The forms *am*, *are*, and *is* are used for the present tense.

The forms *was* and *were* are used for the past tense.

The present participle is *being*.

The past participle is *been*.

The verb *be* can be used as an auxiliary verb:

**to form progressive tenses:**

*What are you doing?*

*We were living in London.*

**to form passive verbs:**

*The world record was broken in the final.*

**beach** *NOUN* beaches
the part of the seashore nearest to the water

**beached** *ADJECTIVE*
a beached whale is one that is stranded on a beach

**beacon** *NOUN* beacons
a light or fire used as a signal or warning

**bead** *NOUN* beads
❶ a small piece of glass, wood or plastic with a hole through it for threading with others on a string or wire, e.g. to make a necklace ❷ a drop of liquid • *beads of sweat*
**WORD ORIGIN** from Old English *gebed* = prayer (because people kept count of the prayers they said by moving the beads on a rosary)

**beady** *ADJECTIVE*
beady eyes are small and bright

**beagle** *NOUN* beagles
a small hound with long ears, used for hunting hares

**beak** *NOUN* beaks
the hard horny part of a bird's mouth

**beaker** *NOUN* beakers (*British*)
❶ a tall drinking mug, often without a handle
❷ a glass container used for pouring liquids in a laboratory

**beam** *NOUN* beams
❶ a long thick bar of wood or metal ❷ a

a b c d e f g h i j k l m n o p q r s t u v w x y z

**beam** *NOUN*
ray or stream of light or other radiation ❸ a happy smile

**beam** *VERB* beams, beaming, beamed
❶ to smile happily ❷ to send out radio or TV signals • *Live pictures of the ceremony were beamed around the world.* ❸ to send out light and warmth • *The sun beamed down on us.*

**bean** *NOUN* beans
❶ a kind of plant with seeds growing in pods ❷ its seed or pod eaten as food ❸ the seed of a coffee plant

**bear** *NOUN* bears
a large heavy animal with thick fur and large teeth and claws

**bear** *VERB* bears, bearing, bore, born or borne
❶ to carry or support the weight of something ❷ to have or show a mark, signature, etc. • *She still bears the scar.* ❸ to accept something and be able to deal with it; to put up with something • *I can't bear all this noise.* ❹ to produce fruit or give birth to a child • *She bore him two sons.*
➤ **bear something in mind** to remember something and take it into account
➤ **bear something out** to support or confirm the truth of something

**bearable** *ADJECTIVE*
that you can accept and deal with; able to be put up with • *The breeze made the heat more bearable.*

**beard** *NOUN* beards
hair on a man's chin

**bearded** *ADJECTIVE*
with a beard

**bearer** *NOUN*
someone who carries or brings something important • *I'm sorry to be the bearer of bad news.*

**bearing** *NOUN* bearings
❶ the way that you stand, walk or behave • *a man of aristocratic bearing* ❷ to have a bearing on something is to be relevant to it or to have an effect on it • *Her comments had no bearing on our decision.*
➤ **get your bearings** to work out where you are in a new place or situation
➤ **lose your bearings** to become confused about where you are

**beast** *NOUN* beasts
❶ any large four-footed animal ❷ (*informal*) a cruel or vicious person

**beastly** *ADJECTIVE*
(*informal*) cruel or unkind

**beat** *VERB* beats, beating, beat, beaten
❶ to hit someone repeatedly, especially with a stick ❷ to defeat someone or do better than them ❸ to shape or flatten something by hitting it repeatedly ❹ to stir a cooking mixture quickly so that it becomes thicker ❺ a heart beats when it makes regular movements • *His heart was beating with excitement.* ❻ a bird or insect beats its wings when it flaps them repeatedly
➤ **beat someone up** to attack someone very violently

**beat** *NOUN* beats
❶ a regular rhythm or stroke • *the beat of your heart* ❷ emphasis in rhythm; a strong rhythm in pop music ❸ a policeman's regular route

**beatific** (say bee-a-**tif**-ik) *ADJECTIVE*
showing great happiness • *a beatific smile*

**beautiful** *ADJECTIVE*
attractive to look at; giving pleasure to your senses or your mind

> **SPELLING**
> There is a tricky bit in **beautiful**–it has three vowels in a row, eau.

**beautifully** *ADVERB*
in a beautiful or pleasing way • *She plays the piano beautifully.*

**beautify** *VERB* beautifies, beautifying, beautified
to make someone or something beautiful

**beauty** *NOUN* beauties
❶ a quality that gives pleasure to your senses or your mind ❷ a beautiful person or thing ❸ an excellent example of something • *The last goal was a beauty.*

**beaver** *NOUN* beavers
an animal with soft brown fur and strong teeth; it builds its home in a deep pool which it makes by damming a stream

**beaver** *VERB* beavers, beavering, beavered
to beaver away at something is to work hard at it • *He's been beavering away on the computer all morning.*

**becalmed** *ADJECTIVE*
a ship that is becalmed is unable to move because there is no wind

**because** *CONJUNCTION*
for the reason that
➤ **because of** for the reason of • *He limped*

*because of his bad leg.*

**SPELLING**

To spell **because** try remembering: big elephants can always understand small elephants.

**beck** *NOUN*
➤ **at someone's beck and call** always ready and waiting to do what he or she asks

**beckon** *VERB* beckons, beckoning, beckoned
to make a sign to someone asking them to come towards you • *She beckoned him inside.*

**become** *VERB* becomes, becoming, became, become
❶ to begin to be something; to come or grow to be something • *It became dark.* • *She wants to become a pilot.* ❷ to make a person look attractive • *Short hair really becomes you.*
➤ **become of** to happen to someone or something • *Whatever became of Jim?*

**bed** *NOUN* beds
❶ a piece of furniture that you sleep or rest on, especially one with a mattress and coverings ❷ an area of ground in a garden where plants are grown ❸ the bottom of the sea or of a river ❹ a layer that other things lie or rest on • *chicken served on a bed of rice* ❺ a layer of rock or soil

**bedclothes** *PLURAL NOUN*
sheets, blankets and duvets for covering a bed

**bedding** *NOUN*
mattresses, pillows and bedclothes

**bedlam** *NOUN*
a scene full of noise and confusion • *It was bedlam as the doors opened on the morning of the sale.* **WORD ORIGIN** from *Bedlam*, the popular name of the Hospital of St Mary of Bethlehem, a London mental hospital in the 14th century

**Bedouin** (say **bed**-oo-in) *NOUN* Bedouin
a member of an Arab people living in tents in the desert regions of Arabia and North Africa

**bedpan** *NOUN* bedpans
a container used as a toilet by a person who is bedridden

**bedraggled** (say bid-**rag**-eld) *ADJECTIVE*
looking untidy or messy, especially after getting very wet

**bedridden** *ADJECTIVE*
too weak or ill to get out of bed

**bedrock** *NOUN*
❶ solid rock beneath soil ❷ the fundamental facts or principles on which an idea or belief is based

**bedroom** *NOUN* bedrooms
a room for sleeping in

**bedside** *NOUN* bedsides
a space beside a bed

**bedsitter, bedsit** *NOUN* bedsitters, bedsits
a room used for both living and sleeping in

**bedspread** *NOUN* bedspreads
a covering spread over a bed during the day

**bedstead** *NOUN* bedsteads
the framework of a bed

**bedtime** *NOUN* bedtimes
the time for going to bed

**bee** *NOUN* bees
a stinging insect with four wings that makes honey

**beech** *NOUN* beeches
a tree with smooth bark and glossy leaves

**beef** *NOUN*
meat from an ox, bull or cow

**beefeater** *NOUN* beefeaters
one of the guards at the Tower of London, who wear a uniform based on Tudor dress **WORD ORIGIN** originally a scornful word for a fat, lazy servant

**beefy** *ADJECTIVE*
having a solid muscular body

**beehive** *NOUN* beehives
a box or other container for bees to live in

**beeline** *NOUN*
➤ **make a beeline for something** to go straight or quickly towards something **WORD ORIGIN** because a bee was believed to fly in a straight line back to its hive

**beep** *VERB* beeps, beeping, beeped
❶ to give out a short high-pitched sound • *His mobile started beeping.* ❷ to sound a car horn as a signal • *A taxi beeped outside.*

**beep** *NOUN* beeps
a short high-pitched sound • *Leave your message after the beep.*

**beer** *NOUN* beers
an alcoholic drink made from malt and hops

**beeswax** *NOUN*
a yellow substance produced by bees, used for polishing wood and making candles

a b c d e f g h i j k l m n o p q r s t u v w x y z

**beet** *NOUN* beet or beets
a plant with a thick root used as a vegetable
or for making sugar

**beetle** *NOUN* beetles
an insect with hard shiny wing covers

**beetling** *ADJECTIVE*
sticking out; overhanging • *beetling brows* • *a
beetling cliff*

**beetroot** *NOUN* beetroot
(*chiefly British*) the dark red root of beet used
as a vegetable

**befall** *VERB* befalls, befalling, befell, befallen
(*formal*)
to happen to someone • *Disaster befell them
on the voyage.*

**befit** *VERB* befits, befitting, befitted
to be suitable or appropriate for someone or
something • *She dressed as befitted a woman
of her status.*

**before** *ADVERB*
at an earlier time • *We've seen this film
before.*

**before** *PREPOSITION & CONJUNCTION*
❶ earlier than • *I was here before you!* ❷ in
front of • *A vast landscape lay before them.*

> **SPELLING**
> Before ends with an e.

**beforehand** *ADVERB*
earlier or before something else happens
• *She had tried to phone me beforehand.*

**befriend** *VERB* befriends, befriending,
befriended
to make friends with someone

**beg** *VERB* begs, begging, begged
❶ to ask other people for money or food
to live on ❷ to ask someone for something
something seriously or desperately • *He
begged for forgiveness.*
➤ **go begging** to be available because no one
else wants it
➤ **I beg your pardon** ❶ I am sorry • *I beg
your pardon. I picked up your bag by mistake.*
❷ I did not hear or understand what you said

**beget** *VERB* begets, begetting, begot,
begotten (*old use*)
❶ to be the father of someone ❷ to produce
or cause something • *Violence only begets
more violence.*

**beggar** *NOUN* beggars
❶ a person who lives by begging in the street
❷ (*informal*) a person • *You lucky beggar!*

**begin** *VERB* begins, beginning, began, begun
❶ to do the earliest or first part of
something; to start doing something • *He
began by thanking everyone for coming.* • *We
began the long walk home.* ❷ to start to
happen or exist • *What time does the concert
begin?* ❸ to have something as its first part
• *The word begins with B.*

**beginner** *NOUN* beginners
a person who is just beginning to learn a
subject or skill

**beginning** *NOUN* beginnings
the first part of something or the time when
it starts

> **SPELLING**
> Begin + ning = beginning. Don't forget
> to double the n in the middle.

**begone** *VERB* (*old use*)
go away immediately • *Begone, witch!*

**begonia** (say big-**oh**-nee-a) *NOUN* begonias
a garden plant with brightly coloured flowers

**begot**
past tense of beget

**begrudge** *VERB* begrudges, begrudging,
begrudged
❶ to resent the fact that someone has
something • *I don't begrudge him his success.*
❷ to resent having to do something • *I
begrudge paying so much for a ticket.*

**beguile** (say big-**yl**) *VERB* beguiles, beguiling,
beguiled
❶ to amuse or fascinate someone ❷ to
deceive someone

**behalf** *NOUN*
➤ **on behalf of** for the benefit of someone
else or as their representative • *We are
collecting money on behalf of cancer
research.*
➤ **on my behalf** for me • *Will you accept the
prize on my behalf?*

> **USAGE**
> Take care not to say *on behalf of* (= for
> someone else) when you mean *on the part
> of* (= by someone). For example, do not
> say *This was a serious mistake on behalf
> of the government* when you mean *on the
> part of the government.*

**behave** *VERB* behaves, behaving, behaved
❶ to act in a particular way • *They behaved
badly.* ❷ to show good manners • *Behave
yourself!*

**behaviour** NOUN
the way that someone behaves or acts • *I apologize for my behaviour yesterday.*
➤ **behavioural** ADJECTIVE

**behead** VERB beheads, beheading, beheaded
to cut the head off a person or thing; to execute a person in this way

**behest** NOUN (*formal*)
➤ at a person's behest done because they have asked or commanded you to do it • *At Laura's behest we took the notice down from the window.*

**behind** ADVERB
❶ at or to the back; at a place people have left • *The others are a long way behind. Don't leave your bag behind.* ❷ not making good progress; late • *I'm behind with my work.*

**behind** PREPOSITION
❶ at or to the back of; on the further side of • *She hid behind a tree.* ❷ having made less progress than • *He is behind the rest of the class in French.* ❸ causing or being the reason for something • *What is behind all this trouble?* ❹ supporting or encouraging a person or thing • *We're all behind you.*
➤ **behind a person's back** kept secret from him or her deceitfully
➤ **behind the times** old-fashioned or out of date

**behind** NOUN behinds (*informal*) a person's bottom

**behindhand** ADVERB & ADJECTIVE
late or slow in doing something

**behold** VERB beholds, beholding, beheld (*old use*)
to see something in front of you • *What a sight to behold!*
➤ **beholder** NOUN

**beige** (say bayzh) NOUN & ADJECTIVE
a very light brown colour

**being** NOUN beings
❶ the state of existing • *Pakistan came into being in 1947.* ❷ a living creature • *alien beings*

**belated** ADJECTIVE
coming very late or too late • *a belated birthday present*
➤ **belatedly** ADVERB

**belay** VERB belays, belaying, belayed
to fasten a rope by winding it round a peg or spike

**belch** VERB belches, belching, belched
❶ to send out wind from your stomach through your mouth noisily ❷ to send out fire or smoke from an opening • *There was a tall chimney belching black smoke.*

**belch** NOUN belches
an act of belching • *He let out a loud belch.*

**belfry** NOUN belfries
a tower or part of a tower in which bells hang

**belie** VERB belies, belying, belied
to give a false idea of something • *His smiling face belied his true feelings.*

**belief** NOUN beliefs
❶ the feeling that something exists or is true • *His belief in UFOs grew stronger.* ❷ something that a person believes • *religious beliefs*

> SPELLING
> The 'ee' sound is spelt ie in belief.

**believable** ADJECTIVE
able to be believed • *All the characters in the novel are believable.*

**believe** VERB believes, believing, believed
to think that something is true or that someone is telling the truth
➤ **believer** NOUN
➤ **believe in** ❶ to think that something exists • *Do you believe in ghosts?* ❷ to think that someone or something is good or can be relied on

> SPELLING
> The 'ee' sound is spelt ie in believe. Don't forget the e after the v.

**belittle** VERB belittles, belittling, belittled
to talk about something as if it were unimportant or of little value • *Her brother was always belittling her achievements.*

**bell** NOUN bells
❶ a cup-shaped metal instrument that makes a ringing sound when struck by the clapper hanging inside it ❷ any device that makes a ringing or buzzing sound to attract attention ❸ a bell-shaped object

**belle** NOUN belles
a beautiful woman

**belligerent** (say bil-ij-er-ent) ADJECTIVE
aggressive; keen to start a fight • *He had a belligerent look in his eye.*
➤ **belligerently** ADVERB

**bellow** VERB bellows, bellowing, bellowed
❶ to shout loudly and deeply • *'Sit down!', he*

bellowed. ❷ to make a loud deep sound, like a bull does

**bellow** NOUN bellows
❶ a deep shout • *a bellow of rage* ❷ the loud deep sound made by a bull or other large animal

**bellows** PLURAL NOUN
a device for pumping air into a fire, organ pipes, etc.

**belly** NOUN bellies
your stomach or abdomen

**belong** VERB belongs, belonging, belonged
❶ to belong to someone is to be owned by them • *Who does this phone belong to?* ❷ to belong to a club or group is to be a member of it ❸ to belong somewhere is to have a special place where it goes • *The butter belongs in the fridge.*

**belongings** PLURAL NOUN
your belongings are the things that you own

**beloved** ADJECTIVE
dearly loved • *his beloved homeland*

**below** ADVERB
at or to a lower position; underneath • *I'll have the top bunk and you can sleep below.*

**below** PREPOSITION
lower than; under • *The temperature was ten degrees below zero.*

**belt** NOUN belts
❶ a strip of cloth or leather etc. that you wear round your waist ❷ a continuous moving band used in engines and machinery ❸ a long narrow area • *a belt of rain* • *the asteroid belt*

**belt** VERB belts, belting, belted
❶ (informal) to hit someone very hard ❷ (informal) to run or travel very fast • *I was belting along on my bike.*

**bemused** ADJECTIVE
puzzled or confused • *He gave her a bemused look.*

**bench** NOUN benches
❶ a long seat ❷ a long table for working at in a workshop or laboratory ❸ the seat where judges or magistrates sit; the judges or magistrates hearing a case

**bend** VERB bends, bending, bent
❶ to make something curved and no longer straight • *It hurts when I bend my knee.* ❷ to be or become curved • *The road bends to the left here.* ❸ to move the top of your body

downwards; to stoop • *She bent down to pick up the cat.*

**bend** NOUN bends
a place where something bends; a curve or turn • *a bend in the road*

**beneath** PREPOSITION
❶ under • *The ship disappeared beneath the waves.* ❷ not good enough for someone • *She felt that cleaning for other people was beneath her.*

**beneath** ADVERB
underneath

**benediction** NOUN benedictions
a blessing

**benefactor** NOUN benefactors
a person who gives money or other help

**beneficial** ADJECTIVE
having a good or helpful effect • *Fresh air is beneficial to health.*

**beneficiary** (say ben-if-**ish**-er-ee) NOUN beneficiaries
a person who benefits from another person's will

**benefit** NOUN benefits
❶ an advantage or good effect that something brings ❷ money that the government pays to help people who are poor, sick or out of work

**benefit** VERB benefits, benefiting, benefited
❶ to receive an advantage from something • *She would benefit from extra training.* ❷ to give an advantage to someone or something • *The rainforests benefit people all over the world.*

**benevolence** NOUN
kindness or being helpful • *a face full of benevolence*

**benevolent** ADJECTIVE
❶ kind and helpful • *a benevolent smile* ❷ formed for charitable purposes • *a benevolent fund*
➤ **benevolently** ADVERB

**benign** (say bin-**yn**) ADJECTIVE
❶ kind and gentle; not hurting anyone • *Fortunately, he was in a benign mood.* ❷ a benign tumour is not dangerous or likely to cause death
➤ **benignly** ADVERB

**bent** ADJECTIVE
curved or crooked
➤ **bent on** determined to do something • *He was clearly bent on revenge.*

**bent** NOUN
a liking or talent for something • *She has quite a bent for acting.*

**benzene** NOUN
a substance obtained from coal tar and used as a solvent, motor fuel and in the manufacture of plastics

**benzine** NOUN
a spirit obtained from petroleum and used in dry cleaning

**bequeath** VERB bequeaths, bequeathing, bequeathed
to leave something to a person in a will

**bequest** NOUN bequests
something left to a person in a will

**bereaved** ADJECTIVE
suffering from the recent death of a close relative
➤ **bereavement** NOUN

**bereft** ADJECTIVE
deprived of or lacking something • *We felt bereft of all hope.*

**beret** (say **bair**-ay) NOUN berets
a round flat cap with no peak

**berg** NOUN bergs
(*S. African*) a mountain

**berry** NOUN berries
any small round juicy fruit without a stone

**berserk** (say ber-**zerk**) ADJECTIVE
➤ **go berserk** to become extremely angry or violent, often in an uncontrolled way • *He'll go berserk when he finds out.*
**WORD ORIGIN** from Icelandic *berserkr* = wild warrior, from *ber-* = bear + *serkr* = coat

**berth** NOUN berths
❶ a sleeping place on a ship or train ❷ a place where a ship can moor
➤ **give someone a wide berth** to avoid someone by keeping at a safe distance

**berth** VERB berths, berthing, berthed
to moor in a berth

**beryl** NOUN beryls
a pale-green precious stone

**beseech** VERB beseeches, beseeching, beseeched or besought
to ask or beg someone earnestly to do something; to implore someone • *Let him go, I beseech you!*

**beset** VERB besets, besetting, beset
to be beset by problems or difficulties is to be

badly affected by them • *The team was beset by injuries all season.*

**beside** PREPOSITION
by the side of; near • *a house beside the sea*
➤ **be beside the point** to have nothing to do with the subject you are discussing
➤ **be beside yourself** to be very excited or upset • *She was beside herself with grief.*

**besides** PREPOSITION & ADVERB
in addition to; also • *Who came besides you?*
• *And besides, it's the wrong colour.*

**besiege** VERB besieges, besieging, besieged
❶ to surround a place in order to capture it
• *The Greeks besieged the city of Troy for ten years.* ❷ to crowd round a person or group
• *Fans besieged the singer after the concert.*

**besotted** ADJECTIVE
so much in love with a person or thing that you cannot think or behave normally

**besought**
past tense of **beseech**

**best** ADJECTIVE
of the most excellent kind; most able to do something • *She's the best swimmer in the class.*

**best** ADVERB
❶ in the best way; most • *Which one do you like best?* ❷ most usefully; most wisely • *We had best go.*

**best** NOUN
❶ the best person or thing; the one that is better than all the others • *He is the best at tennis.* • *We bought the best we could afford.*
❷ to do your best is to do as well as you can

**bestial** (say **best**-ee-al) ADJECTIVE
to do with or like a beast; cruel and disgusting

**best man** NOUN
a man who helps and supports the bridegroom at a wedding

**bestow** VERB bestows, bestowing, bestowed
to give something to someone, especially to show how much they are respected • *It was a title bestowed on him by the king.*

**bestseller** NOUN bestsellers
a book that has sold in large numbers

**bet** NOUN bets
❶ an agreement that you will receive money if you are correct in choosing the winner of a race or game or in saying something will happen and will lose money if you are not correct ❷ the amount of money you risk losing in a bet

a
b
c
d
e
f
g
h
i
j
k
l
m
n
o
p
q
r
s
t
u
v
w
x
y
z

**bet** VERB bets, betting, bet or betted
❶ to make a bet ❷ (*informal*) to think that something is likely to happen or be true • *I bet he will forget.*

**beta** (say **beet**-a) NOUN
the second letter of the Greek alphabet, equivalent to Roman *B, b*

**betide** VERB
➤ **woe betide** there will be trouble for • *Woe betide anyone who gets in her way!*

**betray** VERB betrays, betraying, betrayed
❶ to be disloyal to a person or country; to do harm to someone who trusts you ❷ to reveal something without meaning to • *His voice betrayed the anger he was feeling.*
➤ **betrayer** NOUN

**betrayal** NOUN betrayals
betraying someone or something • *a story of love and betrayal*

**betrothed** ADJECTIVE (*formal*)
engaged to be married
➤ **betrothal** NOUN

**better** ADJECTIVE
❶ more excellent; more satisfactory • *My sister speaks German better than I do.* ❷ no longer ill • *I'm feeling better now.*
➤ **get the better of** to defeat or outwit someone

**better** ADVERB
❶ in a better way; more • *Try to do it better next time.* ❷ if you had better do something, you should do it or ought to do it • *We had better go before it gets dark.*
➤ **be better off** to be more fortunate or have more money

**better** VERB betters, bettering, bettered
to improve on something • *She hopes to better her own record time.*

**between** PREPOSITION & ADVERB
❶ in the space or time that separates two points or limits • *The house stood between two large oak trees.* • *Call me between Tuesday and Friday.* ❷ connecting two or more people, places or things • *The train runs between London and Glasgow.* ❸ shared by • *Divide this money between you.* ❹ separating; comparing • *Can you tell the difference between them?*

> USAGE
> Take care to follow the preposition *between* with the object form of the pronoun (me, her, him, them or us). For example, you would say *between you and me* (not 'between you and I').

**betwixt** PREPOSITION & ADVERB (*old use*)
between

**bevel** VERB bevels, bevelling, bevelled
to give a sloping edge to something • *a mirror with bevelled edges*

**beverage** NOUN beverages
any kind of drink • *hot and cold beverages*

**bevy** NOUN bevies
a large group • *a bevy of beauties*

**bewail** VERB bewails, bewailing, bewailed
to express great sorrow about something

**beware** VERB
to be careful • *Beware of pickpockets.*
> SPELLING
> Beware has no other forms; it is only ever used as a command.

**bewilder** VERB bewilders, bewildering, bewildered
to puzzle or confuse someone completely • *He was bewildered by this sudden change of plan.*
➤ **bewilderment** NOUN

**bewildering** ADJECTIVE
confusing and difficult to understand • *It was a bewildering experience.*

**bewitch** VERB bewitches, bewitching, bewitched
❶ to put a magic spell on someone ❷ to delight or fascinate someone very much

**beyond** PREPOSITION & ADVERB
❶ further than; further on • *Don't go beyond the fence.* • *You can see the next valley and the mountains beyond.* ❷ outside the range of; too difficult for • *The problem is beyond me.*

**Bhagavadgita** NOUN
a sacred book in Hinduism

**bhangra** NOUN
a style of music that combines traditional Punjabi music with rock music

**biannual** ADJECTIVE
happening twice a year
➤ **biannually** ADVERB
> USAGE
> Take care not to confuse this word with biennial.

**bias** *NOUN* biases
❶ a strong feeling in favour of one person or side and against another; a prejudice ❷ a tendency to swerve

**biased** *ADJECTIVE*
showing that you prefer one person or side over another

**bib** *NOUN* bibs
❶ a cloth or covering put under a baby's chin during meals ❷ the part of an apron above the waist

**Bible** *NOUN* Bibles
the sacred book of the Jews (the Old Testament) and of the Christians (the Old and New Testament)

**biblical** *ADJECTIVE*
to do with or mentioned in the Bible

**bibliography** (say bib-lee-**og**-ra-fee) *NOUN* bibliographies
a list of books about a subject or by a particular author

**bicarbonate** *NOUN*
a kind of carbonate

**bicentenary** (say by-sen-**teen**-er-ee) *NOUN* bicentenaries
a 200th anniversary

**biceps** (say **by**-seps) *NOUN* biceps
the large muscle at the front of the arm above the elbow **WORD ORIGIN** Latin, = two-headed (because its end is attached at two points)

**bicker** *VERB* bickers, bickering, bickered
to quarrel over unimportant things; to squabble

**bicycle** *NOUN* bicycles
a two-wheeled vehicle that you ride by pushing down on pedals with your feet

**bid** *NOUN* bids
❶ the offer of an amount you are willing to pay for something, especially at an auction ❷ an attempt • *a bid to break the world record*

**bid** *VERB* bids, bidding, bid
to make a bid • *Someone bid $2 million for the painting.*
➤ **bidder** *NOUN*

**bid** *VERB* bids, bidding, bid (or (*old use*) bade, bid or bidden
❶ to say something as a greeting or farewell • *I bid you all good night.* ❷ to command someone to do something • *He bade me come closer.* **WORD ORIGIN** from two Old

English words; *biddan* = to ask, and *beodan* = to announce or command

**bidding** *NOUN*
if you do someone's bidding, you do what they tell you to do

**bide** *VERB* bides, biding, bided
➤ **bide your time** to wait for the right time to do something

**bidet** (say **bee**-day) *NOUN* bidets
a low washbasin to sit on for washing the lower part of the body **WORD ORIGIN** from French *bidet* = a pony (because you sit astride it)

**biennial** (say by-**en**-ee-al) *ADJECTIVE*
❶ a biennial plant lives for two years, flowering and dying in the second year ❷ happening once every two years
➤ **biennially** *ADVERB*

**biennial** *NOUN* biennials
a plant that lives for two years, flowering and dying in the second year

**USAGE**
Take care not to confuse this word with **biannual**.

**bier** (say beer) *NOUN* biers
a movable stand on which a coffin or a dead body is placed before it is buried

**bifocal** (say by-**foh**-kal) *ADJECTIVE*
bifocal lenses for glasses are made in two sections, with the upper part for looking at distant objects and the lower part for reading

**bifocals** *PLURAL NOUN*
bifocal glasses

**big** *ADJECTIVE* bigger, biggest
❶ more than the normal size; large ❷ important • *the big match* • *a big decision* ❸ more grown-up; elder • *my big sister*

**bigamy** (say **big**-a-mee) *NOUN*
the crime of marrying a person when you are already married to someone else
➤ **bigamist** *NOUN*

**bigot** *NOUN* bigots
a person who holds strong and unreasonable opinions and is not willing to listen to other people's opinions

**bigoted** *ADJECTIVE*
holding strong and unreasonable opinions and not willing to listen to other people's opinions
➤ **bigotry** *NOUN*

**bike** *NOUN* bikes (*informal*)
a bicycle or motorcycle

**bikini** *NOUN* bikinis
a woman's two-piece swimsuit
**WORD ORIGIN** named after the island of *Bikini* in the Pacific Ocean, where an atomic bomb test was carried out in 1946, at about the time the bikini was first worn (both caused great excitement)

**bilateral** *ADJECTIVE*
❶ between two people or groups
• *a bilateral agreement* ❷ affecting both of two sides

**bilberry** *NOUN* bilberries
a small dark-blue edible berry

**bile** *NOUN*
a bitter liquid produced by the liver, helping to digest fats

**bilge** *NOUN* bilges
❶ (the bilges) the bottom of a ship or the water that collects there ❷ (*informal*) nonsense; worthless ideas

**bilingual** (say by-**ling**-wal) *ADJECTIVE*
❶ able to speak two languages well
❷ written in two languages

**bilious** *ADJECTIVE*
feeling sick; sickly

**bill** *NOUN* bills
❶ a piece of paper that shows how much money you owe for goods or services
• *Can we have the bill, please?* • *an electricity bill* ❷ a list of events and performers in a show or concert • *Who's on the bill?* ❸ a poster or notice ❹ the draft of a proposed law to be discussed by parliament
❺ (*North American*) a banknote
❻ a bird's beak

**billabong** *NOUN* billabongs
(in Australia) a river branch that forms a backwater or a stagnant pool
**WORD ORIGIN** an Aboriginal word

**billboard** *NOUN* billboards
a large board near a road where advertisements are displayed

**billet** *NOUN* billets
a temporary lodging for soldiers, especially in a private house

**billet** *VERB* billets, billeting, billeted
to house soldiers in a billet

**billiards** *NOUN*
a game in which three balls are struck with

long sticks (called cues) on a cloth-covered table

**billion** *NOUN* & *ADJECTIVE* billions
❶ a thousand million (1,000,000,000) ❷ (*old use*) a million million (1,000,000,000,000)
➤ **billionth** *ADJECTIVE* & *NOUN*
**USAGE**
Although the word originally meant a million million, nowadays it usually means a thousand million.

**billow** *VERB* billows, billowing, billowed
❶ to fill with air and swell outwards
• *curtains billowing in the breeze* ❷ to move in large clouds through the air • *Smoke billowed from the chimneys.*

**billow** *NOUN* billows
a large rolling mass of cloud, smoke or steam
• *great billows of black smoke*

**billycan** *NOUN* billycans
a pot with a lid, used as a kettle or cooking pot when you are camping
**WORD ORIGIN** from Australian Aboriginal *billa* = water

**billy goat** *NOUN* billy goats
a male goat. Compare with **nanny goat**.

**bin** *NOUN* bins
(*British*) a large or deep container, especially one for rubbish or litter

**binary** (say **by**-ner-ee) *ADJECTIVE*
involving sets of two; consisting of two parts

**binary digit** *NOUN* binary digits
either of the two digits (0 and 1) used in the binary system

**binary number** *NOUN* binary numbers
a number expressed in the binary system

**binary system, binary notation** *NOUN*
a system of expressing numbers by using the digits 0 and 1 only, used in computing

**bind** *VERB* binds, binding, bound
❶ to tie things together or tie someone up
• *They bound the prisoner's hands behind his back.* ❷ to fasten a strip of material round something ❸ to fasten the pages of a book into a cover ❹ to make people feel that they have a close connection • *They shared a secret which had bound them together.*
❺ to make someone agree to do something

**bind** *NOUN* (*informal*) something that you find boring or annoying; a nuisance

**binder** NOUN binders
a cover for holding magazines or loose papers together

**binding** ADJECTIVE
a binding agreement or promise is one that must be carried out or obeyed

**binding** NOUN bindings
the covers and glue that hold the pages of a book together

**binge** NOUN binges (*informal*)
a time spent eating or drinking too much

**bingo** NOUN
a game using cards on which numbered squares are crossed out as the numbers are called out at random

**binoculars** PLURAL NOUN
a device with lenses for both eyes, making distant objects seem nearer
**WORD ORIGIN** from Latin *bini* = two together + *oculus* = eye

**biochemistry** NOUN
the study of the chemical composition and processes of living things
➤ **biochemical** ADJECTIVE
➤ **biochemist** NOUN

**biodegradable** ADJECTIVE
able to be broken down by bacteria in the environment • *All our packaging is biodegradable.*

**biodiversity** NOUN
the existence of a large number of different kinds of animals and plants in an area

**biography** (say by-**og**-ra-fee) NOUN biographies
the story of a person's life
➤ **biographical** ADJECTIVE
➤ **biographer** NOUN

**biological** ADJECTIVE
to do with biology

**biology** NOUN
the scientific study of the life and structure of living things
➤ **biologist** NOUN

**bionic** (say by-**on**-ik) ADJECTIVE
a bionic body part is operated by electronic devices

**biopsy** (say **by**-op-see) NOUN biopsies
an examination of tissue from a living body

**biosphere** NOUN biospheres
all the parts of the Earth which contain living things

**biped** (say **by**-ped) NOUN bipeds
a two-footed animal

**biplane** NOUN biplanes
an aeroplane with two sets of wings, one above the other

**birch** NOUN birches
❶ a deciduous tree with slender branches ❷ a bundle of birch twigs used in the past for flogging people

**bird** NOUN birds
an animal with feathers, two wings and two legs

**birdie** NOUN birdies
❶ (*informal*) a bird ❷ a score in golf of one stroke under par for a hole

**bird of prey** NOUN birds of prey
a bird that feeds on animal flesh, such as an eagle or hawk

**bird's-eye view** NOUN
a view of something from above

**Biro** NOUN Biros (*British*) (*trademark*)
a kind of ballpoint pen **WORD ORIGIN** named after its Hungarian inventor, László *Biró*

**birth** NOUN births
❶ birth is when a baby or young animal comes out from its mother's body at the beginning of its life ❷ a person's family origin • *He is of noble birth.* ❸ the beginning of something • *the birth of television*

**birth control** NOUN
ways of avoiding conceiving a baby

**birthday** NOUN birthdays
the anniversary of the day you were born

**birthmark** NOUN birthmarks
a coloured mark that has been on a person's skin since they were born

**birthplace** NOUN birthplaces
the house or town where someone was born • *We visited Shakespeare's birthplace in Stratford-upon-Avon.*

**birth rate** NOUN birth rates
the number of children born in one year for every 1,000 people

**birthright** NOUN
a right or privilege to which a person is entitled through being born into a particular family or country

a
b
c
d
e
f
g
h
i
j
k
l
m
n
o
p
q
r
s
t
u
v
w
x
y
z

**biscuit** *NOUN* biscuits
a small flat kind of cake that has been baked until it is crisp **WORD ORIGIN** from Latin *bis* = twice + *coctus* = cooked (because originally they were baked and then dried out in a cool oven to make them keep longer)

**bisect** (say by-**sekt**) *VERB* bisects, bisecting, bisected
to divide something into two equal parts
➤ **bisector** *NOUN*

**bishop** *NOUN* bishops
❶ a high-ranking member of the Christian clergy in charge of all the churches in a city or district ❷ a chess piece shaped like a bishop's mitre

**bishopric** *NOUN* bishoprics
the position or diocese of a bishop

**bismuth** *NOUN*
❶ a greyish-white metal ❷ a compound of this used in medicine

**bison** (say **by**-son) *NOUN* bison
a wild ox found in North America and Europe, with a large shaggy head

**bistro** *NOUN* bistros
a small restaurant

**bit** *NOUN* bits
❶ a small piece or amount of something • *Which bit of the film did you like the best?* ❷ the metal part of a horse's bridle that is put into its mouth ❸ the part of a tool that cuts or grips things when twisted ❹ (*in computing*) the smallest unit of information in a computer
➤ **a bit** ❶ a short distance or time • *I'm just going out for a bit.* ❷ slightly • *I'm a bit worried.*
➤ **bit by bit** gradually
➤ **to bits** into small pieces • *She angrily tore the letter to bits.*

**bit** *VERB*
past tense of bite

**bitch** *NOUN* bitches
❶ a female dog, fox or wolf ❷ (*offensive*) a woman who behaves in a spiteful or nasty way

**bitchy** *ADJECTIVE*
talking about other people in a spiteful way • *bitchy remarks*

**bite** *VERB* bites, biting, bit, bitten
❶ to cut or take something with your teeth ❷ to pierce skin with a sting or teeth • *I've been bitten all over by midges.* ❸ fish bite

when they accept an angler's bait
➤ **bite the dust** to die or be killed

**bite** *NOUN* bites
❶ a mouthful cut off by biting • *She took a bite.* ❷ a wound or mark made by biting • *a mosquito bite* ❸ a snack • *Let's grab a quick bite to eat.*

**SPELLING**
The past tense of bite is bit; do not add ed.

**biting** *ADJECTIVE*
a biting wind is cold and unpleasant

**bitter** *ADJECTIVE*
❶ tasting sharp, not sweet ❷ feeling hurt or resentful • *He still feels bitter about the way he was treated.* ❸ causing hurt or sorrow • *a bitter disappointment* ❹ very cold • *a bitter wind*
➤ **bitterness** *NOUN*

**bitterly** *ADVERB*
❶ in an angry and disappointed way • *'I've lost everything,' she said bitterly.* ❷ extremely, unpleasantly • *He was bitterly disappointed.* • *It was a bitterly cold day.*

**bittern** *NOUN* bitterns
a marsh bird, the male of which makes a booming cry

**bitumen** (say **bit**-yoo-min) *NOUN*
a black sticky substance used for covering roads or roofs

**bivalve** *NOUN* bivalves
a shellfish, such as an oyster or mussel, that has a shell with two hinged parts

**bivouac** (say **biv**-oo-ak) *NOUN* bivouacs
a temporary camp without tents

**bivouac** *VERB* bivouacs, bivouacking, bivouacked
to camp in a bivouac

**bizarre** (say biz-**ar**) *ADJECTIVE*
very odd in appearance or effect • *bizarre sea creatures*

**blab** *VERB* blabs, blabbing, blabbed
to let out a secret • *Someone must have blabbed to the police.*

**black** *ADJECTIVE*
❶ of the very darkest colour, like coal or soot ❷ having dark skin; of African or Australian Aboriginal ancestry ❸ black coffee or tea has no milk added to it ❹ very dirty ❺ dismal; not hopeful • *The outlook is black.* ❻ hostile or angry • *He gave me a black look.*

➤ **blackly** ADVERB
➤ **blackness** NOUN

**black** NOUN blacks
a black colour • *People often wear black at funerals.*

**black** VERB blacks, blacking, blacked
to make a thing black • *He was busy blacking his boots.*
➤ **black out** to faint or lose consciousness
➤ **black something out** to cover something so that no light can penetrate • *All the windows were blacked out.*

**blackberry** NOUN blackberries
a sweet black berry

**blackbird** NOUN blackbirds
a European songbird, the male of which is black

**blackboard** NOUN blackboards
a dark board for writing on with chalk

**black box** NOUN black boxes
the flight recorder of an aircraft, which records technical information about its flight

**blacken** VERB blackens, blackening, blackened
❶ to make something black or to become black • *The oak beams had been blackened by smoke.* ❷ to blacken someone's name or reputation is to damage it

**black eye** NOUN black eyes
an eye with a bruise round it

**blackguard** (say **blag**-erd) NOUN blackguards
(old use)
a man who behaves in a wicked or dishonourable way **WORD ORIGIN** originally the *black guard* = the servants who did the dirty jobs

**blackhead** NOUN blackheads
a small black spot in the skin

**black hole** NOUN black holes
a region in outer space with such a strong gravitational field that no matter or radiation can escape from it

**black ice** NOUN
thin transparent ice on roads

**blacklist** NOUN blacklists
a list of people who are disapproved of
➤ **blacklist** VERB

**black magic** NOUN
magic used for evil purposes

**blackmail** VERB blackmails, blackmailing, blackmailed
to demand money from someone by threatening to reveal something that they want to keep secret

**blackmail** NOUN
the crime of blackmailing someone
➤ **blackmailer** NOUN

**black market** NOUN black markets
illegal trading in goods

**blackout** NOUN blackouts
❶ a period of darkness when no light must be shown ❷ a temporary loss of consciousness

**black sheep** NOUN
a member of a family or other group who is seen as a disgrace to it

**blacksmith** NOUN blacksmiths
a person who makes and repairs iron things, especially one who makes and fits horseshoes **WORD ORIGIN** because of the dark colour of iron

**black spot** NOUN black spots
a dangerous place where accidents often happen

**bladder** NOUN bladders
the bag-like part of the body in which urine collects

**blade** NOUN blades
❶ the flat cutting edge of a knife, sword or axe ❷ the flat wide part of an oar, spade or propeller ❸ a long flat narrow leaf of grass ❹ a broad flat bone • *shoulder blade*

**blame** VERB blames, blaming, blamed
❶ to say that somebody or something has caused what is wrong • *My brother broke the window but they blamed me.* ❷ to find fault with someone • *I don't blame you for feeling fed up.*

**blame** NOUN
responsibility for what is wrong • *Why do I always get the blame?*

**blameless** ADJECTIVE
deserving no blame; innocent

**blanch** VERB blanches, blanching, blanched
to turn pale • *He blanched with fear.*

**blancmange** (say bla-**monj**) NOUN blancmanges
(British) a jelly-like pudding made with milk **WORD ORIGIN** from French *blanc* = white + *mange* = eat

**bland** ADJECTIVE
❶ having a mild flavour rather than a strong one ❷ not having any interesting features or qualities • *a bland style of writing*

➤ **blandly** ADVERB
➤ **blandness** NOUN

**blank** ADJECTIVE
❶ empty, with nothing written, printed or recorded on it • *a blank piece of paper*
❷ showing no interest or expression • *His face looked blank.* ❸ empty of thoughts • *My mind's gone blank.*
➤ **blankness** NOUN

**blank** NOUN blanks
❶ an empty space ❷ a blank cartridge
**WORD ORIGIN** from French *blanc* = white

**blank cartridge** NOUN blank cartridges
a cartridge for a gun that makes a noise but does not fire a bullet

**blank cheque** NOUN blank cheques
a cheque with the amount not yet filled in

**blanket** NOUN blankets
❶ a warm cloth covering for a bed ❷ a thick soft layer covering something completely • *a blanket of snow*

**blanket** VERB blankets, blanketing, blanketed
to cover something completely with a thick soft layer • *Snow blanketed the ground.*

**blanket** ADJECTIVE
covering all cases or instances • *a blanket ban*
**WORD ORIGIN** originally = woollen cloth which had not been dyed; from French *blanc* = white

**blankly** ADVERB
without showing any emotion or understanding • *Tom stared at her blankly.*

**blank verse** NOUN
verse written without rhyme, usually in lines of ten syllables

**blare** VERB blares, blaring, blared
to make a loud harsh sound • *Car horns blared.*
➤ **blare** NOUN

**blasé** (say **blah**-zay) ADJECTIVE
not interested in or impressed by something because you are used to it

**blaspheme** (say blas-**feem**) VERB blasphemes, blaspheming, blasphemed
to talk or write in a rude or disrespectful way about God or religion

**blasphemy** (say **blas**-fim-ee) NOUN blasphemies
rude or disrespectful talk about God or religion
➤ **blasphemous** ADJECTIVE

**blast** NOUN blasts
❶ a strong rush of wind or air ❷ a sharp or loud noise • *The referee gave a long blast on his whistle.* ❸ an explosion, especially one caused by a bomb

**blast** VERB blasts, blasting, blasted
❶ to make a hole in something with an explosion; to blow something up • *They had to blast a tunnel through the mountain.* ❷ to hit or kick something with a lot of force • *He blasted the ball over the bar.* ❸ to make a loud noise • *Music was blasting out of the speakers.*
➤ **blast off** to launch by the firing of rockets

**blast furnace** NOUN blast furnaces
a furnace for smelting ore, which works by having hot air driven into it

**blast-off** NOUN
the launch of a rocket or spacecraft • *Apollo 11 was ready for blast-off.*

**blatant** (say **blay**-tant) ADJECTIVE
very obvious • *a blatant lie*
➤ **blatantly** ADVERB
**WORD ORIGIN** from an old word meaning 'noisy'

**blaze** NOUN blazes
a very bright flame, fire or light

**blaze** VERB blazes, blazing, blazed
❶ to burn or shine brightly ❷ to show great feeling • *He was blazing with anger.*
➤ **blaze a trail** to show the way for others to follow

**blazer** NOUN blazers
a kind of jacket, often with a badge or in the colours of a school or team
**WORD ORIGIN** from **blaze** (because originally blazers were made in very bright colours and were thought of as shining or 'blazing')

**bleach** NOUN bleaches
a chemical substance used to make clothes white or to clean things and kill germs

**bleach** VERB bleaches, bleaching, bleached
to make something white or pale by using a chemical or by leaving it in the sun

**bleak** ADJECTIVE
❶ bare and cold • *a bleak hillside* ❷ dreary or miserable • *The future looks bleak.*
➤ **bleakly** ADVERB

**bleary** ADJECTIVE
bleary eyes are tired and do not see clearly
➤ **blearily** ADVERB

**bleat** NOUN bleats
the cry of a lamb, goat or calf

**bleat** VERB bleats, bleating, bleated
to cry with a bleat

**bleed** VERB bleeds, bleeding, bled
to lose blood

**bleep** NOUN bleeps
a short high sound made by a piece of
electronic equipment

**bleep** VERB bleeps, bleeping, bleeped
to make a bleep • *Why is your computer
bleeping?*

**bleeper** NOUN bleepers
(*British*) a small electronic device that bleeps
when the wearer is contacted

**blemish** NOUN blemishes
❶ a mark or flaw that spoils a thing's
appearance ❷ something that spoils a
person's character or reputation
➤ **blemish** VERB

**blench** VERB blenches, blenching, blenched
to back away in fear; to flinch

**blend** VERB blends, blending, blended
❶ to mix things together smoothly or easily
• *Blend the flour and the melted butter
together.* ❷ things blend when they combine
well with each other • *The colours blend well.*
➤ **blend in** to fit in well with your
surroundings

**blend** NOUN blends
a mixture • *The book is a blend of action,
history and horror.*

**blender** NOUN blenders
an electric machine used to mix food or turn
it into liquid

**bless** VERB blesses, blessing, blessed
❶ to ask God to protect a person or thing
❷ to make something holy so that it can be
used in a religious ceremony ❸ to be blessed
with something is to be lucky enough to have
it • *She is blessed with good health.*
➤ **bless you** ❶ something you say when
someone has sneezed ❷ something you say
to thank someone

**blessing** NOUN blessings
❶ a prayer that blesses a person or thing
❷ something that you are grateful for • *It's a
blessing no one was hurt.*

**blight** NOUN blights
❶ a disease that withers plants ❷ something
that spoils or damages something
• *Vandalism is a blight on our community.*

**blight** VERB blights, blighting, blighted
❶ to affect a plant with blight ❷ to spoil

or damage something • *Knee injuries have
blighted his career.*

**blind** ADJECTIVE
❶ without the ability to see ❷ without any
thought or understanding • *blind obedience*
❸ a blind bend or corner is one where you
cannot see clearly ahead
➤ **blindness** NOUN

**blind** VERB blinds, blinding, blinded
❶ to make someone blind ❷ to dazzle
someone with a bright light

**blind** NOUN blinds
❶ a screen for a window ❷ something used
to hide your real intentions • *His journey was
a blind.*

**blind date** NOUN blind dates
a date between people who have not met
before

**blindfold** NOUN blindfolds
a strip of cloth tied round someone's eyes so
that they cannot see

**blindfold** VERB blindfolds, blindfolding,
blindfolded
to cover someone's eyes with a blindfold

**blindfold** ADVERB
with a blindfold covering your eyes
**WORD ORIGIN** from Old English *blindfeld* =
struck blind, from **blind** + **fell** VERB

**blindly** ADVERB
❶ without being able to see what you are
doing • *He groped blindly for the light switch.*
❷ without thinking about what you are doing
• *They were trained to blindly follow orders.*

**blind spot** NOUN blind spots
a subject that you do not understand or know
much about

**bling** NOUN (*informal*)
showy and expensive jewellery and clothes
**WORD ORIGIN** perhaps from the sound of
pieces of jewellery clashing together

**blink** VERB blinks, blinking, blinked
❶ to shut and open your eyes rapidly ❷ a
light blinks when it shines unsteadily

**blink** NOUN blinks
when you shut and open your eyes rapidly
➤ **in the blink of an eye** very rapidly

**blinkers** PLURAL NOUN
leather pieces fixed on a bridle to prevent a
horse from seeing sideways
➤ **blinkered** ADJECTIVE
**WORD ORIGIN** originally a person who was
half-blind; from **blink**

**bliss** NOUN
extreme happiness

**blissful** ADJECTIVE
feeling or causing extreme happiness • *He gave a blissful sigh.*
➤ **blissfully** ADVERB

**blister** NOUN blisters
a swelling like a bubble, especially on skin

**blister** VERB blisters, blistering, blistered
❶ to form blisters ❷ when a surface blisters it swells and cracks • *The paint was starting to blister.*

**blistering** ADJECTIVE
very intense • *the blistering midday heat*

**blithe** ADJECTIVE
casual and carefree
➤ **blithely** ADVERB

**blitz** NOUN blitzes
❶ a sudden violent attack, especially from aircraft ❷ the German bombing of London in 1940 (**WORD ORIGIN**) short for German *Blitzkrieg* (*Blitz* = lightning, *Krieg* = war)

**blizzard** NOUN blizzards
a severe snowstorm

**bloated** ADJECTIVE
swollen by fat, gas or liquid

**bloater** NOUN bloaters
a salted smoked herring

**blob** NOUN blobs
a small round lump or drop of something • *blobs of paint*

**bloc** NOUN blocs
a group of parties or countries who have formed an alliance

**block** NOUN blocks
❶ a solid piece of something ❷ a large building divided into flats or offices ❸ a group of buildings • *I went for a walk round the block.* ❹ an obstacle or obstruction • *a road block*

**block** VERB blocks, blocking, blocked
to get in the way of something; to obstruct something • *Tall buildings blocked our view.* • *The pipe is blocked.*

**blockade** NOUN blockades
the blocking of the entrance to a city or port in order to prevent people and goods from going in or out

**blockade** VERB blockades, blockading, blockaded
to set up a blockade of a place

**blockage** NOUN blockages
something that blocks a pipe or passageway

**block letters** PLURAL NOUN
plain capital letters

**blog** NOUN blogs
a personal website on which someone writes regularly about their own life or opinions

**blog** VERB blogs, blogging, blogged
to write on a blog
➤ **blogging** NOUN

**blogger** NOUN bloggers
someone who keeps a blog or who writes fiction and posts it on the Internet

**bloke** NOUN blokes (*British*) (*informal*)
a man

**blond, blonde** ADJECTIVE
fair-haired; fair

**blond** NOUN blondes
a fair-haired girl or woman

**blood** NOUN
❶ the red liquid that flows through veins and arteries ❷ family background or ancestry • *Do you have any Irish blood?*
➤ in cold blood deliberately and cruelly

**blood bank** NOUN blood banks
a place where supplies of blood and plasma for transfusions are stored

**bloodbath** NOUN bloodbaths
a massacre

**blood donor** NOUN blood donors
a person who gives blood for use in transfusions

**blood group** NOUN blood groups
any of the classes or types of human blood

**bloodhound** NOUN bloodhounds
a large dog that was used to track people by their scent

**bloodshed** NOUN
the killing or wounding of people

**bloodshot** ADJECTIVE
bloodshot eyes are streaked with red

**blood sport** NOUN blood sports
a sport that involves wounding or killing animals

**bloodstream** NOUN
the blood circulating in the body

**bloodthirsty** ADJECTIVE
enjoying killing and violence

**blood vessel** *NOUN* blood vessels
a tube carrying blood in the body; an artery, vein or capillary

**bloody** *ADJECTIVE* bloodier, bloodiest
❶ stained with blood ❷ with much bloodshed • *a bloody battle*

**bloom** *NOUN* blooms
❶ a flower ❷ the fine powder on fresh ripe grapes etc.
➤ **in bloom** producing flowers • *The cherry trees are in bloom.*

**bloom** *VERB* blooms, blooming, bloomed
to produce flowers

**blossom** *NOUN* blossoms
a flower or a mass of flowers, especially on a fruit tree

**blossom** *VERB* blossoms, blossoming, blossomed
❶ to produce flowers ❷ to develop into something • *She blossomed into a fine singer.*

**blot** *NOUN* blots
❶ a spot of ink ❷ a flaw or fault; something ugly • *a blot on the landscape*

**blot** *VERB* blots, blotting, blotted
❶ to make a blot or blots on something ❷ to remove liquid from a surface by pressing paper or cloth on it
➤ **blot something out** ❶ to be in front of something so that it cannot be seen • *Fog blotted out the view.* ❷ to make an effort to forget something unpleasant • *She tried to blot out the memory of what happened.*

**blotch** *NOUN* blotches
an untidy patch of colour
➤ **blotchy** *ADJECTIVE*

**blotter** *NOUN* blotters
a pad of blotting paper; a holder for blotting paper

**blotting paper** *NOUN*
absorbent paper for soaking up ink from writing

**blouse** *NOUN* blouses
a loose piece of clothing like a shirt, worn by women

**blow** *VERB* blows, blowing, blew, blown
❶ to send air out of your mouth or nose • *He blew on his hands to warm them up.* ❷ to move in or with a current of air • *The wind was blowing.* • *His hat blew off.* ❸ to form something or make a sound by blowing • *We were blowing bubbles.* • *The referee blew her whistle.* ❹ a fuse or light bulb blows when it melts or breaks because the electric current is too strong
➤ **blow something up** ❶ to destroy something with an explosion ❷ to fill something with air
➤ **blow up** to be destroyed in an explosion

**blow** *NOUN* blows
❶ a hard knock or hit ❷ a shock or disappointment ❸ the action of blowing

**blowlamp, blowtorch** *NOUN* blowlamps, blowtorches
a portable device for aiming a very hot flame at a surface, used to remove old paint

**blowpipe** *NOUN* blowpipes
a tube for sending out a dart or pellet by blowing

**blubber** *NOUN*
the fat on a whale

**bludge** *VERB* bludges, bludging, bludged
(Australian/NZ) (informal)
❶ to live off someone else's earnings or on state benefits ❷ to avoid work and responsibilities

**bludgeon** (say **bluj**-on) *NOUN* bludgeons
a short stick with a thickened end, used as a weapon

**bludgeon** *VERB* bludgeons, bludgeoning, bludgeoned
to hit someone several times with a heavy stick or other object

**blue** *NOUN* blues
the colour of a cloudless sky
➤ **out of the blue** unexpectedly

**blue** *ADJECTIVE*
❶ of the colour blue ❷ unhappy or depressed
➤ **blueness** *NOUN*

> **SPELLING**
> Blue is a colour. Blew is the past tense of blow. *The sky was blue. The wind blew hard.*

**bluebell** *NOUN* bluebells
a plant with blue bell-shaped flowers

**blueberry** *NOUN* blueberries
a small, blue-black juicy fruit

**blue blood** *NOUN*
royal or aristocratic family

**bluebottle** *NOUN* bluebottles
a large bluish fly

**blueprint** *NOUN* blueprints
a detailed plan for making or doing something **WORD ORIGIN** because copies of plans were made on blue paper

**blues** NOUN
a style of music made up of slow sad songs or tunes • *a blues singer*
➤ **the blues** a very sad feeling; depression
WORD ORIGIN short for *blue devils*, spiteful demons believed to cause depression

**bluff** VERB bluffs, bluffing, bluffed
to try to deceive someone, especially by pretending to be someone else or to be able to do something

**bluff** NOUN bluffs
❶ bluffing; a threat that you make but do not intend to carry out ❷ a cliff with a broad steep front
➤ **call someone's bluff** to challenge someone to do what they have threatened to do

**bluff** ADJECTIVE
frank and direct, in a good-natured way

**bluish** ADJECTIVE
having a blue tinge

**blunder** NOUN blunders
a stupid mistake

**blunder** VERB blunders, blundering, blundered
❶ to make a blunder ❷ to move clumsily and uncertainly • *I could hear him blundering about upstairs.*

**blunderbuss** NOUN blunderbusses
an old type of gun that fired many balls in one shot WORD ORIGIN from Dutch *donderbus* = thunder gun

**blunt** ADJECTIVE
❶ not sharp ❷ saying what you mean without trying to be polite or tactful • *a blunt refusal*
➤ **bluntness** NOUN

**blunt** VERB blunts, blunting, blunted
to make a point or edge blunt

**bluntly** ADVERB
in plain terms, without trying to be polite • *To put it bluntly, you're not welcome here.*

**blur** VERB blurs, blurring, blurred
to make something less clear or distinct

**blur** NOUN blurs
something that you cannot see or remember clearly • *Without his glasses on, everything was a blur.*

**blurb** NOUN blurbs
a short description of a book that is printed on the back and meant to make you want to buy it

**blurred** ADJECTIVE
not clear in outline; out of focus

**blurt** VERB blurts, blurting, blurted
to say something suddenly or tactlessly • *He blurted it out before he had time to think.*

**blush** VERB blushes, blushing, blushed
to become red in the face because you are ashamed or embarrassed

**blush** NOUN blushes
reddening in the face

**bluster** VERB blusters, blustering, blustered
to talk loudly and aggressively, making empty threats

**blustery** ADJECTIVE
blustery weather is when the wind is blowing strongly in gusts

**BMX** ABBREVIATION
a kind of bicycle for use in racing on a dirt track WORD ORIGIN short for *bicycle motocross* (*x* standing for **cross**)

**boa** (say **boh**-a) (or **boa constrictor**) NOUN
boas, boa constrictors
a large South American snake that squeezes its prey so that it suffocates it

**boar** NOUN boars
❶ a wild pig ❷ a male pig

**board** NOUN boards
❶ a long flat piece of wood, used in building ❷ a flat piece of stiff material • *a chopping board* • *a chessboard* ❸ a group of people who run a company or organization ❹ daily meals provided in return for payment or work • *board and lodging*
➤ **on board** on or in a boat, ship, train or aircraft

**board** VERB boards, boarding, boarded
❶ to get on a boat, ship, train or aircraft ❷ to receive meals and accommodation for payment
➤ **board something up** to block something up with fixed boards • *The windows were all boarded up.*

**boarder** NOUN boarders
❶ a pupil who lives at a boarding school during the term ❷ a lodger who receives meals

**board game** NOUN
a game in which you move pieces around a board

**boarding house** NOUN boarding houses
a house where people are provided with rooms and meals for payment

**boarding school** *NOUN* boarding schools
a school where pupils live during the term

**boast** *VERB* boasts, boasting, boasted
❶ to speak with too much pride about yourself and try to impress people ❷ to have something to be proud of • *The city boasts several fine parks.*

**boast** *NOUN* boasts
a boastful statement

**boastful** *ADJECTIVE*
boasting a lot
➤ **boastfully** *ADVERB*

**boat** *NOUN* boats
a vehicle built to travel on water
➤ **in the same boat** in the same situation; suffering the same difficulties

**boater** *NOUN* boaters
a hard flat straw hat

**boating** *NOUN*
going out in a boat (especially a rowing boat) for pleasure

**boatswain** (say boh-sun) *NOUN* boatswains
a ship's officer in charge of rigging, boats and anchors

**bob** *VERB* bobs, bobbing, bobbed
to move quickly up and down • *Small boats were bobbing around in the water.* • *She bobbed down behind the wall again.*

**bobbin** *NOUN* bobbins
a small spool holding thread or wire in a machine

**bobble** *NOUN* bobbles
a small ball of wool, used to decorate a hat or jumper

**bobsleigh, bobsled** *NOUN* bobsleighs, bobsleds
(*British*) a sledge with two sets of runners

**bode** *VERB* bodes, boding, boded
to bode well (or ill) is to be a sign that something good (or bad) will happen • *His silence over the last few days does not bode well.*

**bodice** *NOUN* bodices
the upper part of a dress

**bodily** *ADJECTIVE*
to do with your body • *bodily harm*

**bodily** *ADVERB*
by taking hold of someone's body • *He was picked up bodily and bundled into the car.*

**body** *NOUN* bodies
❶ the whole physical structure of a person or animal; the main part of this apart from the head and limbs ❷ a corpse ❸ the main part of something • *the body of the plane* ❹ an organized group of people • *the school's governing body* ❺ a quantity of something regarded as a unit • *A large body of evidence has built up.* ❻ an object or piece of matter • *Stars and planets are heavenly bodies.*

**bodyguard** *NOUN* bodyguards
a guard whose job is to protect an important person

**Boer** (say boh-er) *NOUN* Boers
❶ an Afrikaner ❷ (*historical*) an early Dutch inhabitant of South Africa

**boffin** *NOUN* boffins (*British*) (*informal*)
a person involved in scientific or technical research

**bog** *NOUN* bogs
an area of wet spongy ground
➤ **bogged down** stuck and unable to make any progress

**bogeyman** *NOUN* bogeymen
an imaginary man used in stories to frighten children

**boggle** *VERB* boggles, boggling, boggled
to be amazed or puzzled • *The mind boggles at the idea.*

**boggy** *ADJECTIVE*
boggy ground is wet and spongy

**bogus** *ADJECTIVE*
not real or genuine • *He gave a name that turned out to be bogus.*

**boil** *VERB* boils, boiling, boiled
❶ to become hot enough to bubble and give off steam ❷ to heat a liquid so that it boils ❸ to cook something in boiling water ❹ to be very hot

**boil** *NOUN* boils
❶ the point at which a liquid starts to boil • *Bring the milk to the boil.* ❷ an inflamed swelling under the skin

**boiler** *NOUN* boilers
a container for heating water or making steam

**boiling point** *NOUN* boiling points
the temperature at which a liquid boils

**boisterous** *ADJECTIVE*
noisy and lively

**bold** ADJECTIVE
❶ brave and confident; not afraid to say what you feel or to take risks • *No one felt bold enough to speak up.* ❷ a bold colour or design is strong and vivid ❸ printed in thick black type
➤ **boldly** ADVERB
➤ **boldness** NOUN

**bole** NOUN boles
the trunk of a tree

**bollard** NOUN bollards
❶ a short post for keeping vehicles off a road ❷ a short thick post on a quayside to which a ship's rope may be tied

**bolster** NOUN bolsters
a long pillow for placing across a bed under other pillows

**bolster** VERB bolsters, bolstering, bolstered
to add extra strength or support to something • *Her win last week has really bolstered her confidence.*

**bolt** NOUN bolts
❶ a sliding bar for fastening a door or window ❷ a thick metal pin for fastening things together ❸ a sliding bar that opens and closes the breech of a rifle ❹ a shaft of lightning ❺ an arrow shot from a crossbow ❻ the action of bolting • *He saw his chance and made a bolt for freedom.*
➤ **a bolt from the blue** a surprise, usually an unpleasant one
➤ **bolt upright** sitting or standing with your back straight

**bolt** VERB bolts, bolting, bolted
❶ to fasten a door or window with a bolt or bolts ❷ to fasten things together with bolts • *A ladder was bolted to the wall.* ❸ to run away or escape • *In a panic, the horse bolted.* ❹ to swallow food quickly • *I just had time to bolt down a pizza.*

**bomb** NOUN bombs
an explosive device
➤ **the bomb** the nuclear bomb

**bomb** VERB bombs, bombing, bombed
to attack a place with bombs

**bombard** VERB bombards, bombarding, bombarded
❶ to attack a place with gunfire or many missiles ❷ to direct a large number of questions or comments at somebody

**bombardment** NOUN bombardments
a heavy attack with guns or missiles

**bombastic** (say bom-**bast**-ik) ADJECTIVE
using pompous words **WORD ORIGIN** from *bombast* = material used for padding; later 'padded' language, with long or unnecessary words

**bomber** NOUN bombers
❶ someone who plants or sets off a bomb ❷ an aeroplane from which bombs are dropped

**bombshell** NOUN bombshells
a great shock

**bona fide** (say **boh**-na **fy**-dee) ADJECTIVE
genuine; without fraud • *Are they bona fide tourists or spies?* **WORD ORIGIN** Latin, = in good faith

**bonanza** NOUN bonanzas
sudden great wealth or luck
**WORD ORIGIN** originally an American word; from Spanish, = good weather, prosperity

**bond** NOUN bonds
❶ a close friendship or connection between two or more people • *the special bond between mother and daughter* ❷ bonds are ropes or chains used to tie someone up ❸ a document stating an agreement

**bond** VERB bonds, bonding, bonded
to become closely linked or connected • *The team has bonded well together.*

**bondage** NOUN
slavery or captivity

**bone** NOUN bones
❶ one of the hard whitish parts that make up the skeleton of a person's or animal's body ❷ the substance from which these parts are made • *Antlers are made of bone.*

**bone** VERB bones, boning, boned
to remove the bones from meat or fish

**bone dry** ADJECTIVE
completely dry

**bonfire** NOUN bonfires
an outdoor fire to burn rubbish or celebrate something **WORD ORIGIN** originally *bone fire* = a fire to dispose of people's or animals' bones

**bonnet** NOUN bonnets
❶ the hinged cover over a car engine ❷ a hat with strings that tie under the chin ❸ a flat cap, often with a bobble, worn by Scottish men

**bonny** ADJECTIVE bonnier, bonniest
(*Scottish*) good-looking or pretty

**bonus** (say **boh**-nus) NOUN bonuses
❶ an extra payment in addition to a person's normal wages ❷ an extra benefit WORD ORIGIN from Latin *bonus* = good

**bon voyage** (say bawn vwah-**yah** zh) EXCLAMATION
said to wish someone a good journey WORD ORIGIN a French phrase = good journey

**bony** ADJECTIVE
❶ so thin that you can see the shape of the bones • *his long bony fingers* ❷ full of bones • *bony fish* ❸ looking or feeling like bone

**boo** EXCLAMATION
❶ shouted out to show that you do not like something ❷ said to take someone by surprise and startle them

**boo** VERB boos, booing, booed
to shout 'boo' in disapproval • *The audience began to boo loudly.*

**booby prize** NOUN booby prizes
a prize given as a joke to someone who comes last in a contest

**booby trap** NOUN booby traps
something designed to hit or injure someone unexpectedly

**book** NOUN books
a set of sheets of paper, usually with printing or writing on them, fastened together inside a cover
➤ **bookseller** NOUN
➤ **bookshop** NOUN
➤ **bookstall** NOUN

**book** VERB books, booking, booked
❶ to reserve a place or ticket in advance ❷ to enter a person in a police record • *The police booked him for speeding.* ❸ to make a note of a player who has committed a foul in a football match

**bookcase** NOUN bookcases
a piece of furniture with shelves for books

**bookkeeping** NOUN
recording details of the money that is spent and received by a business
➤ **bookkeeper** NOUN

**booklet** NOUN booklets
a small thin book with paper covers

**bookmaker** NOUN bookmakers
a person whose business is taking bets, especially bets made on horse races

**bookmark** NOUN bookmarks
❶ something to mark a place in a book ❷ a record of the address of a computer file or Internet page so that you can find it again quickly
➤ **bookmark** VERB

**bookworm** NOUN bookworms
a person who loves reading

**boom** VERB booms, booming, boomed
❶ to make a deep hollow sound • *Outside, thunder boomed and crashed.* ❷ to speak in a loud deep voice • *A voice boomed out from the darkness.* ❸ to be growing and successful • *Business is booming.*

**boom** NOUN booms
❶ a deep hollow sound • *the boom of distant guns* ❷ a period of increased growth or prosperity • *a boom in car sales* ❸ a long pole at the bottom of a sail to keep it stretched ❹ a long pole carrying a microphone or film camera ❺ a chain or floating barrier that can be placed across a river or a harbour entrance

**boomerang** NOUN boomerangs
a curved piece of wood that can be thrown so that it returns to the thrower, originally used by Australian Aborigines WORD ORIGIN an Australian Aboriginal word

**boon** NOUN boons
something that makes life easier

**boon companion** NOUN boon companions
a close friend

**boor** NOUN boors
a rude, bad-mannered person
➤ **boorish** ADJECTIVE

**boost** VERB boosts, boosting, boosted
to increase the strength, value or reputation of a person or thing • *Being in the drama group has really boosted his confidence.*

**boost** NOUN boosts
❶ an increase or improvement ❷ something that encourages or helps someone • *Winning that game gave my confidence a great boost.*

**booster** NOUN boosters
❶ a rocket that gives a spacecraft extra power when it leaves the earth ❷ a second dose of a vaccine which renews the effect of an earlier one

**boot** NOUN boots
❶ a shoe that covers the foot and ankle or leg ❷ the compartment for luggage in a car

**boot** VERB boots, booting, booted
❶ to kick something hard ❷ to boot up a computer is to switch it on and get it ready to use

a b c d e f g h i j k l m n o p q r s t u v w x y z

**bootee** NOUN bootees
a baby's knitted boot

**booth** NOUN booths
an enclosed compartment, e.g. for a public telephone or for voting at elections

**booty** NOUN
valuable goods taken away by soldiers after a battle

**booze** VERB boozes, boozing, boozed (informal)
to drink a lot of alcohol

**booze** NOUN (informal) alcoholic drink

**border** NOUN borders
❶ the line dividing two countries or other areas ❷ a band or line around the edge of something, often for decoration • a white tablecloth with a blue border ❸ a long flower bed

**border** VERB borders, bordering, bordered
to form a border around or along something • The orchard was bordered by a stone wall.

**borderline** NOUN borderlines
a boundary

**borderline** ADJECTIVE
only just belonging to a particular group or category • You're a borderline pass.

**bore** VERB bores, boring, bored
❶ to make someone feel uninterested by being dull ❷ to drill a hole through something ❸ past tense of bear VERB

**bore** NOUN bores
❶ a dull and uninteresting person or thing ❷ the width of the inside of a pipe or gun barrel ❸ a tidal wave with a steep front that moves up some estuaries

**bored** ADJECTIVE
weary and uninterested because something is so dull

USAGE

You can say that you are *bored with* something or *bored by* something: *I'm bored with this game*. It is not acceptable in standard English to say *bored of*.

**boredom** NOUN
a feeling of being bored • She thought she would die of boredom.

**boring** ADJECTIVE
dull and uninteresting

**born** ADJECTIVE
❶ to be born is to have come into existence by birth. (See the note on **borne**.) ❷ having a certain natural quality or ability • a born leader

**borne**
past participle of **bear** VERB

USAGE

The word **borne** is used before by or after have, has or had, e.g. children borne by Eve; she had borne him a son. The word **born** is used after be, e.g. in a son was born.

**borough** (say burra) NOUN boroughs
a town or district that has its own council

**borrow** VERB borrows, borrowing, borrowed
❶ to get something to use for a time, with the intention of giving it back afterwards ❷ to obtain money as a loan ❸ to take something and use it as your own • Some musical terms are borrowed from Italian.
➤ **borrower** NOUN

USAGE

Take care not to confuse **borrow**, which means to use something that belongs to someone else for a short time, with **lend**, which means to let someone use something of yours for a short time.

**bosom** NOUN bosoms
a woman's breasts

**boss** NOUN bosses
❶ (informal) a person who is in charge of a business or group of workers ❷ a round raised knob or stud

**boss** VERB bosses, bossing, bossed
(informal) to order someone about

**bossy** ADJECTIVE
fond of ordering people about
➤ **bossily** ADVERB

**botany** NOUN
the study of plants
➤ **botanical** ADJECTIVE
➤ **botanist** NOUN

**botch** VERB botches, botching, botched
to spoil something by poor or clumsy work

**both** DETERMINER & PRONOUN
the two of them, not only one • Are both films good? • I want them both in the team.

**both** ADVERB
➤ **both ... and** not only ... but also • The house is both small and ugly.

**bother** VERB bothers, bothering, bothered
❶ to cause somebody trouble or worry • I'm

*sorry to bother you.* ❷ to take the time or trouble to do something • *Don't bother to reply.*

**bother** *NOUN*
trouble or worry

**bottle** *NOUN* bottles
❶ a narrow-necked container for liquids
❷ (*informal*) courage • *She showed a lot of bottle.*

**bottle** *VERB* bottles, bottling, bottled
to put or store something in bottles
➤ **bottle something up** if you bottle up your feelings, you keep them to yourself

**bottle bank** *NOUN* bottle banks
(*British*) a large container in which used glass bottles are collected for recycling

**bottleneck** *NOUN* bottlenecks
a narrow place where something, especially traffic, cannot flow freely

**bottom** *NOUN* bottoms
❶ the lowest part of something; the base
❷ the part furthest away • *the bottom of the garden* ❸ your buttocks

**bottom** *ADJECTIVE*
lowest • *the bottom shelf*

**bottomless** *ADJECTIVE*
extremely deep • *a bottomless pit*

**boudoir** (say **boo**-dwar) *NOUN* boudoirs
a woman's bedroom or other private room
WORD ORIGIN French, = place to sulk in

**bough** *NOUN* boughs
a large branch coming from the trunk of a tree

**boulder** *NOUN* boulders
a very large rock

**boulevard** (say **bool**-ev-ard) *NOUN* boulevards
a wide street, often with trees on each side

**bounce** *VERB* bounces, bouncing, bounced
❶ to spring back when thrown against something ❷ to make a ball or other object bounce ❸ to jump up and down repeatedly; to move in a lively manner • *The children were bouncing on their beds.* ❹ a cheque bounces when it is sent back by the bank because there is not enough money in the account

**bounce** *NOUN* bounces
❶ the action of bouncing • *Rose gave a little bounce of delight.* ❷ a lively confident manner • *full of bounce*

**bouncer** *NOUN* bouncers
❶ a person who stands at the door of a club

and stops unwanted people coming in or makes troublemakers leave ❷ a ball in cricket that bounces high

**bouncy** *ADJECTIVE*
❶ lively and full of energy ❷ that bounces well or can make things bounce • *a bouncy ball*

**bound** *VERB* bounds, bounding, bounded
❶ to move or run with large leaps • *She bounded down the stairs.* ❷ to be the boundary of something; to limit something • *Their land is bounded by the river.* ❸ past tense of **bind**

**bound** *NOUN* bounds
a large leap • *With a couple of bounds he had crossed the room.*

**bound** *ADJECTIVE*
❶ obstructed or hindered by something • *The airport is fog-bound.* ❷ going towards a place • *We are bound for Spain.*
➤ **bound to** certain or very likely to • *He is bound to fail.*
➤ **bound up with** closely connected with • *Happiness is bound up with success.*

**boundary** *NOUN* boundaries
❶ a line that marks a limit ❷ a hit to the boundary of a cricket field

SPELLING
There is no e in **boundary**! It ends with **ary**.

**boundless** *ADJECTIVE*
without limits • *his boundless enthusiasm*

**bounds** *PLURAL NOUN*
limits • *This was beyond the bounds of possibility.*
➤ **out of bounds** where you are not allowed to go

**bountiful** *ADJECTIVE*
❶ plentiful; producing a lot • *bountiful harvest* ❷ giving generously

**bounty** *NOUN* bounties
❶ a reward paid for capturing or killing someone ❷ generosity in giving things

**bouquet** (say boh-**kay**) *NOUN* bouquets
a bunch of flowers

**bout** *NOUN* bouts
❶ a boxing or wrestling contest ❷ a period of exercise or work or illness • *a bout of flu*

**boutique** (say boo-**teek**) *NOUN* boutiques
a small shop selling fashionable clothes

**bovine** (say **boh**-vyn) *ADJECTIVE*
❶ to do with or like cattle ❷ dull and stupid

**bow** (rhymes with go) *NOUN* bows
❶ a knot made with two loops and two loose ends ❷ a strip of wood curved by a tight string joining its ends, used for shooting arrows ❸ a wooden rod with horsehair stretched between its ends, used for playing a violin or similar string instrument

**bow** (rhymes with cow) *VERB* bows, bowing, bowed
❶ to bend your body forwards to show respect or as a greeting ❷ to bend a part of your body downwards • *He bowed his head.*

**bow** (rhymes with cow) *NOUN* bows
❶ a movement of bowing your body • *The pianist stood up to take a bow.* ❷ the front end of a ship

**bowels** *PLURAL NOUN*
your intestines **WORD ORIGIN** from Latin *botellus* = little sausage

**bower** *NOUN* bowers
a pleasant shady place under trees

**bowl** *NOUN* bowls
❶ a round open container for food or liquid ❷ the rounded part of a spoon ❸ a heavy ball used in the game of bowls or in bowling

**bowl** *VERB* bowls, bowling, bowled
❶ to send a ball to be played by a batsman in cricket ❷ to get a batsman out by hitting the wicket with the ball ❸ to send a ball rolling along the ground

**bow-legged** *ADJECTIVE*
having legs that curve outwards at the knees

**bowler** *NOUN* bowlers
❶ a person who bowls ❷ (also bowler hat) (*chiefly British*) a man's stiff felt hat with a rounded top

**bowling** *NOUN*
❶ the game of knocking down skittles with a heavy ball ❷ the game of bowls

**bowls** *NOUN*
a game played on a smooth piece of grass, in which you roll heavy wooden balls towards a smaller target ball

**bow tie** *NOUN* bow ties
a tie in the form of a bow, worn by men as part of formal dress

**bow window** *NOUN* bow windows
a curved window

**box** *NOUN* boxes
❶ a container made of wood, cardboard, etc., usually with a top or lid ❷ a rectangular space that you fill in on a form or computer screen ❸ a compartment for seating several people in a theatre ❹ an enclosed area for the jury or witnesses in a law court ❺ a small evergreen shrub
➤ the box (*informal*) television

**box** *VERB* boxes, boxing, boxed
❶ to fight with your fists as a sport ❷ to put something into a box
➤ boxing *NOUN*

**boxer** *NOUN* boxers
❶ a person who boxes ❷ a dog that looks like a bulldog

**Boxing Day** *NOUN*
(*British*) the first weekday after Christmas Day
**WORD ORIGIN** from the old custom of giving presents (*Christmas boxes*) to tradesmen and servants on that day

**box office** *NOUN* box offices
an office for booking seats at a theatre or cinema

**boy** *NOUN* boys
❶ a male child ❷ a young man

**boycott** *VERB* boycotts, boycotting, boycotted
to refuse to use or buy something because you do not approve of it • *They boycotted the buses when the fares went up.*
➤ boycott *NOUN*
**WORD ORIGIN** from the name of Captain *Boycott*, a harsh landlord in Ireland whose tenants in 1880 refused to deal with him

**boyfriend** *NOUN* boyfriends
a person's regular male friend or lover

**boyhood** *NOUN*
the time when a man was boy • *He spent his boyhood in India.*

**boyish** *ADJECTIVE*
like a boy or suitable for a boy • *his boyish enthusiasm*

**bra** *NOUN* bras
a piece of underwear worn by women to support their breasts

**brace** *NOUN* braces
❶ a device for holding things in place ❷ a wire device fitted in your mouth to straighten your teeth ❸ a pair of something • *a brace of pheasants*

**brace** *VERB* braces, bracing, braced
to support something or make it steady • *He braced his back against the wall.*

➤ **brace yourself** to prepare yourself for something unpleasant

**bracelet** *NOUN* bracelets
a small band or chain you wear round your wrist

**braces** *PLURAL NOUN*
straps to hold trousers up, which pass over your shoulders

**bracing** *ADJECTIVE*
making you feel refreshed and healthy • *the bracing sea breeze*

**bracken** *NOUN*
a type of large fern that grows in open country; a mass of these ferns

**bracket** *NOUN* brackets
❶ a mark used in pairs to enclose words or figures. There are round brackets ( ) and square brackets [ ]. ❷ a support attached to a wall to hold up a shelf or light fitting ❸ a group or range between certain limits • *a high income bracket*

**bracket** *VERB* brackets, bracketing, bracketed
❶ to enclose words or figures in brackets
❷ to group things together because they are similar

---
**PUNCTUATION**

Brackets are used in pairs to separate off a word or phrase from the main text.

Parentheses (sometimes called round brackets) surround a comment or information which is not part of the main flow of the sentence. If you take out the word or phrase between the two brackets, the sentence should still make sense on its own:

*Her stomach (which was never very quiet) began to gurgle alarmingly.*

Square brackets are sometimes used by someone other than the original writer of a text to add a short note or explanation:

*He [the president] said that he would not resign.*

---

**brackish** *ADJECTIVE*
brackish water tastes slightly salty

**brae** (say bray) *NOUN* braes (*Scottish*)
a hillside or slope

**brag** *VERB* brags, bragging, bragged
to boast • *He is always bragging about how brilliant he is at football.*

**braggart** *NOUN* braggarts
a person who brags

**Brahmin** *NOUN* Brahmins
a member of the highest Hindu class, originally priests

**braid** *NOUN* braids
❶ a plait of hair ❷ a strip of cloth with a woven decorative pattern, used as trimming

**braid** *VERB* braids, braiding, braided
❶ to plait hair • *Her hair was braided down her back.* ❷ to trim something with braid

**Braille** (rhymes with mail) *NOUN*
a system of representing letters by raised dots which blind people can read by touch
**WORD ORIGIN** named after Louis *Braille*, a blind French teacher who invented it in about 1830

**brain** *NOUN* brains
❶ the organ inside the top of the head that controls the body ❷ your mind or intelligence • *He's got a good brain*

**brainwash** *VERB* brainwashes, brainwashing, brainwashed
to force a person to give up one set of ideas or beliefs and accept new ones

**brainwave** *NOUN* brainwaves
a sudden bright idea • *I've just had a brainwave.*

**brainy** *ADJECTIVE* brainier, brainiest
(*informal*) clever; intelligent

**braise** *VERB* braises, braising, braised
to cook food slowly in a little liquid in a closed container

**brake** *NOUN* brakes
a device for slowing down or stopping a moving vehicle

**brake** *VERB* brakes, braking, braked
to use a brake
---
**SPELLING**
Brake is different from break, which means to divide something into pieces by hitting or dropping it.
---

**bramble** *NOUN* brambles
a blackberry bush or a prickly bush like it

**bran** *NOUN*
ground-up husks of grain which have been sifted out from flour

**branch** *NOUN* branches
❶ a woody arm-like part of a tree or shrub
❷ a local shop, bank or office that belongs

a
b
c
d
e
f
g
h
i
j
k
l
m
n
o
p
q
r
s
t
u
v
w
x
y
z

**branch** *NOUN*
to a large organization ❸ a part of a railway, road or river that leads off from the main part ❹ a part of an academic subject • *Calculus is a branch of mathematics.*

**branch** *VERB* branches, branching, branched
to form a branch or divide into branches • *A footpath branches off from the main track.*
➤ **branch out** to start doing something new • *He has recently branched out into acting.*

**brand** *NOUN* brands
❶ a particular make of goods • *a cheap brand of tea* ❷ a mark made on cattle or sheep by branding ❸ a piece of burning wood

**brand** *VERB* brands, branding, branded
❶ to mark cattle or sheep with a piece of hot iron to identify them ❷ to identify or class someone as something bad • *He will be branded forever as a cheat.* ❸ to sell goods under a particular trademark

**brandish** *VERB* brandishes, brandishing, brandished
to wave something about • *The men leapt out of the boat, brandishing their swords.*

**brand name** *NOUN* brand names
a name given to a product or range of products

**brand new** *ADJECTIVE*
completely new

**brandy** *NOUN* brandies
a strong alcoholic drink, usually made from wine

**brash** *ADJECTIVE*
too confident in a rude or aggressive way

**brass** *NOUN* brasses
❶ a metal that is an alloy of copper and zinc ❷ wind instruments made of brass, such as trumpets and trombones
➤ **brass** *ADJECTIVE*
➤ **brassy** *ADJECTIVE*

**brass band** *NOUN* brass bands
a musical band made up of brass instruments

**brassiere** (say **bras**-ee-air) *NOUN* brassieres
a bra

**brat** *NOUN* brats (*informal*)
a badly behaved child

**bravado** (say brav-**ah**-doh) *NOUN*
a display of boldness to impress people

**brave** *ADJECTIVE*
having or showing courage
➤ **bravely** *ADVERB*

**brave** *VERB* braves, braving, braved
to face and endure something dangerous or unpleasant • *They decided to brave the icy winds outside.*

**brave** *NOUN* braves
a Native American warrior

**bravery** *NOUN*
brave actions; courage • *a medal for bravery*

**bravo** (say **brah**-voh) *EXCLAMATION*
well done!

**brawl** *NOUN* brawls
a noisy quarrel or fight

**brawl** *VERB* brawls, brawling, brawled
to take part in a brawl

**brawn** *NOUN*
physical strength • *In this job you need brains as well as brawn.*

**brawny** *ADJECTIVE*
strong and muscular

**bray** *VERB* brays, braying, brayed
a donkey brays when it makes a loud harsh cry

**bray** *NOUN* brays
the loud harsh cry of a donkey

**brazen** *ADJECTIVE*
❶ bold and shameless • *brazen impudence* ❷ made of brass

**brazen** *VERB* brazens, brazening, brazened
➤ **brazen it out** to behave, after doing something wrong, as if you have nothing to be ashamed of

**brazier** (say **bray**-zee-er) *NOUN* braziers
a metal basket in which coals can be burned to keep people warm outdoors

**breach** *NOUN* breaches
❶ the breaking of an agreement or rule ❷ a gap or broken place in a wall or barrier

**breach** *VERB* breaches, breaching, breached
to break through something; to make a gap • *They finally breached the castle walls.*

**bread** *NOUN* breads
a food made by baking flour and water, usually with yeast
➤ **breadcrumbs** *NOUN*

**breadth** *NOUN*
❶ the distance across something, from one side to another ❷ a wide range • *a breadth of experience*

**breadwinner** *NOUN* breadwinners
the member of a family who earns money to support the others

**break** *VERB* breaks, breaking, broke, broken
❶ to divide something into pieces by hitting or dropping it ❷ to fall into pieces because of being hit ❸ to damage something so that it stops working properly ❹ to fail to keep a promise, rule or law ❺ to stop something for a time; to end something • *She broke her silence.* ❻ weather breaks when it changes suddenly after being hot ❼ a boy's voice breaks when it becomes suddenly deeper at puberty ❽ waves break when they fall in foam on a shore ❾ to go suddenly or with force • *They broke through.* ❿ to appear suddenly • *Dawn had broken.*
➤ **break a record** to do better than anyone else has done before
➤ **break down** ❶ to stop working properly ❷ to collapse
➤ **break off** to stop doing something for a time • *We broke off for lunch.*
➤ **break out** ❶ to begin suddenly, like a disease or fighting ❷ to escape
➤ **break the news** to make something known
➤ **break up** ❶ to break into small parts ❷ a school breaks up when it closes at the end of a term ❸ to end your relationship with someone • *My brother and his girlfriend have broken up.*

**break** *NOUN* breaks
❶ a broken place; a gap ❷ an escape; a sudden dash ❸ a short rest from work ❹ a number of points scored continuously in snooker ❺ the winning of a tennis game against the other player's serve ❻ (*informal*) a piece of luck; a fair chance • *Give me a break.*
➤ **break of day** dawn

SPELLING

Break is different from brake, which is a device for stopping a vehicle.

**breakable** *ADJECTIVE*
easy to break

**breakage** *NOUN* breakages
something that is broken • *Breakages must be paid for.*

**breakdown** *NOUN* breakdowns
❶ a sudden failure to work properly, especially by a car • *We had a breakdown on the motorway.* ❷ a failure or collapse of something • *There has been a breakdown of communication.* ❸ a period of mental illness caused by anxiety or depression ❹ an analysis of accounts or statistics • *Here's a breakdown of last season's football results.*

**breaker** *NOUN* breakers
a large wave breaking on the shore

**breakfast** *NOUN* breakfasts
the first meal of the day (WORD ORIGIN) from **break** + **fast**, because it is the first meal you eat after fasting overnight

**breakneck** *ADJECTIVE*
breakneck speed is dangerously fast

**breakthrough** *NOUN* breakthroughs
an important development or discovery • *a major breakthrough in cancer research*

**breakwater** *NOUN* breakwaters
a wall built out into the sea to protect a coast from heavy waves

**bream** *NOUN* bream
a kind of fish with an arched back

**breast** *NOUN* breasts
❶ one of the two fleshy parts on the upper front of a woman's body that produce milk to feed a baby ❷ a person's or animal's chest

**breastbone** *NOUN* breastbones
the flat bone down the centre of your chest, joined to your ribs

**breastplate** *NOUN* breastplates
a piece of armour covering the chest

**breaststroke** *NOUN*
a way of swimming on your front in which you push your arms forward and bring them round and back

**breath** (say breth) *NOUN* breaths
❶ air that is drawn into your lungs and sent out again ❷ a gentle blowing • *a breath of wind*
➤ **out of breath** breathing with difficulty after exercise; panting
➤ **take your breath away** to surprise or delight you greatly
➤ **under your breath** in a whisper

SPELLING

Breath is a noun and breathe is a verb • *She was out of breath.* • *She found it hard to breathe.*

**breathalyser** *NOUN* breathalysers
a device for measuring the amount of alcohol in a person's breath
➤ **breathalyse** *VERB*

**breathe** (say breeth) *VERB* breathes, breathing, breathed
❶ to take air into your body and send it out again ❷ to say or speak about something • *Don't breathe a word of this.*

a
b
c
d
e
f
g
h
i
j
k
l
m
n
o
p
q
r
s
t
u
v
w
x
y
z

**breather** (say **bree**-ther) *NOUN* breathers
(*informal*) a pause for rest • *Let's take a breather.*

**breathless** *ADJECTIVE*
out of breath
➤ **breathlessly** *ADVERB*

**breathtaking** *ADJECTIVE*
very impressive or beautiful • *breathtaking scenery*

**breech** *NOUN* breeches
the back part of a gun barrel, where the bullets are put in

**breeches** (say **brich**-iz) *PLURAL NOUN*
trousers reaching to just below your knees

**breed** *VERB* breeds, breeding, bred
❶ to produce children or offspring ❷ to keep animals in order to produce young ones from them ❸ to create or produce something • *Poverty breeds illness.* ❹ to be bred in a particular way is to be brought up or trained that way • *These people have been bred to fight.*
➤ **breeder** *NOUN*

**breed** *NOUN* breeds
a variety of animal that has been specially developed • *a breed of dog*

**breeze** *NOUN* breezes
a gentle wind

**breeze block** *NOUN* breeze blocks
(*British*) a lightweight building block made of cinders and cement

**breezy** *ADJECTIVE*
❶ pleasantly windy ❷ relaxed and cheerful
➤ **breezily** *ADVERB*

**brethren** *PLURAL NOUN* (*old use*)
brothers (WORD ORIGIN) the old plural of **brother**

**breve** (say breev) *NOUN* breves
a note in music, lasting eight times as long as a crotchet

**brevity** *NOUN*
being brief or short • *I was surprised by the brevity of her answer.*

**brew** *VERB* brews, brewing, brewed
❶ to make tea or coffee by mixing it with hot water ❷ to make beer by boiling and fermentation ❸ something bad is brewing when it is growing or developing • *Trouble is brewing.*

**brew** *NOUN* brews
a brewed drink

**brewer** *NOUN* brewers
a person who brews beer for sale

**brewery** *NOUN* breweries
a place where beer is brewed

**briar** *NOUN* briars
a thorny bush, especially the wild rose

**bribe** *NOUN* bribes
money or a gift offered to someone to influence them to do something

**bribe** *VERB* bribes, bribing, bribed
to persuade someone to do something by offering them a bribe
➤ **bribery** *NOUN*

**brick** *NOUN* bricks
❶ a small hard block of baked clay used to build walls ❷ a rectangular block of something

**brick** *VERB* bricks, bricking, bricked
➤ **brick something up** to block an entrance or window with bricks

**bricklayer** *NOUN* bricklayers
a worker who builds with bricks

**bridal** *ADJECTIVE*
to do with a bride or a wedding • *a bridal gown*

**bride** *NOUN* brides
a woman on her wedding day

**bridegroom** *NOUN* bridegrooms
a man on his wedding day

**bridesmaid** *NOUN* bridesmaids
a woman or girl who accompanies a bride at her wedding

**bridge** *NOUN* bridges
❶ a structure built over and across a river, railway or road to allow people or vehicles to cross it ❷ a high platform above a ship's deck, for the officer in charge ❸ the bony upper part of your nose ❹ a card game rather like whist

**bridge** *VERB* bridges, bridging, bridged
to make or form a bridge over something
➤ **bridge a gap** to fill a space between two things or bring them closer together • *These novels bridge the gap between children's and adult fiction.*

**bridle** *NOUN* bridles
the part of a horse's harness that fits over its head

**bridle** *VERB* bridles, bridling, bridled
❶ to put a bridle on a horse ❷ to show you are angry or offended by something

**bridleway, bridle path** NOUN bridleways, bridle paths
(*British*) a road suitable for horses but not for vehicles

**brief** ADJECTIVE
lasting for a short time or using only a few words
➤ **in brief** in a few words

**brief** NOUN briefs
instructions and information given to someone before they start a piece of work

**brief** VERB briefs, briefing, briefed
to give someone the instructions and information they need before they start a piece of work

**briefcase** NOUN briefcases
a flat case for carrying documents

**briefing** NOUN briefings
a meeting to give someone instructions or information

**briefly** ADVERB
❶ for a short time • *She glanced briefly at the letter.* ❷ using only a few words • *I'll answer that briefly.*

**briefs** PLURAL NOUN
short knickers or underpants

**brier** NOUN briers
a different spelling of briar

**brigade** NOUN brigades
❶ a large unit of an army ❷ a group of people organized for a special purpose • *the fire brigade*

**brigadier** NOUN brigadiers
an army officer who commands a brigade, higher in rank than a colonel

**brigand** NOUN brigands
a member of a band of robbers

**bright** ADJECTIVE
❶ giving out a strong light; filled with light or sunlight ❷ a bright colour is strong and vivid ❸ clever ❹ cheerful
➤ **brightly** ADVERB
➤ **brightness** NOUN

**brighten** VERB brightens, brightening, brightened
to become brighter or more cheerful; to make something brighter • *Her face brightened when she saw him.*

**brilliance** NOUN
❶ bright light ❷ great intelligence or cleverness

**brilliant** ADJECTIVE
❶ very clever or talented ❷ excellent; very enjoyable ❸ shining very brightly
➤ **brilliantly** ADVERB

**brim** NOUN brims
❶ the edge round the top of a cup, bowl or other container ❷ the bottom part of a hat that sticks out

**brim** VERB brims, brimming, brimmed
to be full of something • *His eyes were brimming with tears.*
➤ **brim over** a container that is brimming over is overflowing

**brimful** ADJECTIVE
full to the brim

**brimstone** NOUN (*old use*)
sulphur

**brine** NOUN
salt water
➤ **briny** ADJECTIVE

**bring** VERB brings, bringing, brought
❶ to carry or take a person or thing with you to a place • *Can I bring a friend to your party?* ❷ to make something come or happen • *Money doesn't always bring happiness.* ❸ to move something somewhere • *She brought the book down off the shelf.*
➤ **bring something about** to make something happen
➤ **bring something off** to achieve something; to do something successfully
➤ **bring someone up** to look after and train children as they grow up
➤ **bring something up** ❶ to mention a subject ❷ to vomit

**brinjal** NOUN brinjals (*Indian & S. African*)
an aubergine or eggplant

**brink** NOUN brinks
❶ the edge of a steep place or of a stretch of water ❷ the point beyond which something will happen • *We were on the brink of war.*

**brisk** ADJECTIVE
❶ quick and lively • *They set off at a brisk pace.* ❷ wanting to get things done quickly and efficiently. • *Her voice became brisk and businesslike.*
➤ **briskly** ADVERB
➤ **briskness** NOUN

**bristle** NOUN bristles
❶ a short stiff hair ❷ one of the stiff pieces of hair, wire or plastic in a brush
➤ **bristly** ADJECTIVE

**bristle** VERB bristles, bristling, bristled
❶ an animal bristles when it raises its bristles in anger or fear ❷ someone bristles when they show indignation
➤ **bristle with** to have a lot of something
• *The room bristled with computer screens.*

**Britain** NOUN
the island made up of England, Scotland and Wales, with the small adjacent islands; Great Britain

USAGE

Note the difference in use between the terms *Britain*, *Great Britain*, the *United Kingdom* and the *British Isles*. Great Britain (or Britain) is used to refer to the island made up of England, Scotland and Wales. The United Kingdom includes Great Britain and Northern Ireland. The British Isles refers to the whole of the island group which includes Great Britain, Ireland and all the smaller nearby islands.

**British Isles** PLURAL NOUN
the island group which includes Great Britain, Ireland and all the smaller nearby islands

USAGE

See note at **Britain**.

**brittle** ADJECTIVE
hard but easy to break or snap
➤ **brittleness** NOUN

**broach** VERB broaches, broaching, broached
❶ to start a discussion of something • *We were unwilling to broach the subject.* ❷ to make a hole in something and draw out liquid

**broad** ADJECTIVE
❶ large across; wide ❷ in general terms; not detailed • *We are in broad agreement.* ❸ strong and unmistakable • *a broad hint* • *a broad accent*
➤ **broad daylight** full daylight; the daytime

**broadband** NOUN
(*in computing*) a system for connecting computers to the Internet at very high speed

**broad bean** NOUN broad beans
a bean with large flat seeds

**broadcast** NOUN broadcasts
a programme sent out on television or the radio

**broadcast** VERB broadcasts, broadcasting, broadcast
to send out a programme on television or the radio
➤ **broadcaster** NOUN

WORD ORIGIN originally = to scatter seeds widely: from **broad** + **cast**

**broaden** VERB broadens, broadening, broadened
to become broader; to make something broader • *Her grin broadened.* • *Travel broadens the mind.*

**broadly** ADVERB
❶ generally; on the whole • *They were broadly right.* ❷ widely • *Tom was smiling broadly now*

**broad-minded** ADJECTIVE
tolerant; not easily shocked

**broadside** NOUN broadsides
❶ a round of firing by all the guns on one side of a ship ❷ a strong verbal attack
➤ **broadside on** sideways on

**brocade** NOUN
a rich fabric woven with raised patterns

**broccoli** NOUN broccoli
a kind of cauliflower with greenish flower heads

SPELLING

Double up the c in **broccoli** (but the l stays single)!

**brochure** (say broh-shoor) NOUN brochures
a booklet or pamphlet containing information
WORD ORIGIN from French, = stitching (because originally the pages were roughly stitched together)

**brogue** (rhymes with rogue) NOUN brogues
❶ a strong kind of shoe ❷ a strong regional accent • *He spoke with an Irish brogue.*

**broil** VERB broils, broiling, broiled
❶ to cook food using a direct heat, such as a grill ❷ to be broiling is to be very hot

**broke** ADJECTIVE (*informal*)
having spent all your money

**broken-hearted** ADJECTIVE
feeling great sadness or grief

**broken home** NOUN broken homes
a family in which the parents are divorced or separated

**broker** NOUN brokers
a person who buys and sells things, especially shares, for other people

**brolly** NOUN brollies (*British*) (*informal*)
an umbrella

**bromide** NOUN
a substance used in medicine to calm the nerves

**bronchial** (say **bronk**-ee-al) ADJECTIVE
to do with the tubes that lead from your windpipe to your lungs

**bronchitis** (say bronk-**y**-tiss) NOUN
a disease that causes inflammation of the bronchial tubes, which makes you cough a lot

**bronze** NOUN bronzes
❶ a metal that is an alloy of copper and tin ❷ something made of bronze ❸ a bronze medal, awarded as third prize ❹ a yellowish-brown colour
➤ **bronze** ADJECTIVE

**Bronze Age** NOUN
the period in human history when tools and weapons were made of bronze

**brooch** (rhymes with coach) NOUN brooches
an ornament with a hinged pin for fastening it on to clothes

**brood** NOUN broods
young birds that were hatched together

**brood** VERB broods, brooding, brooded
❶ to keep thinking and worrying about something • *He was still brooding over his disappointment weeks later.* ❷ to sit on eggs to hatch them

**broody** ADJECTIVE
❶ a broody hen is ready to sit on her eggs ❷ quietly worried and unhappy about something ❸ a woman who is broody is eager to have children

**brook** NOUN brooks
a small stream

**brook** VERB brooks, brooking, brooked
to allow or tolerate something • *She would brook no argument.*

**broom** NOUN brooms
❶ a brush with a long handle, for sweeping floors ❷ a shrub with yellow, white or pink flowers

**broomstick** NOUN broomsticks
the handle of a broom, which in stories witches use to ride on

**broth** NOUN broths
a kind of thin soup

**brothel** NOUN brothels
a house where men pay to have sex with prostitutes

**brother** NOUN brothers
❶ a son of the same parents as another person ❷ a member of a Christian religious order of men
➤ **brotherly** ADJECTIVE

**brotherhood** NOUN brotherhoods
❶ friendliness and companionship between men ❷ a society or association of men

**brother-in-law** NOUN brothers-in-law
the brother of a married person's husband or wife; the husband of a person's sister or brother

**brow** NOUN brows
❶ an eyebrow ❷ your forehead ❸ the top of a hill

**brown** NOUN
a colour between orange and black, like the colour of dark wood

**brown** ADJECTIVE
❶ of the colour brown ❷ having a brown skin; suntanned

**brown** VERB browns, browning, browned
❶ to make something brown, especially by cooking it ❷ to become brown

**brownfield** ADJECTIVE
(*British*) a brownfield site is a piece of land that had buildings on it in the past and that may now be cleared for new buildings to be built

**Brownie** NOUN Brownies
a member of a junior branch of the Guides

**brownie** NOUN brownies
a flat chocolate cake, served in squares

**browse** VERB browses, browsing, browsed
❶ to read or look at something casually ❷ to look for information on the Internet ❸ animals browse when they feed on grass or leaves

**browser** NOUN browsers
(*in computing*) a piece of computer software that allows you to search and look at websites on the Internet

**bruise** NOUN bruises
a dark mark made on the skin by hitting it

**bruise** VERB bruises, bruising, bruised
❶ to make a bruise or bruises appear on a person's skin ❷ to develop a bruise • *I bruise easily.*

**brunch** NOUN (*informal*)
a late-morning meal combining breakfast and lunch **WORD ORIGIN** from **breakfast** and **lunch**

**brunette** NOUN brunettes
a woman with dark-brown hair

**brunt** NOUN
the chief impact of something • *They bore the brunt of the attack.*

**brush** NOUN brushes
❶ an object used for cleaning or painting things or for smoothing the hair, usually with bristles set in a solid base ❷ using a brush • *The floor needs a good brush.* ❸ a fox's bushy tail ❹ an unpleasant experience or encounter • *She told us about her brush with disaster.* ❺ undergrowth, bushes and shrubs that often grow under trees

**brush** VERB brushes, brushing, brushed
❶ to use a brush on something • *I just need to brush my hair.* ❷ to touch something lightly while passing it • *Her hand brushed his arm.*
➤ **brush something aside** to refuse to accept that something is important • *He brushed aside their protests.*
➤ **brush something up** to revise your knowledge of a subject

**brusque** (say bruusk) ADJECTIVE
abrupt and offhand in manner
➤ **brusquely** ADVERB

**Brussels sprout** NOUN Brussels sprouts
the edible buds of a kind of cabbage

**brutal** ADJECTIVE
cruel and violent
➤ **brutally** ADVERB
➤ **brutality** NOUN

**brute** NOUN brutes
❶ a cruel or violent man ❷ an animal

**brute** ADJECTIVE
brute force or strength is purely physical, without using any skill
➤ **brutish** ADJECTIVE

**BSc** ABBREVIATION
Bachelor of Science

**BSE** ABBREVIATION
bovine spongiform encephalopathy; a fatal disease of cattle that affects the nervous system and makes the cow stagger about. BSE is sometimes known as 'mad cow disease'

**bubble** NOUN bubbles
❶ a thin transparent ball of liquid filled with air or gas ❷ a small ball of air in something, such as a fizzy drink

**bubble** VERB bubbles, bubbling, bubbled
❶ to send up bubbles or rise to the surface in bubbles • *The kettle was bubbling now.* ❷ to show great liveliness • *He was bubbling with excitement.*

**bubblegum** NOUN
chewing gum that can be blown into large bubbles

**bubbly** ADJECTIVE bubblier, bubbliest
❶ full of bubbles ❷ cheerful and lively

**buccaneer** NOUN buccaneers
a pirate

**buck** NOUN bucks
❶ a male deer, rabbit or hare ❷ (North American & Australian/NZ) a dollar
➤ **pass the buck** (informal) to pass the responsibility for something to another person

**buck** VERB bucks, bucking, bucked
a horse bucks when it jumps with its back arched
➤ **buck up** (informal)
❶ to cheer up ❷ to hurry up

**bucket** NOUN buckets
a container with a handle, for carrying liquids, sand, etc.
➤ **bucketful** NOUN

**buckle** NOUN buckles
a clip at the end of a belt or strap for fastening it

**buckle** VERB buckles, buckling, buckled
❶ to fasten something with a buckle ❷ to bend or give way under a strain • *The arm of the crane was beginning to buckle.*
➤ **buckle down to something** to start working hard at something

**buckler** NOUN bucklers
a small round shield

**bud** NOUN buds
a flower or leaf before it opens

**Buddhism** (say **buud**-izm) NOUN
a religion that started in Asia and follows the teachings of Siddharta Gautama who lived in India in the 5th century BC and became known as 'the Buddha'
➤ **Buddhist** NOUN

**budding** ADJECTIVE
beginning to develop • *a budding poet*

**buddy** NOUN buddies (informal)
a friend

**budge** VERB budges, budging, budged
if you cannot budge something, you cannot move it at all

**budgerigar** *NOUN* budgerigars
an Australian bird often kept as a pet in a cage

**budget** *NOUN* budgets
❶ a plan for spending money wisely ❷ an amount of money set aside for a purpose
➤ the Budget the Chancellor of the Exchequer's statement of plans for government spending and taxes

**budget** *VERB* budgets, budgeting, budgeted
to plan how much you are going to spend

**budgie** *NOUN* budgies (*informal*)
a budgerigar

**buff** *NOUN* buffs (*informal*)
a person who is very interested in a subject and knows a lot about it • *a film buff*

**buff** *ADJECTIVE*
of a dull yellow colour

**buff** *VERB* buffs, buffing, buffed
to polish something with soft material
**WORD ORIGIN** noun sense comes from the adjective, originally describing people who went to watch fires, from the buff-coloured uniforms once worn by New York firemen

**buffalo** *NOUN* buffalo or buffaloes
a large ox. Different kinds are found in Asia, Africa and North America (where they are also called bison)

**buffer** *NOUN* buffers
❶ something that reduces an impact or protects something ❷ (*British*) a device on a railway engine or wagon or at the end of a track, for reducing the shock if there is a collision ❸ (*in computing*) a memory in which text or data can be stored temporarily

**buffer state** *NOUN* buffer states
a small country between two powerful ones, thought to reduce the chance of these two attacking each other

**buffet** (say **buu**-fay) *NOUN* buffets
❶ a room or counter selling light meals or snacks ❷ a meal where guests serve themselves

**buffet** (say **buf**-it) *VERB* buffets, buffeting, buffeted
to hit or knock something repeatedly • *Strong winds buffeted the aircraft.*

**buffoon** *NOUN* buffoons
a person who acts like a fool

**bug** *NOUN* bugs
❶ a tiny insect ❷ an error in a computer program that prevents it working properly

❸ (*informal*) a germ or virus ❹ a secret hidden microphone

**bug** *VERB* bugs, bugging, bugged
❶ to fit a room with a secret hidden microphone ❷ (*informal*) to pester or annoy someone

**bugbear** *NOUN* bugbears
something you fear or dislike

**buggy** *NOUN* buggies
❶ a kind of chair on wheels for pushing young children around ❷ a small open-topped vehicle used on beaches or golf courses ❸ a light, horse-drawn carriage

**bugle** *NOUN* bugles
a brass instrument like a small trumpet, used for sounding military signals
➤ bugler *NOUN*

**build** *VERB* builds, building, built
❶ to make something by putting parts together ❷ to develop or increase something gradually
➤ build something in to include something in a structure or plan
➤ build up to grow or increase • *The traffic always builds up at this time of the day.*
➤ build something up ❶ to establish something gradually • *He has built up a reputation for getting results.* ❷ to increase something or make it stronger • *You need to build up your strength.*

**build** *NOUN* builds
the shape of someone's body • *She has a slender build.*

**builder** *NOUN* builders
someone who puts up buildings

**building** *NOUN* buildings
❶ a structure with walls and a roof, such as a house or office block ❷ the process of constructing houses and other structures

**building society** *NOUN* building societies
(*British*) an organization that accepts deposits of money and lends to people who want to buy houses

**built-in** *ADJECTIVE*
made into a permanent part of something • *The bedroom has a built-in wardrobe.*

**built-up** *ADJECTIVE*
a built-up area is one with a lot of buildings

**bulb** *NOUN* bulbs
❶ a glass globe that produces electric light ❷ a thick rounded part of a plant from which a stem grows up and roots grow down ❸ a

**bulb** rounded part of something • *the bulb of a thermometer* (WORD ORIGIN) from Greek *bolbos* = onion

**bulbous** *ADJECTIVE*
round and fat in an ugly way • *a bulbous nose*

**bulge** *NOUN* bulges
a rounded swelling; an outward curve

**bulge** *VERB* bulges, bulging, bulged
to swell or stick out in a curve • *His eyes bulged with excitement.*

**bulimia** (say bew-**lim**-ia) *NOUN*
an illness that makes someone alternately overeat and fast, often making themselves vomit after eating
➤ **bulimic** *ADJECTIVE*

**bulk** *NOUN* bulks
❶ the size of something, especially when it is large ❷ the greater part or the majority • *The bulk of the population voted for it.*
➤ **in bulk** in large amounts

**bulk** *VERB* bulks, bulking, bulked
➤ **bulk something out** to increase the size or thickness of something

**bulky** *ADJECTIVE* bulkier, bulkiest
taking up a lot of space

**bull** *NOUN* bulls
❶ a fully-grown male of the cattle family ❷ a male seal, whale or elephant

**bulldog** *NOUN* bulldogs
a dog of a powerful breed with a short thick neck (WORD ORIGIN) because it was used for attacking tethered bulls in the sport of 'bull-baiting'

**bulldoze** *VERB* bulldozes, bulldozing, bulldozed
to clear an area with a bulldozer

**bulldozer** *NOUN* bulldozers
a powerful tractor with a wide metal blade or scoop in front, used for shifting soil or clearing ground

**bullet** *NOUN* bullets
a small piece of shaped metal shot from a rifle or revolver

**bulletin** *NOUN* bulletins
❶ a short announcement of news on radio or television ❷ a regular newsletter or report

**bulletin board** *NOUN* bulletin boards
(*in computing*) a site on a computer system where people can read or write messages

**bullet point** *NOUN* bullet points
an important item in a list, printed with a black dot in front of it

**bulletproof** *ADJECTIVE*
able to keep out bullets

**bullfight** *NOUN* bullfights
in Spain, a public entertainment in which bulls are fought and usually killed, in an arena
➤ **bullfighter** *NOUN*

**bullfinch** *NOUN* bullfinches
a bird with a strong beak and a pink breast

**bullion** *NOUN*
bars of gold or silver

**bullock** *NOUN* bullocks
a young castrated bull

**bullseye** *NOUN* bullseyes
❶ the centre of a target ❷ a hard round peppermint sweet

**bully** *VERB* bullies, bullying, bullied
to use strength or power to hurt or frighten another person

**bully** *NOUN* bullies
someone who bullies people
➤ **bullying** *NOUN*

**bulrush** *NOUN* bulrushes
a tall plant which grows in marshes, with a thick velvety head

**bulwark** *NOUN* bulwarks
a wall of earth built as a defence

**bulwarks** *PLURAL NOUN*
a ship's side above the level of the deck

**bum** *NOUN* bums (*British*) (*informal*)
a person's bottom

**bumble** *VERB* bumbles, bumbling, bumbled
to move or behave or speak clumsily

**bumblebee** *NOUN* bumblebees
a large bee with a loud hum

**bump** *VERB* bumps, bumping, bumped
❶ to knock against something ❷ to move along with jolts
➤ **bump into someone** (*informal*) to meet someone by chance
➤ **bump someone off** (*informal*) to kill someone

**bump** *NOUN* bumps
❶ knocking against something or the sound of this • *He landed with a bump on the floor.*
❷ a swelling or lump • *She had a bump on her forehead.*

**bumper** NOUN bumpers
a bar along the front or back of a motor vehicle to protect it in collisions

**bumper** ADJECTIVE
unusually large or plentiful • *a bumper crop of apples*

**bumpkin** NOUN bumpkins
a country person with awkward manners

**bumptious** (say **bump**-shus) ADJECTIVE
loud and conceited

**bumpy** ADJECTIVE bumpier, bumpiest
having a lot of bumps • *a bumpy road*

**bun** NOUN buns
❶ a small round sweet cake ❷ hair twisted into a round bunch at the back of the head

**bunch** NOUN bunches
a number of things joined or fastened together • *a bunch of grapes* • *a bunch of keys*

**bundle** NOUN bundles
a number of things tied or wrapped together

**bundle** VERB bundles, bundling, bundled
❶ to wrap or tie things into a bundle ❷ to push someone hurriedly or carelessly • *They bundled him into the back of a taxi.*

**bung** NOUN bungs
a stopper for closing a hole in a barrel or jar

**bung** VERB bungs, bunging, bunged (*British*) (*informal*) to bung something somewhere is to put or throw it there carelessly • *Bung those trousers in the washing machine.*
➤ **bunged up** (*informal*) blocked • *My nose is all bunged up today.*

**bungalow** NOUN bungalows
a house without any upstairs rooms
(WORD ORIGIN) from Hindi *bangla* = of Bengal

**bungee jumping** NOUN
the sport of jumping from a height with a special elastic rope (called a **bungee**) tied to your legs to stop you from hitting the ground

**bungle** VERB bungles, bungling, bungled
to make a mess of doing something
➤ **bungler** NOUN

**bunion** NOUN bunions
a swelling at the side of the joint where your big toe joins your foot

**bunk** NOUN bunks
❶ a narrow bed built like a shelf ❷ (also **bunk bed**) one of a pair of single beds mounted one above the other
➤ **do a bunk** (*British*) (*informal*) to run away

**bunk** VERB bunks, bunking, bunked
➤ **bunk off** (*British*) (*informal*) to sneak away from where you are supposed to be, especially school

**bunker** NOUN bunkers
❶ a sandy hollow built as an obstacle on a golf course ❷ an underground shelter for use in wartime ❸ an outdoor container for storing coal

**bunny** NOUN bunnies (*informal*)
a rabbit

**Bunsen burner** NOUN Bunsen burners
a small gas burner used in laboratories
(WORD ORIGIN) named after a German scientist, Robert *Bunsen*, who popularized it

**bunting** NOUN buntings
❶ a kind of small bird ❷ strips of small flags hung up to decorate streets and buildings

**buoy** (say boi) NOUN buoys
a floating object anchored to mark a channel or underwater rocks

**buoy** VERB buoys, buoying, buoyed
❶ to keep something afloat ❷ to encourage someone or keep their spirits up • *They were buoyed up with new hope.*

**buoyant** (say boi-ant) ADJECTIVE
❶ able to float ❷ light-hearted; cheerful • *He was in a buoyant mood.*
➤ **buoyancy** NOUN

**bur** NOUN burs
a different spelling of **burr** (seed case)

**burble** VERB burbles, burbling, burbled
❶ to make a gentle murmuring sound ❷ to speak in a confused way • *He burbled an apology.*

**burden** NOUN burdens
❶ a heavy load that you have to carry ❷ something troublesome that you have to put up with • *He doesn't want to become a burden to his children.*

**burden** VERB burdens, burdening, burdened
❶ to load someone heavily • *She staggered in, burdened with shopping.* ❷ to cause someone worry or trouble • *I'm sorry to burden you with my troubles.*

**bureau** (say bewr-oh) NOUN bureaux
❶ a writing desk with drawers ❷ an office or department • *They will tell you at the Information Bureau.*

**bureaucracy** (say bewr-ok-ra-see) NOUN
the use of too many rules and forms by officials, especially in government

**departments**
➤ **bureaucratic** (say bewr-ok-**rat**-ik) *ADJECTIVE*

**bureaucrat** (say **bewr**-ok-rat) *NOUN*
bureaucrats
a person who works in a government department

**burger** *NOUN* burgers
a hamburger **WORD ORIGIN** short for **hamburger** = from *Hamburg*, a city in Germany; the first syllable was dropped because people thought it referred to ham

**burglar** *NOUN* burglars
a person who breaks into a building in order to steal things

**burglary** *NOUN* burglaries
the crime of breaking into a building and stealing things

**burgle** *VERB* burgles, burgling, burgled
(*British*) to break into a house and steal things
• *Our flat was burgled while we were out.*

**burgundy** *NOUN* burgundies
a rich red or white wine

**burial** *NOUN* burials
burying somebody • *an ancient burial mound*

**burlesque** (say ber-**lesk**) *NOUN* burlesques
a comical imitation that makes fun of something

**burly** *ADJECTIVE* burlier, burliest
having a strong heavy body

**burn** *VERB* burns, burning, burned or burnt
❶ to be on fire; to blaze or glow with fire
• *Firefighters raced to the burning building.*
❷ to damage or destroy something by fire or heat • *He burnt the letters in the fire.* ❸ to hurt yourself with fire or heat • *I burnt my hand on the oven.* ❹ to spoil food by cooking it for too long • *Sorry, I've burnt the toast again.* ❺ to feel very hot • *Her face burnt with embarrassment.*

**burn** *NOUN* burns
❶ a mark or injury made by burning ❷ the firing of a spacecraft's rockets ❸ (*Scottish*) a small stream

**USAGE**
> The word burnt (not burned) is always used when an adjective is required, e.g. in *burnt wood*. As parts of the verb, either burned or burnt may be used, e.g. *the wood had burned* or *had burnt completely*.

**burner** *NOUN* burners
the part of a lamp or cooker that gives out the flame

**burning** *ADJECTIVE*
❶ a burning desire or ambition is one that is very intense ❷ a burning issue or question is one that is very topical and important

**burnish** *VERB* burnishes, burnishing, burnished
to polish a surface by rubbing

**burp** *VERB* burps, burping, burped
to make a noise through your mouth by letting air come up from your stomach

**burp** *NOUN* burps
the act or sound of burping

**burr** *NOUN* burrs
❶ a plant's seed case or flower that clings to hair or clothes ❷ a whirring sound ❸ a strong pronunciation of the letter 'r', as in some regional accents

**burrow** *NOUN* burrows
a hole or tunnel dug by a rabbit or fox as a place to live

**burrow** *VERB* burrows, burrowing, burrowed
❶ to dig a burrow ❷ to push your way through or into something; to search deeply
• *She burrowed in her handbag.*

**bursar** *NOUN* bursars
(*British*) a person who manages the finances and other business of a school or college

**bursary** *NOUN* bursaries
(*British*) a grant given to a student

**burst** *VERB* bursts, bursting, burst
❶ to come apart or tear open suddenly ❷ to break or force something apart ❸ to burst into a room is to go in suddenly in a rush ❹ to start doing something suddenly • *It burst into flames.* • *They burst out laughing.* ❺ to be very full • *She is bursting with energy*

**burst** *NOUN* bursts
❶ a split caused by something bursting ❷ something short and forceful • *a burst of gunfire*

**SPELLING**
> The past tense of burst is also burst; don't add ed.

**bury** *VERB* buries, burying, buried
❶ to put a dead body in the ground ❷ to put something underground ❸ to cover something up or hide it • *The letter was buried at the bottom of a drawer.*

➤ **bury the hatchet** to agree to stop quarrelling or fighting

**bus** *NOUN* buses
a large vehicle for passengers to travel in
**WORD ORIGIN** short for **omnibus**

**busby** *NOUN* busbies
a tall fur cap worn by some regiments on ceremonial occasions

**bush** *NOUN* bushes
❶ a woody plant smaller than a tree; a shrub
❷ wild uncultivated land, especially in Africa and Australia

**bushel** *NOUN* bushels
a measure for grain and fruit equal to 8 gallons (36.4 litres)

**bushman** *NOUN* bushmen
a person who lives or travels in the Australian or African bush

**bushy** *ADJECTIVE* bushier, bushiest
thick and hairy • *bushy eyebrows*

**busily** *ADVERB*
in a busy way

**business** (say **biz**-niss) *NOUN* businesses
❶ buying and selling things; trade ❷ a shop or firm ❸ a person's concern or responsibilities • *Mind your own business.*
❹ an affair or subject • *I'm tired of the whole business.*

**SPELLING**
Don't forget, the i comes after the s in the middle of bus–i–ness.

**businesslike** *ADJECTIVE*
dealing with things in a direct and practical way

**businessman** *NOUN* businessmen
a man or woman who works in business

**businesswoman** *NOUN* businesswomen
a woman who works in business

**busker** *NOUN* buskers
a person who plays music in the street for money
➤ **busking** *NOUN*

**bust** *NOUN* busts
❶ a sculpture of a person's head, shoulders and chest ❷ a woman's breasts or chest

**bust** *VERB* busts, busting, bust
(*informal*) to break something

**bust** *ADJECTIVE* (*informal*)
❶ broken or damaged • *My phone is bust.*
❷ bankrupt

**bustard** *NOUN* bustards
a large bird that can run very fast

**bustle** *VERB* bustles, bustling, bustled
to hurry in a busy or excited way • *He was bustling about in the kitchen.*

**bustle** *NOUN* bustles
❶ hurried or excited activity ❷ padding used to puff out the top of a long skirt at the back

**busy** *ADJECTIVE* busier, busiest
❶ having a lot to do; working on something
❷ full of activity • *The town centre is always busy on Saturdays.* ❸ a busy telephone line or number is one that is engaged
➤ **busyness** *NOUN*

**busy** *VERB* busies, busying, busied
➤ **busy yourself** to do things to occupy yourself; to keep busy • *Bill busied himself making sandwiches.*

**busybody** *NOUN* busybodies
a person who meddles or interferes

**but** *CONJUNCTION*
however; nevertheless • *I wanted to go, but I couldn't.*

**but** *PREPOSITION*
except • *There is no one here but me.*

**but** *ADVERB*
only; no more than • *We can but try.*

**butcher** *NOUN* butchers
❶ a person who cuts up meat and sells it ❷ a person who kills people in a cruel way
➤ **butchery** *NOUN*

**butcher** *VERB* butchers, butchering, butchered
to kill people in a cruel way

**butler** *NOUN* butlers
a male servant in charge of other servants in a large private house

**butt** *NOUN* butts
❶ the thicker end of a weapon or tool ❷ the stub of a cigar or cigarette ❸ a large cask or barrel ❹ someone who is a target for ridicule or teasing • *He was the butt of their jokes.*

**butt** *VERB* butts, butting, butted
an animal butts something when it pushes or hits it with its head and horns
➤ **butt in** to interrupt or interfere

**butter** *NOUN*
a soft fatty food made by churning cream

**butter** *VERB* butters, buttering, buttered
to spread something with butter
➤ **buttery** *ADJECTIVE*

a
b
c
d
e
f
g
h
i
j
k
l
m
n
o
p
q
r
s
t
u
v
w
x
y
z

**buttercup** NOUN buttercups
a wild plant with bright yellow cup-shaped flowers

**butter-fingers** NOUN
a clumsy person who often drops things

**butterfly** NOUN butterflies
❶ an insect with large white or brightly coloured wings ❷ a swimming stroke in which both arms are lifted forwards at the same time

**buttermilk** NOUN
the liquid that is left after butter has been made

**butterscotch** NOUN
a kind of hard toffee

**buttock** NOUN buttocks
either of the two fleshy rounded parts of your bottom

**button** NOUN buttons
❶ a knob or disc sewn on clothes as a fastening or ornament ❷ a small knob that you press to work an electric device

**button** VERB buttons, buttoning, buttoned
to fasten a piece of clothing with a button or buttons

**buttonhole** NOUN buttonholes
❶ a slit through which you push a button to fasten clothes ❷ a flower worn on a lapel

**buttonhole** VERB buttonholes, buttonholing, buttonholed
to come up to someone so that you can talk to them

**buttress** NOUN buttresses
a support built against a wall

**buy** VERB buys, buying, bought
to get something by paying for it

**buy** NOUN buys
something that is bought • *That coat was a good buy.*

**buyer** NOUN buyers
a person who buys something

**buzz** NOUN buzzes
a vibrating humming sound
➤ **get a buzz from something** (*informal*) to find something exciting

**buzz** VERB buzzes, buzzing, buzzed
❶ to make a buzz ❷ to be full of excitement or activity • *The whole place was buzzing with excitement.* ❸ to threaten an aircraft by deliberately flying close to it
➤ **buzz off** (*informal*) to go away

**buzzard** NOUN buzzards
a kind of hawk

**buzzer** NOUN buzzers
a device that makes a buzzing sound as a signal

**by** PREPOSITION
This word is used to show
❶ closeness to something (*Sit by me.*)
❷ direction or route (*We got here by a short cut.*) ❸ the time before which something happens (*Try to get there by 6 o'clock.*)
❹ manner or method (*cooking by gas*)
❺ distance or amount (*You missed it by inches.*)
➤ **by the way** used to introduce a new topic
➤ **by yourself** alone; without help

**by** ADVERB
past • *I can't get by.*
➤ **by and by** soon; later on
➤ **by and large** on the whole
➤ **put something by** to keep something in reserve for future use

**bye** NOUN byes
❶ a run scored in cricket when the ball goes past the batsman without being touched
❷ an opportunity to go to the next round of a tournament without having won the current round, because you have no opponent

**bye-bye** EXCLAMATION (*informal*)
goodbye

**by-election** NOUN by-elections
(*British*) an election to replace a Member of Parliament who has died or resigned

**bygone** ADJECTIVE
belonging to the past
➤ **let bygones be bygones** forgive and forget past disagreements

**by-law** NOUN by-laws
a law that applies only to a particular town or district

**bypass** NOUN bypasses
❶ a road taking traffic round the edge of a town or city rather than going through the centre ❷ an operation on the heart to make an alternative passage for the blood so that it does not flow through a part that is damaged or blocked

**bypass** VERB bypasses, bypassing, bypassed
to avoid something by means of a bypass

**by-product** NOUN by-products
something useful produced while something else is being made

**byre** *NOUN* byres
(*British*) a cowshed

**byroad** *NOUN* byroads
a minor road

**bystander** *NOUN* bystanders
a person standing near but taking no part
when something happens

**byte** *NOUN* bytes
(*in computing*) a unit of information in a
computer

> SPELLING
> Be careful, this sounds the same as bite.

**byway** *NOUN* byways
a minor road or path

**byword** *NOUN* bywords
a person or thing spoken of as a famous
example • *The hotel has become a byword for
luxury and comfort.*

**cab** *NOUN* cabs
❶ a taxi ❷ a compartment for the driver of a
lorry, train, bus or crane

**cabaret** (say **kab**-er-ay) *NOUN* cabarets
an entertainment provided for the customers
in a restaurant or nightclub

**cabbage** *NOUN* cabbages
a vegetable with layers of closely packed
green or purple leaves

**caber** *NOUN* cabers
a tree trunk used in the Scottish Highland
sport of 'tossing the caber'

**cabin** *NOUN* cabins
❶ a wooden hut or shelter ❷ a room for
sleeping on a ship ❸ the part of an aircraft
where the passengers sit ❹ a driver's cab

**Cabinet** *NOUN*
the group of chief ministers, chosen by
the Prime Minister, who meet to decide
government policy

**cabinet** *NOUN* cabinets
a cupboard with drawers or shelves for
storing things

**cable** *NOUN* cables
❶ a thick rope of fibre or wire; a thick chain
❷ a covered group of wires laid underground
for transmitting electrical signals ❸ cable
television ❹ (*old use*)
a telegram sent overseas

**cable car** *NOUN* cable cars
a small cabin suspended on a moving cable,
used for carrying people up and down a
mountainside

**cable television** *NOUN*
a broadcasting service with signals
transmitted by cable to the sets of people
who have paid to receive it

**cacao** (say ka-**kay**-oh) *NOUN* cacaos
a tropical tree with a seed from which cocoa
and chocolate are made

**cache** (say kash) *NOUN* caches
a hidden store of things, especially valuable
things

**cackle** *NOUN* cackles
❶ a loud unpleasant laugh ❷ noisy chatter
❸ the loud clucking noise a hen makes

**cackle** *VERB* cackles, cackling, cackled
❶ to laugh in a loud and unpleasant way
❷ hens cackle when they make loud clucking
noises

**cacophony** (say kak-**off**-on-ee) *NOUN*
cacophonies
a harsh mixture of loud unpleasant sounds
• *a cacophony of car alarms*
➤ **cacophonous** *ADJECTIVE*

**cactus** *NOUN* cacti
a fleshy plant, usually with prickles, from a
hot dry climate

**cad** *NOUN* cads
a dishonourable man

**cadaverous** (say kad-**av**-er-us) *ADJECTIVE*
pale and thin, like a dead body

**caddie** *NOUN* caddies
a person who carries a golfer's clubs during
a game

**caddy** *NOUN* caddies
a small box for holding tea

**cadence** (say **kay**-denss) *NOUN* cadences
❶ rhythm; the rise and fall of the voice
in speaking ❷ the final notes of a musical
phrase

**cadenza** (say ka-**den**-za) *NOUN* cadenzas
an elaborate passage for a solo instrument or
singer, to show the performer's skill

a b c d e f g h i j k l m n o p q r s t u v w x y z

**cadet** NOUN cadets
a young person being trained for the armed forces or the police

**cadge** VERB cadges, cadging, cadged
(*British*) to get something from someone without paying for it • *I managed to cadge a lift into town.*

**cadmium** NOUN
a metal that looks like tin

**Caesarean, Caesarean section** (say siz-**air**-ee-an) NOUN Caesareans, Caesarean sections
a surgical operation for taking a baby out of the mother's womb **WORD ORIGIN** so called because Julius Caesar is said to have been born in this way

**caesura** (say siz-**yoor**-a) NOUN
a short pause in a line of verse

**cafe** (say **kaf**-ay) NOUN cafes
a small restaurant that sells light meals and drinks

**cafeteria** (say kaf-it-**eer**-ee-a) NOUN cafeterias
a self-service cafe

**caffeine** (say **kaf**-een) NOUN
the substance found in tea and coffee that makes you feel more awake and full of energy

**caftan** NOUN caftans
a long loose coat or dress with wide sleeves

**cage** NOUN cages
a container or structure made of bars or wires, in which birds or animals are kept

**caged** ADJECTIVE
kept in a cage • *a caged bird*

**cagoule** (say kag-**ool**) NOUN cagoules
(*British*) a lightweight waterproof jacket

**cairn** NOUN cairns
a pile of loose stones set up as a landmark or monument

**cajole** VERB cajoles, cajoling, cajoled
to persuade someone to do something by saying nice things to them

**cake** NOUN cakes
❶ a sweet food made by baking a mixture of flour, fat, eggs, sugar, etc. ❷ something shaped into a lump or block • *a cake of soap* • *fish cakes*

**caked** ADJECTIVE
covered with something that has dried hard • *boots caked in mud*

**calamine** NOUN
a pink powder used to make a soothing lotion for the skin

**calamity** NOUN calamities
an event that causes a lot of damage or harm
➤ **calamitous** ADJECTIVE

**calcium** NOUN
a chemical substance found in teeth, bones and lime

**calculate** VERB calculates, calculating, calculated
❶ to work something out by using mathematics ❷ if something is calculated to have an effect, it is intended or designed to have that effect • *Her remarks were clearly calculated to hurt me.*

**calculating** ADJECTIVE
planning things carefully so that you get what you want

**calculation** NOUN calculations
something you work out by using mathematics • *I need to do a quick calculation first.*

**calculator** NOUN calculators
a small electronic device for making calculations

**calculus** NOUN
mathematics for working out problems about rates of change **WORD ORIGIN** from Latin *calculus* = small stone (used on an abacus)

**calendar** NOUN calendars
a chart or set of pages showing the dates of the month or year

**SPELLING**
There is a tricky bit in calendar—it ends in ar.

**calf** NOUN calves
❶ a young cow or bull ❷ a young whale, seal or elephant ❸ the fleshy back part of your leg below your knee

**calibrate** (say **kal**-i-brayt) VERB calibrates, calibrating, calibrated
to mark a gauge or instrument with a scale of measurements
➤ **calibration** NOUN

**calibre** (say **kal**-ib-er) NOUN calibres
❶ the diameter of the inside of a tube or gun barrel or of a bullet or shell ❷ ability or quality • *We need more people of your calibre.*

**calico** NOUN
a kind of cotton cloth

**caliper** NOUN calipers
a support for a weak or injured leg

**calipers** PLURAL NOUN
compasses for measuring the width of tubes or of round objects

**caliph** (say **kal**-if or **kay**-lif) NOUN caliphs
the former title of the ruler in certain Muslim countries

**call** VERB calls, calling, called
❶ to name or describe a person or thing • They've decided to call the baby Alexander. • Are you calling me a liar? ❷ to be called something is to have that as your name • What is your dog called? ❸ to shout or speak loudly, e.g. to attract someone's attention ❹ to telephone someone ❺ to tell or ask someone to come to you • The next day he called everyone in for a meeting. ❻ to make a short visit

**call** NOUN calls
❶ a shout or cry to attract someone's attention ❷ a short visit ❸ telephoning someone ❹ a request for someone to come
➤ call a person's bluff to challenge a person to do what they threatened, when you think they are bluffing
➤ call for something to require something • This news calls for a celebration.
➤ call something off to cancel or postpone something
➤ call someone up to summon someone to join the armed forces

**call box** NOUN call boxes
a telephone box

**caller** NOUN callers
a person who telephones or visits someone

**calligram** NOUN calligrams
a poem in which the form of the writing relates to the content of the poem, e.g. a poem about growth shown with the letters getting larger

**calligraphy** (say kal-ig-**raf**-ee) NOUN
the art of beautiful handwriting

**calling** NOUN callings
❶ a person's profession or trade ❷ a strong feeling that you should follow a particular occupation; a vocation

**callous** (say **kal**-us) ADJECTIVE
hard-hearted; not caring about other people's feelings

➤ **callously** ADVERB
➤ **callousness** NOUN

**callow** ADJECTIVE
immature and inexperienced • a callow youth

**callus** NOUN calluses
a small patch of skin that has become thick and hard through being continually pressed or rubbed

**calm** ADJECTIVE
❶ not excited, worried or angry • Try to keep calm. ❷ quiet and still; not windy • a calm sea
➤ **calmness** NOUN

**calm** VERB calms, calming, calmed
to become or make someone calm • Calm down, everyone! (WORD ORIGIN) from Greek kauma = hot time of the day (when people rested)

SPELLING
There is a silent l in calm.

**calmly** ADVERB
in a calm way • 'I'll call the doctor,' she said calmly.

**calorie** NOUN calories
a unit for measuring an amount of heat or the energy produced by food

**calumny** (say **kal**-um-nee) NOUN calumnies
an untrue statement that damages a person's reputation

**calve** VERB calves, calving, calved
to give birth to a calf

**calypso** NOUN calypsos
a West Indian song about current happenings, made up as the singer goes along

**calyx** (say **kay**-liks) NOUN calyces
a ring of leaves (sepals) forming the outer case of a bud

**camaraderie** (say kam-er-**ah**-der-ee) NOUN
trust and comradeship between friends

**camber** NOUN cambers
a slight curved shape from the middle of a road down to the sides

**cambric** NOUN
thin linen or cotton cloth

**camcorder** NOUN camcorders
a combined video camera and sound recorder

**camel** NOUN camels
a large animal with a long neck and either one or two humps on its back, used in desert countries for riding and for carrying goods

**camellia** NOUN camellias
a kind of evergreen flowering shrub
**WORD ORIGIN** Latin, named after Joseph
Camellus, a botanist

**cameo** (say **kam**-ee-oh) NOUN cameos
❶ a small hard piece of stone carved with
a raised design in its upper layer ❷ a short
part in a play or film, usually one played by a
well-known actor

**camera** NOUN cameras
a device for taking photographs, films or
television pictures
➤ **in camera** in a judge's private room; in
private
**WORD ORIGIN** Latin, = vault, chamber

**cameraman, camerawoman** NOUN
cameramen or camerawomen
a person who operates a film or television
camera

**camomile** NOUN camomiles
a plant with sweet-smelling daisy-like flowers

**camouflage** (say **kam**-off-lahzh) NOUN
a way of hiding things by making them look
like part of their surroundings • An animal's
markings are often used for camouflage.

**camouflage** VERB camouflages,
camouflaging, camouflaged
to hide something by camouflage • The
soldiers camouflaged themselves with leaves.

**camp** NOUN camps
a place where people live in tents or huts for
a short time

**camp** VERB camps, camping, camped
❶ to put up a tent or tents • Let's camp here
for the night. ❷ to have a holiday in a tent
➤ **camper** NOUN
➤ **camping** NOUN

**campaign** NOUN campaigns
❶ a planned series of actions, especially
to get people to support you or become
interested in something • an advertising
campaign ❷ a series of battles in one area or
with one purpose

**campaign** VERB campaigns, campaigning,
campaigned
to take part in a campaign • They are
campaigning to save the rainforests.
➤ **campaigner** NOUN

**camphor** NOUN
a strong-smelling white substance used
in medicine and mothballs and in making
plastics

**campsite** NOUN campsites
a place for camping

**campus** NOUN campuses
the grounds and buildings of a university or
college

**can** AUXILIARY VERB past tense could
❶ to be able to • He can play the violin. ❷ to
be allowed to • Can I go now?
**USAGE**
Some people think that **can** should not
be used instead of **may** when asking to
be allowed to do something, e.g. Can I
go to the bathroom? However, in most
situations it is acceptable except in formal
or official writing.

**can** NOUN cans
❶ a sealed tin in which food or drink is
preserved ❷ a metal or plastic container for
liquids

**can** VERB cans, canning, canned
to preserve food in a sealed can

**canal** NOUN canals
❶ an artificial water channel cut through
land so that boats can sail along it or for
irrigating land ❷ a tube through which food
or air passes in a plant or animal body • the
alimentary canal

**canary** NOUN canaries
a small yellow bird that sings

**cancan** NOUN cancans
a lively dance in which the legs are kicked
very high

**cancel** VERB cancels, cancelling, cancelled
❶ to decide that something planned will
not be done or will not take place • My train
has been cancelled. ❷ to stop an order or
instruction for something ❸ to mark a stamp
or ticket etc. so that it cannot be used again
➤ **cancel something out** to have an equal
and opposite effect • The advantages and
disadvantages cancel each other out.

**cancellation** NOUN cancellations
something that has been cancelled • Bad
weather caused the cancellation of the
parade.

**cancer** NOUN cancers
❶ a serious disease in which harmful growths
form in the body ❷ a harmful tumour
➤ **cancerous** ADJECTIVE
**WORD ORIGIN** Latin, = crab, because the
swollen veins around the area of the tumour
were thought to look like the legs of a crab

**candelabrum** (say kan-dil-**ab**-rum) NOUN
candelabra
a candlestick with several branches for
holding candles

**candid** ADJECTIVE
frank and honest
➤ **candidly** ADVERB

**candidate** NOUN candidates
❶ a person who wants to be elected or
chosen for a particular job or position ❷ a
person taking an examination
➤ **candidacy** NOUN
**WORD ORIGIN** from Latin *candidus* = white
(because Roman candidates for office had to
wear a pure white toga)

**candied** ADJECTIVE
coated or preserved in sugar • *candied
cherries*

**candle** NOUN candles
a stick of wax with a wick running through it,
giving light when it is burning

**candlelight** NOUN
the light from a candle • *The hall was lit by
candlelight.*

**candlestick** NOUN candlesticks
a holder for a candle or candles

**candour** (say **kan**-der) NOUN
being candid; frankness and honesty

**candy** NOUN candies
(*North American*) sweets or a sweet

**candyfloss** NOUN candyflosses
(*British*) a fluffy mass of very thin strands of
spun sugar wrapped round a stick

**cane** NOUN canes
❶ the hollow stem of a reed or tall grass ❷ a
long thin stick

**cane** VERB canes, caning, caned
to beat someone with a long thin stick as a
punishment

**canine** (say **kayn**-yn) ADJECTIVE
to do with dogs

**canine** NOUN canines
❶ a dog ❷ a pointed tooth at the front of
the mouth

**canister** NOUN canisters
a round metal container • *a gas canister*

**canker** NOUN
a disease that rots the wood of trees and
plants or causes ulcers and sores on animals

**cannabis** NOUN
hemp smoked as a drug

**cannibal** NOUN cannibals
❶ a person who eats human flesh ❷ an
animal that eats animals of its own kind
➤ **cannibalism** NOUN
**WORD ORIGIN** from Spanish *Canibales*, the
name given to the original inhabitants of the
Caribbean islands, who the Spanish thought ate
people

**cannon** NOUN
❶ cannon a large heavy gun that fires heavy
balls made of metal or stone ❷ cannons
(*chiefly British*) the hitting of two balls in
billiards by the third ball

**cannon** VERB cannons, cannoning, cannoned
(*chiefly British*) to cannon into something is
to collide with it clumsily or heavily • *The two
players cannoned into one another.*
**SPELLING**
Take care not to confuse with **canon**.

**cannon ball** NOUN cannon balls
a large solid ball fired from a cannon

**cannot**
can not

**canny** ADJECTIVE cannier, canniest
clever and cautious; shrewd
➤ **cannily** ADVERB

**canoe** NOUN canoes
a narrow lightweight boat, moved forwards
with paddles

**canoe** VERB canoes, canoeing, canoed
to travel in a canoe
➤ **canoeist** NOUN

**canon** NOUN canons
❶ a general principle; a rule ❷ a clergyman
of a cathedral
**SPELLING**
Take care not to confuse with **cannon**.

**canonize** (also **canonise**) VERB canonizes,
canonizing, canonized
to declare officially that someone is a saint
➤ **canonization** NOUN

**canopy** NOUN canopies
❶ a hanging cover forming a shelter above
a throne or bed ❷ a natural covering, e.g. of
leaves and branches • *The thick jungle canopy
lets very little light through.* ❸ the part of a
parachute that spreads in the air

a b **c** d e f g h i j k l m n o p q r s t u v w x y z

**cant** VERB cants, canting, canted
to slope or tilt

**cant** NOUN
insincere talk about moral behaviour

**can't** (*mainly spoken*)
cannot

> **SPELLING**
>
> Can't = can + not. Add an apostrophe
> between the n and the t.

**cantaloupe** NOUN cantaloupes
a small round orange-coloured melon

**cantankerous** ADJECTIVE
bad-tempered and always complaining • *a cantankerous old man*

**cantata** (say kant-**ah**-ta) NOUN cantatas
a musical composition for singers, usually with a chorus and orchestra

**canteen** NOUN canteens
❶ a restaurant for workers in a factory or office ❷ a case or box containing a set of cutlery ❸ a small water flask carried by a soldier or camper

**canter** NOUN
a gentle gallop by a horse

**canter** VERB canters, cantering, cantered
to go or ride at a gentle gallop
> **WORD ORIGIN** short for 'Canterbury gallop', the gentle pace at which pilgrims were said to travel to Canterbury in the Middle Ages

**cantilever** NOUN cantilevers
a beam or girder fixed at only one end and used to support a bridge

**canton** NOUN cantons
each of the districts into which a country, especially Switzerland, is divided

**canvas** NOUN canvases
❶ a kind of strong coarse cloth ❷ a piece of canvas for painting on; a painting

**canvass** VERB canvasses, canvassing, canvassed
to visit people to ask them for their support, especially in an election
➤ **canvasser** NOUN

**canyon** NOUN canyons
a deep valley, usually with a river running through it

**cap** NOUN caps
❶ a soft hat without a brim but often with a peak ❷ a special headdress, e.g. that worn by a nurse ❸ a cap awarded to members of

a sports team ❹ a cover or top ❺ something that makes a bang when fired in a toy pistol

**cap** VERB caps, capping, capped
❶ to put a cap or cover on something • *The mountain is always capped with snow.* ❷ to award a sports cap to someone chosen to be in a team ❸ to cap a story or joke is to tell one that is better

**capable** ADJECTIVE
able to do something • *She is definitely capable of winning this match.*
➤ **capability** NOUN

**capacious** (say ka-**pay**-shus) ADJECTIVE
roomy; able to hold a large amount • *her capacious handbag*

**capacity** NOUN capacities
❶ the amount that something can hold ❷ ability to do something • *He has a great capacity for work.* ❸ the position that someone occupies • *In my capacity as your guardian I am responsible for you.*

**cape** NOUN capes
❶ a short cloak ❷ a large piece of high land that sticks out into the sea

**caper** VERB capers, capering, capered
to jump about playfully

**caper** NOUN capers
❶ jumping about playfully ❷ (*informal*) an adventure or prank ❸ the pickled bud of a prickly shrub, used in cooking

**capillary** (say ka-**pil**-er-ee) NOUN capillaries
any of the very fine blood vessels that connect veins and arteries

**capillary** ADJECTIVE
to do with or occurring in a very narrow tube; to do with a capillary

**capital** NOUN capitals
❶ a capital city ❷ a capital letter ❸ money or property that can be used to produce more wealth ❹ the top part of a pillar

**capital** ADJECTIVE
(*old use*) very good or excellent

**capital city** NOUN capital cities
the most important city in a country, usually where the government is based

**capitalism** (say **kap**-it-al-izm) NOUN
an economic system in which a country's trade and industry are controlled by private owners for profit and not by the state. Compare with communism.

**capitalist** (say **kap**-it-al-ist) NOUN capitalists
❶ a rich person who has a lot of their wealth

invested ❷ a person who is in favour of capitalism

**capitalize** (also **capitalise**) (say **kap**-it-al-yz) *VERB* capitalizes, capitalizing, capitalized
❶ to write or print a word with a capital letter ❷ to capitalize on something is to use it to your own advantage • *He was able to capitalize on his opponent's mistake.*
➤ **capitalization** *NOUN*

**capital letter** *NOUN* capital letters
a large letter of the kind used at the start of a name or sentence

**capital punishment** *NOUN*
punishing criminals by putting them to death

**capitulate** *VERB* capitulates, capitulating, capitulated
to admit that you are defeated and surrender
➤ **capitulation** *NOUN*

**cappuccino** *NOUN* cappuccinos
milky coffee made frothy by putting steam through it under pressure
**WORD ORIGIN** Italian: named after the Capuchin monks who wore coffee-coloured habits

**caprice** (say ka-**preess**) *NOUN* caprices
a sudden impulsive whim or change of behaviour

**capricious** (say ka-**prish**-us) *ADJECTIVE*
deciding or changing your mind in an impulsive way
➤ **capriciously** *ADVERB*

**capsize** *VERB* capsizes, capsizing, capsized
a boat or ship capsizes when it overturns in the water

**capstan** *NOUN* capstans
a thick post that can be turned to wind up a rope or cable

**capsule** *NOUN* capsules
❶ a hollow pill containing medicine ❷ a plant's seed case that splits open when ripe ❸ a compartment of a spacecraft that can be separated from the main part

**captain** *NOUN* captains
❶ a person in command of a ship or aircraft ❷ the leader of a sports team ❸ an army officer ranking next below a major; a naval officer ranking next below a commodore

**captain** *VERB* captains, captaining, captained
to be the captain of a sports team

**captaincy** *NOUN* captaincies
the position of captain of a team • *He had to resign the captaincy.*

**caption** *NOUN* captions
❶ the words printed next to a picture to describe it ❷ a short title or heading in a newspaper or magazine

**captivate** *VERB* captivates, captivating, captivated
to charm or delight someone • *The children were captivated by the story.*
➤ **captivating** *ADJECTIVE*

**captive** *NOUN* captives
someone who has been taken prisoner

**captive** *ADJECTIVE*
taken prisoner; unable to escape • *They were held captive by masked gunmen.*

**captivity** *NOUN*
❶ the state of being held prisoner • *He was held in captivity for three years.* ❷ the state of being kept in a zoo or wildlife park rather than living in the wild • *These gorillas were bred in captivity.*

**captor** *NOUN* captors
someone who has captured a person or animal

**capture** *VERB* captures, capturing, captured
❶ to catch or imprison a person or animal • *The lion was captured and taken back to the zoo.* ❷ to take control of a place using force • *Rome was captured in 410.* ❸ to make someone interested in something • *The story captured my imagination immediately.* ❹ to succeed in representing or describing something • *A TV cameraman captured the whole scene.* ❺ (in computing) to put data in a form that can be stored in a computer

**capture** *NOUN*
the act of capturing someone or something • *They evaded capture for three days.*

**car** *NOUN* cars
❶ a road vehicle with four wheels that can carry a small number of people ❷ a railway carriage • *dining car*

**carafe** (say ka-**raf**) *NOUN* carafes
a glass bottle holding wine or water for pouring out at the table

**caramel** *NOUN* caramels
❶ a kind of soft toffee made from sugar and butter ❷ burnt sugar used for colouring and flavouring food

**carapace** (say **ka**-ra-payss) *NOUN* carapaces
the hard shell on the back of a tortoise or crustacean

a
b
c
d
e
f
g
h
i
j
k
l
m
n
o
p
q
r
s
t
u
v
w
x
y
z

A
B
C
D
E
F
G
H
I
J
K
L
M
N
O
P
Q
R
S
T
U
V
W
X
Y
Z

**carat** NOUN carats
❶ a measure of weight for precious stones
❷ a measure of the purity of gold • *Pure gold is 24 carats.*

**caravan** NOUN caravans
❶ a vehicle towed by a car and used for living in, especially by people on holiday ❷ a group of people travelling together across desert country
➤ **caravanning** NOUN

**caraway** NOUN
a plant with spicy seeds that are used for flavouring food

**carbohydrate** NOUN carbohydrates
a compound of carbon, oxygen and hydrogen (e.g. sugar or starch), found in food and a source of energy

**carbolic** NOUN
a kind of disinfectant

**carbon** NOUN
❶ an element that is present in all living things and that occurs in its pure form as diamond and graphite ❷ carbon dioxide
• *carbon levels in the atmosphere*

**carbonate** NOUN carbonates
a compound that gives off carbon dioxide when mixed with acid

**carbonated** ADJECTIVE
a carbonated drink has carbon dioxide added to make it fizzy

**carbon copy** NOUN carbon copies
an exact copy of something • *She is a carbon copy of her sister.* **WORD ORIGIN** originally a copy made with carbon paper = thin paper with a coloured coating, placed between sheets of paper to make copies of what is written or typed on the top sheet

**carbon dating** NOUN
the use of a kind of radioactive carbon that decays at a steady rate, to find out how old something

**carbon dioxide** NOUN
a gas formed when things burn or breathed out by humans and animals

**carboniferous** ADJECTIVE
producing coal

**carbon monoxide** NOUN
a poisonous gas found especially in the exhaust fumes of motor vehicles

**carbuncle** NOUN carbuncles
❶ a large boil or abscess in the skin ❷ a bright-red gem

**carburettor** NOUN carburettors
a device for mixing fuel and air in an engine

**carcass** NOUN carcasses
❶ the dead body of an animal ❷ the bony part of a bird's body after the meat has been eaten

**carcinogen** NOUN carcinogens
any substance that can cause cancer

**card** NOUN cards
❶ thick stiff paper or thin cardboard ❷ a small piece of stiff paper for writing or printing on, especially to send messages or greetings or to record information ❸ a small, oblong piece of plastic issued to a customer by a bank or shop for drawing out money and making payments ❹ a playing card
➤ **cards** PLURAL NOUN
a game using playing cards
➤ **be on the cards** to be likely or possible

**cardboard** NOUN
a kind of thin board made of layers of paper or wood fibre

**cardiac** (say kard-ee-ak) ADJECTIVE
to do with the heart

**cardigan** NOUN cardigans
a knitted jumper fastened with buttons down the front **WORD ORIGIN** named after the Earl of *Cardigan*, a commander in the Crimean War; cardigans were first worn by the troops in that war

**cardinal** NOUN cardinals
a senior priest in the Roman Catholic Church

**cardinal** ADJECTIVE
chief or most important • *This is one of the cardinal rules of scientific research.*

**cardinal number** NOUN cardinal numbers
a number for counting things, e.g. one, two, three, etc. Compare with ordinal number.

**cardinal point** NOUN cardinal points
each of the four main points of the compass (North, South, East, West)

**cardiology** NOUN
the study of the heart and its diseases
➤ **cardiological** ADJECTIVE
➤ **cardiologist** NOUN

**care** NOUN cares
❶ serious attention and thought • *Plan your holiday with care.* ❷ caution to avoid

damage or loss • *Glass - handle with care*
❸ protection or supervision • *You can leave the dog in my care.* ❹ worry or anxiety • *She was free from care.*
➤ **take care** to be especially careful
➤ **take care of someone** to look after someone
➤ **take care of something** to deal with something

**care** *VERB* **cares, caring, cared**
❶ to feel interested or concerned about someone or something • *I'm going and I don't care what anybody says.* ❷ to feel affection • *You really care about her, don't you?*
➤ **care for someone** to look after someone • *He cared for his wife when she was ill.*
➤ **care for something** to be fond of something • *I don't much care for fried food.*

**career** *NOUN* **careers**
the series of jobs that someone has as they make progress in their occupation

**career** *VERB* **careers, careering, careered**
to rush along wildly • *We careered down the hill, faster and faster.*

**carefree** *ADJECTIVE*
without worries or responsibilities

**careful** *ADJECTIVE*
❶ thinking about what you are doing so that you do not make a mistake, have an accident, etc. • *Be careful crossing the road.* ❷ giving serious thought and attention to something • *This needs careful planning.*
➤ **carefully** *ADVERB*

SPELLING
Careful + ly = carefully. Don't forget the double l.

**careless** *ADJECTIVE*
not taking enough care to avoid mistakes or harm • *careless work*
➤ **carelessly** *ADVERB*
➤ **carelessness** *NOUN*

**caress** *NOUN* **caresses**
a gentle loving touch

**caress** *VERB* **caresses, caressing, caressed**
to touch someone lovingly

**caret** *NOUN* **carets**
a mark ( ^ ) showing where something is to be inserted in writing or printing

**caretaker** *NOUN* **caretakers**
a person employed to look after a school, block of flats, etc.

**cargo** *NOUN* **cargoes**
goods carried in a ship or aircraft

**Caribbean** *ADJECTIVE*
to do with or from the Caribbean Sea, a part of the Atlantic Ocean east of Central America

**caribou** (say ka-rib-oo) *NOUN* **caribou**
a North American reindeer
WORD ORIGIN from a Native American word meaning 'snow-shoveller' (because the caribou scrapes away the snow to feed on the grass underneath)

**caricature** *NOUN* **caricatures**
an amusing or exaggerated picture or description of someone

**caries** (say **kair**-eez) *NOUN* **caries**
decay in teeth or bones

**carmine** *ADJECTIVE & NOUN*
deep red

**carnage** *NOUN*
the killing of large numbers of people

**carnal** *ADJECTIVE*
to do with the body as opposed to the spirit; not spiritual

**carnation** *NOUN* **carnations**
a garden flower with a sweet smell

**carnival** *NOUN* **carnivals**
a festival, often with a procession of people in fancy dress WORD ORIGIN from Latin *carnis* = of the flesh (because originally this meant the festivities before Lent, when meat was given up until Easter)

**carnivore** (say **kar**-niv-or) *NOUN* **carnivores**
an animal that feeds on the flesh of other animals. Compare with **herbivore**.

**carnivorous** (say kar-**niv**-er-us) *ADJECTIVE*
a carnivorous animal feeds on the flesh of other animals.Compare with **herbivorous**.

**carol** *NOUN* **carols**
a Christmas hymn
➤ **carolling** *NOUN*

**carouse** *VERB* **carouses, carousing, caroused**
to drink alcohol and enjoy yourself with other people WORD ORIGIN from German *gar aus trinken* = drink to the bottom of the glass

**carousel** (say ka-roo-**sel**) *NOUN* **carousels**
❶ a roundabout at a fair ❷ a conveyor belt that goes round in a circle for passengers to collect their baggage at an airport

**carp** *NOUN* **carp**
an edible freshwater fish

**carp** VERB carps, carping, carped
to keep complaining or finding fault

**car park** NOUN car parks
(British) an area where cars may be parked

**carpenter** NOUN carpenters
a person who makes things out of wood
➤ **carpentry** NOUN

**carpet** NOUN carpets
① a thick soft covering for a floor ② a thick layer of something • *a carpet of fallen leaves*
➤ **carpeting** NOUN

**carpeted** ADJECTIVE
① covered with a carpet • *carpeted stairs*
② covered with a thick layer of something • *The forest floor was carpeted with wild flowers.*

**carport** NOUN carports
a shelter with a roof and open sides for a car

**carriage** NOUN carriages
① one of the separate parts of a train, where passengers sit ② a passenger vehicle pulled by horses ③ carrying goods from one place to another or the cost of this • *Carriage is extra.* ④ a moving part carrying or holding something in a machine

**carriageway** NOUN carriageways
(British) the part of a road on which vehicles travel

**carrier** NOUN carriers
a person or thing that carries something

**carrier bag** NOUN carrier bags
(British) a plastic or paper bag with handles

**carrier pigeon** NOUN carrier pigeons
a pigeon used to carry messages

**carrion** NOUN
the decaying flesh of a dead animal

**carrot** NOUN carrots
a plant with a thick orange-coloured root used as a vegetable

**carry** VERB carries, carrying, carried
① to take something from one place to another ② to support the weight of something ③ to take an amount into the next column when adding figures ④ to be heard a long way away • *Sound carries in the mountains.* ⑤ if a motion is carried, it is approved by most people at the meeting • *The motion was carried by ten votes to six.*
➤ **be carried away** to be very excited
➤ **carry on** to continue or keep doing

something • *They ignored me and carried on chatting.*
➤ **carry something out** to do and complete something • *We need to carry out some tests.*

**cart** NOUN carts
an open vehicle for carrying loads

**cart** VERB carts, carting, carted
① (informal) to carry something heavy or tiring • *I've been carting these books around all morning.* ② to carry something in a cart

**carthorse** NOUN carthorses
a large strong horse used for pulling heavy loads

**cartilage** NOUN
tough white flexible tissue attached to a bone

**cartography** NOUN
the art of drawing maps
➤ **cartographer** NOUN

**carton** NOUN cartons
a light cardboard or plastic container

**cartoon** NOUN cartoons
① an amusing drawing, especially one in a newspaper or magazine ② a series of drawings that tell a story ③ an animated film
➤ **cartoonist** NOUN

**cartridge** NOUN cartridges
① a case containing the explosive for a bullet or shell ② a container holding film for a camera, ink for a printer or pen, etc.

**cartwheel** NOUN cartwheels
① a circular movement in which you do a sideways handstand by balancing on each hand in turn with arms and legs spread like spokes of a wheel • *My sister was in the garden doing cartwheels.* ② the wheel of a cart

**carve** VERB carves, carving, carved
① to cut wood or stone in order to make something or to put a pattern or writing on it • *The statue is carved out of marble* ② to cut cooked meat into slices

**carving** NOUN carvings
an object or design that has been carved

**cascade** NOUN cascades
a small waterfall

**cascade** VERB cascades, cascading, cascaded
to pour down in large amounts • *Water cascaded from the roof.*

**case** NOUN cases
① an instance of something existing or occurring • *In every case we found that*

*someone had cheated.* ❷ something that the police are investigating or that is being decided in a law trial • *a murder case* ❸ a set of facts or arguments to support something • *She put forward a good case for equality.* ❹ the form of a word that shows how it is related to other words. *Fred's is the possessive case of Fred; him is the objective case of he.* ❺ a container ❻ a suitcase
➤ **in any case** whatever happens; anyway
➤ **in case** because something may happen • *Take an umbrella in case it rains.*

**casement** *NOUN* casements
a window that opens on hinges at its side

**cash** *NOUN*
❶ money in coin or notes ❷ immediate payment for goods

**cash** *VERB* cashes, cashing, cashed
to cash a cheque is to exchange it for cash

**cash card** *NOUN* cash cards
(*British*) a plastic card used to draw money from a cash dispenser

**cash dispenser** *NOUN* cash dispensers
(*British*) a machine, usually outside a bank or building society, from which people can draw out cash by using a cash card

**cashew** *NOUN* cashews
a kind of small nut

**cashier** *NOUN* cashiers
a person who takes in and pays out money in a bank or takes payments in a shop

**cashmere** *NOUN*
very fine soft wool **WORD ORIGIN** from *Kashmir* in Asia, where it was first produced

**cashpoint** *NOUN* cashpoints
a cash dispenser

**cash register** *NOUN* cash registers
a machine that records and stores the money received in a shop

**casing** *NOUN* casings
a protective case or covering

**casino** *NOUN* casinos
a public building or room for gambling

**cask** *NOUN* casks
a large barrel

**casket** *NOUN* caskets
a small box for jewellery or other valuable objects

**cassava** *NOUN*
a tropical plant with starchy roots that are an important source of food in tropical countries

**casserole** *NOUN* casseroles
❶ a covered dish in which food is cooked and served ❷ a kind of stew cooked in a casserole

**cassette** *NOUN* cassettes
a small sealed case containing recording tape, film, etc.
➤ **cassette player** *NOUN*

**cassock** *NOUN* cassocks
a long piece of clothing worn by clergy and members of a church choir

**cast** *VERB* casts, casting, cast
❶ to throw something with force ❷ to shed something or throw it off ❸ to make a light or shadow fall on something • *The light from the candle cast her shadow on the wall.* ❹ to direct your eyes or thoughts to something • *Cast your mind back to last Sunday.* ❺ to make a vote in an election ❻ to make something out of metal or plaster in a mould ❼ to choose the performers for a play or film

**cast** *NOUN* casts
❶ a shape made by pouring liquid metal or plaster into a mould ❷ all the performers in a play or film

**castanets** *PLURAL NOUN*
two pieces of wood or ivory held in one hand and clapped together to make a clicking sound, especially in Spanish dancing

**castaway** *NOUN* castaways
a shipwrecked person

**caste** *NOUN* castes
(in India) each of the social classes into which Hindus are born

**caster sugar** *NOUN*
(*British*) finely ground white sugar

**casting vote** *NOUN* casting votes
the vote that decides which group wins when the votes on each side are equal

**cast iron** *NOUN*
a hard alloy of iron made by casting it in a mould

**castle** *NOUN* castles
❶ a large fortified building that was built in the past to defend people against attack ❷ a piece in chess, also called a rook
➤ **castles in the air** daydreams or wild hopes

**castor** *NOUN* castors
a small wheel on the leg of a table, chair, etc.

**castor oil** NOUN
oil from the seeds of a tropical plant, used as a laxative

**castrate** VERB castrates, castrating, castrated
to remove the testicles of a male animal. Compare with **spay**.
➤ **castration** NOUN

**casual** ADJECTIVE
❶ happening by chance and not planned • *a casual meeting* ❷ not carefully done or thought out • *It was just a casual remark.* ❸ relaxed and not bothered by something • *She tried to sound casual.* ❹ suitable for informal occasions • *casual clothes* ❺ not permanent • *casual work*

**casually** ADVERB
in a casual way • *'What did he say about me?' she asked as casually as she could.*

**casualty** NOUN casualties
❶ a person who is killed or injured in war or in an accident ❷ a casualty department in a hospital

**casualty department** NOUN casualty departments
(*British*) the department of a hospital that deals with emergency patients

**cat** NOUN cats
❶ a small furry domestic animal ❷ a wild animal of the same family as a domestic cat, e.g. a lion, tiger or leopard
➤ **let the cat out of the bag** to reveal a secret by mistake

**cataclysm** (say **kat**-a-klizm) NOUN cataclysms
a violent upheaval or disaster, such as a flood or war
➤ **cataclysmic** ADJECTIVE

**catacombs** (say **kat**-a-koomz) PLURAL NOUN
underground passages with compartments for tombs

**catalogue** NOUN catalogues
❶ a list of things (e.g. of books in a library), usually arranged in order ❷ a book containing a list of things that can be bought • *our Christmas catalogue*

**catalogue** VERB catalogues, cataloguing, catalogued
to list a collection of things in a catalogue

**catalyst** (say **kat**-a-list) NOUN catalysts
❶ something that starts or speeds up a chemical reaction ❷ something that brings about a change

**catalytic converter** NOUN catalytic converters
a device fitted to a car's exhaust system, with a catalyst for converting the exhaust gases into less harmful ones

**catamaran** NOUN catamarans
a boat with twin parallel hulls

**catapult** NOUN catapults
❶ a forked stick with elastic fastened to each prong, used for shooting small stones ❷ an ancient military weapon for hurling stones

**catapult** VERB catapults, catapulting, catapulted
to hurl something or rush violently • *As the car hit him, he was catapulted into the air.*

**cataract** NOUN cataracts
❶ a large waterfall or rush of water ❷ a cloudy area that forms in the eye and causes blurred vision

**catarrh** (say ka-**tar**) NOUN
inflammation in your nose that makes it drip a watery fluid

**catastrophe** (say ka-**tass**-trof-ee) NOUN catastrophes
a sudden great disaster

**catastrophic** (say kat-a-**strof**-ik) ADJECTIVE
absolutely disastrous • *The earthquake caused catastrophic damage.*
➤ **catastrophically** ADVERB

**catch** VERB catches, catching, caught
❶ to take hold of something ❷ to capture a person or animal ❸ to reach someone who has been ahead of you ❹ to be in time to get on a bus or train ❺ to become infected with an illness ❻ to hear what someone says • *I didn't catch what he said.* ❼ to discover someone doing something wrong • *She was caught smoking in the playground.* ❽ to get something snagged or entangled • *I caught my dress on a nail.* ❾ to hit or strike something • *The blow caught him on the nose.*
➤ **catch fire** to start burning
➤ **catch it** (*informal*) to be scolded or punished
➤ **catch on** (*informal*)
❶ to become popular ❷ to begin to understand something
➤ **catch someone out** to discover someone in a mistake
➤ **catch up with someone** ❶ to reach someone when they have been ahead of you ❷ to reach the same standard or level as someone else

**catch** NOUN catches
❶ catching something, e.g. a ball
❷ something caught or worth catching
• *They had a large catch of fish.* ❸ a hidden
difficulty • *It looks like a good offer, but there
must be a catch.* ❹ a device for fastening a
door or window

**SPELLING**

The past tense of catch is **caught**, and the
'or' sound is spelt **augh**.

**catching** ADJECTIVE
a disease is catching when it is infectious

**catchment area** NOUN catchment areas
❶ the area from which a hospital takes
patients or a school takes pupils ❷ the whole
area from which water drains into a river or
reservoir

**catchphrase** NOUN catchphrases
a well-known phrase, especially one that a
famous person has used

**catchy** ADJECTIVE
a catchy tune is pleasant and easy to
remember

**catechism** (say kat-ik-izm) NOUN catechisms
a set of questions and answers that give the
basic beliefs of a religion

**categorical** (say kat-ig-o-rik-al) ADJECTIVE
completely clear and definite • *a categorical
refusal*
➤ **categorically** ADVERB

**category** NOUN categories
a set of people or things classified as being
similar to each other • *This painting won first
prize in the junior category.*

**cater** VERB caters, catering, catered
❶ to provide food for a lot of people at a
social occasion ❷ to provide what is needed
• *The school caters for children of all abilities.*
➤ **caterer** NOUN

**caterpillar** NOUN caterpillars
the creeping worm-like creature that turns
into a butterfly or moth WORD ORIGIN from
Old French *chatepelose* = hairy cat

**cathedral** NOUN cathedrals
the most important church of a district,
usually with a bishop in charge of it

**Catherine wheel** NOUN Catherine wheels
(*British*) a firework that spins round and
throws out sparks WORD ORIGIN named after
St Catherine of Alexandria, who was martyred
on a spiked wheel

**cathode** NOUN cathodes
the electrode by which electric current leaves
a device. Compare with **anode**.

**cathode ray tube** NOUN cathode ray tubes
a tube used in televisions and computers, in
which a beam of electrons from a cathode
produces an image on a fluorescent screen

**Catholic** ADJECTIVE
belonging to the Roman Catholic Church
➤ **Catholicism** NOUN

**Catholic** NOUN Catholics
a Roman Catholic

**catholic** ADJECTIVE
including a wide range of things • *She has
fairly catholic tastes in music.*

**catkin** NOUN catkins
a spike of small soft flowers on trees such as
hazel and willow

**catnap** NOUN catnaps
a short sleep during the day

**Catseye** NOUN Catseyes (*trademark*)
one of a line of reflecting studs that mark the
centre or edge of a road

**cattle** PLURAL NOUN
cows and bulls kept by farmers for their milk
and beef

**catty** ADJECTIVE cattier, cattiest
saying unkind and spiteful things about
someone

**catwalk** NOUN catwalks
a long narrow platform that models walk
along at a fashion show

**caucus** NOUN caucuses
a small group within a political party,
influencing decisions and policy

**cauldron** NOUN cauldrons
a large deep pot for boiling things in

**cauliflower** NOUN cauliflowers
a cabbage with a large head of white flowers

**cause** NOUN causes
❶ a person or thing that makes something
happen or produces an effect • *The cause of
the accident is a mystery.* ❷ a good reason
• *There is no cause for worry.* ❸ a purpose for
which people work; an organization or charity
• *They were raising money for a good cause.*

**cause** VERB causes, causing, caused
to be the cause of something or to make it
happen • *Do we know what caused the fire?*

a
b
c
d
e
f
g
h
i
j
k
l
m
n
o
p
q
r
s
t
u
v
w
x
y
z

**causeway** NOUN causeways
a raised road across low or marshy ground

**caustic** ADJECTIVE
❶ able to burn or wear things away by chemical action ❷ very critical or sarcastic
• *caustic comments*
➤ **caustically** ADVERB

**cauterize** (also **cauterise**) VERB cauterizes, cauterizing, cauterized
to cauterize a wound is to burn the surface of flesh round it to destroy infection or stop any bleeding

**caution** NOUN cautions
❶ care you take to avoid difficulty or danger ❷ a warning

**caution** VERB cautions, cautioning, cautioned
to give someone a warning • *He cautioned his sister not to tell anyone.*

**cautionary** ADJECTIVE
giving a warning • *a cautionary tale*

**cautious** ADJECTIVE
taking care to avoid difficulty or danger
➤ **cautiously** ADVERB

**cavalcade** NOUN cavalcades
a procession of vehicles or people on horseback

**Cavalier** NOUN Cavaliers
a supporter of King Charles I in the English Civil War (1642–9)

**cavalry** NOUN
soldiers who fight on horseback or in armoured vehicles. Compare with infantry.

**cave** NOUN caves
a large hollow place in the side of a hill or cliff or underground

**cave** VERB caves, caving, caved
➤ **cave in** ❶ to collapse or fall inwards • *The roof of the tunnel had caved in.* ❷ to give way in an argument • *She finally caved in and agreed that he could go.*

**caveat** (say **kav**-ee-at) NOUN caveats
a warning **WORD ORIGIN** Latin, = let a person beware

**caveman** NOUN cavemen
a person living in a cave in prehistoric times

**cavern** NOUN caverns
a large cave

**cavernous** ADJECTIVE
a cavernous room or space is huge and often empty or dark • *He looked around the cavernous hall.*

**caviare** (say **kav**-ee-ar) NOUN
the pickled roe of sturgeon or other large fish

**caving** NOUN
(*British*) exploring caves

**cavity** NOUN cavities
a hollow or hole

**cavort** (say ka-**vort**) VERB cavorts, cavorting, cavorted
to jump or run about excitedly

**caw** NOUN caws
the harsh cry of a crow or other large bird

**CB** ABBREVIATION
citizens' band

**cc** ABBREVIATION
❶ cubic centimetre(s) ❷ used to show that a copy of an email is being sent to another person **WORD ORIGIN** the second meaning is short for 'carbon copy', originally a copy made with carbon paper (= thin paper with a coloured coating) placed between sheets of paper to make copies of what is written or typed on the top sheet

**CD** ABBREVIATION
compact disc

**CD-ROM** ABBREVIATION
compact disc read-only memory; a compact disc on which large amounts of data can be stored and then displayed on a computer screen

**cease** VERB ceases, ceasing, ceased
to stop happening or stop doing something
• *You never cease to amaze me!* • *The company ceased trading in June.*

**ceasefire** NOUN ceasefires
an agreement between the two sides in a conflict for fighting to stop for a time

**ceaseless** ADJECTIVE
not stopping; going on continuously • *the ceaseless cooing of the pigeons*

**cedar** NOUN cedars
an evergreen tree with hard fragrant wood
➤ **cedarwood** NOUN

**cede** (say seed) VERB cedes, ceding, ceded
to give up your rights to something; to surrender something you own • *They had to cede some of their territory.*

**cedilla** (say sid-**il**-a) NOUN cedillas
a mark under c in certain languages to show that it is pronounced as s, e.g. in *façade*
**WORD ORIGIN** from Spanish, = a little z

**ceilidh** (say **kay**-lee) NOUN ceilidhs
an informal gathering for music, singing and dancing, originating from Scotland and Ireland

**ceiling** NOUN ceilings
❶ the flat surface at the top of a room ❷ the highest limit that something can reach • *They imposed a ceiling on car imports.*

SPELLING

In ceiling, e before i is the right way round.

**celandine** NOUN celandines
a small wild plant with yellow flowers

**celebrate** VERB celebrates, celebrating, celebrated
❶ to do something special or enjoyable to show that a day or event is important ❷ to perform a religious ceremony

**celebrated** ADJECTIVE
famous • *a celebrated author*

**celebration** NOUN celebrations
❶ celebrating something • *Her triumph was a cause for celebration.* ❷ a party or other event that celebrates something

**celebrity** NOUN celebrities
❶ a celebrity is a famous person ❷ celebrity is fame or being famous • *He never really enjoyed his celebrity.*

**celery** NOUN
a vegetable with crisp white or green stems

**celestial** (say sil-**est**-ee-al) ADJECTIVE
❶ to do with the sky ❷ to do with heaven; divine
➤ celestial bodies stars or planets

**celibate** (say **sel**-ib-at) ADJECTIVE
remaining unmarried or not having sex, especially for religious reasons
➤ celibacy NOUN

**cell** NOUN cells
❶ a small room where a prisoner is locked up ❷ a small room in a monastery or convent ❸ a microscopic unit of living matter. All plants and animals are made up of cells. ❹ a compartment of a honeycomb ❺ a device for producing electric current chemically ❻ a small group or unit in an organization

**cellar** NOUN cellars
an underground room

**cello** (say **chel**-oh) NOUN cellos
a musical instrument like a large violin, played upright between the knees of a player
➤ cellist NOUN

**Cellophane** NOUN
(*trademark*) a thin transparent wrapping material

**cellular** ADJECTIVE
❶ to do with or containing cells ❷ with an open mesh • *cellular blankets* ❸ a cellular telephone uses a network of radio stations to allow messages to be sent over a wide area

**celluloid** NOUN
a kind of plastic, used in the past for making cinema films

**cellulose** NOUN
tissue that forms the main part of all plants and trees

**Celsius** (say **sel**-see-us) ADJECTIVE
measuring temperature on a scale using 100 degrees, where water freezes at 0° and boils at 100° WORD ORIGIN named after Anders *Celsius*, a Swedish astronomer, who invented it

**Celtic** (say **kel**-tik) ADJECTIVE
to do with the languages or inhabitants of ancient Britain and France before the Romans came or of their descendants, e.g. Irish, Welsh, Gaelic

**cement** NOUN
❶ a mixture of lime and clay used in building, to join bricks together ❷ a strong glue

**cement** VERB cements, cementing, cemented
❶ to build something with cement ❷ to strengthen or join something firmly • *This marriage cemented the relationship between the two countries.*

**cemetery** (say **sem**-et-ree) NOUN cemeteries
a place where dead people are buried

**cenotaph** (say **sen**-o-taf) NOUN cenotaphs
a monument, especially as a war memorial, to people who are buried in other places

**censer** NOUN censers
a container in which incense is burnt

**censor** NOUN censors
a person who examines films, books, letters, etc. and removes or bans anything that is thought to be offensive or unacceptable

**censor** VERB censors, censoring, censored
to ban or remove parts of a film, book, letter, etc. that are thought to be offensive or unacceptable
➤ censorship NOUN
WORD ORIGIN Latin, = magistrate with the power to ban unsuitable people from

a b c d e f g h i j k l m n o p q r s t u v w x y z

ceremonies; from *censere* = to judge

> USAGE
>
> Take care not to confuse with **censure**.

**censorious** (say sen-**sor**-ee-us) *ADJECTIVE*
criticizing something strongly

**censure** (say **sen**-sher) *NOUN*
strong criticism or disapproval of something

**censure** *VERB* censures, censuring, censured
to criticize someone severely and openly

> USAGE
>
> Take care not to confuse with **censor**.

**census** *NOUN* censuses
an official count or survey of the population
of a country or area

**cent** *NOUN* cents
a coin worth one-hundredth of a dollar

**centaur** (say **sen**-tor) *NOUN* centaurs
(in Greek myths) a creature with the upper
body, head and arms of a man and the lower
body of a horse

**centenarian** (say sent-in-**air**-ee-an) *NOUN*
centenarians
a person who is 100 years old or more

**centenary** (say sen-**teen**-er-ee) *NOUN*
centenaries
(*British*) a 100th anniversary of an important
event
> **centennial** (say sen-**ten**-ee-al) *ADJECTIVE*

**centigrade** *ADJECTIVE*
Celsius

**centilitre** *NOUN* centilitres
one-hundredth of a litre

> SPELLING
>
> The 's' sound is spelt with a c in centilitre.
> Do not forget the re at the end.

**centimetre** *NOUN* centimetres
one-hundredth of a metre

> SPELLING
>
> The 's' sound is spelt with a c in
> centimetre. Do not forget the re at the
> end.

**centipede** *NOUN* centipedes
a small crawling creature with a long body
and many legs

**central** *ADJECTIVE*
❶ to do with or at the centre • *a map of
central Europe* ❷ most important or main
• *The film's central character is a fifteen-*
*year-old girl.*
> **centrally** *ADVERB*

**central heating** *NOUN*
a system of heating a building from one
source by circulating hot water or hot air or
steam in pipes or by linked radiators

**centralize** (also **centralise**) *VERB* centralizes,
centralizing, centralized
to bring something under the control of a
central authority
> **centralization** *NOUN*

**centre** *NOUN* centres
❶ the middle point or part ❷ an important
place ❸ a building or place for a special
purpose • *shopping centre* • *sports centre*

**centre** *VERB* centres, centring, centred
to place something at the centre • *Centre the
heading at the top of the page.*
> **centre on something** or **centre around
something** to have something as the
main subject of interest or concern • *Our
discussions centred on the question of
finance.*

**centre forward** *NOUN* centre forwards
the player in the middle of the forward line in
football or hockey

**centre of gravity** *NOUN* centres of gravity
the point in an object around which its mass
is perfectly balanced

**centrifugal** *ADJECTIVE*
moving away from the centre; using
centrifugal force

**centrifugal force** *NOUN*
a force that makes a thing that is travelling
round a central point fly outwards off its
circular path

**centurion** (say sent-**yoor**-ee-on) *NOUN*
centurions
an officer in the ancient Roman army,
originally commanding a hundred men

**century** *NOUN* centuries
❶ a period of one hundred years ❷ a
hundred runs scored by a batsman in an
innings at cricket

**cephalopod** (say **sef**-al-o-pod) *NOUN*
cephalopods
a mollusc (such as an octopus or squid) that
has a head with a ring of tentacles round the
mouth

**ceramic** *ADJECTIVE*
to do with or made of pottery

**ceramics** *PLURAL NOUN*
pottery-making

**cereal** *NOUN* cereals
❶ a grass producing seeds which are used as food, e.g. wheat, barley or rice ❷ a breakfast food made from these seeds
**WORD ORIGIN** from *Ceres*, the Roman goddess of farming

**SPELLING**
Take care not to confuse with **serial**.

**cerebral** (say **se**-rib-ral) *ADJECTIVE*
to do with the brain

**cerebral palsy** *NOUN*
a condition caused by brain damage before birth that makes a person suffer from spasms of the muscles and jerky movements

**ceremonial** *ADJECTIVE*
to do with or used in a ceremony; formal • *a ceremonial occasion*
➤ **ceremonially** *ADVERB*

**ceremonious** *ADJECTIVE*
full of ceremony; elaborately performed • *a ceremonious bow*

**ceremony** *NOUN* ceremonies
❶ a formal religious or public occasion celebrating an important event • *the opening ceremony of the Olympic Games* ❷ the formal actions carried out on an important occasion, e.g. at a wedding or a funeral • *The new hospital was opened with great ceremony.*

**certain** *ADJECTIVE*
❶ something is certain when it is definitely true or going to happen ❷ you are certain about something when you know it is definitely true
➤ **a certain person** or **thing** a person or thing that is known but not named
➤ **for certain** definitely; for sure
➤ **make certain** to make sure

**SPELLING**
There is a tricky bit in **certain** – it ends in **ain**.

**certainly** *ADVERB*
❶ for certain ❷ yes

**certainty** *NOUN* certainties
❶ something that is sure to happen ❷ being sure

**certificate** *NOUN* certificates
an official document giving information about a person or event • *a birth certificate*

**certify** *VERB* certifies, certifying, certified
to declare formally that something is true
➤ **certification** *NOUN*

**cervix** *NOUN* cervices (say **ser**-vis-ees)
the entrance to the womb
➤ **cervical** *ADJECTIVE*

**cessation** *NOUN*
the stopping or ending of something

**cesspit, cesspool** *NOUN* cesspits, cesspools
a covered pit where liquid waste or sewage is stored temporarily

**CFC** *ABBREVIATION*
chlorofluorocarbon; a gas containing chlorine and fluorine that is thought to be harmful to the ozone layer in the Earth's atmosphere

**chafe** *VERB* chafes, chafing, chafed
❶ to make something sore or become sore by rubbing ❷ to become irritated or impatient • *We chafed at the delay.*

**chaff** *NOUN*
husks of corn, separated from the seed

**chaff** *VERB* chaffs, chaffing, chaffed
to tease someone

**chaffinch** *NOUN* chaffinches
a kind of finch

**chagrin** (say **shag**-rin) *NOUN*
a feeling of being annoyed or disappointed

**chain** *NOUN* chains
❶ a row of metal rings fastened together ❷ a connected series of things • *a mountain chain* • *a chain of events* ❸ a number of shops, hotels or other businesses owned by the same company

**chain** *VERB* chains, chaining, chained
to fasten something with a chain or chains • *He chained his bike up outside.*

**chain letter** *NOUN* chain letters
a letter that you are asked to copy and send to several other people, who are supposed to do the same

**chain reaction** *NOUN* chain reactions
a series of happenings in which each causes the next

**chain store** *NOUN* chain stores
one of a number of similar shops owned by the same firm

**chair** *NOUN* chairs
❶ a movable seat, with a back, for one person ❷ the person who is in charge of a meeting

**chair** *VERB* chairs, chairing, chaired
to chair a meeting is to be in charge of it and
run it

**chairman, chairwoman** *NOUN* chairmen or
chairwomen
the person who is in charge of a meeting
➤ **chairmanship** *NOUN*

USAGE
The word chairman may be used of a man
or of a woman, but chairperson is now
often used instead.

**chairperson** *NOUN* chairpersons
a chairman or chairwoman

**chalet** (say **shal**-ay) *NOUN* chalets
❶ a Swiss hut or cottage ❷ a hut in a holiday
camp etc.

**chalice** *NOUN* chalices
a large goblet for holding wine, especially one
from which the Communion wine is drunk in
Christian services

**chalk** *NOUN* chalks
❶ a soft white or coloured stick used for
writing on blackboards or for drawing ❷ soft
white limestone

**chalky** *ADJECTIVE*
containing chalk or like chalk • *Her face was
chalky white.*

**challenge** *NOUN* challenges
❶ a task or activity that is new and exciting
but also difficult • *The role will be the biggest
challenge of his acting career.* ❷ a call to
someone to take part in a contest or to show
their ability or strength

**challenge** *VERB* challenges, challenging,
challenged
❶ to make a challenge to someone • *My
brother challenged me to a game of darts.*
❷ to be a challenge to someone • *This job
doesn't really challenge me.* ❸ to question
whether something is true or correct

**challenger** *NOUN* challengers
a person who makes a challenge, especially
for a sports title

**challenging** *ADJECTIVE*
difficult but also interesting and exciting • *a
challenging job*

**chamber** *NOUN* chambers
❶ (old use) a room ❷ a hall used for meetings
of a parliament or council; the members
of the group using it ❸ a compartment in
machinery etc.

**chamberlain** *NOUN* chamberlains
an official who manages the household of a
sovereign or great noble

**chambermaid** *NOUN* chambermaids
a woman employed to clean bedrooms at a
hotel etc.

**chamber music** *NOUN*
classical music for a small group of players

**chamber pot** *NOUN* chamber pots
a bowl kept in a bedroom and used as a toilet

**chameleon** (say kam-ee-lee-on) *NOUN*
chameleons
a small lizard that can change its colour
to match that of its surroundings
WORD ORIGIN from Greek *khamaileon*, literally
= ground lion

**chamois** *NOUN* chamois
❶ (say **sham**-wa) a small wild antelope living
in the mountains ❷ (say **sham**-ee) a piece
of soft yellow leather used for washing and
polishing things

**champ** *VERB* champs, champing, champed
to munch or bite something noisily

**champagne** (say sham-**payn**) *NOUN*
a bubbly white wine from the region of
Champagne in France

**champion** *NOUN* champions
❶ a person or thing that has defeated all the
others in a sport or competition ❷ someone
who supports a cause by fighting or speaking
for it • *Martin Luther King was a champion of
human rights.*

**champion** *VERB* champions, championing,
championed
to support a cause by fighting or speaking
for it

**championship** *NOUN* championships
a competition to find the best player or team
in a particular sport or game

**chance** *NOUN* chances
❶ an opportunity or possibility • *This is your
only chance to see them.* ❷ the way things
happen without being planned • *I met her by
chance.*
➤ **take a chance** to take a risk

**chance** *VERB* chances, chancing, chanced
❶ to happen by chance • *As she was passing,
she chanced to see him come out of the
house.* ❷ to risk something • *I chanced a
quick look behind me.*

**chancel** *NOUN* chancels
the part of a church nearest to the altar

**chancellor** NOUN chancellors
❶ an important government or legal official
❷ the chief minister of the government in some European countries

**Chancellor of the Exchequer** NOUN
the government minister in charge of a country's finances and taxes

**chancy** ADJECTIVE
risky or uncertain

**chandelier** (say shand-il-**eer**) NOUN chandeliers
a large hanging light with branches for several light bulbs or candles

**change** VERB changes, changing, changed
❶ to make something different or become different • *This town has changed a lot in the last few years.* ❷ to exchange one thing for another • *Could I change this shirt for a larger size?* ❸ to put on different clothes ❹ to go from one train or bus to another • *Change at York for the train to Durham.* ❺ to give smaller units of money or money in another currency, for an amount of money • *Can you change £20?*

**change** NOUN changes
❶ changing; a difference in doing something • *a change in the weather* ❷ coins or notes of small values ❸ money given back to the payer when the price is less than the amount handed over ❹ a fresh set of clothes ❺ something different from what is usual • *Let's walk home for a change.*

**changeable** ADJECTIVE
likely to change; changing frequently • *changeable weather*

**changeling** NOUN changelings
a child who is believed to have been substituted secretly for another, especially by fairies

**channel** NOUN channels
❶ a stretch of water connecting two seas ❷ broadcasting wavelength ❸ a way for water to flow along ❹ the part of a river or sea that is deep enough for ships

**channel** VERB channels, channelling, channelled
❶ to use something for a particular purpose • *She channelled all her energy into her music.* ❷ to make something move along a particular channel, path or route • *Water is channelled from the river to the fields.*

**chant** NOUN chants
❶ a tune to which words with no regular rhythm are fitted, especially one used in church music ❷ a rhythmic call or shout

**chant** VERB chants, chanting, chanted
❶ to sing a chant ❷ to call out words in a rhythm

**chaos** (say **kay**-oss) NOUN
great disorder • *Heavy snow has caused chaos on the roads.*

**chaotic** (say kay-**ot**-ik) ADJECTIVE
in a state of complete confusion and disorder
➤ **chaotically** ADVERB

**chap** NOUN chaps (British) (informal)
a man

**chapatti** NOUN chapattis
a flat cake of unleavened bread, used in Indian cookery

**chapel** NOUN chapels
❶ a small building or room used for Christian worship ❷ a section of a large church, with its own altar

**chaperone** (say **shap**-er-ohn) NOUN chaperones
an older woman in charge of a young one on social occasions
➤ **chaperone** VERB

**chaplain** NOUN chaplains
a member of the clergy who regularly works in a college, hospital, prison, regiment, etc.

**chapped** ADJECTIVE
with skin split or cracked from cold etc. • *chapped lips*

**chapter** NOUN chapters
❶ a section or division of a book ❷ the clergy of a cathedral or members of a monastery

**char** VERB chars, charring, charred
to make something black by burning

**char** NOUN chars
(British) (old use) a charwoman

**character** NOUN characters
❶ a person in a story, film or play ❷ all the qualities that make a person or thing what he, she or it is • *The book gives a fascinating insight into Madonna's character.* ❸ a letter of the alphabet or other written symbol

**characteristic** NOUN characteristics
a quality that forms part of a person's or thing's character

**characteristic** ADJECTIVE
typical of a person or thing • *This style of dancing is characteristic of the region.*
➤ **characteristically** ADVERB

**characterize** (also **characterise**) *VERB*
characterizes, characterizing, characterized
❶ to be a characteristic of something
• *The country's recent history has been characterized by upheaval and conflict.* ❷ to describe a person's character in a certain way
• *His friends characterized him as ambitious.*
➤ **characterization** *NOUN*

**charade** (say sha-**rahd**) *NOUN* charades
❶ a scene in the game of **charades**, in which people try to guess a word from other people's acting ❷ a pretence • *I'm sorry, I can't keep this charade up any longer.*

**charcoal** *NOUN*
a black substance made by burning wood slowly. Charcoal can be used for drawing with.

**charge** *NOUN* charges
❶ the price asked for something ❷ an accusation that someone has committed a crime • *He is facing three charges of burglary.* ❸ a rushing attack ❹ the amount of electricity in something ❺ the amount of explosive needed to fire a gun ❻ a person or thing in someone's care
➤ **in charge** in control; deciding what will happen to a person or thing
➤ **take charge** to take control of something and become responsible for it

**charge** *VERB* charges, charging, charged
❶ to ask a particular price for something
❷ to accuse someone of committing a crime ❸ to rush forward in an attack • *The bull put its head down and charged.* ❹ to give an electric charge to something • *My phone needs charging.* ❺ to give someone a responsibility or task

**charger** *NOUN* chargers
❶ a piece of equipment for charging a battery with electricity • *a mobile phone charger* ❷ (old use) a cavalry horse

**chariot** *NOUN* chariots
a horse-drawn vehicle with two wheels, used in ancient times for fighting and racing
➤ **charioteer** *NOUN*

**charisma** (say ka-**riz**-ma) *NOUN*
the special quality that makes a person attractive or influential

**charismatic** (say ka-riz-**mat**-ik) *ADJECTIVE*
having charisma • *She was a charismatic leader.*

**charitable** *ADJECTIVE*
❶ giving money and help to people who need it; to do with a charity • *a charitable*
donation ❷ kind in your attitude to other people • *Let's be charitable and assume she just made a mistake.*
➤ **charitably** *ADVERB*

**charity** *NOUN* charities
❶ an organization set up to help people who are poor, ill or disabled or have suffered a disaster ❷ giving money or help to people who need it ❸ kindness and sympathy towards others; being unwilling to think badly of people

**charlatan** (say **shar**-la-tan) *NOUN* charlatans
a person who falsely claims to be an expert

**charm** *NOUN* charms
❶ the power to please or delight people; attractiveness • *The story has great charm.*
❷ a magic spell ❸ a small object that is believed to bring good luck • *a lucky charm*
❹ an ornament worn on a bracelet

**charm** *VERB* charms, charming, charmed
❶ to give pleasure or delight to people ❷ to put a spell on someone; bewitch
➤ **charmer** *NOUN*

**charming** *ADJECTIVE*
pleasant and attractive

**chart** *NOUN* charts
❶ a map for people sailing ships or flying aircraft ❷ an outline map showing special information • *a weather chart* ❸ a diagram, list or table giving information in an orderly way
➤ **the charts** a list of the CDs and records that have sold the most copies

**chart** *VERB* charts, charting, charted
to make a chart or map of something • *Cook explored and charted the coast of New Zealand.*

**charter** *NOUN* charters
❶ an official document stating the rights or aims of an organization or group of people
❷ hiring an aircraft, ship or vehicle

**charter** *VERB* charters, chartering, chartered
to hire an aircraft, ship or vehicle

**chartered accountant** *NOUN* chartered accountants
an accountant who is qualified according to the rules of a professional association that has a royal charter

**charwoman** *NOUN* charwomen (British) (old use)
a woman employed as a cleaner

**chary** (say **chair**-ee) *ADJECTIVE*
cautious about doing or giving something

**chase** VERB chases, chasing, chased
to go quickly after a person or thing in order to capture or catch them up or drive them away

**chase** NOUN chases
chasing someone or something • *an exciting car chase*

**chasm** (say kazm) NOUN chasms
a deep opening in the ground

**chassis** (say shas-ee) NOUN chassis
the framework under a car etc., on which other parts are mounted

**chaste** ADJECTIVE
not expressing sexual feelings • *a chaste kiss on the cheek*

**chasten** (say chay-sen) VERB chastens, chastening, chastened
to make someone realize that they have behaved badly or done something wrong • *He looked chastened and immediately apologized.*

**chastise** VERB chastises, chastising, chastised
to punish or scold someone severely
➤ **chastisement** NOUN

**chastity** (say chas-ti-ti) NOUN
the state of not having sex with anyone

**chat** NOUN chats
a friendly informal conversation

**chat** VERB chats, chatting, chatted
❶ to have a friendly informal conversation ❷ to exchange messages with other people on the Internet

**chateau** (say shat-oh) NOUN chateaux
a castle or large country house in France

**chat room** NOUN chat rooms
an area on the Internet where people can have a conversation by sending messages to each other

**chattel** NOUN chattels
(*old use*) something you own that can be moved from place to place, as distinct from a house or land

**chatter** VERB chatters, chattering, chattered
❶ to talk quickly about unimportant things; to keep on talking ❷ your teeth chatter when they make a rattling sound because you are cold or frightened
➤ **chatterer** NOUN

**chatter** NOUN
chattering talk or sound

**chatterbox** NOUN chatterboxes
a talkative person

**chatty** ADJECTIVE
❶ liking to talk a lot in a friendly way ❷ in an informal style • *a chatty letter*

**chauffeur** (say shoh-fer) NOUN chauffeurs
a person employed to drive a car

**chauvinism** (say shoh-vin-izm) NOUN
❶ prejudiced belief that your own country is superior to any other ❷ the belief of some men that men are superior to women
➤ **chauvinist** NOUN
➤ **chauvinistic** ADJECTIVE
**WORD ORIGIN** from the name of Nicolas *Chauvin*, a French soldier in Napoleon's army, noted for his extreme patriotism

**cheap** ADJECTIVE
❶ low in price; not expensive ❷ of poor quality; of low value
➤ **cheapness** NOUN

**cheaply** ADVERB
for a low price

**cheat** VERB cheats, cheating, cheated
❶ to try to do well in an exam or game by breaking the rules ❷ to trick or deceive someone so they lose something • *He had cheated her out of her fortune.*

**cheat** NOUN cheats
a person who cheats

**check** VERB checks, checking, checked
❶ to make sure that something is correct or in good condition ❷ to make something stop or go slower

**check** NOUN checks
❶ checking something ❷ stopping or slowing; a pause ❸ (*North American*) a bill in a restaurant ❹ the situation in chess when a king may be captured ❺ a pattern of squares
**WORD ORIGIN** the oldest meaning is the chess meaning, which comes from Persian *shah* = king

**checked** ADJECTIVE
marked with a pattern of squares • *a checked shirt*

**checkmate** NOUN
the winning situation in chess, where one player's king is threatened and cannot be moved out of danger **WORD ORIGIN** from Persian *shah mat* = the king is dead

**checkout** NOUN checkouts
a place where goods are paid for in a self-service shop

a
b
c
d
e
f
g
h
i
j
k
l
m
n
o
p
q
r
s
t
u
v
w
x
y
z

**check-up** NOUN check-ups
a routine medical or dental examination

**Cheddar** NOUN
a kind of cheese, originally made in Cheddar in Somerset

**cheek** NOUN cheeks
❶ the side of your face below your eye ❷ rude or disrespectful talk or behaviour

**cheeky** ADJECTIVE
rude or disrespectful
➤ **cheekily** ADVERB

**cheer** NOUN cheers
❶ a shout of praise or pleasure or encouragement ❷ good cheer is being cheerful and enjoying yourself

**cheer** VERB cheers, cheering, cheered
❶ to give a cheer ❷ to comfort or encourage someone • *They were all cheered by the good news.*
➤ **cheer up** to become more cheerful

**cheerful** ADJECTIVE
❶ looking or sounding happy ❷ pleasantly bright or colourful
➤ **cheerfully** ADVERB
➤ **cheerfulness** NOUN

**cheerio** EXCLAMATION (*informal*)
goodbye

**cheerless** ADJECTIVE
gloomy or dreary • *a dark and cheerless room*

**cheers** EXCLAMATION (*informal*)
❶ a word that people say to each other as they lift up their glasses to drink ❷ goodbye ❸ thank you

**cheery** ADJECTIVE
bright and cheerful • *a cheery grin*

**cheese** NOUN cheeses
a solid food made from milk

**cheesecake** NOUN cheesecakes
a dessert made of a mixture of sweetened curds on a layer of biscuit

**cheetah** NOUN cheetahs
a large spotted animal of the cat family that can run extremely fast

**chef** (say shef) NOUN chefs
the cook in a hotel or restaurant

**chemical** ADJECTIVE
to do with or produced by chemistry

**chemical** NOUN chemicals
a substance obtained by or used in chemistry

**chemist** NOUN chemists
❶ a person who makes or sells medicines ❷ a shop selling medicines, cosmetics, etc. ❸ an expert in chemistry

**chemistry** NOUN
❶ the way that substances combine and react with one another ❷ the study of substances and their reactions etc.

**chemotherapy** NOUN
the treatment of disease, especially cancer, by the use of chemical substances

**cheque** NOUN cheques
a printed form on which you write instructions to a bank to pay out money from your account

**chequered** ADJECTIVE
marked with a pattern of squares

**cherish** VERB cherishes, cherishing, cherished
❶ to look after a person or thing lovingly ❷ to keep something in your mind for a long time • *He cherished the memory of those days in Paris.*

**cherry** NOUN cherries
a small soft round fruit with a stone

**cherub** NOUN cherubim or cherubs
an angel, often pictured as a chubby child with wings
➤ **cherubic** (say che-**roo**-bik) ADJECTIVE

**chess** NOUN
a game for two players with sixteen pieces each (called **chessmen**) on a board of 64 squares (a **chessboard**)

**chest** NOUN chests
❶ the front part of the body between the neck and the waist ❷ a large strong box for storing things in

**chestnut** NOUN chestnuts
❶ a tree that produces hard brown nuts ❷ the nut of this tree ❸ an old joke or story

**chest of drawers** NOUN chests of drawers
a piece of furniture with drawers for storing clothes etc.

**chevron** (say **shev**-ron) NOUN chevrons
a V-shaped stripe

**chew** VERB chews, chewing, chewed
to grind food between your teeth

**chewing gum** NOUN
a sticky flavoured type of sweet for chewing

**chewy** *ADJECTIVE*
chewy food is tough and needs a lot of
chewing

**chic** (say sheek) *ADJECTIVE*
stylish and elegant

**chick** *NOUN* chicks
a very young bird

**chicken** *NOUN* chickens
❶ a young hen ❷ a hen's flesh used as food

**chicken** *ADJECTIVE* (*informal*) afraid to do
something; cowardly

**chicken** *VERB* chickens, chickening, chickened
➤ **chicken out** (*informal*) to refuse to take
part in something because you are afraid

**chickenpox** *NOUN*
a disease that produces red spots on the skin

**chickpea** *NOUN* chickpeas
the yellow seed of a plant of the pea family,
eaten as a vegetable

**chicory** *NOUN*
a plant whose leaves are used in salads

**chide** *VERB* chides, chiding, chided, chidden
to tell someone off

**chief** *NOUN* chiefs
❶ a leader or ruler of a people, especially of
a Native American tribe ❷ a person with the
highest rank or authority • *the chief of police*

**chief** *ADJECTIVE*
❶ most important; main • *Caesar defeated
his chief rival, Pompey and took power.*
❷ having the highest rank or authority • *the
company's chief executive*

**chiefly** *ADVERB*
mainly or mostly • *Liam is the one who is
chiefly to blame.*

**chieftain** *NOUN* chieftains
the chief of a tribe or clan

**chiffon** (say **shif**-on) *NOUN*
a very thin, almost transparent, fabric

**chilblain** *NOUN* chilblains
a sore swollen place, usually on a hand or
foot, caused by cold weather

**child** *NOUN* children
❶ a young person; a boy or girl ❷ someone's
son or daughter

**childhood** *NOUN* childhoods
the time when a person is a child

**childish** *ADJECTIVE*
❶ like a child; unsuitable for a grown person

• *childish handwriting* ❷ silly and immature
• *Don't be so childish!*
➤ **childishly** *ADVERB*

**childless** *ADJECTIVE*
having no children

**childlike** *ADJECTIVE*
having the good qualities that a child has
• *His childlike enthusiasm delighted us all.*

**childminder** *NOUN* childminders
(*British*) a person who is paid to look after
children while their parents are out at work

**chill** *NOUN* chills
❶ unpleasant coldness • *There's a chill in the
air.* ❷ an illness that makes you shiver

**chill** *VERB* chills, chilling, chilled
❶ to make a person or thing cold
❷ (*informal*) to relax completely • *We've just
been chilling in front of the TV.*

**chilli** *NOUN* chillies
the hot-tasting pod of a red pepper

**chilli con carne** *NOUN*
a stew of chilli-flavoured minced beef and
beans

**chilly** *ADJECTIVE*
❶ rather cold ❷ unfriendly • *We got a chilly
reception.*

**chime** *NOUN* chimes
a series of ringing sounds made by a set of
bells or clock

**chime** *VERB* chimes, chiming, chimed
to make a chime • *The church clock chimed
nine o'clock.*
➤ **chime in** to join in a conversation by
saying something

**chimney** *NOUN* chimneys
a tall pipe or structure that carries smoke
away from a fire

**chimney pot** *NOUN* chimney pots
a pipe fitted to the top of a chimney

**chimney sweep** *NOUN* chimney sweeps
a person who cleans soot from inside
chimneys

**chimpanzee** *NOUN* chimpanzees
an intelligent African ape, smaller than a
gorilla

**chin** *NOUN* chins
the lower part of the face below the mouth

**china** *NOUN*
thin delicate pottery

**chink** NOUN chinks
❶ a narrow opening that lets light through
• *He looked through a chink in the curtains.*
❷ a chinking sound • *There was a chink of coins as the money changed hands.*

**chink** VERB chinks, chinking, chinked
to make a sound like glasses or coins being struck together

**chintz** NOUN
a shiny cotton cloth used for making curtains etc.

**chip** NOUN chips
❶ a thin piece cut or broken off something hard ❷ a fried oblong strip of potato ❸ a place where a small piece has been knocked off something ❹ a small counter used in gambling games ❺ a microchip
➤ **a chip off the old block** a child who is very like his or her father or mother
➤ **have a chip on your shoulder** to feel resentful or defensive about something

**chip** VERB chips, chipping, chipped
❶ to knock a small piece off something by accident ❷ to cut a potato into chips
➤ **chip in** to make a suggestion or comment during a conversation that other people are having

**chipboard** NOUN
board made from chips of wood pressed and stuck together

**chipolata** NOUN chipolatas
(*British*) a small spicy sausage

**chiropody** (say ki-**rop**-od-ee) NOUN
(*chiefly British*) medical treatment of the feet, e.g. corns
➤ **chiropodist** NOUN
WORD ORIGIN from Greek *cheir* = hand + *podos* = of the foot (because chiropodists originally treated both hands and feet)

**chirp** VERB chirps, chirping, chirped
to make short sharp sounds like a small bird
➤ **chirp** NOUN

**chirpy** ADJECTIVE
lively and cheerful

**chisel** NOUN chisels
a tool with a sharp end for shaping wood or stone

**chisel** VERB chisels, chiselling, chiselled
to shape or cut wood or stone with a chisel

**chivalry** (say **shiv**-al-ree) NOUN
❶ the code of good behaviour and brave fighting that medieval knights used to follow
❷ behaviour that is considerate and helpful,

especially by men towards women
➤ **chivalrous** ADJECTIVE

**chive** NOUN chives
a small herb with leaves that taste like onions

**chivvy** VERB chivvies, chivvying, chivvied
(*British*) to try to make someone hurry
WORD ORIGIN probably from *Chevy Chase*, the scene of a skirmish which was the subject of an old ballad

**chlorine** (say **klor**-een) NOUN
a greenish-yellow gas used to disinfect water etc.

**chloroform** (say **klo**-ro-form) NOUN
a liquid that gives off a vapour that makes people unconscious

**chlorophyll** (say **klo**-ro-fil) NOUN
the substance that makes plants green

**choc ice** NOUN choc ices
(*British*) a bar of ice cream covered with chocolate

**chock** NOUN chocks
a block or wedge used to prevent an aircraft from moving

**chock-a-block** ADJECTIVE
(*British*) full of people or things crowded or packed together • *The town is always chock-a-block with tourists.*

**chock-full** ADJECTIVE
crammed full of good things • *This issue is chock-full of exciting stories.*

**chocolate** NOUN chocolates
❶ a solid brown food or powder made from roasted cacao seeds ❷ a drink made with this powder ❸ a sweet made of or covered with chocolate
SPELLING
There are two tricky bits in chocolate—it has an o in the middle and it ends in late.

**choice** NOUN choices
❶ the opportunity to choose between things
• *I'm afraid we have no choice.* ❷ the range of things from which someone can choose
• *There is now a wide choice of TV channels.*
❸ a person or thing that someone has chosen
• *This is my choice.*

**choice** ADJECTIVE
of the best quality • *choice bananas*

**choir** NOUN choirs
a group of people trained to sing together, especially in a church
➤ **choirboy** NOUN ➤ **choirgirl** NOUN

**choke** VERB chokes, choking, choked
❶ to be unable to breathe properly because something is blocking your windpipe ❷ to stop someone breathing properly by blocking their windpipe ❸ to block up or clog something • *The roads were choked with traffic.*

**choke** NOUN chokes
a device controlling the flow of air into the engine of a motor vehicle

**cholera** (say kol-er-a) NOUN
an infectious disease that is often fatal

**cholesterol** (say kol-**est**-er-ol) NOUN
a fatty substance that can clog the arteries

**choose** VERB chooses, choosing, chose, chosen
to decide which you want from among a number of people or things

**choosy** ADVERB
(*informal*) careful or fussy about what you choose

**chop** VERB chops, chopping, chopped
❶ to cut something into pieces with a knife • *Chop the carrots up into small pieces.* ❷ to cut or hit something with a heavy blow • *He chopped a branch off the tree.*

**chop** NOUN chops
❶ a chopping blow ❷ a small thick slice of meat, usually on a rib

**chopper** NOUN choppers
❶ a chopping tool; a small axe ❷ (*informal*) a helicopter

**choppy** ADJECTIVE choppier, choppiest
the sea is choppy when it is not smooth but full of small waves

**chopsticks** PLURAL NOUN
a pair of thin sticks used for lifting Chinese and Japanese food to your mouth

**chop suey** NOUN chop sueys
a Chinese dish of meat fried with bean sprouts and vegetables served with rice

**choral** ADJECTIVE
to do with or sung by a choir or chorus

**chord** (say kord) NOUN chords
❶ a number of musical notes sounded together ❷ a straight line joining two points on a curve

> **SPELLING**
> **Chord** is different from **cord**, which means a piece of thin rope.

**chore** (say chor) NOUN chores
a regular or dull task

**choreography** (say ko-ree-**og**-ra-fee) NOUN
the art of writing the steps for ballets or stage dances
➤ **choreographer** NOUN

**chorister** (say **ko**-rist-er) NOUN choristers
a member of a choir

**chortle** VERB chortles, chortling, chortled
to chuckle loudly

**chortle** NOUN chortles
a loud chuckle **WORD ORIGIN** a mixture of **chuckle** and **snort**: invented by Lewis Carroll

**chorus** NOUN choruses
❶ the words repeated after each verse of a song or poem ❷ a piece of music sung by a group of people ❸ a group singing together

**chorus** VERB choruses, chorusing, chorused
to all say something at the same time • *'We'll help!' chorused the girls.*

**chow mein** NOUN
a Chinese dish of fried noodles with shredded meat or shrimps etc. and vegetables

**christen** VERB christens, christening, christened
❶ to baptize a child and give them a name ❷ to give a name or nickname to a person or thing

**christening** NOUN christenings
the church ceremony at which a child is baptized

**Christian** NOUN Christians
a person who believes in Jesus Christ and his teachings

**Christian** ADJECTIVE
to do with Christians or their beliefs
➤ **Christianity** NOUN

**Christian name** NOUN Christian names
a name given to a person at his or her christening; a person's first name

**Christmas** NOUN Christmases
the day (25 December) when Christians commemorate the birth of Jesus Christ; the days round it

**Christmas pudding** NOUN Christmas puddings
(*British*) a dark pudding containing dried fruit etc., eaten at Christmas

**Christmas tree** NOUN Christmas trees
an evergreen or artificial tree decorated at Christmas

**chromatic scale** *NOUN* chromatic scales
a musical scale going up or down in semitones

**chrome** (say krohm) *NOUN*
chromium **WORD ORIGIN** from Greek *chroma* = colour (because its compounds have brilliant colours)

**chromium** (say **kroh**-mee-um) *NOUN*
a shiny silvery metal

**chromosome** (say **kroh**-mos-ohm) *NOUN*
chromosomes
a tiny thread-like part of an animal cell or plant cell, carrying genes

**chronic** *ADJECTIVE*
lasting for a long time • *a chronic illness*
➤ **chronically** *ADVERB*

**chronicle** *NOUN* chronicles
a record of events in the order that they happened

**chronological** *ADJECTIVE*
arranged in the order that things happened • *Here are the main events of her life in chronological order.*
➤ **chronologically** *ADVERB*

**chronology** (say kron-**ol**-oj-ee) *NOUN*
the arrangement of events in the order in which they happened, e.g. in history or geology

**chronometer** (say kron-**om**-it-er) *NOUN*
chronometers
a very exact device for measuring time

**chrysalis** *NOUN* chrysalises
the hard cover a caterpillar makes round itself before it changes into a butterfly or moth

**chrysanthemum** *NOUN* chrysanthemums
a garden flower that blooms in autumn

**chubby** *ADJECTIVE* chubbier, chubbiest
plump and healthy

**chuck** *VERB* chucks, chucking, chucked
(*informal*)
to throw something roughly or carelessly • *Someone had chucked a brick through the window.*

**chuck** *NOUN* chucks
❶ the part of a drill that holds the bit ❷ the gripping part of a lathe

**chuckle** *NOUN* chuckles
a quiet laugh

**chuckle** *VERB* chuckles, chuckling, chuckled
to laugh quietly

**chug** *VERB* chugs, chugging, chugged
to move making the sound of an engine running slowly • *The train chugged out of the station.*

**chum** *NOUN* chums (*informal*)
a friend
➤ **chummy** *ADJECTIVE*

**chunk** *NOUN* chunks
a thick piece of something • *a huge chunk of ice*

**chunky** *ADJECTIVE*
thick and big • *a bike with chunky tyres*

**chupatty** (say chup-**at**-ee) *NOUN* chupatties
a different spelling of **chapatti**

**church** *NOUN* churches
❶ a building where Christians go to worship
❷ a religious service in a church • *I will see you after church.* ❸ a particular Christian religion, e.g. the Church of England

**churchyard** *NOUN* churchyards
the ground round a church, often used as a graveyard

**churlish** *ADJECTIVE*
rude and bad-tempered

**churn** *NOUN* churns
❶ a large can in which milk is carried from a farm ❷ a machine in which milk is beaten to make butter

**churn** *VERB* churns, churning, churned
❶ to stir something or move it around vigorously • *Vast crowds had churned the field into a sea of mud.* ❷ your stomach churns when you feel very nervous or excited ❸ to make butter in a churn
➤ **churn things out** to produce large quantities of something very quickly • *She has been churning out bestsellers for many years.*

**chute** (say shoot) *NOUN* chutes
a steep channel for people or things to slide down

**SPELLING**

Chute is different from **shoot** • *Shoot at the target.*

**chutney** *NOUN* chutneys
a strong-tasting mixture of fruit, peppers, etc., eaten with meat or cheese

**CID** *ABBREVIATION*
Criminal Investigation Department

**cider** *NOUN* ciders
an alcoholic drink made from apples

**cigar** *NOUN* cigars
a roll of compressed tobacco leaves for
smoking

**cigarette** *NOUN* cigarettes
a small roll of shredded tobacco in thin paper
for smoking

**cinder** *NOUN* cinders
a small piece of partly burnt coal or wood

**cine camera** (say sin-ee) *NOUN* cine cameras
a camera used for taking moving pictures

**cinema** *NOUN* cinemas (*chiefly British*)
❶ a place where films are shown ❷ the
business or art of making films • *a classic of
Russian cinema*

**cinnamon** (say sin-a-mon) *NOUN*
a yellowish-brown spice

**cinquain** (say sin-kayn) *NOUN* cinquains
a poem of five lines with a total of 22
syllables arranged in the pattern 2, 4, 6, 8, 2

**cipher** (say sy-fer) *NOUN* ciphers
a secret system of writing used for sending
messages; a code

**circle** *NOUN* circles
❶ a perfectly round flat shape or thing ❷ the
balcony of a cinema or theatre ❸ a number
of people with similar interests • *She's well
known in theatrical circles.*

**circle** *VERB* circles, circling, circled
to move round something in a circle • *The
plane circled the town several times before it
landed.* • *Vultures circled overhead.*

> SPELLING
>
> There is le at the end of circle.

**circuit** (say ser-kit) *NOUN* circuits
❶ a circular line or journey ❷ a track for
motor racing ❸ the path of an electric
current

**circuitous** (say ser-kew-it-us) *ADJECTIVE*
going a long way round, not direct • *a
circuitous route*

**circular** *ADJECTIVE*
❶ shaped like a circle; round ❷ moving round
in a circle • *a circular tour of the town*

**circular** *NOUN* circulars
a letter or advertisement sent to a number of
people

**circulate** *VERB* circulates, circulating,
circulated
❶ to go round something continuously
• *Blood circulates in the body.* ❷ to spread

or be passed from one person to another
• *Rumours about the president's health
began to circulate.* ❸ to send something
round to a number of people

**circulation** *NOUN* circulations
❶ the movement of blood around the body
❷ the number of copies of each issue of
a newspaper or magazine that are sold or
distributed

**circumcise** *VERB* circumcises, circumcising,
circumcised
to cut off the fold of skin at the tip of the
penis
➤ circumcision *NOUN*

**circumference** *NOUN* circumferences
the line or distance round something,
especially round a circle

> SPELLING
>
> The 's' sound is spelt with a c in
> circumference. Do not forget the ence
> at the end.

**circumflex accent** *NOUN* circumflex accents
a mark ( ˆ ) over a vowel

**circumnavigate** *VERB* circumnavigates,
circumnavigating, circumnavigated
to sail completely round something • *Francis
Drake circumnavigated the globe between
1577 and 1580.*
➤ circumnavigation *NOUN*

**circumscribe** *VERB* circumscribes,
circumscribing, circumscribed
to limit or restrict something • *Her powers
are circumscribed by many regulations.*

**circumspect** *ADJECTIVE*
cautious and watchful
➤ circumspection *NOUN*

**circumstance** *NOUN* circumstances
a fact or condition connected with an event
or person or action • *She did brilliantly in the
circumstances.*

**circumstantial** (say ser-kum-stan-shal)
*ADJECTIVE*
circumstantial evidence consists of facts
that strongly suggest something but do not
actually prove it

**circumvent** *VERB* circumvents, circumventing,
circumvented
to find a way of avoiding something • *We
managed to circumvent the rules.*

**circus** *NOUN* circuses
a travelling show usually performed in a tent,

with clowns, acrobats and sometimes trained animals **WORD ORIGIN** Latin, = ring, because a circus is usually held in a ring-shaped arena in a tent

**cirrus** (say si-rus) NOUN cirri
cloud made up of light wispy streaks

**cistern** NOUN cisterns
a tank for storing water

**citadel** NOUN citadels
a fortress protecting a city

**cite** (say sight) VERB cites, citing, cited
to quote or name something as an example
• *Many reasons have been cited for the rise in these injuries.*
➤ **citation** NOUN

**citizen** NOUN citizens
a person belonging to a particular city or country

**citizenry** NOUN
all the citizens

**citizens' band** NOUN
a range of special radio frequencies on which people can speak to one another over short distances

**citizenship** NOUN
the rights or duties of a citizen • *She has applied for American citizenship.*

**citrus fruit** NOUN citrus fruits
a lemon, orange, grapefruit or other sharp-tasting fruit

**city** NOUN cities
a large important town, often having a cathedral
➤ **the City** the oldest part of London, now a centre of commerce and finance

**civic** ADJECTIVE
to do with a city or its citizens • *civic leaders*
• *civic pride*

**civics** NOUN
the study of the rights and duties of citizens

**civil** ADJECTIVE
❶ polite and courteous ❷ to do with citizens
❸ to do with civilians; not military • *civil aviation*
➤ **civilly** ADVERB

**civil engineering** NOUN
the work of designing or maintaining roads, bridges, dams, etc.
➤ **civil engineer** NOUN

**civilian** NOUN civilians
a person who is not serving in the armed forces

**civility** NOUN civilities
polite and courteous behaviour • *I expect to be treated with a little more civility.*

**civilization** (also **civilisation**) NOUN
civilizations
❶ a society or culture at a particular time in history • *ancient civilizations* ❷ a developed or organized way of life • *We were far from civilization.*

**civilize** (also **civilise**) VERB civilizes, civilizing, civilized
❶ to bring culture and education to a primitive community ❷ to improve a person's behaviour and manners

**civil partnership** NOUN civil partnerships
(in some countries) a legal union of a couple of the same sex, with rights similar to those of marriage
➤ **civil partner** NOUN

**civil rights** PLURAL NOUN
the rights of citizens, especially to have freedom, equality and the right to vote

**civil service** NOUN
all the officials who work for the government to run its affairs
➤ **civil servant** NOUN

**civil war** NOUN civil wars
war between groups of people of the same country

**clack** NOUN clacks
a short sharp sound like that of plates struck together

**clack** VERB clacks, clacking, clacked
to make this sound • *Her heels clacked on the marble floor.*

**clad** ADJECTIVE
to be clad in something is to be wearing it or covered by it • *He was clad in magnificent robes.*

**claim** VERB claims, claiming, claimed
❶ to state something without being able to prove it • *They claimed they had been at home all evening.* ❷ to ask for something to which you believe you have a right • *A wallet was handed in yesterday but no one has claimed it yet.*

**claim** NOUN claims
❶ a statement that something is true, without any proof ❷ a statement that you

have a right to something ❸ a piece of
ground claimed by someone for mining etc.

**claimant** *NOUN* **claimants**
someone who makes a claim for something,
especially money

**clairvoyant** *NOUN* **clairvoyants**
a person who is said to be able to predict
future events or know about things that are
happening out of sight
➤ **clairvoyance** *NOUN*

**clam** *NOUN* **clams**
a large shellfish

**clamber** *VERB* **clambers, clambering,
clambered**
to climb with difficulty, using your hands and
feet • *We clambered over the slippery rocks.*

**clammy** *ADJECTIVE*
damp and slimy • *clammy hands*

**clamorous** *ADJECTIVE*
making a loud confused noise

**clamour** *NOUN* **clamours**
❶ a loud confused noise • *the clamour of car
horns* ❷ a loud protest or demand

**clamour** *VERB* **clamours, clamouring,
clamoured**
to make a loud protest or demand • *The
children were clamouring for attention.*

**clamp** *NOUN* **clamps**
a device for holding things tightly

**clamp** *VERB* **clamps, clamping, clamped**
❶ to fix something with a clamp ❷ to hold
something firmly in position • *She clamped
her hand over his mouth.*
➤ **clamp down on something** to become
stricter about something or put a stop to it

**clan** *NOUN* **clans**
a group of families sharing the same ancestor,
especially in Scotland

**clandestine** (say klan-**dest**-in) *ADJECTIVE*
done secretly; kept secret

**clang** *NOUN* **clangs**
a loud ringing sound

**clang** *VERB* **clangs, clanging, clanged**
to make a loud ringing sound • *The gate
clanged shut behind them.*

**clank** *NOUN* **clanks**
a sound like heavy pieces of metal banging
together

**clank** *VERB* **clanks, clanking, clanked**
to make a sound like heavy pieces of metal

banging together • *I could hear clanking
chains.*

**clap** *VERB* **claps, clapping, clapped**
❶ to strike the palms of the hands together
loudly, especially as applause ❷ to slap
someone in a friendly way • *I clapped him on
the shoulder.* ❸ to put someone somewhere
quickly or with force • *They clapped him into
jail.*

**clap** *NOUN* **claps**
❶ a sudden sharp noise • *a clap of thunder*
❷ a round of clapping • *We all gave the
winners a clap.* ❸ a friendly slap

**clapper** *NOUN* **clappers**
the hanging piece inside a bell that strikes
against the bell to make it sound

**claptrap** *NOUN*
insincere or foolish talk

**claret** *NOUN* **clarets**
a kind of red wine

**clarify** *VERB* **clarifies, clarifying, clarified**
to make something clear or easier to
understand • *I hope this clarifies the
situation.*
➤ **clarification** *NOUN*

**clarinet** *NOUN* **clarinets**
a woodwind instrument
➤ **clarinettist** *NOUN*

**clarion** *NOUN* **clarions**
an old type of trumpet

**clarity** *NOUN*
the quality of being clear or easy to
understand • *The report is written with clarity
and precision.*

**clash** *VERB* **clashes, clashing, clashed**
❶ to make a loud sound like that of cymbals
banging together ❷ two events clash when
they happen inconveniently at the same time
❸ people clash when they have a fight or
argument • *Gangs of rival supporters clashed
outside the stadium.* ❹ colours clash when
they do not go well together

**clash** *NOUN* **clashes**
❶ a loud sound like that of cymbals banging
together • *the clash of swords* ❷ a fight or
argument

**clasp** *NOUN* **clasps**
❶ a device for fastening things, with
interlocking parts ❷ a tight grasp

**clasp** *VERB* **clasps, clasping, clasped**
❶ to grasp or hold someone or something

a
b
c
d
e
f
g
h
i
j
k
l
m
n
o
p
q
r
s
t
u
v
w
x
y
z

tightly • *She clasped his hand in hers.* ❷ to fasten something with a clasp

**class** *NOUN* classes
❶ a group of children or students who are taught together ❷ a group of similar people, animals or things ❸ people of the same social or economic level ❹ a level of quality • *first class*

**class** *VERB* classes, classing, classed
to put something in a particular class or group; to classify something • *These gorillas are classed as an endangered species.*

**classic** *ADJECTIVE*
❶ generally agreed to be excellent or important ❷ very typical or common • *a classic case of overconfidence*

**classic** *NOUN* classics
a book, film or song that is well known and generally agreed to be excellent or important

**classical** *ADJECTIVE*
❶ to do with ancient Greek or Roman literature or art ❷ serious or conventional in style and of lasting value • *classical music*

**classics** *NOUN*
the study of ancient Greek and Latin languages and literature

**classified** *ADJECTIVE*
❶ put into classes or groups ❷ classified information is officially secret and available only to certain people

**classify** *VERB* classifies, classifying, classified
to arrange things in classes or groups • *The books in the library are classified according to subject.*
➤ **classification** *NOUN*

**classmate** *NOUN* classmates
someone in the same class at school

**classroom** *NOUN* classrooms
a room where a class of children or students is taught

**clatter** *VERB* clatters, clattering, clattered
to make a sound like hard objects rattling together • *I heard horses' hooves clattering on the cobbles outside.*

**clatter** *NOUN*
a clattering noise

**clause** *NOUN* clauses
❶ a single part of a treaty, law or contract ❷ (*in grammar*) a part of a sentence, with its own verb

---GRAMMAR---

A **clause** is a part of a sentence that contains a verb. A sentence can contain one or more main clauses, linked by a conjunction such as *and*, *but* or *or* or by a semicolon:

*Ladybirds eat aphids.*

*We approached cautiously; the lioness was beginning to stir.*

A **subordinate clause** begins with a conjunction such as *because*, *if* or *when*, and it can come before or after the main clause. A subordinate clause should not be used without a main clause:

*Because they eat aphids, ladybirds are useful in the garden.*

*I'll never speak to you again if you lose that ring.*

A **relative clause** explains or describes something that has just been mentioned, and is introduced by *that*, *which*, *who*, *whom*, *whose*, *when* or *where*. A relative clause can either specify which person or thing you are talking about:

*Of all Tolkien's books, the one which I like best is 'The Hobbit'.*

or can simply add further information, in which case you put a comma before it, and another comma after it if it appears in the middle of a sentence:

*The book, which Tolkien wrote for his children, was an instant success.*

In the first of these two examples, but not the second, you can use *that* instead of *which*; you can also say *the one I like best is* The Hobbit.

See also the panels on **conjunctions and connectives**, **which and that**, and **commas**.

**claustrophobia** *NOUN*
an extreme fear of being inside an enclosed space
➤ **claustrophobic** *ADJECTIVE*

**claw** *NOUN* claws
❶ a sharp nail on a bird's or animal's foot ❷ a claw-like part or device used for grasping things

**claw** *VERB* claws, clawing, clawed
to grasp, pull or scratch something with a claw or hand

**clay** *NOUN*
a kind of stiff sticky earth that becomes hard when baked, used for making bricks and pottery
➤ **clayey** *ADJECTIVE*

**clean** *ADJECTIVE*
❶ without any dirt or marks or stains
❷ fresh; not yet used • *Start on a clean page.*
❸ done or played in a fair way according to the rules • *a clean fight* ❹ not rude or indecent • *a clean joke* ❺ a clean catch is one made skilfully with no fumbling

**clean** *VERB* cleans, cleaning, cleaned
to make something clean

**clean** *ADVERB* (*informal*) completely • *I clean forgot it was your birthday.*

**cleaner** *NOUN* cleaners
❶ a person who cleans things, especially rooms etc. ❷ something used for cleaning things

**cleanliness** (say klen-li-nis) *NOUN*
being clean or keeping things clean

**cleanly** (say kleen-lee) *ADVERB*
easily or smoothly in one movement; neatly • *The rock split cleanly in two.*

**cleanse** (say klenz) *VERB* cleanses, cleansing, cleansed
❶ to clean something ❷ to make something pure
➤ **cleanser** *NOUN*

**clear** *ADJECTIVE*
❶ transparent; not muddy or cloudy ❷ easy to see or hear • *He spoke with a clear voice.*
❸ easy to understand, without doubt • *It was clear to me that he was lying.* ❹ free from obstacles or unwanted things ❺ a clear conscience is one that doesn't make you feel guilty ❻ complete • *Give three clear days' notice.*
➤ **clearness** *NOUN*

**clear** *ADVERB*
❶ in a way that is easy to see or hear; distinctly • *We heard you loud and clear.*
❷ completely • *He got clear away.* ❸ at a distance from something; not too close to something • *Stand clear of the doors.*

**clear** *VERB* clears, clearing, cleared
❶ to make something clear or become clear ❷ to show that someone is innocent or reliable ❸ to jump over something

without touching it ❹ to get approval or authorization for something • *The plane was cleared for take-off.*
➤ **clear something away** to remove used plates etc. after a meal
➤ **clear off or out** (*informal*) to go away
➤ **clear up** ❶ to make things tidy • *Make sure you clear up before you leave.* ❷ to become better or brighter • *The weather seems to be clearing up.*
➤ **clear something up** to solve something • *Thank you for clearing up that little mystery.*

**clearance** *NOUN* clearances
❶ official permission to do something • *Only the staff who have clearance to work there are allowed in.* ❷ getting rid of unwanted goods • *The shoe shop is having a clearance sale.* ❸ the space between one thing and another that is passing under or beside it

**clearing** *NOUN* clearings
an open space in a forest

**clearly** *ADVERB*
❶ in a way that is easy to see, hear or understand • *Please speak clearly after the tone.* ❷ without doubt; obviously • *They were clearly going to win.*

**cleavage** *NOUN*
the hollow between a woman's breasts

**cleave** *VERB* cleaves, cleaving; past tense cleaved, clove or cleft; past participle cleft or cloven
❶ to divide something by chopping it; to split something • *She cleaved the log in two with an axe.* ❷ to make a way through something • *yachts cleaving through the water*

**cleave** *VERB* cleaves, cleaving, cleaved
(*old use*) to cling to something • *Her tongue seemed to cleave to the roof of her mouth.*

**cleaver** *NOUN* cleavers
a butcher's chopping tool

**clef** *NOUN* clefs
a symbol on a stave in music, showing the pitch of the notes • *treble clef* • *bass clef*

**cleft**
past tense of **cleave** *VERB*

**cleft** *NOUN* clefts
a split in something • *There was a deep cleft in the mountain side.*

**clemency** *NOUN*
gentleness or mildness; mercy

a b c d e f g h i j k l m n o p q r s t u v w x y z

**clench** VERB clenches, clenching, clenched
to close your teeth or fingers tightly

**clergy** NOUN
the people who have been ordained as priests or ministers of the Christian Church
➤ **clergyman** NOUN
➤ **clergywoman** NOUN

**clerical** ADJECTIVE
❶ to do with the routine work in an office, such as filing and writing letters ❷ to do with the clergy

**clerk** (say klark) NOUN clerks
a person employed to keep records or accounts, deal with papers in an office, etc.

**clever** ADJECTIVE
❶ quick at learning and understanding things ❷ showing intelligence and imagination
• That's a clever idea.
➤ **cleverly** ADVERB
➤ **cleverness** NOUN

**cliché** (say **klee**-shay) NOUN clichés
a phrase or idea that is used so often that it has little meaning

**click** NOUN clicks
a short sharp sound

**click** VERB clicks, clicking, clicked
❶ to make a short sharp sound ❷ to press a button on a computer mouse

**client** NOUN clients
a person who gets help or advice from a professional person such as a lawyer, accountant, architect, etc.; a customer

**clientele** (say klee-on-**tel**) NOUN
customers

**cliff** NOUN cliffs
a steep rock face, especially on a coast

**cliffhanger** NOUN cliffhangers
a tense and exciting ending to an episode of a story

**climate** NOUN climates
the normal weather conditions of an area
• Palm trees grow best in a hot climate.
➤ **climatic** (say kly-**mat**-ik) ADJECTIVE

**climax** NOUN climaxes
the most interesting or important point of a story, series of events, etc.
WORD ORIGIN from Greek klimax = ladder

**climb** VERB climbs, climbing, climbed
❶ to go up towards the top of something ❷ to move somewhere with difficulty or effort • I managed to climb out of the window. ❸ to go higher • The plane climbed steadily. ❹ to grow upwards
➤ **climb down** to admit that you have been wrong

**climb** NOUN climbs
an act of climbing • It's a long climb to the top of the hill.

SPELLING
Don't forget the silent b at the end of climb.

**climber** NOUN climbers
someone who climbs mountains as a sport

**clinch** VERB clinches, clinching, clinched
❶ to settle something definitely • We hope to clinch the deal today. ❷ boxers clinch when they clasp each other during a fight
➤ **clinch** NOUN

**cling** VERB clings, clinging, clung
to hold on tightly • She clung to the rope with all her strength.

**cling film** NOUN
(British) a thin clinging transparent film, used as a covering for food

**clinic** NOUN clinics
a place where people see doctors etc. for treatment or advice

**clinical** ADJECTIVE
❶ to do with the medical treatment of patients ❷ cool and unemotional
➤ **clinically** ADVERB

**clink** NOUN clinks
a thin sharp sound like glasses being struck together

**clink** VERB clinks, clinking, clinked
to make a thin sharp sound like glasses being struck together • The coins clinked in his pocket.

**clip** NOUN clips
❶ a fastener for keeping things together, usually worked by a spring ❷ a short piece of film shown on its own ❸ (informal) a hit on the head

**clip** VERB clips, clipping, clipped
❶ to fasten something with a clip ❷ to cut something with shears or scissors ❸ (informal) to hit someone or something
• My front wheel must have clipped the pavement.

**clipper** NOUN clippers
an old type of fast sailing ship

**clippers** *PLURAL NOUN*
an instrument for cutting hair

**clique** (say kleek) *NOUN* cliques
a small group of people who stick together and keep others out

**clitoris** *NOUN* clitorises
the small sensitive piece of flesh near the opening of a woman's vagina

**cloak** *NOUN* cloaks
a sleeveless piece of outdoor clothing that hangs loosely from the shoulders

**cloak** *VERB* cloaks, cloaking, cloaked
to cover or conceal something

**cloaked** *ADJECTIVE*
wearing a cloak • *a cloaked figure*

**cloakroom** *NOUN* cloakrooms
❶ a place where people can leave coats and bags while visiting a building ❷ a toilet

**clobber** *VERB* clobbers, clobbering, clobbered (*informal*)
to hit someone hard again and again

**cloche** (say klosh) *NOUN* cloches
a glass or plastic cover to protect outdoor plants

**clock** *NOUN* clocks
❶ a device that shows what the time is ❷ a measuring device with a dial or digital display

**clock** *VERB* clocks, clocking, clocked
(*informal*) to notice or recognize someone • *I clocked her standing at the back of the hall.*
➤ **clock in** or **out** to register the time you arrive at work or leave work
➤ **clock something up** to reach a certain speed or total

**clockwise** *ADVERB & ADJECTIVE*
moving round a circle in the same direction as a clock's hands

**clockwork** *NOUN*
a mechanism with a spring that has to be wound up
➤ **like clockwork** or **regular as clockwork** very regularly

**clod** *NOUN* clods
a lump of earth or clay

**clog** *NOUN* clogs
a shoe with a wooden sole

**clog** *VERB* clogs, clogging, clogged
to block something up • *The roads were clogged with traffic.*

**cloister** *NOUN* cloisters
a covered path along the side of a church or monastery etc., round a courtyard

**clone** *NOUN* clones
an animal or plant made from the cells of another animal or plant and therefore exactly like it

**clone** *VERB* clones, cloning, cloned
to produce a clone of an animal or plant

**close** (say klohss) *ADJECTIVE*
❶ near • *Our hotel is close to the beach.*
❷ detailed or careful • *Now pay close attention.* ❸ that you know well and have a strong friendship with; related to you directly • *She is one of my closest friends.* • *close relatives* ❹ a close fit is tight, with little space to spare ❺ a close contest or fight is one in which competitors are nearly equal ❻ warm and stuffy, without fresh air
➤ **closeness** *NOUN*

**close** (say klohss) *ADVERB*
at a close distance • *Two men were walking close behind.*

**close** (say klohss) *NOUN* closes (*British*)
❶ a street that is closed at one end ❷ an enclosed area, especially round a cathedral

**close** (say klohz) *VERB* closes, closing, closed
❶ to shut something ❷ to be no longer open • *The supermarket closes at 6 o'clock.* ❸ to end a meeting or activity
➤ **close in** ❶ to get nearer someone you are chasing ❷ if the days are closing in, they are getting shorter

**close** (say klohz) *NOUN*
the close of an activity is when it ends • *The scores were level at the close of play.*

**closed** *ADJECTIVE*
not open; shut • *Keep your mouth closed.* • *The supermarket is closed.*

**closely** *ADVERB*
❶ carefully, with attention • *His friends were watching closely.* ❷ in a way that is very similar or shows a strong connection • *The insect closely resembles a stick.* ❸ so that people or things are close together • *Books were closely packed on the shelves.* • *She climbed out of the window, closely followed by her brother.*

**closet** *NOUN* closets (*North American*)
a cupboard or storeroom

**closet** *VERB* closets, closeting, closeted
to shut yourself away in a private room

**close-up** NOUN close-ups
a photograph or piece of film taken at close range

**closure** NOUN closures
the closing of something permanently • *The local library is threatened with closure.*

**clot** NOUN clots
❶ a small mass of blood, cream, etc. that has become solid ❷ (*informal*) a stupid person

**clot** VERB clots, clotting, clotted
to form clots

**cloth** NOUN cloths
❶ woven material or felt ❷ a piece of this material ❸ a tablecloth

> SPELLING
>
> Do not confuse **cloths**, which are pieces of material, with **clothes**, which are things that you wear.

**clothe** VERB clothes, clothing, clothed
to put clothes on someone • *He was clothed from head to toe in green.*

**clothes** PLURAL NOUN
things worn to cover the body

> SPELLING
>
> Do not confuse **clothes**, which are things that you wear, with **cloths**, which are pieces of material.

**clothing** NOUN
clothes

**clotted cream** NOUN
(*chiefly British*) cream thickened by being scalded

**cloud** NOUN clouds
❶ a mass of condensed water vapour floating in the sky ❷ a mass of smoke, dust, etc., in the air

**cloud** VERB clouds, clouding, clouded
❶ to become difficult to see through • *His eyes clouded with tears.* ❷ if a person's face clouds, their expression becomes more serious, worried or angry
➤ **cloud over** to become full of clouds

**cloudburst** NOUN cloudbursts
a sudden heavy rainstorm

**cloudless** ADJECTIVE
without clouds

**cloudy** ADJECTIVE cloudier, cloudiest
❶ full of clouds • *a cloudy sky* ❷ a cloudy liquid is not clear or transparent
➤ **cloudiness** NOUN

**clout** VERB clouts, clouting, clouted (*informal*)
to hit someone roughly
➤ **clout** NOUN

**clove** NOUN cloves
❶ the dried bud of a tropical tree, used as a spice ❷ one of the separate sections in a bulb of garlic • *a clove of garlic*

**clove** VERB
past tense of cleave

**cloven**
past participle of cleave
➤ **cloven hoof** a hoof that is divided, like those of cows and sheep

**clover** NOUN
a small plant usually with three leaves on each stalk
➤ **in clover** in ease and luxury

**clown** NOUN clowns
❶ a performer who does amusing tricks and actions, especially in a circus ❷ a person who does silly things

**clown** VERB clowns, clowning, clowned
to fool about and do silly things

**cloying** ADJECTIVE
sickeningly sweet

**club** NOUN clubs
❶ a heavy stick used as a weapon ❷ a stick with a shaped head used to hit the ball in golf ❸ a group of people who meet because they are interested in the same thing; the building where they meet ❹ a playing card with black clover leaves on it

**club** VERB clubs, clubbing, clubbed
to hit someone with a heavy stick
➤ **club together** to join with other people in order to pay for something • *They clubbed together to buy a van.*

**cluck** VERB clucks, clucking, clucked
to make a hen's throaty cry
➤ **cluck** NOUN

**clue** NOUN clues
something that helps you to solve a puzzle or a mystery
➤ **not have a clue** (*informal*) to be stupid or helpless
> WORD ORIGIN originally a ball of thread: in Greek legend, the warrior Theseus had to go into a maze (the Labyrinth); as he went in he unwound a ball of thread, and found his way out by winding it up again

**clump** NOUN clumps
a cluster or mass of things • *a small clump of trees*

**clump** VERB clumps, clumping, clumped
❶ to walk with a heavy tread • *She could hear him clumping around upstairs.* ❷ to form a cluster or mass

**clumsy** ADJECTIVE clumsier, clumsiest
❶ careless and likely to knock things over or drop things ❷ not skilful or tactful • *a clumsy apology*
➤ **clumsily** ADVERB
➤ **clumsiness** NOUN

**cluster** NOUN clusters
a group of people or things that stand or grow close together • *a little cluster of buildings*

**cluster** VERB clusters, clustering, clustered
to form a cluster • *We all clustered around the computer screen.*

**clutch** VERB clutches, clutching, clutched
to grasp something tightly • *He clutched his mother's hand in fear.*

**clutch** NOUN clutches
❶ a tight grasp ❷ a device for connecting and disconnecting the engine of a motor vehicle from its gears ❸ a set of eggs laid at the same time

**clutter** NOUN
a lot of things lying about untidily

**clutter** VERB clutters, cluttering, cluttered
to fill a place with clutter • *Piles of books and papers cluttered her desk.*

**Co.** ABBREVIATION
Company

**c/o** ABBREVIATION
care of

**coach** NOUN coaches
❶ a comfortable bus used for long journeys ❷ a carriage of a railway train ❸ a large horse-drawn carriage with four wheels ❹ an instructor who gives training in sports ❺ a teacher giving private tuition in a subject

**coach** VERB coaches, coaching, coached
to instruct or train somebody, especially in sports

**coagulate** VERB coagulates, coagulating, coagulated
to change from liquid to semi-solid; to clot
➤ **coagulation** NOUN

**coal** NOUN
a hard black mineral substance used for burning to supply heat; a piece of this
➤ **coalfield** NOUN

**coalesce** (say koh-a-**less**) VERB coalesces, coalescing, coalesced
to combine and form one whole thing

**coalition** NOUN coalitions
a temporary alliance, especially of two or more political parties in order to form a government

**coarse** ADJECTIVE
❶ not smooth or delicate; rough • *coarse cloth* ❷ made up of large particles; not fine • *coarse salt* ❸ rude or vulgar
➤ **coarsely** ADVERB
➤ **coarseness** NOUN

**coast** NOUN coasts
the seashore or the land close to it
➤ **the coast is clear** there is no chance of being seen or hindered

**coast** VERB coasts, coasting, coasted
to ride downhill without using power

**coastal** ADJECTIVE
by the coast or near the coast • *a coastal resort*

**coastguard** NOUN coastguards
a person whose job is to keep watch on the coast, detect or prevent smuggling, etc.

**coastline** NOUN coastlines
the shape or outline of a coast

**coat** NOUN coats
❶ a piece of clothing with sleeves, worn over other clothes ❷ the hair or fur on an animal's body ❸ a layer of something that covers a surface • *The walls will need two coats of paint.*

**coat** VERB coats, coating, coated
to cover a thing with a layer of something • *The furniture was coated with dust.*

**coating** NOUN coatings
a thin layer that covers something • *nuts with a coating of chocolate*

**coat of arms** NOUN coats of arms
a design on a shield, used as an emblem by a family, city, etc.

**coax** VERB coaxes, coaxing, coaxed
to persuade someone gently or patiently to do something • *I managed to coax her into the water.*

**cob** NOUN cobs
❶ the central part of an ear of maize, on which the corn grows ❷ (*British*) a round loaf of bread ❸ a sturdy horse for riding ❹ a male swan (The female is a pen.)

a b c d e f g h i j k l m n o p q r s t u v w x y z

**cobalt** NOUN
a hard silvery-white metal
(WORD ORIGIN) from German *Kobalt* = demon (because it was believed to harm the silver ore with which it was found)

**cobber** NOUN cobbers (*informal*)
(*Australian/NZ*) a friend or companion

**cobble** NOUN cobbles
cobbles are a surface of cobblestones on a street

**cobble** VERB cobbles, cobbling, cobbled
to cobble something together is to make it quickly and without much care
➤ cobbled ADJECTIVE

**cobbler** NOUN cobblers
someone who mends shoes

**cobblestone** NOUN cobblestones
a small smooth rounded stone sometimes used in large numbers to pave roads in towns

**cobra** (say **koh**-bra) NOUN cobras
a poisonous snake that can rear up
(WORD ORIGIN) from Portuguese *cobra de capello* = snake with a hood

**cobweb** NOUN cobwebs
the thin sticky net made by a spider to trap insects (WORD ORIGIN) from Old English *coppe* = spider, + web

**cocaine** NOUN
a drug made from the leaves of a tropical plant called *coca*

**cock** NOUN cocks
❶ a male chicken ❷ a male bird ❸ a lever in a gun

**cock** VERB cocks, cocking, cocked
❶ to make a gun ready to fire by raising the cock ❷ to turn part of your body upwards or in a particular direction • *The dog cocked its ears.* • *She cocked her head to one side and looked at me.*

**cockatoo** NOUN cockatoos
a crested parrot

**cocked hat** NOUN cocked hats
a triangular hat worn with some uniforms

**cockerel** NOUN cockerels
a young male chicken

**cocker spaniel** NOUN cocker spaniels
a kind of small spaniel with long hanging ears

**cockle** NOUN cockles
an edible shellfish

**cockney** NOUN cockneys
❶ a person born in the East End of London
❷ the dialect or accent of cockneys
(WORD ORIGIN) originally = a small, misshapen egg, believed to be a cock's egg (because country people believed townspeople were feeble)

**cockpit** NOUN cockpits
the compartment where the pilot of an aircraft sits

**cockroach** NOUN cockroaches
a dark brown beetle-like insect, often found in dirty houses

**cocksure** ADJECTIVE
too confident

**cocktail** NOUN cocktails
❶ a mixed alcoholic drink ❷ a dish consisting of small pieces of shellfish or mixed fruit
• *a prawn cocktail* (WORD ORIGIN) originally = a racehorse that was not a thoroughbred (because carthorses had their tails cut so that they stood up like a cock's tail)

**cocky** ADJECTIVE cockier, cockiest (*informal*)
too self-confident and cheeky
➤ cockiness NOUN

**cocoa** NOUN cocoas
❶ a hot drink made from a powder of crushed cacao seeds ❷ this powder

**coconut** NOUN coconuts
❶ a large round nut that grows on a kind of palm tree ❷ its white lining, used in sweets and cookery (WORD ORIGIN) from Spanish *coco* = grinning face (because the base of the nut looks like a monkey's face)

**cocoon** NOUN cocoons
❶ the covering round a chrysalis ❷ a protective wrapping

**cocoon** VERB cocoons, cocooning, cocooned
to protect something by wrapping it up • *He lay in his tent, cocooned in a sleeping bag.*

**cod** NOUN cod
a large edible sea fish

**coddle** VERB coddles, coddling, coddled
to treat someone in a way that protects them too much

**code** NOUN codes
❶ a system of words, letters or numbers used instead of the real letters or words to make a message or information secret • *The message was written in code.* ❷ a set of signals or signs used in sending messages • *Morse code* ❸ a set of numbers used for an area in

making telephone calls • *Do you know the code for Stockholm?* ❹ a set of laws or rules • *the Highway Code* • *a code of behaviour*

**code** *VERB* codes, coding, coded
to put a message into code
➤ **coded** *ADJECTIVE*

**codify** *VERB* codifies, codifying, codified
to arrange laws or rules into a code or system

**co-education** *NOUN*
educating boys and girls together
➤ **co-educational** *ADJECTIVE*

**coefficient** *NOUN* coefficients
a number by which another number is multiplied; a factor

**coerce** (say koh-**erss**) *VERB* coerces, coercing, coerced
to make someone do something by using threats or force
➤ **coercion** *NOUN*

**coexist** *VERB* coexists, coexisting, coexisted
to exist together or at the same time
➤ **coexistence** *NOUN*

**coffee** *NOUN* coffees
❶ a hot drink made from the roasted ground seeds (**coffee beans**) of a tropical plant
❷ these seeds

**coffer** *NOUN* coffers
a large strong box for holding money and valuables
➤ **coffers** the funds or financial resources of an organization

**coffin** *NOUN* coffins
a long box in which a body is buried or cremated

**cog** *NOUN* cogs
one of a number of tooth-like parts round the edge of a wheel, fitting into and pushing those on another wheel

**cogent** (say koh-jent) *ADJECTIVE*
a cogent argument is strong and convincing

**cogitate** *VERB* cogitates, cogitating, cogitated
to think deeply about something
➤ **cogitation** *NOUN*

**cognac** (say **kon**-yak) *NOUN* cognacs
brandy, especially from Cognac in France

**cogwheel** *NOUN* cogwheels
a wheel with cogs

**cohere** *VERB* coheres, cohering, cohered
things cohere when they stick to each other

in a mass
➤ **cohesive** *ADJECTIVE*

**coherent** (say koh-**heer**-ent) *ADJECTIVE*
clear, reasonable and making sense • *a coherent explanation*
➤ **coherently** *ADVERB*

**cohesion** *NOUN*
the ability to combine or fit together well to form a whole • *There are some good individual players, but the team lacks cohesion.*

**coil** *NOUN* coils
something wound into a spiral or series of loops • *a coil of rope*

**coil** *VERB* coils, coiling, coiled
to wind something into a coil • *The snake coiled itself around his leg.*

**coin** *NOUN* coins
a piece of metal, usually round, used as money

**coin** *VERB* coins, coining, coined
❶ to manufacture coins ❷ to invent a word or phrase

**coinage** *NOUN* coinages
❶ coins; a system of money ❷ a new word or phrase that someone has invented

**coincide** *VERB* coincides, coinciding, coincided
❶ to happen at the same time as something else • *The end of term coincides with my birthday.* ❷ to be the same • *My opinion coincided with hers.*

**coincidence** *NOUN* coincidences
the happening of similar events at the same time by chance

**coke** *NOUN*
the solid fuel left when gas and tar have been extracted from coal

**colander** *NOUN* colanders
a bowl-shaped container with holes in it, used for straining water from vegetables etc. after cooking

**cold** *ADJECTIVE*
❶ having or at a low temperature; not warm ❷ not friendly or loving; showing no kindness or understanding • *She gave him a cold, hard look.*
➤ **coldness** *NOUN*
➤ **get cold feet** to have doubts about doing something bold or ambitious
➤ **give someone the cold shoulder** to be deliberately unfriendly

a b c d e f g h i j k l m n o p q r s t u v w x y z

**cold** NOUN colds
❶ lack of warmth; low temperature; cold weather ❷ an infectious illness that makes your nose run, your throat sore, etc.

**cold-blooded** ADJECTIVE
❶ having a body temperature that changes according to the surroundings ❷ showing no feelings or pity for other people • *cold-blooded murder*

**coldly** ADVERB
in an unfriendly or distant way • *'Nothing's the matter,' she said coldly.*

**cold war** NOUN
a situation where nations are enemies without actually fighting

**colic** NOUN
pain in a baby's stomach

**collaborate** VERB collaborates, collaborating, collaborated
to work together on a job • *It is the first time he has collaborated with another songwriter.*
➤ **collaboration** NOUN
➤ **collaborator** NOUN

**collage** (say kol-**ah** zh) NOUN collages
a picture made by fixing small objects to a surface

**collapse** VERB collapses, collapsing, collapsed
❶ to break down or fall in suddenly, often after breaking apart • *Several buildings collapsed in the earthquake.* ❷ to fall down because of being very weak or ill ❸ to fold up • *The table collapses for easy storage.*

**collapse** NOUN collapses
❶ collapsing • *The walls were strengthened to protect them from collapse.* ❷ a failure or breakdown • *The peace talks were on the verge of collapse.*

**collapsible** ADJECTIVE
able to be folded up • *a collapsible umbrella*

**collar** NOUN collars
❶ the part of a piece of clothing that goes round your neck ❷ a band that goes round the neck of a dog, cat, horse, etc.

**collar** VERB collars, collaring, collared
(*informal*) to seize or catch someone

**collarbone** NOUN collarbones
the bone joining the breastbone and shoulder blade

**collate** VERB collates, collating, collated
to collect and arrange pieces of information in an organized way • *We collated the results*
in the form of a graph.
➤ **collation** NOUN

**collateral** ADJECTIVE
additional but less important

**collateral** NOUN
money or property that is used as a guarantee that a loan will be repaid

**colleague** NOUN colleagues
a person you work with

**collect** (say kol-**ekt**) VERB collects, collecting, collected
❶ to bring people or things together from various places • *We are collecting signatures for a petition.* ❷ to get and keep together examples of things as a hobby • *She collects rare coins.* ❸ to come together • *A crowd collected to see what was going on.* ❹ to ask for money or contributions etc. from people • *We're collecting for charity.* ❺ to go to fetch someone or something • *Don't forget to collect your coat from the cleaners.*

**collection** NOUN collections
❶ a number of things someone has collected • *a coin collection* ❷ collecting something • *What time is the rubbish collection?* ❸ money collected for a charity or some other purpose

**collective** ADJECTIVE
to do with a group taken as a whole • *It was a collective decision.*

**collective noun** NOUN collective nouns
a noun that is singular in form but refers to many individuals taken as a unit, e.g. *army, herd, choir*

**collector** NOUN collectors
someone who collects things as a hobby or as part of their job • *a stamp collector* • *a ticket collector*

**college** NOUN colleges
a place where people can continue learning after they have left school

**collide** VERB collides, colliding, collided
to crash into something • *The car collided head-on with the van.*

**collie** NOUN collies
a dog with a long pointed face

**colliery** NOUN collieries
(*British*) a coal mine and its buildings

**collision** NOUN collisions
an accident in which two moving vehicles or people crash into each other • *a collision between two trains*

**colloquial** (say col-**oh**-kwee-al) *ADJECTIVE*
suitable for conversation but not for formal speech or writing

**cologne** (say kol-**ohn**) *NOUN*
eau de Cologne or a similar liquid

**colon** *NOUN* colons
❶ a punctuation mark (:), often used to introduce lists or an explanation ❷ the largest part of the intestine

> **PUNCTUATION**
>
> You use a colon to introduce an example or explanation within a sentence. The part of a sentence after a colon should illustrate, explain or expand on what comes before it:
>
> *These words were scratched in blood: 'Do not return without the gold.'*
>
> *It wasn't much of a holiday: two weeks of constant rain in a leaky tent.*
>
> A colon can also be used to introduce a list of people or items, or a range of options.
>
> *The following players are injured: Messi, Neymar and Suarez.*
>
> *The bags come in four colours: red, blue, yellow and green.*

**colonel** (say **ker**-nel) *NOUN* colonels
an army officer in charge of a regiment

> **SPELLING**
>
> The 'er' sound in colonel is spelt olo.

**colonial** *ADJECTIVE*
to do with a colony

**colonialism** *NOUN*
the policy of acquiring and keeping colonies

**colonist** *NOUN* colonists
a person who goes to live in a colony abroad

**colonize** (also **colonise**) *VERB* colonizes, colonizing, colonized
to establish a colony in a country • *The Portuguese colonized Brazil in 1500.*
➤ **colonization** *NOUN*

**colonnade** *NOUN* colonnades
a row of columns

**colony** *NOUN* colonies
❶ an area of land that the people of another country settle in and control ❷ the people of a colony ❸ a group of people or animals of the same kind living close together • *a colony of ants*

**coloration** *NOUN*
colouring • *The blue coloration is typical of the rock of the region.*

**colossal** *ADJECTIVE*
extremely large; enormous

**colossus** *NOUN* colossi
❶ a huge statue ❷ a person of immense importance **WORD ORIGIN** from the bronze statue of Apollo at Rhodes, called the *Colossus of Rhodes*

**colour** *NOUN* colours
❶ the effect produced by waves of light of a particular wavelength ❷ the use of various colours, not only black and white • *All the pictures in the book are in colour.* ❸ the colour of someone's skin ❹ a substance used to colour things ❺ the special flag of a ship or regiment

**colour** *VERB* colours, colouring, coloured
❶ to put colour on something, using paint, crayons, etc. ❷ to blush ❸ to influence what someone says or believes • *Don't let your judgement be coloured by personal feelings.*

> **SPELLING**
>
> The 'er' sound is spelt our in colour.

**colour-blind** *ADJECTIVE*
unable to see the difference between certain colours

**coloured** *ADJECTIVE*
having colour

**colourful** *ADJECTIVE*
❶ with bright colours ❷ lively; with vivid details • *The book is full of colourful characters.*

**colouring** *NOUN*
❶ a substance that you add to something, especially food, to give it a special colour ❷ a person's colouring is the colour of their skin and hair

**colourless** *ADJECTIVE*
without colour • *a colourless gas*

**colt** *NOUN* colts
a young male horse

**column** *NOUN* columns
❶ a pillar ❷ something long or tall and narrow • *a column of smoke* ❸ a vertical section of a page ❹ a regular article or feature in a newspaper or magazine

> **SPELLING**
>
> Don't forget the silent n at the end of column.

a b c d e f g h i j k l m n o p q r s t u v w x y z

**columnist** NOUN columnists
a journalist who writes regularly for one newspaper or magazine

**coma** (say koh-ma) NOUN comas
a state of deep unconsciousness, especially in someone who is ill or injured • *He fell into a deep coma.*

**comb** NOUN combs
❶ a strip of wood, plastic or metal with a row of teeth, used to tidy hair or hold it in place ❷ something used like this, e.g. to separate strands of wool ❸ the red crest on a fowl's head ❹ a honeycomb

**comb** VERB combs, combing, combed
❶ to tidy your hair with a comb ❷ to search a place thoroughly • *Police have been combing the beach for clues.*

**combat** NOUN combats
fighting, especially in a war • *He was killed in combat.*

**combat** VERB combats, combating, combated
to combat something bad or unpleasant is to fight it and try to get rid of it • *These measures will help police combat crime.*

**combatant** (say kom-ba-tant) NOUN combatants
someone who takes part in a fight

**combination** NOUN combinations
❶ a number of people or things that have been joined or mixed together • *What an unusual combination of flavours!* ❷ joining or mixing things • *The element silicon is always found in combination with something else.* ❸ a series of numbers or letters used to open a combination lock

**combination lock** NOUN combination locks
a lock that you can open only by setting a dial or dials to positions shown by numbers or letters

**combine** (say komb-yn) VERB combines, combining, combined
to join or mix things together; to come together to form something • *Now combine all the ingredients in a bowl.* • *Hydrogen and oxygen combine to form water.*

**combine harvester** NOUN combine harvesters
(British) a machine that both reaps and threshes grain

**combustible** ADJECTIVE
able to be set on fire and burn

**combustion** NOUN
the process of burning, a chemical process in which substances combine with oxygen in air and produce heat

**come** VERB comes, coming, came, come
❶ to move or travel to the place where you are • *Come here!* ❷ to arrive at or reach a place or condition or result • *They came to a city.* • *We came to a decision.* ❸ to happen • *How did you come to lose it?* ❹ to occur or be present • *The answer comes on the next page.* ❺ to result • *That's what comes of being careless.*
➤ **come about** to happen
➤ **come across someone** to meet someone by chance
➤ **come by something** to obtain something
➤ **come in for something** to receive a share of something
➤ **come round** or **come to** to become conscious again
➤ **come to pass** to happen
➤ **come to something** to add up to an amount

**comedian** NOUN comedians
someone who entertains people by making them laugh

**comedy** NOUN comedies
❶ a play or film etc. that makes people laugh ❷ humour

**comely** ADJECTIVE
(old use) good-looking

**comet** NOUN comets
an object moving across the sky with a bright tail of light (WORD ORIGIN) from Greek *kometes* = long-haired (star)

**comfort** NOUN comforts
❶ a feeling of being physically relaxed and satisfied • *These shoes are designed for extra comfort.* ❷ soothing somebody who is worried or unhappy • *She tried to offer a few words of comfort.* ❸ a person or thing that gives comfort • *the comforts of home*

**comfort** VERB comforts, comforting, comforted
to make a person feel less worried or unhappy

**comfortable** ADJECTIVE
❶ at ease; free from worry or pain ❷ pleasant to use or wear; making you feel relaxed • *comfortable shoes*
➤ **comfortably** ADVERB

**comfy** ADJECTIVE (informal)
comfortable

**comic** NOUN comics
❶ a children's magazine full of comic strips
❷ a comedian

**comic** ADJECTIVE
making people laugh; funny

**comical** ADJECTIVE
making people laugh; funny
➤ **comically** ADVERB

**comic strip** NOUN comic strips
a series of drawings telling a story, especially
a funny one

**comma** NOUN commas
a punctuation mark (,) used to mark a pause
in a sentence or to separate items in a list

> **PUNCTUATION**
>
> Commas are used:
>
> to mark a pause in a sentence, especially
> to separate a subordinate clause from the
> main clause:
>
> *When you go out, don't forget to lock the
> door.*
>
> *Smiling to herself, she walked out of the
> room.*
>
> before a coordinating conjunction such as
> *or*, *and* or *but* to separate the two clauses
> in a multi-clause sentence:
>
> *I like swimming, but I love ice skating.*
>
> *It's a lovely house, and it's very near the
> station.*
>
> to separate items in a list or series:
>
> *Make sure you bring pens, pencils, a ruler
> and a notebook.*
>
> in pairs if a subordinate clause is inserted
> into the middle of the main clause:
>
> *After three weeks, if you have been
> practising regularly, you should find that
> your technique has improved.*
>
> *The robot, who was called Buzz, could
> speak several languages.*
>
> after an adverb or an adverbial if you are
> using it at the start of a sentence:
>
> *Luckily, no one saw her fall over.*
>
> *To his horror, he saw the ball hit the back
> of the net.*
>
> to separate the name of a person or group
> of people you are addressing directly from

> the rest of the sentence:
>
> *OK, Sam, what shall we do next?*
>
> *Ladies and gentlemen, thank you for
> coming.*

**command** NOUN commands
❶ a statement telling someone to do
something; an order ❷ to be in command is
to have authority or control over someone
❸ a command of a subject or language is a
good knowledge of it and an ability to use it
well • *She has a good command of Spanish.*

**command** VERB commands, commanding,
commanded
❶ to give a command to someone; to
order someone to do something ❷ to have
authority over a group of people ❸ to
deserve and get something • *They command
our respect.*

> **GRAMMAR**
>
> A **command** is a sentence that gives an
> order or instruction. A command is usually
> written in the imperative and the verb is
> the first word of the sentence. The subject
> is understood as 'you'. A command can
> end with a full stop or, if it is an urgent
> one, an exclamation mark:
>
> *Write down your answers.*
>
> *Come over here.*
>
> *Don't move!*
>
> A single verb can form a command, like
> *Run!* or *Stop!*
>
> See also the panel on sentences.

**commandant** (say kom-an-dant) NOUN
commandants
a military officer in charge of a fortress etc.

**commandeer** VERB commandeers,
commandeering, commandeered
to take or seize something for military
purposes or for your own use

**commander** NOUN commanders
a person in command of a group of people

**commandment** NOUN commandments
a sacred command, especially one of the Ten
Commandments given to Moses

**commando** NOUN commandos
a soldier trained for making dangerous raids

**commemorate** VERB commemorates, commemorating, commemorated
to be a celebration or reminder of some past event or person • *A plaque commemorates the battle.*
➤ **commemoration** NOUN
➤ **commemorative** ADJECTIVE

**commence** VERB commences, commencing, commenced (*formal*)
to begin • *The ceremony commenced.*
➤ **commencement** NOUN

**commend** VERB commends, commending, commended
❶ to praise someone • *He was commended for bravery.* ❷ (*formal*) to entrust a person or thing to someone • *We commend him to your care.*
➤ **commendation** NOUN

**commendable** ADJECTIVE
deserving praise

**comment** NOUN comments
an opinion given about something or to explain something

**comment** VERB comments, commenting, commented
to make a comment

**commentary** VERB commentaries
❶ a description of an event by someone who is watching it, especially for radio or television ❷ a set of explanatory comments on a text

**commentator** NOUN commentators
a person who gives a radio or television commentary
➤ **commentate** VERB

**commerce** NOUN
the business of buying and selling goods and services; trade

**commercial** ADJECTIVE
❶ to do with commerce ❷ paid for by advertising • *a commercial radio station* ❸ making a profit • *The film was not a commercial success.*
➤ **commercially** ADVERB

**commercial** NOUN commercials
a broadcast advertisement

**commiserate** VERB commiserates, commiserating, commiserated
to sympathize with someone
➤ **commiseration** NOUN

**commission** NOUN commissions
❶ a task formally given to someone • *a commission to paint a portrait* ❷ an

appointment to be an officer in the armed forces ❸ a group of people given authority to do or investigate something ❹ extra money that a person gets for selling goods
➤ **out of commission** not in working order

**commission** VERB commissions, commissioning, commissioned
to give someone a task or assignment
• *Michelangelo was commissioned to paint the Sistine chapel ceiling in 1508.*

**commissionaire** NOUN commissionaires (*British*) an attendant in uniform at the entrance to a theatre, large shop, offices, etc.

**commissioner** NOUN commissioners
❶ an official appointed by commission ❷ a member of a commission

**commit** VERB commits, committing, committed
❶ to commit a crime is to do something against the law ❷ to commit yourself to something is to promise to do it or to devote all your energy to doing it • *I can't commit myself to helping you tomorrow.* ❸ to promise that you will make your time etc. available for a particular purpose • *Don't commit all your spare time to helping him.* ❹ to place a person in someone's care or custody • *He was committed to prison.*

**commitment** NOUN commitments
❶ the work, belief and loyalty that a person gives to something because they think it is important • *I admire your commitment to protecting the environment.* ❷ something that regularly takes up some of your time
• *work commitments*

**committee** NOUN committees
a group of people appointed to deal with something

SPELLING

Committee has a double m, a double t and a double e.

**commode** NOUN commodes
a box or chair into which a chamber pot is fitted

**commodious** ADJECTIVE
having plenty of space; roomy

**commodity** NOUN commodities
a product or material that can be bought and sold

**commodore** NOUN commodores
❶ a naval officer ranking next below a rear admiral ❷ the commander of part of a fleet

**common** ADJECTIVE
❶ ordinary or usual; occurring frequently • *a common weed* • *Traffic jams are common where we live.* ❷ affecting all or most people • *They worked for the common good.* ❸ shared • *Music is their common interest.* ❹ vulgar; showing a lack of education
➤ **in common** shared by two or more people or things • *We've got a lot in common.*

**common** NOUN commons
a piece of land that everyone can use

**commoner** NOUN commoners
a member of the ordinary people, not of the nobility

**commonly** ADVERB
usually or frequently • *X-rays are commonly used in hospitals.*

**commonplace** ADJECTIVE
not exciting or unusual; ordinary

**common room** NOUN common rooms
(*chiefly British*) a room for students or teachers at a school or college to use when they are not involved in lessons

**common sense** NOUN
normal good sense in thinking or behaviour

**commonwealth** NOUN
❶ a group of countries cooperating together ❷ a country made up of an association of states • *the Commonwealth of Australia*
➤ **the Commonwealth** ❶ an association of Britain and various other countries that used to be part of the British Empire, including Canada, Australia and New Zealand ❷ the republic set up in Britain by Oliver Cromwell, lasting from 1649 to 1660

**commotion** NOUN
great noise or excitement; an uproar • *Suddenly he heard a commotion outside.*

**communal** (say kom-yoo-nal) ADJECTIVE
shared by several people • *a communal kitchen*

**commune** (say kom-yoon) NOUN communes
❶ a group of people living together and sharing everything ❷ a district of local government in France and some other countries

**commune** (say ko-**mewn**) VERB communes, communing, communed
to share your thoughts and feelings with someone or with nature without speaking

**communicate** VERB communicates, communicating, communicated

❶ to pass news or information to other people ❷ rooms communicate when there is a door leading from one to the other

**communication** NOUN communications
❶ communicating with other people ❷ a written or spoken message
➤ **communications** PLURAL NOUN
ways of sending messages or information between people and places, e.g. telephones, television and the Internet

**communicative** ADJECTIVE
willing to talk

**communion** NOUN
religious fellowship
➤ **Communion** or **Holy Communion** the Christian ceremony in which bread and wine are blessed and given to worshippers

**communiqué** (say ko-**mew**-nik-ay) NOUN communiqués
an official message giving a report

**communism** NOUN
a political system in which property is shared by everyone and the state controls the country's industry and resources. Compare with **capitalism**.

**communist** NOUN communists
a person who believes in communism

**community** NOUN communities
❶ the people living in one area ❷ a group with similar interests or origins

**commute** VERB commutes, commuting, commuted
❶ to travel a fairly long way by train, bus or car to and from your daily work ❷ to alter a punishment to something less severe

**commuter** NOUN commuters
a person who commutes to and from work

**compact** ADJECTIVE
❶ neat and small • *a compact camera* ❷ closely or neatly packed together

**compact** NOUN compacts
❶ a small flat container for face powder ❷ an agreement or contract

**compact** VERB compacts, compacting, compacted
to press something firmly together • *The snow on the pavement soon became compacted.*

**compact disc** NOUN compact discs
a small plastic disc on which music or information is stored as digital signals and is read by a laser beam

a
b
c
d
e
f
g
h
i
j
k
l
m
n
o
p
q
r
s
t
u
v
w
x
y
z

**companion** NOUN companions
❶ a person who you spend time with or travel with ❷ a guidebook or reference book • *The Oxford Companion to Music*
**WORD ORIGIN** literally = someone you eat bread with: from Latin *panis* = bread

**companionable** ADJECTIVE
friendly and sociable

**companionship** NOUN
being with someone and enjoying their friendship

**company** NOUN companies
❶ a business firm ❷ a group of people who perform together • *a theatre company* ❸ having people with you; being with someone • *She was lonely and longed for some company.* • *I enjoy Matt's company.* ❹ visitors • *We've got company.* ❺ a section of a battalion

**comparable** (say kom-per-a-bul) ADJECTIVE
able to be compared, similar • *These two cases are not really comparable.*

**comparative** ADJECTIVE
compared with something else • *They live in comparative comfort.*

**comparative** NOUN comparatives
the form of an adjective or adverb that expresses 'more' • *The comparative of 'big' is 'bigger' and the comparative of 'bad' is 'worse'.*

**GRAMMAR**

Comparative adjectives and adverbs are used to compare and contrast people, things or actions. The comparative shows which of two things is greater or more: *Cheetahs run faster than antelopes.*

For many adjectives, and some adverbs, the comparative is formed by adding -er (or -r if the word already ends in e). Note that some adjectives double their final letter, and those ending in -y change to -i before adding -er:

*This flower is bigger and paler than the others.*

*His next film was even scarier.*

*The guests arrived sooner than expected.*

For longer adjectives, and for adverbs ending in -ly, the comparative is formed with *more*:

*Hot-air balloons are a more interesting*

way to travel.

*She started typing more furiously than ever.*

However, some common adjectives and adverbs have irregular comparatives which in some cases are different words, e.g. *good* / *well* (*better*), *bad* / *badly* (*worse*), and *far* (*farther* or *further*).

You will find guidance in this dictionary on irregular comparatives.

See also the panel on superlatives.

**comparatively** ADVERB
compared to something else or what is usual; relatively • *Fortunately, the disease is comparatively rare nowadays.*

**compare** VERB compares, comparing, compared
❶ to put or consider things together so that you can see in what ways they are similar or different ❷ to form the comparative and superlative of an adjective or adverb
➤ compare notes to share information
➤ compare with something ❶ to be similar to something ❷ to be as good as something • *Our art gallery cannot compare with Tate Modern.*

**USAGE**

When compare is used with an object, it can be followed by either to or with. As a general rule, you use to when you are showing the similarity between two things: *She compared me to a pig.* You use with when you are looking at the similarities and differences between things: *Just compare this year's exam results with last year's.*

**comparison** NOUN comparisons
comparing things

**compartment** NOUN compartments
❶ one of the spaces into which something is divided; a separate room or enclosed space ❷ a division of a railway carriage

**compass** NOUN compasses
an instrument that shows direction, with a magnetized needle pointing to the north
➤ compasses or pair of compasses a device for drawing circles, usually with two rods hinged together at one end

**compassion** NOUN
pity or mercy you show to someone who is

suffering
> **compassionate** ADJECTIVE
> **compassionately** ADVERB

**compatible** ADJECTIVE
❶ able to live or exist together without trouble ❷ able to be used together • *This printer is not compatible with my computer.*
> **compatibility** NOUN

**compatriot** (say kom-**pat**-ri-ot) NOUN
a person from the same country as another

**compel** VERB compels, compelling, compelled
to force someone to do something • *He felt compelled to read on further.*

**compelling** ADJECTIVE
forcing you to pay attention or believe something • *a compelling story* • *compelling evidence*

**compendium** NOUN compendiums or compendia
❶ an encyclopedia or handbook in one volume ❷ a set of different board games in one box

**compensate** VERB compensates, compensating, compensated
❶ to give a person money etc. to make up for a loss or injury ❷ to have a balancing effect • *This victory compensates for our earlier defeats.*

**compensation** NOUN compensations
❶ money paid to someone to make up for a loss or injury ❷ a thing that reduces the bad effect of something • *It may be a boring job, but there are compensations.*

**compère** (say **kom**-pair) NOUN compères
(*British*) a person who introduces the performers in a show or broadcast
> **compère** VERB

**compete** VERB competes, competing, competed
❶ to take part in a competition • *She competed in the 1992 Barcelona Olympics.*
❷ to try to be better or more successful than someone else • *These small shops just can't compete with the supermarkets.*

**competent** ADJECTIVE
having the skill or knowledge to do something in a satisfactory way
> **competently** ADVERB
> **competence** NOUN

**competition** NOUN competitions
❶ a game or race or other contest in which people try to win ❷ trying to be better or

more successful than someone else • *There was fierce competition for the job.* ❸ the people who compete with you • *Before the race she tried to size up the competition.*

**competitive** ADJECTIVE
❶ a competitive person enjoys competing with other people ❷ involving competition between people or firms • *competitive sport*

**competitor** NOUN competitors
someone who competes; a rival

**compile** VERB compiles, compiling, compiled
to put together a book, list, etc. by collecting together information from various places • *He has compiled a collection of children's poems.*
> **compiler** NOUN
> **compilation** NOUN

**complacent** ADJECTIVE
smugly satisfied with the way things are and feeling that no change or action is necessary
> **complacently** ADVERB
> **complacency** NOUN

**complain** VERB complains, complaining, complained
to say that you are annoyed or unhappy about something

**complaint** NOUN complaints
❶ a statement complaining about something
❷ a minor illness

**complement** NOUN complements
❶ the quantity needed to fill or complete something • *The ship had its full complement of sailors.* ❷ the word or words used after verbs such as be and become to complete the sense. In *She was brave* and *He became king of England*, the complements are *brave* and *king of England*

**complement** VERB complements, complementing, complemented
one thing complements another when they go well together or when one makes the other complete • *The hat complements the outfit.*

**SPELLING**
Take care not to confuse with a compliment, which is when you tell someone that you approve of something.

**complementary** ADJECTIVE
going together well or going together to make a whole • *Our skills are different but complementary.*

139

A
B
C
D
E
F
G
H
I
J
K
L
M
N
O
P
Q
R
S
T
U
V
W
X
Y
Z

**complementary angle** NOUN
complementary angles
either of two angles that add up to 90°

**complementary medicine** NOUN
(*British*) medical methods that are not
considered part of ordinary medicine, but
may be used alongside it, e.g. acupuncture
and homoeopathy

**complete** ADJECTIVE
❶ having all its parts, with nothing missing
❷ finished, with everything done • *The work
should be complete by Friday.* ❸ thorough; in
every way • *a complete stranger*
➤ **completeness** NOUN

**complete** VERB completes, completing,
completed
❶ to finish something or make it complete
❷ to complete a form is to write on it all the
information you are asked for

**completely** ADVERB
in every way; totally • *Many buildings were
completely destroyed by the earthquake.*

SPELLING

Complete + ly = completely. Don't forget
to keep the e after the t.

**completion** NOUN
making a thing complete; finishing something
• *The new hospital is near to completion.*

**complex** ADJECTIVE
❶ made up of many different parts • *complex
machinery* ❷ difficult or complicated • *a
complex problem*
➤ **complexity** NOUN

**complex** NOUN complexes
❶ a set of buildings made up of related parts
• *a sports complex* ❷ a group of feelings
or ideas that influence a person's behaviour
or make them worry about something • *an
inferiority complex*

**complexion** NOUN complexions
❶ the natural colour and appearance of the
skin of the face ❷ the way things seem • *That
puts a different complexion on the matter.*

**compliant** ADJECTIVE
willing to obey
➤ **compliance** NOUN

**complicate** VERB complicates, complicating,
complicated
to make something more difficult to
understand or deal with • *To complicate
matters further, there are no trains today.*

**complicated** ADJECTIVE
❶ made up of many different parts
❷ difficult to understand or deal with

**complication** NOUN complications
❶ something that complicates things or adds
difficulties ❷ a new illness that you get when
you are already ill

**complicity** NOUN
being involved in a crime or something bad

**compliment** NOUN compliments
something you say or do to show that you
approve of a person or thing • *It was the first
time he had ever paid her a compliment.*
➤ **compliments** PLURAL NOUN
formal greetings given in a message

**compliment** VERB compliments,
complimenting, complimented
to pay someone a compliment; to
congratulate someone

SPELLING

Take care not to confuse with
complement, which is when things go
well together.

**complimentary** ADJECTIVE
❶ expressing a compliment ❷ given free of
charge • *complimentary tickets*

**comply** VERB complies, complying, complied
to obey an order, rule or request • *You must
comply fully with these instructions.*

**component** NOUN components
each of the parts of which a thing is made up

**compose** VERB composes, composing,
composed
❶ to write music ❷ to write a letter, speech
or poem ❸ to be composed of several people
or things is to contain or include them • *The
class is composed of 20 students.* ❹ to
compose yourself is to become calm after
being excited or angry

**composed** ADJECTIVE
calm and in control of your feelings • *a
composed manner*

**composer** NOUN composers
a person who composes music

**composite** (say kom-poz-it) ADJECTIVE
made up of a number of parts or different
styles

**composition** NOUN compositions
❶ composing music or poetry ❷ something
composed, especially a piece of music ❸ an
essay or story written as a school exercise

**❹** the composition of a substance is the way that it is made up • *the chemical composition of the soil*

**compost** NOUN
**❶** decayed leaves and grass etc. used as a fertilizer **❷** a soil-like mixture for growing seedlings, cuttings, etc.

**composure** NOUN
calmness of manner • *He needed a minute to regain his composure.*

**compound** ADJECTIVE
made of two or more parts or ingredients

**compound** NOUN compounds
**❶** a compound substance **❷** (*in grammar*) a word or expression made from other words joined together, e.g. 'football' and 'newspaper' **❸** a fenced area containing buildings

**compound** VERB compounds, compounding, compounded
to make something worse • *His irritation was compounded by the fact that she was late.*

**comprehend** VERB comprehends, comprehending, comprehended
to understand something

**comprehensible** ADJECTIVE
able to be understood

**comprehension** NOUN comprehensions
**❶** understanding something **❷** an exercise that tests how well you understand something written or spoken in another language

**comprehensive** ADJECTIVE
including all or many kinds of people or things • *a comprehensive list of local restaurants*

**comprehensive** NOUN comprehensives
(*British*) a comprehensive school

**comprehensive school** NOUN
comprehensive schools
(*British*) a secondary school for all or most of the children in an area

**compress** (say kom-**press**) VERB compresses, compressing, compressed
**❶** to press or squeeze something together or into a smaller space • *He compressed his lips tightly.* **❷** to alter the form of computer data to reduce the amount of space needed to store it
➤ **compression** NOUN
➤ **compressor** NOUN

**compress** (say **kom**-press) NOUN compresses
a soft pad or cloth pressed on the body to stop bleeding or cool inflammation etc.

**comprise** VERB comprises, comprising, comprised
to include or consist of • *The pentathlon comprises five events.*

> **USAGE**
> Be careful not to use *comprise of*. The correct usage is: *The country comprises 20 states.*

**compromise** (say **kom**-prom-yz) NOUN compromises
settling a dispute by each side accepting less than it wanted or asked for

**compromise** VERB compromises, compromising, compromised
to accept less than you wanted or asked for in order to settle a dispute

**compulsion** NOUN compulsions
a strong and uncontrollable desire to do something

**compulsive** ADJECTIVE
having or resulting from a strong and uncontrollable desire • *a compulsive liar*

> **USAGE**
> See note at **compulsory**.

**compulsory** ADJECTIVE
something is compulsory when you have to do it and cannot choose • *Wearing seat belts is compulsory.*

> **USAGE**
> Take care not to confuse **compulsory** with **compulsive**. An action is compulsory if a law or rules say that you must do it, but compulsive if you want to do it and cannot resist it.

**compunction** NOUN
a guilty feeling • *She felt no compunction about hitting the burglar.*

**compute** VERB computes, computing, computed
to calculate something
➤ **computation** NOUN

**computer** NOUN computers
an electronic machine for making calculations, storing and analysing information put into it or controlling machinery automatically

a b c d e f g h i j k l m n o p q r s t u v w x y z

**computerize** (also **computerise**) *VERB*
computerizes, computerizing, computerized
to use computers to do a job or to store information • *The library catalogue has now been computerized.*
➤ **computerization** *NOUN*

**computing** *NOUN*
the use of computers

**comrade** *NOUN* comrades
a companion who shares in your activities
➤ **comradeship** *NOUN*

**con** *VERB* cons, conning, conned (*informal*)
to swindle someone

**concave** *ADJECTIVE*
curved like the inside of a ball or circle. (The opposite is **convex**.)

**conceal** *VERB* conceals, concealing, concealed
to hide something or keep it secret • *She couldn't conceal her astonishment.*
➤ **concealment** *NOUN*

**concede** *VERB* concedes, conceding, conceded
❶ to admit that something is true ❷ to admit that you have been defeated ❸ to give up a possession or right • *They conceded us the right to cross their land.*

**conceit** *NOUN*
too much pride in your abilities and achievements • *I can't believe the conceit of the man!*

**conceited** *ADJECTIVE*
too proud of yourself and your abilities

**conceivable** *ADJECTIVE*
able to be imagined or believed
➤ **conceivably** *ADVERB*

**conceive** *VERB* conceives, conceiving, conceived
❶ to become pregnant; to form a baby in the womb ❷ to form an idea or plan in your mind • *I can't conceive what that must feel like.*

**concentrate** *VERB* concentrates, concentrating, concentrated
❶ to give your full attention or effort to something ❷ to bring something together in one place • *Industry is concentrated in the north of the country.*

**concentrated** *ADJECTIVE*
a concentrated liquid has been made stronger by removing water • *concentrated orange juice*

**concentration** *NOUN* concentrations
❶ concentrating on something ❷ the amount dissolved in each part of a liquid

**concentration camp** *NOUN* concentration camps
a prison camp where political prisoners are kept together, especially one set up by the Nazis during World War II

**concentric** *ADJECTIVE*
having the same centre • *concentric circles*

**concept** *NOUN* concepts
an idea • *It is a difficult concept to grasp.*

**conception** *NOUN* conceptions
❶ conceiving a baby ❷ forming an idea in your mind

**concern** *VERB* concerns, concerning, concerned
❶ to be important to or affect someone • *This doesn't concern you, so go away.* ❷ to worry someone ❸ to be about something; to have something as its subject • *The story concerns a group of rabbits.*

**concern** *NOUN* concerns
❶ something that is important to you or that affects you; a responsibility ❷ a worry or a feeling of worry • *My main concern is that we'll run out of time.* ❸ a business

**concerned** *ADJECTIVE*
❶ worried or anxious ❷ involved in or affected by something

**concerning** *PREPOSITION*
on the subject of; about • *laws concerning seat belts*

**concert** *NOUN* concerts
a performance of music

**concerted** *ADJECTIVE*
done in cooperation with others • *We made a concerted effort.*

**concertina** *NOUN* concertinas
a portable musical instrument with bellows, played by squeezing

**concerto** (say kon-**chert**-oh) *NOUN* concertos
a piece of music for a solo instrument and an orchestra

**concession** *NOUN* concessions
❶ something that you agree to let someone have or do in order to end an argument or to be helpful ❷ a reduction in price for a certain category of person
➤ **concessionary** *ADJECTIVE*

**conciliate** VERB conciliates, conciliating, conciliated
❶ to win over an angry or hostile person by friendliness ❷ to help people who disagree to come to an agreement
➤ **conciliation** NOUN

**concise** ADJECTIVE
brief; giving a lot of information in a few words • *clear and concise instructions*
➤ **concisely** ADVERB

**conclave** NOUN conclaves
a private meeting

**conclude** VERB concludes, concluding, concluded
❶ to decide about something; to form an opinion by reasoning • *The jury concluded that he was guilty.* ❷ to end or to bring something to an end • *This film concludes the 'Lord of the Rings' trilogy.*

**conclusion** NOUN conclusions
❶ an ending ❷ an opinion formed by reasoning

**conclusive** ADJECTIVE
putting an end to all doubt • *The evidence is conclusive.*
➤ **conclusively** ADVERB

**concoct** VERB concocts, concocting, concocted
❶ to make something by putting ingredients together ❷ to invent something or make it up • *We'll have to concoct an excuse.*
➤ **concoction** NOUN

**concord** NOUN
friendly agreement or harmony

**concourse** NOUN concourses
an open area through which people pass, e.g. at an airport

**concrete** NOUN
cement mixed with sand and gravel, used in building

**concrete** ADJECTIVE
❶ based on facts, not ideas or guesses • *We need concrete evidence, not theories.* ❷ definite and clear, not general • *I don't have any concrete plans.*

**concrete poem** NOUN concrete poems
a poem printed in a special way, so that the words form a pattern on the page that has something to do with the meaning of the poem

**concur** VERB concurs, concurring, concurred
to agree
➤ **concurrence** NOUN

**concussion** NOUN
a temporary injury to the brain caused by a hard knock
➤ **concussed** ADJECTIVE

**condemn** VERB condemns, condemning, condemned
❶ to say that you strongly disapprove of something ❷ to convict or sentence a criminal • *He was condemned to death.* ❸ to be condemned to something unpleasant is to have to suffer it • *She was condemned to a lonely life.* ❹ to declare that a building is not fit to be used
➤ **condemnation** NOUN

**condensation** NOUN
❶ water from humid air collecting as tiny drops on a cold surface ❷ the process of changing from gas or vapour to liquid

**condense** VERB condenses, condensing, condensed
❶ to make a liquid denser or more compact ❷ to put something into fewer words or less space • *I have condensed the first three chapters into one.* ❸ to change from gas or vapour to liquid • *Steam condenses on windows.*
➤ **condenser** NOUN

**condescend** VERB condescends, condescending, condescended
❶ to behave towards someone in a way which shows that you think you are superior to them ❷ to allow yourself to do something that you think is unworthy of you or beneath you
➤ **condescension** NOUN

**condescending** ADJECTIVE
behaving towards someone in a way which shows that you think you are superior to them • *a condescending smile*

**condiment** NOUN condiments
a seasoning (e.g. salt or pepper) for food

**condition** NOUN conditions
❶ the state or fitness of a person or thing • *This bike is in good condition.* ❷ the situation or surroundings that affect people • *measures to improve working conditions in factories* ❸ something required as part of an agreement
➤ **on condition that** only if; on the understanding that something will be done

**condition** VERB conditions, conditioning, conditioned
❶ to bring something into a healthy or proper condition ❷ to train someone to behave in a particular way or become used to a particular situation

**conditional** ADJECTIVE
containing a condition; depending on something else

**conditioner** NOUN conditioners
a substance you put on your hair to keep it in good condition

**condole** VERB condoles, condoling, condoled
to express sympathy

**condolence** NOUN condolences
an expression of sympathy, especially for someone who is bereaved • *a letter of condolence*

**condom** NOUN condoms
a rubber sheath worn on the penis during sexual intercourse as a contraceptive and as a protection against sexual disease or infection

**condone** VERB condones, condoning, condoned
to accept or ignore wrongdoing • *I'm sorry, but I can't condone this sort of deception.*

**condor** NOUN condors
a kind of large vulture

**conducive** ADJECTIVE
helping to cause or produce something • *Noisy surroundings are not conducive to work.*

**conduct** (say kon-**dukt**) VERB conducts, conducting, conducted
❶ to manage something or carry it out • *She conducted a series of important experiments.* ❷ to lead or guide someone to a place • *We were conducted around the ruins of the temple.* ❸ to be the conductor of an orchestra or choir ❹ to allow heat, light, sound or electricity to pass along or through something ❺ to behave in a particular way • *They conducted themselves with dignity.*

**conduct** (say **kon**-dukt) NOUN
a person's behaviour

**conduction** NOUN
the conducting of heat or electricity etc

**conductor** NOUN conductors
❶ a person who directs the performance of an orchestra or choir by movements of the arms ❷ something that conducts heat or electricity etc. ❸ a person who collects the fares on a bus etc.

**conduit** (say **kon**-dit) NOUN conduits
❶ a pipe or channel for liquid ❷ a tube protecting electric wire

**cone** NOUN cones
❶ an object that is circular at one end and narrows to a point at the other end ❷ an ice cream cornet ❸ the dry cone-shaped fruit of a pine, fir or cedar tree

**confection** NOUN confections
something made of various things, especially sweet ones, put together

**confectioner** NOUN confectioners
someone who makes or sells sweets
➤ **confectionery** NOUN

**confederacy** NOUN confederacies
a union of states; a confederation

**confederate** ADJECTIVE
allied; joined by an agreement or treaty

**confederate** NOUN confederates
❶ a member of a confederacy ❷ an ally or accomplice

**confederation** NOUN confederations
❶ the process of joining in an alliance ❷ a group of people, organizations or states joined together by an agreement or treaty

**confer** VERB confers, conferring, conferred
❶ to have a discussion before deciding something ❷ to grant a right or privilege to someone • *Thank you for conferring this honour upon me.*

**conference** NOUN conferences
a meeting at which formal discussions take place

**confess** VERB confesses, confessing, confessed
to state openly that you have done something wrong or have a weakness; to admit something • *I confess that I don't like her very much.*

**confession** NOUN confessions
❶ admitting that you have done wrong • *He made a full confession to the police.* ❷ (in the Roman Catholic Church) an act of telling a priest that you have sinned

**confessional** NOUN confessionals
a small room where a priest hears confessions

**confessor** NOUN confessors
a priest who hears confessions

**confetti** NOUN
tiny pieces of coloured paper thrown by

wedding guests at the bride and bridegroom
**WORD ORIGIN** Italian, = sweets (which were traditionally thrown at Italian weddings)

**confidant** NOUN (confidante is used of a woman) confidants, confidantes
a person you confide in

**confide** VERB confides, confiding, confided
to tell someone a secret • *I decided to confide in my sister.*

**confidence** NOUN confidences
❶ a feeling of being sure that you are right or can do something ❷ firm trust in someone or something ❸ something told as a secret
➤ in confidence as a secret or private matter
➤ in a person's confidence trusted with his or her secrets

**confidence trick** NOUN confidence tricks
swindling a person after persuading him or her to trust you

**confident** ADJECTIVE
showing or feeling confidence • *She is confident that she will win.*
➤ confidently ADVERB

**confidential** ADJECTIVE
meant to be kept secret
➤ confidentially ADVERB
➤ confidentiality NOUN

**configuration** NOUN configurations
the way in which the parts of something or a group of things are arranged. • *the configuration of the continents*

**confine** VERB confines, confining, confined
❶ to keep something within limits; to restrict something • *Please confine your remarks to the subject being discussed.* ❷ to keep someone in a place and not let them leave

**confined** ADJECTIVE
a confined space is narrow or enclosed

**confinement** NOUN confinements
❶ being forced to stay somewhere • *He spent two weeks in solitary confinement.* ❷ (old use) the time of giving birth to a baby

**confines** (say **kon**-fynz) PLURAL NOUN
the limits or boundaries of an area

**confirm** VERB confirms, confirming, confirmed
❶ to show definitely that something is true or correct ❷ to make an arrangement definite • *Please write to confirm your order.* ❸ to make a person a full member of the Christian Church

**confirmation** NOUN confirmations
❶ a statement showing that something is

true, correct or definite • *You will receive confirmation of your booking by email.* ❷ a ceremony in which a person is made a full member of the Christian Church

**confiscate** VERB confiscates, confiscating, confiscated
to take something away from someone as a punishment
➤ confiscation NOUN

**conflagration** NOUN conflagrations
a great and destructive fire

**conflict** (say **kon**-flikt) NOUN conflicts
a fight, struggle or disagreement

**conflict** (say kon-**flikt**) VERB conflicts, conflicting, conflicted
two things conflict when they contradict or disagree with one another • *His account of the incident conflicts with hers.*

**confluence** NOUN confluences
the place where two rivers meet

**conform** VERB conforms, conforming, conformed
to keep to accepted rules, customs or ideas
➤ conformity NOUN

**confound** VERB confounds, confounding, confounded
to astonish or confuse someone

**confront** VERB confronts, confronting, confronted
❶ to confront someone is to challenge them face to face for a fight or argument ❷ to confront a problem or difficulty is to deal with it rather than ignoring it • *She has learned to confront her fears.* ❸ if a problem or difficulty confronts you, you have to deal with it • *He was confronted with a very difficult decision.*

**confrontation** NOUN confrontations
meeting someone face to face for a fight or argument

**confuse** VERB confuses, confusing, confused
❶ to make a person puzzled or muddled ❷ to mistake one person or thing for another • *I often confuse Ollie with his brother.*
➤ confused ADJECTIVE

**confusing** ADJECTIVE
difficult to understand; not clear

**confusion** NOUN
❶ not being able to think clearly or not knowing what to do • *He stared in confusion at the exam paper.* ❷ mistaking one thing for

a b c d e f g h i j k l m n o p q r s t u v w x y z

another • *To avoid confusion, I've written my name on my bag.*

**congeal** (say kon-**jeel**) *VERB* congeals, congealing, congealed
to become jelly-like instead of liquid, especially in cooling • *congealed blood*

**congenial** *ADJECTIVE*
pleasant through being similar to yourself or suiting your tastes • *a congenial companion*

**congenital** (say kon-**jen**-it-al) *ADJECTIVE*
existing in a person from birth • *a congenital heart defect*

**congested** *ADJECTIVE*
❶ a congested place is crowded or blocked up with traffic or people • *congested streets*
❷ your breathing or a part of your body are congested when they become blocked with mucus • *congested lungs*

**congestion** *NOUN*
❶ when a place is crowded and full of traffic or people ❷ when your nose is blocked with mucus and you cannot breathe properly

**conglomerate** *NOUN* conglomerates
a large business group formed by merging several different companies

**conglomeration** *NOUN* conglomerations
a mass of different things put together

**congratulate** *VERB* congratulates, congratulating, congratulated
to tell a person that you are pleased about what they have achieved or something good that has happened to them
➤ **congratulatory** *ADJECTIVE*

**congratulations** *PLURAL NOUN*
what you say to congratulate someone

**congregate** *VERB* congregates, congregating, congregated
to come together in a crowd or group
• *Young people congregate in the square each evening.*

**congregation** *NOUN* congregations
a group of people who have come together to take part in religious worship

**Congress** *NOUN*
the parliament of the USA

**congress** *NOUN* congresses
a large meeting or conference

**congruent** *ADJECTIVE*
(*in mathematics*) having exactly the same shape and size • *congruent triangles*
➤ **congruence** *NOUN*

**conical** *ADJECTIVE*
cone-shaped • *a conical hat*

**conifer** (say **kon**-if-er) *NOUN* conifers
an evergreen tree with cones
➤ **coniferous** *ADJECTIVE*

**conjecture** *NOUN* conjectures
guesswork or a guess

**conjecture** *VERB* conjectures, conjecturing, conjectured
to guess about something

**conjoined twins** *PLURAL NOUN*
twins who are born with their bodies joined together

**conjugal** (say **kon**-jug-al) *ADJECTIVE*
to do with marriage

**conjugate** *VERB* conjugates, conjugating, conjugated
to give all the different forms of a verb
➤ **conjugation** *NOUN*

**conjunction** *NOUN* conjunctions
a word that joins words, phrases or sentences, e.g. *and*, *but* and *because*
➤ **in conjunction with** together with; combined with • *The course book is designed to be used in conjunction with our website.*

---

**GRAMMAR**

Conjunctions and other connectives are used to link ideas in a piece of writing.

Conjunctions are used to join words, clauses or phrases in a sentence.

Coordinating conjunctions such as *and*, *but* and *or* join words or clauses which are of equal importance:

*Would you prefer tea <u>and</u> biscuits, <u>or</u> coffee <u>and</u> cake?*

Subordinating conjunctions such as *although*, *because*, *if*, *until*, *unless* and *when* are used to introduce a subordinate clause:

*She felt weak <u>because</u> she was tired and hungry.*

*The computer won't work <u>unless</u> you switch it on.*

Other connectives are adverbs or phrases used as adverbials. They often come at the start of a sentence and connect it with a previous sentence or paragraph. Common examples of adverbials used in this way are the adverbs *moreover*, *nevertheless*, *finally* and *furthermore*, and the phrases *on the other hand*, *in addition to this*, and *later that day.*

*The goods arrived late. <u>Furthermore</u>, the parcel was damaged.*

*He left in the morning. <u>Later that day</u>, he was back.*

**conjure** *VERB* conjures, conjuring, conjured
to perform tricks that look like magic
➤ **conjuror** *NOUN*
➤ **conjure something up** to produce an image or impression in your mind • *Mention of the Arctic conjures up visions of snow.*

**conker** *NOUN* conkers (*British*)
the hard shiny brown nut of the horse chestnut tree
➤ **conkers** a game between players who each have a conker threaded on a string
**WORD ORIGIN** from a dialect word = snail shell (because conkers was originally played with snail shells)

SPELLING
Be careful, this sounds the same as **conquer**.

**connect** *VERB* connects, connecting, connected
❶ to join things together; to link one thing with another • *Have you connected the printer to the computer?* ❷ to think of things or people as being associated with each other • *There was no evidence to connect him with the murder.*

**connection** *NOUN* connections
❶ a link or relationship between things • *We all know there is a connection between smoking and cancer.* ❷ a place where two wires, pipes, etc are joined together • *a loose connection* ❸ a train, bus, etc. that leaves a station soon after another arrives, so that passengers can change from one to the other

**connective** *NOUN* connectives
a word that joins words, clauses or sentences. Some connectives (e.g. *but, and* and *because*) are conjunctions, while some (e.g. *however* and *in addition*) are adverbials.

**conning tower** *NOUN* conning towers
the part on top of a submarine, containing the periscope

**connive** (say kon-**yv**) *VERB* connives, conniving, connived
➤ **connive at something** to ignore something wrong or quietly approve of it
➤ **connivance** *NOUN*

**connoisseur** (say kon-a-**ser**) *NOUN* connoisseurs
a person with great experience and appreciation of something • *a connoisseur of wine*

**conquer** *VERB* conquers, conquering, conquered
❶ to defeat and take control of a country and its people ❷ to succeed in controlling a difficult feeling • *She's trying to conquer her fear of flying.*
➤ **conqueror** *NOUN*

SPELLING
The 'k' sound is spelt **qu** in the middle of **conquer**.

**conquest** *NOUN* conquests
❶ a victory over someone ❷ conquered territory

**conscience** (say **kon**-shens) *NOUN* consciences
knowing what is right and wrong, especially in your own actions

**conscientious** (say kon-shee-**en**-shus) *ADJECTIVE*
careful and honest about doing your work properly • *She is a conscientious student.*
➤ **conscientiously** *ADVERB*

**conscientious objector** *NOUN* conscientious objectors
a person who refuses to serve in the armed forces because he or she believes it is morally wrong

**conscious** (say **kon**-shus) *ADJECTIVE*
❶ awake and knowing what is happening ❷ aware of something • *I was not conscious of the time.* ❸ done deliberately • *a conscious decision*
➤ **consciously** *ADVERB*
➤ **consciousness** *NOUN*

SPELLING
There is a tricky bit in **conscious** – it has **sci** in the middle.

**conscript** (say kon-**skript**) *VERB* conscripts, conscripting, conscripted
to make a person join the armed forces
➤ **conscription** *NOUN*

**conscript** (say **kon**-skript) *NOUN* conscripts
a person who has been conscripted

**consecrate** *VERB* consecrates, consecrating, consecrated
to officially say that a thing, especially a building, is holy
➤ **consecration** *NOUN*

**consecutive** ADJECTIVE
following one after another • *Borg won five consecutive Wimbledon titles.*
➤ **consecutively** ADVERB

**consensus** NOUN consensuses
general agreement; the opinion of most people • *There was a growing consensus that the rule should be changed.*

**consent** NOUN
agreement to what someone wishes; permission • *You can only go on the trip if your parents give their consent.*

**consent** VERB consents, consenting, consented
to say that you are willing to do or allow what someone wishes

**consequence** NOUN consequences
❶ something that happens as the result of an event or action ❷ the importance that something has • *It is of no consequence.*

**consequent** ADJECTIVE
happening as a result

**consequently** ADVERB
as a result

**conservation** NOUN
❶ the preservation of the natural environment ❷ not allowing something valuable from being spoilt or wasted • *the conservation of energy*

**conservationist** NOUN conservationists
a person who believes in preserving the natural environment

**Conservative** NOUN Conservatives
a person who supports the Conservative Party, a British political party that favours private enterprise and freedom from state control
➤ **Conservative** ADJECTIVE

**conservative** ADJECTIVE
❶ liking traditional ways and disliking changes ❷ lower than what is probably the real amount • *a conservative estimate*
➤ **conservatism** NOUN

**conservatory** NOUN conservatories
a room with a glass roof and large windows, built against an outside wall of a house with a connecting door from the house

**conserve** VERB conserves, conserving, conserved
to prevent something valuable from being changed, spoilt or wasted

**consider** VERB considers, considering, considered
❶ to think carefully about or give attention to something, especially in order to make a decision ❷ to have something as an opinion; to think something • *I consider myself very lucky.*

**considerable** ADJECTIVE
fairly great or large • *a considerable amount*

**considerably** ADVERB
very much; a lot • *The new house is considerably larger than our last one.*

**considerate** ADJECTIVE
always thinking of other people's needs, wishes or feelings
➤ **considerately** ADVERB

**consideration** NOUN considerations
❶ careful thought or attention ❷ considerate behaviour ❸ a fact that must be kept in mind
➤ **take something into consideration** to think carefully about something when you are making a decision or giving an opinion

**considering** PREPOSITION
taking something into consideration • *The car runs well, considering its age.*

**consign** VERB consigns, consigning, consigned
to put something somewhere in order to get rid of it • *I consigned her letter to the bin.*

**consignment** NOUN consignments
a batch of goods etc. sent to someone

**consist** VERB consists, consisting, consisted
to be made up or formed of • *The band consists of a singer, two guitarists and a drummer.*

**consistency** NOUN consistencies
❶ how thick or smooth a liquid is • *The mixture should have a creamy consistency.*
❷ being consistent • *The team needs to play with more consistency.*

**consistent** ADJECTIVE
❶ keeping to a regular pattern, style or standard; not changing • *She's our most consistent player.* ❷ agreeing with something else; not contradictory • *These results are consistent with earlier findings.*
➤ **consistently** ADVERB

**consolation** NOUN consolations
❶ consolation is giving comfort or sympathy to someone ❷ a consolation is something that comforts someone who is unhappy or disappointed

**consolation prize** NOUN consolation prizes
a prize given to a competitor who has just missed winning one of the main prizes

**console** (say kon-**sohl**) VERB consoles, consoling, consoled
to comfort someone who is unhappy or disappointed

**console** (say **kon**-sohl) NOUN consoles
a panel or unit containing the controls for electrical or other equipment

**consolidate** VERB consolidates, consolidating, consolidated
❶ to make something secure and strong • *They consolidated their lead with a second goal.* ❷ to combine two or more organizations, funds, etc. into one
➤ **consolidation** NOUN

**consonant** NOUN consonants
a letter that is not a vowel • *B, c, d, f, etc. are consonants.*

**consort** (say **kon**-sort) NOUN consorts
a husband or wife, especially of a monarch

**consort** (say kon-**sort**) VERB consorts, consorting, consorted
to consort with someone is to be often in their company • *He was known to consort with criminals.*

**consortium** NOUN consortia
a group of companies working together

**conspicuous** ADJECTIVE
easy to see or notice; standing out very clearly • *I felt very conspicuous in my new suit.*
➤ **conspicuously** ADVERB

**conspiracy** NOUN conspiracies
a secret plan made by a group of people to do something illegal

**conspirator** NOUN conspirators
a person who takes part in a conspiracy

**conspiratorial** ADJECTIVE
showing that you share a secret with someone • *He gave her a conspiratorial wink.*

**conspire** VERB conspires, conspiring, conspired
to take part in a conspiracy

**constable** NOUN constables
a police officer of the lowest rank

**constabulary** NOUN constabularies
(*British*) a police force

**constancy** NOUN
being faithful or loyal

**constant** ADJECTIVE
❶ not changing; happening all the time
❷ faithful or loyal

**constant** NOUN constants
❶ a thing that does not vary ❷ (*in science and mathematics*) a number or value that does not change

**constantly** ADVERB
all the time; again and again • *The situation is constantly changing.*

**constellation** NOUN constellations
a group of stars

**constipated** ADJECTIVE
unable to empty the bowels easily or regularly
➤ **constipation** NOUN

**constituency** NOUN constituencies
a district represented by a Member of Parliament elected by the people who live there

**constituent** NOUN constituents
❶ one of the parts that form a whole thing
• *Hydrogen and oxygen are the constituents of water.* ❷ someone who lives in a particular constituency
➤ **constituent** ADJECTIVE

**constitute** VERB constitutes, constituting, constituted
❶ to make up or form something • *These 50 states constitute the USA.* ❷ to be considered to be something • *What he did surely constitutes bullying.*

**constitution** NOUN constitutions
❶ the group of laws or principles that state how a country is to be organized and governed ❷ the condition of your body in terms of its general physical health • *She has a strong constitution.*
➤ **constitutional** ADJECTIVE

**constrain** VERB constrains, constraining, constrained
to force someone to act in a certain way

**constraint** NOUN constraints
❶ something that limits you; a restriction
❷ forcing someone to act in a certain way

**constrict** VERB constricts, constricting, constricted
to become tighter and narrower or to make something do this • *She felt her throat constrict with fear.*
➤ **constriction** NOUN

**construct** VERB constructs, constructing, constructed
to make something by placing parts together;

a b c d e f g h i j k l m n o p q r s t u v w x y z

to build something from parts • *When was the bridge constructed?*
➤ **constructor** NOUN

**construction** NOUN constructions
❶ constructing something • *Our new school is still under construction.* ❷ something constructed; a building ❸ two or more words put together to form a phrase or clause or sentence

**constructive** ADJECTIVE
helpful and positive • *constructive suggestions*

**construe** VERB construes, construing, construed
to interpret or explain something difficult

**consul** NOUN consuls
❶ a government official appointed to live in a foreign city to help people from his or her own country who visit there ❷ either of the two chief magistrates in ancient Rome

**consulate** NOUN consulates
the building where a consul works

**consult** VERB consults, consulting, consulted
❶ to go to a person or book etc. for information or advice ❷ to discuss something with someone before taking a decision

**consultant** NOUN consultants
❶ a person who is qualified to give expert advice ❷ a senior hospital doctor who is an expert in one type of medicine

**consultation** NOUN consultations
❶ a discussion between people before a decision is taken ❷ meeting someone to get information or advice or looking for it in a book • *a consultation with a doctor*

**consume** VERB consumes, consuming, consumed
❶ to eat or drink something ❷ to use something up • *Much time was consumed in waiting.* ❸ to destroy something • *Fire consumed the building.*

**consumer** NOUN consumers
a person who buys or uses goods or services

**consummate** (say kon-**sum**-at) ADJECTIVE
perfect; highly skilled • *a consummate artist*

**consummate** (say kon-**sum**-ayt)
VERB consummates, consummating, consummated
to make something complete or perfect
➤ **consummation** NOUN

**consumption** NOUN
❶ the using up of something, especially food

or fuel • *Gas consumption increases in cold weather.* ❷ (old use) tuberculosis of the lungs

**contact** NOUN contacts
❶ communication with someone, by speaking or writing to them regularly • *I've lost contact with my uncle.* ❷ if two things are in contact with one another, they are touching • *Don't let the glue come into contact with your skin.* ❸ a person to communicate with when you need information or help

**contact** VERB contacts, contacting, contacted
to get in touch with a person • *You can contact me on this email address.*

**contact lens** NOUN contact lenses
a tiny plastic lens worn against the eyeball, instead of glasses

**contagion** NOUN contagions
a contagious disease

**contagious** ADJECTIVE
a contagious disease is one that spreads by contact with an infected person

**contain** VERB contains, containing, contained
❶ to have something inside • *This book contains a great deal of information.* ❷ to consist of • *A litre contains a hundred centilitres.* ❸ to restrain or hold back a strong feeling • *Try to contain your laughter.*

**container** NOUN containers
❶ a box or bottle etc. designed to contain something ❷ a large box-like object of standard design in which goods are transported

**contaminate** VERB contaminates, contaminating, contaminated
to make a thing dirty or impure or diseased; to pollute something • *The drinking water may have become contaminated.*
➤ **contamination** NOUN

**contemplate** VERB contemplates, contemplating, contemplated
❶ to look at something thoughtfully ❷ to consider or think about doing something • *We are contemplating a visit to London.*
➤ **contemplative** ADJECTIVE

**contemplation** NOUN
thinking deeply about something • *She sat in quiet contemplation.*

**contemporary** ADJECTIVE
❶ living or happening in the same period • *Dickens was contemporary with Thackeray.* ❷ belonging to the present time; modern • *contemporary art*

**contemporary** *NOUN* **contemporaries**
a person who is about the same age as another or is living at the same time • *She was my contemporary at college.*

**contempt** *NOUN*
a feeling of despising a person or thing

**contemptible** *ADJECTIVE*
deserving contempt • *Hurting her feelings like that was a contemptible thing to do.*

**contemptuous** *ADJECTIVE*
feeling or showing contempt • *She gave me a contemptuous look.*
➤ **contemptuously** *ADVERB*

**contend** *VERB* **contends, contending, contended**
❶ to contend with a problem or difficulty is to have to deal with it • *The players also had to contend with wind and rain.* ❷ to compete in a contest ❸ to declare or claim that something is true • *We contend that he is innocent.*

**contender** *NOUN* **contenders**
a person who may win a competition • *She is a contender for a gold medal.*

**content** (say kon-**tent**) *ADJECTIVE*
happy or satisfied

**content** (say kon-**tent**) *NOUN*
a happy or satisfied feeling

**content** (say kon-**tent**) *NOUN*
❶ the amount of a substance in something • *milk with a low fat content* ❷ the subject and ideas dealt with in a book, television programme, speech, etc. • *The content of the essay is good, but there are too many spelling mistakes.*

**content** (say kon-**tent**) *VERB* **contents, contenting, contented**
to make a person happy or satisfied

**contented** *ADJECTIVE*
happy with what you have; satisfied
➤ **contentedly** *ADVERB*

**contention** *NOUN* **contentions**
❶ a point of view or opinion that someone puts forward or arguing ❷ strong disagreement or arguing

**contentment** *NOUN*
a feeling of being happy or satisfied

**contents** (say **kon**-tents) *PLURAL NOUN*
❶ the contents of a box or other container are what is inside it ❷ the contents of a book, magazine, etc. are the things you read in it

**contest** (say **kon**-test) *NOUN* **contests**
a competition; a struggle in which rivals try to obtain something or to be the best

**contest** (say kon-**test**) *VERB* **contests, contesting, contested**
❶ to try to win a competition, election, etc. • *The final was fiercely contested.* ❷ to dispute something or argue that it is wrong or not legal • *Several players contested the referee's decision.*

**contestant** *NOUN* **contestants**
a person taking part in a contest; a competitor

**context** *NOUN* **contexts**
❶ the words that come before and after a particular word or phrase and help to fix its meaning ❷ the background to an event that helps to explain it

**continent** *NOUN* **continents**
one of the main masses of land in the world • *The continents are Europe, Asia, Africa, North America, South America, Australia and Antarctica.*
➤ **continental** *ADJECTIVE*
➤ **the Continent** the mainland of Europe, from the point of view of people living in the British Isles

**contingency** *NOUN* **contingencies**
something that may happen but cannot be known for certain

**contingent** *NOUN* **contingents**
a group that forms part of a larger group or gathering • *The French contingent arrived next.*

**contingent** *ADJECTIVE*
one thing is contingent on another when the first depends on the second • *His future is contingent on success in this exam.*

**continual** *ADJECTIVE*
happening all the time, usually with breaks in between • *Stop this continual quarrelling!*
➤ **continually** *ADVERB*

**USAGE**
Take care not to confuse with **continuous**. You use **continual** to describe something that happens very frequently (*there were continual interruptions*) while you use **continuous** to describe something that happens without a pause (*there is a continuous hum from the fridge*).

a b c d e f g h i j k l m n o p q r s t u v w x y z

151

**continuance** NOUN
(*formal*) continuing something

**continue** VERB continues, continuing, continued
❶ to do something without stopping ❷ to begin again after stopping • *The game will continue after lunch.*
➤ **continuation** NOUN

**continuous** ADJECTIVE
going on and on; without a break
➤ **continuously** ADVERB
➤ **continuity** NOUN

USAGE
See note at **continual**.

**contort** VERB contorts, contorting, contorted
to twist or force something out of the usual shape • *His face was contorted with pain.*
➤ **contortion** NOUN

**contortionist** NOUN contortionists
a person who can twist his or her body into unusual positions

**contour** NOUN contours
❶ a line on a map joining the points that are the same height above sea level ❷ an outline

**contraband** NOUN
smuggled goods

**contraception** NOUN
the use of contraceptives to prevent pregnancy; birth control

**contraceptive** NOUN contraceptives
a substance or device that prevents pregnancy

**contract** (say kon-trakt) NOUN contracts
❶ a formal agreement to do something ❷ a document stating the terms of an agreement

**contract** (say kon-**trakt**) VERB contracts, contracting, contracted
❶ to become smaller or shorter • *Heated metal contracts as it cools.* ❷ to get an illness • *She contracted measles.* ❸ to make a contract

**contraction** NOUN contractions
❶ getting smaller or shorter • *the contraction of a muscle* ❷ a shortened form of a word or words. *Can't* is a contraction of *cannot.*

GRAMMAR
When a word is made shorter by dropping one or more letters, this is called a contraction.

Contractions are used a great deal when writing direct speech, and also in informal writing.

Contractions are written as a single word and use an apostrophe to show where letters have been left out.

*I've finished my homework.*

*I don't think I can come.*

*What's the matter?*

*I'd like to help if I can.*

It is fine to use contractions in informal writing, but in most formal writing, including most school work, you should use the full form of the words.

**contractor** NOUN contractors
a person or company that has a contract to do work for someone else, especially in the building industry

**contradict** VERB contradicts, contradicting, contradicted
❶ to say that something said is not true or that someone is wrong ❷ to say the opposite of something • *These rumours contradict previous ones.*

**contradiction** NOUN contradictions
a statement that is opposite to or different from another one • *There were a number of contradictions in what he told the police.*

**contradictory** ADJECTIVE
being opposite to or not matching something else • *Contradictory reports appeared in the newspapers.*

**contraflow** NOUN contraflows
(*British*) a special arrangement of traffic when a motorway is being repaired, with traffic going in both directions using the carriageway on the other side

**contralto** NOUN contraltos
a female singer with a low voice

**contraption** NOUN contraptions
a strange-looking or complicated device or machine

**contrary** ADJECTIVE
❶ (say kon-tra-ree) completely different or opposed to something • *Contrary to popular belief, many cats dislike milk.* ❷ (say kon-**trair**-ee) awkward and obstinate

**contrary** (say **kon**-tra-ree) NOUN
the opposite

➤ **on the contrary** the opposite is true; certainly not

**contrast** (say kon-trahst) *NOUN* contrasts
❶ a difference clearly seen when things are compared ❷ something showing a clear difference compared with something else

**contrast** (say kon-**trahst**) *VERB* contrasts, contrasting, contrasted
❶ to compare two things in order to show that they are clearly different ❷ to be clearly different when compared

**contravene** *VERB* contravenes, contravening, contravened
to do something that breaks a rule or law
➤ **contravention** *NOUN*

**contribute** *VERB* contributes, contributing, contributed
❶ to give money or help jointly with others ❷ to write something for a newspaper or magazine etc. ❸ to help to cause something • *Fatigue contributed to the accident.*
➤ **contributor** *NOUN*
➤ **contributory** *ADJECTIVE*

**contribution** *NOUN* contributions
money or help that someone gives jointly with others

**contrite** *ADJECTIVE*
very sorry for having done wrong

**contrivance** *NOUN* contrivances
an ingenious device

**contrive** *VERB* contrives, contriving, contrived
❶ to find a way of doing something although it is difficult • *She contrived to get away without anyone seeing her.* ❷ to plan or make something cleverly

**control** *VERB* controls, controlling, controlled
❶ to have the power to make other people or things do what you want ❷ to operate a machine ❸ to hold something, especially anger, in check
➤ **controller** *NOUN*

**control** *NOUN*
controlling a person or thing; authority
➤ **in control** having control of something
➤ **out of control** no longer able to be controlled
➤ **under control** being dealt with successfully

**controls** *PLURAL NOUN*
the switches, buttons, etc. used to control a machine

**control tower** *NOUN* control towers
the building at an airport where people control air traffic by radio

**controversial** *ADJECTIVE*
likely to cause people to have strong opinions and disagree about it • *a controversial issue*

**controversy** (say **kon**-tro-ver-see or kon-**trov**-er-see) *NOUN* controversies
a long argument or disagreement

**contusion** *NOUN* contusions
a bruise

**conundrum** *NOUN* conundrums
a riddle or difficult question

**conurbation** *NOUN* conurbations
a large urban area where towns have spread into each other

**convalesce** *VERB* convalesces, convalescing, convalesced
to be recovering from an illness
➤ **convalescence** *NOUN*
➤ **convalescent** *ADJECTIVE & NOUN*

**convection** *NOUN*
the passing on of heat within liquid, air or gas by circulation of the warmed parts

**convector** *NOUN* convectors
a heater that circulates warm air by convection

**convene** *VERB* convenes, convening, convened
to bring people together or come together for a meeting • *An emergency meeting was convened.*

**convenience** *NOUN* conveniences
❶ the quality of being easy to use or of making it easy for you to do something ❷ something that is convenient ❸ a public toilet
➤ **at your convenience** whenever you find it convenient; as it suits you

**convenience food** *NOUN* convenience foods
food sold in a form that is already partly prepared and so is easy to use

**convenient** *ADJECTIVE*
easy to use or deal with or reach
➤ **conveniently** *ADVERB*

**convent** *NOUN* convents
a place where nuns live and work

**convention** *NOUN* conventions
❶ an accepted way of doing things • *social conventions such as shaking hands* ❷ a large meeting or conference

a
b
c
d
e
f
g
h
i
j
k
l
m
n
o
p
q
r
s
t
u
v
w
x
y
z

**conventional** ADJECTIVE
❶ done or doing things in the normal or accepted way; traditional ❷ conventional weapons are those that are not nuclear
➤ **conventionally** ADVERB

**converge** VERB converges, converging, converged
to come to or towards the same point from different directions • *The two roads converge at the town square.*

**conversant** ADJECTIVE (formal)
familiar with something • *Are you conversant with the rules of this game?*

**conversation** NOUN conversations
an informal talk between two or more people

**conversational** ADJECTIVE
informal; as used in conversation • *She has a conversational style of writing.*

**converse** (say kon-**verss**) VERB converses, conversing, conversed
to have a conversation • *They conversed in low voices.*

**converse** (say **kon**-verss) NOUN
the opposite of something • *In fact, the converse is true.*
➤ **conversely** ADVERB

**conversion** NOUN conversions
❶ changing something from one form, system or use to another • *a conversion table for miles and kilometres* ❷ changing your religion

**convert** (say kon-**vert**) VERB converts, converting, converted
❶ to change something from one form, system or use to another • *Your body converts food into energy.* ❷ to change to a different religion ❸ to kick a goal after scoring a try at rugby football
➤ **converter** NOUN

**convert** (say **kon**-vert) NOUN converts
a person who has changed his or her religion

**convertible** ADJECTIVE
able to be converted

**convertible** NOUN convertibles
a car with a roof that can be folded down or taken off

**convex** ADJECTIVE
curved like the outside of a ball or circle. (The opposite is **concave**.)

**convey** VERB conveys, conveying, conveyed
❶ to communicate a message, idea or feeling • *Please convey my apologies to your mother.*

• *The tone of his voice conveyed his disgust.*
❷ to transport people or goods

**conveyance** NOUN conveyances
❶ transporting people or goods ❷ (formal) a vehicle for transporting people

**conveyancing** NOUN
transferring the legal ownership of land or property from one person to another

**conveyor belt** NOUN conveyor belts
a continuous moving belt for moving objects from one place to another

**convict** (say kon-**vikt**) VERB convicts, convicting, convicted
to convict someone of a crime is to decide at their trial that they are guilty of it

**convict** (say **kon**-vikt) NOUN convicts
a convicted person who is in prison

**conviction** NOUN convictions
❶ being convicted of a crime • *He had several previous convictions for burglary.*
❷ being firmly convinced of something ❸ a firm opinion or belief
➤ **carry conviction** to be convincing

**convince** VERB convinces, convincing, convinced
to make someone feel certain that something is true; to persuade someone to do something

**convincing** ADJECTIVE
❶ able to make someone believe that something is true • *a convincing argument*
❷ a convincing victory is a complete and clear one

**convivial** ADJECTIVE
sociable and lively

**convoluted** ADJECTIVE
❶ complicated and difficult to follow • *a convoluted explanation* ❷ having lots of twists and curves

**convoy** NOUN convoys
a group of ships or vehicles travelling together

**convulse** VERB convulses, convulsing, convulsed
to be convulsed is to have violent movements of the body that you cannot control • *The boys were convulsed with laughter.*
➤ **convulsive** ADJECTIVE

**convulsion** NOUN convulsions
a violent movement of the body that you cannot control

**coo** VERB coos, cooing, cooed
to make a soft murmuring sound like a dove
➤ **coo** NOUN

**cook** VERB cooks, cooking, cooked
to make food ready to eat by heating it
➤ **cook something up** (*informal*) if you cook up a story or plan, you invent it

**cook** NOUN cooks
a person who cooks

**cooker** NOUN cookers
(*British*) a piece of equipment for cooking food

**cookery** NOUN
(*chiefly British*) the skill of cooking food

**cookie** NOUN cookies
(*North American*) a sweet biscuit

**cool** ADJECTIVE
❶ fairly cold; not hot or warm ❷ calm and not easily excited ❸ not friendly or enthusiastic ❹ (*informal*) very good or fashionable • *Hey, cool shoes!*
➤ **coolness** NOUN

**cool** VERB cools, cooling, cooled
to become cool or make something cool
➤ **cooler** NOUN

**coolly** ADVERB
❶ in a calm way ❷ in a slightly unfriendly way

**coop** NOUN coops
a cage for poultry

**cooped up** ADJECTIVE
having to stay in a place which is small and uncomfortable

**cooperate** VERB cooperates, cooperating, cooperated
❶ to work helpfully with other people ❷ to be helpful by doing what someone asks
➤ **cooperative** ADJECTIVE

**cooperation** NOUN
❶ working helpfully with other people ❷ being helpful by doing what someone asks

**co-opt** VERB co-opts, co-opting, co-opted
invite someone to become a member of a committee etc.

**coordinate** VERB coordinates, coordinating, coordinated
to organize people or things to work properly together
➤ **coordinator** NOUN

**coordinate** NOUN coordinates
either of the pair of numbers or letters used to fix the position of a point on a graph or map

**coordination** NOUN
❶ organizing people or things to work properly together ❷ the ability to control the movements of your body well

**coot** NOUN coots
a waterbird with a horny white patch on its forehead

**cop** VERB cops, copping, copped
➤ **cop it** to get into trouble or be punished

**cop** NOUN cops (*informal*)
a police officer

**cope** VERB copes, coping, coped
to manage or deal with something successfully • *I really can't cope with this heat.*

**copier** NOUN copiers
a machine for copying pages

**co-pilot** NOUN co-pilots
a second pilot who helps the main pilot in an aircraft

**coping** NOUN
the top row of stones or bricks in a wall, usually slanted so that rainwater will run off

**copious** ADJECTIVE
plentiful; in large amounts • *She made copious notes at the lecture.*
➤ **copiously** ADVERB

**copper** NOUN coppers
❶ a reddish-brown metal used to make wire, coins, etc. ❷ a reddish-brown colour ❸ (*British*) coppers are brown coins of low value made of copper or bronze ❹ (*British*) (*informal*) a policeman
➤ **copper** ADJECTIVE

**copperplate** NOUN
a style of neat round handwriting
**WORD ORIGIN** because the books of examples of this writing for learners to copy were printed from copper plates

**coppice** NOUN coppices
a small group of trees

**copra** NOUN
dried coconut kernels

**copse** NOUN copses
a small group of trees

**copulate** VERB copulates, copulating, copulated
to have sexual intercourse
➤ **copulation** NOUN

a
b
c
d
e
f
g
h
i
j
k
l
m
n
o
p
q
r
s
t
u
v
w
x
y
z

**copy** NOUN copies
❶ a thing made to look like another ❷ something written or typed out again from its original form ❸ a single book, newspaper, CD, etc. that is one of many produced at the same time

**copy** VERB copies, copying, copied
❶ to make a copy of something ❷ to do the same as someone else; to imitate someone ❸ to copy a computer file or program or piece of text is to make another one that is exactly the same, usually one that you store somewhere else

**copyright** NOUN
the legal right to print a book, reproduce a picture, record a piece of music, etc.

**coquette** (say ko-**ket**) NOUN coquettes
a woman who flirts
➤ **coquettish** ADJECTIVE

**coral** NOUN
❶ a hard red, pink or white substance formed by the skeletons of tiny sea creatures massed together ❷ a pink colour

**cord** NOUN cords
❶ strong thick string made of twisted threads or strands ❷ a piece of flex ❸ a cord-like structure in the body • the spinal cord

SPELLING

Cord is different from chord, which means a number of musical notes sounded together.

**cordial** NOUN cordials
a fruit-flavoured drink

**cordial** ADJECTIVE
warm and friendly • We got a cordial welcome.
➤ **cordially** ADVERB
➤ **cordiality** NOUN

**cordon** NOUN cordons
a line of police, soldiers or vehicles placed round an area to guard or enclose it

**cordon** VERB cordons, cordoning, cordoned
➤ **cordon something off** to stop people entering an area by surrounding it with a ring of police, soldiers or vehicles • Police have cordoned off the street.

**cordon bleu** (say kor-dawn **bler**) ADJECTIVE
of the highest class in cookery

**cords** PLURAL NOUN
trousers made of corduroy

**corduroy** NOUN
a thick cotton cloth with velvety ridges

**core** NOUN cores
❶ the hard central part of an apple or pear etc., containing the seeds ❷ the part in the middle of something ❸ the Earth's core ❹ the most important or basic part of something • This is the core of the problem.

**corgi** NOUN corgis
a small dog with short legs and upright ears

**cork** NOUN corks
❶ the lightweight bark of a kind of oak tree ❷ a stopper for a bottle, made of cork or other material

**cork** VERB corks, corking, corked
to close a bottle or other container with a cork

**corkscrew** NOUN corkscrews
❶ a device for removing corks from bottles ❷ a spiral

**corm** NOUN corms
a part of a plant rather like a bulb

**cormorant** NOUN cormorants
a large black seabird

**corn** NOUN
❶ the seed of wheat and similar plants ❷ a plant, such as wheat, grown for its grain ❸ a small hard painful lump on the foot

**cornea** NOUN corneas
the transparent covering over the pupil of the eye

**corned beef** NOUN
tinned beef preserved with salt

**corner** NOUN corners
❶ the angle or area where two lines or sides or walls meet or where two streets join ❷ a free hit or kick from the corner of a hockey or football field ❸ a remote or distant region • a quiet corner of the world

**corner** VERB corners, cornering, cornered
❶ to drive someone into a corner or other position from which it is difficult to escape • He finally cornered me in the kitchen. ❷ to go round a corner or a bend in the road ❸ to corner the market is to get possession of all or most of something that people want

**cornerstone** NOUN cornerstones
❶ a stone built into the corner at the base of a building ❷ a vitally important part that everything else depends on

**cornet** NOUN cornets
❶ a cone-shaped wafer for holding ice cream ❷ a musical instrument rather like a trumpet but shorter and wider

**cornflakes** *PLURAL NOUN*
toasted maize flakes eaten as a breakfast cereal

**cornflour** *NOUN*
(*British*) flour made from maize or rice, used in sauces and milk puddings

**cornflower** *NOUN* cornflowers
a plant with blue flowers that grows wild in fields of corn

**cornice** *NOUN* cornices
a band of ornamental moulding on walls just below a ceiling or at the top of a building

**cornucopia** *NOUN*
❶ a plentiful supply of good things ❷ a horn-shaped container overflowing with fruit and flowers **WORD ORIGIN** from Latin *cornu* = horn + *copiae* = of plenty

**corny** *ADJECTIVE* cornier, corniest (*informal*)
a corny joke or remark is one that is silly or repeated so often that it no longer has much effect

**corona** (say kor-**oh**-na) *NOUN* coronas
a circle of light round something

**coronary** *NOUN* coronaries
short for **coronary thrombosis**, blockage of an artery carrying blood to the heart

**coronation** *NOUN* coronations
the ceremony of crowning a king or queen

**coroner** *NOUN* coroners
an official who holds an inquiry into the cause of a death thought to be from unnatural causes

**coronet** *NOUN* coronets
a small crown

**corporal** *NOUN* corporals
a soldier ranking next below a sergeant

**corporal punishment** *NOUN*
punishment by hitting or beating someone

**corporate** *ADJECTIVE*
shared by members of a group, especially in business • *corporate responsibility*

**corporation** *NOUN* corporations
❶ a large business company ❷ a group of people elected to govern a town

**corps** (say kor) *NOUN* corps (say korz)
❶ a special army unit • *the Medical Corps* ❷ a large group of soldiers ❸ a set of people doing the same job • *the diplomatic corps*

**corps de ballet** (say kor der **bal**-ay) *NOUN*
the whole group of dancers (not the soloists) in a ballet

**corpse** *NOUN* corpses
a dead body

**corpulent** *ADJECTIVE*
having a bulky body; fat

**corpuscle** *NOUN* corpuscles
one of the red or white cells in blood

**corral** (say kor-**ahl**) *NOUN* corrals (*North American*)
an enclosure for horses or cattle on a farm or ranch

**correct** *ADJECTIVE*
❶ true or accurate; without any mistakes ❷ correct behaviour is behaving properly or in a way that people approve of
➤ **correctness** *NOUN*

**correct** *VERB* corrects, correcting, corrected
❶ to make a thing correct by altering or adjusting it • *She quickly corrected a couple of spelling mistakes.* ❷ to mark the mistakes in something ❸ to tell someone what mistake they have just made • *'It's Tom, not Tim,' he corrected me.*
➤ **corrective** *ADJECTIVE*

**correction** *NOUN* corrections
❶ a change made in something in order to correct it • *I've made a few small corrections to your letter.* ❷ correcting something • *Some of the punctuation may need correction.*

**correctly** *ADVERB*
in the right way, without any mistakes • *He guessed my age correctly.*

**correspond** *VERB* corresponds, corresponding, corresponded
❶ to agree or match • *Your story corresponds with his.* ❷ to be similar or equivalent • *Their assembly corresponds to our parliament.* ❸ people correspond when they write letters to each other

**correspondence** *NOUN*
❶ letters or writing letters ❷ similarity or agreement between things

**SPELLING**
Don't forget the double r in correspondence.

**correspondent** NOUN correspondents
❶ a person who writes letters to someone else ❷ a person employed to gather news and send reports to a newspaper or broadcasting station

**corridor** NOUN corridors
a passage in a building

**corroborate** VERB corroborates, corroborating, corroborated
to help to confirm a statement etc. • *Can anyone corroborate your story?*
➤ **corroboration** NOUN

**corrode** VERB corrodes, corroding, corroded
to destroy metal gradually by chemical action
➤ **corrosion** NOUN

**corrosive** ADJECTIVE
able to corrode something • *corrosive acid*

**corrugated** ADJECTIVE
shaped into alternate ridges and grooves • *a roof made of corrugated iron*

**corrupt** ADJECTIVE
❶ dishonest; willing to accept bribes
❷ wicked or immoral ❸ (*in computing*) corrupt data is unreliable because of errors or faults

**corrupt** VERB corrupts, corrupting, corrupted
❶ to cause someone to become dishonest or wicked ❷ (*in computing*) a bug or other fault corrupts data when it makes it unreliable or impossible to read

**corruption** NOUN
dishonest behaviour by people in authority

**corsair** NOUN corsairs
❶ a pirate ship ❷ a pirate

**corset** NOUN corsets
a close-fitting piece of underwear worn to shape or support the body

**cortège** (say kort-**ay** zh) NOUN cortèges
a funeral procession

**cosh** NOUN coshes
(*British*) a thick heavy stick used as a weapon

**cosine** NOUN cosines
in a right-angled triangle, the ratio of the length of a side adjacent to one of the acute angles to the length of the hypotenuse. Compare with **sine**.

**cosmetic** NOUN cosmetics
a substance put on the face to make it look more attractive, e.g. lipstick or face powder

**cosmetic surgery** NOUN
surgery carried out to make people look more attractive

**cosmic** ADJECTIVE
❶ to do with the universe ❷ to do with outer space • *cosmic rays*

**cosmonaut** NOUN cosmonauts
a Russian astronaut

**cosmopolitan** ADJECTIVE
from many countries; containing people from many countries • *a cosmopolitan city*

**cosmos** (say koz-moss) NOUN
the universe

**Cossack** NOUN Cossacks
a member of a people of south Russia, famous as horsemen

**cosset** VERB cossets, cosseting, cosseted
to pamper someone or treat them very kindly and lovingly

**cost** NOUN costs
❶ the amount of money needed to buy, do or make something ❷ the effort or loss needed to achieve something • *She saved them at the cost of her own life.*
➤ **at all costs** or **at any cost** no matter what the cost or difficulty may be

**cost** VERB costs, costing, cost
❶ to have a certain amount as the price or charge ❷ to cause the loss of something • *This war has cost many lives.* ❸ past tense is **costed** to estimate the cost of something

**costermonger** NOUN costermongers
(*British*) (*old use*) a person who sells fruit and vegetables from a barrow in the street

**costly** ADJECTIVE costlier, costliest
expensive

**cost of living** NOUN
the average amount each person in a country spends on food, clothing and housing

**costume** NOUN costumes
❶ a set or style of clothes, especially for a particular purpose or of a particular place or period ❷ the clothes worn by an actor

**cosy** ADJECTIVE cosier, cosiest
warm and comfortable
➤ **cosily** ADVERB
➤ **cosiness** NOUN

**cosy** NOUN cosies
a cover placed over a teapot or boiled egg to keep it hot

**cot** NOUN cots
(*British*) a baby's bed with high sides

**cottage** NOUN cottages
a small simple house, especially in the country

**cottage cheese** NOUN
soft white cheese made from curds of skimmed milk

**cottage pie** NOUN cottage pies
(*British*) a dish of minced meat covered with mashed potato and baked

**cottager** NOUN cottagers
a person who lives in a country cottage

**cotton** NOUN
❶ a soft white substance covering the seeds of a tropical plant; the plant itself ❷ thread made from this substance ❸ cloth made from cotton thread

**cotton wool** NOUN
soft fluffy wadding originally made from cotton

**couch** NOUN couches
❶ a long soft seat like a sofa but with only one end raised ❷ a sofa or settee

**couch** VERB couches, couching, couched
to express something in words of a certain kind • *The request was couched in polite terms.*

**cougar** (say koo-ger) NOUN cougars
(*North American*) a puma

**cough** (say kof) VERB coughs, coughing, coughed
to send out air from the lungs with a sudden sharp sound

**cough** NOUN coughs
❶ the act or sound of coughing ❷ an illness that makes you cough

**could**
past tense of **can** VERB

**couldn't** (*mainly spoken*)
could not
> SPELLING
> Couldn't = could + not. Add an **apostrophe** between the **n** and the **t**.

**council** NOUN councils
a group of people chosen or elected to organize or discuss something, especially those elected to organize the affairs of a town or county

**council house** NOUN council houses
(*British*) a house owned and let to tenants by a town council

**councillor** NOUN councillors
a member of a town or county council

**council tax** NOUN council taxes
a tax paid to a local authority to pay for local services, based on the estimated value of your house or flat

**counsel** NOUN counsels
❶ (*formal*) advice given by someone • *Thank you, I will follow your counsel.* ❷ a barrister or group of barristers representing someone in a lawsuit
> SPELLING
> Counsel is different from council, which means a group of people chosen to run something.

**counsel** VERB counsels, counselling, counselled
to give advice to someone

**counsellor** NOUN counsellors
a person whose job is to give advice

**count** VERB counts, counting, counted
❶ to find the total of something by using numbers ❷ to say a sequence of numbers in their proper order ❸ to include something in a total • *There are six of us, counting the dog.* ❹ to be important • *It's what you do that counts.* ❺ to regard or consider something in a particular way • *I should count it an honour to be invited.*
> count on someone or something to rely on a person or thing

**count** NOUN counts
❶ a number reached by counting • *On the count of three, let go of the rope.* ❷ each of the points being considered, e.g. in accusing someone of crimes • *He was found guilty on all counts.* ❸ a foreign nobleman

**countdown** NOUN countdowns
counting numbers backwards to zero before an event, especially the launching of a space rocket

**countenance** NOUN countenances
a person's face or the expression on a person's face

**countenance** VERB countenances, countenancing, countenanced
to give approval to or allow something • *Will they countenance this plan?*

**counter** NOUN counters
❶ a flat surface over which customers are served in a shop, bank or office ❷ a small round playing piece used in certain board games ❸ a device for counting things

**counter** VERB counters, countering, countered
❶ to reply to someone by trying to prove that what they said is not true • *'No, I never said that,' Chris countered.* ❷ to try to reduce or prevent the bad effects of something

**counter** ADVERB
contrary to something • *This is counter to what we really want.*

**counteract** VERB counteracts, counteracting, counteracted
to act against something and reduce or prevent its effects

**counter-attack** VERB counter-attacks, counter-attacking, counter-attacked
to attack in response to an enemy's attack
➤ counter-attack NOUN

**counterbalance** NOUN counterbalances
a weight or influence that balances another
➤ counterbalance VERB

**counterfeit** (say **kownt**-er-feet) ADJECTIVE
fake; not genuine • *They were using counterfeit money.*

**counterfeit** NOUN counterfeits
a forgery or imitation

**counterfeit** VERB counterfeits, counterfeiting, counterfeited
to forge or make an imitation of something

**counterfoil** NOUN counterfoils
(*British*) a section of a cheque or receipt etc. that is torn off and kept as a record

**counterpane** NOUN counterpanes
a bedspread

**counterpart** NOUN counterparts
a person or thing that corresponds to another • *Their President is the counterpart of our Prime Minister.*

**counterpoint** NOUN
a method of combining melodies in harmony

**countersign** VERB countersigns, countersigning, countersigned
to add another signature to a document to give it authority

**counterweight** NOUN
a counterbalancing weight or influence

**countess** NOUN countesses
the wife or widow of a count or earl; a female count

**countless** ADJECTIVE
too many to count • *I have told you countless times.*

**countrified** ADJECTIVE
like the countryside

**country** NOUN countries
❶ the land occupied by a nation ❷ all the people of a country ❸ the countryside

**country dance** NOUN country dances
a folk dance

**countryman** NOUN countrymen
❶ a man who lives in the countryside ❷ a man who comes from the same country as you do

**countryside** NOUN
an area with fields, woods, villages, etc. away from towns

**countrywoman** NOUN countrywomen
❶ a woman who lives in the countryside ❷ a woman who comes from the same country as you do

**county** NOUN counties
each of the main areas that a country is divided into for local government

**coup** (say koo) NOUN coups
❶ the sudden overthrow of a government; a coup d'état ❷ a sudden action taken to win power; a clever victory WORD ORIGIN French, = a blow

**coup de grâce** (say koo der **grahs**) NOUN
a stroke or blow that puts an end to something WORD ORIGIN French, = mercy-blow

**coup d'état** (say koo day-**tah**) NOUN coups d'état
the sudden overthrow of a government WORD ORIGIN French, = blow of State

**couple** NOUN couples
two people or things considered together; a pair

**couple** VERB couples, coupling, coupled
to fasten or link two things together • *The fog, coupled with the amount of traffic, made driving very difficult.*

**couplet** NOUN couplets
a pair of lines in rhyming verse

**coupon** NOUN coupons
a piece of paper that gives you the right to receive or do something

**courage** NOUN
the ability to face danger or difficulty or pain even when you are afraid; bravery

**courageous** ADJECTIVE
ready to face danger or difficulty or pain even when you are afraid

**courgette** (say koor-zh et) NOUN courgettes
(British) a kind of small vegetable marrow

**courier** (say koor-ee-er) NOUN couriers
❶ a messenger who takes goods or documents ❷ a person employed to guide and help a group of tourists

**course** NOUN courses
❶ the direction followed by something • The ship's course was to the west. ❷ a series of events or actions; a way of proceeding • Your best course is to start again. ❸ a series of lessons or exercises in learning something ❹ part of a meal • the meat course ❺ a racecourse or golf course
➤ in the course of something during something • He mentioned it in the course of the conversation.
➤ of course without a doubt; as we expected

**course** VERB courses, coursing, coursed
to move or flow freely • Tears coursed down his cheeks.

**court** NOUN courts
❶ the royal household ❷ a law court; the judges and lawyers in a law court ❸ an enclosed area for games such as tennis or netball ❹ a courtyard

**court** VERB courts, courting, courted
❶ to try to get someone's support ❷ (old use) to try to win someone's love

**courteous** (say ker-tee-us) ADJECTIVE
polite and helpful
➤ courteously ADVERB

**courtesy** (say ker-tiss-ee) NOUN
polite behaviour towards other people • She didn't even have the courtesy to say she was sorry.

**courtier** NOUN courtiers (old use)
one of a king's or queen's companions at court

**courtly** ADJECTIVE
dignified and polite

**court martial** NOUN courts martial
❶ a court for trying members of the armed services who have broken military law ❷ a trial in this court

**court-martial** VERB court-martials, court-martialling, court-martialled
to try a person by a court martial

**courtship** NOUN
❶ (old use) a period of courting someone in the hope of marrying them ❷ the mating ritual of some birds and animals • a courtship display

**courtyard** NOUN courtyards
a space surrounded by walls or buildings

**cousin** NOUN cousins
a child of your uncle or aunt

**cove** NOUN coves
a small bay

**coven** (say kuv-en) NOUN covens
a group of witches

**covenant** (say kuv-en-ant) NOUN covenants
a formal agreement or contract

**Coventry** NOUN
➤ send a person to Coventry to refuse to speak to him or her
( WORD ORIGIN ) possibly because, during the English Civil War, Cavalier prisoners were sent to Coventry (a city in the Midlands): the citizens supported the Roundheads, and would not speak to the Cavaliers

**cover** VERB covers, covering, covered
❶ to place one thing over or round another; to conceal something ❷ to deal with or include a particular subject • The book covers all aspects of photography. ❸ to travel a certain distance • We covered ten miles a day. ❹ to aim a gun at or near somebody • I've got you covered. ❺ to protect something by insurance or a guarantee • These goods are covered against fire or theft. ❻ to be enough money to pay for something • Do you have enough to cover your fare?
➤ cover something up to conceal an awkward fact or piece of information

**cover** NOUN covers
❶ a thing used for covering something else; a lid, wrapper, envelope, etc. ❷ the binding of a book ❸ a place where you can hide or take shelter • We took cover from the rain under a tree.

**coverage** NOUN
the amount of time or space given to reporting an event in a newspaper or broadcast

**coverlet** NOUN coverlets
a bedspread

**covert** (say **kuv**-ert) NOUN coverts
an area of thick bushes in which birds and animals hide

**covert** (say koh-**vert**) ADJECTIVE
done secretly • *a covert police operation*

**cover-up** NOUN cover-ups
an attempt to conceal information about something, especially a crime or mistake

**covet** (say **kuv**-it) VERB covets, coveting, coveted
to wish to have something that belongs to someone else • *She had always coveted her sister's room.*
➤ **covetous** ADJECTIVE

**covey** (say **kuv**-ee) NOUN coveys
a group of partridges

**cow** NOUN cows
❶ the fully-grown female of cattle ❷ the fully-grown female of certain large animals, e.g. the elephant, whale or seal

**cow** VERB cows, cowing, cowed
to frighten someone into doing what you want them to • *Everyone looked cowed and weary.*

**coward** NOUN cowards
a person who has no courage and shows fear in a shameful way
➤ **cowardice** NOUN

**cowardly** ADJECTIVE
behaving like a coward; lacking courage

**cowboy** NOUN cowboys
a man in charge of grazing cattle on a ranch in the USA

**cower** VERB cowers, cowering, cowered
to crouch or shrink back in fear

**cowl** NOUN cowls
❶ a monk's hood ❷ a hood-shaped covering, e.g. on a chimney

**cowshed** NOUN cowsheds
a shed for cattle

**cowslip** NOUN cowslips
a wild plant with small yellow flowers in spring

**cox** NOUN coxes
a person who steers a rowing boat

**coxswain** (say **kok**-swayn or **kok**-sun) NOUN coxswains
❶ a cox ❷ a sailor with special duties

**coy** ADJECTIVE
pretending to be shy or modest
➤ **coyly** ADVERB

**coyote** (say koi-**oh**-ti) NOUN coyotes
a North American mammal, similar to but smaller than a wolf

**crab** NOUN crabs
a shellfish with ten legs, the first pair being a set of pincers

**crab apple** NOUN crab apples
a small sour apple

**crack** NOUN cracks
❶ a line on the surface of something where it has broken but not come completely apart ❷ a narrow gap ❸ a sudden sharp noise • *the crack of a pistol shot* ❹ a hard knock or blow • *a crack on the head* ❺ (*informal*) a joke; a wisecrack ❻ a drug made from cocaine

**crack** ADJECTIVE (*informal*) first-class • *He is a crack shot.*

**crack** VERB cracks, cracking, cracked
❶ to make a crack in something ❷ to split without breaking • *The plate has cracked.* ❸ to make a sudden sharp noise ❹ to break down • *He finally cracked under the strain.* ❺ to solve a problem • *Have you cracked the code yet?*
➤ **crack a joke** to tell a joke
➤ **crack down on something** (*informal*) to stop something that is illegal or against rules
➤ **get cracking** (*informal*) to get busy

**cracker** NOUN crackers
❶ a paper tube that bangs when pulled apart ❷ a thin biscuit

**crackle** VERB crackles, crackling, crackled
to make small cracking sounds • *The fire crackled in the grate.*
➤ **crackle** NOUN

**crackling** NOUN
crisp skin on roast pork

**cradle** NOUN cradles
❶ a small cot for a baby ❷ a supporting framework

**cradle** VERB cradles, cradling, cradled
to hold someone or something gently and protectively • *She was cradling a kitten in her arms.*

**craft** NOUN crafts
❶ a job that needs skill, especially with the hands ❷ skill in doing your work • *He is a master of the craft of cooking.* ❸ cunning or trickery ❹ craft a ship or boat; an aircraft or spacecraft

**craftsman, craftswoman** NOUN craftsmen
or craftswomen
a person who is good at a craft
➤ **craftsmanship** NOUN

**crafty** ADJECTIVE craftier, craftiest
cunning or deceitful
➤ **craftily** ADVERB
➤ **craftiness** NOUN

**crag** NOUN crags
a steep piece of rough rock

**craggy** ADJECTIVE
❶ steep and rocky • *a craggy coastline* ❷ a
craggy face is strong and has deep lines in it
• *his craggy features*

**cram** VERB crams, cramming, crammed
❶ to push many things into something so
that it is very full • *I managed to cram all
my clothes into one bag.* ❷ to learn as many
facts as you can in a short time just before an
examination

**cramp** NOUN cramps
pain caused by a muscle tightening suddenly

**cramp** VERB cramps, cramping, cramped
to hinder someone's freedom or growth

**cramped** ADJECTIVE
in a space that is too small or tight • *The four
of us felt cramped sleeping in the same room.*

**cranberry** NOUN cranberries
a small sour red berry used for making jelly
and sauce

**crane** NOUN cranes
❶ a machine for lifting and moving heavy
objects ❷ a large wading bird with long legs
and a long slender neck

**crane** VERB cranes, craning, craned
to crane your neck is to stretch it to try to see
something

**crane fly** NOUN crane flies
a flying insect with very long thin legs

**cranium** NOUN craniums
the skull

**crank** NOUN cranks
❶ an L-shaped part used for changing the
direction of movement in machinery ❷ a
person with strange or fanatical ideas

**crank** VERB cranks, cranking, cranked
to turn or move something using a crank

**cranky** ADJECTIVE (*informal*)
❶ strange or fanatical • *cranky ideas* ❷ bad-
tempered

**cranny** NOUN crannies
a narrow hole or space; a crevice

**crash** NOUN crashes
❶ the loud noise of something breaking or
colliding ❷ an accident in which a vehicle hits
something violently and is badly damaged • *a
car crash* ❸ a sudden drop or failure

**crash** VERB crashes, crashing, crashed
❶ a vehicle crashes when it hits something
violently and is badly damage • *We crashed
into the car in front.* ❷ to move or fall with
a crash • *The tree crashed to the ground.*
❸ a computer system crashes when it stops
working suddenly

**crash** ADJECTIVE
done rapidly and intensively • *a crash course*

**crash helmet** NOUN crash helmets
a padded helmet worn by cyclists and
motorcyclists to protect the head

**crash landing** NOUN crash landings
an emergency landing of an aircraft, which
usually damages it
➤ **crash-land** VERB

**crass** ADJECTIVE
very stupid or insensitive • *crass remarks*

**crate** NOUN crates
❶ a packing case made of strips of wood
❷ an open container with compartments for
carrying bottles

**crater** NOUN craters
❶ the mouth of a volcano ❷ a wide hole
in the ground caused by an explosion or by
something hitting it • *the Moon's craters*

**cravat** NOUN cravats
a short wide scarf worn by men round the
neck and tucked into an open-necked shirt
**WORD ORIGIN** from French *Cravate* = Croatian
(because Croatian soldiers wore linen cravats)

**crave** VERB craves, craving, craved
❶ to want something very strongly
❷ (*formal*) to beg for something • *I humbly
crave forgiveness.*

**craven** ADJECTIVE
cowardly

**craving** NOUN cravings
a strong desire; a longing

**crawl** VERB crawls, crawling, crawled
❶ to move with the body close to the ground
or other surface or on hands and knees
❷ traffic crawls when it moves slowly ❸ a
place is crawling with unpleasant things or

people when there are a lot of them there
• *The floor was crawling with insects.*

**crawl** NOUN
❶ a crawling movement ❷ a very slow pace
❸ an overarm swimming stroke

**crayon** NOUN crayons
a stick or pencil of coloured wax etc. for
drawing

**craze** NOUN crazes
a brief enthusiasm for something

**crazed** ADJECTIVE
driven insane

**crazy** ADJECTIVE crazier, craziest
❶ insane ❷ very foolish • *this crazy idea*
➤ **crazily** ADVERB
➤ **craziness** NOUN

**crazy paving** NOUN
(*British*) paving made of pieces of stone of
different shapes and sizes fitted together

**creak** NOUN creaks
a harsh squeak like that of a stiff door hinge

**creak** VERB creaks, creaking, creaked
to make a creak

**creaky** ADJECTIVE
making creaks • *creaky floorboards*

**cream** NOUN creams
❶ the fatty part of milk ❷ a yellowish-white
colour ❸ a food containing or looking like
cream • *chocolate cream* ❹ a soft substance
• *face cream* ❺ the best people or things
• *the cream of the world's tennis players*

**cream** VERB creams, creaming, creamed
to make something creamy; to beat a mixture
until it is soft like cream
➤ **cream something off** to remove the best
part of something • *The big clubs cream off
the best young players.*

**creamy** ADJECTIVE creamier, creamiest
❶ smooth and thick like cream ❷ pale
yellowish-white in colour • *creamy skin*

**crease** NOUN creases
❶ a line made in something by folding,
pressing or crushing it ❷ a line on a cricket
pitch marking a batsman's or bowler's
position

**crease** VERB creases, creasing, creased
to make a crease or creases in something

**create** VERB creates, creating, created
❶ to make or produce something, especially
something that no one has made before ❷ to
bring something into existence; to make

something happen • *The bad weather created
huge problems for us.*

**creation** NOUN creations
❶ the act of creating something
❷ something that has been created

**creative** ADJECTIVE
showing imagination and thought as well as
skill • *his creative use of language*
➤ **creativity** NOUN

**creator** NOUN creators
a person who creates something
➤ **the Creator** a name for God

**creature** NOUN creatures
a living being, especially an animal

**crèche** (say kresh) NOUN crèches
a place where babies and young children are
looked after while their parents are at work

**credence** NOUN
if you give credence to something, you
believe that it is true • *He gave no credence
to their story.*

**credentials** PLURAL NOUN
❶ documents showing a person's identity,
qualifications, etc. ❷ a person's past
achievements that make them suitable for
something

**credible** ADJECTIVE
able to be believed; convincing
➤ **credibly** ADVERB
➤ **credibility** NOUN

> **USAGE**
> Take care not to confuse with **credulous**.

**credit** NOUN credits
❶ a source of pride or honour • *He is a credit
to the school.* ❷ praise or acknowledgement
given for some achievement or good quality
• *I must give you credit for persistence.*
❸ an arrangement allowing a person to buy
something and not pay for it until later on
❹ an amount of money in an account at a
bank etc. or entered in a financial account as
paid in. Compare with **debit**. ❺ belief or trust
• *I put no credit in this rumour.*
➤ **credits** a list of people who have helped to
produce a film or television programme

**credit** VERB credits, crediting, credited
❶ to believe something ❷ to believe or
say that a person has done or achieved
something • *Columbus is credited with the
discovery of America.* ❸ to enter something
as a credit in a financial account. Compare
with **debit**.

**creditable** ADJECTIVE
deserving praise • *That was a very creditable result.*
➤ **creditably** ADVERB

**credit card** NOUN credit cards
a plastic card that you can use to buy something and pay for it later on

**creditor** NOUN creditors
a person to whom money is owed

**credulous** ADJECTIVE
too ready to believe things; gullible

USAGE
Take care not to confuse with credible.

**creed** NOUN creeds
a set or formal statement of religious beliefs

**creek** NOUN creeks
❶ (*British*) a narrow inlet ❷ (*North American & Australian*) a small stream
➤ up the creek (*informal*) in difficulties

**creep** VERB creeps, creeping, crept
❶ to move quietly and slowly • *She crept into the room so as not to wake him.* ❷ to move along close to the ground ❸ to appear or increase gradually • *A slight feeling of suspicion crept over me.* ❹ your flesh creeps when it prickles with fear

**creep** NOUN creeps
(*informal*) an unpleasant person, especially one who is always trying to get other people's approval
➤ the creeps (*informal*) a feeling or fear or disgust • *There's something about him that gives me the creeps.*

SPELLING
The past tense of creep is crept. Do not add ed.

**creeper** NOUN creepers
a plant that grows along the ground or up a wall

**creepy** ADJECTIVE creepier, creepiest
(*informal*) slightly frightening and sinister

**cremate** VERB cremates, cremating, cremated
to burn a dead body to ashes
➤ **cremation** NOUN

**crematorium** NOUN crematoria
a place where dead people are cremated

**crème de la crème** (say krem der la krem) NOUN
the very best of something

**creosote** NOUN
an oily brown liquid painted on wood to prevent it from rotting

**crêpe** (say krayp) NOUN crêpes
a thin pancake

**crêpe paper** NOUN
paper with a wrinkled surface

**crescendo** (say krish-**end**-oh) NOUN crescendos
a gradual increase in loudness

**crescent** NOUN crescents
❶ a narrow curved shape coming to a point at each end ❷ a curved street forming an arc
WORD ORIGIN originally = the new moon: from Latin *crescens* = growing

**cress** NOUN
a plant with hot-tasting leaves, used in salads and sandwiches

**crest** NOUN crests
❶ a tuft of hair, skin or feathers on an animal's or bird's head ❷ the top of a hill or wave ❸ a design used as the symbol of a family or organization
➤ **crested** ADJECTIVE

**crestfallen** ADJECTIVE
disappointed or dejected

**cretin** (say **kret**-in) NOUN cretins (*offensive*)
a stupid person

**crevasse** (say kri-**vass**) NOUN crevasses
a deep open crack, especially in a glacier

**crevice** NOUN crevices
a narrow opening, especially in a rock or wall

**crew** NOUN crews
❶ the people working in a ship or aircraft ❷ a group working together • *a film crew*

**crew** VERB
past tense of crow VERB

**crib** NOUN cribs
❶ a baby's cot ❷ a framework holding fodder for animals ❸ a model representing the Nativity of Jesus Christ ❹ a piece of paper with answers to questions on it, used dishonestly by a student in an examination ❺ cribbage

**crib** VERB cribs, cribbing, cribbed
to copy someone else's work

**cribbage** NOUN
a card game

**crick** NOUN cricks
painful stiffness in the neck or back

**cricket** NOUN
❶ a game played outdoors between teams with a ball, bats and two wickets ❷ a brown insect like a grasshopper
➤ **cricketer** NOUN

**crime** NOUN crimes
❶ breaking the law • *They say crime does not pay.* ❷ an act that breaks the law • *Arson is a very serious crime.*

**criminal** NOUN criminals
a person who has committed a crime or crimes

**criminal** ADJECTIVE
to do with crime or criminals
➤ **criminally** ADVERB

**criminology** NOUN
the study of crime

**crimp** VERB crimps, crimping, crimped
to press something into small ridges

**crimson** ADJECTIVE
deep red
➤ **crimson** NOUN
**WORD ORIGIN** from Arabic *kirmiz* = an insect which was used to make crimson dye

**cringe** VERB cringes, cringing, cringed
❶ to shrink back in fear; to cower ❷ to feel embarrassed • *I cringe when I think of the stories I used to write.*

**crinkle** VERB crinkles, crinkling, crinkled
to make something have creases or wrinkles in it • *The boy crinkled his nose.*
➤ **crinkly** ADJECTIVE

**crinoline** NOUN crinolines
a long skirt worn over a framework that makes it stand out

**cripple** NOUN cripples
a person who is permanently lame

**cripple** VERB cripples, crippling, crippled
❶ to make a person lame ❷ to weaken or damage something seriously

**crisis** NOUN crises
an important and dangerous or difficult situation • *The country was facing a financial crisis.*

**crisp** ADJECTIVE
❶ very dry so that it breaks with a snap ❷ fresh and stiff • *a crisp £10 note* ❸ cold and dry • *a crisp winter morning* ❹ brisk and sharp • *He has a crisp manner.*
➤ **crispness** NOUN

**crisp** NOUN crisps
a very thin fried slice of potato, usually sold in packets

**crisply** ADVERB
in a brisk and sharp way • *'Take a seat,'* she said crisply.

**criss-cross** ADJECTIVE & ADVERB
with crossing lines

**criss-cross** VERB criss-crosses, criss-crossing, criss-crossed
to form a pattern of crossing lines

**criterion** (say kry-teer-ee-on) NOUN criteria
a standard or principle by which something is judged or decided

**USAGE**

Note that **criteria** is a plural. You should say *this criterion* and *these criteria*, and not *'this criteria'*.

**critic** NOUN critics
❶ a person who gives opinions on books, plays, films, music, etc. ❷ a person who criticizes

**critical** ADJECTIVE
❶ pointing out faults or weaknesses in a person or thing • *Why do you always have to be so critical?* ❷ to do with or at a crisis; very serious • *The patient is in a critical condition.* ❸ to do with critics or criticism

**critically** ADVERB
❶ extremely and seriously • *She is critically ill.* ❷ in a critical way

**criticism** NOUN criticisms
❶ pointing out faults and weaknesses ❷ the work of a critic

**criticize** (also **criticise**) VERB criticizes, criticizing, criticized
to say that a person or thing has faults or weaknesses

**croak** NOUN croaks
a deep hoarse sound like that of a frog

**croak** VERB croaks, croaking, croaked
to make a croak

**crochet** (say kroh-shay) NOUN
a kind of needlework done by using a hooked needle to loop a thread into patterns
➤ **crochet** VERB crochets, crocheting, crocheted

**crock** NOUN crocks
❶ a piece of crockery ❷ (British) (informal) an old person or an old car in a bad condition

**crockery** NOUN
dishes, plates, cups, etc.

**crocodile** NOUN crocodiles
❶ a large tropical reptile with a thick skin, long tail and huge jaws ❷ a long line of schoolchildren walking in pairs
➤ **crocodile tears** sorrow that is not sincere (so called because the crocodile was said to weep while it ate its victim)

**crocus** NOUN crocuses
a small plant with yellow, purple or white flowers

**croft** NOUN crofts
(British) a small rented farm in Scotland
➤ **crofter** NOUN

**croissant** (say **krwah**-sahn) NOUN croissants
a flaky crescent-shaped bread roll
(WORD ORIGIN) French, = crescent

**crone** NOUN crones
a very old woman

**crony** NOUN cronies
a close friend or companion

**crook** NOUN crooks
❶ (informal) a thief or other criminal ❷ a shepherd's stick with a curved end ❸ a bend at the elbow

**crook** VERB crooks, crooking, crooked
to crook a finger is to bend or curl it

**crook** ADJECTIVE (Australian/NZ) (informal)
bad or unwell

**crooked** ADJECTIVE
❶ bent or twisted; not straight ❷ dishonest or criminal

**croon** VERB croons, crooning, crooned
to sing softly and gently

**crop** NOUN crops
❶ a plant grown in large quantities for food • a good crop of wheat ❷ a very short haircut ❸ a whip with a loop instead of a lash ❹ a pouch in a bird's throat, where it stores food

**crop** VERB crops, cropping, cropped
❶ to cut something or bite the top off it • Sheep were cropping the grass. ❷ to produce a crop
➤ **crop up** to happen or appear unexpectedly • His name just cropped up in conversation.

**cropper** NOUN
➤ **come a cropper** (informal)
❶ to have a bad fall ❷ to fail badly

**croquet** (say **kroh**-kay) NOUN
a game played on a lawn with wooden balls and mallets

**crore** NOUN crore
(Indian) ten million; one hundred lakhs

**crosier** (say **kroh**-zee-er) NOUN crosiers
a bishop's staff shaped like a shepherd's crook

**cross** NOUN crosses
❶ a mark or shape made like + or x ❷ an upright post with another piece of wood across it, used in ancient times for crucifixion; **the Cross** the cross on which Christ was crucified, used as a symbol of Christianity ❸ a mixture of two different things • She gave a cross between a groan and a laugh.

**cross** VERB crosses, crossing, crossed
❶ to go across something • She crossed the room to meet him. ❷ to cross your arms, legs or fingers is to put one over the other ❸ to draw a line or lines across something ❹ to make the sign or shape of a cross ❺ to cross animals or plants of different kinds is to produce a new animal or plant from them
➤ **cross something out** to draw a line across something because it is unwanted or wrong

**cross** ADJECTIVE
❶ annoyed or bad-tempered ❷ going from one side to another • There were cross winds on the bridge.
➤ **crossly** ADVERB

**crossbar** NOUN crossbars
a horizontal bar between two uprights

**crossbow** NOUN crossbows
a powerful bow with a mechanism for pulling and releasing the string

**cross-breed** VERB cross-breeds, cross-breeding, cross-bred
to breed by mating an animal with one of a different kind
➤ **cross-breed** NOUN
Compare with **hybrid**.

**crosse** NOUN crosses
a hooked stick with a net across it, used in lacrosse

**cross-examine** VERB cross-examines, cross-examining, cross-examined
to question a witness called by the other side in a law court, to check the evidence they have already given
➤ **cross-examination** NOUN

**cross-eyed** ADJECTIVE
with eyes that look or seem to look towards the nose

a b c d e f g h i j k l m n o p q r s t u v w x y z

**crossfire** NOUN
lines of gunfire that cross each other

**cross-hatch** VERB cross-hatches, cross-hatching, cross-hatched
to shade part of a drawing with two sets of parallel lines crossing each other
➤ **cross-hatching** NOUN

**crossing** NOUN crossings
a place where people can cross a road or railway

**cross-legged** ADJECTIVE & ADVERB
with ankles crossed and knees spread apart

**cross-question** VERB cross-questions, cross-questioning, cross-questioned
to question someone carefully in order to test answers they have already given

**cross-reference** NOUN cross-references
a note telling readers to look at another part of a book etc. for more information

**crossroads** NOUN crossroads
a place where two or more roads cross one another

**cross-section** NOUN cross-sections
❶ a drawing of something as if it has been cut through ❷ a typical sample from a larger group

**crosswise** ADVERB & ADJECTIVE
with one thing crossing another

**crossword** NOUN crosswords
a puzzle in which words have to be guessed from clues and then written into the blank squares in a diagram

**crotch** NOUN crotches
the part between the legs where they join the body; a similar angle in a forked part

**crotchet** NOUN crotchets
a note in music, which usually represents one beat (written ♩)

**crotchety** ADJECTIVE
bad-tempered or irritable

**crouch** VERB crouches, crouching, crouched
to lower your body, with your arms and legs bent • *He crouched down beside her.*

**croup** (say kroop) NOUN
a disease causing a hard cough and difficulty in breathing

**crow** NOUN crows
❶ a large black bird ❷ a shrill cry like that of a cock
➤ **as the crow flies** in a straight line

**crow** VERB crows, crowing, crowed or crew
❶ to make a shrill cry as a cock does ❷ to boast or be triumphant • *He's crowing because he beat me at table tennis.*

**crowbar** NOUN crowbars
an iron bar used as a lever

**crowd** NOUN crowds
a large number of people in one place

**crowd** VERB crowds, crowding, crowded
❶ to come together in large numbers; to form a crowd • *Photographers crowded around outside.* ❷ to make a place uncomfortably full of people • *Tourists crowded the streets.* • *Somehow we all crowded into their small living room.*

**crowded** ADJECTIVE
full of people • *a crowded bus*

**crown** NOUN crowns
❶ an ornamental headdress worn by a king or queen ❷ (often **Crown**) the king or queen • *This land belongs to the Crown.* ❸ the highest part • *the crown of the road* ❹ a former coin worth 5 shillings (25p)
➤ **Crown Prince** or **Crown Princess** the heir to the throne

**crown** VERB crowns, crowning, crowned
❶ to place a crown on someone as a symbol of royal power or victory ❷ to form or cover or decorate the top of something • *The mountain was crowned with snow.* ❸ to reward something; to make a successful end to something • *Our efforts were crowned with victory.* ❹ (*informal*) to hit someone on the head

**Crown Court** NOUN Crown Courts
a law court where criminal cases are tried

**crow's nest** NOUN crow's nests
a lookout platform high up on a ship's mast

**crucial** (say kroo-shal) ADJECTIVE
extremely important because it will affect other things • *a crucial decision* • *It is crucial that we get this right.*

**crucible** NOUN crucibles
a melting pot for metals

**crucifix** NOUN crucifixes
a model of a cross with a figure of Christ on it

**crucify** VERB crucifies, crucifying, crucified
to put a person to death by nailing or tying their hands and feet to a cross
➤ **crucifixion** NOUN

**crude** ADJECTIVE
❶ in a natural state; not yet processed or

refined • *crude oil* ❷ not well finished; rough and simple • *a crude carving* ❸ rude or coarse
➤ **crudely** ADVERB

**cruel** ADJECTIVE crueller, cruellest
deliberately causing pain or suffering to others
➤ **cruelly** ADVERB

**cruelty** NOUN cruelties
cruel behaviour • *He has campaigned against cruelty to animals.*

**cruet** NOUN cruets
a set of small containers for salt, pepper, oil, etc. for use at the table

**cruise** NOUN cruises
a voyage on a ship, taken as a holiday

**cruise** VERB cruises, cruising, cruised
❶ to sail or travel at a gentle or steady speed ❷ to have a cruise

**cruiser** NOUN cruisers
❶ a fast warship ❷ a large motor boat

**crumb** NOUN crumbs
a tiny piece of bread, cake or biscuit

**crumble** VERB crumbles, crumbling, crumbled
❶ to break something into small pieces • *We crumbled up some bread and threw it to the birds.* ❷ to fall or break into small pieces
• *The castle walls were beginning to crumble.*

**crumble** NOUN crumbles (*British*) a dessert made with fruit cooked with a crumbly topping • *apple crumble*

**crumbly** ADJECTIVE
that easily breaks into small pieces • *crumbly cheese*

**crumpet** NOUN crumpets
a soft flat cake made with yeast, eaten toasted with butter

**crumple** VERB crumples, crumpling, crumpled
to crush something or become crushed, into creases or folds • *He crumpled the letter into a ball and threw it away.* • *The front of the car crumpled when it hit the wall.*

**crunch** VERB crunches, crunching, crunched
to crush something noisily, for example between your teeth or under your feet • *We crunched through the snow.*

**crunch** NOUN crunches
a crunching sound
➤ **the crunch** (*informal*) a crucial event or turning point

**crunchy** ADJECTIVE
crunchy food is firm and crisp and makes a noise when you bite it • *a crunchy apple*

**Crusade** NOUN Crusades
a military expedition made by Christians in the Middle Ages to recover the Holy Land from the Muslims who had conquered it
➤ **Crusader** NOUN

**crusade** NOUN crusades
a campaign against something you believe is wrong or to achieve something you believe is right

**crush** VERB crushes, crushing, crushed
❶ to press or squeeze something so that it gets broken or harmed ❷ to break something into very small pieces or powder • *Now crush the garlic.* ❸ to defeat someone completely
• *The army soon crushed the rebellion.*

**crush** NOUN crushes
❶ a crowd of people pressed together ❷ a drink made with crushed fruit

**crust** NOUN crusts
❶ the hard outer layer of something, especially bread ❷ the rocky outer layer of the earth

**crustacean** (say krust-**ay**-shon) NOUN crustaceans
an animal with a shell that lives in water, e.g. a crab, lobster or shrimp

**crusty** ADJECTIVE crustier, crustiest
❶ having a crisp crust ❷ bad-tempered or irritable

**crutch** NOUN crutches
a support like a long walking stick for helping a lame person to walk

**cry** NOUN cries
❶ a loud wordless sound expressing pain, grief, joy, etc. ❷ a shout • *No one heard her cries for help.* ❸ the special sound made by a bird or animal ❹ crying • *Have a good cry.*

**cry** VERB cries, crying, cried
❶ to shed tears; to weep ❷ to call out loudly
➤ **cry off** to say that you cannot do something that you had promised to do

**crypt** NOUN crypts
a room under a church, used as a chapel or burial place

**cryptic** ADJECTIVE
having a hidden meaning that is not easy to understand • *a cryptic remark*
➤ **cryptically** ADVERB

**cryptogram** NOUN cryptograms
something written in code

**crystal** NOUN crystals
❶ a transparent colourless mineral rather like glass ❷ very clear high-quality glass ❸ a small solid piece of a substance with a symmetrical shape • ice crystals

**crystalline** ADJECTIVE
made of crystals or having the structure of crystals

**crystallize** (also **crystallise**) VERB crystallizes, crystallizing, crystallized
❶ to form into crystals ❷ to become definite in form • The solution to the problem began to crystallize.
➤ **crystallization** NOUN

**crystallized fruit** NOUN
fruit preserved in sugar

**Cub, Cub Scout** NOUN Cubs, Cub Scouts
a member of the junior branch of the Scout Association

**cub** NOUN cubs
a young lion, tiger, fox, bear, etc.

**cubbyhole** NOUN cubbyholes
a small compartment or snug place

**cube** NOUN cubes
❶ an object that has six equal square sides, like a box or dice ❷ the number you get by multiplying a number by itself twice • The cube of 3 is 3 x 3 x 3 = 27.

**cube** VERB cubes, cubing, cubed
❶ to multiply a number by itself twice • 4 cubed is 4 x 4 x 4 = 64. ❷ to cut something into small cubes

**cube root** NOUN cube roots
the number that gives a particular number if it is multiplied by itself twice • The cube root of 27 is 3 (3 x 3 x 3 = 27).

**cubic** ADJECTIVE
shaped like a cube
➤ **cubic metre, cubic centimetre, etc.**, the volume of a cube with sides one metre, centimetre etc. long, used as a unit of measurement for volume

**cubicle** NOUN cubicles
a small room made by separating off part of a larger room

**cuboid** (say kew-boid) NOUN cuboids
an object with six rectangular sides

**cuckoo** NOUN cuckoos
a bird that makes a sound like 'cuck-oo' and lays its eggs in other birds' nests

**cucumber** NOUN cucumbers
a long green-skinned vegetable eaten raw or pickled

**cud** NOUN
half-digested food that a cow brings back from its first stomach to chew again

**cuddle** VERB cuddles, cuddling, cuddled
to put your arms closely round a person in a loving way

**cuddle** NOUN cuddles
to give someone a cuddle is to put your arms closely round them in a loving way

**cuddly** ADJECTIVE
soft and pleasant to cuddle • a cuddly toy

**cudgel** NOUN cudgels
a short thick stick used as a weapon

**cudgel** VERB cudgels, cudgelling, cudgelled
to beat someone with a cudgel

**cue** NOUN cues
❶ something said or done that acts as a signal for an actor to say something or come on stage ❷ a long stick for striking the ball in billiards or snooker

**cuff** NOUN cuffs
❶ the end of a sleeve that fits round the wrist ❷ a light hit or slap with the hand
➤ **off the cuff** without rehearsal or preparation • I'm just speaking off the cuff here.

**cuff** VERB cuffs, cuffing, cuffed
to hit someone lightly with your hand

**cufflink** NOUN cufflinks
each of a pair of fasteners for shirt cuffs, used instead of buttons

**cuisine** (say kwiz-een) NOUN cuisines
a style or method of cooking • French cuisine

**cul-de-sac** NOUN culs-de-sac
a street or passage closed at one end; a dead end (WORD ORIGIN) French, = bottom of a sack

**culinary** ADJECTIVE
to do with cooking

**cull** VERB culls, culling, culled
❶ to collect information or ideas from different places • I've culled lines from several poems. ❷ to pick out and kill a number of animals from a group to reduce the population

**cull** *NOUN* culls
the act of culling a group of animals • *a deer cull*

**culminate** *VERB* culminates, culminating, culminated
to reach its highest point or final result
• *Their long struggle for freedom culminated in victory.*
➤ **culmination** *NOUN*

**culprit** *NOUN* culprits
the person who has done something wrong

**cult** *NOUN* cults
❶ a small religious group with special beliefs and practices ❷ a film, TV programme, rock group, etc. that is very popular with a particular group of people

**cultivate** *VERB* cultivates, cultivating, cultivated
❶ to use land to grow crops ❷ to try to make something grow or develop • *He has made an effort to cultivate a more caring image.*
➤ **cultivation** *NOUN*
➤ **cultivator** *NOUN*

**cultivated** *ADJECTIVE*
having good manners and education

**cultural** *ADJECTIVE*
❶ to do with the customs and traditions of a people • *There are cultural differences between the two communities.* ❷ to do with literature, art, music, etc. • *a cultural event*

**culture** *NOUN* cultures
❶ appreciation and understanding of literature, art, music, etc. ❷ the customs and traditions of a people • *West Indian culture* ❸ (*in science*) a quantity of bacteria or cells grown for study

**cultured** *ADJECTIVE*
educated to appreciate literature, art, music, etc.

**cultured pearl** *NOUN* cultured pearls
a pearl formed by an oyster when a speck of grit is put into its shell

**culvert** *NOUN* culverts
a tunnel taking a stream or drain under a road or railway

**cumbersome** *ADJECTIVE*
difficult or awkward to carry or use

**cumin** *NOUN*
a plant with spicy seeds that are used for flavouring foods

**cummerbund** *NOUN* cummerbunds
a broad sash worn round the waist

**cumulative** *ADJECTIVE*
increasing by continuous additions

**cumulus** *NOUN* cumuli
a type of cloud consisting of rounded heaps on a horizontal base

**cunning** *ADJECTIVE*
❶ clever at deceiving people ❷ cleverly designed or planned • *a cunning trick*

**cunning** *NOUN*
❶ skill in deceiving people; craftiness ❷ skill or ingenuity

**cup** *NOUN* cups
❶ a small bowl-shaped container for drinking from ❷ anything shaped like a cup ❸ a trophy shaped like a cup with a stem, given as a prize

**cup** *VERB* cups, cupping, cupped
to form your hands into the curved shape of a cup • *He cupped his hands to drink from the river.*

**cupboard** *NOUN* cupboards
a piece of furniture or compartment with a door, for storing things

**cupful** *NOUN* cupfuls
as much as a cup will hold • *a cupful of water*

**cupola** (say kew-pol-a) *NOUN* cupolas
a small dome on a roof

**cur** *NOUN* curs
a scruffy or bad-tempered dog

**curable** *ADJECTIVE*
a curable illness is one that can be cured

**curate** *NOUN* curates
a member of the clergy who helps a vicar

**curator** (say kewr-ay-ter) *NOUN* curators
a person in charge of a museum or other collection

**curb** *VERB* curbs, curbing, curbed
to keep something in check; to restrain something • *You need to curb your impatience.*

**curb** *NOUN* curbs
a limit or restraint on something • *Put a curb on spending.*

> **SPELLING**
> Take care not to confuse with **kerb**, which is the edge of a pavement.

a b c d e f g h i j k l m n o p q r s t u v w x y z

**curd** NOUN (or **curds**) PLURAL NOUN
a thick substance formed when milk turns sour

**curdle** VERB curdles, curdling, curdled
to form into curds or lumps
➤ **make someone's blood curdle** to horrify or terrify someone

**cure** VERB cures, curing, cured
❶ to get rid of someone's illness ❷ to stop something bad • *He finally cured the rattling noise in his car.* ❸ to treat meat or fish in order to preserve it • *Fish can be cured in smoke.*

**cure** NOUN cures
❶ something that cures a person or thing; a remedy • *They are trying to find a cure for cancer.* ❷ a return to good health; being cured • *We cannot promise a cure.*

**curfew** NOUN curfews
a time or signal after which people must remain indoors until the next day
**WORD ORIGIN** from old French *cuevrefeu*, literally = cover fire (from an old law saying that all fires should be covered or put out by a certain time each evening)

**curio** NOUN curios
a rare or unusual object

**curiosity** NOUN curiosities
❶ curiosity is being curious ❷ a curiosity is something unusual and interesting

**curious** ADJECTIVE
❶ wanting to find out about things; inquisitive • *She was curious to know what was in the box.* ❷ strange or unusual • *There was a curious silence.*
➤ **curiously** ADVERB

**curl** NOUN curls
a curve or coil, e.g. of hair

**curl** VERB curls, curling, curled
❶ to form into curls ❷ to move in a curve or spiral • *Smoke curled up into the sky.*
➤ **curl up** to pull your arms, legs and head close to your body • *The cat curled up in front of the fire.*

**curler** NOUN curlers
a device for curling the hair

**curlew** NOUN curlews
a wading bird with a long curved bill

**curling** NOUN
a game played on ice with large flat stones

**curly** ADJECTIVE
full of curls

**currant** NOUN currants
❶ a small black dried grape used in cookery
❷ a small round red, black or white berry
**WORD ORIGIN** from old French *raisins de Couarantz* = grapes from Corinth (a city in Greece)

**SPELLING**
Take care not to confuse with current, which means a flow of water, air or electricity.

**currency** NOUN currencies
❶ the money in use in a country ❷ the general use of something • *Some words have no currency now.*

**current** ADJECTIVE
happening or being used now

**current** NOUN currents
❶ water or air etc. moving in one direction
❷ the flow of electricity along a wire etc. or through something

**SPELLING**
Take care not to confuse with currant, which means a dried grape.

**current affairs** PLURAL NOUN
political events in the news at the moment

**currently** ADVERB
at present; at the moment • *The road is currently being repaired.*

**curriculum** NOUN curricula
the subjects forming a course of study in a school or university

**curriculum vitae** (say **vee**-ty) NOUN curricula vitae
a brief account of a person's education, career, etc., which he or she sends when applying for a job

**curry** NOUN curries
food cooked with spices that make it taste hot
➤ **curried** ADJECTIVE

**curry** VERB curries, currying, curried
➤ **curry favour** to try to win someone's approval or support by flattering them

**curse** NOUN curses
❶ a call or prayer for a person or thing to be harmed; the evil produced by this
❷ something very unpleasant • *the curse of poverty* ❸ an angry or offensive word or expression

**curse** VERB curses, cursing, cursed
❶ to say offensive words; to swear ❷ to use a

curse against a person or thing
➤ **be cursed with something** to suffer from something

**cursor** *NOUN* cursors
a movable indicator, usually a flashing light or arrow, on a computer screen, showing where new data will go

**cursory** *ADJECTIVE*
hasty and not thorough • *a cursory inspection*

**curt** *ADJECTIVE*
brief and hasty or rude • *a curt reply*
➤ **curtly** *ADVERB*
➤ **curtness** *NOUN*

**curtail** *VERB* curtails, curtailing, curtailed
❶ to cut something short • *The lesson was curtailed.* ❷ to reduce something • *We must curtail our spending.*
➤ **curtailment** *NOUN*

**curtain** *NOUN* curtains
❶ a piece of material hung at a window or door ❷ the large cloth screen hung at the front of a stage

**curtsy** *NOUN* curtsies
a movement of respect made by women and girls, putting one foot behind the other and bending the knees

**curtsy** *VERB* curtsies, curtsying, curtsied
to make a curtsy

**curvature** *NOUN* curvatures
a curving or bending, especially of the earth's horizon • *the curvature of the earth*

**curve** *NOUN* curves
a line or shape that bends gradually and smoothly

**curve** *VERB* curves, curving, curved
to bend gradually and smoothly; to form a curve
➤ **curvy** *ADJECTIVE*

**curved** *ADJECTIVE*
forming a curve • *a curved blade*

**cushion** *NOUN* cushions
❶ a bag, usually of cloth, filled with soft material so that it is comfortable to sit on or lean against ❷ anything soft or springy that protects or supports something • *The hovercraft travels on a cushion of air.*

**cushion** *VERB* cushions, cushioning, cushioned
to protect someone from the effects of a knock or shock etc. • *A pile of boxes cushioned his fall.*

**cushy** *ADJECTIVE* (*informal*)
pleasant and easy • *a cushy job*

**custard** *NOUN* custards
❶ a sweet yellow sauce made with milk ❷ a pudding made with beaten eggs and milk

**custodian** *NOUN* custodians
a person who is responsible for looking after something; a keeper

**custody** *NOUN*
❶ the legal right or duty to take care of a person or thing ❷ to be in custody is to be in prison awaiting trial
➤ **take someone into custody** to arrest someone

**custom** *NOUN* customs
❶ the usual way of behaving or doing something ❷ regular business from customers

**customary** *ADJECTIVE*
according to custom; usual
➤ **customarily** *ADVERB*

**custom-built** *ADJECTIVE*
made according to a customer's order

**customer** *NOUN* customers
a person who buys goods or services from a shop or business

**customs** *PLURAL NOUN*
❶ the place at a port or airport where officials examine your luggage to check that you are not carrying anything illegal ❷ taxes charged on goods brought into a country

**cut** *VERB* cuts, cutting, cut
❶ to divide or separate something by using a knife, axe, scissors, etc. ❷ to wound someone with a sharp object or weapon ❸ to make a thing shorter or smaller; to remove part of something • *They are cutting all their prices.* ❹ to divide a pack of playing cards ❺ to hit a ball with a chopping movement ❻ to go through or across something ❼ to switch off electrical power or an engine ❽ in a film, to move from one shot or scene to another ❾ to make a sound recording
➤ **cut a corner** to go across a corner rather than around it
➤ **cut and dried** already decided
➤ **cut and paste** to remove text on a computer screen from one place and put it somewhere else
➤ **cut in** to interrupt someone
➤ **cut something off** to stop the supply of something

➤ **cut something out** to stop doing something

**cut** *NOUN* cuts
❶ cutting; the result of cutting • *Your hair could do with a cut.* ❷ a small wound ❸ (*informal*) a share of profits
➤ **be a cut above something** to be superior

**cute** *ADJECTIVE* (*informal*)
pretty or attractive

**cuticle** (say **kew**-tik-ul) *NOUN* cuticles
the skin round a nail

**cutlass** *NOUN* cutlasses
a short sword with a broad curved blade

**cutlery** *NOUN*
knives, forks and spoons used for eating

**cutlet** *NOUN* cutlets
a thick slice of meat for cooking

**cut-out** *NOUN* cut-outs
a shape cut out of paper, cardboard, etc.

**cut-price** *ADJECTIVE*
for sale at a reduced price

**cutter** *NOUN* cutters
❶ a person or thing that cuts ❷ a small fast sailing ship

**cutting** *NOUN* cuttings
❶ something cut out of a newspaper or magazine ❷ a piece cut from a plant to form a new plant ❸ a steep-sided passage cut through high ground for a road or railway

**cuttlefish** *NOUN* cuttlefish
a sea creature with ten arms, which sends out a black liquid when attacked

**cyanide** *NOUN*
a very poisonous chemical

**cycle** *NOUN* cycles
❶ a bicycle or motorcycle ❷ a series of events that are regularly repeated in the same order • *Rainfall is part of the water cycle.*

**cycle** *VERB* cycles, cycling, cycled
to ride a bicycle or tricycle

**cyclical, cyclic** *ADJECTIVE*
repeated regularly in the same order

**cyclist** *NOUN* cyclists
a person who rides a bicycle

**cyclone** *NOUN* cyclones
a violent tropical storm in which strong winds rotate round a calm central area
➤ **cyclonic** *ADJECTIVE*

**cygnet** (say **sig**-nit) *NOUN* cygnets
a young swan

**cylinder** *NOUN* cylinders
an object with straight sides and circular ends

**cylindrical** *ADJECTIVE*
shaped like a cylinder

**cymbal** *NOUN* cymbals
a percussion instrument consisting of a metal plate that is hit to make a ringing sound
SPELLING
Take care not to confuse with **symbol**.

**cynic** (say **sin**-ik) *NOUN* cynics
a person who believes that people's reasons for doing things are usually selfish or bad,
➤ **cynicism** *NOUN*

**cynical** *ADJECTIVE*
believing that people's reasons for doing things are usually selfish or bad

**cypress** *NOUN* cypresses
an evergreen tree with dark leaves

**cyst** (say sist) *NOUN* cysts
an abnormal swelling in the body containing fluid or soft matter

**czar** (say zar) *NOUN* czars
a different spelling of **tsar**

# Dd

**dab** *NOUN* dabs
❶ a quick gentle touch, usually with something wet ❷ a small amount of something put on a surface • *a dab of paint*

**dab** *VERB* dabs, dabbing, dabbed
to touch something quickly and gently • *I dabbed my eyes with a handkerchief.*

**dabble** *VERB* dabbles, dabbling, dabbled
❶ to splash something about in water ❷ to do something as a hobby or not very seriously • *I dabble in astronomy.*

**dachshund** (say **daks**-huund) *NOUN* dachshunds
a small dog with a long body and very short legs WORD ORIGIN German = badger-dog (because dachshunds were once used to dig badgers from their sets)

**dad**, **daddy** *NOUN* dads, daddies (*informal*)
father

**daddy-long-legs** *NOUN* daddy-long-legs
a crane fly

**daffodil** *NOUN* daffodils
a yellow flower that grows from a bulb

**daft** *ADJECTIVE* (*British*) (*informal*)
silly or stupid

**dag** *NOUN* dags (*informal*)
(*Australian/NZ*) a dirty or untidy person
**WORD ORIGIN** shortening of *daglock* = a piece
of dung-coated wool on a sheep's hindquarters

**dagger** *NOUN* daggers
a pointed knife with two sharp edges, used as
a weapon
➤ **look daggers at someone** to glare angrily
at someone

**dahlia** (say **day**-lee-a) *NOUN* dahlias
a garden plant with brightly-coloured flowers
**WORD ORIGIN** named after Andreas *Dahl*, a
Swedish botanist

**daily** *ADVERB & ADJECTIVE*
every day

**dainty** *ADJECTIVE* daintier, daintiest
small, delicate and pretty
➤ **daintily** *ADVERB*
➤ **daintiness** *NOUN*

**dairy** *NOUN* dairies
a place where milk, butter, etc. are produced
or sold

**dairy** *ADJECTIVE*
to do with the production of milk; made from
milk • *dairy farming* • *dairy products*

**dais** (say **day**-iss) *NOUN* daises
a low platform, especially at the end of a
room

**daisy** *NOUN* daisies
a small flower with white petals and a yellow
centre **WORD ORIGIN** from *day's eye* (because
the daisy opens in daylight and closes at night)

**dale** *NOUN* dales
a valley

**dally** *VERB* dallies, dallying, dallied
to dawdle or waste time

**dam** *NOUN* dams
a barrier built across a river to hold water
back

**dam** *VERB* dams, damming, dammed
to hold water back with a dam

**damage** *NOUN*
harm or injury done to something • *The storm
caused a lot of damage.*

**damage** *VERB* damages, damaging, damaged
to harm or spoil something

**damages** *PLURAL NOUN*
money paid as compensation for an injury or
loss

**Dame** *NOUN* Dames
the title of a woman who has been given the
equivalent of a knighthood

**dame** *NOUN* dames
a comic middle-aged woman in a pantomime,
usually played by a man

**damn** *VERB* damns, damning, damned
❶ to condemn someone to eternal
punishment in hell ❷ to swear at someone or
curse them

**damn** *EXCLAMATION*
(*informal*) said to show you are angry or
annoyed

**damnation** *NOUN*
being condemned to hell

**damned** *ADJECTIVE*
hateful or annoying

**damp** *ADJECTIVE*
slightly wet; not quite dry
➤ **damply** *ADVERB*
➤ **dampness** *NOUN*

**damp** *NOUN*
moisture in the air or on a surface or all
through something

**damp** *VERB* damps, damping, damped
❶ to make something slightly wet ❷ to
reduce the strength of something • *The
defeat damped their enthusiasm.*

**damp course** *NOUN* damp courses
(*British*) a layer of material built into a wall to
prevent dampness in the ground from rising

**dampen** *VERB* dampens, dampening,
dampened
❶ to make something damp ❷ to reduce
the strength of something • *Even the awful
weather didn't dampen their spirits.*

**damper** *NOUN* dampers
❶ a felt pad that presses against a piano
string to stop it vibrating ❷ a metal plate that
can be moved to increase or decrease the
amount of air flowing into a fire or furnace
➤ **put a damper on something** to reduce
people's enthusiasm or enjoyment

**damsel** NOUN damsels (*old use*)
a young woman

**damson** NOUN damsons
a small dark purple plum

**dance** VERB dances, dancing, danced
to move about in time to music

**dance** NOUN dances
❶ a set of movements used in dancing ❷ a piece of music for dancing to ❸ a party or gathering where people dance

**dancer** NOUN dancers
a person who dances

**dandelion** NOUN dandelions
a yellow wild flower with jagged leaves
**WORD ORIGIN** from French *dent-de-lion* = tooth of a lion (because the jagged edges of the leaves looked like lions' teeth)

**dandruff** NOUN
tiny white flakes of dead skin in a person's hair

**D and T** ABBREVIATION
design and technology

**dandy** NOUN dandies
a man who likes to look very smart

**danger** NOUN dangers
❶ the possibility of suffering harm or death or that something bad might happen • *Are they in any danger?* • *There's a danger they might be sold out.* ❷ a bad effect that happens as a result of doing something • *the dangers of overeating*

**dangerous** ADJECTIVE
likely to kill or harm you
➤ **dangerously** ADVERB

**dangle** VERB dangles, dangling, dangled
❶ to swing or hang down loosely • *A single light bulb dangled from the ceiling.* ❷ to hold or carry something so that it swings loosely • *She dangled her legs over the side of the bed.*

**dank** ADJECTIVE
damp and chilly • *a dank dungeon*

**dapper** ADJECTIVE
dressed neatly and smartly

**dappled** ADJECTIVE
marked with patches of a different colour or with patches of shade

**dare** VERB dares, daring, dared
❶ to be brave or bold enough to do something • *He didn't dare look down.* ❷ to challenge a person to do something risky • *I dare you to climb up there.*

**dare** NOUN dares
a challenge to do something risky

**daredevil** NOUN daredevils
a person who enjoys doing dangerous things

**daring** ADJECTIVE
bold or courageous

**daring** NOUN
adventurous courage

**dark** ADJECTIVE
❶ with little or no light ❷ not light in colour • *a dark suit* ❸ having dark hair ❹ sinister or unpleasant • *dark deeds*

**dark** NOUN
❶ absence of light • *Cats can see in the dark.* ❷ the time when it becomes dark • *She went out after dark.*
➤ **be in the dark** to have no information about something

**darken** VERB darkens, darkening, darkened
❶ to become dark or darker • *The sky suddenly darkened.* ❷ to make something dark or darker • *a darkened room*

**darkly** ADJECTIVE
in a threatening or unpleasant way • *He scowled at me darkly.*

**darkness** NOUN
being dark, without any light • *The room was suddenly plunged into total darkness.*

**darkroom** NOUN darkrooms
a room kept dark for developing and printing photographs

**darling** NOUN darlings
someone who is loved very much

**darn** VERB darns, darning, darned
to mend a hole by weaving threads across it

**darn** NOUN darns
a place that has been darned

**dart** NOUN darts
❶ an object with a sharp point, thrown at a target ❷ a sudden swift movement ❸ a tapering tuck stitched in something to make it fit

**dart** VERB darts, darting, darted
❶ to run suddenly and quickly ❷ you dart a look or glance at someone when you look at them suddenly and briefly

**darts** NOUN
a game in which darts are thrown at a circular board (**dartboard**)

**dash** VERB dashes, dashing, dashed
❶ to run quickly; to rush ❷ to throw a thing violently against something hard • *The storm dashed the ship against the rocks.* ❸ to destroy a hope or expectation

**dash** NOUN dashes
❶ a short quick run; a rush ❷ a small amount of something • *Add a dash of cream.* ❸ a short line (–) used in writing or printing

> PUNCTUATION
>
> Dashes are used, especially in informal writing, to mark a break in the flow of a sentence.
>
> They can be used on their own, to add a final comment, question or summary:
>
> *I have only two words to say to you—'Never again'!*
>
> *Would you like your bagel split, toasted, buttered—or none of the above?*
>
> They can be used in pairs before and after an interruption in a narrative or conversation. For example, they can show a change of subject, or a break or hesitation in thought:
>
> *Maybe I'll just say—oh, I don't know—that I'm allergic to cats.*
>
> or they can be used to elaborate or explain a point:
>
> *The creature was vast—over ten feet tall—and was staring at me.*
>
> Dashes are quite informal and should be avoided in formal writing.

**dashboard** NOUN dashboards
a panel with dials and controls in front of the driver of a vehicle WORD ORIGIN originally a board on the front of a carriage to keep out mud, which dashed against it

**dashing** ADJECTIVE
attractive in an exciting and stylish way • *a dashing young officer*

**dastardly** ADJECTIVE
(old use) wicked and cruel • *What a dastardly trick!*

**data** (say **day**-ta) NOUN
pieces of information

> USAGE
>
> Strictly speaking, this word is a plural noun (the singular is *datum*), so it should be used with a plural verb: *Here are the data.* However, the word is widely used as if it were a singular noun: *Here is the data.*

**database** NOUN databases
a store of information held in a computer

**date** NOUN dates
❶ the time when something happens or happened, stated as the day, month and year (or any of these) ❷ an appointment to meet someone, especially at the start of a romantic relationship ❸ a small sweet brown fruit that grows on a kind of palm tree

**date** VERB dates, dating, dated
❶ to give a date to something • *The letter is dated 3 June 2013.* ❷ to have existed from a particular time • *The church dates from 1684.* ❸ to seem old-fashioned • *Some fashions date very quickly.*

**daub** VERB daubs, daubing, daubed
to paint or smear something clumsily
➤ **daub** NOUN

**daughter** NOUN daughters
a girl or woman who is someone's child

**daughter-in-law** NOUN daughters-in-law
a son's wife

**daunt** VERB daunts, daunting, daunted
to make someone feel worried and not confident about doing something • *Don't be daunted by the length of the book – it's a good read.*

**daunting** ADJECTIVE
a daunting task makes you feel worried because it seems so difficult

**dauntless** ADJECTIVE
brave and determined

**dauphin** (say **daw**-fin) NOUN dauphins
the title of the eldest son of each of the kings of France between 1349 and 1830

**dawdle** VERB dawdles, dawdling, dawdled
to walk or do things slowly and lazily

**dawn** NOUN dawns
❶ the time when the sun rises ❷ the beginning of something • *the dawn of civilization*

**dawn** VERB dawns, dawning, dawned
❶ to begin to grow light in the morning ❷ to begin to be realized • *The truth dawned on them.*

**day** NOUN days
❶ the 24 hours between midnight and the next midnight ❷ the light part of this time; the daytime ❸ a period of time • *in Queen Victoria's day*

**daybreak** NOUN
the first light of day; dawn

**daydream** NOUN daydreams
pleasant thoughts of something you would like to happen

**daydream** VERB daydreams, daydreaming, daydreamed
to have daydreams

**daylight** NOUN
❶ the light of day; sunlight ❷ dawn

**daytime** NOUN
the time of daylight

**day-to-day** ADJECTIVE
ordinary; happening every day

**daze** NOUN
➤ **in a daze** unable to think or see clearly

**dazed** ADJECTIVE
unable to think or see clearly

**dazzle** VERB dazzles, dazzling, dazzled
❶ a light dazzles you when it is so bright that you cannot see clearly because of it ❷ to amaze or impress a person by a splendid display

**DC** ABBREVIATION
direct current

**deacon** NOUN deacons
❶ a member of the clergy ranking below a priest in Catholic, Anglican and Orthodox Christian Churches ❷ a church officer who is not a member of the clergy in some Christian Churches
➤ **deaconess** NOUN

**dead** ADJECTIVE
❶ no longer alive ❷ not at all lively • *This town is dead at the weekend.* ❸ no longer working or in use • *The phone went dead.* ❹ exact or complete • *The arrow hit the target in the dead centre.* • *We came to a dead stop.*

**deaden** VERB deadens, deadening, deadened
to make a pain, feeling or sound weaker

**dead end** NOUN dead ends
❶ a road or passage with one end closed ❷ a situation where there is no chance of making progress

**dead heat** NOUN dead heats
a race in which two or more winners finish exactly together

**deadline** NOUN deadlines
a time by which you have to finish something
**WORD ORIGIN** originally this meant a line round an American military prison; if prisoners went beyond it they could be shot

**deadlock** NOUN deadlocks
a situation in which two sides cannot reach an agreement

**deadly** ADJECTIVE & ADVERB deadlier, deadliest
❶ likely to kill ❷ complete or completely
• *There was a deadly hush in the room.* • *He was deadly serious.*

**deaf** ADJECTIVE
❶ unable to hear ❷ refusing to listen • *She was deaf to all advice.*
➤ **deafness** NOUN

**deafen** VERB deafens, deafening, deafened
to make someone unable to hear by making a very loud noise • *We were deafened by the roar of the aircraft above.*

**deafening** ADJECTIVE
extremely loud

**deal** VERB deals, dealing, dealt
❶ to hand something out ❷ to give out cards for a card game ❸ to do business; to buy and sell goods • *He deals in scrap metal.* ❹ to deal someone or something a blow is to hit or harm them • *The man dealt Tom a heavy blow on the nose.*
➤ **deal with something** ❶ to be concerned with something • *This chapter deals with whales and dolphins.* ❷ to do what is needed • *I'll deal with the washing-up.*

**deal** NOUN deals
❶ an agreement or bargain ❷ someone's turn to deal at cards
➤ **a good deal** or **a great deal** a large amount

**dealer** NOUN dealers
❶ someone who buys and sells things ❷ the person who deals in a game of cards

**dean** NOUN deans
❶ an important member of the clergy in a cathedral ❷ the head of a university, college or department
➤ **deanery** NOUN

**dear** ADJECTIVE
❶ loved very much ❷ a polite greeting in letters • *Dear Sir* ❸ expensive

**dearly** ADVERB
very much; a lot • *She loved her husband dearly.*

**dearth** (say derth) NOUN dearths
a dearth of something is a lack or shortage of it

**death** NOUN deaths
dying; the end of life

**deathly** ADJECTIVE & ADVERB
like death • *There was a deathly silence.*

**death trap** NOUN death traps
a very dangerous place

**debar** VERB debars, debarring, debarred
to ban someone from doing or taking part in something • *He was debarred from the contest.*

**debase** VERB debases, debasing, debased
to reduce the quality or value of something
➤ **debasement** NOUN

**debatable** ADJECTIVE
not certain; that people might argue about

**debate** NOUN debates
a formal discussion about a subject

**debate** VERB debates, debating, debated
❶ to discuss or argue about something ❷ to think about something before deciding what to do • *I was debating whether to go or not.*

**debilitating** ADJECTIVE
making you very weak • *a debilitating disease*

**debit** NOUN debits
an entry in an account showing how much money is owed. Compare with **credit**.

**debit** VERB debits, debiting, debited
to enter an amount as a debit in an account; to remove money from an account

**debonair** (say deb-on-**air**) ADJECTIVE
fashionable and and confident
**WORD ORIGIN** from French *de bon air* = of good disposition

**debris** (say **deb**-ree) NOUN
scattered broken pieces that are left after something has been destroyed

**debt** (say det) NOUN debts
something, especially money, that you owe someone
➤ **in debt** owing money

➤ **in someone's debt** grateful to someone who has done you a favour

**debtor** (say **det**-or) NOUN debtors
a person who owes money to someone

**debut** (say **day**-bew) NOUN debuts
someone's first public appearance as a performer

**decade** (say **dek**-ayd) NOUN decades
a period of ten years

**decadent** (say **dek**-a-dent) ADJECTIVE
falling to a lower standard of morality or behaviour, especially in order to enjoy pleasure
➤ **decadence** NOUN

**decaffeinated** ADJECTIVE
decaffeinated coffee or tea has had caffeine removed from it

**decamp** VERB decamps, decamping, decamped
to go away suddenly or secretly

**decant** (say dik-**ant**) VERB decants, decanting, decanted
to pour wine or other liquid gently from one container into another

**decanter** (say dik-**ant**-er) NOUN decanters
a decorative glass bottle into which wine etc. is poured for serving

**decapitate** VERB decapitates, decapitating, decapitated
to cut someone's head off; to behead someone
➤ **decapitation** NOUN

**decathlon** NOUN decathlons
an athletic contest in which each competitor takes part in ten events

**decay** VERB decays, decaying, decayed
❶ to go bad or rot ❷ to become less good or less strong

**decay** NOUN
going bad or rotting • *tooth decay*

**decease** (say dis-**eess**) NOUN (formal)
a person's death

**deceased** ADJECTIVE (formal)
dead

**deceit** (say dis-**eet**) NOUN deceits
making a person believe something that is not true • *I'm tired of his lies and deceit.*

**deceitful** ADJECTIVE
dishonest; trying to make someone believe

a b c **d** e f g h i j k l m n o p q r s t u v w x y z

something that is not true
➤ **deceitfully** ADVERB

**deceive** VERB deceives, deceiving, deceived
to make a person believe something that is
not true

SPELLING

In deceive, e before i is the right way
round.

**December** NOUN
the twelfth month of the year
WORD ORIGIN from Latin *decem* = ten,
because it was the tenth month of the ancient
Roman calendar

**decency** NOUN
respectable and honest behaviour

**decent** ADJECTIVE
❶ respectable and honest ❷ of a good
enough standard or quality ❸ (*informal*)
kind or generous
➤ **decently** ADVERB

**deception** NOUN deceptions
❶ deceiving someone ❷ something that
deceives people

**deceptive** ADJECTIVE
not what it seems to be; giving a false
impression • *Appearances can be deceptive.*
➤ **deceptively** ADVERB

**decibel** (say **dess**-ib-el) NOUN decibels
a unit for measuring the loudness of sound

**decide** VERB decides, deciding, decided
❶ to make up your mind; to make a choice
❷ to settle a contest or argument • *Next
week's match will decide the championship.*
➤ **decider** NOUN

SPELLING

The 's' sound is spelt with a c in decide.

**decided** ADJECTIVE
❶ noticeable or definite • *a decided
advantage* ❷ having clear and definite
opinions

**decidedly** ADVERB
definitely and in an obvious way • *She was
looking decidedly worried.*

**deciduous** (say dis-**id**-yoo-us) ADJECTIVE
a deciduous tree is one that loses its leaves in
autumn

**decimal** ADJECTIVE
decimal numbers or fractions are expressed in
tens or tenths

**decimal** NOUN decimals
a decimal fraction

**decimal currency** NOUN decimal currencies
a currency in which each unit is ten or one
hundred times the value of the one next
below it

**decimal fraction** NOUN decimal fractions
a fraction with tenths shown as numbers
after a dot (¼ is 0.25; 1½ is 1.5)

**decimalize** (also **decimalise**) VERB
decimalizes, decimalizing, decimalized
❶ to express a number as a decimal ❷ to
change something, especially coinage, to a
decimal system
➤ **decimalization** NOUN

**decimal point** NOUN decimal points
the dot in a decimal fraction

**decimate** (say **dess**-im-ayt) VERB decimates,
decimating, decimated
to kill or destroy a large part of something
• *The famine decimated the population.*
WORD ORIGIN from Latin *decimare* = kill
every tenth man (this was the ancient Roman
punishment for an army guilty of mutiny or
other serious crime)

**decipher** (say dis-**y**-fer) VERB deciphers,
deciphering, deciphered
❶ to work out the meaning of a coded
message ❷ to work out the meaning of
something that is hard to read • *I can't
decipher his handwriting.*
➤ **decipherment** NOUN

**decision** NOUN decisions
❶ a decision is what someone has decided
❷ decision is deciding or making a judgment
about something • *The moment of decision
had arrived.*

**decisive** (say dis-**y**-siv) ADJECTIVE
❶ that settles or ends something • *a decisive
battle* ❷ able to make decisions quickly and
firmly
➤ **decisively** ADVERB

**deck** NOUN decks
❶ a floor or level on a ship or bus ❷ a pack of
playing cards ❸ a part of a music system for
playing discs or tapes

**deck** VERB decks, decking, decked
to decorate a place with something • *The
front of the house was decked with flags and
balloons.*

**deckchair** NOUN deckchairs
a folding chair with a canvas or plastic seat

**WORD ORIGIN** because they were first used on the decks of passenger ships

**declaim** VERB declaims, declaiming, declaimed
to speak or say something loudly and dramatically • *She declaimed the famous opening speech of the play.*
➤ **declamation** NOUN

**declaration** NOUN declarations
an official or public statement about something

**declare** VERB declares, declaring, declared
❶ to say something clearly or firmly • *He always declared that he is innocent.* ❷ to tell customs officials that you have goods on which you ought to pay duty ❸ to end a cricket innings before all the batsmen are out
➤ **declare war** to announce that you are starting a war against someone

**decline** VERB declines, declining, declined
❶ to refuse something politely • *She declined his offer of help.* ❷ to become weaker or smaller • *In the last few years his popularity has declined.* ❸ to state the forms of a noun, pronoun or adjective that correspond to particular cases, numbers and genders

**decline** NOUN declines
a gradual decrease or loss of strength • *a decline in the birth rate*

**decode** VERB decodes, decoding, decoded
to work out the meaning of something written in code
➤ **decoder** NOUN

**decompose** VERB decomposes, decomposing, decomposed
to decay or rot
➤ **decomposition** NOUN

**decompression** NOUN
reducing air pressure

**decontamination** NOUN
getting rid of poisonous chemicals or radioactive material from a place, clothes, etc.

**decor** (say **day**-kor) NOUN
the style of furnishings and decorations used in a room

**decorate** VERB decorates, decorating, decorated
❶ to make something look more beautiful or colourful ❷ to put fresh paint or paper on walls ❸ to give somebody a medal or other award

**decoration** NOUN decorations
❶ something used to decorate a room,

table, etc. on special occasions • *Christmas decorations* ❷ the process of decorating a room or building ❸ a medal or other award given as an honour

**decorative** ADJECTIVE
attractive to look at • *a decorative design*

**decorator** NOUN decorators
a person whose job is to paint and decorate rooms and buildings

**decorous** (say **dek**-er-us) ADJECTIVE
polite and dignified
➤ **decorously** ADVERB

**decorum** (say dik-**or**-um) NOUN
polite and dignified behaviour

**decoy** (say **dee**-koi) NOUN decoys
something used to tempt a person or animal into a trap or into danger

**decoy** (say dik-**oi**) VERB decoys, decoying, decoyed
to tempt a person or animal into a trap or danger

**decrease** VERB decreases, decreasing, decreased
❶ to become smaller or fewer ❷ to make something smaller or fewer in number

**decrease** NOUN decreases
decreasing; the amount by which something decreases

**decree** NOUN decrees
an official order or decision

**decree** VERB decrees, decreeing, decreed
to give an official order that something must happen

**decrepit** (say dik-**rep**-it) ADJECTIVE
old and weak

**dedicate** VERB dedicates, dedicating, dedicated
❶ to devote all your time or energy to something • *She dedicated her life to nursing.* ❷ to name a person as a mark of respect or friendship, e.g. at the beginning of a book • *This book is dedicated to my parents.*

**dedication** NOUN dedications
❶ hard work and effort ❷ a message at the beginning of a book, naming a person as a mark of respect or friendship

**deduce** VERB deduces, deducing, deduced
to work something out from facts that you already know are true • *From her name I deduced that she was Polish.*

**deduct** VERB deducts, deducting, deducted
to subtract an amount from a total • *The examiner may deduct marks for bad spelling.*

**deduction** NOUN deductions
❶ something you work out from facts that you already know are true • *a brilliant piece of deduction* ❷ an amount taken away from a total

**deed** NOUN deeds
❶ something that someone has done; an act • *tales of his many brave deeds* ❷ a legal document that shows who owns something

**deem** VERB deems, deeming, deemed (*formal*)
to consider something in a certain way • *I should deem it an honour to be invited.*

**deep** ADJECTIVE
❶ going a long way down or back or in • *a deep well* • *deep cupboards* ❷ measured from top to bottom or front to back • *a hole two metres deep* ❸ a deep feeling is intense or strong • *deep suspicion* ❹ a deep colour is dark and intense • *a deep red* ❺ low-pitched, not shrill • *a deep voice*

**deepen** VERB deepens, deepening, deepened
to become deeper or more intense • *The darkness deepened.*

**deep-freeze** NOUN deep-freezes
a freezer

**deeply** ADVERB
very or very much • *She was deeply upset.* • *I deeply regret what happened.*

**deer** NOUN deer
a fast-running graceful animal, the male of which usually has antlers

SPELLING
Deer is spelt the same in the singular and plural.

**deface** VERB defaces, defacing, defaced
to spoil the surface of something, e.g. by scribbling on it

**defame** VERB defames, defaming, defamed
to attack or damage a person's good reputation; to slander or libel someone
➤ **defamation** (say def-a-**may**-shon) NOUN
➤ **defamatory** (say dif-**am**-a-ter-ee) ADJECTIVE

**default** VERB defaults, defaulting, defaulted
to fail to do what you have agreed to do, especially to pay back a loan
➤ **defaulter** NOUN

**default** NOUN defaults
❶ failure to do something, especially to pay back a loan ❷ (*in computing*) what a computer does unless you give it another command
➤ **by default** because something has failed to happen • *The other team didn't arrive in time, so we won by default.*

**defeat** VERB defeats, defeating, defeated
❶ to win a victory over someone ❷ to baffle someone or be too difficult for them • *The instructions completely defeated me.*

**defeat** NOUN defeats
❶ being defeated; a lost game or battle • *It's our first defeat of the season.* ❷ defeating someone • *William's defeat of Harold at the Battle of Hastings*

**defecate** (say def-ik-ayt) VERB defecates, defecating, defecated
to get rid of faeces from your body
➤ **defecation** NOUN

**defect** (say dee-fect) NOUN defects
a fault or flaw in something

**defect** (say dif-ekt) VERB defects, defecting, defected
to desert your own country or cause and join the other side
➤ **defection** NOUN
➤ **defector** NOUN

**defective** ADJECTIVE
having defects; incomplete • *defective goods*

**defence** NOUN defences
❶ protecting someone or something from an attack or from criticism • *His friends immediately rushed to his defence.* ❷ all the soldiers, weapons, etc. that a country uses to protect itself from attack • *spending on defence* ❸ something that defends or protects you • *High walls were built around the city as a defence against enemy attacks.* ❹ the case put forward by or on behalf of a defendant in a trial; the lawyers who put forward this case ❺ the players in a defending position in a game

**defenceless** ADJECTIVE
having no defences; not able to defend yourself

**defend** VERB defends, defending, defended
❶ to protect someone, especially against an attack or accusation ❷ to argue in support of something • *How can you defend such behaviour?* ❸ to try to prove that an accused person is not guilty ❹ to try to stop the other team from scoring
➤ **defender** NOUN

**defendant** *NOUN* defendants
a person accused of something in a law court

**defensible** *ADJECTIVE*
able to be defended

**defensive** *ADJECTIVE*
❶ used or done to defend something;
protective ❷ anxious about being criticized
• *There's no need to be so defensive.*
➤ **defensively** *ADVERB*
➤ **on the defensive** ready to defend yourself
against criticism

**defer** *VERB* defers, deferring, deferred
❶ to put something off to a later time; to
postpone something • *She deferred her
departure until Saturday.* ❷ to give way to a
person's wishes or authority • *I defer to your
superior knowledge.*

**deference** (say **def**-er-ens) *NOUN*
polite respect
➤ **deferential** (say def-er-**en**-shal) *ADJECTIVE*
➤ **deferentially** *ADVERB*

**defiance** *NOUN*
open disobedience • *a look of defiance*

**defiant** *ADJECTIVE*
openly showing that you refuse to obey
someone • *a defiant laugh*
➤ **defiantly** *ADVERB*

**deficiency** *NOUN* deficiencies
❶ a lack or shortage • *a vitamin deficiency*
❷ a defect or failing
➤ **deficient** *ADJECTIVE*

**deficit** (say **def**-iss-it) *NOUN* deficits
❶ the amount by which a total is smaller
than what is required ❷ the amount by which
spending is greater than income

**defile** *VERB* defiles, defiling, defiled
to make a thing dirty or impure

**define** *VERB* defines, defining, defined
❶ to explain what a word or phrase means
❷ to show clearly what something is • *We
need to define the problem before we can
solve it.* ❸ to show a thing's outline

**definite** *ADJECTIVE*
❶ clearly stated; exact • *Let's fix a definite
time.* ❷ certain or settled • *Is it definite that
we are going to move?*

SPELLING
There is a tricky bit in **definite**—it ends
in ite.

**definite article** *NOUN* definite articles
the word 'the'. See also the panels at **the** and
at **determiner**

**definitely** *ADVERB*
without doubt; certainly

SPELLING
There is no a in **definitely**.

**definition** *NOUN* definitions
❶ a statement of what a word or phrase
means or of what a thing is ❷ being distinct;
clearness of outline (e.g. in a photograph)
• *The face lacks definition.*

**definitive** (say dif-**in**-it-iv) *ADJECTIVE*
❶ finally settling something; conclusive • *a
definitive victory* ❷ not able to be bettered
• *the definitive history of French cinema*

**deflate** *VERB* deflates, deflating, deflated
❶ to let out air from a tyre or balloon etc.
❷ to make someone feel less proud or less
confident • *All the criticism left him feeling a
bit deflated.* ❸ to reduce or reverse inflation
➤ **deflation** *NOUN*

**deflect** *VERB* deflects, deflecting, deflected
to make something turn aside • *He deflected
the blow with his shield.*
➤ **deflection** *NOUN*
➤ **deflector** *NOUN*

**deforest** *VERB* deforests, deforesting,
deforested
to clear away the trees from an area

**deforestation** *NOUN*
the cutting down of a lot of trees in an area

**deform** *VERB* deforms, deforming, deformed
to spoil a thing's shape or appearance
➤ **deformation** *NOUN*

**deformed** *ADJECTIVE*
not properly shaped because it has grown
wrongly
➤ **deformity** *NOUN*

**defraud** *VERB* defrauds, defrauding,
defrauded
to get money from someone by fraud

**defray** *VERB* defrays, defraying, defrayed
to provide money to pay costs or expenses

**defrost** *VERB* defrosts, defrosting, defrosted
❶ to thaw out frozen food ❷ to remove
the ice and frost from a refrigerator or
windscreen

**deft** *ADJECTIVE*
skilful and quick • *She painted a fish with a*

few deft strokes.
➤ **deftly** ADVERB
➤ **deftness** NOUN

**defunct** ADJECTIVE
no longer in use or existing

**defuse** VERB defuses, defusing, defused
❶ to remove the fuse from a bomb so that
it cannot explode ❷ to make a situation less
dangerous or tense • *Her joke defused the
situation and we all relaxed.*

**defy** VERB defies, defying, defied
❶ to refuse to obey someone or something;
to openly resist something • *They defied the
law.* ❷ to challenge a person to do something
you believe cannot be done • *I defy you to
prove this.* ❸ to prevent something being
done • *The door defied all efforts to open it.*

**degenerate** VERB degenerates, degenerating,
degenerated
to become worse or lower in standard • *The
game degenerated into a series of fouls.*
➤ **degeneration** NOUN

**degenerate** ADJECTIVE
having become immoral or bad
➤ **degeneracy** NOUN

**degrade** VERB degrades, degrading, degraded
❶ to humiliate or dishonour someone ❷ to
reduce a chemical substance to a simpler
molecular form
➤ **degradation** (say deg-ra-**day**-shon) NOUN

**degree** NOUN degrees
❶ a unit for measuring temperature ❷ a unit
for measuring angles ❸ extent or amount
• *I agree with you to some degree.* • *a high
degree of skill* ❹ an award to someone at a
university or college who has successfully
finished a course

**dehydrated** ADJECTIVE
❶ someone who is dehydrated has lost a lot
of water from their body ❷ a dehydrated
substance has had all its moisture removed
➤ **dehydration** NOUN

**de-ice** VERB de-ices, de-icing, de-iced
to remove ice from a windscreen etc.
➤ **de-icer** NOUN

**deign** (say dayn) VERB deigns, deigning,
deigned
to do something that you think is below your
dignity • *She did not deign to reply.*

**deity** (say **dee**-it-ee or **day**-it-ee) NOUN deities
a god or goddess • *ancient Egyptian deities*

**déjà vu** (say day-zha **vew**) NOUN
a feeling that you have already experienced
what is happening now **WORD ORIGIN** French
= already seen

**dejected** ADJECTIVE
sad or disappointed
➤ **dejectedly** ADVERB
➤ **dejection** NOUN

**delay** VERB delays, delaying, delayed
❶ to make someone or something late ❷ to
postpone something until later ❸ to wait or
hesitate before doing something

**delay** NOUN delays
❶ delaying or waiting • *Do it without delay.*
❷ the amount of time by which something is
delayed • *a two-hour delay*

**delectable** ADJECTIVE
delightful or delicious

**delegate** (say **del**-ig-at) NOUN delegates
a person who represents others and acts on
their instructions

**delegate** (say **del**-ig-ayt) VERB delegates,
delegating, delegated
❶ to choose someone to carry out a task
or duty that you are responsible for • *I'm
going to delegate this job to my assistant.*
❷ to appoint someone as a delegate • *We
delegated Jones to represent us.*

**delegation** (say del-ig-**ay**-shon) NOUN
delegations
❶ a group of delegates • *the delegation from
South Africa* ❷ delegating

**delete** (say dil-**eet**) VERB deletes, deleting,
deleted
to cross out or remove something written or
printed or stored on a computer • *He deleted
the email without reading it.*
➤ **deletion** NOUN

**deliberate** (say dil-**ib**-er-at) ADJECTIVE
❶ done on purpose; intentional ❷ slow
and careful • *She entered the room with
deliberate steps.*

**deliberate** (say dil-**ib**-er-ayt) VERB deliberates,
deliberating, deliberated
to think over or discuss something carefully
before reaching a decision

**deliberately** ADVERB
on purpose • *I didn't break it deliberately.*

**deliberation** NOUN deliberations
thinking carefully about something before
reaching a decision

**delicacy** NOUN delicacies
❶ a delicious food • *Try this – it's a local delicacy.* ❷ being delicate • *We must handle the matter with great delicacy.*

**delicate** ADJECTIVE
❶ fine and graceful • *delicate embroidery* ❷ fragile and easily damaged ❸ pleasant and not strong or intense • *a delicate shade of pink* ❹ becoming ill easily ❺ using or needing great care • *a delicate situation*
➤ **delicately** ADVERB

**delicatessen** NOUN delicatessens
a shop that sells cooked meats, cheeses, salads, etc. (WORD ORIGIN) from German = delicacies to eat

**delicious** ADJECTIVE
tasting or smelling very pleasant
➤ **deliciously** ADVERB

**delight** VERB delights, delighting, delighted
❶ to please someone greatly ❷ to take great pleasure in something • *He delights in playing tricks on people.*

**delight** NOUN delights
great pleasure

**delighted** ADJECTIVE
extremely pleased • *I'd be delighted to come.*

**delightful** ADJECTIVE
giving great pleasure; very pleasant
➤ **delightfully** ADVERB

**delinquent** (say dil-**ing**-kwent) NOUN delinquents
a young person who breaks the law
➤ **delinquent** ADJECTIVE
➤ **delinquency** NOUN

**delirious** (say di-**li**-ri-us) ADJECTIVE
❶ in a state of mental confusion and agitation during a feverish illness ❷ extremely excited or enthusiastic
➤ **deliriously** ADVERB

**delirium** (say dil-**irri**-um) NOUN
❶ a state of mental confusion and agitation during a feverish illness ❷ wild excitement

**deliver** VERB delivers, delivering, delivered
❶ to take letters or goods to the person or place they are addressed to ❷ to give a speech or lecture ❸ to help with the birth of a baby ❹ to aim or strike a blow or an attack ❺ to rescue someone or set them free
➤ **deliverer** NOUN

**deliverance** NOUN
being rescued or set free

**delivery** NOUN deliveries
❶ delivering letters or goods • *Your order is ready for delivery.* • *We have two deliveries a day.* ❷ the way a person gives a speech or lecture ❸ giving birth to a baby ❹ a ball bowled in cricket

**dell** NOUN dells
a small valley with trees

**delphinium** NOUN delphiniums
a garden plant with tall spikes of flowers, usually blue

**delta** NOUN deltas
a triangular area at the mouth of a river where it spreads into branches (WORD ORIGIN) shaped like the Greek letter delta (= D), written Δ

**delude** VERB deludes, deluding, deluded
to deceive someone into believing something that is not true

**deluge** NOUN deluges
❶ a large flood ❷ a heavy fall of rain ❸ something coming in great numbers • *a deluge of questions*

**deluge** VERB deluges, deluging, deluged
to be deluged with something is to be overwhelmed by a great number of them • *We have been deluged with replies.*

**delusion** NOUN delusions
a false belief

**de luxe** ADJECTIVE
of very high quality

**delve** VERB delves, delving, delved
❶ to delve into a subject is to study it closely • *I've been delving into the history of the local area.* ❷ to search for something inside a bag or container

**demand** VERB demands, demanding, demanded
❶ to ask for something firmly or forcefully ❷ to need something • *This work demands great skill.*

**demand** NOUN demands
❶ a firm or forceful request ❷ a desire to have or buy something • *There was a great demand for tickets.*
➤ **in demand** wanted or needed

**demanding** ADJECTIVE
❶ needing skill or effort • *a demanding job* ❷ needing a lot of attention • *a demanding child*

**demarcation** (say dee-mar-**kay**-shon) NOUN
marking the boundary or limits of something

**demean** VERB demeans, demeaning, demeaned
to lower a person's dignity • *I wouldn't demean myself to ask for it!*

**demeanour** (say dim-**een**-er) NOUN demeanours
a person's behaviour or manner • *Suddenly his whole demeanour changed.*

**demented** ADJECTIVE
driven mad; crazy

**demerara** (say dem-er-**air**-a) NOUN
light-brown cane sugar

**demerit** NOUN demerits
a fault or defect

**demigod** NOUN demigods
a partly divine being

**demise** (say dim-**yz**) NOUN (*formal*)
❶ a person's death ❷ the end or failure of something

**demisemiquaver** NOUN demisemiquavers
(*chiefly British*) a note in music, equal in length to one-eighth of a crotchet

**demist** VERB demists, demisting, demisted
(*British*) to remove misty condensation from a windscreen etc.

**demo** NOUN demos (*informal*)
a demonstration

**democracy** NOUN democracies
❶ government of a country by representatives elected by all the people ❷ a country governed in this way

**Democrat** NOUN Democrats
a member of the Democratic Party in the USA

**democrat** NOUN democrats
a person who believes in or supports democracy

**democratic** ADJECTIVE
❶ based on the system of democracy • *democratic elections* ❷ taking account of the views of all people involved • *We've reached a democratic decision.*
➤ **democratically** ADVERB

**demolish** VERB demolishes, demolishing, demolished
❶ to pull or knock down a building ❷ to destroy something completely • *She demolished his argument in one sentence.*
➤ **demolition** NOUN

**demon** NOUN demons
❶ a devil or evil spirit ❷ a fierce or forceful person
➤ **demonic** (say dim-**on**-ik) ADJECTIVE

**demonstrate** VERB demonstrates, demonstrating, demonstrated
❶ to show that something is true; to prove something ❷ to show someone how to do something or how something works ❸ to take part in a demonstration
➤ **demonstrator** NOUN

**demonstration** NOUN demonstrations
❶ demonstrating; showing how to do or work something ❷ a march or meeting held to show everyone what you think about something

**demonstrative** (say dim-**on**-strat-iv) ADJECTIVE
❶ showing feelings or affections openly ❷ (*in grammar*) pointing out the person or thing referred to. *This*, *that*, *these* and *those* are demonstrative adjectives and pronouns.

**demoralize** (also **demoralise**) VERB
demoralizes, demoralizing, demoralized
to make someone lose confidence or the courage to continue doing something

**demote** VERB demotes, demoting, demoted
to move someone to a lower position or rank than they had before
➤ **demotion** NOUN

**demur** (say dim-**er**) VERB demurs, demurring, demurred
to raise objections to something • *At first he demurred, but finally he agreed.*

**demure** ADJECTIVE
shy and modest
➤ **demurely** ADVERB

**den** NOUN dens
❶ a wild animal's lair ❷ a place where something illegal happens • *a gambling den* ❸ a secret place where children go to play

**denial** NOUN denials
a statement that something is not true

**denim** NOUN
a kind of strong, usually blue, cotton cloth used to make jeans etc. WORD ORIGIN from French *serge de Nim* = serge from Nîmes (a town in southern France)

**denizen** (say **den**-iz-en) NOUN denizens
an inhabitant • *Monkeys are denizens of the jungle.*

**denomination** NOUN denominations
❶ a person's name or title ❷ a branch of a Church or religion • *Baptists, Methodists and other denominations* ❸ a unit of money • *coins of small denomination*

**denominator** NOUN denominators
the number below the line in a fraction, showing how many parts the whole is divided into, e.g. 4 in ¼. Compare with **numerator**.

**denote** VERB denotes, denoting, denoted
to mean or indicate something • *In road signs, P denotes a car park.*

**dénouement** (say day-**noo**-mahn) NOUN dénouements
the final outcome of a plot or story, which is revealed at the end (WORD ORIGIN) French = unravelling

**denounce** VERB denounces, denouncing, denounced
to speak strongly against someone or something; to accuse someone of something • *They denounced him as a spy.*
➤ **denunciation** NOUN

**dense** ADJECTIVE
❶ thick and not easy to see through • *dense fog* ❷ packed closely together • *a dense forest* ❸ (*informal*) stupid

**densely** ADVERB
thickly; closely together • *a densely populated area*

**density** NOUN densities
❶ how thick or tightly packed something is ❷ (*in science*) the proportion of mass to volume • *Water has greater density than air.*

**dent** NOUN dents
a hollow left in a surface where something has pressed or hit it

**dent** VERB dents, denting, dented
to make a dent in something

**dental** ADJECTIVE
to do with your teeth or with dentistry

**dentist** NOUN dentists
a person who is trained to treat people's teeth and gums
➤ **dentistry** NOUN

**dentures** PLURAL NOUN
a set of false teeth

**denunciation** NOUN denunciations
denouncing someone or something

**deny** VERB denies, denying, denied
❶ to say that something is not true • *Do*

you deny it? ❷ to refuse to give or allow something • *She could not deny his request.*
➤ **deny yourself** to go without pleasures

**deodorant** (say dee-**oh**-der-ant) NOUN deodorants
a substance that removes unpleasant smells

**deodorize** (also **deodorise**) VERB deodorizes, deodorizing, deodorized
to remove unpleasant smells
➤ **deodorization** NOUN

**depart** VERB departs, departing, departed
to go away or leave • *The next train to the airport departs from platform 2.*

**department** NOUN departments
one section of a large organization or shop
➤ **departmental** ADJECTIVE

**department store** NOUN department stores
a large shop that sells many different kinds of goods

**departure** NOUN departures
leaving or going away from a place • *He delayed his departure until the following morning.*

**depend** VERB depends, depending, depended
❶ to rely on someone or something • *We depend on your help.* ❷ to be controlled or decided by something else • *It all depends on the weather.*

**dependable** ADJECTIVE
that you can depend on; reliable

**dependant** NOUN dependants
a person who depends on another, especially financially • *She has two dependants, a son and a daughter.*

> **SPELLING**
> Note that the spelling ends ant for this noun but ent for the adjective **dependent**.

**dependence** NOUN
being dependent on someone or something • *The country needs to reduce its dependence on imported oil.*

> **SPELLING**
> There is no a in **dependence**. Do not forget the ce at the end.

**dependency** NOUN dependencies
a country that is controlled by another

**dependent** ADJECTIVE
❶ relying on someone else financially • *She has two dependent children.* • *He was*

a
b
c
d
e
f
g
h
i
j
k
l
m
n
o
p
q
r
s
t
u
v
w
x
y
z

*dependent on his father.* ❷ controlled by or needing something • *Unlike other balloons, an airship is not dependent on the wind.*

SPELLING

Note that the spelling ends ent for this adjective but ant for the noun dependant.

**depict** VERB depicts, depicting, depicted
❶ to show something in a painting or drawing etc. ❷ to describe something in words • *The novel depicts life in the village a century ago.*
➤ depiction NOUN

**deplete** (say dip-**leet**) VERB depletes, depleting, depleted
to reduce the supply of something by using up large amounts • *Fish stocks have been severely depleted.*
➤ depletion NOUN

**deplorable** ADJECTIVE
extremely bad or shocking • *Their rudeness was deplorable.*

**deplore** VERB deplores, deploring, deplored
to strongly dislike something because you think it is wrong

**deploy** VERB deploys, deploying, deployed
❶ to place troops or weapons in good positions so that they are ready to be used effectively ❷ to use something effectively • *He deployed his arguments well.*
➤ deployment NOUN

**deport** VERB deports, deporting, deported
to send an unwanted foreign person out of a country
➤ deportation NOUN

**deportment** NOUN
a person's way of standing and walking

**depose** VERB deposes, deposing, deposed
to remove a person from power

**deposit** NOUN deposits
❶ an amount of money paid into a bank or other account ❷ a sum of money paid as a first instalment ❸ a layer of solid matter in or on the earth • *New deposits of copper were found.*

**deposit** VERB deposits, depositing, deposited
❶ to put something down • *She deposited the books on the desk.* ❷ to pay money as a deposit
➤ depositor NOUN

**deposition** NOUN depositions
a written piece of evidence, given under oath

**depot** (say **dep**-oh) NOUN depots
❶ a place where things are stored ❷ a place where buses or trains are kept and repaired

**depraved** ADJECTIVE
behaving wickedly; of bad character
➤ depravity NOUN

**deprecate** (say **dep**-rik-ayt) VERB deprecates, deprecating, deprecated
to say that you disapprove of something
➤ deprecation NOUN
➤ deprecatory (say dep-rik-**ayt**-er-i) ADJECTIVE

**depreciate** (say dip-**ree**-shee-ayt) VERB depreciates, depreciating, depreciated
to become lower in value over a period of time
➤ depreciation NOUN

**depress** VERB depresses, depressing, depressed
❶ to make someone feel very sad and gloomy ❷ to lower the value of something • *Threat of war depressed prices* ❸ to press something down • *Depress the lever.*
➤ depressive ADJECTIVE

**depressed** ADJECTIVE
feeling very sad and without hope

**depressing** ADJECTIVE
making you feel sad or gloomy

**depression** NOUN depressions
❶ a feeling of great sadness or hopelessness, often with physical symptoms ❷ a long period when trade is very slack because no one can afford to buy things, with widespread unemployment ❸ a shallow hollow in the ground or on a surface ❹ an area of low air pressure which may bring rain

**deprive** VERB deprives, depriving, deprived
to take or keep something away from someone • *The prisoners were deprived of food.*
➤ deprivation NOUN

**deprived** ADJECTIVE
not having enough of the things that are essential for a comfortable life, e.g. food, money, etc. • *a deprived area*

**depth** NOUN depths
❶ being deep; how deep something is • *What is the depth of the river here?* ❷ how strong or intense something is • *I was surprised by the depth of his feelings.* ❸ the deepest or lowest part • *the depths of the sea*
➤ in depth thoroughly
➤ out of your depth ❶ in water that is too

**deputation** NOUN deputations
a group of people sent as representatives of others

**depute** (say dip-**yoot**) VERB deputes, deputing, deputed
to appoint a person to do something • *We deputed John to take the message.*

**deputize** (also **deputise**) VERB deputizes, deputizing, deputized
to act as someone's deputy

**deputy** NOUN deputies
a person appointed to help someone else in their job and to take their place when they are away

**derail** VERB derails, derailing, derailed
to cause a train to come off the tracks
➤ **derailment** NOUN

**deranged** ADJECTIVE
insane; wild and out of control
➤ **derangement** NOUN

**derby** (say **dar**-bi) NOUN derbies
a sports match between two teams from the same city or area (WORD ORIGIN) from the name of the Earl of *Derby*, who in 1780 founded the famous horse race called the Derby which is run at Epsom in Surrey

**derelict** (say **derri**-likt) ADJECTIVE
abandoned and left to fall into ruin • *an old derelict mill*
➤ **dereliction** NOUN

**deride** VERB derides, deriding, derided
to laugh at someone or something with contempt or scorn

**derision** NOUN
scorn or ridicule • *She gave a snort of derision.*
➤ **derisive** (say dir-**y**-siv) ADJECTIVE
➤ **derisively** ADVERB

**derisory** ADJECTIVE
❶ so small that it is ridiculous • *a derisory offer* ❷ scornful

**derivation** NOUN derivations
the origin of a word from another language or from another word

**derivative** ADJECTIVE
derived from something; not original
➤ **derivative** NOUN

**derive** VERB derives, deriving, derived
❶ to obtain something from a source • *She*
derived great enjoyment from music. ❷ to originate from a language or from another word • *Some English words are derived from Latin words.*

**dermatology** NOUN
the study of the skin and its diseases
➤ **dermatologist** NOUN

**dermis** NOUN
the layer of skin below the epidermis

**derogatory** (say di-**rog**-at-er-ee) ADJECTIVE
scornful or critical • *derogatory remarks*

**derrick** NOUN derricks
❶ a kind of crane for lifting things ❷ a tall framework holding the machinery used in drilling an oil well (WORD ORIGIN) originally a gallows; Derrick was the surname of a London hangman

**derv** NOUN
(*British*) diesel fuel for lorries and other heavy vehicles (WORD ORIGIN) from the initials of 'diesel-engined road vehicle'

**dervish** NOUN dervishes
a member of a Muslim religious group who vowed to live a life of poverty

**descant** NOUN descants
a tune sung or played above the main tune

**descend** VERB descends, descending, descended
❶ to go or come down • *The plane started to descend.* • *She descended the stairs slowly.*
❷ to surprise someone with a sudden visit • *I hope you don't mind us descending on you like this.*
➤ **be descended from someone** to have someone as an ancestor; to come by birth from a certain person or family

**descendant** NOUN descendants
a person who is descended from someone

**descending** ADJECTIVE
going down from the highest to the lowest • *I have listed the scores in descending order.*

**descent** NOUN descents
❶ the process of going down; a climb down
• *The plane began its descent.* ❷ a way down; a downward path or slope • *The descent is steep.* ❸ a person's family origin • *She is of French descent.*

**describe** VERB describes, describing, described
❶ to say what someone or something is like
• *How would you describe the painting?* • *Can you describe what happened?* ❷ to move or draw something in a particular pattern or

shape • *The orbit of the Earth around the Sun describes an ellipse.*

**description** NOUN descriptions
❶ describing someone or something ❷ an account or picture in words

**descriptive** ADJECTIVE
giving a description; full of details • *a descriptive poem*

**desecrate** (say **dess**-ik-rayt) VERB desecrates, desecrating, desecrated
to treat a sacred thing without respect
➤ **desecration** NOUN

**desert** (say **dez**-ert) NOUN deserts
a large area of dry land, often covered with sand

**desert** (say diz-**ert**) VERB deserts, deserting, deserted
❶ to leave a person or place without intending to return ❷ to run away from the army
➤ **desertion** NOUN

SPELLING
Desert is different from dessert, which means food eaten at the end of a meal.

**deserted** ADJECTIVE
empty or abandoned • *The streets were deserted.*

**deserter** NOUN deserters
a soldier who runs away from the army

**desert island** NOUN desert islands
an uninhabited island

**deserts** (say diz-**erts**) PLURAL NOUN
what a person deserves • *He got his deserts.*

**deserve** VERB deserves, deserving, deserved
to have a right to something; to be worthy of something • *Everyone deserves a second chance.*
➤ **deservedly** ADVERB

**desiccated** ADJECTIVE
dried, in order to preserve it • *desiccated coconut*

**design** NOUN designs
❶ the way something is made or arranged ❷ a drawing that shows how something is to be made ❸ lines and shapes that form a decoration; a pattern ❹ a plan or scheme in the mind
➤ **have designs on something** to plan to get hold of something

**design** VERB designs, designing, designed
❶ to draw a design for something ❷ to plan or intend something for a special purpose • *The course is designed for beginners.*

SPELLING
There is a silent g before the n in design.

**designate** VERB designates, designating, designated
❶ to mark or describe a thing as something particular • *They designated the river as the boundary.* ❷ *These arrows designate the emergency exits.* ❷ to appoint someone to a position • *She designated me as her successor.*

**designate** ADJECTIVE
appointed to a job but not yet doing it • *the bishop designate*
➤ **designation** NOUN

**designer** NOUN designers
someone who designs things, especially clothes

**desirable** ADJECTIVE
worth having or doing • *It would be desirable to repeat the experiment if possible.*
➤ **desirability** NOUN

**desire** NOUN desires
a feeling of wanting something very much
➤ **desirous** ADJECTIVE

**desire** VERB desires, desiring, desired
to want something very much

**desist** (say diz-**ist**) VERB desists, desisting, desisted
(*formal*) to stop doing something

**desk** NOUN desks
❶ a piece of furniture with a flat top and often drawers, used when writing or doing work ❷ a counter at which a cashier or receptionist sits

**desktop** NOUN desktops
❶ a screen on a computer that shows the icons of the programs that you can use ❷ a computer that is designed to be used on a desk

**desolate** ADJECTIVE
❶ lonely and sad ❷ uninhabited or barren • *a desolate landscape*
➤ **desolation** NOUN

**despair** NOUN
a feeling of hopelessness

**despair** VERB despairs, despairing, despaired
to lose all hope • *She despaired of ever seeing him again.*

**despatch** VERB despatches, despatching, despatched
a different spelling of **dispatch**
➤ **despatch** NOUN

**desperado** (say dess-per-**ah**-doh) NOUN
desperadoes
a reckless criminal

**desperate** ADJECTIVE
❶ extremely serious or hopeless • *a desperate situation* ❷ needing or wanting something very much • *She is desperate to get a ticket.* ❸ reckless and ready to do anything
➤ **desperation** NOUN

> **SPELLING**
> There is a tricky bit in desperate—it has an e in the middle.

**desperately** ADVERB
❶ in a desperate way • *She tried desperately to grab the rope.* ❷ very much; extremely • *He was desperately unlucky not to win.*

**despicable** ADJECTIVE
very unpleasant or evil; deserving to be despised

**despise** VERB despises, despising, despised
to hate someone or something or have no respect for them

**despite** PREPOSITION
in spite of • *They went out despite the rain.*

**despondent** ADJECTIVE
sad or gloomy
➤ **despondently** ADVERB
➤ **despondency** NOUN

**despot** (say **dess**-pot) NOUN despots
a tyrant
➤ **despotism** NOUN
➤ **despotic** (say dis-**pot**-ik) ADJECTIVE

**dessert** (say diz-**ert**) NOUN desserts
fruit or a sweet food served as the last course of a meal

> **SPELLING**
> Dessert is different from desert, which means an area of very dry land.

**dessertspoon** NOUN dessertspoons
a medium-sized spoon used for eating puddings etc.

**destination** NOUN destinations
the place to which a person or thing is travelling or being sent

**destined** ADJECTIVE
intended by fate; meant to happen • *They felt they were destined to win.*

**destiny** NOUN destinies
what will happen or has happened to someone or something, in a way that seems to be beyond human control; fate • *She felt that it was her destiny to be a great singer.*

**destitute** ADJECTIVE
left without anything; living in extreme poverty
➤ **destitution** NOUN

**destroy** VERB destroys, destroying, destroyed
to damage something so badly that it can no longer be used or no longer exists • *The building was destroyed by fire.*

**destroyer** NOUN destroyers
a fast warship

**destruction** NOUN
destroying something or being destroyed
• *The war brought death and destruction to the city.*

**destructive** ADJECTIVE
causing a lot of harm or damage
• *Earthquakes can be very destructive.*

**desultory** (say **dess**-ul-ter-ee) ADJECTIVE
half-hearted, without enthusiasm or a definite plan • *a desultory conversation*
**WORD ORIGIN** from Latin *desultorius* = like an acrobat (someone who leaps about)

**detach** VERB detaches, detaching, detached
to unfasten or separate something • *Detach the coupon from the bottom of the page.*
➤ **detachable** ADJECTIVE

**detached** ADJECTIVE
❶ separated; not connected ❷ a detached house is one that is not joined to another ❸ able to stand back from a situation and not get emotionally involved in it • *As a journalist, I need to remain detached.*

**detachment** NOUN detachments
❶ the ability to stand back from a situation and not get emotionally involved in it ❷ a small group of soldiers sent away from a larger group for a special duty

**detail** NOUN details
❶ a very small part of a design, plan or decoration ❷ a small piece of information
➤ **in detail** describing or dealing with everything fully

**detailed** ADJECTIVE
giving many details • *a detailed description*

**detain** VERB detains, detaining, detained
❶ to keep someone waiting • *I'll try not to detain you for long.* ❷ to keep someone at a place

**detainee** NOUN detainees
a person who is officially detained or kept in custody

**detect** VERB detects, detecting, detected
to discover or notice something • *A bat's ears can detect sounds that are too high for us to hear.*
➤ **detection** NOUN

**detective** NOUN detectives
a person, especially a police officer, who investigates crimes

**detector** NOUN detectors
a device that detects something • *a smoke detector*

**detention** NOUN detentions
❶ detaining or being detained ❷ being made to stay late in school as a punishment

**deter** VERB deters, deterring, deterred
to discourage or prevent a person from doing something • *Nothing would deter Will from his plan.*

**detergent** NOUN detergents
a substance used for cleaning or washing things

**deteriorate** (say dit-**eer**-ee-er-ayt) VERB
deteriorates, deteriorating, deteriorated
to become worse • *The weather was starting to deteriorate.*
➤ **deterioration** NOUN

**determination** NOUN
the firm intention to achieve what you have decided to achieve

**determine** VERB determines, determining, determined
❶ to decide something • *His punishment is still to be determined.* ❷ to cause or influence something • *Where you live can determine your state of health.* ❸ to find out or calculate something • *Can you determine the height of the mountain?*

**determined** ADJECTIVE
full of determination; with your mind firmly made up

**determiner** NOUN determiners
(*in grammar*) a word (such as *a*, *the*, *many*) that introduces a noun and gives you some information about it

**GRAMMAR**

Nouns often have a determiner in front of them. Determiners tell you 'which one', 'how many', or 'how much'. The most common determiners are the words *the*, known as the definite article, and *a* or *an*, known as the indefinite article. The following words are also determiners when they come before a noun:

*this*, *that*, *these*, and *those* (known as demonstratives), e.g. <u>*this*</u> *weekend*, <u>*those*</u> *boots*;

*my*, *your*, *his*, *her*, *its*, *our*, and *their* (known as possessives), e.g. *That's* <u>*my*</u> *idea; It's* <u>*your*</u> *problem*;

*what*, *which*, and *whose* (known as interrogatives), e.g. <u>*What*</u> *flavours do you have?* <u>*Which*</u> *team won?*

Other determiners, such as *all*, *another*, *any*, *both*, *each*, *every*, *few*, *many*, *some*, and *several*, are used to express quantity, e.g. <u>*Both*</u> *socks are missing;* <u>*Few*</u> *people have climbed this mountain.* Note that *any* and *some* can refer to either a number of separate things (<u>*any*</u> *coins*, <u>*some*</u> *biscuits*), or to an amount of something (<u>*any*</u> *money*, <u>*some*</u> *cake*).

Numbers can also be determiners when they come before a noun, e.g. <u>*one*</u> *slice*, <u>*thirty*</u> *euros*, as can the words *next* and *last*, e.g. <u>*next*</u> *season*, <u>*last*</u> *summer*.

See also the panels on the and a and the panel on possessives.

**deterrent** NOUN deterrents
something that may deter people, e.g. a nuclear weapon that deters countries from making war on the one that has it
➤ **deterrence** NOUN

**detest** VERB detests, detesting, detested
to strongly dislike a person or thing • *They absolutely detest each other.*
➤ **detestable** ADJECTIVE
➤ **detestation** NOUN

**detonate** (say **det**-on-ayt) VERB detonates, detonating, detonated
to explode or make a bomb or mine explode
➤ **detonation** NOUN
➤ **detonator** NOUN

**detour** (say **dee**-toor) NOUN detours
a roundabout route you use instead of the normal one

**detract** VERB detracts, detracting, detracted
to make something seem less good or
valuable • *Not even the rain could detract
from our enjoyment.*
➤ **detraction** NOUN

**detriment** (say det-rim-ent) NOUN
something is to the detriment of a thing if
it is harmful or damaging to it • *She worked
long hours, to the detriment of her health.*

**detrimental** (say det-rim-**en**-tal) ADJECTIVE
harmful or damaging • *The sun can have a
detrimental effect on the skin.*

**deuce** NOUN deuces
a score in tennis where both sides have 40
points and must gain two consecutive points
to win

**devalue** VERB devalues, devaluing, devalued
❶ to reduce a thing's value ❷ to reduce the
value of a country's currency in relation to
other currencies or to gold
➤ **devaluation** NOUN

**devastate** VERB devastates, devastating,
devastated
❶ to ruin or cause great destruction to
something • *Floods devastated the region.*
❷ to overwhelm someone with shock or grief
• *The tragedy has devastated the community.*
➤ **devastating** ADJECTIVE
➤ **devastation** NOUN

**develop** VERB develops, developing, developed
❶ to create or improve something gradually
• *Over the years she developed her own
singing style.* ❷ to become bigger or better;
to grow • *Children develop at different rates.*
❸ to come gradually into existence • *A storm
was developing in the distance.* ❹ to begin to
have or use something • *They developed bad
habits.* ❺ to use an area of land for building
houses, shops, factories, etc. ❻ to treat
photographic film with chemicals so that
pictures appear
➤ **developer** NOUN

SPELLING
There is no e at the end of develop.

**developing country** NOUN developing
countries
a poor country that is building up its industry
and trying to improve its living conditions

**development** NOUN developments
❶ developing or being developed ❷ a recent
event that changes a situation • *Have there
been any further developments since I
last saw you?* ❸ an area of land with new
buildings on it

SPELLING
Be careful: there is only one p and one l in
development.

**deviate** (say dee-vee-ayt) VERB deviates,
deviating, deviated
to turn aside from a course or from what is
usual or true
➤ **deviation** NOUN

**device** NOUN devices
a tool or piece of equipment used for a
particular purpose • *a device for opening tins*
➤ **leave someone to their own devices** to
leave someone to do as they wish

**devil** NOUN devils
❶ an evil spirit ❷ a wicked, cruel or annoying
person

**devilish** ADJECTIVE
extremely cruel or cunning • *a devilish plan*

**devilment** NOUN
mischief

**devious** (say dee-vee-us) ADJECTIVE
❶ cunning and dishonest; underhand • *He
got rich by devious means.* ❷ a devious route
is roundabout and not direct
➤ **deviously** ADVERB

**devise** VERB devises, devising, devised
to invent a way of doing something • *He
devised a new method of painting.*

**devoid** ADJECTIVE
lacking or without something • *His work is
devoid of merit.*

**devolution** NOUN
handing over power from central government
to local or regional government

**devolve** VERB devolves, devolving, devolved
a task or power devolves on a deputy or
successor when it is passed on to them

**devote** VERB devotes, devoting, devoted
to devote yourself or your time to something
is to spend all your time doing it • *He devotes
all his free time to music.*

**devoted** ADJECTIVE
very loving or loyal

**devotee** (say dev-o-**tee**) NOUN devotees
a person who likes something very much; an
enthusiast • *a devotee of science fiction*

**devotion** NOUN
great love or loyalty

**devotions** *PLURAL NOUN*
prayers

**devour** *VERB* devours, devouring, devoured
❶ to eat or swallow something hungrily or greedily ❷ to read or look at something eagerly • *She devours two or three books a week.*

**devout** *ADJECTIVE*
deeply religious
➤ **devoutly** *ADVERB*

**dew** *NOUN*
tiny drops of water that form during the night on the ground and other surfaces in the open air
➤ **dewdrop** *NOUN*
➤ **dewy** *ADJECTIVE*

SPELLING
Be careful, this sounds the same as due.

**dexterity** (say deks-**terri**-tee) *NOUN*
skill in handling things WORD ORIGIN from Latin *dexter* = on the right-hand side, because the right hand was thought of as the stronger hand

**dhal** *NOUN*
an Indian dish of cooked lentils

**dhoti** *NOUN* dhotis
a loincloth worn by male Hindus

**diabetes** (say dy-a-**bee**-teez) *NOUN*
a disease in which there is too much sugar in a person's blood
➤ **diabetic** (say dy-a-**bet**-ik) *ADJECTIVE & NOUN*

**diabolical** *ADJECTIVE*
❶ like a devil; very wicked ❷ very bad or annoying • *The traffic was diabolical.*

**diadem** (say **dy**-a-dem) *NOUN* diadems
a crown or headband worn by a royal person

**diagnose** *VERB* diagnoses, diagnosing, diagnosed
to find out and say what disease a person has or what is wrong • *My brother was diagnosed with diabetes.*

**diagnosis** *NOUN* diagnoses
saying what is wrong with someone who is ill after examining them • *The doctor made a diagnosis of asthma.*
➤ **diagnostic** *ADJECTIVE*

**diagonal** (say dy-**ag**-on-al) *NOUN* diagonals
a straight line joining opposite corners • *Fold the paper in half along the diagonal.*

**diagonal** *ADJECTIVE*
slanting; crossing from corner to corner
➤ **diagonally** *ADVERB*

**diagram** *NOUN* diagrams
a kind of drawing or picture that shows the parts of something or how it works

**dial** *NOUN* dials
❶ a circular object with numbers or letters round it, used for measuring something ❷ a round control on a radio, cooker, etc. that you turn to change something

**dial** *VERB* dials, dialling, dialled
to press the numbers on a telephone dial or keypad in order to call a telephone number

**dialect** *NOUN* dialects
the words and pronunciations used by people in one district but not in the rest of a country

**dialogue** *NOUN* dialogues
❶ the words spoken by characters in a play, film or story ❷ a conversation

**dialysis** (say dy-**al**-iss-iss) *NOUN*
a way of removing harmful substances from a person's blood by letting it flow through a machine

**diameter** (say dy-**am**-it-er) *NOUN* diameters
❶ a line drawn straight across a circle or sphere and passing through its centre ❷ the length of this line

**diametrically** *ADVERB*
something that is diametrically opposite is completely opposite • *My sister and I took diametrically opposite views about the matter.*

**diamond** *NOUN* diamonds
❶ a very hard precious stone, a form of carbon, that looks like clear glass ❷ a shape with four equal sides and four angles that are not right angles ❸ a playing card with red diamond shapes on it

SPELLING
There is a tricky bit in diamond – there is an a after the i.

**diamond wedding** *NOUN* diamond weddings
a couple's 60th wedding anniversary

**diaper** *NOUN* diapers
(*North American*) a baby's nappy

**diaphanous** (say dy-**af**-an-us) *ADJECTIVE*
diaphanous fabric is thin, light and almost transparent

**diaphragm** (say **dy**-a-fram) *NOUN* diaphragms
❶ the muscular layer inside your body that

separates your chest from your abdomen
and is used in breathing ❷ a dome-shaped
contraceptive device that fits over the neck
of the womb

**diarist** NOUN diarists
a person who keeps a diary

**diarrhoea** (say dy-a-ree-a) NOUN
too frequent and too watery emptying of the
bowels

**diary** NOUN diaries
a book in which someone writes down what
happens each day

**diatribe** NOUN diatribes
a strong verbal attack

**dice** NOUN dice
a small cube marked with dots (1 to 6) on its
sides, used in games

USAGE

Dice was originally the plural of the noun
die, but now it is often used as a singular,
with the plural dice.

**dice** VERB dices, dicing, diced
❶ to cut meat, vegetables, etc. into small
cubes ❷ to play gambling games using dice

**dictate** VERB dictates, dictating, dictated
❶ to speak or read something aloud for
someone else to write down ❷ to give orders
in a bossy way

**dictates** (say **dik**-tayts) PLURAL NOUN
rules or principles that must be obeyed • the
dictates of fashion

**dictation** NOUN dictations
❶ a test in which students write down what
is being read to them, especially in a language
lesson ❷ speaking or reading something
aloud for someone else to write down

**dictator** NOUN dictators
a ruler who has complete power over the
people of a country
➤ **dictatorship** NOUN

**dictatorial** (say dik-ta-**tor**-ee-al) ADJECTIVE
always telling people what to do and ignoring
their views

**diction** NOUN
❶ a person's way of speaking words • clear
diction ❷ a writer's choice of words

**dictionary** NOUN dictionaries
a book that contains words in alphabetical
order so that you can find out how to spell
them and what they mean; a similar product
for use on a computer

**diddle** VERB diddles, diddling, diddled
(informal)
to cheat or swindle someone

**didgeridoo** NOUN didgeridoos
an Australian Aboriginal musical instrument
which consists of a long thin pipe that you
blow into to make a low humming sound

**didn't** (mainly spoken)
did not

SPELLING

Didn't = did + not. Add an apostrophe
between the n and the t.

**die** VERB dies, dying, died
❶ to stop living or existing ❷ to stop working
or burning • The engine spluttered and died.
➤ **be dying for** or **to** (informal) to want to
have or do something very much • We are all
dying to see you again.
➤ **die down** to gradually become less strong
• The wind died down at last.
➤ **die out** to gradually disappear or become
extinct • The tiger is beginning to die out.

**die** NOUN
❶ singular of **dice** ❷ dies a device that
stamps a design on coins etc. or that cuts or
moulds metal

SPELLING

Change the ie to y and add ing to make
dying.

**diehard** NOUN diehards
a person who obstinately refuses to give up
old ideas or policies

**diesel** (say **dee**-zel) NOUN diesels
❶ an engine that works by burning oil in
compressed air ❷ fuel for this kind of engine
WORD ORIGIN named after Rudolf Diesel, a
German engineer, who invented it

**diet** NOUN diets
❶ special meals that someone eats in order
to be healthy or to lose weight ❷ the sort of
foods usually eaten by a person or animal • a
vegetarian diet ❸ the parliament of certain
countries, such as Japan

**diet** VERB diets, dieting, dieted
to keep to a diet

**dietitian** (say dy-it-**ish**-an) NOUN dietitians
an expert in diet and nutrition

**differ** VERB differs, differing, differed
❶ to be different • The two accounts differ
in some important details. ❷ to disagree in
opinion • The two writers differ on this point.

**difference** NOUN differences
❶ being different; the way in which things differ • *There's a big difference between reading about China and actually going there.* ❷ the remainder left after one number is subtracted from another • *The difference between 8 and 3 is 5.* ❸ a disagreement

**different** ADJECTIVE
❶ unlike; not the same • *You look completely different with short hair.* ❷ separate or distinct • *I called on three different occasions.*

> USAGE

It is regarded as more acceptable to say *different from* rather than *different to*, which is common in less formal use. The phrase *different than* is used in American English but not in standard British English.

> SPELLING

Remember, there is a silent er in the middle of different and it ends in ent; there is no a.

**differential** NOUN differentials
❶ a difference in wages between one group of workers and another ❷ a differential gear

**differential gear** NOUN differential gears
a system of gears that makes a vehicle's driving wheels revolve at different speeds when going round corners

**differentiate** VERB differentiates, differentiating, differentiated
❶ to be a difference between things; to make one thing different from another • *What are the features that differentiate one breed from another?* ❷ to recognize differences between things • *We do not differentiate between them.*
> **differentiation** NOUN

**differently** ADVERB
in a different way • *You'll feel differently about it tomorrow.*

**difficult** ADJECTIVE
❶ needing a lot of effort or skill; not easy to do or understand ❷ not easy to please or satisfy • *a difficult child*

**difficulty** NOUN difficulties
❶ being difficult ❷ something that causes a problem

**diffident** (say **dif**-id-ent) ADJECTIVE
shy and not self-confident; hesitating to put yourself or your ideas forward

> **diffidently** ADVERB
> **diffidence** NOUN

**diffract** VERB diffracts, diffracting, diffracted
to break up a beam of light
> **diffraction** NOUN

**diffuse** (say dif-**yooz**) VERB diffuses, diffusing, diffused
❶ to spread something widely or thinly • *The Internet is being used to diffuse knowledge.* ❷ if a gas or liquid diffuses in a substance, it becomes slowly mixed with that substance
> **diffusion** NOUN

**diffuse** (say dif-**yooss**) ADJECTIVE
❶ spread widely; not concentrated • *diffuse light* ❷ using many words; not concise

**dig** VERB digs, digging, dug
❶ to break up soil and move it; to make a hole or tunnel by moving soil ❷ to poke or jab something sharply • *Its claws dug into my hand* ❸ to seek or discover something by investigating • *We dug up some facts.*

**dig** NOUN digs
❶ a place where archaeologists dig to look for ancient remains ❷ a sharp poke • *She gave me a dig in the ribs.* ❸ an unpleasant remark

**digest** (say dy-**jest**) VERB digests, digesting, digested
❶ to soften and break down food in the stomach so that the body can absorb it ❷ to take information into your mind and think it over • *The boy digested this news in silence for a few minutes.*
> **digestible** ADJECTIVE

**digest** (say **dy**-jest) NOUN digests
a summary of news or information

**digestion** NOUN
the process of digesting food

**digestive** ADJECTIVE
to do with digestion • *the digestive system*

**digestive biscuit** NOUN digestive biscuits
a wholemeal biscuit

**digger** NOUN diggers
❶ a machine for digging ❷ (*informal*) (*Australian/NZ*) a friendly form of address for a man

**digit** (say **dij**-it) NOUN digits
❶ any of the numbers from 0 to 9 ❷ a finger or toe

**digital** ADJECTIVE
❶ to do with or using digits ❷ a digital watch or clock shows the time with a row of figures

**➌** a digital image or sound is represented as a series of binary digits **➍** a digital camera or recorder records digital sound and images
➤ **digitally** ADVERB

**digitize** (also **digitise**) VERB digitizes, digitizing, digitized
to convert information to a digital form so that it can be used on a computer

**dignified** ADJECTIVE
having or showing dignity • a dignified manner

**dignitary** NOUN dignitaries
an important official • a number of local dignitaries

**dignity** NOUN
a calm and serious manner
➤ **beneath your dignity** not considered worthy enough for you to do

**digraph** NOUN digraphs
a group of two letters forming one sound, e.g. th and ey

**digress** VERB digresses, digressing, digressed
to stray from the main subject • But I digress. Back to the story...
➤ **digression** NOUN

**dike** NOUN dikes
a different spelling of dyke

**dilapidated** ADJECTIVE
falling to pieces; in disrepair • a dilapidated fence
➤ **dilapidation** NOUN

**dilate** VERB dilates, dilating, dilated
to become or to make something wider or larger • His eyes dilated with fear.
➤ **dilation** NOUN

**dilatory** (say **dil**-at-er-ee) ADJECTIVE
slow in doing something; not prompt

**dilemma** (say dil-**em**-a) NOUN dilemmas
a situation where someone has to choose between two or more possible actions, either of which would bring difficulties

USAGE

Take care not to use dilemma to mean simply a problem or difficult situation. There should be some idea of choosing between two (or perhaps more) things.

**diligence** NOUN
careful and thorough work or effort • He prepared for the exam with great diligence.

**diligent** (say **dil**-ij-ent) ADJECTIVE
careful and hard-working • a diligent student
➤ **diligently** ADVERB

**dilute** VERB dilutes, diluting, diluted
to make a liquid weaker by adding water or other liquid
➤ **dilution** NOUN

**dilute** ADJECTIVE
diluted • a dilute acid

**dim** ADJECTIVE dimmer, dimmest
**➊** not bright or clear; only faintly lit **➋** not distinct or vivid • I have only a dim memory of the plot. **➌** (informal) stupid
➤ **dimness** NOUN

**dim** VERB dims, dimming, dimmed
to become or make something dim • As the curtain rose, the lights dimmed.
➤ **dimmer** NOUN

**dime** NOUN dimes
(North American) a ten-cent coin

**dimension** NOUN dimensions
**➊** a measurement such as length, width, area or volume • What are the dimensions of the room? **➋** the size or extent of something • a problem of considerable dimensions
➤ **dimensional** ADJECTIVE

**diminish** VERB diminishes, diminishing, diminished
**➊** to become smaller or less important • The world's resources are rapidly diminishing. **➋** to make something smaller or less important • The bad news did not diminish her enthusiasm.
➤ **diminution** NOUN

**diminutive** (say dim-**in**-yoo-tiv) ADJECTIVE
very small

**dimly** ADVERB
**➊** not brightly or clearly • a dimly lit passage **➋** not distinctly or vividly • I was dimly aware of the sound of a car in the distance.

**dimple** NOUN dimples
a small hollow or dent, especially in the skin of a person's cheek or chin
➤ **dimpled** ADJECTIVE

**din** NOUN
a loud annoying noise

**dine** VERB dines, dining, dined (formal)
to have dinner

**diner** NOUN diners
**➊** a person who is dining **➋** (North American) a small, inexpensive restaurant

a
b
c
d
e
f
g
h
i
j
k
l
m
n
o
p
q
r
s
t
u
v
w
x
y
z

**dinghy** (say **ding**-ee) NOUN dinghies
a kind of small boat

**dingo** NOUN dingoes
an Australian wild dog

**dingy** (say **din**-jee) ADJECTIVE
dark and dirty-looking • a dingy hotel room

**dinkum** ADJECTIVE (informal)
(Australian/NZ) genuine, real or honest
➤ **fair dinkum** used for emphasis or to query
whether something is true

**dinner** NOUN dinners
❶ the main meal of the day, eaten either in
the middle of the day or in the evening
❷ a formal evening meal in honour of
something

**dinosaur** (say **dy**-noss-or) NOUN dinosaurs
a prehistoric reptile, often of enormous size
**WORD ORIGIN** from Greek deinos = terrible +
sauros = lizard

**dint** NOUN
➤ **by dint of** by means of; using • I got
through the exam by dint of a good memory
and a lot of luck.

**diocese** (say **dy**-oss-iss) NOUN dioceses
a district under the care of a bishop in the
Christian Church
➤ **diocesan** (say dy-**oss**-iss-an) ADJECTIVE

**dioxide** NOUN
an oxide with two atoms of oxygen to one of
another element • carbon dioxide

**dip** VERB dips, dipping, dipped
❶ to put something into a liquid and then
take it out again • Dip the brush in the paint.
❷ to go or slope downwards • The road dips
steeply after the hill. • The sun dipped below
the horizon. ❸ to move or point something
downwards • The plane dipped its wings.

**dip** NOUN dips
❶ dipping ❷ a downward slope ❸ a quick
swim ❹ a creamy mixture into which you can
dip pieces of food

**diphtheria** (say dif-**theer**-ee-a) NOUN
a serious disease that causes inflammation in
the throat

**diphthong** (say **dif**-thong) NOUN diphthongs
a compound vowel sound made up of two
sounds, e.g. oi in point, (made up of 'aw' +
'ee') or ou in loud ('ah' + 'oo')

**diploma** NOUN diplomas
a certificate awarded by a college etc. for skill
in a particular subject

**diplomacy** NOUN
❶ the work of making agreements with other
countries ❷ skill in dealing with other people
without upsetting or offending them; tact

**diplomat** NOUN diplomats
❶ a person who represents their country
officially abroad ❷ a tactful person

**diplomatic** ADJECTIVE
❶ to do with diplomats or diplomacy
• a diplomatic career ❷ tactful; careful not to
offend people • a diplomatic reply
➤ **diplomatically** ADVERB

**dipper** NOUN dippers
❶ a kind of bird that dives for its food
❷ a ladle

**dire** ADJECTIVE
dreadful or serious • The refugees are in dire
need of food and shelter.

**direct** ADJECTIVE
❶ as straight as possible; not changing
direction • a direct flight to Hong Kong
❷ with no one or nothing in between • You
should protect your skin from direct sunlight.
❸ going straight to the point; frank ❹ exact
or complete • the direct opposite

**direct** VERB directs, directing, directed
❶ to tell or show someone the way ❷ to
guide or aim something in a certain direction
• The advert is directed at young people.
❸ to control or manage someone or
something • She has directed many films.
❹ to order someone to do something
• He directed his troops to advance.

**direct current** NOUN
electric current flowing only in one direction

**direction** NOUN directions
❶ the line along which something moves
or faces • She glanced in his direction.
❷ managing or controlling someone or
something • The mural was painted by the
students under the direction of the art
teacher.

**directions** PLURAL NOUN
information on how to use or do something
or how to get somewhere

**directive** NOUN directives
an official command

**directly** ADVERB
❶ by a direct route or in a direct line • The
man turned and looked directly at me.
❷ immediately; without delay • I want you to
come directly.

**directness** NOUN
being frank and straightforward in what you say • *He replied with his usual directness.*

**direct object** NOUN direct objects
(*in grammar*) the word that receives the action of the verb. In *she hit him*, 'him' is the direct object.

**director** NOUN directors
❶ a person who is in charge of something, especially one of a group of people managing a company ❷ a person who decides how a film, programme or play should be made or performed

**directory** NOUN directories
❶ a book containing a list of people with their telephone numbers, addresses, etc.
❷ (*in computing*) a file containing a group of other files

**direct speech** NOUN
someone's words written down exactly in the way they were said

**GRAMMAR**

Direct speech shows the exact words that a person or character says. The spoken words—and any punctuation that goes with them, such as full stops, exclamation marks or question marks—are enclosed in quotation marks:

*'Wait! Can you at least tell me your name?' I shouted at the retreating figure.*

Any description of who is speaking (e.g. *she said, I exclaimed*) is separated from the spoken words by a comma or commas:

*'We are planning', said a NASA spokesperson, 'to send a manned expedition to Mars.'*

Reported speech is also called **indirect speech**. It describes or reports what a person or character says without using their exact words. You do not use quotation marks in reported speech and the tense of the verb (*were* in this example) follows that of the reporting verb (*said* in the example):

*A NASA spokesperson <u>said</u> that they <u>were</u> planning to send a manned expedition to Mars.*

You can also leave out the word *that* at the beginning of the reported speech:

*A NASA spokesperson <u>said</u> they <u>were</u> planning to send a manned expedition to Mars.*

See also the panel on **quotation marks**.

**dirge** NOUN dirges
a slow sad song

**dirk** NOUN dirks
a kind of dagger

**dirt** NOUN
❶ anything that is not clean, such as mud or dust • *His face and hands were covered in dirt.* ❷ loose earth or soil

**dirty** ADJECTIVE dirtier, dirtiest
❶ covered with dirt; not clean ❷ unfair or dishonourable • *That was a dirty trick.*
❸ indecent or obscene

**disability** NOUN disabilities
a physical or mental condition that restricts someone's movements or senses

**disable** VERB disables, disabling, disabled
to stop something from working properly

**disabled** ADJECTIVE
unable to use part of your body because of illness or injury

**disadvantage** NOUN disadvantages
something that hinders you or is unhelpful
➤ disadvantageous ADJECTIVE

**disadvantaged** ADJECTIVE
in a bad social or economic situation
• *disadvantaged children*

**disagree** VERB disagrees, disagreeing, disagreed
❶ to have or express a different opinion from someone ❷ to have a bad effect • *Rich food disagrees with me.*

**disagreeable** ADJECTIVE
unpleasant

**disagreement** NOUN disagreements
a situation in which people have different opinions about something and often also argue • *They had a few disagreements with their neighbours.*

**disappear** VERB disappears, disappearing, disappeared
❶ to stop being visible; to vanish ❷ to stop happening or existing • *Her nervousness soon disappeared.*
➤ disappearance NOUN

**disappoint** VERB disappoints, disappointing, disappointed

A
B
C
D
E
F
G
H
I
J
K
L
M
N
O
P
Q
R
S
T
U
V
W
X
Y
Z

to make you sad by failing to do or be what you hoped for or expected • *I'm sorry to disappoint you, but I can't come after all.*
➤ **disappointed** ADJECTIVE

**disappointing** ADJECTIVE
not as good as you hoped or expected • *a disappointing result*

**disappointment** NOUN disappointments
❶ a feeling of being disappointed ❷ a person or thing that disappoints you • *The film was a big disappointment.*

**disapproval** NOUN
a feeling that someone is behaving badly
• *She could hear the disapproval in his voice.*

**disapprove** VERB disapproves, disapproving, disapproved
to think that something is wrong or bad, especially the way someone is behaving

**disarm** VERB disarms, disarming, disarmed
❶ to reduce the size of armed forces ❷ to take away someone's weapons ❸ to overcome a person's anger or doubt • *Her friendliness disarmed their suspicions.*
➤ **disarming** ADJECTIVE

**disarmament** NOUN
reduction of a country's armed forces or weapons

**disarray** NOUN
disorder or confusion • *Our plans were thrown into disarray by her sudden arrival.*

**disassemble** VERB disassembles, disassembling, disassembled
to take something to pieces

**disaster** NOUN disasters
❶ an event or accident that causes a lot of harm or damage; a very bad misfortune
• *earthquakes, floods and other natural disasters* ❷ a complete failure • *The first night of the play was a disaster.*

**disastrous** ADJECTIVE
causing great harm or failing completely
• *This mistake had disastrous results.*
➤ **disastrously** ADVERB

**disband** VERB disbands, disbanding, disbanded
a group or organization disbands when it breaks up • *The choir disbanded last year.*

**disbelief** NOUN
a feeling of not being able to believe something • *The others stared at him in disbelief.*
➤ **disbelieve** VERB

**disc** NOUN discs
❶ any round flat object ❷ a CD or DVD ❸ a layer of cartilage between vertebrae in your spine

**discard** VERB discards, discarding, discarded
to get rid of something because it is useless or unwanted

**discern** (say dis-**sern**) VERB discerns, discerning, discerned
to see or recognize something that is not obvious • *I discerned a note of anger in his voice.*
➤ **discernible** ADJECTIVE
➤ **discernment** NOUN

**discerning** ADJECTIVE
showing good judgement about the quality of something • *a discerning film-goer*

**discharge** VERB discharges, discharging, discharged
❶ to allow a person to leave a place • *She was discharged from hospital yesterday.*
❷ to send something out • *The engine was discharging black smoke.* ❸ to discharge a debt or promise is to pay it off or do what has been agreed

**discharge** NOUN discharges
❶ an act of discharging someone or something ❷ something that is discharged

**disciple** NOUN disciples
❶ a follower or pupil of a leader or of a religion or philosophy ❷ any of the original followers of Jesus Christ

**disciplinarian** NOUN disciplinarians
a person who believes in strict discipline

**discipline** NOUN disciplines
❶ training people to obey rules and behave well and punishing them if they do not ❷ self-control; the ability to work or behave in a controlled way ❸ a subject for study
➤ **disciplinary** (say **dis**-ip-lin-er-ee) ADJECTIVE

**discipline** VERB disciplines, disciplining, disciplined
❶ to train yourself to work or behave in a controlled way • *He disciplined himself to practise the piano every morning.* ❷ to punish someone

**disc jockey** NOUN disc jockeys
a person who introduces and plays records on the radio or at a club

**disclaim** VERB disclaims, disclaiming, disclaimed
to say that you are not responsible for something or have no knowledge of

something • *They disclaimed all responsibility for the bomb.*
➤ **disclaimer** *NOUN*

**disclose** *VERB* discloses, disclosing, disclosed
you disclose a fact or information when you reveal it or make it known
➤ **disclosure** *NOUN*

**disco** *NOUN* discos
an event where pop music is played for people to dance to

**discolour** *VERB* discolours, discolouring, discoloured
to spoil or change the colour of something
➤ **discoloration** *NOUN*

**discomfit** *VERB* discomfits, discomfiting, discomfited
to make a person feel uneasy or embarrassed

**discomfiture** *NOUN*
a feeling of unease or embarrassment

**discomfort** *NOUN*
❶ slight pain ❷ being uneasy or embarrassed • *She was clearly enjoying my discomfort.*

**disconcert** (say dis-kon-**sert**) *VERB* disconcerts, disconcerting, disconcerted
to make a person feel uneasy or worried • *His answer disconcerted her.*

**disconnect** *VERB* disconnects, disconnecting, disconnected
to break a connection; to detach something • *The phone has been disconnected.*
➤ **disconnection** *NOUN*

**disconnected** *ADJECTIVE*
not joined together in a logical way or order • *a disconnected narrative*

**disconsolate** (say dis-**kon**-sol-at) *ADJECTIVE*
unhappy and disappointed

**discontent** *NOUN*
a feeling of being unhappy and not satisfied • *There were a few murmurs of discontent.*
➤ **discontented** *ADJECTIVE*

**discontinue** *VERB* discontinues, discontinuing, discontinued
to stop doing or producing something

**discord** *NOUN* discords
❶ disagreement; quarrelling ❷ musical notes sounded together and producing a harsh or unpleasant sound
➤ **discordant** *ADJECTIVE*

**discotheque** (say **dis**-ko-tek) *NOUN*
discotheques
(*old use*) a disco

**discount** *NOUN* discounts
an amount by which a price is reduced

**discount** *VERB* discounts, discounting, discounted
to ignore or disregard something • *We cannot discount the possibility.*

**discourage** *VERB* discourages, discouraging, discouraged
❶ to take away someone's enthusiasm or confidence • *Don't be discouraged – try again!* ❷ to try to persuade someone not to do something • *His parents tried to discourage him from being an actor.*
➤ **discouragement** *NOUN*

**discourse** *NOUN* discourses
a formal speech or piece of writing about something

**discourse** *VERB* discourses, discoursing, discoursed
to speak or write at length about something

**discourteous** *ADJECTIVE*
not courteous or polite; rude
➤ **discourteously** *ADVERB*
➤ **discourtesy** *NOUN*

**discover** *VERB* discovers, discovering, discovered
❶ to find or find out something, especially by searching ❷ to be the first person to find something • *Herschel discovered the planet Uranus.*
➤ **discoverer** *NOUN*

**discovery** *NOUN* discoveries
❶ discovering something or being discovered • *Columbus is famous for the discovery of America.* ❷ something that is discovered • *This drug was an important discovery in the history of medicine.*

**discredit** *VERB* discredits, discrediting, discredited
❶ to cause an idea or theory to be doubted ❷ to damage someone's reputation

**discredit** *NOUN*
damage to someone's reputation
➤ **discreditable** *ADJECTIVE*

**discreet** *ADJECTIVE*
❶ being careful in what you say and not giving away secrets • *I'll make a few discreet enquiries.* ❷ not likely to attract attention
➤ **discreetly** *ADVERB*

**SPELLING**
Take care not to confuse with discrete.

**discrepancy** (say dis-**krep**-an-see) NOUN
discrepancies
lack of agreement between things which
should be the same • *There are several
discrepancies in the two accounts.*

**discrete** ADJECTIVE
(*formal*) separate; distinct from each other
• *We divided the data into six discrete
categories.*

**discretion** (say dis-**kresh**-on) NOUN
❶ being discreet; keeping secrets • *I hope
I can count on your discretion.* ❷ freedom
to decide things and take action according
to your own judgement • *You can use your
discretion.*

**discriminate** VERB discriminates,
discriminating, discriminated
❶ to notice and understand the differences
between things; to prefer one thing to
another ❷ to treat people differently or
unfairly because of their race, gender or
religion

**discrimination** NOUN
❶ different or unfair treatment of people
because of their race, gender or religion
❷ the ability to notice and understand the
differences between things

**discus** NOUN discuses
a thick heavy disc thrown in athletic contests

**discuss** VERB discusses, discussing, discussed
to talk with other people about a subject or
to write about it in detail

**discussion** NOUN discussions
❶ a conversation about a subject ❷ a piece
of writing in which the writer examines a
subject from different points of view

**disdain** NOUN
scorn or contempt • *She stared at him with
cold disdain.*
➤ **disdainful** ADJECTIVE
➤ **disdainfully** ADVERB

**disdain** VERB disdains, disdaining, disdained
❶ to regard or treat someone or something
with disdain ❷ to not do something because
of disdain • *She disdained to reply.*

**disease** NOUN diseases
an unhealthy condition; an illness
➤ **diseased** ADJECTIVE

**disembark** VERB disembarks, disembarking,
disembarked
to get off a ship or aircraft
➤ **disembarkation** NOUN

**disembodied** ADJECTIVE
a disembodied voice comes from an invisible
or unknown source

**disembowel** VERB disembowels,
disembowelling, disembowelled
to take out the bowels or inside parts of
something

**disengage** VERB disengages, disengaging,
disengaged
to disconnect or detach something

**disentangle** VERB disentangles, disentangling,
disentangled
to free something from tangles or confusion
• *I disentangled my coat from the bushes.*

**disfavour** NOUN
disapproval or dislike

**disfigure** VERB disfigures, disfiguring,
disfigured
to spoil a person's or thing's appearance • *His
face was disfigured by a long red scar.*
➤ **disfigurement** NOUN

**disgorge** VERB disgorges, disgorging,
disgorged
to pour or send something out • *The pipe
disgorged its contents.*

**disgrace** NOUN
❶ shame; loss of approval or respect
• *You have brought disgrace to your
family.* ❷ something that is shameful or
unacceptable • *The bus service is a disgrace.*

**disgrace** VERB disgraces, disgracing, disgraced
to bring disgrace upon someone

**disgraceful** ADJECTIVE
shameful or unacceptable
➤ **disgracefully** ADVERB

**disgruntled** ADJECTIVE
discontented or in a bad mood
**WORD ORIGIN** from an old word *gruntle* =
grunt softly

**disguise** VERB disguises, disguising, disguised
❶ to make a person or thing look different
so that people will not recognize them ❷ to
conceal your feelings • *She could not disguise
her amazement.*

**disguise** NOUN disguises
something you wear or use to change your
appearance so that nobody recognizes you

**disgust** NOUN
a feeling that something is very unpleasant or
disgraceful

**disgust** VERB disgusts, disgusting, disgusted
to make someone feel disgust
➤ **disgusted** ADJECTIVE

**disgusting** ADJECTIVE
making you feel disgust; very unpleasant
• *What a disgusting smell!*

**dish** NOUN dishes
❶ a plate or bowl for food ❷ food prepared for eating • *We're having a vegetarian dish tonight.* ❸ a bowl-shaped aerial for receiving broadcasting signals transmitted by satellite

**dish** VERB dishes, dishing, dished (*informal*)
➤ **dish something out** to give out portions of something to people

**dishcloth** NOUN dishcloths
a cloth you use for washing dishes

**dishearten** VERB disheartens, disheartening, disheartened
to cause a person to lose hope or confidence
➤ **disheartened** ADJECTIVE

**dishevelled** (say dish-ev-eld) ADJECTIVE
untidy in appearance • *He looked tired and dishevelled.*

**dishonest** ADJECTIVE
not honest or truthful
➤ **dishonestly** ADVERB
➤ **dishonesty** NOUN

**dishonour** NOUN
loss of honour or respect; disgrace
➤ **dishonour** VERB
➤ **dishonourable** ADJECTIVE

**dishwasher** NOUN dishwashers
a machine for washing dishes etc. automatically

**disillusion** VERB disillusions, disillusioning, disillusioned
you disillusion someone if you show them that something they like to think is true is wrong or mistaken
➤ **disillusioned** ADJECTIVE
➤ **disillusionment** NOUN

**disinclination** NOUN
unwillingness to do something

**disinclined** ADJECTIVE
unwilling to do something • *He was disinclined to believe anything she said.*

**disinfect** VERB disinfects, disinfecting, disinfected
to destroy the germs in something
➤ **disinfection** NOUN

**disinfectant** NOUN disinfectants
a substance used for disinfecting things

**disinherit** VERB disinherits, disinheriting, disinherited
to deprive a person of the right to inherit something

**disintegrate** VERB disintegrates, disintegrating, disintegrated
to break up into small parts or pieces • *The spacecraft exploded and disintegrated.*
➤ **disintegration** NOUN

**disinterested** ADJECTIVE
not influenced by the hope of gaining something yourself; impartial • *She gave us some disinterested advice.*

USAGE
If you mean 'not interested' or 'bored', use uninterested.

**disjointed** ADJECTIVE
disjointed talk or writing is not well joined together and so is difficult to understand

**disk** NOUN disks
a flat circular object on which computer data can be stored

**dislike** VERB dislikes, disliking, disliked
to not like someone or something

**dislike** NOUN dislikes
a feeling of not liking someone or something

**dislocate** VERB dislocates, dislocating, dislocated
a bone is dislocated when it moves or is forced from its proper position in one of your joints
➤ **dislocation** NOUN

**dislodge** VERB dislodges, dislodging, dislodged
to move or force something from its place
• *The wind dislodged several roof tiles.*

**disloyal** ADJECTIVE
not loyal
➤ **disloyalty** NOUN

**dismal** ADJECTIVE
❶ gloomy or dreary • *dismal surroundings*
❷ of poor quality • *a dismal first-half performance*
➤ **dismally** ADVERB
WORD ORIGIN from Latin *dies mali* = unlucky days

**dismantle** VERB dismantles, dismantling, dismantled
to take something to pieces • *He was busy dismantling the wardrobe.*

a b c **d** e f g h i j k l m n o p q r s t u v w x y z

**dismay** NOUN
a feeling of strong disappointment and surprise • *I realized to my dismay that we were going to miss our plane.*
➤ **dismayed** ADJECTIVE

**dismember** VERB dismembers, dismembering, dismembered
to tear or cut the limbs from a body

**dismiss** VERB dismisses, dismissing, dismissed
❶ to send someone away ❷ to tell someone that you will no longer employ them ❸ to put something out of your thoughts because it is not worth thinking about • *He dismissed the idea as nonsense.*
➤ **dismissal** NOUN

**dismissive** ADJECTIVE
saying or showing that you think something is not worth taking seriously • *a dismissive gesture*
➤ **dismissively** ADVERB

**dismount** VERB dismounts, dismounting, dismounted
to get off a horse or bicycle

**disobedient** ADJECTIVE
not obedient
➤ **disobedience** NOUN

**disobey** VERB disobeys, disobeying, disobeyed
to refuse to do what you are told to do • *He was punished for disobeying orders.*

**disorder** NOUN disorders
❶ untidiness or lack of order ❷ an illness • *an eating disorder* ❸ violent behaviour by a large number of people
➤ **disorderly** ADJECTIVE

**disorganized** (also **disorganised**) ADJECTIVE
muddled and badly organized
➤ **disorganization** NOUN

**disown** VERB disowns, disowning, disowned
to refuse to acknowledge that a person has any connection with you • *Her family disowned her for marrying a foreigner.*

**disparage** (say dis-**pa**-rij) VERB disparages, disparaging, disparaged
to criticize something or say that it is unimportant
➤ **disparagement** NOUN

**disparity** NOUN disparities
difference or inequality • *the wide disparity between rich and poor*

**dispassionate** ADJECTIVE
calm and impartial; not emotional
➤ **dispassionately** ADVERB

**dispatch** VERB dispatches, dispatching, dispatched
❶ to send someone or something off to a destination ❷ to kill a person or animal

**dispatch** NOUN dispatches
❶ dispatching ❷ a report or message sent ❸ to do something with dispatch is to do it promptly and efficiently

**dispatch box** NOUN dispatch boxes
a container for carrying official documents

**dispatch rider** NOUN dispatch riders
(*British*) a messenger who travels by motorcycle

**dispel** VERB dispels, dispelling, dispelled
❶ to drive or clear something away • *Wind dispels fog.* ❷ to get rid of a fear or doubt

**dispensary** NOUN dispensaries
a place where medicines are dispensed

**dispense** VERB dispenses, dispensing, dispensed
❶ to distribute something to a number of people ❷ a machine dispenses money or goods when it gives them out to customers ❸ to prepare medicine according to prescriptions
➤ **dispensation** NOUN
➤ **dispense with something** to do without something

**dispenser** NOUN dispensers
a device that supplies a quantity of something • *a cash dispenser*

**disperse** VERB disperses, dispersing, dispersed
❶ to separate and go off in different directions; to scatter • *The fog began to disperse.* ❷ to force a crowd to break up • *Police dispersed the protesters.*
➤ **dispersal** NOUN
➤ **dispersion** NOUN

**displace** VERB displaces, displacing, displaced
❶ to take a person's or thing's place • *Last year she displaced him as captain.* ❷ to force someone or something to move from their usual place • *Thousands of people have been displaced by the fighting.*
➤ **displacement** NOUN

**display** VERB displays, displaying, displayed
❶ to show or arrange something so that it can be clearly seen ❷ to show a quality or emotion • *They displayed great courage.*

**display** NOUN displays
❶ the displaying of something ❷ a collection of things displayed in a shop window,

museum, etc. ❸ an electronic device for visually presenting data

**displease** VERB displeases, displeasing, displeased
to annoy or offend someone
➤ **displeasure** NOUN

**disposable** ADJECTIVE
made to be thrown away after it has been used • *disposable nappies*

**disposal** NOUN
getting rid of something • *bomb disposal*
➤ **at your disposal** available for you to use • *The computer is at your disposal all afternoon.*

**dispose** VERB disposes, disposing, disposed
❶ to dispose of something is to get rid of it • *Please dispose of all your rubbish.* ❷ to be disposed to do something is to be ready or willing to do it • *They were not at all disposed to help us.*
➤ **be well disposed to someone** to be friendly towards someone

**disposition** NOUN dispositions
a person's nature or qualities • *She has a cheerful disposition.*

**disproportionate** ADJECTIVE
out of proportion; too large or too small

**disprove** VERB disproves, disproving, disproved
to show that something is not true • *The theory has now been disproved.*

**dispute** VERB disputes, disputing, disputed
❶ to argue about something ❷ to question the truth of something • *We dispute their claim.*

**dispute** NOUN disputes
a disagreement or argument
➤ **in dispute** being argued about • *The cause of the accident is not in dispute.*

**disqualify** VERB disqualifies, disqualifying, disqualified
to bar someone from a competition because they have broken the rules or are not properly qualified to take part
➤ **disqualification** NOUN

**disquiet** NOUN
anxiety or worry
➤ **disquieting** ADJECTIVE

**disregard** VERB disregards, disregarding, disregarded
to take no notice of something; to ignore

something • *Please disregard my earlier instructions.*

**disregard** NOUN
the act of ignoring something • *He ran into the burning building with complete disregard for his own safety.*

**disrepair** NOUN
bad condition caused by not doing repairs
• *The old mill is in a state of disrepair.*

**disreputable** ADJECTIVE
not respectable in character

**disrepute** NOUN
bad reputation • *He has been charged with bringing the game into disrepute.*

**disrespect** NOUN
lack of respect; rudeness
➤ **disrespectful** ADJECTIVE
➤ **disrespectfully** ADVERB

**disrupt** VERB disrupts, disrupting, disrupted
to stop something running smoothly; to throw something into confusion • *Fog disrupted traffic.*
➤ **disruption** NOUN

**disruptive** ADJECTIVE
causing so much disorder that a lesson, meeting, etc. cannot continue

**dissatisfied** ADJECTIVE
not satisfied or pleased
➤ **dissatisfaction** NOUN

**dissect** (say dis-**sekt**) VERB dissects, dissecting, dissected
to cut something up so that you can examine it
➤ **dissection** NOUN

**disseminate** VERB disseminates, disseminating, disseminated
to spread ideas or information widely
➤ **dissemination** NOUN

**dissent** NOUN
a difference of opinion; disagreement

**dissent** VERB dissents, dissenting, dissented
to express a difference of opinion about something

**dissertation** NOUN dissertations
a long essay on an academic subject, written as part of a university degree

**disservice** NOUN
a harmful action done by someone who was intending to help

**dissident** NOUN dissidents
a person who disagrees, especially someone

who opposes their government
➤ **dissident** ADJECTIVE
➤ **dissidence** NOUN

**dissipate** VERB dissipates, dissipating, dissipated
❶ to disappear or scatter • *The fog gradually dissipated.* ❷ to waste or squander something
➤ **dissipation** NOUN

**dissolute** ADJECTIVE
having an immoral way of life

**dissolution** NOUN dissolutions
❶ putting an end to a marriage or partnership ❷ formally ending a parliament or assembly

**dissolve** VERB dissolves, dissolving, dissolved
❶ to mix something with a liquid so that it becomes part of the liquid ❷ to break up and become mixed with a liquid • *Wait for the tablet to dissolve.* ❸ to put an end to a marriage or partnership ❹ to formally end a parliament or assembly • *Parliament was dissolved and a general election was held.*

**dissuade** VERB dissuades, dissuading, dissuaded
to persuade someone not to do something • *I tried to dissuade him from going.*

**distaff** NOUN distaffs
a stick holding raw wool for spinning into yarn

**distance** NOUN distances
❶ the amount of space between two places or things ❷ being far away in space or time • *The island looked magical from a distance.*
➤ **in the distance** far away but visible

**distant** ADJECTIVE
❶ far away • *distant stars* ❷ not closely related • *distant cousins* ❸ not friendly or sociable • *She sounded cold and distant on the phone.*
➤ **distantly** ADVERB

**distaste** NOUN
a feeling of dislike for something • *She looked at his clothes with distaste.*

**distasteful** ADJECTIVE
unpleasant or offensive

**distemper** NOUN
❶ a disease of dogs and certain other animals ❷ a kind of paint

**distend** VERB distends, distending, distended
to make something swell outwards because of pressure from inside
➤ **distension** NOUN

**distil** VERB distils, distilling, distilled
to purify a liquid by boiling it and condensing the vapour
➤ **distillation** NOUN

**distillery** NOUN distilleries
a place where whisky or other alcoholic spirit is made
➤ **distiller** NOUN

**distinct** ADJECTIVE
❶ easily heard or seen; noticeable • *There has been a distinct improvement.* ❷ clearly separate or different • *A rabbit is quite distinct from a hare.*
➤ **distinctness** NOUN

USAGE
See note at **distinctive**.

**distinction** NOUN distinctions
❶ a difference between things ❷ excellence or honour • *She is a writer of distinction.* ❸ an award for excellence; a high mark in an examination

**distinctive** ADJECTIVE
clearly different from others and therefore easy to recognize • *The school has a distinctive uniform.*
➤ **distinctively** ADVERB

USAGE
Take care not to confuse this word with **distinct**. A distinct mark is a clear mark; a distinctive mark is one that is not found anywhere else.

**distinctly** ADVERB
❶ clearly or noticeably • *I can see Mars distinctly through my binoculars.* ❷ particularly; definitely • *His behaviour has been distinctly odd recently.*

**distinguish** VERB distinguishes, distinguishing, distinguished
❶ to make or notice differences between things • *You need to distinguish between facts and opinions.* ❷ to see or hear something clearly • *I was too far away to distinguish what they were saying.* ❸ if you distinguish yourself you do something that brings you honour or respect • *He distinguished himself by his bravery.*
➤ **distinguishable** ADJECTIVE

**distinguished** ADJECTIVE
❶ excellent and famous ❷ dignified in appearance

**distort** VERB distorts, distorting, distorted
❶ to pull or twist something out of its normal

shape • *His face was distorted with anger.*
❷ to give a false account or impression of
something • *The film deliberately distorts the truth.*
➤ **distortion** NOUN

**distract** VERB distracts, distracting, distracted
to take a person's attention away from what they are doing

**distracted** ADJECTIVE
greatly upset by worry or distress; distraught

**distraction** NOUN distractions
❶ something that distracts a person's attention ❷ an amusement or entertainment
❸ great worry or distress

**distraught** (say dis-**trawt**) ADJECTIVE
greatly upset by worry or distress

**distress** NOUN distresses
great sorrow, pain or trouble
➤ **in distress** in danger and needing help

**distress** VERB distresses, distressing, distressed
to make someone feel very upset or worried
• *It distressed her to see him looking so ill.*

**distribute** VERB distributes, distributing, distributed
❶ to give or share something out to a number of people • *The money was distributed among all the local schools.* ❷ to spread or scatter something around • *Make sure your weight is evenly distributed.*
➤ **distributor** NOUN

**distribution** NOUN
❶ the way that something is shared out or spread over an area • *The map shows the distribution of rainfall in Africa.* ❷ giving or delivering something to a number of people or places • *the distribution of food supplies*

**district** NOUN districts
part of a town or country

**distrust** NOUN
lack of trust; suspicion
➤ **distrustful** ADJECTIVE

**distrust** VERB distrusts, distrusting, distrusted
to have no trust in someone or something

**disturb** VERB disturbs, disturbing, disturbed
❶ to spoil someone's peace or rest • *Sorry, I didn't mean to disturb you.* ❷ to make someone feel upset or worried ❸ to move a thing from its position • *He noticed that the papers on his desk had been disturbed.*

**disturbance** NOUN disturbances
❶ something that makes you stop what you

are doing • *We have a lot to do so we don't want any disturbances.* ❷ fighting or noisy behaviour in a public place • *There were several disturbances in the streets.*

**disuse** NOUN
the state of being no longer used • *The farm buildings had fallen into disuse.*

**disused** ADJECTIVE
no longer used • *a disused railway line*

**ditch** NOUN ditches
a trench dug to hold water or carry it away or to serve as a boundary

**ditch** VERB ditches, ditching, ditched
❶ (*informal*) to abandon or get rid of something • *The thieves ditched the car and ran off.* ❷ to bring an aircraft down in a forced landing on the sea

**dither** VERB dithers, dithering, dithered
to hesitate nervously • *Stop dithering and make up your mind!*

**ditto** NOUN
used in a list with the meaning 'the same again'

**ditty** NOUN ditties
a short simple song

**divan** NOUN divans
a bed or couch without a raised back or sides

**dive** VERB dives, diving, dived
❶ to jump into water with your arms and head first ❷ to swim under water using breathing equipment ❸ to move down quickly • *The engines failed and the plane dived.*

**dive** NOUN dives
❶ diving into water ❷ a quick downwards movement

**diver** NOUN divers
❶ someone who dives ❷ a person who works under water in a special suit with an air supply ❸ a bird that dives for its food

**diverge** VERB diverges, diverging, diverged
to go aside or in different directions • *The two paths diverge at this point.*
➤ **divergent** ADJECTIVE
➤ **divergence** NOUN

**divers** (say **dy**-verz) ADJECTIVE (*old use*)
various or several

**diverse** (say dy-**verss**) ADJECTIVE
varied; of several different kinds • *people from diverse backgrounds*

a
b
c
d
e
f
g
h
i
j
k
l
m
n
o
p
q
r
s
t
u
v
w
x
y
z

**diversify** VERB diversifies, diversifying, diversified
to become varied; to involve yourself in different kinds of things
➤ **diversification** NOUN

**diversion** NOUN diversions
❶ diverting something from its course ❷ something intended to take people's attention away from something • *You look in the room, while I create a diversion.* ❸ an alternative route for traffic when a road is closed ❹ something amusing or entertaining

**diversity** NOUN
the wide variety of something • *the region's vast diversity of animal species*

**divert** VERB diverts, diverting, diverted
❶ to make something change its direction or path • *All traffic is being diverted while the road is under repair.* ❷ to entertain or amuse someone
➤ **diverting** ADJECTIVE

**divest** VERB divests, divesting, divested
to take something away from someone • *They divested him of power.*

**divide** VERB divides, dividing, divided
❶ to separate something into smaller parts; to split something up ❷ to share something out • *We'll divide the money between us.* ❸ to find how many times one number is contained in another • *Divide six by three and you get two (6 ÷ 3 = 2).* ❹ to cause people to disagree • *This issue has divided the party.*

**dividend** NOUN dividends
❶ a share of a business's profit ❷ a number that is to be divided by another. Compare with divisor.

**dividers** PLURAL NOUN
a pair of compasses for measuring distances

**divine** ADJECTIVE
❶ belonging to or coming from God ❷ like a god ❸ (*informal*) excellent; extremely beautiful
➤ **divinely** ADVERB

**divine** VERB divines, divining, divined
to discover something by guessing or instinct

**divinity** NOUN divinities
❶ being divine ❷ a god or goddess ❸ the study of religion

**division** NOUN divisions
❶ the process of dividing numbers or things ❷ a dividing line or partition ❸ one of the parts into which something is divided ❹ a difference of opinion within a group of people

**divisive** (say div-**y**-siv) ADJECTIVE
causing disagreement within a group

**divisor** NOUN divisors
a number by which another is to be divided. Compare dividend.

**divorce** NOUN divorces
the legal ending of a marriage

**divorce** VERB divorces, divorcing, divorced
two people divorce when they end their marriage by law

**divulge** VERB divulges, divulging, divulged
to reveal information • *He promised not to divulge the secret formula.*

**Diwali** (say di-**wah**-lee) NOUN
a Hindu religious festival at which lamps are lit, held in October or November
**WORD ORIGIN** from Sanskrit *dipavali* = row of lights

**DIY** ABBREVIATION
do-it-yourself; the activity of doing your own house repairs and improvements instead of paying someone to do them • *a DIY store*

**dizzy** ADJECTIVE dizzier, dizziest
having or causing the feeling that everything is spinning round; giddy
➤ **dizzily** ADVERB
➤ **dizziness** NOUN

**DJ** ABBREVIATION
disc jockey

**DNA** ABBREVIATION
deoxyribonucleic acid; a substance in chromosomes that stores genetic information

**do** VERB does, doing, did, done
This word has many different uses, most of which mean performing or dealing with something (*Do your best. I can't do this. She is doing well at school.*) or being suitable or enough (*This will do*). The verb is also used with other verbs:
❶ in questions (*Do you want this?*) ❷ in statements with 'not' (*He does not want it.*) ❸ for emphasis (*I do like nuts.*) ❹ to avoid repeating a verb that has just been used (*We work as hard as they do.*)
➤ do away with something to get rid of something
➤ do something up ❶ to fasten something • *Do your coat up.* ❷ to repair or redecorate

208

a room or house • *We're doing up the spare room.*

**GRAMMAR**

The auxiliary verb do is used:

**in questions and in short answers:**

*Do you want to watch this film?*

*No, I don't, thanks.*

*Did he pass his exams?*

*Yes, he did.*

**in negative statements:**

*I don't want to watch this film.*

*He didn't pass his exams.*

**in negative imperatives:**

*Do not walk on the grass.*

*Don't be silly.*

**for emphasis:**

*I do want to watch this film.*

*He did pass his exam!*

**do** *NOUN* dos (*informal*) a party or other social event

**docile** (say **doh-**syl) *ADJECTIVE*
quiet, obedient and easy to control • *She was a shy docile child.*
➤ docility *NOUN*

**dock** *NOUN* docks
❶ a part of a harbour where ships are loaded, unloaded or repaired ❷ the place in a law court where the prisoner on trial sits or stands ❸ a weed with broad leaves

**dock** *VERB* docks, docking, docked
❶ a ship docks when it comes into a dock ❷ when two spacecraft dock, they join together in space ❸ to cut short an animal's tail ❹ to reduce or take away part of someone's wages or the number of points they have

**docker** *NOUN* dockers
a worker in a port who loads and unloads ships

**docket** *NOUN* dockets
a document or label listing the contents of a package

**dockyard** *NOUN* dockyards
an open area with docks and equipment for building or repairing ships

**doctor** *NOUN* doctors
❶ a person who is trained to treat sick or injured people ❷ a person who holds an advanced degree (a **doctorate**) at a university • *Doctor of Music*

**doctrine** *NOUN* doctrines
a belief held by a religious, political or other group

**document** *NOUN* documents
❶ a written or printed paper giving information or evidence about something ❷ (*in computing*) a computer file that contains text or images and that has a name • *Save the document before logging off.*
➤ documentation *NOUN*

**documentary** *ADJECTIVE*
❶ consisting of documents • *documentary evidence* ❷ showing real events or situations

**documentary** *NOUN* documentaries
a film or television programme giving information about real events

**doddery, doddering** *ADJECTIVE*
shaking and walking unsteadily because of old age

**dodge** *VERB* dodges, dodging, dodged
❶ to move quickly to avoid someone or something • *He ran across the road, dodging the traffic.* ❷ to avoid doing something • *She tried to dodge the question.*

**dodge** *NOUN* dodges
(*informal*) a trick; a clever way of doing something

**dodgem** *NOUN* dodgems
(*British*) a small electrically driven car at a funfair, in which each driver tries to bump some cars and dodge others
**WORD ORIGIN** from dodge + *'em* (them)

**dodgy** *ADJECTIVE* (*British*) (*informal*)
❶ awkward or tricky ❷ not working properly ❸ dishonest or unreliable

**dodo** *NOUN* dodos
a large heavy bird that used to live on an island in the Indian Ocean but has been extinct for over 200 years **WORD ORIGIN** from Portuguese *doudo* = fool (because the bird had no fear of people)

**doe** *NOUN* does
a female deer, rabbit or hare

**doer** *NOUN* doers
a person who does things • *He's a doer not a talker.*

**doesn't** (*mainly spoken*)
does not

> **SPELLING**
>
> Doesn't = does + not.
> Add an **apostrophe** between the n and
> the t.

**doff** VERB doffs, doffing, doffed
to take off your hat, especially to show
respect for someone **WORD ORIGIN** from *do
off*; compare **don**

**dog** NOUN dogs
a four-legged animal that barks, often kept
as a pet

**dog** VERB dogs, dogging, dogged
to follow someone closely or persistently
• *Reporters dogged his footsteps.*

**doge** (say dohj) NOUN doges
the elected ruler of the former republics of
Venice and Genoa

**dog-eared** ADJECTIVE
a dog-eared book has the corners of its pages
bent from constant use

**dogfish** NOUN dogfish
a kind of small shark

**dogged** (say **dog**-id) ADJECTIVE
determined and persistent; not giving up
easily
> **doggedly** ADVERB

**doggerel** NOUN
bad or comic verse • *a piece of doggerel*

**dogma** NOUN dogmas
a belief or principle that a Church or other
authority declares is true and must be
accepted

**dogmatic** ADJECTIVE
expressing ideas in a very firm authoritative
way
> **dogmatically** ADVERB

**dogsbody** NOUN dogsbodies (*British*) (*informal*)
a person who is given boring or unimportant
jobs to do

**doh** NOUN
a name for the keynote of a scale in music or
the note C

**doily** NOUN doilies
a small ornamental table-mat, made of paper
or lace **WORD ORIGIN** named after a Mr *Doily*
or *Doyley*, who sold household linen in the 17th
century

**doldrums** PLURAL NOUN
the ocean regions near the equator where
there is little or no wind
> **in the doldrums** feeling depressed and
unable to do anything

**dole** VERB NOUN doles, doling, doled (*informal*)
money paid by the state to unemployed
people • *He lost his job and had to go on the
dole.*
> **dole something out** to distribute
something among a group of people

**doleful** ADJECTIVE
sad or sorrowful • *a doleful expression*
> **dolefully** ADVERB

**doll** NOUN dolls
a toy model of a person, especially a baby or
child

**dollar** NOUN dollars
a unit of money in the USA and some other
countries

**dollop** NOUN dollops (*informal*)
a lump of something soft • *a dollop of cream*

**dolly** NOUN dollies (*informal*)
a doll

**dolphin** NOUN dolphins
a sea animal like a small whale with a beak-
like snout

**domain** (say dom-**ayn**) NOUN domains
❶ a kingdom ❷ an area of knowledge or
interest ❸ a group of Internet addresses that
end with the same letters, such as .com

**dome** NOUN domes
a roof shaped like the top half of a ball
> **domed** ADJECTIVE

**domestic** ADJECTIVE
❶ to do with your home or household ❷ to
do with your own country; not foreign or
international • *a domestic flight* ❸ domestic
animals are kept by people and are not wild
> **domestically** ADVERB

**domesticated** ADJECTIVE
domesticated animals are trained to live with
and be kept by humans

**domicile** (say **dom**-iss-syl) NOUN domiciles
(*formal*)
the place where someone lives; a residence
> **domiciled** ADJECTIVE

**dominant** ADJECTIVE
more important or powerful than others
• *Arabic is the dominant language of the*

*Middle East.*
➤ **dominance** NOUN

**dominate** VERB dominates, dominating, dominated
❶ to control someone or something by being stronger or more powerful ❷ to be the highest or most noticeable thing in a place • *The mountain dominates the whole landscape.*
➤ **domination** NOUN

**domineer** VERB domineers, domineering, domineered
to behave in a forceful or arrogant way towards others
➤ **domineering** ADJECTIVE

**dominion** NOUN dominions
❶ authority to rule others; control ❷ an area over which someone rules

**domino** NOUN dominoes
a small flat oblong piece of wood or plastic with dots (1 to 6) or a blank space at each end, used in the game of dominoes

**don** VERB dons, donning, donned
(*formal*) to put on a piece of clothing
• *Donning his cloak, he went outside.*
**WORD ORIGIN** from *do on*; compare **doff**

**donate** VERB donates, donating, donated
to present money or a gift to a charity or organization
➤ **donation** NOUN

**donga** NOUN dongas (*S. African*)
❶ a ditch caused by erosion ❷ a dry water channel

**donkey** NOUN donkeys
an animal that looks like a small horse with long ears

**donor** NOUN donors
someone who gives something • *a blood donor*

**don't** (*mainly spoken*)
do not

> **SPELLING**
> Don't = do + not. Add an apostrophe between the n and the t.

**doodle** VERB doodles, doodling, doodled
to scribble or draw something absent-mindedly

**doodle** NOUN doodles
a drawing made by doodling

**doom** NOUN
a grim fate that you cannot avoid, especially

death or destruction • *a sense of impending doom*

**doom** VERB dooms, dooming, doomed
to make it certain that someone will suffer a grim fate

**doomed** ADJECTIVE
❶ certain to suffer a grim fate ❷ bound to fail or be destroyed • *The plan was doomed from the start.*

**doomsday** NOUN
the day of the Last Judgement; the end of the world

**door** NOUN doors
a movable barrier on hinges (or one that slides or revolves), used to open or close an entrance; the entrance itself
➤ **doorknob** NOUN
➤ **doormat** NOUN

**doorstep** NOUN doorsteps
the step or piece of ground just outside a door

**door-to-door** ADJECTIVE
done at each house in turn

**doorway** NOUN doorways
the opening into which a door fits

**dope** NOUN dopes (*informal*)
❶ a drug, especially one taken or given illegally ❷ a stupid person

**dope** VERB dopes, doping, doped (*informal*) to give a drug to a person or animal

**dopey** ADJECTIVE (*informal*)
❶ stupid or silly ❷ not fully awake

**dormant** ADJECTIVE
❶ sleeping ❷ living or existing but not active; not extinct • *a dormant volcano*

**dormitory** NOUN dormitories
a room for several people to sleep in, especially in a school or institution

**dormouse** NOUN dormice
an animal like a large mouse that hibernates in winter

**dorp** NOUN dorps
(*S. African*) a village or small country town in South Africa

**dorsal** ADJECTIVE
to do with or on the back • *Some fish have a dorsal fin.*

**dosage** NOUN dosages
❶ the giving of medicine in doses ❷ the size of a dose

**dose** _NOUN_ doses
the amount of a medicine that you are meant to take at one time

**dose** _VERB_ doses, dosing, dosed
to give a dose of medicine to a person or animal

**dossier** (say **doss**-ee-er or **doss**-ee-ay) dossiers
a set of documents containing information about a person or event

**dot** _NOUN_ dots
a small round mark or spot
➤ **on the dot** exactly on time

**dot** _VERB_ dots, dotting, dotted
❶ to mark something with dots ❷ an area is dotted with things when they are scattered all over it • _The hillside was dotted with sheep._

**dotage** (say **doh**-tij) _NOUN_
someone is in their dotage when they are old, weak and not able to think clearly

**dote** _VERB_ dotes, doting, doted
➤ **dote on someone** to be very fond of someone

**dotty** _ADJECTIVE_ dottier, dottiest (_British_) (_informal_)
slightly mad or eccentric
➤ **dottiness** _NOUN_

**double** _ADJECTIVE_
❶ twice as much; twice as many ❷ having two things or parts that form a pair • _a double-barrelled shotgun_ ❸ suitable for two people • _a double bed_

**double** _NOUN_ doubles
❶ a double quantity or thing ❷ a person or thing that looks exactly like another • _He's his father's double._
➤ **doubles** a game of tennis or badminton between two pairs of players

**double** _VERB_ doubles, doubling, doubled
❶ to become twice as much or as many • _The price has doubled in the last two years._ ❷ to make something twice as much or as many • _Think of a number and double it._ ❸ to bend or fold something in two
➤ **double back** to turn and go back the same way you have come • _The fox doubled back on its tracks._
➤ **double up** to bend over because you are in pain or laughing so much

**double bass** _NOUN_ double basses
a musical instrument with strings, like a large cello

**double-click** _VERB_ double-clicks, double-clicking, double-clicked
to press a button on a computer mouse twice quickly

**double-cross** _VERB_ double-crosses, double-crossing, double-crossed
to deceive or cheat someone who thinks you are working with them

**double-decker** _NOUN_ double-deckers
a bus with two floors, one above the other

**doublet** _NOUN_ doublets
a man's close-fitting jacket worn in the 15th-17th centuries

**doubly** _ADVERB_
twice as much; more than usual • _It's doubly important that you should go._

**doubt** _NOUN_ doubts
a feeling of not being sure about something

**doubt** _VERB_ doubts, doubting, doubted
to feel unsure about something; to think that something is unlikely • _I never doubted that she would come._
➤ **doubter** _NOUN_

SPELLING

There is a silent b before the t in doubt.

**doubtful** _ADJECTIVE_
❶ feeling doubt; unsure ❷ not certain to happen • _It is doubtful whether we'll finish on time._

**doubtfully** _ADVERB_
in a doubtful way • _'I suppose it'll be all right,' she said doubtfully._

**doubtless** _ADVERB_
certainly; without any doubt • _Doubtless she'll have a good excuse for being late._

**dough** _NOUN_
❶ a thick mixture of flour and water used for making bread or pastry ❷ (_informal_) money
➤ **doughy** _ADJECTIVE_

SPELLING

The 'oh' sound is spelt ough in dough.

**doughnut** _NOUN_ doughnuts
a round or ring-shaped bun that has been fried and covered in sugar

SPELLING

The 'oh' sound is spelt ough in doughnut.

**doughty** (say **dow**-tee) _ADJECTIVE_
brave and determined

**dour** (say doo-er) *ADJECTIVE*
stern and gloomy-looking
➤ **dourly** *ADVERB*

**douse** *VERB* douses, dousing, doused
❶ to pour water or other liquid over something ❷ to put out a light or fire • *She doused each of the lamps.*

**dove** *NOUN* doves
a kind of pigeon, often used as a symbol of peace

**dovetail** *NOUN* dovetails
a wedge-shaped joint used to join two pieces of wood

**dovetail** *VERB* dovetails, dovetailing, dovetailed
❶ to join pieces of wood with a dovetail ❷ to fit neatly together • *My plans dovetailed with hers.* **WORD ORIGIN** because the wedge shape looks like a dove's tail

**dowager** *NOUN* dowagers
a woman who holds a title or property after her husband has died • *the dowager duchess*

**dowdy** *ADJECTIVE* dowdier, dowdiest
shabby and unfashionable; not stylish
➤ **dowdily** *ADVERB*

**dowel** *NOUN* dowels
a headless wooden or metal pin for holding together two pieces of wood or stone
➤ **dowelling** *NOUN*

**down** *ADVERB*
❶ to or in a lower place or position or level • *It fell down.* • *Can you turn the volume down?* ❷ in writing • *Take down these instructions.* ❸ to a source or place • *The police tracked them down.*

**down** *PREPOSITION*
downwards through or along or into • *Pour it down the drain.* • *He walked down the corridor.*

**down** *ADJECTIVE*
❶ unhappy or depressed • *He's feeling down at the moment.* ❷ not connected or working properly • *All the computers are down.*
➤ **be down to** someone to be someone's responsibility • *It's down to you to feed the rabbits.*

**down** *VERB* downs, downing, downed
to finish a drink

**down** *NOUN* downs
❶ very fine soft feathers or hair ❷ a grass-covered hill • *the South Downs*

**downcast** *ADJECTIVE*
❶ looking downwards • *downcast eyes* ❷ sad or dejected

**downfall** *NOUN* downfalls
a person's fall from power or prosperity; the thing that causes this • *His enemies began to plot his downfall.* • *Greed was her downfall.*

**downgrade** *VERB* downgrades, downgrading, downgraded
to reduce a person or thing to a lower grade or rank • *She has been downgraded to vice-captain.*

**downhill** *ADVERB & ADJECTIVE*
down a slope

**downland** *NOUN*
open countryside of gently rolling hills

**download** *VERB* downloads, downloading, downloaded
to transfer data or programs to your computer from the Internet or a large computer system

**download** *NOUN* downloads
a computer program or file that you have downloaded

**downpour** *NOUN* downpours
a heavy fall of rain

**downright** *ADVERB & ADJECTIVE*
complete or completely • *a downright lie* • *That was downright rude.*

**Down's syndrome** *NOUN*
a medical condition caused by a chromosome defect that causes intellectual impairment and physical abnormalities such as short stature and a broad flattened skull

**downstairs** *ADVERB & ADJECTIVE*
to or on a lower floor

**downstream** *ADJECTIVE & ADVERB*
in the direction in which a stream or river flows

**down-to-earth** *ADJECTIVE*
sensible and practical

**downward** *ADJECTIVE & ADVERB*
going towards what is lower • *a downward movement*
➤ **downwards** *ADVERB*

**downy** *ADJECTIVE*
covered in very fine soft feathers or hair

**dowry** *NOUN* dowries
property or money brought by a bride to her husband when she marries him

**doze** VERB dozes, dozing, dozed
to sleep lightly

**doze** NOUN
a short light sleep
➤ **dozy** ADJECTIVE

**dozen** NOUN dozens
a set of twelve

**drab** ADJECTIVE drabber, drabbest
❶ not colourful ❷ dull or uninteresting • *a drab life*
➤ **drabness** NOUN

**Draconian** (say drak-**oh**-nee-an) ADJECTIVE
very harsh or strict • *Draconian laws*
**WORD ORIGIN** named after *Draco*, who established very severe laws in ancient Athens

**draft** NOUN drafts
❶ a rough plan of a piece of writing, not the final version ❷ a written order for a bank to pay out money

**draft** VERB drafts, drafting, drafted
❶ to make a rough plan of something you are going to write ❷ to select someone for a special duty • *She was drafted to our office in Paris.*

**drag** VERB
❶ to pull something heavy along ❷ to search a river or lake with nets and hooks ❸ to continue slowly in a boring manner • *The morning seemed to drag.*

**drag** NOUN
❶ (*informal*) something that is tedious or a nuisance ❷ women's clothes worn by men

**dragon** NOUN dragons
❶ a mythological monster, usually with wings and able to breathe out fire ❷ a fierce person, especially a woman

**dragonfly** NOUN dragonflies
an insect with a long thin body and two pairs of transparent wings

**dragoon** NOUN dragoons
a member of certain cavalry regiments

**dragoon** VERB dragoons, dragooning, dragooned
to force someone into doing something

**drain** NOUN drains
❶ a pipe or ditch for taking away water or other liquid ❷ something that takes away your strength or resources

**drain** VERB drains, draining, drained
❶ to make an area dry by taking the water away • *The land will have to be drained before it can be used for farming.* ❷ to flow or trickle away • *The water drained away.* • *All the colour drained from his face.* ❸ to pour off liquid in which something has been cooked • *Drain the pasta thoroughly.* ❹ to take away your strength gradually; to exhaust someone • *I felt drained of energy.*

**drainage** NOUN
a system of drains for taking water away

**drainpipe** NOUN drainpipes
a pipe used for carrying water or sewage from a building

**drake** NOUN drakes
a male duck

**drama** NOUN dramas
❶ a play ❷ writing or performing plays ❸ a series of exciting or emotional events

**dramatic** ADJECTIVE
❶ to do with drama ❷ exciting and impressive • *the film's dramatic opening scene* ❸ sudden and very noticeable • *a dramatic change*
➤ **dramatics** PLURAL NOUN
➤ **dramatically** ADVERB

**dramatis personae** (say **dram**-a-tis per-**sohn**-eye) PLURAL NOUN
the characters in a play **WORD ORIGIN** Latin = persons of the drama

**dramatist** NOUN dramatists
a person who writes plays

**dramatize** (also **dramatise**) VERB dramatizes, dramatizing, dramatized
❶ to make a story into a play • *The novel has been dramatized for TV.* ❷ to make something seem more exciting than it really is • *The newspaper was accused of dramatizing the facts.*
➤ **dramatization** NOUN

**drape** VERB drapes, draping, draped
to arrange cloth or clothing loosely over something • *He draped his coat over the back of the chair.*

**draper** NOUN drapers (*British*) (*old use*)
a shopkeeper who sells cloth or clothes

**drapery** NOUN draperies
cloth arranged in loose folds

**drastic** ADJECTIVE
having a strong or violent effect • *a drastic course of action*
➤ **drastically** ADVERB

**draught** (say drahft) NOUN draughts
❶ a current of cold air indoors ❷ a swallow

of liquid

**SPELLING**

A draught is a current of air. A draft is a first version of something, and to draft something means to make a first version of it.

**draughts** *NOUN*
(*British*) a game played with 24 round pieces on a chessboard

**draughtsman** *NOUN* draughtsmen
❶ a person who makes drawings or is good at drawing ❷ (*British*) a piece used in the game of draughts

**draughty** *ADJECTIVE* draughtier, draughtiest
a draughty room or building is one that lets in currents of cold air

**draw** *VERB* draws, drawing, drew, drawn
❶ to produce a picture or outline by making marks on a surface ❷ to pull something along • *She drew her chair up to the table.* ❸ to take something out • *A woman was drawing water from the well.* • *He drew his sword.*
❹ to attract people or their attention • *The fair drew large crowds.* ❺ to end a game or contest with the same score on both sides ❻ to move or come gradually • *The ship drew nearer.* ❼ to draw curtains is to open or close them ❽ to get a prize or ticket in a raffle or lottery
➤ draw a conclusion to form an opinion about something by thinking about the evidence

**draw** *NOUN* draws
❶ a game or match that ends with the same score on both sides ❷ a raffle or similar competition in which the winner is chosen by picking tickets or numbers at random ❸ an attraction ❹ the drawing out of a gun • *He was quick on the draw.*

**SPELLING**

The past tense of draw is drew and the past participle is drawn.

**drawback** *NOUN* drawbacks
a disadvantage

**drawbridge** *NOUN* drawbridges
a bridge over a moat, hinged at one end so that it can be raised or lowered

**drawer** *NOUN* drawers
❶ a sliding box-like compartment in a piece of furniture ❷ a person who draws something

**drawing** *NOUN* drawings
❶ a picture drawn with a pencil, pen or

crayon ❷ making pictures in this way • *My brother is good at drawing.*

**drawing pin** *NOUN* drawing pins
(*British*) a short pin with a flat top that you use for fastening paper to a surface

**drawing room** *NOUN* drawing rooms (*old use*)
a sitting room **WORD ORIGIN** short for *withdrawing room* = a private room in a hotel etc., to which guests could withdraw

**drawl** *VERB* drawls, drawling, drawled
to speak very slowly or lazily

**drawl** *NOUN* drawls
a drawling way of speaking

**dray** *NOUN* drays
a strong low flat cart for carrying heavy loads

**dread** *NOUN*
great fear or worry

**dread** *VERB* dreads, dreading, dreaded
to fear something very much • *I'm dreading the exam results.*
➤ **dreaded** *ADJECTIVE*

**dreadful** *ADJECTIVE* (*informal*)
very bad or unpleasant • *We've had dreadful weather.*

**dreadfully** *ADVERB*
(*chiefly British*) extremely; or very badly • *I'm dreadfully sorry.*

**dreadlocks** *PLURAL NOUN*
hair worn in many ringlets or plaits, especially by Rastafarians

**dream** *NOUN* dreams
❶ a series of pictures or events in your mind while you are asleep ❷ something you imagine; an ambition or ideal • *His dream is to be famous.*

**dream** *VERB* dreams, dreaming, dreamt or dreamed
❶ to have a dream or dreams ❷ to have an ambition • *She dreams of being an astronomer.* ❸ to think something might happen • *I never dreamt she would leave.*
➤ **dream something up** to invent or imagine a plan or idea
➤ **dreamer** *NOUN*

**dreamy** dreamier, dreamiest *ADJECTIVE*
looking as though you are not paying attention but thinking about something pleasant • *a dreamy expression*
➤ **dreamily** *ADVERB*

**dreary** *ADJECTIVE* drearier, dreariest
❶ dull or boring ❷ gloomy or depressing

a
b
c
d
e
f
g
h
i
j
k
l
m
n
o
p
q
r
s
t
u
v
w
x
y
z

A

B

C

**D**

E

F

G

H

I

J

K

L

M

N

O

P

Q

R

S

T

U

V

W

X

Y

Z

➤ **drearily** ADVERB
➤ **dreariness** NOUN

**dredge** VERB dredges, dredging, dredged
to drag something up, especially by scooping
at the bottom of a river or the sea
➤ **dredger** NOUN

**dregs** PLURAL NOUN
the last drops of a liquid at the bottom of a
glass, barrel, etc., together with any sediment

**drench** VERB drenches, drenching, drenched
to make someone or something wet all
through; to soak someone or something
• *They got drenched in the rain.*

**dress** NOUN dresses
❶ a woman's or girl's piece of clothing which
has a skirt and also covers the top part of the
body ❷ clothes or costume • *fancy dress*

**dress** VERB dresses, dressing, dressed
❶ to put clothes on someone or yourself
❷ to clean a wound and put a dressing on it
❸ to put a dressing on a salad

**dressage** (say **dress**-ahzh) NOUN
the training of a horse to perform various
manoeuvres in order to show its obedience

**dresser** NOUN dressers
❶ a sideboard with shelves at the top for
displaying plates etc. ❷ a person who dresses
in a particular way • *He is a a stylish dresser.*

**dressing** NOUN dressings
❶ a bandage, plaster or ointment etc. for a
wound ❷ a sauce of oil, vinegar, etc. for a
salad

**dressing gown** NOUN dressing gowns
(*British*) a loose light indoor coat you wear
when you are not fully dressed

**dressmaker** NOUN dressmakers
a person who makes women's clothes
➤ **dressmaking** NOUN

**dress rehearsal** NOUN dress rehearsals
the final rehearsal of a play at which the cast
wear their costumes

**dribble** VERB dribbles, dribbling, dribbled
❶ to let saliva trickle out of your mouth
❷ liquid dribbles when it flows in drops
• *Juice dribbled down his chin.* ❸ to move the
ball forward in football or hockey with slight
touches of your feet or stick
➤ **dribble** NOUN

**drier** NOUN driers
a device for drying hair or laundry

**drift** VERB drifts, drifting, drifted
❶ to be carried gently along by water or air
• *The boat drifted out to sea.* ❷ to move
along slowly and casually • *People started to
drift out of the hall.* ❸ to live casually with
no definite plan or purpose • *He drifted into
teaching.*
➤ **drift off** to gradually fall asleep

**drift** NOUN drifts
❶ a drifting movement ❷ a mass of snow
or sand piled up by the wind ❸ the general
meaning of what someone says • *I'm afraid I
don't get your drift.*

**driftwood** NOUN
wood floating on the sea or washed ashore
by it

**drill** NOUN drills
❶ a tool for making holes; a machine for
boring holes or wells ❷ repeated exercises,
e.g. in military training ❸ (*informal*) a set way
of doing something • *You should know the
drill by now.*

**drill** VERB drills, drilling, drilled
❶ to make a hole or well with a drill ❷ to
teach someone to do something by making
them do repeated exercises

**drily** ADVERB
you speak drily when you say something
funny in a clever and sarcastic way • *'I can
hardly contain my excitement,' he said drily.*

**drink** VERB drinks, drinking, drank, drunk
❶ to swallow liquid ❷ to drink a lot of
alcoholic drinks
➤ **drinker** NOUN

**drink** NOUN drinks
❶ a liquid for drinking; an amount of liquid
swallowed • *Can I have a drink of water?*
❷ an alcoholic drink

**drip** VERB drips, dripping, dripped
❶ to fall in drops • *Water dripped from his
hair.* ❷ to let liquid fall in drops • *The tap was
dripping.*

**drip** NOUN drips
❶ liquid falling in drops; the sound it makes
❷ a piece of medical equipment for dripping
liquid or a drug into the veins of a sick person

**drip-dry** ADJECTIVE
made of material that dries easily and does
not need ironing

**dripping** NOUN
fat melted from roasted meat and allowed
to set

216

**drive** *VERB* drives, driving, drove, driven
❶ to operate a motor vehicle or a train; to go or take someone to a place in a car ❷ to make something or someone move • *The dogs drove the sheep into the field.* ❸ to force or compel someone to do something • *Hunger drove them to steal.* ❹ to force someone into a state • *She is driving me crazy.* ❺ to force something into place by hitting it • *He drove a nail into the wall.* ❻ to move or fall rapidly • *The rain was driving down in torrents.*
➤ **driver** *NOUN*

SPELLING
The past tense of drive is drove and the past participle is driven.

**drive** *NOUN* drives
❶ a journey in a vehicle ❷ a hard stroke in cricket or golf ❸ a track for vehicles through the grounds of a house ❹ energy or enthusiasm ❺ an organized effort • *a sales drive* ❻ the part of a computer that reads and stores information on disks

**drive-in** *ADJECTIVE*
that you can use without getting out of your car • *a drive-in restaurant*

**drivel** *NOUN*
silly talk; nonsense

**drizzle** *NOUN*
very fine rain

**drizzle** *VERB* drizzles, drizzling, drizzled
to rain gently

**droll** *ADJECTIVE*
amusing in an odd way

**dromedary** *NOUN* dromedaries
a camel with one hump, bred for riding on

**drone** *VERB* drones, droning, droned
❶ to make a deep humming sound ❷ to talk for a long time in a boring way

**drone** *NOUN* drones
❶ a droning sound ❷ a male bee

**drool** *VERB* drools, drooling, drooled
to dribble continuously
➤ **drool over something** to show great pleasure in looking at something you like • *He's been drooling over car catalogues all afternoon.*

**droop** *VERB* droops, drooping, drooped
to bend or hang down weakly • *The tulips were beginning to droop.*

**drop** *NOUN* drops
❶ a tiny amount of liquid ❷ a fall or decrease • *There has been a sharp drop in prices.* ❸ a distance down from a high point to a lower point • *a sheer drop of 40 metres to the sea*

**drop** *VERB* drops, dropping, dropped
❶ to let something fall • *She almost dropped one of the eggs.* ❷ to fall downwards ❸ to become lower or less • *The temperature suddenly dropped.* ❹ to abandon or stop dealing with something • *Let's just drop the subject.* ❺ to leave a passenger, parcel, etc. at a destination • *Can you drop me at the station?*
➤ **drop in** to visit someone casually
➤ **drop off** to fall asleep
➤ **drop out** to stop taking part in something

**droplet** *NOUN* droplets
a small drop

**droppings** *PLURAL NOUN*
the dung of animals or birds

**drought** (say drout) *NOUN* droughts
a long period of dry weather

**drove** *NOUN* droves
a moving herd or flock
➤ **droves** a large number of people • *Tourists started coming to the village in droves.*

**drown** *VERB* drowns, drowning, drowned
❶ to die or kill someone by suffocation under water ❷ to make so much noise that another sound cannot be heard • *She turned up the radio to drown out the noise from next door.* ❸ to cover something completely in liquid • *The fruit was drowned in cream.*

**drowsy** *ADJECTIVE*
sleepy
➤ **drowsily** *ADVERB*
➤ **drowsiness** *NOUN*

**drubbing** *NOUN* drubbings
a severe defeat

**drudge** *NOUN* drudges
a person who does hard or boring work
➤ **drudgery** *NOUN*

**drug** *NOUN* drugs
❶ a substance used in medicine ❷ a substance that affects your senses or your mind, e.g. a narcotic or stimulant, especially one causing addiction • *a drug addict*

**drug** *VERB* drugs, drugging, drugged
to give a drug to someone, especially to make them unconscious

a
b
c
d
e
f
g
h
i
j
k
l
m
n
o
p
q
r
s
t
u
v
w
x
y
z

**Druid** (say **droo**-id) NOUN Druids
a priest of an ancient Celtic religion in Britain
and France

**drum** NOUN drums
❶ a musical instrument made of a cylinder
with a skin or parchment stretched over
one or both ends ❷ a cylindrical object or
container • *an oil drum*

**drum** VERB drums, drumming, drummed
❶ to play a drum or drums ❷ to tap
repeatedly on something • *He drummed his
fingers on the table.* ❸ you drum a lesson
or fact into someone when you make them
remember it by constant repetition
➤ **drum something up** to try hard to get
more support or business

**drummer** NOUN drummers
a person who plays the drums

**drumstick** NOUN drumsticks
❶ a stick for beating a drum ❷ the lower part
of a cooked bird's leg

**drunk** ADJECTIVE
not able to control your behaviour because of
drinking too much alcohol

**drunk** NOUN drunks
a person who is drunk

**drunkard** NOUN drunkards
a person who is often drunk

**drunken** ADJECTIVE
❶ drunk • *a drunken man* ❷ caused by
drinking alcohol • *a drunken brawl*

**dry** ADJECTIVE drier, driest
❶ without water or moisture ❷ thirsty
❸ boring or dull ❹ funny in a clever and not
obvious way • *dry wit*
➤ **dryness** NOUN

**dry** VERB dries, drying, dried
❶ to make something dry ❷ to become dry

**dryad** NOUN dryads
a wood nymph

**dry-cleaning** NOUN
a method of cleaning clothes using a liquid
that evaporates quickly

**dry dock** NOUN dry docks
a dock that can be emptied of water so that
ships can float in and then be repaired

**DT** ABBREVIATION
design technology

**dual** ADJECTIVE
having two parts or aspects; double • *This
building has a dual purpose.*

SPELLING
Take care not to confuse this word with
duel.

**dual carriageway** NOUN dual carriageways
(*British*) a road with a dividing strip between
lanes of traffic in opposite directions

**dub** VERB dubs, dubbing, dubbed
❶ to change or add new sound to the
soundtrack of a film or to a recording • *It is
a Spanish film dubbed into English.* ❷ to give
a person or thing a nickname or title ❸ to
make a man a knight by touching him on the
shoulder with a sword

**dubious** (say **dew**-bee-us) ADJECTIVE
❶ doubtful or suspicious about something
• *I'm dubious about our chances of winning.*
❷ not to be relied on; probably not honest
• *dubious business dealings*
➤ **dubiously** ADVERB

**ducal** ADJECTIVE
to do with a duke

**ducat** (say **duk**-at) NOUN ducats
a former gold coin used in Europe

**duchess** NOUN duchesses
a duke's wife or widow

**duchy** NOUN duchies
the territory of a duke • *the duchy of
Cornwall*

**duck** NOUN ducks
❶ a swimming bird with a flat beak; the
female of this bird ❷ a batsman's score of
nought at cricket

**duck** VERB ducks, ducking, ducked
❶ to bend down quickly to avoid being hit or
seen ❷ to push someone's head under water
for a short time ❸ to avoid doing something
• *He tried to duck out of apologizing.*

**duckling** NOUN ducklings
a young duck

**duct** NOUN ducts
a tube or channel through which liquid, gas,
air or cables can pass

**ductile** ADJECTIVE
ductile metal is able to be drawn out into fine
strands

**dud** NOUN duds (*informal*)
something that is useless or a fake or fails to
work

**dudgeon** (say **duj**-on) *NOUN*
➤ **in high dudgeon** very resentful or indignant

**due** *ADJECTIVE*
❶ expected; scheduled to do something or to arrive • *The train is due in ten minutes.* ❷ owing; needing to be paid • *Payment for the trip is due next week.* ❸ that ought to be given; rightful • *Treat her with due respect.*
➤ **due to** as a result of; caused by

**due** *ADVERB*
exactly or directly • *We sailed due east.*

**due** *NOUN* dues
❶ something you deserve or have a right to; proper respect • *Give him his due.* ❷ a fee • *harbour dues*

**duel** *NOUN* duels
a fight between two people, especially with pistols or swords
➤ **duelling** *NOUN*
➤ **duellist** *NOUN*

> **SPELLING**
> Take care not to confuse this word with **dual**.

**duet** *NOUN* duets
a piece of music for two players or singers

**duff** *ADJECTIVE* (*British*) (*informal*)
worthless or broken

**duffel coat** *NOUN* duffel coats
a thick overcoat with a hood, fastened with toggles

**duffer** *NOUN* duffers (*informal*)
a person who is stupid or not good at doing something

**dugout** *NOUN* dugouts
❶ an underground shelter ❷ a shelter at the side of a sports field for a team's coaches and substitutes ❸ a canoe made by hollowing out a tree trunk

**duke** *NOUN* dukes
a member of the highest rank of noblemen
➤ **dukedom** *NOUN*

**dulcet** (say **dul**-sit) *ADJECTIVE*
sweet-sounding **WORD ORIGIN** from Latin *dulcis* = sweet

**dulcimer** *NOUN* dulcimers
a musical instrument with strings that are struck by two small hammers

**dull** *ADJECTIVE*
❶ not bright or clear • *dull weather* ❷ not interesting or exciting; boring • *a dull concert*
❸ not sharp • *a dull pain* • *a dull thud*
❹ stupid; slow to understand
➤ **dully** *ADVERB*
➤ **dullness** *NOUN*

**duly** *ADVERB*
in the due or proper way; as expected • *We duly assembled at 7.30 as agreed.*

**dumb** *ADJECTIVE*
❶ without the ability to speak ❷ silent; unable or unwilling to speak • *We were struck dumb with amazement.* ❸ (*informal*) stupid or foolish • *What a dumb thing to do!*
➤ **dumbly** *ADVERB*
➤ **dumbness** *NOUN*

**dumbfounded** *ADJECTIVE*
unable to say anything because you are so astonished

**dummy** *NOUN* dummies
❶ a model of a person used to display clothes ❷ a rubber teat given to a baby to suck ❸ an imitation of something

**dump** *NOUN* dumps
❶ a place where rubbish is left or stored ❷ (*informal*) a dull or unattractive place

**dump** *VERB* dumps, dumping, dumped
❶ to get rid of something you do not want ❷ to put something down carelessly • *You can dump your bags in the hall.*

**dumpling** *NOUN* dumplings
a ball of dough cooked in a stew or baked with fruit inside

**dumps** *PLURAL NOUN* (*informal*)
➤ **in the dumps** feeling depressed or unhappy

**dumpy** *ADJECTIVE*
short and fat

**dunce** *NOUN* dunces
a person who is slow at learning
**WORD ORIGIN** from John *Duns* Scotus, a Scottish philosopher in the Middle Ages (because his opponents said that his followers could not understand new ideas)

**dune** *NOUN* dunes
a mound of loose sand shaped by the wind

**dung** *NOUN*
solid waste matter excreted by an animal

**dungarees** *PLURAL NOUN*
trousers with a piece in front covering your chest, held up by straps over your shoulders

**dungeon** (say **dun**-jon) *NOUN* dungeons
an underground cell for prisoners

a b c **d** e f g h i j k l m n o p q r s t u v w x y z

**dunk** *VERB* dunks, dunking, dunked
to dip something into liquid

**duo** (say **dew**-oh) *NOUN* duos
a pair of people, especially playing music

**duodenum** (say dew-o-**deen**-um) *NOUN* duodenums
the part of the small intestine that is just below the stomach
➤ duodenal *ADJECTIVE*
WORD ORIGIN from Latin *duodecim* = twelve (because its length is about twelve times the breadth of a finger)

**dupe** *VERB* dupes, duping, duped
to deceive or trick someone

**duplicate** (say **dyoop**-lik-at) *NOUN* duplicates
❶ something that is exactly the same as something else ❷ an exact copy • *a duplicate key*

**duplicate** (say **dyoop**-lik-ayt) *VERB* duplicates, duplicating, duplicated
❶ to make an exact copy of something ❷ to do something that has already been done
• *There's no point in duplicating the work we did last year.*
➤ duplication *NOUN*
➤ duplicator *NOUN*

**duplicity** (say dew-**plis**-it-ee) *NOUN*
deceitful behaviour

**durable** *ADJECTIVE*
strong and likely to last • *a durable material*
➤ durability *NOUN*

**duration** *NOUN*
the length of time something lasts

**duress** (say dewr-**ess**) *NOUN*
the use of force or threats to make someone do something against their will • *He signed the confession under duress.*

**during** *PREPOSITION*
throughout or within a period of time
• *During the summer holidays we went swimming every day.* • *He died during the night.*

**dusk** *NOUN* dusks
the darker stage of twilight

**dusky** *ADJECTIVE*
dark or shadowy

**dust** *NOUN*
tiny particles of earth or other solid material

**dust** *VERB* dusts, dusting, dusted
❶ to wipe away dust ❷ to sprinkle something with powder • *Dust the cake with sugar.*

**dustbin** *NOUN* dustbins
(*British*) a bin for household rubbish

**duster** *NOUN* dusters
a cloth for dusting things

**dustman** *NOUN* dustmen
(*British*) a person employed to empty dustbins and take away household rubbish

**dustpan** *NOUN* dustpans
a pan into which dust is brushed from a floor

**dusty** *ADJECTIVE* dustier, dustiest
covered with or full of dust

**dutiful** *ADJECTIVE*
doing your duty; obedient • *a dutiful daughter*
➤ dutifully *ADVERB*

**duty** *NOUN* duties
❶ what you ought to do or must do ❷ a task that must be done, often as part of your job ❸ a tax charged on imports and on certain other things
➤ on or off duty at work (or not at work)
• *What time do you go off duty?*

**duty-free** *ADJECTIVE*
duty-free goods are goods on which duty is not charged

**duvet** (say **doo**-vay) *NOUN* duvets
(*British*) a thick soft quilt used instead of other bedclothes

**DVD** *ABBREVIATION*
digital video disc; a disc used for storing large amounts of audio or video information, especially films

**dwarf** *NOUN* dwarfs or dwarves
❶ a very small person or thing ❷ a creature in stories like a small human being, sometimes with magical powers

**dwarf** *VERB* dwarfs, dwarfing, dwarfed
to make something seem small by contrast
• *The ocean liner dwarfed the tugs that were towing it.*

**dwell** *VERB* dwells, dwelling, dwelt
(*formal*) to dwell in a place is to live there
➤ dweller *NOUN*
➤ dwell on something to think or talk about something for a long time

**dwelling** *NOUN* dwellings
a house or other place to live in

**dwindle** *VERB* dwindles, dwindling, dwindled
to get smaller or less gradually • *Their savings dwindled away to nothing.*

**dye** *NOUN* dyes
a substance used to change the colour of something

**dye** *VERB* dyes, dyeing, dyed
to change the colour of something with dye • *She died her hair green.*

**dyke** *NOUN* dykes
❶ a long wall or embankment to hold back water and prevent flooding ❷ a ditch for draining water from land

**dynamic** *ADJECTIVE*
❶ a dynamic person is energetic and forceful
❷ a dynamic force produces motion
➤ **dynamically** *ADVERB*

**dynamics** *NOUN*
❶ the scientific study of force and motion
❷ (*in music*) the different levels of loudness and softness in a piece of music

**dynamite** *NOUN*
❶ a powerful explosive ❷ something likely to make people very excited or angry
• *This discovery was dynamite.*

**dynamo** *NOUN* dynamos
(*chiefly British*) a machine that makes electricity

**dynasty** (say **din**-a-stee) *NOUN* dynasties
a line of rulers or powerful people all from the same family
➤ **dynastic** *ADJECTIVE*

**dysentery** (say **dis**-en-tree) *NOUN*
a disease causing severe diarrhoea

**dyslexia** (say dis-**leks**-ee-a) *NOUN*
special difficulty in being able to read and spell, caused by a brain condition
➤ **dyslexic** *ADJECTIVE*

**dyspepsia** (say dis-**pep**-see-a) *NOUN*
indigestion
➤ **dyspeptic** *ADJECTIVE*

**dystrophy** (say **dis**-trof-ee) *NOUN*
a disease that weakens the muscles

# Ee

**E.** *ABBREVIATION*
east; eastern

**each** *DETERMINER & PRONOUN*
every one of two or more people or things
• *Each player gets seven cards.* • *Each of us wanted to help.*

> **USAGE**
> Take care to use the pronoun each with a singular verb and singular pronouns:
> • *Each has chosen her own outfit.*

**eager** *ADJECTIVE*
wanting very much to do or have something; very keen • *We were all eager to hear his news.*
➤ **eagerly** *ADVERB*
➤ **eagerness** *NOUN*

**eagle** *NOUN* eagles
a large bird of prey with very strong sight

**ear** *NOUN* ears
❶ the organ of the body that is used for hearing ❷ the ability to recognize and repeat sounds • *She has a good ear for music.* ❸ the spike of seeds at the top of a stalk of corn

**earache** *NOUN*
pain inside the ear

**eardrum** *NOUN* eardrums
a membrane in the ear that vibrates when sounds reach it

**earl** *NOUN* earls
a British nobleman
➤ **earldom** *NOUN*

**early** *ADJECTIVE & ADVERB* earlier, earliest
❶ before the usual or expected time
• *We arrived ten minutes early.* ❷ near the beginning of something • *The murder happens early in the book.* • *an early goal*
❸ near the beginning of the day • *I have to get up early tomorrow.*
➤ **earliness** *NOUN*

**earmark** *VERB* earmarks, earmarking, earmarked
to put something aside for a particular purpose **WORD ORIGIN** from the custom of marking an animal's ear to identify it

a b c d e f g h i j k l m n o p q r s t u v w x y z

**earn** VERB earns, earning, earned
❶ to get money as an income for doing work
❷ to win or receive something because you deserve it • *Your hard work has earned you a place in the team.*

**earnest** ADJECTIVE
very serious and sincere • *an earnest young man*
➤ **earnestly** ADVERB
➤ **earnestness** NOUN
➤ **in earnest** ❶ more seriously or with more determination • *The building work will begin in earnest next week.* ❷ meaning what you say

**earnings** PLURAL NOUN
money earned

**earphones** PLURAL NOUN
a listening device that fits over or in your ears

**earring** NOUN earrings
an ornament worn on your ear

**earshot** NOUN
the distance within which a sound can be heard • *The others were safely out of earshot.*

**earth** NOUN earths
❶ the planet that we live on ❷ the ground; soil ❸ the hole or burrow where a fox or badger lives ❹ connection to the ground to complete an electrical circuit

**earth** VERB earths, earthing, earthed
to connect an electrical circuit to the ground

**earthenware** NOUN
pottery made of coarse baked clay

**earthly** ADJECTIVE
to do with life on earth rather than with life after death

**earthquake** NOUN earthquakes
a violent movement of part of the earth's surface

**earthworm** NOUN earthworms
a worm that lives in the soil

**earthy** ADJECTIVE
❶ like earth or soil • *a damp earthy smell*
❷ crude and vulgar

**earwig** NOUN earwigs
a crawling insect with pincers at the end of its body (WORD ORIGIN) so named because it was once thought to crawl into people's ears

**ease** NOUN
❶ a lack of difficulty or trouble • *She climbed the tree with ease.* ❷ to be at ease with

someone is to feel comfortable and relaxed with them

**ease** VERB eases, easing, eased
❶ to make something less painful or troublesome • *This should ease the pain.* ❷ to move something gently into position • *He eased the key into the lock.* ❸ to become less severe • *The pressure eased.*

**easel** NOUN easels
a stand for supporting a painting or a blackboard (WORD ORIGIN) from Dutch *ezel* = donkey (which carries a load)

**easily** ADVERB
❶ without difficulty; with ease ❷ by far • *This was easily the best victory of her career.* ❸ very likely • *He could easily be lying.*

**east** NOUN
❶ the direction where the sun rises ❷ the eastern part of a country, city or other area

**east** ADJECTIVE & ADVERB
towards or in the east; coming from the east
➤ **easterly** ADJECTIVE
➤ **eastern** ADJECTIVE
➤ **easterner** NOUN
➤ **easternmost** ADJECTIVE

**Easter** NOUN
the Sunday (in March or April) when Christians commemorate the resurrection of Christ; the days around it

**eastward** ADJECTIVE & ADVERB
towards the east
➤ **eastwards** ADVERB

**easy** ADJECTIVE easier, easiest
able to be done or used or understood without trouble

**easy** ADVERB
➤ **take it easy** to relax or calm down

**easy chair** NOUN easy chairs
a comfortable armchair

**eat** VERB eats, eating, ate, eaten
❶ to chew and swallow something as food ❷ to have a meal • *When do we eat?* ❸ to use something up; to destroy something gradually • *Extra expenses ate up our savings.* • *Acid rain will eat away the stonework of buildings.*

**eatable** ADJECTIVE
fit to be eaten

**eau de Cologne** (say oh der kol-**ohn**) NOUN
a light perfume first made at Cologne, in Germany

**eaves** *PLURAL NOUN*
the overhanging edges of a roof

**eavesdrop** *VERB* eavesdrops, eavesdropping, eavesdropped
to listen secretly to a private conversation
• *They caught her eavesdropping outside the window.*
➤ **eavesdropper** *NOUN*
**WORD ORIGIN** as if you are listening outside a wall, where water drops from the eaves

**ebb** *NOUN* ebbs
the movement of the tide when it is going out, away from the land
➤ **at a low ebb** at a low point; in a poor state
• *Our confidence was at a low ebb.*

**ebb** *VERB* ebbs, ebbing, ebbed
❶ the tide ebbs when it flows away from the land ❷ your strength or courage ebbs when it weakens or fades

**ebony** *NOUN*
a hard black wood

**e-book** *NOUN* e-books
a book in electronic form that you can read on a screen

**ebullient** (say i-**bul**-ient) *ADJECTIVE*
cheerful, full of high spirits
➤ **ebullience** *NOUN*

**eccentric** (say ik-**sen**-trik) *ADJECTIVE*
behaving strangely
➤ **eccentrically** *ADVERB*
➤ **eccentricity** (say ek-sen-**triss**-it-ee) *NOUN*

**ecclesiastical** (say ik-lee-zee-**ast**-ik-al) *ADJECTIVE*
to do with the Christian Church or the clergy

**echo** *NOUN* echoes
a sound that is heard again as it is reflected off something

**echo** *VERB* echoes, echoing, echoed
❶ to make an echo • *Her footsteps echoed down the corridor.* ❷ to repeat a sound or what someone has said • *'A surprise?' he echoed.*

**eclair** (say ay-**klair**) *NOUN* eclairs
a finger-shaped cake of pastry with a creamy filling

**eclipse** *NOUN* eclipses
the blocking of the sun's or moon's light when the moon or the earth is in the way

**eclipse** *VERB* eclipses, eclipsing, eclipsed
❶ to block the light and cause an eclipse ❷ to seem better or more important than

others • *Her performance eclipsed the rest of the team.*

**ecology** (say ee-**kol**-o-jee) *NOUN*
the study of living things in relation to each other and to where they live
➤ **ecological** *ADJECTIVE*
➤ **ecologically** *ADVERB*
➤ **ecologist** *NOUN*

**economic** (say ee-kon-**om**-ik) *ADJECTIVE*
❶ to do with the economy or economics ❷ making enough money; profitable
• *The mine was closed because it was not economic.*

**economical** *ADJECTIVE*
using money and resources in a careful way that avoids waste • *It would be more economical to buy a bigger pack.*
➤ **economically** *ADVERB*

**economics** *NOUN*
the study of how money is used and how goods and services are provided and used
➤ **economist** *NOUN*

**economize** (also **economise**) *VERB*
economizes, economizing, economized
to be economical; to use or spend less • *We need to economize on fuel.*

**economy** *NOUN* economies
❶ the system of trade and industry that a country uses to produce wealth ❷ careful use of money or resources ❸ a way of saving money • *You need to make economies.*

**ecosystem** (say ee-koh-sis-tum) *NOUN*
ecosystems
all the plants and animals in a particular area considered in terms of their relationship with their environment

**ecstasy** (say **ek**-sta-see) *NOUN*
❶ a feeling of great delight ❷ an illegal drug that makes people feel very energetic and can cause hallucinations
**SPELLING**
Ecstasy ends with *asy*; not many words end with this pattern.

**ecstatic** (say ik-**stat**-ik) *ADJECTIVE*
extremely happy
➤ **ecstatically** *ADVERB*

**eczema** (say **eks**-im-a) *NOUN*
a skin disease that causes rough itching patches

**eddy** *NOUN* eddies
a swirling patch of water, air or smoke

**eddy** *VERB* eddies, eddying, eddied
to swirl

**edge** *NOUN* edges
❶ the part along the side or end of something ❷ the sharp part of a knife or axe or other cutting instrument
➤ **be on edge** to be tense and irritable

**edge** *VERB* edges, edging, edged
❶ to move gradually and carefully • *We edged closer to get a better view.* ❷ to put something around the edge of something • *The cloth was edged with lace.* ❸ to be the edge or border of something

**edgeways** *ADVERB*
➤ **not get a word in edgeways** to not be able to say something because someone else is talking a lot

**edgy** *ADJECTIVE*
tense and irritable
➤ **edginess** *NOUN*

**edible** *ADJECTIVE*
suitable for eating, not poisonous • *edible fruits*

**edict** (say ee-dikt) *NOUN* edicts
an official command

**edifice** (say ed-if-iss) *NOUN* edifices
a large building

**edify** *VERB* edifies, edifying, edified
to be an improving influence on a person's mind
➤ **edification** *NOUN*

**edit** *VERB* edits, editing, edited
❶ to make written material ready for publishing ❷ to make changes to text on a computer screen ❸ to be the editor of a newspaper or other publication ❹ to choose and put the parts of a film or tape recording into order

**edition** *NOUN* editions
❶ the form in which something is published • *a paperback edition* ❷ all the copies of a book etc. published at the same time • *the first edition* ❸ an individual television or radio programme in a series

**editor** *NOUN* editors
❶ the person in charge of a newspaper or a section of it ❷ a person who edits something

**editorial** *ADJECTIVE*
to do with editing or editors

**editorial** *NOUN* editorials
a newspaper article giving the editor's comments on something

**educate** *VERB* educates, educating, educated
to provide people with education
➤ **educator** *NOUN*

**educated** *ADJECTIVE*
showing a high standard of knowledge and culture, as a result of a good education

**education** *NOUN*
the process of training people's minds and abilities so that they acquire knowledge and develop skills

**educational** *ADJECTIVE*
to do with education; teaching you something • *an educational toy*
➤ **educationally** *ADVERB*

**eel** *NOUN* eels
a long fish that looks like a snake

**eerie** *ADJECTIVE* eerier, eeriest
strange in a frightening or mysterious way
• *an eerie silence*
➤ **eerily** *ADVERB*

**efface** *VERB* effaces, effacing, effaced
to rub something out or make it disappear
➤ **effacement** *NOUN*

**effect** *NOUN* effects
❶ a change that is produced by an action or cause; a result • *Some chemicals have a harmful effect on the environment.* ❷ an impression that is produced by something • *The stage lighting gives the effect of a moonlit scene.*
➤ **come into effect** a law or rule comes into effect when it begins to be used
➤ **take effect** to begin to work or come into operation • *The pills will take effect soon.*

**effect** *VERB* effects, effecting, effected
to make something happen • *We want to effect a change.*

SPELLING
> Effect is different from affect, which is a verb meaning to have an effect on or to harm.

**effective** *ADJECTIVE*
❶ producing the effect that is wanted
❷ impressive and striking
➤ **effectively** *ADVERB*
➤ **effectiveness** *NOUN*

**effectual** *ADJECTIVE*
producing the result that is wanted
➤ **effectually** *ADVERB*

**effeminate** *ADJECTIVE*
an effeminate man looks or behaves like a woman

**effervesce** (say ef-er-**vess**) *VERB* effervesces, effervescing, effervesced
liquid effervesces when it fizzes or gives off bubbles of gas
➤ **effervescent** *ADJECTIVE*
➤ **effervescence** *NOUN*

**efficacious** (say ef-ik-**ay**-shus) *ADJECTIVE*
able to produce the result that is wanted • *an efficacious remedy*
➤ **efficacy** (say **ef**-ik-a-see) *NOUN*

**efficient** *ADJECTIVE*
able to work well without making mistakes or wasting time
➤ **efficiently** *ADVERB*
➤ **efficiency** *NOUN*

**effigy** *NOUN* effigies
a model or sculptured figure

**effort** *NOUN* efforts
❶ the use of physical or mental energy; the energy used • *You have all put a lot of effort into this project.* ❷ something difficult or tiring • *It was an effort to stay awake.* ❸ an attempt • *This painting is a good effort.*

**effortless** *ADJECTIVE*
done with little or no effort
➤ **effortlessly** *ADVERB*

**effusive** *ADJECTIVE*
showing a great deal of affection or enthusiasm
➤ **effusively** *ADVERB*

**e.g.** *ABBREVIATION*
for example (**WORD ORIGIN**) short for Latin *exempli gratia* = for the sake of an example

**egg** *NOUN* eggs
❶ an oval or round object produced by the female of birds, fishes, reptiles and insects, which may develop into a new individual if fertilized ❷ a hen's or duck's egg used as food ❸ an ovum

**egg** *VERB* eggs, egging, egged
❶ egg someone on to encourage someone to do something with taunts or dares • *He didn't want to dance but his friends egged him on.*

**eggplant** *NOUN* eggplants
(*North American*) an aubergine

**ego** (say **eeg**-oh) *NOUN* egos
the opinion that you have of yourself and your own importance • *Winning the award really boosted her ego.* (**WORD ORIGIN**) Latin = I

**egotist** (say **eg**-oh-tist) *NOUN* egotists
a conceited person who is always talking about himself or herself
➤ **egotism** *NOUN*
➤ **egotistic** *ADJECTIVE*

**Eid** (say eed) *NOUN*
a Muslim festival marking the end of the fast of Ramadan

**eiderdown** *NOUN* eiderdowns
a quilt stuffed with soft material

**eight** *NOUN & ADJECTIVE* eights
the number 8
➤ **eighth** *ADJECTIVE & NOUN*

**eighteen** *NOUN & ADJECTIVE* eighteens
the number 18
➤ **eighteenth** *ADJECTIVE & NOUN*

**eighty** *NOUN & ADJECTIVE* eighties
the number 80
➤ **eightieth** *ADJECTIVE & NOUN*

**eisteddfod** (say eye-**ste** th-vod) *NOUN* eisteddfods or eisteddfodau
an annual Welsh gathering of poets and musicians for competitions

**either** *DETERMINER & PRONOUN*
❶ one or the other of two • *Either team can win.* • *Either of those dates will do.* ❷ both of two • *There are fields on either side of the river.*

**either** *ADVERB*
also; similarly • *If you won't go, I won't either.*

**either** *CONJUNCTION*
(used with *or*) the first of two possibilities • *He is either ill or drunk.* • *Either come right in or go away.*

**ejaculate** *VERB* ejaculates, ejaculating, ejaculated
❶ to produce semen from the penis ❷ (*formal*) to suddenly say something
➤ **ejaculation** *NOUN*

**eject** *VERB* ejects, ejecting, ejected
❶ to force someone to leave • *Several protesters were ejected from the hall.* ❷ to send something out forcefully ❸ a pilot ejects when they are deliberately thrown out of an aircraft in a special seat in an emergency ❹ to remove a disk or tape from a machine, usually by pressing a button
➤ **ejection** *NOUN*
➤ **ejector** *NOUN*

**eke** (say eek) *VERB* ekes, eking, eked
➤ eke something out to manage to make something last as long as possible by only using small amounts of it

**elaborate** (say il-**ab**-er-at) ADJECTIVE
having many parts or details; complicated
• *an elaborate pattern*
➤ **elaborately** ADVERB

**elaborate** (say il-**ab**-er-ayt) VERB elaborates, elaborating, elaborated
to explain or work something out in detail
• *Could you elaborate on that idea?*
➤ **elaboration** NOUN

**elapse** VERB elapses, elapsing, elapsed
an amount of time elapses when it passes
• *Six years elapsed before they met again.*

**elastic** NOUN
cord or material woven with strands of rubber so that it can stretch

**elastic** ADJECTIVE
able to be stretched or squeezed and then go back to its original length or shape
➤ **elasticity** NOUN

**elated** ADJECTIVE
feeling very pleased and excited
➤ **elation** NOUN

**elbow** NOUN elbows
the joint in the middle of your arm, where ir bends

**elbow** VERB elbows, elbowing, elbowed
to push or prod someone with your elbow
• *She elbowed me out of the way.*

**elder** ADJECTIVE
older • *my elder brother*

**elder** NOUN elders
❶ an older person • *Respect your elders!*
• *a council of village elders* ❷ an official in some Christian Churches ❸ a tree with white flowers and black berries

**elderberry** NOUN elderberries
a small black berry, the fruit of the elder tree

**elderly** ADJECTIVE
rather old

**eldest** ADJECTIVE
oldest

**elect** VERB elects, electing, elected
❶ to choose someone by voting ❷ to choose or decide to do something

**elect** ADJECTIVE
chosen by a vote but not yet in office • *the president elect*

**election** NOUN elections
a time when people choose someone to do a political or official job by voting

**elector** NOUN electors
a person who has the right to vote in an election
➤ **electoral** ADJECTIVE

**electorate** NOUN electorates
all the people who have a right to vote in an election

**electric** ADJECTIVE
❶ to do with or worked by electricity ❷ very tense or exciting • *The atmosphere inside the hall was electric.* WORD ORIGIN from Greek *elektron* = amber (which is easily given a charge of static electricity)

**electrical** ADJECTIVE
to do with or worked by electricity • *an electrical fault*
➤ **electrically** ADVERB

**electric chair** NOUN
an electrified chair used for capital punishment in the USA

**electrician** NOUN electricians
a person whose job is to fit and repair electrical equipment

**electricity** NOUN
a form of energy carried by certain particles of matter (electrons and protons), used for lighting and heating and for making machines work

**electrify** VERB electrifies, electrifying, electrified
❶ to supply something with electric power to make it work ❷ to give an electric charge to something • *an electrified fence* ❸ to make someone feel very excited • *Her singing electrified the audience.*
➤ **electrification** NOUN

**electrocute** VERB electrocutes, electrocuting, electrocuted
to kill someone with electricity that goes through the body
➤ **electrocution** NOUN

**electrode** NOUN electrodes
a solid conductor through which electricity enters or leaves a battery or other piece of electrical equipment

**electromagnet** NOUN electromagnets
a magnet worked by electricity
➤ **electromagnetic** ADJECTIVE

**electron** NOUN electrons
a particle of matter with a negative electric charge

**electronic** ADJECTIVE
  ❶ worked by microchips, etc. that control an electric current ❷ done using a computer or the Internet • *electronic banking*
  ➤ **electronically** ADVERB

**electronics** NOUN
the use or study of electronic devices

**elegant** ADJECTIVE
graceful and stylish • *an elegant young woman*
  ➤ **elegantly** ADVERB
  ➤ **elegance** NOUN

**elegy** (say **el**-ij-ee) NOUN elegies
a sad or sorrowful poem

**element** NOUN elements
  ❶ each of about 100 substances that cannot be split up into simpler substances, composed of atoms that have the same number of protons ❷ each of the parts that make up a whole thing ❸ a basic or elementary principle • *the elements of algebra* ❹ a wire or coil that gives out heat in an electric fire or cooker ❺ the environment or circumstances that suit you best • *Karen is really in her element at parties.*
  ➤ **the elements** the forces of weather, such as rain, wind and cold

**elementary** ADJECTIVE
dealing with the simplest stages of something; easy

**elephant** NOUN elephants
a very large animal with a trunk, large ears and tusks

**elephantine** (say el-if-**ant**-yn) ADJECTIVE
  ❶ very large ❷ clumsy and slow-moving

**elevate** VERB elevates, elevating, elevated
  ❶ to lift or raise something to a higher position • *The injured leg should be elevated.* ❷ to give someone a higher position or rank • *He was elevated to the Board of Directors.*

**elevation** NOUN elevations
  ❶ moving to a higher position or rank ❷ the height of a place above sea level ❸ a drawing of a building seen from the side

**elevator** NOUN elevators
  ❶ something that raises things ❷ (*North American*) a lift

**eleven** NOUN & ADJECTIVE elevens
the number 11
  ➤ **eleventh** ADJECTIVE & NOUN

**elf** NOUN elves
in fairy stories, a small being with pointed ears and magic powers
  ➤ **elfin** ADJECTIVE

**elicit** (say ill-**iss**-it) VERB elicits, eliciting, elicited
to manage to get information or a reaction from someone

> **SPELLING**
> Take care not to confuse with illicit.

**eligible** (say **el**-ij-ib-ul) ADJECTIVE
qualified or suitable for something • *You have to be under 16 to be eligible for a prize.*
  ➤ **eligibility** NOUN

**eliminate** VERB eliminates, eliminating, eliminated
  ❶ to get rid of someone or something ❷ to defeat someone and stop them going further in a competition • *Our team was eliminated in the first round.*
  ➤ **elimination** NOUN

**elision** (say il-**li** zh-on) NOUN
omitting part of a word in pronouncing it, e.g. in saying *I'm* for *I am*

**elite** (say ay-**leet**) NOUN
a group of people given privileges which are not given to others

**elixir** (say il-**iks**-er) NOUN elixirs
a liquid that is believed to have magic powers, such as restoring youth to someone who is old (WORD ORIGIN) from Arabic *al-iksir* = substance that would cure illness and change metals into gold

**Elizabethan** (say il-iz-a-**beeth**-an) ADJECTIVE
from the time of Queen Elizabeth I (1558-1603)
  ➤ **Elizabethan** NOUN

**elk** NOUN elks
a large kind of deer

**ellipse** (say il-**ips**) NOUN ellipses
an oval shape

> **SPELLING**
> Do not forget to double the l in ellipse.

**ellipsis** NOUN
omitting a word or words from a sentence, usually so that the sentence can still be understood

**elliptical** (say il-**ip**-tik-al) ADJECTIVE
  ❶ shaped like an ellipse • *The planets move in an elliptical orbit around the Sun.* ❷ with some words omitted • *an elliptical phrase*
  ➤ **elliptically** ADVERB

**elm** NOUN elms
a tall tree with rough leaves

**elocution** (say el-o-**kew**-shon) NOUN
the art of speaking clearly and correctly

**elongated** ADJECTIVE
made longer; lengthened • *He often paints people with elongated faces and bodies.*

**elope** VERB elopes, eloping, eloped
two people elope if they run away secretly to get married
➤ **elopement** NOUN

**eloquent** ADJECTIVE
speaking well and expressing ideas clearly and effectively
➤ **eloquently** ADVERB
➤ **eloquence** NOUN

**else** ADVERB
❶ besides; other • *Nobody else knows.*
❷ otherwise; if not • *I must run or else I'll be late.*

**elsewhere** ADVERB
somewhere else

**elucidate** (say il-**oo**-sid-ayt) VERB elucidates, elucidating, elucidated
to make something clear by explaining it
➤ **elucidation** NOUN

**elude** (say il-**ood**) VERB eludes, eluding, eluded
❶ to avoid being caught by someone • *The fox eluded the hounds.* ❷ to be too difficult for you to remember or understand • *I'm afraid the name eludes me.*

**elusive** ADJECTIVE
difficult to find, catch or remember

**emaciated** (say im-**ay**-see-ay-tid) ADJECTIVE
very thin from illness or starvation
➤ **emaciation** NOUN

**email** NOUN emails
❶ a system of sending messages and data from one computer to another by means of a network ❷ a message sent in this way
**email** VERB emails, emailing, emailed
to send an email to someone

**emanate** (say **em**-an-ayt) VERB emanates, emanating, emanated
to come out of a place or thing • *Strange music emanated from the tent.*

**emancipate** (say im-**an**-sip-ayt) VERB emancipates, emancipating, emancipated
to set someone free from slavery or other restrictions
➤ **emancipation** NOUN

**embalm** VERB embalms, embalming, embalmed
to preserve a corpse from decay by using spices or chemicals

**embankment** NOUN embankments
a long bank of earth or stone to hold back water or support a road or railway

**embargo** NOUN embargoes
an official ban, especially on trade with a country

**embark** VERB embarks, embarking, embarked
to go on board a ship or aircraft • *Passengers with cars must embark first.*
➤ **embarkation** NOUN
➤ embark on something to begin something new or difficult • *They were about to embark on a dangerous mission.*

**embarrass** VERB embarrasses, embarrassing, embarrassed
to make someone feel shy, awkward or ashamed • *Please don't embarrass me in front of my friends again.*

> SPELLING
> There is a double r and a double s in embarrass.

**embarrassed** ADJECTIVE
feeling shy, awkward or ashamed • *I've never felt so embarrassed in my life!*

**embarrassing** ADJECTIVE
making you feel shy, awkward or ashamed • *an embarrassing mistake*

**embarrassment** NOUN
the feeling you have when you are embarrassed

**embassy** NOUN embassies
❶ an ambassador and his or her staff ❷ the building where they work

**embed** VERB embeds, embedding, embedded
to fix something firmly in something solid • *The axe was embedded in the door.*

**embellish** VERB embellishes, embellishing, embellished
to decorate something or add extra details to it • *The story has been embellished over time.*
➤ **embellishment** NOUN

**embers** PLURAL NOUN
small pieces of glowing coal or wood in a dying fire

**embezzle** VERB embezzles, embezzling, embezzled
to take money dishonestly that was left in

your care
➤ **embezzlement** NOUN

**emblazon** VERB emblazons, emblazoning, emblazoned
❶ to decorate something with a coat of arms
❷ to decorate something with bright or eye-catching designs or words • The words 'Top Secret' were emblazoned in red on the cover.

**emblem** NOUN emblems
a symbol that represents something • The dove is an emblem of peace.
➤ **emblematic** ADJECTIVE

**embody** VERB embodies, embodying, embodied
❶ to express principles or ideas in a visible form • The marathon embodies the true spirit of the Olympics. ❷ to include or contain something • Parts of the old treaty are embodied in the new one.
➤ **embodiment** NOUN

**emboss** VERB embosses, embossing, embossed
to decorate a flat surface with a raised design

**embrace** VERB embraces, embracing, embraced
❶ to hold someone closely in your arms
❷ to accept or adopt a cause or belief
• The country has embraced democracy.
❸ to include a number of things • The talks embraced a wide range of issues.

**embrace** NOUN embraces
a hug • He held her in a warm embrace.

**embroider** VERB embroiders, embroidering, embroidered
❶ to decorate cloth by sewing designs or pictures into it ❷ to add made-up details to a story to make it more interesting

**embroidery** NOUN
designs or pictures sewn into cloth; the art of decorating cloth in this way

**embroil** VERB embroils, embroiling, embroiled
to involve someone in an argument or quarrel
• He became embroiled in a dispute with his neighbours.

**embryo** (say **em**-bree-oh) NOUN embryos
❶ a baby or young animal as it starts to grow in the womb; a young bird growing in an egg ❷ anything in its earliest stages of development
➤ **embryonic** (say em-bree-**on**-ik) ADJECTIVE

**emerald** NOUN emeralds
❶ a bright-green precious stone ❷ a bright green colour

**emerge** VERB emerges, emerging, emerged
❶ to come out or appear • A man emerged from the shadows. ❷ to become known • No new evidence has emerged.
➤ **emergence** NOUN

**emergency** NOUN emergencies
a sudden serious happening that needs to be dealt with very quickly

**emery paper** NOUN
paper with a gritty coating like sandpaper

**emetic** (say im-**et**-ik) NOUN emetics
a medicine used to make a person vomit

**emigrate** VERB emigrates, emigrating, emigrated
to leave your own country and go and live in another • His family emigrated to Canada when he was 14.
➤ **emigration** NOUN
➤ **emigrant** NOUN

USAGE
People are emigrants from the country they leave and immigrants in the country where they settle.

SPELLING
There is only one m in emigrate.

**eminent** ADJECTIVE
famous and respected • an eminent scientist
➤ **eminence** NOUN

**eminently** ADVERB
(formal) very • She is eminently suitable for the job.

**emir** (say em-**eer**) NOUN emirs
a Muslim ruler

**emission** NOUN emissions
❶ emitting something ❷ something that is emitted, especially fumes or radiation

**emit** VERB emits, emitting, emitted
to send out light, heat, fumes or sound • The box began to emit a clicking sound.

**emotion** NOUN emotions
a strong feeling in the mind, such as love, anger or hate

**emotional** ADJECTIVE
❶ causing strong feelings • an emotional speech ❷ expressing your feelings openly
• I didn't mean to get so emotional. ❸ to do with people's feelings • emotional problems
➤ **emotionally** ADVERB

**emotive** ADJECTIVE
causing emotion or strong feelings • *It is an emotive issue.*

**empathy** NOUN
the ability to understand and share in someone else's feelings
➤ **empathize** VERB

**emperor** NOUN emperors
a man who rules an empire

**emphasis** (say em-fa-sis) NOUN emphases
❶ special importance given to something
❷ stress put on a word or part of a word

**emphasize** (also **emphasise**) VERB
emphasizes, emphasizing, emphasized
to put emphasis on something • *I would like to emphasize the importance of backing up your work.*

**emphatic** (say im-**fat**-ik) ADJECTIVE
using or showing emphasis • *He agreed, with an emphatic nod of the head.*
➤ **emphatically** ADVERB

**empire** NOUN empires
❶ a group of countries controlled by one person or government ❷ a large business organization controlled by one person or group

**empirical** ADJECTIVE
based on observation or experiment, not on theory

**employ** VERB employs, employing, employed
❶ to pay a person to work for you ❷ to make use of something • *Our doctor employs the most modern methods.*

**employee** NOUN employees
someone who is employed in a job

**employer** NOUN employers
a person or organization that has people working for them

**employment** NOUN
having a paid job • *He hoped to find employment abroad.*

**emporium** (say em-**por**-ee-um) NOUN emporia or emporiums
a large shop

**empower** VERB empowers, empowering, empowered
to give someone the power or authority to do something

**empress** NOUN empresses
❶ a woman who rules an empire ❷ an emperor's wife

**empty** ADJECTIVE
❶ with nothing in it • *an empty glass* ❷ with nobody in it • *an empty bus* ❸ with no meaning or no effect • *empty promises*
➤ **emptiness** NOUN

**empty** VERB empties, emptying, emptied
❶ to remove the contents from something
❷ to become empty • *After the show, the hall quickly emptied.*

**emu** NOUN emus
a large Australian bird rather like an ostrich

**emulate** VERB emulates, emulating, emulated
to try to do as well as someone or something, especially by imitating them • *He hopes to emulate his brother's sporting achievements.*
➤ **emulation** NOUN

**emulsion** NOUN emulsions
❶ a creamy or slightly oily liquid ❷ a kind of water-based paint ❸ the coating on photographic film which is sensitive to light

**enable** VERB enables, enabling, enabled
to give someone the means or ability to do something • *The software enables you to create an animated film.*

**enact** VERB enacts, enacting, enacted
❶ to make a law by a formal process
• *Parliament enacted new laws against drugs.*
❷ to perform a play or act out a scene • *We enacted scenes from the history of the town.*

**enamel** NOUN enamels
❶ a shiny substance for coating metal
❷ paint that dries hard and shiny ❸ the hard shiny surface of teeth

**enamel** VERB enamels, enamelling, enamelled
to coat or decorate a surface with enamel

**encamp** VERB encamps, encamping, encamped
to settle in a camp

**encampment** NOUN encampments
a camp, especially a military one

**encapsulate** VERB encapsulates, encapsulating, encapsulated
to express an idea or set of ideas concisely

**encase** VERB encases, encasing, encased
to surround or cover something completely
• *His leg was encased in a plaster cast.*

**enchant** VERB enchants, enchanting, enchanted
❶ to put someone under a magic spell ❷ to fill someone with intense delight
➤ **enchanter** NOUN
➤ **enchantress** NOUN

**enchanted** ADJECTIVE
placed under a magic spell • *an enchanted castle*

**enchanting** ADJECTIVE
attractive or delightful • *It was an enchanting scene.*

**enchantment** NOUN
❶ being under a magic spell ❷ a feeling of intense delight

**encircle** VERB encircles, encircling, encircled
to surround someone or something • *The island is encircled by a coral reef.*

**enclave** NOUN enclaves
a country's territory lying entirely within the boundaries of another country

**enclose** VERB encloses, enclosing, enclosed
❶ to put a wall or fence round an area; to shut something in on all sides • *The garden was enclosed by a high wall.* ❷ to put something into an envelope or packet with something else • *She enclosed a couple of photos with her letter.*

**enclosure** NOUN enclosures
❶ a piece of ground with a wall or fence round it ❷ something enclosed with a letter or packet

**encompass** VERB encompasses, encompassing, encompassed
❶ to contain or include a number of things • *The course encompasses a range of subjects.* ❷ to surround something

**encore** (say on-kor) NOUN encores
an extra item performed at a concert after previous items have been applauded

**encounter** VERB encounters, encountering, encountered
❶ to meet someone unexpectedly ❷ to experience something • *We encountered some difficulties.*

**encounter** NOUN encounters
❶ an unexpected meeting ❷ a battle

**encourage** VERB encourages, encouraging, encouraged
❶ to give someone confidence or hope ❷ to urge or try to persuade someone to do something ❸ to help something to develop or happen more easily • *The school has launched a poster campaign to encourage healthy eating.*
➤ **encouragement** NOUN

**encroach** VERB encroaches, encroaching, encroached
to take or use too much of something • *The extra work would encroach on their free time.*
➤ **encroachment** NOUN

**encrusted** ADJECTIVE
covered with a layer or crust • *a crown encrusted with diamonds*

**encrypt** VERB encrypts, encrypting, encrypted
to put information into a special code in order to stop people reading it if they are not allowed to
➤ **encryption** NOUN

**encumber** VERB encumbers, encumbering, encumbered
to be a burden to someone; to hamper someone
➤ **encumbrance** NOUN

**encyclopedia** NOUN encyclopedias
a book or set of books containing information about many subjects

**encyclopedic** ADJECTIVE
giving information about many different subjects

**end** NOUN ends
❶ the last part of something or the point where it stops ❷ the half of a sports pitch or court defended or occupied by one team or player ❸ destruction or death ❹ a person's goal or purpose • *He knew she was just using him for her own ends.*

**end** VERB ends, ending, ended
❶ to come to an end ❷ to bring something to an end

**endanger** VERB endangers, endangering, endangered
to cause danger to someone or something • *Smoking seriously endangers your health.*

**endangered species** NOUN endangered species
a species in danger of extinction

**endear** VERB endears, endearing, endeared
if you endear yourself to someone, you make them fond of you
➤ **endearing** ADJECTIVE

**endearment** NOUN endearments
a word or phrase that expresses love or affection

**endeavour** (say in-dev-er) VERB endeavours, endeavouring, endeavoured
to try hard to do something • *I will endeavour to find out what happened.*

**endeavour** NOUN endeavours
an attempt

**ending** NOUN endings
the last or final part of something • *I like a story with a happy ending.*

**endless** ADJECTIVE
❶ never stopping; having no end • *an endless stream of questions* ❷ an endless belt or loop has the ends joined to make a continuous strip for use in machinery
➤ **endlessly** ADVERB

**endorse** VERB endorses, endorsing, endorsed
❶ to give your approval or support to something ❷ to sign your name on the back of a cheque or document ❸ to make an official entry on a licence about an offence committed by its holder
➤ **endorsement** NOUN

**endow** VERB endows, endowing, endowed
❶ to provide money to establish something • *She endowed a library in the village where she was born.* ❷ to be endowed with an ability or quality is to possess it • *He was endowed with great talent.*
➤ **endowment** NOUN

**endurance** NOUN
the ability to put up with difficulty or pain for a long period

**endure** VERB endures, enduring, endured
❶ to suffer or put up with difficulty or pain • *She could not endure the thought of parting.* ❷ to continue to exist; to last
➤ **endurable** ADJECTIVE

**enemy** NOUN enemies
❶ a person who hates someone else and wants to harm them ❷ a nation or army that is at war with another

**energetic** ADJECTIVE
full of or needing energy • *an energetic dance*
➤ **energetically** ADVERB

**energy** NOUN energies
❶ strength to do things, liveliness ❷ the ability of matter or radiation to do work. Energy is measured in joules ❸ power obtained from fuel and other resources and used for light and heat or to operate machinery

**enfold** VERB enfolds, enfolding, enfolded
to surround or be wrapped round something • *He enfolded her in his arms.*

**enforce** VERB enforces, enforcing, enforced
to make people obey a law or rule • *This new law will be hard to enforce.*
➤ **enforcement** NOUN
➤ **enforceable** ADJECTIVE

**engage** VERB engages, engaging, engaged
❶ to attract and keep a person's interest or attention • *They engaged her in conversation.* ❷ to give someone a job • *They engaged her as a cook.* ❸ to begin a battle against someone • *We engaged the enemy.*

**engaged** ADJECTIVE
❶ someone who is engaged has promised to marry another person ❷ in use; occupied • *I phoned earlier but the line was engaged.*

**engagement** NOUN engagements
❶ a promise to marry someone ❷ an arrangement to meet someone or do something ❸ a battle

**engaging** ADJECTIVE
attractive or charming

**engine** NOUN engines
❶ a machine that provides power ❷ a vehicle that pulls a railway train; a locomotive

**engineer** NOUN engineers
an expert in engineering

**engineer** VERB engineers, engineering, engineered
❶ to arrange for something to happen • *He engineered a meeting between them.* ❷ to plan and construct something • *The car is beautifully engineered.*

**engineering** NOUN
the design and building or control of machinery or of structures such as roads and bridges

**engrave** VERB engraves, engraving, engraved
to cut words or a design onto a hard surface such as metal or stone • *His name is engraved on the cup.*
➤ **engraver** NOUN

**engraving** NOUN engravings
a picture or design that has been cut into metal or stone

**engrossed** ADJECTIVE
so interested in something that you give it all your attention • *He was engrossed in his book.*

**engulf** VERB engulfs, engulfing, engulfed
to flow over something and cover it completely • *The vehicle was engulfed in flames.*

**enhance** VERB enhances, enhancing, enhanced
to improve something or make it more attractive or valuable • *This film is sure to*

*enhance her reputation as a director.*
➤ **enhancement** NOUN

**enigma** (say in-**ig**-ma) NOUN enigmas
something very difficult to understand; a
puzzle

**enigmatic** (say en-ig-**mat**-ik) ADJECTIVE
mysterious and puzzling
➤ **enigmatically** ADVERB

**enjoy** VERB enjoys, enjoying, enjoyed
❶ to get pleasure from something ❷ to enjoy
yourself is to have a good time

**enjoyable** ADJECTIVE
giving pleasure • *an enjoyable afternoon*

**enjoyment** NOUN enjoyments
a feeling of pleasure; something that you
enjoy doing • *She gets a lot of enjoyment
from painting.*

**enlarge** VERB enlarges, enlarging, enlarged
to make something bigger • *I'm going to have
this photo enlarged.*
➤ **enlargement** NOUN

**enlighten** VERB enlightens, enlightening,
enlightened
to give someone more knowledge or
information about something
➤ **enlightenment** NOUN

**enlist** VERB enlists, enlisting, enlisted
❶ to join the armed forces ❷ to enlist
someone's help or support is to ask for and
get it
➤ **enlistment** NOUN

**enliven** VERB enlivens, enlivening, enlivened
to make something more lively or interesting

**en masse** (say ahn **mass**) ADVERB
all together; in large numbers • *The crowds
turned out en masse, despite the weather.*

**enmity** NOUN
the feeling of being someone's enemy;
hostility

**enormity** NOUN enormities
❶ great wickedness • *the enormity of this
crime* ❷ great size; hugeness • *We began to
realize the enormity of the task.*

> USAGE

Some people regard the use in sense 2
as incorrect, though it is very common.
Words you can use instead include *extent*
and *magnitude*.

**enormous** ADJECTIVE
very large; huge
➤ **enormousness** NOUN

**enormously** ADVERB
hugely; a lot • *I enjoyed the party
enormously.*

**enough** DETERMINER, NOUN & ADVERB
as much or as many as necessary • *I've saved
enough money for a new bike.* • *I have had
enough.* • *Are you warm enough?*

> SPELLING

The 'uff' sound at the end of enough is
spelt ough.

**enquire** VERB enquires, enquiring, enquired
(chiefly British)
❶ to ask for information • *He enquired if I
was well.* ❷ to enquire into something is to
find out about it

> USAGE

See the note at inquire.

**enquiry** NOUN enquiries (chiefly British)
❶ a question ❷ an investigation

**enrage** VERB enrages, enraging, enraged
to make someone very angry

**enraptured** ADJECTIVE
filled with great pleasure

**enrich** VERB enriches, enriching, enriched
❶ to improve the quality of something
• *Fertilizer is used to enrich the soil.* ❷ to
make someone or something richer

**enrol** VERB enrols, enrolling, enrolled
to arrange for yourself or someone else to
join a course or school • *You need to enrol
before the end of August.*
➤ **enrolment** NOUN

**en route** (say ahn **root**) ADVERB
on the way

**ensconce** VERB ensconces, ensconcing,
ensconced
to be ensconced in a place is to be settled
there comfortably • *Dad was already
ensconced in an armchair.*

**ensemble** (say on-**somb**l) NOUN ensembles
❶ a group of musicians or actors who
perform together ❷ a matching outfit of
clothes ❸ a group of things that go together

**enshrine** VERB enshrines, enshrining,
enshrined
to preserve an idea or memory with love or

respect • *His memory is enshrined in our hearts.*

**ensign** NOUN ensigns
a military or naval flag

**enslave** VERB enslaves, enslaving, enslaved
to make a slave of someone; to force someone into slavery
➤ **enslavement** NOUN

**ensue** VERB ensues, ensuing, ensued
to happen afterwards or as a result • *An argument ensued.*
➤ **ensuing** ADJECTIVE

**ensure** VERB ensures, ensuring, ensured
to make sure that something happens or is done • *Please ensure that all lights are switched off.*

SPELLING

Take care not to confuse with insure, which means to protect something with insurance.

**entail** VERB entails, entailing, entailed
to involve something or make it necessary • *This job will probably entail a few late nights.*

**entangle** VERB entangles, entangling, entangled
two or more things are entangled when they are tangled together • *A bird was entangled in the net.*
➤ **entanglement** NOUN

**entente** (say on-**tont**) NOUN ententes
a friendly understanding between countries

**enter** VERB enters, entering, entered
❶ to come or go into a place ❷ to join an organization • *He entered the army when he was 18.* ❸ to key something into a computer • *Now enter your password.* ❹ to put something into a list or book ❺ to put your name down to take part in a competition or examination

**enterprise** NOUN enterprises
❶ being bold and adventurous ❷ a difficult or important task or project • *Deep-sea diving is still a hazardous enterprise.* ❸ business activity • *private enterprise*

**enterprising** ADJECTIVE
willing to take on new or adventurous projects

**entertain** VERB entertains, entertaining, entertained
❶ to amuse and interest someone ❷ to have

people as guests and give them food and drink ❸ to consider something • *He refused to entertain the idea.*

**entertainer** NOUN entertainers
someone whose job is to amuse and please an audience, such as a singer or comedian

**entertainment** NOUN entertainments
❶ entertaining people; being entertained ❷ something performed in front of an audience to amuse or interest them

**enthral** (say in-**thrawl**) VERB enthrals, enthralling, enthralled
to hold someone's complete attention; to fascinate someone

**enthusiasm** NOUN enthusiasms
a strong liking, interest or excitement
➤ **enthusiast** NOUN

**enthusiastic** ADJECTIVE
full of enthusiasm • *You don't sound very enthusiastic about the idea.*
➤ **enthusiastically** ADVERB

**entice** VERB entices, enticing, enticed
to persuade someone to do something or go somewhere by offering them something pleasant • *We tried to entice the dog away from the door.*
➤ **enticement** NOUN
➤ **enticing** ADJECTIVE

**entire** ADJECTIVE
whole or complete • *He read the entire book in two days.*

**entirely** ADVERB
completely; in every way • *I entirely agree with you.*

**entirety** (say in-**ty**-rit-ee) NOUN
the whole of something
➤ **in its entirety** in its complete form

**entitle** VERB entitles, entitling, entitled
to give someone the right to have or do something • *This coupon entitles you to a free ticket.*
➤ **entitlement** NOUN

**entitled** ADJECTIVE
having as a title • *a short poem entitled 'Spring'*

**entity** NOUN entities
something that exists as a distinct and separate thing • *A language is a living entity.*

**entomb** (say in-**toom**) VERB entombs, entombing, entombed
to place a body in a tomb
➤ **entombment** NOUN

**entomology** (say en-tom-**ol**-o-jee) *NOUN*
the study of insects
➤ **entomologist** *NOUN*

**entourage** (say on-toor-**ah** zh) *NOUN*
the people who accompany an important
person

**entrails** *PLURAL NOUN*
the intestines of a person or animal

**entrance** (say **en**-trans) *NOUN* entrances
❶ the way into a place ❷ coming or going
into a place • *Her entrance is the signal for
applause.*

**entrance** (say in-**trahns**) *VERB* entrances,
entrancing, entranced
to fill someone with delight and wonder

**entrant** *NOUN* entrants
someone who takes part in an examination or
competition

**entreat** *VERB* entreats, entreating, entreated
to beg or plead with someone to do
something

**entreaty** *NOUN* entreaties
a serious and emotional request

**entrench** *VERB* entrenches, entrenching,
entrenched
❶ to fix or establish something firmly so
that it is difficult to change • *These ideas are
deeply entrenched in his mind.* ❷ to settle in
a well-defended position
➤ **entrenchment** *NOUN*

**entrepreneur** (say on-tru-pren-er) *NOUN*
entrepreneurs
a person who starts a new business or sets up
business deals, especially risky ones, in order
to make a profit
➤ **entrepreneurial** *ADJECTIVE*

**entrust** *VERB* entrusts, entrusting, entrusted
to make someone responsible for doing
something or looking after someone • *He
entrusted the task to his nephew.*

**entry** *NOUN* entries
❶ coming or going into a place; the right
to enter a place • *The sign said 'No Entry'.*
❷ something entered in a list, diary or
reference book ❸ something entered in
a competition • *Send your entries to this
address.*

**entwine** *VERB* entwines, entwining, entwined
to twist or wind something round something
else • *They strolled through the park, with
arms entwined.*

**enumerate** *VERB* enumerates, enumerating,
enumerated
to list things one by one

**envelop** (say en-**vel**-op) *VERB* envelops,
enveloping, enveloped
to cover or wrap round something
completely • *The mountain was enveloped
in mist.*

**envelope** (say **en**-vel-ohp) *NOUN* envelopes
a wrapper or covering, especially a folded
cover for a letter

**enviable** *ADJECTIVE*
likely to be envied

**envious** *ADJECTIVE*
feeling envy; wanting something that
someone else has
➤ **enviously** *ADVERB*

**environment** *NOUN* environments
❶ your surroundings, especially as they affect
your life • *a happy home environment* ❷ the
natural world of the land, sea and air

> **SPELLING**
> There is a tricky bit in environment—it
> has an n before the m in the middle.

**environmental** *ADJECTIVE*
to do with the environment • *the
environmental effects of pollution*
➤ **environmentally** *ADVERB*

**environmentalist** *NOUN* environmentalists
a person who wishes to protect or improve
the environment

**environmentally-friendly** *ADJECTIVE*
not harmful to the environment

**environs** (say in-**vy**-ronz) *PLURAL NOUN*
the surrounding districts • *They all lived in the
environs of Liverpool.*

**envisage** (say in-**viz**-ij) *VERB* envisages,
envisaging, envisaged
to picture something in the mind; to imagine
something • *It is difficult to envisage such a
change.*

**envoy** *NOUN* envoys
an official representative, especially one sent
by one government to another

**envy** *NOUN*
❶ a feeling of discontent you have when
someone possesses things that you would
like to have for yourself ❷ something causing

this feeling • *Their car is the envy of all their friends.*

**envy** *VERB* envies, envying, envied
to feel envy towards someone

**enzyme** *NOUN* enzymes
a kind of substance that assists chemical processes such as digestion

**epaulette** (say **ep**-al-et) *NOUN* epaulettes
an ornamental flap on the shoulder of a coat

**ephemeral** (say if-**em**-er-al) *ADJECTIVE*
lasting only a very short time

**epic** *NOUN* epics
❶ a long poem or story about heroic deeds or history ❷ a spectacular film

**epicentre** *NOUN* epicentres
the point where an earthquake reaches the earth's surface

**epidemic** *NOUN* epidemics
an outbreak of a disease that spreads quickly among the people of an area

**epidermis** *NOUN*
the outer layer of the skin

**epigram** *NOUN* epigrams
a short witty saying

**epilepsy** *NOUN*
a disease of the nervous system which causes convulsions
➤ **epileptic** *ADJECTIVE & NOUN*

**epilogue** (say **ep**-il-og) *NOUN* epilogues
a short section at the end of a book or play

**Epiphany** (say ip-**if**-an-ee) *NOUN*
a Christian festival on 6 January, commemorating the showing of the infant Christ to the 'wise men' from the East

**episcopal** (say ip-**iss**-kop-al) *ADJECTIVE*
❶ to do with a bishop or bishops ❷ an episcopal church is governed by bishops

**episode** *NOUN* episodes
❶ one event in a series of happenings ❷ one programme in a television or radio serial

**epistle** *NOUN* epistles
a letter, especially one forming part of the New Testament

**epitaph** *NOUN* epitaphs
words written on a tomb or describing a person who has died

**epithet** *NOUN* epithets
a word or phrase used to describe someone

and often forming part of their name, e.g. 'the Great' in *Alfred the Great*

**epitome** (say ip-**it**-om-ee) *NOUN*
a person or thing that is a perfect example of something • *She is the epitome of kindness.*

**epoch** (say **ee**-pok) *NOUN* epochs
a period of time in the past during which important events happened
➤ **epoch-making** *ADJECTIVE*
very important in history

**eponym** (say **ep**-o-nim) *NOUN* eponyms
a word that is derived from the name of a person

**equable** (say **ek**-wa-bul) *ADJECTIVE*
❶ calm and not likely to get annoyed • *She has an equable manner.* ❷ an equable climate is moderate, neither too hot nor too cold

**equal** *ADJECTIVE*
❶ the same in amount, size or value ❷ having the necessary strength, courage or ability to do something • *He was equal to the task.*

**equal** *NOUN* equals
a person or thing that is equal to another • *She has no equal.*

**equal** *VERB* equals, equalling, equalled
❶ to be the same in amount, size or value
❷ to be as good as someone or something • *No one has yet equalled this score.*

**equality** *NOUN*
being equal

**equalize** (also **equalise**) *VERB* equalizes, equalizing, equalized
❶ to make things equal ❷ to score a goal that makes the score equal

**equalizer** (also **equaliser**) *NOUN* equalizers
a goal or point that makes the score equal

**equally** *ADVERB*
in the same way or to the same extent • *You are all equally to blame.*

> **SPELLING**
> Don't forget to double the l in equally.

**equanimity** (say ekwa-**nim**-it-ee) *NOUN*
calmness of mind or temper

**equate** *VERB* equates, equating, equated
to think that two things are equal or equivalent

**equation** *NOUN* equations
(*in mathematics*) a statement that two amounts etc. are equal, e.g. $3 + 4 = 2 + 5$

**equator** NOUN equators
an imaginary line round the Earth at an equal distance from the North and South Poles

**equatorial** (say ek-wa-**tor**-ee-al) ADJECTIVE
to do with or near the equator • *equatorial rainforests*

**equerry** (say **ek**-wer-ee) NOUN equerries
a personal attendant of a member of the British royal family

**equestrian** (say ik-**wes**-tree-an) ADJECTIVE
to do with horse riding • *equestrian events at the Olympic Games*

**equidistant** (say ee-kwi-**dis**-tant) ADJECTIVE
at an equal distance

**equilateral** (say ee-kwi-**lat**-er-al) ADJECTIVE
an equilateral triangle has all its sides equal

**equilibrium** (say ee-kwi-**lib**-ree-um) NOUN
❶ a balance between different forces or influences ❷ a calm and balanced state of mind

**equine** (say **ek**-wyn) ADJECTIVE
to do with or like a horse

**equinox** (say **ek**-win-oks) NOUN equinoxes
the time of year when day and night are equal in length (about 20 March in spring and about 22 September in autumn)

**equip** VERB equips, equipping, equipped
to supply someone or something with what is needed • *The drama studio is well equipped.*

**equipment** NOUN
the things needed for a particular purpose

**equity** (say **ek**-wit-ee) NOUN
fairness
➤ **equitable** ADJECTIVE

**equivalent** ADJECTIVE
equal in importance, meaning or value • *12km is equivalent to 7.5 miles.*

**equivalent** NOUN equivalents
a thing that is equivalent to something else • *The Golden Honey Awards are the beekeepers' equivalent of the Oscars.*

**equivocal** (say ik-**wiv**-ok-al) ADJECTIVE
able to be interpreted in two ways and deliberately vague; ambiguous
➤ **equivocally** ADVERB

**era** (say **eer**-a) NOUN eras
a period of history • *the era of silent films*

**eradicate** VERB eradicates, eradicating, eradicated
to get rid of something completely; to remove all traces of something • *Some diseases, like smallpox, have now been eradicated.*
➤ **eradication** NOUN

**erase** VERB erases, erasing, erased
❶ to rub something out ❷ to wipe out a recording on magnetic tape
➤ **eraser** NOUN

**ere** (say air) PREPOSITION & CONJUNCTION (old use)
before

**erect** ADJECTIVE
standing straight up

**erect** VERB erects, erecting, erected
to set up or build something • *Huge TV screens were erected above the stage.*
➤ **erection** NOUN

**erection** NOUN
❶ the process of erecting something ❷ a building or structure that has been erected ❸ the swelling and hardening of a man's penis when he becomes sexually excited

**ermine** NOUN ermines
❶ a kind of weasel with brown fur that turns white in winter ❷ this valuable white fur

**erode** VERB erodes, eroding, eroded
to wear away the surface of something over time • *Water has eroded the rocks.*

**erosion** NOUN
the wearing away of the earth's surface by the action of water and wind

**erotic** ADJECTIVE
arousing sexual feelings
➤ **erotically** ADVERB

**err** (say er) VERB errs, erring, erred
to make a mistake or be incorrect

**errand** NOUN errands
a short journey to take a message or fetch something • *He used to run errands for his grandmother.*

**errant** (say **e**-rant) ADJECTIVE
❶ misbehaving ❷ wandering; travelling in search of adventure • *a knight errant*

**erratic** (say ir-**at**-ik) ADJECTIVE
not regular or reliable • *Most babies have erratic sleep patterns to begin with.*
➤ **erratically** ADVERB

**erroneous** (say ir-**oh**-nee-us) ADJECTIVE
incorrect; based on wrong information • *an erroneous conclusion*
➤ **erroneously** ADVERB

**error** NOUN errors
a mistake
➤ **in error** by mistake

**erudite** (say **e-rew-dyt**) ADJECTIVE
having great knowledge or learning
➤ **erudition** NOUN

**erupt** VERB erupts, erupting, erupted
❶ a volcano erupts when it shoots out lava
❷ to start suddenly and powerfully; to break
out • *Violence erupted outside the gates.*

**eruption** NOUN eruptions
❶ when a volcano erupts ❷ a sudden
bursting out • *a huge eruption of
laughter*

**escalate** VERB escalates, escalating, escalated
to become greater, more serious or more
intense • *The riots escalated into a war.*
➤ **escalation** NOUN

**escalator** NOUN escalators
a staircase with an endless line of steps
moving up or down

**escapade** (say es-ka-**payd**) NOUN escapades
a reckless adventure

**escape** VERB escapes, escaping, escaped
❶ to get yourself free; to get out or away
• *They managed to escape from the burning
building.* ❷ to avoid something unpleasant
• *He escaped punishment.* ❸ to be forgotten
or not noticed • *Her name escapes me for the
moment.*

**escape** NOUN escapes
❶ escaping from somewhere or something
• *an escape of prisoners* ❷ a way to escape
• *She knew there was no escape.*

**escapism** NOUN
escaping from the difficulties of life by
thinking about or doing more pleasant
things
➤ **escapist** ADJECTIVE

**escarpment** NOUN escarpments
a steep slope at the edge of some high level
ground

**escort** (say **ess**-kort) NOUN escorts
a person or group accompanying a person
or thing, especially to protect or guard them
• *an armed escort*

**escort** (say iss-**kort**) VERB escorts, escorting,
escorted
to act as an escort to someone or
something

**Eskimo** NOUN Eskimos or Eskimo
a member of a people living near the Arctic

coast of North America, Greenland and
Siberia

USAGE
It is becoming less common to refer
to these peoples as Eskimos. Many
people who live in northern Canada and
Greenland prefer the term Inuit. The
name for those who live in Alaska and
Asia is Yupik.

**especial** ADJECTIVE
special or particular • *This should be of
especial interest to you.*

**especially** ADVERB
specially; more than anything else • *She loves
animals, especially dogs.*

**espionage** (say **ess**-pee-on-ahzh) NOUN
spying on other countries or organizations

**esplanade** NOUN esplanades
a flat open area where people can walk,
especially by the sea

**espresso** NOUN espressos
strong black coffee made by forcing steam
through ground coffee beans

**esprit de corps** (say ess-pree der **kor**) NOUN
loyalty to your group **WORD ORIGIN** French =
spirit of the body

**espy** VERB espies, espying, espied
to catch sight of someone or something

**Esq.** ABBREVIATION
(short for **Esquire**)
a title written after a man's surname
where no title is used before his name
**WORD ORIGIN** an *esquire* was originally a
knight's attendant; from Latin *scutarius* =
shield-bearer

**essay** (say **ess**-ay) NOUN essays
a short piece of writing on one subject

**essay** (say ess-**ay**) VERB essays, essaying,
essayed (*formal*) to attempt to do something

**essence** NOUN essences
❶ the most important quality or element
of something • *His paintings capture the
essence of France.* ❷ a concentrated liquid
• *vanilla essence*

**essential** ADJECTIVE
completely necessary; that you cannot do
without • *A car is essential in the country.*

**essential** NOUN essentials
something that you cannot do without

**essentially** ADVERB
basically; when you consider the basic or most important part of something • *The plots of both films are essentially the same.*

**establish** VERB establishes, establishing, established
❶ to set up a business, government or relationship on a firm basis ❷ to show that something is true; to prove something • *He managed to establish his innocence.*
➤ **the established Church** a country's national Church, officially recognized as such by law

**establishment** NOUN establishments
❶ establishing something ❷ a business firm or other institution
➤ **the Establishment** the people in a country in positions of power and influence

**estate** NOUN estates
❶ an area of land with a set of houses or factories on it ❷ a large area of land owned by one person ❸ all that a person owns when he or she dies

**estate agent** NOUN estate agents
(*British*) a person whose business is selling or letting houses and land

**estate car** NOUN estate cars
(*British*) a car with a door or doors at the back and rear seats that can be removed or folded away

**esteem** VERB esteems, esteeming, esteemed
to respect and admire someone very much • *She is a highly esteemed scientist.*

**esteem** NOUN
respect and admiration • *Please accept this gift as a token of our esteem.*

**ester** NOUN esters
a kind of chemical compound

**estimable** ADJECTIVE
worthy of respect and admiration • *an estimable young man*

**estimate** (say **ess**-tim-at) NOUN estimates
a rough calculation or guess about an amount or value

**estimate** (say **ess**-tim-ayt) VERB estimates, estimating, estimated
to make an estimate • *I estimate that the work will take three weeks.*

**estimation** NOUN
a person's opinion or judgement • *Who is to blame in your estimation?*

**estranged** ADJECTIVE
no longer friendly or in contact with someone who was once close to you • *He became estranged from his family.*
➤ **estrangement** NOUN

**estuary** (say **ess**-tew-er-ee) NOUN estuaries
the mouth of a river where it reaches the sea and the tide flows in and out

**etc.** ABBREVIATION
(short for et cetera)
and other similar things; and so on
**WORD ORIGIN** from Latin *et* = and + *cetera* = the other things

**etch** VERB etches, etching, etched
❶ to engrave a picture with acid on a metal plate, especially for printing ❷ if something is etched on your mind or memory, it has made a deep impression and you will never forget it
➤ **etcher** NOUN

**etching** NOUN etchings
a picture printed from an etched metal plate

**eternal** ADJECTIVE
lasting for ever; not ending or changing
➤ **eternally** ADVERB

**eternity** NOUN
❶ time that goes on for ever ❷ (*informal*) a very long time • *The bus took an eternity to arrive.*

**ether** (say **ee**-ther) NOUN
❶ a colourless liquid that evaporates easily into fumes that are used as an anaesthetic ❷ the upper air

**ethereal** (say ith-**eer**-ee-al) ADJECTIVE
light and delicate • *ethereal music*
➤ **ethereally** ADVERB

**ethical** (say **eth**-ik-al) ADJECTIVE
❶ to do with ethics ❷ morally right; honourable
➤ **ethically** ADVERB

**ethics** (say **eth**-iks) PLURAL NOUN
standards of right behaviour; moral principles

**ethnic** ADJECTIVE
belonging to a particular national or racial group within a larger set of people • *different ethnic communities*

**ethnic cleansing** NOUN
the mass killing of people from other ethnic or religious groups within a certain area

**etiquette** (say **et**-ik-et) NOUN
the rules of correct behaviour

**etymology** (say et-im-**ol**-oj-ee) NOUN
etymologies
❶ a description of the origin and history of a particular word ❷ the study of the origins of words
➤ **etymological** ADJECTIVE

**EU** ABBREVIATION
European Union

**eucalyptus** (say yoo-kal-**ip**-tus) NOUN
eucalyptuses
❶ a kind of evergreen tree ❷ a strong-smelling oil obtained from its leaves

**Eucharist** (say **yoo**-ker-ist) NOUN
the Christian sacrament in which bread and wine are consecrated and swallowed, commemorating the Last Supper of Christ and his disciples

**eulogy** (say **yoo**-loj-ee) NOUN eulogies
a speech or piece of writing in praise of a person or thing

**eunuch** (say **yoo**-nuk) NOUN eunuchs
a man who has been castrated

**euphemism** (say **yoo**-fim-izm) NOUN
euphemisms
a mild word or phrase used instead of an offensive or frank one; 'to pass away' is a euphemism for 'to die'
➤ **euphemistic** ADJECTIVE
➤ **euphemistically** ADVERB

**euphonium** (say yoof-**oh**-nee-um) NOUN
euphoniums
a large brass wind instrument

**euphoria** (say yoo-**for**-ee-a) NOUN
a feeling of general happiness

**Eurasian** ADJECTIVE
having European and Asian parents or ancestors
➤ **Eurasian** NOUN

**eureka** (say yoor-**eek**-a) EXCLAMATION
a cry of triumph at a great discovery
**WORD ORIGIN** Greek = 'I have found it', said to have been uttered by the Greek mathematician Archimedes, who was excited by his new idea about the volume and density of matter

**euro** NOUN euros or euro
the single currency introduced in the EU in 1999. Its symbol is €.

**European** ADJECTIVE
to do with Europe or its people
➤ **European** NOUN

**euthanasia** (say yooth-an-**ay**-zee-a) NOUN
causing someone to die gently and without pain when they are suffering from a painful incurable disease

**evacuate** VERB evacuates, evacuating, evacuated
to move people away from a dangerous place • Police evacuated nearby buildings.
• Thousands of children were evacuated from the war zone.
➤ **evacuation** NOUN

**evacuee** NOUN evacuees
a person who has been evacuated

**evade** VERB evades, evading, evaded
❶ to avoid being caught or meeting someone • They managed to evade capture for six months. ❷ to avoid dealing with something
• I asked her directly but she evaded the question.

**evaluate** VERB evaluates, evaluating, evaluated
to estimate the value or quality of something; to assess something • We evaluated each of the websites.
➤ **evaluation** NOUN

**Evangelist** NOUN Evangelists
any of the writers (Matthew, Mark, Luke, John) of the four Gospels

**evangelist** NOUN evangelists
a person who preaches the Christian faith enthusiastically
➤ **evangelical** ADJECTIVE

**evaporate** VERB evaporates, evaporating, evaporated
❶ to change from liquid into steam or vapour ❷ to disappear completely • It didn't take long for their enthusiasm to evaporate.

**evaporation** NOUN
the process of changing from liquid into steam or vapour

**evasion** NOUN evasions
❶ evading someone or something ❷ an evasive answer or excuse

**evasive** ADJECTIVE
trying to avoid answering something; not frank or straightforward
➤ **evasively** ADVERB

**eve** NOUN eves
❶ the day or evening before an important day or event • Christmas Eve ❷ (old use) evening

**even** ADJECTIVE
❶ level and smooth ❷ not changing or varying; regular ❸ calm and not easily upset • *an even temper* ❹ equal or equally balanced • *Our scores were even.* • *an even contest* ❺ able to be divided exactly by two • *Six and fourteen are even numbers.*
Compare with **odd.**
➤ **evenness** NOUN
➤ **get even** to take revenge on someone

**even** VERB evens, evening, evened
❶ to make something even • *That goal evened the score.* ❷ things even up or even out when they become even

**even** ADVERB
used to emphasize a word or statement • *She ran even faster.* • *I couldn't even stand, let alone walk.*
➤ **even so** although that is correct

**even** NOUN
(*old use*) evening

**even-handed** ADJECTIVE
fair and impartial

**evening** NOUN evenings
the time at the end of the day between the late afternoon and bedtime

**evenly** ADVERB
in a smooth, regular or equal way • *The match was evenly balanced.* • *Spread the cake mixture evenly in the tin.*

**event** NOUN events
❶ something that happens, especially something important ❷ a race or competition that forms part of a sports contest

**eventful** ADJECTIVE
full of happenings • *It's been an eventful day.*

**eventual** ADJECTIVE
happening in the end • *his eventual success*

**eventuality** (say iv-en-tew-**al**-it-ee) NOUN
eventualities
something that may happen

**eventually** ADVERB
finally; in the end • *We eventually managed to get the door open.*

**ever** ADVERB
❶ at any time • *It's the best present I've ever had.* ❷ always; at all times • *Scientists are ever hopeful of finding signs of life on other planets.* ❸ (*informal*) used for emphasis • *Why ever didn't you tell me?*

**evergreen** ADJECTIVE
an evergreen tree or shrub has green leaves all through the year

**evergreen** NOUN evergreens
an evergreen tree or shrub

**everlasting** ADJECTIVE
lasting for ever or for a very long time

**every** DETERMINER
❶ each without any exceptions • *We enjoyed every minute.* ❷ used for saying how often something happens • *Take one tablet every four hours.*
➤ **every other day or week**, etc. each alternate one; every second one • *The magazine is published every other Friday.*

USAGE
Take care to use a singular verb with *every*, e.g. *Every one of the eggs has hatched* (not 'have hatched').

SPELLING
Every has **er** in the middle, ev-er-y.

**everybody** PRONOUN
every person; everyone

**everyday** ADJECTIVE
ordinary or usual • *The Internet is now part of everyday life.*

**everyone** PRONOUN
every person; all people • *Everyone likes her.*
SPELLING
Everyone has **er** in the middle, ev-er-y-one.

**everything** PRONOUN
❶ all things; all ❷ the only or most important thing • *Winning is not everything.*

**everywhere** ADVERB
in every place

**evict** VERB evicts, evicting, evicted
to make people move out from where they are living
➤ **eviction** NOUN

**evidence** NOUN
❶ anything that gives people reason to believe something • *There was no evidence of a struggle in the room.* ❷ statements made or objects produced in a law court to prove something

**evident** ADJECTIVE
obvious; clearly seen or understood • *It is evident that he is lying.*

a b c d e f g h i j k l m n o p q r s t u v w x y z

**evidently** ADVERB
obviously or clearly • *She had evidently changed her mind.*

**evil** ADJECTIVE
morally bad; wicked
➤ **evilly** ADVERB

**evil** NOUN evils
❶ wickedness ❷ something bad or harmful • *the evils of war*

**evoke** VERB evokes, evoking, evoked
to bring a memory or feeling into your mind • *The photographs evoked happy memories.*
➤ **evocation** NOUN
➤ **evocative** ADJECTIVE

**evolution** (say ee-vol-**oo**-shon) NOUN
❶ gradual change into something different ❷ the development of animals and plants from earlier or simpler forms of life
➤ **evolutionary** ADJECTIVE

**evolve** VERB evolves, evolving, evolved
❶ to develop gradually or naturally • *His style of painting evolved over the next 20 years.* ❷ animals and plants evolve when they develop from earlier or simpler forms of life • *Birds evolved from reptiles.*

**ewe** (say yoo) NOUN ewes
a female sheep

**ewer** (say **yoo**-er) NOUN ewers
a large water jug

**ex-** PREFIX
former • *ex-wife* • *ex-president*

**exacerbate** (say eks-**ass**-er-bayt) VERB
exacerbates, exacerbating, exacerbated
to make a pain or disease or other problem worse

**exact** ADJECTIVE
❶ completely correct • *I can't tell you the exact number of people who are coming.* ❷ clearly stated; giving all the details • *exact instructions*
➤ **exactness** NOUN

**exact** VERB exacts, exacting, exacted
❶ to demand and get something from someone • *She was keen to exact a promise from him.* ❷ to exact revenge on someone is to take revenge on them

**exacting** ADJECTIVE
needing a lot of effort and care • *an exacting task*

**exactly** ADVERB
❶ in an exact manner; precisely • *Tell me exactly what happened.* ❷ used for agreeing

with someone • *'You mean you've lost all your money?' 'Exactly.'*

**exaggerate** VERB exaggerates, exaggerating, exaggerated
to make something seem bigger, better or worse than it really is • *Come on, there's no need to exaggerate.*

**exaggeration** NOUN exaggerations
making something seem bigger, better or worse than it really is • *He has a reputation for exaggeration and making things up.*

**exalt** (say ig-**zawlt**) VERB exalts, exalting, exalted
❶ to raise someone in rank or status ❷ to praise someone or something highly
➤ **exaltation** NOUN

**exam** NOUN exams (informal)
an examination

**examination** NOUN examinations
❶ a test of a person's knowledge or skill ❷ examining something; an inspection • *a medical examination*

**examine** VERB examines, examining, examined
❶ to look at something closely or in detail • *Tom bent down and examined the footprints.* ❷ to test a person's knowledge or skill

**examinee** NOUN examinees
a person being tested in an examination

**examiner** NOUN examiners
a person who sets or marks an examination

**example** NOUN examples
❶ anything that shows what others of the same kind are like or how they work ❷ a person or thing good enough to be worth imitating • *Her courage is an example to us all.*
➤ **for example** as an example

**exasperate** VERB exasperates, exasperating, exasperated
to annoy someone very much
➤ **exasperation** NOUN

**excavate** VERB excavates, excavating, excavated
❶ to dig in the ground in order to find things from the past • *Archaeologists excavated the site with great care.* ❷ to uncover something by digging • *The statue was excavated in 1931.*
➤ **excavation** NOUN
➤ **excavator** NOUN

**exceed** VERB exceeds, exceeding, exceeded
❶ to be more than a particular number or
amount • *The weight should not exceed 20
kilos.* ❷ to go beyond the limit of what is
normal or allowed • *He has exceeded his
authority.*

SPELLING
The 's' sound is spelt with a c in exceed.

**exceedingly** ADVERB
very; extremely • *an exceedingly difficult
problem*

**excel** VERB excels, excelling, excelled
to be better than others at doing something
• *She excels at foreign languages.*

**excellence** NOUN
the quality of being extremely good • *The
school has a reputation for academic
excellence.*

**Excellency** NOUN Excellencies
the title of high officials such as ambassadors
and governors

**excellent** ADJECTIVE
extremely good
➤ **excellently** ADVERB

**except** PREPOSITION
not including; apart from • *The museum
is open every day except Mondays.* • *I can
answer all of the questions except for the
last one.*

**except** VERB excepts, excepting, excepted
to not include someone or something; to
leave someone or something out • *I blame
you all, no one is excepted.*

SPELLING
The 's' sound is spelt with a c in except.
Take care not to confuse with the verb
accept.

**excepting** PREPOSITION
except for; apart from

**exception** NOUN exceptions
a person or thing that is left out or does not
follow the general rule
➤ **take exception to something** to object
strongly to something
➤ **with the exception of** except for; apart
from

**exceptional** ADJECTIVE
❶ very unusual ❷ outstandingly good • *He
showed exceptional talent for art when he
was young.*
➤ **exceptionally** ADVERB

**excerpt** (say **ek**-serpt) NOUN excerpts
a passage taken from a book, speech or film

**excess** NOUN excesses
too much of something • *Tests showed an
excess of alcohol in the driver's blood.*
➤ **in excess of** more than

**excessive** ADJECTIVE
too much or too great
➤ **excessively** ADVERB

**exchange** VERB exchanges, exchanging,
exchanged
to give something and receive something else
for it

**exchange** NOUN exchanges
❶ exchanging things ❷ a place where things
(especially stocks and shares) are bought and
sold • *a stock exchange* ❸ a place where
telephone lines are connected to each other
when a call is made

**exchequer** NOUN exchequers
a national treasury into which public funds
(such as taxes) are paid WORD ORIGIN from
Latin *scaccarium* = chessboard (because the
Norman kings kept their accounts by means of
counters placed on a chequered tablecloth)

**excise** (say **eks**-yz) NOUN
a tax charged on certain goods and licences

**excitable** ADJECTIVE
easily excited

**excite** VERB excites, exciting, excited
❶ to make someone eager and enthusiastic
about something • *The thought of finding
the hidden treasure excited them.* ❷ to cause
a feeling or reaction • *The invention excited
great interest.*

SPELLING
The 's' sound is spelt with a c in excite.

**excited** ADJECTIVE
feeling eager and enthusiastic about
something
➤ **excitedly** ADVERB

**excitement** NOUN excitements
a strong feeling of eagerness or pleasure

**exciting** ADJECTIVE
causing strong feelings or pleasure and
interest • *That's very exciting news.*

**exclaim** VERB exclaims, exclaiming, exclaimed
to shout or cry out in eagerness or surprise

**exclamation** NOUN exclamations
❶ exclaiming ❷ a word or words cried out expressing joy, pain or surprise

GRAMMAR

An exclamation often expresses a strong feeling such as delight or anger, and can be used as a strong command or warning.

Exclamations do not always have a subject and verb, and may be a single word; they should end with an exclamation mark:

*What a good a good answer!*

*Put that down!*

*Oh, no!*

*Good!*

See also the panels on exclamation marks and sentences.

**exclamation mark** NOUN exclamation marks
the punctuation mark (!) placed after an exclamation

PUNCTUATION

You use an exclamation mark to indicate shouting, surprise or excitement in direct speech:

*'Stop! Don't drink! The goblet is poisoned!'*

*'Wow! That's a real mammoth's tooth!'*

It can also be used to express surprise, alarm or excitement in a story, or in a character's thoughts:

*The sun was coming up. She must hurry! Soon the spell would wear off!*

*Swimming with sharks! That would be something to remember!*

An exclamation mark can be used at the end of a sentence to show that it is a command, giving an order or an instruction:

*Come in! Sit down!*

See also the panel on exclamations.

**exclude** VERB excludes, excluding, excluded
❶ to keep someone or something out of a place ❷ to leave something out • *Do not exclude the possibility of rain.*
➤ exclusion NOUN

**exclusive** ADJECTIVE
❶ allowing only a few people to be involved

• *an exclusive club* ❷ not shared with others
• *This newspaper has an exclusive report.*
➤ exclusively ADVERB
➤ exclusive of excluding, not including • *This is the price exclusive of meals.*

**excommunicate** VERB excommunicates, excommunicating, excommunicated
to cut a person off from membership of a Church
➤ excommunication NOUN

**excrement** (say eks-krim-ent) NOUN
waste matter excreted from the bowels

**excrescence** (say iks-kress-ens) NOUN
excrescences
❶ a growth or lump on a plant or animal's body ❷ an ugly addition or part

**excrete** VERB excretes, excreting, excreted
to get rid of waste matter from the body
➤ excretion NOUN
➤ excretory ADJECTIVE

**excruciating** (say iks-kroo-shee-ayt-ing) ADJECTIVE
extremely painful
➤ excruciatingly ADVERB

**excursion** NOUN excursions
a short journey made for pleasure

**excusable** ADJECTIVE
able to be excused

**excuse** (say iks-kewz) VERB excuses, excusing, excused
❶ to forgive someone ❷ to allow someone not to do something • *Please may I be excused swimming?* ❸ to allow someone to leave a room, table or meeting

**excuse** (say iks-kewss) NOUN excuses
a reason given to explain why something wrong has been done

**execrable** (say eks-ik-rab-ul) ADJECTIVE
very bad or unpleasant

**execute** VERB executes, executing, executed
❶ to put someone to death as a punishment ❷ to perform or produce something • *She executed the somersault perfectly.*
➤ execution NOUN

**executioner** NOUN executioners
a person whose job is to execute people

**executive** (say ig-zek-yoo-tiv) NOUN
executives
a senior person with authority in a business or government organization

**executive** ADJECTIVE
having the authority to carry out plans or
laws

**executor** (say ig-**zek**-yoo-ter) NOUN executors
a person appointed to carry out the
instructions in someone's will

**exemplary** (say ig-**zem**-pler-ee) ADJECTIVE
very good; being a good example to others
• *His conduct was exemplary.*

**exemplify** VERB exemplifies, exemplifying,
exemplified
to be a typical example of something • *This
painting exemplifies the style of his early
work.*

**exempt** ADJECTIVE
not having to do something that others have
to do • *Charities are exempt from paying tax.*

**exempt** VERB exempts, exempting, exempted
to make someone or something exempt
➤ exemption NOUN

**exercise** NOUN exercises
❶ using your body to make it strong and
healthy ❷ a piece of work done for practice

**exercise** VERB exercises, exercising, exercised
❶ to do exercises ❷ to give exercise to an
animal ❸ to use something • *You must
exercise more patience.*

**exert** VERB exerts, exerting, exerted
to use power, strength or influence • *The
moon exerts a force on the earth that causes
the tides.*
➤ exert yourself to make an effort

**exertion** NOUN exertions
physical effort or exercise • *He was tired
after the exertions of the morning.*

**exeunt** (say **eks**-ee-unt) VERB
a stage direction meaning 'they leave the
stage' WORD ORIGIN Latin = they go out

**exhale** VERB exhales, exhaling, exhaled
to breathe out • *He took a deep breath and
exhaled slowly.*
➤ exhalation NOUN

**exhaust** VERB exhausts, exhausting,
exhausted
❶ to make someone very tired ❷ to use
something up completely • *Within three days
they had exhausted their supply of food.*

**exhaust** NOUN exhausts
❶ the waste gases or steam from an engine
❷ the pipe through which they are sent out

**exhaustion** NOUN
being very tired

**exhaustive** ADJECTIVE
thorough; including everything possible • *We
made an exhaustive search.*

**exhibit** VERB exhibits, exhibiting, exhibited
to show or display something in public
➤ exhibitor NOUN

**exhibit** NOUN exhibits
something on display in a gallery or museum

**exhibition** NOUN exhibitions
a collection of things put on display for
people to look at, for example at a museum
or gallery

**exhilarate** (say ig-**zil**-er-ayt) VERB exhilarates,
exhilarating, exhilarated
to make someone very happy and excited
• *She felt exhilarated by the storm.*
➤ exhilarating ADJECTIVE
➤ exhilaration NOUN

**exhort** (say ig-**zort**) VERB exhorts, exhorting,
exhorted
to try hard to persuade someone to do
something
➤ exhortation NOUN

**exhume** (say ig-**zewm**) VERB exhumes,
exhuming, exhumed
to dig up a body that has been buried
➤ exhumation NOUN

**exile** VERB exiles, exiling, exiled
to banish someone from a country

**exile** NOUN exiles
❶ to be in exile is to be forced to live away
from your own country • *He was in exile for
ten years.* ❷ someone who has been banished
from their own country

**exist** VERB exists, existing, existed
❶ to be present as part of what is real • *Do
ghosts exist?* ❷ to stay alive • *They existed on
berries and water.*

**existence** NOUN
❶ existing or being • *This is the oldest human
skeleton in existence.* ❷ a way of living • *For
several years he led a lonely existence.*

**existing** ADJECTIVE
that is already there or being used • *His time
shattered the existing world record.*

**exit** NOUN exits
❶ the way out of a building ❷ going off the
stage • *The actress made her exit.*

**exit** VERB
an actor or performer exits when they leave
the stage WORD ORIGIN Latin = he or she goes
out

a
b
c
d
e
f
g
h
i
j
k
l
m
n
o
p
q
r
s
t
u
v
w
x
y
z

**exodus** NOUN exoduses
the departure of many people

**exonerate** VERB exonerates, exonerating, exonerated
to say or prove that a person is not to blame for something

**exorbitant** ADJECTIVE
much too great; excessive • *exorbitant prices*

**exorcize** (also **exorcise**) VERB exorcizes, exorcizing, exorcized
to drive out an evil spirit
➤ **exorcism** NOUN
➤ **exorcist** NOUN

**exotic** ADJECTIVE
❶ very unusual and colourful • *exotic clothes* ❷ from a foreign country, especially a distant or tropical one • *exotic plants*
➤ **exotically** ADVERB

**expand** VERB expands, expanding, expanded
❶ to become larger or fuller • *Metals expand when they are heated.* ❷ to make something larger or fuller

**expanse** NOUN expanses
a wide area of open land, sea or sky

**expansion** NOUN
becoming larger or making something larger

**expansive** ADJECTIVE
❶ covering a wide area ❷ friendly and willing to talk a lot • *She was in an expansive mood.*

**expatriate** (say eks-**pat**-ree-at) NOUN expatriates
a person living away from his or her own country

**expect** VERB expects, expecting, expected
❶ to think or believe that something will happen or that someone will come • *I expect that it will rain this afternoon.* ❷ to think that something ought to happen • *She expects obedience.*

**expectant** ADJECTIVE
❶ expecting something to happen; hopeful ❷ an expectant mother is a woman who is pregnant
➤ **expectantly** ADVERB
➤ **expectancy** NOUN

**expectation** NOUN expectations
❶ expecting something; being hopeful ❷ something you expect to happen or get

**expecting** ADJECTIVE (informal)
a woman who is expecting is pregnant

**expedient** (say iks-**pee**-dee-ent) ADJECTIVE
❶ suitable or convenient ❷ useful and practical though perhaps unfair
➤ **expediency** NOUN

**expedient** NOUN expedients
a convenient means of achieving something

**expedite** (say **eks**-pid-dyt) VERB expedites, expediting, expedited
to make something happen more quickly
**WORD ORIGIN** from Latin *expedire* = free someone's feet

**expedition** NOUN expeditions
❶ a journey or voyage made in order to do something • *a climbing expedition* ❷ (formal) speed or promptness
➤ **expeditionary** ADJECTIVE

**expel** VERB expels, expelling, expelled
❶ to send or force something out • *This fan expels stale air.* ❷ to make a person leave a school or country
➤ **expulsion** NOUN

**expend** VERB expends, expending, expended
to use or spend time, money or energy doing something • *I have already expended a lot of energy on this show.*

**expendable** ADJECTIVE
no longer useful or necessary and so not worth keeping or saving

**expenditure** NOUN expenditures
the spending of money or the amount spent

**expense** NOUN expenses
the cost of doing something • *The garden was transformed at great expense.*

**expensive** ADJECTIVE
costing a lot
➤ **expensively** ADVERB

**experience** NOUN experiences
❶ what you learn from doing or seeing things ❷ something that has happened to you

**experience** VERB experiences, experiencing, experienced
to have something happen to you • *It was the first time she had experienced failure.*

**experienced** ADJECTIVE
having a lot of skill or knowledge from much experience

**experiment** NOUN experiments
a test made in order to find out what happens or to prove something

**experiment** VERB experiments, experimenting, experimented
❶ to carry out an experiment ❷ to try out

new things
➤ **experimentation** NOUN

**experimental** ADJECTIVE
to do with experiments or trying out
new ideas • *The machine is still at the
experimental stage.*
➤ **experimentally** ADVERB

**expert** NOUN experts
a person with great knowledge or skill in
something

**expert** ADJECTIVE
having great knowledge or skill • *He's an
expert cook.*
➤ **expertly** ADVERB

**expertise** (say eks-per-**teez**) NOUN
expert ability or knowledge

**expire** VERB expires, expiring, expired
❶ to come to an end or stop being usable
• *Your season ticket has expired.* ❷ to die
➤ **expiration** NOUN
➤ **expiry** NOUN

**explain** VERB explains, explaining, explained
❶ to make something clear to someone else;
to show its meaning ❷ to give or be a reason
for something • *That explains his absence.*

**explanation** NOUN explanations
a statement or fact that explains something
or gives a reason for it

**explanatory** (say iks-**plan**-at-er-ee) ADJECTIVE
giving an explanation • *an explanatory note*

**explicit** (say iks-**pliss**-it) ADJECTIVE
stated or stating something openly and
exactly. Compare with **implicit**.
➤ **explicitly** ADVERB

**explode** VERB explodes, exploding, exploded
❶ to burst or suddenly release energy with a
loud noise ❷ to cause a bomb to go off ❸ to
burst into anger or laughter suddenly • *He
exploded with rage.* ❹ to increase suddenly
or quickly (WORD ORIGIN) originally = to drive a
player off the stage by clapping or hissing; from
**ex-** + Latin *plaudere* = clap

**exploit** (say **eks**-ploit) NOUN exploits
a brave or exciting deed

**exploit** (say iks-**ploit**) VERB exploits,
exploiting, exploited
❶ to exploit someone is to treat them
unfairly for your own advantage ❷ to exploit
resources is to use or develop them
➤ **exploitation** NOUN

**exploration** NOUN
exploring a place • *space exploration*

**exploratory** (say iks-**plo**rra-ter-ee) ADJECTIVE
for the purpose of exploring

**explore** VERB explores, exploring, explored
❶ to travel through a place in order to
learn about it ❷ to examine a subject or
idea carefully • *We need to explore all the
possibilities before we decide.*

**explorer** NOUN explorers
someone who explores a remote place to find
out what is there

**explosion** NOUN explosions
❶ the exploding of a bomb; the noise made
by exploding • *Two people were killed in the
explosion.* ❷ a sudden great increase • *a
population explosion*

**explosive** ADJECTIVE
able to explode • *Hydrogen is highly
explosive.*

**explosive** NOUN explosives
a substance that is used for causing
explosions

**exponent** NOUN exponents
❶ someone who is very good at an activity
• *a major exponent of landscape painting*
❷ a person who puts forward an idea or
theory ❸ (*in mathematics*) the raised number
etc. written to the right of another (e.g. 3 in
$2^3$ ) showing how many times the first one is
to be multiplied by itself

**export** VERB exports, exporting, exported
to send goods abroad to be sold • *Peru
exports copper, lead and zinc.*
➤ **exporter** NOUN

**export** NOUN exports
❶ exporting goods ❷ something that is
exported

**expose** VERB exposes, exposing, exposed
❶ to reveal or uncover something ❷ to put
someone in a situation where they could be
harmed • *Some people were exposed to high
levels of radiation.* ❸ to allow light to reach a
photographic film so as to take a picture

**expostulate** VERB expostulates,
expostulating, expostulated
to argue or protest strongly about something
➤ **expostulation** NOUN

**exposure** NOUN exposures
❶ the harmful effects of being exposed to
cold weather without enough protection
❷ exposing film to the light so as to take a
picture or a piece of film exposed in this way

a b c d e f g h i j k l m n o p q r s t u v w x y z

**expound** *VERB* expounds, expounding, expounded
to describe or explain something in detail

**express** *ADJECTIVE*
❶ going or sent quickly ❷ clearly stated
• *This was done against my express orders.*

**express** *NOUN* expresses
a fast train stopping at only a few stations

**express** *VERB* expresses, expressing, expressed
to put ideas or feelings into words; to make your feelings known • *He expressed his opinion on the matter very clearly.*

**expression** *NOUN* expressions
❶ the look on a person's face that shows his or her feelings ❷ a word or phrase ❸ a way of speaking or of playing music that shows your feelings ❹ expressing something • *this expression of opinion*

**expressive** *ADJECTIVE*
showing your thoughts and feelings • *an expressive gesture*

**expressly** *ADVERB*
❶ clearly and plainly • *This was expressly forbidden.* ❷ specially • *The exhibition is designed expressly for children*

**expulsion** *NOUN* expulsions
expelling someone or something or being expelled

**exquisite** (say **eks-kwiz**-it) *ADJECTIVE*
very beautiful or delicate • *The flowers are painted in exquisite detail.*
➤ **exquisitely** *ADVERB*

**extend** *VERB* extends, extending, extended
❶ to spread or stretch out • *Our land extends as far as the river.* ❷ to make something become longer or larger • *The table can be extended to seat more people.* ❸ to offer or give something • *I would like to extend a warm welcome to our guests.*

**extension** *NOUN* extensions
❶ a section added on to a building ❷ an extra period that is allowed for something to be done ❸ one of a set of telephones in an office or house

**extensive** *ADJECTIVE*
❶ covering a large area • *extensive gardens* ❷ large in scope; wide-ranging • *an extensive internet search*
➤ **extensively** *ADVERB*

**extent** *NOUN* extents
❶ the area or length over which something extends ❷ the amount, level or scope of

something • *We don't yet know the full extent of the damage.*

**extenuating** *ADJECTIVE*
making a crime seem less great by providing a partial excuse • *There were extenuating circumstances.*
➤ **extenuation** *NOUN*

**exterior** *ADJECTIVE*
outer • *the exterior walls of the house*

**exterior** *NOUN* exteriors
❶ the outside of something ❷ a person's outward appearance

**exterminate** *VERB* exterminates, exterminating, exterminated
to kill all the members of a group of people or animals
➤ **extermination** *NOUN*
➤ **exterminator** *NOUN*

**external** *ADJECTIVE*
on or from the outside of something • *an external fuel tank*
➤ **externally** *ADVERB*

**extinct** *ADJECTIVE*
❶ not existing any more • *The dodo is an extinct bird.* ❷ an extinct volcano is no longer burning or active

**extinction** *NOUN*
becoming extinct • *The giant panda is in danger of extinction.*

**extinguish** *VERB* extinguishes, extinguishing, extinguished
❶ to put out a fire or light ❷ to put an end to something • *Our hopes of victory were soon extinguished.*

**extinguisher** *NOUN* extinguishers
a portable device for sending out water, chemicals or gases to put out a fire

**extol** *VERB* extols, extolling, extolled
to praise someone or something enthusiastically

**extort** *VERB* extorts, extorting, extorted
to obtain something by force or threats
➤ **extortion** *NOUN*

**extortionate** *ADJECTIVE*
an extortionate price or fee is much too high

**extra** *ADJECTIVE*
additional; more than is usual • *There is an extra charge for taking your bike on the train.*

**extra** *ADVERB*
more than usually • *extra strong mints*

**extra** *NOUN* extras
 **❶** an extra person or thing **❷** a person acting as part of a crowd in a film or play

**extract** (say iks-**trakt**) *VERB* extracts, extracting, extracted
 **❶** to take something out; to remove something **❷** to obtain information from someone, usually with difficulty
 ➤ **extractor** *NOUN*

**extract** (say **eks**-trakt) *NOUN* extracts
 **❶** a passage taken from a book, film, piece of music, etc. **❷** a substance separated or obtained from another • *a plant extract*

**extraction** *NOUN*
 **❶** extracting something **❷** a person's family history • *He is of Chinese extraction.*

**extradite** *VERB* extradites, extraditing, extradited
 to hand over an accused person to the police of the country where the crime was committed
 ➤ **extradition** (say eks-tra-**dish**-on) *NOUN*

**extraordinary** *ADJECTIVE*
 very unusual or strange
 ➤ **extraordinarily** *ADVERB*

**extrasensory** *ADJECTIVE*
 outside the range of the known human senses

**extraterrestrial** *ADJECTIVE*
 from beyond the earth's atmosphere; from outer space

**extraterrestrial** *NOUN* extraterrestrials
 a being from outer space

**extravagant** *ADJECTIVE*
 **❶** spending or using too much of something **❷** too much; more than is reasonable
 • *extravagant praise*
 ➤ **extravagantly** *ADVERB*
 ➤ **extravagance** *NOUN*

**extravaganza** *NOUN* extravaganzas
 a very spectacular show

**extreme** *ADJECTIVE*
 **❶** very great or intense • *extreme cold* **❷** furthest away • *the extreme north* **❸** going to great lengths in actions or opinions; not moderate • *It seemed a bit extreme to call the police.*

**extreme** *NOUN* extremes
 **❶** something extreme **❷** either end of something

**extremely** *ADVERB*
 very • *They are extremely pleased.*

**extremist** *NOUN* extremists
 a person who holds extreme (not moderate) opinions in political or other matters

**extremity** (say iks-**trem**-it-ee) *NOUN* extremities
 **❶** an extreme point; the very end of something **❷** your extremities are your hands and feet **❸** an extreme need, feeling or danger

**extricate** (say **eks**-trik-ayt) *VERB* extricates, extricating, extricated
 to free someone or something from a difficult position or situation • *He managed to extricate himself from the wreckage.*
 ➤ **extrication** *NOUN*

**extrovert** *NOUN* extroverts
 a person who is generally lively and confident and likes company. (The opposite is **introvert**.)

**extrude** *VERB* extrudes, extruding, extruded
 to push or squeeze something out
 ➤ **extrusion** *NOUN*

**exuberant** (say ig-**zew**-ber-ant) *ADJECTIVE*
 very lively and cheerful
 ➤ **exuberantly** *ADVERB*
 ➤ **exuberance** *NOUN*

**exude** *VERB* exudes, exuding, exuded
 **❶** to give off moisture or a smell **❷** to display a feeling or quality openly • *She exuded confidence.*

**exult** *VERB* exults, exulting, exulted
 to show great pleasure and excitement about something • *'Ha! I win!' exulted Leah.*
 ➤ **exultation** *NOUN*

**exultant** *ADJECTIVE*
 very pleased and excited about something

**eye** *NOUN* eyes
 **❶** the organ of the body that is used for seeing **❷** the power of seeing • *She has sharp eyes.* **❸** the small hole in a needle **❹** the centre of a storm

**eye** *VERB* eyes, eyeing, eyed
 to look at something with interest

**eyeball** *NOUN* eyeballs
 the ball-shaped part of the eye inside the eyelids

**eyebrow** *NOUN* eyebrows
 the fringe of hair growing on your face above each eye

**eye-catching** *ADJECTIVE*
 striking or attractive

a b c d e f g h i j k l m n o p q r s t u v w x y z

**eyelash** NOUN eyelashes
one of the short hairs that grow on an eyelid

**eyelid** NOUN eyelids
either of the two folds of skin that can close over the eyeball

**eyepiece** NOUN eyepieces
the lens of a telescope or microscope that you put to your eye

**eyesight** NOUN
the ability to see

**eyesore** NOUN eyesores
something that is ugly to look at

**eyewitness** NOUN eyewitnesses
a person who actually saw an accident or crime

**eyrie** (say **ee-ree**) NOUN eyries
the nest of an eagle or other bird of prey

**fable** NOUN fables
a short story that teaches a lesson about how people should behave, often with animals as characters

**fabric** NOUN fabrics
❶ cloth ❷ the basic framework of something, especially the walls, floors and roof of a building

**fabricate** VERB fabricates, fabricating, fabricated
❶ to construct or manufacture something ❷ to invent a story or excuse
➤ **fabrication** NOUN

**fabulous** ADJECTIVE
❶ wonderful; really good • *She has a fabulous voice.* ❷ incredibly great • *fabulous wealth* ❸ told of in fables and myths
➤ **fabulously** ADVERB

**facade** (say fas-**ahd**) NOUN facades
❶ the front of a building ❷ an outward appearance, especially a deceptive one • *His good humour was just a facade.*

**face** NOUN faces
❶ the front part of the head ❷ the expression on a person's face ❸ the front or

upper side of something • *Put the cards face down.* ❹ a flat surface • *A cube has six faces.*

**face** VERB faces, facing, faced
❶ to look or have the front towards something • *Our room faced the sea.* ❷ to have to deal with something difficult or dangerous • *Explorers face many dangers.* ❸ to cover a surface with a layer of different material

**facelift** NOUN facelifts
surgery to remove wrinkles by tightening the skin of the face, done to make someone look younger

**facet** (say **fas**-it) NOUN facets
❶ one of the many sides of a cut stone or jewel ❷ one aspect of a situation or problem • *There are many facets to this argument.*

**facetious** (say fas-**ee**-shus) ADJECTIVE
trying to be funny at an unsuitable time • *facetious remarks*
➤ **facetiously** ADVERB

**facial** (say **fay**-shal) ADJECTIVE
to do with the face • *an odd facial expression*

**facilitate** (say fas-**il**-it-ayt) VERB facilitates, facilitating, facilitated
to make something easier to do

**facility** (say fas-**il**-it-ee) NOUN facilities
❶ a building or service that provides you with the means to do things • *The college has excellent sports facilities.* ❷ ease or skill in doing something • *She has a facility for languages.*

**facsimile** (say fak-**sim**-il-ee) NOUN facsimiles
an exact reproduction of a document

**fact** NOUN facts
something that is known to have happened or to be true
➤ **as a matter of fact** or **in fact** really; actually
➤ **the facts of life** information about how babies are conceived

**faction** NOUN factions
a small united group within a larger one, especially in politics

**factor** NOUN factors
❶ something that helps to bring about a result • *Hard work was a big factor in her success.* ❷ a number by which a larger number can be divided exactly • *2 and 3 are factors of 6*

**factory** NOUN **factories**
a large building where machines are used to make things in large quantities

**factual** ADJECTIVE
based on facts; containing facts • *I wrote down a factual account of what happened.*
➤ **factually** ADVERB

**faculty** NOUN **faculties**
❶ any of the powers of the body or mind (e.g. sight, speech, understanding) ❷ a department teaching a particular subject in a university or college • *the faculty of music*

**fad** NOUN **fads**
a fashion or interest that only lasts a short time

**fade** VERB **fades, fading, faded**
❶ to lose colour, freshness or strength • *Jeans fade when you wash them.* ❷ to disappear gradually • *The laughter faded away.* ❸ to make a sound etc. become gradually weaker (*fade it out*) or stronger (*fade it in* or *up*)

**faeces** (say fee-seez) PLURAL NOUN
solid waste matter passed out of the body

**fag** NOUN **fags** (British) (informal)
❶ something that is tiring or boring ❷ a cigarette
➤ **fagged out** tired out; exhausted

**faggot** NOUN **faggots**
❶ a meat ball made with chopped liver and baked ❷ a bundle of sticks bound together, used for firewood

**Fahrenheit** ADJECTIVE
measuring temperature on a scale where water freezes at 32° and boils at 212°
**WORD ORIGIN** named after G. D. *Fahrenheit*, a German scientist, who invented the mercury thermometer

**fail** VERB **fails, failing, failed**
❶ to try to do something but not be able to do it ❷ to become weak or useless; to stop working • *The brakes failed.* ❸ to not do something when you should • *He failed to warn me of the danger.* ❹ to not get enough marks to pass an examination ❺ to judge that someone has not passed an examination

**fail** NOUN **fails**
a mark which does not pass an examination • *Alex got four passes and one fail.*
➤ **without fail** for certain; whatever happens • *I'll be there without fail.*

**failing** NOUN **failings**
a weakness or a fault

**failure** NOUN **failures**
❶ a lack of success; not being able to do something • *All his efforts ended in failure.* ❷ not doing something that you were expected to do • *I was disappointed at his failure to turn up.* ❸ a person or thing that has failed

**faint** ADJECTIVE
❶ pale or dim; not clear or distinct • *a faint sound in the distance* ❷ slight • *a faint hope* ❸ feeling weak and dizzy; nearly unconscious
➤ **faintness** NOUN

**faint** VERB **faints, fainting, fainted**
to become unconscious for a short time

**SPELLING**
Take care not to confuse with **feint**, which means a pretended attack.

**faintly** ADVERB
❶ not in a clear or strong way • *He smiled faintly.* ❷ slightly • *She looked faintly embarrassed.*

**fair** ADJECTIVE
❶ just or reasonable; treating everyone equally • *a fair decision* • *a fair contest* ❷ fair hair or skin is light in colour and a fair person has hair that is light in colour ❸ fair weather is fine and without clouds ❹ of a reasonable size, amount or number • *a fair number of people* ❺ quite good • *We've got a fair chance of winning.* ❻ (old use) beautiful
➤ **fairness** NOUN

**fair** ADVERB
fairly, according to the rules • *Play fair!*

**fair** NOUN **fairs**
❶ an outdoor entertainment with rides, amusements and stalls ❷ an exhibition or market • *a craft fair*

**fairground** NOUN **fairgrounds**
an open outdoor space where a fair is held

**fairly** ADVERB
❶ justly; according to the rules • *She promised to treat everyone fairly.* ❷ quite or rather • *It is fairly hard.*

**fairy** NOUN **fairies**
an imaginary very small creature with magic powers

**fairyland** NOUN
the imaginary land where fairies live

**fairy tale** NOUN **fairy tales**
a story about fairies or magic

**faith** NOUN **faiths**
❶ strong belief or trust • *We have great faith*

**A**

*in her.* ❷ a religion
➤ **in good faith** with honest intentions

**B**

**faithful** ADJECTIVE
❶ loyal and trustworthy ❷ true to the facts;
accurate • *a faithful account* ❸ sexually loyal
to one partner
➤ **faithfully** ADVERB
➤ **faithfulness** NOUN
➤ **Yours faithfully** see **yours**

**C**

**D**

**E**

**fake** NOUN fakes
something that looks genuine but is not; a
forgery

**F**

**fake** ADJECTIVE
not real or genuine • *fake diamonds*

**G**

**fake** VERB fakes, faking, faked
❶ to make something that looks genuine, in
order to deceive people ❷ to pretend to have
something • *He used to fake illness to miss
games.*

**H**

**I**

**J**

**fakir** (say **fay**-keer) NOUN fakirs
a Muslim or Hindu religious beggar regarded
as a holy man

**K**

**falcon** NOUN falcons
a kind of hawk often used in the sport of
hunting other birds or game
➤ **falconry** NOUN

**L**

**M**

**N**

**fall** VERB falls, falling, fell, fallen
❶ to come or go down without being pushed
or thrown • *Leaves were falling from the
trees.* ❷ to decrease or become lower • *Prices
fell.* ❸ to be captured or overthrown • *The
city fell.* ❹ to die in battle ❺ to happen
• *Silence fell.* ❻ to become • *She fell asleep.*
➤ **fall back** to retreat
➤ **fall back on something** to use something
for support or in an emergency
➤ **fall for someone** to be attracted to a
person
➤ **fall for something** to be taken in by a trick
or deception
➤ **fall in** to collapse • *The roof fell in.*
➤ **fall in love** to begin to love someone
➤ **fall out** to quarrel and stop being friends
➤ **fall through** to fail • *Our plans fell
through.*

**O**

**P**

**Q**

**R**

**S**

**T**

**U**

**V**

**W**

**fall** NOUN falls
❶ the action of falling ❷ (*North American*)
autumn, when leaves fall

**X**

SPELLING
The past tense of **fall** is **fell** and the past
participle is **fallen**.

**Y**

**Z**

**fallacy** (say **fal**-a-see) NOUN fallacies
a false or mistaken idea or belief that many
people believe is true

**fallible** (say **fal**-ib-ul) ADJECTIVE
liable to make mistakes; not infallible • *All
people are fallible.*
➤ **fallibility** NOUN

**Fallopian tube** NOUN Fallopian tubes
one of the two tubes in a woman's body
along which the eggs travel from the ovaries
to the uterus

**fallout** NOUN
particles of radioactive material carried in the
air after a nuclear explosion

**fallow** ADJECTIVE
fallow land is ploughed but left without
crops in order to make it fertile again
WORD ORIGIN from Old English *falu* = pale
brown (because of the colour of the bare earth)

**fallow deer** NOUN fallow deer
a kind of light-brown deer

**falls** PLURAL NOUN
a waterfall

**false** ADJECTIVE
❶ untrue or incorrect ❷ not genuine;
artificial • *false teeth* ❸ treacherous or
deceitful
➤ **falsely** ADVERB

**falsehood** NOUN falsehoods
❶ a lie ❷ telling lies

**falsetto** NOUN falsettos
a man's voice forced into speaking or singing
higher than is natural

**falsify** VERB falsifies, falsifying, falsified
to alter a document or evidence dishonestly
➤ **falsification** NOUN

**falter** VERB falters, faltering, faltered
❶ to hesitate when you move or speak ❷ to
become weaker; to begin to give way • *His
courage began to falter.*

**fame** NOUN
being famous • *His fame spread throughout
Europe.*

**famed** ADJECTIVE
very well known • *The restaurant is famed for
its seafood.*

**familiar** ADJECTIVE
❶ well-known; often seen or experienced
• *His yellow van was a familiar sight in the
village.* ❷ knowing something well • *Are you
familiar with this book?* ❸ very friendly

➤ **familiarly** ADVERB
➤ **familiarity** NOUN

**familiarize** (also **familiarise**) VERB
familiarizes, familiarizing, familiarized
to make yourself familiar with something

**family** NOUN families
❶ parents and their children, sometimes including grandchildren and other relations
❷ a group of related plants or animals • *Lions belong to the cat family.* ❸ a group of things that are alike in some way • *a family of languages*

**family planning** NOUN
the use of contraceptives to control pregnancies; birth control

**family tree** NOUN family trees
a diagram showing how people in a family are related

**famine** NOUN famines
a very bad shortage of food in an area

**famished** ADJECTIVE
very hungry

**famous** ADJECTIVE
known to very many people

**famously** ADVERB (*informal*)
very well • *They get on famously.*

**fan** NOUN fans
❶ a device or machine for making air move about in order to cool people or things ❷ an enthusiastic admirer or supporter

**fan** VERB fans, fanning, fanned
to send a current of air on something
➤ **fan out** to spread out in the shape of a fan
• *The police fanned out across the field.*

**fanatic** NOUN fanatics
a person who is very enthusiastic or too enthusiastic about something
➤ **fanaticism** NOUN

**fanatical** ADJECTIVE
very enthusiastic or too enthusiastic about something • *He's fanatical about keeping things tidy.*
➤ **fanatically** ADVERB

**fanciful** ADJECTIVE
❶ imagined; not based on reality or reason
• *What a fanciful idea!* ❷ imagining things
• *a fanciful child*

**fancy** NOUN fancies
❶ a liking or desire for something
❷ something that you imagine

**fancy** ADJECTIVE
decorated or elaborate; not plain • *fancy stitching*

**fancy** VERB fancies, fancying, fancied
❶ to have a liking or desire for something
• *Do you fancy getting a bite to eat?* ❷ to imagine something ❸ to believe or suppose something • *I fancy it's raining.*

**fancy dress** NOUN
unusual costume worn for a party, often to make you look like a famous person

**fanfare** NOUN fanfares
a short piece of loud music played on trumpets, especially as part of a ceremony

**fang** NOUN fangs
a long sharp tooth

**fanlight** NOUN fanlights
a window above a door

**fantasia** (say fan-**tay**-zee-a) NOUN fantasias
an imaginative piece of music or writing

**fantasize** (also **fantasise**) VERB fantasizes, fantasizing, fantasized
to imagine something pleasant or strange that you would like to happen

**fantastic** ADJECTIVE
❶ (*informal*) excellent ❷ strange or unusual; showing a lot of imagination • *a story full of fantastic creatures*
➤ **fantastically** ADVERB

**fantasy** NOUN fantasies
❶ something pleasant that you imagine but is not likely to happen; imagining things ❷ a very imaginative story that is not based on real life

**far** ADVERB
❶ at or to a great distance • *We didn't go far.* ❷ much; by a great amount • *This is far better.*
➤ **by far** by a great amount

**far** ADJECTIVE
❶ distant or remote • *We could see the hills in the far distance.* ❷ the far side or end of something is the side or end facing you or furthest away • *A boy was standing on the far side of the river.*

**farce** NOUN farces
❶ a comedy in which the humour is exaggerated ❷ a situation or series of events that is ridiculous or a pretence • *The trial was a complete farce.*
➤ **farcical** ADJECTIVE
**WORD ORIGIN** French, literally = stuffing (the

name given to a comic interlude between acts of a play)

**fare** NOUN **fares**
❶ the price charged for a passenger to travel ❷ food and drink • *There was only very plain fare.*

**fare** VERB **fares, faring, fared**
to get on or make progress • *How did they fare?*

**farewell** EXCLAMATION & NOUN **farewells**
goodbye

**far-fetched** ADJECTIVE
unlikely to be true, difficult to believe • *It all sounds rather far-fetched to me.*

**farm** NOUN **farms**
❶ an area of land and its buildings used for growing crops or keeping animals for food or other use ❷ a farmhouse

**farm** VERB **farms, farming, farmed**
❶ to grow crops or keep animals for food etc. ❷ to use land for growing crops

**farmer** NOUN **farmers**
a person who owns or manages a farm

**farmhouse** NOUN **farmhouses**
the main house on a farm, where the farmer lives

**farmyard** NOUN **farmyards**
the yard or area round farm buildings

**farrier** (say fa-ree-er) NOUN **farriers**
a smith who shoes horses

**farther** ADVERB & ADJECTIVE
at or to a greater distance; more distant

USAGE

Farther and farthest are used only if you are talking about distance (e.g. *She lives farther from the school than I do*), but even in such cases many people prefer to use further. Only further can be used to mean 'additional', e.g. in *Phone this number for further details*. If you are not sure which is right, use further.

**farthest** ADVERB & ADJECTIVE
at or to the greatest distance; most distant

USAGE

See the note at farther.

**farthing** NOUN **farthings**
a former British coin worth one-quarter of a penny

**fascinate** VERB **fascinates, fascinating, fascinated**
to be very attractive or interesting to someone • *Ancient Egypt has always fascinated me.*
➤ **fascinating** ADJECTIVE

SPELLING

There is a tricky bit in **fascinate**—the 's' sound is spelt **sc**.

**fascination** NOUN
great interest in something • *She watched him with increasing fascination.*

**Fascist** (say fash-ist) NOUN **Fascists**
a person who supports a type of government in which a country is ruled by a powerful dictator and people are not allowed to hold opposing political views
➤ **Fascism** NOUN
WORD ORIGIN from Latin *fasces*, the bundle of rods with an axe through it, carried before a magistrate in ancient Rome as a symbol of his power to punish people

**fashion** NOUN **fashions**
❶ the style of clothes or other things that most people like at a particular time ❷ a way of doing something • *He's been behaving in a very strange fashion.*

**fashion** VERB **fashions, fashioning, fashioned**
to make something in a particular shape or style • *She fashioned a pot from the clay.*

**fashionable** ADJECTIVE
following the fashion of the time; popular
➤ **fashionably** ADVERB

**fast** ADJECTIVE **faster, fastest**
❶ moving or done quickly • *She's a fast runner.* • *Thank you for your fast response.*
❷ allowing fast movement • *a fast road*
❸ showing a time later than the correct time • *Your watch is fast.* ❹ firmly fixed or attached • *He made the boat fast before he got out.* ❺ a fast colour or dye is not likely to fade or run

**fast** ADVERB
❶ quickly • *How fast can you run?* ❷ firmly • *His leg was stuck fast in the mud.*
➤ **fast asleep** in a deep sleep

**fast** VERB **fasts, fasting, fasted**
to go without food, especially for religious or medical reasons

**fast** NOUN **fasts**
a period of fasting

**fasten** VERB fastens, fastening, fastened
❶ to fix one thing firmly to another ❷ to close or lock something firmly

**fastener, fastening** NOUN fasteners or fastenings
a device used to fasten something

**fast food** NOUN
restaurant food that is quickly prepared and served

**fastidious** ADJECTIVE
❶ fussy and hard to please ❷ very careful about small details of dress or cleanliness
➤ **fastidiously** ADVERB
➤ **fastidiousness** NOUN

**fat** NOUN fats
❶ the white greasy part of meat ❷ oil or grease used in cooking

**fat** ADJECTIVE fatter, fattest
❶ having a very thick round body ❷ thick • a fat book
➤ **fatness** NOUN

**fatal** ADJECTIVE
❶ causing or ending in death • a fatal accident ❷ likely to have bad results • He then made a fatal mistake.
➤ **fatally** ADVERB

**fatalist** NOUN fatalists
a person who accepts whatever happens and thinks it could not have been avoided
➤ **fatalism** NOUN
➤ **fatalistic** ADJECTIVE

**fatality** (say fa-**tal**-it-ee) NOUN fatalities
a death caused by an accident, war or other disaster

**fate** NOUN fates
❶ a person's fate is what will happen or has happened to them • She sat outside, waiting to find out her fate. ❷ a power that is thought to make things happen • It was fate that brought them together again after 20 years.

**fated** ADJECTIVE
destined by fate; doomed

**fateful** ADJECTIVE
bringing events that are important and often disastrous • How well she remembered that fateful day.
➤ **fatefully** ADVERB

**father** NOUN fathers
❶ a male parent ❷ the title of certain priests

**father** VERB fathers, fathering, fathered
to become a father • He fathered six children.

**father-in-law** NOUN fathers-in-law
the father of a married person's husband or wife

**fatherly** ADJECTIVE
typical of a father • a piece of fatherly advice

**fathom** NOUN fathoms
a unit used to measure the depth of water, equal to 1.83 metres or 6 feet

**fathom** VERB fathoms, fathoming, fathomed
to understand something difficult; to work something out • I can't fathom how you did it.

**fatigue** NOUN
❶ extreme tiredness ❷ weakness in metals, caused by stress
➤ **fatigued** ADJECTIVE

**fatten** VERB fattens, fattening, fattened
to feed a person or animal to make them fatter

**fatty** ADJECTIVE
fatty meat or food contains a lot of fat

**fatuous** ADJECTIVE
a fatuous remark is pointless and silly
➤ **fatuously** ADVERB

**fatwa** NOUN fatwas
a ruling on a religious matter given by an Islamic authority

**faucet** NOUN faucets
(North American) a tap

**fault** NOUN faults
❶ anything that makes a person or thing imperfect; a flaw or mistake ❷ the responsibility for something wrong • It wasn't your fault. ❸ a break in a layer of rock, caused by movement of the earth's crust ❹ an incorrect serve in tennis
➤ **at fault** responsible for a mistake or failure

**fault** VERB faults, faulting, faulted
to find faults in something • I cannot fault this book – it's brilliant.

**faultless** ADJECTIVE
without a fault; perfect
➤ **faultlessly** ADVERB

**faulty** ADJECTIVE
having a fault or faults; not working or made properly • a faulty light switch

**faun** NOUN fauns
an ancient Roman god with a man's body and goat's legs, horns and tail **WORD ORIGIN** from the name of *Faunus*, an ancient Roman country god (see **fauna**)

**fauna** NOUN
the animals of a certain area or period of time. Compare with **flora**. • *the flora and fauna of South America* **WORD ORIGIN** from the name of *Fauna*, an ancient Roman country goddess, sister of Faunus (see **faun**)

**favour** NOUN favours
❶ something kind or helpful that you do for someone ❷ approval or liking • *The idea found favour with most people.*
➤ **be in favour of** to agree with or support something • *I'm in favour of longer holidays!*

**favour** VERB favours, favouring, favoured
❶ to approve of or prefer something • *I favour the second explanation.* ❷ to help or support one person or group more than others • *Fortune seemed to favour him.*

**favourable** ADJECTIVE
❶ helpful or advantageous • *Conditions are favourable for skiing.* ❷ showing or earning approval • *favourable comments* • *I hope I made a favourable impression on them.*
➤ **favourably** ADVERB

**favourite** ADJECTIVE
liked more than others

**favourite** NOUN favourites
❶ a person or thing that you like most ❷ a competitor that is generally expected to win

**SPELLING**
The 'er' sound is spelt **our** in the middle of **favourite**.

**favouritism** NOUN
unfairly being kinder to one person than to others

**fawn** NOUN fawns
❶ a young deer ❷ a light-brown colour

**fawn** VERB fawns, fawning, fawned
to get someone to like you by flattering or praising them too much

**fax** NOUN faxes
❶ a machine that sends an exact copy of a document electronically ❷ a copy produced by this

**fax** VERB faxes, faxing, faxed
to send a copy of a document using a fax machine

**faze** VERB fazes, fazing, fazed (*informal*)
to make someone feel confused or shocked, so that they do not know what to do • *She wasn't fazed by his comments.*

**fear** NOUN fears
a feeling that you are in danger or that something unpleasant may happen

**fear** VERB fears, fearing, feared
❶ to feel fear; to be afraid of someone or something ❷ to be anxious or sad about something • *I fear we may be late.*

**fearful** ADJECTIVE
❶ afraid or worried • *He was fearful of going out alone.* ❷ causing fear or horror • *It was a fearful sight.* ❸ (*informal*) very great or bad • *We made a fearful mess.*
➤ **fearfully** ADVERB

**fearless** ADJECTIVE
without fear
➤ **fearlessly** ADVERB
➤ **fearlessness** NOUN

**fearsome** ADJECTIVE
frightening or dreadful

**feasible** ADJECTIVE
❶ able to be done; possible • *a feasible plan* ❷ likely or probable • *a feasible explanation*
➤ **feasibly** ADVERB
➤ **feasibility** NOUN

**feast** NOUN feasts
❶ a large splendid meal for a lot of people ❷ a religious festival

**feast** VERB feasts, feasting, feasted
to eat a feast or a large amount
➤ **feast your eyes on something** to gaze at something with great pleasure

**feat** NOUN feats
a deed or achievement that shows a lot of skill, strength or courage • *a remarkable feat of endurance*

**feather** NOUN feathers
one of the very light coverings that grow from a bird's skin

**feathered** ADJECTIVE
covered with or having feathers • *a feathered headdress*

**featherweight** NOUN featherweights
a boxer weighing between 54 and 57 kg

**feathery** ADJECTIVE
light and soft; like a feather • *feathery green leaves*

**feature** NOUN features
❶ any part of the face (e.g. mouth, nose, eyes) • *He has rugged features.* ❷ an important or noticeable part of something; a characteristic ❸ a special newspaper article or programme that deals with a particular

subject ❹ the main film in a cinema programme

**feature** VERB features, featuring, featured
❶ to include something as an important part • *The film features an all-star cast.* ❷ to play an important part in something • *Elves feature in many of his books.*

**February** NOUN
the second month of the year
**WORD ORIGIN** named after *februa*, the ancient Roman feast of purification held in this month
**SPELLING**
February can be difficult to spell—the letter r appears twice.

**feckless** ADJECTIVE
not having the determination to achieve anything in life

**fed**
past tense of **feed**
➤ **fed up** (*informal*) depressed, unhappy or bored

**federal** ADJECTIVE
to do with a system in which several states are ruled by a central government but have the power to make some of their own laws

**federation** NOUN federations
a group of states that have joined together under a central government

**fee** NOUN fees
a charge for something

**feeble** ADJECTIVE
weak; without strength or force • *a feeble excuse*
➤ **feebly** ADVERB
➤ **feebleness** NOUN

**feed** VERB feeds, feeding, fed
❶ to give food to a person or animal ❷ to take and eat food • *Sheep feed on grass.* ❸ to put something into a machine • *We fed all the figures into the database.*
➤ **feeder** NOUN

**feed** NOUN
food for animals or babies

**feedback** NOUN
❶ the response you get from people to something you have done ❷ the harsh noise produced when some of the sound from an amplifier goes back into it

**feel** VERB feels, feeling, felt
❶ to touch something to find out what it is like ❷ to think or have something as an

opinion • *I feel that she was badly treated.* ❸ to experience an emotion • *I feel a lot happier now.* ❹ to be affected by something • *Suddenly he felt very cold.* ❺ to give a certain sensation • *It feels damp in here.*
➤ **feel like something** to want something • *I don't feel like going out.*

**feel** NOUN
what something is like when you touch it • *I like the feel of silk.*
**SPELLING**
The past tense of feel is felt.

**feeler** NOUN feelers
❶ either of the two long thin parts that stick out from an insect's or crustacean's body, used for feeling ❷ a cautious question or suggestion to test people's reactions

**feeling** NOUN feelings
❶ the ability to feel things; the sense of touch • *She lost the feeling in her right hand.* ❷ what a person feels in the mind; emotion • *I didn't mean to hurt your feelings.* ❸ what you think about something • *I have a feeling that we are going to win.*

**feign** (say fayn) VERB feigns, feigning, feigned
to pretend to have a feeling or to be ill • *He feigned surprise when she walked in.*

**feint** (say faynt) NOUN feints
a pretended attack or punch meant to deceive an opponent

**feint** VERB feints, feinting, feinted
to pretend to attack or hit someone
**SPELLING**
Take care not to confuse with **faint**, which means pale, slight or dizzy.

**felicity** NOUN
❶ great happiness ❷ a pleasing manner or style • *He expressed himself with great felicity.*
➤ **felicitous** ADJECTIVE

**feline** (say feel-yn) ADJECTIVE
to do with cats; cat-like

**fell**
past tense of **fall**

**fell** VERB fells, felling, felled
❶ to cut down a tree ❷ to knock someone down with a hard blow

**fell** NOUN fells
a piece of wild hilly country, especially in the north of England

**fellow** *NOUN* fellows
❶ a friend or companion; one who belongs to the same group ❷ a man or boy ❸ a member of a learned society

**fellow** *ADJECTIVE*
of the same group or kind • *Her fellow students supported her.*

**fellowship** *NOUN* fellowships
❶ friendship between people ❷ a group of friends; a society

**felon** (say fel-on) *NOUN* felons
a criminal

**felony** (say fel-on-ee) *NOUN* felonies
a serious crime

**felt**
past tense of **feel**

**felt** *NOUN*
a thick fabric made of wool fibres pressed together

**female** *ADJECTIVE*
of the sex that can bear offspring or produce eggs or fruit

**female** *NOUN* females
a female person, animal or plant

**feminine** *ADJECTIVE*
❶ to do with or like women; thought to be suitable for a woman ❷ belonging to the class of words (in some languages) which includes the words referring to women
➤ **femininity** *NOUN*

**feminist** *NOUN* feminists
a person who believes that women should have the same rights and opportunities as men
➤ **feminism** *NOUN*

**femur** (say fee-mer) *NOUN* femurs
the thigh bone

**fen** *NOUN* fens
an area of low-lying marshy or flooded ground

**fence** *NOUN* fences
❶ a barrier made of wood or wire etc. round an area ❷ a structure for a horse to jump over ❸ a person who buys stolen goods and sells them again

**fence** *VERB* fences, fencing, fenced
❶ to put a fence round or along something ❷ to fight with long narrow swords (called foils) as a sport
➤ **fencer** *NOUN*
➤ **fencing** *NOUN*

**fend** *VERB* fends, fending, fended
➤ **fend for yourself** to take care of yourself
➤ **fend someone** or **something off** to defend yourself from a person or thing that is attacking you • *She managed to fend off all their awkward questions.*

**fender** *NOUN* fenders
❶ something placed round a fireplace to stop coals from falling into the room ❷ something hung over the side of a boat to protect it from knocks

**fennel** *NOUN*
a herb with yellow flowers whose seeds and root are used for flavouring

**feral** *ADJECTIVE*
wild and untamed • *feral cats*

**ferment** (say fer-ment) *VERB* ferments, fermenting, fermented
to bubble and change chemically by the action of a substance such as yeast • *The wine is starting to ferment.*
➤ **fermentation** *NOUN*

> **SPELLING**
> Take care not to confuse **ferment** with **foment**, which means to stir up trouble.

**ferment** (say fer-ment) *NOUN*
a state of great excitement or agitation • *The crowd was in a ferment.*

**fern** *NOUN* ferns
a plant with feathery leaves and no flowers

**ferocious** *ADJECTIVE*
fierce or savage • *a ferocious beast*
➤ **ferociously** *ADVERB*

**ferocity** *NOUN*
violence or fierceness • *He hadn't expected the ferocity of the attack.*

**ferret** *NOUN* ferrets
a small weasel-like animal used for catching rabbits and rats
➤ **ferrety** *ADJECTIVE*

**ferret** *VERB* ferrets, ferreting, ferreted
❶ to hunt with a ferret ❷ to search or rummage about for something • *She ferreted around in her bag for her phone.*

**ferric, ferrous** *ADJECTIVE*
containing iron

**ferry** *NOUN* ferries
a boat or ship used for carrying people or things across a short stretch of water

**ferry** VERB ferries, ferrying, ferried
to carry people or things across water or for a short distance • *The fisherman agreed to ferry us across to the island.*

**fertile** ADJECTIVE
❶ fertile soil is rich and produces good crops ❷ people or animals that are fertile can produce babies or young animals ❸ a fertile brain or imagination is able to produce ideas

**fertility** NOUN
being fertile • *a goddess of fertility*

**fertilize** (also **fertilise**) VERB fertilizes, fertilizing, fertilized
❶ to add substances to the soil to make it more fertile ❷ to put pollen into a plant or sperm into an egg or female animal so that it develops seed or young
➤ **fertilization** NOUN

**fertilizer** (also **fertiliser**) NOUN fertilizers
chemicals or manure added to the soil to make it more fertile

**fervent** ADJECTIVE
showing warm or strong feelings about something • *She is one of his most fervent admirers.*
➤ **fervently** ADVERB
➤ **fervour** NOUN

**fester** VERB festers, festering, festered
❶ a wound festers if it becomes septic and fills with pus ❷ to cause resentment for a long time • *The hatred between them has been festering for years.*

**festival** NOUN festivals
❶ a time of celebration, especially for religious reasons ❷ an organized series of concerts, films, performances, etc., especially one held every year

**festive** ADJECTIVE
❶ to do with a festival ❷ suitable for a festival; joyful • *We were all in a festive mood.*

**festivity** NOUN festivities
❶ festivities are the parties and other events that are held to celebrate something • *The festivities went on until dawn.* ❷ festivity is being happy and celebrating something • *There was an air of festivity in the village.*

**festoon** VERB festoons, festooning, festooned
to hang decorations, such as chains of flowers or paper, across something • *The streets were festooned with coloured flags.*

**fetch** VERB fetches, fetching, fetched
❶ to go for something and bring it back • *Can you fetch a cloth from the kitchen?* • *There was no time to fetch a doctor.* ❷ to be sold for a particular price • *The painting is expected to fetch \$20,000.*

**fete** (say fayt) NOUN fetes
an outdoor event with stalls, games and things for sale, often held to raise money • *a school fete*

**fete** VERB fetes, feting, feted
to honour a person with celebrations

SPELLING

A **fete** is an outdoor entertainment with stalls. **Fate** is a power that is thought to make things happen.

**fetlock** NOUN fetlocks
the part of a horse's leg above and behind the hoof

**fetter** NOUN fetters
a chain or shackle put round a prisoner's ankle

**fetter** VERB fetters, fettering, fettered
to put fetters on a prisoner

**fettle** NOUN
➤ **in fine fettle** in good health

**feud** (say fewd) NOUN feuds
a long-lasting quarrel, especially between two families

**feud** VERB feuds, feuding, feuded
to keep up a quarrel for a long time • *feuding families*

**feudal** (say few-dal) ADJECTIVE
to do with the system used in the Middle Ages in which people could farm land in exchange for work done for the owner
➤ **feudalism** NOUN

**fever** NOUN fevers
❶ an abnormally high body temperature, usually with an illness ❷ excitement or agitation
➤ **fevered** ADJECTIVE

**feverish** ADJECTIVE
❶ having a fever or high temperature ❷ showing great excitement or agitation • *months of feverish activity*
➤ **feverishly** ADVERB

a b c d e f g h i j k l m n o p q r s t u v w x y z

**few** *DETERMINER*
not many

> USAGE

Take care not to confuse **fewer** and **less**. You should use **fewer** when you mean 'not so many', and **less** when you mean 'not so much':• *Venus has fewer craters than the Earth and also less water.*

**few** *PRONOUN*
a small number of people or things
➤ **quite a few** or **a good few** a fairly large number

**fez** *NOUN* fezzes
a high flat-topped red hat with a tassel, worn by men in some Muslim countries
**WORD ORIGIN** named after *Fez*, a town in Morocco, where fezzes were made

**fiancé** (say fee-**ahn**-say) *NOUN* fiancés
a woman's fiancé is the man who she is engaged to be married to

**fiancée** (say fee-**ahn**-say) *NOUN* fiancées
a man's fiancée is the woman who he is engaged to be married to

**fiasco** (say fee-**as**-koh) *NOUN* fiascos
a complete and embarrassing failure

**fib** *NOUN* fibs
a lie about something unimportant

**fib** *VERB* fibs, fibbing, fibbed
to tell a lie about something unimportant
➤ **fibber** *NOUN*

**fibre** *NOUN* fibres
❶ a very thin thread ❷ a substance made of thin threads ❸ parts of certain foods that your body cannot digest but that move the rest of the food quickly through your body
• *Wholemeal bread is high in fibre.*

**fibreglass** *NOUN*
❶ fabric made from glass fibres ❷ plastic containing glass fibres

**fibrous** *ADJECTIVE*
made up of lots of fibres • *fibrous roots*

**fickle** *ADJECTIVE*
constantly changing your mind; not staying loyal to one person or group
➤ **fickleness** *NOUN*

**fiction** *NOUN* fictions
❶ writings about events that have not really happened; stories and novels ❷ something made up or untrue

**fictional** *ADJECTIVE*
existing only in a story, not in real life • *a fictional character*

**fictitious** *ADJECTIVE*
made up by someone and not true or real
• *This friend she kept talking about turned out to be completely fictitious.*

**fiddle** *NOUN* fiddles
❶ (*informal*) a violin ❷ (*informal*) a swindle

**fiddle** *VERB* fiddles, fiddling, fiddled
❶ (*informal*) to play the violin ❷ to keep touching or playing with something, using your fingers • *Stop fiddling with your keys.*
❸ (*informal*) to alter accounts or records dishonestly
➤ **fiddler** *NOUN*

**fiddly** *ADJECTIVE*
(*British*) small and awkward to use or do • *The buttons on my coat are quite fiddly.*

**fidelity** *NOUN*
❶ faithfulness or loyalty ❷ accuracy; the exactness with which sound is reproduced

**fidget** *VERB* fidgets, fidgeting, fidgeted
to make small restless movements because you are bored or nervous
➤ **fidgety** *ADJECTIVE*

**fidget** *NOUN* fidgets
a person who fidgets

**field** *NOUN* fields
❶ a piece of land with grass or crops growing on it ❷ an area of interest or study • *recent advances in the field of genetics* ❸ those who are taking part in a race or outdoor game ❹ (*in computing*) one area of a database, where one particular type of information is stored

**field** *VERB* fields, fielding, fielded
❶ to stop or catch the ball in cricket or other ball games ❷ to be on the side not batting in cricket ❸ to put a team into a match • *They fielded their best players.*
➤ **fielder** *NOUN*

> SPELLING

The 'ee' sound in **field** is spelt ie.

**field events** *PLURAL NOUN*
athletic sports other than track races, such as jumping and throwing events

**Field Marshal** *NOUN* Field Marshals
an army officer of the highest rank

**fieldwork** *NOUN*
practical work or research done in various places outside, not in a school, college or

laboratory • *We went to the coast to do some geography fieldwork.*

**fiend** (say feend) *NOUN* fiends
❶ an evil spirit or devil ❷ a very wicked or cruel person ❸ a person who is enthusiastic about doing or having something • *She is a fresh-air fiend.*

**fiendish** *ADJECTIVE*
❶ very wicked or cruel ❷ extremely difficult or complicated • *a fiendish puzzle*
➤ **fiendishly** *ADVERB*

**fierce** *ADJECTIVE*
❶ angry and violent and likely to attack you • *a fierce dog* ❷ strong or intense • *fierce heat*
➤ **fierceness** *NOUN*

**fiercely** *ADVERB*
❶ in a fierce way • *The man glared fiercely at us.* ❷ strongly or intensely • *The fire was now burning fiercely.*

**fiery** *ADJECTIVE*
❶ full of flames or heat ❷ easily made angry • *His sister had a fiery temper.* ❸ full of emotion and passion

**fife** *NOUN* fifes
a small shrill flute

**fifteen** *NOUN & ADJECTIVE* fifteens
the number 15
➤ **fifteenth** *ADJECTIVE & NOUN*

**fifth** *ADJECTIVE & NOUN* fifths
next after the fourth
➤ **fifthly** *ADVERB*

**fifty** *NOUN & ADJECTIVE* fifties
the number 50
➤ **fiftieth** *ADJECTIVE & NOUN*

**fifty-fifty** *ADJECTIVE & ADVERB*
❶ shared equally between two people or groups • *We'll split the money fifty-fifty.* ❷ evenly balanced • *a fifty-fifty chance*

**fig** *NOUN* figs
a soft fruit full of small seeds

**fight** *NOUN* fights
❶ a struggle against someone using hands or weapons ❷ an attempt to achieve or overcome something • *the fight against crime*

**fight** *VERB* fights, fighting, fought
❶ to have a fight ❷ to try to achieve or overcome something • *He has spent the last ten years fighting for justice.* • *They fought the fire all night.*

**fighter** *NOUN* fighters
❶ someone who fights ❷ a fast military plane that attacks other aircraft

**figment** *NOUN* figments
➤ **a figment of your imagination** something that you only imagine and is not real

**figurative** *ADJECTIVE*
figurative language uses words or phrases for special effect and not in their literal meanings
➤ **figuratively** *ADVERB*

**figure** *NOUN* figures
❶ the symbol of a number ❷ an amount or value ❸ a diagram or illustration ❹ a shape • *a five-sided figure* ❺ the shape of a person's, especially a woman's, body ❻ a person • *a leading figure in the music industry* ❼ a representation of a person or animal in painting, sculpture, etc.

**figure** *VERB* figures, figuring, figured
❶ to appear or take part in something • *She figures in some of the stories about King Arthur.* ❷ (informal, chiefly North American) to think that something is probably true • *I figured that the best thing to do was to wait.*
➤ **figure something out** to work something out • *Can you figure out the answer?*

**figurehead** *NOUN* figureheads
❶ a carved figure decorating the prow of a sailing ship ❷ a person who is head of a country or organization but has no real power

**figure of speech** *NOUN* figures of speech
a word or phrase used for special effect and not intended literally, e.g. 'flood' in *a flood of emails*

**filament** *NOUN* filaments
a thread or thin wire, especially one in a light bulb

**filch** *VERB* filches, filching, filched
to steal something slyly

**file** *NOUN* files
❶ a folder or box for keeping papers in order ❷ a collection of data stored under one name in a computer ❸ a line of people one behind the other ❹ a metal tool with a rough surface that is rubbed on things to shape them or make them smooth

**file** *VERB* files, filing, filed
❶ to put something into a file ❷ to walk in a line one behind the other • *They filed out of the classroom.* ❸ to shape or smooth

something with a file • *She sat there, filing her nails.*

**filial** (say fil-ee-al) ADJECTIVE
(*formal*) to do with a son or daughter

**filigree** NOUN
delicate lace-like decoration made from twisted metal wire

**filings** PLURAL NOUN
tiny pieces of metal rubbed off by a metal file • *iron filings*

**fill** VERB fills, filling, filled
❶ to make something full or to become full • *I'll just fill the kettle. • The room was filling quickly.* ❷ to block up a hole or cavity ❸ to appoint a person to a vacant post
➤ **fill someone in** to give someone the information they need
➤ **fill something in** to put answers or other information in a form or document

**fill** NOUN
enough to make you full • *We ate our fill.*

**filler** NOUN fillers
a substance used to fill holes or cracks in wood or plaster

**fillet** NOUN fillets
a piece of fish or meat without bones

**fillet** VERB fillets, filleting, filleted
remove the bones from fish or meat

**filling** NOUN fillings
❶ something used to fill a hole or gap, e.g. in a tooth ❷ something put in pastry to make a pie or between layers of bread to make a sandwich

**filling station** NOUN filling stations
a place where petrol is sold from pumps

**filly** NOUN fillies
a young female horse

**film** NOUN films
❶ a story or event recorded by a camera as a series of moving pictures and shown in cinemas, on television, etc. ❷ a rolled strip or sheet of thin plastic coated with material that is sensitive to light, used, especially in the past, for taking photographs or cinema images ❸ a very thin layer of something • *a film of grease*

**film** VERB films, filming, filmed
to record moving pictures using a camera; to make a film of a story • *She was put in charge of filming the school play.*

**filmy** ADJECTIVE filmier, filmiest
thin and almost transparent

**filter** NOUN filters
a device for holding back dirt or other unwanted material from a liquid or gas that passes through it

**filter** VERB filters, filtering, filtered
❶ to pass something through a filter ❷ to move gradually • *They filtered into the hall. • News began to filter out.*

**filth** NOUN
disgusting dirt

**filthy** ADJECTIVE filthier, filthiest
❶ extremely dirty ❷ obscene or offensive

**fin** NOUN fins
❶ a thin flat part sticking out from a fish's body, that helps it to swim ❷ a flat part that sticks out from an aircraft or rocket and helps it to balance

**final** ADJECTIVE
❶ coming at the end; last ❷ that cannot be argued with or changed • *The judge's decision is final. • You must go and that's final!*

**final** NOUN finals
the last in a series of contests, that decides the overall winner

**finale** (say fin-ah-lee) NOUN finales
the final section of a piece of music or entertainment

**finalist** NOUN finalists
a person or team taking part in a final

**finality** NOUN
the quality of being final and impossible to change • *There was a note of finality in his voice.*

**finalize** (also **finalise**) VERB finalizes, finalizing, finalized
to put something into its final form

**finally** ADVERB
❶ after a long time; at last • *We finally got there around midnight.* ❷ as the last thing • *Finally, I would like to thank my parents.*

SPELLING
Finally = final + ly. Don't forget to double the l.

**finance** NOUN
❶ the use or management of money ❷ the money used to pay for something
➤ **finances** PLURAL NOUN
someone's finances are the money and other funds they have

**finance** VERB finances, financing, financed
to provide the money for something
➤ **financier** NOUN

**financial** ADJECTIVE
to do with finance
➤ **financially** ADVERB

**finch** NOUN finches
a small bird with a short stubby bill

**find** VERB finds, finding, found
❶ to get or see something by looking for it or by chance ❷ to learn something by experience • *He found that digging was hard work.* ❸ something is found in a particular place when it lives, grows or exists there • *This species is found only in Australia.* ❹ to decide and give a verdict • *The jury found him guilty.*
➤ **find something out** to get or discover some information

**find** NOUN finds
something interesting or valuable that has been found

**findings** PLURAL NOUN
the conclusions reached from an investigation

**fine** ADJECTIVE
❶ of high quality; excellent ❷ dry and clear; sunny • *fine weather* ❸ very thin or delicate • *The curtains were made of fine material.* ❹ consisting of small particles ❺ in good health; well • *I'm fine.*
➤ **fineness** NOUN

**fine** ADVERB
❶ finely • *a bunch of parsley, chopped fine* ❷ (informal) very well • *That will suit me fine.*

**fine** NOUN fines
money which has to be paid as a punishment

**fine** VERB fines, fining, fined
to make someone pay a fine

**fine arts** PLURAL NOUN
painting, sculpture and music

**finely** ADVERB
❶ into very small grains or pieces • *Slice the tomato finely.* ❷ carefully and delicately • *a finely embroidered shirt*

**finery** NOUN
fine clothes or decorations

**finesse** (say fin-**ess**) NOUN
skill and elegance in doing something

**finger** NOUN fingers
❶ one of the long thin parts sticking out from the hand ❷ something shaped like a finger • *chocolate fingers*

**finger** VERB fingers, fingering, fingered
to touch or feel something with your fingers
• *He fingered his watch chain nervously.*

**fingernail** NOUN fingernails
the hard covering at the end of a finger

**fingerprint** NOUN fingerprints
a mark made by the tiny ridges on your fingertip, used as a way of identifying someone

**fingertip** NOUN fingertips
the tip of a finger
➤ **have something at your fingertips** to be very familiar with a subject and ready to talk about it

**finicky** ADJECTIVE
fussy about details; hard to please

**finish** VERB finishes, finishing, finished
❶ to complete something or reach the end of it • *Have you finished your essay yet?* ❷ to come to an end • *What time does the film finish?*

**finish** NOUN finishes
❶ the last stage of something; the end ❷ the surface or coating on woodwork etc.

**finite** (say **fy**-nyt) ADJECTIVE
limited; not infinite • *We have only a finite supply of coal.*

**finite verb** NOUN finite verbs
a verb that agrees with its subject in person and number; 'was', 'went' and 'says' are finite verbs; 'going' and 'to say' are not

**fiord** (say fee-**ord**) NOUN fiords
a different spelling of fjord

**fir** NOUN firs
an evergreen tree with needle-like leaves, that produces cones

**fire** NOUN fires
❶ the flames, heat and light produced when something burns ❷ coal and wood etc. burning in a grate or furnace to give heat ❸ a device using electricity or gas to heat a room ❹ the shooting of guns • *Hold your fire!*
➤ **on fire** burning
➤ **set fire to something** to set something alight and start it burning

**fire** VERB fires, firing, fired
❶ to set fire to something ❷ to bake pottery or bricks in a kiln ❸ to shoot a gun; to send out a bullet or missile ❹ to tell someone that you will no longer employ them ❺ to produce a strong feeling in someone • *The talk had fired her with enthusiasm.*

**firearm** NOUN firearms
a gun that you can carry; a rifle, pistol or revolver

**firebrand** NOUN firebrands
a person who stirs up trouble

**fire brigade** NOUN fire brigades
(*British*) a team of people organized to fight fires

**fire drill** NOUN fire drills
a rehearsal of the procedure that needs to be followed in case of a fire

**fire engine** NOUN fire engines
a large vehicle that carries firefighters and equipment to put out large fires

**fire escape** NOUN fire escapes
a special staircase by which people may escape from a burning building

**fire extinguisher** NOUN fire extinguishers
a metal cylinder from which water or foam can be sprayed to put out a fire

**firefighter** NOUN firefighters
a member of a fire brigade

**firefly** NOUN fireflies
a kind of beetle that gives off a glowing light

**fireman** NOUN firemen
a man who is a member of a fire brigade

**fireplace** NOUN fireplaces
an opening in the wall of a room for holding a fire

**fireproof** ADJECTIVE
able to stand fire or great heat without burning • *a fireproof door*

**fireside** NOUN firesides
the part of the room near a fireplace

**firewood** NOUN
wood for use as fuel

**firework** NOUN fireworks
a device containing chemicals that burn or explode attractively or noisily

**firing squad** NOUN firing squads
a group of soldiers given the duty of shooting a condemned person

**firm** NOUN firms
a business organization

**firm** ADJECTIVE
❶ not giving way when pressed; hard or solid ❷ steady; not shaking or moving ❸ definite and not likely to change • *a firm belief*
➤ **firmness** NOUN

**firm** ADVERB
firmly • *They are standing firm on their decision.*

**firm** VERB firms, firming, firmed
to make something firm or definite • *We'll firm up the date later.*

**firmament** NOUN (*poetical use*)
the sky with its clouds and stars

**firmly** ADVERB
❶ in a strong or definite way • *'No, you can't come,' he said firmly.* ❷ in a fixed or steady way • *She kept her eyes firmly on the road ahead.*

**first** ADJECTIVE
coming before all others in time or order or importance

**first** ADVERB
before everything else • *We should have read the instructions first.*

**first** NOUN firsts
a person or thing that is first
➤ **at first** at the beginning; to start with

**first aid** NOUN
treatment given to an injured person before a doctor comes

**first-class** ADJECTIVE
❶ using the best class of a service • *first-class post* ❷ excellent

**first-hand** ADJECTIVE & ADVERB
obtained directly, rather than from other people or from books • *first-hand experience* • *She had experienced poverty first-hand.*

**firstly** ADVERB
as the first thing • *Firstly, let me introduce myself.*

**firth** NOUN firths
an estuary or inlet of the sea on the coast of Scotland

**fish** NOUN fish or fishes
an animal with gills and fins that always lives and breathes in water

**fish** VERB fishes, fishing, fished
❶ to try to catch fish ❷ to search for something; to try to get something • *He is only fishing for compliments.*
➤ **fish something out** to pull something out of a place after searching for it

**fisherman** NOUN fishermen
a person who catches fish either as a job or as a sport

**fishery** NOUN fisheries
❶ the part of the sea where fishing is carried on ❷ the business of fishing

**fishmonger** NOUN fishmongers
a shopkeeper who sells fish

**fishy** ADJECTIVE fishier, fishiest
❶ smelling or tasting of fish ❷ (informal) causing doubt or suspicion • Parts of his story sound fishy to me.

**fission** NOUN
❶ splitting something ❷ splitting the nucleus of an atom so as to release energy

**fissure** (say fish-er) NOUN fissures
a narrow opening made where something splits

**fist** NOUN fists
a tightly closed hand with the fingers bent into the palm

**fit** ADJECTIVE fitter, fittest
❶ suitable or good enough • a meal fit for a king ❷ healthy, in good physical condition • Dancing is a good way to keep fit. ❸ ready or likely • They worked till they were fit to collapse.
➤ see or think fit to decide or choose to do something

**fit** VERB fits, fitting, fitted
❶ to be the right size and shape for something ❷ to be suitable for something • Her speech fitted the occasion perfectly. ❸ to put something into place • We need to fit a new lock on the door. ❹ to alter something to make it the right size and shape ❺ to make someone suitable for something • His training fits him for the job.
➤ fitter NOUN

**fit** NOUN fits
❶ the way something fits • These trousers are a good fit. ❷ a sudden illness, especially one that makes you move violently or become unconscious ❸ a sudden outburst • a fit of rage

**fitful** ADJECTIVE
happening in short periods, not steadily • a fitful sleep
➤ fitfully ADVERB

**fitness** NOUN
❶ being healthy and in good physical condition • Fitness is important in most sports. ❷ being suitable for something • No one doubts her fitness for the job.

**fitting** ADJECTIVE
proper or appropriate • This statue is a fitting memorial to an extraordinary woman.

**fitting** NOUN fittings
having a piece of clothing fitted • I needed several fittings.

**fittings** PLURAL NOUN
pieces of furniture or equipment in a room or building

**five** NOUN & ADJECTIVE fives
the number 5

**fiver** NOUN fivers (informal)
a five-pound note; £5

**fix** VERB fixes, fixing, fixed
❶ to fasten or place something firmly ❷ to make something permanent and unable to change ❸ to decide or arrange something • We fixed a date for the party. ❹ to repair something that is broken • I need to get my bike fixed.
➤ fix something up to arrange or organize something

**fix** NOUN fixes
❶ (informal) an awkward situation • I'm in a fix. ❷ finding the position of something, by using a compass, radar, etc.

**fixation** NOUN fixations
a strong interest or a concentration on one idea; an obsession
➤ fixated ADJECTIVE

**fixative** NOUN fixatives
a substance used to keep something in position or make it permanent

**fixed** ADJECTIVE
not changing • fixed prices • a fixed expression

**fixedly** ADVERB
with a fixed expression • She looked at me fixedly but said nothing.

**fixture** NOUN fixtures
❶ something fixed in its place, such as a cupboard or washbasin ❷ a sports event planned for a particular day

**fizz** VERB fizzes, fizzing, fizzed
to make a hissing or spluttering sound; to produce a lot of small bubbles

**fizzle** VERB fizzles, fizzling, fizzled
to make a slight fizzing sound
➤ fizzle out to come to a disappointing end • The game fizzled out in the second half.

a
b
c
d
e
f
g
h
i
j
k
l
m
n
o
p
q
r
s
t
u
v
w
x
y
z

**fizzy** ADJECTIVE
a fizzy drink has a lot of small bubbles

**fjord** (say fee-**ord**) NOUN fjords
an inlet of the sea between high cliffs, as in
Norway

**flabbergasted** ADJECTIVE
greatly astonished

**flabby** ADJECTIVE
fat and soft, not firm
➤ **flabbiness** NOUN

**flag** NOUN flags
❶ a piece of cloth with a coloured pattern or
shape on it, used as the symbol of a country
or organization or as a signal ❷ a small piece
of paper or plastic that looks like a flag ❸ a
flagstone

**flag** VERB flags, flagging, flagged
to become weak or droop because of
tiredness
➤ **flag someone down** to signal a driver to
stop by waving

**flagon** NOUN flagons
a large bottle or container for drink,
especially wine

**flagpole, flagstaff** NOUN flagpoles,
flagstaffs
a pole used for flying a flag

**flagrant** (say **flay**-grant) ADJECTIVE
very bad and noticeable • flagrant
disobedience
➤ **flagrantly** ADVERB
➤ **flagrancy** NOUN
WORD ORIGIN from Latin flagrans = blazing

**flagship** NOUN flagships
❶ a main ship in a navy's fleet, which has the
fleet's admiral on board ❷ a company's best
or most important product or store

**flagstone** NOUN flagstones
a flat slab of stone used for paving

**flail** NOUN flails
an old-fashioned tool for threshing grain

**flail** VERB flails, flailing, flailed
to flail your arms or legs is to wave them
about wildly

**flair** NOUN
a natural ability or talent • Ian has a flair for
languages.
SPELLING
Take care not to confuse flair with flare,
which means a bright flame.

**flak** NOUN
❶ shells fired by anti-aircraft guns ❷ strong
criticism WORD ORIGIN short for German
Fliegerabwehrkanone = aircraft defence
cannon

**flake** NOUN flakes
❶ a very light thin piece of something ❷ a
small flat piece of falling snow
➤ **flaky** ADJECTIVE

**flake** VERB flakes, flaking, flaked
to come off in flakes • The paint is beginning
to flake.

**flamboyant** ADJECTIVE
very showy in appearance or manner • a
flamboyant costume WORD ORIGIN from
French, meaning 'flaming, blazing'

**flame** NOUN flames
a tongue-shaped portion of fire or burning
gas

**flame** VERB flames, flaming, flamed
❶ to produce flames ❷ to become bright red
• Her cheeks flamed with rage.

**flamenco** (say fla-**menk**-oh) NOUN flamencos
a lively Spanish style of guitar playing and
dance WORD ORIGIN from Spanish, = Flemish,
'like a gypsy'

**flaming** ADJECTIVE
❶ burning brightly • flaming torches
❷ bright red or orange • a flaming sunset

**flamingo** NOUN flamingoes
a wading bird with long legs, a long neck and
pinkish feathers

**flammable** ADJECTIVE
able to be set on fire
USAGE
See the note at **inflammable**.

**flan** NOUN flans
a pastry or sponge shell with no cover over
the filling

**flank** NOUN flanks
the side of something, especially an animal's
body or an army

**flank** VERB flanks, flanking, flanked
to be positioned at the side of something • He
stepped off the boat, flanked by two guards.

**flannel** NOUN flannels
❶ a soft cloth for washing your face ❷ a soft
woollen material

**flap** VERB flaps, flapping, flapped
❶ to move loosely back and forth in the wind
or air • The sails were flapping in the breeze.

❷ to make something move back and forth in the air • *The parrot flapped her wings and flew to her perch.* ❸ (*informal*) to panic or fuss about something

**flap** *NOUN* flaps
❶ a part that is fixed at one edge onto something else, often to cover an opening ❷ the action or sound of flapping ❸ (*informal*) a panic or fuss • *Don't get in a flap.*

**flapjack** *NOUN*
a cake made from oats and golden syrup

**flare** *VERB* flares, flaring, flared
❶ to blaze with a sudden bright flame ❷ to become angry suddenly ❸ to become gradually wider • *The bull flared its nostrils.*
➤ **flare up** to start suddenly or to suddenly get worse • *Her asthma flared up over the weekend.*

**flare** *NOUN* flares
❶ a sudden bright flame or light, especially one fired into the sky as a signal ❷ a gradual widening, especially in skirts or trousers

SPELLING

Take care not to confuse **flare** with **flair**, which means a talent for something.

**flash** *NOUN* flashes
❶ a sudden bright flame or light ❷ a device for making a sudden bright light for taking photographs ❸ a sudden display of anger, wit, etc. ❹ a short item of news
➤ **in a flash** immediately or very quickly • *The idea came to him in a flash.*

**flash** *VERB* flashes, flashing, flashed
❶ to make a flash of light ❷ to appear or move suddenly and quickly • *The train flashed past us.*

**flashback** *NOUN* flashbacks
going back in a film or story to something that happened earlier • *The hero's childhood was shown in flashbacks.*

**flashy** *ADJECTIVE*
showy and expensive • *a flashy car*

**flask** *NOUN* flasks
❶ a bottle with a narrow neck ❷ a vacuum flask

**flat** *ADJECTIVE* flatter, flattest
❶ with no curves or bumps; smooth and level ❷ spread out; lying at full length • *Lie flat on the ground.* ❸ a flat tyre has no air inside ❹ flat feet do not have the normal arch underneath ❺ firm and absolute • *a flat refusal* ❻ dull; showing no interest or

emotion • *She spoke in a flat voice.* ❼ a drink that is flat is no longer fizzy ❽ (*British*) a flat battery is unable to produce any more electric current ❾ (*in music*) one semitone lower than the natural note • *E flat*
➤ **flatness** *NOUN*

**flat** *ADVERB*
❶ so as to be flat • *Press it flat.* ❷ (*informal*) exactly and no more • *He won the race in ten seconds flat.* ❸ (*in music*) below the correct pitch
➤ **flat out** as fast as possible

**flat** *NOUN* flats
❶ (*chiefly British*) a set of rooms for living in, usually on one floor of a building ❷ (*in music*) a note one semitone lower than the natural note; the sign (♭) that indicates this ❸ a punctured tyre

**flatly** *ADVERB*
❶ in a definite way, leaving no room for doubt • *They flatly refused to go.* ❷ in a way that shows no interest or emotion

**flatten** *VERB* flattens, flattening, flattened
❶ to make something flat ❷ to become flat

**flatter** *VERB* flatters, flattering, flattered
❶ to praise someone more than they deserve ❷ to make a person or thing seem better or more attractive than they really are • *The portrait flatters him, don't you think?*
➤ **flatterer** *NOUN*

**flattery** *NOUN*
flattering someone • *I don't think flattery will work on her.*

**flaunt** *VERB* flaunts, flaunting, flaunted
to display something proudly in a way that annoys people; to show something off • *He liked to flaunt his expensive clothes and cars.*

**flavour** *NOUN* flavours
the taste of something

**flavour** *VERB* flavours, flavouring, flavoured
to give something a flavour; to season food
➤ **flavouring** *NOUN*

**flaw** *NOUN* flaws
something that makes a person or thing imperfect
➤ **flawed** *ADJECTIVE*

**flawless** *ADJECTIVE*
without a flaw; perfect
➤ **flawlessly** *ADVERB*

**flax** *NOUN*
a plant that produces fibres from which linen is made and seeds from which linseed oil is obtained

**flaxen** ADJECTIVE
pale yellow like flax fibres • *flaxen hair*

**flay** VERB flays, flaying, flayed
❶ to strip the skin from an animal ❷ to whip or beat someone

**flea** NOUN fleas
a small jumping insect that sucks blood

**flea market** NOUN flea markets
a street market that sells cheap or second-hand goods

**fleck** NOUN flecks
❶ a very small patch of colour • *His hair was dark, with flecks of grey.* ❷ a very small piece of something • *flecks of dirt*

**flecked** ADJECTIVE
with small spots of colour • *green eyes flecked with brown*

**fledged** ADJECTIVE
young birds are fledged when they have grown feathers and are able to fly

**fledgeling** NOUN fledgelings
a young bird that is just fledged

**flee** VERB flees, fleeing, fled
to run or hurry away from something • *As the fire approached, people fled their homes.*

**fleece** NOUN fleeces
❶ the woolly hair of a sheep or similar animal ❷ a warm piece of clothing made from a soft fabric

**fleece** VERB fleeces, fleecing, fleeced
❶ to shear the fleece from a sheep ❷ to swindle a person out of some money

**fleecy** ADJECTIVE
made of soft material like fleece; soft and light • *fleecy clouds*

**fleet** NOUN fleets
a number of ships, aircraft or vehicles owned by one country or company

**fleet** ADJECTIVE
able to run or move swiftly

**fleeting** ADJECTIVE
passing quickly; brief • *I caught a fleeting glimpse of him.*

**Flemish** ADJECTIVE
to do with Flanders in Belgium or its people or language
➤ **Flemish** NOUN

**flesh** NOUN
❶ the soft substance of the bodies of people and animals, consisting of muscle and fat ❷ the body as opposed to the mind or soul ❸ the pulpy part of fruits and vegetables
➤ **fleshy** ADJECTIVE

**flex** VERB flexes, flexing, flexed
to bend or stretch a limb or muscle

**flex** NOUN flexes (British) flexible insulated wire for carrying electric current

**flexible** ADJECTIVE
❶ easy to bend or stretch without breaking ❷ able to be changed or adapted • *Our plans are flexible.*
➤ **flexibility** NOUN

**flick** NOUN flicks
a quick light hit or movement

**flick** VERB flicks, flicking, flicked
❶ to hit or move something with a flick ❷ to flick through a book or magazine etc. is to turn its pages quickly, without reading carefully

**flicker** VERB flickers, flickering, flickered
❶ to burn or shine unsteadily ❷ to move quickly to and fro

**flicker** NOUN flickers
a flickering light or movement

**flick knife** NOUN flick knives
(British) a knife with a blade that springs out when a button is pressed

**flier** NOUN fliers
a different spelling of flyer

**flight** NOUN flights
❶ flying • *The picture shows an owl in flight.* ❷ a journey in an aircraft ❸ a series of stairs ❹ a group of flying birds or aircraft ❺ the feathers or fins on a dart or arrow ❻ fleeing; an escape

**flight recorder** NOUN flight recorders
an electronic device in an aircraft that records technical information about its flight. It may be used after an accident to help find the cause.

**flighty** ADJECTIVE flightier, flightiest
silly and frivolous

**flimsy** ADJECTIVE flimsier, flimsiest
❶ made of something thin or weak; fragile • *a flimsy bookcase* ❷ not convincing • *a flimsy excuse*

**flinch** VERB flinches, flinching, flinched
to make a sudden movement backwards because you are afraid or in pain

**fling** *VERB* flings, flinging, flung
to throw something violently or carelessly • *He flung his shoes under the bed.*

**fling** *NOUN* flings
❶ a short time of enjoyment • *a final fling before the exams* ❷ a brief romantic affair ❸ a vigorous dance • *the Highland fling*

**flint** *NOUN* flints
❶ a very hard kind of stone ❷ a piece of flint or hard metal used to produce sparks
➤ **flinty** *ADJECTIVE*

**flip** *VERB* flips, flipping, flipped
❶ to turn something over with a quick movement • *She flipped open her sketchbook.* ❷ (*informal*) to become crazy or very angry

**flip** *NOUN* flips
a flipping movement

**flippant** *ADJECTIVE*
not being serious when you should be • *a flippant comment*
➤ **flippantly** *ADVERB*
➤ **flippancy** *NOUN*

**flipper** *NOUN* flippers
❶ a limb that water animals use for swimming ❷ a kind of flat rubber shoe, shaped like a duck's foot, that you wear on your feet to help you to swim

**flirt** *VERB* flirts, flirting, flirted
❶ to behave as though you are attracted to someone, in a playful rather than a serious way ❷ to take an interest in an idea without being too serious about it
➤ **flirt with danger or death** to risk danger
➤ **flirtation** *NOUN*

**flirt** *NOUN* flirts
a person who flirts
➤ **flirtatious** *ADJECTIVE*
➤ **flirtatiously** *ADVERB*

**flit** *VERB* flits, flitting, flitted
to fly or move lightly and quickly • *A moth flitted across the room.*

**flitter** *VERB* flitters, flittering, flittered
to flit about

**float** *VERB* floats, floating, floated
❶ to stay or move on the surface of a liquid or in air ❷ to make something move on the surface of a liquid ❸ to launch a business by getting financial support from the sale of shares

**float** *NOUN* floats
❶ a device designed to float ❷ a vehicle with a platform used for delivering milk or for carrying a display in a parade or carnival ❸ a

small amount of money kept for paying small bills or giving change

**floating voter** *NOUN* floating voters
(*British*) a person who has not yet decided who to vote for in an election

**flock** *NOUN* flocks
❶ a number of birds flying or resting together ❷ a number of sheep or goats kept together ❸ a tuft of wool or cotton

**flock** *VERB* flocks, flocking, flocked
to gather or move in a crowd or in large numbers • *People flocked to hear him sing.*

**floe** *NOUN* floes
a sheet of floating ice

**flog** *VERB* flogs, flogging, flogged
❶ to beat a person or animal hard with a whip or stick as a punishment ❷ (*British*) (*informal*) to sell something
➤ **flogging** *NOUN*

**flood** *NOUN* floods
❶ a large amount of water spreading over a place that is usually dry ❷ a large number of things • *a flood of requests* ❸ the movement of the tide when it is coming in towards the land

**flood** *VERB* floods, flooding, flooded
❶ to cover an area with a flood ❷ a river floods when its waters flow over the banks ❸ to come in large quantities • *Letters flooded in.*

**floodlight** *NOUN* floodlights
a lamp that makes a broad bright beam to light up a stadium or a public building
➤ **floodlit** *ADJECTIVE*

**floor** *NOUN* floors
❶ the part of a room that people walk on ❷ a storey of a building; all the rooms at the same level

**USAGE**

In Britain, the *ground floor* of a building is the one at street level, and the one above it is the *first floor*. In the USA, the *first floor* is the one at street level, and the one above it is the *second floor*.

**floor** *VERB* floors, flooring, floored
❶ to knock a person down ❷ to baffle someone

**floorboard** *NOUN* floorboards
one of the boards forming the floor of a room

**flop** *VERB* flops, flopping, flopped
❶ to fall or sit down clumsily ❷ to hang or

sway heavily and loosely • *Her hair flopped over her eyes.* ❸ (*informal*) to be a failure

**flop** NOUN flops
❶ a flopping movement or sound ❷ (*informal*) a failure or disappointment

**floppy** ADJECTIVE
hanging loosely; not firm or rigid • *Our dog has huge floppy ears.*

**flora** NOUN
the plants of a particular area or period. Compare with **fauna**. (WORD ORIGIN) from the name of *Flora*, the ancient Roman goddess of flowers; her name comes from Latin *flores* = flowers

**floral** ADJECTIVE
decorated with a pattern of flowers or made of flowers • *a floral dress*

**florid** (say flo-rid) ADJECTIVE
❶ red and flushed • *a florid complexion* ❷ elaborate and ornate • *florid language*

**florin** NOUN florins
a former British coin worth two shillings (10p) (WORD ORIGIN) from Italian *fiore* = flower; the name was originally given to an Italian coin which had a lily on one side

**florist** NOUN florists
a person who sells flowers

**floss** NOUN
❶ silky thread or fibres ❷ a soft medicated thread pulled between the teeth to clean them
➤ **flossy** ADJECTIVE

**flotation** NOUN flotations
floating something

**flotilla** (say flot-il-a) NOUN flotillas
a fleet of boats or small ships

**flotsam** NOUN
wreckage or cargo found floating after a shipwreck
➤ **flotsam and jetsam** odds and ends

**flounce** VERB flounces, flouncing, flounced
to go in an impatient or annoyed manner • *She flounced out of the room.*

**flounce** NOUN flounces
❶ a flouncing movement ❷ a wide frill on a skirt or dress

**flounder** VERB flounders, floundering, floundered
❶ to move clumsily and with difficulty • *He was floundering around in the water.* ❷ to

make mistakes or become confused when trying to do something

**flounder** NOUN flounder
a small flat edible sea fish

**flour** NOUN
a fine powder of wheat or other grain, used in cooking
➤ **floury** ADJECTIVE

**flourish** VERB flourishes, flourishing, flourished
❶ to grow or develop strongly • *These plants flourish in a damp climate.* ❷ to be successful; to prosper • *Over the next few years the town flourished.* ❸ to wave something about dramatically • *She proudly flourished two tickets for the concert.*

**flourish** NOUN flourishes
a showy or dramatic sweeping movement, curve or passage of music • *He took out his pen with a flourish.*

**flout** VERB flouts, flouting, flouted
to disobey a rule or instruction openly and scornfully • *She shaved her head one day, just because she loved to flout convention.*

**flow** VERB flows, flowing, flowed
❶ to move along smoothly or continuously ❷ to gush out • *Water flowed from the tap.* ❸ to hang loosely • *flowing hair* ❹ the tide flows when it comes in towards the land

**flow** NOUN flows
❶ a flowing movement or mass ❷ a steady continuous stream of something • *a flow of ideas* ❸ the movement of the tide when it is coming in towards the land • *the ebb and flow of the tide*

**flow chart** NOUN flow charts
a diagram that shows how the different stages of a process or parts of a system are connected

**flower** NOUN flowers
❶ the part of a plant from which seed and fruit develops ❷ a blossom and its stem used for decoration, usually in groups

**flower** VERB flowers, flowering, flowered
to produce flowers

**flowerpot** NOUN flowerpots
a pot in which a plant may be grown

**flowery** ADJECTIVE
❶ full of flowers ❷ flowery language is elaborate and fully of fancy phrases • *a flowery style of writing*

**flu** NOUN
influenza

**fluctuate** VERB fluctuates, fluctuating, fluctuated
to keep changing, especially by rising and falling • *Prices fluctuated.*
➤ **fluctuation** NOUN

**flue** NOUN flues
a pipe or tube that takes smoke and fumes away from a stove or boiler

**fluent** (say floo-ent) ADJECTIVE
❶ skilful at speaking clearly and without hesitating ❷ able to speak a foreign language easily and well
➤ **fluently** ADVERB
➤ **fluency** NOUN

**fluff** NOUN
the small soft pieces that come off wool and cloth

**fluff** VERB fluffs, fluffing, fluffed (*informal*) to make a mistake
➤ **fluff something up** to make a pillow or cushion softer and rounder by patting it

**fluffy** ADJECTIVE
having a mass of soft fur or fibres

**fluid** NOUN fluids
a substance that is able to flow freely as liquids and gases do

**fluid** ADJECTIVE
❶ able to flow freely and smoothly • *He drew his sword in a single fluid movement.* ❷ not fixed and able to be changed • *My plans for Christmas are fluid.*
➤ **fluidity** NOUN

**fluke** NOUN flukes
a success that you achieve by unexpected good luck

**flummox** VERB flummoxes, flummoxing, flummoxed (*informal*)
to baffle someone

**fluorescent** (say floo-er-**ess**-ent) ADJECTIVE
❶ creating light from radiation • *a fluorescent lamp* ❷ very bright and shining in the dark • *a fluorescent yellow armband*
➤ **fluorescence** NOUN

**fluoridation** NOUN
adding fluoride to drinking water in order to help prevent tooth decay

**fluoride** NOUN
a chemical substance that is thought to prevent tooth decay

**flurry** NOUN flurries
❶ a sudden whirling gust of wind, rain or snow ❷ a short period of activity or excitement

**flush** VERB flushes, flushing, flushed
❶ to become red in the face; to blush ❷ to clean or remove something with a fast flow of water

**flush** NOUN flushes
❶ a slight blush ❷ a fast flow of water ❸ a hand of playing cards of the same suit

**flush** ADJECTIVE
❶ level with the surrounding surface • *The doors are flush with the walls.* ❷ (*informal*) having plenty of money

**fluster** NOUN
➤ **in a fluster** nervous and confused

**flustered** ADJECTIVE
nervous and confused • *She was looking hot and flustered.*

**flute** NOUN flutes
a musical instrument consisting of a long pipe with holes that are stopped by fingers or keys, which you play by blowing across a hole at one end

**flutter** VERB flutters, fluttering, fluttered
❶ to flap wings quickly • *A butterfly fluttered in through the window.* ❷ to move or flap quickly and lightly • *Flags fluttered in the breeze.*

**flutter** NOUN flutters
a fluttering movement
➤ **in a flutter** nervous and excited

**flux** NOUN fluxes
continual change or flow

**fly** VERB flies, flying, flew, flown
❶ to move through the air by means of wings or in an aircraft ❷ to move quickly or suddenly, especially through the air • *A large stone came flying through the window.* • *The door flew open.* ❸ to wave in the air • *Flags were flying.* ❹ to make something fly • *They were flying model aircraft.* ❺ a period of time flies when it passes quickly • *The weekend has just flown by.*

**fly** NOUN flies
❶ a small flying insect with two wings ❷ a real or artificial fly used as bait in fishing ❸ the front opening of a pair of trousers

**flyer** NOUN flyers
❶ a person or vehicle that flies ❷ a small poster advertising an event

**flying saucer** NOUN flying saucers
a mysterious saucer-shaped object that some people say they have seen in the sky and believe to be an alien spacecraft

**flying squad** NOUN flying squads
(*British*) a team of police officers organized so that they can move rapidly

**flyleaf** NOUN flyleaves
a blank page at the beginning or end of a book

**flyover** NOUN flyovers
a bridge that carries one road over another

**flywheel** NOUN flywheels
a heavy wheel in a machine that helps it to run smoothly and at a steady speed

**foal** NOUN foals
a young horse

**foal** VERB foals, foaling, foaled
to give birth to a foal

**foam** NOUN
❶ a white mass of tiny bubbles on a liquid; froth ❷ a spongy kind of rubber or plastic
➤ **foamy** ADJECTIVE

**foam** VERB foams, foaming, foamed
to form a white mass of tiny bubbles; to froth • *Water foamed around the rocks.*

**fob** NOUN fobs
❶ a chain for a pocket watch ❷ a tab on a key ring

**fob** VERB fobs, fobbing, fobbed
➤ **fob someone off** to get rid of someone by an excuse or a trick

**focal** ADJECTIVE
to do with or at a focus

**focal point** NOUN focal points
❶ the point on a lens at which rays seem to meet ❷ something that is a centre of interest or attention

**focus** NOUN focuses or foci
❶ the distance from an eye or lens at which an object appears clearest ❷ the point at which rays seem to meet ❸ something that is a centre of interest or attention
➤ **in focus** appearing clearly
➤ **out of focus** not appearing clearly; blurred

**focus** VERB focuses, focusing, focused
❶ to adjust the focus of your eye or a lens so that objects appear clearer ❷ to concentrate on something • *She focused her attention on the problem.* WORD ORIGIN Latin, = hearth (the central point of a household)

**fodder** NOUN
food for horses and farm animals

**foe** NOUN foes (*old use*)
an enemy

**foetus** (say **fee**-tus) NOUN foetuses
a developing embryo, especially an unborn human baby
➤ **foetal** ADJECTIVE

**fog** NOUN
thick mist

**fogey** NOUN fogeys
➤ **old fogey** a person with old-fashioned ideas

**foggy** ADJECTIVE
full of fog • *It was a foggy night.*

**foghorn** NOUN foghorns
a loud horn for warning ships in fog

**foible** (say **foy**-bel) NOUN foibles
a slight peculiarity in someone's character or tastes

**foil** NOUN foils
❶ a very thin sheet of metal ❷ a person or thing that makes another look better in contrast ❸ a long narrow sword used in the sport of fencing

**foil** VERB foils, foiling, foiled
to prevent something from being successful • *We foiled his evil plan.*

**foist** VERB foists, foisting, foisted
to force a person to accept something that they do not want • *They foisted the job on me at the last minute.*

**fold** VERB folds, folding, folded
❶ to bend or wrap one part of something over another part • *He folder the letter and put it in the envelope.* ❷ to bend or move in this way • *The table folds up flat.* ❸ you fold your arms when you put one of your arms over the other one and hold them against your chest

**fold** NOUN folds
❶ a line where something is folded ❷ an enclosure for sheep

**folder** NOUN folders
❶ a folding cover for loose papers ❷ a place where a set of files are grouped together in a computer

**foliage** NOUN
the leaves of a tree or plant

**folk** PLURAL NOUN
people

272

**folk dance** NOUN folk dances
a dance in the traditional style of a country

**folklore** NOUN
old beliefs and legends

**folk music** NOUN
the traditional music of a country

**folk song** NOUN folk songs
a song in the traditional style of a country

**follow** VERB follows, following, followed
❶ to go or come after someone or something
❷ to do a thing after something else ❸ to act according to someone's instructions, advice or example • *I followed the instructions carefully.* ❹ to go along a road or path • *Follow this road for a mile.* ❺ to take an interest in the progress of events or a sport or team ❻ to understand someone or something • *Did you follow what he said?* ❼ to result from something ❽ to receive the messages that a particular person sends on social networking websites such as Twitter

**follower** NOUN followers
a person who follows or supports someone or something

**following** PREPOSITION
after, as a result of • *Following the burglary, we had new locks fitted.*

**folly** NOUN follies
foolishness; a foolish action • *It would be folly to ignore their warnings*

**foment** (say fo-**ment**) VERB foments, fomenting, fomented
to stir up trouble or difficulty deliberately

**fond** ADJECTIVE
❶ loving or liking a person or thing • *She's fond of reading.* ❷ pleasant and affectionate • *I have fond memories of my grandmother.*
➤ **fondly** ADVERB
➤ **fondness** NOUN

**fondle** VERB fondles, fondling, fondled
to touch or stroke someone or something lovingly

**font** NOUN fonts
❶ a basin (often of carved stone) in a Christian church, to hold water for baptism
❷ a set of characters used in printing and computer documents

**food** NOUN foods
any substance that a plant or animal can take into its body to help it to grow and be healthy

**food chain** NOUN food chains
a series of plants and animals each of which serves as food for the one above it in the series

**foodstuff** NOUN foodstuffs
something that can be used as food

**food technology** NOUN
the study of foods, what they are made of and how they are prepared

**fool** NOUN fools
❶ a stupid person; someone who acts unwisely ❷ a jester or clown ❸ (*British*) a creamy pudding with crushed fruit in it
• *gooseberry fool*
➤ **fool's errand** a useless errand
➤ **fool's paradise** happiness that comes only from being mistaken about something

**fool** VERB fools, fooling, fooled
to trick or deceive someone
➤ **fool about** or **around** to behave in a silly or stupid way

**foolhardy** ADJECTIVE
bold but foolish; reckless
➤ **foolhardiness** NOUN

**foolish** ADJECTIVE
without good sense or judgement; unwise
➤ **foolishly** ADVERB
➤ **foolishness** NOUN

**foolproof** ADJECTIVE
easy to use or do without anything going wrong • *My plan is foolproof.*

**foot** NOUN feet
❶ the lower part of your leg below the ankle
❷ any similar part, e.g. one used by certain animals to move or attach themselves to things ❸ the lowest part or end of something
• *the foot of the hill* ❹ a measure of length, 12 inches (30.48 centimetres) • *a ten-foot pole* • *It is ten feet long.* ❺ a unit of rhythm in a line of poetry, e.g. each of the four divisions in *Jack / and Jill / went up / the hill*
➤ **on foot** walking • *We came back on foot.*

**footage** NOUN
an amount of film showing something
• *footage of the first moon landing*

**foot-and-mouth disease** NOUN
a serious contagious disease that affects cattle, sheep and other animals

**football** NOUN footballs
❶ a game played by two teams of eleven players who try to kick a ball into their opponents' goal ❷ the round ball used in this game

a
b
c
d
e
f
g
h
i
j
k
l
m
n
o
p
q
r
s
t
u
v
w
x
y
z

**footballer** NOUN footballers
a person who plays football

**foothill** NOUN foothills
a low hill near the bottom of a mountain or range of mountains

**foothold** NOUN footholds
❶ a place to put your foot when climbing ❷ a small but firm position from which further progress can be made

**footing** NOUN
❶ having your feet firmly placed on something • *He lost his footing and slipped.* ❷ the status or nature of a relationship • *We must try to get on a more friendly footing with our neighbours.*

**footlights** PLURAL NOUN
a row of lights along the front of the floor of a stage

**footman** NOUN footmen
a male servant who opens doors, serves at table, etc.

**footnote** NOUN footnotes
a note printed at the bottom of the page

**footpath** NOUN footpaths
a path for people to walk along, especially one in the countryside

**footprint** NOUN footprints
a mark made by a foot or shoe

**footsore** ADJECTIVE
having feet that are painful or sore from walking

**footstep** NOUN footsteps
❶ a step taken in walking or running ❷ the sound of a step being taken

**footstool** NOUN footstools
a stool for resting your feet on when you are sitting

**footwear** NOUN
shoes, boots and other coverings for the feet

**for** PREPOSITION
This word is used to show
❶ purpose or direction (*This letter is for you; We set out for home.*) ❷ distance or time (*They walked for three miles; We've been waiting for hours.*) ❸ price or exchange (*We bought it for £5; New lamps for old.*) ❹ cause or reason (*She was fined for speeding.*) ❺ defence or support (*He fought for his country; Are you for us or against us?*) ❻ what something refers to or relates to (*She has a good ear for music; What's*

*the Russian for 'goodbye'?*) ❼ similarity or correspondence (*We took him for a fool.*)
➤ **for ever** for all time; always

**for** CONJUNCTION
because • *They hesitated, for they were afraid.*

**forage** VERB forages, foraging, foraged
to go searching for something, especially food or fuel

**foray** NOUN forays
a sudden attack or raid

**forbear** VERB forbears, forbearing, forbore, forborne
❶ to avoid or refrain from doing something something • *We forbore to mention it.* ❷ to be patient or tolerant
➤ **forbearance** NOUN

**forbid** VERB forbids, forbidding, forbade, forbidden
❶ to order someone not to do something ❷ to refuse to allow something • *Smoking is forbidden in this station.*

**forbidding** ADJECTIVE
looking stern or unfriendly

**force** NOUN forces
❶ strength or power ❷ (*in science*) an influence, which can be measured, that causes something to move ❸ an organized group of police, soldiers or workers
➤ **in** or **into force** being used; having effect
• *The new law comes into force next week.*
➤ **the forces** a country's armed forces

**force** VERB forces, forcing, forced
❶ to get someone to do something by using force or power ❷ to break something open by force

**forceful** ADJECTIVE
strong and vigorous
➤ **forcefully** ADVERB

**forceps** NOUN forceps
pincers or tongs used by dentists or surgeons

**forcible** ADJECTIVE
done by force; forceful
➤ **forcibly** ADVERB

**ford** NOUN fords
a shallow place where you can walk across a river

**ford** VERB fords, fording, forded
to cross a river at a ford

**fore** ADJECTIVE & ADVERB
at or towards the front

**fore** NOUN
the front part
➤ **to the fore** to or at the front; in a leading
position • *This latest incident has brought the
issue to the fore.*

**forearm** NOUN **forearms**
the arm from the elbow to the wrist or
fingertips

**forearm** VERB **forearms, forearming,
forearmed**
to be forearmed is to be prepared in advance
against possible danger

**forebears** PLURAL NOUN
your forebears are your ancestors

**foreboding** NOUN
a feeling that trouble is coming • *He was
filled with a sense of foreboding.*

**forecast** NOUN **forecasts**
a statement that tells in advance what is likely
to happen • *a weather forecast*

**forecast** VERB **forecasts, forecasting, forecast**
to say in advance what is likely to happen
• *The weather report forecasts snow for
tomorrow.*
➤ **forecaster** NOUN

**forecastle** (say **foh-ksul**) NOUN **forecastles**
the forward part of certain ships

**forecourt** NOUN **forecourts**
an open area in front of a large building or
petrol station

**forefathers** PLURAL NOUN
your forefathers are your ancestors (both
male and female)

**forefinger** NOUN **forefingers**
the finger next to your thumb

**forefoot** NOUN **forefeet**
an animal's front foot

**forefront** NOUN
the leading position; the position at the front
• *They were at the forefront of the Green
movement.*

**foregoing** ADJECTIVE
preceding; previously mentioned • *the
foregoing discussion*

SPELLING

Note the spelling of this word. It has an
'e' in it, whereas **forgo**, meaning 'give up',
does not.

**foregone conclusion** NOUN **foregone
conclusions**
a result that is certain to happen

**foreground** NOUN
the part of a scene, picture or view that is
nearest to you

**forehand** NOUN **forehands**
a stroke made in tennis etc. with the palm of
the hand turned forwards

**forehead** (say **forrid** or **for-hed**) NOUN
**foreheads**
the part of your face above your eyes

**foreign** ADJECTIVE
❶ belonging to or in another country
❷ not belonging naturally to a place or to
someone's nature • *Lying is foreign to her
nature.*

**foreigner** NOUN **foreigners**
a person from another country

**foreleg** NOUN **forelegs**
an animal's front leg

**foreman** NOUN **foremen**
❶ a worker in charge of a group of other
workers ❷ a member of a jury who is in
charge of the jury's discussions and who
speaks on its behalf

**foremost** ADJECTIVE & ADVERB
first in position or rank; most important
• *Athens became the foremost naval power in
the Greek world.* • *First and foremost, thank
you for coming.*

**forensic** (say **fer-en-sik**) ADJECTIVE
❶ to do with or used in law courts ❷ using
scientific tests to find out about a crime

**forensic medicine** NOUN
medical knowledge needed in legal matters or
in solving crimes

**forerunner** NOUN **forerunners**
a person or thing that comes before another;
a sign of what is to come

**foresee** VERB **foresees, foreseeing, foresaw,
foreseen**
to realize that something is likely to happen
• *She could foresee many difficulties ahead.*

**foreseeable** ADJECTIVE
a foreseeable event is one that you should
realize is likely to happen
➤ **for the foreseeable future** for as long as
can be seen or planned at the moment

a b c d e f g h i j k l m n o p q r s t u v w x y z

A
B
C
D
E
**F**
G
H
I
J
K
L
M
N
O
P
Q
R
S
T
U
V
W
X
Y
Z

**foreshadow** VERB foreshadows, foreshadowing, foreshadowed
to be a sign of something that is to come

**foreshorten** VERB foreshortens, foreshortening, foreshortened
to draw or paint an object with some lines shortened to give an effect of distance or depth

**foresight** NOUN
the ability to realize what is likely to happen in the future and be prepared for it

**foreskin** NOUN foreskins
the fold of skin covering the end of a penis

**forest** NOUN forests
trees and undergrowth covering a large area
➤ **forested** ADJECTIVE

**forestall** VERB forestalls, forestalling, forestalled
to prevent something from happening or someone from doing something by taking action first

**forestry** NOUN
planting forests and looking after them
➤ **forester** NOUN

**foretaste** NOUN foretastes
an experience of something that is to come in the future

**foretell** VERB foretells, foretelling, foretold
to know or say what will happen in the future; to predict something • *Everything happened as the witch had foretold.*

**forethought** NOUN
careful thought and planning for the future

**forever** ADVERB
❶ for all time or for a long time
❷ continually or constantly • *He is forever complaining.*

**forewarn** VERB forewarns, forewarning, forewarned
to warn someone beforehand

**forewoman** NOUN forewomen
❶ a female worker in charge of other workers
❷ a female member of a jury who is in charge of the jury's discussions and who speaks on its behalf

**foreword** NOUN forewords
a short introduction at the beginning of a book

**forfeit** (say **for**-fit) VERB forfeits, forfeiting, forfeited
to pay or give up something as a penalty • *If*

*you cancel your flight, you will forfeit your deposit.*
➤ **forfeiture** NOUN

**forfeit** NOUN forfeits
something forfeited

**forge** NOUN forges
a place where metal is heated and shaped; a blacksmith's workshop

**forge** VERB forges, forging, forged
❶ to shape metal by heating and hammering it ❷ to copy a banknote, document or painting in order to deceive people
➤ **forger** NOUN
➤ **forge ahead** to move forward with a strong effort

**forgery** NOUN forgeries
❶ the crime of copying something in order to deceive people ❷ a copy of something made to deceive people • *The painting was proved to be a forgery.*

**forget** VERB forgets, forgetting, forgot, forgotten
❶ to fail to remember something • *I've forgotten what I was going to say.* ❷ to stop thinking or worrying about something • *Try to forget about your troubles for a while.*
➤ **forget yourself** to behave rudely or thoughtlessly

**forgetful** ADJECTIVE
frequently forgetting things
➤ **forgetfulness** NOUN

**forget-me-not** NOUN forget-me-nots
a plant with small blue flowers
**WORD ORIGIN** because in the Middle Ages the flower was worn by lovers

**forgive** VERB forgives, forgiving, forgave, forgiven
to stop feeling angry towards someone for something they have done

**forgiveness** NOUN
forgiving someone • *He begged for forgiveness for what he had done.*

**forgo** VERB forgoes, forgoing, forwent, forgone
to decide to give something up; to go without something • *We may have to forgo lunch.*
**SPELLING**
Note the spelling of this word. It does not have an 'e' in it, whereas **foregoing**, meaning 'preceding', does.

**fork** NOUN forks
❶ a small device with prongs for lifting food

to your mouth ❷ a large device with prongs used for digging or lifting things ❸ a place where a road or river separates into two or more parts • *a fork in the road*

**fork** VERB **forks, forking, forked**
❶ to lift or dig something with a fork ❷ a road or river forks when it separates into two or more branches ❸ to follow one fork of a road or river • *Fork left.*
➤ **fork out for something** (*informal*) to pay out money for something

**forklift truck** NOUN **forklift trucks**
a truck with two metal bars at the front for lifting and moving heavy loads

**forlorn** ADJECTIVE
left alone and unhappy
➤ **forlornly** ADVERB
➤ **forlorn hope** the only faint hope left

**form** NOUN **forms**
❶ the shape, appearance or condition of something • *They could see a shadowy form in front of them.* • *The letters have been published in book form.* ❷ a kind or type of something • *Swimming is a good form of exercise.* ❸ a class in school ❹ a piece of paper with spaces to be filled in

**form** VERB **forms, forming, formed**
❶ to shape or construct something; to create something • *We have formed a book club.*
❷ to come into existence or develop • *Icicles formed on the window.*

**formal** ADJECTIVE
❶ strictly following the accepted rules or customs; not casual • *a formal occasion* • *formal dress* ❷ rather serious and stiff in your manner ❸ official or ceremonial • *The formal opening of the bridge takes place tomorrow.*

**formality** NOUN **formalities**
❶ formal behaviour ❷ something done to obey a rule or custom

**formally** ADVERB
in a formal way • *They bowed formally.*

**format** NOUN **formats**
❶ the shape and size of something ❷ the way something is arranged or organized ❸ (*in computing*) the way data is organized for processing or storage by a computer

**format** VERB **formats, formatting, formatted**
(*in computing*) to organize data in a particular format

**formation** NOUN **formations**
❶ the act of forming something • *This chapter is about the formation of ice crystals.*
❷ something that has been formed • *a rock formation* ❸ a special arrangement or pattern
• *The aircraft were flying in formation.*

**formative** ADJECTIVE
having an important and lasting influence on how a person develops • *His formative years were spent in Australia.*

**former** ADJECTIVE
of an earlier time • *In former times the house had been an inn.* • *Bill Clinton, the former US President*
Compare with **latter**.
➤ **the former** the first of two people or things just mentioned

**formerly** ADVERB
at an earlier time; previously

**formidable** (say for-mid-a-bul) ADJECTIVE
❶ difficult to deal with or do • *a formidable task* ❷ impressive and frightening • *a formidable opponent*
➤ **formidably** ADVERB

**formula** NOUN **formulae** or **formulas**
❶ a set of chemical symbols showing what a substance consists of ❷ a rule or statement expressed in symbols or numbers ❸ a list of the ingredients you need to make something ❹ a fixed wording for a speech or ceremony ❺ one of the groups into which racing cars are placed according to the size of their engines • *Formula One*

**formulate** VERB **formulates, formulating, formulated**
to express an idea or plan clearly and exactly

**forsake** VERB **forsakes, forsaking, forsook, forsaken**
❶ to give something up; to leave a place ❷ to abandon someone

**fort** NOUN **forts**
a building that has been strongly built against attack

**forth** ADVERB
❶ out; into view • *They set forth at dawn.*
❷ onwards or forwards • *from this day forth*
➤ **and so forth** and so on

**forthcoming** ADJECTIVE
❶ due to happen soon • *forthcoming events*
❷ made available when needed • *Money for the trip was not forthcoming.* ❸ willing to talk or give information

**forthright** ADJECTIVE
frank and outspoken

**forthwith** ADVERB
immediately

**fortification** NOUN fortifications
❶ fortifying something ❷ a wall or building constructed to make a place strong against attack

**fortify** VERB fortifies, fortifying, fortified
❶ to make a place strong against attack, especially by building fortifications ❷ to make someone feel stronger • *He fortified himself against the cold with hot soup.*

**fortissimo** ADVERB
(*in music*) to be played very loudly

**fortitude** NOUN
courage in bearing pain or trouble

**fortnight** NOUN fortnights
a period of two weeks
➤ **fortnightly** ADVERB & ADJECTIVE
WORD ORIGIN from Old English *feowertene niht* = fourteen nights

**fortress** NOUN fortresses
a castle or town that has been strongly built against attack

**fortuitous** (say for-**tew**-it-us) ADJECTIVE
happening by chance; accidental • *The timing of his return was entirely fortuitous.*
➤ **fortuitously** ADVERB

USAGE
Note that **fortuitous** does not mean the same as **fortunate**.

**fortunate** ADJECTIVE
having or caused by good luck; lucky

**fortunately** ADVERB
by good luck • *Fortunately the train hadn't left when we got to the station.*

**fortune** NOUN fortunes
❶ luck, especially good luck ❷ a large amount of money
➤ **tell someone's fortune** to predict what will happen to someone in the future

**forty** NOUN & ADJECTIVE forties
the number 40
➤ **fortieth** ADJECTIVE & NOUN
➤ **forty winks** a short sleep; a nap

**forum** NOUN forums
❶ the public square in an ancient Roman city ❷ a place or meeting where people can exchange and discuss ideas • *The website provides a forum for young musicians to share their experiences.*

**forward** ADJECTIVE
❶ going forwards ❷ placed in the front
❸ too eager or bold

**forward** ADVERB
forwards or ahead

**forward** NOUN forwards
a player in the front line of a team in football, hockey, etc.

**forward** VERB forwards, forwarding, forwarded
to send on a letter, parcel or email to a new address

**forwards** ADVERB
❶ to or towards the front ❷ in the direction you are facing

**fossick** VERB fossicks, fossicking, fossicked (*Australian/NZ*)
❶ to turn things over or move them about while looking for something ❷ to search for gold or precious stones in streams or old mines

**fossil** NOUN fossils
the remains or traces of a prehistoric animal or plant that has been buried in the ground for a very long time and become hardened in rock

**fossil fuel** NOUN fossil fuels
a natural fuel such as coal or gas formed in the geological past

**fossilized** (also **fossilised**) ADJECTIVE
formed into a fossil • *fossilized dinosaur bones*

**foster** VERB fosters, fostering, fostered
❶ to take care of and bring up a child who is not your own ❷ to help something to grow or develop • *Reading to young children can foster a long-lasting love of books.*
➤ **foster child** NOUN
➤ **foster parent** NOUN
➤ **foster family** NOUN

**foul** ADJECTIVE
❶ disgusting; tasting or smelling unpleasant
❷ foul weather is wet and stormy ❸ unfair; breaking the rules of a game • *That was a foul shot.*
➤ **foulness** NOUN

**foul** NOUN fouls
an action that breaks the rules of a game

**foul** VERB fouls, fouling, fouled
❶ to commit a foul against a player in a game
❷ to make something foul or unpleasant
• *Smoke had fouled the air.*

**foul play** NOUN
a violent crime, especially murder

**found**
past tense of **find**

**found** VERB founds, founding, founded
❶ to start or set up an organization or institution, especially by providing money • *The museum was founded in 1683.* ❷ to be founded on something is to be based on it • *This novel is founded on fact.*

**foundation** NOUN foundations
❶ a building's foundations are the solid base under the ground on which it is built ❷ the basis for something ❸ the founding of an organization or institution ❹ a fund of money set aside for a charitable purpose

**founder** NOUN founders
a person who founds something • *the founder of the hospital*

**founder** VERB founders, foundering, foundered
❶ to fill with water and sink • *The ship foundered on the rocks.* ❷ to fail completely • *Their plans foundered.*

**foundling** NOUN foundlings
a child found abandoned, whose parents are not known

**foundry** NOUN foundries
a factory or workshop where metal or glass is made

**fount** NOUN founts (*poetical use*)
a fountain

**fountain** NOUN fountains
an ornamental structure in which a jet of water shoots up into the air

**fountain pen** NOUN fountain pens
a pen that can be filled with a supply of ink

**four** NOUN & ADJECTIVE fours
the number 4
➤ **on all fours** on your hands and knees

**fourteen** NOUN & ADJECTIVE fourteens
the number 14
➤ **fourteenth** ADJECTIVE & NOUN

**fourth** ADJECTIVE
next after the third
➤ **fourthly** ADVERB

**fourth** NOUN fourths
❶ the fourth person or thing ❷ one of four equal parts; a quarter

**fowl** NOUN fowls
a bird, especially one kept on a farm for its eggs or meat

**fox** NOUN foxes
a wild animal that looks like a dog with a long furry tail
➤ **foxy** ADJECTIVE

**fox** VERB foxes, foxing, foxed
to deceive or puzzle someone • *The last question really foxed me.*

**foxglove** NOUN foxgloves
a tall plant with flowers like the fingers of gloves

**foyer** (say **foy**-ay) NOUN foyers
the entrance hall of a theatre, cinema or hotel

**fraction** NOUN fractions
❶ a number that is not a whole number, e.g. ½ or 0.5 ❷ a tiny part or amount of something • *It took me a fraction of a second to realize my mistake.*

**fractionally** ADVERB
by a small amount; very slightly • *The ball was fractionally over the line.*

**fractious** (say **frak**-shus) ADJECTIVE
irritable or bad-tempered • *a fractious toddler*

**fracture** NOUN fractures
the breaking of something, especially of a bone

**fracture** VERB fractures, fracturing, fractured
to break something, especially a bone

**fragile** ADJECTIVE
easy to break or damage • *Be careful, this bowl is fragile.*
➤ **fragility** NOUN

**fragment** NOUN fragments
❶ a small piece broken off ❷ a small part of something • *He overheard fragments of their conversation.*
➤ **fragmentary** ADJECTIVE
➤ **fragmented** ADJECTIVE

**fragrance** NOUN fragrances
a pleasant smell or perfume

**fragrant** ADJECTIVE
having a pleasant smell

**frail** ADJECTIVE
not strong or healthy; physically weak • *a frail old man*

**frailty** NOUN frailties
weakness in someone's body or character

**frame** NOUN frames
❶ a holder that fits round the outside of a picture or mirror ❷ a rigid structure that supports something • *the frame of a bicycle* ❸ a human or animal body • *He has a small frame.* ❹ each of the single photographs that a cinema film or video is made from
➤ **frame of mind** the way you think or feel for a while

**frame** VERB frames, framing, framed
❶ to put a frame on or round something ❷ to express something in a particular way • *They framed the question badly.* ❸ to make an innocent person seem guilty by arranging false evidence

**framework** NOUN frameworks
❶ a frame supporting something ❷ a basic plan or system

**franc** NOUN francs
a unit of money in Switzerland and formerly in France, Belgium and some other countries (until replaced by the euro)

**franchise** NOUN franchises
❶ the right to vote in elections ❷ a licence to sell a firm's goods or services in a certain area

**frank** ADJECTIVE
honest and saying exactly what you think • *I'll be frank with you.*
➤ **frankness** NOUN

**frank** VERB franks, franking, franked
to mark a letter or parcel automatically in a machine to show that postage has been paid

**frankincense** NOUN
a sweet-smelling gum burnt as incense

**frankly** ADVERB
in an honest and direct way • *Please tell me frankly what you think.*

**frantic** ADJECTIVE
❶ wildly anxious or frightened • *She was frantic with worry.* ❷ done in a hurried and urgent way • *a frantic search for survivors*
➤ **frantically** ADVERB

**fraternal** (say fra-**tern**-al) ADJECTIVE
to do with brothers; brotherly

**fraternity** NOUN fraternities
❶ a brotherly feeling ❷ a group of people who have the same interests or occupation • *the medical fraternity*

**fraternize** (also **fraternise**) VERB fraternizes, fraternizing, fraternized
to be friendly towards a group of people and

spend time with them • *She was accused of fraternizing with the enemy.*

**fraud** NOUN frauds
❶ the crime of getting money by tricking people ❷ a dishonest trick ❸ a person who is not what they pretend to be

**fraudulent** (say **fraw**-dew-lent) ADJECTIVE
involving fraud; deceitful or dishonest
➤ **fraudulently** ADVERB

**fraught** ADJECTIVE
❶ filled with problems or difficulties • *The situation is fraught with danger.* ❷ tense or upset • *I'm feeling rather fraught this morning.*

**fray** VERB frays, fraying, frayed
❶ material frays or becomes frayed when some of the threads become loose and start to come apart • *Your shirt collar is frayed.* ❷ a person's temper or nerves fray when they become strained or upset

**fray** NOUN
a fight or conflict • *They were ready for the fray.*

**freak** NOUN freaks
❶ a very strange or abnormal person, animal or thing ❷ a person with a very strong interest in something • *She is a fitness freak.*

**freakish** ADJECTIVE
very unusual or strange • *freakish weather*

**freckle** NOUN freckles
a small brown spot on the skin
➤ **freckled** ADJECTIVE

**free** ADJECTIVE freer, freest
❶ able to do what you want to do or go where you want to go ❷ not costing anything ❸ not fixed • *Leave one end free.* ❹ not having or being affected by something • *The main roads are still free of snow.* ❺ available; not being used or occupied ❻ not already having things to do • *Are you free next Saturday?* ❼ generous • *She is very free with her money.*

**free** VERB frees, freeing, freed
to set someone or something free

**freedom** NOUN freedoms
❶ the right to do or say what you like • *freedom of speech* ❷ being free; not being a prisoner • *He was finally given his freedom after 25 years in jail.*

**freehand** ADJECTIVE & ADVERB
a freehand drawing is done without a ruler

or compasses or without tracing it • *Draw a circle freehand.*

**freehold** NOUN
(*chiefly British*) possessing land or a house as its absolute owner, not as a tenant renting from a landlord

**freely** ADVERB
❶ without being controlled or limited • *the country's first freely elected president* • *I freely admit that I made a mistake.* ❷ without anything stopping the movement or flow of something • *The wheel can now turn freely.*

**free-range** ADJECTIVE
❶ free-range hens are not kept in small cages but are allowed to move about freely ❷ free-range eggs are ones laid by these hens

**free verse** NOUN
poetry that does not rhyme or have a regular rhythm

**freeway** NOUN freeways
(*North American*) a dual-carriageway main road

**freewheel** VERB freewheels, freewheeling, freewheeled
to ride a bicycle without pedalling

**freeze** VERB freezes, freezing, froze, frozen
❶ to turn into ice or to become covered with ice • *The pond froze last night.* ❷ to feel very cold ❸ to freeze food is to store it at a low temperature to preserve it ❹ to suddenly stand completely still ❺ to keep wages or prices at a fixed level

**freeze** NOUN freezes
❶ a period of freezing weather ❷ the freezing of wages or prices

**freezer** NOUN freezers
a refrigerator in which food can be frozen quickly and stored

**freezing** ADJECTIVE
very cold • *I'm freezing.* • *It's freezing outside.*

**freezing point** NOUN freezing points
the temperature at which a liquid freezes

**freight** (say frayt) NOUN
goods carried by road or in a ship or aircraft

**freighter** (say fray-ter) NOUN freighters
a ship or aircraft used for carrying goods

**French window** NOUN French windows
a long window that serves as a door on an outside wall

**frenzied** ADJECTIVE
wildly excited or angry • *a frenzied attack*
➤ **frenziedly** ADVERB

**frenzy** NOUN
wild and uncontrolled excitement or anger
• *He had worked the crowd up into a frenzy.*

**frequency** NOUN frequencies
❶ being frequent; happening often ❷ how often something happens ❸ the number of vibrations made each second by a wave of sound, radio or light

**frequent** (say freek-went) ADJECTIVE
happening often

**frequent** (say frik-went) VERB frequents, frequenting, frequented
to visit a place or be seen there, often • *They frequented the club.*

**frequently** ADVERB
often • *I frequently forget my keys.*

**fresco** NOUN frescoes or frescos
a picture painted on a wall or ceiling before the plaster is dry **WORD ORIGIN** from Italian *affresco* = on the fresh (plaster)

**fresh** ADJECTIVE
❶ newly made or produced or arrived; not stale • *fresh bread* ❷ not tinned or preserved • *fresh fruit* ❸ fresh air is cool and refreshing ❹ fresh water is not salty ❺ full of energy and not tired
➤ **freshness** NOUN

**freshen** VERB freshens, freshening, freshened
❶ to make something fresh ❷ to become fresh

**freshly** ADVERB
newly or recently • *freshly baked bread*

**freshwater** ADJECTIVE
living in rivers or lakes, not the sea
• *freshwater fish*

**fret** VERB frets, fretting, fretted
to worry or be upset about something
➤ **fretful** ADJECTIVE
➤ **fretfully** ADVERB

**fret** NOUN frets
a bar or ridge on the fingerboard of a guitar etc.

**fretsaw** NOUN fretsaws
a very narrow saw used for cutting patterns in thin wood

**fretwork** NOUN
cutting decorative patterns in wood; wood cut in this way

a b c d e f g h i j k l m n o p q r s t u v w x y z

**friar** NOUN friars
a man who is a member of a Roman Catholic religious order and has vowed to live a life of poverty

**friary** NOUN friaries
a building where friars live

**friction** NOUN
❶ the rubbing of one thing against another ❷ (*in science*) the resistance that one surface or object meets when it moves over another ❸ bad feeling between people; quarrelling

**Friday** NOUN
the day of the week following Thursday
(WORD ORIGIN) from Old English *Frigedaeg* = day of Frigga, a Norse goddess

**fridge** NOUN fridges
(*British*) a refrigerator

**friend** NOUN friends
❶ a person you like and who likes you ❷ a person you send messages to on a social networking site ❸ a helpful or kind person
(SPELLING)
There is a silent i before the e in **friend**.

**friendless** ADJECTIVE
without any friends

**friendly** ADJECTIVE friendlier, friendliest
❶ behaving like a friend; kind and pleasant ❷ helpful and easy to use; not harmful • *environmentally-friendly farming methods*
➤ **friendliness** NOUN

**friendly** NOUN friendlies
(*British*) a sports match that is not part of a formal competition

**friendship** NOUN friendships
friendly feelings between people; being friends

**frieze** (say freez) NOUN friezes
a strip of designs or pictures round the top of a wall or building

**frigate** NOUN frigates
a small warship

**fright** NOUN frights
❶ sudden great fear ❷ (*informal*) a person or thing that looks ridiculous

**frighten** VERB frightens, frightening, frightened
to make someone afraid
➤ **be frightened of** to be afraid of someone or something • *When I was young I was frightened of spiders.*
➤ **frightening** ADJECTIVE

**frightful** ADJECTIVE
(*British*) awful; very great or bad
➤ **frightfully** ADVERB

**frigid** ADJECTIVE
❶ extremely cold ❷ unfriendly; not affectionate
➤ **frigidly** ADVERB

**frill** NOUN frills
❶ a decorative gathered or pleated trimming on a dress, shirt, curtain, etc. ❷ something extra that is pleasant but unnecessary • *a simple hotel with no frills*
➤ **frilled** ADJECTIVE
➤ **frilly** ADJECTIVE

**fringe** NOUN fringes
❶ a decorative edging with many threads hanging down loosely ❷ a straight line of hair hanging down over your forehead ❸ the edge of something • *These hills mark the northern fringe of the desert.*

**fringe** VERB
➤ **be fringed with something** to have something as a border or around the edge • *The lake was fringed with pine trees.*

**frisk** VERB frisks, frisking, frisked
❶ to jump or run about playfully ❷ to search someone by running your hands over his or her clothes

**frisky** ADJECTIVE
playful or lively

**fritter** NOUN fritters
a slice of meat, potato or fruit coated in batter and fried

**fritter** VERB fritters, frittering, frittered
if you fritter away your time or money, you waste it on trivial things

**frivolous** ADJECTIVE
without a serious purpose; light-hearted when you should be serious
➤ **frivolity** NOUN

**frizzy** ADJECTIVE
frizzy hair is in tight stiff curls

**fro** ADVERB
➤ **to and fro** backwards and forwards

**frock** NOUN frocks
(*British*) a girl's or woman's dress

**frog** NOUN frogs
a small jumping animal that can live both in water and on land
➤ **have a frog in your throat** to be hoarse and unable to speak clearly

**frogman** NOUN **frogmen**
a swimmer equipped with a rubber suit,
flippers and breathing apparatus for
swimming and working underwater

**frolic** NOUN **frolics**
a lively cheerful game or entertainment
➤ **frolicsome** ADJECTIVE

**frolic** VERB **frolics, frolicking, frolicked**
to play about in a lively cheerful way

**from** PREPOSITION
This word is used to show
❶ a starting point in space or time or order
(*We flew from London to Paris. We work
from 9 to 5 o'clock. Count from one to ten.*)
❷ distance (*We are a mile from home.*)
❸ source or origin (*Get water from the tap.*)
❹ separation or release (*Take the gun from
him. She was freed from prison.*) ❺ difference
(*How do you tell one twin from the other?*)
❻ cause (*We were all suffering from
exhaustion.*)

**frond** NOUN **fronds**
a leaf-like part of a fern, palm tree, etc.

**front** NOUN **fronts**
❶ the part or side that comes first or is the
most important or furthest forward ❷ a road
or promenade along the seashore ❸ the place
where fighting is happening in a war ❹ in
weather systems, the forward edge of an
approaching mass of air
➤ **in front** at or near the front

**front** ADJECTIVE
of the front; in front • *We sat in the front
row.*

**frontage** NOUN **frontages**
the front of a building; the land beside this

**frontier** NOUN **frontiers**
the boundary between two countries or
regions

**frontispiece** NOUN **frontispieces**
an illustration opposite the title page of a
book

**frost** NOUN **frosts**
❶ powdery ice that forms on things
in freezing weather ❷ weather with a
temperature below freezing point

**frost** VERB **frosts, frosting, frosted**
➤ **frost up** or **over** to become covered with
frost

**frostbite** NOUN
harm done to the body by very cold weather
➤ **frostbitten** ADJECTIVE

**frosted glass** NOUN
glass made cloudy so that you cannot see
clearly through it

**frosting** NOUN
sugar icing for cakes

**frosty** ADJECTIVE **frostier, frostiest**
❶ so cold that there is frost • *It was a frosty
morning.* ❷ unfriendly and unwelcoming
• *She gave us a frosty look.*
➤ **frostily** ADVERB

**froth** NOUN
a white mass of tiny bubbles on a liquid

**froth** VERB **froths, frothing, frothed**
to form a froth • *The dog was frothing at the
mouth.*
➤ **frothy** ADJECTIVE

**frown** VERB **frowns, frowning, frowned**
to wrinkle your forehead because you are
angry or worried

**frown** NOUN **frowns**
a frowning movement or look

**frozen** ADJECTIVE
❶ frozen food is stored at a low temperature
in order to preserve it ❷ very cold • *My
feet are frozen!* ❸ with a layer of ice on the
surface • *a frozen pond*

**frugal** (say **froo**-gal) ADJECTIVE
❶ spending very little money ❷ small and
meagre; costing very little money • *a frugal
meal*
➤ **frugally** ADVERB
➤ **frugality** NOUN

**fruit** NOUN **fruits** or **fruit**
❶ the seed container that grows on a tree or
plant and is often used as food ❷ the result
of doing something • *It will be years before
we see the fruits of all this work.*

**fruit** VERB **fruits, fruiting, fruited**
a tree or plant fruits when it produces fruit

SPELLING

The 'oo' sound is spelt **ui** in **fruit**.

**fruitful** ADJECTIVE
producing good results • *fruitful discussions*
➤ **fruitfully** ADVERB

**fruition** (say froo-**ish**-on) NOUN
the achievement of what was hoped or
worked for • *Our plans never came to
fruition.*

**fruitless** ADJECTIVE
producing no results • *a fruitless search*
➤ **fruitlessly** ADVERB

**fruit machine** NOUN fruit machines
(*British*) a gambling machine worked by
putting a coin in a slot

**fruity** ADJECTIVE
❶ like or containing fruit ❷ a fruity voice is
deep and rich

**frustrate** VERB frustrates, frustrating,
frustrated
❶ to make someone annoyed and upset
because they are prevented from doing
something • *The delay was beginning to
frustrate me.* ❷ to prevent something from
being successful • *All our plans have been
frustrated.*

**frustrating** ADJECTIVE
making you annoyed or upset because you
cannot do what you want • *It's been a very
frustrating day.*

**frustration** NOUN
a feeling of annoyance when you have been
prevented from doing something

**fry** VERB fries, frying, fried
to cook food in very hot fat
➤ **fryer** NOUN

**fry** PLURAL NOUN
very young fishes

**frying pan** NOUN frying pans
a shallow pan for frying things

**fuchsia** (say few-sha) NOUN fuchsias
an ornamental plant with flowers that hang
down WORD ORIGIN named after Leonard
*Fuchs*, a German botanist

**fudge** NOUN
a soft sugary sweet

**fudge** VERB fudges, fudging, fudged
to avoid giving clear and accurate
information or a clear answer • *People accuse
us of fudging the issue.*

**fuel** NOUN fuels
something that is burnt to produce heat or
power

**fuel** VERB fuels, fuelling, fuelled
❶ to supply something with fuel ❷ to
strengthen a feeling or belief • *His answers
only fuelled my suspicions.*

**fug** NOUN (*British*) (*informal*)
a stuffy or smoky atmosphere in a room
➤ **fuggy** ADJECTIVE

**fugitive** (say few-jit-iv) NOUN fugitives
a person who is running away from
something, especially from the police

**fugue** (say fewg) NOUN fugues
a piece of music in which tunes are repeated
in a complicated pattern

**fulcrum** NOUN fulcrums or fulcra
the point on which something balances or
turns

**fulfil** VERB fulfils, fulfilling, fulfilled
❶ to do what is required; to carry something
out • *You must fulfil your promises.* ❷ to
make something come true • *It fulfilled an
ancient prophecy.* ❸ to give you a feeling of
satisfaction

**fulfilment** NOUN
the feeling of satisfaction you have when you
have achieved something

**full** ADJECTIVE
❶ containing as much or as many as possible
• *The cinema was full.* ❷ having many people
or things • *She's full of ideas.* ❸ complete
• *Tell me the full story.* ❹ the greatest
possible • *at full speed* ❺ fitting loosely; with
many folds • *a full skirt*
➤ **fullness** NOUN
➤ **in full** with nothing left out • *We have
paid in full.*
➤ **to the full** completely or thoroughly

**full** ADVERB
completely and directly • *It hit him full in the
face.*

**full-blown** ADJECTIVE
fully developed

**full moon** NOUN full moons
the moon when you can see the whole of it as
a bright disc

**full stop** NOUN full stops
(*British*) the dot (.) used as a punctuation
mark at the end of a sentence or an
abbreviation or after an initial

PUNCTUATION

A **full stop** (called a **period** in American
English) is used to show where a sentence
ends, when the sentence is neither a
question nor an exclamation:

*I am the tallest in my class.*

*You can text me later.*

It can also be used to indicate a complete
break between single words or phrases
that are not complete sentences:

*There was nothing left of the cake. Not a
crumb. Not a particle. Nothing.*

Full stops go within quotation marks in direct speech:

*He said, 'I'll meet you outside the cinema.'*

A full stop is also used after an initial or to mark an abbreviation (e.g. *Mon.* = Monday). This is no longer necessary for common abbreviations, like *Mr, Mrs,* and *Dr.*

**full-time** ADJECTIVE & ADVERB
for all the normal working hours of the day
• *a full-time job* • *She works full-time.*

**fully** ADVERB
completely • *He has fully recovered from his illness.*

**fully-fledged** ADJECTIVE
fully trained or developed • *a fully-fledged engineer*

**fumble** VERB fumbles, fumbling, fumbled
to handle or feel for something something clumsily • *I fumbled in the dark for the light switch.*

**fume** VERB fumes, fuming, fumed
❶ to give off fumes ❷ to be very angry

**fumes** PLURAL NOUN
strong-smelling smoke or gas

**fun** NOUN
amusement or enjoyment
➤ **make fun of someone** to laugh at someone in an unkind way or make other people do this

**function** NOUN functions
❶ what someone or something is there to do • *The function of the heart is to pump blood round the body.* ❷ an important event or party ❸ a basic operation in a computer or calculator ❹ (*in mathematics*) a variable quantity whose value depends on the value of other variable quantities • *X is a function of Y and Z.*

**function** VERB functions, functioning, functioned
to perform a function; to work properly
• *Only one engine was still functioning.*

**functional** ADJECTIVE
❶ working properly ❷ practical and useful without being decorative or luxurious

**fund** NOUN funds
❶ an amount of money collected or kept for a special purpose ❷ a stock or supply • *He has a fund of stories and jokes.*

**fund** VERB funds, funding, funded
to supply someone or something with money

**fundamental** ADJECTIVE
basic; involving the central and most important part of something
➤ **fundamentally** ADVERB

**funeral** NOUN funerals
the ceremony when a dead person is buried or cremated

**funereal** (say few-**neer**-ee-al) ADJECTIVE
gloomy or depressing

**funfair** NOUN funfairs
(*British*) a fair consisting of amusements and sideshows

**fungus** NOUN fungi (say **fung**-eye)
a living thing without leaves or flowers that grows on plants or on decayed material, such as mushrooms and toadstools

**funk** VERB funks, funking, funked
(*British*) (*old-fashioned use*) to be afraid of doing something and avoid it

**funk** NOUN
a style of popular music with a strong rhythm, based on jazz and blues

**funnel** NOUN funnels
❶ a metal chimney on a ship or steam engine ❷ a tube that is wide at the top and narrow at the bottom to help you pour things into a narrow opening

**funny** ADJECTIVE funnier, funniest
❶ that makes you laugh or smile ❷ strange or odd • *a funny smell*
➤ **funnily** ADVERB

**funny bone** NOUN funny bones
part of your elbow which produces a tingling feeling if you knock it

**fur** NOUN furs
❶ the soft hair that covers some animals ❷ animal skin with the fur on it, used for clothing; fabric that looks like animal fur

**furious** ADJECTIVE
❶ very angry ❷ violent or intense • *They were travelling at a furious speed.*

**furiously** ADVERB
❶ angrily ❷ with great energy or speed • *We worked furiously to get it finished on time.*

**furl** VERB furls, furling, furled
to roll up a sail, flag or umbrella

**furlong** NOUN furlongs
one-eighth of a mile, 220 yards (201 metres)

a b c d e f g h i j k l m n o p q r s t u v w x y z

**WORD ORIGIN** from Old English *furlang* = 'furrow long'; the length of a furrow in a common field

**furnace** NOUN **furnaces**
a type of large oven that produces great heat for making glass or melting metals

**furnish** VERB
❶ to put furniture in a room or building
❷ to provide someone with something • *She furnished him with all the facts he needed.*

**furnishings** PLURAL NOUN
furniture, curtains and fittings for a room or house

**furniture** NOUN
tables, chairs and other movable things that you need in a house, school or office

**furore** (say few-**ror**-ee) NOUN
an excited or angry uproar

**furrow** NOUN **furrows**
❶ a long cut in the ground made by a plough
❷ a deep wrinkle in the skin

**furrow** VERB **furrows, furrowing, furrowed**
to make furrows in something • *Tom furrowed his brow.*

**furry** ADJECTIVE
like fur; covered with fur

**further** ADVERB & ADJECTIVE
❶ at or to a greater distance; more distant
❷ more; additional • *We made further enquiries.*
**USAGE**
See the note at **farther.**

**further** VERB **furthers, furthering, furthered**
to help something to progress • *It was a chance for her to further her career.*

**further education** NOUN
(*British*) education for people above school age

**furthermore** ADVERB
also; moreover

**furthest** ADVERB & ADJECTIVE
at or to the greatest distance; most distant
**USAGE**
See the note at **farther.**

**furtive** ADJECTIVE
stealthy; trying not to be seen • *He gave a furtive glance over his shoulder.*
➤ **furtively** ADVERB

**fury** NOUN **furies**
wild anger; rage • *She was speechless with fury.*

**furze** NOUN
gorse shrubs

**fuse** NOUN **fuses**
❶ a safety device containing a short piece of wire that melts if too much electricity is passed through it ❷ a length of material that burns easily, used for setting off an explosive

**fuse** VERB **fuses, fusing, fused**
❶ an electrical device fuses when it stops working because a fuse has melted ❷ to fuse things is to blend them together, especially through melting

**fuselage** (say few-zel-ahzh) NOUN **fuselages**
the main body of an aircraft

**fusillade** (say few-zil-**ayd**) NOUN **fusillades**
❶ an outburst of rapid gunfire ❷ a rapid series of questions

**fusion** NOUN
❶ the action of blending or uniting things
❷ the uniting of atomic nuclei, usually releasing energy

**fuss** NOUN **fusses**
❶ unnecessary excitement or worry about something • *What's all the fuss about?*
❷ angry complaints about something
➤ **make a fuss of someone** to treat someone with great kindness and attention

**fuss** VERB **fusses, fussing, fussed**
to be too anxious about something that is not important • *She fusses when I go out on my bike.*

**fussy** ADJECTIVE **fussier, fussiest**
❶ worrying too much about something that is not important ❷ choosing very carefully; hard to please • *My brother is a fussy eater.*
❸ full of unnecessary details or decorations • *a fussy design*
➤ **fussily** ADVERB

**fusty** ADJECTIVE **fustier, fustiest**
smelling stale or stuffy

**futile** (say few-tyl) ADJECTIVE
useless or pointless; having no chance of success • *He knew it was futile to argue with her.*
➤ **futility** NOUN

**futon** (say foo-ton) NOUN **futons**
a seat with a mattress that rolls out to form a bed

**future** NOUN
❶ the time that will come • *Who knows what will happen in the future?* ❷ what is going to happen to someone or something in the time to come • *She has a bright future.* ❸ (*in grammar*) the use of verbs and phrases such as 'will', 'shall', 'be going to', or 'be about to' to talk about something happening in the future

**GRAMMAR**
See also the panel at **tense**.

**future** ADJECTIVE
belonging or referring to the future

**futuristic** ADJECTIVE
very modern, as if belonging to the future rather than the present • *futuristic buildings*

**fuzz** NOUN
something soft and fluffy like soft hair

**fuzzy** ADJECTIVE
❶ a fuzzy picture or image is blurred and not clear ❷ covered with short soft hair or fur
➤ **fuzziness** NOUN

**gabble** VERB gabbles, gabbling, gabbled
to talk so quickly that it is difficult to hear the words • *She was nervous and started to gabble.*

**gable** NOUN gables
the pointed triangular part at the top of an outside wall, between two sloping roofs
➤ **gabled** ADJECTIVE

**gad** VERB gads, gadding, gadded
➤ **gad about** (*informal*)
to have a lot of fun in different places

**gadget** NOUN gadgets
any small useful tool or device
➤ **gadgetry** NOUN

**Gaelic** (say **gay**-lik) NOUN
the Celtic languages of Scotland and Ireland

**gaffe** NOUN gaffes
an obvious and embarrassing mistake

**gag** NOUN gags
❶ something put into a person's mouth or tied over it to prevent them speaking ❷ a joke

**gag** VERB gags, gagging, gagged
❶ to put a gag on a person ❷ to prevent someone from making comments • *We cannot gag the press.* ❸ to retch

**gaggle** NOUN gaggles
❶ a flock of geese ❷ a group of noisy people
• *a gaggle of tourists*

**gaiety** NOUN
being cheerful and having fun

**gaily** ADVERB
in a cheerful way

**gain** VERB gains, gaining, gained
❶ to get something that you did not have before ❷ a clock or watch gains when it shows a time later than the correct time ❸ (*literary*) to reach or arrive at a place • *At last we gained the shore.*
➤ **gain on someone** to come closer to someone when you are chasing them or in a race

**gain** NOUN gains
something that you gain; a profit or improvement

**gait** NOUN gaits
a way of walking or running • *He walked with a shuffling gait.*

**gaiter** NOUN gaiters
a leather or cloth covering for the lower part of the leg

**gala** (say **gah**-la) NOUN galas
❶ a festival or celebration ❷ a set of sports contests, especially in swimming

**galaxy** NOUN galaxies
a very large group of stars
➤ **galactic** (say ga-**lak**-tik) ADJECTIVE
**WORD ORIGIN** originally = the Milky Way: from Greek *galaxias* = milky

**gale** NOUN gales
a very strong wind

**gall** (say gawl) NOUN
being bold or cheeky enough to do something
• *I don't know how he had the gall to say it was his idea.*

**gall** VERB galls, galling, galled
to annoy or upset someone, especially because something is unfair • *It galls me that I ended up getting the blame.*

**gallant** (say **gal**-lant) ADJECTIVE
❶ brave or heroic • *a gallant effort* ❷ courteous towards women
➤ **gallantly** ADVERB
➤ **gallantry** NOUN

**gall bladder** NOUN gall bladders
an organ attached to the liver, in which bile is stored

**galleon** NOUN galleons
a large Spanish sailing ship used in the 16th and 17th centuries

**gallery** NOUN galleries
❶ a room or building for showing works of art ❷ the highest balcony in a cinema or theatre ❸ a long room or passage ❹ a platform jutting out from the wall in a church or hall

**galley** NOUN galleys
❶ an ancient type of ship driven by oars ❷ the kitchen in a ship or aircraft

**galling** (say **gawl**-ing) ADJECTIVE
annoying and upsetting because of being unfair

**gallivant** VERB gallivants, gallivanting, gallivanted
to go about in search of pleasure

**gallon** NOUN gallons
a unit used to measure liquids, 8 pints or 4.546 litres

**gallop** NOUN gallops
❶ the fastest pace that a horse can go ❷ a fast ride on a horse

**gallop** VERB gallops, galloping, galloped
to go or ride at a gallop

**gallows** NOUN gallows
a framework with a noose for hanging criminals

**galore** ADVERB
in great numbers; in a large amount • There will be bargains galore.

**galoshes** PLURAL NOUN
a pair of waterproof shoes worn over ordinary shoes

**galvanize** (also **galvanise**) VERB galvanizes, galvanizing, galvanized
❶ to shock or stimulate someone into sudden activity • The urgency of his voice galvanized them into action. ❷ to coat iron with zinc to protect it from rust **WORD ORIGIN** named after an Italian scientist, Luigi Galvani, who discovered that muscles move because of electricity in the body

**gambit** NOUN gambits
❶ a kind of opening move in chess ❷ an action or remark intended to gain an advantage

**gamble** VERB gambles, gambling, gambled
❶ to bet on the result of a game, race or other event ❷ to take risks in the hope of gaining something • I wouldn't gamble on the weather staying fine.
➤ **gambler** NOUN

**gamble** NOUN gambles
❶ a bet or chance • a gamble on the lottery ❷ something you do that is a risk • He knew that playing when he had an injury was a gamble.

**gambol** VERB gambols, gambolling, gambolled
to jump or skip about in play

**game** NOUN games
❶ something that you can play, usually with rules • a game of football • a computer game ❷ a section of a long game such as tennis or whist ❸ a scheme or plan; a trick • Whatever his game is, he won't succeed. ❹ wild animals or birds hunted for sport or food
➤ **give the game away** to reveal a secret

**game** ADJECTIVE
willing to do or try something • Are you game for a swim?
➤ **gamely** ADVERB

**gamekeeper** NOUN gamekeepers
a person employed to protect game birds and animals, especially from poachers

**gameplay** NOUN
the design of a computer game and how it is played

**games** PLURAL NOUN
❶ a meeting for sporting contests • the Olympic Games ❷ athletics or sports as a subject taught at school

**gaming** NOUN
❶ gambling ❷ playing computer games

**gamma** NOUN
the third letter of the Greek alphabet, equivalent to Roman G, g

**gamma rays** PLURAL NOUN
very short X-rays emitted by radioactive substances

**gammon** NOUN
(British) a kind of ham

**gamut** (say **gam**-ut) NOUN
the whole range or scope of anything • He ran the whole gamut of emotions from joy to despair.

**gander** NOUN ganders
a male goose

**gang** NOUN gangs
❶ a group of people who do things together ❷ a group of young people who cause trouble and fight other groups ❸ a group of criminals

**gang** VERB gangs, ganging, ganged
➤ **gang up on someone** to form a group to fight or oppose someone

**gangling** ADJECTIVE
tall, thin and awkward-looking

**gangplank** NOUN gangplanks
a plank placed so that people can walk on or off a boat

**gangrene** (say **gang**-green) NOUN
decay of body tissue in a living person

**gangster** NOUN gangsters
a member of a gang of violent criminals

**gangway** NOUN gangways
❶ a gap left for people to pass between rows of seats, e.g. in a theatre or aircraft ❷ a movable bridge placed so that people can walk onto or off a ship

**gannet** NOUN gannets
a large seabird which catches fish by flying above the sea and then diving in

**gaol** (say jayl) NOUN gaols
(British) a different spelling of jail
➤ **gaol** VERB
➤ **gaoler** NOUN

**gap** NOUN gaps
❶ a break or opening in something continuous such as a hedge or fence ❷ an interval or break ❸ a wide difference in ideas

**gape** VERB gapes, gaping, gaped
❶ to stare in amazement with your mouth open ❷ to be wide open • *a gaping wound*

**garage** (say **ga**-rahzh or **ga**-rij) NOUN garages
❶ a building for keeping a motor vehicle or vehicles ❷ a place where petrol is sold and vehicles are repaired and serviced

**garb** NOUN
special clothing • *a man dressed in prison garb*

**garbage** NOUN
(esp. North American) rubbish, especially household rubbish

**garbed** ADJECTIVE
(old use) or (poetical use) dressed in a particular way • *They were garbed in robes of pure white.*

**garbled** ADJECTIVE
a garbled message or story is mixed up so that it is difficult to understand
(**WORD ORIGIN**) from Arabic *garbala* = sift, select (because the real facts are 'sifted out')

**garden** NOUN gardens
a piece of ground where flowers, fruit or vegetables are grown
➤ **gardener** NOUN
➤ **gardening** NOUN

**gargantuan** (say gar-**gan**-tew-an) ADJECTIVE
gigantic (**WORD ORIGIN**) from *Gargantua*, the name of a giant in a book by the French writer Rabelais

**gargle** VERB gargles, gargling, gargled
to hold a liquid at the back of the mouth and push air through it to wash the inside of the throat
➤ **gargle** NOUN

**gargoyle** NOUN gargoyles
an ugly or comical face or figure carved on a building, especially on a waterspout
(**WORD ORIGIN**) from French *gargouille* = throat (because the water passes through the throat of the figure)

**garish** (say **gair**-ish) ADJECTIVE
too bright or highly coloured; gaudy
➤ **garishly** ADVERB

**garland** NOUN garlands
a wreath of flowers worn or hung as a decoration

**garland** VERB garlands, garlanding, garlanded
to decorate something with a garland

**garlic** NOUN
a plant with a bulb divided into smaller bulbs (called cloves), which have a strong smell and taste and are used for flavouring food

**garment** NOUN garments
a piece of clothing

**garner** VERB garners, garnering, garnered
(formal)
to gather or collect something • *He managed to garner plenty of information.*

**garnet** NOUN garnets
a dark red stone used as a gem

**garnish** VERB garnishes, garnishing, garnished
to decorate something, especially food
• *Garnish the fish with slices of lemon.*

**garnish** NOUN
something used to decorate food or give it extra flavour

a b c d e f g h i j k l m n o p q r s t u v w x y z

**garret** NOUN garrets
a dingy attic room

**garrison** NOUN garrisons
❶ troops who stay in a town or fort to defend it ❷ the building they live in
➤ **garrison** VERB

**garrulous** (say ga-rool-us) ADJECTIVE
extremely talkative

**garter** NOUN garters
a band of elastic to hold up a sock or stocking

**gas** NOUN gases
❶ a substance, such as oxygen, that can move freely and is not liquid or solid at ordinary temperatures ❷ a gas that can be burned, used for lighting, heating or cooking ❸ (North American) (informal) short for gasoline

**gas** VERB gasses, gassing, gassed
❶ to kill or injure someone with gas ❷ (informal) to chatter idly

**gas chamber** NOUN gas chambers
a room that can be filled with poisonous gas to kill people or animals

**gaseous** (say gas-ee-us) ADJECTIVE
in the form of a gas

**gash** NOUN gashes
a long deep cut or wound

**gash** VERB gashes, gashing, gashed
to make a gash in something

**gasket** NOUN gaskets
a flat ring or strip of soft material for sealing a joint between metal surfaces in machinery

**gasoline** NOUN
(North American) petrol

**gasometer** (say gas-om-it-er) NOUN gasometers
a large round tank in which gas is stored

**gasp** VERB gasps, gasping, gasped
❶ to breathe in suddenly when you are shocked or surprised ❷ to struggle to breathe with your mouth open when you are tired or ill ❸ to speak in a breathless way

**gasp** NOUN gasps
a sudden deep breath, especially one caused by shock or surprise

**gassy** ADJECTIVE
fizzy

**gastric** ADJECTIVE
to do with the stomach

**gastronomy** (say gas-tron-om-ee) NOUN
the art or practice of good eating
➤ **gastronomic** ADJECTIVE

**gastropod** NOUN gastropods
an animal (e.g. a snail or slug) that moves by means of a fleshy 'foot' on its stomach
**WORD ORIGIN** from Greek gaster = stomach + podos = of the foot

**gate** NOUN gates
❶ a movable barrier, usually on hinges, used as a door in a wall or fence ❷ a barrier for controlling the flow of water in a dam or lock ❸ a place where you wait before you board an aircraft ❹ the number of people attending a football match or other sports event

**gateau** (say gat-oh) NOUN gateaus or gateaux
a large rich cream cake

**gatecrash** VERB gatecrashes, gatecrashing, gatecrashed
to go to a private party without being invited
➤ **gatecrasher** NOUN

**gateway** NOUN gateways
❶ an opening containing a gate ❷ a way to reach something • the gateway to success

**gather** VERB gathers, gathering, gathered
❶ to come together • A crowd soon gathered round. ❷ to bring people or things together • He gathered up all his papers. ❸ to collect something; to obtain something gradually • We've been gathering information. ❹ to collect crops as harvest; to pick plants or fruit • Gather the corn when it is ripe. • She was out gathering mushrooms. ❺ to understand or learn something • I gather you've been on holiday. ❻ to pull cloth into folds by running a thread through it
➤ **gather speed** to move gradually faster

**gathering** NOUN gatherings
an assembly or meeting of people; a party

**gaudy** ADJECTIVE
very showy and bright • gaudy jewellery
➤ **gaudily** ADVERB

**gauge** (say gayj) NOUN gauges
❶ a measuring instrument • a fuel gauge ❷ a standard measurement ❸ the distance between the rails on a railway track

**gauge** VERB gauges, gauging, gauged
❶ to measure something ❷ to estimate or form a judgement about something • It was difficult to gauge the mood of the audience.

**gaunt** ADJECTIVE
lean and haggard • His face was gaunt and unshaven.

**gauntlet** NOUN gauntlets
a glove with a wide cuff covering the wrist
➤ **run the gauntlet** to have to face criticism or hostility from a lot of people
➤ **throw down the gauntlet** to offer a challenge
WORD ORIGIN 'Running the gauntlet' was once a former military and naval punishment in which the victim was made to pass between two rows of men who struck him as he passed

**gauze** NOUN
❶ thin transparent woven material ❷ fine wire mesh
➤ **gauzy** ADJECTIVE

**gay** ADJECTIVE
❶ homosexual ❷ cheerful ❸ brightly coloured
➤ **gayness** NOUN

USAGE

Nowadays the most common meaning of *gay* is 'homosexual'. The other two meanings are older and are becoming less and less common in everyday use. *Gayness* is the noun from meaning 1 of *gay*. The noun that relates to the other two meanings is **gaiety**.

**gaze** VERB gazes, gazing, gazed
to look at something steadily for a long time
• *She gazed at him in amazement.*

**gaze** NOUN gazes
a long steady look

**gazelle** NOUN gazelles or gazelle
a small antelope, usually fawn and white, from Africa or Asia

**gazette** NOUN gazettes
❶ a newspaper ❷ an official journal of an organization WORD ORIGIN from Italian *gazzetta de la novità* = a halfpenny worth of news (a *gazetta* was a Venetian coin of small value)

**gazetteer** (say gaz-it-**eer**) NOUN gazetteers
a dictionary or list of place names
WORD ORIGIN originally = journalist; the first list of this kind was called *The Gazetteer's or Newsman's Interpreter*, and was intended to help journalists

**GCSE** ABBREVIATION
(*British*) General Certificate of Secondary Education

**gear** NOUN gears
❶ a set of toothed wheels in a motor vehicle that turn power from the engine into movement of the wheels ❷ equipment or apparatus • *camping gear* ❸ (*informal*) clothing

**gear** VERB gears, gearing, geared
to gear one thing to another is to make it match or be suitable for the other thing
• *Health care should be geared to people's needs, not to whether they can pay.*
➤ **be geared up** to be fully prepared or equipped for something • *We were all geared up to play cricket, but then it rained.*

**gearbox** NOUN gearboxes
a set of gears in a casing

**Geiger counter** (say **gy**-ger) NOUN Geiger counters
an instrument that detects and measures radioactivity WORD ORIGIN named after a German scientist, H. W. *Geiger*

**gel** NOUN gels
a jelly-like substance, especially one used to give a style to hair

**gelatin, gelatine** NOUN
a clear jelly-like substance made by boiling animal tissue and used to make jellies and other foods and in photographic film
➤ **gelatinous** (say jil-**at**-in-us) ADJECTIVE

**geld** VERB gelds, gelding, gelded
to castrate a male animal

**gelding** NOUN geldings
a castrated horse or other male animal

**gelignite** (say **jel**-ig-nyt) NOUN
a kind of explosive

**gem** NOUN gems
❶ a precious stone ❷ an excellent person or thing

**gender** NOUN genders
❶ the group in which a noun is classed in the grammar of some languages, e.g. masculine, feminine or neuter ❷ a person's sex • *Jobs should be open to all, regardless of race or gender.*

**gene** (say jeen) NOUN genes
the part of a living cell that controls which characteristics (such as the colour of hair or eyes) are inherited from parents

**genealogy** (say jeen-ee-**al**-o-jee) NOUN genealogies
❶ a list or diagram showing how people are descended from an ancestor ❷ the study of family history and ancestors

**genera** (say **jen**-e-ra) PLURAL NOUN
plural of **genus**

**general** ADJECTIVE
❶ to do with or involving most people or things • *This drug is now in general use.*
❷ not detailed; broad • *I've got the general idea.* ❸ chief or head • *the general manager*
➤ **in general** in most cases; usually

**general** NOUN generals
a senior army officer

**general election** NOUN general elections
an election of Members of Parliament for the whole country

**generalize** (also **generalise**) VERB
generalizes, generalizing, generalized
to make a statement that is true in most cases
➤ **generalization** NOUN

**generally** ADVERB
❶ by or to most people • *He is generally considered to be the greatest player ever.*
❷ usually • *She generally cycles to school.*
❸ in a general sense; without regard to details • *I was speaking generally.*

**general practitioner** NOUN general practitioners
a doctor who treats all kinds of diseases and is the first doctor that people see when they are ill

**generate** VERB generates, generating, generated
to produce or create something • *There are various ways of generating electricity.*

**generation** NOUN generations
❶ generating something ❷ a single stage in a family • *Three generations were included: children, parents and grandparents.* ❸ all the people born at about the same time • *our parents' generation*

**generator** NOUN generators
a machine for converting mechanical energy into electricity

**generic** (say jin-e-rik) ADJECTIVE
belonging to a whole class, group or genus

**generosity** NOUN
the quality of being generous • *He was known for his generosity.*

**generous** ADJECTIVE
❶ willing to give things or share them
❷ given freely; larger than usual • *a generous helping*
➤ **generously** ADVERB

**genesis** NOUN
the beginning or origin of something

**genetic** (say jin-et-ik) ADJECTIVE
❶ to do with genes ❷ to do with characteristics inherited from parents or ancestors
➤ **genetically** ADVERB

**genetics** NOUN
the study of genes and genetic behaviour

**genial** (say jee-nee-al) ADJECTIVE
friendly and cheerful • *a genial manner*
➤ **genially** ADVERB
➤ **geniality** (say jee-nee-al-it-ee) NOUN

**genie** (say jee-nee) NOUN genii (say jee-nee-y)
in Arabian tales, a spirit with strange powers, especially one who can grant wishes

**genital** (say jen-it-al) ADJECTIVE
to do with the reproductive organs of a person or animal

**genitals** (say jen-it-alz) PLURAL NOUN
external reproductive organs

**genius** NOUN geniuses
❶ an unusually clever person; a person with very great creativity or natural ability
❷ unusual cleverness; very great creativity or natural ability • *He has a real genius for music.*

**genocide** (say jen-o-syd) NOUN
the deliberate killing of large numbers of people from a particular nation or ethnic group

**genome** (say jen-ohm) NOUN genomes
(*in science*) the complete set of genes in one cell of a living thing • *the human genome*

**genre** (say zhahnr) NOUN genres
a particular kind or style of art or literature, e.g. epic, romance or western

**gent** NOUN gents (*informal*)
a gentleman; a man

**genteel** (say jen-teel) ADJECTIVE
trying to seem polite and refined
➤ **gentility** (say jen-til-it-ee) NOUN

**gentile** NOUN gentiles
a person who is not Jewish

**gentle** ADJECTIVE
❶ mild or kind; not rough ❷ not harsh or severe • *a gentle breeze*
➤ **gentleness** NOUN

**gentleman** NOUN gentlemen
❶ a well-mannered or honourable man ❷ a man of good social position ❸ (*in polite use*) a man

**gently** ADVERB
in a gentle way • *She kissed him gently on the forehead.* • *'We have to go now,' he said gently.*

**gentry** PLURAL NOUN (old use)
upper-class people

**genuine** ADJECTIVE
❶ real; not faked or pretending ❷ sincere and honest
➤ **genuinely** ADVERB
➤ **genuineness** NOUN
WORD ORIGIN from Latin *genu* = knee (because a father would take a baby onto his knee to show that he accepted it as his)

**genus** (say jee-nus) NOUN genera (say jen-er-a)
a group of similar animals or plants • *Lions and tigers belong to the same genus.*

**geo-** PREFIX
earth WORD ORIGIN from Greek *ge* = earth

**geographical** ADJECTIVE
to do with geography or where something is • *The Roman empire covered a vast geographical area.*
➤ **geographically** ADVERB

**geography** (say jee-og-ra-fee) NOUN
the study of the earth's surface and of its climate, peoples and products
➤ **geographer** NOUN

**geology** (say jee-ol-o-jee) NOUN
the study of the structure of the earth's crust and its layers
➤ **geological** ADJECTIVE
➤ **geologically** ADVERB
➤ **geologist** NOUN

**geometric, geometrical** ADJECTIVE
consisting of regular shapes and lines • *a geometric pattern*

**geometry** (say jee-om-it-ree) NOUN
the study of lines, angles, surfaces and solids in mathematics

**Georgian** ADJECTIVE
belonging to the time of the British kings George I-IV (1714-1830) or George V-VI (1910-52)

**geranium** NOUN geraniums
a garden plant with red, pink or white flowers

**gerbil** (say jer-bil) NOUN gerbils
a small brown rodent with long hind legs, often kept as a pet

**geriatric** (say je-ree-at-rik) ADJECTIVE
to do with the care of old people and their health

**germ** NOUN germs
❶ a micro-organism, especially one that can cause disease ❷ a tiny living structure from which a plant or animal may develop ❸ part of the seed of a cereal plant ❹ a first stage from which something might develop • *Rick had the germ of an idea.*

**Germanic** NOUN
❶ a group of languages spoken in northern Europe and Scandinavia ❷ an unrecorded language believed to be the ancestor of this group

**German measles** NOUN
rubella

**German shepherd dog** NOUN German shepherd dogs
a large strong dog, often used by the police

**germicide** NOUN germicides
a substance that kills germs

**germinate** VERB germinates, germinating, germinated
when a seed germinates, it begins to develop and roots and shoots grow from it
➤ **germination** NOUN

**gerund** (say je-rund) NOUN gerunds
(*in grammar*) a form of a verb (in English ending in *-ing*) that functions as a noun, e.g. *telling* in *do you mind my telling her?*

**gestation** (say jes-tay-shun) NOUN
the process of carrying a foetus in the womb between conception and birth; the time this takes

**gesticulate** (say jes-tik-yoo-layt) VERB gesticulates, gesticulating, gesticulated
to make movements with your hands and arms in order to express something • *The farmer began gesticulating wildly and shouting.*
➤ **gesticulation** NOUN

**gesture** (say jes-cher) NOUN gestures
❶ a movement that expresses what a person feels ❷ an action that shows goodwill • *It would be a nice gesture to send her some flowers.*

**gesture** VERB gestures, gesturing, gestured
to tell a person something by making a gesture • *She gestured me to be quiet.*

**get** VERB gets, getting, got
❶ to obtain or receive something • *She*

got first prize. **②** to become • *Don't get angry!* **③** to reach a place • *We got there by midnight.* **④** to put or move something into position • *I can't get my shoe on.* **⑤** to make or prepare something • *Will you get the tea?* **⑥** to persuade or order someone to do something • *How did you get her to say yes?* **⑦** to catch or suffer from an illness **⑧** (*informal*) to understand something • *I don't get that joke.*
> **get away with something** **①** to escape with something **②** to avoid being punished for what you have done
> **get by** (*informal*) to manage
> **get on** **①** to make progress **②** to be friendly with someone
> **get out of something** to avoid having to do something
> **get over something** to recover from an illness or shock
> **get up** **①** to stand up **②** to get out of bed in the morning
> **get your own back** (*informal*) to have your revenge
> **have got to** must • *We have got to go now.*

**getaway** *NOUN* **getaways**
an escape after committing a crime • *They made their getaway in a stolen car.*

**geyser** (say **gee**-zer or **gy**-zer) *NOUN* **geysers**
**①** a natural spring that shoots up columns of hot water **②** a kind of water heater

**ghastly** *ADJECTIVE*
**①** very unpleasant or bad • *It's all been a ghastly mistake.* **②** looking pale and ill

**gherkin** (say **ger**-kin) *NOUN* **gherkins**
a small cucumber used for pickling

**ghetto** (say **get**-oh) *NOUN* **ghettos**
an area of a city, often a slum area, where a group of people live who are treated unfairly in comparison with others

**ghost** *NOUN* **ghosts**
the spirit of a dead person that a living person believes they can see or hear

**SPELLING**
There is a silent **h** after the **g** in **ghost**.

**ghostly** *ADJECTIVE*
looking or sounding like a ghost • *ghostly shadows*

**ghoul** (say **gool**) *NOUN* **ghouls**
an evil spirit in stories that eats dead bodies
**WORD ORIGIN** from Arabic *gul* = a demon that eats dead bodies

**ghoulish** (say **gool**-ish) *ADJECTIVE*
enjoying watching ot thinking about things to do with death, murder and suffering
> **ghoulishly** *ADVERB*

**giant** *NOUN* **giants**
**①** (in myths or fairy tales) a creature like a huge man **②** a man, animal or plant that is much larger than the usual size

**giant** *ADJECTIVE*
much larger than the usual size

**gibber** (say **jib**-er) *VERB* **gibbers, gibbering, gibbered**
to speak very quickly without making sense, especially when shocked or terrified

**gibberish** (say **jib**-er-ish) *NOUN*
meaningless speech; nonsense • *You were talking gibberish in your sleep.*

**gibbet** (say **jib**-it) *NOUN* **gibbets**
**①** a gallows **②** an upright post with an arm from which a criminal's body was hung after execution, as a warning to others

**gibbon** *NOUN* **gibbons**
a small ape from south-east Asia. Gibbons have very long arms to help them swing through the trees where they live

**giblets** (say **jib**-lits) *PLURAL NOUN*
the parts of the inside of a bird, such as the heart, liver, etc., that are taken out before it is cooked

**giddy** *ADJECTIVE*
**①** feeling that everything is spinning round and that you might fall **②** causing this feeling • *We looked down from the giddy height of the cliff.*
> **giddily** *ADVERB*
> **giddiness** *NOUN*

**gift** *NOUN* **gifts**
**①** a present **②** a natural talent • *She has a gift for music.*

**gifted** *ADJECTIVE*
having a special talent or ability • *a gifted songwriter*

**gig** *NOUN* **gigs** (*informal*)
a live performance by a musician, comedian, etc.

**gigabyte** (say **gi**-ga-byt) *NOUN* **gigabytes**
(*in computing*) a unit of information equal to one thousand million bytes or (more precisely) 230 bytes

**gigantic** (say jy-**gan**-tik) *ADJECTIVE*
extremely large; huge

**giggle** VERB giggles, giggling, giggled
to laugh in a silly way

**giggle** NOUN giggles
❶ a silly laugh ❷ (informal) something amusing; a bit of fun

**gild** VERB gilds, gilding, gilded
to cover something with a thin layer of gold or gold paint

**gills** PLURAL NOUN
the part of the body through which fish and certain other water animals breathe

**gilt** NOUN
a thin covering of gold or gold paint

**gilt** ADJECTIVE
gilded; gold-coloured

**gimlet** NOUN gimlets
a small tool with a screw-like tip for boring holes

**gimmick** NOUN gimmicks
something unusual or silly done or used just to attract people's attention

**gin** NOUN gins
❶ a clear alcoholic drink flavoured with juniper berries ❷ a machine for separating the fibres of the cotton plant from its seeds

**ginger** NOUN
❶ the hot-tasting root of a tropical plant or a flavouring made from this root, used especially in drinks and Eastern cooking ❷ a reddish-yellow colour

**ginger** ADJECTIVE
reddish-yellow • ginger hair

**ginger** VERB gingers, gingering, gingered
to make something more lively or exciting • This will ginger things up!

**gingerbread** NOUN
a ginger-flavoured cake or biscuit

**gingerly** ADVERB
in a cautious or careful way • He gingerly tiptoed towards the door.

**gipsy** NOUN gipsies
a different spelling of **gypsy**

**giraffe** NOUN giraffe or giraffes
an African animal with long legs and a very long neck, the world's tallest mammal

**gird** (say gerd) VERB girds, girding, girded
❶ to fasten something with a belt or band • He girded on his sword. ❷ to prepare for an effort • It is time to gird yourself for action.

**girder** NOUN girders
a metal beam supporting part of a building or a bridge

**girdle** NOUN girdles
❶ a belt or cord worn round the waist ❷ a woman's elastic corset covering from the waist to the thigh

**girl** NOUN girls
❶ a female child ❷ a young woman

**girlfriend** NOUN girlfriends
a person's regular female friend or lover

**girlhood** NOUN
the time when a woman was a girl • She used to tell us stories of her girlhood.

**girlish** ADJECTIVE
like a girl or suitable for a girl • a girlish giggle

**giro** (say jy-roh) NOUN
a system of sending money directly from one bank account or post office account to another

**girth** NOUN girths
❶ the measurement round something, especially a person's waist • a man of enormous girth ❷ a band passing under a horse's body to hold the saddle in place

**gist** (say jist) NOUN
the essential points or general sense of what someone says

**give** VERB gives, giving, gave, given
❶ to let someone have something ❷ to make or do something • He gave a little laugh. ❸ to present or perform something • They gave a concert to raise money. ❹ be flexible or springy; to bend or collapse when pressed • The branch began to give under my weight.
➤ **giver** NOUN
➤ **give in** to accept that you have been defeated
➤ **give up** ❶ to stop trying ❷ to end a habit
➤ **give something up** to stop doing or using something

**given** ADJECTIVE
named or stated in advance • Work out how much you can do in a given time.

**gizzard** NOUN gizzards
a bird's second stomach, in which food is ground up

**glacé** (say glas-ay) ADJECTIVE
iced with sugar; crystallized

**glacial** (say glay-shal) ADJECTIVE
❶ made of ice or formed by glaciers • a

a
b
c
d
e
f
g
h
i
j
k
l
m
n
o
p
q
r
s
t
u
v
w
x
y
z

glacial landscape ❷ icy or very cold • *glacial winds*

**glaciation** (say glay-see-**ay**-shun) *NOUN*
the process or state of being covered with glaciers or ice sheets
➤ **glaciated** *ADJECTIVE*

**glacier** (say **glas**-ee-er) *NOUN* glaciers
a mass of ice that moves very slowly down a mountain valley

**glad** *ADJECTIVE*
❶ pleased or happy; expressing joy ❷ giving pleasure or happiness • *We've heard the glad news.* ❸ to be glad of something is to be grateful for it or pleased with it
➤ **gladness** *NOUN*

**gladden** *VERB* gladdens, gladdening, gladdened
to make a person glad

**glade** *NOUN* glades
an open space in a forest

**gladiator** (say **glad**-ee-ay-ter) *NOUN* gladiators
a man trained to fight for public entertainment in ancient Rome
➤ **gladiatorial** (say glad-ee-at-**or**-ee-al) *ADJECTIVE*

**gladly** *ADVERB*
with pleasure or willingly • *I gladly accept your invitation.*

**glamorize** (also **glamorise**) *VERB* glamorizes, glamorizing, glamorized
to make something seem glamorous or romantic

**glamorous** *ADJECTIVE*
excitingly attractive • *glamorous movie stars*

**glamour** *NOUN*
exciting attractiveness or romantic charm • *the glamour of Hollywood*

**glance** *VERB* glances, glancing, glanced
❶ to look at something briefly ❷ to strike something at an angle and slide off it • *The ball glanced off his bat.*

**glance** *NOUN* glances
a quick look • *The sisters exchanged glances.*

**gland** *NOUN* glands
an organ of the body that separates substances from the blood so that they can be used or passed out of the body
➤ **glandular** *ADJECTIVE*

**glare** *VERB* glares, glaring, glared
❶ to stare angrily or fiercely at someone ❷ to shine with a bright or dazzling light

**glare** *NOUN* glares
❶ an angry stare ❷ a strong light

**glaring** *ADJECTIVE*
very obvious • *a glaring error*

**glass** *NOUN* glasses
❶ a hard brittle substance that is usually transparent ❷ a container made of glass for drinking from ❸ (*old use*) a mirror

**glasses** *PLURAL NOUN*
a pair of lenses in a frame, worn over the eyes to help improve eyesight

**glassy** *ADJECTIVE*
❶ like glass; smooth and shiny • *a glassy lake* ❷ dull; without liveliness or expression • *He gave a glassy stare.*

**glaze** *VERB* glazes, glazing, glazed
❶ to fit a window or building with glass ❷ to give a shiny surface to pottery or food ❸ your eyes glaze when they lose expression or interest

**glaze** *NOUN* glazes
a shiny surface or coating, especially on pottery or food

**glazier** (say **glay**-zee-er) *NOUN* glaziers
a person whose job is to fit glass in windows

**gleam** *NOUN* gleams
❶ a beam of soft light, especially one that comes and goes ❷ a small amount of hope, humour, etc.

**gleam** *VERB* gleams, gleaming, gleamed
to shine brightly, especially after cleaning or polishing

**glean** *VERB* gleans, gleaning, gleaned
❶ to gather information bit by bit • *I gleaned as much information as I could from the Internet.* ❷ to pick up grain left by harvesters

**glee** *NOUN*
great delight • *He rubbed his hands in glee.*
➤ **gleeful** *ADJECTIVE*
➤ **gleefully** *ADVERB*

**glen** *NOUN* glens
a narrow valley, especially in Scotland

**glib** *ADJECTIVE*
speaking or writing fluently but not sincerely or thoughtfully
➤ **glibly** *ADVERB*

**glide** *VERB* glides, gliding, glided
❶ to move along smoothly • *The dancers glided across the floor.* ❷ to fly without using an engine ❸ birds glide when they fly without

beating their wings
➤ **glide** NOUN

**glider** NOUN gliders
an aircraft without an engine that flies by
floating on warm air currents called thermals

**glimmer** NOUN glimmers
❶ a faint light that flickers ❷ a small sign or
trace of something • *a glimmer of hope*

**glimmer** VERB glimmers, glimmering,
glimmered
to shine with a faint, flickering light • *The
candle glimmered in the corner.*

**glimpse** NOUN glimpses
a brief view of something • *He caught a
glimpse of her in the crowd.*

**glimpse** VERB glimpses, glimpsing, glimpsed
to see something briefly

**glint** NOUN glints
a very brief flash of light

**glint** VERB glints, glinting, glinted
to shine with small flashes of light • *His sword
glinted in the moonlight.*

**glisten** (say **glis**-en) VERB glistens, glistening,
glistened
to shine like something wet or oily • *Her eyes
glistened with tears.*

**glitter** VERB glitters, glittering, glittered
to shine with tiny flashes of light; to sparkle
• *The river glittered in the sunlight.*

**glitter** NOUN
tiny sparkling pieces used for decoration

**gloaming** NOUN
(*Scottish*) the evening twilight

**gloat** VERB gloats, gloating, gloated
to be pleased in an unkind way that you have
succeeded or that someone else has failed or
had problems

**global** ADJECTIVE
❶ to do with the whole world; worldwide
❷ to do with the whole of a system
➤ **globally** ADVERB

**globalization** (also **globalisation**) NOUN
the fact that different economies and
cultures around the world are becoming
connected and similar to each other because
of improved communication and the
influence of very large companies

**global warming** NOUN
the increase in the temperature of the earth's
atmosphere, caused by the greenhouse effect

**globe** NOUN globes
❶ something shaped like a ball, especially one
with a map of the whole world on it ❷ the
world • *She has travelled all over the globe.*
❸ a hollow round glass object

**globular** (say **glob**-yoo-ler) ADJECTIVE
shaped like a globe

**globule** (say **glob**-yool) NOUN globules
a small rounded drop

**gloom** NOUN
❶ darkness • *He peered into the gathering
gloom.* ❷ sadness or despair

**gloomy** ADJECTIVE gloomier, gloomiest
❶ almost dark; not well lit • *a gloomy
corridor* ❷ depressed or depressing
➤ **gloomily** ADVERB
➤ **gloominess** NOUN

**glorify** VERB glorifies, glorifying, glorified
❶ to give great praise or great honour to
someone ❷ to make a thing seem more
splendid or attractive than it really is • *It is a
film that glorifies war.*

**glorious** ADJECTIVE
splendid or magnificent
➤ **gloriously** ADVERB

**glory** NOUN glories
❶ fame and honour you get for achieving
something • *The team was welcomed home
in a blaze of glory.* ❷ praise and worship of
God ❸ beauty or magnificence

**glory** VERB glories, glorying, gloried
to rejoice over an achievement and take great
pride in it • *They gloried in victory.*

**gloss** NOUN glosses
the shine on a smooth surface

**gloss** VERB glosses, glossing, glossed
➤ **gloss over something** to mention a fault
or mistake only briefly to make it seem less
serious than it really is

**glossary** NOUN glossaries
a list of difficult words with their meanings
explained • *There is a glossary at the back of
the book.*

**gloss paint** NOUN gloss paints
a paint with a glossy finish

**glossy** ADJECTIVE glossier, glossiest
smooth and shiny • *glossy hair*

**glove** NOUN gloves
a covering for the hand, usually with separate
divisions for each finger and thumb
➤ **gloved** ADJECTIVE

a
b
c
d
e
f
g
h
i
j
k
l
m
n
o
p
q
r
s
t
u
v
w
x
y
z

**glow** NOUN
❶ brightness and warmth without flames ❷ a warm or cheerful feeling • *We felt a glow of pride.*

**glow** VERB glows, glowing, glowed
to shine with a soft, warm light • *Her watch glows in the dark.*

**glower** (rhymes with flower) VERB glowers, glowering, glowered
to stare with an angry look; to scowl

**glowing** ADJECTIVE
very enthusiastic or favourable • *a glowing report*

**glow-worm** NOUN glow-worms
a kind of beetle whose tail gives out a green light

**glucose** NOUN
a form of sugar found in fruit juice and honey

**glue** NOUN glues
a sticky substance used for joining things together
➤ **gluey** ADJECTIVE

**glue** VERB glues, gluing, glued
❶ to stick something with glue ❷ to be glued to something is to pay close attention to it for a long period • *Our eyes were glued to the screen all evening.*

**glum** ADJECTIVE
miserable or depressed • *Hey, don't look so glum.*
➤ **glumly** ADVERB

**glut** NOUN gluts
more of something than is needed • *a glut of action films in cinemas*

**gluten** (say gloo-ten) NOUN
a sticky protein substance in flour

**glutinous** (say gloo-tin-us) ADJECTIVE
glue-like or sticky

**glutton** NOUN gluttons
a person who eats too much
➤ **gluttonous** ADJECTIVE
➤ **a glutton for punishment** a person who seems to enjoy doing something difficult or unpleasant

**gluttony** NOUN
eating too much

**glycerine** (say glis-er-een) NOUN
a thick sweet colourless liquid used in ointments and medicines and in explosives

**gm** ABBREVIATION
gram

**GMT** ABBREVIATION
Greenwich Mean Time

**gnarled** (say narld) ADJECTIVE
twisted and knobbly, like an old tree • *the old man's gnarled hands*

> SPELLING

There is a silent **g** in **gnarled, gnash, gnat, gnaw, gnome** and **gnu.**

**gnash** (say nash) VERB gnashes, gnashing, gnashed
to grind your teeth together, especially because you are angry

**gnat** (say nat) NOUN gnats
a tiny fly that bites

**gnaw** (say naw) VERB gnaws, gnawing, gnawed
to keep on biting something hard so that it wears away

**gnome** (say nohm) NOUN gnomes
a kind of dwarf in fairy tales, usually living underground

**gnu** (say noo) NOUN gnu or gnus
a large ox-like antelope

**go** VERB goes, going, went, gone
This word has many uses, including
❶ to move or travel from one place to another • *Where are you going?* ❷ to leave • *I must go.* ❸ to disappear or be used up • *Has your headache gone yet?* • *Most of their money went on rent.* ❹ to lead from one place to another • *This road goes to the coast.* ❺ to become • *The milk has gone sour.* ❻ to make a sound • *The gun went bang.* ❼ to work properly • *This clock doesn't go.* ❽ to belong in some place or position • *Plates go on that shelf.* ❾ to be sold • *The house went very cheaply.*
➤ **go off** ❶ to explode ❷ to become stale
➤ **go off something** to stop liking something
➤ **go on** to continue or happen
➤ **go out** to stop burning or shining
➤ **go through** to experience something unpleasant or difficult

**go** NOUN goes
❶ a turn or try • *May I have a go?*
❷ (*informal*) energy or liveliness • *She is full of go.*
➤ **make a go of something** to be successful at something
➤ **on the go** active; always working or moving

**goad** NOUN goads
a stick with a pointed end for prodding cattle to move onwards

**goad** *VERB* goads, goading, goaded
to stir someone into action by being annoying
• *He goaded me into fighting.*

**go-ahead** *NOUN*
permission to do something • *We have been given the go-ahead to paint a mural in the gym.*

**goal** *NOUN* goals
❶ the area between two posts where a ball must go to score a point in football, hockey, etc. ❷ a successful shot at goal, scoring a point ❸ something that you are trying to reach or achieve

**goalkeeper** *NOUN* goalkeepers
the player in football or hockey who stands in the goal and tries to keep the ball out

**goat** *NOUN* goats
a mammal with horns and a beard, closely related to the sheep. Domestic goats are kept for their milk.

**gobble** *VERB* gobbles, gobbling, gobbled
to eat something quickly and greedily • *We soon gobbled up all the sandwiches.*

**gobbledegook** *NOUN* (*informal*)
pompous and technical language that is difficult to understand, especially in official documents

**go-between** *NOUN* go-betweens
a person who acts as a messenger or negotiator between others

**goblet** *NOUN* goblets
a drinking glass with a long stem and a base

**goblin** *NOUN* goblins
a mischievous ugly elf in stories

**God** *NOUN*
the creator of the universe in many religions

**god** *NOUN* gods
a male being that is worshipped • *Mars was a Roman god.*

**godchild** *NOUN* godchildren
a child that a godparent promises to see brought up as a Christian
➤ **god-daughter** *NOUN*
➤ **godson** *NOUN*

**goddess** *NOUN* goddesses
a female being that is worshipped

SPELLING

There is a double **d** and double **s** in **goddess**.

**godly** *ADJECTIVE* godlier, godliest
sincerely religious
➤ **godliness** *NOUN*

**godparent** *NOUN* godparents
a person at a child's christening who promises to see that it is brought up as a Christian
➤ **godfather** *NOUN*
➤ **godmother** *NOUN*

**godsend** *NOUN* godsends
a piece of unexpected good luck

**gogga** *NOUN* goggas (*informal*)
(*S. African*) an insect or any small flying or crawling creature

**goggle** *VERB* goggles, goggling, goggled
to stare with wide-open eyes

**goggles** *PLURAL NOUN*
large glasses that you wear to protect your eyes from wind, water, dust, etc.

**going**
present participle of **go**
➤ **be going to do something** to be ready or likely to do it

**going** *NOUN*
➤ **good going** quick progress • *It was good going to get home before dark.*

**go-kart** *NOUN* go-karts
a kind of small lightweight racing car

**gold** *NOUN* golds
❶ a precious yellow metal ❷ a deep yellow colour ❸ a gold medal, awarded as first prize

**gold** *ADJECTIVE*
❶ made of gold ❷ deep yellow in colour

**golden** *ADJECTIVE*
❶ made of gold ❷ coloured like gold ❸ precious or excellent • *It was a golden opportunity.*

**golden wedding** *NOUN* golden weddings
a couple's fiftieth wedding anniversary

**goldfinch** *NOUN* goldfinches
a bird with yellow feathers in its wings

**goldfish** *NOUN* goldfish
a small red or orange fish, often kept as a pet

**gold leaf** *NOUN*
gold that has been beaten into a very thin sheet

**goldsmith** *NOUN* goldsmiths
a person who makes things in gold

**golf** *NOUN*
an outdoor game played by hitting a small white ball with a club into a series of holes on

299

a
b
c
d
e
f
g
h
i
j
k
l
m
n
o
p
q
r
s
t
u
v
w
x
y
z

a specially prepared ground (a **golf course**) and taking as few strokes as possible
➤ **golfing** NOUN

**golfer** NOUN golfers
a person who plays golf

**gondola** (say gond-ol-a) NOUN gondolas
a boat with high pointed ends used on the canals in Venice

**gondolier** NOUN gondoliers
the person who moves a gondola along with a pole

**gone**
past participle of go

**gone** ADJECTIVE
not present any longer; completely used or finished • She stood at the gate for a moment and then she was gone. • The milk's all gone.

**gong** NOUN gongs
a large metal disc that makes an echoing sound when it is hit

**good** ADJECTIVE better, best
❶ having the right qualities; of the kind that people like • a good book ❷ kind • It was good of you to help us. ❸ well-behaved • Be a good boy. ❹ skilled or talented • a good pianist ❺ healthy; giving benefit • Exercise is good for you. ❻ thorough • Give it a good clean. ❼ large; considerable • It's a good distance from the shops.

**good** NOUN
❶ something good • They tried to do good to others. ❷ benefit or advantage • It's for your own good.
➤ **for good** for ever
➤ **no good** useless

USAGE
In standard English, good cannot be used as an adverb. You can say She's a good player but not She played good. The adverb that goes with good is well.

**goodbye** EXCLAMATION
a word used when you leave someone or at the end of a phone call

**Good Friday** NOUN
the Friday before Easter, when Christians commemorate the Crucifixion of Christ

**good-looking** ADJECTIVE
attractive or handsome

**goodness** NOUN
❶ being good ❷ the good part of something

**goods** PLURAL NOUN
❶ things that are bought and sold ❷ things that are carried on trains or lorries

**goodwill** NOUN
a kindly or helpful feeling towards another person

**goody** NOUN goodies (informal)
❶ something good or attractive, especially to eat ❷ a good person, especially one of the heroes in a story

**gooey** ADJECTIVE
sticky or slimy

**goose** NOUN geese
a long-necked water bird with webbed feet, larger than a duck

**gooseberry** NOUN gooseberries
❶ a small green fruit that grows on a prickly bush ❷ (informal) an unwanted extra person when two people want to be alone together

**goose pimples, goosebumps** PLURAL NOUN
skin that has turned rough with small bumps on it because a person is cold or afraid
WORD ORIGIN because it looks like the skin of a plucked goose

**gore** VERB gores, goring, gored
to wound a person or animal by piercing them with a horn or tusk • He was gored to death by a bull.

**gore** NOUN
thickened blood from a cut or wound

**gorge** NOUN gorges
a narrow valley with steep sides

**gorge** VERB gorges, gorging, gorged
to eat something greedily; to stuff yourself with food • We gorged ourselves on cakes.

**gorgeous** ADJECTIVE
very attractive or beautiful
➤ **gorgeously** ADVERB

**gorilla** NOUN gorillas
a large powerful African ape, the largest of all the apes
SPELLING
Take care not to confuse with guerrilla, which is a person in an unofficial army.

**gorse** NOUN
a prickly bush with small yellow flowers

**gory** ADJECTIVE
❶ involving a lot of violence and bloodshed • a gory film ❷ covered with blood

**gosh** *EXCLAMATION*
an exclamation of surprise

**gosling** *NOUN* goslings
a young goose

**gospel** *NOUN*
❶ the teachings of Jesus Christ ❷ something you can safely believe to be true • *You can take what she says as gospel.*
➤ the Gospels the first four books of the New Testament, telling of the life and teachings of Jesus Christ
**WORD ORIGIN** from Old English *god* = good + *spel* = news

**gospel music** *NOUN*
a style of black American religious singing

**gossamer** *NOUN*
❶ fine cobwebs made by small spiders ❷ any fine delicate material **WORD ORIGIN** from *goose summer*, a period of fine weather in the autumn (when geese were eaten), when gossamer is very common

**gossip** *VERB* gossips, gossiping, gossiped
to talk a lot about other people

**gossip** *NOUN* gossips
❶ talk, especially rumours, about other people ❷ a person who enjoys gossiping
➤ gossipy *ADJECTIVE*
**WORD ORIGIN** from Old English *godsibb* = close friend (literally = god-brother or sister), someone to gossip with

**got**
past tense of get
➤ have got something to possess or be carrying something • *Have you got a pen?*
➤ have got to must

**Gothic** *NOUN*
the style of building common in the 12th-16th centuries, with pointed arches and much decorative carving

**gouge** (say gowj) *VERB* gouges, gouging, gouged
to scoop or force something out by pressing • *Glaciers gouged out valleys from the hills.*

**goulash** (say goo-lash) *NOUN*
a Hungarian meat stew seasoned with paprika

**gourd** (say goord) *NOUN* gourds
the rounded hard-skinned fruit of a climbing plant

**gourmet** (say goor-may) *NOUN* gourmets
a person who knows about and enjoys good food and drink

**gout** *NOUN*
a disease that causes painful swelling in the legs and feet
➤ gouty *ADJECTIVE*

**govern** *VERB* governs, governing, governed
to be in charge of the public affairs of a country or region

**governess** *NOUN* governesses
a woman employed to teach children in a private household

**government** *NOUN* governments
❶ the group of people who are in charge of the public affairs of a country ❷ the process of governing

**governor** *NOUN* governors
❶ a person who governs a state or a colony etc. ❷ a member of the group of people who manage a school or other institution ❸ the person in charge of a prison

**gown** *NOUN* gowns
❶ a woman's long dress ❷ a loose robe worn by lawyers, members of a university, etc.

**GP** *ABBREVIATION*
general practitioner (a doctor who treats all kinds of diseases and is the first doctor that people see when they are ill)

**grab** *VERB* grabs, grabbing, grabbed
to take hold of something firmly or suddenly

**grace** *NOUN*
❶ beauty, especially of movement ❷ dignity or good manners • *At least he had the grace to apologize.* ❸ extra time that is allowed for something • *His teacher gave him a week's grace to finish his project.* ❹ a short prayer of thanks before or after a meal ❺ the title of a duke, duchess or archbishop • *His Grace the Duke of Kent*

**grace** *VERB* graces, gracing, graced
to bring honour or dignity to something • *The mayor himself graced the occasion with his presence.*

**graceful** *ADJECTIVE*
beautiful and elegant in movement or shape • *a graceful dancer*
➤ gracefully *ADVERB*
➤ gracefulness *NOUN*

**gracious** *ADJECTIVE*
generous and pleasant • *I am pleased to accept your gracious offer.*
➤ graciously *ADVERB*
➤ graciousness *NOUN*

a
b
c
d
e
f
g
h
i
j
k
l
m
n
o
p
q
r
s
t
u
v
w
x
y
z

**grade** NOUN **grades**
❶ a mark showing the quality of a student's work ❷ a step in a scale of quality or value or rank

**grade** VERB **grades, grading, graded**
to sort or divide things into grades • *The eggs are then graded by size.*

**gradient** (say gray-dee-ent) NOUN **gradients**
a slope or the steepness of a slope

**gradual** ADJECTIVE
happening slowly but steadily

**gradually** ADVERB
slowly but steadily; bit by bit • *The weather gradually improved.*

**graduate** (say grad-yoo-ayt) VERB **graduates, graduating, graduated**
❶ to get a university or college degree ❷ to divide something into graded sections; to mark something with units of measurement • *The jug is graduated in millimetres.*

**graduate** (say grad-yoo-at) NOUN **graduates**
a person who has a university or college degree

**graduation** NOUN
graduating from a university or college; a ceremony at which degrees are given out • *It was her first job after graduation.*

**graffiti** NOUN
words or drawings scribbled or sprayed on a wall **WORD ORIGIN** Italian, = scratchings

**USAGE**
Strictly speaking, this word is a plural noun and should be used with a plural verb: *There are graffiti all over the wall.* However, the word is widely used nowadays as if it were a singular noun and most people do not regard this as wrong: *There is graffiti all over the wall.*

**graft** NOUN **grafts**
❶ a shoot from one plant or tree fixed into another to form a new growth ❷ a piece of living tissue transplanted by a surgeon to replace what is diseased or damaged • *a skin graft* ❸ (*British*) (*informal*) hard work

**graft** VERB **grafts, grafting, grafted**
to insert or transplant something as a graft

**grain** NOUN **grains**
❶ a small hard seed or similar particle ❷ cereal plants when they are growing or after being harvested ❸ a very small amount • *There is a grain of truth in the story.* ❹ the

pattern of lines made by the fibres in a piece of wood or paper

**grainy** ADJECTIVE
❶ a grainy photograph or film is not clear because the image looks like it is made up of small spots • *The film is shot in grainy black and white.* ❷ with grains in it • *grainy mustard*

**gram** NOUN **grams**
a unit of mass or weight in the metric system

**grammar** NOUN **grammars**
❶ the rules for putting words together to form sentences ❷ a book about these rules
**SPELLING**
The 'er' sound at the end of **grammar** is spelt **ar**.

**grammar school** NOUN **grammar schools**
a secondary school for children with high academic ability

**grammatical** ADJECTIVE
following the rules of grammar
➤ **grammatically** ADVERB

**gramophone** NOUN **gramophones**
(*old use*) a record player

**granary** NOUN **granaries**
a storehouse for grain

**grand** ADJECTIVE
❶ large and impressive ❷ most important or highest-ranking ❸ (*informal*) very good or pleasant • *You've done a grand job!*
➤ **grandly** ADVERB

**grandad** NOUN **grandads** (*informal*)
grandfather

**grandchild** NOUN **grandchildren**
the child of a person's son or daughter
➤ **granddaughter** NOUN
➤ **grandson** NOUN

**grandeur** (say grand-yer) NOUN
impressive beauty; splendour • *the grandeur of the Rocky Mountains*

**grandfather** NOUN **grandfathers**
the father of a person's father or mother

**grandfather clock** NOUN **grandfather clocks**
a clock in a tall wooden case

**grandiose** (say grand-ee-ohss) ADJECTIVE
larger or more complicated than is necessary; trying to seem impressive • *a grandiose palace*

**grandma** NOUN (*informal*)
grandmother

**grandmother** NOUN grandmothers
the mother of a person's father or mother

**grandpa** NOUN (*informal*)
grandfather

**grandparent** NOUN grandparents
a grandfather or grandmother

**grand piano** NOUN grand pianos
a large piano with the strings fixed
horizontally

**grandstand** NOUN grandstands
a building with a roof and rows of seats for
spectators at a racecourse or sports ground

**grand total** NOUN
the sum of other totals

**grange** NOUN granges
a large country house

**granite** NOUN
a very hard kind of rock used for building

**granny** NOUN grannies (*informal*)
grandmother

**granny knot** NOUN granny knots
a reef knot with the strings crossed the
wrong way and therefore likely to slip

**grant** VERB grants, granting, granted
❶ to give or allow someone what they have
asked for • *We have decided to grant your
request.* ❷ to admit something or agree that
it is true • *They are a bit odd, I grant you.*
➤ **take for granted** ❶ to assume that
something is true or will happen ❷ to be so
used to having something that you no longer
appreciate it

**grant** NOUN grants
a sum of money awarded for a special
purpose

**Granth** (say grunt) NOUN
the sacred scriptures of the Sikhs

**granulated sugar** NOUN
white sugar in the form of small grains

**granule** NOUN granules
a small grain; a small hard piece of something

**grape** NOUN grapes
a small green or purple berry that grows in
bunches on a vine. Grapes are used to make
wine

**grapefruit** NOUN grapefruit
a large round yellow citrus fruit

**grapevine** NOUN grapevines
❶ a vine on which grapes grow ❷ a way by
which news spreads unofficially, with people
passing it on from one to another • *I heard on
the grapevine that you are getting married.*

**graph** NOUN graphs
a diagram showing how two quantities or
variables are related

**grapheme** NOUN graphemes
a letter or combination of letters which can
be used to represent a sound, for example *f*
and *ph* to represent the same sound at the
beginning of the words *face* and *phase*

**graphic** ADJECTIVE
❶ to do with drawing or painting • *a graphic
artist* ❷ very detailed and lively • *a graphic
description of the battle*
➤ **graphically** ADVERB

**graphics** PLURAL NOUN
diagrams, lettering and drawings, especially
pictures that are produced by a computer

**graphite** NOUN
a soft black form of carbon used for the
lead in pencils, as a lubricant and in nuclear
reactors

**graph paper** NOUN
paper printed with small squares, used for
drawing graphs

**grapnel** NOUN grapnels
a heavy metal device with claws for hooking
things

**grapple** VERB grapples, grappling, grappled
❶ to struggle or wrestle with someone ❷ to
seize or hold something firmly ❸ to try to
deal with a problem • *I've been grappling
with this essay all day.*

**grasp** VERB grasps, grasping, grasped
❶ to seize something and hold it firmly ❷ to
understand something

**grasp** NOUN
❶ a person's understanding of something • *a
good grasp of electronics* ❷ a firm hold • *The
sword slipped from his grasp and fell to the
floor.*

**grasping** ADJECTIVE
greedy for money or possessions

**grass** NOUN grasses
❶ a plant with green blades and stalks that
are eaten by animals ❷ ground covered with
grass; lawn

**grasshopper** NOUN grasshoppers
a jumping insect that makes a shrill noise

**grassland** NOUN grasslands
a wide area covered in grass with few trees

**grass roots** PLURAL NOUN
the ordinary people in a political party or
other group

**grassy** ADJECTIVE
covered with grass • *grassy slopes*

**grate** NOUN grates
❶ a metal framework that keeps fuel in a
fireplace ❷ a fireplace

**grate** VERB grates, grating, grated
❶ to shred something into small pieces by
rubbing it on a rough surface ❷ to make a
harsh sound by rubbing on something • *Her
nails grated against the window.*
➤ **grate on someone** to have an irritating
effect on someone • *His voice really grates
on me.*

**grateful** ADJECTIVE
feeling or showing that you want to thank
someone for what they have done for you
➤ **gratefully** ADVERB

**grater** NOUN graters
a device with a jagged surface for grating
food

**gratify** VERB gratifies, gratifying, gratified
❶ to give pleasure to someone ❷ to satisfy a
feeling or desire • *Please gratify our curiosity.*
➤ **gratifying** ADJECTIVE
➤ **gratification** NOUN

**grating** NOUN gratings
a framework of metal bars placed across an
opening

**gratis** (say grah-tiss) ADVERB & ADJECTIVE
free of charge • *You can have the leaflet
gratis.* **WORD ORIGIN** Latin, = out of kindness

**gratitude** NOUN
a feeling of being grateful • *I would like to
express my gratitude.*

**gratuitous** (say gra-tew-it-us) ADJECTIVE
done without good reason; uncalled for
➤ **gratuitously** ADVERB

**grave** NOUN graves
the place where a dead person is buried

**grave** ADJECTIVE
serious or solemn • *She told him he was in
grave danger.*

**grave accent** (rhymes with starve) NOUN
grave accents

a backward-sloping mark over a vowel, as in
*vis-à-vis*

**gravel** NOUN
small stones mixed with coarse sand, used to
make paths
➤ **gravelled** ADJECTIVE

**gravelly** ADJECTIVE
❶ a gravelly voice is deep and rough-
sounding ❷ containing many small stones
• *gravelly soil*

**gravely** ADVERB
seriously or solemnly • *He is gravely ill.* • *She
nodded gravely.*

**gravestone** NOUN gravestones
a stone monument put over a grave

**graveyard** NOUN graveyards
a burial ground

**gravitate** VERB gravitates, gravitating,
gravitated
to move or be attracted towards something

**gravitation** NOUN
the force of gravity
➤ **gravitational** ADJECTIVE

**gravity** NOUN
❶ the force that pulls all objects in the
universe towards each other ❷ the force that
pulls everything towards the earth ❸ the
seriousness or importance of something • *I
don't think you understand the gravity of the
situation.*

**gravy** NOUN
a hot brown sauce made from meat juices

**graze** VERB grazes, grazing, grazed
❶ animals graze when they feed on growing
grass ❷ to scrape your skin slightly • *I grazed
my elbow on the wall.* ❸ to touch something
lightly in passing

**graze** NOUN grazes
a raw place where skin has been scraped

**grease** NOUN
❶ any thick oily substance ❷ melted fat

**grease** VERB greases, greasing, greased
to put grease on something

**greasy** ADJECTIVE greasier, greasiest
oily like grease • *greasy hair*

**great** ADJECTIVE
❶ very large; much above average • *The
party was a great success.* ❷ very important
or talented • *a great composer* ❸ (informal)
very good or enjoyable • *It's great to see you
again.* ❹ older or younger by one generation

• *great-grandfather*
➤ **greatness** NOUN

**Great Britain** NOUN
the island made up of England, Scotland and Wales, with the small islands close to it

USAGE
See the note at **Britain**.

**greatly** ADVERB
very much • *I am greatly relieved to see you.*

**grebe** (say greeb) NOUN grebes
a kind of diving bird

**greed** NOUN
being greedy • *Nothing would satisfy his greed for power.*

**greedy** ADJECTIVE greedier, greediest
wanting more food, money or other things than you need
➤ **greedily** ADVERB

**green** NOUN greens
❶ the colour of grass, leaves, etc. ❷ an area of grassy land • *the village green* • *a putting green*

**green** ADJECTIVE
❶ of the colour green ❷ concerned with protecting the natural environment ❸ inexperienced and likely to make mistakes
➤ **greenness** NOUN

**green belt** NOUN green belts
an area kept as open land round a city

**greenery** NOUN
green leaves or plants

**greenfield** ADJECTIVE
(*British*) a greenfield site is a piece of land that has not yet had buildings on it, though there may be plans to build on it. Compare with **brownfield**.

**greenfly** NOUN greenfly
a small green insect that feeds on and damages plants

**greengrocer** NOUN greengrocers
(*British*) a person who keeps a shop that sells fruit and vegetables
➤ **greengrocery** NOUN

**greenhouse** NOUN greenhouses
a glass building where plants are protected from cold

**greenhouse effect** NOUN
the warming up of the earth's surface when heat from the sun is trapped in the earth's atmosphere by gases such as carbon dioxide and methane

**greenhouse gas** NOUN greenhouse gases
any of the gases, especially carbon dioxide and methane, that are found in the earth's atmosphere and contribute to the greenhouse effect

**greens** PLURAL NOUN
green vegetables, such as cabbage and spinach

**Greenwich Mean Time** (say **gren**-ich) NOUN
the time on the line of longitude which passes through Greenwich in London, used as a basis for calculating time throughout the world

**greet** VERB greets, greeting, greeted
❶ to say hello to someone or to welcome them when they arrive ❷ to receive something in a certain way • *They greeted the song with applause.* ❸ to be the first thing that you notice • *A strange sight greeted our eyes.*

**greeting** NOUN greetings
words or actions used to greet someone

**greetings** PLURAL NOUN
good wishes • *a greetings card*

**gregarious** (say grig-**air**-ee-us) ADJECTIVE
❶ fond of company ❷ living in flocks or communities WORD ORIGIN from Latin *gregis* = of a herd

**grenade** (say grin-**ayd**) NOUN grenades
a small bomb thrown by hand
WORD ORIGIN from old French *pome grenate* = pomegranate (because of the shape of the grenade)

**grey** NOUN greys
the colour between black and white, like ashes or dark clouds

**grey** ADJECTIVE
of the colour grey
➤ **greyness** NOUN

**greyhound** NOUN greyhounds
a slender dog with smooth hair and long legs, used in racing

**grid** NOUN grids
❶ a framework or pattern of bars or lines crossing each other ❷ a network of cables or wires for carrying electricity over a large area

**griddle** NOUN griddles
a round iron plate for cooking things on

**gridiron** NOUN gridirons
a framework of bars for cooking on

a
b
c
d
e
f
g
h
i
j
k
l
m
n
o
p
q
r
s
t
u
v
w
x
y
z

**grid reference** NOUN grid references
a set of numbers that allows you to describe the exact position of something on a map

**grief** NOUN
deep sorrow, especially because a close relative or friend has died
➤ **come to grief** to suffer a disaster

**grievance** NOUN grievances
something that people are unhappy or angry about

**grieve** VERB grieves, grieving, grieved
❶ to feel deep sorrow, especially because a close relative or friend has died ❷ to make a person feel very sad • *It grieves me to have to tell you this.*

**grievous** (say gree-vus) ADJECTIVE
very serious • *a grievous error*
➤ **grievously** ADVERB

**griffin** NOUN griffins
a creature in fables, with an eagle's head and wings on a lion's body

**grill** NOUN grills
❶ (*British*) a heated element on a cooker, for sending heat downwards ❷ food cooked under this ❸ a grille

**grill** VERB grills, grilling, grilled
❶ (*British*) to cook food under a grill ❷ to question someone closely and severely • *The police grilled him for an hour.*

**grille** NOUN grilles
a metal grating covering a window or similar opening

**grim** ADJECTIVE grimmer, grimmest
❶ stern or severe • *She looked grim.*
❷ unpleasant or unattractive • *a grim prospect*
➤ **grimly** ADVERB
➤ **grimness** NOUN

**grimace** (say grim-ayss or grim-as) NOUN
grimaces
a twisted expression on the face made in pain or disgust

**grimace** VERB grimaces, grimacing, grimaced
to make a grimace

**grime** NOUN
dirt in a layer on a surface or on the skin

**grimy** ADJECTIVE
very dirty • *grimy windows*

**grin** NOUN grins
a broad smile showing your teeth

**grin** VERB grins, grinning, grinned
to smile broadly showing your teeth

**grind** VERB grinds, grinding, ground
❶ to crush something into tiny pieces or powder ❷ to sharpen or smooth something by rubbing it on a rough surface ❸ to grind your teeth is to rub the upper and lower teeth harshly together, often as sign of anger or impatience
➤ **grinder** NOUN
➤ **grind to a halt** to stop suddenly with a loud noise

**grindstone** NOUN grindstones
a thick round rough revolving stone for sharpening or grinding things
➤ **keep your nose to the grindstone** to keep working hard

**grip** VERB grips, gripping, gripped
❶ to hold something firmly ❷ to hold a person's attention • *The opening chapter really gripped me.*

**grip** NOUN grips
❶ a firm hold ❷ a handle, especially on a sports racket or bat ❸ a travelling bag ❹ control or power • *The country was in the grip of revolution.*
➤ **get to grips with something** to begin to deal with something successfully

**gripe** VERB gripes, griping, griped (*informal*)
to grumble or complain

**gripe** NOUN gripes (*informal*) a complaint

**gripping** ADJECTIVE
very interesting and exciting in a way that holds your attention • *This book is a gripping read.*

**grisly** ADJECTIVE grislier, grisliest
causing horror or disgust; gruesome • *a grisly murder*

**grist** NOUN
corn for grinding
➤ **grist to the mill** experience or knowledge that you can make use of

**gristle** NOUN
tough rubbery tissue in meat
➤ **gristly** ADJECTIVE

**grit** NOUN
❶ tiny pieces of stone or sand ❷ courage and determination to do something difficult
➤ **gritty** ADJECTIVE

**grit** VERB grits, gritting, gritted
to spread a road or path with grit
➤ **grit your teeth** ❶ to clench your teeth when in pain or trouble ❷ to use your

courage or determination to continue in the face of difficulty

**grizzle** VERB grizzles, grizzling, grizzled
(*British*) (*informal*) a baby or young child grizzles when it cries or whimpers

**grizzled** ADJECTIVE
streaked with grey hairs • *his grizzled beard*

**grizzly** ADJECTIVE
grey-haired

**grizzly bear** NOUN grizzly bears
a large fierce bear of North America

**groan** VERB groans, groaning, groaned
❶ to make a long deep sound in pain, distress or disapproval ❷ to creak loudly under a heavy load

**groan** NOUN groans
the sound of groaning

**grocer** NOUN grocers
a person who keeps a shop that sells food and household goods **WORD ORIGIN** originally = wholesaler; from Latin *grossus* = gross (because a wholesaler buys goods *in the gross* = in large quantities)

**groceries** PLURAL NOUN
goods sold by a grocer

**grocery** NOUN groceries
a grocer's shop

**groggy** ADJECTIVE groggier, groggiest
dizzy and unsteady, especially after illness or injury
➤ **groggily** ADVERB

**groin** NOUN
the hollow between your thigh and the trunk of the body

**groom** NOUN grooms
❶ a person whose job is to look after horses ❷ a bridegroom

**groom** VERB grooms, grooming, groomed
❶ to clean and brush a horse or other animal ❷ to make something, especially hair or a beard, neat and trim ❸ to prepare or train a person for a certain job or position • *Evans is being groomed for the captaincy.*

**groove** NOUN grooves
a long narrow furrow or channel cut in the surface of something
➤ **grooved** ADJECTIVE

**grope** VERB gropes, groping, groped
to feel about for something you cannot see
• *He groped around for the light switch.*

**gross** (say grohss) ADJECTIVE
❶ fat and ugly ❷ very obvious or shocking • *gross stupidity* ❸ having bad manners; crude or vulgar ❹ (*informal*) disgusting ❺ total; without anything being deducted • *our gross income*
Compare with **net**.

**gross** NOUN gross
twelve dozen (144) of something • *ten gross*

**grossly** ADVERB
to an extremely bad degree • *That is grossly unfair.*

**grotesque** (say groh-*tesk*) ADJECTIVE
very strange and ugly • *The dancers wore grotesque masks.*
➤ **grotesquely** ADVERB

**grotto** NOUN grottoes
❶ an attractive cave ❷ an artificial cave, especially one that is brightly decorated

**ground** NOUN grounds
❶ the solid surface of the earth ❷ a sports field ❸ land of a certain kind • *marshy ground* ❹ the amount of a subject that is dealt with • *The course covers a lot of ground.*

**ground** VERB grounds, grounding, grounded
❶ to prevent a plane from flying • *All aircraft are grounded because of the fog.* ❷ to stop a child from going out, as a punishment • *You're grounded for a week!* ❸ an idea or story is grounded on something when it is based on it • *This theory is grounded on reliable evidence.*

**ground** past tense of **grind**

**ground control** NOUN
the people and machinery that control and monitor an aircraft or spacecraft from the ground

**grounding** NOUN
basic training or instruction

**groundless** ADJECTIVE
having no good reason or cause • *Your fears are groundless.*

**grounds** PLURAL NOUN
❶ the gardens of a large house ❷ small solid pieces that sink to the bottom of a drink • *coffee grounds* ❸ good reasons • *There are grounds for suspicion.*

**groundsheet** NOUN groundsheets
(*British*) a piece of waterproof material for spreading on the ground inside a tent

a
b
c
d
e
f
g
h
i
j
k
l
m
n
o
p
q
r
s
t
u
v
w
x
y
z

**groundsman** NOUN groundsmen
(*chiefly British*) a person whose job is to look
after a sports ground

**groundwork** NOUN
work that lays the basis for something

**group** NOUN groups
❶ a number of people, animals or things that
come together or belong together in some
way ❷ a band of musicians

**group** VERB groups, grouping, grouped
to put people or things together in a group
or groups; to gather into a group • *Scientists
group together living things that share
certain features.*

**grouse** NOUN grouse
a bird with feathered feet, hunted as game

**grouse** VERB grouses, grousing, groused
(*informal*)
to grumble or complain

**grove** NOUN groves
a small wood or group of trees

**grovel** VERB grovels, grovelling, grovelled
❶ to crawl on the ground, especially in
a show of fear or humility ❷ to act in an
excessively humble way, for example by
apologizing a lot

**grow** VERB grows, growing, grew, grown
❶ to become bigger or greater ❷ a plant or
seed grows when it develops in the ground
❸ to put a plant in the ground or a pot and
look after it • *She grows roses.* ❹ to become
• *He grew rich.* • *By now it was growing dark.*
➤ **grow on someone** something grows on
you when you gradually start to like it • *This
music is definitely growing on me.*
➤ **grow up** to become an adult

**grower** NOUN growers
a person who grows plants or fruit for sale
• *orange growers*

**growl** VERB growls, growling, growled
to make a deep angry sound in the throat

**growl** NOUN growls
the sound of growling

**grown-up** NOUN grown-ups
an adult person
➤ **grown-up** ADJECTIVE

**growth** NOUN growths
❶ growing or developing ❷ something that
has grown ❸ a lump that has grown on or
inside a person's body; a tumour

**grub** NOUN grubs
❶ a tiny worm-like creature that will become
an insect; a larva ❷ (*informal*) food

**grub** VERB grubs, grubbing, grubbed
❶ to turn things over or move them about
while looking for something • *The dog was
grubbing around under a bush.* ❷ to dig
something up by the roots

**grubby** ADJECTIVE grubbier, grubbiest
rather dirty

**grudge** NOUN grudges
unfriendly feelings towards someone because
you are angry about what has happened in
the past • *She isn't the sort of person who
bears a grudge.*

**grudge** VERB grudges, grudging, grudged
to be unhappy that someone has something
or that you have to do something • *I don't
grudge him his success – he deserves it.*

**grudging** ADJECTIVE
given or done although you do not want to
• *grudging thanks*
➤ **grudgingly** ADVERB

**gruelling** ADJECTIVE
difficult and exhausting • *It was a gruelling
race.*

**gruesome** ADJECTIVE
horrible or shocking • *He told me the
gruesome story of how she died.*

**gruff** ADJECTIVE
having a rough unfriendly voice or manner
➤ **gruffly** ADVERB
➤ **gruffness** NOUN

**grumble** VERB grumbles, grumbling, grumbled
to complain in a bad-tempered way

**grumble** NOUN grumbles
a bad-tempered complaint

**grumpy** ADJECTIVE
bad-tempered
➤ **grumpily** ADVERB
➤ **grumpiness** NOUN

**grunt** VERB grunts, grunting, grunted
to make a gruff snorting sound like a pig

**grunt** NOUN grunts
the sound of grunting

**guarantee** NOUN guarantees
a formal promise to do something or to repair
something you have sold if it breaks or goes
wrong

**guarantee** VERB guarantees, guaranteeing,
guaranteed
❶ to give a guarantee; to make a formal

promise ❷ to make it certain that something will happen • *Money cannot guarantee happiness.*

**guard** VERB guards, guarding, guarded
❶ to protect a place or thing from danger; to keep something safe ❷ to watch over a prisoner and prevent them from escaping
➤ **guard against something** to try to prevent something happening

**guard** NOUN guards
❶ guarding or protecting people or things • *Keep the prisoners under close guard.*
❷ someone who guards a person or place
❸ a group of soldiers or police officers etc. acting as a guard ❹ a railway official in charge of a train ❺ a protecting device or screen • *a fireguard*
➤ **on guard** alert for possible danger or difficulty

SPELLING
There is a silent u in guard.

**guardian** NOUN guardians
❶ someone who guards or protects something ❷ a person who is legally in charge of a child whose parents cannot look after him or her
➤ **guardianship** NOUN

**guerrilla** (say ger-il-a) NOUN guerrillas
a member of a small unofficial army who fights by making surprise attacks

SPELLING
Take care not to confuse with gorilla, which is an ape.

**guess** NOUN guesses
an opinion or answer that you give without making careful calculations or without being certain

**guess** VERB guesses, guessing, guessed
to make a guess
➤ **guesser** NOUN

**guesswork** NOUN
something you do or think by guessing • *The police had a few facts but the rest was guesswork.*

**guest** NOUN guests
❶ a person who is invited to your house for a meal or a visit or to a special event • *We have guests staying this weekend.* • *wedding guests* ❷ a person staying at a hotel ❸ a person who takes part in another's show as a visiting performer

**guest house** NOUN guest houses
a kind of small hotel

**guffaw** VERB guffaws, guffawing, guffawed
to laugh noisily

**guffaw** NOUN guffaws
a noisy laugh

**guidance** NOUN
help and advice • *He learned to cook under the guidance of the head chef.*

**Guide** NOUN Guides
a member of the Guide Association, an organization for girls

**guide** NOUN guides
❶ a person who shows others the way or points out interesting sights ❷ a book giving information about a place or subject

**guide** VERB guides, guiding, guided
to show someone the way or how to do something

**guidebook** NOUN guidebooks
a book of information about a place, for travellers or visitors

**guided missile** NOUN guided missiles
an explosive rocket that is guided to its target by remote control or by equipment inside it

**guide dog** NOUN guide dogs
a dog trained to lead a blind person

**guidelines** PLURAL NOUN
statements that give general advice about how something should be done

**guild** (say gild) NOUN guilds
a society of people with similar skills or interests

**guilder** (say gild-er) NOUN guilders
a unit of money used in the Netherlands before the introduction of the euro

**guile** (rhymes with mile) NOUN
craftiness and deceit
➤ **guileless** ADJECTIVE

**guillotine** (say gil-ot-een) NOUN guillotines
❶ a machine with a heavy blade for beheading criminals, used in the past in France ❷ a machine with a long sharp blade for cutting paper

**guillotine** VERB guillotines, guillotining, guillotined
to cut off someone's head with a guillotine
WORD ORIGIN named after Dr *Guillotin*, who suggested its use in France during the Revolution in 1789

a b c d e f g h i j k l m n o p q r s t u v w x y z

**guilt** NOUN
❶ an unpleasant feeling you have when you have done wrong or are to blame for something bad that has happened ❷ the fact that you have committed a crime or done wrong • *Everyone was convinced of her guilt.*

**guilty** ADJECTIVE
❶ having done wrong • *He was found guilty of murder.* ❷ feeling or showing guilt • *a guilty conscience* • *a guilty look*
➤ **guiltily** ADVERB

**guinea** (say **gin**-ee) NOUN **guineas**
❶ a former British gold coin worth 21 shillings (£1.05) ❷ this amount of money (WORD ORIGIN) originally = a coin used by British traders in Africa: named after *Guinea* in west Africa

**guinea pig** NOUN **guinea pigs**
❶ a small furry animal without a tail, kept as a pet ❷ a person who is used to try out something new (WORD ORIGIN) from *Guinea* in west Africa, probably by mistake for Guiana, in South America, where the guinea pig comes from

**guise** (say **guys**) NOUN **guises**
an outward disguise or pretence • *He returned to his father's kingdom in the guise of a servant.*

**guitar** NOUN **guitars**
a musical instrument played by plucking its strings
➤ **guitarist** NOUN

**gulf** NOUN **gulfs**
❶ a large area of the sea that is partly surrounded by land ❷ a wide gap; a great difference • *the gulf between rich and poor*

**gull** NOUN **gulls**
a seagull

**gullet** NOUN **gullets**
the tube from the throat to the stomach

**gullible** ADJECTIVE
easily deceived or persuaded to believe something

**gully** NOUN **gullies**
a narrow channel that carries water

**gulp** VERB **gulps, gulping, gulped**
❶ to swallow something hastily or greedily ❷ to make a loud swallowing noise, especially because of fear

**gulp** NOUN **gulps**
❶ the act of gulping food or drink ❷ a large mouthful of liquid

**gum** NOUN **gums**
❶ the firm flesh in which your teeth are rooted ❷ a sticky substance produced by some trees and shrubs, used as glue ❸ a sweet made with gum or gelatin • *a fruit gum* ❹ chewing gum ❺ a gum tree

**gum** VERB **gums, gumming, gummed**
to cover or stick something with gum

**gummy** ADJECTIVE
sticky like gum

**gumption** NOUN (*informal*)
common sense

**gum tree** NOUN **gum trees**
a eucalyptus

**gun** NOUN **guns**
❶ a weapon that fires shells or bullets from a metal tube ❷ a starting pistol ❸ a device that forces a substance out of a tube • *a grease gun*

**gun** VERB **guns, gunning, gunned**
➤ **gun someone down** to shoot and kill someone with a gun (WORD ORIGIN) probably from the Swedish girl's name *Gunnhildr*, from *gunnr* = war

**gunboat** NOUN **gunboats**
a small warship

**gunfire** NOUN
the rapid firing of guns

**gunman** NOUN **gunmen**
a criminal with a gun

**gunner** NOUN **gunners**
a person in the armed forces who operates a large gun

**gunnery** NOUN
the making or use of large guns

**gunpowder** NOUN
an explosive made from a powdered mixture of potassium nitrate, charcoal and sulphur

**gunshot** NOUN **gunshots**
the sound of a gun being fired

**gunwale** (say **gun**-al) NOUN **gunwales**
the upper edge of the side of a boat

**gurdwara** NOUN **gurdwaras**
a Sikh temple

**gurgle** VERB **gurgles, gurgling, gurgled**
to make a low bubbling sound • *Water gurgled through the pipes.*

**gurgle** NOUN **gurgles**
a low bubbling sound

**guru** NOUN **gurus**
① a spiritual teacher in Hinduism and Sikhism
② an influential teacher; an expert on a subject whose ideas people follow

**gush** VERB **gushes, gushing, gushed**
① to flow out suddenly or quickly ② to talk too enthusiastically or emotionally
➤ **gush** NOUN

**gust** NOUN **gusts**
a short sudden rush of wind

**gust** VERB **gusts, gusting, gusted**
to blow in gusts

**gusto** NOUN
great enjoyment and enthusiasm

**gusty** ADJECTIVE
with the wind blowing in gusts • *a gusty breeze*

**gut** NOUN **guts**
the lower part of the digestive system; the intestine

**gut** VERB **guts, gutting, gutted**
① to remove the guts from a dead fish or other animal ② to remove or destroy the inside of something • *The fire completely gutted the factory.*

**guts** PLURAL NOUN
① the digestive system; the insides of a person or thing ② (*informal*) courage and determination

**gutted** ADJECTIVE (*British*) (*informal*)
extremely disappointed or upset

**gutter** NOUN **gutters**
a long narrow channel at the side of a street or along the edge of a roof, for carrying away rainwater

**gutter** VERB **gutters, guttering, guttered**
a candle gutters when it burns unsteadily so that melted wax runs down

**guttural** (say gut-er-al) ADJECTIVE
a guttural voice is throaty and harsh-sounding

**guy** NOUN **guys**
① a figure representing Guy Fawkes, burnt on 5 November in memory of the Gunpowder Plot which planned to blow up Parliament on that day in 1605 ② (*informal*) a man ③ (also **guy-rope**) a rope used to hold something in place, especially a tent

**guzzle** VERB **guzzles, guzzling, guzzled**
to eat or drink greedily
➤ **guzzler** NOUN

**gym** (say jim) NOUN **gyms** (*informal*)
① a gymnasium ② gymnastics

**gymkhana** (say jim-kah-na) NOUN **gymkhanas**
a series of horse-riding contests and other sports events

**gymnasium** NOUN **gymnasiums**
a large room or building with equipment for doing physical exercise **WORD ORIGIN** from Greek *gymnos* = naked (because in ancient Greece men exercised naked)

**gymnast** NOUN **gymnasts**
a person trained in gymnastics

**gymnastics** PLURAL NOUN
exercises performed to develop the muscles or to show the performer's agility
➤ **gymnastic** ADJECTIVE

**gynaecology** (say guy-ni-kol-o-ji) NOUN
the branch of medicine concerned with the female reproductive system

**gypsy** NOUN **gypsies**
a member of a community of people, also called travellers, who live in caravans or similar vehicles and travel from place to place **WORD ORIGIN** from *Egyptian*, because gypsies were originally thought to have come from Egypt

**gyrate** (say jy-rayt) VERB **gyrates, gyrating, gyrated**
to move round in circles or spirals • *They began gyrating to the music.*
➤ **gyration** NOUN

**gyroscope** (say jy-ro-skohp) NOUN **gyroscopes**
a device used in navigation, that keeps steady because of a heavy wheel spinning inside it

# Hh

**habit** NOUN **habits**
① something that you do regularly or often; a settled way of behaving ② something that is hard to give up • *a smoking habit* ③ a piece of clothing like a long dress worn by a monk or nun

**habitat** NOUN **habitats**
where an animal or plant lives or grows naturally • *We were taken to see elephants in their natural habitat.*

a b c d e f g h i j k l m n o p q r s t u v w x y z

**habitation** NOUN habitations
❶ a place to live in ❷ living in a place • *There was no sign of human habitation.*

**habitual** ADJECTIVE
done regularly; usual or typical of someone
• *her habitual afternoon walk*
➤ **habitually** ADVERB

**hack** VERB hacks, hacking, hacked
❶ to chop or cut something roughly • *They began hacking their way through the dense forest.* ❷ (*informal*) to break into a computer system

**hacker** NOUN hackers
a person who breaks into a computer system, especially that of a company or government

**hackles** PLURAL NOUN
➤ **make someone's hackles rise** to make someone angry or indignant
WORD ORIGIN *hackles* are the long feathers on some birds' necks, which the bird raises when alarmed

**hackneyed** ADJECTIVE
used so often that it is no longer interesting

**hacksaw** NOUN hacksaws
a saw for cutting metal

**haddock** NOUN haddock
a sea fish like cod but smaller, used as food

**hadn't** (*mainly spoken*)
had not
SPELLING
Hadn't = had + not. Add an apostrophe between the n and the t.

**haemoglobin** (say heem-a-**gloh**-bin) NOUN
the red substance that carries oxygen in the blood

**haemophilia** (say heem-o-**fil**-ee-a) NOUN
a disease that causes people to bleed dangerously from even a slight cut
➤ **haemophiliac** NOUN

**haemorrhage** (say **hem**-er-ij) NOUN
severe bleeding, especially inside a person's body

**hag** NOUN hags
an ugly old woman

**haggard** ADJECTIVE
looking ill or very tired

**haggis** NOUN haggises
a Scottish food made from sheep's offal

**haggle** VERB haggles, haggling, haggled
to argue about a price or agreement

**haiku** (say **hy**-koo) NOUN haiku
a Japanese form of poem, written in three lines of five, seven and five syllables

**hail** NOUN
❶ frozen drops of rain ❷ a hail of bullets or arrows is a large number of them coming quickly

**hail** VERB hails, hailing, hailed
❶ it is hailing when rain is falling in frozen drops ❷ to call out or wave to someone to get their attention
➤ **hail from somewhere** to come from a particular place • *He hails from Ireland.*

**hail** EXCLAMATION (*old use*)
an exclamation of greeting • *Hail, Caesar!*

**hailstone** NOUN hailstones
a frozen drop of rain

**hair** NOUN hairs
❶ a soft covering that grows on the heads and bodies of people and animals ❷ one of the threads that make up this covering
➤ **keep your hair on** (*informal*) stay calm and do not lose your temper
➤ **split hairs** to make petty or unimportant distinctions of meaning

**hairbrush** NOUN hairbrushes
a brush for tidying your hair

**haircut** NOUN haircuts
❶ cutting a person's hair when it gets too long ❷ the style in which someone's hair is cut

**hairdresser** NOUN hairdressers
a person whose job is to cut and arrange people's hair

**hairdryer** NOUN
an electrical device for drying the hair with warm air

**hairpin** NOUN hairpins
a U-shaped pin for keeping hair in place

**hair-raising** ADJECTIVE
terrifying but also exciting • *a hair-raising chase across the rooftops*

**hairstyle** NOUN hairstyles
a way or style of arranging your hair

**hairy** ADJECTIVE
❶ with a lot of hair ❷ (*informal*) dangerous and frightening • *a hairy experience*

**hajj** NOUN
the pilgrimage to Mecca which all Muslims are expected to make at least once

**hake** *NOUN* hake
a sea fish used as food

**halal** *ADJECTIVE*
halal meat is prepared according to Muslim law

**halcyon** (say hal-see-on) *ADJECTIVE*
halcyon days are happy and peaceful days that you long for from the past
**WORD ORIGIN** from Greek *alkyon* = a bird which was once believed to build its nest on the sea, which magically stayed calm

**hale** *ADJECTIVE*
➤ **hale and hearty** strong and healthy

**half** *NOUN* halves
one of the two equal parts or amounts into which something is or can be divided

**half** *ADVERB*
partly; not completely • *This meat is only half cooked.*
➤ **not half** (informal) extremely • *Was she cross? Not half!*

**half-baked** *ADJECTIVE* (informal)
not properly planned or thought out

**half-brother** *NOUN* half-brothers
a brother to whom you are related by one parent but not by both parents

**half-hearted** *ADJECTIVE*
not very keen or enthusiastic
➤ **half-heartedly** *ADVERB*

**half-life** *NOUN* half-lives
the time taken for the radioactivity of a substance to fall to half its original value

**half mast** *NOUN*
a point about halfway up a flagpole, to which a flag is lowered as a mark of respect for a person who has died

**halfpenny** (say hayp-nee) *NOUN* halfpennies
for individual coins or halfpence for a sum of money, a former British coin worth half a penny

**half-sister** *NOUN* half-sisters
a sister to whom you are related by one parent but not by both parents

**half-term** *NOUN* half-terms
(in British schools) a short holiday in the middle of a school term

**half-time** *NOUN*
the point or interval halfway through a game

**halfway** *ADJECTIVE* & *ADVERB*
at a point half the distance or amount between two places or times • *He stopped halfway up the stairs.*

**half-witted** *ADJECTIVE*
(informal) stupid
➤ **half-wit** *NOUN*

**halibut** *NOUN* halibut
a large flat fish used as food
**WORD ORIGIN** from *holy* + *butt*, a dialect word = flatfish (because it was eaten on Christian holy days, when meat was forbidden)

**hall** *NOUN* halls
❶ a space or passage just inside the front entrance of a house ❷ a large room or building used for meetings, concerts or social events ❸ a large country house

**hallelujah** *EXCLAMATION* & *NOUN* hallelujahs
alleluia

**hallmark** *NOUN* hallmarks
❶ an official mark made on gold, silver and platinum to show its quality ❷ a typical quality or feature by which you can recognize a person or thing • *The book has all the hallmarks of a classic.*

**hallo** *EXCLAMATION*
a different spelling of hello

**hallowed** *ADJECTIVE*
honoured as being holy

**Hallowe'en** *NOUN*
31 October, traditionally a time when ghosts and witches are believed to appear
**WORD ORIGIN** from *All Hallow Even*, the evening before the Christian festival honouring all the *hallows* = saints

**hallucination** *NOUN* hallucinations
something you think you can see or hear that is not really there, usually because of illness or drugs
➤ **hallucinate** *VERB*

**halo** *NOUN* haloes
a circle of light round something, especially round the head of a saint or other holy person in paintings

**halt** *VERB* halts, halting, halted
to stop or to make something stop • *The parade halted briefly at the square.* • *The judge decided to halt the trial.*

**halt** *NOUN* halts
❶ a stop or standstill • *Work came to a halt when the digger broke down.* ❷ a small stopping place on a railway

**halter** NOUN halters
a rope or strap put round a horse's head so that it can be led or fastened to something

**halting** ADJECTIVE
slow and uncertain • *He has a halting walk.*
➤ **haltingly** ADVERB

**halve** VERB halves, halving, halved
❶ to reduce something to half its size or amount • *We need to halve our expenses.*
❷ to divide something into halves • *Halve the peach and remove the stone.*

**ham** NOUN hams
❶ meat from a pig's leg ❷ (*informal*) an actor who acts in a very exaggerated way ❸ (*informal*) someone who operates a radio to send and receive messages as a hobby

**hamburger** NOUN hamburgers
a flat round cake of minced beef served fried, often in a bread roll **WORD ORIGIN** named after Hamburg in Germany (not after **ham**)

**hamlet** NOUN hamlets
a small village

**hammer** NOUN hammers
a tool with a heavy metal head used for hitting nails into things

**hammer** VERB hammers, hammering, hammered
❶ to hit something with a hammer ❷ to knock loudly • *Someone was hammering on the door.* ❸ (*informal*) to criticize or defeat someone

**hammock** NOUN hammocks
a bed made of a strong net or piece of cloth hung up above the ground or floor

**hamper** NOUN hampers
a large box-shaped basket with a lid

**hamper** VERB hampers, hampering, hampered
to hinder someone or prevent them from moving or working freely • *Later in the match he was hampered by his shoulder injury.*

**hamster** NOUN hamsters
a small furry animal with cheek pouches for carrying grain

**hamstring** NOUN hamstrings
any of the five tendons at the back of a person's knee

**hand** NOUN hands
❶ the end part of the arm below the wrist ❷ a pointer on a clock or dial ❸ a worker; a member of a ship's crew • *All hands on deck!* ❹ the cards held by one player in a card game ❺ side or direction • *the right-hand side* • *on the other hand* ❻ help or assistance • *Give me a hand with these boxes.*
➤ **at hand** nearby
➤ **by hand** using your hand or hands
➤ **give someone** or **receive a big hand** to applaud someone or be applauded
➤ **hands down** winning easily
➤ **in good hands** in the care or control of someone who can be trusted
➤ **in hand** being dealt with
➤ **on hand** available; ready to help
➤ **out of hand** out of control

**hand** VERB hands, handing, handed
to give or pass something to someone • *Hand it over.*
➤ **hand something down** to pass something from one generation to the next

**handbag** NOUN handbags
a small bag for holding a purse and other personal items

**handbook** NOUN handbooks
a small book that gives useful facts about something

**handcuff** NOUN handcuffs
one of a pair of metal rings linked by a chain, for fastening wrists together

**handcuff** VERB handcuffs, handcuffing, handcuffed
to put handcuffs on someone

**handful** NOUN handfuls
❶ as much as you can hold in one hand ❷ a few people or things • *There were only a handful of people in the audience.* ❸ (*informal*) a difficult or awkward person or task

**handicap** NOUN handicaps
❶ a disadvantage ❷ (*offensive*) a physical or mental disability
➤ **handicapped** ADJECTIVE

**USAGE**
Do not use *handicapped* to describe people with disabilities as this is offensive.

**handicraft** NOUN handicrafts
artistic work done with your hands, e.g. woodwork or needlework

**handily** ADVERB
in a handy way

**handiwork** NOUN
❶ something made by hand ❷ something done • *Is this mess your handiwork?*

**handkerchief** *NOUN* **handkerchiefs**
a small square of cloth for wiping your nose
or face

**handle** *NOUN* **handles**
the part of a thing by which you can hold,
carry or control it

**handle** *VERB* **handles, handling, handled**
❶ to touch or feel something with your
hands ❷ to deal with or manage something
• *I thought you handled the situation very
well.*
➤ **handler** *NOUN*

**handlebar** *NOUN* (or **handlebars**) *PLURAL NOUN*
the bar, with a handle at each end, that steers
a bicycle or motorcycle

**handout** *NOUN* **handouts**
❶ money given to a needy person ❷ a sheet
of information given out in a lesson, lecture,
etc.

**handrail** *NOUN* **handrails**
a narrow rail for people to hold as a support

**handset** *NOUN* **handsets**
❶ the part of a telephone that you hold up
to speak into and listen to ❷ a hand-held
control device for a piece of electronic
equipment

**handshake** *NOUN* **handshakes**
shaking hands with someone as a greeting or
to show you agree to something

**handsome** *ADJECTIVE*
❶ attractive or good-looking ❷ large and
generous • *a handsome offer*
➤ **handsomely** *ADVERB*

**hands-on** *ADJECTIVE*
involving actual experience of using
equipment or doing something • *The science
museum has many hands-on activities you
can try.*

**handstand** *NOUN* **handstands**
balancing on your hands with your feet in
the air

**handwriting** *NOUN*
writing done by hand; a person's style of
writing

**handwritten** *ADJECTIVE*
written by hand, not typed or printed • *a
handwritten sign*

**handy** *ADJECTIVE* **handier, handiest**
❶ convenient or useful; within easy reach • *a
handy little tool* • *Have you got a pen handy?*
❷ good at using the hands

**handyman** *NOUN* **handymen**
a person who does household repairs or odd
jobs

**hang** *VERB* **hangs, hanging, hung**
❶ to fix the top part of something to a hook
or nail etc. so that the lower part is free; to
be supported in this way • *Coats hung from
pegs along one wall.* ❷ to stick wallpaper to a
wall ❸ to decorate something with drapery or
hanging ornaments etc. • *The tree was hung
with lights.* ❹ to lean or lie over something
• *Her clothes hung over a chair.* ❺ to remain
in the air or as something unpleasant
• *Smoke hung over the city.* • *The threat is
still hanging over him.* ❻ with past tense &
past participle **hanged** to execute someone
by hanging them from a rope that tightens
round the neck • *He was hanged in 1950.*
➤ **hang about** to wait around doing nothing
➤ **hang back** to hesitate to go forward or to
do something
➤ **hang on** (*informal*) to wait • *Hang on! I'm
not ready yet.*
➤ **hang on to something** to hold something
tightly
➤ **hang up** to end a telephone conversation

**hang** *NOUN*
➤ **get the hang of** (*informal*) to learn how to
do or use something

**hangar** *NOUN* **hangars**
a large shed where aircraft are kept

**hanger** *NOUN* **hangers**
a curved piece of wood, plastic or wire with
a hook at the top, for hanging clothes from
a rail

**hang-glider** *NOUN* **hang-gliders**
a framework like a large kite from which a
person can hang and glide through the air
➤ **hang-gliding** *NOUN*

**hangman** *NOUN* **hangmen**
a man whose job it is to hang people
condemned to death

**hangover** *NOUN* **hangovers**
a headache and sick feeling after drinking too
much alcohol

**hank** *NOUN* **hanks**
a coil or piece of wool or thread

**hanker** *VERB* **hankers, hankering, hankered**
to hanker after something is to feel a longing
for it

**hanky** *NOUN* **hankies** (*informal*)
a handkerchief

a
b
c
d
e
f
g
h
i
j
k
l
m
n
o
p
q
r
s
t
u
v
w
x
y
z

**Hanukkah** (say **hah**-noo-ka) *NOUN*
the eight-day Jewish festival of lights
beginning in December

**haphazard** *ADJECTIVE*
done or chosen at random, with no particular
order or plan • *The books were piled on the
shelf in a haphazard fashion.*
➤ **haphazardly** *ADVERB*

**hapless** *ADJECTIVE*
having no luck

**happen** *VERB* happens, happening, happened
❶ to take place; to occur ❷ to do something
by chance • *I happened to see him in the
street.*

**happening** *NOUN* happenings
something that happens; an event

**happily** *ADVERB*
❶ in a happy way • *The children were playing
happily outside.* ❷ it is lucky that • *Happily,
no one was hurt.*

**happy** *ADJECTIVE* happier, happiest
❶ pleased or contented ❷ willing to do
something • *I'd be happy to help.* ❸ fortunate
• *a happy coincidence*
➤ **happiness** *NOUN*

**harangue** (say ha-**rang**) *VERB* harangues,
haranguing, harangued
to speak to someone at length in a loud
aggressive way, often to criticize them

**harangue** *NOUN*
a long aggressive speech criticizing someone

**harass** (say ha-**ras**) *VERB* harasses, harassing,
harassed
to trouble or annoy someone continually
➤ **harassment** (say **ha**-ras-ment) *NOUN*

**harassed** *ADJECTIVE*
tired and anxious because you have too much
to do • *a harassed-looking waiter*

**harbour** *NOUN* harbours
a place where ships can shelter or unload

**harbour** *VERB* harbours, harbouring,
harboured
❶ to keep something in your mind for a long
time • *I think she still harbours a grudge
against them.* ❷ to give shelter to someone,
especially a criminal

**hard** *ADJECTIVE*
❶ firm or solid; not soft ❷ strong and
violent • *a hard punch* ❸ difficult to do or
understand • *These questions are too hard.*
❹ severe or harsh ❺ causing suffering • *hard
luck* ❻ using or needing great effort • *a*

*hard worker* • *a hard climb* ❼ hard drugs are
strong and addictive ❽ hard water contains
minerals that prevent soap from making
much lather
➤ **hardness** *NOUN*
➤ **hard of hearing** slightly deaf
➤ **hard up** (*informal*) short of money

**hard** *ADVERB*
❶ so as to be hard • *The ground froze hard.*
❷ with great effort or force • *We worked
hard.* • *It is raining hard.* ❸ with difficulty
• *hard-earned cash*

**hardback** *NOUN* hardbacks
a book bound in stiff covers

**hardboard** *NOUN*
stiff board made of compressed wood pulp

**hard disk** *NOUN* hard disks
a disk fixed inside a computer, able to store
large amounts of data

**harden** *VERB* hardens, hardening, hardened
❶ to make something hard or to become
hard • *Wait for the varnish to harden.* ❷ to
become more serious and unfriendly • *Her
face hardened immediately.*
➤ **hardener** *NOUN*

**hard-hearted** *ADJECTIVE*
unkind or unsympathetic

**hardly** *ADVERB*
only just; only with difficulty • *She can hardly
walk.*

**hardship** *NOUN* hardships
difficult conditions that cause discomfort or
suffering • *a life of hardship*

**hard shoulder** *NOUN* hard shoulders
(*British*) a strip at the edge of a motorway
where vehicles can stop in an emergency

**hardware** *NOUN*
❶ tools and other pieces of equipment
that you use in the house and garden
• *a hardware shop* ❷ the machinery of
a computer as opposed to the software.
Compare with **software**.

**hard-wearing** *ADJECTIVE*
able to stand a lot of wear

**hardwood** *NOUN* hardwoods
hard heavy wood from deciduous trees, e.g.
oak and teak

**hardy** *ADJECTIVE* hardier, hardiest
able to endure cold or difficult conditions • *a
hardy plant*

**hare** NOUN hares
a fast-running animal like a large rabbit

**hare** VERB hares, haring, hared
(British) to hare about or hare off is to rush away at great speed

**harem** (say har-eem) NOUN harems
the part of a Muslim palace or house where the women live; the women living there

**hark** VERB harks, harking, harked
(old use) to listen
➤ **hark back to something** to return to an earlier subject

**harm** VERB harms, harming, harmed
to damage or injure someone or something

**harm** NOUN
damage or injury

**harmful** ADJECTIVE
causing harm or likely to cause harm
• harmful rays from the sun

**harmless** ADJECTIVE
not able or likely to cause harm • These spiders are completely harmless.
➤ **harmlessly** ADVERB

**harmonic** ADJECTIVE
to do with harmony in music

**harmonica** NOUN harmonicas
a mouth organ

**harmonious** ADJECTIVE
❶ combining together in a pleasant, attractive or effective way ❷ sounding pleasant ❸ peaceful and friendly

**harmonize** (also **harmonise**) VERB
harmonizes, harmonizing, harmonized
❶ to combine together in a pleasant, attractive or effective way • He believed that buildings should harmonize with their environment. ❷ musicians or singers harmonize when they play or sing together with notes that combine in a pleasant way with the main tune

**harmony** NOUN harmonies
❶ a pleasant combination of musical notes played or sung at the same time ❷ being friendly to each other and not quarrelling

**harness** NOUN harnesses
the straps put round a horse's head and neck for controlling it

**harness** VERB harnesses, harnessing, harnessed
❶ to put a harness on a horse ❷ to control and use something • Could we harness the power of the wind?

**harp** NOUN harps
a musical instrument made of strings stretched across a frame and plucked with the fingers
➤ **harpist** NOUN

**harp** VERB harps, harping, harped
to harp on about something is to keep on talking about it in a tiresome way • He keeps harping on about all the work he has to do.

**harpoon** NOUN NOUN harpoons
a spear attached to a rope, used for catching whales or large fish

**harpoon** VERB harpoons, harpooning, harpooned
to spear a whale or fish with a harpoon

**harpsichord** NOUN harpsichords
an instrument like a piano but with strings that are plucked (not struck) when keys are pressed

**harrow** NOUN harrows
a heavy device pulled over the ground to break up the soil

**harrowing** ADJECTIVE
very upsetting or distressing

**harry** VERB harries, harrying, harried
to keep bothering or harassing someone
• She has been harried by reporters all week.

**harsh** ADJECTIVE
❶ rough and unpleasant ❷ severe or cruel
➤ **harshly** ADVERB
➤ **harshness** NOUN

**hart** NOUN harts
a male deer. Compare with **hind**.

**harvest** NOUN harvests
❶ the time when farmers gather in the corn, fruit or vegetables that they have grown ❷ the crop that is gathered in

**harvest** VERB harvests, harvesting, harvested
to gather in a crop
➤ **harvester** NOUN

**hash** NOUN
❶ a mixture of small pieces of meat and vegetables, usually fried ❷ (chiefly British) the symbol #
➤ **make a hash of something** (informal) to make a mess of something or bungle it

**hashtag** NOUN hashtags
a word or phrase with the symbol # in front of it, used on websites such as Twitter to identify the subject of a message

**hasn't** (*mainly spoken*)
has not

> SPELLING
> **Hasn't = has + not.** Add an **apostrophe** between the **n** and the **t**.

**hassle** (*informal*) NOUN
something that is difficult or troublesome

**hassle** VERB **hassles, hassling, hassled**
to annoy or pester someone

**haste** NOUN
doing something in a short time or too quickly • *The letter had clearly been written in haste.*
> **make haste** to move or act quickly

**hasten** VERB **hastens, hastening, hastened**
❶ to be quick to do or say something
• *She hastened to apologize.* ❷ to make something happen or be done earlier or more quickly

**hasty** ADJECTIVE
hurried; done too quickly • *a hasty decision*
> **hastily** ADVERB

**hat** NOUN **hats**
a covering for the head, worn out of doors
> **keep something under your hat** to keep something a secret

**hatch** NOUN **hatches**
an opening in a floor, wall or door, usually with a covering

**hatch** VERB **hatches, hatching, hatched**
❶ to break out of an egg ❷ to keep an egg warm until a baby bird comes out ❸ to plan something • *They hatched a plot.* ❹ to shade part of a drawing with close parallel lines

**hatchback** NOUN **hatchbacks**
a car with a sloping back hinged at the top

**hatchet** NOUN **hatchets**
a small axe

**hate** VERB **hates, hating, hated**
to dislike someone or something very strongly

**hate** NOUN **hates**
❶ extreme dislike ❷ something you dislike very much

**hateful** ADJECTIVE
extremely unkind or unpleasant; horrible
• *It was a hateful thing to say.*

**hatred** NOUN
extreme dislike

**hatter** NOUN **hatters**
a person who makes hats

**hat-trick** NOUN **hat-tricks**
getting three goals, wickets or victories one after the other

**haughty** ADJECTIVE **haughtier, haughtiest**
proud of yourself and looking down on other people
> **haughtily** ADVERB
> **haughtiness** NOUN

**haul** VERB **hauls, hauling, hauled**
to pull or drag something with great effort

**haul** NOUN **hauls**
❶ an amount taken or obtained by an effort
• *Police recovered a large haul of weapons.*
❷ a distance to be covered • *It was a long haul to the summit.*

**haulage** NOUN (*British*)
❶ transporting goods by road ❷ a charge for this

**haunches** PLURAL NOUN
the buttocks and top part of the thighs

**haunt** VERB **haunts, haunting, haunted**
❶ a ghost haunts a place or person when it appears often ❷ to visit a place often ❸ to stay for a long time in your mind
• *The memory haunts me still.*

**haunt** NOUN **haunts**
a place that you often visit

**haunted** ADJECTIVE
a haunted place is one that people think is visited by ghosts

**haunting** ADJECTIVE
so beautiful and sad that it stays in your mind
• *a haunting tune*

**have** VERB **has, having, had**
This word has many uses, including
❶ to possess or own something • *We have two dogs.* ❷ to contain something • *This tin has sweets in it.* ❸ to experience something
• *He had a shock.* ❹ to be obliged or forced to do something • *We have to go now.* ❺ to allow something to happen • *I won't have him bullied.* ❻ to receive or accept something
• *Will you have a sweet?* ❼ to get something done; to organize something • *I'm having my phone mended.* • *We're having a party next week.* ❽ (*informal*) to be had is to be cheated or deceived
> **have someone on** (*informal*) to fool someone

**have** *AUXILIARY VERB*
used to form the past tense of verbs, e.g. *He has gone*

> **GRAMMAR**
>
> The auxiliary verb **have** is used in perfect tenses (**have** + **past participle** of the main verb):
>
> *Have you watched this film before?*
>
> *He had already arrived.*
>
> *It has rained all night.*
>
> *The sea had swept everything away.*
>
> In writing, take care to follow modal verbs like *could*, *might* and *would* with *have*, not *of*:
>
> *If I'd got there in time, I could have helped.*
>
> *It might have been Jack who scored, but I'm not sure.*

**haven** *NOUN* havens
a safe place for people or animals • *The river banks are a haven for wildlife.*

**haven't** (*mainly spoken*)
have not

> **SPELLING**
>
> Have + not = haven't.
> Add an **apostrophe** between the **n** and the **t**.

**haversack** *NOUN* haversacks
a strong bag carried on your back or over your shoulder

**havoc** *NOUN*
great destruction or disorder • *The floods caused havoc throughout the country.*
➤ **play havoc with something** to disrupt something completely

**hawk** *NOUN* hawks
a bird of prey with very strong eyesight

**hawk** *VERB* hawks, hawking, hawked
to carry goods about and try to sell them
➤ **hawker** *NOUN*

**hawthorn** *NOUN* hawthorns
a thorny tree with small red berries (called *haws*)

**hay** *NOUN*
dried grass for feeding to animals

**hay fever** *NOUN*
an allergy to pollen that causes irritation of the nose, throat and eyes

**haystack** *NOUN* haystacks
a large neat pile of hay packed for storing

**haywire** *ADJECTIVE* (*informal*)
out of control • *My computer's gone haywire.*
**WORD ORIGIN** because wire for tying up hay bales was often used for makeshift repairs

**hazard** *NOUN* hazards
❶ a danger or risk ❷ an obstacle on a golf course

**hazard** *VERB* hazards, hazarding, hazarded
to put something at risk
➤ **hazard a guess** to make a guess
**WORD ORIGIN** from Persian or Turkish *zar* = dice

**hazardous** *ADJECTIVE*
dangerous or risky • *a hazardous expedition*

**haze** *NOUN*
thin mist

**hazel** *NOUN* hazels
❶ a bush with small nuts ❷ a light brown colour
➤ **hazelnut** *NOUN*

**hazy** *ADJECTIVE*
❶ misty • *hazy sunshine* ❷ vague or uncertain • *I have a hazy memory of the party.*
➤ **hazily** *ADVERB*
➤ **haziness** *NOUN*

**H-bomb** *NOUN* H-bombs
a hydrogen bomb

**he** *PRONOUN*
❶ the male person or animal being talked about ❷ a person (male or female) • *He who hesitates is lost.*

**head** *NOUN* heads
❶ the part of the body containing the brains, eyes and mouth ❷ your brains or mind; intelligence • *Use your head!* ❸ a talent or ability • *She has a good head for figures.*
❹ heads is the side of a coin on which someone's head is shown • *Heads or tails?*
❺ a person • *It costs £5 a head.* ❻ the top or front of something • *a pinhead* • *at the head of the procession* ❼ the person in charge of an organization or group of people ❽ a headteacher
➤ **come to a head** to reach a crisis point
➤ **keep your head** to stay calm and not panic
➤ **off the top of your head** without preparation or thinking carefully

**head** VERB heads, heading, headed
❶ to be at the top or front of something
• *Spain heads the table after two games.*
❷ to be in charge of or lead something ❸ to
hit a ball with your head ❹ to start to go in
a particular direction • *We headed for the
coast.*
➤ **head someone off** to force someone to
turn aside by getting in front of them

**headache** NOUN headaches
❶ a pain in the head ❷ (*informal*) a worrying
problem

**headdress** NOUN headdresses
a covering or decoration for the head

**header** NOUN headers
a shot or pass made with the head in football

**heading** NOUN headings
a word or words put at the top of a piece of
printing or writing

**headland** NOUN headlands
a large piece of high land that sticks out into
the sea

**headlight** NOUN headlights
a powerful light at the front of a car, engine,
etc.

**headline** NOUN headlines
a heading in a newspaper, printed in large
type
➤ **the headlines** the main items of news

**headlong** ADVERB & ADJECTIVE
❶ falling head first ❷ in a hasty or
thoughtless way • *He's always rushing
headlong into trouble.*

**headmaster** NOUN headmasters
(*chiefly British*) a male headteacher

**headmistress** NOUN headmistresses
(*chiefly British*) a female headteacher

**head-on** ADVERB & ADJECTIVE
with the front parts hitting each other • *a
head-on collision*

**headphones** PLURAL NOUN
a pair of earphones on a band that fits over
the head

**headquarters** NOUN & PLURAL NOUN
the place from which an organization is
controlled

**headstone** NOUN headstones
a stone set up on a grave, with the name of
the person buried there

**headstrong** ADJECTIVE
determined to do what you want

**headteacher** NOUN headteachers
the person in charge of a school

**headway** NOUN
➤ **make headway** to make good progress

**heal** VERB heals, healing, healed
❶ a wound or injury heals when it gets better
• *The cut should heal up in a few days.* ❷ to
make a wound or injury better ❸ (*old use*) to
cure someone who is ill
➤ **healer** NOUN

**health** NOUN
❶ the condition of a person's body or mind
• *His health is bad.* ❷ being healthy and not
ill • *in sickness and in health*

**health food** NOUN health foods
food that contains only natural substances
and is thought to be good for your health

**healthy** ADJECTIVE healthier, healthiest
❶ being well; free from illness ❷ producing
good health • *Fresh air is healthy.*
➤ **healthily** ADVERB

**heap** NOUN heaps
a pile, especially an untidy one
➤ **heaps** PLURAL NOUN
(*informal*) a great amount; plenty • *There's
heaps of time.*

**heap** VERB heaps, heaping, heaped
❶ to put things in a pile • *Heap all the leaves
up over there.* ❷ to put large amounts on
something • *She heaped his plate with food.*
❸ to give a lot of something, such as praise or
criticism, to someone • *The press heaped the
team with praise.*

**hear** VERB hears, hearing, heard
❶ to take in sounds through the ears ❷ to
receive news or information ❸ to listen to
and try a case in a law court ❹ to hear from
someone is to get a phone call, letter or email
from them
➤ **hearer** NOUN
➤ **hear! hear!** (in a debate) I agree
➤ **not hear of** to refuse to allow something
• *He wouldn't hear of my paying for it.*

SPELLING
The past tense of **hear** is **heard**.

**hearing** NOUN hearings
❶ the ability to hear ❷ a chance to give your
opinion or to defend yourself • *Please give
me a fair hearing.* ❸ a trial in a law court

**hearing aid** NOUN hearing aids
a device to help a partially deaf person to hear

**hearsay** NOUN
something you have heard from another person or as a rumour, which may or may not be true

**hearse** NOUN hearses
a vehicle for taking the coffin to a funeral

**heart** NOUN hearts
❶ the organ in your chest that pumps the blood around your body ❷ a person's feelings or emotions; sympathy ❸ enthusiasm or courage • *We must take heart.* ❹ the middle or most important part of something • *Let's get to the heart of the problem.* ❺ a curved shape representing a heart ❻ a playing card with red heart shapes on it
➤ **break a person's heart** to make someone very unhappy
➤ **by heart** by using only your memory • *She knows the whole speech by heart.*

**heart attack** NOUN heart attacks
a sudden failure of the heart to work properly, which results in great pain or sometimes death

**heartbroken** ADJECTIVE
very unhappy

**hearten** VERB heartens, heartening, heartened
to make a person feel encouraged • *He was heartened by her words of support.*
➤ **heartening** ADJECTIVE

**heart failure** NOUN
gradual failure of the heart to work properly, especially as a cause of death

**heartfelt** ADJECTIVE
felt deeply and sincerely • *my heartfelt thanks*

**hearth** NOUN hearths
the floor of a fireplace or the area in front of it

**heartily** ADVERB
❶ in an enthusiastic way • *The boy laughed heartily.* ❷ completely • *I am heartily sick of this place.*

**heartland** NOUN
the central or most important region

**heartless** ADJECTIVE
cruel or without pity

**hearty** ADJECTIVE
❶ strong and healthy ❷ enthusiastic and sincere • *He offered his hearty congratulations.* ❸ a hearty meal is large and filling
➤ **heartiness** NOUN

**heat** NOUN heats
❶ hotness or (in scientific use) the form of energy that causes things to be hot ❷ hot weather ❸ strong feeling, especially anger ❹ a race or contest to decide who will take part in the final
➤ **on heat** a female mammal is on heat when it is ready for mating

**heat** VERB heats, heating, heated
❶ to make something hot ❷ to become hot

**heater** NOUN heaters
a device for heating a room or vehicle

**heath** NOUN heaths
an area of flat open land with low shrubs

**heathen** NOUN heathens
a person who does not believe in any of the world's chief religions

**heather** NOUN
an evergreen plant with small purple, pink or white flowers

**heatwave** NOUN heatwaves
a long period of hot weather

**heave** VERB heaves, heaving, heaved (when used of ships hove)
❶ to lift or move something heavy ❷ (*informal*) to throw something ❸ to rise and fall • *Her shoulders heaved with laughter.* ❹ if your stomach heaves, you feel like vomiting
➤ **heave into view** a ship heaves into view when appears on the horizon
➤ **heave a sigh** to utter a deep sigh
➤ **heave to** a ship heaves to when it stops without mooring or anchoring

**heave** NOUN heaves
an act of heaving; a strong pull or shove • *With a mighty heave, he lifted the sack onto the truck.*

**heaven** NOUN heavens
❶ the place where, in some religions, good people are thought to go when they die and where God and angels are thought to live ❷ a very pleasant place or state
➤ **the heavens** the sky

**heavenly** ADJECTIVE
❶ to do with heaven ❷ a heavenly body is

a star or planet in the sky ❸ (*informal*) very pleasing

**heavily** ADVERB
❶ to a great degree; in large amounts • *It was raining heavily.* ❷ with a lot of force or effort • *She fell heavily to the ground.* ❸ in a slow and sad way • *He sighed heavily.*

**heavy** ADJECTIVE heavier, heaviest
❶ weighing a lot; difficult to lift or carry ❷ used to ask or say how much something weighs • *How heavy is that bag?* ❸ great in amount or force • *heavy rain* • *a heavy penalty* ❹ needing much effort • *heavy work* ❺ full of sadness or worry • *with a heavy heart*
➤ **heaviness** NOUN

**heavy industry** NOUN heavy industries
industry producing metal, large machines, etc.

**heavyweight** NOUN heavyweights
❶ a heavy person ❷ a boxer of the heaviest weight
➤ **heavyweight** ADJECTIVE

**Hebrew** NOUN
the language of the Jews in ancient Palestine and modern Israel

**heckle** VERB heckles, heckling, heckled
to interrupt a speaker with awkward questions
➤ **heckler** NOUN

**hectare** (say **hek**-tar) NOUN hectares
a unit of area equal to 10,000 square metres or nearly 2.5 acres

**hectic** ADJECTIVE
full of frantic activity • *It's been a hectic morning.*

**hector** VERB hectors, hectoring, hectored
to talk to someone in a bullying way
**WORD ORIGIN** from a gang of young bullies in London in the 17th century who named themselves after Hector, a hero in Greek legend

**hedge** NOUN hedges
a row of bushes forming a barrier or boundary

**hedge** VERB hedges, hedging, hedged
❶ to surround a field or other area with a hedge ❷ to avoid giving a definite answer
➤ **hedge your bets** to avoid committing yourself when you are faced with a difficult choice

**hedgehog** NOUN hedgehogs
a small animal covered with long prickles

**hedgerow** NOUN hedgerows
a hedge of bushes bordering a field

**heed** VERB heeds, heeding, heeded
to pay attention to someone or something

**heed** NOUN
➤ **take** or **pay heed** to give your attention to something

**heedless** ADJECTIVE
taking no notice of something • *Heedless of the danger, she started climbing up the rocks.*

**hee-haw** NOUN hee-haws
a donkey's bray

**heel** NOUN heels
❶ the back part of the foot ❷ the part of a sock or shoe round or under your heel
➤ **take to your heels** to run away

**heel** VERB heels, heeling, heeled
❶ to repair the heel of a shoe ❷ a ship heels when it leans over to one side

**hefty** ADJECTIVE heftier, heftiest
large and strong
➤ **heftily** ADVERB

**Hegira** (say **hej**-ir-a) NOUN
the flight of Muhammad from Mecca in AD 622. The Muslim era is reckoned from this date.

**heifer** (say **hef**-er) NOUN heifers
a young cow

**height** NOUN heights
❶ how high something is; the distance from the base to the top or from head to foot ❷ a high place • *My brother is afraid of heights.* ❸ the highest or most intense part • *at the height of the holiday season*
**SPELLING**
There is a tricky bit in **height**—it begins with **hei**.

**heighten** VERB heightens, heightening, heightened
❶ to become or make something more intense • *Their excitement heightened as the kick-off approached.* ❷ to make something higher

**heinous** (say **hay**-nus or **hee**-nus) ADJECTIVE
very bad or wicked • *a heinous crime*

**heir** (say air) NOUN heirs
a person who inherits money or a title

**heir apparent** NOUN heirs apparent
an heir whose right to inherit cannot be set

aside even if someone with a stronger right is born

**heiress** (say air-ess) NOUN **heiresses**
a female heir, especially to great wealth

**heirloom** (say air-loom) NOUN **heirlooms**
a valued possession that has been handed down in a family for several generations

**heir presumptive** NOUN **heirs presumptive**
an heir whose right to inherit may be set aside if someone with a stronger right is born

**helicopter** NOUN **helicopters**
a kind of aircraft with a large horizontal propeller or rotor

**heliotrope** NOUN **heliotropes**
a plant with small fragrant purple flowers

**helium** (say hee-lee-um) NOUN
a light colourless gas that does not burn and is sometimes used to fill balloons

**helix** (say hee-liks) NOUN **helices** (say hee-liss-ee7)
a spiral

**hell** NOUN
❶ a place where, in some religions, wicked people are thought to be punished after they die ❷ a very unpleasant place or situation ❸ (informal) an exclamation of anger
➤ **hell for leather** (informal) at high speed

**hellish** ADJECTIVE (informal)
very difficult or unpleasant

**hello** EXCLAMATION
a word used to greet someone or to attract their attention

**helm** NOUN **helms**
the handle or wheel used to steer a ship
➤ **helmsman** NOUN

**helmet** NOUN **helmets**
a strong hat or covering worn to protect the head

**help** VERB **helps, helping, helped**
❶ to do something useful for someone ❷ to make something better or easier • This will help you to sleep. ❸ if you cannot help doing something, you cannot avoid it • I can't help coughing. ❹ to serve food or drink to someone
➤ **helper** NOUN

**help** NOUN
❶ helping someone • I need your help. ❷ a person or thing that helps • Thank you, you've been a great help.

**helpful** ADJECTIVE
giving help; useful
➤ **helpfully** ADVERB

**helping** NOUN **helpings**
a portion of food at a meal

**helpless** ADJECTIVE
not able to do things or look after yourself
➤ **helplessly** ADVERB
➤ **helplessness** NOUN

**helpline** NOUN **helplines**
a telephone service giving advice on problems

**helter-skelter** ADVERB
in great haste

**helter-skelter** NOUN **helter-skelters**
a tall spiral slide at a fair

**hem** NOUN **hems**
the edge of a piece of cloth that is folded over and sewn down

**hem** VERB **hems, hemming, hemmed**
to put a hem on something
➤ **hem someone in** to surround someone and prevent them from leaving

**hemisphere** NOUN **hemispheres**
❶ half a sphere ❷ half the earth, divided into north and south • Australia is in the southern hemisphere.
➤ **hemispherical** ADJECTIVE

**hemlock** NOUN
a poisonous plant or poison made from it

**hemp** NOUN
❶ a plant that produces coarse fibres from which cloth and ropes are made ❷ the drug cannabis, made from this plant
➤ **hempen** ADJECTIVE

**hen** NOUN **hens**
❶ a female bird ❷ a female fowl

**hence** ADVERB
❶ as a result; therefore ❷ from now on ❸ (old use) from here

**henceforth** ADVERB
from now on

**henchman** NOUN **henchmen**
a trusty supporter

**henna** NOUN
a reddish-brown dye, especially used for colouring hair

**hepatitis** NOUN
a disease causing inflammation of the liver

**heptagon** NOUN **heptagons**
a flat shape with seven sides and seven angles

a b c d e f g h i j k l m n o p q r s t u v w x y z

**heptathlon** NOUN heptathlons
an athletic contest in which each competitor takes part in seven events

**her** PRONOUN
the form of **she** used as the object of a verb or after a preposition • *He took the books from her.*

**her** DETERMINER
belonging to her • *That is her book.*

**herald** NOUN heralds
❶ an official in former times who made announcements and carried messages for a king or queen ❷ a person or thing that is a sign of something to come • *Spring is the herald of summer.*

**herald** VERB heralds, heralding, heralded
to show that something is coming • *Voices outside heralded their arrival.*

**heraldry** NOUN
the study of coats of arms
➤ **heraldic** (say hir-**al**-dik) ADJECTIVE

**herb** NOUN herbs
a plant used for flavouring or for making medicine

**herbaceous** (say her-**bay**-shus) ADJECTIVE
containing many flowering plants • *a herbaceous border*

**herbal** ADJECTIVE
made of or using herbs • *a herbal remedy*

**herbivore** (say **her**-biv-or) NOUN herbivores
an animal that feeds on plants and not on the flesh of other animals. Compare with **carnivore**.

**herbivorous** (say her-**biv**-er-us) ADJECTIVE
a herbivorous animal feeds on plants and not on the flesh of other animals. Compare with **carnivorous**.

**Herculean** (say her-kew-**lee**-an) ADJECTIVE
needing great strength or effort • *a Herculean task* **WORD ORIGIN** from *Hercules*, a hero in ancient Greek legend

**herd** NOUN herds
❶ a group of cattle or other animals that feed together ❷ a mass of people; a mob

**herd** VERB herds, herding, herded
❶ to gather or move in a large group • *We all herded onto the bus.* ❷ to move people or animals together in a large group • *The visitors were herded into two large halls.* ❸ to look after a herd of animals • *a shepherd herding his flock*

**herdsman** NOUN herdsmen
a person who looks after a herd of animals

**here** ADVERB
in or to this place
➤ **here and there** in various places or directions

**hereafter** ADVERB
from now on; in future

**hereby** ADVERB
as a result of this act or statement. • *I hereby swear to tell the truth.*

**hereditary** ADJECTIVE
passed down to a child from a parent • *a hereditary disease*

**heredity** (say hir-**ed**-it-ee) NOUN
the process of inheriting physical or mental characteristics from parents or ancestors

**heresy** (say **herri**-see) NOUN heresies
an opinion or belief that disagrees with those that are generally accepted, especially in Christianity

**heretic** (say **herri**-tik) NOUN heretics
a person who supports a heresy
➤ **heretical** (say hi-**ret**-ik-al) ADJECTIVE

**heritage** NOUN
things that have been passed from one generation to another; a country's history and traditions • *Music is part of our cultural heritage.*

**hermetically** ADVERB
so as to be airtight • *The tin is hermetically sealed.*

**hermit** NOUN hermits
a person who lives alone and keeps away from people, often for religious reasons

**hermitage** NOUN hermitages
a hermit's home

**hernia** NOUN hernias
a condition in which an internal part of the body pushes through a weak point in another part

**hero** NOUN heroes
❶ a man or boy who is admired for doing something very brave or great ❷ the chief male character in a story, play or film

**heroic** ADJECTIVE
showing great courage or determination • *a heroic effort*
➤ **heroically** ADVERB

**heroin** NOUN
a very strong drug, made from morphine

**heroine** NOUN heroines
❶ a woman or girl who is admired for doing something very brave or great ❷ the chief female character in a story, play or film

**heroism** NOUN
great courage

**heron** NOUN herons
a wading bird with long legs and a long neck

**herring** NOUN herring or herrings
a sea fish used as food

**hers** POSSESSIVE PRONOUN
belonging to her • Those books are hers.
**SPELLING**
There is never an apostrophe in hers.

**herself** PRONOUN
she or her and nobody else. The word is used to refer back to the subject of a sentence (e.g. She cut herself.) or for emphasis (e.g. She herself has said it.)
➤ by herself alone; on her own

**hertz** NOUN hertz
a unit of frequency of electromagnetic waves, equal to one cycle per second
**WORD ORIGIN** named after a German scientist, H. R. Hertz, who discovered radio waves

**hesitant** ADJECTIVE
slow to speak or do something because you are not sure if you should or not
➤ hesitantly ADVERB
➤ hesitancy NOUN

**hesitate** VERB hesitates, hesitating, hesitated
to pause before doing or saying something, because you are uncertain or worried

**hesitation** NOUN hesitations
a pause before doing or saying something, because you are uncertain or worried • She agreed without a moment's hesitation.

**hessian** NOUN
(chiefly British) a type of strong coarse cloth, used for making sacks

**heterogeneous** (say het-er-o-**jeen**-ee-us) ADJECTIVE
consisting of people or things of different kinds

**heterosexual** ADJECTIVE
attracted to people of the opposite sex; not homosexual
➤ heterosexual NOUN

**hew** VERB hews, hewing, hewn
to chop or cut wood or stone with an axe or other tool

**hexagon** NOUN hexagons
a flat shape with six sides and six angles
➤ hexagonal ADJECTIVE

**hey** EXCLAMATION
an exclamation used to attract attention or to express surprise or interest

**heyday** NOUN
the time of a person's or thing's greatest success or popularity

**hi** EXCLAMATION
an exclamation used as a friendly greeting

**hiatus** (say hy-ay-tus) NOUN hiatuses
a gap in something that is otherwise continuous

**hibernate** VERB hibernates, hibernating, hibernated
an animal hibernates when it spends the winter in a state like deep sleep
➤ hibernation NOUN

**hiccup** NOUN hiccups
❶ a high gulping sound made when your breath is briefly interrupted ❷ a brief hitch or setback

**hiccup** VERB hiccups, hiccuping, hiccuped
to make a sound of hiccups
**SPELLING**
There is a double c in hiccups.

**hickory** NOUN hickories
a tree rather like the walnut tree

**hide** VERB hides, hiding, hid, hidden
❶ to get into a place where you cannot be seen ❷ to keep a person or thing from being seen ❸ to keep a thing secret

**hide** NOUN hides
❶ an animal's skin ❷ (British) a camouflaged shelter used to observe wildlife at close quarters

**hide-and-seek** NOUN
a game in which one person looks for others who are hiding

**hidebound** ADJECTIVE
narrow-minded; having old-fashioned attitudes and ideas **WORD ORIGIN** originally used of underfed cattle, with skin stretched tight over their bones, later of a tree whose bark was so tight it could not grow

**hideous** ADJECTIVE
very ugly or unpleasant
➤ **hideously** ADVERB

**hideout** NOUN hideouts
a place where someone hides

**hiding** NOUN hidings
❶ being hidden • *She went into hiding.* ❷ a thrashing or beating

**hierarchy** (say **hyr**-ark-ee) NOUN hierarchies
an organization that ranks people one above another according to the power or authority that they hold

**hieroglyphics** (say hyr-o-**glif**-iks) PLURAL NOUN
pictures or symbols used in ancient Egypt to represent words

**hi-fi** NOUN hi-fis (*informal*)
equipment for playing CDs or other recorded music

**higgledy-piggledy** ADVERB & ADJECTIVE
completely mixed up; not in any order
• *Books were piled higgledy-piggledy on the table.*

**high** ADJECTIVE higher, highest
❶ reaching a long way upwards • *high hills* ❷ far above the ground or above sea level • *high clouds* ❸ measuring from top to bottom • *The post is two metres high.* ❹ above average level in importance, quality or amount • *high rank* • *high prices* ❺ a high note is one at the top end of a musical scale ❻ meat is high when it is beginning to go bad ❼ (*informal*) affected by a drug
➤ **it is high time** it is past the time when something should have happened • *It's high time we left.*

**high** ADVERB
❶ far above the ground or a long way up
• *They flew high above us.* ❷ at or to a high level • *The temperature is going to rise even higher this week.*

**highbrow** ADJECTIVE
having serious or intellectual tastes
**WORD ORIGIN** from *highbrowed* = having a high forehead (thought to be a sign of intelligence)

**Higher** NOUN Highers
the advanced level of the Scottish Certificate of Education

**higher education** NOUN
education at a university or college

**high explosive** NOUN high explosives
a powerful explosive

**high fidelity** NOUN
reproducing recorded sound with very little distortion

**high jump** NOUN
an athletic contest in which competitors try to jump over a high bar

**highlands** PLURAL NOUN
mountainous country • *the Scottish Highlands*
➤ **highland** ADJECTIVE
➤ **highlander** NOUN

**highlight** NOUN highlights
❶ the most interesting part of something
• *The highlight of the holiday was the trip to Pompeii.* ❷ a light area in a painting or photograph ❸ highlights are light-coloured streaks in a person's hair

**highlight** VERB highlights, highlighting, highlighted
❶ to draw special attention to something
• *The test was designed to highlight students' strengths and weaknesses.* ❷ to mark part of a text with a different colour so that people give it more attention • *Click on the highlighted word to go to the section you want.*

**highlighter** NOUN highlighters
a felt-tip pen that you use to spread bright colour over lines of text to draw attention to them

**highly** ADVERB
❶ extremely; to a high degree • *He is highly intelligent.* • *a highly paid job* ❷ very well or favourably • *We think highly of her.*

**highly-strung** ADJECTIVE
nervous and easily upset

**Highness** NOUN Highnesses
the title of a prince or princess

**high-pitched** ADJECTIVE
high in sound

**high-rise** ADJECTIVE
a high-rise building is tall with many storeys

**high school** NOUN high schools
a secondary school

**high spirits** PLURAL NOUN
cheerful and lively behaviour
➤ **high-spirited** ADJECTIVE

**high street** NOUN high streets
(*British*) a town's main street

**high-tech** *ADJECTIVE*
using the most advanced technology, especially electronic devices and computers

**highway** *NOUN* highways
a main road or route for vehicles

**highwayman** *NOUN* highwaymen
a man who robbed travellers on highways in former times

**hijab** *NOUN* hijabs
a head covering worn in public by some Muslim women

**hijack** *VERB* hijacks, hijacking, hijacked
to seize control of an aircraft or vehicle by force during a journey
➤ **hijack** *NOUN*
➤ **hijacker** *NOUN*

**hike** *NOUN* hikes
a long walk in the countryside

**hike** *VERB* hikes, hiking, hiked
to go on a hike
➤ **hiker** *NOUN*

**hilarious** *ADJECTIVE*
very funny
➤ **hilariously** *ADVERB*

**hilarity** *NOUN*
great amusement and laughter • *My new hairstyle was the cause of much hilarity.*

**hill** *NOUN* hills
a piece of land that is higher than the ground around it

**hillock** *NOUN* hillocks
a small hill or mound

**hillside** *NOUN* hillsides
a piece of land forming the side of a hill

**hilly** *ADJECTIVE*
having a lot of hills • *The country's very hilly around here.*

**hilt** *NOUN* hilts
the handle of a sword, dagger or knife
➤ **to the hilt** to a high degree; completely
• *I'll defend you to the hilt.*

**him** *PRONOUN*
the form of **he** used as the object of a verb or after a preposition

**himself** *PRONOUN*
he or him and nobody else. The word is used to refer back to the subject of a sentence (e.g. *He has hurt himself*) or for emphasis (e.g. *He himself has told us*)
➤ **by himself** alone; on his own

**hind** *ADJECTIVE*
at the back • *the hind legs*

**hind** *NOUN* hinds
a female deer. Compare with **hart**.

**hinder** *VERB* hinders, hindering, hindered
to get in your way or make things difficult for you • *Bad weather hindered our journey.*

**Hindi** *NOUN*
one of the languages of India

**hindmost** *ADJECTIVE*
furthest behind

**hindquarters** *PLURAL NOUN*
an animal's hind legs and rear parts

**hindrance** *NOUN*
a person or thing that gets in your way or makes it difficult for you to do something
• *She was more of a hindrance than a help.*

**hindsight** *NOUN*
looking back on an event with knowledge or understanding that you did not have at the time

**Hindu** *NOUN* Hindus
a person who believes in Hinduism, which is one of the religions of India

**hinge** *NOUN* hinges
a joining device on which a lid or door etc. turns when it opens

**hinge** *VERB* hinges, hinging, hinged
❶ to be hinged is to be fixed with a hinge
❷ to hinge on something is to depend on it
• *Everything hinges on this meeting.*

**hint** *NOUN* hints
❶ a slight indication or suggestion • *Give me a hint of what you want.* ❷ a useful idea or piece of advice • *household hints*

**hint** *VERB* hints, hinting, hinted
to suggest something without actually saying it • *She hinted at the plot of her next book.*

**hinterland** *NOUN* hinterlands
the district lying inland beyond a coast or port

**hip** *NOUN* hips
❶ your hips are the bony parts at the side of your body between your waist and your thighs ❷ the fruit of the wild rose

**hip hop** *NOUN*
a type of popular dance music with spoken words and a steady beat, played on electronic instruments

**hippie** NOUN hippies (*informal*)
a young person who joins with others to live in an unconventional way, often based on ideas of peace and love. Hippies first appeared in the 1960s.

**hippo** NOUN hippos (*informal*)
a hippopotamus

**hippopotamus** NOUN hippopotamuses
a very large African animal that lives near water (WORD ORIGIN) from Greek *hippos ho potamios* = horse of the river

**hire** VERB hires, hiring, hired
① to pay to have use of something for a time • *We hired a boat for the afternoon.* ② to lend something in return for payment • *He hires out bicycles.* ③ to pay someone to do a job for you

**hire** NOUN
➤ **for hire** available for people to hire
• *Do you have bicycles for hire?*

**hire purchase** NOUN
(*British*) buying something by paying for it in instalments

**his** DETERMINER & POSSESSIVE PRONOUN
belonging to him • *That is his book.* • *That book is his.*

**hiss** VERB hisses, hissing, hissed
① to make a sound like a continuous *s* • *The cat hissed at me.* ② to say something in a quiet angry voice • *'Stay away from me!' she hissed.*

**hiss** NOUN hisses
the sound of hissing • *There were boos and hisses from the audience.*

**histogram** NOUN histograms
a chart showing amounts as rectangles of varying sizes

**historian** NOUN historians
a person who writes or studies history

**historic** ADJECTIVE
famous or important in history; likely to be remembered • *a historic town* • *a historic meeting*
USAGE
Take care not to confuse with **historical**.

**historical** ADJECTIVE
① to do with history ② that actually existed or took place in the past • *The novel is based*
on historical events.
➤ **historically** ADVERB
USAGE
Take care not to confuse with **historic**.

**history** NOUN histories
① what happened in the past • *an important moment in history* ② the study of past events ③ a description of important events

**hit** VERB hits, hitting, hit
① to come forcefully against a person or thing. or to give them a blow ② to have a bad effect on a place or group of people • *Famine has hit the poorer countries.* ③ something hits you when you suddenly realize or feel it • *Then it hit me where I'd seen him before.* ④ to reach something • *I can't hit that high note.*
➤ **hit it off** to get on well with someone
➤ **hit on something** to discover something suddenly or by chance

**hit** NOUN hits
① hitting; a knock or stroke ② a shot that hits the target ③ a success ④ a successful song or show ⑤ a result of a search on a computer, especially on the Internet • *How many hits did you get?*

**hit-and-run** ADJECTIVE
a hit-and-run driver is one who injures someone in an accident and drives off without stopping

**hitch** VERB hitches, hitching, hitched
① to raise or pull something with a slight jerk • *She hitched up her skirt and waded into the river.* ② to fasten something with a loop or hook ③ to hitch-hike

**hitch** NOUN hitches
① a slight difficulty causing delay ② a knot

**hitch-hike** VERB hitch-hikes, hitch-hiking, hitch-hiked
to travel by getting lifts from passing vehicles
➤ **hitch-hiker** NOUN

**hi-tech** ADJECTIVE
a different spelling of **high-tech**

**hither** ADVERB
(*old use*) to or towards this place

**hitherto** ADVERB
until this time

**HIV** ABBREVIATION
human immunodeficiency virus; a virus that causes Aids

**hive** NOUN hives
❶ a beehive ❷ the bees living in a beehive
➤ **a hive of activity** or **industry** a place full
of people working busily

**hoard** NOUN hoards
a carefully saved store of money, treasure,
food, etc.

**hoard** VERB hoards, hoarding, hoarded
to collect and store away large quantities of
something
➤ **hoarder** NOUN

SPELLING

Hoard is different from horde, which
means a large group or crowd.

**hoarding** NOUN hoardings
(*British*) a tall fence covered with
advertisements

**hoar frost** NOUN
the white frost that forms on the ground in
the morning after a cold night

**hoarse** ADJECTIVE
having a rough or croaking voice • *He was
hoarse from shouting.*
➤ **hoarsely** ADVERB
➤ **hoarseness** NOUN

**hoary** ADJECTIVE
❶ white or grey from age • *hoary hair* ❷ old
and overused • *hoary jokes*

**hoax** NOUN hoaxes
a trick played on someone in which they are
told about something that is not true
➤ **hoax** VERB
➤ **hoaxer** NOUN

**hob** NOUN hobs
a flat surface on the top of a cooker, for
cooking or heating food

**hobble** VERB hobbles, hobbling, hobbled
to walk with difficulty because your feet or
legs hurt

**hobby** NOUN hobbies
something you enjoy doing in your spare time

**hobby horse** NOUN hobby horses
❶ a stick with a horse's head, used as a toy
❷ a subject that a person likes to talk about
whenever they get the chance

**hobgoblin** NOUN hobgoblins
a mischievous or evil spirit

**hobnob** VERB hobnobs, hobnobbing,
hobnobbed
to spend a lot of time with someone famous

or important • *She's been hobnobbing with
rock stars.*

**hock** NOUN hocks
the middle joint of an animal's hind leg

**hockey** NOUN
a game played by two teams with curved
sticks and a hard ball

**hoe** NOUN hoes
a gardening tool with a long handle and a
metal blade, used for scraping up weeds and
making soil loose

**hoe** VERB hoes, hoeing, hoed
to scrape or dig the ground with a hoe

**hog** NOUN hogs
❶ a male pig ❷ (*informal*) a greedy person
➤ **go the whole hog** (*informal*) to do
something completely or thoroughly

**hog** VERB hogs, hogging, hogged (*informal*) to
take more than your fair share of something

**Hogmanay** NOUN
New Year's Eve in Scotland

**hoi polloi** NOUN
the ordinary people; the masses
WORD ORIGIN Greek, = the many

**hoist** VERB hoists, hoisting, hoisted
to lift something up, especially by using ropes
or pulleys • *The crew soon hoisted the sails.*
• *He hoisted the boy onto his shoulders.*

**hold** VERB holds, holding, held
❶ to have something in your hands ❷ to keep
something in a certain position • *Hold your
head up straight.* ❸ to contain or have room
for a certain amount • *The jug holds two
pints.* ❹ to support something • *This plank
won't hold my weight.* ❺ to stay the same;
to continue • *Will the fine weather hold?*
❻ to have or possess something • *She holds
the world high jump record.* ❼ to believe
or consider something • *We shall hold you
responsible.* ❽ to arrange something or cause
it to take place • *The 2012 Olympics were held
in London.* ❾ to keep someone somewhere
or stop them getting away • *The police are
holding three men for the robbery.*
➤ **hold forth** to make a long speech
➤ **hold it** stop; wait a minute
➤ **hold out** ❶ to refuse to give in ❷ to last
or continue
➤ **hold someone up** ❶ to hinder or delay
someone ❷ to stop and rob someone by
threats or force
➤ **hold with something** to approve of
something • *We don't hold with bullying.*

**➤ hold your tongue** (*informal*) to stop talking

**hold** NOUN holds
❶ holding something; a grasp • *Don't lose hold of the rope.* ❷ a place where you can put your hand or foot when climbing ❸ the part of a ship where cargo is stored, below the deck
**➤ get hold of someone** to make contact with a person
**➤ get hold of something** ❶ to grasp something ❷ to obtain something

**holdall** NOUN holdalls
(*British*) a large portable bag or case

**holder** NOUN holders
a person or thing that holds something • *the world record holder*

**hold-up** NOUN hold-ups
❶ a brief delay ❷ a robbery with threats or force

**hole** NOUN holes
❶ a hollow place; a gap or opening made in something ❷ an animal's burrow ❸ one of the small holes into which you have to hit the ball in golf ❹ (*informal*) an unpleasant place
**➤ holey** ADJECTIVE
**➤ in a hole** in an awkward situation

**hole** VERB holes, holing, holed
❶ to make a hole or holes in something, especially a boat or ship ❷ to hit a golf ball into one of the holes

**SPELLING**

Hole is different from whole, which means all of something.

**Holi** NOUN
a Hindu festival held in the spring

**holiday** NOUN holidays (*chiefly British*)
❶ a day or time when people do not go to work or to school ❷ a time when you go away to enjoy yourself **WORD ORIGIN** from *holy* + *day* (because holidays were originally religious festivals)

**holiness** NOUN
being holy or sacred
**➤ His Holiness** the title of the pope

**hollow** ADJECTIVE
❶ with an empty space inside; not solid ❷ loud and echoing • *hollow footsteps* ❸ not sincere • *a hollow promise*
**➤ hollowly** ADVERB

**hollow** NOUN hollows
a hollow or sunken place

**hollow** VERB hollows, hollowing, hollowed
to make a thing hollow • *We always hollow out a pumpkin at Halloween.*

**holly** NOUN
an evergreen bush with shiny prickly leaves and red berries

**hollyhock** NOUN hollyhocks
a plant with large flowers on a very tall stem

**holocaust** NOUN holocausts
large-scale destruction, especially by fire or in a war • *the nuclear holocaust*
**➤ the Holocaust** the mass murder of Jews by the Nazis from 1939 to 1945
**WORD ORIGIN** from Greek *holos* + *kaustos* = completely burnt

**hologram** NOUN holograms
a type of photograph made by laser beams that produces a three-dimensional image

**holster** NOUN holsters
a leather case in which a pistol or revolver is carried

**holy** ADJECTIVE holier, holiest
❶ to do with God or a particular religion • *the holy city of Mecca* ❷ a holy person is religious and leads a pure life

**homage** NOUN homages
an act or expression of respect or honour • *We paid homage to his achievements.*

**home** NOUN homes
❶ the place where you live ❷ the place where you were born or where you feel you belong ❸ a place where those who need help are looked after • *an old people's home* ❹ the place to be reached in a race or in certain games

**home** ADJECTIVE
❶ to do with your own home or country • *home industries* ❷ played on a team's own ground • *a home match*

**home** ADVERB
❶ to or at home • *Is she home yet?* ❷ to the point aimed at • *Push the bolt home.*
**➤ bring something home to someone** to make a person realize something

**home** VERB homes, homing, homed
**➤ home in on something** to aim at something and move straight towards it • *The missile homed in on its target.*

**home economics** NOUN
the study of cookery and how to run a home

**homeland** NOUN homelands
a person's native country

**homeless** ADJECTIVE
having no home
➤ **homelessness** NOUN

**homely** ADJECTIVE
simple and ordinary • *a homely meal*

**home-made** ADJECTIVE
made at home, not bought from a shop

**homeopath** NOUN homeopaths
a person who practises homeopathy

**homeopathy** NOUN
the treatment of disease by tiny doses of
drugs that in a healthy person would produce
symptoms of the disease
➤ **homeopathic** ADJECTIVE

**home page** NOUN home pages
an introductory page on a website

**homesick** ADJECTIVE
sad or upset because you are away from
home
➤ **homesickness** NOUN

**homestead** NOUN homesteads
a farmhouse, usually with the land and
buildings round it

**homeward** ADJECTIVE & ADVERB
going towards home • *the long homeward
journey*
➤ **homewards** ADVERB

**homework** NOUN
school work that you have to do at home

**homicide** NOUN homicides
the crime of killing another person
➤ **homicidal** ADJECTIVE

**homily** NOUN homilies
a lecture about behaviour

**homing** ADJECTIVE
❶ trained or having the natural ability, to
find its way home from a long distance away
• *a homing pigeon* ❷ programmed to find
and hit its target • *a missile fitted with a
homing device*

**homogeneous** (say hom-o-**jeen**-ee-us)
ADJECTIVE
formed of people or things of the same kind

**homograph** NOUN homographs
a word that is spelt like another but has a
different meaning or origin, e.g. *bat* (a flying
animal) and *bat* (for hitting a ball)

**homonym** (say **hom**-o-nim) NOUN homonyms
a homograph or homophone

**homophone** NOUN homophones
a word with the same sound as another but a
different spelling and meaning, e.g. *son, sun*

**Homo sapiens** NOUN
human beings regarded as a species of animal

**homosexual** ADJECTIVE
attracted to people of the same sex; not
heterosexual
➤ **homosexual** NOUN
➤ **homosexuality** NOUN

**honest** ADJECTIVE
not stealing or cheating or telling lies;
truthful

**honestly** ADVERB
❶ in an honest way • *I can't believe he got
that money honestly.* ❷ speaking truthfully
• *I honestly don't mind.*

**honesty** NOUN
being honest and truthful • *I appreciate your
honesty.*

**honey** NOUN
a sweet sticky food made by bees

**honeycomb** NOUN honeycombs
a wax structure of small six-sided sections
made by bees to hold their honey and eggs

**honeycombed** ADJECTIVE
with many holes or tunnels

**honeymoon** NOUN honeymoons
a holiday spent together by a newly-married
couple

**honeysuckle** NOUN
a climbing plant with fragrant yellow or pink
flowers

**honk** NOUN honks
a loud sound like that made by a goose or an
old-fashioned car horn

**honk** VERB honks, honking, honked
to make a honking sound

**honorary** ADJECTIVE
❶ given or received as an honour • *an
honorary degree* ❷ unpaid • *the honorary
treasurer of the club*

USAGE
Take care not to confuse with
**honourable**.

**honour** NOUN honours
❶ great respect or reputation ❷ a person
or thing that brings honour ❸ something
a person is proud to do • *It is an honour to
meet you.* ❹ honesty and loyalty • *a man*

a
b
c
d
e
f
g
h
i
j
k
l
m
n
o
p
q
r
s
t
u
v
w
x
y
z

of honour ❺ an award given as a mark of respect
➤ **in honour of** out of respect for • *A banquet was held in honour of her visit.*

**honour** VERB honours, honouring, honoured
❶ to feel or show honour for a person ❷ to keep to the terms of an agreement or promise

**honourable** ADJECTIVE
able to be trusted and always trying to do the right thing; deserving honour and respect
➤ **honourably** ADVERB

**USAGE**

Take care not to confuse with **honorary**.

**hood** NOUN hoods
❶ a covering of soft material for the head and neck ❷ a folding roof or cover
➤ **hooded** ADJECTIVE

**hoodie** NOUN hoodies
❶ a jacket or sweatshirt with a hood that goes over the head ❷ a person who wears a hoodie

**hoodwink** VERB hoodwinks, hoodwinking, hoodwinked
to deceive someone **WORD ORIGIN** originally = to blindfold with a hood: from **hood** + an old sense of *wink* = close the eyes

**hoof** NOUN hoofs or hooves
the hard horny part of the feet of horses and some other animals

**hook** NOUN hooks
a bent or curved piece of metal or plastic for hanging things on or for catching hold of something
➤ **be let off the hook** (informal) to escape punishment

**hook** VERB hooks, hooking, hooked
❶ to fasten something with or on a hook ❷ to catch fish with a hook ❸ to hit a ball in a curving path
➤ **be hooked on something** (informal) to be addicted to something

**hookah** NOUN hookahs
an oriental tobacco pipe with a long tube passing through a jar of water

**hooked** ADJECTIVE
hook-shaped • *a hooked nose*

**hooligan** NOUN hooligans
a rough and violent young person
➤ **hooliganism** NOUN

**hoop** NOUN hoops
a large ring made of metal, wood or plastic

**hoopla** NOUN
a game in which people try to throw hoops round an object, which they then win as a prize

**hooray** EXCLAMATION
a different spelling of **hurray**

**hoot** NOUN hoots
❶ the sound made by an owl or a vehicle's horn or a steam whistle ❷ a cry of scorn or disapproval ❸ a loud laugh ❹ something funny

**hoot** VERB hoots, hooting, hooted
❶ to make the sound of a hoot ❷ to laugh loudly
➤ **hooter** NOUN

**Hoover** NOUN Hoovers (trademark) (British)
a vacuum cleaner

**hoover** VERB hoovers, hoovering, hoovered
to clean a carpet with a vacuum cleaner

**hop** VERB hops, hopping, hopped
❶ to jump on one foot ❷ an animal hops when it springs from all its feet at once ❸ (informal) to move quickly • *Hop in and I'll give you a lift.*
➤ **hop it** (informal) to go away

**hop** NOUN hops
❶ a hopping movement ❷ a climbing plant used to give beer its flavour

**hope** NOUN hopes
❶ the feeling of wanting something to happen and thinking that it will happen ❷ a person or thing that gives hope • *You are our only hope.*

**hope** VERB hopes, hoping, hoped
to feel hope; to want and expect something • *I hope that you feel better soon.*

**hopeful** ADJECTIVE
❶ feeling hope ❷ likely to be good or successful • *The future did not seem very hopeful.*

**hopefully** ADVERB
❶ in a hopeful way • *'Can I come too?' she asked hopefully.* ❷ it is to be hoped; I hope that • *Hopefully we will be there by lunchtime.*

**hopeless** ADJECTIVE
❶ without hope ❷ very bad at something
➤ **hopelessly** ADVERB
➤ **hopelessness** NOUN

**hopper** NOUN hoppers
a large funnel-shaped container for grain or sand

**hopscotch** NOUN
a game of hopping into squares drawn on the ground

**horde** NOUN hordes
a large group or crowd • *hordes of tourists*

SPELLING

Horde is different from hoard, which means a hidden store of something.

**horizon** NOUN horizons
the line where the earth and the sky seem to meet

**horizontal** ADJECTIVE
level or flat; going across from side to side, not up and down. (The opposite is **vertical**.)
➤ **horizontally** ADVERB

**hormone** NOUN hormones
a substance produced by glands in the body and carried by the blood to stimulate other organs in the body
➤ **hormonal** ADJECTIVE

**horn** NOUN horns
❶ a hard substance that grows into a point on the head of a bull, cow, ram, etc. ❷ a brass musical instrument played by blowing ❸ a device for making a warning sound

**horned** ADJECTIVE
having horns • *a horned helmet*

**hornet** NOUN hornets
a large kind of wasp

**hornpipe** NOUN hornpipes
a sailors' lively dance or the music for this

**horny** ADJECTIVE
hard like horn • *a horny beak*

**horoscope** NOUN horoscopes
an astrologer's forecast of what is going to happen to someone in the future

**horrendous** ADJECTIVE
extremely unpleasant WORD ORIGIN from Latin *horrendus* = making your hair stand on end

**horrible** ADJECTIVE
❶ shocking or horrifying • *a horrible murder* ❷ very unpleasant or nasty • *Don't be so horrible!*
➤ **horribly** ADVERB

**horrid** ADJECTIVE
nasty or unkind; horrible

**horrific** ADJECTIVE
shocking or horrifying • *a horrific accident*
➤ **horrifically** ADVERB

**horrify** VERB horrifies, horrifying, horrified
to make someone feel shocked or disgusted
• *He was horrified when he discovered the truth.*

**horror** NOUN horrors
❶ great fear or disgust ❷ a person or thing causing horror ❸ (*informal*) a badly behaved child

**hors-d'oeuvre** (say or-**dervr**) NOUN hors-d'oeuvres
food served as an appetizer at the start of a meal

**horse** NOUN horses
❶ a large four-legged animal used for riding on and for pulling carts etc. ❷ a padded wooden block for vaulting over in gymnastics

**horseback** NOUN
➤ **on horseback** riding on a horse

**horse chestnut** NOUN horse chestnuts
a large tree that produces dark-brown nuts (conkers)

**horseman** NOUN horsemen
a man who rides a horse, especially a skilled rider

**horsemanship** NOUN
skill in riding horses

**horseplay** NOUN
rough play

**horsepower** NOUN
a unit for measuring the power of an engine, equal to 746 watts WORD ORIGIN because the unit was based on the amount of work a horse could do

**horseshoe** NOUN horseshoes
a U-shaped piece of metal nailed to a horse's hoof

**horsewoman** NOUN horsewomen
a woman who rides a horse, especially a skilled rider

**horticulture** NOUN
the art of planning and looking after gardens
➤ **horticultural** ADJECTIVE

**hose** NOUN hoses
❶ a flexible tube for taking water to something ❷ (*old use*) men's breeches
• *doublet and hose*

**hose** VERB hoses, hosing, hosed
to water or spray something with a hose

**hosiery** NOUN
socks, stockings and tights sold in shops

a
b
c
d
e
f
g
h
i
j
k
l
m
n
o
p
q
r
s
t
u
v
w
x
y
z

**hospice** (say hosp-iss) *NOUN* hospices
a nursing home for people who are very ill or dying

**hospitable** *ADJECTIVE*
welcoming and friendly to guests and visitors
➤ **hospitably** *ADVERB*

**hospital** *NOUN* hospitals
a place where ill or injured people are given medical treatment

**hospitality** *NOUN*
welcoming guests and visitors and giving them food and entertainment

**host** *NOUN* hosts
❶ a person who has guests and looks after them ❷ the presenter of a television or radio programme ❸ a large number of people or things ❹ in the Christian Church, the bread consecrated at Communion

**host** *VERB* hosts, hosting, hosted
to organize a party, event, etc. and look after the people who come • *London hosted the 2012 Olympic Games.*

**hostage** *NOUN* hostages
a person who is held prisoner until the people who are holding them get what they want
• *The hijackers took the crew hostage.*

**hostel** *NOUN* hostels
a building where travellers, students or other groups can stay or live

**hostess** *NOUN* hostesses
a woman who has guests and looks after them

**hostile** *ADJECTIVE*
❶ unfriendly and angry • *a hostile glance* ❷ opposed to something ❸ to do with an enemy • *hostile aircraft*

**hostility** *NOUN*
unfriendliness and strong dislike • *She did not speak but I could sense her hostility.*

**hot** *ADJECTIVE* hotter, hottest
❶ having great heat or a high temperature ❷ giving a burning sensation in the mouth; spicy ❸ passionate or excitable • *He has a hot temper.*
➤ **hotness** *NOUN*
➤ **be in hot water** (*informal*) to be in trouble or disgrace

**hot** *VERB* hots, hotting, hotted
➤ **hot up** (*British*) (*informal*) to become hotter or more exciting

**hot cross bun** *NOUN* hot cross buns
a spicy bun marked with a cross, eaten at Easter

**hot dog** *NOUN* hot dogs
a hot sausage in a long bread roll

**hotel** *NOUN* hotels
a building where people pay to stay for the night when they are travelling or on holiday

**hotfoot** *ADVERB*
in eager haste • *She had just arrived hotfoot from Madrid.*

**hothead** *NOUN* hotheads
an impetuous person
➤ **hot-headed** *ADJECTIVE*

**hothouse** *NOUN* hothouses
a heated greenhouse

**hotly** *ADVERB*
strongly or forcefully • *He hotly denied that he'd done it.*

**hotplate** *NOUN* hotplates
a heated surface for cooking food or keeping it hot

**hotpot** *NOUN* hotpots
(*British*) a kind of stew

**hot-water bottle** *NOUN* hot-water bottles
a container that is filled with hot water and used to warm a bed

**hound** *NOUN* hounds
a dog used in hunting or racing

**hound** *VERB* hounds, hounding, hounded
to keep on chasing and bothering someone

**hour** *NOUN* hours
❶ one of the twenty four parts into which a day is divided; sixty minutes ❷ a particular time • *Why are you up at this hour?*
➤ **hours** *PLURAL NOUN*
a fixed period for work • *Office hours are 9 a.m. to 5 p.m.*

SPELLING
Be careful, this sounds the same as **our** which means 'belonging to us'.

**hourglass** *NOUN* hourglasses
a glass container with a very narrow part in the middle through which sand runs from the top half to the bottom half, taking one hour

**hourly** *ADVERB & ADJECTIVE*
every hour • *Trains run hourly.* • *an hourly bus service*

**house** (say howss) *NOUN* **houses**
❶ a building made for people to live in, usually designed for one family ❷ a building or establishment for a special purpose • *the opera house* ❸ a building for a government assembly; the assembly itself • *the House of Commons* ❹ one of the divisions in some schools for sports competitions and other events ❺ a family or dynasty • *the royal house of Tudor*

**house** (say howz) *VERB* **houses, housing, housed**
to provide a place for someone to live or a place where something can be kept • *The hangar was big enough to house two large aircraft.*

**houseboat** *NOUN* **houseboats**
a barge-like boat for living in

**household** *NOUN* **households**
all the people who live together in the same house

**householder** *NOUN* **householders**
a person who owns or rents a house

**housekeeper** *NOUN* **housekeepers**
a person employed to look after a household

**housekeeping** *NOUN*
❶ looking after a household ❷ the money for food and the other things that you need at home

**housemaid** *NOUN* **housemaids**
a woman servant in a house, especially one who cleans rooms

**house plant** *NOUN* **house plants**
a plant grown indoors

**house-proud** *ADJECTIVE*
very careful to keep a house clean and tidy

**house-trained** *ADJECTIVE*
an animal that is house-trained is trained to be clean in the house

**house-warming** *NOUN* **house-warmings**
a party to celebrate moving into a new home

**housewife** *NOUN* **housewives**
a woman who does the housekeeping for her family and does not have a paid job

**housework** *NOUN*
the regular work that has to be done in a house, such as cleaning and cooking

**housing** *NOUN* **housings**
❶ buildings in which people live ❷ a stiff cover or guard for a piece of machinery

**housing estate** *NOUN* **housing estates**
(*British*) a set of houses planned and built together in one area

**hove**
past tense of **heave** (when used of ships)

**hovel** *NOUN* **hovels**
a small shabby house

**hover** *VERB* **hovers, hovering, hovered**
❶ to stay in one place in the air ❷ to wait about near someone or something • *He hovered nervously outside the door.*

**hovercraft** *NOUN* **hovercraft**
a vehicle that travels just above the surface of land or water, supported by a strong current of air sent downwards from its engines

**how** *ADVERB*
❶ in what way; by what means • *How did you do it?* ❷ to what extent or amount etc. • *How high can you jump?* ❸ in what condition • *How are you?* ❹ used for emphasis • *How odd!*
➤ **how about** would you like • *How about a game of football?*
➤ **how do you do?** a formal greeting

**however** *ADVERB*
❶ in whatever way; to whatever extent • *You will never catch him, however hard you try.* ❷ all the same; nevertheless • *Later, however, he decided to go.*

**however** *CONJUNCTION*
in any way • *You can do it however you like.*

**howl** *NOUN* **howls**
a long loud sad-sounding cry or sound, such as that made by a dog or wolf

**howl** *VERB* **howls, howling, howled**
❶ to make a howl ❷ to weep loudly

**howler** *NOUN* **howlers**
(*informal*) a silly and embarrassing mistake

**HQ** *ABBREVIATION*
headquarters

**hub** *NOUN* **hubs**
❶ the central part of a wheel ❷ the central point of interest or activity

**hubbub** *NOUN*
a loud confused noise of voices

**huddle** *VERB* **huddles, huddling, huddled**
❶ people huddle when they crowd together, often for warmth • *We huddled together round the fire.* ❷ to curl up your body closely

**huddle** *NOUN* **huddles**
a small group of people crowded together

**hue** NOUN hues
a colour or tint
➤ **hue and cry** a public outcry of alarm or protest

**huff** VERB huffs, huffing, huffed
to breathe out noisily • *He climbed up the hill, huffing and puffing.*
➤ **in a huff** offended or sulking about something • *She went away in a huff.*
➤ **huffy** ADJECTIVE

**hug** VERB hugs, hugging, hugged
❶ to clasp someone tightly in your arms ❷ to keep close to something • *The little boat hugged the shore.*

**hug** NOUN hugs
clasping someone tightly in your arms

**huge** ADJECTIVE
extremely large; enormous
➤ **hugeness** NOUN

**hugely** ADVERB
extremely; very much • *The singer is hugely popular.*

**hulk** NOUN hulks
❶ the body or wreck of an old ship ❷ a large clumsy person or thing

**hulking** ADJECTIVE
large and heavy in appearance

**hull** NOUN hulls
the main framework of a ship

**hullabaloo** NOUN hullabaloos
an uproar or commotion

**hullo** EXCLAMATION
a different spelling of hello

**hum** VERB hums, humming, hummed
❶ to sing a tune with your lips closed ❷ to make a low continuous sound like that of a bee

**hum** NOUN hums
a humming sound • *the hum of distant traffic*

**human** ADJECTIVE
to do with human beings

**human** NOUN humans
a human being

**human being** NOUN human beings
a person; a man, woman or child

**humane** (say hew-**mayn**) ADJECTIVE
showing kindness and a wish to cause as little suffering or pain as possible
➤ **humanely** ADVERB

**humanist** NOUN humanists
a person who believes that people can live using reason and understanding of others, rather than using religious belief
➤ **humanism** NOUN

**humanitarian** ADJECTIVE
concerned with people's welfare and the reduction of suffering
➤ **humanitarian** NOUN

**humanity** NOUN
❶ human beings as a whole; people ❷ being human ❸ compassion and understanding
➤ **humanities** PLURAL NOUN
arts subjects such as history, literature and music, not sciences

**humble** ADJECTIVE
❶ modest; not proud or showy ❷ not special or important • *He comes from a humble background.*
➤ **humbly** ADVERB

**humble** VERB humbles, humbling, humbled
to make someone feel humble or humiliated

**humbug** NOUN humbugs
❶ insincere or dishonest talk or behaviour ❷ a hard peppermint sweet

**humdrum** ADJECTIVE
dull and boring; commonplace • *a humdrum existence.*

**humid** (say **hew**-mid) ADJECTIVE
humid air is warm and damp
➤ **humidity** NOUN

**humiliate** VERB humiliates, humiliating, humiliated
to make a person feel ashamed or foolish in front of other people
➤ **humiliation** NOUN

**humility** NOUN
being humble

**hummingbird** NOUN hummingbirds
a small tropical bird that makes a humming sound by beating its wings rapidly

**humorist** NOUN humorists
a humorous writer

**humorous** ADJECTIVE
amusing or funny

**humour** NOUN
❶ being amusing; what makes people laugh ❷ the ability to enjoy things that are funny • *a sense of humour* ❸ a person's mood • *She is in a good humour today.*

**humour** VERB humours, humouring, humoured
to keep a person happy by doing what they want or agreeing with them

**hump** NOUN humps
❶ a rounded lump or mound ❷ an abnormal outward curve at the top of a person's back

**hump** VERB humps, humping, humped
to carry something heavy with difficulty • We've been humping furniture around all day.

**humpback bridge** NOUN humpback bridges
(British) a small bridge that steeply curves upwards in the middle

**humus** (say hew-mus) NOUN
rich earth made by decayed plants

**hunch** NOUN hunches
a feeling that you can guess what is going to happen • I have a hunch that she won't come.

**hunch** VERB hunches, hunching, hunched
to hunch your shoulders is to raise them so that your back is rounded

**hunchback** NOUN hunchbacks
(old use) someone with a hump on their back
➤ **hunchbacked** ADJECTIVE

**hundred** NOUN & ADJECTIVE hundreds
the number 100
➤ **hundredth** ADJECTIVE & NOUN

**hundredweight** NOUN hundredweight
a unit of weight equal to 112 pounds (about 50.8 kilograms)

**hunger** NOUN
❶ the feeling that you have when you need to eat ❷ a strong desire for something • a hunger for knowledge

**hunger** VERB hungers, hungering, hungered
to hunger for something is to want it very much

**hunger strike** NOUN hunger strikes
refusing to eat, as a way of making a protest

**hungry** ADJECTIVE hungrier, hungriest
❶ wanting or needing to eat ❷ wanting something very much • He was hungry for power.
➤ **hungrily** ADVERB

**hunk** NOUN hunks
❶ a large piece of something • a hunk of bread ❷ (informal) a muscular, good-looking man

**hunt** VERB hunts, hunting, hunted
❶ to chase and kill animals for food or as a sport • Owls hunt at night. ❷ to search for something • I've hunted everywhere, but I can't find it.

**hunt** NOUN hunts
❶ hunting or searching • The hunt for clues has begun. ❷ a group of hunters

**hunter, huntsman** NOUN hunters or huntsmen
someone who hunts for sport

**hurdle** NOUN hurdles
❶ an upright frame that runners jump over in hurdling ❷ a difficulty or problem that you need to overcome

**hurdling** NOUN
racing in which the runners jump over hurdles
➤ **hurdler** NOUN

**hurl** VERB hurls, hurling, hurled
to throw something with great force

**hurly-burly** NOUN
a rough bustle of activity

**hurray, hurrah** EXCLAMATION
a shout of joy or approval; a cheer

**hurricane** NOUN hurricanes
a storm with violent wind

**hurriedly** ADVERB
in a hurry • We hurriedly got dressed.

**hurry** VERB hurries, hurrying, hurried
❶ to move or do something quickly ❷ to try to make someone be quick
➤ **hurried** ADJECTIVE

**hurry** NOUN
hurrying; a need to hurry • She got up late and left in a hurry. • It's all right, there's no hurry.

**hurt** VERB hurts, hurting, hurt
❶ to cause pain or injury to someone ❷ to feel painful • My leg hurts. ❸ to upset or offend someone • I'm sorry if I hurt your feelings.

**hurt** NOUN
physical or mental pain or injury

**hurtful** ADJECTIVE
upsetting and unkind • a hurtful remark

**hurtle** VERB hurtles, hurtling, hurtled
to move rapidly, sometimes in an uncontrolled way • The train hurtled along.

**husband** NOUN husbands
the man someone is married to

337

a b c d e f g h i j k l m n o p q r s t u v w x y z

**husbandry** NOUN
farming • *animal husbandry*

**hush** VERB hushes, hushing, hushed
to become silent or quiet or to make someone do this • *Hush now and try to sleep.*
➤ **hush something up** to prevent something from becoming generally known

**hush** NOUN
silence or quiet • *A hush descended over the crowd.*

**hush-hush** ADJECTIVE (*informal*)
highly secret or confidential

**husk** NOUN husks
the dry outer covering of some seeds and fruits

**husky** ADJECTIVE huskier, huskiest
a husky voice is low-pitched and slightly hoarse
➤ **huskily** ADVERB
➤ **huskiness** NOUN

**husky** NOUN huskies
a large powerful dog used in the Arctic for pulling sledges

**hustle** VERB hustles, hustling, hustled
❶ to push or shove someone roughly • *He grabbed her arm and hustled her out of the room.* ❷ to hurry

**hut** NOUN huts
a small roughly-made house or shelter

**hutch** NOUN hutches
a box or cage for a rabbit or other pet animal

**hyacinth** NOUN hyacinths
a sweet-smelling flower that grows from a bulb WORD ORIGIN because, in Greek legend, the flower sprang from the blood of *Hyacinthus*, a youth who was accidentally killed by Apollo

**hybrid** NOUN hybrids
❶ a plant or animal produced by combining two different species or varieties ❷ something that combines parts or characteristics of two different things

**hydra** NOUN hydras
a microscopic freshwater animal with a tubular body

**hydrangea** (say hy-**drayn**-ja) NOUN hydrangeas
a shrub with pink, blue or white flowers growing in large clusters

**hydrant** NOUN hydrants
an outdoor water tap with a nozzle that a fire hose can be attached to

**hydraulic** ADJECTIVE
worked by the force of water or other fluid • *hydraulic brakes*

**hydrochloric acid** NOUN
a strong colourless acid containing hydrogen and chlorine

**hydroelectric** ADJECTIVE
using water power to produce electricity
➤ **hydroelectricity** NOUN

**hydrofoil** NOUN hydrofoils
a boat designed to skim over the surface of water

**hydrogen** NOUN
a lightweight gas that combines with oxygen to form water

**hydrogen bomb** NOUN hydrogen bombs
a very powerful bomb using energy created by the fusion of hydrogen nuclei

**hydrophobia** NOUN
abnormal fear of water, as in someone suffering from rabies

**hyena** NOUN hyenas
a wild animal that looks like a wolf and makes a shrieking howl

**hygiene** (say hy-jeen) NOUN
keeping things clean in order to remain healthy and prevent disease

**hygienic** ADJECTIVE
clean and healthy and free of germs
➤ **hygienically** ADVERB

**hymn** NOUN hymns
a Christian religious song, usually one praising God
➤ **hymn book** NOUN

**hype** NOUN (*informal*)
extravagant publicity or advertising

**hyperactive** ADJECTIVE
unable to relax and always moving about or doing things

**hyperbola** (say hy-**per**-bol-a) NOUN hyperbolas
(*in mathematics*) a kind of curve

**hyperbole** (say hy-**per**-bol-ee) NOUN hyperboles
a dramatic exaggeration that is not meant to be taken literally, e.g. 'I've got a stack of work a mile high.'

**hyperlink** *NOUN* **hyperlinks**
a place in a computer document that is linked to another computer document • *Click on the hyperlink.*

**hypermarket** *NOUN* **hypermarkets**
(*British*) a very large supermarket, usually outside a town

**hypertext** *NOUN* **hypertexts**
a computer document that contains links that allow the user to move from one document to another

**hyphen** *NOUN* **hyphens**
a short dash (-) used to join words or parts of words together (e.g. in *hitch-hiker*)

> **PUNCTUATION**
>
> A **hyphen** is used to join two or more words which make up a compound noun or adjective. A hyphen is shorter than a dash and does not have a space on either side of it. Sometimes, the hyphen is part of a fixed compound, like *close-up*, *free range* or *great-aunt*, but hyphens can join any pair or group of words to form a new compound: an *ultra-squidgy sandwich*; *that morning-after-the-night-before feeling.*
>
> A hyphen is sometimes used to join prefixes to words, especially where there would be a confusing combination of letters without it, as in *co-education* and *re-enter.*
>
> Hyphens are often useful to make things clearer. Note, for example, the difference between *a cross-section of the audience* (= a typical sample) and *a cross section of the audience* (= an annoyed group). You do not need a hyphen for compound adjectives when they follow a noun (*an out-of-date hairstyle* but *a hairstyle which looks out of date*).
>
> Hyphens are also used in compound numbers and fractions, such as *thirty-two* and *four-fifths.*
>
> A hyphen is also used to divide the two parts of a word that is split between the end of one line and the beginning of the next line.

**hyphenate** *VERB* **hyphenates, hyphenating, hyphenated**
to write a word or group of words with a hyphen

**hypnosis** (say hip-**noh**-sis) *NOUN*
a condition like a deep sleep in which a person can be made to follow the commands of someone else

**hypnotic** *ADJECTIVE*
❶ having a regular, repeated sound or movement which makes you feel sleepy • *the hypnotic ticking of the clock* ❷ to do with hypnosis

**hypnotize** (also **hypnotise**) *VERB* **hypnotizes, hypnotizing, hypnotized**
to put someone in a state of hypnosis
> ➤ **hypnotism** *NOUN*
> ➤ **hypnotist** *NOUN*

**hypochondriac** (say hy-po-**kon**-dree-ak) *NOUN* **hypochondriacs**
a person who constantly imagines that they are ill even though there is nothing wrong with them
> ➤ **hypochondria** *NOUN*
> **WORD ORIGIN** from Greek *hypochondrios* = under the breastbone (because the organs there were once thought to be the source of depression and anxiety)

**hypocrite** (say **hip**-o-krit) *NOUN* **hypocrites**
someone who pretends to be a better person than they really are
> ➤ **hypocrisy** (say hip-**ok**-riss-ee) *NOUN*
> ➤ **hypocritical** *ADJECTIVE*

**hypodermic** *ADJECTIVE*
a hypodermic needle or syringe is one used to inject something under the skin

**hypotenuse** (say hy-**pot**-i-newz) *NOUN* **hypotenuses**
the side opposite the right angle in a right-angled triangle

**hypothermia** *NOUN*
the condition of having a body temperature well below normal

**hypothesis** (say hy-**poth**-i-sis) *NOUN* **hypotheses**
a suggestion or guess that tries to explain something but has not yet been proved to be true or correct

**hypothetical** (say hy-po-**thet**-ikal) *ADJECTIVE*
based on a theory or possibility, not on proven facts • *a hypothetical example*

**hysteria** *NOUN*
wild uncontrollable excitement or emotion • *There was mass hysteria when the band came on stage.* **WORD ORIGIN** from Greek *hystera* = womb (because people used to

believe that the womb was the source of
hysteria, and that only women suffered from it)

**hysterical** ADJECTIVE
❶ in a state of hysteria ❷ (*informal*)
extremely funny
➤ **hysterically** ADVERB

**hysterics** (say hiss-**te**-riks) PLURAL NOUN
a fit of hysteria
➤ **in hysterics** (*informal*) laughing a lot

**I** PRONOUN
a word used by a person to refer to himself
or herself

**ice** NOUN ices
❶ solid frozen water ❷ an ice cream

**ice** VERB ices, icing, iced
❶ to become covered with ice • *The pond has
iced over.* ❷ to put icing on a cake

**ice age** NOUN ice ages
a period in the past when most of the earth's
surface was covered with ice

**iceberg** NOUN icebergs
a large mass of ice floating in the sea with
most of it under water

**ice cap** NOUN ice caps
a permanent covering of ice and snow at the
North or South Pole

**ice cream** NOUN ice creams
a sweet creamy frozen food

**ice hockey** NOUN
a form of hockey played on ice

**ice lolly** NOUN ice lollies
(*British*) frozen juice on a small stick

**ice rink** NOUN ice rinks
a place made for skating

**icicle** NOUN icicles
a pointed hanging piece of ice formed when
dripping water freezes

**icily** ADVERB
in a very unfriendly way • '*I don't care what
you think,*' he said icily.

**icing** NOUN
a sugary liquid mixture for decorating cakes

**icon** (say **eye**-kon) NOUN icons
❶ a small symbol or picture on a computer
screen, representing a program, window, etc.
that you can select ❷ a sacred painting or
mosaic of a holy person

**ICT** ABBREVIATION
information and communication technology

**icy** ADJECTIVE icier, iciest
❶ covered with ice ❷ very cold • *an icy wind*
❸ very unfriendly • *an icy stare*

**Id** NOUN
a different spelling of Eid

**idea** NOUN ideas
❶ a plan or thought that you form in your
mind ❷ an opinion or belief ❸ what you
know about something • *I have no idea what
you are talking about.*

**ideal** ADJECTIVE
perfect; completely suitable

**ideal** NOUN ideals
❶ a person or thing that seems to be a
perfect example of something ❷ a high
standard or principle that people try to follow

**idealist** NOUN idealists
a person who has high ideals and wishes to
achieve them
➤ **idealism** NOUN
➤ **idealistic** ADJECTIVE

**ideally** ADVERB
if things were perfect • *Ideally, I would train
every day.*

**identical** ADJECTIVE
exactly the same • *All the desks were
identical.* • *identical twins*
➤ **identically** ADVERB

**identification** NOUN
❶ any document, such as a passport or
driving licence, that proves who you are
❷ identifying someone or something

**identify** VERB identifies, identifying,
identified
❶ to recognize a person or thing as being
who or what they are • *The police have
identified the car used in the robbery.*
❷ to treat something as being identical to
something else • *Don't identify wealth with
happiness.* ❸ to think of yourself as sharing
someone else's feelings or experiences • *We
can identify with the hero of this play.*
➤ **identifiable** ADJECTIVE

**identity** NOUN identities
who or what a person or thing is • *Can you guess the identity of our mystery guest?*

**ideology** (say eye-dee-**ol**-o-jee) NOUN ideologies
a set of beliefs and aims, especially in politics
• *a socialist ideology*
➤ **ideological** ADJECTIVE

**idiocy** NOUN
stupid behaviour

**idiom** NOUN idioms
a phrase that means something different from the meanings of the words in it, e.g. *in hot water* (= in trouble) or *hell for leather* (= at great speed)

**idiosyncrasy** (say id-ee-o-**sink**-ra see) NOUN idiosyncrasies
one person's own way of behaving or doing something
➤ **idiosyncratic** ADJECTIVE

**idiot** NOUN idiots
a stupid or foolish person

**idiotic** ADJECTIVE
stupid or foolish • *That was an idiotic thing to say.*
➤ **idiotically** ADVERB

**idle** ADJECTIVE
❶ doing no work; lazy ❷ not being used
• *The machines were idle.* ❸ useless; with no real purpose • *idle gossip* • *an idle threat*
➤ **idly** ADVERB
➤ **idleness** NOUN

**idle** VERB idles, idling, idled
❶ to be idle or lazy • *We idled away the afternoon.* ❷ an engine idles when it is working slowly
➤ **idler** NOUN

**idol** NOUN idols
❶ a statue or image that is worshipped as a god ❷ a famous person who is widely admired

**idolatry** NOUN
❶ worship of idols ❷ great admiration for someone
➤ **idolatrous** ADJECTIVE

**idolize** (also **idolise**) VERB idolizes, idolizing, idolized
to admire or love someone very much • *She idolized her older brother.*

**idyll** (say **id**-il) NOUN idylls
❶ a beautiful or peaceful scene or situation

❷ a poem describing a peaceful or romantic scene

**idyllic** (say id-**il**-ik) ADJECTIVE
beautiful and peaceful • *an idyllic scene*

**i.e.** ABBREVIATION
that is • *The world's highest mountain (i.e. Mount Everest) is in the Himalayas.*
**WORD ORIGIN** short for Latin *id est* = that is

**if** CONJUNCTION
❶ on condition that; supposing that • *I'll tell you if you promise to keep it a secret.* ❷ even though • *I'll finish this job if it kills me.*
❸ whether • *Do you know if lunch is ready?*
➤ **if only** I wish • *If only I were taller!*

**igloo** NOUN igloos
an Inuit round house built of blocks of hard snow

**igneous** ADJECTIVE
igneous rock is formed when hot liquid rock from a volcano cools and becomes hard

**ignite** VERB ignites, igniting, ignited
❶ to set fire to something ❷ to catch fire
• *The petrol suddenly ignited and there was an explosion.*

**ignition** NOUN ignitions
❶ igniting ❷ the part of a motor engine that starts the fuel burning

**ignoble** ADJECTIVE
not noble; shameful

**ignominious** ADJECTIVE
humiliating; bringing disgrace or shame • *an ignominious defeat*
➤ **ignominy** NOUN

**ignoramus** NOUN ignoramuses
an ignorant person

**ignorance** NOUN
a lack of information or knowledge • *They were kept in ignorance of her plans.*

**ignorant** ADJECTIVE
❶ not knowing about something ❷ knowing very little
➤ **ignorantly** ADVERB

**ignore** VERB ignores, ignoring, ignored
to take no notice of a person or thing • *She ignored him and carried on reading.*

**iguana** (say ig-**wah**-na) NOUN iguanas
a large tree-climbing tropical lizard

**ilk** NOUN
➤ **of that ilk** (*informal*) of that kind

341

**ill** ADJECTIVE
① unwell; in bad health ② bad or harmful
• *There were no ill effects.*

**ill** ADVERB
badly • *The animals had been ill-treated.*
➤ **ill at ease** uncomfortable or embarrassed

**illegal** ADJECTIVE
not legal; against the law
➤ **illegally** ADVERB

**illegible** ADJECTIVE
illegible writing is not clear enough to read
➤ **illegibly** ADVERB

**illegitimate** ADJECTIVE
(old use) an illegitimate child is born of
parents who are not married to each other
➤ **illegitimacy** NOUN

**ill-fated** ADJECTIVE
bound to fail or have bad luck • *an ill-fated
expedition*

**illicit** ADJECTIVE
done in a way that is against the law; not
allowed
➤ **illicitly** ADVERB

SPELLING
Take care not to confuse with **elicit**.

**illiterate** ADJECTIVE
unable to read or write
➤ **illiteracy** NOUN

**illness** NOUN illnesses
① being ill • *He missed two weeks of school
through illness.* ② a particular form of bad
health; a disease

**illogical** ADJECTIVE
not logical; not reasoning correctly
➤ **illogically** ADVERB

**ills** PLURAL NOUN
problems and difficulties • *the ills of the
modern world*

**illuminate** VERB illuminates, illuminating,
illuminated
① to light something up ② to decorate
streets or buildings with lights ③ to decorate
a manuscript with coloured designs ④ to help
to explain something or make it clearer
➤ **illumination** NOUN

**illusion** NOUN illusions
① something that seems to be real or actually
happening but is not, especially something
that deceives the eye • *an optical illusion*
② a false idea or belief • *He had no illusions
about the danger he was in.*

**illusionist** NOUN illusionists
an entertainer who performs tricks that
deceive the eye

**illustrate** VERB illustrates, illustrating,
illustrated
① to show or explain something by pictures
or examples • *To illustrate my point, let me
tell you a little story.* ② to illustrate a book is
to put illustrations in it

**illustration** NOUN illustrations
① a picture in a book etc. ② an example that
helps to explain something ③ illustrating
something

**illustrator** NOUN illustrators
a person who produces the illustrations in a
book

**illustrious** ADJECTIVE
famous and respected

**ill will** NOUN
unkind feelings towards a person

**image** NOUN images
① a picture or statue of a person or thing
② what you see in a mirror or through a lens
③ a person or thing that looks very much
like another • *He is the image of his father.*
④ a word or phrase that describes something
in an imaginative way ⑤ a person's or
company's public reputation

**imagery** NOUN
a writer's or speaker's use of words to produce
pictures in the mind of the reader or hearer

**imaginable** ADJECTIVE
able to be imagined • *It was the worst smell
imaginable.*

**imaginary** ADJECTIVE
existing only in your mind; not real • *When
she was a little girl she had an imaginary
friend.*

**imagination** NOUN imaginations
the ability to imagine things, especially in a
creative or inventive way • *He has a lively
imagination.*

**imaginative** ADJECTIVE
having or showing imagination • *Her stories
are full of imaginative ideas.*

**imagine** VERB imagines, imagining, imagined
① to form pictures or ideas in your mind
• *Close your eyes and imagine you are on a
beach.* ② to suppose or think something • *I
don't imagine there'll be any tickets left.*

**imam** NOUN imams
a Muslim religious leader

**imbalance** NOUN
a lack of balance

**imbecile** (say **imb**-i-seel) NOUN imbeciles
a very stupid person
➤ **imbecility** NOUN

**imbibe** VERB imbibes, imbibing, imbibed
(formal)
❶ to drink alcohol ❷ to absorb information
or ideas

**imitate** VERB imitates, imitating, imitated
to copy or mimic something
➤ **imitator** NOUN
➤ **imitative** ADJECTIVE

**imitation** NOUN imitations
❶ a copy of something else • He does a good
imitation of his father. ❷ copying something
• A child learns to talk by imitation.

**immaculate** ADJECTIVE
❶ perfectly clean; spotless • an immaculate
white shirt ❷ without any faults or mistakes
• an immaculate performance
➤ **immaculately** ADVERB

**immaterial** ADJECTIVE
not important; not mattering at all • It is
immaterial whether he goes or stays.

**immature** ADJECTIVE
❶ not fully grown or developed ❷ behaving
in a silly or childish way
➤ **immaturity** NOUN

**immediate** ADJECTIVE
❶ happening or done without any delay
❷ nearest; with nothing or no one between
• our immediate neighbours

**immediately** ADVERB
at once; without any delay • You must come
immediately.

**immemorial** ADJECTIVE
➤ **from time immemorial** further back in
time than anyone can remember

**immense** ADJECTIVE
extremely large or great; huge
➤ **immensity** NOUN

**immensely** ADVERB
extremely; very much • I am immensely
grateful.

**immerse** VERB immerses, immersing,
immersed
❶ to put something completely into a liquid
❷ to be immersed in something is to be

concentrating fully on it • She was immersed
in her work.
➤ **immersion** NOUN

**immersion heater** NOUN immersion heaters
a device that heats up water by means of an
electric element immersed in the water in a
tank

**immigrant** NOUN immigrants
a person who has come into a country to live
there

USAGE
If you mean someone who has left a
country to live somewhere else, use
emigrant.

**immigration** NOUN
the process by which people come into a
country to live there
➤ **immigrate** VERB

**imminent** ADJECTIVE
likely to happen at any moment • an
imminent storm
➤ **imminence** NOUN

**immobile** ADJECTIVE
not moving or not able to move • He stood
immobile by the door.
➤ **immobility** NOUN

**immobilize** (also **immobilise**) VERB
immobilizes, immobilizing, immobilized
to stop a thing from moving or working

**immodest** ADJECTIVE
❶ not behaving or dressing decently or
modestly ❷ conceited

**immoral** ADJECTIVE
morally wrong; wicked
➤ **immorality** NOUN

**immortal** ADJECTIVE
❶ living for ever; not mortal ❷ famous for
all time
➤ **immortal** NOUN
➤ **immortality** NOUN

**immortalize** (also **immortalise**) VERB
immortalizes, immortalizing, immortalized
to make someone famous for all time

**immovable** ADJECTIVE
unable to be moved

**immune** ADJECTIVE
❶ not able to catch a disease ❷ not affected
by something • I'm immune to flattery.
❸ protected from something and able to
avoid it • No one should be immune from

prosecution.
➤ **immunity** NOUN

**immune system** NOUN immune systems
the body's means of resisting infection

**immunize** (also **immunise**) VERB immunizes, immunizing, immunized
to make a person immune from a disease etc., e.g. by vaccination
➤ **immunization** NOUN

**immutable** (say i-**mewt**-a-bul) ADJECTIVE
that cannot be changed

**imp** NOUN imps
❶ a small devil ❷ a mischievous child

**impact** NOUN impacts
❶ the force of one thing hitting another
❷ an influence or effect • *the impact of the Internet on our lives*

**impair** VERB impairs, impairing, impaired
to damage or weaken something • *Ear infections can impair hearing.*
➤ **impairment** NOUN

**impala** (say im-**pah**-la) NOUN impala
a small African antelope

**impale** VERB impales, impaling, impaled
to pierce or fix something on a sharp pointed object

**impart** VERB imparts, imparting, imparted
❶ to impart news or information is to tell it to someone • *She imparted the good news to her brother.* ❷ to give something a certain taste, smell or quality • *The lamp imparted a warm glow to the room.*

**impartial** ADJECTIVE
not favouring one side more than the other; treating everyone equally
➤ **impartially** ADVERB
➤ **impartiality** NOUN

**impassable** ADJECTIVE
not able to be travelled along or over • *The road is impassable because of flooding.*

**impasse** (say **am**-pahss) NOUN impasses
a situation in which no progress can be made; a deadlock

**impassive** ADJECTIVE
not showing any emotion • *His face remained impassive as the charges were read out.*
➤ **impassively** ADVERB

**impasto** (say im-**past**-oh) NOUN
(*in art*) the technique of applying paint so thickly that it stands out from the surface of the picture

**impatient** ADJECTIVE
❶ not able to wait for something without getting annoyed • *The passengers were getting impatient at the delay.* ❷ eager to do something and not wanting to wait • *She was impatient to get home.*
➤ **impatiently** ADVERB
➤ **impatience** NOUN

**impeach** VERB impeaches, impeaching, impeached
to bring an important person to trial for a serious crime against their country
➤ **impeachment** NOUN

**impeccable** ADJECTIVE
without any mistakes or faults; perfect • *He has impeccable manners.*
➤ **impeccably** ADVERB

**impede** VERB impedes, impeding, impeded
to hinder someone or get in their way
**WORD ORIGIN** from Latin *impedire* = shackle the feet

**impediment** NOUN impediments
❶ a hindrance ❷ a fault or defect • *He has a slight speech impediment.*

**impel** VERB impels, impelling, impelled
to urge or drive someone to do something
• *Curiosity impelled her to investigate.*

**impending** ADJECTIVE
about to happen; imminent • *a feeling of impending disaster*

**impenetrable** ADJECTIVE
❶ impossible to get through or see through
• *impenetrable darkness* ❷ impossible to understand

**imperative** ADJECTIVE
❶ (*in grammar*) expressing a command or instruction ❷ essential • *Speed is imperative.*

**imperative** NOUN imperatives (*in grammar*)
the form of a verb used in making commands (e.g. 'come' in *Come here!*)

**imperceptible** ADJECTIVE
too small or gradual to be noticed
➤ **imperceptibly** ADVERB

**imperfect** ADJECTIVE
❶ with faults or problems; not perfect • *She speaks imperfect English.* ❷ the imperfect tense of a verb shows a continuous action in the past, e.g. *She was singing.*
➤ **imperfectly** ADVERB
➤ **imperfection** NOUN

**imperial** ADJECTIVE
❶ to do with an empire or its rulers

**imperial** ❷ imperial weights and measures are the non-metric ones formerly in use in Britain and still used for some purposes • *an imperial gallon*

**imperious** ADJECTIVE
haughty and bossy • *an imperious command*

**impermeable** ADJECTIVE
not allowing liquid or gas to pass through it • *impermeable rock*

**impersonal** ADJECTIVE
❶ not showing friendly human feelings • *Her manner was cold and impersonal.* ❷ not referring to any particular person

**impersonate** VERB impersonates, impersonating, impersonated
to pretend to be another person
➤ **impersonation** NOUN
➤ **impersonator** NOUN

**impertinent** ADJECTIVE
rude to someone and not showing them proper respect • *impertinent questions*
➤ **impertinently** ADVERB
➤ **impertinence** NOUN

**imperturbable** ADJECTIVE
always calm and not easily worried
➤ **imperturbably** ADVERB

**impervious** ADJECTIVE
❶ not affected by something and not noticing it • *He seems impervious to criticism.* ❷ not allowing water, heat, etc. to pass through • *The rock is impervious to water.*

**impetuous** ADJECTIVE
acting hastily without thinking

**impetus** NOUN
❶ the force that makes an object start moving and that keeps it moving ❷ the influence that causes something to develop more quickly • *The ceasefire gave an impetus to peace talks.*

**impinge** VERB impinges, impinging, impinged
to have an effect or influence on something • *The economic recession impinged on all aspects of our lives.*

**impish** ADJECTIVE
mischievous • *an impish grin*

**implacable** ADJECTIVE
not able to be calmed; relentless • *an implacable enemy*
➤ **implacably** ADVERB

**implant** VERB implants, implanting, implanted
to fix something into a person's body by means of an operation

**implant** NOUN implants
an organ or piece of tissue implanted into a person's body

**implement** NOUN implements
a tool or device you use for something

**implement** VERB implements, implementing, implemented
to put a plan or idea into action • *We shall implement these plans next month.*

**implicate** VERB implicates, implicating, implicated
to involve a person in a crime etc. or to show that a person is involved • *His evidence implicates his sister.*

**implication** NOUN implications
❶ something that someone suggests without actually saying it ❷ a possible effect or result of something

**implicit** (say im-**pliss**-it) ADJECTIVE
❶ suggested but not stated openly. Compare with **explicit.** • *implicit criticism* ❷ absolute or unquestioning • *She expects implicit obedience.*
➤ **implicitly** ADVERB

**implode** VERB implodes, imploding, imploded
to burst or explode inwards
➤ **implosion** NOUN

**implore** VERB implores, imploring, implored
to beg someone to do something • *She implored him to stay.*

**imply** VERB implies, implying, implied
to suggest something without actually saying it • *Are you implying that I'm lazy?*

**USAGE**
If you mean to work something out from what someone says or does, use **infer.**

**impolite** ADJECTIVE
not polite; having bad manners

**import** VERB imports, importing, imported
to bring in goods from another country

**import** NOUN imports
❶ importing goods ❷ something that is imported ❸ (*formal*) meaning or importance • *The message was of great import.*

**importance** NOUN
being important • *She explained the importance of training properly.*

**important** ADJECTIVE
❶ having a great effect or value ❷ having great authority or influence
➤ **importantly** ADVERB

**impose** VERB imposes, imposing, imposed
❶ to make someone have to put up with or accept something • *The building plans were imposed on the village against everyone's wishes.* ❷ to make people have to pay something • *A new tax was imposed on fuel.*
➤ **impose on someone** to take unfair advantage of someone • *I hate to impose on you, but can you lend me some money?*

**imposing** ADJECTIVE
grand and impressive • *The embassy is an imposing building.*

**imposition** NOUN impositions
❶ an unfair burden or inconvenience • *I'd like to stay if it's not too much of an imposition.* ❷ imposing something

**impossible** ADJECTIVE
❶ not possible ❷ (*informal*) very annoying; unbearable • *He really is impossible!*
➤ **impossibly** ADVERB
➤ **impossibility** NOUN

**impostor** NOUN impostors
a person who dishonestly pretends to be someone else

**impotent** ADJECTIVE
❶ powerless; unable to take action • *She blazed with impotent rage.* ❷ a man is impotent when he is unable to have an erection
➤ **impotently** ADVERB
➤ **impotence** NOUN

**impound** VERB impounds, impounding, impounded
to confiscate something or take possession of it

**impoverished** ADJECTIVE
❶ poor • *impoverished students* ❷ poor in quality • *impoverished soil*

**impracticable** ADJECTIVE
not able to be done in practice

**impractical** ADJECTIVE
not practical or sensible • *Many of his ideas are impractical.*

**imprecise** ADJECTIVE
not precise

**impregnable** ADJECTIVE
strong enough to be safe against attack • *an impregnable fortress*

**impregnated** ADJECTIVE
something is impregnated with a substance when the substance has spread all the way through it • *The air was impregnated with the scent.*

**impresario** NOUN impresarios
a person who organizes concerts, shows, etc.

**impress** VERB impresses, impressing, impressed
❶ to make a person admire something or think it is very good ❷ to impress something on someone is to make them realize its importance • *He impressed on them the need for secrecy.* ❸ to press a mark into something

**impression** NOUN impressions
❶ an effect produced on the mind • *The book made a big impression on me.* ❷ a vague idea you have about something • *I got the impression that she didn't like me.* ❸ an imitation of a person or a sound ❹ a reprint of a book

**impressionable** ADJECTIVE
easily influenced or affected

**Impressionism** NOUN
a style of painting that gives the general effect of a scene but without details

**impressionist** NOUN impressionists
an entertainer who does impressions of famous people
➤ **Impressionist** a painter in the style of Impressionism

**impressive** ADJECTIVE
making a strong impression; seeming to be very good
➤ **impressively** ADVERB

**imprint** NOUN imprints
a mark pressed into or on something

**imprison** VERB imprisons, imprisoning, imprisoned
to put someone in prison; to shut someone up in a place
➤ **imprisonment** NOUN

**improbable** ADJECTIVE
unlikely
➤ **improbably** ADVERB
➤ **improbability** NOUN

**impromptu** ADJECTIVE
done without any rehearsal or preparation • *We ended up having an impromptu party in the garden.*

**improper** ADJECTIVE
❶ unsuitable or wrong ❷ rude or indecent

➤ **improperly** ADVERB
➤ **impropriety** (say im-pro-**pry**-it-ee) NOUN

**improper fraction** NOUN improper fractions
a fraction that is greater than 1, with the
numerator greater than the denominator,
e.g. ¾

**improve** VERB improves, improving, improved
to make something better or to become
better

**improvement** NOUN improvements
making something better or becoming better
• There is still room for improvement.

**improvise** VERB improvises, improvising,
improvised
❶ to perform something by making it up
as you go along, rather than following a
score or script ❷ to make something quickly
with whatever is available • We managed
to improvise some shelves out of planks of
wood and bricks.
➤ **improvisation** NOUN

**imprudent** ADJECTIVE
unwise or rash

**impudent** ADJECTIVE
cheeky or disrespectful
➤ **impudently** ADVERB
➤ **impudence** NOUN

**impulse** NOUN impulses
❶ a sudden desire or urge to do something
• I did it on impulse. ❷ (in science) a force
acting on something for a very short time
• electrical impulses

**impulsive** ADJECTIVE
done or acting on impulse, not after careful
thought
➤ **impulsively** ADVERB

**impunity** (say im-**pewn**-it-ee) NOUN
freedom from any risk of being punished

**impure** ADJECTIVE
not pure

**impurity** NOUN impurities
a small amount of something in a substance
that makes it not pure • The filter removes
impurities from the water.

**impute** VERB imputes, imputing, imputed
(formal) to claim that someone has
something or is responsible for something
➤ **imputation** NOUN

**in** PREPOSITION
This word is used to show position or
condition, e.g.

❶ at or inside something (I was in the
kitchen; He fell in a puddle.) ❷ within the
limits of something (I will see you in an hour.)
❸ arranged as; consisting of (a serial in four
parts) ❹ a member of (He is in the army.)
❺ by means of (We paid in cash.)
➤ **in all** in total number; altogether

**in** ADVERB
❶ so as to be in something or inside (Get in.)
❷ inwards (The top caved in.) ❸ at home;
indoors (Is anybody in?) ❹ having arrived (The
train will be in soon.)
➤ **be in for something** to be likely to get
something • You're in for a shock.
➤ **be in on something** (informal) to be aware
of or sharing in something • We were all in on
the secret.

**inability** NOUN
being unable to do something • His main
problem is his inability to concentrate.

**inaccessible** ADJECTIVE
not able to be reached • The beach is
inaccessible by car.

**inaccurate** ADJECTIVE
not accurate
➤ **inaccuracy** NOUN

**inactive** ADJECTIVE
not active or working
➤ **inaction** NOUN
➤ **inactivity** NOUN

**inadequate** ADJECTIVE
❶ not enough; not good enough ❷ not able
to cope or deal with something
➤ **inadequately** ADVERB
➤ **inadequacy** NOUN

**inadvertently** ADVERB
by accident; without intending to • He
inadvertently picked up her phone when he
left.
➤ **inadvertent** ADJECTIVE

**inadvisable** ADJECTIVE
not advisable; unwise

**inalienable** ADJECTIVE
that cannot be taken away • an inalienable
right

**inane** ADJECTIVE
silly; without sense • an inane grin
➤ **inanely** ADVERB
➤ **inanity** NOUN

**inanimate** ADJECTIVE
❶ not living • inanimate objects ❷ showing
no sign of life

**inappropriate** ADJECTIVE
not appropriate or suitable

**inarticulate** ADJECTIVE
❶ not able to speak or express yourself clearly • *He was inarticulate with rage.* ❷ not expressed in words • *an inarticulate cry*

**inattentive** ADJECTIVE
not listening or paying attention
➤ **inattention** NOUN

**inaudible** ADJECTIVE
not loud enough to be heard • *Her voice was almost inaudible.*
➤ **inaudibly** ADVERB

**inaugurate** VERB inaugurates, inaugurating, inaugurated
❶ to start or introduce something new and important ❷ to formally establish a person in office • *The new President will be inaugurated next month.*
➤ **inaugural** ADJECTIVE
➤ **inauguration** NOUN

**inauspicious** ADJECTIVE
not auspicious; unlikely to be successful

**inborn** ADJECTIVE
present in a person or animal from birth • *an inborn ability*

**inbox** NOUN inboxes
the place on a computer where new email messages are shown

**inbred** ADJECTIVE
❶ inborn ❷ produced by inbreeding

**inbreeding** NOUN
breeding from closely related individuals over many generations

**incalculable** ADJECTIVE
not able to be calculated or predicted

**in camera** ADVERB
in a judge's private room, not in public
**WORD ORIGIN** Latin, = in the room

**incandescent** ADJECTIVE
❶ giving out a bright light when heated; shining ❷ very angry • *She was incandescent with rage.*
➤ **incandescence** NOUN

**incantation** NOUN incantations
a set of words spoken as a spell or charm

**incapable** ADJECTIVE
not able to do something • *They seem incapable of understanding how serious the situation is.*

**incapacitate** VERB incapacitates, incapacitating, incapacitated
to make a person too ill or weak to be able to do things normally

**incapacity** NOUN
inability; lack of sufficient strength or power

**incarcerate** VERB incarcerates, incarcerating, incarcerated
to shut in or imprison a person
➤ **incarceration** NOUN

**incarnate** ADJECTIVE
having a body or human form • *She looked at him as if he were the devil incarnate.*

**incarnation** NOUN incarnations
❶ a period of life in a particular form • *one of the incarnations of the god Vishnu* ❷ a perfect example of a certain quality • *She is the incarnation of style.*
➤ **the Incarnation** in Christian teaching, God's taking a human form as Jesus Christ

**incendiary** ADJECTIVE
an incendiary bomb or device is one that is designed to start a fire

**incense** (say **in**-sens) NOUN
a substance making a spicy smell when it is burnt

**incense** (say in-**sens**) VERB incenses, incensing, incensed
to make a person very angry • *They were incensed by the decision.*

**incentive** NOUN incentives
something that encourages a person to do something or to work harder

**inception** NOUN
the beginning of something

**incessant** ADJECTIVE
continuing for a long time without a pause • *He kept up an incessant stream of chatter.*
➤ **incessantly** ADVERB

**incest** NOUN
sexual intercourse between two people who are so closely related that they cannot marry each other
➤ **incestuous** ADJECTIVE

**inch** NOUN inches
a measure of length, one-twelfth of a foot (about 2½ centimetres)

**inch** VERB inches, inching, inched
to move slowly and gradually • *I inched along the ledge.*

**incidence** NOUN
the extent or frequency of something • *What is the incidence of heart disease in the population?*

**incident** NOUN incidents
an event, especially an unusual or unpleasant one • *One particular incident sticks in my mind.*

**incidental** ADJECTIVE
happening as a minor part of something else
• *incidental expenses*

**incidentally** ADVERB
by the way • *Incidentally, we're out of printer paper.*

**incinerate** VERB incinerates, incinerating, incinerated
to destroy something by burning it
➤ **incineration** NOUN

**incinerator** NOUN incinerators
a device for burning rubbish

**incipient** (say in-**sip**-ee-ent) ADJECTIVE
just beginning • *incipient decay*

**incise** VERB incises, incising, incised
to cut or engrave something into a surface
• *A floral design is incised along the edge of the bowl.*

**incision** NOUN incisions
a cut, especially one made in a surgical operation

**incisive** ADJECTIVE
clear and sharp • *incisive comments*

**incisor** (say in-**sy**-zer) NOUN incisors
each of the sharp-edged front teeth in the upper and lower jaws

**incite** VERB incites, inciting, incited
to urge a person to do something; to stir people up • *They were accused of inciting a riot.*
➤ **incitement** NOUN

**incivility** NOUN
rudeness or discourtesy

**inclement** ADJECTIVE (formal)
cold, wet or stormy • *inclement weather*

**inclination** NOUN inclinations
❶ a feeling that makes you want to do something • *He did not show the slightest inclination to help.* ❷ a tendency to do something ❸ a slope or the angle of a slope

**incline** (say in-**klyn**) VERB inclines, inclining, inclined

❶ to lean or slope ❷ to bend the head or body forward, as in a nod or bow ❸ to influence someone to act or think in a certain way • *Her frank manner inclines me to believe her.*
➤ **be inclined** to have a tendency or willingness to do something • *The door is inclined to bang.* • *I'm inclined to agree with you.*

**incline** (say **in**-klyn) NOUN inclines
a slope

**include** VERB includes, including, included
to make or consider something as part of a group of things • *The tour of the castle includes a visit to the dungeon.*
➤ **inclusion** NOUN

**inclusive** ADJECTIVE
including everything; including all the things mentioned • *Read pages 20 to 28 inclusive.*

**incognito** (say in-kog-**neet**-oh or in-**kog**-nit-oh) ADJECTIVE & ADVERB
with your name or identity concealed • *The film star was travelling incognito.*

**incoherent** ADJECTIVE
not speaking or reasoning in a way that can be understood

**income** NOUN incomes
money received regularly from doing work or from investments

**income tax** NOUN
tax charged on income

**incoming** ADJECTIVE
❶ arriving or being received • *an incoming flight* • *incoming texts* ❷ about to take over from someone else • *the incoming chairman*

**incomparable** (say in-**komp**-er-abul) ADJECTIVE
so good or great that it does not have an equal • *incomparable beauty*

**incompatible** ADJECTIVE
not able to exist or be used together

**incompetent** ADJECTIVE
not able or skilled enough to do something properly
➤ **incompetence** NOUN

**incomplete** ADJECTIVE
not complete

**incomprehensible** ADJECTIVE
not able to be understood • *The instructions are incomprehensible.*
➤ **incomprehension** NOUN

a b c d e f g h i j k l m n o p q r s t u v w x y z

**inconceivable** ADJECTIVE
not able to be imagined; most unlikely

**inconclusive** ADJECTIVE
not leading to a definite decision or result
• *inconclusive evidence*

**incongruous** ADJECTIVE
out of place or unsuitable
➤ **incongruously** ADVERB
➤ **incongruity** NOUN

**inconsiderable** ADJECTIVE
small or unimportant • *a not inconsiderable sum of money*

**inconsiderate** ADJECTIVE
not considerate towards other people

**inconsistent** ADJECTIVE
not consistent • *The witnesses' accounts of what happened are inconsistent.*
➤ **inconsistently** ADVERB
➤ **inconsistency** NOUN

**inconsolable** ADJECTIVE
not able to be consoled; overcome with sadness

**inconspicuous** ADJECTIVE
not attracting attention or clearly visible • *I tried to make myself as inconspicuous as possible.*
➤ **inconspicuously** ADVERB

**incontinent** ADJECTIVE
not able to control the bladder or bowels
➤ **incontinence** NOUN

**incontrovertible** ADJECTIVE
not able to be denied or disputed

**inconvenience** NOUN inconveniences
difficulty or problems caused by something
• *We are sorry for the inconvenience.*

**inconvenience** VERB inconveniences, inconveniencing, inconvenienced
to cause slight difficulty for someone

**inconvenient** ADJECTIVE
not convenient; awkward • *Have I come at an inconvenient time?*

**incorporate** VERB incorporates, incorporating, incorporated
to include something as a part of something larger • *He incorporated several of her ideas into his story.*
➤ **incorporation** NOUN

**incorrect** ADJECTIVE
not correct; wrong
➤ **incorrectly** ADVERB

**incorrigible** ADJECTIVE
not able to be reformed or changed • *an incorrigible liar*

**incorruptible** ADJECTIVE
❶ not able to decay ❷ not able to be bribed

**increase** VERB increases, increasing, increased
❶ to become larger or more • *His excitement increased.* ❷ to make something larger or more • *We increased our speed.*

**increase** NOUN increases
increasing; the amount by which a thing increases

**increasingly** ADVERB
more and more • *He was becoming increasingly anxious.*

**incredible** ADJECTIVE
❶ very difficult to believe • *an incredible story* ❷ (*informal*) extremely good or big

**incredibly** ADVERB
❶ extremely • *I felt incredibly nervous.*
❷ in a way that is very difficult to believe
• *Incredibly, no one was hurt.*

**incredulous** ADJECTIVE
finding it difficult to believe someone; doubtful that something is true • *She was incredulous when I told her that I had won the lottery.*
➤ **incredulously** ADVERB
➤ **incredulity** NOUN

**increment** (say in-krim-ent) NOUN increments
an increase; an added amount

**incriminate** VERB incriminates, incriminating, incriminated
to make it seem as if a person is guilty of a crime or doing something wrong • *Her evidence appears to incriminate her brother.*
➤ **incriminating** ADJECTIVE

**incrustation** NOUN incrustations
a crust or deposit that forms on a surface

**incubate** VERB incubates, incubating, incubated
❶ to hatch eggs by keeping them warm ❷ to cause bacteria or a disease to develop
➤ **incubation** NOUN

**incubation period** NOUN incubation periods
the time it takes for symptoms of a disease to be seen in an infected person

**incubator** NOUN incubators
❶ a device in which a baby born prematurely can be kept warm and supplied with oxygen
❷ a device for incubating eggs

**incumbent** ADJECTIVE
if it is incumbent on you to do something, it is your duty to do it • *It is incumbent on you to warn people of the danger.*

**incumbent** NOUN incumbents
a person who holds a particular office or position

**incur** VERB incurs, incurring, incurred
to bring something upon yourself • *I hope you don't incur too much expense.*

**incurable** ADJECTIVE
not able to be cured
➤ **incurably** ADVERB

**incurious** ADJECTIVE
feeling or showing no curiosity about something

**incursion** NOUN incursions
a raid or brief invasion

**indebted** ADJECTIVE
owing money or gratitude to someone

**indecent** ADJECTIVE
something that is indecent is rude or shocking because it involves sex or the body
➤ **indecently** ADVERB
➤ **indecency** NOUN

**indecipherable** ADJECTIVE
not able to be deciphered

**indecision** NOUN
being unable to make up your mind; hesitation

**indecisive** ADJECTIVE
not able to make decisions easily

**indeed** ADVERB
❶ used to strengthen a meaning • *It's very cold indeed.* ❷ really and truly; in fact • *I am indeed surprised.*

**indefinable** ADJECTIVE
not able to be defined or described clearly

**indefinite** ADJECTIVE
not definite or fixed • *He's gone away for an indefinite period.*

**indefinite article** NOUN indefinite articles
the word 'a' or 'an'. See also the panels on **a** and on **determiners**.

**indefinitely** ADVERB
for an indefinite or unlimited time

**indelible** ADJECTIVE
impossible to rub out or remove
➤ **indelibly** ADVERB

**indelicate** ADJECTIVE
❶ slightly indecent ❷ tactless
➤ **indelicacy** NOUN

**indent** VERB indents, indenting, indented
to start a line of writing or printing further in from the margin than other lines • *Always indent the first line of a new paragraph.*

**indentation** NOUN indentations
a dent or notch made in something

**independence** NOUN
❶ the freedom to live your life without being dependent on someone else ❷ the freedom of a country from foreign rule and the ability to govern itself

**independent** ADJECTIVE
❶ not dependent on any other person or thing for help, money or support ❷ an independent country is one that governs itself ❸ not connected or involved with something
➤ **independently** ADVERB

**indescribable** ADJECTIVE
unable to be described
➤ **indescribably** ADVERB

**indestructible** ADJECTIVE
unable to be destroyed
➤ **indestructibility** NOUN

**indeterminate** ADJECTIVE
not fixed or decided exactly; left vague

**index** NOUN
❶ indexes an alphabetical list of things, especially at the end of a book ❷ a number showing how prices or wages have changed from a previous level ❸ (*in mathematics*) indices the raised number etc. written to the right of another (e.g. 3 in $2^3$) showing how many times the first one is to be multiplied by itself

**index** VERB indexes, indexing, indexed
to make an index to a book etc.; to put something into an index

**index finger** NOUN index fingers
the finger next to your thumb; the forefinger

**Indian** ADJECTIVE
❶ to do with India or its people ❷ to do with Native Americans
➤ **Indian** NOUN

USAGE
The preferred term for the descendants of the original inhabitants of North and South America is *Native American*. *American Indian* is usually acceptable but the term *Red Indian* is offensive and should not be used.

**Indian summer** *NOUN* Indian summers
a period of warm weather in autumn

**indicate** *VERB* indicates, indicating, indicated
❶ to point something out or make it known
❷ to be a sign of something ❸ when drivers
indicate, they signal which direction they are
turning by using their indicators

**indication** *NOUN* indications
a sign of something • *He gave no indication
that he was thinking of quitting.*

**indicative** *ADJECTIVE*
being a sign of something • *Her remarks were
indicative of the change in her attitude.*

**indicative** *NOUN*
the form of a verb used in making a
statement (e.g. 'he said' or 'He is coming.'),
not in a command, question or wish

**indicator** *NOUN* indicators
❶ a thing that indicates or points to
something ❷ a flashing light used to signal
that a motor vehicle is turning ❸ *(in science)*
a chemical compound (such as litmus) that
changes colour in the presence of a particular
substance or condition

**indict** (say ind-**yt**) *VERB* indicts, indicting,
indicted
to charge a person with having committed a
serious crime
➤ **indictment** *NOUN*

**indie** *ADJECTIVE*
used to describe popular music that is
produced by small independent companies
• *indie bands*

**indifferent** *ADJECTIVE*
❶ not caring about something; not interested
in something at all ❷ not very good
• *indifferent weather*
➤ **indifferently** *ADVERB*
➤ **indifference** *NOUN*

**indigenous** (say in-**dij**-in-us) *ADJECTIVE*
growing or originating in a particular country;
native • *The koala bear is indigenous to
Australia.*

**indigent** (say **in**-dij-ent) *ADJECTIVE*
poor or needy

**indigestible** *ADJECTIVE*
difficult or impossible to digest

**indigestion** *NOUN*
pain or discomfort caused by difficulty in
digesting food

**indignant** *ADJECTIVE*
angry at something you think is wrong or
unfair
➤ **indignantly** *ADVERB*

**indignation** *NOUN*
anger about something you think is wrong or
unfair

**indignity** *NOUN* indignities
treatment that makes a person feel
undignified or humiliated; an insult

**indigo** *NOUN*
a deep-blue colour

**indirect** *ADJECTIVE*
not direct or straight
➤ **indirectly** *ADVERB*

**indirect speech** *NOUN*
a speaker's words given in a changed form
reported by someone else, as in *He said that
he would come.* (reporting the words 'I will
come.')

**indiscreet** *ADJECTIVE*
❶ not discreet; revealing secrets or too much
information ❷ not cautious; rash
➤ **indiscreetly** *ADVERB*
➤ **indiscretion** *NOUN*

**indiscriminate** *ADJECTIVE*
showing no discrimination; not making a
careful choice
➤ **indiscriminately** *ADVERB*

**indispensable** *ADJECTIVE*
that you cannot do without; essential • *A
good waterproof jacket is indispensable here.*
➤ **indispensability** *NOUN*

**indisposed** *ADJECTIVE*
slightly unwell so that you are unable to do
something
➤ **indisposition** *NOUN*

**indisputable** *ADJECTIVE*
definitely true; that cannot be shown to be
wrong

**indistinct** *ADJECTIVE*
not distinct or clear • *indistinct shapes in the
darkness*
➤ **indistinctly** *ADVERB*
➤ **indistinctness** *NOUN*

**indistinguishable** *ADJECTIVE*
not able to be told apart • *From a distance
the two colours are indistinguishable.*

**individual** *ADJECTIVE*
❶ of or for one person ❷ single or separate
• *Count each individual word.*

**individual** *NOUN* individuals
one person, animal or plant

**individuality** *NOUN*
the things that make one person or thing different from another; distinctive identity

**individually** *ADVERB*
separately; one by one • *The coach talked to each of us individually.*

**indivisible** *ADJECTIVE*
not able to be divided or separated

**indoctrinate** *VERB* indoctrinates, indoctrinating, indoctrinated
to fill a person's mind with particular ideas or beliefs, so that they come to accept them without thinking
➤ **indoctrination** *NOUN*

**indolent** *ADJECTIVE*
lazy
➤ **indolently** *ADVERB*
➤ **indolence** *NOUN*

**indomitable** *ADJECTIVE*
not able to be overcome or conquered • *She was a woman of indomitable courage.*

**indoor** *ADJECTIVE*
used, placed or done inside a building
• *indoor games*

**indoors** *ADVERB*
inside a building

**indubitable** (say in-**dew**-bit-a-bul) *ADJECTIVE*
not able to be doubted; certain
➤ **indubitably** *ADVERB*

**induce** *VERB* induces, inducing, induced
❶ to persuade someone to do something
• *Nothing could induce him to change his mind.* ❷ to produce or cause something
• *Some substances induce sleep.* ❸ if a pregnant woman is induced, the birth is brought on artificially with the use of drugs
➤ **induction** *NOUN*

**inducement** *NOUN* inducements
something that is offered to someone to persuade them to do something

**indulge** *VERB* indulges, indulging, indulged
to allow a person to have or do whatever they want
➤ **indulge in something** to allow yourself to have or do something that you enjoy • *On the journey we indulged in jokes and bad puns.*

**indulgent** *ADJECTIVE*
allowing someone to have or do whatever

they want; kind and lenient
➤ **indulgence** *NOUN*

**industrial** *ADJECTIVE*
to do with industry; working or used in industry

**industrial action** *NOUN*
(*chiefly British*) ways for workers to protest, such as striking or working to rule

**industrialist** *NOUN* industrialists
a person who owns or manages an industrial business

**industrialized** (also **industrialised**) *ADJECTIVE*
an industrialized country or district has many industries
➤ **industrialization** *NOUN*

**Industrial Revolution** *NOUN*
the expansion of British industry by the use of machines in the late 18th and early 19th century

**industrious** *ADJECTIVE*
working hard
➤ **industriously** *ADVERB*

**industry** *NOUN* industries
❶ making or producing goods, especially in factories ❷ a particular branch of this or any business activity • *the motor industry* • *the tourist industry* ❸ hard work and effort • *We were impressed by his industry.*

**inebriated** *ADJECTIVE*
drunk

**inedible** *ADJECTIVE*
not suitable for eating

**ineffective** *ADJECTIVE*
not producing the effect or result that you want
➤ **ineffectively** *ADVERB*

**ineffectual** *ADJECTIVE*
not achieving anything

**inefficient** *ADJECTIVE*
not working well and wasting time or energy
➤ **inefficiently** *ADVERB*
➤ **inefficiency** *NOUN*

**inelegant** *ADJECTIVE*
not elegant

**ineligible** *ADJECTIVE*
not eligible

**inept** *ADJECTIVE*
lacking any skill • *an inept wizard*
➤ **ineptly** *ADVERB*
➤ **ineptitude** *NOUN*

**inequality** *NOUN* inequalities
not being equal

**inert** *ADJECTIVE*
not moving or reacting • *He lay inert on the ground.*

**inert gas** *NOUN* inert gases
a gas that almost never combines with other substances

**inertia** (say in-er-sha) *NOUN*
❶ being unwilling to move or take action ❷ (*in science*) the tendency for a moving thing to keep moving in a straight line

**inescapable** *ADJECTIVE*
unavoidable • *an inescapable conclusion*

**inestimable** *ADJECTIVE*
too great or precious to be able to be estimated • *His advice was of inestimable value.*

**inevitable** *ADJECTIVE*
something is inevitable when it cannot be avoided and is sure to happen • *War seemed to be inevitable.*
➤ **inevitably** *ADVERB*
➤ **inevitability** *NOUN*

**inexcusable** *ADJECTIVE*
not able to be excused or justified

**inexhaustible** *ADJECTIVE*
so great that it cannot be used up completely • *Ben has an inexhaustible supply of jokes.*

**inexorable** (say in-eks-er-a-bul) *ADJECTIVE*
not able to be stopped; relentless
➤ **inexorably** *ADVERB*

**inexpensive** *ADJECTIVE*
not expensive; cheap
➤ **inexpensively** *ADVERB*

**inexperience** *NOUN*
lack of experience
➤ **inexperienced** *ADJECTIVE*

**inexplicable** *ADJECTIVE*
impossible to explain
➤ **inexplicably** *ADVERB*

**in extremis** (say eks-treem-iss) *ADVERB*
at the point of death; in very great difficulties

**infallible** *ADJECTIVE*
❶ never wrong ❷ never failing • *an infallible remedy*
➤ **infallibly** *ADVERB*
➤ **infallibility** *NOUN*

**infamous** (say in-fam-us) *ADJECTIVE*
famous for being bad or wicked • *an*

*infamous bank robber*
➤ **infamy** *NOUN*

**infancy** *NOUN*
❶ the time when you are a baby or young child ❷ an early stage of development • *Cinema was still in its infancy.*

**infant** *NOUN* infants
a baby or young child

**infantile** *ADJECTIVE*
❶ very childish and silly ❷ to do with babies or young children

**infantry** *NOUN*
soldiers who fight on foot. Compare with **cavalry**.

**infatuated** *ADJECTIVE*
filled with an unreasonably strong feeling of love that does not last long
➤ **infatuation** *NOUN*

**infect** *VERB* infects, infecting, infected
to pass on a disease or bacteria to a person, animal or plant • *We must clean the wound before it becomes infected.*

**infection** *NOUN* infections
❶ infecting someone or something • *A dirty water supply can be a source of infection.* ❷ an infectious disease or condition

**infectious** *ADJECTIVE*
❶ an infectious disease is able to be spread by air, water, etc. Compare with **contagious**. ❷ quickly spreading to others • *His enthusiasm is infectious.*

**infer** *VERB* infers, inferring, inferred
to form an opinion or work something out from what someone says or does, even though they do not actually say it • *I infer from your passport that you are going on holiday.*
➤ **inference** *NOUN*

USAGE
If you mean to suggest something without actually saying it, use **imply**.

**inferior** *ADJECTIVE*
less good or less important; low or lower in position, quality, etc.
➤ **inferiority** *NOUN*

**inferior** *NOUN* inferiors
a person who is lower in position or rank than someone else

**infernal** *ADJECTIVE*
❶ (*informal*) awful; very annoying • *Stop that*

354

*infernal noise.* ❷ to do with or like hell • *the infernal regions*

**inferno** *NOUN* infernos
a raging fire

**infertile** *ADJECTIVE*
not fertile • *infertile soil*
➤ **infertility** *NOUN*

**infest** *VERB* infests, infesting, infested
insects or other pests infest a place when they are numerous and troublesome there
➤ **infestation** *NOUN*
➤ **infested** *ADJECTIVE*

**infidel** (say in-fid-el) *NOUN* infidels (*old use*)
a person who does not believe in a religion

**infidelity** *NOUN*
being unfaithful to your husband, wife or partner

**infiltrate** *VERB* infiltrates, infiltrating, infiltrated
to get into a place or organization gradually and without being noticed
➤ **infiltration** *NOUN*
➤ **infiltrator** *NOUN*

**infinite** *ADJECTIVE*
❶ endless; without a limit ❷ too great to be measured

**infinitely** *ADVERB*
very much; with no limit • *This book is infinitely better than any of his others.*

**infinitesimal** *ADJECTIVE*
extremely small
➤ **infinitesimally** *ADVERB*

**infinitive** *NOUN* infinitives
(*in grammar*) the form of a verb that does not change to indicate a particular tense, number or person, in English used with or without to, e.g. *go* in 'Let him go.' or 'Allow him to go.'

**infinity** *NOUN*
an infinite number, distance or time • *The landscape seemed to stretch into infinity.*

**infirm** *ADJECTIVE*
weak, especially from old age or illness
➤ **infirmity** *NOUN*

**infirmary** *NOUN* infirmaries
❶ a hospital ❷ a place where sick people are cared for in a school, monastery, etc.

**inflame** *VERB* inflames, inflaming, inflamed
❶ to produce strong feelings or anger in people ❷ a part of the body is inflamed when it becomes painfully red and swollen

**inflammable** *ADJECTIVE*
able to be set on fire

> **USAGE**
> This word means the same as flammable. If you want to say that something is not able to be set on fire, use non-flammable.

**inflammation** *NOUN*
painful redness or swelling in a part of the body

**inflammatory** *ADJECTIVE*
likely to make people angry • *inflammatory remarks*

**inflatable** *ADJECTIVE*
able to be inflated • *an inflatable mattress*

**inflate** *VERB* inflates, inflating, inflated
❶ to fill something with air or gas so that it expands ❷ to increase something too much

**inflation** *NOUN*
a general rise in prices and fall in the purchasing power of money

**inflect** *VERB* inflects, inflecting, inflected
❶ (*in grammar*) to change the ending or form of a word to show its tense or its grammatical relation to other words, e.g. *sing* changes to *sang* or *sung*, *child* changes to *children* ❷ to alter the voice in speaking

**inflection** *NOUN* inflections
❶ (*in grammar*) an ending or form of a word used to inflect it, e.g. *-ed* in *killed* and *-es* in *bunches* ❷ the rise and fall in your voice when you are speaking

**inflexible** *ADJECTIVE*
not able to be bent, changed or persuaded
➤ **inflexibly** *ADVERB*
➤ **inflexibility** *NOUN*

**inflict** *VERB* inflicts, inflicting, inflicted
to make someone suffer something • *They inflicted a heavy defeat on us last season.*

**influence** *NOUN* influences
❶ the power to affect other people or things • *He had a huge influence on landscape painting.* ❷ a person or thing with this power • *She is a good influence on her brother.*

**influence** *VERB* influences, influencing, influenced
to have an influence on a person or thing • *The tides are influenced by the moon.*

**influential** *ADJECTIVE*
having great influence • *a hugely influential writer*

a b c d e f g h i j k l m n o p q r s t u v w x y z

**influenza** NOUN
an infectious disease that causes fever, catarrh and pain

**influx** NOUN
a flowing in, especially of people or things coming in • *the summer influx of tourists*

**inform** VERB informs, informing, informed
to tell someone something or give them information about it • *Please inform us of any change of address.*

**informal** ADJECTIVE
not formal; casual and relaxed • *The restaurant has an informal atmosphere.*
➤ **informally** ADVERB
➤ **informality** NOUN

> **USAGE**
> In this dictionary, words marked *informal* are used in everyday speaking but not when you are writing or speaking formally.

**informant** NOUN informants
a person who gives information

**information** NOUN
facts or knowledge about something • *The website has lots of information on the history of aircraft.*

**information technology** NOUN
the study or use of ways of storing, arranging and giving out information, especially computers and telecommunications

**informative** ADJECTIVE
giving a lot of useful information • *an entertaining and informative programme*

**informed** ADJECTIVE
knowing about something

**informer** NOUN informers
a person who gives information against someone, especially to the police

**infra-red** ADJECTIVE
below or beyond red in the spectrum

**infrastructure** NOUN infrastructures
the basic services and systems that a country needs in order for its society and economy to work properly, such as buildings, roads, transport and power supplies

**infrequent** ADJECTIVE
not happening often
➤ **infrequently** ADVERB

**infringe** VERB infringes, infringing, infringed
❶ to break a rule, law or agreement ❷ to reduce or limit a person's rights
➤ **infringement** NOUN

**infuriate** VERB infuriates, infuriating, infuriated
to make a person very angry

**infuse** VERB infuses, infusing, infused
❶ to fill someone or something with a feeling or quality • *His novels are infused with sadness.* ❷ to soak or steep tea, herbs, etc. in a liquid to extract the flavour
➤ **infusion** NOUN

**ingenious** ADJECTIVE
❶ cleverly made or done • *an ingenious plan*
❷ clever at inventing things
➤ **ingeniously** ADVERB

**ingenuity** NOUN
cleverness in inventing things or solving problems

**ingenuous** ADJECTIVE
without cunning; innocent
➤ **ingenuously** ADVERB

**ingot** NOUN ingots
a lump of gold or silver that is cast in a brick shape

**ingrained** ADJECTIVE
❶ ingrained feelings or habits are deeply fixed in people's minds ❷ ingrained dirt marks a surface deeply

**ingratiate** VERB ingratiates, ingratiating, ingratiated
➤ **ingratiate yourself** to get yourself into favour with someone, especially by flattering them or always agreeing with them

**ingratitude** NOUN
lack of gratitude

**ingredient** NOUN ingredients
one of the parts of a mixture; one of the things used in a recipe

**inhabit** VERB inhabits, inhabiting, inhabited
to live in a place • *Many rare species inhabit the island.*

**inhabitant** NOUN inhabitants
a person or animal that lives in a place • *the oldest inhabitant of the village*

**inhale** VERB inhales, inhaling, inhaled
to breathe in • *He opened a window and inhaled deeply.*
➤ **inhalation** NOUN

**inhaler** NOUN inhalers
a device used for relieving asthma by inhaling medicine into your mouth

**inherent** (say in-**heer**-ent) ADJECTIVE
existing in something as one of its natural
or permanent qualities • *I pointed out the
inherent stupidity of this idea.*
➤ **inherently** ADVERB

**inherit** VERB inherits, inheriting, inherited
❶ to receive money, property or a title when
its previous owner dies ❷ to get certain
qualities or characteristics from your parents
or predecessors • *She has inherited her
father's love of music.*
➤ **inheritor** NOUN

**inheritance** NOUN
inheriting something; the money, property,
etc. that you inherit

**inhibit** VERB inhibits, inhibiting, inhibited
to hinder or restrain something

**inhibition** NOUN inhibitions
a feeling of embarrassment or worry that
prevents you from doing something or
expressing your emotions
➤ **inhibited** ADJECTIVE

**inhospitable** ADJECTIVE
❶ unfriendly to visitors ❷ an inhospitable
place is difficult to live in because it gives no
shelter from the weather

**inhuman** ADJECTIVE
cruel; without pity or kindness
➤ **inhumanity** NOUN

**inhumane** ADJECTIVE
not humane

**inimitable** ADJECTIVE
impossible to imitate

**iniquitous** ADJECTIVE
very unjust
➤ **iniquity** NOUN

**initial** NOUN initials
the first letter of a word or name

**initial** VERB initials, initialling, initialled
to mark or sign something with the initials of
your names

**initial** ADJECTIVE
at the beginning • *the initial stages*

**initially** ADVERB
at the beginning; at first • *Initially, everything
went well.*

**initiate** VERB initiates, initiating, initiated
❶ to start something • *He pressed the button
to initiate the launch sequence.* ❷ to admit
a person as a member of a society or group,

often with special ceremonies
➤ **initiation** NOUN

**initiative** (say in-**ish**-a-tiv) NOUN
❶ the power or right to get something
started ❷ the ability to make decisions and
take action on your own without being told
what to do
➤ **take the initiative** to take action yourself
to start something happening

**inject** VERB injects, injecting, injected
❶ to put a medicine or drug into the body
by means of a hollow needle ❷ to put liquid
into something by means of a syringe etc.
❸ to add a new quality • *Try to inject some
humour into the story.*
➤ **injection** NOUN

**injunction** NOUN injunctions
a command given with authority, e.g. by a
law court

**injure** VERB injures, injuring, injured
to harm or hurt someone • *He injured his
knee playing football.*
➤ **injured** ADJECTIVE

**injury** NOUN injuries
harm or damage done to someone • *They
escaped with only minor injuries.*
➤ **injurious** (say in-**joor**-ee-us) ADJECTIVE

**injustice** NOUN injustices
lack of justice; unjust treatment
➤ **do someone an injustice** to judge
someone unfairly

**ink** NOUN inks
a black or coloured liquid used in writing and
printing

**inkling** NOUN inklings
a slight idea or suspicion • *I had no inkling of
what was going to happen.*

**inky** ADJECTIVE
❶ stained with ink ❷ black like ink • *inky
darkness*

**inland** ADJECTIVE & ADVERB
in or towards the middle part of a country,
away from the coast • *The village lies twenty
kilometres inland.*

**Inland Revenue** NOUN
(formerly in the UK) the government
department responsible for collecting income
tax and some other taxes

**in-laws** PLURAL NOUN (informal)
relatives by marriage, especially the parents
of your husband or wife

**inlay** VERB inlays, inlaying, inlaid
to set pieces of wood or metal into a surface to form a design • *The lid of the box was inlaid with silver.*

**inlay** NOUN inlays
a design formed by inlaying

**inlet** NOUN inlets
a strip of water reaching into the land from a sea or lake

**inmate** NOUN inmates
one of the people kept in a prison or mental hospital

**in memoriam** PREPOSITION
in memory of

**inmost** ADJECTIVE
most inward

**inn** NOUN inns
a hotel or public house, especially in the country
➤ **innkeeper** NOUN

**innards** PLURAL NOUN (*informal*)
the internal organs of a person or animal; the inner parts of a machine

**innate** ADJECTIVE
an innate ability or quality is one that you were born with

**inner** ADJECTIVE
inside; nearer to the centre • *an inner courtyard*

**innermost** ADJECTIVE
❶ nearest to the centre; furthest inside
❷ most secret or private • *She could not talk about her innermost feelings to anyone.*

**innings** NOUN innings
the time when a cricket team or player is batting

**innocence** NOUN
❶ not being guilty of doing something wrong
❷ lack of experience of the world, especially of bad things

**innocent** ADJECTIVE
❶ not guilty of doing something wrong
❷ lacking experience of the world, especially of bad things ❸ harmless • *an innocent remark*
➤ **innocently** ADVERB

**innocuous** ADJECTIVE
harmless

**innovation** NOUN innovations
❶ introducing new things or new methods

❷ a completely new process or way of doing things that has just been introduced
➤ **innovator** NOUN

**innovative** ADJECTIVE
an innovative design or way of doing something is new and clever

**innuendo** NOUN innuendoes
indirect reference to something insulting or rude

**innumerable** ADJECTIVE
too many to be counted

**inoculate** VERB inoculates, inoculating, inoculated
to inject or treat someone with a vaccine or serum as a protection against a disease
➤ **inoculation** NOUN

**inoffensive** ADJECTIVE
not likely to upset or offend anyone • *a shy, inoffensive young man*

**inordinate** ADJECTIVE
excessive • *He spends an inordinate amount of time watching TV.*
➤ **inordinately** ADVERB

**inorganic** ADJECTIVE
not of living organisms; of mineral origin

**in-patient** NOUN in-patients
a patient who stays at a hospital for treatment

**input** NOUN
what you put into something, especially data put into a computer

**input** VERB inputs, inputting, input or inputted
to put data into a computer

**inquest** NOUN inquests
an official inquiry to find out how a person died

**inquire** VERB inquires, inquiring, inquired
❶ to investigate something carefully ❷ to ask for information

USAGE
You can spell this word inquire or enquire in either of its meanings. It is probably more common for inquire to be used for 'investigate' and enquire to be used for 'ask for information', but there is no real need to follow this distinction.

**inquiry** NOUN inquiries
❶ an official investigation ❷ a question

**inquisition** NOUN inquisitions
a detailed questioning or investigation

➤ **inquisitor** NOUN
➤ **the Inquisition** a council of the Roman Catholic Church in the Middle Ages, especially the very severe one in Spain, set up to discover and punish heretics

**inquisitive** ADJECTIVE
always asking questions or trying to find out things • *Don't be so inquisitive – it's none of your business.*
➤ **inquisitively** ADVERB

**inroads** PLURAL NOUN
➤ **make inroads on** or **into something** to take away or use up large quantities of something

**inrush** NOUN **inrushes**
a sudden rushing in

**insane** ADJECTIVE
not sane; mad
➤ **insanely** ADVERB
➤ **insanity** NOUN

**insanitary** ADJECTIVE
unclean and likely to be harmful to health

**insatiable** (say in-**say**-sha-bul) ADJECTIVE
impossible to satisfy • *an insatiable appetite*

**inscribe** VERB **inscribes, inscribing, inscribed**
to write or carve words or symbols on something • *The names of the previous winners are inscribed on the trophy.*

**inscription** NOUN **inscriptions**
words written or carved on a monument, coin, stone, etc. or written in the front of a book

**inscrutable** ADJECTIVE
mysterious; impossible to interpret • *an inscrutable smile*

**insect** NOUN **insects**
a small animal with six legs, no backbone and a body divided into three parts (head, thorax, abdomen)

**insecticide** NOUN **insecticides**
a substance for killing insects

**insectivorous** ADJECTIVE
feeding on insects and other small invertebrate creatures
➤ **insectivore** NOUN

**insecure** ADJECTIVE
❶ not secure or safe ❷ lacking confidence about yourself
➤ **insecurely** ADVERB
➤ **insecurity** NOUN

**insensible** ADJECTIVE
❶ unconscious ❷ unaware of something • *He was insensible of her needs.*

**insensitive** ADJECTIVE
not sensitive or thinking about other people's feelings
➤ **insensitively** ADVERB
➤ **insensitivity** NOUN

**inseparable** ADJECTIVE
❶ liking to be constantly together • *inseparable friends* ❷ not able to be separated

**insert** VERB **inserts, inserting, inserted**
to put a thing into something else or between two things • *He inserted a coin into the slot.* • *Where do you want to insert that paragraph?*
➤ **insertion** NOUN

**inshore** ADVERB & ADJECTIVE
near or nearer to the shore • *The boat came inshore.*

**inside** NOUN **insides**
the inner side, surface or part
➤ **inside out** with the inside turned to face outwards
➤ **insides** (*informal*) a person's stomach and bowels

**inside** ADJECTIVE
on or coming from the inside; in or nearest to the middle • *an inside pocket*

**inside** ADVERB & PREPOSITION
on or to the inside of something; in • *Come inside.* • *It's inside that box.*

**insidious** ADJECTIVE
causing harm gradually, without being noticed
➤ **insidiously** ADVERB

**insight** NOUN **insights**
❶ the ability to see the truth about things • *With a flash of insight, she realized what had really happened that day.* ❷ an understanding of something • *The book gives us a good insight into life as a pirate.*

**insignia** SINGULAR NOUN & PLURAL NOUN
a badge or symbol that shows that you belong to something or hold a particular office

**insignificant** ADJECTIVE
not important or influential • *She felt small and insignificant.*
➤ **insignificance** NOUN

a
b
c
d
e
f
g
h
i
j
k
l
m
n
o
p
q
r
s
t
u
v
w
x
y
z

**insincere** ADJECTIVE
not sincere
➤ **insincerely** ADVERB
➤ **insincerity** NOUN

**insinuate** VERB insinuates, insinuating, insinuated
❶ to hint something unpleasant • *What are you insinuating?* ❷ to introduce a thing or yourself gradually or craftily into a place

**insinuation** NOUN insinuations
an unpleasant hint or suggestion that someone makes

**insipid** ADJECTIVE
❶ lacking flavour ❷ not lively or interesting
➤ **insipidity** NOUN

**insist** VERB insists, insisting, insisted
to be very firm in saying or asking for something • *He insisted that he was innocent.* • *I insist on seeing the manager.*

**insistent** ADJECTIVE
❶ insisting on doing or having something ❷ continuing for a long time in a way that you cannot ignore • *an insistent tapping on the window*
➤ **insistence** NOUN

**insolent** ADJECTIVE
very rude and disrespectful • *an insolent stare*
➤ **insolently** ADVERB
➤ **insolence** NOUN

**insoluble** ADJECTIVE
❶ impossible to solve • *an insoluble problem* ❷ impossible to dissolve

**insolvent** ADJECTIVE
unable to pay your debts
➤ **insolvency** NOUN

**insomnia** NOUN
being unable to sleep • *Do you ever suffer from insomnia?*
➤ **insomniac** NOUN

**inspect** VERB inspects, inspecting, inspected
to examine something carefully to check that everything is as it should be • *The teacher walked around inspecting their work.*
➤ **inspection** NOUN

**inspector** NOUN inspectors
❶ a person whose job is to inspect or supervise things ❷ a police officer ranking next above a sergeant

**inspiration** NOUN inspirations
❶ a sudden brilliant idea ❷ a person or thing that fills you with ideas or enthusiasm

**inspire** VERB inspires, inspiring, inspired
to fill a person with ideas, enthusiasm or creative feeling • *The applause inspired us with confidence.*

**instability** NOUN
lack of stability

**install** VERB installs, installing, installed
❶ to put something in position and ready to use • *They have installed a new computer system.* ❷ to put a person into an important position with a ceremony • *He was installed as pope.*
➤ **installation** NOUN

**instalment** NOUN instalments
❶ each of a series of payments made for something over a period of time • *You can pay by monthly instalments.* ❷ each part of a television serial or of a series of publications

**instance** NOUN instances
an example
➤ **for instance** for example

**instant** ADJECTIVE
❶ happening immediately • *It was an instant success.* ❷ instant food or drink is designed to be prepared quickly and easily • *instant coffee*

**instant** NOUN instants
a moment • *I don't believe it for an instant.*
➤ **this instant** at once • *Come here this instant!*

**instantaneous** ADJECTIVE
happening immediately • *The effect was instantaneous.*
➤ **instantaneously** ADVERB

**instantly** ADVERB
without delay; immediately

**instead** ADVERB
in place of something else

**instep** NOUN insteps
the top of the foot between the toes and the ankle

**instigate** VERB instigates, instigating, instigated
to make something start to happen; to stir something up • *The were accused of instigating the rebellion.*
➤ **instigation** NOUN
➤ **instigator** NOUN

**instil** VERB instils, instilling, instilled
to put ideas into a person's mind gradually

**instinct** NOUN instincts
a natural tendency or ability • *Birds learn to fly by instinct.* • *I didn't have time to think – I just acted on instinct.*

**instinctive** ADJECTIVE
following instinct, not thought • *His instinctive reaction was to run.*
➤ **instinctively** ADVERB

**institute** NOUN institutes
a society or organization; the building used by this

**institute** VERB institutes, instituting, instituted
to establish or introduce something • *The new head instituted many innovations and changes.*

**institution** NOUN institutions
❶ an institute; a public organization, e.g. a hospital or university ❷ an established habit or custom • *Going out for a walk on Sunday was a family institution.* ❸ instituting something

**instruct** VERB instructs, instructing, instructed
❶ to teach a person a subject or skill ❷ to tell a person what they must do

**instruction** NOUN instructions
❶ teaching a subject or skill ❷ an order or piece of information • *Follow the instructions carefully.*
➤ **instructional** ADJECTIVE

**instructive** ADJECTIVE
giving useful information or knowledge

**instructor** NOUN instructors
a person who teaches a practical skill or sport • *a driving instructor*

**instrument** NOUN instruments
❶ a device for producing musical sounds ❷ a tool used for delicate or scientific work ❸ a measuring device

**instrumental** ADJECTIVE
❶ performed on musical instruments, without singing ❷ to be instrumental in doing something is to play an important part in it • *She was instrumental in getting me a job.*

**instrumentalist** NOUN instrumentalists
a person who plays a musical instrument

**insubordinate** ADJECTIVE
disobedient or rebellious
➤ **insubordination** NOUN

**insufferable** ADJECTIVE
annoying and difficult to bear • *an insufferable bore*

**insufficient** ADJECTIVE
not enough • *There is insufficient evidence.*

**insular** ADJECTIVE
❶ to do with or like an island ❷ narrow-minded

**insulate** VERB insulates, insulating, insulated
to cover or protect something to prevent heat, cold or electricity from passing in or out
➤ **insulation** NOUN
➤ **insulator** NOUN

**insulin** NOUN
a substance that controls the amount of sugar in the blood. The lack of insulin causes diabetes.

**insult** (say in-**sult**) VERB insults, insulting, insulted
to speak to or treat someone in a rude way that offends them

**insult** (say **in**-sult) NOUN insults
an insulting remark or action

**insuperable** ADJECTIVE
unable to be overcome • *an insuperable difficulty*

**insurance** NOUN
an agreement to compensate someone for a loss, damage or injury etc., in return for a payment (called a **premium**) made in advance

**insure** VERB insures, insuring, insured
to protect something with insurance • *Is your jewellery insured?*

SPELLING
Take care not to confuse with **ensure**, which means to make sure that something happens.

**insurgent** NOUN insurgents
someone who rebels against a ruler or government
➤ **insurgent** ADJECTIVE

**insurmountable** ADJECTIVE
unable to be overcome • *insurmountable difficulties*

**insurrection** NOUN insurrections
a rebellion

**intact** ADJECTIVE
not damaged; complete • *Only a few buildings remained intact after the earthquake.*

**intake** NOUN intakes
❶ taking something in • *a sharp intake of breath* ❷ the number of people or things taken in • *We have a high intake of students this year.*

**intangible** ADJECTIVE
difficult to describe or measure; not able to be touched • *intangible benefits*

**integer** NOUN integers
a whole number (e.g. 0, 3, 19), not a fraction

**integral** (say **in**-tig-ral) ADJECTIVE
that is an essential part of a whole thing • *An engine is an integral part of a car.*

**integrate** VERB integrates, integrating, integrated
❶ to make parts into a whole; to combine things ❷ to bring people together harmoniously into a single community
➤ **integration** NOUN

**integrity** (say in-**teg**-rit-ee) NOUN
being honest and behaving well • *a person of great integrity*

**intellect** NOUN intellects
the ability to think and work things out with your mind

**intellectual** ADJECTIVE
❶ to do with or using the intellect ❷ having a good intellect and a liking for knowledge
➤ **intellectually** ADVERB

**intellectual** NOUN intellectuals
an intellectual person

**intelligence** NOUN
❶ being intelligent ❷ information, especially of military value; the people who collect and study this information

**intelligent** ADJECTIVE
able to learn and understand things; having great mental ability
➤ **intelligently** ADVERB

**SPELLING**
There is a double l in **intelligent**.

**intelligible** ADJECTIVE
able to be understood • *The message was barely intelligible.*

**intend** VERB intends, intending, intended
❶ to have something in mind as what you want to do • *We finished later than we intended.* ❷ to plan that something should have a particular meaning or purpose • *It was intended to be a joke.*

**intense** ADJECTIVE
❶ very strong or great • *The heat was intense.* ❷ feeling things very strongly and seriously • *He's a very intense young man.*
➤ **intensely** ADVERB

**intensify** VERB intensifies, intensifying, intensified
to make something more intense or to become more intense • *The fighting intensified.*

**intensity** NOUN
the intensity of something is how strong or great it is • *The storm increased in intensity with every passing second.*

**intensive** ADJECTIVE
concentrated; using a lot of effort over a short time • *two weeks of intensive training*
➤ **intensively** ADVERB

**intensive care** NOUN
medical treatment of a patient who is dangerously ill, with constant supervision

**intent** NOUN intents
what someone intends; an intention

**intent** ADJECTIVE
showing great attention and interest • *She was so intent upon her work that she didn't hear me come in.*
➤ **intent on something** eager or determined to do something

**intention** NOUN intentions
what someone intends; a purpose or plan

**intentional** ADJECTIVE
deliberate, not accidental
➤ **intentionally** ADVERB

**intently** ADVERB
with great attention and interest • *The boys listened intently.*

**inter** VERB inters, interring, interred
to bury a corpse

**interact** VERB interacts, interacting, interacted
❶ to talk to or mix with other people • *It is interesting to watch how young children interact.* ❷ to have an effect upon one another • *In a chemical reaction, two or more chemicals interact with each other.*
➤ **interaction** NOUN

**interactive** ADJECTIVE
(*in computing*) allowing information to be sent immediately in either direction between a computer system and its user

**interbreed** VERB interbreeds, interbreeding, interbred
animals interbreed when they breed with each other

**intercede** VERB intercedes, interceding, interceded
to speak or act on behalf of another person or as a peacemaker
➤ **intercession** NOUN

**intercept** VERB intercepts, intercepting, intercepted
to stop or catch a person or thing that is going from one place to another • *Police intercepted him on the way to the airport.*
➤ **interception** NOUN

**interchange** VERB interchanges, interchanging, interchanged
❶ to put each of two things into the other's place ❷ to exchange things

**interchange** NOUN interchanges
❶ interchanging • *a lively interchange of ideas* ❷ a road junction where vehicles can move from one motorway etc. to another

**interchangeable** ADJECTIVE
things are interchangeable when they can be changed or swapped around

**intercom** NOUN intercoms
a system of communication between rooms or compartments, operating rather like a telephone

**intercourse** NOUN
❶ communication or dealings between people ❷ sexual intercourse

**interdependent** ADJECTIVE
dependent upon each other

**interest** NOUN interests
❶ a feeling of wanting to know about or be involved with something ❷ a thing that interests someone • *Science fiction is one of my interests.* ❸ an advantage or benefit • *She looks after her own interests.* ❹ money paid regularly in return for money lent or deposited

**interest** VERB interests, interesting, interested
to attract a person's interest • *Sport doesn't interest me very much.*
➤ **interested** ADJECTIVE

SPELLING
There is a tricky bit in interest—there is an e after the first t.

**interesting** ADJECTIVE
catching and holding your attention • *That's*

*an interesting idea.*
➤ **interestingly** ADVERB

**interface** NOUN interfaces
a connection between two parts of a computer system

**interfere** VERB interferes, interfering, interfered
❶ to take part in something that has nothing to do with you ❷ to get in the way of something • *She never allowed her personal feelings to interfere with her work.*

**interference** NOUN
❶ interfering in something ❷ a crackling or distorting of a radio or television signal

**interim** NOUN
an interval of time between two events

**interim** ADJECTIVE
in use for the time being until something more permanent is arranged • *an interim report*

**interior** NOUN interiors
the inside of something; the central or inland part of a country • *the interior of the cave*

**interior** ADJECTIVE
inner • *interior walls*

**interject** VERB interjects, interjecting, interjected
to break in with a remark while someone is speaking

**interjection** NOUN interjections
a word or words exclaimed expressing joy or pain or surprise, such as *oh!* or *wow!* or *good heavens!*

**interlock** VERB interlocks, interlocking, interlocked
things interlock when they fit into each other

**interloper** NOUN interlopers
an intruder

**interlude** NOUN interludes
❶ an interval ❷ something happening in an interval or between other events

**intermediary** NOUN intermediaries
someone who tries to settle a dispute by negotiating with both sides; a mediator

**intermediate** ADJECTIVE
coming between two things in time, place or order • *an intermediate stage* • *intermediate students*

**interminable** ADJECTIVE
seeming to go on for ever; long and boring

• *an interminable speech*
➤ **interminably** ADVERB

**intermission** NOUN intermissions
an interval between parts of a film or show

**intermittent** ADJECTIVE
happening at intervals; not continuous
• *intermittent showers*
➤ **intermittently** ADVERB

**intern** VERB interns, interning, interned
to imprison someone in a special camp or
area, usually in wartime

**internal** ADJECTIVE
inside; within something • *internal injuries*
➤ **internally** ADVERB

**internal-combustion engine** NOUN
internal-combustion engines
an engine that produces power by burning
fuel inside the engine itself

**international** ADJECTIVE
to do with or belonging to more than one
country; agreed between nations • *an
international trade organization*
➤ **internationally** ADVERB

**international** NOUN internationals
❶ a sports contest between teams
representing different countries ❷ a sports
player who plays for his or her country

**Internet** NOUN
a computer network that allows users all over
the world to communicate and exchange
information

**internment** NOUN
being interned in wartime

**interplanetary** ADJECTIVE
between planets

**interpolate** VERB interpolates, interpolating,
interpolated
to add a remark during a conversation
➤ **interpolation** NOUN

**interpose** VERB interposes, interposing,
interposed
❶ to add a question or remark into a
conversation • *'Just a minute,' Kerry
interposed. 'How do you know?'* ❷ to place
something between two things

**interpret** VERB interprets, interpreting,
interpreted
❶ to explain what something means ❷ to
translate what someone says into another
language as they are speaking ❸ to perform
music, a part in a play, etc. in a way that

shows your feelings about its meaning
➤ **interpretation** NOUN

**interpreter** NOUN interpreters
a person whose job is to translate what
someone is saying immediately into another
language

**interregnum** NOUN interregnums or
interregna
an interval between the reign of one ruler
and that of his or her successor

**interrogate** VERB interrogates, interrogating,
interrogated
to question someone closely or aggressively
• *The prisoner was interrogated for six hours.*
➤ **interrogation** NOUN
➤ **interrogator** NOUN

**interrogative** ADJECTIVE
questioning; expressing a question

**interrupt** VERB interrupts, interrupting,
interrupted
❶ to stop someone while they are in the
middle of speaking or concentrating by saying
something to them • *They kept interrupting
me with silly questions.* ❷ to stop something
continuing for a short time • *The match was
interrupted several times by rain.*

**interruption** NOUN interruptions
interrupting someone or something • *It was
the only quiet place where he could work
without interruption.*

**intersect** VERB intersects, intersecting,
intersected
❶ lines or roads intersect when they cross
each other • *The lines intersect at right
angles.* ❷ to divide a thing by passing or lying
across it

**intersection** NOUN intersections
a place where lines or roads cross each other

**intersperse** VERB intersperses, interspersing,
interspersed
to be interspersed with things is to have them
mixed in here and there • *Her speech was
interspersed with jokes.*

**interval** NOUN intervals
❶ a time between two events or parts of
a play or show ❷ (*in music*) the musical
difference between the pitches of two notes
➤ **at intervals** with some time or distance
between each one

**intervene** VERB intervenes, intervening,
intervened
❶ to come between two events • *in the*

*intervening years* ❷ to interrupt a discussion or fight to try and stop it or change its result
➤ **intervention** NOUN

**interview** NOUN interviews
a meeting with someone to ask him or her questions or to obtain information

**interview** VERB interviews, interviewing, interviewed
to have an interview with someone
➤ **interviewer** NOUN

**intestine** NOUN intestines
the long tube along which food passes while being absorbed by the body, between the stomach and the anus
➤ **intestinal** ADJECTIVE

**intimacy** NOUN
having a very close friendship or relationship with someone

**intimate** (say **in**-tim-at) ADJECTIVE
❶ very friendly with someone ❷ private and personal • *intimate thoughts* ❸ detailed • *He has an intimate knowledge of the country.*
➤ **intimately** ADVERB

**intimate** (say **in**-tim-ayt) VERB intimates, intimating, intimated
to hint at something • *She has not yet intimated what her plans are.*
➤ **intimation** NOUN

**intimidate** VERB intimidates, intimidating, intimidated
to frighten a person into doing something by using threats
➤ **intimidation** NOUN

**into** PREPOSITION
❶ used to express movement to the inside of something (*Go into the house.*) ❷ used to express a change of condition or state (*It broke into pieces. She went into politics.*) ❸ used to show division (*4 into 20 = 20 divided by 4*)

**intolerable** ADJECTIVE
too much to bear • *The heat was intolerable.*
➤ **intolerably** ADVERB

**intolerant** ADJECTIVE
not tolerant or willing to put up with people
➤ **intolerantly** ADVERB
➤ **intolerance** NOUN

**intonation** NOUN intonations
the tone or pitch of the voice in speaking

**intone** VERB intones, intoning, intoned
to recite something in a chanting voice

**intoxicate** VERB intoxicates, intoxicating, intoxicated
❶ to make someone very drunk ❷ to make someone wildly excited
➤ **intoxicated** ADJECTIVE
➤ **intoxication** NOUN

**intransitive** ADJECTIVE
an intransitive verb is one that is used without a direct object after it, e.g. *hear* in *We can hear.* (but not in *We can hear you.*) Compare with transitive.
➤ **intransitively** ADVERB

**intravenous** (say in-tra-**veen**-us) ADJECTIVE
an intravenous injection is made directly into a vein

**intrepid** ADJECTIVE
fearless and brave • *an intrepid explorer*
➤ **intrepidly** ADVERB
➤ **intrepidity** NOUN

**intricate** ADJECTIVE
very complicated, with a lot of fine details
• *an intricate pattern*
➤ **intricately** ADVERB
➤ **intricacy** NOUN

**intrigue** (say in-**treeg**) VERB intrigues, intriguing, intrigued
to interest someone very much and make them curious • *The subject intrigues me.*
➤ **intriguing** ADJECTIVE

**intrigue** (say **in**-treeg) NOUN intrigues
❶ plotting; an underhand plot ❷ (*old use*) a secret love affair

**intrinsic** ADJECTIVE
being part of the essential nature or character of something • *The coin has little intrinsic value.*

**introduce** VERB introduces, introducing, introduced
❶ to bring an idea or practice into use • *The new law was introduced in 2011.* ❷ to make a person known to other people • *Come with me and I'll introduce you to my brother.* ❸ to announce a broadcast, speaker, etc.

**introduction** NOUN introductions
❶ introducing someone or something • *the introduction of computers into the classroom* ❷ an explanation put at the beginning of a book, speech, etc.
➤ **introductory** ADJECTIVE

**introspective** ADJECTIVE
examining your own thoughts and feelings
➤ **introspection** NOUN

**introvert** NOUN introverts
a shy person who does not like to talk about their own thoughts and feelings with other people. (The opposite is **extrovert**.)
➤ **introverted** ADJECTIVE

**intrude** VERB intrudes, intruding, intruded
to come in or join in without being wanted • I hope I am not intruding.
➤ **intrusion** NOUN
➤ **intrusive** ADJECTIVE

**intruder** NOUN intruders
someone who forces their way into a place where they are not supposed to be

**intuition** NOUN
the power to know or understand things without having to think hard or without being taught
➤ **intuitive** ADJECTIVE
➤ **intuitively** ADVERB

**Inuit** (say in-yoo-it) NOUN Inuit
❶ a member of a people living in northern Canada and Greenland; an Eskimo ❷ the language of the Inuit

USAGE

See the note at **Eskimo**.

**inundate** VERB inundates, inundating, inundated
to send someone so many things that they cannot deal with them all • We've been inundated with letters about the programme.

**inure** (say in-yoor) VERB inures, inuring, inured
to accustom someone to something unpleasant • I've become inured to criticism by now.

**invade** VERB invades, invading, invaded
❶ to attack and enter a country ❷ to crowd into a place • Tourists invade Oxford in summer.
➤ **invader** NOUN

**invalid** (say in-va-leed) NOUN invalids
a person who is ill or who is weakened by illness

**invalid** (say in-val-id) ADJECTIVE
not valid; not able to be used legally • This passport is invalid.
➤ **invalidity** NOUN

**invalidate** VERB invalidates, invalidating, invalidated
to make a thing invalid
➤ **invalidation** NOUN

**invaluable** ADJECTIVE
having a value that is too great to be measured; extremely valuable • invaluable information

**invariable** ADJECTIVE
not variable; never changing

**invariably** ADVERB
without exception; always • She invariably arrives late.

**invasion** NOUN invasions
❶ attacking and entering a country ❷ crowding into a place • an invasion of ants

**invective** NOUN
abusive words

**inveigle** (say in-vay-gul) VERB inveigles, inveigling, inveigled
to coax or entice someone to do something

**invent** VERB invents, inventing, invented
❶ to be the first person to make or think of a particular thing ❷ to make up a false story • She had to invent an excuse quickly.

**invention** NOUN inventions
❶ a thing that has been made or designed by someone for the first time ❷ inventing something • The invention of the telephone changed the world.

**inventive** ADJECTIVE
having clever new ideas • She has an inventive mind.

**inventor** NOUN inventors
a person who has invented something

**inventory** (say in-ven-ter-ee) NOUN inventories
a detailed list of goods or furniture

**inverse** ADJECTIVE
opposite or reverse
➤ **inversely** ADVERB

**invert** VERB inverts, inverting, inverted
to turn something upside down
➤ **inversion** NOUN

**invertebrate** NOUN invertebrates
an animal without a backbone
➤ **invertebrate** ADJECTIVE

**inverted commas** PLURAL NOUN
punctuation marks (" " or ' ') which are put round quotations and spoken words

PUNCTUATION

Inverted commas (also known as **quotation marks** or **speech marks**) are used in pairs and can surround a single word or phrase or a longer piece of text. The punctuation always goes inside the inverted commas. They are used:

in direct speech to show which words are being spoken:

*'Look!' said a voice behind me. 'Look at the sky!'*

to highlight a word to which you are referring:

*The words 'turn back' were scratched on the door.*

to show that a word is being used in a slightly odd way, for example because it is a slang word:

*Disneyland wasn't my idea of a place to 'chill' on holiday.*

to show that something is the title of a poem, story, piece of music, etc.

*She stood up and recited Kipling's poem 'If'.*

to enclose direct quotations from a speech, book, play or film:

*Which film contains the famous line, 'Toto, I've a feeling we're not in Kansas anymore'?*

Pairs of inverted commas can be single ( ' ' ) or double ( " " ), but are never mixed. You can, however, use a pair of double inverted commas within a pair of single inverted commas:

*'When I say, "Action", start the gladiator scene again.'*

See also the panel on **direct and reported speech**.

**invest** VERB invests, investing, invested
❶ to use money to make a profit, e.g. by lending it in return for interest to be paid or by buying stocks and shares or property
❷ to give someone an honour, medal or special title in a formal ceremony
➤ **investor** NOUN

**investigate** VERB investigates, investigating, investigated
to find out as much as you can about something • *Police are investigating the robbery.*
➤ **investigator** NOUN
➤ **investigative** ADJECTIVE

**investigation** NOUN investigations
a careful search for information about something • *a murder investigation*

**investiture** NOUN investitures
the ceremony of investing someone with an honour etc.

**investment** NOUN investments
❶ an amount of money invested
❷ something in which money is invested
• *Property is a good investment.*

**inveterate** ADJECTIVE
always doing something and not likely to stop
• *an inveterate gambler*

**invigilate** VERB invigilates, invigilating, invigilated
(*British*) to supervise the people taking an examination
➤ **invigilation** NOUN
➤ **invigilator** NOUN

**invigorate** VERB invigorates, invigorating, invigorated
to make someone feel healthy and full of energy • *He felt invigorated after his swim.*
➤ **invigorating** ADJECTIVE

**invincible** ADJECTIVE
not able to be defeated
➤ **invincibility** NOUN

**invisible** ADJECTIVE
not visible; not able to be seen • *These creatures are so tiny that they are invisible to the human eye.*
➤ **invisibly** ADVERB
➤ **invisibility** NOUN

**invitation** NOUN invitations
a request for a person to do or come to something

**invite** VERB invites, inviting, invited
❶ to ask a person to come or do something
❷ to be likely to cause something unpleasant to happen • *You are inviting disaster.*

**inviting** ADJECTIVE
attractive or tempting
➤ **invitingly** ADVERB

**invoice** NOUN invoices
a list of goods sent or work done, with the prices charged

**invoke** VERB invokes, invoking, invoked
❶ to mention a law or someone's authority to support what you are doing ❷ to call upon a god in prayer asking for help etc.
➤ **invocation** NOUN

**involuntary** ADJECTIVE
not deliberate; done without thinking • *an involuntary shudder*
➤ **involuntarily** ADVERB

**involve** VERB involves, involving, involved
❶ to have or include something as a necessary part • *The job involved a lot of effort.* ❷ to make or let someone share or take part in something • *We want to involve everybody in the celebrations.*
➤ **involvement** NOUN

**involved** ADJECTIVE
❶ taking part in something; closely connected with something • *I didn't want to get involved in their argument.* ❷ long and complicated • *The book has an involved plot.*

**invulnerable** ADJECTIVE
not able to be harmed

**inward** ADJECTIVE
❶ on the inside ❷ going or facing inwards

**inward** ADVERB
inwards

**inwardly** ADVERB
in your thoughts; privately • *He groaned inwardly.*

**inwards** ADVERB
towards the inside • *A concave lens curves inwards.*

**iodine** NOUN
a chemical substance used as an antiseptic

**ion** NOUN ions
an electrically charged particle

**ionosphere** (say eye-**on**-os-feer) NOUN
a region of the upper atmosphere, containing ions

**iota** NOUN iotas
a tiny amount of something • *There's not an iota of truth in what she says.*
**WORD ORIGIN** the name of *i*, the ninth and smallest letter of the Greek alphabet

**IOU** NOUN IOUs
a signed note acknowledging that you owe someone some money **WORD ORIGIN** short for 'I owe you'

**IQ** ABBREVIATION
intelligence quotient; a number showing how a person's intelligence compares with that of an average person

**irascible** (say ir-**as**-ib-ul) ADJECTIVE
easily becoming angry; irritable

**irate** (say eye-**rayt**) ADJECTIVE
angry • *irate customers*

**iridescent** ADJECTIVE
showing rainbow-like colours
➤ **iridescence** NOUN

**iris** NOUN irises
❶ the coloured part of your eyeball ❷ a plant with long pointed leaves and large flowers

**irk** VERB irks, irking, irked
to annoy someone

**irksome** ADJECTIVE
annoying or tiresome

**iron** NOUN irons
❶ a hard grey metal ❷ a device with a flat base that is heated for smoothing clothes or cloth ❸ a tool made of iron • *a branding iron*
➤ **iron** ADJECTIVE

**iron** VERB irons, ironing, ironed
to smooth clothes or cloth with an iron
➤ **iron something out** to sort out a difficulty or problem

**Iron Age** NOUN
the time when tools and weapons were made of iron

**ironic** (say eye-**ron**-ik) ADJECTIVE
❶ an ironic situation is strange because the opposite happens to what you might expect ❷ you are being ironic when you say the opposite of what you mean
➤ **ironical** ADJECTIVE
➤ **ironically** ADVERB

**ironmonger** NOUN ironmongers
(*British*) a shopkeeper who sells tools and other metal objects
➤ **ironmongery** NOUN

**irons** PLURAL NOUN
shackles or fetters

**irony** NOUN ironies
❶ saying the opposite of what you mean in order to emphasize it or as a joke, e.g. saying 'What a lovely day.' when it is pouring with rain ❷ a situation that is the opposite of what you might have expected • *The irony of it is that I tripped while telling someone else to be careful.*

**irrational** ADJECTIVE
not rational; illogical • *an irrational fear*
➤ **irrationally** ADVERB

**irrefutable** (say ir-**ef**-yoo-ta-bul) ADJECTIVE
unable to be proven wrong • *The evidence is irrefutable.*

**irregular** ADJECTIVE
❶ not regular; uneven • *His visits became more and more irregular.* • *an irregular shape*
❷ not following the normal rules or usual custom
➤ **irregularly** ADVERB
➤ **irregularity** NOUN

**irrelevant** (say ir-**el**-iv-ant) ADJECTIVE
not relevant; not having anything to do with what is being discussed
➤ **irrelevantly** ADVERB
➤ **irrelevance** NOUN

**irreparable** (say ir-**ep**-er-a-bul) ADJECTIVE
unable to be repaired • *irreparable damage*
➤ **irreparably** ADVERB

**irreplaceable** ADJECTIVE
unable to be replaced

**irrepressible** ADJECTIVE
unable to be repressed; always lively and cheerful
➤ **irrepressibly** ADVERB

**irreproachable** ADJECTIVE
blameless or faultless
➤ **irreproachably** ADVERB

**irresistible** ADJECTIVE
too strong or attractive or tempting to resist
• *I had an irresistible urge to laugh.*
➤ **irresistibly** ADVERB

**irresolute** ADJECTIVE
feeling uncertain; hesitant
➤ **irresolutely** ADVERB

**irrespective** ADJECTIVE
not taking something into account • *Prizes are awarded to winners, irrespective of age.*

**irresponsible** ADJECTIVE
not thinking enough about the effects of your actions
➤ **irresponsibly** ADVERB
➤ **irresponsibility** NOUN

**irretrievable** ADJECTIVE
not able to be retrieved
➤ **irretrievably** ADVERB

**irreverent** ADJECTIVE
not reverent or respectful
➤ **irreverently** ADVERB
➤ **irreverence** NOUN

**irrevocable** (say ir-**ev**-ok-a-bul) ADJECTIVE
unable to be changed • *an irrevocable decision*
➤ **irrevocably** ADVERB

**irrigate** VERB irrigates, irrigating, irrigated
to supply land with water so that crops can grow
➤ **irrigation** NOUN

**irritable** ADJECTIVE
easily annoyed; bad-tempered
➤ **irritably** ADVERB
➤ **irritability** NOUN

**irritate** VERB irritates, irritating, irritated
❶ to annoy someone ❷ to make a part of your body itch or feel sore • *This soap irritates my skin.*
➤ **irritating** ADJECTIVE
➤ **irritant** NOUN

**irritation** NOUN irritations
❶ being annoyed • *There was a hint of irritation in her voice.* ❷ something that annoys you

**Islam** NOUN
the religion of Muslims
➤ **Islamic** ADJECTIVE

**island** NOUN islands
❶ a piece of land surrounded by water ❷ something that resembles an island because it is isolated or detached • *a traffic island*

**islander** NOUN islanders
someone who lives on an island

**isle** (rhymes with mile) NOUN isles (*poetic & in names*)
an island

**isn't** (*mainly spoken*)
is not

> **SPELLING**
>
> Isn't = is + not. Add an apostrophe between the n and the t.

**isobar** (say **eye**-so-bar) NOUN isobars
a line on a map connecting places that have the same atmospheric pressure

**isolate** VERB isolates, isolating, isolated
to place or keep a person or thing apart from other people or things • *Patients with the disease need to be isolated.*
➤ **isolated** ADJECTIVE

**isolation** NOUN
being separate or alone • *He lived in complete isolation from the outside world.*

**isosceles** (say eye-**soss**-il-eez) ADJECTIVE
an isosceles triangle has two sides of equal length

a b c d e f g h i j k l m n o p q r s t u v w x y z

**isotope** NOUN isotopes
(*in science*) a form of an element that differs from other forms in the structure of its nucleus but has the same chemical properties as the other forms WORD ORIGIN from Greek *isos* = same + *topos* = place (because they appear in the same place in the table of chemical elements)

**ISP** ABBREVIATION
Internet service provider, a company providing individual users with a connection to the Internet

**issue** VERB issues, issuing, issued
❶ to supply something or give it out to people • *We issued one blanket to each refugee.* ❷ to send something out • *They issued a gale warning.* ❸ to put something out for sale; to publish something ❹ to come or go out; to flow out • *Black smoke issued from the chimneys.*

**issue** NOUN issues
❶ a subject for discussion or concern • *There were two main issues the jury had to consider.* ❷ a particular edition of a newspaper or magazine • *Look out for the free poster in next week's issue.* ❸ issuing something • *The issue of passports has been held up.* ❹ (*formal*) the birth of children • *He died without issue.*
➤ **take issue with someone** to disagree with someone

**isthmus** (say **iss**-mus) NOUN isthmuses
a narrow strip of land connecting two larger pieces of land

**IT** ABBREVIATION
information technology

**it** PRONOUN
❶ the thing being talked about ❷ used in statements about the weather, the time or a distance • *It is raining.* • *It is six miles to York.* ❸ used to refer to a phrase • *It is a pity that she was so tired.* ❹ used as an indefinite object • *Run for it!*

**italic** (say it-**al**-ik) ADJECTIVE
printed with sloping letters (called **italics**) like this

**itch** VERB itches, itching, itched
❶ to have or feel a tickling sensation in the skin that makes you want to scratch it ❷ to long to do something • *I am itching to get started.*

**itch** NOUN itches
❶ an itching feeling ❷ a longing

**itchy** ADJECTIVE itchier, itchiest
making you want to scratch your skin
• *My nose is itchy.*
➤ **itchiness** NOUN

**item** NOUN items
❶ one thing in a list or group of things ❷ one piece of news, article, etc., in a newspaper or bulletin

**itinerant** (say it-**in**-er-ant) ADJECTIVE
travelling from place to place • *itinerant musicians*

**itinerary** (say eye-**tin**-er-er-ee) NOUN
itineraries
a list of places to be visited on a journey; a route

**its** DETERMINER
belonging to it • *The cat was licking its paw.*
SPELLING
Take care not to confuse this word **its**, meaning 'belonging to it', with the word **it's**, meaning 'it is' or 'it has'.

**it's** (*mainly spoken*)
❶ it is • *It's very hot.* ❷ it has • *It's broken all records.*
SPELLING
Take care not to confuse this word **it's**, meaning 'it is' or 'it has', with the word **its**, meaning 'belonging to it'.

**itself** PRONOUN
it and nothing else. The word is used to refer back to the subject of a sentence (e.g. *The cat has hurt itself.*) or for emphasis (e.g. *The house itself is quite small.*).
➤ **by itself** on its own; alone

**ivory** NOUN
❶ the hard creamy-white substance that forms elephants' tusks ❷ a creamy-white colour

**ivy** NOUN ivies
a climbing evergreen plant with shiny leaves

# Jj

**jab** *VERB* jabs, jabbing, jabbed
❶ to poke someone roughly with your finger or something pointed • *She jabbed me in the ribs with her elbow.* ❷ to push a thing roughly into something else • *He jabbed his gun into my back.*

**jab** *NOUN* jabs
❶ a rough push or hit with something pointed or a fist ❷ (*informal*) an injection

**jabber** *VERB* jabbers, jabbering, jabbered
to speak quickly and not clearly; to chatter • *They were all jabbering excitedly.*
➤ **jabber** *NOUN*

**jack** *NOUN* jacks
❶ a device for lifting something heavy off the ground, especially a car ❷ a playing card with a picture of a young man ❸ a small white ball that players aim at in the game of bowls
➤ **jack of all trades** someone who can do many different kinds of work

**jack** *VERB* jacks, jacking, jacked
to lift something with a jack
➤ **jack it in** (*informal*) to give up or abandon something
**WORD ORIGIN** the name *Jack* was given to various sorts of tool (as though it was a person helping you)

**jackal** *NOUN* jackals
a wild animal rather like a dog

**jackaroo** *NOUN* jackaroos (*informal*)
(*Australian*) a young male trainee worker on a sheep or cattle station

**jackass** *NOUN* jackasses
❶ a male donkey ❷ (*informal*) a stupid person

**jackdaw** *NOUN* jackdaws
a kind of small crow

**jacket** *NOUN* jackets
❶ a short coat, usually reaching to your hips ❷ a cover to keep the heat in a water tank or boiler ❸ a paper wrapper for a book ❹ the skin of a potato that is baked without being peeled

**jack-in-the-box** *NOUN* jack-in-the-boxes
a toy figure that springs out of a box when the lid is lifted

**jackknife** *VERB* jackknifes, jackknifing, jackknifed
an articulated lorry jackknifes if it folds against itself in an accidental skidding movement

**jackpot** *NOUN* jackpots
an amount of prize money that increases until someone wins it
➤ **hit the jackpot** ❶ to win a large prize ❷ to have remarkable luck or success
**WORD ORIGIN** originally = a kitty which could be won only by playing a pair of jacks or cards of higher value

**Jacobean** *ADJECTIVE*
from the reign of James I of England (1603-25)

**Jacobite** *NOUN* Jacobites
a supporter of the exiled Stuarts after the abdication of James II of England (1688)

**Jacuzzi** (say ja-koo-zi) *NOUN* Jacuzzis
(*trademark*)
a large bath in which underwater jets of water massage your body
**WORD ORIGIN** named after its inventor Candido *Jacuzzi*

**jade** *NOUN*
a hard green stone that is carved to make ornaments and jewellery

**jaded** *ADJECTIVE*
tired and bored after doing the same thing for too long **WORD ORIGIN** from an old word *jade* = a worn-out horse

**jagged** (say jag-id) *ADJECTIVE*
a jagged line or outline has an uneven edge with sharp points

**jaguar** *NOUN* jaguars
a large fierce South American animal of the cat family rather like a leopard

**jail** *NOUN* jails
a prison

**jail** *VERB* jails, jailing, jailed
to put someone in prison

**jailer** *NOUN* jailers
a person in charge of a jail

**Jain** (say Jane) *NOUN* Jains
a follower of Jainism

a
b
c
d
e
f
g
h
i
j
k
l
m
n
o
p
q
r
s
t
u
v
w
x
y
z

**Jainism** (say **jayn**-izm) NOUN
an ancient philosophy originating in India and closely linked to Hinduism

**jam** NOUN jams
❶ a sweet food made of fruit boiled with sugar until it is thick ❷ a lot of people, cars or logs etc. crowded together so that movement is difficult
➤ **in a jam** (*informal*)
in a difficult situation

**jam** VERB jams, jamming, jammed
❶ to become or make something fixed and difficult to move • *The paper keeps jamming in the printer.* ❷ to squeeze something into a space where there is not much room • *Six of us were jammed into one small car.* ❸ to push something with a lot of force • *He jammed his fingers in his ears.* • *I jammed the brakes on.* ❹ to block a broadcast by causing interference with the transmission

**jamb** (say jam) NOUN jambs
a side post of a doorway or window frame

**jamboree** NOUN jamborees
a large party or celebration

**jangle** VERB jangles, jangling, jangled
❶ to make a loud harsh ringing sound • *His keys jangled in his pocket.* ❷ your nerves are jangling when you feel anxious
➤ **jangle** NOUN

**janitor** NOUN janitors
a caretaker

**January** NOUN
the first month of the year
(WORD ORIGIN) named after *Janus*, a Roman god of gates and beginnings, usually shown with two faces that look in opposite directions

**jar** NOUN jars
a container made of glass or pottery

**jar** VERB jars, jarring, jarred
❶ to cause an unpleasant jolt or shock • *I jarred my neck when I fell.* ❷ to make a harsh sound, especially in an annoying way • *Her voice really jars on me.*

**jargon** NOUN
words or expressions used by a profession or group that are difficult for other people to understand • *The guide is full of computer jargon.*

**jasmine** NOUN
a shrub with yellow or white flowers

**jaundice** NOUN
a disease in which the skin becomes yellow

**jaunt** NOUN jaunts
a short trip for fun

**jaunty** ADJECTIVE jauntier, jauntiest
lively and cheerful • *She gave them a jaunty little wave as she left.*
➤ **jauntily** ADVERB

**javelin** NOUN javelins
a lightweight spear used for throwing in athletics competitions

**jaw** NOUN jaws
❶ either of the two bones that form the framework of the mouth ❷ the lower part of the face; the mouth and teeth of a person or animal ❸ the part of a tool that grips something

**jay** NOUN jays
a noisy brightly-coloured bird

**jaywalker** NOUN jaywalkers
a person who dangerously walks across a road without looking out for traffic
➤ **jaywalking** NOUN

**jazz** NOUN
a kind of music with strong rhythm, often improvised
➤ **jazz something up** to make something more lively or interesting

**jealous** ADJECTIVE
❶ angry or upset because someone you love seems to be showing interest in someone else ❷ unhappy or resentful because you feel that someone is more successful or luckier than you or has something that you would like to have ❸ careful in keeping something • *He is very jealous of his privacy.*
➤ **jealously** ADVERB

SPELLING
There is a tricky bit in **jealous**—it begins with **jea**.

**jealousy** NOUN jealousy
a jealous feeling • *I felt sick with jealousy.*

**jeans** PLURAL NOUN
trousers made of denim or another strong cotton fabric

**Jeep** NOUN Jeeps (*trademark*)
a small sturdy motor vehicle with four-wheel drive, especially one used in the army
(WORD ORIGIN) from *G.P.*, short for 'general purpose'

**jeer** VERB jeers, jeering, jeered
to laugh rudely at someone and shout insults at them

**jeer** VERB jeers
a rude or scornful remark

**jelly** NOUN jellies
❶ a soft transparent food with a fruit flavour
❷ any soft slippery substance
➤ **jellied** ADJECTIVE

**jellyfish** NOUN jellyfish
a sea animal with a body like jelly and
stinging tentacles

**jemmy** NOUN jemmies
a burglar's crowbar

**jeopardize** (also **jeopardise**) (say jep-er-dyz)
VERB jeopardizes, jeopardizing, jeopardized
to put something at risk • *This could
jeopardize the whole mission.*

**jeopardy** (say jep-er-dee) NOUN
danger of harm or failure • *The future of the
factory is now in jeopardy.*

**jerk** VERB jerks, jerking, jerked
❶ to make a sudden sharp movement • *The
train jerked forwards.* ❷ to pull something
suddenly

**jerk** NOUN jerks
❶ a sudden sharp movement ❷ (*informal*) a
stupid person

**jerkin** NOUN jerkins
a sleeveless jacket

**jerky** ADJECTIVE
moving with sudden sharp movements
➤ **jerkily** ADVERB

**jersey** NOUN jerseys
❶ a pullover with sleeves ❷ a plain machine-
knitted material used for making clothes
**WORD ORIGIN** originally = a woollen cloth
made in *Jersey*, one of the Channel Islands

**jest** NOUN jests
a joke
➤ **in jest** as a joke

**jest** VERB jests, jesting, jested
to make jokes

**jester** NOUN jesters
a professional entertainer at a royal court in
the Middle Ages

**jet** NOUN jets
❶ a stream of water, gas, flame, etc. shot out
from a narrow opening ❷ a spout or nozzle
from which a jet comes ❸ an aircraft driven
by engines that send out a high-speed jet of
hot gases at the back ❹ a hard black mineral
substance ❺ a deep glossy black colour

**jet** VERB jets, jetting, jetted
❶ to come out or send something out in a
strong stream ❷ (*informal*) to travel in a jet
aircraft

**jet lag** NOUN
extreme tiredness that a person feels after a
long flight between different time zones

**jetsam** NOUN
goods thrown overboard from a
ship in difficulty and washed ashore
**WORD ORIGIN** from **jettison**

**jettison** VERB jettisons, jettisoning, jettisoned
❶ to throw something overboard ❷ to
release or drop something from an aircraft or
spacecraft in flight ❸ to get rid of something
that you no longer want

**jetty** NOUN jetties
a small landing stage for boats

**Jew** NOUN Jews
❶ a member of a people descended from
the ancient tribes of Israel ❷ someone who
believes in Judaism
➤ **Jewish** ADJECTIVE

**jewel** NOUN jewels
❶ a precious stone ❷ an ornament
containing precious stones
➤ **jewelled** ADJECTIVE

**jeweller** NOUN jewellers
a person who sells or makes jewellery

**jewellery** NOUN
jewels and similar ornaments for wearing

**jib** NOUN jibs
❶ a triangular sail stretching forward from a
ship's front mast ❷ the arm of a crane

**jib** VERB jibs, jibbing, jibbed
to be unwilling to do or accept something

**jibe** NOUN jibes
a remark that is meant to hurt someone's
feelings or make them look silly

**jibe** VERB jibes, jibing, jibed
to make hurtful remarks; to mock someone

**jiffy** NOUN (*informal*)
a brief moment • *I'll be ready in a jiffy.*

**jig** NOUN jigs
❶ a lively jumping dance ❷ a device that
holds something in place while you work on
it with tools

**jig** VERB jigs, jigging, jigged
to move up and down quickly and jerkily

**jiggle** VERB jiggles, jiggling, jiggled
to move around with short quick movements
• *Stop jiggling around!*

**jigsaw** NOUN jigsaws
❶ a puzzle made of differently shaped pieces that you have to fit together to make a picture ❷ a saw that can cut curved shapes

**jihad** NOUN jihads
(among Muslims) a war or struggle against unbelievers or a spiritual struggle

**jilt** VERB jilts, jilting, jilted
to abandon a boyfriend or girlfriend, especially after promising to marry them

**jingle** VERB jingles, jingling, jingled
❶ metal objects jingle when they make a tinkling sound like small bells ❷ to shake metal objects together so that they make a tinkling sound like small bells • *She jingled the coins in her pocket.*

**jingle** NOUN jingles
❶ a jingling sound ❷ a catchy verse or tune, especially one used in advertising

**jingoism** NOUN
an extremely strong and unreasonable belief that your country is superior to others
➤ **jingoistic** ADJECTIVE
WORD ORIGIN from the saying *by jingo!*, used in a patriotic song in the 19th century

**jinx** NOUN jinxes
a person or thing that is thought to bring bad luck WORD ORIGIN probably a variation of *jynx* = wryneck, a bird used in witchcraft

**jitters** PLURAL NOUN (*informal*)
a feeling of extreme nervousness

**jittery** ADJECTIVE (*informal*)
extremely nervous and anxious • *The horses were getting jittery.*

**job** NOUN jobs
❶ work that someone does regularly to earn a living ❷ a piece of work that needs to be done ❸ (*informal*) a difficult task • *You'll have a job to lift that box.* ❹ (*informal*) a thing; a state of affairs • *It's a good job you're here.*
➤ **just the job** (*informal*) exactly what you want

**jobcentre** NOUN jobcentres
a government office with information about available jobs

**jockey** NOUN jockeys
a person who rides horses in races

**jocular** ADJECTIVE
joking or humorous
➤ **jocularly** ADVERB
➤ **jocularity** NOUN

**jodhpurs** (say jod-perz) PLURAL NOUN
trousers for horse riding, fitting closely from the knee to the ankle WORD ORIGIN named after *Jodhpur*, a city in India, where similar trousers are worn

**joey** NOUN joeys
(*Australian*) a young animal, especially a kangaroo, still young enough to be carried in its mother's pouch

**jog** VERB jogs, jogging, jogged
❶ to run or trot slowly, especially for exercise ❷ to give something a slight knock or push
➤ **jogger** NOUN
➤ **jog someone's memory** to help someone to remember something

**jog** NOUN jogs
a slow run or trot

**joggle** VERB joggles, joggling, joggled
to shake slightly or move jerkily

**joie de vivre** (say zhwah der **veevr**) NOUN
a feeling of great enjoyment of life
WORD ORIGIN French, = joy of life

**join** VERB joins, joining, joined
❶ two things join when they come together ❷ to put things together; to fasten or connect things ❸ to take part with others in doing something or going somewhere • *Do you mind if I join you?* ❹ to become a member of a group or organization • *Join the Navy.*
➤ **join in** to take part in something
➤ **join up** to become a member of the armed forces

**join** NOUN joins
a place where things join

**joiner** NOUN joiners
a person whose job is to make doors, window frames, etc. and furniture out of wood
➤ **joinery** NOUN

**joint** NOUN joints
❶ a place where two things are joined ❷ the place where two bones fit together ❸ a large piece of meat cut ready for cooking ❹ (*informal*) a cannabis cigarette

**joint** ADJECTIVE
shared or done by two or more people, groups or countries • *The song was a joint effort.*
➤ **jointly** ADVERB

**joist** NOUN joists
any of the long beams supporting a floor or ceiling

**joke** NOUN jokes
❶ something said or done to make people laugh ❷ a ridiculous person or thing

**joke** VERB jokes, joking, joked
❶ to make jokes ❷ to tease someone or not be serious • *I'm only joking.*

**joker** NOUN jokers
❶ someone who likes making jokes ❷ an extra playing card with a picture of a jester on it

**jolly** ADJECTIVE jollier, jolliest
cheerful and good-humoured
➤ **jollity** NOUN

**jolly** ADVERB (*British*) (*informal*) very • *jolly good*

**jolly** VERB jollies, jollying, jollied (*British*) (*informal*)
➤ **jolly someone along** to keep someone in a cheerful mood

**jolt** VERB jolts, jolting, jolted
❶ to shake or dislodge something with a sudden sharp movement ❷ to move along jerkily, e.g. on a rough road ❸ to give someone a shock

**jolt** NOUN jolts
❶ a jolting movement ❷ a shock

**jostle** VERB jostles, jostling, jostled
to push someone roughly, especially in a crowd • *People jostled to get a better view*

**jot** VERB jots, jotting, jotted
to jot something down is to write it down quickly

**jot** NOUN jots
a tiny amount • *He doesn't care a jot about other people.*

**jotter** NOUN jotters
(*British*) a notepad or notebook

**joule** (say jool) NOUN joules
(*in science*) a unit of work or energy
**WORD ORIGIN** named after an English scientist, James *Joule*

**journal** NOUN journals
❶ a newspaper or magazine ❷ a diary

**journalist** NOUN journalists
a person who writes for a newspaper or magazine or who prepares news broadcasts on television or radio
➤ **journalism** NOUN
➤ **journalistic** ADJECTIVE

**journey** NOUN journeys
❶ going from one place to another ❷ the distance or time taken to travel somewhere • *The town was two days' journey away.*

**journey** VERB journeys, journeying, journeyed
to make a journey • *They journeyed for seven long months.*

**joust** (say jowst) VERB jousts, jousting, jousted
to fight on horseback with lances, as knights did in medieval times
➤ **joust** NOUN

**jovial** ADJECTIVE
cheerful and good-humoured
➤ **jovially** ADVERB
➤ **joviality** NOUN
**WORD ORIGIN** from Latin *jovialis* = to do with Jupiter (because people born under the planet's influence were said to be cheerful)

**jowl** NOUN jowls
❶ the jaw or cheek ❷ loose skin on the neck

**joy** NOUN joys
❶ a feeling of great pleasure or happiness ❷ a thing that causes joy ❸ satisfaction or success • *Any joy with the crossword?*

**joyful** ADJECTIVE
very happy • *a joyful occasion*
➤ **joyfully** ADVERB
➤ **joyfulness** NOUN

**joyous** ADJECTIVE
full of joy; causing joy
➤ **joyously** ADVERB

**joyride** NOUN joyrides
a drive in a stolen car for amusement
➤ **joyrider** NOUN
➤ **joyriding** NOUN

**joystick** NOUN joysticks
❶ the control lever of an aircraft ❷ a device for moving a cursor or image on a computer screen, especially in computer games

**jubilant** ADJECTIVE
very happy because you have won or succeeded
➤ **jubilantly** ADVERB
➤ **jubilation** NOUN

**jubilee** (say joo-bil-ee) NOUN jubilees
a special anniversary of an important event

**USAGE**
A *silver jubilee* is the 25th anniversary, a *golden jubilee* is the 50th anniversary, and a *diamond jubilee* is a 60th anniversary.

**WORD ORIGIN** from Hebrew *yobel* = a year when slaves were freed and property returned

a
b
c
d
e
f
g
h
i
j
k
l
m
n
o
p
q
r
s
t
u
v
w
x
y
z

to its owners, held in ancient Israel every 50 years

**Judaism** (say **joo**-day-izm) NOUN
the religion of the Jewish people

**judder** VERB judders, juddering, juddered
(*British*) to shake noisily or violently • *The van juddered to a halt.*

**judge** NOUN judges
❶ a person appointed to hear cases in a law court and decide what should be done ❷ a person who decides the winner of a contest or competition ❸ someone who is good at forming opinions or making decisions about things • *She's a good judge of character.*

**judge** VERB judges, judging, judged
❶ to act as a judge ❷ to form and give an opinion ❸ to estimate something • *He judged the distance carefully.*

**judgement** NOUN judgements
❶ judging ❷ the decision made by a law court ❸ someone's opinion • *In my judgement, you're making a big mistake.*
❹ the ability to make decisions wisely ❺ something considered as a punishment from God • *It's a judgement on you!*

> SPELLING
>
> There is a tricky bit in **judgement** – there is an **e** after the **g**.

**judicial** ADJECTIVE
to do with law courts, judges or legal judgements • *the British judicial system*

> USAGE
>
> Take care not to confuse with **judicious**.

**judiciary** (say joo-**dish**-er-ee) NOUN judiciaries
all the judges in a country

**judicious** (say joo-**dish**-us) ADJECTIVE
having or showing good sense or good judgement
> **judiciously** ADVERB

> USAGE
>
> Take care not to confuse with **judicial**.

**judo** NOUN
a Japanese method of self-defence without using weapons **WORD ORIGIN** from Japanese *ju* = gentle + *do* = way

**jug** NOUN jugs
a container for holding and pouring liquids, with a handle and a lip

**juggernaut** NOUN juggernauts
(*British*) a huge lorry **WORD ORIGIN** named

after a huge wagon bearing the image of the Hindu god *Jagannatha*, dragged through the streets at an annual festival

**juggle** VERB juggles, juggling, juggled
❶ to toss and catch a number of objects skilfully for entertainment, keeping one or more in the air at any time ❷ to try to deal with several jobs or activities at the same time
> **juggler** NOUN

**jugular** ADJECTIVE
to do with your throat or neck • *the jugular veins*

**juice** NOUN juices
❶ the liquid from fruit, vegetables or other food ❷ a liquid produced by the body • *the digestive juices*

> SPELLING
>
> Juice is a tricky word to spell: the 'oo' sound is spelt **ui** and the '**s**' sound is spelt with a **c**.

**juicy** ADJECTIVE juicier, juiciest
full of juice

**jukebox** NOUN jukeboxes
a machine that automatically plays a record you have selected when you put a coin in

**July** NOUN
the seventh month of the year
**WORD ORIGIN** named after *Julius* Caesar, who was born in this month

**jumble** VERB jumbles, jumbling, jumbled
to mix things up in a confused and untidy way

**jumble** NOUN
a confused mixture of things; a muddle • *a jumble of books and paper*

**jumble sale** NOUN jumble sales
(*British*) a sale of second-hand goods to raise money

**jumbo** NOUN jumbos
❶ something very large ❷ a jumbo jet
**WORD ORIGIN** the name of a very large elephant in London Zoo

**jumbo jet** NOUN jumbo jets
a very large jet aircraft

**jump** VERB jumps, jumping, jumped
❶ to move up suddenly from the ground into the air ❷ to go over something by jumping
• *The horse jumped the fence.* ❸ to move suddenly in surprise • *Oh, it's only you – you made me jump.* ❹ to get into or out of a

vehicle quickly • *A taxi stopped and we jumped in.* ❺ to pass over something; to miss out part of a book etc. ❻ to pass quickly to a higher level

➤ **jump at something** to accept something eagerly
➤ **jump on someone** to start criticizing someone
➤ **jump the gun** to start before you should
➤ **jump the queue** to go in front of people before it is your turn

**jump** NOUN jumps
❶ a jumping movement ❷ an obstacle to jump over ❸ a sudden rise or change

**jumper** NOUN jumpers
a pullover with sleeves

**jumpy** ADJECTIVE
nervous and edgy

**junction** NOUN junctions
a place where roads or railway lines meet

**juncture** NOUN junctures
a point of time while something is happening • *At this juncture there was a knock on the door.*

**June** NOUN
the sixth month of the year
**WORD ORIGIN** named after the Roman goddess Juno

**jungle** NOUN jungles
a thick tangled forest, especially in the tropics

**junior** ADJECTIVE
❶ younger ❷ for young children • *a junior school* ❸ lower in rank or importance • *junior officers*

**junior** NOUN juniors
a junior person

**juniper** NOUN junipers
an evergreen shrub

**junk** NOUN junks
❶ old worthless things that should be thrown away • *The attic is full of junk.* ❷ a Chinese sailing boat

**junk food** NOUN
food that is not nourishing

**junkie** NOUN junkies (*informal*)
a drug addict

**junk mail** NOUN
unwanted advertising material sent by post or email

**jurisdiction** NOUN
authority; official power, especially to interpret and apply the law

**juror** NOUN jurors
a member of a jury

**jury** NOUN juries
❶ a group of people (usually twelve) appointed to give a verdict about a case in a law court ❷ a group of people chosen to judge a competition

**just** ADJECTIVE
❶ fair and right; giving proper consideration to everyone's claims • *a just decision* ❷ deserved; right in amount etc. • *a just reward*
➤ **justly** ADVERB

**just** ADVERB
❶ exactly • *It's just what I wanted.* ❷ only; simply • *I just wanted to see him.* ❸ barely; by only a small amount • *The ball hit her just below the knee.* ❹ at this moment or only a little while ago • *She has just gone.*

**justice** NOUN justices
❶ being just; fair treatment • *a struggle for justice* ❷ the system by which courts deal with people who break the law • *a court of justice* ❸ a judge or magistrate

**justifiable** ADJECTIVE
that you can accept because there is good reason for it • *Her actions were entirely justifiable.*

**justify** VERB justifies, justifying, justified
❶ to show that something is fair, just or reasonable • *Can you justify your decision?* ❷ to arrange lines of printed text so that one or both edges are straight
➤ **justification** NOUN

**jut** VERB juts, jutting, jutted
to stick out • *Rocky cliffs jutted out into the sea.*

**jute** NOUN
fibre from tropical plants, used for making sacks etc.

**juvenile** ADJECTIVE
❶ to do with or for young people ❷ childish

**juvenile** NOUN juveniles
a young person, not old enough to be legally considered an adult

**juvenile delinquent** NOUN juvenile delinquents
a young person who has broken the law

**juxtapose** *VERB* **juxtaposes, juxtaposing, juxtaposed**
to juxtapose two or more things is to put them next to each other to show how they are different
➤ **juxtaposition** *NOUN*

# Kk

**kale** *NOUN*
a kind of cabbage with curly leaves

**kaleidoscope** (say kal-y-dos-kohp) *NOUN* **kaleidoscopes**
❶ a tube that you look through to see brightly coloured patterns which change as you turn the end of the tube ❷ something full of colour and variety
➤ **kaleidoscopic** *ADJECTIVE*
**WORD ORIGIN** from Greek *kalos* = beautiful + *eidos* = form + *skopein* = look at

**kangaroo** *NOUN* **kangaroos**
an Australian animal that jumps along on its strong hind legs. (See **marsupial**.)

**kaolin** *NOUN*
fine white clay used in making porcelain and in medicine **WORD ORIGIN** from Chinese *gao ling* = high hill (because it was first found on a hill in northern China)

**karaoke** *NOUN*
a form of entertainment in which people sing well-known songs against a pre-recorded backing **WORD ORIGIN** Japanese = empty orchestra

**karate** (say ka-**rah**-tee) *NOUN*
a Japanese method of self-defence in which the hands and feet are used as weapons
**WORD ORIGIN** from Japanese *kara* = empty + *te* = hand

**karoo** *NOUN* **karoos**
(*S. African*) a dry plateau in southern Africa

**kayak** *NOUN* **kayaks**
a small canoe with a covering that fits round the canoeist's waist

**KB, Kb** *ABBREVIATION*
kilobytes

**kebab** *NOUN* **kebabs**
small pieces of meat or vegetables cooked on a skewer

**keel** *NOUN* **keels**
the long piece of wood or metal along the bottom of a boat
➤ **on an even keel** well balanced and steady

**keel** *VERB* **keels, keeling, keeled**
➤ **keel over** to fall down or overturn • *The ship keeled over.*

**keen** *ADJECTIVE*
❶ enthusiastic or eager • *a keen swimmer* ❷ to be keen on a person or thing is to like or be interested in them ❸ very sharp • *a keen edge* ❹ piercingly cold • *a keen wind*
➤ **keenly** *ADVERB*
➤ **keenness** *NOUN*

**keen** *VERB* **keens, keening, keened**
to wail in grief for a dead person

**keep** *VERB* **keeps, keeping, kept**
❶ to have something and look after it or not get rid of it ❷ to stay or cause something to stay in the same condition etc. • *Keep still.* • *I'll keep it hot.* ❸ to do something continually or repeatedly • *They kept laughing at her.* ❹ food or drink keeps when it lasts without going bad • *How long will this milk keep?* ❺ to keep a promise or your word is to respect and not break it ❻ to keep a diary is to make regular entries in it
➤ **keep up** to make the same progress as others
➤ **keep something up** to continue doing something • *Keep up the good work!*

**keep** *NOUN* **keeps**
❶ the food, clothes, etc. that a person needs to live • *She earns her keep.* ❷ a strong tower in a castle
➤ **for keeps** (*informal*) to keep for always • *Is this football mine for keeps?*

**SPELLING**
The past tense of **keep** is **kept**.

**keeper** *NOUN* **keepers**
❶ a person who looks after an animal, building, etc. • *the park keeper* ❷ a goalkeeper or wicketkeeper

**keeping** *NOUN*
something is in your keeping when you are looking after it • *The diaries are in safe keeping.*
➤ **be in keeping with something** to fit in with something or be suitable • *Modern furniture is not in keeping with such an old house.*

**keepsake** NOUN keepsakes
a gift to be kept in memory of the person who gave it

**keg** NOUN kegs
a small barrel

**kelp** NOUN
a large type of seaweed

**kelvin** NOUN kelvins
the SI unit of thermodynamic temperature
**WORD ORIGIN** named after a British scientist, Lord *Kelvin*, who invented it

**kennel** NOUN kennels
a shelter for a dog

**kennels** NOUN
a place where dogs are bred or where they can be looked after while their owners are away

**kenning** NOUN kennings
a type of expression or riddle from Anglo-Saxon times, in which something is described without using its name, e.g. *oar steed* meaning 'ship'

**kerb** NOUN kerbs
the edge of a pavement
SPELLING
Take care not to confuse with **curb**, which is a verb meaning to put a limit on something.

**kerchief** NOUN kerchiefs (old use)
❶ a square scarf worn on the head ❷ a handkerchief

**kernel** NOUN kernels
the part inside the shell of a nut
SPELLING
Do not confuse this word with **colonel**.

**kerosene** (say ke-ro-seen) NOUN
paraffin

**kestrel** NOUN kestrels
a small falcon

**ketchup** NOUN
a thick sauce made from tomatoes and vinegar

**kettle** NOUN kettles
a container with a spout and handle, for boiling water

**kettledrum** NOUN kettledrums
a drum consisting of a large metal bowl with skin or plastic over the top

**key** NOUN keys
❶ a piece of metal shaped so that it will open a lock ❷ a device for winding up a clock or clockwork toy ❸ a small lever or button to be pressed by a finger, e.g. on a piano, typewriter or computer ❹ a system of notes in music • *the key of C major* ❺ a fact or clue that explains or solves something • *the key to the mystery* ❻ a list of symbols used in a map or table

**key** VERB keys, keying, keyed
➤ **key something in** to type information into a computer using a keyboard • *Now key in your password.*

**keyboard** NOUN keyboards
the set of keys on a piano, computer, etc.

**keyhole** NOUN keyholes
the hole through which a key is put into a lock

**keyhole surgery** NOUN
surgery carried out through a very small cut in the patient's body, using special instruments

**keynote** NOUN keynotes
❶ the note on which a key in music is based • *The keynote of C major is C.* ❷ the main idea or theme in something that is said, written or done

**keypad** NOUN keypads
a small keyboard or set of buttons used to operate a telephone, television, etc.

**keystone** NOUN keystones
the central wedge-shaped stone in an arch, locking the others together

**keyword** NOUN keywords
a word that you type into a computer search engine so that it will search for that word on the Internet

**kg** ABBREVIATION
kilogram

**khaki** NOUN
a dull yellowish-brown colour, used for military uniforms **WORD ORIGIN** from Urdu *khaki* = dust-coloured

**Khalsa** NOUN
members of the Sikh religion who vow to wear five signs of their faith known as the five Ks

**kibbutz** NOUN kibbutzim
a farming commune in Israel

**kick** *VERB* **kicks, kicking, kicked**
❶ to hit or move a person or thing with your foot ❷ to move your legs about vigorously ❸ a gun kicks if it moves back sharply when it is fired
➤ **kick off** ❶ to start a football match ❷ (*informal*) to start doing something
➤ **kick someone out** to get rid of someone
➤ **kick up a fuss** (*informal*) to protest strongly about something
➤ **kick yourself** to be annoyed with yourself

**kick** *NOUN* **kicks**
❶ a kicking movement ❷ the sudden backwards movement a gun makes when it is fired ❸ (*informal*) a feeling of great excitement or pleasure • *She gets a real kick out of climbing.* ❹ (*informal*) an interest or activity • *He's on a health kick.*

**kick-off** *NOUN* **kick-offs**
the start of a football match

**kid** *NOUN* **kids**
❶ (*informal*) a child ❷ a young goat ❸ fine leather made from goatskin

**kid** *VERB* **kids, kidding, kidded** (*informal*) to tease or fool someone in fun • *Don't worry, I'm only kidding.*

**kiddie** *NOUN* **kiddies** (*informal*)
a child

**kidnap** *VERB* **kidnaps, kidnapping, kidnapped**
to take someone away by force, especially in order to obtain a ransom
➤ **kidnapper** *NOUN*

**kidney** *NOUN* **kidneys**
either of the two organs in the body that remove waste products from the blood and turn them into urine

**kidney bean** *NOUN* **kidney beans**
a dark red bean with a curved shape like a kidney

**kill** *VERB* **kills, killing, killed**
❶ to make a person or animal die ❷ to destroy or put an end to something ❸ (*informal*) to cause a person pain or mental suffering • *My feet are killing me.*
➤ **kill time** to spend time idly while waiting

**kill** *NOUN* **kills**
❶ killing an animal • *Lions often make a kill in the evening.* ❷ an animal that has been hunted and killed

**killer** *NOUN* **killers**
a person, animal or thing that kills

**killing** *NOUN* **killings**
an act causing death; a murder
➤ **make a killing** to make a lot of money

**kiln** *NOUN* **kilns**
an oven for hardening pottery or bricks, or for drying hops

**kilo** *NOUN* **kilos**
a kilogram

**kilobyte** *NOUN* **kilobytes**
(*in computing*) a unit of memory or data equal to 1,024 bytes

**kilogram** *NOUN* **kilograms**
a unit of mass or weight equal to 1,000 grams (about 2.2 pounds)

> **SPELLING**
> There is only one m in **kilogram**.

**kilometre** (say kil-o-meet-er or kil-**om**-it-er)
*NOUN* **kilometres**
a unit of length equal to 1,000 metres (about ⅔ of a mile)

> **SPELLING**
> There is a tricky bit in **kilometre** – it is spelt re at the end and not er.

**kilowatt** *NOUN* **kilowatts**
a unit of electrical power equal to 1,000 watts

**kilt** *NOUN* **kilts**
a kind of pleated skirt worn by men as part of traditional Scottish dress
➤ **kilted** *ADJECTIVE*

**kimono** *NOUN* **kimonos**
a long loose Japanese robe with wide sleeves
**WORD ORIGIN** from Japanese *ki* = wearing + *mono* = thing

**kin** *NOUN*
a person's relatives
➤ **kinsman** *NOUN*
➤ **kinswoman** *NOUN*
➤ **next of kin** a person's closest relative

**kind** *NOUN* **kinds**
a class of similar things or animals; a sort or type • *What kind of music do you like?*

**kind** *ADJECTIVE*
friendly and helpful; considerate
➤ **kindness** *NOUN*
➤ **in kind** ❶ in the same way • *She repaid his insults in kind.* ❷ payment in kind is given in the form of goods or services, not in money
➤ **kind of** (*informal*) in a way; to some extent • *I felt kind of sorry for him.*

**kindergarten** NOUN kindergartens
a school or class for very young children

**kind-hearted** ADJECTIVE
kind and sympathetic

**kindle** VERB kindles, kindling, kindled
❶ to start a flame; to set light to something
❷ to begin burning

**kindling** NOUN
small pieces of wood used for lighting fires

**kindly** ADVERB
❶ in a kind manner ❷ please • *Kindly close the door.*

**kindly** ADJECTIVE kindlier, kindliest
kind or friendly • *a kindly smile*
➤ **kindliness** NOUN

**kindred** NOUN
a person's family and relatives

**kindred** ADJECTIVE
related or similar • *chemistry and kindred subjects*
➤ **kindred spirit** someone whose tastes or attitudes are similar to your own

**kinetic** ADJECTIVE
to do with or produced by movement
• *kinetic energy*

**king** NOUN kings
❶ a man who is the ruler of a country through inheriting the position ❷ a person or thing regarded as supreme • *The lion is the king of beasts.* ❸ the most important piece in chess ❹ a playing card with a picture of a king
➤ **kingly** ADJECTIVE
➤ **kingship** NOUN

**kingdom** NOUN kingdoms
❶ a country ruled by a king or queen ❷ a division of the natural world • *the animal kingdom*

**kingfisher** NOUN kingfishers
a small bird with blue feathers that dives to catch fish

**king-size, king-sized** ADJECTIVE
extra large

**kink** NOUN kinks
❶ a short twist in a rope, wire or length of hair ❷ a peculiarity

**kiosk** NOUN kiosks
❶ a telephone booth ❷ a small hut or stall where newspapers, sweets, etc. are sold

**kip** NOUN kips (*British informal*)
a sleep • *I need to get some kip.*
➤ **kip** VERB

**kipper** NOUN kippers
a smoked herring

**kirk** NOUN kirks (*Scottish*)
a church

**kiss** NOUN kisses
touching someone with your lips as a sign of affection or greeting

**kiss** VERB kisses, kissing, kissed
to give someone a kiss

**kiss of life** NOUN
blowing air from your mouth into someone else's to help them start breathing again, especially after an accident

**kit** NOUN kits
❶ equipment or clothes that you need to do a sport, a job or some other activity • *a drum kit* ❷ a set of parts sold ready to be fitted together • *a model aircraft kit*

**kitchen** NOUN kitchens
a room in which meals are prepared and cooked

**kitchenette** NOUN kitchenettes
a small kitchen

**kite** NOUN kites
❶ a light framework covered with cloth or paper that you fly in the wind on the end of a long piece of string ❷ a large hawk

**kith and kin** PLURAL NOUN
friends and relatives

**kitten** NOUN kittens
a very young cat

**kitty** NOUN kitties
❶ a fund of money for use by several people ❷ an amount of money that you can win in a card game

**kiwi** (say kee-wee) NOUN kiwis
❶ a New Zealand bird that cannot fly
❷ (*informal*) (**Kiwi**) someone who comes from or lives in New Zealand

**kiwi fruit** NOUN kiwi fruits
a fruit with thin hairy skin, green flesh and black seeds (**WORD ORIGIN**) named after the kiwi, because the fruit was exported from New Zealand

**kleptomania** NOUN
an uncontrollable urge to steal things
➤ **kleptomaniac** NOUN

**kloof** NOUN kloofs
(S. African) a narrow valley or mountain pass, usually wooded

**km** ABBREVIATION
kilometre

**knack** NOUN
a special skill or talent • There's a knack to putting up a deckchair.

**knapsack** NOUN knapsacks
a bag carried on the back by soldiers, hikers, etc.

**knave** NOUN knaves
❶ (old use) a dishonest man; a rogue ❷ a jack in a pack of playing cards

**knead** VERB kneads, kneading, kneaded
to press and stretch something soft (especially dough) with your hands

**knee** NOUN knees
the joint in the middle of your leg

**kneecap** NOUN kneecaps
the small bone covering the front of your knee joint

**kneel** VERB kneels, kneeling, knelt
to be or get yourself in a position where you are resting on your knees

**knell** NOUN knells
the sound of a bell rung solemnly after a death or at a funeral

**knickerbockers** PLURAL NOUN
loose-fitting short trousers gathered in at the knees **WORD ORIGIN** from D. *Knickerbocker*, the imaginary author of a book in which people were shown wearing these kinds of trousers

**knickers** PLURAL NOUN
underpants worn by women and girls

**knick-knack** NOUN knick-knacks
a small ornament

**knife** NOUN knives
a cutting instrument or weapon consisting of a sharp blade set in a handle

**knife** VERB knifes, knifing, knifed
to stab someone with a knife

SPELLING
There is a silent **k** at the beginning of **knife**.

**knight** NOUN knights
❶ a man who has been given the rank that allows him to put 'Sir' before his name ❷ a warrior of high social rank in the Middle Ages, usually mounted and in armour ❸ a piece in chess, with a horse's head
➤ **knighthood** NOUN

**knight** VERB knights, knighting, knighted
to make someone a knight

SPELLING
**Knight** is different from **night**, which is the time when it is dark.

**knit** VERB knits, knitting, knitted or knit
❶ to make something by looping together wool or other yarn, using long needles or a machine ❷ broken bones knit together when they join back together and heal
➤ **knit your brow** to frown

**knitting** NOUN
❶ the activity of making things by knitting ❷ something that is being knitted

**knitting needle** NOUN knitting needles
a long thick needle used in knitting

**knob** NOUN knobs
❶ the round handle of a door or drawer ❷ a round lump on something ❸ a round button or switch on a dial or machine ❹ a small round piece of something • a knob of butter

**knobbly** ADJECTIVE
having many small hard lumps or bumps • knobbly knees

**knock** VERB knocks, knocking, knocked
❶ to make a noise by hitting a thing hard • Someone's knocking at the door. ❷ to hit something hard or bump into it, especially by accident • Sorry, I knocked the vase over. ❸ to produce something by hitting • We need to knock a hole in the wall. ❹ (informal) to criticize someone or something • People are always knocking this country.
➤ **knock off** (informal) to stop working
➤ **knock something off** ❶ to deduct something from a price ❷ (informal) to steal something
➤ **knock someone out** to make a person unconscious, especially by a blow to the head

**knock** NOUN knocks
the act or sound of knocking

SPELLING
There is a silent **k** at the beginning of **knock**.

**knocker** NOUN knockers
a hinged metal device for knocking on a door

**knockout** NOUN knockouts
❶ knocking someone out ❷ a contest in which the loser in each round has to drop

382

out ❸ (*informal*) an extremely attractive or outstanding person or thing

**knoll** *NOUN* knolls
a small round hill; a mound

**knot** *NOUN* knots
❶ a fastening made by tying or looping two ends of string, rope or cloth together ❷ a lump where hair or threads have become tangled together ❸ a round spot on a piece of wood where a branch once joined it ❹ a small group of people standing close together ❺ a unit for measuring the speed of ships and aircraft, equal to 2,025 yards (1,852 metres or 1 nautical mile) per hour

**knot** *VERB* knots, knotting, knotted
❶ to tie or fasten something with a knot
❷ to become tangled up

**SPELLING**

There is a silent **k** at the start of **knot**. A **knot** is a place where a piece of string or rope is twisted round. **Not** is used to show that something is negative, e.g. *Samir was not happy.*

**knotty** *ADJECTIVE* knottier, knottiest
❶ full of knots ❷ difficult or puzzling • *a knotty problem*

**know** *VERB* knows, knowing, knew, known
❶ to have something in your mind that you have learned or discovered ❷ to recognize or be familiar with a person or place • *I've known him for years.* ❸ to understand or realize something • *She knows how to please people.*
➤ **be known as something** to be called or named something

**SPELLING**

There is a silent **k** at the start of **know**.

**know-all** *NOUN* know-alls
(*British*) a person who behaves as if they know everything

**know-how** *NOUN*
practical knowledge or skill for a particular job

**knowing** *ADJECTIVE*
showing that you know or are aware of something • *a knowing look*

**knowingly** *ADVERB*
❶ in a knowing way • *He winked at me knowingly.* ❷ deliberately • *She would never have done such a thing knowingly.*

**knowledge** *NOUN*
❶ information and skills you have through experience and education ❷ knowing about a particular thing • *She did it without my knowledge.* ❸ all that is known
➤ **to my knowledge** as far as I know

**knowledgeable** *ADJECTIVE*
knowing a lot about something; well-informed
➤ **knowledgeably** *ADVERB*

**knuckle** *NOUN* knuckles
a joint in your finger

**knuckle** *VERB* knuckles, knuckling, knuckled
➤ **knuckle down** to begin to work hard
➤ **knuckle under** to accept someone else's authority

**koala** (say koh-**ah**-la) *NOUN* koalas
a furry Australian animal that looks like a small bear

**koppie** (say **kop**-i) *NOUN* koppies
(*S. African*) a small hill

**Koran, Qur'an** (say kor-**ahn**) *NOUN*
the sacred book of Islam **WORD ORIGIN** from Arabic *kur'an* = reading

**kosher** (say **koh**-sher) *ADJECTIVE*
keeping to Jewish laws about the preparation of food • *kosher meat*

**kraal** (say krahl) *NOUN* kraals (*S. African*)
❶ a traditional African village of huts ❷ an enclosure for sheep and cattle

**krill** *NOUN*
a mass of tiny shrimp-like creatures, the chief food of certain whales

**krypton** *NOUN*
an inert gas that is present in the earth's atmosphere and is used in fluorescent lamps

**kudos** (say **kew**-doss) *NOUN*
honour and glory

**kung fu** *NOUN*
a Chinese method of self-defence, similar to karate

**kW** *ABBREVIATION*
kilowatt

**L** *ABBREVIATION*
learner, a person learning to drive a car

**lab** *NOUN* labs (*informal*)
a laboratory

**label** *NOUN* labels
a small piece of paper, cloth or metal fixed on or beside something to show what it is or what it costs or its owner, destination, etc.

**label** *VERB* labels, labelling, labelled
❶ to put a label on something ❷ to describe something in a particular way • *He was soon labelled as a troublemaker.*

**laboratory** *NOUN* laboratories
a room or building equipped for scientific experiments

**laborious** *ADJECTIVE*
❶ needing or using a lot of hard work ❷ explaining something at great length and with obvious effort
➤ **laboriously** *ADVERB*

**Labour** *NOUN*
the Labour Party, a British political party formed to represent the interests of working people and believing in social equality and socialism

**labour** *NOUN* labours
❶ hard work ❷ a task ❸ workers ❹ the contractions of the womb when a baby is being born

**labour** *VERB* labours, labouring, laboured
❶ to work hard at something ❷ to explain or discuss something at great length and with obvious effort • *I will not labour the point.*

**labourer** *NOUN* labourers
a person who does hard manual work, especially outdoors

**Labrador** *NOUN* Labradors
a large black or light-brown dog
**WORD ORIGIN** named after Labrador, a district in Canada, where it was bred

**laburnum** *NOUN* laburnums
a tree with hanging yellow flowers

**labyrinth** *NOUN* labyrinths
a complicated arrangement of passages or paths; a maze • *a labyrinth of tunnels*

**WORD ORIGIN** from Greek, originally referring to the maze in Greek mythology that the Minotaur lived in

**lace** *NOUN* laces
❶ net-like material with decorative patterns of holes in it ❷ a piece of thin cord or leather for fastening a shoe, etc.

**lace** *VERB* laces, lacing, laced
❶ to fasten something with a lace ❷ to thread a cord through something ❸ to add spirits to a drink

**lacerate** *VERB* lacerates, lacerating, lacerated
to injure flesh by cutting or tearing it
➤ **laceration** *NOUN*

**lack** *NOUN*
being without something or not having enough of it • *The trip was cancelled because of lack of interest.*

**lack** *VERB* lacks, lacking, lacked
to be without something • *He lacks courage.*

**lackadaisical** *ADJECTIVE*
lacking energy or determination; careless
**WORD ORIGIN** from *lack-a-day*, an old phrase expressing grief or surprise

**lackey** *NOUN* lackeys
a servant; a person who behaves or is treated like a servant

**lacking** *ADJECTIVE*
not having any or enough of something • *The story is lacking in humour.*

**laconic** *ADJECTIVE*
using few words; terse • *a laconic reply*
➤ **laconically** *ADVERB*
**WORD ORIGIN** from Greek *Lakon* = a native of Laconia, an area in Greece (because the Laconians were famous for their terse speech)

**lacquer** *NOUN*
a hard glossy varnish
➤ **lacquered** *ADJECTIVE*

**lacrosse** *NOUN*
a game using a stick with a net on it (called a *crosse*) to catch and throw a ball

**lactate** *VERB* lactates, lactating, lactated
female mammals lactate when they produce milk

**lacy** *ADJECTIVE*
made of lace or like lace • *lacy wings*

**lad** *NOUN* lads
a boy or young man

**ladder** *NOUN* ladders
❶ two upright pieces of wood or metal and

crosspieces (**rungs**), used for climbing up or down ❷ (*British*) a vertical ladder-like flaw in a pair of tights or stockings where a stitch has become undone

**ladder** *VERB* ladders, laddering, laddered
(*British*) to get a ladder in a pair of tights or stockings

**laden** *ADJECTIVE*
carrying something heavy or a lot of something • *She appeared at the door, laden with bags.* • *The trees were laden with apples.*

**ladle** *NOUN* ladles
a large deep spoon with a long handle, used for lifting and pouring liquids

**ladle** *VERB* ladles, ladling, ladled
to lift and pour a liquid with a ladle

**lady** *NOUN* ladies
❶ a polite word for a woman ❷ a well-mannered woman ❸ a woman of good social position
➤ **Lady** *NOUN*
the title of a noblewoman

**ladybird** *NOUN* ladybirds
(*British*) a small flying beetle, usually red with black spots

**lady-in-waiting** *NOUN* ladies-in-waiting
a woman of good social position who attends a queen or princess

**ladylike** *ADJECTIVE*
behaving in a well mannered and refined way that was traditionally thought to be suitable for a woman

**ladyship** *NOUN*
a title used in speaking to or about a woman of the rank of 'Lady'

**lag** *VERB* lags, lagging, lagged
❶ to go too slowly and fail to keep up with others • *The little boy was lagging behind.* ❷ (*British*) to wrap a pipe or boiler in insulating material (*lagging*) to prevent loss of heat

**lag** *NOUN* lags
a delay

**lager** (say **lah**-ger) *NOUN* lagers
a light beer

**laggard** *NOUN* laggards
a person who lags behind

**lagoon** *NOUN* lagoons
a salt-water lake separated from the sea by sandbanks or reefs

**laid**
past tense of **lay**

**laid-back** *ADJECTIVE* (*informal*)
relaxed and easy-going

**lain**
past participle of **lie**

**lair** *NOUN* lairs
a sheltered place where a wild animal lives

**laity** (say **lay**-it-ee) *NOUN*
lay people, not the clergy

**lake** *NOUN* lakes
a large area of water entirely surrounded by land

**lakh** (say **lak**) *NOUN* lakh
(*Indian*) a hundred thousand (rupees etc.)

**lama** *NOUN* lamas
a Buddhist priest or monk in Tibet and Mongolia

**lamb** *NOUN* lambs
❶ a young sheep ❷ meat from a lamb
➤ **lambswool** *NOUN*

**lame** *ADJECTIVE*
❶ not able to walk normally because of an injury to the leg or foot ❷ weak and not very convincing • *a lame excuse*
➤ **lameness** *NOUN*

**lamely** *ADVERB*
in a weak and unconvincing way • *'I must have made a mistake,' I said lamely.*

**lament** *VERB* laments, lamenting, lamented
to express grief or disappointment about something • *She lamented the loss of her local library.*

**lament** *NOUN* laments
a statement, song or poem expressing grief or regret
➤ **lamentation** *NOUN*

**lamentable** (say **lam**-in-ta-bul) *ADJECTIVE*
disappointing or regrettable

**laminated** *ADJECTIVE*
made of thin layers or sheets joined one upon the other • *laminated plastic*

**lamp** *NOUN* lamps
a device for producing light from electricity, gas or oil
➤ **lamplight** *NOUN*

**lamp post** *NOUN* lamp posts
a tall post in a street or path, with a lamp at the top

**lamprey** NOUN lampreys
a small eel-like water animal

**lampshade** NOUN lampshades
a cover for the bulb of an electric lamp, to
soften the light

**lance** NOUN lances
a long spear

**lance** VERB lances, lancing, lanced
to cut open a boil on someone's skin with a
surgical knife

**lance corporal** NOUN lance corporals
a soldier ranking between a private and a
corporal

**lancet** NOUN lancets
❶ a pointed two-edged knife used by
surgeons ❷ a tall narrow pointed window or
arch

**land** NOUN lands
❶ the part of the earth's surface not covered
by sea ❷ the ground or soil; an area of
country • *forest land* ❸ the area occupied by
a nation; a country

**land** VERB lands, landing, landed
❶ to arrive on land from a ship or aircraft
❷ to reach the ground after jumping or
falling • *Where did the arrow land?* ❸ to
come down through the air and settle on
something • *A fly landed on his arm.* ❹ to
bring a fish out of the water ❺ to succeed in
getting something • *She landed an excellent
job.* ❻ to give someone something unpleasant
to do • *I got landed with all the boring jobs.*
➤ **land up** to finish in a certain place or
position • *They landed up in jail.*

**landed** ADJECTIVE
❶ owning land ❷ consisting of land • *landed
estates*

**landing** NOUN landings
❶ the level area at the top of a flight of
stairs ❷ bringing an aircraft to the ground
• *The pilot made a smooth landing.* ❸ a place
where people can get on and off a boat

**landing stage** NOUN landing stages
(*British*) a platform on which people and
goods are taken on and off a boat

**landlady** NOUN landladies
❶ a woman who lets rooms to lodgers ❷ a
woman who runs a pub

**landline** NOUN landlines
a telephone connection that uses wires
carried on poles or under the ground • *I'll call
you later on the landline.*

**landlocked** ADJECTIVE
almost or entirely surrounded by land
• *Switzerland is completely landlocked.*

**landlord** NOUN landlords
❶ a person who lets a house, room or land to
a tenant ❷ a person who runs a pub

**landlubber** NOUN landlubbers (*informal*)
a person who is not used to travelling on the
sea WORD ORIGIN from an old word *lubber* =
an awkward, clumsy person

**landmark** NOUN landmarks
❶ an object that is easily seen in a landscape
❷ an important event in the history or
development of something

**landmine** NOUN landmines
an explosive mine laid on or just under the
surface of the ground

**landowner** NOUN landowners
a person who owns a large amount of land

**landscape** NOUN landscapes
❶ a view of a particular area of countryside
or town ❷ a picture of a scene in the
countryside

**landscape gardening** NOUN
laying out a garden to imitate natural scenery

**landslide** NOUN landslides
❶ a landslip ❷ an overwhelming victory in an
election • *She won the General Election by a
landslide.*

**landslip** NOUN landslips
(*chiefly British*) a huge mass of soil and rocks
sliding down a slope

**landward** ADJECTIVE & ADVERB
towards the land
➤ **landwards** ADVERB

**lane** NOUN lanes
❶ a narrow road, especially in the country
❷ a strip of road for a single line of traffic
❸ a strip of track or water for one athlete or
swimmer in a race

**language** NOUN languages
❶ the words we speak and write ❷ the words
used in a particular country or by a particular
group of people ❸ a system of signs or
symbols giving information, especially in
computing WORD ORIGIN from Latin *lingua*
= tongue

**language laboratory** NOUN language
laboratories
a room equipped with audio equipment for
learning a foreign language

**languid** ADJECTIVE
lacking energy and moving slowly, sometimes in an elegant way • *a languid wave of the hand*
➤ **languidly** ADVERB
➤ **languor** NOUN

**languish** VERB languishes, languishing, languished
❶ to be forced to suffer miserable conditions for a long time • *He has been languishing in prison for three years.* ❷ to become weaker

**lank** ADJECTIVE
lank hair is long and limp

**lanky** ADJECTIVE lankier, lankiest
a lanky person is awkwardly thin and tall

**lanolin** NOUN
a kind of ointment, made of fat from sheep's wool

**lantern** NOUN lanterns
a transparent case for holding a light and shielding it from the wind

**lanyard** NOUN lanyards
a short cord for fastening or holding something

**lap** NOUN laps
❶ the level place formed by the top of your legs when you are sitting down with your knees together ❷ going once round a racetrack ❸ one section of a journey • *the last lap*

**lap** VERB laps, lapping, lapped
❶ to overtake another competitor in a race to go one or more laps ahead ❷ a cat or other animal laps a liquid when it drinks it by scooping it up in its tongue ❸ waves lap when they make a gentle splash on rocks or the shore

**lapel** (say la-**pel**) NOUN lapels
a flap folded back at the front edge of a coat or jacket

**lapse** NOUN lapses
❶ a slight mistake or failure • *a lapse of concentration* ❷ an amount of time that has passed • *After a lapse of six months work began again.*

**lapse** VERB lapses, lapsing, lapsed
❶ to pass or slip gradually into a state • *He lapsed into unconsciousness.* ❷ to be no longer valid, through not being renewed • *My insurance policy has lapsed.*

**laptop** NOUN laptops
a portable computer for use while travelling

**lapwing** NOUN lapwings
a black and white bird with a crested head and a shrill cry

**larceny** NOUN
the crime of stealing other people's possessions

**larch** NOUN larches
a tall deciduous tree that bears small cones

**lard** NOUN
a white greasy substance prepared from pig fat and used in cooking

**larder** NOUN larders
a cupboard or small room for storing food

**large** ADJECTIVE
of more than the ordinary or average size; big
➤ **largeness** NOUN
➤ **at large** ❶ free to roam about, not captured • *The escaped prisoners are still at large.* ❷ in general, as a whole • *She is respected by the country at large.*

**largely** ADVERB
to a great extent; mostly • *You are largely responsible for the accident.*

**largesse** (say lar-**jess**) NOUN
money or gifts generously given

**lark** NOUN larks
❶ a small sandy-brown bird; the skylark ❷ (informal) something amusing; a bit of fun • *We did it for a lark.*

**lark** VERB larks, larking, larked
➤ **lark about** (British) (informal)
to have fun playing jokes or tricks

**larrikin** NOUN larrikins
(Australian/NZ) a young person who behaves in a wild and mischievous way

**larva** NOUN larvae
an insect in the first stage of its life, after it comes out of the egg
➤ **larval** ADJECTIVE
WORD ORIGIN Latin, = ghost or mask

**laryngitis** NOUN
inflammation of the larynx, causing hoarseness

**larynx** (say la-**rinks**) NOUN larynxes
the part of your throat that contains the vocal cords

**lasagne** (say laz-**an**-ya) NOUN
pasta in the form of flat sheets, usually cooked with minced meat and cheese sauce

a b c d e f g h i j k l m n o p q r s t u v w x y z

**laser** *NOUN* lasers
a device that makes a very strong narrow beam of light or other electromagnetic radiation **WORD ORIGIN** from the initials of 'light amplification (by) stimulated emission (of) radiation', which is a technical description of what a laser does

**lash** *NOUN* lashes
❶ a stroke with a whip or stick ❷ the cord or cord-like part of a whip ❸ an eyelash

**lash** *VERB* lashes, lashing, lashed
❶ to strike a person or animal with a whip or stick ❷ to hit something with great force • *Wind and rain lashed the windows.* ❸ to tie something tightly with a rope or cord • *During the storm they lashed the boxes to the mast.*
➤ **lash down** rain lashes down when it is raining heavily
➤ **lash out** to speak or hit out angrily at someone

**lashings** *PLURAL NOUN*
(*British*) (*informal*) plenty of food or drink • *lashings of custard*

**lass** *NOUN* lasses
a girl or young woman
➤ **lassie** *NOUN*

**lassitude** *NOUN*
tiredness; lack of energy

**lasso** *NOUN* lassoes or lassos
a rope with a sliding noose at the end, used for catching cattle

**lasso** *VERB* lassoes, lassoing, lassoed
to catch an animal with a lasso

**last** *ADJECTIVE*
❶ coming after all others; final • *We caught the last bus home.* ❷ latest; most recent • *Where were you last night?* ❸ least likely • *She is the last person I'd have chosen.*
➤ **the last straw** a final thing that makes a problem unbearable

**last** *ADVERB*
at the end; after everything or everyone else • *He came last in the race.*

**last** *VERB* lasts, lasting, lasted
❶ to continue; to go on existing or living or being usable • *The good weather lasted until September.* • *Those shoes didn't last very long.* ❷ to be enough for your needs • *The food will last us for three days.*

**last** *NOUN*
❶ a person or thing that is last • *I was the last to arrive.* ❷ lasts
a block of wood or metal shaped like a foot,
used in making and repairing shoes
➤ **at last** or **at long last** finally; after much delay
➤ **to the last** to the end • *He was brave to the last.*

**lasting** *ADJECTIVE*
able to last for a long time • *a lasting peace*

**lastly** *ADVERB*
in the last place; finally • *Lastly, I would like to thank my parents.*

**last post** *NOUN*
a military bugle call sounded at sunset and at military funerals

**last rites** *PLURAL NOUN*
a Christian ceremony given to a person who is close to death

**latch** *NOUN* latches
a small bar fastening a door or gate, lifted by a lever or spring
➤ **latchkey** *NOUN*

**latch** *VERB* latches, latching, latched
to fasten a door or gate with a latch
➤ **latch on to someone** to meet someone and follow them around all the time
➤ **latch on to something** to understand something • *It took them a while to latch on to what she was talking about.*

**late** *ADJECTIVE & ADVERB*
❶ after the usual or expected time • *Sorry I'm late.* ❷ near the end • *late in the afternoon* ❸ who has died recently • *the late king*
➤ **of late** recently

**lately** *ADVERB*
recently • *She has been very busy lately.*

**latent** (say lay-tent) *ADJECTIVE*
existing but not yet developed, active or visible • *her latent talent*

**latent heat** *NOUN*
the heat needed to change a solid into a liquid or vapour, or a liquid into a vapour, without a change in temperature

**later** *ADVERB*
after in time; afterwards • *Two days later we set off again.*

**lateral** *ADJECTIVE*
❶ to do with the side or sides of something • *the lateral branches of a tree* ❷ sideways • *lateral movement*
➤ **laterally** *ADVERB*

**lateral thinking** *NOUN*
solving problems by thinking about them

in an unusual and creative (and apparently illogical) way

**latest** ADJECTIVE
very recent or new • *Have you heard the latest news?*

**latest** NOUN
the most recent or the newest thing or piece of news • *This is the very latest in smartphone technology.*
➤ **at the latest** no later than the time mentioned • *I'll ring you on Friday at the latest.*

**latex** NOUN
the milky juice of various plants and trees, especially the rubber tree

**lath** NOUN laths
a narrow thin strip of wood

**lathe** (say layth) NOUN lathes
a machine for holding and turning pieces of wood while they are being shaped

**lather** NOUN
the thick foam you get when you mix soap with water

**lather** VERB lathers, lathering, lathered
❶ to cover something with lather ❷ to form a lather

**Latin** NOUN
the language of the ancient Romans

**Latin America** NOUN
the parts of Central and South America where the main language is Spanish or Portuguese
**WORD ORIGIN** because these languages developed from Latin

**latitude** NOUN latitudes
❶ the distance of a place from the equator, measured in degrees ❷ freedom to choose what you do or the way that you do it

**latrine** (say la-treen) NOUN latrines
a toilet in a camp or barracks

**latter** ADJECTIVE
later or more recent • *the latter part of the year*
Compare with **former**.
➤ **the latter** the second of two people or things just mentioned

**latterly** ADVERB
recently; not long ago

**lattice** NOUN lattices
a framework of crossed strips or bars with spaces between

**laud** (rhymes with ford) VERB lauds, lauding, lauded (*formal*)
to praise someone or something

**laudable** ADJECTIVE
deserving praise • *a laudable aim*

**laugh** VERB laughs, laughing, laughed
to make the sounds that show you are happy or think something is funny

**laugh** NOUN laughs
❶ the sound of laughing ❷ (*informal*) something that is fun or amusing

**laughable** ADJECTIVE
deserving to be laughed at

**laughing stock** NOUN laughing stocks
a person or thing that is the object of ridicule and scorn

**laughter** NOUN
laughing or the sound of laughing

**launch** VERB launches, launching, launched
❶ to send a ship from the land into the water ❷ to send a rocket or spacecraft into space ❸ to set a thing moving by throwing or pushing it ❹ to make a new product available for the first time • *Our new model will be launched in April.* ❺ to start something off • *They planned to launch an attack the next day.*

**launch** NOUN launches
❶ the launching of a ship or spacecraft ❷ a large motor boat

**launch pad** NOUN launch pads
a platform from which a rocket is launched

**launder** VERB launders, laundering, laundered
to wash and iron clothes etc.

**launderette** NOUN launderettes
(*British*) a place fitted with washing machines that people pay to use

**laundry** NOUN laundries
❶ a place where clothes, sheets, etc. are washed and ironed for customers ❷ clothes, sheets, etc. to be washed or sent to a laundry

**laureate** (say lorri-at) ADJECTIVE
➤ **Poet Laureate** a person appointed to write poems for national occasions
**WORD ORIGIN** from **laurel**, because a laurel wreath was worn in ancient times as a sign of victory

**laurel** NOUN laurels
an evergreen shrub with smooth shiny leaves

**lava** NOUN
molten rock that flows from a volcano; the solid rock formed when it cools

**lavatory** NOUN lavatories
❶ a toilet ❷ a room containing a toilet
(WORD ORIGIN) from Latin *lavatorium* = a basin or bath for washing

**lavender** NOUN
❶ a shrub with sweet-smelling purple flowers
❷ a light-purple colour

**lavish** ADJECTIVE
❶ generous ❷ plentiful
➤ **lavishly** ADVERB

**lavish** VERB lavishes, lavishing, lavished
to give large or generous amounts of something • *They lavished praise upon him.*

**law** NOUN laws
❶ a rule or set of rules that everyone must obey ❷ the profession of being a lawyer
❸ (*informal*) the police ❹ a scientific statement of something that always happens
• *the law of gravity*

**law-abiding** ADJECTIVE
obeying the law

**law court** NOUN law courts
a room or building in which a judge or magistrate hears evidence and decides whether someone has broken the law

**lawful** ADJECTIVE
allowed or accepted by the law • *She was the lawful heiress.*
➤ **lawfully** ADVERB

**lawless** ADJECTIVE
❶ without proper laws • *a lawless country*
❷ not obeying the law
➤ **lawlessness** NOUN

**lawn** NOUN lawns
❶ an area of closely-cut grass in a garden or park ❷ very fine cotton material

**lawnmower** NOUN lawnmowers
a machine for cutting the grass of lawns

**lawn tennis** NOUN
tennis played on an outdoor grass or hard court

**lawsuit** NOUN lawsuits
a dispute or claim that is brought to a law court to be settled

**lawyer** NOUN lawyers
a person who is qualified to give advice in matters of law

**lax** ADJECTIVE
slack; not strict enough • *Discipline was lax.*

**laxative** NOUN laxatives
a medicine that you take to empty your bowels

**lay** VERB lays, laying, laid
❶ to put something down in a particular place or way ❷ to lay a table is to arrange things on it for a meal ❸ to place blame or responsibility on someone • *He laid the blame on his sister.* ❹ to form or prepare something
• *We laid our plans.* ❺ to lay an egg is to produce it
➤ **lay off** (*informal*) to stop doing something
➤ **lay someone off** to stop employing someone for a while
➤ **lay something on** to supply or provide something
➤ **lay someone out** ❶ to knock a person unconscious ❷ to prepare a corpse for burial
➤ **lay something out** to arrange or prepare something

**lay** VERB
past tense of **lie**

USAGE
Lay is different from **lie**, which means to be in a flat position. However, the past tense of **lie** is **lay**: *Go and lie down. I lay down. Lay the parcel by the floor. I laid it on the floor.*

**lay** ADJECTIVE
❶ not belonging to the clergy • *a lay preacher* ❷ not professionally qualified • *lay opinion*

**lay** NOUN lays
(*old use*) a poem meant to be sung; a ballad

**layabout** NOUN layabouts
(*British*) (*informal*) a person who lazily avoids working for a living

**lay-by** NOUN lay-bys
a place where vehicles can stop beside a main road

**layer** NOUN layers
a single thickness or coating

**layman, layperson** NOUN laymen or laypeople
❶ a person who does not have specialized knowledge or training (e.g. as a doctor or lawyer) ❷ a person who is not ordained as a member of the clergy

**layout** NOUN layouts
the way in which the parts of something are

arranged • *The home page of his website has a new layout.*

**laywoman** *NOUN* laywomen
❶ a woman who does not have specialized knowledge or training (e.g. as a doctor or lawyer) ❷ a woman who is not ordained as a member of the clergy

**laze** *VERB* lazes, lazing, lazed
to spend time in a lazy way

**lazy** *ADJECTIVE* lazier, laziest
not wanting to work; doing little work
➤ **lazily** *ADVERB*
➤ **laziness** *NOUN*

**lea** *NOUN* leas (*poetical use*)
a meadow

**leach** *VERB* leaches, leaching, leached
to remove a soluble substance from soil or rock by making water percolate through it

**lead** (say leed) *VERB* leads, leading, led
❶ to take or guide someone, especially by going in front ❷ to be winning in a race or contest; to be ahead ❸ to be in charge of a group of people ❹ to be a way or route • *This path leads to the beach.* ❺ to play the first card in a card game ❻ to live or experience a particular kind of life • *He leads a dull life.*
➤ **lead to something** to result in or cause something • *Their carelessness led to the accident.*

**lead** (say leed) *NOUN* leads
❶ a leading place, part or position • *She took the lead on the final bend.* ❷ a good example or guidance for others to follow • *We should be taking a lead on this issue.* ❸ a clue to be followed ❹ a strap or cord for leading a dog or other animal ❺ an electrical wire attached to something

**lead** (say leed) *ADJECTIVE*
the most important of a number or group
• *the lead singer*

**lead** (say led) *NOUN* leads
❶ a soft heavy grey metal ❷ the writing substance (graphite) in a pencil

**lead** (say led) *ADJECTIVE*
made of or like lead

> **SPELLING**
> The past tense of **lead** is led.

**leaden** (say led-en) *ADJECTIVE*
❶ made of lead ❷ heavy and slow ❸ lead-coloured; dark grey • *leaden skies*

**leader** *NOUN* leaders
❶ the person in charge of a group of people;

a chief ❷ the person who is winning ❸ a newspaper article giving the editor's opinion

**leadership** *NOUN*
being a leader; the ability to be a good leader

**leaf** *NOUN* leaves
❶ a flat, usually green, part of a plant, growing out from its stem, branch or root ❷ the paper forming one page of a book ❸ a very thin sheet of metal • *gold leaf* ❹ a flap that makes a table larger
➤ **leafless** *ADJECTIVE*
➤ **turn over a new leaf** to make a fresh start and improve your behaviour

**leaf** *VERB* leafs, leafing, leafed
➤ **leaf through something** to turn the pages of a book, etc. quickly one by one

**leaflet** *NOUN* leaflets
a piece of paper printed with information

**leafy** *ADJECTIVE*
having a lot of leaves or trees • *a leafy bush* • *leafy streets*

**league** *NOUN* leagues
❶ a group of teams who compete against each other for a championship ❷ a group of people or nations who agree to work together ❸ an old measure of distance, about 3 miles
➤ **in league with someone** working or plotting together

**leak** *NOUN* leaks
❶ a hole or crack through which liquid or gas accidentally escapes ❷ the revealing of secret information

**leak** *VERB* leaks, leaking, leaked
❶ to get out or let something out through a leak • *The roof is leaking.* ❷ to reveal secret information
➤ **leakage** *NOUN*

**leaky** *ADJECTIVE*
a leaky pipe or tap has a leak

**lean** *VERB* leans, leaning, leaned or leant
❶ to bend your body towards or over something • *She leaned out of the window and waved.* ❷ to put something or be in a sloping position • *Don't lean your bike against the window.* ❸ to rest against something ❹ to lean on someone is to rely or depend on them for help

**lean** *ADJECTIVE*
❶ lean meat has little or no fat ❷ a lean person or body is thin with little or no body fat

**leaning** NOUN leanings
a tendency or preference • *He has a leaning towards the sciences.*

**leap** VERB leaps, leaping, leaped or leapt
❶ to jump high or a long way ❷ to increase sharply in amount or value

**leap** NOUN leaps
❶ a high or long jump ❷ a sudden increase in amount or value

**SPELLING**
The past tense of **leap** is **leapt** or **leaped**.

**leapfrog** NOUN
a game in which each player jumps with legs apart over another who is bending down

**leap year** NOUN leap years
a year with an extra day in it (29 February)
**WORD ORIGIN** probably because the dates from March onwards 'leap' a day of the week; a date which would fall on a Monday in an ordinary year will be on Tuesday in a leap year

**learn** VERB learns, learning, learned or learnt
❶ to get knowledge or skill through study or training • *She's learning to play the guitar.* ❷ to find out about something • *I was sorry to learn that he was ill.*

**USAGE**
Take care not to use **learn** to mean 'to teach'.

**learned** (say ler-nid) ADJECTIVE
a learned person has gained a lot of knowledge through study

**learner** NOUN learners
a person who is learning something, especially how to drive a car

**learning** NOUN
knowledge you get by studying

**lease** NOUN leases
an agreement to allow someone to use a building or land for a fixed period in return for payment
➤ **leaseholder** NOUN
➤ **a new lease of life** a chance to be healthy, active or usable again

**lease** VERB leases, leasing, leased
to allow or obtain the use of something by lease

**leash** NOUN leashes
a dog's lead

**least** DETERMINER & ADVERB
smallest in amount or degree; less than all the others • *the least amount of time* • *the least expensive bike*
➤ **at least** ❶ not less than what is mentioned • *It will take at least two weeks to do.* ❷ anyway • *He's at home or at least I think he is.*

**least** PRONOUN
the smallest amount or degree • *The least I could do was to offer to pay for his ticket.*

**leather** NOUN
material made from animal skins

**leathery** ADJECTIVE
tough like leather • *leathery skin*

**leave** VERB leaves, leaving, left
❶ to go away from a person or place ❷ to stop belonging to a group or working somewhere ❸ to allow something to stay where it is or as it is • *You left the door open.* ❹ to go away without taking something • *I left my phone at home.* ❺ to let someone deal with something • *Leave the washing-up to me.* ❻ to put something somewhere so that it can be collected or passed on later • *Would you like to leave a message?*
➤ **leave off** to stop doing something
➤ **leave something out** to omit something or not include it
➤ **be left over** to remain when other things have been used

**leave** NOUN
❶ permission ❷ official permission to be away from work; the time for which this permission lasts • *three days' leave*

**SPELLING**
The past tense of **leave** is **left**.

**leaven** (say lev-en) NOUN
a substance, especially yeast, used to make dough rise

**leaven** VERB leavens, leavening, leavened
to add leaven to dough

**lectern** NOUN lecterns
a stand to hold a Bible or other large book or notes for reading

**lecture** NOUN lectures
❶ a talk about a subject to an audience or a class ❷ a long serious talk to someone that warns them about something or tells them off

**lecture** VERB lectures, lecturing, lectured
to give a lecture
➤ **lecturer** NOUN

**led**
past tense of **lead**

**ledge** NOUN ledges
a narrow shelf • *a window ledge* • *a mountain ledge*

**ledger** NOUN ledgers
an account book

**lee** NOUN lees
the sheltered side or part of something, away from the wind

**leech** NOUN leeches
a small blood-sucking worm that lives in water

**leek** NOUN leeks
a long green and white vegetable of the onion family

**leer** VERB leers, leering, leered
to look at someone in a lustful or unpleasant way
➤ **leer** NOUN

**leeward** ADJECTIVE
on the lee side

**leeway** NOUN
extra space or time available
➤ **make up leeway** to make up lost time or to regain a lost position

**left** ADJECTIVE & ADVERB
❶ on or towards the west if you think of yourself as facing north ❷ in favour of socialist or radical views

**left** NOUN
the left-hand side or part of something

**left** VERB
past tense of **leave**

**left-hand** ADJECTIVE
on the left side of something • *the top left-hand corner of the page*

**left-handed** ADJECTIVE
using the left hand in preference to the right hand

**leftovers** PLURAL NOUN
food not eaten at a meal

**leg** NOUN legs
❶ one of the limbs on a person's or animal's body on which they stand or move ❷ one of the parts of a pair of trousers that cover your leg ❸ each of the supports of a chair or other piece of furniture ❹ one part of a journey ❺ one of a pair of matches played between the same teams in a round of a competition

**legacy** NOUN legacies
❶ something left to a person in a will ❷ a thing received from someone who did

something before you or because of earlier events • *The conflict has left a legacy of distrust.*

**legal** ADJECTIVE
❶ allowed by the law ❷ to do with the law or lawyers
➤ **legally** ADVERB
➤ **legality** NOUN

**legalize** (also **legalise**) VERB legalizes, legalizing, legalized
to make a thing legal

**legate** NOUN legates
an official representative, especially of the Pope

**legend** NOUN legends
❶ an old story handed down from the past, which may or may not be true. Compare with **myth**. ❷ a very famous person

**legendary** ADJECTIVE
❶ to do with legends or happening in legends • *legendary heroes* ❷ very famous or well known for a long time • *Her temper is legendary.*

**leggings** PLURAL NOUN
❶ tight-fitting stretchy trousers, worn by women ❷ protective outer coverings for each leg from knee to ankle

**legible** ADJECTIVE
legible writing is clear enough to read
➤ **legibly** ADVERB
➤ **legibility** NOUN

**legion** NOUN legions
❶ a division of the ancient Roman army ❷ a group of soldiers or former soldiers

**legionnaire** NOUN legionnaires
a member of an association of former soldiers

**legionnaires' disease** NOUN
a serious form of pneumonia caused by bacteria WORD ORIGIN so-called because of an outbreak at a meeting of the American Legion of ex-servicemen in 1976

**legislate** VERB legislates, legislating, legislated
to make laws
➤ **legislator** NOUN

**legislation** NOUN
making laws; a set of laws passed by a parliament

**legislative** ADJECTIVE
having the authority to make laws • *a legislative assembly*

a b c d e f g h i j k l m n o p q r s t u v w x y z

**legislature** NOUN legislatures
a country's parliament or law-making assembly

**legitimate** ADJECTIVE
❶ allowed by a law or rule ❷ (old use) a legitimate child is born of parents who are married to each other
➤ **legitimately** ADVERB
➤ **legitimacy** NOUN

**leisure** NOUN
time that is free from work, when you can do what you like • His busy life leaves little time for leisure.
➤ **at leisure** having leisure; not hurried
➤ **at your leisure** when you have time

**leisurely** ADJECTIVE
done with plenty of time; unhurried • We took a leisurely stroll by the river.

**lemming** NOUN lemmings
a small mouse-like animal of Arctic regions that migrates in large numbers and is said to run headlong into the sea and drown

**lemon** NOUN lemons
❶ an oval yellow citrus fruit with a sour taste ❷ a pale yellow colour

**lemonade** NOUN
a lemon-flavoured drink

**lemur** (say lee-mer) NOUN lemurs
a monkey-like animal

**lend** VERB lends, lending, lent
❶ to allow a person to use something of yours for a short time ❷ to provide someone with money that they must repay over time, usually in return for payments (called interest) ❸ to give or add a quality • She lent dignity to the occasion.
➤ **lender** NOUN
➤ **lend a hand** to give help or assistance

USAGE
Take care not to confuse lend, which means to let someone use something of yours for a short time, with borrow, which means to use something that belongs to someone else for a short time.

**length** NOUN lengths
❶ how long something is ❷ a piece of cloth, rope or wire cut from a larger piece ❸ the distance of a swimming pool from one end to the other
➤ **at length** ❶ after a long time ❷ taking a long time; in detail • We discussed the matter at length.

➤ **go to great lengths** to take a lot of trouble or effort over something

SPELLING
There is a silent g in length.

**lengthen** VERB lengthens, lengthening, lengthened
❶ to make something longer • He started to lengthen his stride. ❷ to become longer • The shadows were lengthening.

**lengthways, lengthwise** ADVERB
from end to end; along the longest part
• Slice the carrots lengthways.

**lengthy** ADJECTIVE
going on for a long time • He gave a lengthy speech.

**lenient** (say lee-nee-ent) ADJECTIVE
not as strict as expected, especially when punishing someone
➤ **leniently** ADVERB
➤ **leniency** NOUN

**lens** NOUN lenses
❶ a curved piece of glass or plastic used to focus things ❷ the transparent part of the eye, immediately behind the pupil
WORD ORIGIN Latin, = lentil (because a lens has a shape like a lentil)

**Lent** NOUN
a period of about six weeks before Easter when some Christians give up something they enjoy

**lent**
past tense of lend

**lentil** NOUN lentils
a kind of small bean

**leopard** (say lep-erd) NOUN leopards
a large spotted mammal of the cat family, also called a panther

**leotard** (say lee-o-tard) NOUN leotards
a close-fitting piece of clothing worn for dance, exercise and gymnastics
WORD ORIGIN named after a French trapeze artist, J. Leotard, who designed it

**leper** NOUN lepers
a person who has leprosy

**lepidopterous** ADJECTIVE
to do with the group of insects that includes butterflies and moths

**leprechaun** (say lep-rek-awn) NOUN leprechauns
in Irish folklore, an elf who looks like a little

old man **WORD ORIGIN** from Irish, = a small body

**leprosy** NOUN
an infectious disease that makes parts of the body waste away
➤ **leprous** ADJECTIVE
**WORD ORIGIN** from Greek *lepros* = scaly (because white scales form on the skin)

**lesbian** NOUN lesbians
a homosexual woman **WORD ORIGIN** named after the Greek island of *Lesbos* (because Sappho, a poetess who lived there about 600 BC, was said to be homosexual)

**less** DETERMINER & ADVERB
smaller in amount; not so much • *My new computer makes less noise than the old one.* • *It is less important.*

> **USAGE**
>
> Take care not to confuse **less** and **fewer**. You should use **fewer** when you mean 'not so many', and **less** when you mean 'not so much' • *Venus has fewer craters than the Earth and also less water.*

**less** PRONOUN
a smaller amount • *I have less than you.*

**less** PREPOSITION
minus; deducting • *She earned $20,000, less tax.*

**lessen** VERB lessens, lessening, lessened
to make something less or to become less • *Her fear gradually lessened.*

**lesser** ADJECTIVE
not so great as the other • *the lesser evil*

**lesson** NOUN lessons
❶ an amount of teaching given at one time ❷ something to be learnt by a pupil or student ❸ an example or experience from which you should learn • *Let this be a lesson to you!* ❹ a passage from the Bible read aloud as part of a Christian church service

**lest** CONJUNCTION (old use)
so that something should not happen • *Remind us, lest we forget.*

**let** VERB lets, letting, let
❶ to allow someone to do something • *Let me see it.* ❷ to allow something to happen and not prevent it • *Don't let the paper get wet.* ❸ used to make a suggestion • *Let's go for a walk.* ❹ to allow or cause a person or thing to come or go or pass • *Let me out!* ❺ to allow someone to use a house or building in return for payment (**rent**)

➤ **let someone down** to disappoint someone or fail to do what you said you would
➤ **let something down** to let down a tyre or balloon is to let the air out of it
➤ **let someone off** to excuse someone from a duty or punishment
➤ **let something off** to make something explode
➤ **let on** (*informal*) to reveal a secret
➤ **let up** (*informal*)
❶ to relax or do less work ❷ to become less intense • *The rain didn't let up.*

**lethal** (say lee-thal) ADJECTIVE
deadly; causing death • *a lethal blow*

**lethargy** (say leth-er-jee) NOUN
extreme lack of energy or interest in doing anything
➤ **lethargic** (say lith-ar-jik) ADJECTIVE

**letter** NOUN letters
❶ a symbol representing a sound used in speech ❷ a written message, usually sent by post
➤ **to the letter** paying strict attention to every detail

**letter box** NOUN letter boxes
❶ a slot in a door, through which letters are delivered ❷ a postbox

**lettering** NOUN
letters drawn or painted • *The inscription was in gold lettering.*

**lettuce** NOUN lettuces
a garden plant with broad crisp leaves used in salads

**leukaemia** (say lew-kee-mee-a) NOUN
a disease in which there are too many white corpuscles in the blood

**level** ADJECTIVE
❶ flat or horizontal • *Put the tent up on level ground.* ❷ at the same height or position as something else • *Are these pictures level?*

**level** NOUN levels
❶ height, depth or position • *Fix the shelves at eye level.* ❷ a standard or grade of achievement • *a high level of skill* ❸ a stage of a computer game that you reach • *What level are you on?* ❹ a level surface ❺ a device that shows whether something is level
➤ **on the level** (*informal*) honest; telling the truth

**level** VERB levels, levelling, levelled
❶ to make something level or to become level • *United levelled the score with a late*

**goal. ❷** to aim a gun or missile **❸** to direct an accusation at a person

**level crossing** NOUN level crossings
(*British*) a place where a road crosses a railway at the same level

**lever** NOUN levers
**❶** a bar that turns on a fixed point (the **fulcrum**) in order to lift something or force something open **❷** a bar used as a handle to operate machinery • *a gear lever*

**lever** VERB levers, levering, levered
to lift or move something by means of a lever

**leverage** NOUN
**❶** the force you need when you use a lever **❷** influence over people

**leveret** NOUN leverets
a young hare

**levitation** NOUN
rising into the air and floating there
➤ **levitate** VERB

**levity** NOUN
being humorous, especially at an unsuitable time • *He was shocked at her levity.*

**levy** VERB levies, levying, levied
to collect a tax or other payment by the use of authority or force

**levy** NOUN levies
an amount of money paid in tax

**lewd** ADJECTIVE
indecent or crude

**lexicography** NOUN
the writing of dictionaries
➤ **lexicographer** NOUN

**liability** NOUN liabilities
**❶** being legally responsible for something **❷** a debt or obligation **❸** a disadvantage or handicap • *Our goalkeeper has become a liability.*

**liable** ADJECTIVE
**❶** likely to do or suffer something • *She is liable to colds.* • *The cliff is liable to crumble.* **❷** legally responsible for something

**liaise** (say lee-**ayz**) VERB liaises, liaising, liaised
to work closely with someone and keep them informed

**liaison** (say lee-**ay**-zon) NOUN liaisons
**❶** communication and cooperation between people or groups **❷** a person who is a link or go-between **❸** a romantic affair

**liar** NOUN liars
a person who tells lies

**libel** (say **ly**-bel) NOUN libels
an untrue written, printed or broadcast statement that damages a person's reputation. Compare with **slander**.
➤ **libellous** ADJECTIVE

**libel** VERB libels, libelling, libelled
to make a libel against someone

**liberal** ADJECTIVE
**❶** tolerant of other people's point of view or behaviour • *Your parents are more liberal than mine.* **❷** supporting individual freedom and gradual political and social change **❸** giving or given freely and generously • *a liberal sprinkling of sugar*
➤ **liberality** NOUN

**liberal** NOUN liberals
a person with liberal views

**Liberal Democrat** NOUN Liberal Democrats
a member of the Liberal Democrat party in the UK, a political party favouring moderate reforms

**liberally** ADVERB
in large amounts or generously • *Pour the cream on liberally.*

**liberate** VERB liberates, liberating, liberated
to liberate a person or animal is to set them free
➤ **liberation** NOUN
➤ **liberator** NOUN

**liberty** NOUN liberties
the freedom to go where you want or do what you want
➤ **take liberties** to behave too casually or in too familiar a way
➤ **take the liberty** to do something without asking permission • *I took the liberty of helping myself to a drink.*

**librarian** NOUN librarians
a person in charge of or working in a library
➤ **librarianship** NOUN

**library** (say **ly**-bra-ree) NOUN libraries
**❶** a place where books are kept for people to use or borrow **❷** a collection of books, records, films, etc.

**libretto** NOUN librettos
the words of an opera or other long musical work

**lice**
plural of **louse**

**licence** NOUN licences
**①** an official document allowing someone to do or use or own something • *a driving licence* **②** special freedom to avoid the usual rules or customs

> SPELLING
>
> **Licence** is a noun and **license** is a verb • *a TV licence* • *The ship is licensed to carry passengers.*

**license** VERB licenses, licensing, licensed
to give a licence to a person; to authorize someone to do something • *The restaurant is not licensed to sell alcohol.*

**lichen** (say **ly**-ken) NOUN lichens
a dry-looking plant that grows on rocks, walls or trees

**lick** VERB licks, licking, licked
**①** to move your tongue over something **②** a wave or flame licks a surface when it touches it lightly **③** (*informal*) to defeat someone

**lick** NOUN licks
**①** licking something • *Can I have a lick of your ice cream?* **②** a small amount of paint • *The kitchen could do with a lick of paint.*
> **at a lick** (*informal*) at a fast pace

**lid** NOUN lids
**①** a cover for a box, pot or jar **②** an eyelid

**lido** (say **leed**-oh) NOUN lidos
(*British*) a public open-air swimming pool or pleasure beach (WORD ORIGIN) from Lido, the name of a beach near Venice

**lie** VERB lies, lying, lay, lain
**①** to be or get in a flat or resting position • *He lay on the grass.* • *The cat has lain here all night.* **②** to be or remain a certain way • *The island lies near the coast.* • *The machinery lay idle.*
> **lie low** to keep yourself hidden

> USAGE
>
> See the note at **lay**.

**lie** VERB lies, lying, lied
to say something that you know is untrue

**lie** NOUN lies
something you say that you know is not true
> **the lie of the land** **①** the features of an area **②** the way a situation is developing

**liege, liege lord** (say leej) NOUN lieges or liege lords (*old use*)
a person who is entitled to receive feudal service or allegiance

**lieu** (say lew) NOUN
> **in lieu** instead • *He accepted a cheque in lieu of cash.*

**lieutenant** (say lef-**ten**-ant) NOUN lieutenants
**①** an officer in the army or navy **②** a deputy or chief assistant

**life** NOUN lives
**①** the period between birth and death or the period that a person has been alive **②** being alive and able to function and grow **③** living things • *Is there life on Mars?* **④** liveliness • *She is full of life.* **⑤** a biography **⑥** the length of time that something exists or functions • *The battery has a life of two years.*

**lifebelt** NOUN lifebelts
a ring of material that will float, used to support someone's body in water

**lifeboat** NOUN lifeboats
a boat for rescuing people at sea

**lifebuoy** NOUN lifebuoys
a device to support someone's body in water

**life cycle** NOUN life cycles
the series of changes in the life of a living thing • *The diagram shows the life cycle of a frog.*

**life form** NOUN life forms
any living thing • *an alien life form*

**lifeguard** NOUN lifeguards
someone whose job is to rescue swimmers who are in difficulty

**life jacket** NOUN life jackets
a jacket of material that will float, used to support someone's body in water

**lifeless** ADJECTIVE
**①** dead or appearing to be dead • *his lifeless body* **②** with no signs of life or living things • *The place seemed lifeless.*
> **lifelessly** ADVERB

**lifelike** ADJECTIVE
looking exactly like a real person or thing

**lifelong** ADJECTIVE
continuing for the whole of someone's life • *a lifelong love of reading*

**lifespan** NOUN lifespans
the length of someone's life

**lifestyle** NOUN lifestyles
the way of life of a person or a group of people

**lifetime** NOUN lifetimes
the time for which someone is alive • *His diary was not published during his lifetime.*

**lift** VERB lifts, lifting, lifted
❶ to pick something up or move it to a higher position • *The box is too heavy to lift.* ❷ to rise or go upwards • *The balloon lifted off the ground.* ❸ to remove or abolish something • *The ban has been lifted.* ❹ (*informal*) to steal something

**lift** NOUN lifts
❶ a device in a building for taking people or goods from one floor or level to another ❷ a ride in someone else's vehicle • *Can you give me a lift to the station?* ❸ a movement upwards

**lift-off** NOUN lift-offs
the vertical take-off of a rocket or spacecraft

**ligament** NOUN ligaments
a piece of the tough flexible tissue that holds your bones together

**light** NOUN lights
❶ radiation that stimulates the sense of sight and makes things visible ❷ something that provides light, especially an electric lamp • *Can you switch on the light?* ❸ a flame
➤ **bring something to light** to make something known
➤ **come to light** to become known
➤ **in the light of something** taking something into consideration

**light** ADJECTIVE
❶ full of light; not dark ❷ pale • *light blue* ❸ having little weight; not heavy ❹ small in amount or force; not severe • *light rain* • *a light punishment* ❺ needing little effort • *light work* ❻ cheerful, not sad • *with a light heart* ❼ not serious or profound • *light music*
➤ **lightness** NOUN

**light** ADVERB
➤ **travel light** to travel without much luggage

**light** VERB lights, lighting, lit or lighted
❶ to start a thing burning or to begin to burn • *The fire won't light.* ❷ to provide light for something • *The stage was lit by a bright spotlight.*
➤ **light on** or **upon something** to see or find something by accident • *His eyes lit upon a small boat on the horizon.*
➤ **light up** ❶ to become bright with lights ❷ if a person's face lights up, it becomes bright with happiness or excitement
➤ **light something up** to make something bright with lights

USAGE
Say *He lit the lamps; the lamps were lit* (not 'lighted'), but *She carried a lighted candle* (not 'a lit candle').

**lighten** VERB lightens, lightening, lightened
❶ to make something lighter in weight or less heavy; to become less heavy ❷ to make something brighter or less dark; to become less dark

**lighter** NOUN lighters
a device for lighting cigarettes etc.

**light-hearted** ADJECTIVE
❶ cheerful and free from worry ❷ not serious

**lighthouse** NOUN lighthouses
a tower with a bright light at the top to guide or warn ships

**lighting** NOUN
lights or the way that a place is lit • *street lighting*

**lightly** ADVERB
❶ gently, with very little force • *He touched her lightly on the arm.* ❷ only a little; not much • *It began to snow lightly.* ❸ not seriously; without serious thought • *We do not take our customers' complaints lightly.*

**lightning** NOUN
a flash of bright light produced by natural electricity during a thunderstorm
➤ **like lightning** with very great speed

SPELLING
**Lightning** can be tricky to spell – there is no e in the middle.

**lightning conductor** NOUN lightning conductors
(*British*) a metal rod or wire fixed on a building to divert lightning into the earth

**lightweight** ADJECTIVE
less than average weight • *a bicycle with a lightweight frame*

**lightweight** NOUN lightweights
❶ a person who is not heavy ❷ a boxer weighing between 57.1 and 59 kg

**light year** NOUN light years
a unit of distance equal to the distance that light travels in one year (about 9.5 million million km)

**like** VERB likes, liking, liked
❶ to think a person or thing is pleasant or satisfactory; to enjoy doing something ❷ to

wish to do something • *I'd like to come.* ❸ to click a button to show that you agree with or like something on a social media website

**like** *PREPOSITION*
❶ similar to; in the manner of • *He swims like a fish.* ❷ in a suitable state for • *It looks like rain.* • *I feel like a cup of tea.* ❸ such as • *She's good at things like art and music.*

**like** *ADJECTIVE*
similar; having some or all of the qualities of another person or thing • *We are of like mind about it.*

**like** *NOUN* **likes**
❶ a similar person or thing • *We shall not see his like again.* ❷ a symbol on a social media website that shows that someone agrees with or likes something

**likeable** *ADJECTIVE*
pleasant and easy to like

**likelihood** *NOUN*
the chance of something happening; how likely something is to happen • *There's not much likelihood of finding anything.*

**likely** *ADJECTIVE* **likelier, likeliest**
❶ probable; expected to happen or be true • *Rain is likely.* ❷ expected to be suitable or successful • *This is the most likely spot for our picnic.*

**liken** *VERB* **likens, likening, likened**
to compare one person or thing to another • *He likened the human heart to a pump.*

**likeness** *NOUN* **likenesses**
❶ a similarity in appearance; a resemblance ❷ a portrait

**likewise** *ADVERB*
similarly; in the same way • *I intend to apologize and suggest you do likewise.*

**liking** *NOUN*
a feeling that you like something • *She has a liking for large earrings.*

**lilac** *NOUN*
❶ a bush with fragrant purple or white flowers ❷ pale purple

**lilt** *NOUN*
a light pleasant rhythm in a voice or tune
➤ **lilting** *ADJECTIVE*

**lily** *NOUN* **lilies**
a garden plant with trumpet-shaped flowers, growing from a bulb

**limb** *NOUN* **limbs**
❶ a leg, arm or wing ❷ a large branch of a tree

➤ **out on a limb** isolated; without any support

**limber** *VERB* **limbers, limbering, limbered**
➤ **limber up** to do exercises in preparation for a sport or athletic activity

**limbo** *NOUN*
a West Indian dance in which you bend backwards to pass under a low bar
➤ **in limbo** in an uncertain situation where you are waiting for something to happen • *Lack of money has left our plans in limbo.* **WORD ORIGIN** The phrase 'in limbo' comes from the name of a place formerly believed by Christians to exist on the borders of hell, where the souls of people who were not baptized waited for God's judgement.

**lime** *NOUN* **limes**
❶ a green fruit like a small round lemon ❷ a drink made from lime juice ❸ a tree with yellow flowers ❹ a white chalky substance (calcium oxide) used in making cement and as a fertilizer

**limelight** *NOUN*
➤ **in the limelight** receiving a lot of publicity and attention **WORD ORIGIN** from **lime** (calcium oxide) which gives a bright light when heated and was formerly used to light up the stage of a theatre

**limerick** *NOUN* **limericks**
a type of amusing poem with five lines
**WORD ORIGIN** named after *Limerick*, a town in Ireland

**limestone** *NOUN*
a kind of rock from which lime (calcium oxide) is obtained

**limit** *NOUN* **limits**
❶ the greatest amount allowed • *the speed limit* ❷ a line, point or level where something ends • *She had reached the limit of her patience.* • *the city limits*

**limit** *VERB* **limits, limiting, limited**
to keep something within a limit • *You are limited to one choice each.* • *We did all we could to limit the damage.*

**limitation** *NOUN* **limitations**
a thing that stops someone or something from going beyond a certain point • *There are no limitations on what we can do.*

**limited** *ADJECTIVE*
kept within limits; not great • *a limited choice* • *limited experience*

**limited company** *NOUN* **limited companies**
(*British*) a business company whose

a
b
c
d
e
f
g
h
i
j
k
l
m
n
o
p
q
r
s
t
u
v
w
x
y
z

shareholders would have to pay only some of
its debts

**limousine** (say lim-oo-**zeen**) NOUN limousines
a large luxurious car **WORD ORIGIN** originally,
a hooded cape worn in *Limousin*, a district in
France; the name was given to the cars because
early ones had a canvas roof to shelter the
driver

**limp** VERB limps, limping, limped
to walk with difficulty because of an injury to
your leg or foot

**limp** NOUN limps
a limping walk

**limp** ADJECTIVE
❶ not stiff or firm • *limp celery* ❷ without
strength or energy • *a limp handshake*
➤ **limply** ADVERB

**limpet** NOUN limpets
a small shellfish that attaches itself firmly to
rocks

**limpid** ADJECTIVE
a liquid is limpid if it is clear or transparent

**linchpin** NOUN linchpins
the person or thing that is vital to the success
of something

**line** NOUN lines
❶ a long thin mark on paper or another
surface ❷ a row or series of people or things;
a row of words ❸ a length of rope, string or
wire used for a special purpose • *a fishing
line* ❹ a railway; a railway track ❺ a company
operating a transport service of ships,
aircraft or buses ❻ a way of doing things or
behaving; a type of business • *What line are
you in?* ❼ a telephone connection ❽ several
generations of a family • *He comes from a
long line of musicians.*
➤ **in line** ❶ forming a straight line ❷ under
control

**line** VERB lines, lining, lined
❶ to mark something with lines • *Use lined
paper.* ❷ to form something into a line or
lines; to form a line along something • *Line
them up.* • *Crowds lined the streets to watch
the race.* ❸ to cover the inside of something
with a different material

**lineage** (say **lin**-ee-ij) NOUN lineages
ancestry; a line of descendants from an
ancestor

**linear** (say **lin**-ee-er) ADJECTIVE
❶ arranged in a line ❷ to do with a line or
length

**linen** NOUN
❶ cloth made from flax ❷ shirts, sheets and
tablecloths etc. (which were formerly made
of linen)

**liner** NOUN liners
a large passenger ship

**linger** VERB lingers, lingering, lingered
to stay for a long time, as if unwilling to
leave; to be slow to leave • *The smell of her
perfume lingered in the room.*

**lingerie** (say **lan**-zher-ee) NOUN
women's underwear

**lingo** NOUN lingos or lingoes (*informal*)
a foreign language

**linguist** NOUN linguists
an expert in languages or someone who can
speak several languages well

**linguistics** NOUN
the study of languages
➤ **linguistic** ADJECTIVE

**liniment** NOUN
a lotion for rubbing on parts of the body that
ache

**lining** NOUN linings
a layer of material that covers the inside of
something

**link** NOUN links
❶ one of the rings or loops of a chain ❷ a
connection or relationship ❸ a connection
between documents on the Internet • *Click
on the link at the bottom of the page.*

**link** VERB links, linking, linked
❶ to join things together; to connect people
or things • *The new bridge will link the island
to the mainland.* ❷ to link up is to become
connected • *The two spacecraft linked up in
orbit.*

**links** NOUN & PLURAL NOUN
a golf course, especially one near the sea
**WORD ORIGIN** from Old English *hlinc* = sandy
ground near the seashore

**linnet** NOUN linnets
a kind of finch

**lino** NOUN
(*British*) (*informal*) linoleum

**linocut** NOUN linocuts
a print made from a design cut into a block of
thick linoleum

**linoleum** NOUN
a stiff shiny floor covering

**linseed** NOUN
the seed of flax, from which oil is obtained

**lint** NOUN
a soft material for covering wounds

**lintel** NOUN lintels
a horizontal piece of wood or stone above a door or other opening

**lion** NOUN lions
a large strong flesh-eating animal of the cat family found in Africa and India

**lioness** NOUN lionesses
a female lion

**lip** NOUN lips
❶ either of the two fleshy edges of the mouth ❷ the edge of something hollow, such as a cup or crater ❸ the pointed part at the top of a jug or saucepan from which you pour things

**lip-read** VERB lip-reads, lip-reading, lip-read
to understand what a person says by watching the movements of their lips, not by hearing their voice

**lipstick** NOUN lipsticks
a stick of a waxy substance for colouring the lips

**liquefy** VERB liquefies, liquefying, liquefied
to make something liquid or to become liquid
➤ **liquefaction** NOUN

**liqueur** (say lik-yoor) NOUN liqueurs
a strong sweet alcoholic drink

**liquid** NOUN liquids
a substance like water or oil that flows freely but (unlike a gas) has a constant volume

**liquid** ADJECTIVE
in the form of a liquid; flowing freely

**liquidate** VERB liquidates, liquidating, liquidated
to close down a business and divide its value between its creditors
➤ **liquidation** NOUN
➤ **liquidator** NOUN

**liquidize** (also **liquidise**) VERB liquidizes, liquidizing, liquidized
(British) to make something, especially food, into a liquid or pulp
➤ **liquidizer** NOUN

**liquor** NOUN
❶ alcoholic drink ❷ juice produced in cooking; liquid in which food has been cooked

**liquorice** (say lick-er-iss) NOUN
❶ a black substance used in medicine and as a sweet ❷ the plant from whose root this substance is obtained

**lisp** NOUN lisps
a fault in speech in which s and z are pronounced like th

**lisp** VERB lisps, lisping, lisped
to speak with a lisp

**list** NOUN lists
❶ a number of names, items or figures written or printed one after another ❷ leaning over to one side

**list** VERB lists, listing, listed
❶ to make a list of people or things ❷ a boat or ship lists when it leans over to one side

**listen** VERB listens, listening, listened
to pay attention in order to hear something
• Listen to me. • I like listening to music.
➤ **listener** NOUN

**listless** ADJECTIVE
too tired to be active or enthusiastic
➤ **listlessly** ADVERB

**lit**
past tense of **light** VERB

**litany** NOUN litanies
a formal prayer with fixed responses

**literacy** NOUN
the ability to read and write

**literal** ADJECTIVE
❶ meaning exactly what is said, not metaphorical or exaggerated ❷ word for word • a literal translation

**literally** ADVERB
really; exactly as stated • The noise made me literally jump out of my seat.

**literary** (say lit-er-er-i) ADJECTIVE
to do with literature; interested in literature

**literate** ADJECTIVE
able to read and write

**literature** NOUN
books and other writings, especially those that are widely read and thought to be well written

**lithe** ADJECTIVE
flexible and supple • He was tall and lithe.

**litigation** NOUN litigations
a lawsuit; the process of carrying on a lawsuit

**litmus** NOUN
a blue substance that is turned red by acids and can be turned back to blue by alkalis

**litmus paper** NOUN
paper stained with litmus

**litre** NOUN litres
a measure of liquid, about 1¾ pints

SPELLING

There is a tricky bit in **litre** – it is spelt **re** at the end and not **er**.

**litter** NOUN litters
❶ rubbish or untidy things left lying about ❷ the young animals born to one mother at one time ❸ absorbent material put down on a tray for a cat to urinate and defecate in indoors ❹ a kind of stretcher

**litter** VERB litters, littering, littered
to be scattered all over a place, making it untidy • The floor was littered with books and papers.

**little** ADJECTIVE
❶ small in size or amount; not great or big • a little house ❷ short in time or distance • A little while later the phone rang.

**little** DETERMINER & PRONOUN less, least
not much • I have very little money left. • I understood little of what he said.
➤ **a little** ❶ a small amount • Could I have a little milk, please? ❷ slightly • I'm feeling a little tired.
➤ **little by little** gradually; by a small amount at a time

**little** ADVERB less, least
not much; only slightly • I eat very little.

**liturgy** NOUN liturgies
a fixed form of public worship used in Christian churches
➤ **liturgical** ADJECTIVE

**live** (rhymes with give) VERB lives, living, lived
❶ to have life; to be alive ❷ to have your home somewhere • She lives in Glasgow.
❸ to pass your life in a certain way • He lived as a hermit.
➤ **live something down** if you cannot live down a mistake or embarrassment, you cannot make people forget it
➤ **live on something** to use something as food; to depend on something for your living • The islanders lived mainly on fish.

**live** (rhymes with hive) ADJECTIVE
❶ alive ❷ a live wire or connection is connected to a source of electric current ❸ a live television programme is broadcast while

it is actually happening, not from a recording ❹ a live coal is still burning

**livelihood** NOUN livelihoods
a way of earning money or providing enough food to support yourself

**lively** ADJECTIVE livelier, liveliest
full of life, energy and excitement • The town is quite lively at night.
➤ **liveliness** NOUN

**liven** VERB livens, livening, livened
to make something lively or to become lively • The match livened up in the second half.

**liver** NOUN livers
❶ a large organ of the body, found in your abdomen, that processes digested food and purifies the blood ❷ an animal's liver used as food

**livery** NOUN liveries
❶ a uniform worn by male servants in a household ❷ the distinctive colours used by a railway, bus company or airline

**livery stable** NOUN livery stables
a place where horses are kept for their owner or where horses may be hired

**livestock** NOUN
farm animals

**live wire** NOUN live wires
a person who is lively and full of energy

**livid** ADJECTIVE
❶ bluish-grey • a livid bruise ❷ furiously angry

**living** ADJECTIVE
alive now • her only living relative

**living** NOUN
❶ the way that a person lives • a good standard of living ❷ a way of earning money or providing enough food to support yourself • What do you do for a living?

**living room** NOUN living rooms
a room for general use during the day

**lizard** NOUN lizards
a reptile with a rough or scaly skin, four legs and a long tail

**llama** (say lah-ma) NOUN llamas
a South American animal with woolly fur, like a camel but with no hump

**lo** EXCLAMATION (old use)
see; behold

**load** NOUN loads
❶ something that is being carried ❷ the

quantity that can be carried ❸ the total amount of electric current supplied ❹ (*informal*) a large amount • *It's a load of nonsense.*
➤ **loads** (*informal*) a lot; plenty • *We've got loads of time.*

**load** VERB **loads, loading, loaded**
❶ to put a load in or on something • *I'll go and load the back of the car.* ❷ to load someone with something is to give them large amounts of it • *They loaded him with gifts.* ❸ to load dice is to put a weight into them to make them land in a certain way ❹ to load a gun is to put a bullet or shell into it ❺ to load a camera is to put a film into it ❻ to enter programs or data into a computer

**loaf** NOUN **loaves**
a shaped mass of bread baked in one piece
➤ **use your loaf** to think or use your common sense

**loaf** VERB **loafs, loafing, loafed**
to spend time idly; to loiter or stand about
➤ **loafer** NOUN

**loam** NOUN
rich soil containing clay, sand and decayed leaves
➤ **loamy** ADJECTIVE

**loan** NOUN **loans**
something lent, especially money
➤ **on loan** being lent • *This painting is on loan from the National Gallery.*

**loan** VERB **loans, loaning, loaned**
to lend something

**loath** (rhymes with both) ADJECTIVE
unwilling to do something • *I was loath to go.*

**loathe** (rhymes with clothe) VERB **loathes, loathing, loathed**
to feel great hatred and disgust for someone or something • *They loathe each other.*
➤ **loathing** NOUN

**loathsome** ADJECTIVE
making you feel great hatred and disgust; repulsive

**lob** VERB **lobs, lobbing, lobbed**
to throw, hit or kick a ball high into the air, especially in a high arc

**lob** NOUN **lobs**
a lobbed ball in tennis or football

**lobby** NOUN **lobbies**
❶ an entrance hall ❷ a group of people who try to influence politicians or officials or persuade them of something • *the anti-hunting lobby*

**lobby** VERB **lobbies, lobbying, lobbied**
to try to persuade a politician or other person to support your cause, by speaking to them in person or writing letters **WORD ORIGIN** the lobby of the Houses of Parliament is where members of the public can meet MPs

**lobe** NOUN **lobes**
❶ a rounded fairly flat part of a leaf or an organ of the body ❷ the rounded soft part at the bottom of your ear
➤ **lobed** ADJECTIVE

**lobster** NOUN **lobsters**
a large shellfish with eight legs and two long claws

**local** ADJECTIVE
belonging to a particular place or a small area • *Where is your local library?*
➤ **locally** ADVERB

**local** NOUN **locals** (*informal*)
❶ someone who lives in a particular district ❷ the pub nearest to a person's home

**local anaesthetic** NOUN **local anaesthetics**
an anaesthetic affecting only the part of the body where it is applied

**local government** NOUN
the system of administration of a town or county by people elected by those who live there

**locality** NOUN **localities**
a place and the area that surrounds it • *There is no airport in the locality.*

**localized** (also **localised**) ADJECTIVE
restricted to a particular place • *localized showers*

**locate** VERB **locates, locating, located**
to discover where something is • *I have located the fault.*
➤ **be located** to be situated in a particular place • *The cinema is located in the High Street.*

**location** NOUN **locations**
the place where something is situated • *What is the exact location of the submarine?*
➤ **on location** filmed in natural surroundings, not in a studio

**loch** NOUN **lochs**
a lake in Scotland

**lock** NOUN **locks**
❶ a fastening that is opened with a key or other device ❷ a section of a canal or river fitted with gates and sluices so that boats can be raised or lowered to the level beyond

403

each gate ❸ the distance that a vehicle's front wheels can turn ❹ a wrestling hold that keeps an opponent's arm or leg from moving ❺ a clump of hair
➤ **lock, stock, and barrel** completely

**lock** VERB locks, locking, locked
❶ to fasten something by means of a lock • Have you locked the door? ❷ to put or keep something in a safe place that can be fastened with a lock • The diamonds are locked away in a safe. ❸ to become fixed in one place; to jam • The brakes locked and the car skidded.

**locker** NOUN lockers
a small cupboard for keeping things safe, often in a changing room

**locket** NOUN lockets
a small ornamental case for holding a portrait or lock of hair, worn on a chain round the neck

**locks** PLURAL NOUN
the hair on a person's head

**locksmith** NOUN locksmiths
a person whose job is to make and mend locks

**locomotion** NOUN
movement or the ability to move

**locomotive** NOUN locomotives
a railway engine

**locum** NOUN locums
(British) a doctor or member of the clergy who takes the place of another who is temporarily away

**locus** (say **loh**-kus) NOUN loci (say **loh**-ky)
(in mathematics) the path traced by a moving point or made by points placed in a certain way

**locust** NOUN locusts
a kind of grasshopper that travels in large swarms which eat all the plants in an area

**lodestone** NOUN lodestones
a kind of stone that can be used as a magnet

**lodge** NOUN lodges
❶ a small house, especially at the gates of a park ❷ a porter's room at the entrance to a college or other building ❸ a beaver's or otter's lair

**lodge** VERB lodges, lodging, lodged
❶ to stay somewhere as a lodger ❷ to provide a person with somewhere to live temporarily ❸ to become stuck or caught somewhere • The ball lodged in the tree.

➤ **lodge a complaint** to make an official complaint

**lodger** NOUN lodgers
(chiefly British) a person who pays to live in another person's house

**lodgings** PLURAL NOUN
a room or rooms, not in a hotel, rented for living in

**loft** NOUN lofts
a room or storage space under the roof of a house or barn

**lofty** ADJECTIVE
❶ high or tall • lofty towers ❷ a lofty aim or ambition is a noble one that deserves praise ❸ a lofty attitude or manner is a very arrogant one • her lofty disdain for other people
➤ **loftily** ADVERB

**log** NOUN logs
❶ a large piece of a tree that has fallen or been cut down; a piece cut off this ❷ a detailed record kept of a voyage or flight

**log** VERB logs, logging, logged
to enter facts in a log
➤ **log in** or **on** to gain access to a computer system
➤ **log out** or **off** to finish using a computer system

**loganberry** NOUN loganberries
a dark-red fruit like a blackberry
**WORD ORIGIN** named after an American lawyer H. R. Logan, who first grew it

**logarithm** NOUN logarithms
one of a series of numbers set out in tables which make it possible to do sums by adding and subtracting instead of multiplying and dividing

**logbook** NOUN logbooks
❶ a book in which a log of a voyage is kept ❷ the registration document of a motor vehicle

**log cabin** NOUN log cabins
a hut built of logs

**loggerheads** PLURAL NOUN
➤ **at loggerheads** disagreeing or quarrelling

**logic** NOUN
❶ reasoning; a system or method of reasoning • I don't see the logic of your argument. ❷ the principles used in designing a computer

**logical** ADJECTIVE
using logic or worked out by logic; reasonable

or sensible • *That was the logical thing to do.*
➤ **logically** ADVERB

**login** NOUN logins
the process of starting to use a computer system; the name or password you use to do this • *Enter your login name.*

**logo** (say **loh**-goh or **log**-oh) NOUN logos
a printed symbol used by a business company as its emblem

**loin** NOUN loins
the side and back of the body between the ribs and the hip bone

**loincloth** NOUN loincloths
a piece of cloth wrapped round the hips, worn by men in some hot countries as their only piece of clothing

**loiter** VERB loiters, loitering, loitered
to stand about idly for no obvious reason
➤ **loiterer** NOUN

**loll** VERB lolls, lolling, lolled
❶ to lean lazily against something • *He lolled back in his chair by the fire.* ❷ to hang loosely • *The dog's tongue lolled from its mouth.*

**lollipop** NOUN lollipops
a large round hard sweet on a stick

**lollipop woman, lollipop man** NOUN
lollipop women, lollipop men
an official who uses a circular sign on a stick to signal traffic to stop so that children can cross a road

**lolly** NOUN lollies (*informal*)
❶ a lollipop or an ice lolly ❷ money

**lone** ADJECTIVE
solitary; on its own • *a lone rider*

**lonely** ADJECTIVE lonelier, loneliest
❶ sad because you are on your own or have no friends ❷ far from inhabited places; not often visited or used • *a lonely road*
➤ **loneliness** NOUN

**lonesome** ADJECTIVE
lonely

**long** ADJECTIVE
❶ measuring a lot from one end to the other ❷ taking a lot of time • *a long holiday* ❸ having a certain length • *The river is 10 miles long.*

**long** ADVERB
❶ for a long time • *Have you been waiting long?* ❷ at a long time before or after • *They left long ago.* ❸ throughout a time • *all night*

*long*
➤ **as long as** or **so long as** provided that; on condition that • *I'll come as long as I can bring my dog.*
➤ **before long** soon
➤ **no longer** not any more

**long** VERB longs, longing, longed
to want something very much • *She had always longed for a brother.*

**long-distance** ADJECTIVE
travelling or covering a long distance • *a long-distance runner*

**long division** NOUN
dividing one number by another and writing down all the calculations

**longevity** (say lon-**jev**-it-ee) NOUN
long life

**longhand** NOUN
ordinary writing, contrasted with shorthand or typing

**longing** NOUN longings
a strong desire for something or someone

**longitude** NOUN longitudes
the distance east or west, measured in degrees, from the Greenwich meridian

**longitudinal** ADJECTIVE
❶ to do with longitude ❷ to do with length; measured lengthways

**long jump** NOUN
an athletic contest in which competitors jump as far as possible along the ground in one leap

**long-range** ADJECTIVE
covering a long distance or period of time • *a long-range missile* • *a long-range weather forecast*

**longship** NOUN longships
a long narrow warship, with oars and a sail, used by the Vikings

**long-sighted** ADJECTIVE
(*chiefly British*) able to see distant things clearly but not things close to you

**long-suffering** ADJECTIVE
putting up with things patiently

**long-term** ADJECTIVE
to do with or happening over a long period of time

**long wave** NOUN
a radio wave of a wavelength above one

kilometre and a frequency less than 300 kilohertz

**long-winded** ADJECTIVE
talking or writing at too great a length and therefore boring

**loo** NOUN loos (British) (informal)
a toilet

**loofah** NOUN loofahs
a rough sponge made from a dried gourd

**look** VERB looks, looking, looked
❶ to use your eyes; to turn your eyes in a particular direction ❷ to face in a particular direction ❸ to have a certain appearance; to seem a certain way • *You look sad.*
➤ **look after someone** to protect or take care of someone
➤ **look after something** to be in charge of something
➤ **look down on someone** to regard someone with contempt
➤ **look for something** to try to find something
➤ **look forward to something** to be waiting eagerly for something to happen
➤ **look into something** to investigate something
➤ **look out** to be careful
➤ **look something up** to search for information about something
➤ **look up** to improve in prospects • *Things are looking up.*
➤ **look up to someone** to admire or respect someone

**look** NOUN looks
❶ the act of looking; a gaze or glance • *Take a look at this.* ❷ the expression on a person's face • *She gave me a surprised look.* ❸ an appearance or general impression • *I don't like the look of this place.*

**look-alike** NOUN look-alikes
someone who looks very like a famous person

**looking glass** NOUN looking glasses (old use)
a glass mirror

**lookout** NOUN lookouts
❶ looking out or watching for something • *Keep a lookout for snakes.* ❷ a place from which you can keep watch ❸ a person whose job is to keep watch ❹ (informal) a person's own fault or concern • *If he wastes his money, that's his lookout.*

**loom** VERB looms, looming, loomed
to appear suddenly; to seem large or close and threatening • *An iceberg loomed up through the fog.*

**loom** NOUN looms
a machine for weaving cloth

**loony** ADJECTIVE loonier, looniest (informal)
mad or crazy

**loop** NOUN loops
the shape made by a curve crossing itself; a piece of string, ribbon or wire made into this shape

**loop** VERB loops, looping, looped
❶ to make string etc. into a loop ❷ to enclose something in a loop

**loophole** NOUN loopholes
❶ a way of avoiding a law, rule or promise without actually breaking it ❷ a narrow opening in the wall of a castle, for shooting arrows through

**loose** ADJECTIVE looser, loosest
❶ not tight or firmly fixed • *a loose tooth*
❷ not tied up or shut in • *The dog got loose.*
❸ not packed in a box or packet ❹ not exact • *a loose translation*
➤ **at a loose end** with nothing to do
➤ **on the loose** free after escaping

> SPELLING
>
> **Loose** is different from **lose**. **Loose** is when something is not tight and **lose** is when you misplace something.

**loose** VERB looses, loosing, loosed
❶ to fire an arrow, bullet, etc. • *He rapidly loosed a second arrow.* ❷ to loosen something ❸ to untie or release someone or something

**loose-leaf** ADJECTIVE
with each sheet of paper separate and able to be removed • *a loose-leaf folder*

**loosely** ADVERB
not tightly or firmly • *She tied the scarf loosely round her waist.*

**loosen** VERB loosens, loosening, loosened
❶ to make something loose or looser • *He loosened his grip on the rope.* ❷ to become loose

**loot** NOUN
stolen things; goods taken from an enemy

**loot** VERB loots, looting, looted
❶ to rob a place violently, especially during a war or riot ❷ to take something as loot
➤ **looter** NOUN

**lop** VERB lops, lopping, lopped
to lop a branch or twig is to cut it off from a tree or bush

**lope** *VERB* lopes, loping, loped
to run with a long bounding stride
➤ **lope** *NOUN*

**lopsided** *ADJECTIVE*
with one side lower or smaller than the other
• *She had a lopsided smile.*

**loquacious** (say lok-**way**-shus) *ADJECTIVE*
talkative
➤ **loquacity** (say lok-**wass**-it-ee) *NOUN*

**lord** *NOUN* lords
❶ a nobleman, especially one who is allowed
to use the title 'Lord' in front of his name ❷ a
master or ruler
➤ **Our Lord** in Christianity, Jesus Christ
➤ **the Lord** God

**lord** *VERB* lords, lording, lorded
➤ **lord it over someone** to behave in
a superior or domineering way towards
someone • *At school Liam always used to
lord it over the rest of us.*

**lordly** *ADJECTIVE* lordlier, lordliest
❶ to do with a lord ❷ proud or haughty

**Lord Mayor** *NOUN* Lord Mayors
the title of the mayor of some large cities

**lordship** *NOUN*
a title used in speaking to or about a man of
the rank of 'Lord'

**lore** *NOUN*
a set of traditional facts or beliefs about
something • *forest lore and legends*

**lorgnette** (say lorn-**yet**) *NOUN* lorgnettes
a pair of spectacles held on a long handle
**WORD ORIGIN** French, from *lorgner* = to squint

**lorry** *NOUN* lorries
(*British*) a large strong motor vehicle for
carrying heavy goods or troops

**lose** *VERB* loses, losing, lost
❶ to be without something that you once
had, especially because you cannot find it
❷ to fail to keep or obtain something • *We
lost control.* ❸ to be defeated in a contest or
argument ❹ to cause the loss of something
• *That one mistake lost us the game.* ❺ a
clock or watch loses time if it shows a time
that is earlier than the correct one
➤ **lose your life** to be killed
➤ **lose your way** to not know where you are
or which is the right path

**loser** *NOUN* losers
❶ a person who is defeated ❷ (*informal*) a
person who is never successful

**loss** *NOUN* losses
❶ losing something ❷ something that has
been lost
➤ **be at a loss** to not know what to do or say

**lost**
past tense and past participle of **lose**

**lost** *ADJECTIVE*
❶ not knowing where you are or not able to
find your way • *I think we're lost.* ❷ missing
or strayed • *a lost dog*
➤ **lost cause** an idea or policy that is failing
➤ **be lost in something** to be engrossed in a
task or activity • *She was lost in thought.*

**lot** *NOUN* lots
❶ a large number or amount • *You have a lot
of friends.* • *There's lots of time.* ❷ something
for sale at an auction ❸ a piece of land ❹ a
person's fate or situation in life • *She was
unhappy with her lot.*
➤ **a lot** very much • *I feel a lot better.*
➤ **draw lots** to draw cards or other objects
from a set in turn in order to choose or
decide something by chance • *We drew lots
to see who should go first.*
➤ **the lot** or **the whole lot** everything; all

**SPELLING**
A lot is two words, not one.

**loth** *ADJECTIVE*
a different spelling of **loath**

**lotion** *NOUN* lotions
a liquid for putting on the skin

**lottery** *NOUN* lotteries
a way of raising money by selling numbered
tickets and giving prizes to people who hold
winning numbers, which are chosen by a
method depending on chance

**lotto** *NOUN*
a game like bingo

**lotus** *NOUN* lotuses
a kind of tropical water lily

**loud** *ADJECTIVE*
❶ easily heard; producing a lot of noise
❷ unpleasantly bright; gaudy • *The room was
painted in loud colours.*
➤ **loudly** *ADVERB*
➤ **loudness** *NOUN*

**loudspeaker** *NOUN* loudspeakers
a device that changes electrical signals into
sound, for reproducing music or voices

**lounge** *NOUN* lounges
a sitting room

**lounge** VERB lounges, lounging, lounged
to sit or stand in a lazy and relaxed way • *He was lounging in an armchair by the fire.*

**louse** NOUN lice
a small insect that lives as a parasite on animals or plants

**lousy** ADJECTIVE lousier, lousiest
❶ full of lice ❷ (*informal*) very bad or unpleasant

**lout** NOUN louts
a bad-mannered man

**lovable** ADJECTIVE
easy to love • *a lovable little dog*

**love** NOUN loves
❶ great liking or affection ❷ sexual affection or passion ❸ a loved person; a sweetheart ❹ a score of nil in tennis
➤ in love feeling strong love for someone
➤ make love to have sexual intercourse

**love** VERB loves, loving, loved
❶ to feel love for a person ❷ to like something very much

**love affair** NOUN love affairs
a romantic or sexual relationship between two people in love

**loveless** ADJECTIVE
without love

**lovelorn** ADJECTIVE
pining with love, especially when abandoned by a lover

**lovely** ADJECTIVE lovelier, loveliest
❶ beautiful ❷ very pleasant or enjoyable
➤ loveliness NOUN

**lover** NOUN lovers
❶ someone who loves something • *an art lover* ❷ a person who someone is having a sexual relationship with but is not married to

**lovesick** ADJECTIVE
longing for someone you love, especially someone who does not love you

**loving** ADJECTIVE
feeling or showing love or affection • *a loving family*
➤ lovingly ADVERB

**low** ADJECTIVE
❶ only reaching a short way up; not high ❷ below average in importance, quality or amount • *low prices* • *people of low rank* ❸ unhappy • *I'm feeling low.* ❹ not high-pitched; not loud • *low notes* • *a low voice*
➤ lowness NOUN

**low** ADVERB
at or to a low level or position • *The plane was flying low.*

**low** VERB lows, lowing, lowed
to moo like a cow

**low-down** NOUN
the true facts or relevant information • *Go to our website for the low-down on disability sport in your area.*

**lower** ADJECTIVE & ADVERB
less high

**lower** VERB lowers, lowering, lowered
to make something lower or move it down
• *They lowered the boat into the water.*

**lower case** NOUN
small letters, not capitals

**lowlands** PLURAL NOUN
low-lying country
➤ lowland ADJECTIVE
➤ lowlander NOUN

**lowly** ADJECTIVE lowlier, lowliest
low in importance or rank; humble • *a lowly peasant*

**loyal** ADJECTIVE
always firmly supporting your friends, group or country
➤ loyally ADVERB

**loyalist** NOUN loyalists
a person who is loyal to the government during a revolt

**loyalty** NOUN loyalties
❶ being loyal • *She showed great loyalty to her friends.* ❷ a strong feeling that you want to be loyal to someone • *You have got to decide where your loyalties lie.*

**lozenge** NOUN lozenges
❶ a small flavoured tablet, especially one containing medicine ❷ a diamond-shaped design

**Ltd.** ABBREVIATION
limited (used after the name of a company)

**lubricant** NOUN lubricants
oil or grease for lubricating machinery

**lubricate** VERB lubricates, lubricating, lubricated
to oil or grease something so that it moves smoothly
➤ lubrication NOUN

**lucid** ADJECTIVE
❶ clear and easy to understand • *a lucid explanation* ❷ thinking clearly; not confused

in your mind
➤ **lucidly** ADVERB
➤ **lucidity** NOUN

**luck** NOUN
❶ the way things happen by chance without being planned • *There's no skill in this game – it's all a matter of luck.* ❷ good fortune • *She phoned to wish me luck.*

**luckily** ADVERB
by a lucky chance; fortunately • *Luckily it stayed warm all day.*

**luckless** ADJECTIVE
unlucky

**lucky** ADJECTIVE luckier, luckiest
having, bringing or resulting from good luck
• *He was lucky to be alive.* • *a lucky escape*

**lucrative** (say loo-kra-tiv) ADJECTIVE
profitable; earning you a lot of money

**ludicrous** ADJECTIVE
ridiculous or laughable
➤ **ludicrously** ADVERB

**ludo** NOUN
(*British*) a game played with dice and counters on a board WORD ORIGIN Latin, = I play

**lug** VERB lugs, lugging, lugged
to drag or carry something heavy • *I had to lug my suitcase up all those stairs.*

**lug** NOUN lugs
❶ an ear-like part on an object, by which it may be carried or fixed ❷ (*informal*) an ear

**luggage** NOUN
suitcases and bags for holding things to take on a journey

**lugubrious** (say lug-oo-bree-us) ADJECTIVE
gloomy or mournful
➤ **lugubriously** ADVERB

**lukewarm** ADJECTIVE
❶ only slightly warm; tepid ❷ not very enthusiastic • *lukewarm applause*

**lull** VERB lulls, lulling, lulled
❶ to soothe or calm someone; to send someone to sleep ❷ to give someone a false feeling of being safe

**lull** NOUN lulls
a short period of quiet or inactivity • *There was a lull in the fighting.*

**lullaby** NOUN lullabies
a song that you sing to send a baby to sleep

**lumbago** NOUN
pain in the muscles of the lower back

**lumbar** ADJECTIVE
to do with the lower back area

**lumber** NOUN
❶ unwanted furniture or other goods; junk ❷ (*North American*) timber

**lumber** VERB lumbers, lumbering, lumbered
❶ to move in a heavy clumsy way • *We could hear someone lumbering about upstairs.* ❷ to leave someone with an unwanted or unpleasant task • *I'm sorry you got lumbered with all the washing-up.*

**lumberjack** NOUN lumberjacks
a person whose job is to cut or carry timber

**luminescent** ADJECTIVE
giving out light
➤ **luminescence** NOUN

**luminous** ADJECTIVE
glowing in the dark • *luminous green eyes*
➤ **luminosity** NOUN

**lump** NOUN lumps
❶ a solid piece of something ❷ a swelling

**lump** VERB lumps, lumping, lumped
to lump things together is to put or treat them in a group because you regard them as alike in some way
➤ **lump it** (*informal*) to put up with something you dislike

**lump sum** NOUN lump sums
a single payment, especially one covering a number of items

**lumpy** ADJECTIVE lumpier, lumpiest
full of lumps or covered in lumps • *This bed is very lumpy.*

**lunacy** NOUN lunacies
insanity or great foolishness

**lunar** ADJECTIVE
to do with the moon WORD ORIGIN from Latin *luna* = moon

**lunar month** NOUN lunar months
the period between new moons; four weeks

**lunatic** NOUN lunatics
an insane person
➤ **lunatic** ADJECTIVE
WORD ORIGIN from Latin *luna* = moon (because it was once thought that people could be affected by changes of the moon)

**lunch** NOUN lunches
a meal eaten in the middle of the day
➤ **lunch** VERB

**luncheon** NOUN luncheons (*formal*)
lunch

a b c d e f g h i j k l m n o p q r s t u v w x y z

**lung** NOUN lungs
either of the two parts of the body, in your chest, used in breathing

**lunge** VERB lunges, lunging, lunged
to thrust your body forward suddenly

**lunge** NOUN lunges
a sudden forward movement • *He made a lunge for the phone.*

**lupin** NOUN lupins
a garden plant with tall spikes of flowers

**lurch** VERB lurches, lurching, lurched
❶ to stagger; to lean suddenly to one side ❷ if you heart or stomach lurches, you have a sudden feeling of fear or excitement

**lurch** NOUN lurches
a sudden staggering or leaning movement • *The train moved forward with a lurch.*
➤ **leave someone in the lurch** to desert someone when they are in difficulty

**lure** VERB lures, luring, lured
to tempt a person or animal into a trap; to entice someone

**lure** NOUN lures
the attractive qualities of something • *the lure of adventure*

**lurid** (say **lewr**-id) ADJECTIVE
❶ in very bright colours; gaudy ❷ sensational and shocking • *the lurid details of the murder*
➤ **luridly** ADVERB

**lurk** VERB lurks, lurking, lurked
to wait where you cannot be seen

**luscious** (say **lush**-us) ADJECTIVE
tasting delicious • *luscious fruit*

**lush** ADJECTIVE
growing thickly and strongly • *lush grass*

**lust** NOUN lusts
powerful desire, especially sexual desire
➤ **lustful** ADJECTIVE

**lust** VERB lusts, lusting, lusted
to have a powerful desire for a person or thing • *people who lust after power*

**lustre** NOUN
brightness or brilliance • *Her eyes had lost their lustre.*
➤ **lustrous** ADJECTIVE

**lusty** ADJECTIVE lustier, lustiest
strong and vigorous • *a lusty cheer*
➤ **lustily** ADVERB

**lute** NOUN lutes
a stringed musical instrument with a pear-

shaped body, popular in the 14th-17th centuries

**luxuriant** ADJECTIVE
growing thickly and strongly • *luxuriant vegetation*

**luxuriate** VERB luxuriates, luxuriating, luxuriated
to luxuriate in something is to enjoy it as a luxury • *We've been luxuriating in the warm sunshine.*

**luxurious** ADJECTIVE
full of luxury; expensive and comfortable • *a luxurious hotel*
➤ **luxuriously** ADVERB

**luxury** NOUN luxuries
❶ something expensive that you enjoy but do not really need ❷ expensive and comfortable surroundings • *a life of luxury*

**lychgate** NOUN lychgates
a churchyard gate with a roof over it
**WORD ORIGIN** from Old English *lic* = corpse (because the coffin-bearers would shelter there until it was time to enter the church)

**Lycra** NOUN (*trademark*)
a thin stretchy material used especially for sports clothing

**lying**
present participle of **lie**

**lymph** (say limf) NOUN
a colourless fluid from the flesh or organs of the body, containing white blood cells
➤ **lymphatic** ADJECTIVE

**lynch** VERB lynches, lynching, lynched
to join together to execute someone without a proper trial, especially by hanging them
**WORD ORIGIN** named after William *Lynch*, an American judge who allowed this kind of punishment in about 1780

**lynx** NOUN lynxes
a wild animal like a very large cat with thick fur and very sharp sight

**lyre** NOUN lyres
an ancient musical instrument like a small harp

**lyric** (say **li**-rik) NOUN lyrics
❶ a short poem that expresses the poet's feelings ❷ lyrics are the words of a popular song

**lyrical** ADJECTIVE
❶ like a song ❷ expressing poetic feelings ❸ expressing yourself enthusiastically

# Mm

**MA** *ABBREVIATION*
Master of Arts

**ma** *NOUN* (*informal*)
mother

**ma'am** (say mam) *NOUN*
a word used when speaking politely
to a woman (especially the Queen)
**WORD ORIGIN** short for **madam**

**mac** *NOUN* macs (*British*) (*informal*)
a raincoat

**macabre** (say mak-ahbr) *ADJECTIVE*
gruesome; strange and horrible

**macadam** *NOUN*
layers of broken stone rolled flat to make a
firm road surface **WORD ORIGIN** named after
a Scottish engineer, J. *McAdam*, who first laid
such roads

**macaroni** *NOUN*
pasta in the form of short narrow tubes

**macaroon** *NOUN* macaroons
a small sweet cake or biscuit made with
ground almonds

**macaw** (say ma-**kaw**) *NOUN* macaws
a brightly coloured parrot from Central and
South America

**mace** *NOUN* maces
an ornamental staff carried or placed in front
of an official

**Mach** (say mahk) *NOUN*
➤ **Mach number** the ratio of the speed of a
moving object to the speed of sound. Mach
one is the speed of sound, Mach two is twice
the speed of sound and so on.
**WORD ORIGIN** named after the Austrian
scientist Ernst *Mach* (1838-1916)

**machete** (say mash-et-ee) *NOUN* machetes
a broad heavy knife used as a tool or weapon

**machinations** (say mash-in-**ay**-shonz) *PLURAL
NOUN*
clever schemes or plots

**machine** *NOUN* machines
a piece of equipment made of moving parts
that work together to do a job

**machine gun** *NOUN* machine guns
a gun that can keep firing bullets quickly one
after another

**machine-readable** *ADJECTIVE*
machine-readable data is in a form that a
computer can process

**machinery** *NOUN*
❶ machines • *farm machinery* ❷ the moving
parts of a machine • *He was tinkering with
the machinery of the motor.* ❸ an organized
system for doing something • *the machinery
of local government*

**macho** (say mach-oh) *ADJECTIVE*
showing off masculine strength

**mackerel** *NOUN* mackerel
a sea fish used as food

**mackintosh** *NOUN* mackintoshes (*British*) (*old
use*)
a raincoat **WORD ORIGIN** named after the
Scottish inventor of a waterproof material, C.
*Macintosh*

**mad** *ADJECTIVE* madder, maddest
❶ having something wrong with the mind;
insane ❷ extremely foolish ❸ very keen • *She
is mad about football.* ❹ (*informal*) very
excited or annoyed
➤ **madness** *NOUN*
➤ **madman** *NOUN*
➤ **like mad** (*informal*) with great speed,
energy or enthusiasm

**madam** *NOUN*
a word used when speaking politely to a
woman • *Can I help you, madam?*

**madcap** *ADJECTIVE*
foolish and rash • *a madcap scheme*

**mad cow disease** *NOUN*
BSE

**madden** *VERB* maddens, maddening,
maddened
to make a person mad or angry

**maddening** *ADJECTIVE*
annoying • *She has some really maddening
habits.*

**madly** *ADVERB*
extremely; very much • *They are madly in
love.*

**madonna** *NOUN* madonnas
a picture or statue of the Virgin Mary

**madrigal** *NOUN* madrigals
a song for several voices singing different
parts together

**maelstrom** (say **mayl**-strom) NOUN
maelstroms
❶ a great whirlpool ❷ a state of great
confusion WORD ORIGIN originally the name
of a whirlpool off the Norwegian coast: from
Dutch *malen* = whirl + *stroom* = stream

**maestro** (say **my**-stroh) NOUN maestros
a master, especially a musician

**mafia** NOUN
❶ a large organization of criminals in Italy,
Sicily and the United States of America ❷ any
group of people who act together in a sinister
way

**magazine** NOUN magazines
❶ a paper-covered publication that comes
out regularly, with articles, stories or features
by several writers ❷ the part of a gun that
holds the cartridges ❸ a store for weapons
and ammunition or for explosives ❹ a
device that holds film for a camera or slides
for a projector WORD ORIGIN from Arabic
*makhazin* = storehouses, the original meaning
in English. The word then came to be used for
a store for weapons and ammunition, and later
the part of a gun.

**magenta** (say ma-**jen**-ta) NOUN
a colour between bright red and purple
WORD ORIGIN named after *Magenta*, a town
in north Italy, where Napoleon III won a battle
in the year when the dye was first developed
(1859)

**maggot** NOUN maggots
the larva of some kinds of fly
➤ **maggoty** ADJECTIVE

**Magi** (say **mayj**-eye) PLURAL NOUN
the 'wise men' from the East who brought
offerings to the infant Jesus at Bethlehem
WORD ORIGIN from old Persian *magus* =
priest; later = astrologer or wizard

**magic** NOUN
❶ the art of making impossible things
happen by a mysterious or supernatural
power ❷ mysterious tricks performed
for entertainment ❸ a mysterious and
enchanting quality • *the magic of Greece*
**magic** ADJECTIVE
❶ used in or using magic • *a magic potion*
❷ having a special or mysterious quality. • *It
was a magic moment.*

**magical**
❶ to do with magic or using magic
❷ wonderful or marvellous • *a magical
evening*
➤ **magically** ADVERB

**magician** NOUN magicians
❶ a person who does magic tricks ❷ a wizard

**magistrate** NOUN magistrates
an official who hears and judges minor cases
in a local court

**magma** NOUN
a molten substance beneath the earth's crust

**magnanimous** (say mag-**nan**-im-us) ADJECTIVE
generous and forgiving, not petty-minded
➤ **magnanimously** ADVERB
➤ **magnanimity** NOUN

**magnate** NOUN magnates
a wealthy influential person, especially in
business

**magnesia** NOUN
a white powder that is a compound of
magnesium, used in medicine

**magnesium** NOUN
a silvery-white metal that burns with a very
bright flame

**magnet** NOUN magnets
a piece of iron or steel that can attract iron
and that points north and south when it is
hung up

**magnetic** ADJECTIVE
❶ having or using the powers of a magnet
❷ having the power to attract people • *a
magnetic personality*
➤ **magnetically** ADVERB

**magnetic tape** NOUN magnetic tapes
a plastic strip coated with a magnetic
substance, for recording sound or pictures or
storing computer data

**magnetism** NOUN
❶ the properties and effects of magnetic
substances ❷ great personal charm and
attraction

**magnetize** (also **magnetise**) VERB
magnetizes, magnetizing, magnetized
to make something into a magnet
➤ **magnetization** NOUN

**magneto** (say mag-**neet**-oh) NOUN magnetos
a small electric generator using magnets

**magnificent** ADJECTIVE
❶ looking grand or splendid • *She rode
a magnificent black horse.* ❷ very good;
excellent
➤ **magnificently** ADVERB
➤ **magnificence** NOUN

**magnify** VERB magnifies, magnifying,
magnified

❶ to make something look bigger than it really is, as a lens or microscope does ❷ to exaggerate something
➤ **magnification** NOUN
➤ **magnifier** NOUN

**magnifying glass** NOUN magnifying glasses
a lens that magnifies things

**magnitude** NOUN magnitudes
the magnitude of something is how large or important it is • *At first we didn't realize the magnitude of the problem.*

**magnolia** NOUN magnolias
a tree with large white or pale-pink flowers
**(WORD ORIGIN)** named after a French botanist, P. *Magnol*

**magpie** NOUN magpies
a noisy bird with black and white feathers, related to the crow

**maharajah** NOUN maharajahs
the title of certain Indian princes

**mah-jong** NOUN
a Chinese game for four people, played with pieces called tiles

**mahogany** NOUN
a hard brown wood

**maid** NOUN maids
❶ a female servant ❷ (*old use*) a girl

**maiden** NOUN maidens (*old use*)
a girl
➤ **maidenhood** NOUN

**maiden** ADJECTIVE
❶ a maiden aunt is one who is not married
❷ a ship's maiden voyage is its first voyage after being built

**maiden name** NOUN maiden names
a woman's family name before she marries

**maiden over** NOUN maiden overs
a cricket over in which no runs are scored

**mail** NOUN mails
❶ letters and parcels sent by post ❷ email; an email • *I had a mail from Danny this morning.*
❸ armour made of metal rings joined together • *a suit of chain mail*

**mail** VERB mails, mailing, mailed
to send something by post or by email

**mailing list** NOUN mailing lists
a list of names and addresses of people to whom an organization sends information from time to time

**mail order** NOUN
a system for buying and selling goods by post

**maim** VERB maims, maiming, maimed
to injure a person so badly that part of their body is damaged for life

**main** ADJECTIVE
largest or most important

**main** NOUN
❶ the main pipe or cable in a public system carrying water, gas, or (usually called mains) electricity to a building ❷ (*old use*) the seas
• *Drake sailed the Spanish main.*
➤ **in the main** for the most part; on the whole

**main clause** NOUN main clauses
a clause that can be used as a complete sentence. Compare with subordinate clause.

**mainframe** NOUN mainframes
a large powerful computer that a lot of people can use at the same time

**mainland** NOUN
the main part of a country or continent, not the islands round it

**mainly** ADVERB
chiefly or mostly • *They eat mainly fruit and nuts.*

**mainmast** NOUN mainmasts
the tallest and most important mast on a ship

**mainstay** NOUN
the chief support or main part • *Cocoa is the mainstay of the country's economy.*

**mainstream** NOUN
the most widely accepted ideas or opinions about something • *Music should be part of the mainstream of education.*

**maintain** VERB maintains, maintaining, maintained
❶ to make something continue at the same standard or level • *The pilot maintained a constant flying speed.* ❷ to keep a thing in good condition • *Wind turbines can be costly to maintain.* ❸ to keep saying that something is true • *I still maintain that I did the right thing.* ❹ to provide money for a person to live on

**maintenance** NOUN
❶ maintaining or keeping something in good condition ❷ money for food and clothing ❸ money to be paid by a husband or wife to the other partner after a divorce

**maize** NOUN
(*British*) a tall kind of corn with large seeds on cobs

**majestic** ADJECTIVE
① stately and dignified ② very impressive
➤ **majestically** ADVERB

**majesty** NOUN majesties
① the title of a king or queen • *Her Majesty the Queen* ② being majestic

**major** ADJECTIVE
① greater; very important or serious • *major roads* • *a major operation* ② of the musical scale that has a semitone after the 3rd and 7th notes. Compare with **minor**.

**major** NOUN majors
an army officer ranking next above a captain

**major** VERB majors, majoring, majored (North American & Australian/NZ) to specialize in a particular subject at college or university • *He's majoring in psychology.*

**majority** NOUN majorities
① the greatest part of a group of people or things. Compare with **minority**. • *The vast majority of the people who live in China speak Chinese.* ② the amount by which the winner in an election beats the loser • *She had a majority of 25 over her opponent.* ③ the age at which a person becomes an adult according to the law, now usually 18 • *He attained his majority.*

**make** VERB makes, making, made
① to bring something into existence, especially by putting things together ② to cause something to happen • *You made me jump!* • *Make him repeat it.* ③ to gain or earn an amount of money • *She makes £30,000 a year.* ④ to achieve or reach something • *He made 25 runs.* • *The swimmer just made the shore.* ⑤ to estimate or reckon something • *What do you make the time?* ⑥ to result in or add up to something • *4 and 6 make 10* ⑦ to perform an action • *Can I make a suggestion?* ⑧ to arrange something for use • *I'll just make the beds.* ⑨ to cause someone to be successful or happy • *Her visit made my day.*
➤ **make do** to manage with something that is not what you really want
➤ **make for somewhere** to go towards a place
➤ **make love** ① to have sexual intercourse ② (*old use*) to try to win someone's love
➤ **make off** to go away quickly
➤ **make out** to claim or pretend that something is true

➤ **make something out** to manage to see, hear or understand something
➤ **make up** ① to be friendly again after a disagreement ② to put on make-up
➤ **make something up** ① to build something or put it together • *Elements are made up of atoms.* ② to invent a story or excuse
➤ **make up for something** to compensate for something
➤ **make up your mind** to decide about something

**make** NOUN makes
a brand of goods; something made by a particular firm

SPELLING

The past tense of **make** is **made**.

**make-believe** NOUN
pretending or imagining things

**make-over** NOUN make-overs
changes in your make-up, hairstyle and the way you dress to make you look and feel more attractive

**maker** NOUN makers
the person or firm that has made something

**makeshift** ADJECTIVE
used for the time being because you have nothing better • *We used a box as a makeshift table.*

**make-up** NOUN
① creams and powders put on your face to make it look more attractive or different ② the way something is made up ③ a person's character

**maladjusted** ADJECTIVE
unable to fit in or cope with other people or your own circumstances

**malady** NOUN maladies
an illness or disease

**malapropism** NOUN malapropisms
a comical confusion of words, e.g. using *hooligan* instead of *hurricane*
WORD ORIGIN named after Mrs *Malaprop* in Sheridan's play *The Rivals*, who made mistakes of this kind

**malaria** NOUN
a feverish disease spread by mosquitoes
➤ **malarial** ADJECTIVE
WORD ORIGIN from Italian *mala aria* = bad air, which was once thought to cause the disease

**male** ADJECTIVE
of the sex that reproduces by fertilizing egg cells produced by the female

**male** NOUN males
a male person, animal or plant

**male chauvinist** NOUN male chauvinists
a man who thinks that women are not as
good as men

**malefactor** (say **mal**-if-ak-ter) NOUN
malefactors
a criminal or wrongdoer

**malevolent** (say ma-**lev**-ol-ent) ADJECTIVE
showing a desire to harm other people
➤ **malevolently** ADVERB
➤ **malevolence** NOUN

**malformed** ADJECTIVE
faultily formed

**malfunction** NOUN malfunctions
faulty functioning • *a computer malfunction*

**malfunction** VERB malfunctions,
malfunctioning, malfunctioned
to fail to work properly

**malice** NOUN
a desire to harm other people; spite • *His eyes
glinted with malice.*

**malicious** ADJECTIVE
intending to do harm • *malicious gossip*
➤ **maliciously** ADVERB

**malign** (say mal-**y**'n) ADJECTIVE
❶ harmful and sinister • *a malign influence*
❷ showing malice
➤ **malignity** (say mal-**ig**-nit-ee) NOUN

**malign** VERB maligns, maligning, maligned
to say unpleasant and untrue things about
someone

**malignant** ADJECTIVE
❶ a malignant tumour is one that is growing
uncontrollably ❷ full of malice
➤ **malignantly** ADVERB
➤ **malignancy** NOUN

**malinger** VERB malingers, malingering,
malingered
to pretend to be ill in order to avoid work
➤ **malingerer** NOUN

**mall** (say mal or mawl) NOUN malls
a large covered shopping centre

**mallard** NOUN mallard or mallards
a kind of wild duck of North America, Europe
and parts of Asia

**malleable** ADJECTIVE
❶ able to be pressed or hammered into shape
❷ easy to influence
➤ **malleability** NOUN

**mallet** NOUN mallets
❶ a large hammer, usually made of wood
❷ an implement with a long handle, used in
croquet or polo for striking the ball

**malnutrition** NOUN
bad health because you do not have enough
food or the right kind of food
➤ **malnourished** ADJECTIVE

**malt** NOUN
dried barley used in brewing, making vinegar,
etc.
➤ **malted** ADJECTIVE

**maltreat** VERB maltreats, maltreating,
maltreated
to ill-treat a person or animal
➤ **maltreatment** NOUN

**mama, mamma** NOUN (old use)
mother

**mammal** NOUN mammals
any animal of which the female gives birth to
live babies which are fed with milk from her
own body
➤ **mammalian** (say mam-**ay**-lee-an) ADJECTIVE

**mammoth** NOUN mammoths
an extinct elephant with a hairy skin and
curved tusks

**mammoth** ADJECTIVE
huge • *a mammoth effort*

**man** NOUN men
❶ a grown-up male human being ❷ an
individual person ❸ people in general;
mankind • *Early man lived by hunting.* ❹ a
piece used in chess or some other board game

**man** VERB mans, manning, manned
to provide a place or machine with the people
to run or work it • *Man the pumps!*

**manacle** NOUN manacles
a fetter or handcuff

**manacle** VERB manacles, manacling,
manacled
to put manacles on someone

**manage** VERB manages, managing, managed
❶ to succeed in doing or dealing with
something difficult • *She finally managed
to open the door.* ❷ to be in charge of a
business or part of it or a group of people

**manageable** ADJECTIVE
not too big or too difficult to deal with

**management** NOUN
❶ managing something ❷ managers; the
people in charge of a business

a b c d e f g h i j k l m n o p q r s t u v w x y z

**manager** NOUN managers
a person who manages something
➤ **managerial** (say man-a-**jeer**-ee-al)
ADJECTIVE

**manageress** NOUN manageresses
(British) a woman manager, especially of a
shop or hotel

**mandarin** NOUN mandarins
❶ an important official ❷ a kind of small
orange

**mandate** NOUN mandates
authority given to someone to carry
out a certain task or policy • An elected
government has a mandate to govern the
country.

**mandatory** ADJECTIVE
obligatory or compulsory

**mandible** NOUN mandibles
❶ a jaw, especially the lower one ❷ either
part of a bird's beak or the similar part in
insects etc. Compare with maxilla.

**mandolin** NOUN mandolins
a musical instrument rather like a guitar

**mane** NOUN manes
the long hair on a horse's or lion's neck

**manfully** ADVERB
using a lot of effort in a brave or determined
way

**manganese** NOUN
a hard brittle metal

**mange** NOUN
a skin disease of dogs etc.

**manger** NOUN mangers
a trough in a stable for horses or cattle to
feed from

**mangle** VERB mangles, mangling, mangled
to damage something by crushing or cutting
it roughly • The motorway was covered with
the mangled wreckage of cars.

**mango** NOUN mangoes
a tropical fruit with yellow pulp

**mangrove** NOUN mangroves
a tropical tree growing in mud and swamps,
with many tangled roots above the ground

**mangy** ADJECTIVE
❶ having mange ❷ scruffy or dirty

**manhandle** VERB manhandles, manhandling,
manhandled
to handle or push a person or thing roughly

• Two burly men manhandled him out of the
door.

**manhole** NOUN manholes
a space or opening, usually with a cover, by
which a person can get into a sewer or boiler
etc. to inspect or repair it

**manhood** NOUN
❶ the condition of being a man • When he
reached manhood he moved away from the
village. ❷ manly qualities

**mania** NOUN manias
❶ violent madness ❷ a great enthusiasm for
something • a mania for fast cars

**maniac** NOUN maniacs
a person who acts in a wild or violent way

**manic** ADJECTIVE
❶ to do with or suffering from mania
❷ (informal) full of excited activity or
nervous energy • Things are a bit manic here
at the moment.

**manicure** NOUN manicures
care and treatment of the hands and nails
➤ **manicured** ADJECTIVE
➤ **manicurist** NOUN

**manifest** ADJECTIVE
clear and obvious
➤ **manifestly** ADVERB

**manifest** VERB manifests, manifesting,
manifested
to manifest a feeling or sign is to show it
clearly

**manifestation** NOUN manifestations
a sign that something is happening

**manifesto** NOUN manifestos
a public statement of a group's or person's
policy or principles

**manifold** ADJECTIVE
of many kinds; very varied

**manipulate** VERB manipulates, manipulating,
manipulated
❶ to handle or arrange something skilfully
• He began to manipulate the controls and
levers. ❷ to get someone to do what you
want by treating them cleverly • She uses her
charm to manipulate people.
➤ **manipulation** NOUN
➤ **manipulator** NOUN

**mankind** NOUN
human beings in general

**manly** ADJECTIVE
❶ suitable for a man ❷ brave and strong
➤ **manliness** NOUN

**manner** NOUN
❶ the way something happens or is done ❷ a person's way of behaving
➤ **all manner of** many different kinds of
• *They asked me all manner of strange questions.*

**mannerism** NOUN mannerisms
a person's own particular gesture or way of speaking

**manners** PLURAL NOUN
how a person behaves with other people; politeness

**mannish** ADJECTIVE
a woman is mannish when she is like a man

**manoeuvre** (say man-oo-ver) NOUN manoeuvres
a difficult or skilful or cunning action
• *Parking the car in that small space was a tricky manoeuvre.*

**manoeuvre** VERB manoeuvres, manoeuvring, manoeuvred
❶ to move something skilfully into position
• *She manoeuvred the boat through the gap in the rocks.* ❷ to move carefully and skilfully
➤ **manoeuvrable** ADJECTIVE

**man-of-war** NOUN men-of-war
a warship

**manor** NOUN manors (British)
❶ a manor house ❷ the land belonging to a manor house

**manor house** NOUN manor houses
(British) a large important house in the country

**manpower** NOUN
the number of people who are working or needed or available for work on something

**manse** NOUN manses
a church minister's house, especially in Scotland

**mansion** NOUN mansions
a large stately house

**manslaughter** NOUN
the crime of killing a person unlawfully but without meaning to

**mantelpiece** NOUN mantelpieces
a shelf above a fireplace

**mantilla** NOUN mantillas
a lace veil worn by Spanish women over the hair and shoulders

**mantle** NOUN mantles
❶ a cloak ❷ a covering • *There was a mantle of snow on the hills.*

**mantra** NOUN mantras
a word or phrase that is constantly repeated to help people meditate, originally in Hinduism and Buddhism

**manual** ADJECTIVE
worked by or done with the hands • *a manual typewriter* • *manual work*
➤ **manually** ADVERB

**manual** NOUN manuals
a handbook or book of instructions

**manufacture** VERB manufactures, manufacturing, manufactured
to make things in large quantities using machines

**manufacture** NOUN
the process of making things in large quantities using machines

**manufacturer** NOUN manufacturers
a business that manufactures things

**manure** NOUN
animal dung added to the soil as fertilizer

**manuscript** NOUN manuscripts
something written or typed but not printed
(WORD ORIGIN) from Latin *manu* = by hand ı *scriptum* = written

**Manx** ADJECTIVE
to do with the Isle of Man

**many** DETERMINER more, most
❶ great in number; numerous • *Many people are afraid of spiders.* ❷ used to talk about the size of a number • *How many tickets do you want?*

**many** PRONOUN
a large number of people or things • *Many were found.*

**Maori** (rhymes with flowery) NOUN Maoris
❶ a member of the people who were living in New Zealand before European settlers arrived ❷ their language

**map** NOUN maps
a diagram of part or all of the earth's surface or of the sky

**map** VERB maps, mapping, mapped
to make a map of an area

a
b
c
d
e
f
g
h
i
j
k
l
m
n
o
p
q
r
s
t
u
v
w
x
y
z

> **map something out** to plan the details of something

**maple** NOUN maples
a tree with broad leaves

**maple syrup** NOUN
a sweet substance made from the sap of some kinds of maple

**mar** VERB mars, marring, marred
to spoil something • *The game was marred by crowd trouble.*

**marathon** NOUN marathons
a long-distance running race, especially one covering 26 miles 385 yards (42.195 km) (WORD ORIGIN) named after *Marathon* in Greece, from which a messenger is said to have run to Athens (about 40 kilometres) to announce that the Greeks had defeated the Persian army

**marauding** ADJECTIVE
a marauding army or pack of animals goes about attacking people or stealing things
> **marauder** NOUN

**marble** NOUN marbles
❶ a small glass ball used in games ❷ a kind of limestone polished and used in sculpture or building

**March** NOUN
the third month of the year
(WORD ORIGIN) named after *Mars*, the Roman god of war

**march** VERB marches, marching, marched
❶ to walk with regular steps ❷ to make someone walk somewhere • *He marched them up the hill.*
> **marcher** NOUN

**march** NOUN marches
❶ a large group of people marching, sometimes to protest about something ❷ a journey by marching ❸ music suitable for marching to

**marchioness** NOUN marchionesses
the wife or widow of a marquis

**mare** NOUN mares
a female horse or donkey

**margarine** (say mar-ja-**reen**) NOUN
a substance used like butter, made from animal or vegetable fats

**marge** NOUN (*British*) (*informal*)
margarine

**margin** NOUN margins
❶ an edge or border ❷ the blank space between the edge of a page and the writing or pictures on it ❸ the difference between two scores or prices etc. • *She won by a narrow margin.*

**marginal** ADJECTIVE
❶ very slight • *a marginal difference* ❷ in a margin • *marginal notes*

**marginally** ADVERB
very slightly; by a small amount • *I did marginally better this time.*

**marginal seat** NOUN marginal seats
a constituency where an MP was elected with only a small majority and may be defeated in the next election

**marigold** NOUN marigolds
a yellow or orange garden flower

**marijuana** (say ma-ri-**hwah**-na) NOUN
a drug made from hemp

**marina** NOUN marinas
a harbour for yachts, motor boats, etc.

**marinade** NOUN marinades
a flavoured liquid in which meat or fish is soaked before being cooked

**marinate** VERB marinates, marinating, marinated
to soak meat or fish in a marinade

**marine** (say ma-**reen**) ADJECTIVE
to do with the sea; living in the sea • *marine life*

**marine** NOUN marines
a member of the troops who are trained to serve at sea as well as on land

**mariner** (say **ma**-rin-er) NOUN mariners
a sailor

**marionette** NOUN marionettes
a puppet that you work by strings or wires
(WORD ORIGIN) French, = little Mary

**marital** ADJECTIVE
to do with marriage

**maritime** ADJECTIVE
❶ to do with the sea or ships ❷ found near the sea

**marjoram** NOUN
a herb with a mild flavour, used in cooking

**mark** NOUN marks
❶ a spot, dot, line or stain on something ❷ a number or letter put on a piece of work to show how good it is ❸ a distinguishing feature ❹ a sign or symbol • *They all stood as a mark of respect.* ❺ a target ❻ a unit

of money used in Germany before the
introduction of the euro
➤ **on your marks!** a command to runners to
get ready to begin a race
➤ **be up to the mark** to reach the normal or
expected standard

**mark** VERB marks, marking, marked
❶ to put a mark on something ❷ to give a
mark to a piece of work ❸ to keep close to
an opposing player in football etc. ❹ to pay
attention to something • *Mark my words!*
➤ **mark time** ❶ to march on the spot
without moving forward ❷ to occupy your
time without making any progress

**marked** ADJECTIVE
clear or noticeable • *a marked improvement*
➤ **markedly** ADVERB

**marker** NOUN markers
a thing that shows the position of something
• *a boundary marker*

**market** NOUN markets
❶ a place where things are bought and
sold, usually from stalls in the open air ❷ a
demand for goods • *There is hardly any
market for typewriters now.*
➤ **on the market** offered for sale

**market** VERB markets, marketing, marketed
to offer things for sale

**marketing** NOUN
the branch of business concerned with
advertising and selling the product

**marketplace** NOUN marketplaces
the place in a town where a market is held or
used to be held

**market research** NOUN
the study of what people need or want to buy

**marksman, markswoman** NOUN marksmen
or markswomen
an expert in shooting at a target
➤ **marksmanship** NOUN

**marmalade** NOUN
jam made from oranges, lemons or other
citrus fruit

**marmoset** NOUN marmosets
a kind of small monkey

**maroon** VERB maroons, marooning, marooned
to abandon someone in a deserted place
that they cannot leave • *The sailors were
marooned on a little island.*

**maroon** NOUN
dark red

**marquee** (say mar-kee) NOUN marquees
a large tent used for a party or exhibition

**marquis** NOUN marquises
a nobleman ranking next above an earl

**marriage** NOUN marriages
❶ the legal relationship between a husband
and wife or a similar legal relationship
between any couple ❷ a wedding

**marrow** NOUN marrows
❶ a large gourd eaten as a vegetable ❷ the
soft substance inside bones

**marry** VERB marries, marrying, married
❶ to marry someone is to be legally joined in
marriage with them ❷ to marry two people is
to perform a marriage ceremony
➤ **married** ADJECTIVE

**marsh** NOUN marshes
a low-lying area of very wet ground
➤ **marshy** ADJECTIVE

**marshal** NOUN marshals
❶ an official who helps to organize or control
a large public event ❷ an army officer of very
high rank • *a Field Marshal* ❸ a police official
in the USA

**marshal** VERB marshals, marshalling,
marshalled
❶ to gather things together and arrange
them neatly • *He spent some time
marshalling his thoughts.* ❷ to control or
organize a large group of people

**marshmallow** NOUN marshmallows
a soft spongy sweet, usually pink or white

**marsupial** (say mar-soo-pee-al) NOUN
marsupials
an animal such as a kangaroo, wallaby or
koala. The female has a pouch on the front of
its body in which its babies are carried.

**martial** ADJECTIVE
to do with war; warlike **WORD ORIGIN** Latin, =
belonging to Mars, the Roman god of war

**martial arts** PLURAL NOUN
fighting sports, such as judo and karate

**martial law** NOUN
government of a country by the armed forces
during a crisis

**martin** NOUN martins
a bird rather like a swallow
**WORD ORIGIN** probably after St *Martin* of
Tours, who gave half his cloak to a beggar
(because of the bird's markings, which look like
a torn cloak)

**martinet** *NOUN* martinets
a very strict person **(WORD ORIGIN)** named after a French army officer, J. *Martinet*, who imposed harsh discipline on his troops

**martyr** *NOUN* martyrs
a person who is killed or made to suffer because of their beliefs, especially religious beliefs
➤ **martyrdom** *NOUN*

**martyr** *VERB* martyrs, martyring, martyred
to kill someone or make them suffer as a martyr

**marvel** *NOUN* marvels
a wonderful thing

**marvel** *VERB* marvels, marvelling, marvelled
to be filled with wonder or astonishment by something • *The whole town marvelled at her bravery.*

**marvellous** *ADJECTIVE*
extremely good; wonderful
➤ **marvellously** *ADVERB*

**Marxism** *NOUN*
the Communist theories of the German writer Karl Marx (1818-83)
➤ **Marxist** *NOUN & ADJECTIVE*

**marzipan** *NOUN*
a soft sweet food made of ground almonds, eggs and sugar

**mascara** *NOUN*
a cosmetic for darkening the eyelashes

**mascot** *NOUN* mascots
a person, animal or object that is believed to bring good luck

**masculine** *ADJECTIVE*
❶ to do with or like men; thought to be suitable for a man ❷ belonging to the class of words (in some languages) which includes the words referring to men
➤ **masculinity** *NOUN*

**mash** *VERB* mashes, mashing, mashed
to crush something into a soft mass

**mash** *NOUN* mashes
❶ a soft mixture of cooked grain or bran etc. ❷ (*informal*) mashed potatoes

**mask** *NOUN* masks
a covering that you wear over your face to disguise or protect it

**mask** *VERB* masks, masking, masked
❶ to cover your face with a mask ❷ to disguise or conceal something • *She masked her anger with a smile.*

**mason** *NOUN* masons
a person who builds or works with stone

**masonry** *NOUN*
❶ the parts of a building that are made of stone • *He was injured by falling masonry.* ❷ a mason's work

**masquerade** *NOUN* masquerades
a pretence

**masquerade** *VERB* masquerades, masquerading, masqueraded
to pretend to be something • *He masqueraded as a police officer.*

**Mass** *NOUN* Masses
the Communion service in a Roman Catholic church

**mass** *NOUN* masses
❶ a large amount of something • *They had gathered a mass of evidence.* ❷ a heap or other collection of matter • *A huge mass of snow and rocks blocked the path.* ❸ (*in science*) the quantity of physical matter that a thing contains
➤ **the masses** the ordinary people

**mass** *ADJECTIVE*
involving a large number of people • *mass murder*

**mass** *VERB* masses, massing, massed
to collect into a mass • *People were massing in the square.*

**massacre** *NOUN* massacres
the deliberate and brutal killing of a large number of people

**massacre** *VERB* massacres, massacring, massacred
to kill a large number of people deliberately

**massage** (say **mas**-ahzh) *VERB* massages, massaging, massaged
to rub and press the body to make it less stiff or less painful

**massage** *NOUN* massages
massaging someone's body

**massive** *ADJECTIVE*
large and heavy; huge
➤ **massively** *ADVERB*

**mass media** *PLURAL NOUN*
the main media of news information, especially newspapers and broadcasting

**mass production** *NOUN*
manufacturing goods in large quantities
➤ **mass-produced** *ADJECTIVE*

**mast** *NOUN* masts
a tall pole that holds up a ship's sails or a flag or an aerial

**master** *NOUN* masters
❶ a man who is in charge of something ❷ a person who is extremely skilled at doing something, such as a great artist or composer ❸ (*old use*) a male teacher ❹ something from which copies are made ❺ (*old use*) a title put before a boy's name

**master** *VERB* masters, mastering, mastered
❶ to master a subject or a skill is to learn it thoroughly ❷ to master a fear or difficulty is to control it • *She succeeded in mastering her fear of heights.* ❸ to overcome someone

**masterful** *ADJECTIVE*
having control; domineering
➤ **masterfully** *ADVERB*

**master key** *NOUN* master keys
a key that will open several different locks

**masterly** *ADJECTIVE*
very skilful • *a masterly performance*

**mastermind** *NOUN* masterminds
❶ a very clever person ❷ the person who plans and organizes a scheme or crime

**mastermind** *VERB* masterminds, masterminding, masterminded
to plan and organize a scheme or crime

**Master of Arts** *NOUN* Masters of Arts
a person who has taken the next degree after Bachelor of Arts

**master of ceremonies** *NOUN* masters of ceremonies
a person who introduces the speakers at a formal event or the entertainers at a variety show

**Master of Science** *NOUN* Masters of Science
a person who has taken the next degree after Bachelor of Science

**masterpiece** *NOUN* masterpieces
❶ an excellent piece of work ❷ a person's best piece of work

**mastery** *NOUN*
complete control or thorough knowledge or skill in something • *The battle was fought for mastery of the seas.*

**masticate** *VERB* masticates, masticating, masticated (*formal*)
to chew food
➤ **mastication** *NOUN*

**mastiff** *NOUN* mastiffs
a large kind of dog

**masturbate** *VERB* masturbates, masturbating, masturbated
to get sexual pleasure by touching the genitals
➤ **masturbation** *NOUN*

**mat** *NOUN* mats
❶ a small carpet ❷ a doormat ❸ a small piece of material put on a table to protect the surface

**matador** *NOUN* matadors
a bullfighter who fights on foot

**match** *NOUN* matches
❶ a small thin stick with a head made of a substance that gives a flame when rubbed on something rough ❷ a game or contest between two teams or players ❸ one person or thing that is equal to or similar to another • *Can you find a match for this sock?* ❹ a marriage

**match** *VERB* matches, matching, matched
❶ to be equal or similar to another person or thing • *This book doesn't match the standard of her earlier ones.* ❷ to go well with something so that they look good together • *That shirt matches your jacket.* ❸ to find something that is similar or corresponding ❹ to put teams or players together to compete against each other

**matchbox** *NOUN* matchboxes
a small box for matches

**matchstick** *NOUN* matchsticks
the thin wooden part of a match

**mate** *NOUN* mates
❶ a friend or companion ❷ each of a pair of birds or animals that produce young together ❸ an officer on a merchant ship ❹ checkmate in chess

**mate** *VERB* mates, mating, mated
❶ a pair of animals or birds mate when they come together in order to breed ❷ to mate a pair of animals is to bring them together in order to breed

**material** *NOUN* materials
❶ anything used for making something else ❷ cloth or fabric

**material** *ADJECTIVE*
❶ to do with possessions, money, etc. • *material comforts* ❷ important or relevant • *The changes made little material difference.*

**materialism** *NOUN*
the belief that possessions are very important

a
b
c
d
e
f
g
h
i
j
k
l
m
n
o
p
q
r
s
t
u
v
w
x
y
z

➤ **materialist** NOUN
➤ **materialistic** ADJECTIVE

**materialize** (also **materialise**) VERB
materializes, materializing, materialized
❶ to become visible; to appear • *The ghost didn't materialize.* ❷ to become a fact; to happen • *The trip he had been promised failed to materialize.*

**maternal** ADJECTIVE
❶ to do with a mother ❷ motherly

**maternity** NOUN
motherhood

**maternity** ADJECTIVE
to do with having a baby • *maternity ward*

**matey** ADJECTIVE
(British) (informal) friendly and sociable

**mathematical** ADJECTIVE
to do with or using mathematics
• *mathematical calculations*
➤ **mathematically** ADVERB

**mathematician** (say math-em-a-**tish**-an)
NOUN mathematicians
an expert in mathematics

**mathematics** NOUN
the study of numbers, measurements and shapes

**maths** NOUN (British) (informal)
mathematics

**matinee** NOUN matinees
an afternoon performance at a theatre or cinema **WORD ORIGIN** French *matinée*, literally = morning, because the performances used to be in the morning as well as the afternoon

**matins** NOUN
the church service of morning prayer

**matriarch** (say **may**-tree-ark) NOUN
matriarchs
a woman who is head of a family or tribe. Compare with **patriarch**.
➤ **matriarchal** ADJECTIVE

**matrimony** NOUN
marriage
➤ **matrimonial** ADJECTIVE

**matrix** (say **may**-triks) NOUN matrices, (say **may**-tri-seez)
❶ (in *mathematics*) a set of quantities arranged in rows and columns ❷ a mould or framework in which something is made or allowed to develop

**matron** NOUN matrons
❶ an older married woman ❷ a woman in charge of nursing in a school etc. or (formerly) of the nursing staff in a hospital
➤ **matronly** ADJECTIVE

**matt** ADJECTIVE
not shiny • *matt paint*

**matted** ADJECTIVE
matted hair or fur is tangled into a mass

**matter** NOUN matters
❶ something you can touch or see, not the spirit or mind or qualities etc. ❷ a substance • *Peat consists mainly of vegetable matter.* ❸ things of a certain kind • *printed matter* ❹ something you can think about or do • *It's a serious matter.* ❺ a quantity • *in a matter of minutes*
➤ **as a matter of course** as the natural or expected thing • *I always lock my bike up, as a matter of course*
➤ **as a matter of fact** in fact
➤ **no matter** it is not important
➤ **what is the matter?** what is wrong?

**matter** VERB matters, mattering, mattered
to be important • *Nobody's hurt and that's all that matters.*

**matter-of-fact** ADJECTIVE
keeping to facts; not imaginative or emotional • *She talked about death in a very matter-of-fact way.*

**matting** NOUN
rough material for covering floors

**mattress** NOUN mattresses
soft or springy material in a fabric covering, used on or as a bed

**mature** ADJECTIVE
❶ fully grown or developed ❷ behaving in a sensible adult manner
➤ **maturely** ADVERB

**mature** VERB matures, maturing, matured
to become fully grown or developed • *It takes a few years for the wine to mature.*

**maturity** NOUN
❶ being fully grown or developed • *The forest will take 100 years to reach maturity.* ❷ behaving in a sensible adult manner

**maudlin** ADJECTIVE
sentimental in a silly or tearful way
**WORD ORIGIN** from an old pronunciation of St Mary Magdalen (because pictures usually show her weeping)

**maul** VERB mauls, mauling, mauled
to injure someone by violent handling or clawing • *He was mauled by a lion.*

**mausoleum** (say maw-sol-**ee**-um) NOUN mausoleums
a magnificent tomb WORD ORIGIN named after the tomb of *Mausolus*, a king in the 4th century BC in what is now Turkey

**mauve** (say mohv) NOUN
pale purple

**maverick** NOUN mavericks
a person who belongs to a group but often disagrees with its beliefs or acts on his or her own WORD ORIGIN originally = an unbranded calf: named after an American rancher, S. A. *Maverick*, who did not brand his cattle

**maw** NOUN maws
the jaws, mouth or stomach of a hungry or fierce animal

**maxilla** NOUN maxillae, (say mak-si-lee)
the upper jaw; a similar part in a bird or insect etc. Compare with **mandible**.

**maxim** NOUN maxims
a short saying giving a general truth or rule of behaviour, e.g. 'Waste not, want not'

**maximize** (also **maximise**) VERB maximizes, maximizing, maximized
to make something as great, large or effective as possible

**maximum** NOUN maxima or maximums
the greatest possible number or amount. (The opposite is **minimum**.) • *The bus can carry a maximum of 40 people.*

**maximum** ADJECTIVE
the greatest possible • *The maximum speed is 50 km per hour.*

**May** NOUN
the fifth month of the year
WORD ORIGIN named after *Maia*, a Roman goddess

**may** AUXILIARY VERB may, might
used to express
❶ permission (*You may go now*) ❷ possibility (*It may be true*) ❸ wish (*Long may she reign*)
❹ uncertainty (*whoever it may be*)

**maybe** ADVERB
perhaps; possibly

**Mayday** NOUN Maydays
an international radio signal calling for help
WORD ORIGIN from French *m'aider* = help me

**mayfly** NOUN mayflies
an insect that lives for only a short time, in spring

**mayhem** NOUN
violent confusion or damage • *The mob caused mayhem.*

**mayonnaise** NOUN
a creamy sauce made from eggs, oil, vinegar, etc., eaten with salad

**mayor** NOUN mayors
the person in charge of the council in a town or city
➤ **mayoress** NOUN

**maypole** NOUN maypoles
a decorated pole round which people dance on 1 May

**maze** NOUN mazes
a network of paths, especially one designed as a puzzle in which to try and find your way

**Mb** ABBREVIATION
megabyte(s)

**MC** ABBREVIATION
master of ceremonies

**MD** ABBREVIATION
Doctor of Medicine

**ME** NOUN
(*British*) long-lasting fever, weakness and pain in the muscles following a viral infection
WORD ORIGIN abbreviation of the scientific name, *myalgic encephalomyelitis*

**me** PRONOUN
the form of I used as the object of a verb or after a preposition

**mead** NOUN
an alcoholic drink made from honey and water

**meadow** (say med-oh) NOUN meadows
a field of grass

**meagre** ADJECTIVE
scanty in amount; barely enough • *a meagre diet of bread and water*

**meal** NOUN meals
❶ food served and eaten at one sitting
❷ coarsely-ground grain

**mealie** NOUN mealies
(*S. African*) a maize plant or cob

**mealtime** NOUN mealtimes
a regular time for having a meal

A

**mealy-mouthed** ADJECTIVE
too polite or timid to say what you really
mean

B

C

**mean** VERB means, meaning, meant (say ment)
❶ to have something as an equivalent or
explanation; to have a certain meaning • *I'm
not sure what this word means.* ❷ to intend
to do something • *I meant to tell you, but
I forgot.* ❸ to be serious • *Don't open that
door – I mean it!* ❹ to show that something
is likely • *Dark clouds mean rain.* ❺ to have
something as a result • *It means I'll have to
get the early train.*

D

E

F

G

**mean** ADJECTIVE meaner, meanest
❶ not generous; miserly ❷ unkind or spiteful
• *That was a mean trick.* ❸ poor in quality or
appearance • *They lived in a mean little hovel.*
➤ **meanly** ADVERB
➤ **meanness** NOUN

H

I

**mean** NOUN means
a point or number midway between two
extremes; the average of a set of numbers

J

K

**mean** ADJECTIVE
midway between two points; average • *We
worked out the mean temperature.*

L

**meander** (say mee-**an**-der) VERB meanders,
meandering, meandered
❶ a river or road that meanders has a lot
of bends in it ❷ to walk or travel slowly or
without any definite direction
➤ **meander** NOUN
(WORD ORIGIN) named after the *Meander,* a
river in Turkey (now Mendere or Menderes)

M

N

O

P

**meaning** NOUN meanings
what something means

Q

**meaningful** ADJECTIVE
expressing an important meaning • *He gave
her a meaningful look.*

R

S

**meaningless** ADJECTIVE
with no meaning or purpose • *a meaningless
phrase*

T

**means** NOUN
a way of achieving something or producing a
result • *a means of transport*
➤ **by all means** certainly; of course
➤ **by means of** by this method; using this
➤ **by no means** not at all

U

V

W

X

**means** PLURAL NOUN
money or other wealth
➤ **live beyond your means** to spend more
than you can afford

Y

Z

**meantime** NOUN
➤ **in the meantime** in the time between two
events or while something else is happening

**meanwhile** ADVERB
in the time between two events or while
something else is happening

**measles** NOUN
an infectious disease that causes small red
spots on the skin

**measly** ADJECTIVE (*informal*)
not adequate or generous • *I only got a
measly three points.*

**measure** VERB measures, measuring,
measured
❶ to find the size, amount or extent of
something by comparing it with a fixed unit
or with an object of known size ❷ to be a
certain size • *The room measures 4 metres
by 5.*

**measure** NOUN measures
❶ a unit used for measuring • *A kilometre
is a measure of length.* ❷ a device used
in measuring ❸ the size or quantity of
something ❹ something done for a particular
purpose • *We took measures to stop
vandalism.*

**measurement** NOUN measurements
❶ the process of measuring something ❷ a
size or amount found by measuring • *She
took some measurements with a ruler.*

**meat** NOUN
animal flesh used as food
➤ **meaty** ADJECTIVE

**mecca** NOUN
a place which attracts people with a
particular interest • *Wimbledon is a mecca
for tennis fans.* (WORD ORIGIN) from *Mecca* in
Saudi Arabia, a holy city and place of pilgrimage
for Muslims

**mechanic** NOUN mechanics
a person who maintains or repairs machinery

**mechanical** ADJECTIVE
❶ to do with machines ❷ produced or
worked by machines ❸ done or doing
something without thinking about it

**mechanically** ADVERB
without thinking about it • *'That's good,' she
replied mechanically.*

**mechanics** NOUN
❶ the study of movement and force ❷ the
study or use of machines

**mechanism** *NOUN* mechanisms
❶ the moving parts of a machine ❷ the way a machine works ❸ the process by which something is done

**mechanized** (also **mechanised**) *ADJECTIVE*
equipped with machines
➤ **mechanization** *NOUN*

**medal** *NOUN* medals
a piece of metal shaped like a coin, star or cross, given to a person for bravery or for achieving something • *She won two Olympic gold medals.*

**medallion** *NOUN* medallions
a large medal, usually worn round the neck as an ornament

**medallist** *NOUN* medallists
a winner of a medal

**meddle** *VERB* meddles, meddling, meddled
❶ to interfere in something without being asked ❷ to tinker with something • *Don't meddle with it.*
➤ **meddlesome** *ADJECTIVE*

**media**
plural of medium noun
➤ **the media** newspapers, radio and television, which convey information and ideas to the public. (see medium)

**median** *ADJECTIVE*
in the middle

**median** *NOUN* medians
❶ a median point or line ❷ (*in mathematics*) the middle number in a set of numbers that have been arranged in order. The median of 2, 3, 5, 8, 9, 14 and 15 is 8 ❸ a straight line passing from a point of a triangle to the centre of the opposite side

**mediate** *VERB* mediates, mediating, mediated
to negotiate between the opposing sides in a dispute
➤ **mediation** *NOUN*
➤ **mediator** *NOUN*

**medical** *ADJECTIVE*
to do with the treatment of disease
➤ **medically** *ADVERB*

**medicated** *ADJECTIVE*
treated with a medicinal substance
• *medicated shampoo*

**medication** *NOUN*
❶ a medicine ❷ treatment using medicine

**medicinal** (say med-**iss**-in-al) *ADJECTIVE*
helping to cure an illness • *medicinal plants*
➤ **medicinally** *ADVERB*

**medicine** *NOUN* medicines
❶ a substance, usually swallowed, used to try to cure a disease ❷ the study and treatment of diseases

**medieval** (say med-ee-**ee**-val) *ADJECTIVE*
belonging to or to do with the Middle Ages

SPELLING
There is a tricky bit in **medieval** – it is spelt al at the end and not il.

**mediocre** (say mee-dee-**oh**-ker) *ADJECTIVE*
not very good; of only medium quality
➤ **mediocrity** *NOUN*

**meditate** *VERB* meditates, meditating, meditated
❶ to think deeply or seriously about something ❷ to think deeply in silence for religious reasons or to make your mind calm
➤ **meditation** *NOUN*
➤ **meditative** *ADJECTIVE*

**Mediterranean** *ADJECTIVE*
to do with the Mediterranean Sea (which lies between Europe and Africa) or the countries round it WORD ORIGIN from Latin *Mare Mediterraneum* = sea in the middle of land, from *medius* = middle + *terra* = land

**medium** *ADJECTIVE*
neither large nor small; average

**medium** *NOUN*
❶ media a thing in which something exists, moves or is expressed • *Air is the medium in which sound travels.* • *Television is used as a medium for advertising.*
(see media) ❷ mediums a person who claims to be able to communicate with the dead

**medium wave** *NOUN*
(*chiefly British*) a radio wave of a frequency between 300 kilohertz and 3 megahertz

**medley** *NOUN* medleys
❶ an assortment or mixture of things • *a medley of flavours* ❷ a collection of songs or tunes played as a continuous piece

**meek** *ADJECTIVE* meeker, meekest
quiet and obedient
➤ **meekly** *ADVERB*
➤ **meekness** *NOUN*

**meet** *VERB* meets, meeting, met
❶ to come together from different places • *We all met in London.* ❷ to see someone for the first time and get to know them • *I*

met her at a party. ❸ to go to a place and wait there for someone to arrive • *I'll meet you off the train.* ❹ to touch, join or come into contact • *They came to a spot where two rivers met.* ❺ to meet the cost of something is to pay it ❻ to satisfy or fulfil something • *I hope this meets your needs.*

➤ **meet with something** to get a particular reaction or result • *My suggestion was met with howls of protest.*

**meet** NOUN meets
a gathering of riders and hounds for a hunt

**meeting** NOUN meetings
❶ a time when a number of people come together in order to discuss or decide something ❷ coming together

**megabyte** NOUN megabytes
(*in computing*) a unit of information roughly equal to one million bytes

**megalomaniac** NOUN megalomaniacs
a person who has an exaggerated idea of their own importance
➤ **megalomania** NOUN

**megaphone** NOUN megaphones
a funnel-shaped device for amplifying a person's voice

**melancholy** ADJECTIVE
sad and gloomy

**melancholy** NOUN
sadness or depression • *There was an air of melancholy about her.*

**melee** (say **mel**-ay) NOUN melees
a situation in which a lot of people are rushing or pushing each other in a confused way

**mellow** ADJECTIVE mellower, mellowest
❶ not harsh; soft and rich in flavour, colour or sound ❷ having become kinder and more sympathetic with age

**mellow** VERB mellows, mellowing, mellowed
❶ to make something softer or less harsh or to become this ❷ a person mellows when they become kinder and more sympathetic with age

**melodic** ADJECTIVE
to do with melody; pleasant to listen to

**melodious** ADJECTIVE
like a melody; pleasant to listen to • *a melodious voice*

**melodrama** NOUN melodramas
a play full of dramatic excitement and strong emotion

**melodramatic** ADJECTIVE
behaving in an exaggerated way that is full of emotion • *Don't be so melodramatic – of course you're not going to die!*

**melody** NOUN melodies
a tune, especially one that is pleasant to listen to

**melon** NOUN melons
a large sweet fruit with a yellow or green skin

**melt** VERB melts, melting, melted
❶ to make something liquid by heating it • *Melt the butter in a saucepan.* ❷ to become liquid by heating • *The snow has melted.* ❸ to disappear slowly • *The crowd just melted away.* ❹ to become softer • *Her heart melted at these words.*

**melting pot** NOUN melting pots
a place where people of many different races and cultures live and influence each other

**member** NOUN members
❶ a person or thing that belongs to a particular society or group ❷ a part of something

**Member of Parliament** NOUN Members of Parliament
a person elected to represent the people of an area in Parliament

**membership** NOUN
being a member of a particular society or group • *Visit our website to apply for membership.*

**membrane** NOUN membranes
a thin skin or similar covering

**memento** NOUN mementoes
a souvenir

**memo** (say **mem**-oh) NOUN memos
a note from one person to another in the same firm

**memoir** (say **mem**-wahr) NOUN memoirs
a biography, especially one written by someone who knew the person

**memoirs** PLURAL NOUN
an autobiography

**memorable** ADJECTIVE
❶ worth remembering • *It was a memorable holiday.* ❷ easy to remember • *He has a memorable name.*
➤ **memorably** ADVERB

**memorandum** NOUN memoranda or memorandums
(*formal*) a memo

**memorial** NOUN memorials
something set up to remind people of a person or event • *a war memorial*
➤ **memorial** ADJECTIVE

**memorize** (also **memorise**) VERB memorizes, memorizing, memorized
to learn something so that you can remember it exactly

**memory** NOUN memories
❶ the ability to remember things
❷ something that you remember from the past ❸ the part of a computer where information is stored
➤ **in memory of someone** in order to remind people of someone who has died

**menace** NOUN menaces
❶ a threat or danger ❷ a troublesome person or thing

**menace** VERB menaces, menacing, menaced
to threaten someone with harm or danger

**menacing** ADJECTIVE
threatening to cause harm or danger • *There was something menacing in the tone of his voice.*

**menagerie** NOUN menageries
a small zoo

**mend** VERB mends, mending, mended
❶ to repair something broken ❷ to make something better • *He promised he would mend his ways.*
➤ **mender** NOUN

**mend** NOUN
➤ **on the mend** getting better after an illness

**meneer** NOUN
(*S. African*) a title in Afrikaans meaning 'Mr' or 'sir'

**menial** (say **meen**-ee-al) ADJECTIVE
needing little or no skill or thought • *menial tasks*

**menial** NOUN menials
a person who does menial work; a servant

**meningitis** NOUN
a disease causing inflammation of the membranes (*meninges*) round the brain and spinal cord

**menopause** NOUN
the time of life when a woman gradually stops menstruating

**menstruate** VERB menstruates, menstruating, menstruated
to bleed from the womb about once a month, as girls and women normally do from their teens until middle age
➤ **menstruation** NOUN
➤ **menstrual** ADJECTIVE

**mental** ADJECTIVE
❶ to do with or in the mind • *mental arithmetic* ❷ (*informal*) mad

**mentality** NOUN mentalities
a person's mental ability or attitude

**mentally** ADVERB
in your mind; to do with the mind • *She mentally added up how much she had spent.*

**menthol** NOUN
a solid white peppermint-flavoured substance

**mention** VERB mentions, mentioning, mentioned
to speak or write about a person or thing briefly; to refer to a person or thing

**mention** NOUN mentions
an example of mentioning someone or something • *Our school got a mention in the local paper.*

**mentor** NOUN mentors
an experienced and trusted adviser
(WORD ORIGIN) named after *Mentor* in Greek legend, who advised Odysseus' son

**menu** (say **men**-yoo) NOUN menus
❶ a list of the food available in a restaurant or served at a meal ❷ (*in computing*) a list of possible actions, shown on a screen, from which you choose what you want a computer to do

**MEP** ABBREVIATION
Member of the European Parliament

**mercantile** ADJECTIVE
to do with trade or trading

**mercenary** ADJECTIVE
interested only in the money you can get for the work you do

**mercenary** NOUN mercenaries
a soldier who fights for any army or country that will pay them

**merchandise** NOUN
goods for sale

**merchant** NOUN merchants
a person involved in trade

**merchant bank** NOUN merchant banks
(*British*) a bank that gives loans and advice to businesses

**merchant navy** NOUN
(*British*) the ships and sailors that carry goods for trade

**merciful** ADJECTIVE
showing mercy
➤ **mercifully** ADVERB

**merciless** ADJECTIVE
showing no mercy; cruel
➤ **mercilessly** ADVERB

**mercurial** ADJECTIVE
❶ having sudden changes of mood ❷ to do with mercury

**mercury** NOUN
a heavy silvery metal that is usually liquid, used in thermometers

**mercy** NOUN mercies
❶ kindness or pity shown towards someone instead of harming them or punishing them ❷ something to be thankful for
➤ **at the mercy of someone** or **something** having no power against someone or something • *We were at the mercy of the weather.*

**mere** ADJECTIVE
not more than • *He's a mere child.*

**mere** NOUN meres
(*British*) (*poetical use*) a lake

**merely** ADVERB
only; simply • *He merely smiled and walked away.*

**merest** ADJECTIVE
very small or slight • *the merest trace of colour*

**merge** VERB merges, merging, merged
when two or more things merge they combine together to form a single thing • *The sea and the sky seemed to merge.*

**merger** NOUN mergers
the combining of two business companies into one

**meridian** NOUN meridians
a line on a map or globe from the North Pole to the South Pole. The meridian that passes through Greenwich is shown on maps as 0° longitude.

**meringue** (say mer-**ang**) NOUN meringues
a crisp cake made from egg white and sugar

**merino** NOUN merinos
a kind of sheep with fine soft wool

**merit** NOUN merits
❶ a quality that deserves praise • *I can see the merits of this argument.* ❷ excellence
➤ **meritorious** ADJECTIVE

**merit** VERB merits, meriting, merited
to deserve something • *This suggestion merits further discussion.*

**mermaid** NOUN mermaids
a mythical sea creature with a woman's body but with a fish's tail instead of legs
➤ **merman** NOUN

**merriment** NOUN
happy talk, enjoyment and the sound of people laughing

**merry** ADJECTIVE merrier, merriest
cheerful and lively
➤ **merrily** ADVERB

**merry-go-round** NOUN merry-go-rounds
a roundabout at a fair

**mesh** NOUN meshes
❶ the open spaces in a net, sieve or other criss-cross structure ❷ material made like a net

**mesh** VERB meshes, meshing, meshed
gears mesh when they fit together as they move

**mesmerize** (also **mesmerise**) VERB
mesmerizes, mesmerizing, mesmerized
❶ (*old use*) to hypnotize someone ❷ to fascinate or hold a person's attention completely • *The audience were mesmerized by his performance.*
➤ **mesmeric** ADJECTIVE
**WORD ORIGIN** named after an Austrian doctor, F. A. *Mesmer*, who made hypnosis famous

**mess** NOUN messes
❶ a dirty or untidy condition or thing ❷ a difficult or confused situation ❸ in the armed forces, a dining room
➤ **make a mess of something** to do something very badly

**mess** VERB messes, messing, messed
➤ **mess about** to behave stupidly or idly
➤ **mess something up** ❶ to make a thing dirty or untidy ❷ to bungle or ruin something • *They messed up our plans.*
➤ **mess with something** to interfere or tinker with something

**message** NOUN messages
❶ a piece of information sent from one person to another • *I left a message on her voicemail.* ❷ the main theme or moral of a

book, film, etc. • *It is a funny film but it also has a serious message.*

**messenger** *NOUN* messengers
a person who carries a message

**Messiah** (say mis-**y**-a) *NOUN* Messiahs
❶ the saviour expected by the Jews ❷ Jesus Christ, who Christians believe was this saviour

**Messrs** (plural of Mr)

**messy** *ADJECTIVE* messier, messiest
❶ dirty and untidy ❷ difficult and complicated • *I'm afraid it's a messy situation.*
➤ **messily** *ADVERB*
➤ **messiness** *NOUN*

**metabolism** (say mit-**ab**-ol-izm) *NOUN*
the process by which food is built up into living material in a plant or animal or used to supply it with energy
➤ **metabolic** *ADJECTIVE*

**metal** *NOUN* metals
a chemical substance, usually hard, that conducts heat and electricity and melts when it is heated. Gold, silver, copper, iron and uranium are metals.

**metallic** *ADJECTIVE*
made of or like metal • *a metallic sound*

**metallurgy** (say mit-**al**-er-jee) *NOUN*
❶ the study of metals ❷ the craft of making and using metals
➤ **metallurgist** *NOUN*

**metamorphic** *ADJECTIVE*
formed or changed by heat or pressure
• *Marble is a metamorphic rock.*

**metamorphosis** (say met-a-**mor**-fo-sis) *NOUN*
metamorphoses (say met-a-**mor**- fo-seez)
❶ a complete change made by some living things, such as a caterpillar changing into a butterfly ❷ a change of form or character
➤ **metamorphose** *VERB*

**metaphor** *NOUN* metaphors
using a word or phrase in a way that describes one thing as if it were something else, e.g. 'He was a little monkey' and 'Her heart leapt for joy'

SPELLING

The 'f' sound is spelt ph in metaphor.

**metaphorical** *ADJECTIVE*
to do with or using metaphors • *metaphorical language*
➤ **metaphorically** *ADVERB*

**mete** *VERB* metes, meting, meted
➤ **mete something out** to give someone a punishment or bad treatment • *Severe penalties were meted out.*

**meteor** (say **meet**-ee-er) *NOUN* meteors
a piece of rock or metal that moves through space and burns up when it enters the earth's atmosphere

**meteoric** (say meet-ee-**o**-rik) *ADJECTIVE*
❶ to do with meteors ❷ becoming very successful very rapidly • *They have had a meteoric rise to fame.*

**meteorite** *NOUN* meteorites
the remains of a meteor that has landed on the earth

**meteorology** *NOUN*
the study of the conditions of the atmosphere, especially in order to forecast the weather
➤ **meteorological** *ADJECTIVE*
➤ **meteorologist** *NOUN*

**meter** *NOUN* meters
a device for measuring something, especially the amount of something used • *a gas meter*
➤ **meter** *VERB*

SPELLING

Meter is different from metre: • *an electricity meter* • *The table measures two metres.*

**methane** (say **mee**-thayn) *NOUN*
an inflammable gas produced by decaying matter

**method** *NOUN* methods
❶ a procedure or way of doing something ❷ good organization or orderly behaviour

**methodical** *ADJECTIVE*
doing things in a careful and well-organized way • *He is a methodical worker.*
➤ **methodically** *ADVERB*

**Methodist** *NOUN* Methodists
a member of a Christian religious group started by John and Charles Wesley in the 18th century
➤ **Methodism** *NOUN*

**methodology** *NOUN* methodologies
the methods and main principles that you use when you are studying a particular subject or doing a particular kind of work

**meths** *NOUN* (*British*) (*informal*)
methylated spirit

**methylated spirit, spirits** NOUN
a liquid fuel made from alcohol

**meticulous** ADJECTIVE
very careful and precise • *She keeps meticulous records.*
➤ **meticulously** ADVERB

**metre** NOUN metres
❶ a unit of length in the metric system, about 39½ inches ❷ rhythm in poetry

SPELLING
Metre is different from meter: • *The table measures two metres.* • *an electricity meter*

**metric** ADJECTIVE
❶ to do with the metric system ❷ to do with metre in poetry
➤ **metrically** ADVERB

**metrical** ADJECTIVE
in, or to do with, rhythmic metre, not prose
• *metrical psalms*

**metric system** NOUN
a measuring system based on decimal units (the metre, litre and gram)

**metric ton** NOUN metric tons
1,000 kilograms

**metronome** NOUN metronomes
a device that makes a regular clicking noise to help you keep in time when practising music

**metropolis** NOUN metropolises
the chief city of a country or region

**metropolitan** ADJECTIVE
❶ to do with a metropolis ❷ to do with a city and its suburbs

**mettle** NOUN
courage or strength of character • *The next game will be a real test of their mettle.*
➤ **be on your mettle** to be ready to show your courage or ability

**mew** VERB mews, mewing, mewed
to make a cat's cry

**mew** NOUN mews
a cat's cry

**mews** NOUN mews
(*British*) a row of houses in a small street or square, converted from former stables
WORD ORIGIN first used of royal stables in London, built on the site of hawks' cages (called mews)

**miaow** (say mee-**ow**) VERB miaows, miaowing, miaowed
to make a cat's cry

**miaow** NOUN miaows
a cat's cry

**miasma** (say mee-**az**-ma) NOUN miasmas
unpleasant or unhealthy air

**mica** NOUN
a mineral substance used to make electrical insulators

**mice**
plural of **mouse**

**microbe** NOUN microbes
a tiny organism that can only be seen with a microscope; a microorganism

**microchip** NOUN microchips
a very small piece of silicon etc. made to work like a complex wired electric circuit

**microcomputer** NOUN microcomputers
a small computer with a microprocessor as its central processing unit

**microcosm** NOUN microcosms
a world in miniature; something regarded as resembling something else on a very small scale

**microfiche** NOUN microfiches
a piece of film on which pages of information are photographed in greatly reduced size

**microfilm** NOUN
a length of film on which written or printed material is photographed in greatly reduced size

**micron** NOUN microns
a unit of measurement equal to one millionth of a metre

**microorganism** NOUN microorganisms
a microscopic creature, e.g. a bacterium or virus

**microphone** NOUN microphones
an electrical device that picks up sound waves for recording them or making them louder

**microprocessor** NOUN microprocessors
the central processing unit of a computer, consisting of one or more microchips

**microscope** NOUN microscopes
an instrument with lenses that magnify tiny objects or details

**microscopic** ADJECTIVE
❶ extremely small; too small to be seen

without the aid of a microscope • *microscopic creatures* ❷ to do with a microscope

**microwave** *NOUN* microwaves
❶ a very short electromagnetic wave ❷ a microwave oven

**microwave** *VERB* microwaves, microwaving, microwaved
to cook food in a microwave oven

**microwave oven** *NOUN* microwave ovens
an oven that uses microwaves to heat or cook food very quickly

**mid** *ADJECTIVE*
❶ in the middle of • *mid-July* ❷ middle • *He's in his mid thirties.*

**mid-air** *NOUN*
the area above the ground; open sky
• *The bird caught the insects in mid-air.*

**midday** *NOUN*
the middle of the day; noon

**middle** *NOUN* middles
❶ the place or part of something that is at the same distance from all its sides or edges or from both its ends ❷ someone's waist
➤ **in the middle of something** during or halfway through a process or activity • *I'm just in the middle of cooking.*

**middle** *ADJECTIVE*
❶ placed or happening in the middle ❷ moderate in size or rank etc.

**middle-aged** *ADJECTIVE*
aged between about 45 and 65
➤ **middle age** *NOUN*

**Middle Ages** *NOUN*
the period in history from about AD 1000 to 1400

**middle class, classes** *NOUN*
the class of people between the upper class and the working class, including business and professional people such as teachers, doctors and lawyers
➤ **middle-class** *ADJECTIVE*

**Middle East** *NOUN*
the countries from Egypt to Iran inclusive

**Middle English** *NOUN*
the English language from about 1150 to 1500

**middleman** *NOUN* middlemen
❶ a trader who buys from a producer and sells to a consumer ❷ a go-between or intermediary

**middle school** *NOUN* middle schools
a school for children aged from about 9 to 13

**middling** *ADJECTIVE*
of medium size or quality

**midge** *NOUN* midges
a small insect like a gnat

**midget** *NOUN* midgets
an extremely small person or thing
➤ **midget** *ADJECTIVE*

**midland** *ADJECTIVE*
❶ to do with the middle part of a country ❷ to do with the Midlands

**Midlands** *PLURAL NOUN*
the central part of a country, especially the central counties of England

**midnight** *NOUN*
twelve o'clock at night

**midriff** *NOUN* midriffs
the front part of the body just above the waist

**midshipman** *NOUN* midshipmen
a sailor ranking next above a cadet

**midst** *NOUN*
➤ **in the midst of** in the middle of or surrounded by • *The country is in the midst of a recession.*
➤ **in our midst** among us • *There is a traitor in our midst.*

**midsummer** *NOUN*
the middle part of summer

**Midsummer's Day** *NOUN*
24 June

**midway** *ADVERB*
halfway between two points

**midwife** *NOUN* midwives
a person trained to look after a woman who is giving birth to a baby
➤ **midwifery** (say mid-wif-ri) *NOUN*

**midwinter** *NOUN*
the middle part of winter

**mien** (say meen) *NOUN* (old or poetical use)
a person's manner and expression • *a tall youth of noble mien*

**might** *NOUN*
great strength or power
➤ **with all your might** using all your strength and determination

**might** *AUXILIARY VERB*
❶ the past tense of may (*We told her she*

431

might go.) ❷ used to express possibility (*It might be true.*)

**mightily** ADVERB
❶ very; very much • *We were mightily impressed.* ❷ with great strength or effort • *They fought mightily.*

**mighty** ADJECTIVE
very strong or powerful • *a mighty blow*

**migraine** (say mee-grayn or my-grayn) NOUN migraines
a severe kind of headache

**migrant** NOUN migrants
a person or animal that migrates or has migrated

**migrate** VERB migrates, migrating, migrated
❶ to leave one place or country and settle in another ❷ birds and animals migrate when they move periodically from one area to another
➤ **migratory** ADJECTIVE

**migration** NOUN migrations
moving in large numbers from one area to another • *seasonal migration of birds*

**mike** NOUN mikes (*informal*)
a microphone

**mild** ADJECTIVE milder, mildest
❶ not harsh or severe • *a mild infection* ❷ not great or extreme; slight • *a look of mild surprise* ❸ gentle and kind ❹ not strongly flavoured • *a mild curry* ❺ mild weather is quite warm and pleasant
➤ **mildness** NOUN

**mildew** NOUN
a tiny fungus that forms a white coating on things kept in damp conditions
➤ **mildewed** ADJECTIVE

**mildly** ADVERB
❶ slightly • *She was mildly irritated by this.* ❷ in a gentle manner

**mile** NOUN miles
a measure of distance equal to 1,760 yards (about 1.6 kilometres)

**mileage** NOUN mileages
the number of miles you have travelled

**milestone** NOUN milestones
❶ a stone of a kind that used to be fixed beside a road to mark the distance between towns ❷ an important stage or event in history or in a person's life

**militant** ADJECTIVE
❶ eager to fight ❷ forceful or aggressive • *a militant protest*
➤ **militant** NOUN
➤ **militancy** NOUN

**military** ADJECTIVE
to do with soldiers or the armed forces
➤ **the military** a country's armed forces

**militate** VERB militates, militating, militated
to be a strong influence against something; to make something difficult or unlikely • *The weather militated against the success of our plans.*

**militia** (say mil-**ish**-a) NOUN militias
a military force, especially one raised from civilians

**milk** NOUN
❶ a white liquid that female mammals produce in their bodies to feed their babies ❷ the milk of cows, used as food by human beings ❸ a milky liquid, e.g. that in a coconut
**milk** VERB milks, milking, milked
to get the milk from a cow or other animal

**milkman** NOUN milkmen
a man who delivers milk to customers' houses

**milkshake** NOUN milkshakes
a cold frothy drink made from milk whisked with sweet fruit flavouring

**milk tooth** NOUN milk teeth
one of the first set of teeth of a child or animal, which will be replaced by adult teeth

**milky** ADJECTIVE milkier, milkiest
❶ like milk; white • *milky white skin* ❷ made with a lot of milk • *milky coffee*

**Milky Way** NOUN
the broad band of stars formed by our galaxy

**mill** NOUN mills
❶ machinery for grinding corn to make flour; a building containing this machinery ❷ a grinding machine • *a coffee mill* ❸ a factory for processing certain materials • *a paper mill*
**mill** VERB mills, milling, milled
❶ to grind or crush something in a mill ❷ to cut markings round the edge of a coin
➤ **mill about** or **around** to move in a confused crowd • *There were a lot of people milling about outside.*

**millennium** NOUN millenniums
a period of 1,000 years

**miller** NOUN millers
a person who runs a flour mill

**millet** NOUN
a kind of cereal with tiny seeds

**milligram** NOUN milligrams
one-thousandth of a gram

**millilitre** NOUN millilitres
one-thousandth of a litre

> SPELLING
>
> Take care: millilitre is spelt re at the end and not er.

**millimetre** NOUN millimetres
one-thousandth of a metre

> SPELLING
>
> Take care: millimetre is spelt re at the end and not er.

**milliner** NOUN milliners
a person who makes or sells women's hats
> **millinery** NOUN
> WORD ORIGIN originally = a person from *Milan*, an Italian city where fashionable accessories and hats were made

**million** NOUN & ADJECTIVE millions
one thousand thousand (1,000,000)
> **millionth** ADJECTIVE & NOUN

**millionaire** NOUN millionaires
a person who has at least a million pounds or dollars; an extremely rich person

> SPELLING
>
> Double up the l in millionaire (but the n stays single).

**millipede** NOUN millipedes
a small crawling creature like a centipede, with many legs WORD ORIGIN from Latin *mille* = thousand + *pedes* = feet

**millstone** NOUN millstones
either of a pair of large circular stones between which corn is ground
> **a millstone around someone's neck** a heavy responsibility or burden

**milometer** NOUN milometers
(*British*) an instrument for measuring how far a vehicle has travelled

**mime** NOUN mimes
acting with movements of the body, not using words

**mime** VERB mimes, miming, mimed
to use mime to act or express something
• *She mimed washing her hands.*

**mimic** VERB mimics, mimicking, mimicked
to imitate someone, especially to amuse people
> **mimicry** NOUN

**mimic** NOUN mimics
a person who is good at imitating others

**mimosa** NOUN mimosas
a tropical tree or shrub with small ball-shaped flowers

**minaret** NOUN minarets
the tall tower of a mosque

**mince** VERB minces, mincing, minced
❶ to cut meat or other food into very small pieces in a machine ❷ to walk in an affected way with short quick steps
> **mincer** NOUN
> **not to mince words or matters** to speak bluntly

**mince** NOUN (*British*) minced meat

**mincemeat** NOUN
(*chiefly British*) a sweet mixture of currants, raisins, apple, etc. used in pies

**mince pie** NOUN mince pies
(*chiefly British*) a pie containing mincemeat

**mind** NOUN minds
❶ the ability to think, feel, understand and remember, originating in the brain • *He has a brilliant mind.* ❷ a person's thoughts, opinion or intention • *Have you made your mind up?* • *I changed my mind.*
> **in two minds** not able to decide
> **out of your mind** insane or very foolish

**mind** VERB minds, minding, minded
❶ to look after a person or animal for a while • *He was minding the baby.* ❷ to be careful about something • *Mind the step.* ❸ to be sad or upset about something; to object to something • *We don't mind waiting.*
> **minder** NOUN

**mindful** ADJECTIVE
taking thought or care • *He was mindful of his reputation.*

**mindless** ADJECTIVE
done without thinking; stupid or pointless

**mine** POSSESSIVE PRONOUN
belonging to me • *He is a friend of mine.*

**mine** NOUN mines
❶ a place where coal, metal or precious stones are dug out of the ground ❷ an explosive placed in or on the ground or in the sea to destroy people or things that come close to it

**mine** VERB mines, mining, mined
❶ to dig something from a mine ❷ to lay explosive mines in a place

**minefield** NOUN minefields
❶ an area where explosive mines have been laid ❷ something with hidden dangers or problems

**miner** NOUN miners
a person who works in a mine

**mineral** NOUN minerals
❶ a substance that is formed naturally in rocks and in the ground, such as iron, salt and coal ❷ a cold fizzy non-alcoholic drink

**mineralogy** (say min-er-**al**-o-jee) NOUN
the study of minerals
➤ **mineralogist** NOUN

**mineral water** NOUN
water from a natural spring, containing mineral salts or gases

**minestrone** (say mini-**stroh**-nee) NOUN
an Italian soup containing vegetables and pasta

**mingle** VERB mingles, mingling, mingled
to mix or blend with other things • *Tears ran down her face, mingling with the seawater.* • *The sounds of laughter and singing mingled in the evening air.*

**mingy** ADJECTIVE mingier, mingiest (*informal*)
not generous; mean

**miniature** ADJECTIVE
❶ very small ❷ copying something on a very small scale • *a miniature railway*

**miniature** NOUN miniatures
❶ a very small portrait ❷ a small-scale model

> SPELLING
> Take care with this word—there is an **a** after mini.

**minibus** NOUN minibuses
a small bus, seating about ten people

**minim** NOUN minims
a note in music, lasting twice as long as a crotchet (written ♩)

**minimal** ADJECTIVE
very little; as little as possible • *The damage to the car was minimal.*

**minimize** (also **minimise**) VERB minimizes, minimizing, minimized
to make something as small as possible • *Good hygiene helps to minimize the risk of infection.*

**minimum** NOUN minima or minimums
the lowest possible number or amount. (The opposite is **maximum**.) • *Keep the noise to a minimum.*

**minimum** ADJECTIVE
least or smallest • *What is the minimum amount of sleep you need?*

**minion** NOUN minions
a very humble or obedient assistant or servant

**minister** NOUN ministers
❶ a person in charge of a government department ❷ a member of the clergy
➤ **ministerial** ADJECTIVE

**minister** VERB ministers, ministering, ministered
to attend to people's needs

**ministry** NOUN ministries
❶ a government department • *the Ministry of Defence* ❷ the work of the clergy

**mink** NOUN mink or minks
❶ an animal rather like a stoat ❷ this animal's valuable brown fur or a coat made from it

**minnow** NOUN minnows
a tiny freshwater fish

**minor** ADJECTIVE
❶ not very important, especially when compared to something else • *a minor problem* ❷ of the musical scale that has a semitone after the second note. Compare with **major**.

**minor** NOUN minors
a person under the age of legal responsibility

**minority** NOUN minorities
❶ the smallest part of a group of people or things • *There was a minority who wanted to leave.* ❷ a small group that is different from others. Compare with **majority**.

**minstrel** NOUN minstrels
a travelling singer and musician in the Middle Ages

**mint** NOUN mints
❶ a plant with fragrant leaves that are used for flavouring things ❷ a sweet flavoured with peppermint ❸ the place where a country's coins are made
➤ **in mint condition** in perfect condition, as though it had never been used

**mint** VERB mints, minting, minted
to make coins by stamping metal

**minuet** NOUN minuets
a slow stately dance

**minus** PREPOSITION
with the next number or thing subtracted
• *Ten minus four equals six (10 - 4 = 6).*

**minus** ADJECTIVE
less than zero • *temperatures of minus ten degrees (-10°)*

**minuscule** ADJECTIVE
extremely small

**minute** (say **min**-it) NOUN minutes
❶ one-sixtieth of an hour ❷ a very short time; a moment • *I'll be ready in a minute.*
❸ one-sixtieth of a degree (used in measuring angles)

**minute** (say my-**newt**) ADJECTIVE
❶ very small • *a minute insect* ❷ very detailed • *a minute examination*

**minutely** ADVERB
in a very detailed way • *He examined the envelope minutely.*

**minutes** PLURAL NOUN
a written summary of what was said at a meeting

**minx** NOUN minxes (old use)
a cheeky or mischievous girl

**miracle** NOUN miracles
❶ a wonderful event that seems to be impossible and is believed to have a supernatural or divine cause ❷ something fortunate and surprising • *It's a miracle that no one was killed in the crash.*

**miraculous** ADJECTIVE
completely unexpected and very lucky • *She made a miraculous recovery.*
➤ **miraculously** ADVERB

**mirage** (say **mi**-rahzh) NOUN mirages
an illusion; something that seems to be there but is not, especially when a lake seems to appear in a desert

**mire** NOUN
❶ a swamp ❷ deep mud

**mirror** NOUN mirrors
a device or surface of reflecting material, usually glass

**mirror** VERB mirrors, mirroring, mirrored
to reflect something in or like a mirror • *She saw herself mirrored in the window.*

**mirth** NOUN
merriment or laughter • *His eyes twinkled with mirth.*
➤ **mirthful** ADJECTIVE
➤ **mirthless** ADJECTIVE

**misadventure** NOUN misadventures
a piece of bad luck

**misapprehension** NOUN misapprehensions
a wrong idea or impression of something

**misbehave** VERB misbehaves, misbehaving, misbehaved
to behave badly
➤ **misbehaviour** NOUN

**miscalculate** VERB miscalculates, miscalculating, miscalculated
to calculate something incorrectly • *I had miscalculated how long it would take.*
➤ **miscalculation** NOUN

**miscarriage** NOUN miscarriages
❶ a woman has a miscarriage when she gives birth to a baby before it has developed enough to survive ❷ failure to achieve the right result • *a miscarriage of justice*
➤ **miscarry** VERB

**miscellaneous** (say mis-el-**ay**-nee-us) ADJECTIVE
of various kinds; mixed • *miscellaneous musical instruments*

**miscellany** (say mis-**el**-an-ee) NOUN miscellanies
a collection or mixture of different things

**mischance** NOUN
misfortune; bad luck

**mischief** NOUN
❶ naughty or troublesome behaviour ❷ trouble caused by this

**mischievous** ADJECTIVE
liking to behave badly or cause trouble • *a mischievous grin*
➤ **mischievously** ADVERB

**misconception** NOUN misconceptions
a wrong or mistaken idea

**misconduct** NOUN
bad behaviour by someone in a responsible position • *professional misconduct*

**misconstrue** VERB misconstrues, misconstruing, misconstrued
to understand or interpret something wrongly

**miscreant** (say **mis**-kree-ant) NOUN miscreants
a wrongdoer or criminal

**misdeed** NOUN misdeeds
a wrong or wicked act

**misdemeanour** NOUN misdemeanours
an action which is wrong or illegal, but not very serious; a petty crime

**miser** NOUN misers
a person who hoards money and spends as little as possible
➤ **miserly** ADJECTIVE
➤ **miserliness** NOUN

**miserable** ADJECTIVE
❶ full of misery; very unhappy or uncomfortable ❷ unpleasant; making you feel depressed • *What miserable weather!*
➤ **miserably** ADVERB

**misery** NOUN miseries
❶ great unhappiness or discomfort or suffering, especially lasting for a long time ❷ (*informal*) a person who is always unhappy or complaining

**misfire** VERB misfires, misfiring, misfired
❶ a gun or engine misfires when it fails to fire or start ❷ a plan or idea or joke misfires when it goes wrong or has the wrong effect

**misfit** NOUN misfits
a person who does not fit in well with other people or with their surroundings

**misfortune** NOUN misfortunes
❶ bad luck ❷ an unlucky event or accident

**misgiving** NOUN misgivings
a feeling of doubt, or slight fear or mistrust • *I had serious misgivings about leaving him on his own.*

**misguided** ADJECTIVE
guided by mistaken ideas or beliefs

**mishap** (say **mis**-hap) NOUN mishaps
an unlucky accident

**misinterpret** VERB misinterprets, misinterpreting, misinterpreted
to interpret something incorrectly
➤ **misinterpretation** NOUN

**misjudge** VERB misjudges, misjudging, misjudged
to judge something wrongly; to form a wrong idea or opinion about someone or something • *I think I may have misjudged him.*
➤ **misjudgement** NOUN

**mislay** VERB mislays, mislaying, mislaid
to lose something for a short time because you cannot remember where you put it

**mislead** VERB misleads, misleading, misled
to give someone a wrong idea or impression deliberately

**mismanagement** NOUN
bad management

**misplaced** ADJECTIVE
❶ put in the wrong place ❷ inappropriate or unjustified • *misplaced loyalty*

**misprint** NOUN misprints
a mistake in printing, such as a spelling mistake

**mispronounce** VERB mispronounces, mispronouncing, mispronounced
to pronounce a word or name incorrectly
➤ **mispronunciation** NOUN

**misquote** VERB misquotes, misquoting, misquoted
to quote someone or something incorrectly
➤ **misquotation** NOUN

**misread** VERB misreads, misreading, misread (say mis-**red**)
to read or interpret something incorrectly • *She had completely misread the situation.*

**misrepresent** VERB misrepresents, misrepresenting, misrepresented
to represent someone or something in a false or misleading way
➤ **misrepresentation** NOUN

**misrule** NOUN
bad government

**Miss** NOUN Misses
a title put before a girl's or unmarried woman's name

**miss** VERB misses, missing, missed
❶ to fail to hit, reach, catch, see, hear or find something ❷ to be sad because someone or something is not with you ❸ to miss a train, bus or plane is to arrive too late to catch it ❹ to miss a lesson or other activity is to fail to attend it • *How many classes have you missed?* ❺ to notice that something is not where it should be
➤ **miss something out** to leave something out
➤ **miss out on something** to not get the benefit or enjoyment from something that others have had

**miss** NOUN misses
missing something • *Was that shot a hit or a miss?*
➤ **give something a miss** to decide not to do or have something

**misshapen** ADJECTIVE
distorted or badly shaped

436

**missile** NOUN missiles
**①** a weapon that is fired a long distance and explodes when it hits its target **②** an object that is thrown at someone in order to hurt them

**missing** ADJECTIVE
**①** lost; not in the proper place **②** absent

**mission** NOUN missions
**①** an important job that someone is sent to do or feels they must do **②** a place or building where missionaries work **③** a military or scientific expedition • *a space mission*

**missionary** NOUN missionaries
a person who is sent to another country to spread a religious faith

**misspell** VERB misspells, misspelling, misspelt or misspelled
to spell a word wrongly

**mist** NOUN mists
**①** damp cloudy air near the ground **②** condensed water vapour on a window, mirror, etc.

**mist** VERB mists, misting, misted
to become covered with mist • *My goggles kept misting up.*

**mistake** NOUN mistakes
**①** something done wrongly **②** an incorrect opinion
➤ by mistake by accident; without intending to • *I picked up your bag by mistake.*

**mistake** VERB mistakes, mistaking, mistook, mistaken
**①** to choose or identify a person or thing wrongly • *We mistook her for her sister.* **②** to misunderstand something • *Don't mistake my meaning.*

**mistaken** ADJECTIVE
**①** incorrect • *a case of mistaken identity* **②** having an incorrect opinion • *You are mistaken if you believe that.*
➤ mistakenly ADVERB

**mister** NOUN (*informal*)
a form of address to a man

**mistime** VERB mistimes, mistiming, mistimed
to do or say something at a wrong time

**mistletoe** NOUN
a plant with white berries that grows as a parasite on trees

**mistreat** VERB mistreats, mistreating, mistreated
to treat a person or thing in a cruel or unkind way • *He was accused of mistreating his horse.*

**mistress** NOUN mistresses
**①** a woman who is in charge of something **②** a woman teacher **③** the woman owner of a dog or other animal **④** a woman who is a man's lover but not his wife

**mistrust** VERB mistrusts, mistrusting, mistrusted
to feel no trust in someone or something
➤ mistrust NOUN

**misty** ADJECTIVE mistier, mistiest
**①** full of mist • *a misty morning* **②** not clear or distinct • *misty memories* **③** misty eyes are full of tears
➤ mistily ADVERB
➤ mistiness NOUN

**misunderstand** VERB misunderstands, misunderstanding, misunderstood
to get a wrong idea or impression of something • *You misunderstand what I said.*

**misunderstanding** NOUN misunderstandings
a situation in which someone gets a wrong idea or impression of something • *I think there's been a misunderstanding.*

**misuse** (say mis-yooz) VERB misuses, misusing, misused
**①** to use something incorrectly **②** to treat someone badly

**misuse** (say mis-yooss) NOUN
using something incorrectly • *the misuse of power*

**mite** NOUN mites
**①** a tiny spider-like creature that lives on plants, animals, carpets, etc. **②** a small child

**mitigate** VERB mitigates, mitigating, mitigated
to make a thing less intense or less severe • *These measures are designed to mitigate the effects of air pollution.*
➤ mitigation NOUN

**mitigating circumstances** PLURAL NOUN
facts that may partially excuse wrongdoing

**mitre** NOUN mitres
**①** the tall tapering hat that a bishop wears **②** a joint of two pieces of wood or cloth with their ends tapered so that together they form a right angle

**mitten** NOUN mittens
a kind of glove without separate parts for the fingers

a b c d e f g h i j k l m n o p q r s t u v w x y z

**mix** VERB mixes, mixing, mixed
**①** to put different things together so that they make a single substance or thing; to blend or combine things • *Mix all the ingredients together in a bowl.* **②** to get together with other people
➤ **mix things up** **①** to mix things together thoroughly **②** to confuse two things in your mind

**mix** NOUN mixes
a mixture

**mixed** ADJECTIVE
**①** containing two or more kinds of things or people • *I have mixed feelings about what happened.* **②** for both sexes • *mixed doubles*

**mixed farming** NOUN
farming of both crops and animals

**mixer** NOUN mixers
a machine used for mixing something • *a food mixer*

**mixture** NOUN mixtures
something made of different things mixed together

**mix-up** NOUN
a confusion or misunderstanding

**mnemonic** (say nim-**on**-ik) NOUN mnemonics
a verse or saying that helps you to remember something WORD ORIGIN from Greek *mnemonikos* = for the memory

SPELLING
There is a silent **m** at the beginning of mnemonic.

**moan** VERB moans, moaning, moaned
**①** to make a long low sound of pain or suffering **②** to complain or grumble

**moan** NOUN moans
**①** a long low sound of pain or suffering **②** a complaint or grumble

**moat** NOUN moats
a deep wide ditch round a castle, usually filled with water

**mob** NOUN mobs
a large disorderly crowd

**mob** VERB mobs, mobbing, mobbed
people mob someone when they crowd round them • *The band was mobbed by fans as they left the hotel.* WORD ORIGIN from Latin *mobile vulgus* = excitable crowd

**mobile** ADJECTIVE
able to move or be moved or carried easily
➤ **mobility** NOUN

**mobile** NOUN mobiles
**①** a mobile phone **②** a decoration for hanging up so that its parts move in currents of air

**mobile phone** NOUN mobile phones
a phone you can carry around with you

**mobilize** (also **mobilise**) VERB mobilizes, mobilizing, mobilized
to assemble people or things for a particular purpose, especially for war
➤ **mobilization** NOUN

**moccasin** NOUN moccasins
a soft leather shoe

**mock** VERB mocks, mocking, mocked
**①** to make fun of a person or thing **②** to imitate someone or something to make people laugh

**mock** ADJECTIVE
**①** imitation, not real • *He held up his hands in mock surprise.* **②** a mock exam is one done as a practice before the real one

**mockery** NOUN
**①** ridicule or contempt **②** a ridiculous imitation

**mock-up** NOUN mock-ups
a model of something, made in order to test or study it

**modal verb** NOUN
a verb such as *can*, *may* or *will* that is used with another verb to express possibility, permission, intention, etc.

**mode** NOUN modes
**①** the way a thing is done; a type of something • *different modes of transport* **②** one of the ways in which a machine can work • *The game has a two-player mode.* **③** what is fashionable

**model** NOUN models
**①** a copy of an object, usually on a smaller scale **②** a particular design **③** a person who poses for an artist or displays clothes by wearing them **④** a person or thing that is worth copying

**model** VERB models, modelling, modelled
**①** to make a model of something; to make something out of wood or clay **②** to design or plan something using another thing as an example • *The building is modelled on a Roman villa.* **③** to work as an artist's model or a fashion model

**modem** (say **moh**-dem) *NOUN* modems
a device that links a computer to a telephone
line for transmitting data

**moderate** (say **mod**-er-at) *ADJECTIVE*
❶ medium; not too little and not too much
• *a moderate climate* ❷ not extreme or
unreasonable • *moderate opinions*
➤ **moderately** *ADVERB*

**moderate** (say **mod**-er-ayt) *VERB* moderates,
moderating, moderated
to become or make something less strong or
extreme

**moderation** *NOUN*
being moderate
➤ **in moderation** in moderate amounts

**modern** *ADJECTIVE*
❶ belonging to the present or recent times
❷ in fashion now

**modernize** (also **modernise**) *VERB*
modernizes, modernizing, modernized
to make a thing more modern
➤ **modernization** *NOUN*

**modest** *ADJECTIVE*
❶ not boasting about how good you are
❷ quite small in size or amount • *a modest
income* ❸ dressing or behaving in a decent
or shy way
➤ **modestly** *ADVERB*
➤ **modesty** *NOUN*

**modicum** *NOUN*
a small amount

**modification** *NOUN* modifications
a slight change in something

**modify** *VERB* modifies, modifying, modified
❶ to change something slightly ❷ to describe
a word or limit its meaning • *Adjectives
modify nouns.*

**modulate** *VERB* modulates, modulating,
modulated
❶ to vary the pitch or tone of your voice or a
sound ❷ to alter an electronic wave to allow
signals to be sent
➤ **modulation** *NOUN*

**module** *NOUN* modules
❶ a separate section or part of something
larger, such as a spacecraft or building ❷ a
unit or section of a course of study

**modus operandi** (say moh-dus op-er-**and**-
ee) *NOUN*
a particular method of working

**mogul** (say **moh**-gul) *NOUN* moguls (*informal*)
an important or influential person
**WORD ORIGIN** the *Moguls* were the ruling
family in northern India in the 16th-19th
centuries

**mohair** *NOUN*
fine silky wool from an angora goat

**moist** *ADJECTIVE*
slightly wet • *Her eyes were moist with tears.*

**moisten** *VERB* moistens, moistening,
moistened
to make something moist • *He moistened his
lips before he spoke.*

**moisture** *NOUN*
water in tiny drops in the air or on a surface

**moisturizer** (also **moisturiser**) *NOUN*
a cream used to make the skin less dry

**molar** *NOUN* molars
any of the wide teeth at the back of the jaw,
used in chewing

**molasses** *NOUN*
dark syrup from raw sugar

**mole** *NOUN* moles
❶ a small furry animal that burrows under
the ground ❷ a spy working within an
organization and passing information to
another organization or country ❸ a small
dark spot on skin

**molecular** (say mo-**lek**-yoo-ler) *ADJECTIVE*
to do with molecules • *the molecular
structure of penicillin*

**molecule** *NOUN* molecules
the smallest part into which a substance can
be divided without changing its chemical
nature; a group of atoms

**molehill** *NOUN* molehills
a small pile of earth thrown up by a
burrowing mole

**molest** *VERB* molests, molesting, molested
❶ to annoy or pester someone ❷ to illegally
touch or attack someone in a sexual way
➤ **molestation** *NOUN*

**mollify** *VERB* mollifies, mollifying, mollified
to make a person feel less angry or upset
• *She seemed slightly mollified by his
apology.*

**mollusc** *NOUN* molluscs
any of a group of animals including snails,
slugs and mussels, with soft bodies, no
backbones, and, in some cases, external shells

a
b
c
d
e
f
g
h
i
j
k
l
m
n
o
p
q
r
s
t
u
v
w
x
y
z

**molten** ADJECTIVE
melted; made liquid by great heat • *Molten lava flowed down the side of the volcano.*

**moment** NOUN moments
❶ a very short time • *Wait a moment.* ❷ a particular time • *I'll call you the moment she arrives.*
➤ **at the moment** now

**momentary** ADJECTIVE
lasting for only a moment • *There was a momentary pause.*
➤ **momentarily** ADVERB

**momentous** (say mo-**ment**-us) ADJECTIVE
very important • *a momentous occasion*

**momentum** NOUN
❶ the ability something has to keep developing or increasing • *The protests gathered momentum.* ❷ the ability an object has to keep moving as a result of the speed it already has • *The stone gathered momentum as it rolled downhill.* ❸ (*in science*) the quantity of motion of a moving object, measured as its mass multiplied by its velocity

**monarch** NOUN monarchs
a king, queen, emperor or empress ruling a country

**monarchy** NOUN monarchies
❶ a country ruled by a monarch
❷ government by a monarch
➤ **monarchist** NOUN

**monastery** NOUN monasteries
a building where monks live and work

**monastic** ADJECTIVE
to do with monks or monasteries

**Monday** NOUN
the day of the week following Sunday
**WORD ORIGIN** from Old English *monandaeg* = day of the moon

**monetary** ADJECTIVE
to do with money

**money** NOUN
❶ coins and banknotes ❷ wealth or riches

**mongoose** NOUN mongooses
a small tropical animal rather like a stoat, that can kill snakes

**mongrel** (say **mung**-rel) NOUN mongrels
a dog of mixed breeds

**monitor** NOUN monitors
❶ a device for watching or testing how something is working ❷ a screen that displays data and images produced by a computer ❸ a
pupil who is given a special responsibility in a school

**monitor** VERB monitors, monitoring, monitored
to regularly watch or test what is happening with something • *Pollution levels in the lake are closely monitored.*

**monk** NOUN monks
a member of a community of men who live according to the rules of a religious organization. Compare with **nun**.

**monkey** NOUN monkeys
❶ an animal with long arms, hands with thumbs and often a tail ❷ a mischievous person, especially a child

**monochrome** ADJECTIVE
done in one colour or in black and white

**monocle** NOUN monocles
a lens worn over one eye, like half of a pair of glasses

**monogram** NOUN monograms
a design made up of a letter or letters, especially a person's initials
➤ **monogrammed** ADJECTIVE

**monograph** NOUN monographs
a scholarly book or article on one particular subject

**monolith** NOUN monoliths
a large single upright block of stone

**monolithic** ADJECTIVE
❶ to do with or like a monolith ❷ huge and difficult to move or change

**monologue** NOUN monologues
a long speech by one person

**monoplane** NOUN monoplanes
a type of aeroplane with only one set of wings

**monopolize** (also **monopolise**) VERB
monopolizes, monopolizing, monopolized
to take the whole of something for yourself
• *One girl monopolized my attention.*

**monopoly** NOUN monopolies
❶ complete control by a single company over selling a product or supplying a service
❷ complete possession, control or use of something by one group

**monorail** NOUN monorails
a railway that uses a single rail, not a pair of rails

**monosyllable** *NOUN* monosyllables
a word with only one syllable
➤ **monosyllabic** *ADJECTIVE*

**monotone** *NOUN*
a level unchanging tone of voice in speaking or singing • *He spoke in a flat monotone.*

**monotonous** *ADJECTIVE*
boring because it does not change
• *monotonous work*
➤ **monotonously** *ADVERB*

**monotony** *NOUN*
being always the same and therefore dull and boring • *the monotony of his job in the factory*

**monoxide** *NOUN* monoxides
an oxide with one atom of oxygen

**monsoon** *NOUN* monsoons
❶ a strong wind in and near the Indian Ocean, bringing heavy rain in summer ❷ the rainy season brought by this wind

**monster** *NOUN* monsters
❶ a large frightening creature ❷ a huge thing ❸ a wicked or cruel person

**monster** *ADJECTIVE*
very large; huge

**monstrosity** *NOUN* monstrosities
a monstrous thing

**monstrous** *ADJECTIVE*
❶ like a monster; huge ❷ very shocking or outrageous • *a monstrous crime*

**montage** (say mon-tahzh) *NOUN*
a picture, film, or other work of art made by putting together separate pieces or pieces from different works

**month** *NOUN* months
each of the twelve parts into which a year is divided (**WORD ORIGIN** from Old English; related to **moon** (because time was measured by the changes in the moon's appearance)

**monthly** *ADJECTIVE & ADVERB*
happening or done once a month

**monument** *NOUN* monuments
a statue, building or column put up to remind people of some person or event

**monumental** *ADJECTIVE*
❶ built as a monument ❷ very large or important • *It was a monumental achievement.*

**moo** *VERB* moos, mooing, mooed
to make the low deep sound of a cow

**moo** *NOUN* moos
the low deep sound a cow makes

**mood** *NOUN* moods
the way someone feels • *She is in a cheerful mood.*

**moody** *ADJECTIVE* moodier, moodiest
❶ gloomy or sullen • *He lapsed into a moody silence.* ❷ having sudden changes of mood for no apparent reason
➤ **moodily** *ADVERB*
➤ **moodiness** *NOUN*

**moon** *NOUN* moons
❶ the natural satellite of the earth that can be seen in the sky at night ❷ a satellite of any planet • *the moons of Jupiter*

**moon** *VERB* moons, mooning, mooned
to go about in a dreamy way, often because you are in love

**moonbeam** *NOUN* moonbeams
a ray of moonlight

**moonlight** *NOUN*
the light from the moon
➤ **moonlit** *ADJECTIVE*

**Moor** *NOUN* Moors
a member of a Muslim people of north-west Africa who controlled southern Spain between the 8th and 15th centuries
➤ **Moorish** *ADJECTIVE*

**moor** *NOUN* moors
(*chiefly British*) an area of rough land covered with heather, bracken and bushes

**moor** *VERB* moors, mooring, moored
to fasten a boat to a fixed object with a rope or cable

**moorhen** *NOUN* moorhens
a small waterbird

**mooring** *NOUN* moorings
a place where a boat can be moored

**moorland** *NOUN* moorlands
(*chiefly British*) land that consists of moors

**moose** *NOUN* moose
a North American elk

**moot** *ADJECTIVE*
➤ **a moot point** a question that is undecided or debatable

**mop** *NOUN* mops
❶ a bunch or pad of soft material fastened on the end of a stick, used for cleaning floors etc. ❷ a thick mass of hair

**mop** *VERB* mops, mopping, mopped
to clean or wipe something with a mop or

a
b
c
d
e
f
g
h
i
j
k
l
m
n
o
p
q
r
s
t
u
v
w
x
y
z

sponge
➤ **mop something up** ❶ to wipe or soak up liquid ❷ to deal with the last parts of something • *The army is mopping up the last of the rebels.*

**mope** *VERB* mopes, moping, moped
to be miserable and not interested in doing anything • *She's been moping about in the house all day.*

**moped** (say moh-ped) *NOUN* mopeds
a kind of small motorcycle that can be pedalled

**moraine** *NOUN* moraines
a mass of stones and earth carried down by a glacier

**moral** *ADJECTIVE*
❶ to do with what is right and wrong in behaviour ❷ good or virtuous
➤ **morally** *ADVERB*
➤ **morality** *NOUN*
➤ **moral support** help in the form of encouragement

**moral** *NOUN* morals
a lesson in right behaviour taught by a story or event

**morale** (say mor-ahl) *NOUN*
the level of confidence and good spirits in a person or group of people • *Morale was high after the victory.*

**moralize** (also **moralise**) *VERB* moralizes, moralizing, moralized
to talk or write about right and wrong behaviour
➤ **moralist** *NOUN*

**morals** *PLURAL NOUN*
standards of behaviour

**morass** (say mo-rass) *NOUN* morasses
❶ a marsh or bog ❷ a confused mass

**morbid** *ADJECTIVE*
❶ thinking about gloomy or unpleasant things such as death • *She has a morbid interest in funerals.* ❷ (*in medicine*) unhealthy • *a morbid growth*
➤ **morbidly** *ADVERB*

**more** *DETERMINER* (comparative of **much** and **many**)
greater in amount or degree • *We need more money.*

**more** *PRONOUN*
a greater amount • *I want more.*

**more** *ADVERB*
❶ to a greater extent • *This is more important.* • *You must work more.* ❷ again • *I don't want to do it any more.*
➤ **more or less** ❶ approximately ❷ nearly or practically

**moreover** *ADVERB*
besides; in addition to what has been said

**Mormon** *NOUN* Mormons
a member of a religious group founded in the USA

**morn** *NOUN* (*poetical use*)
morning

**morning** *NOUN* mornings
the early part of the day, before noon or before lunchtime

**morocco** *NOUN*
a kind of leather originally made in Morocco from goatskins

**moron** *NOUN* morons (*informal*)
a very stupid person
➤ **moronic** *ADJECTIVE*

**morose** (say mo-rohss) *ADJECTIVE*
bad-tempered and miserable
➤ **morosely** *ADVERB*
➤ **moroseness** *NOUN*

**morpheme** *NOUN* morphemes
the smallest unit of meaning that a word can be divided into, e.g. *go* and *-ing* in the word *going*

**morphine** (say mor-feen) *NOUN*
a drug made from opium, used to lessen pain (WORD ORIGIN) named after *Morpheus*, the Roman god of dreams

**morris dance** *NOUN* morris dances
a traditional English dance performed in costume by men with ribbons and bells (WORD ORIGIN) originally *Moorish dance* (because it was thought to have come from the Moors)

**morrow** *NOUN* (*poetical use*)
the following day

**Morse code** *NOUN*
a signalling code using short and long sounds or flashes of light (dots and dashes) to represent letters (WORD ORIGIN) named after its American inventor, S. F. B. *Morse*

**morsel** *NOUN* morsels
a small piece of food

**mortal** *ADJECTIVE*
❶ not living for ever • *All of us are mortal.* ❷ causing death; fatal • *a mortal wound*

❸ deadly or extreme • *mortal enemies*
➤ **mortally** ADVERB

**mortal** NOUN mortals
a human being, as compared to a god or immortal spirit

**mortality** NOUN
❶ the state of being mortal and bound to die ❷ the number of people who die over a period of time • *a low rate of infant mortality*

**mortar** NOUN mortars
❶ a mixture of sand, cement and water used in building to stick bricks together ❷ a hard bowl in which substances are pounded with a pestle ❸ a short cannon for firing shells at a high angle

**mortar board** NOUN mortar boards
an academic cap with a stiff square top
**WORD ORIGIN** because it looks like the board used by workmen to hold mortar

**mortgage** (say mor-gij) NOUN mortgages
an arrangement to borrow money to buy a house, with the house as security for the loan

**mortgage** VERB mortgages, mortgaging, mortgaged
to take out a loan, with your house as security

**mortify** VERB mortifies, mortifying, mortified
to humiliate someone or make them feel very ashamed • *I was mortified to realize she had heard every word I said.*
➤ **mortification** NOUN

**mortise** NOUN mortises
a slot made in a piece of wood for another piece to be joined to it. Compare with **tenon**.

**mortise lock** NOUN mortise locks
a lock set into a door

**mortuary** NOUN mortuaries
a place where dead bodies are kept before being buried or cremated

**mosaic** (say mo-zay-ik) NOUN mosaics
a picture or design made from small coloured pieces of stone or glass

**mosque** (say mosk) NOUN mosques
a building where Muslims worship

**mosquito** NOUN mosquitoes
a kind of gnat that sucks blood

**moss** NOUN mosses
a plant that grows in damp places and has no flowers

**mossy** ADJECTIVE
covered in moss

**most** DETERMINER
(superlative of **much** and **many**)

**most** PRONOUN
the greatest amount • *Most of the food was eaten.*

**most** ADVERB
❶ to the greatest extent; more than any other • *It seemed the most natural thing in the world.* • *I liked this book most.* ❷ very or extremely • *It was most amusing.*

**mostly** ADVERB
mainly; in most ways • *The Sun is mostly made of hydrogen gas.*

**motel** NOUN motels
a hotel for people who are travelling by car, with space for parking cars near the rooms

**moth** NOUN moths
an insect rather like a butterfly, that usually flies at night

**mother** NOUN mothers
a female parent
➤ **motherhood** NOUN

**mother** VERB mothers, mothering, mothered
to look after someone in a motherly way

**Mothering Sunday** NOUN
(*British*) Mother's Day

**mother-in-law** NOUN mothers-in-law
the mother of a married person's husband or wife

**motherly** ADJECTIVE
kind and gentle; like a mother

**mother-of-pearl** NOUN
a pearly substance lining the shells of mussels etc.

**Mother's Day** NOUN
the fourth Sunday in Lent, when many people give cards or presents to their mothers

**motif** (say moh-teef) NOUN motifs
a repeated design or theme

**motion** NOUN motions
❶ a way of moving; movement • *The motion of the boat made me feel sick.* ❷ a formal suggestion at a meeting that people discuss and vote on
➤ **go through the motions** to do or say something because you have to, without much interest

**motion** VERB motions, motioning, motioned
to signal to someone with a gesture • *She motioned him to sit beside her.*

**motionless** ADJECTIVE
not moving

**motivate** VERB motivates, motivating, motivated
❶ to give a person a motive or reason to do something • *She seems to be motivated by a sense of duty.* ❷ to make a person determined to achieve something • *He is good at motivating his players.*
➤ **motivation** NOUN

**motive** NOUN motives
what makes a person do something • *The police couldn't discover a motive for the murder.*

**motive** ADJECTIVE
producing movement • *The engine provides motive power.*

**motley** ADJECTIVE
made up of various sorts of things or people that do not seem to belong together • *They were a motley bunch.*

**motor** NOUN motors
a machine providing power to drive machinery etc.; an engine

**motor** ADJECTIVE
having a motor; to do with vehicles that have motors • *motor vehicles* • *the motor industry*

**motor** VERB motors, motoring, motored
to travel by car

**motorbike** NOUN motorbikes
a motorcycle

**motorcade** NOUN motorcades
a procession of cars

**motorcycle** NOUN motorcycles
a two-wheeled road vehicle with an engine
➤ **motorcyclist** NOUN

**motorist** NOUN motorists
a person who drives a car

**motorized** (also **motorised**) ADJECTIVE
equipped with a motor or with motor vehicles

**motor neuron disease** NOUN
a disease of the nerves that control movement, so that the muscles get weaker and weaker until the person dies

**motorway** NOUN motorways
a wide road for fast long-distance traffic

**mottled** ADJECTIVE
marked with spots or patches of colour

**motto** NOUN mottoes
❶ a short saying used as a guide for behaviour • *'Better safe than sorry' is my*
motto. ❷ a short verse or riddle found inside a cracker

**mould** NOUN moulds
❶ a hollow container of a particular shape, in which a liquid or soft substance is put to set into this shape ❷ a fine furry growth of very small fungi

**mould** VERB moulds, moulding, moulded
❶ to make something have a particular shape • *First, mould the clay into a ball.* ❷ to strongly influence how someone develops • *He moulded them into a superb team.*

**moulder** VERB moulders, mouldering, mouldered
to rot away or decay into dust

**mouldy** ADJECTIVE
covered with mould • *The cheese has gone mouldy.*

**moult** VERB moults, moulting, moulted
to shed feathers, hair or skin while a new growth forms

**mound** NOUN mounds
❶ a pile of earth or stones etc. ❷ a small hill

**mount** VERB mounts, mounting, mounted
❶ to go up something • *She slowly mounted the stairs.* ❷ to get on a horse or bicycle ❸ to increase in amount • *Our costs are mounting.* ❹ to mount a picture or photograph is to put it in a frame or album in order to display it ❺ to organize something • *The gallery is to mount an exhibition of young British artists.*

**mount** NOUN mounts
❶ a mountain • *Mount Everest* ❷ something on which an object is mounted ❸ a horse for riding

**mountain** NOUN mountains
❶ a very high hill ❷ a large heap, pile, or quantity • *We have a mountain of work to do.*

**mountaineer** NOUN mountaineers
a person who climbs mountains
➤ **mountaineering** NOUN

**mountainous** ADJECTIVE
❶ having many mountains • *a mountainous region* ❷ huge • *mountainous waves*

**mounted** ADJECTIVE
on horseback • *mounted police*

**mourn** VERB mourns, mourning, mourned
to be sad, especially because someone has died • *When he died, he was mourned all over the world.*

**mourner** NOUN mourners
mourners are the people who go to a funeral, especially the family and friends of the person who has died

**mournful** ADJECTIVE
sad and sorrowful • *a mournful song*
➤ **mournfully** ADVERB

**mouse** NOUN mice
❶ a small animal with a long thin tail and a pointed nose ❷ (*in computing*) mouses or mice a small device which you move around on a mat to control the movements of a cursor on a computer screen

**mousetrap** NOUN mousetraps
a trap for catching and killing mice

**moussaka** NOUN
a dish of minced meat, aubergine, etc., with a cheese sauce

**mousse** (say mooss) NOUN mousses
❶ a creamy pudding flavoured with fruit or chocolate ❷ a frothy creamy substance put on the hair so that it can be styled more easily

**moustache** (say mus-**tahsh**) NOUN moustaches
a strip of hair that a man grows above his upper lip

**mousy** ADJECTIVE mousier, mousiest
❶ mousy hair is a dull light brown in colour ❷ a mousy person is timid and feeble

**mouth** NOUN mouths
❶ the opening in your face that you use for eating and speaking ❷ the place where a river enters the sea ❸ an opening or outlet

**mouth** VERB mouths, mouthing, mouthed
to form words carefully with your lips, especially without saying them aloud • *'Time to go,' she mouthed.*

**mouthful** NOUN mouthfuls
an amount of food you put in your mouth

**mouth organ** NOUN mouth organs
(*British*) a small musical instrument that you play by blowing and sucking while passing it along your lips

**mouthpiece** NOUN mouthpieces
the part of a musical instrument or other device that you put to your mouth

**movable** ADJECTIVE
able to be moved • *model soldiers with movable arms and legs*

**move** VERB moves, moving, moved
❶ to go or take something from one place to another; to change a person's or thing's position ❷ to affect a person's feelings • *Their sad story moved us deeply.* ❸ to put forward a formal suggestion (**a motion**) to be discussed and voted on at a meeting
➤ **mover** NOUN

**move** NOUN moves
❶ a movement or action ❷ a player's turn to move a piece in a game such as chess
➤ **get a move on** (*informal*) to hurry up
➤ **on the move** moving or making progress

**movement** NOUN movements
❶ moving or being moved ❷ a group of people working together to achieve something ❸ (*in music*) one of the main divisions of a symphony or other long musical work

**movie** NOUN movies (*North American*) (*informal*)
a cinema film **WORD ORIGIN** short for *moving picture*

**moving** ADJECTIVE
making someone feel strong emotion, especially sorrow or pity • *It was a very moving story.*

**mow** VERB mows, mowing, mowed, mown
to cut down grass or cereal crops
➤ **mower** NOUN
➤ **mow someone down** to kill someone with a car or gun

**mozzarella** NOUN
a kind of Italian cheese used in cooking, originally made from buffalo's milk

**MP** ABBREVIATION
Member of Parliament

**Mr** (say **mist**-er) NOUN Messrs
a title put before a man's name

**Mrs** (say **mis**-iz) NOUN Mrs
a title put before a married woman's name

**MS** ABBREVIATION
multiple sclerosis

**Ms** (say miz) NOUN
a title put before a woman's name, regardless of whether she is married or not

**MSc** ABBREVIATION
Master of Science

**MSP** ABBREVIATION
Member of the Scottish Parliament

a b c d e f g h i j k l m n o p q r s t u v w x y z

**Mt** *ABBREVIATION*
mount or mountain

**much** *ADJECTIVE* **more, most**
existing in a large amount • *There is much work to do.*

**much** *PRONOUN*
a large amount of something • *That's not very much.*

**much** *ADVERB*
❶ greatly or considerably • *I feel much better today.* • *He came, much to my surprise.* ❷ approximately • *These are much the same.*

**muck** *NOUN*
❶ farmyard manure ❷ (*informal*) dirt or filth

**muck** *VERB*
➤ **muck about** (*informal*) to mess about
➤ **muck something out** to clean out the place where an animal is kept
➤ **muck something up** (*informal*)
❶ to make something dirty ❷ to spoil or make a mess of something

**mucky** *ADJECTIVE* **muckier, muckiest**
dirty or filthy

**mucous** (say **mew**-kus) *ADJECTIVE*
❶ like mucus ❷ covered with mucus • *a mucous membrane*

**mucus** (say **mew**-kus) *NOUN*
the moist sticky substance on the inner surface of the throat etc.

**mud** *NOUN*
wet soft earth

**muddle** *VERB* **muddles, muddling, muddled**
❶ to jumble or mix things up ❷ to confuse things in your mind • *I always get those two names muddled up.*

**muddle** *NOUN* **muddles**
confusion or disorder • *My papers are all in a muddle.*

**muddy** *ADJECTIVE* **muddier, muddiest**
full of or covered with mud • *muddy boots*

**mudguard** *NOUN* **mudguards**
a curved cover over the top part of a bicycle wheel to protect the rider from the mud and water thrown up by the wheel

**muesli** (say **mooz**-lee) *NOUN*
(*chiefly British*) a breakfast food made of mixed cereals, dried fruit and nuts

**muezzin** (say moo-**ez**-in) *NOUN* **muezzins**
a Muslim crier who calls the hours of prayer from a minaret

**muff** *NOUN* **muffs**
a short tube-shaped piece of warm material into which the hands are pushed from opposite ends

**muff** *VERB* **muffs, muffing, muffed**
(*informal*) to bungle something

**muffin** *NOUN* **muffins**
❶ a flat bun eaten toasted and buttered ❷ a small sponge cake, usually containing fruit, chocolate chips, etc.

**muffle** *VERB* **muffles, muffling, muffled**
❶ to cover or wrap something to protect it or keep it warm ❷ to deaden the sound of something • *a muffled scream*

**muffler** *NOUN* **mufflers**
a warm scarf

**mug** *NOUN* **mugs**
❶ a kind of large straight-sided cup ❷ (*British*) (*informal*) a fool; a person who is easily fooled or cheated ❸ (*informal*) a person's face

**mug** *VERB* **mugs, mugging, mugged**
to attack and rob someone in the street
➤ **mugger** *NOUN*

**muggy** *ADJECTIVE* **muggier, muggiest**
muggy weather is unpleasantly warm and damp

**mulberry** *NOUN* **mulberries**
a purple or white fruit rather like a blackberry

**mule** *NOUN* **mules**
an animal that is the offspring of a donkey and a mare, known for being stubborn
➤ **mulish** *ADJECTIVE*

**mull** *VERB* **mulls, mulling, mulled**
➤ **mull something over** to think about something carefully • *I'll have to mull it over before making a decision.*

**mulled** *ADJECTIVE*
mulled wine is heated with sugar and spices

**mullet** *NOUN* **mullet**
a kind of fish used as food

**multi-** *PREFIX*
many (as in *multicoloured* = with many colours)

**multicultural** *ADJECTIVE*
made up of people of many different races, religions and cultures

**multifarious** (say multi-**fair**-ee-us) *ADJECTIVE*
of many kinds; very varied

**multilateral** ADJECTIVE
a multilateral agreement or treaty is made between three or more people, organizations, or countries

**multimedia** ADJECTIVE
using more than one medium of communication • *a multimedia show with pictures, lights and music*

**multimedia** NOUN
a computer program with sound and still and moving pictures linked to the text

**multimillionaire** NOUN multimillionaires
a person with a fortune of several million pounds or dollars

**multinational** NOUN multinationals
a large business company which works in several countries

**multiple** ADJECTIVE
having many parts or elements • *a monster with multiple heads*

**multiple** NOUN multiples
a number that contains another number (a **factor**) an exact amount of times with no remainder • *8 and 12 are multiples of 4.*

**multiple sclerosis** NOUN
a disease of the nervous system which makes a person unable to control their movements and may affect their sight

**multiplex** NOUN multiplexes
a large cinema complex that has many screens

**multiplication** NOUN
the process of multiplying one number by another

**multiplicity** NOUN
a great variety or large number

**multiply** VERB multiplies, multiplying, multiplied
❶ to add a number to itself a given quantity of times • *Five multiplied by four equals twenty* (5 x 4 = 20). ❷ to make things many or to become many; to increase • *His doubts started to multiply.*

**multiracial** ADJECTIVE
consisting of people of many different races

**multitude** NOUN multitudes
a very large number of people or things • *a multitude of birds*
➤ **multitudinous** ADJECTIVE

**mum** NOUN mums (*British*) (*informal*)
mother

**mum** ADJECTIVE (*informal*)
saying nothing • *He promised to keep mum.*

**mumble** VERB mumbles, mumbling, mumbled
to speak indistinctly so that you are not easy to hear • *Stop mumbling and speak up!*
➤ **mumble** NOUN
➤ **mumbler** NOUN

**mumbo-jumbo** NOUN
(*informal*) talk or ceremony that has no real meaning

**mummify** VERB mummifies, mummifying, mummified
in ancient Egypt, to preserve a corpse as a mummy

**mummy** NOUN mummies
❶ (*British*) (*informal*) mother ❷ in ancient Egypt, a corpse wrapped in cloth and treated with oils etc. before being buried so that it does not decay

**mumps** NOUN
an infectious disease that makes the neck swell painfully

**munch** VERB munches, munching, munched
to chew food steadily and often noisily • *He sat there munching his toast.*

**mundane** ADJECTIVE
ordinary, not exciting

**municipal** (say mew-**nis**-ip-al) ADJECTIVE
to do with a town or city that has its own local government • *municipal buildings*

**munificent** ADJECTIVE (*formal*)
extremely generous
➤ **munificently** ADVERB
➤ **munificence** NOUN

**munitions** PLURAL NOUN
military weapons, ammunition and equipment

**mural** NOUN murals
a large picture painted on a wall

**murder** VERB murders, murdering, murdered
to kill a person unlawfully and deliberately
➤ **murderer** NOUN
➤ **murderess** NOUN

**murder** NOUN murders
the murdering of someone • *They were found guilty of murder.*

**murderous** ADJECTIVE
likely to murder someone or looking as though you might • *There was a murderous look in his eyes.*

a
b
c
d
e
f
g
h
i
j
k
l
m
n
o
p
q
r
s
t
u
v
w
x
y
z

**murky** ADJECTIVE murkier, murkiest
dark and gloomy • He peered into the murky
water.
➤ **murk** NOUN

**murmur** VERB murmurs, murmuring,
murmured
❶ to speak in a soft voice • She murmured
something in her sleep. ❷ to make a low
continuous sound • The wind murmured in
the trees.

**murmur** NOUN murmurs
a sound of soft voices

**muscle** NOUN muscles
❶ a band or bundle of fibrous tissue that can
contract and relax and so produce movement
in parts of the body ❷ the power of muscles;
strength (WORD ORIGIN) from Latin *musculus*
= little mouse (because a flexed muscle was
thought to have the shape of a mouse hiding
under a mat)

SPELLING
Take care: the s sound is spelt **sc**.

**muscular** ADJECTIVE
❶ to do with the muscles ❷ having well-
developed muscles

**muse** VERB muses, musing, mused
❶ to think deeply about something; to
ponder ❷ to say something to yourself in a
thoughtful way • 'I wonder where he's gone?'
mused Lisa.

**museum** NOUN museums
a place where interesting, old or valuable
objects are displayed for people to see
(WORD ORIGIN) from Greek *mouseion* = place of
Muses (goddesses of the arts and sciences)

**mush** NOUN
a soft thick mass • The vegetables had turned
to mush.

**mushroom** NOUN mushrooms
an edible fungus with a stem and a dome-
shaped top

**mushroom** VERB mushrooms, mushrooming,
mushroomed
to grow or appear suddenly in large numbers
• Blocks of flats mushroomed in the city

**mushy** ADJECTIVE
❶ soft and thick, like mush ❷ too emotional
or sentimental • a mushy film

**music** NOUN
❶ a pattern of pleasant or interesting
sounds made by instruments or by the voice

❷ printed or written symbols which stand for
musical sounds

**musical** ADJECTIVE
❶ to do with music ❷ producing music
❸ good at music or interested in it
➤ **musically** ADVERB

**musical** NOUN musicals
a play or film containing a lot of songs

**musician** NOUN musicians
someone who plays a musical instrument

**musk** NOUN
a strong-smelling substance used in perfumes
➤ **musky** ADJECTIVE

**musket** NOUN muskets
a kind of gun with a long barrel, used in the
past by soldiers

**musketeer** NOUN musketeers
a soldier armed with a musket

**Muslim** NOUN Muslims
someone who follows the religion of Islam

**muslin** NOUN
very thin cotton cloth (WORD ORIGIN) named
after *Mosul*, a city in Iraq, where it was first
made

**mussel** NOUN mussels
a black shellfish

**must** AUXILIARY VERB
used to show
❶ that someone has to do something or
that it is necessary that something happens
(I must go home soon.) ❷ that something is
certain (You must be joking!)

**mustang** NOUN mustangs
a wild horse of the United States of America
and Mexico

**mustard** NOUN
a yellow paste or powder used to give food a
hot taste

**muster** VERB musters, mustering, mustered
❶ to find as much of something as you can
• He was trying to muster up the courage to
speak to her. ❷ to gather people together in
one place; to assemble

**muster** NOUN musters
an assembly of people or things
➤ **pass muster** to be up to the required
standard

**mustn't** (mainly spoken)
must not

**musty** ADJECTIVE mustier, mustiest
smelling or tasting mouldy or stale
➤ **mustiness** NOUN

**mutant** NOUN mutants
a living creature that is different from others
of the same type because of changes in its
genes
➤ **mutant** ADJECTIVE

**mutation** NOUN mutations
a change in the form of a living creature
because of changes in its genes
➤ **mutate** VERB

**mute** ADJECTIVE
❶ silent; not speaking or able to speak ❷ not
pronounced • The g in 'gnat' is mute.

**mute** NOUN mutes
❶ a person who cannot speak ❷ a device
fitted to a musical instrument to deaden its
sound

**muted** ADJECTIVE
quiet; not strongly expressed • muted
applause

**mutely** ADVERB
without speaking • I shook my head mutely.

**mutilate** VERB mutilates, mutilating,
mutilated
to damage something by breaking or cutting
off part of it
➤ **mutilation** NOUN

**mutineer** NOUN mutineers
a person who takes part in a mutiny

**mutinous** ADJECTIVE
taking part in a mutiny; refusing to obey
orders • The crew became mutinous.
➤ **mutinously** ADVERB

**mutiny** NOUN mutinies
rebellion against authority, especially refusal
by soldiers or sailors to obey orders

**mutiny** VERB mutinies, mutinying, mutinied
to take part in a mutiny

**mutter** VERB mutters, muttering, muttered
❶ to speak in a low voice ❷ to grumble
➤ **mutter** NOUN

**mutton** NOUN
meat from a sheep

**mutual** (say **mew**-tew-al) ADJECTIVE
❶ given or done to each other • They have
mutual respect for one another. ❷ shared by
two or more people • a mutual friend
➤ **mutually** ADVERB

**muzzle** NOUN muzzles
❶ an animal's nose and mouth ❷ a cover put
over an animal's nose and mouth so that it
cannot bite ❸ the open end of a gun

**muzzle** VERB muzzles, muzzling, muzzled
❶ to put a muzzle on an animal ❷ to
silence someone; to prevent a person from
expressing opinions

**my** DETERMINER
belonging to me

**myriad** (say **mirr**i-ad) ADJECTIVE
very many; countless • She gazed at the
myriad stars in the sky above.

**myriad** NOUN
a huge number of people or things • a myriad
of colours

**myrrh** (say mer) NOUN
a substance used in perfumes, incense, and
medicine

**myrtle** NOUN myrtles
an evergreen shrub with dark leaves and
white flowers

**myself** PRONOUN
I or me and nobody else. The word is used to
refer back to the subject of a sentence (e.g.
I have hurt myself.) or for emphasis (e.g. I
myself will not be coming.).
➤ **by myself** alone; on my own

**mysterious** ADJECTIVE
full of mystery; puzzling • her mysterious
disappearance
➤ **mysteriously** ADVERB

**mystery** NOUN mysteries
something that cannot be explained or
understood; something puzzling • Exactly
why the ship sank is a mystery.

**mystic** NOUN mystics
a person who seeks to obtain spiritual contact
with God by deep religious meditation

**mystic** ADJECTIVE
mystical

**mystical** ADJECTIVE
having spiritual powers or qualities that are
difficult to understand or explain • Watching
the sun set over the island was an almost
mystical experience.
➤ **mystically** ADVERB

**mystify** VERB mystifies, mystifying, mystified
to puzzle or bewilder someone • I'm
completely mystified about how this
happened.
➤ **mystification** NOUN

a
b
c
d
e
f
g
h
i
j
k
l
m
n
o
p
q
r
s
t
u
v
w
x
y
z

**mystique** (say mis-**teek**) *NOUN*
an air of mystery or secret power

**myth** (say mith) *NOUN* myths
❶ an old story containing ideas about ancient times or about supernatural beings. Compare with **legend**. ❷ an untrue story or belief

**mythical** *ADJECTIVE*
❶ imaginary; found only in myths • *a mythical animal* ❷ to do with myths

**mythological** *ADJECTIVE*
to do with myths • *mythological stories*

**mythology** *NOUN*
myths or the study of myths

**myxomatosis** (say miks-om-at-**oh**-sis) *NOUN*
a disease that kills rabbits

**N.** *ABBREVIATION*
❶ north ❷ northern

**nab** *VERB* nabs, nabbing, nabbed (*informal*)
to catch or arrest someone; to seize or grab something

**nag** *VERB* nags, nagging, nagged
❶ to pester a person by keeping on criticizing, complaining or asking for things ❷ to keep on hurting or bothering you • *a nagging pain*

**nag** *NOUN* nags
(*informal*) a horse

**nail** *NOUN* nails
❶ the hard covering over the end of a finger or toe ❷ a small sharp piece of metal hammered in to fasten pieces of wood together

**nail** *VERB* nails, nailing, nailed
❶ to fasten something with a nail or nails
❷ (*informal*) to catch or arrest someone

**naive** (say nah-**eev**) *ADJECTIVE*
showing a lack of experience or good judgement; innocent and trusting
➤ **naively** *ADVERB*
➤ **naivety** *NOUN*

**naked** *ADJECTIVE*
❶ without any clothes or coverings on
❷ obvious; not hidden • *the naked truth*
➤ **nakedness** *NOUN*

**naked eye** *NOUN*
the eye when it is not helped by a telescope, binoculars or microscope • *These creatures are too tiny to see with the naked eye.*

**name** *NOUN* names
❶ the word or words by which a person, animal, place or thing is known ❷ a person's reputation

**name** *VERB* names, naming, named
❶ to give a name to a person or thing
• *Braille is named after its inventor, Louis Braille.* ❷ to say what someone or something is called • *Can you name all the planets?* ❸ to say what you want something to be • *Name your price.*
➤ **name the day** to decide when something, especially a wedding, is to take place or happen • *Have you two named the day yet?*

**nameless** *ADJECTIVE*
❶ without a name • *a nameless grave* ❷ not named or identified • *The culprit shall remain nameless.*

**namely** *ADVERB*
that is to say • *My two favourite subjects are sciences, namely chemistry and biology.*

**namesake** *NOUN* namesakes
a person or thing with the same name as another

**nanny** *NOUN* nannies
❶ a person, usually a woman, who looks after young children ❷ (*informal*) grandmother

**nanny goat** *NOUN* nanny goats
a female goat. Compare with **billy goat**.

**nap** *NOUN* naps
a short sleep
➤ **catch a person napping** to catch a person unprepared for something or not alert

**napalm** (say **nay**-pahm) *NOUN*
a substance made of petrol, used in some incendiary bombs

**nape** *NOUN* napes
the back part of your neck

**napkin** *NOUN* napkins
❶ a piece of cloth or paper used at meals to protect your clothes or for wiping your lips or fingers ❷ (*old use*) a nappy

**nappy** *NOUN* nappies
(*British*) a piece of cloth or other fabric put round a baby's bottom

**narcissistic** *ADJECTIVE*
extremely vain **WORD ORIGIN** from *Narcissus*,

a youth in Greek legend who fell in love with his own reflection and was turned into a flower

**narcissus** NOUN narcissi
a garden flower like a daffodil

**narcotic** NOUN narcotics
a drug that makes a person sleepy or unconscious
➤ **narcotic** ADJECTIVE

**narrate** VERB narrates, narrating, narrated
to tell a story or give an account of something • *Each chapter is narrated by a different character.*
➤ **narration** NOUN

**narrative** NOUN narratives
a spoken or written account of something

**narrator** NOUN narrators
the person who is telling a story

**narrow** ADJECTIVE
❶ not wide or broad ❷ uncomfortably close; with only a small margin of error or safety • *We all had a narrow escape.*

**narrow** VERB narrows, narrowing, narrowed
to make something narrower or to become narrower • *He narrowed his eyes.* • *As they drove on, the road narrowed.*

**narrowly** ADVERB
only by a small amount • *The car narrowly missed a cyclist.*

**narrow-minded** ADJECTIVE
not willing to accept other people's beliefs and ways

**nasal** ADJECTIVE
❶ to do with the nose ❷ sounding as if the breath comes out through the nose • *a nasal voice*
➤ **nasally** ADVERB

**nasturtium** (say na-**ster**-shum) NOUN
nasturtiums
a garden plant with round leaves and red, yellow or orange flowers (**WORD ORIGIN**) from Latin *nasus* = nose + *torquere* = to twist (because of its sharp smell)

**nasty** ADJECTIVE nastier, nastiest
❶ horrid or unpleasant • *a nasty smell*
❷ cruel or unkind • *a nasty remark*
➤ **nastily** ADVERB
➤ **nastiness** NOUN

**nation** NOUN nations
a large community of people most of whom have the same ancestors, language, history and customs and who usually live in the same part of the world under one government

**national** ADJECTIVE
to do with or belonging to a nation or country • *national dress* • *a national newspaper*
➤ **nationally** ADVERB

**national** NOUN nationals
a citizen of a particular country

**national anthem** NOUN national anthems
a nation's official song, which is played or sung on important occasions

**national curriculum** NOUN
the subjects that must be taught by state schools in England and Wales

**nationalist** NOUN nationalists
❶ a person who is very patriotic ❷ a person who wants their country to be independent and not to form part of another country • *Scottish Nationalists*
➤ **nationalism** NOUN
➤ **nationalistic** ADJECTIVE

**nationality** NOUN nationalities
the condition of belonging to a particular nation • *What is your nationality?*

**nationalize** (also **nationalise**) VERB
nationalizes, nationalizing, nationalized
to put an industry or business under the ownership or control of the state
➤ **nationalization** NOUN

**national park** NOUN national parks
an area of natural beauty which is protected by the government and which the public may visit

**nationwide** ADJECTIVE & ADVERB
over the whole of a country • *a nationwide campaign*

**native** NOUN natives
a person born in a particular place • *He is a native of Sweden.*

**native** ADJECTIVE
❶ your native country or city is the place where you were born ❷ your native language is the language that you first learned to speak ❸ grown or originating in a particular place • *a plant native to China* ❹ that you have naturally without having to learn it • *native cunning*

**Native American** NOUN Native Americans
one of the original inhabitants of North and South America

a
b
c
d
e
f
g
h
i
j
k
l
m
n
o
p
q
r
s
t
u
v
w
x
y
z

**USAGE**

The preferred term for the descendants of the original inhabitants of North and South America is *Native American*. *American Indian* is usually acceptable but the term *Red Indian* is offensive and should not be used.

**nativity** NOUN nativities
a person's birth
➤ **the Nativity** the birth of Jesus Christ

**natter** VERB natters, nattering, nattered
(*informal*) to chat informally

**natty** ADJECTIVE nattier, nattiest (*informal*)
neat in appearance
➤ **nattily** ADVERB

**natural** ADJECTIVE
❶ produced or done by nature, not by people or machines ❷ normal; not surprising • *It's only natural to be nervous before an exam.* ❸ having a quality or ability that you were born with • *a natural leader* ❹ a natural note is neither sharp nor flat
➤ **naturalness** NOUN

**natural** NOUN naturals
❶ a person who is naturally good at something ❷ a natural note in music; a sign (♮) that shows this

**natural gas** NOUN
gas found underground or under the sea, not made from coal

**natural history** NOUN
the study of plants and animals

**naturalist** NOUN naturalists
an expert in natural history

**naturalize** (also **naturalise**) VERB naturalizes, naturalizing, naturalized
❶ to give a person full rights as a citizen of a country although they were not born there ❷ to cause a plant or animal to grow or live naturally in a country that is not its own
➤ **naturalization** NOUN

**naturally** ADVERB
❶ in a natural way • *The gas is produced naturally.* ❷ as you would expect • *We were naturally disappointed to lose.*

**natural science** NOUN
the study of physics, chemistry and biology

**natural selection** NOUN
Charles Darwin's theory that only the plants and animals best suited to their surroundings will survive and breed

**nature** NOUN natures
❶ everything in the world that was not made by people, such as plants and animals ❷ the qualities and characteristics of a person or thing • *She has a loving nature.* ❸ a kind or sort of thing • *He likes things of that nature.*

**nature reserve** NOUN nature reserves
an area of land which is managed in a way that preserves the wild animals and plants that live there

**nature trail** NOUN nature trails
a path in a country area with signs telling you about the plants and animals that live there

**naught** NOUN (*old use*)
nothing

**naughty** ADJECTIVE naughtier, naughtiest
❶ badly behaved or disobedient ❷ slightly rude or indecent • *naughty pictures*
➤ **naughtily** ADVERB
➤ **naughtiness** NOUN

**nausea** (say naw-zee-a) NOUN
a feeling of sickness or disgust
➤ **nauseating** ADJECTIVE

**nauseous** ADJECTIVE
feeling that you are going to be sick; sickening

**nautical** ADJECTIVE
to do with ships or sailors • *a nautical term*

**nautical mile** NOUN nautical miles
a measure of distance used at sea, equal to 2,025 yards (1.852 kilometres)

**naval** ADJECTIVE
to do with a navy • *a naval officer*

**nave** NOUN naves
the main central part of a church (the other parts are the chancel, aisles and transepts)

**navel** NOUN navels
the small hollow in the centre of the abdomen, where the umbilical cord was attached

**navigable** ADJECTIVE
suitable for ships and boats to sail in • *a navigable river*

**navigate** VERB navigates, navigating, navigated
❶ to sail in or through a river or sea etc. • *The ship navigated the Suez Canal.* ❷ to make sure that a ship, aircraft or vehicle is going in the right direction ❸ to find your way around a website

➤ **navigation** NOUN
➤ **navigator** NOUN

**navvy** NOUN navvies
(*British*) a labourer digging a road, railway or canal **WORD ORIGIN** short for 'navigator', a person who constructs a 'navigation' (= canal)

**navy** NOUN navies
❶ a country's warships and the people trained to use them ❷ (also **navy blue**) a very dark blue, the colour of naval uniform

**nay** ADVERB (*old use*)
no

**Nazi** (say **nah**-tsee) NOUN Nazis
a member of the National Socialist Party in Germany in Hitler's time, with Fascist beliefs
➤ **Nazism** NOUN

**NB** ABBREVIATION
take note that **WORD ORIGIN** Latin *nota bene* = note well

**NE** ABBREVIATION
❶ north-east ❷ north-eastern

**Neanderthal** (say nee-**an**-der-tahl) NOUN Neanderthals
an early type of human who lived in Europe during the Stone Age

**near** ADVERB & ADJECTIVE
not far away
➤ **near by** not far away • *They live near by.*

**near** PREPOSITION
not far away from • *The bus stops near our house.*

**near** VERB nears, nearing, neared
to come close to something • *The ship neared the harbour.*

**nearby** ADJECTIVE
near; not far away • *a nearby house*

**nearly** ADVERB
almost; not quite • *We have nearly finished.*

**neat** ADJECTIVE neater, neatest
❶ arranged carefully; tidy and in order • *a neat desk* ❷ clever or skilful • *a neat trick* ❸ drunk without anything added • *neat whisky* ❹ (*North American*) (*informal*) excellent
➤ **neatness** NOUN

**neaten** VERB neatens, neatening, neatened
to make something neat

**neatly** ADVERB
❶ in a tidy or carefully arranged way • *neatly folded clothes* ❷ in a clever or skilful way • *She neatly avoided answering the question.*

**nebula** NOUN nebulae
a bright or dark patch in the sky, caused by a distant galaxy or a cloud of dust or gas

**nebulous** ADJECTIVE
unclear or vague • *nebulous ideas*

**necessarily** ADVERB
in a way that cannot be avoided • *The number of tickets available is necessarily limited.*
➤ **not necessarily** not always or not definitely • *Expensive restaurants are not necessarily better than cheaper ones.*

**necessary** ADJECTIVE
needed for something; essential
**SPELLING**
Double up the s in **necessary** (but the c stays single).

**necessitate** VERB necessitates, necessitating, necessitated
to make a thing necessary • *This route up the mountain necessitated a tricky climb.*

**necessity** NOUN necessities
❶ need; great importance • *the necessity of buying food and clothing* ❷ something necessary

**neck** NOUN necks
❶ the part of the body that joins the head to the shoulders ❷ the part of a piece of clothing round your neck ❸ a narrow part of something, especially of a bottle
➤ **neck and neck** almost exactly together in a race or contest

**necklace** NOUN necklaces
a piece of jewellery worn round the neck

**necktie** NOUN neckties
a strip of material worn passing under the collar of a shirt and knotted in front

**nectar** NOUN
❶ a sweet liquid collected by bees from flowers ❷ a delicious drink
**WORD ORIGIN** from Greek *nektar* = the drink of the gods

**nectarine** NOUN nectarines
a kind of peach with a thin smooth skin

**nectary** NOUN nectaries
the nectar-producing part of a plant

**née** (say nay) ADJECTIVE
born, used to give a married woman's maiden name • *Mrs Smith, née Jones*
**WORD ORIGIN** French = born

a b c d e f g h i j k l m **n** o p q r s t u v w x y z

**need** VERB needs, needing, needed
❶ to be without something you should have; to require something • *We need two more chairs.* ❷ (as an auxiliary verb) to have to do something • *You need not answer.*

**need** NOUN needs
❶ something needed; a necessary thing ❷ a situation where something is necessary • *There is no need to shout.* ❸ great poverty or hardship

**needle** NOUN needles
❶ a very thin pointed piece of steel used in sewing ❷ either of a pair of metal, plastic or bamboo rods used in knitting ❸ a thin spike on a tree or plant • *pine needles* ❹ the pointer of a meter or compass

**needless** ADJECTIVE
not necessary because it could have been avoided • *It was a needless waste of time.*
➤ **needlessly** ADVERB

**needlework** NOUN
sewing or embroidery

**needy** ADJECTIVE needier, neediest
very poor; lacking things necessary for life
➤ **neediness** NOUN

**ne'er** ADVERB (poetical use)
never

**nefarious** (say nif-**air**-ee-us) ADJECTIVE
wicked or criminal • *his nefarious plans*

**negate** VERB negates, negating, negated
❶ to make something ineffective ❷ to disprove or deny something
➤ **negation** NOUN

**negative** ADJECTIVE
❶ that says 'no' • *a negative answer* ❷ looking only at the bad aspects of a situation • *Don't be so negative.* ❸ showing no sign of what is being tested for • *Her pregnancy test was negative.* ❹ less than zero; minus ❺ to do with the kind of electric charge carried by electrons
➤ **negatively** ADVERB

USAGE
The opposite of meaning 1 is **affirmative**; the opposite of the other meanings is **positive**.

**negative** NOUN negatives
❶ a negative statement ❷ a photograph or film with the dark parts light and the light parts dark, from which a positive print (with the dark and light or colours correct) can be made

**neglect** VERB neglects, neglecting, neglected
❶ to fail to look after or pay attention to a person or thing • *The buildings have been neglected for many years.* ❷ to fail or forget to do something • *He neglected to shut the door.*

**neglect** NOUN
neglecting or being neglected
➤ **neglectful** ADJECTIVE

**negligence** NOUN
lack of proper care or attention; carelessness
➤ **negligent** ADJECTIVE
➤ **negligently** ADVERB

**negligible** ADJECTIVE
not big or important enough to be worth bothering about • *Fortunately, the damage was negligible.*

**negotiable** ADJECTIVE
able to be changed after being discussed
• *The salary is negotiable.*

**negotiate** VERB negotiates, negotiating, negotiated
❶ to bargain or discuss something with others in order to reach an agreement ❷ to arrange something after discussion • *They negotiated a treaty.* ❸ to get over or past an obstacle or difficulty • *We first had to negotiate a five-metre wall.*
➤ **negotiator** NOUN

**negotiation** NOUN negotiations
negotiations are discussions people have to reach an agreement about something

**neigh** VERB neighs, neighing, neighed
to make the high-pitched cry of a horse

**neigh** NOUN neighs
the high-pitched cry of a horse

**neighbour** NOUN neighbours
someone who lives next door or near to you

SPELLING
The 'ay' sound is spelt **eigh** at the start of **neighbour**, and the 'er' sound at the end is spelt **our**.

**neighbourhood** NOUN neighbourhoods
❶ the surrounding district or area ❷ a part of a town where people live • *a quiet neighbourhood*

**neighbouring** ADJECTIVE
near each other • *neighbouring villages*

**neighbourly** ADVERB
friendly and helpful to people who live near you

**neither** (say **ny**-ther or **nee**-ther) DETERMINER & PRONOUN
not either • *Neither parent was there.*
• *Neither of them likes cabbage.*

**neither** ADVERB CONJUNCTION
➤ **neither ... nor** not one thing and not the other • *She neither knew nor cared.*

USAGE

Correct use is *Neither of them likes it.*
*Neither he nor his children like it.* Use a singular verb (e.g. *likes*) unless one of its subjects is plural (e.g. *children*).

**nemesis** (say **nem**-i-sis) NOUN
a punishment that is deserved and cannot be avoided (WORD ORIGIN) named after *Nemesis,* goddess of retribution in Greek mythology

**Neolithic** (say nee-o-**lith**-ik) ADJECTIVE
belonging to the later part of the Stone Age

**neon** NOUN
a gas that glows when electricity passes through it, used in glass tubes to make illuminated signs

**nephew** NOUN nephews
the son of a person's brother or sister

**nepotism** (say **nep**-ot-izm) NOUN
showing favouritism to relatives in appointing them to jobs (WORD ORIGIN) from Latin *nepos* = nephew

**nerve** NOUN nerves
❶ any of the fibres in your body that carry messages to and from your brain, so that parts of your body can feel and move ❷ courage and calmness in a dangerous situation • *Don't lose your nerve.* ❸ cheek or impudence • *You've got a nerve!*
➤ **get on someone's nerves** to irritate someone
➤ **nerves** nervousness or anxiety • *I always suffer from nerves before exams.*

**nerve** VERB nerves, nerving, nerved
to give someone the courage to do something • *He nerved himself to look down.*

**nerve centre** NOUN nerve centres
the place from which a system or organization is controlled

**nerve-racking** ADJECTIVE
making you feel anxious or stressed

**nervous** ADJECTIVE
❶ anxious about something or afraid of something • *I always get nervous just before a match.* ❷ easily worried or frightened • *She's quite a nervous girl.* ❸ to do with the nerves • *a nervous illness*
➤ **nervousness** NOUN

**nervous breakdown** NOUN nervous breakdowns
a state of severe depression and anxiety, making it difficult to cope with life

**nervously** ADVERB
in a way that shows you are nervous • *He smiled nervously.*

**nervous system** NOUN nervous systems
the system, consisting of the brain, spinal cord and nerves, which sends electrical messages from one part of your body to another

**nervy** ADJECTIVE nervier, nerviest
nervous or anxious

**nest** NOUN nests
❶ a structure or place in which a bird lays its eggs and feeds its young ❷ a place where some small creatures, especially mice and wasps, live ❸ a set of similar things that fit inside each other • *a nest of tables*

**nest** VERB nests, nesting, nested
❶ to have or make a nest • *Gulls were nesting on the cliffs.* ❷ to fit inside something

**nest egg** NOUN nest eggs
a sum of money saved up for future use
(WORD ORIGIN) originally = an egg left in the nest to encourage a hen to lay more

**nestle** VERB nestles, nestling, nestled
❶ to curl up comfortably or put something in a comfortable position • *She nestled her head on his shoulder.* ❷ to be in a sheltered position • *A little village nestled at the foot of the hill.*

**nestling** NOUN nestlings
a bird that is too young to leave the nest

**net** NOUN nets
❶ material made of pieces of thread, cord or wire joined together in a criss-cross pattern with holes between ❷ something made of this • *a fishing net*
➤ **the Net** the Internet

**net** ADJECTIVE
remaining when nothing more is to be deducted. Compare with **gross**. • *The net weight, without the box, is 100 grams.*

**net** VERB nets, netting, netted
❶ to catch something with a net; to kick a ball into a net ❷ to gain or produce an amount as a net profit

**netball** NOUN
a game in which two teams try to throw a ball into a high net hanging from a ring

**nether** ADJECTIVE
lower • *the nether regions*

**netting** NOUN
a piece of net

**nettle** NOUN nettles
a wild plant with leaves that sting when they are touched

**nettle** VERB nettles, nettling, nettled
to annoy someone • *Her remarks clearly nettled him.*

**network** NOUN networks
❶ a net-like arrangement or pattern of intersecting lines or parts • *the railway network* ❷ an organization with many connecting parts that work together • *a spy network* ❸ a group of radio or television stations which broadcast the same programmes ❹ a set of computers which are linked to each other

**neuralgia** (say newr-**al**-ja) NOUN
pain along a nerve, especially in your face or head

**neurology** NOUN
the study of nerves and their diseases
➤ **neurological** ADJECTIVE
➤ **neurologist** NOUN

**neuron, neurone** NOUN neurons or neurones
a cell that is part of the nervous system and sends messages to and from your brain

**neurotic** (say newr-**ot**-ik) ADJECTIVE
always very worried about something

**neuter** ADJECTIVE
in some languages, belonging to the class of words which are neither masculine nor feminine, such as *Fenster* in German

**neuter** VERB neuters, neutering, neutered
to remove an animal's sex organs so that it cannot breed

**neutral** ADJECTIVE
❶ not supporting either side in a war or quarrel ❷ not very distinctive • *a neutral colour such as grey* ❸ neither acid nor alkaline
➤ **neutrality** NOUN

**neutral** NOUN neutrals
❶ a neutral person or country ❷ a gear that is not connected to the driving parts of an engine

**neutralize** (also **neutralise**) VERB neutralizes, neutralizing, neutralized
❶ to stop something from having any effect ❷ to make a substance chemically neutral
➤ **neutralization** NOUN

**neutron** NOUN neutrons
a particle of matter with no electric charge

**never** ADVERB
❶ at no time; not ever ❷ not at all • *I never realized she was so unhappy.*

**nevertheless** ADVERB
in spite of this; although this is a fact

**new** ADJECTIVE
❶ not existing before; just made, invented, discovered or received ❷ fresh; not used before • *Start on a new page.* ❸ different or changed • *We've just moved to a new house.*
➤ **newness** NOUN

**new** ADVERB
recently • *new-laid eggs*

**New Age** ADJECTIVE
to do with a way of living and thinking that includes belief in astrology and alternative medicine and concern for environmental and spiritual matters rather than possessions

**newborn** ADJECTIVE
recently born • *a newborn baby*

**newcomer** NOUN newcomers
a person who has arrived recently

**newfangled** ADJECTIVE
disliked because it is new in method or style

**newly** ADVERB
recently • *a newly discovered comet*

**new moon** NOUN new moons
the moon at the beginning of its cycle, when only a thin crescent can be seen

**news** NOUN
❶ information about recent events or a broadcast report of this ❷ a piece of new information • *That's news to me.*

**newsagent** NOUN newsagents
(*British*) a shopkeeper who sells newspapers

**newsflash** NOUN newsflashes
a short news broadcast which interrupts a programme because something important has happened

**newsgroup** NOUN newsgroups
a place on the Internet where people discuss a particular subject and exchange information about it

**newsletter** NOUN newsletters
a short, informal report sent regularly to members of an organization

**newspaper** NOUN newspapers
❶ a daily or weekly publication on large sheets of paper, containing news reports, reviews and articles ❷ the sheets of paper forming a newspaper • *Wrap it in newspaper.*

**newsy** ADJECTIVE (*informal*)
full of news • *a newsy email*

**newt** NOUN newts
a small animal rather like a lizard, that lives near or in water **WORD ORIGIN** from Old English: originally *an ewt*

**newton** NOUN newtons
a unit for measuring force
**WORD ORIGIN** named after the English scientist, Isaac *Newton*

**New Year's Day** NOUN
the first day of the year, which in the modern Western calendar is 1 January

**next** ADJECTIVE
nearest; coming immediately after • *on the next day* • *When does the next bus leave?*

**next** ADVERB
❶ after this; then • *What happened next?* ❷ in the next place in order • *Jo was the next oldest after Ali.*
➤ **next** to close beside someone or something • *He sat down next to me.*

**next door** ADVERB & ADJECTIVE
in the next house or building • *Who lives next door?*

**NGO** ABBREVIATION
non-governmental organization (a charity or association that is independent of government or business)

**nib** NOUN nibs
the pointed metal part of a pen

**nibble** VERB nibbles, nibbling, nibbled
to eat something by taking small, quick or gentle bites • *He sat at the table nibbling a biscuit.*

**nice** ADJECTIVE nicer, nicest
❶ kind and friendly ❷ pleasant or enjoyable ❸ precise or careful • *Dictionaries make nice distinctions between meanings of words.*
➤ **nicely** ADVERB
➤ **niceness** NOUN
**WORD ORIGIN** originally = stupid: from Latin *nescius* = ignorant

**nicety** (say **ny-sit-ee**) NOUN niceties
❶ a small detail or difference pointed out ❷ precision or accuracy

**niche** (say nich or neesh) NOUN niches
❶ a small recess, especially in a wall • *The vase stood in a niche.* ❷ a suitable place or position • *She found her niche in the drama club.*

**nick** NOUN nicks
❶ a small cut or notch ❷ (*informal*) a police station or prison
➤ **in good nick** (*informal*) in good condition
➤ **in the nick of time** only just in time

**nick** VERB nicks, nicking, nicked
❶ to make a nick in something ❷ (*informal*) to steal something ❸ (*informal*) to arrest someone

**nickel** NOUN nickels
❶ a silvery-white metal ❷ (*North American*) a 5-cent coin

**nickname** NOUN nicknames
an informal name given to a person instead of his or her real name **WORD ORIGIN** originally *an eke-name*: from Middle English *eke* = addition + **name**

**nicotine** NOUN
a poisonous substance found in tobacco
**WORD ORIGIN** from the name of J. *Nicot*, who introduced tobacco into France in 1560

**niece** NOUN nieces
the daughter of a person's brother or sister

**niggardly** ADJECTIVE
mean or stingy

**niggle** VERB niggles, niggling, niggled
to be a small but constant worry • *The question niggled away at the back of his mind.*
➤ **niggling** ADJECTIVE

**nigh** ADVERB & PREPOSITION (*poetical use*)
near or nearly

**night** NOUN nights
❶ the dark hours between sunset and sunrise ❷ a particular night or evening • *the first night of the play*
**SPELLING**
**Night** is different from **knight**, which is a noble warrior.

**nightcap** NOUN nightcaps
❶ (*old use*) a knitted cap worn in bed ❷ a drink, especially an alcoholic one, which you have before going to bed

a b c d e f g h i j k l m n o p q r s t u v w x y z

**nightclub** NOUN nightclubs
a place that is open at night where people go to drink and dance

**nightdress** NOUN nightdresses
a loose dress that girls or women wear in bed

**nightfall** NOUN
the coming of darkness at the end of the day

**nightie** NOUN nighties (informal)
a nightdress

**nightingale** NOUN nightingales
a small brown bird that sings sweetly

**nightlife** NOUN
the places of entertainment that you can go to at night • a popular resort with plenty of nightlife

**nightly** ADJECTIVE & ADVERB
happening every night • nightly patrols

**nightmare** NOUN nightmares
❶ a frightening dream ❷ an unpleasant experience • The journey was a nightmare.
➤ **nightmarish** ADJECTIVE
**WORD ORIGIN** from night + Middle English mare = an evil spirit

**nil** NOUN
nothing or nought • We lost three-nil.
**WORD ORIGIN** from Latin nihil = nothing

**nimble** ADJECTIVE
able to move quickly and easily; agile • You need nimble fingers for that job.
➤ **nimbly** ADVERB

**nine** NOUN & ADJECTIVE nines
the number 9

**ninepins** NOUN
the game of skittles played with nine objects

**nineteen** NOUN & ADJECTIVE nineteens
the number 19
➤ **nineteenth** ADJECTIVE & NOUN

**ninety** NOUN & ADJECTIVE nineties
the number 90
➤ **ninetieth** ADJECTIVE & NOUN

**ninth** ADJECTIVE & NOUN ninths
❶ next after eighth ❷ one of nine equal parts of a thing

**nip** VERB nips, nipping, nipped
❶ to pinch or bite someone quickly
❷ (informal) to go somewhere quickly • I'm just nipping out to the shops.

**nip** NOUN nips
❶ a quick pinch or bite ❷ sharp coldness

• There's a nip in the air. ❸ a small drink of a spirit • a nip of brandy

**nipper** NOUN nippers (informal)
a young child

**nipple** NOUN nipples
the small part that sticks out at the front of a person's breast, from which babies suck milk

**nippy** ADJECTIVE nippier, nippiest (informal)
❶ quick or nimble ❷ rather cold

**nirvana** NOUN
in Buddhism and Hinduism, the highest state of knowledge and understanding, achieved by meditation

**nit** NOUN nits
a parasitic insect or its egg, found in people's hair

**nit-picking** NOUN
pointing out very small faults or mistakes

**nitrate** NOUN nitrates
❶ a chemical compound containing nitrogen
❷ potassium or sodium nitrate, used as a fertilizer

**nitric acid** (say ny-trik) NOUN
a very strong colourless acid containing nitrogen

**nitrogen** (say ny-tro-jen) NOUN
a gas that makes up about four-fifths of the air

**nitwit** NOUN nitwits (informal)
a stupid person

**no** DETERMINER
not any • We have no money.

**no** EXCLAMATION
used to deny or refuse something • 'Will you come?' 'No.'

**no** ADVERB
not at all • She is no better.

**No., no.** ABBREVIATION Nos. or nos.
number

**nobility** NOUN
❶ being noble ❷ the aristocracy

**noble** ADJECTIVE nobler, noblest
❶ of high social rank; aristocratic ❷ having a very good character or qualities • a noble king ❸ stately or impressive • a noble building
➤ **nobly** ADVERB

**noble** NOUN nobles
a person of high social rank

**nobleman, noblewoman** *NOUN* noblemen, noblewomen
a man or woman of high social rank

**nobody** *PRONOUN*
no person; no one

**nobody** *NOUN* nobodies (*informal*) an unimportant person

**nocturnal** *ADJECTIVE*
❶ happening at night ❷ active at night • *Badgers are nocturnal animals.*

**nocturne** *NOUN* nocturnes
a piece of music with the quiet dreamy feeling of night

**nod** *VERB* nods, nodding, nodded
to move your head up and down, especially as a way of agreeing with someone or as a greeting
➤ **nod off** to fall asleep

**nod** *NOUN* nods
a movement of your head up and down

**node** *NOUN* nodes
a small round swelling

**nodule** *NOUN* nodules
a small node

**noise** *NOUN* noises
a sound, especially one that is loud or unpleasant

**noiseless** *ADJECTIVE*
making no noise • *She moved with noiseless steps.*
➤ **noiselessly** *ADVERB*

**noisome** (say **noi**-sum) *ADJECTIVE*
smelling unpleasant; harmful • *a noisome dungeon*

**noisy** *ADJECTIVE* noisier, noisiest
making a lot of noise or full of noise • *a noisy classroom*
➤ **noisily** *ADVERB*

**nomad** *NOUN* nomads
a member of a tribe that moves from place to place looking for pasture for their animals

**nomadic** *ADJECTIVE*
moving from place to place • *a nomadic tribe*

**no man's land** *NOUN*
an area that does not belong to anybody, especially the land between opposing armies

**nom de plume** *NOUN* noms de plume
a name used by a writer instead of their real name; a pseudonym (WORD ORIGIN) French, = pen-name (this phrase is not used in French)

**nominal** *ADJECTIVE*
❶ in name only • *He is the nominal ruler, but the real power is held by the generals.*
❷ small or insignificant • *We charged them only a nominal fee.*
➤ **nominally** *ADVERB*

**nominate** *VERB* nominates, nominating, nominated
to formally suggest that someone should be a candidate in an election or should be given a job or award • *His latest novel has been nominated for several book prizes.*
➤ **nomination** *NOUN*

**nominee** *NOUN* nominees
a person who is nominated

**non-** *PREFIX*
not (as in *non-stop*) • *non-existent*

**nonagenarian** *NOUN* nonagenarians
a person aged between 90 and 99

**nonchalant** (say **non**-shal-ant) *ADJECTIVE*
calm and casual; showing no anxiety or excitement • *He tried to sound nonchalant.*
➤ **nonchalantly** *ADVERB*
➤ **nonchalance** *NOUN*

**non-committal** *ADJECTIVE*
not saying what you think or what you plan to do • *a non-committal reply*

**Nonconformist** *NOUN* Nonconformists
a member of a Protestant Church (e.g. Baptist, Methodist) that does not conform to all the customs of the Church of England

**nondescript** *ADJECTIVE*
having no special or distinctive qualities and therefore difficult to describe

**none** *PRONOUN*
❶ not any • *Sorry, we've got none left.* ❷ no one • *None can tell.*

**none** *ADVERB*
not at all • *He is none too bright.* • *She seemed none the worse for the experience.*

**nonentity** (say non-**en**-tit-ee) *NOUN* nonentities
an unimportant person

**nonetheless** *ADVERB*
in spite of this; although this is a fact

**non-existent** *ADJECTIVE*
not existing or unreal

**non-fiction** *NOUN*
writings that are not fiction; books about real people and things and true events

**non-flammable** ADJECTIVE
not able to be set on fire

USAGE
See note at **inflammable**.

**nonplussed** ADJECTIVE
puzzled or confused

**nonsense** NOUN
❶ words put together in a way that does not mean anything ❷ stupid ideas or behaviour
➤ **nonsensical** (say non-**sens**-ik-al) ADJECTIVE

**non sequitur** (say non **sek**-wit-er) NOUN non sequiturs
a conclusion that does not follow from the evidence given

**non-stop** ADJECTIVE & ADVERB
❶ not stopping • *They talked non-stop for hours.* ❷ not stopping between two main stations • *a non-stop train*

**noodles** PLURAL NOUN
pasta made in narrow strips, used in soups and stir-fries

**nook** NOUN nooks
a small sheltered place or corner
➤ **every nook and cranny** every part of a place

**noon** NOUN
twelve o'clock midday

**no one** PRONOUN
no person; nobody

SPELLING
No one is two separate words.

**noose** NOUN nooses
a loop in a rope that gets smaller when the rope is pulled

**nor** CONJUNCTION
and not • *She cannot do it; nor can I.*

**norm** NOUN norms
❶ a standard or average type, amount or level ❷ normal or expected behaviour • *social norms*

**normal** ADJECTIVE
❶ usual or ordinary ❷ natural and healthy; not suffering from an illness
➤ **normality** NOUN

**normally** ADVERB
❶ usually • *The journey normally takes an hour.* ❷ in the usual way • *Just breathe normally.*

**Norman** NOUN Normans
a member of the people of Normandy in northern France, who conquered England in 1066
➤ **Norman** ADJECTIVE
WORD ORIGIN from Old Norse *northmathr* = man from the north (because the Normans were partly descended from the Vikings)

**north** NOUN
❶ the direction to the left of a person who faces east ❷ the northern part of a country, city or other area

**north** ADJECTIVE & ADVERB
towards or in the north; coming from the north
➤ **northerly** ADJECTIVE
➤ **northern** ADJECTIVE
➤ **northerner** NOUN
➤ **northernmost** ADJECTIVE

**north-east** NOUN, ADJECTIVE & ADVERB
midway between north and east
➤ **north-easterly** ADJECTIVE
➤ **north-eastern** ADJECTIVE

**northward** ADJECTIVE & ADVERB
towards the north
➤ **northwards** ADVERB

**north-west** NOUN, ADJECTIVE & ADVERB
midway between north and west
➤ **north-westerly** ADJECTIVE
➤ **north-western** ADJECTIVE

**Nos., nos.**
plural of No. or no

**nose** NOUN noses
❶ the part of the face that is used for breathing and for smelling things ❷ the front end or part of something

**nose** VERB noses, nosing, nosed
to go forward cautiously • *Ships nosed through the ice.*
➤ **nose about** or **around** (*informal*) to look for private information about someone; to pry

**nosebag** NOUN nosebags
a bag containing fodder, for hanging on a horse's head

**nosedive** NOUN nosedives
a steep downward dive, especially by an aircraft
➤ **nosedive** VERB

**nosegay** NOUN nosegays
a small bunch of flowers

**nostalgia** (say nos-**tal**-ja) *NOUN*
a feeling of pleasure, mixed with sadness, when you remember happy times in the past
➤ **nostalgic** *ADJECTIVE*
➤ **nostalgically** *ADVERB*
**WORD ORIGIN** originally = homesickness: from Greek *nostos* = return home + *algos* = pain

**nostril** *NOUN* nostrils
either of the two openings in the nose
**WORD ORIGIN** from Old English *nosthryl* = nose-hole

**nosy** *ADJECTIVE* nosier, nosiest (*informal*)
always wanting to know other people's business
➤ **nosiness** *NOUN*
**WORD ORIGIN** from *sticking your nose in* = being inquisitive

**not** *ADVERB*
used to change the meaning of something to its opposite or absence

**notable** *ADJECTIVE*
worth noticing; remarkable or famous • *It was a notable achievement.* • *The area is notable for its wildlife.*

**notably** *ADVERB*
especially or remarkably • *Many important people, most notably the Prime Minister, have given their support.*

**notation** *NOUN* notations
a system of symbols representing numbers, quantities or musical notes

**notch** *NOUN* notches
a small V-shape cut into a surface

**notch** *VERB* notches, notching, notched
to cut a notch or notches in a surface
➤ **notch something up** to score or achieve a certain score or figure • *He has already notched up 20 goals this season.*

**note** *NOUN* notes
❶ something written down as a reminder or as a comment or explanation ❷ a short letter ❸ a banknote ❹ a single sound in music ❺ any of the keys on a piano or other keyboard instrument ❻ a sound or quality that indicates something • *There was a note of warning in his voice.*
➤ **take note of something** to pay attention to something and be sure to remember it

**note** *VERB* notes, noting, noted
❶ to make a note about something; to write something down ❷ to notice or pay attention to something • *Note the instructions on the label.*

**notebook** *NOUN* notebooks
❶ a book with blank pages on which to write notes ❷ a small computer that you can carry around with you

**noted** *ADJECTIVE*
famous, especially for a particular reason • *an area noted for its mild climate*

**notepaper** *NOUN*
paper for writing letters

**nothing** *PRONOUN*
❶ no thing; not anything • *There was nothing to do.* ❷ no amount; nought
➤ **for nothing** ❶ without payment; free ❷ without a result • *His hard work was all for nothing.*

**nothing** *ADVERB*
not at all; in no way • *It's nothing like as good as her first book.*

**notice** *NOUN* notices
❶ something written or printed and displayed for people to see ❷ attention • *It escaped my notice.* ❸ warning that something is going to happen ❹ a formal announcement that you are about to end an agreement or leave a job at a specified time • *You will need to give a month's notice.*

**notice** *VERB* notices, noticing, noticed
to see or become aware of something • *Did you notice the tattoo on his arm?*

**noticeable** *ADJECTIVE*
easily seen or noticed • *The scar is barely noticeable now.*
➤ **noticeably** *ADVERB*

**noticeboard** *NOUN* noticeboards
(*British*) a board on which notices may be displayed

**notify** *VERB* notifies, notifying, notified
to tell someone about something formally or officially • *We had better notify the police.*
➤ **notification** *NOUN*

**notion** *NOUN* notions
an idea, especially one that is vague or incorrect

**notorious** *ADJECTIVE*
well known for something bad • *a notorious criminal*
➤ **notoriously** *ADVERB*
➤ **notoriety** (say noh-ter-y-it-ee) *NOUN*

**notwithstanding** *PREPOSITION*
in spite of

a b c d e f g h i j k l m n o p q r s t u v w x y z

**nougat** (say noo-gah) NOUN
a chewy sweet made from nuts, sugar or honey and egg white

**nought** (say nawt) NOUN
(*British*) the figure 0

**noun** NOUN nouns
a word that stands for a person, place or thing. **Common nouns** are words such as *boy, dog, river, sport, table*, which are used of a whole kind of people or things; **proper nouns** are words such as *Jennifer, Thames* and *London* which name a particular person or thing.

GRAMMAR

Nouns are used to name people, places or things and tell you who or what a sentence is about.

Common nouns describe a whole group or category of people or things: for example, *footballer, lizard, picture, television, day*. They can be divided into

concrete nouns, which are used to talk about things which can be physically seen or touched (e.g. *baby, penguin, telescope*), and abstract nouns, which are used to talk about things which cannot be physically touched or seen, such as a state, idea, process or feeling (e.g. *beauty, horror, mystery*).

Proper nouns give the name of a specific person, place or thing. They include personal names and titles (e.g. *Alexander, Shakespeare, the Queen*), place names and names of geographical features (e.g. *Rome, Antarctica, Saturn, the Grand Canyon*), the names of organizations and religions (e.g. *the United Nations, Buddhism*), the days of the week, months of the year and festivals (e.g. *Tuesday, July, Diwali, Hallowe'en*). Proper nouns always begin with a capital letter; common nouns only begin with a capital when they start a sentence: *Penguins are non-flying birds that live in Antarctica.*

Nouns that can be made plural are called countable nouns. Most common nouns are countable.

Nouns that cannot be made plural are called uncountable nouns (e.g. *rice, music, anger* and *information*).

**nourish** VERB nourishes, nourishing, nourished
to keep a person, animal or plant alive and well by means of food
➤ **nourishing** ADJECTIVE

**nourishment** NOUN
food that a person, animal or plant needs to stay alive and well

**nova** (say noh-va) NOUN novae (say noh-vee) or novas
a star that suddenly becomes much brighter for a short time

**novel** NOUN novels
a story that fills a whole book

**novel** ADJECTIVE
of a new and unusual kind • *a novel experience*

**novelist** NOUN novelists
a person who writes novels

**novelty** NOUN novelties
❶ the quality of being new, different and interesting • *The novelty of living in a cave soon wore off.* ❷ something new and unusual ❸ a cheap toy or ornament

**November** NOUN
the eleventh month of the year
WORD ORIGIN from Latin *novem* = nine, because it was the ninth month of the ancient Roman calendar

**novice** NOUN novices
❶ a beginner ❷ a person preparing to be a monk or nun

**now** ADVERB
❶ at the present time; this moment • *They will be at home by now.* ❷ by this time
❸ immediately • *You must go now.* ❹ I wonder or I am telling you • *Now why didn't I think of that?*
➤ **for now** until a later time
➤ **now and again** or **now and then** sometimes; occasionally

**now** CONJUNCTION
as a result of or at the same time as something • *Now that you have come, we'll start.*

**nowadays** ADVERB
at the present time, as contrasted with years ago

**nowhere** ADVERB
not anywhere; in or to no place • *There's nowhere to sit.*

**noxious** ADJECTIVE
unpleasant and harmful • *noxious fumes*

**nozzle** *NOUN* **nozzles**
the spout of a hose, pipe or tube

**nuance** (say **new**-ahns) *NOUN* **nuances**
a slight difference or shade of meaning

**nub** *NOUN* **nubs**
❶ a small knob or lump ❷ the central point
of a problem

**nuclear** *ADJECTIVE*
❶ to do with a nucleus, especially of an
atom ❷ using the energy that is created by
reactions in the nuclei of atoms • *nuclear
power* • *nuclear weapons*

**nucleus** *NOUN* **nuclei**
❶ the central part of an atom or biological
cell ❷ the part in the centre of something,
round which other things are grouped • *The
queen bee is the nucleus of the hive.*

**nude** *ADJECTIVE*
not wearing any clothes; naked
➤ **nudity** *NOUN*

**nude** *NOUN* **nudes**
a painting or sculpture of a naked human
figure
➤ **in the nude** not wearing any clothes

**nudge** *VERB* **nudges, nudging, nudged**
❶ to poke a person gently with your elbow
❷ to push something slightly or gradually

**nudge** *NOUN* **nudges**
a slight push or poke

**nugget** *NOUN* **nuggets**
❶ a rough lump of something, especially
gold, found in the earth ❷ a small but
valuable fact

**nuisance** *NOUN* **nuisances**
a person or thing that is annoying or causes
trouble

**null** *ADJECTIVE*
➤ **null and void** not legally valid • *The
agreement is null and void.*

**nullify** *VERB* **nullifies, nullifying, nullified**
to make a thing no longer valid; to cancel an
agreement or arrangement
➤ **nullification** *NOUN*

**numb** *ADJECTIVE*
not able to feel anything • *My fingers were
numb with cold.*
➤ **numbly** *ADVERB*
➤ **numbness** *NOUN*

**numb** *VERB* **numbs, numbing, numbed**
to make you unable to feel anything • *We
were all numbed by the dreadful news.*

**number** *NOUN* **numbers**
❶ a symbol or word that tells you how many
of something there are; a numeral or figure
❷ a series of numbers given to a thing to
identify it • *a telephone number* ❸ a quantity
of people or things • *He found a large
number of people waiting outside.* ❹ one
issue of a magazine or newspaper ❺ a song
or piece of music

USAGE

Note that *a number of*, meaning 'a
quantity of' or 'several', should be
followed by a plural verb • *A number of
problems remain.*

**number** *VERB* **numbers, numbering, numbered**
❶ to give something a number or mark it
with a number • *The houses are numbered
from 1 to 34.* ❷ to amount to a certain figure
• *The crowd numbered 10,000.*

GRAMMAR

**Numbers** tell you how many of something
there are.

A **cardinal number** is a number that
expresses a quantity and is used for
counting things, e.g. *one, two, three*, etc.

An **ordinal number** is a number that
shows a thing's position in a series, e.g.
*first, fifth, twentieth*, etc.

**numberless** *ADJECTIVE*
too many to count

**numeracy** *NOUN*
a good basic knowledge of mathematics
➤ **numerate** *ADJECTIVE*

**numeral** *NOUN* **numerals**
a symbol that represents a certain number;
a figure

**numerator** *NOUN* **numerators**
the number above the line in a fraction,
showing how many parts are to be taken, e.g.
2 in ⅖. Compare with **denominator**.

**numerical** (say new-**merri**-kal) *ADJECTIVE*
to do with or consisting of numbers • *The
pages are not in numerical order.*
➤ **numerically** *ADVERB*

**numerous** *ADJECTIVE*
many; lots of • *There are numerous websites
on the subject.*

**numismatics** (say new-miz-**mat**-iks) *NOUN*
the study of coins
➤ **numismatist** *NOUN*

**nun** NOUN nuns
a member of a community of women who live according to the rules of a religious organization. Compare with **monk**.

**nunnery** NOUN nunneries
a convent

**nuptial** ADJECTIVE
to do with marriage or a wedding

**nuptials** PLURAL NOUN
a wedding

**nurse** NOUN nurses
❶ a person trained to look after people who are ill or injured ❷ a woman employed to look after young children

**nurse** VERB nurses, nursing, nursed
❶ to look after someone who is ill or injured ❷ to take care of an injury or illness • *I got up slowly, nursing my bruised shoulder.* ❸ to feed a baby at the breast ❹ to have a feeling for a long time • *She's been nursing a grudge against him for years* ❺ to hold something carefully in your hands • *He sat nursing his mug of coffee.*

**nursemaid** NOUN nursemaids
a young woman employed to look after young children

**nursery** NOUN nurseries
❶ a place where young children are looked after or play ❷ a place where young plants are grown and usually for sale

**nursery rhyme** NOUN nursery rhymes
a simple rhyme or song of the kind that young children like

**nursery school** NOUN nursery schools
a school for children below primary school age

**nursing home** NOUN nursing homes
a small hospital or home for invalids

**nurture** VERB nurtures, nurturing, nurtured
❶ to take care of and educate a young child while he or she is growing ❷ to help something to grow or develop • *He has nurtured the talent of many young footballers.* ❸ to cherish an idea or hope • *She nurtured a hope of becoming famous.*

**nurture** NOUN
a child's upbringing and education

**nut** NOUN nuts
❶ a fruit with a hard shell ❷ a kernel ❸ a small piece of metal with a hole in the middle, for screwing onto a bolt ❹ (*informal*) the head ❺ (*informal*) a mad or eccentric person

**nutcrackers** PLURAL NOUN
pincers for cracking nuts

**nutmeg** NOUN
the hard seed of a tropical tree, grated and used in cooking

**nutrient** (say new-tree-ent) NOUN nutrients
a substance that is needed to keep a plant or animal alive and to help it grow • *Plants take minerals and other nutrients from the soil.*

**nutriment** (say new-trim-ent) NOUN
nourishing food

**nutrition** (say new-trish-on) NOUN
the food that you eat and the way that it affects your health; nourishment
➤ **nutritional** ADJECTIVE
➤ **nutritionally** ADVERB

**nutritious** (say new-**trish**-us) ADJECTIVE
nutritious food has substances in it that help you to stay healthy • *a nutritious meal*

**nuts** ADJECTIVE
(*informal*) mad or eccentric

**nutshell** NOUN nutshells
the shell of a nut
➤ **in a nutshell** stated very briefly

**nutty** ADJECTIVE
❶ tasting of nuts or full of nuts ❷ (*informal*) slightly crazy

**nuzzle** VERB nuzzles, nuzzling, nuzzled
to rub gently against someone with the nose or face • *The dog began nuzzling my hand.*

**NW** ABBREVIATION
❶ north-west ❷ north-western

**nylon** NOUN
a synthetic, strong, lightweight cloth or fibre

**nymph** (say nimf) NOUN nymphs
❶ in myths, a young goddess living in the sea or woods etc. ❷ the immature form of insects such as the dragonfly

**NZ** ABBREVIATION
New Zealand

**Oo**

**O** *EXCLAMATION*
oh

**oaf** *NOUN* oafs
a stupid or clumsy man

**oak** *NOUN* oaks
a large deciduous tree with seeds called acorns
➤ **oaken** *ADJECTIVE*

**oar** *NOUN* oars
a pole with a flat blade at one end, used for rowing a boat
➤ **oarsman** *NOUN*

**oasis** (say oh-**ay**-sis) *NOUN* oases
a fertile place in a desert, with a spring or well of water

**oath** *NOUN* oaths
❶ a solemn promise to do something or that something is true, sometimes appealing to God as witness ❷ a swear word
➤ **on** or **under oath** having sworn to tell the truth in a law court

**oatmeal** *NOUN*
ground oats, used to make porridge or in baking

**oats** *PLURAL NOUN*
a cereal used to make food for animals and for people

**obedient** *ADJECTIVE*
doing what you are told; willing to obey
➤ **obediently** *ADVERB*
➤ **obedience** *NOUN*

**obeisance** (say o-**bay**-sans) *NOUN* obeisances
a deep bow or curtsy showing respect

**obelisk** *NOUN* obelisks
a tall pillar set up as a monument

**obese** (say o-**beess**) *ADJECTIVE*
very fat; overweight

**obesity** (say o-**beess**-it-ee) *NOUN*
being too fat in a way that is unhealthy • *the problem of obesity in children*

**obey** *VERB* obeys, obeying, obeyed
to do what you are told to do • *Soldiers are trained to obey orders.*

**obituary** *NOUN* obituaries
an announcement in a newspaper of a person's death, often with a short account of their life

**object** (say **ob**-jikt) *NOUN* objects
❶ something solid that can be seen or touched ❷ a purpose or intention • *Making money is his sole object in life.* ❸ a person or thing to which some action or feeling is directed • *She has become an object of pity.*
❹ (*in grammar*) the word or words naming the person or thing that is affected by the action of a verb or preposition, e.g. *him* in *The dog bit him.* and *I threw the ball to him.*

**object** (say ob-**jekt**) *VERB* objects, objecting, objected
to say that you are not in favour of something or do not agree • *I'd like to come too, if you don't object.*
➤ **objector** *NOUN*

**objection** *NOUN* objections
❶ objecting to something ❷ a reason for objecting • *I have a couple of objections to your plan.*

**objectionable** *ADJECTIVE*
unpleasant or nasty

**objective** *NOUN* objectives
what you are trying to reach or do; an aim
• *My main objective is to tell a good story.*

**objective** *ADJECTIVE*
❶ not influenced by personal feelings or opinions • *He tried to give an objective account of what happened.*
Compare with **subjective.** ❷ having real existence outside someone's mind • *Is there any objective evidence to prove his claims?*
➤ **objectively** *ADVERB*
➤ **objectivity** *NOUN*

**objet d'art** (say ob-zhay **dar**) *NOUN* objets d'art
a small artistic object

**obligation** *NOUN* obligations
❶ being obliged to do something ❷ what you are obliged to do; a duty
➤ **under an obligation** owing gratitude to someone who has helped you

**obligatory** (say ob-**lig**-a-ter-ee) *ADJECTIVE*
something is obligatory when you must do it because of a law or rule

**oblige** *VERB* obliges, obliging, obliged
❶ to force someone to do something • *I felt obliged to invite her to the party.* ❷ to help someone by doing what they ask • *Can you*

*oblige me with a loan?*
➤ **be obliged to someone** to feel gratitude to a person who has helped you

**obliging** ADJECTIVE
polite and helpful

**oblique** (say ob-**leek**) ADJECTIVE
❶ slanting ❷ not saying something straightforwardly • *an oblique reply*
➤ **obliquely** ADVERB

**obliterate** VERB obliterates, obliterating, obliterated
to remove all traces of something by destroying it completely or covering it up
• *The snow had obliterated their footprints.*
➤ **obliteration** NOUN
**WORD ORIGIN** from Latin *obliterare* = cross out, from *littera* = letter

**oblivion** NOUN
❶ being forgotten ❷ being unconscious

**oblivious** ADJECTIVE
completely unaware of what is happening around you • *She seemed oblivious to the danger.*

**oblong** ADJECTIVE
rectangular in shape and longer than it is wide

**oblong** NOUN oblongs
a rectangular shape that is longer than it is wide

**obnoxious** ADJECTIVE
very unpleasant or offensive

**oboe** NOUN oboes
a high-pitched woodwind instrument
➤ **oboist** NOUN

**obscene** (say ob-**seen**) ADJECTIVE
indecent in a very offensive way
➤ **obscenity** NOUN

**obscure** ADJECTIVE
❶ difficult to see or to understand; not clear
❷ not well known
➤ **obscurely** ADVERB

**obscure** VERB obscures, obscuring, obscured
to make a thing difficult to see or to understand • *Clouds obscured the sun.*

**obscurity** NOUN
❶ being not well known • *He spent most of his life working in obscurity.* ❷ the quality of being difficult to understand

**obsequious** (say ob-**seek**-wee-us) ADJECTIVE
showing too much respect or too willing to obey or serve someone

➤ **obsequiously** ADVERB
➤ **obsequiousness** NOUN

**observance** NOUN
obeying or keeping a law, custom or religious festival

**observant** ADJECTIVE
quick at observing or noticing things
➤ **observantly** ADVERB

**observation** NOUN observations
❶ noticing or watching something carefully
❷ a comment or remark • *She made a few observations about the weather.*

**observatory** NOUN observatories
a building with telescopes and other instruments for observing the stars or weather

**observe** VERB observes, observing, observed
❶ to see and notice something • *I observed her putting the letter into her bag.* ❷ to watch something carefully • *The puffins were observed throughout the breeding season.* ❸ to obey a law or rule ❹ to keep or celebrate a custom or religious festival ❺ to make a remark
➤ **observer** NOUN

**obsessed** ADJECTIVE
to be obsessed with something is to be continually thinking about it • *He is obsessed with dinosaurs.*

**obsession** NOUN obsessions
something you cannot stop thinking about
• *She seems to have an obsession with aliens.*

**obsessive** ADJECTIVE
showing that a person thinks too much about something in a way that is not normal • *his obsessive cleanliness*

**obsolete** ADJECTIVE
not used any more; out of date

**obstacle** NOUN obstacles
something that stands in the way or makes it difficult to do something

**obstetrics** NOUN
the branch of medicine and surgery that deals with the birth of babies

**obstinate** ADJECTIVE
❶ refusing to change your ideas or ways, even though they may be wrong ❷ difficult to overcome or remove • *an obstinate problem*
➤ **obstinately** ADVERB
➤ **obstinacy** NOUN

**obstreperous** (say ob-**strep**-er-us) ADJECTIVE
noisy and unruly

**obstruct** VERB obstructs, obstructing,
obstructed
to stop a person or thing from getting past;
to hinder the progress of something • *A fallen
tree was obstructing the road.*
➤ **obstructive** ADJECTIVE

**obstruction** NOUN obstructions
❶ obstructing something ❷ something that
obstructs or hinders progress

**obtain** VERB obtains, obtaining, obtained
to get or be given something • *You need to
obtain permission to take photos there.*
➤ **obtainable** ADJECTIVE

**obtrude** VERB obtrudes, obtruding, obtruded
to force yourself or your ideas on someone;
to be obtrusive
➤ **obtrusion** NOUN

**obtrusive** ADJECTIVE
unpleasantly noticeable

**obtuse** ADJECTIVE
slow to understand something
➤ **obtuseness** NOUN

**obtuse angle** NOUN obtuse angles
an angle of more than 90° but less than 180°.
Compare with **acute angle**.

**obverse** NOUN
the side of a coin or medal showing the head
or chief design (the other side is the **reverse**)

**obvious** ADJECTIVE
easy to see or understand

**obviously** ADVERB
it is obvious that; clearly • *There has
obviously been a mistake.*

**occasion** NOUN occasions
❶ the time when something happens
❷ a special event ❸ a suitable time or
opportunity • *I will speak to him about it if
the occasion arises.*
➤ **on occasion** from time to time

**occasion** VERB occasions, occasioning,
occasioned (*formal*) to cause something to
happen

**occasional** ADJECTIVE
❶ happening from time to time but not
regularly or frequently ❷ for special
occasions • *occasional music*

**occasionally** ADVERB
sometimes, but not often • *We text each
other occasionally.*

**occult** ADJECTIVE
to do with the supernatural or magic • *occult
powers*

**occupant** NOUN occupants
someone who is in a place or building • *The
other occupants of the car got out.*
➤ **occupancy** NOUN

**occupation** NOUN occupations
❶ a person's job or profession ❷ something
you do to pass your time ❸ capturing a
country by military force

**occupational** ADJECTIVE
caused by an occupation • *an occupational
disease*

**occupational therapy** NOUN
creative work designed to help people to
recover from certain illnesses
➤ **occupational therapist** NOUN

**occupy** VERB occupies, occupying, occupied
❶ to live or work in a place or building;
to inhabit somewhere ❷ to fill a space or
position • *A large table occupied most of the
room.* ❸ to keep someone busy or interested
• *This game should occupy them for a few
hours.* ❹ to capture a country by force and
place troops there
➤ **occupier** NOUN

**occur** VERB occurs, occurring, occurred
❶ to happen or take place • *An earthquake
occurred on the island in 1953.* ❷ to exist or
be found somewhere • *These plants occur in
ponds.* ❸ to come into a person's mind • *Just
then an idea occurred to me.*

**occurrence** NOUN occurrences
❶ something that happens; an incident or
event ❷ occurring

**ocean** NOUN oceans
the seas that surround the continents of the
earth, especially one of the large named areas
of this • *the Pacific Ocean*
➤ **oceanic** ADJECTIVE
**WORD ORIGIN** from *Oceanus*, the river that the
ancient Greeks thought surrounded the world

**ocelot** (say **oss**-il-ot) NOUN ocelots
a leopard-like animal of Central and South
America

**ochre** (say **oh**-ker) NOUN
❶ a yellow, red or brownish mineral used as a
pigment ❷ pale brownish-yellow

**o'clock** ADVERB
used after the number of the hour when you

are saying what time it is • *Lunch is at one o'clock.* **WORD ORIGIN** short for *of the clock*

**octagon** NOUN **octagons**
a flat shape with eight sides and eight angles
➤ **octagonal** ADJECTIVE

**octave** NOUN **octaves**
the interval of eight steps between one musical note and the next note of the same name above or below it

**octet** NOUN **octets**
a group of eight instruments or singers

**October** NOUN
the tenth month of the year
**WORD ORIGIN** from Latin *octo* = eight, because it was the eighth month of the ancient Roman calendar

**octogenarian** NOUN **octogenarians**
a person aged between 80 and 89

**octopus** NOUN **octopuses**
a sea creature with eight long tentacles
**WORD ORIGIN** from Greek *okto* = eight + *pous* = foot

**ocular** ADJECTIVE
to do with your eyes or vision

**oculist** NOUN **oculists**
a doctor who treats diseases of the eye

**odd** ADJECTIVE
❶ strange or unusual ❷ an odd number is one that cannot be divided exactly by two Compare with **even**. ❸ left over from a pair or set • *I've got one odd sock.* ❹ of various kinds; not regular • *odd jobs*
➤ **oddness** NOUN

**oddity** NOUN **oddities**
a strange person or thing

**oddly** ADVERB
❶ strangely • *She's been behaving very oddly recently.* ❷ surprisingly • *Oddly enough, the most expensive tickets sold fastest.*

**oddments** PLURAL NOUN
scraps or pieces left over from a larger piece or set

**odds** PLURAL NOUN
❶ the chances that a certain thing will happen ❷ the proportion of money that you will win if a bet is successful • *When the odds are 10 to 1, you will win £10 if you bet £1.*
➤ **be at odds with someone** or **something** to disagree or conflict with someone or something

➤ **odds and ends** small things of various kinds

**ode** NOUN **odes**
a poem addressed to a person or thing

**odious** (say oh-dee-us) ADJECTIVE
extremely unpleasant; hateful

**odour** NOUN **odours**
a smell, especially an unpleasant one
➤ **odorous** ADJECTIVE
➤ **odourless** ADJECTIVE

**odyssey** (say od-iss-ee) NOUN **odysseys**
a long adventurous journey
**WORD ORIGIN** named after the *Odyssey*, a Greek poem telling of the wanderings of Odysseus

**o'er** PREPOSITION & ADVERB (*poetical use*)
over; above

**oesophagus** (say ee-sof-a-gus) NOUN
**oesophagi**
the tube leading from the throat to the stomach; the gullet

**oestrogen** (say ees-tro-jen) NOUN
a hormone which develops and maintains female sexual and physical characteristics

**of** PREPOSITION
❶ belonging to • *the mother of the child*
❷ concerning; about • *news of the disaster*
❸ made from • *built of stone* ❹ from • *north of the town*
**SPELLING**
Of is different from **off** • *I've never heard of it.* • *He fell off his bike.*

**off** PREPOSITION
❶ not on; away or down from • *He fell off the ladder.* ❷ not taking or wanting • *She is off her food.* ❸ deducted from • *£5 off the price*

**off** ADVERB
❶ away or down from something • *His hat blew off.* ❷ not working or happening • *The heating is off.* • *The match is off because of snow.* ❸ to the end; completely • *I'll finish it off tonight.* ❹ as regards money or supplies • *How are you off for cash?* ❺ food that is off is beginning to go bad ❻ behind or at the side of a stage • *There were noises off.*

**offal** NOUN
the organs of an animal, such as liver and kidneys, sold as food

**off-colour** ADJECTIVE
slightly unwell

**offence** *NOUN* offences
❶ a crime or something illegal ❷ a feeling of annoyance or resentment
➤ **give offence** to hurt someone's feelings
➤ **take offence** to be upset by what someone has said or done

**offend** *VERB* offends, offending, offended
❶ to cause offence to someone; to hurt a person's feelings ❷ to commit a crime or do something wrong
➤ **offender** *NOUN*

**offensive** *ADJECTIVE*
❶ causing offence; insulting ❷ disgusting
• *an offensive smell* ❸ used for attacking
• *offensive weapons*
➤ **offensively** *ADVERB*

**offensive** *NOUN* offensives
a forceful attack or campaign
➤ **be on the offensive** to be ready to attack or criticize someone first

**offer** *VERB* offers, offering, offered
❶ to hold something out or present it so that people can accept it if they want to ❷ to say that you are willing to do or give something or to pay a certain amount

**offer** *NOUN* offers
❶ offering something • *Thank you for your offer of help.* ❷ an amount of money offered ❸ a specially reduced price

**offering** *NOUN* offerings
something that is offered

**offhand** *ADJECTIVE*
rather casual and rude, without thought or consideration • *an offhand manner*

**offhand** *ADVERB*
without previous thought or preparation • *I don't know offhand how much it cost.*

**office** *NOUN* offices
❶ a room or building where people work, usually sitting at desks ❷ a place where people can go for tickets, information or some other service • *a lost property office* ❸ a government department • *the Foreign and Commonwealth Office* ❹ an important job or position
➤ **be in office** to hold an official position

**officer** *NOUN* officers
❶ a person who is in charge of others, especially in the armed forces ❷ a member of the police force ❸ an official

**official** *ADJECTIVE*
❶ approved or done by someone with authority • *an official announcement* ❷ done as part of your job or position • *official duties*

**official** *NOUN* officials
a person who holds a position of authority

**officially** *ADVERB*
❶ publicly and by someone in a position of authority • *The new school will be officially opened next month.* ❷ according to a set of rules • *I'm not officially supposed to be here.*

**officiate** *VERB* officiates, officiating, officiated
to be in charge of a meeting or event

**officious** *ADJECTIVE*
too ready to give orders; bossy
➤ **officiously** *ADVERB*

**USAGE**

Take care not to confuse with **official**, which means approved of or done by someone in authority.

**offing** *NOUN*
➤ **in the offing** likely to happen soon

**off-licence** *NOUN* off-licences
(*British*) a shop with a licence to sell alcoholic drinks to be drunk away from the shop

**off-putting** *ADJECTIVE*
making you less keen on something • *There was a rather off-putting smell coming from the kitchen.*

**offset** *VERB* offsets, offsetting, offset
to cancel out or make up for something • *The failures were offset by some successes.*

**offshoot** *NOUN* offshoots
❶ a side shoot on a plant ❷ a by-product

**offshore** *ADJECTIVE*
❶ in the sea some distance from the shore
• *an offshore island* ❷ from the land towards the sea • *an offshore breeze*

**offside** *ADJECTIVE & ADVERB*
a player in football or other sports is offside when they are in a position where the rules do not allow them to play the ball

**offspring** *NOUN* offspring
a person's child or children; the young of an animal

**oft** *ADVERB* (*old use*)
often

**often** *ADVERB*
many times; in many cases

**ogle** *VERB* ogles, ogling, ogled
to stare at someone whom you find attractive

**ogre** NOUN ogres
❶ a cruel giant in fairy tales and legends ❷ a terrifying person

**oh** EXCLAMATION
❶ a cry of pain, surprise or delight ❷ used for emphasis • *Oh yes I will!*

**ohm** NOUN ohms
a unit of electrical resistance
**WORD ORIGIN** named after a German scientist, G. S. *Ohm*, who studied electric currents

**oil** NOUN oils
❶ a thick slippery liquid that will not dissolve in water ❷ a kind of petroleum used as fuel ❸ oil paint

**oil** VERB oils, oiling, oiled
to put oil on something, especially to make it work smoothly • *I need to oil the chain on my bike.*

**oilfield** NOUN oilfields
an area where oil is found in the ground or under the sea

**oil paint** NOUN oil paints
paint made with oil

**oil painting** NOUN oil paintings
a painting done with oil paints

**oil rig** NOUN oil rigs
a structure set up to support the equipment for drilling for oil

**oilskin** NOUN oilskins
cloth made waterproof by treatment with oil

**oil well** NOUN oil wells
a hole drilled in the ground or under the sea to get oil

**oily** ADJECTIVE
❶ containing or like oil; covered or soaked with oil ❷ behaving in an insincerely polite way
➤ oiliness NOUN

**ointment** NOUN ointments
a cream or slippery paste for putting on sore skin and cuts

**OK, okay** ADVERB & ADJECTIVE (informal)
all right **WORD ORIGIN** perhaps from the initials of *oll* (or *orl*) *korrect*, a humorous spelling of *all correct*, first used in the USA in 1839

**old** ADJECTIVE
❶ having lived for a long time ❷ made or existing from a long time ago • *an old tradition* ❸ of a particular age • *I'm ten years old.* ❹ former or original • *I liked my old*
*school better than the one I go to now.*
➤ **of old** long ago; in the distant past

**old age** NOUN
the time when a person is old

**olden** ADJECTIVE
of former times

**Old English** NOUN
the English language from about 700 to 1150, also called *Anglo-Saxon*

**old-fashioned** ADJECTIVE
of the kind that was usual a long time ago; no longer fashionable

**Old Norse** NOUN
the language spoken by the Vikings, the ancestor of modern Scandinavian languages

**olfactory** ADJECTIVE
to do with your sense of smell

**oligarchy** NOUN oligarchies
a country ruled by a small group of people
➤ oligarch NOUN

**olive** NOUN olives
❶ an evergreen tree with a small bitter fruit ❷ this fruit, from which an oil (*olive oil*) is made ❸ a shade of green like an unripe olive

**olive branch** NOUN olive branches
something you do or offer that shows you want to make peace **WORD ORIGIN** from a story in the Bible, where the dove brings Noah an olive branch as a sign that God is no longer angry with mankind

**Olympic Games, Olympics** PLURAL NOUN
a series of international sports contests held every four years in a different part of the world
➤ **Olympic** ADJECTIVE
**WORD ORIGIN** from the name of *Olympia*, a city in Greece where they were held in ancient times

**ombudsman** NOUN ombudsmen
an official whose job is to investigate complaints against government organizations

**omega** (say oh-meg-a) NOUN
the last letter of the Greek alphabet, equivalent to Roman *o* **WORD ORIGIN** from Greek *o mega* = big O

**omelette** NOUN omelettes
eggs beaten together and cooked in a pan, often with a filling

**omen** NOUN omens
an event regarded as a sign of what is going to happen

**ominous** ADJECTIVE
suggesting that trouble is coming • *There was another ominous rumble of thunder.*
➤ **ominously** ADVERB

**omission** NOUN omissions
❶ something that has been missed out or not done ❷ missing something out or failing to do it

**omit** VERB omits, omitting, omitted
❶ to miss something out • *We can omit the last two verses.* ❷ to fail to do something • *He omitted to mention that they were staying the night.*

**omnibus** NOUN omnibuses
❶ a book containing several stories or books that were previously published separately ❷ a single edition of several radio or television programmes previously broadcast separately ❸ (*old use*) a bus **WORD ORIGIN** Latin, = for everybody

**omnipotent** ADJECTIVE
having unlimited power or very great power

**omniscient** (say om-**niss**-ee-ent) ADJECTIVE
knowing everything
➤ **omniscience** NOUN

**omnivore** (say **om**-niv-or) NOUN omnivores
an animal that feeds on both plants and the flesh of other animals. Compare with **carnivore, herbivore.**

**omnivorous** (say om-**niv**-er-us) ADJECTIVE
an omnivorous animal feeds on both plants and the flesh of other animals. Compare with **carnivorous, herbivorous.**

**on** PREPOSITION
❶ supported by, covering or attached to something • *There was no sign on the door.* • *We sat on the floor.* ❷ during; at the time of • *I'll see you on Monday.* ❸ close to; towards • *The army advanced on Paris.* ❹ by reason of • *Two men were arrested on suspicion of murder.* ❺ concerning; about • *a book on butterflies* ❻ in a state of; using or showing • *The house was on fire.*

**on** ADVERB
❶ so that it is on something • *Put the lid on.* ❷ further forward • *Move on.* ❸ working; in action • *Is the central heating on?*
➤ **on and off** occasionally; not all the time

**once** ADVERB
❶ for one time or on one occasion only • *They came only once.* ❷ at an earlier time; formerly • *They once lived here.*

**once** CONJUNCTION
as soon as • *You can go once I have taken your names.*

**oncoming** ADJECTIVE
approaching or coming towards you • *oncoming traffic*

**one** ADJECTIVE
❶ single; only • *This was my one chance.* ❷ identical; the same • *We are all of one mind.* ❸ a certain • *You must come for lunch one day.*

**one** NOUN
❶ the smallest whole number, 1 ❷ a person or thing alone
➤ **one another** each other

**one** PRONOUN
❶ a person or thing previously mentioned • *There are lots of films on but I can't find one I want to see.* ❷ a person; any person • *One likes to help.*
➤ **oneself** PRONOUN

**onerous** (say **ohn**-er-us or **on**-er-us) ADJECTIVE
difficult to bear or do • *an onerous task*

**one-sided** ADJECTIVE
❶ with one side or person in a contest or conversation being much stronger or doing a lot more than the other • *a one-sided match* ❷ showing only one point of view in an unfair way • *This is a very one-sided account of the conflict.*

**one-way** ADJECTIVE
where traffic is allowed to travel in one direction only • *a one-way street*

**ongoing** ADJECTIVE
continuing to exist or be in progress • *It's an ongoing project.*

**onion** NOUN onions
a round vegetable with a strong flavour

**online** ADJECTIVE & ADVERB
connected to a computer or to the Internet

**onlooker** NOUN onlookers
a spectator

**only** ADJECTIVE
being the one person or thing of a kind; sole • *She's the only person we can trust.*
➤ **only child** a child who has no brothers or sisters

**only** ADVERB
❶ no more than; and that is all • *There are only three cakes left.* ❷ nothing other than • *I only eat pizza.*

**only** CONJUNCTION
but then; however • *He makes promises, only he never keeps them.*

**onomatopoeia** (say on-om-at-o-**pee**-a) NOUN
forming or using words that sound like the thing they stand for, e.g. *cuckoo, plop, sizzle*
➤ **onomatopoeic** ADJECTIVE

**onrush** NOUN
a surging rush forward

**onset** NOUN
❶ the beginning of something • *the onset of winter* ❷ the first part of a syllable, e.g. *d* in *dog*

**onshore** ADJECTIVE
from the sea towards the land • *an onshore breeze*

**onslaught** NOUN onslaughts
a fierce attack

**onto, on to** PREPOSITION
to a position on

**onus** (say **oh**-nus) NOUN
the duty or responsibility of doing something • *The onus is on the prosecution to prove he did it.*

**onward** ADVERB & ADJECTIVE
going forward; further on
➤ **onwards** ADVERB

**onyx** NOUN
a stone rather like marble, with different colours in layers

**ooze** VERB oozes, oozing, oozed
❶ to flow or trickle out of something slowly ❷ a wound, crack or other opening oozes when liquid flows out of it slowly • *The wound oozed blood.*

**ooze** NOUN
mud at the bottom of a river or sea

**opal** NOUN opals
a kind of stone with a rainbow sheen
➤ **opalescent** ADJECTIVE

**opaque** (say o-**payk**) ADJECTIVE
not able to be seen through; not transparent or translucent • *opaque glass*

**open** ADJECTIVE
❶ allowing people or things to go in and out; not closed or fastened ❷ not covered or blocked up ❸ spread out; unfolded • *She greeted us with open arms.* ❹ not limited or restricted • *an open championship* ❺ letting in visitors or customers ❻ with wide empty spaces • *open country* ❼ honest and frank;

not secret or secretive • *Be open about the danger.* ❽ not decided • *an open mind* ❾ willing or likely to receive something • *I'm open to suggestions.*
➤ **openness** NOUN
➤ **in the open** ❶ outside ❷ not secret
➤ **in the open air** not inside a house or building
➤ **open-air** ADJECTIVE

**open** VERB opens, opening, opened
❶ to make something open or more open ❷ to become open or more open ❸ to begin; to start something • *I'd like to open the meeting by welcoming everybody.* ❹ a shop or office opens when it starts business for the day • *What time do you open?*

**opencast** ADJECTIVE
(*British*) an opencast mine is worked by removing layers of earth from the surface, not underground

**opener** NOUN openers
a device for opening a bottle or can

**opening** NOUN openings
❶ a space or gap; a place where something opens ❷ the beginning of something ❸ an opportunity, especially for a job

**openly** ADVERB
without trying to hide anything • *No one dared to criticize him openly.*

**open-minded** ADJECTIVE
ready to listen to other people's ideas and opinions; not having fixed ideas

**opera** NOUN
❶ operas
a play in which all or most of the words are sung to music; works of this kind ❷ plural of **opus**

**operate** VERB operates, operating, operated
❶ to make a machine work ❷ to work or be in action • *How does this machine operate?* ❸ to perform a surgical operation on someone

**operatic** ADJECTIVE
to do with opera • *an operatic composer*

**operating system** NOUN operating systems
the software that controls a computer's basic functions

**operation** NOUN operations
❶ something done to the body by a surgeon to take away or repair a part of it ❷ a carefully planned activity involving a lot of people • *a rescue operation* ❸ a piece of work performed by a machine • *The computer*

can perform this operation in a fraction of a second.
➤ **in operation** working or in use • *When does the new system come into operation?*
➤ **operational** ADJECTIVE

**operative** ADJECTIVE
❶ working or functioning ❷ to do with surgical operations

**operator** NOUN operators
a person who works something, especially a telephone switchboard or exchange

**operetta** NOUN operettas
a short opera on a light or humorous theme

**ophthalmic** (say off-**thal**-mik) ADJECTIVE
to do with or for your eyes

**ophthalmic optician** NOUN ophthalmic opticians
(*British*) a person who is qualified to test people's eyesight and prescribe glasses and contact lenses

**opinion** NOUN opinions
what you think of something; a belief or judgement • *I have recently changed my opinion of her.*

**opinionated** ADJECTIVE
having strong opinions and holding them whatever anybody says

**opinion poll** NOUN opinion polls
an estimate of what people think, made by questioning a sample of them

**opium** NOUN
a powerful drug made from the juice of certain poppies, used in the past in medicine

**opossum** NOUN opossums
a small furry marsupial that lives in trees, with different kinds in America and Australia

**opponent** NOUN opponents
a person or group opposing another in a contest or war

**opportune** ADJECTIVE
❶ an opportune time is convenient or suitable for a purpose ❷ done or happening at a suitable time
➤ **opportunely** ADVERB
**WORD ORIGIN** from Latin *ob* = towards, against + *portus* = harbour (originally used of wind blowing a ship towards a harbour)

**opportunity** NOUN opportunities
a good chance to do a particular thing
• *I'd like to take this opportunity to thank everyone for coming.*

**oppose** VERB opposes, opposing, opposed
to argue or fight against someone or something; to resist something
➤ **as opposed to** in contrast with; rather than • *This game relies on skill as opposed to luck.*
➤ **be opposed to something** to be strongly against something • *We are opposed to parking in the town centre.*

**opposite** ADJECTIVE
❶ placed on the other or further side; facing • *on the opposite side of the road* ❷ moving away from or towards each other • *The trains were travelling in opposite directions.*
❸ completely different • *My efforts to calm him down had the opposite effect.*

**opposite** NOUN opposites
an opposite person or thing • *'Happy' is the opposite of 'sad'.*

**opposite** ADVERB
in an opposite position or direction • *I'll sit opposite.*

**opposite** PREPOSITION
opposite to • *They live opposite the school.*

**opposition** NOUN
❶ opposing something; resistance ❷ the people who oppose something
➤ **the Opposition** the chief political party opposing the one that is in power

**oppress** VERB oppresses, oppressing, oppressed
❶ to govern or treat someone cruelly or unjustly ❷ to weigh someone down with worry or sadness • *The gloomy atmosphere at home oppressed him.*
➤ **oppressed** ADJECTIVE
➤ **oppressor** NOUN

**oppression** NOUN
governing or treating people cruelly or unjustly • *a struggle against oppression*

**oppressive** ADJECTIVE
❶ cruel or harsh • *an oppressive regime* ❷ worrying and difficult to bear • *an oppressive silence* ❸ oppressive weather is unpleasantly hot and humid

**opt** VERB opts, opting, opted
to choose something • *I opted for the chicken salad.*
➤ **opt out** to decide not to take part in something

**optic** ADJECTIVE
to do with your eyes or sight • *the optic nerve*

a b c d e f g h i j k l m n o p q r s t u v w x y z

**optical** ADJECTIVE
to do with sight; aiding sight • *optical instruments*
➤ **optically** ADVERB

**optical illusion** NOUN optical illusions
a deceptive appearance that makes you think you see something that is not really there

**optician** NOUN opticians
a person who tests people's eyesight and makes or sells glasses and contact lenses

**optics** NOUN
the study of sight and of light as connected with this

**optimist** NOUN optimists
a person who expects that things will turn out well. Compare with **pessimist**.
➤ **optimism** NOUN

**optimistic** ADJECTIVE
expecting things to turn out well • *I'm not very optimistic about our chances.*
➤ **optimistically** ADVERB

**optimum** ADJECTIVE
best; most favourable
➤ **optimum** NOUN
➤ **optimal** ADJECTIVE

**option** NOUN options
❶ the right or power to choose something
• *You have the option of staying.*
❷ something chosen or that may be chosen
• *Your options are to travel by bus or by train.*

**optional** ADJECTIVE
that you can choose, not compulsory
➤ **optionally** ADVERB

**opulent** ADJECTIVE
wealthy or luxurious
➤ **opulence** NOUN

**opus** (say oh-pus) NOUN opuses or opera
a numbered musical composition • *Beethoven opus 15*

**or** CONJUNCTION
used to show that there is a choice or an alternative • *Do you want a cake or a biscuit?*

**oracle** NOUN oracles
❶ a shrine where the ancient Greeks consulted one of their gods for advice or a prophecy ❷ a wise or knowledgeable adviser
➤ **oracular** (say or-**ak**-yoo-ler) ADJECTIVE

**oral** ADJECTIVE
❶ spoken, not written ❷ to do with or using your mouth
➤ **orally** ADVERB

**oral** NOUN orals
a spoken examination or test
**WORD ORIGIN** from Latin *oris* = of the mouth

**SPELLING**
Take care not to confuse with **aural**, which means to do with the ear or hearing.

**orange** NOUN oranges
❶ a round juicy citrus fruit with reddish-yellow peel ❷ a reddish-yellow colour

**orange** ADJECTIVE
reddish-yellow in colour

**orangutan** NOUN orangutans
a large ape of Borneo and Sumatra
**WORD ORIGIN** from Malay *orang hutan* = man of the forest (Malay is spoken in Malaysia)

**oration** NOUN orations
a long formal speech

**orator** NOUN orators
a person who is good at making speeches in public
➤ **oratorical** ADJECTIVE

**oratorio** NOUN oratorios
a piece of music for voices and an orchestra, usually on a religious subject

**oratory** NOUN
❶ the art of making speeches in public
❷ eloquent speech

**orb** NOUN orbs
a sphere or globe

**orbit** NOUN orbits
❶ the curved path taken by something moving round a planet, moon or star ❷ the range of someone's influence or control
➤ **orbital** ADJECTIVE

**orbit** VERB orbits, orbiting, orbited
to move in an orbit round something • *The satellite has been orbiting the earth since 1986.*

**orchard** NOUN orchards
a piece of ground planted with fruit trees

**orchestra** NOUN orchestras
a large group of people playing various musical instruments together
➤ **orchestral** ADJECTIVE

**orchestrate** VERB orchestrates, orchestrating, orchestrated
❶ to compose or arrange music for an orchestra ❷ to coordinate things deliberately
• *a carefully orchestrated campaign*
➤ **orchestration** NOUN

**orchid** NOUN orchids
a kind of plant with brightly coloured, often unevenly shaped, flowers

**ordain** VERB ordains, ordaining, ordained
❶ to make a person a member of the clergy in the Christian Church • *He was ordained in 1981.* ❷ to declare or order something by law

**ordeal** NOUN ordeals
a difficult or horrific experience

**order** NOUN orders
❶ a command to do something ❷ a request for something to be supplied • *The waiter came to take our order.* ❸ the way things are arranged • *in alphabetical order* ❹ a neat arrangement, with everything in the right place • *We were busy getting the house in order.* ❺ a situation in which people are behaving properly and obeying the rules • *The police managed to restore order.* ❻ a kind or sort of thing • *She showed courage of the highest order.* ❼ a group of monks or nuns who live by certain religious rules
➤ **in order that** or **in order to** for the purpose of
➤ **out of order** broken or not working

**order** VERB orders, ordering, ordered
❶ to command someone to do something ❷ to ask for something to be supplied to you ❸ to put something into order; to arrange things neatly • *He needed a few minutes to order his thoughts.*

**orderly** ADJECTIVE
❶ arranged neatly or well • *an orderly desk* ❷ well-behaved and obedient • *an orderly demonstration*
➤ **orderliness** NOUN

**orderly** NOUN orderlies
❶ an assistant in a hospital ❷ a soldier whose job is to assist an officer

**ordinal number** NOUN ordinal numbers
a number that shows a thing's position in a series, e.g. first, fifth, twentieth, etc. Compare with **cardinal number**.

**ordinance** NOUN ordinances
a command or decree

**ordinarily** ADVERB
usually or normally • *Ordinarily, I wouldn't have minded.*

**ordinary** ADJECTIVE
normal or usual; not special
➤ **out of the ordinary** unusual

**ordination** NOUN ordinations
ordaining someone or being ordained, as a member of the Christian clergy

**ordnance** NOUN
weapons and other military equipment

**Ordnance Survey** NOUN
an official survey organization that makes detailed maps of the British Isles
**WORD ORIGIN** because the maps were originally made for the army

**ore** NOUN ores
rock with metal or other useful substances in it • *iron ore*

**oregano** (say o-ri-**gah**-noh) NOUN
the dried leaves of wild marjoram used as a herb in cooking

**organ** NOUN organs
❶ a musical instrument from which sounds are produced by air forced through pipes, played by keys and pedals ❷ a part of the body with a particular function • *the digestive organs*

**organdie** NOUN
a kind of thin fabric, usually stiffened

**organic** ADJECTIVE
❶ to do with or formed from living things • *organic matter* ❷ organic food is grown or produced without using chemical fertilizers or pesticides • *organic farming* ❸ to do with the organs of the body • *organic diseases*
➤ **organically** ADVERB

**organism** NOUN organisms
a living thing; an individual animal or plant

**organist** NOUN organists
a person who plays the organ

**organization** (also **organisation**) NOUN organizations
❶ an organized group of people, such as a business, charity or government department ❷ the organizing of something
➤ **organizational** ADJECTIVE

**organize** (also **organise**) VERB organizes, organizing, organized
❶ to plan and prepare something • *We organized a picnic.* ❷ to put things in order • *I'm trying to organize all my notebooks.* ❸ to form people into a group to work together

**organizer** (also **organiser**) NOUN organizers
❶ a person who arranges an event or activity ❷ a thing used for organizing

a
b
c
d
e
f
g
h
i
j
k
l
m
n
o
p
q
r
s
t
u
v
w
x
y
z

**orgasm** NOUN orgasms
the moment during sexual activity when feelings of sexual pleasure are at their strongest

**Orient** NOUN
the countries of the East, especially east Asia

**orient** VERB orients, orienting, oriented
to orientate something

**oriental** ADJECTIVE
(old use) to do with the countries east of the Mediterranean Sea, especially China and Japan

**orientate** VERB orientates, orientating, orientated (chiefly British)
❶ to place something or face in a certain direction ❷ to get your bearings • *I'm just trying to orientate myself.*
➤ orientation NOUN
WORD ORIGIN originally = turn to face the east

**orienteering** NOUN
the sport of finding your way across rough country with a map and compass

**orifice** (say o-rif-iss) NOUN orifices
an opening in your body

**origami** (say o-rig-**ah**-mee) NOUN
the art of folding paper into decorative shapes WORD ORIGIN from Japanese ori = fold + kami = paper

**origin** NOUN origins
❶ the start of something; the point or cause from which something began • *a book about the origins of life on earth* ❷ a person's family background • *a man of humble origins* ❸ the point where two or more axes on a graph meet

**original** ADJECTIVE
❶ existing from the start; earliest • *the original inhabitants* ❷ new and interesting; different from others of its type • *an original idea* ❸ producing new ideas; inventive • *an original thinker* ❹ made or created first, before copies • *an original painting by a local artist*

**original** NOUN originals
a document, painting or other work which was the first one made and is not a copy

**originality** NOUN
the quality of being new and interesting • *His stories show great originality.*

**originally** ADVERB
at first, before anything changed • *My family originally came from Pakistan.*

**originate** VERB originates, originating, originated
❶ to have its origin; to begin to happen or appear • *Buddhism originated in India.* ❷ to create something • *Who originated this theory?*
➤ originator NOUN

**ornament** NOUN ornaments
an object you display or wear as a decoration

**ornament** VERB ornaments, ornamenting, ornamented
to decorate something with beautiful things • *The tree was ornamented with coloured glass balls and tiny flags.*
➤ ornamentation NOUN

**ornamental** ADJECTIVE
used as an ornament; decorative rather than useful • *an ornamental fountain*

**ornate** ADJECTIVE
elaborately decorated • *an ornate box*
➤ ornately ADVERB

**ornithology** NOUN
the study of birds
➤ ornithologist NOUN
➤ ornithological ADJECTIVE

**orphan** NOUN orphans
a child whose parents are dead
➤ orphaned ADJECTIVE

**orphanage** NOUN orphanages
a home for orphans

**orthodox** ADJECTIVE
❶ holding beliefs that are correct or generally accepted ❷ conventional or normal
➤ orthodoxy NOUN

**Orthodox Church** NOUN
the Christian Churches of eastern Europe

**orthopaedics** (say orth-o-**pee**-diks) NOUN
the treatment of deformities and injuries to bones and muscles
➤ orthopaedic ADJECTIVE

**oscillate** VERB oscillates, oscillating, oscillated
to keep moving to and fro; to vibrate • *The needle on the dial began to oscillate.*
➤ oscillation NOUN

**osier** (say **oh**-zee-er) NOUN osiers
a willow with flexible twigs used in making baskets

**osmosis** NOUN
the passing of fluid through a porous partition into another more concentrated fluid

**ostensible** ADJECTIVE
apparently true, but actually concealing the true reason • *Their ostensible reason for travelling was to visit friends.*
➤ **ostensibly** ADVERB

**ostentatious** ADJECTIVE
making a showy display of something to impress people • *ostentatious gold jewellery*
➤ **ostentatiously** ADVERB
➤ **ostentation** NOUN

**osteopath** NOUN osteopaths
a person who treats certain diseases by pressing and moving a patient's bones and muscles
➤ **osteopathy** NOUN
➤ **osteopathic** ADJECTIVE

**ostracize** (also **ostracise**) VERB ostracizes, ostracizing, ostracized
to exclude someone from your group and completely ignore them
➤ **ostracism** NOUN
**WORD ORIGIN** from Greek *ostrakon* = piece of pottery (because people voted to banish someone by writing their name on this)

**ostrich** NOUN ostriches
a large long-legged African bird that can run very fast but cannot fly. It is said to bury its head in the sand when pursued, in the belief that it then cannot be seen.

**other** ADJECTIVE
❶ different; not the same • *Play some other tune.* ❷ remaining • *Try the other shoe.* ❸ additional • *my other friends* ❹ just recent or past • *I saw him the other day.*
➤ **other than** apart from; except

**other** PRONOUN others
the other person or thing • *Where are the others?*

**otherwise** ADVERB
❶ if things happen differently; if you do not • *Write it down, otherwise you'll forget.* ❷ in other ways • *It rained, but otherwise the holiday was good.* ❸ differently • *We could not do otherwise.*

**otter** NOUN otters
a fish-eating animal with webbed feet, a flat tail and thick brown fur, living near water

**ottoman** NOUN ottomans
❶ a long padded seat ❷ a storage box with a padded top

**ought** AUXILIARY VERB
used with other words to show
❶ what you should or must do • *We ought to*
feed them. • *You ought to take more exercise.*
❷ what is likely to happen • *At this speed, we ought to be there by noon.*

**oughtn't** (mainly spoken)
ought not

**ounce** NOUN ounces
❶ a unit of weight equal to 1/16 of a pound (about 28 grams) ❷ a tiny amount • *There was not an ounce of strength left in him.*

**our** DETERMINER
belonging to us
**SPELLING**
Be careful, this sounds the same as **hour** which means 'sixty minutes'.

**ours** POSSESSIVE PRONOUN
belonging to us • *These seats are ours.*
**SPELLING**
There is never an apostrophe in *ours*.

**ourselves** PRONOUN
we or us and nobody else. The word is used to refer back to the subject of a sentence (e.g. *We blame ourselves.*) or for emphasis (e.g. *We made all the costumes ourselves.*).
➤ **by ourselves** alone; on our own

**oust** VERB ousts, ousting, ousted
to drive someone out from a position or office • *The rebels ousted the government from power.*

**out** ADVERB
❶ away from or not in a particular place or position or state; not at home • *She phoned while you were out.* ❷ into the open; into existence or sight • *The sun came out.* ❸ no longer burning or shining • *The fire has gone out.* ❹ in error • *Your estimate was 10% out.* ❺ to or at an end; completely • *The concert is sold out.* • *I'm worn out.* ❻ loudly or boldly • *He cried out.* ❼ no longer batting in cricket
➤ **be out to do something** to be seeking or wanting to do something • *They are out to make trouble.*
➤ **be out of something** to have no more of something left
➤ **out of date** ❶ old-fashioned ❷ no longer valid
➤ **out of doors** in the open air
➤ **out of the way** remote or distant

**out-and-out** ADJECTIVE
thorough or complete • *He is an out-and-out villain.*

a
b
c
d
e
f
g
h
i
j
k
l
m
n
o
p
q
r
s
t
u
v
w
x
y
z

**outback** NOUN
the remote inland districts of Australia

**outboard motor** NOUN outboard motors
a motor fitted to the outside of a boat's stern

**outbreak** NOUN outbreaks
the start of something unpleasant, such as a disease or war

**outburst** NOUN outbursts
a sudden bursting out of anger or laughter

**outcast** NOUN outcasts
a person who has been rejected by family, friends or society

**outcome** NOUN outcomes
the result of what happens or has happened

**outcrop** NOUN outcrops
a large piece of rock from a lower level that sticks out on the surface of the ground

**outcry** NOUN outcries
a strong protest • *There was an outcry over the rise in rail fares.*

**outdated** ADJECTIVE
out of date • *outdated ideas*

**outdistance** VERB outdistances, outdistancing, outdistanced
to get far ahead of someone in a race

**outdo** VERB outdoes, outdoing, outdid, outdone
to do better than another person • *They tried to outdo each other in making up silly words.*

**outdoor** ADJECTIVE
done or used outdoors

**outdoors** ADVERB
in the open air

**outer** ADJECTIVE
outside or external; nearer to the outside
• *the outer walls*

**outermost** ADJECTIVE
nearest to the outside; furthest from the centre

**outer space** NOUN
the universe beyond the earth's atmosphere

**outfit** NOUN outfits
❶ a set of clothes worn together ❷ a set of equipment ❸ (*informal*) a team or organization

**outflow** NOUN outflows
❶ flowing out; what flows out ❷ a pipe for liquid flowing out

**outgoing** ADJECTIVE
❶ soon to leave or retire from office • *the outgoing chairman* ❷ sociable and friendly
• *Vicky is cheerful and outgoing.*

**outgoings** PLURAL NOUN
what you have to spend; expenditure

**outgrow** VERB outgrows, outgrowing, outgrew, outgrown
❶ to grow out of clothes or habits • *She has outgrown those red shoes.* ❷ to grow faster or larger than another person or thing

**outgrowth** NOUN outgrowths
something that grows out of another thing
• *Feathers are outgrowths on a bird's skin.*

**outhouse** NOUN outhouses
a small building, such as a shed or barn, that belongs to a house but is separate from it

**outing** NOUN outings
a journey for pleasure

**outlandish** ADJECTIVE
looking or sounding strange or foreign • *an outlandish costume*

**outlast** VERB outlasts, outlasting, outlasted
to last longer than something else

**outlaw** NOUN outlaws
a robber or bandit who is hiding to avoid being caught and is not protected by the law

**outlaw** VERB outlaws, outlawing, outlawed
to make something illegal

**outlay** NOUN outlays
the amount of money spent on something

**outlet** NOUN outlets
❶ a way for something to get out • *The tank has an outlet at the bottom.* ❷ a way of expressing strong feelings ❸ a place from which goods are sold or distributed

**outline** NOUN outlines
❶ a line round the outside of something, showing its boundary or shape ❷ a summary

**outline** VERB outlines, outlining, outlined
❶ to make an outline of something ❷ to summarize something

**outlive** VERB outlives, outliving, outlived
to live or last longer than another person or thing • *He outlived his wife by three years.*

**outlook** NOUN outlooks
❶ a view on which people look out • *a pleasant outlook over the lake* ❷ a person's mental attitude to something • *She has an optimistic outlook on life.* ❸ what seems

likely to happen in the future • *The outlook is bleak.*

**outlying** *ADJECTIVE*
far from the centre; remote • *the outlying districts*

**outmanoeuvre** *VERB* outmanoeuvres, outmanoeuvring, outmanoeuvred
to use skill or cunning to gain an advantage over someone

**outmoded** *ADJECTIVE*
out of date

**outnumber** *VERB* outnumbers, outnumbering, outnumbered
to be greater in number than another group • *The girls outnumber the boys in our team.*

**outpatient** *NOUN* outpatients
a person who visits a hospital for treatment but does not stay there

**outpost** *NOUN* outposts
a small town or camp that is in a remote place

**output** *NOUN* outputs
❶ the amount produced, especially by a factory or business ❷ the information or results produced by a computer

**outrage** *NOUN* outrages
❶ a strong feeling of shock and anger ❷ something that shocks people by being very wicked or cruel

**outrage** *VERB* outrages, outraging, outraged
to shock and anger people greatly • *He was outraged at the way he had been treated.*

**outrageous** *ADJECTIVE*
making people feel very angry or shocked • *outrageous behaviour*
➤ **outrageously** *ADVERB*

**outrider** *NOUN* outriders
a person riding on a motorcycle as an escort or guard

**outrigger** *NOUN* outriggers
a framework attached to the side of a boat, e.g. to prevent a canoe from capsizing

**outright** *ADVERB*
❶ completely; not gradually • *This drug should be banned outright.* ❷ frankly • *We told him outright what we thought about it.*

**outright** *ADJECTIVE*
thorough or complete • *an outright victory*

**outrun** *VERB* outruns, outrunning, outran, outrun
to run faster or further than someone else

**outset** *NOUN*
➤ **at** or **from the outset** at or from the beginning of something • *It was clear from the outset that it was a bad idea.*

**outside** *NOUN* outsides
the outer side, surface or part of something
➤ **at the outside** at the most • *a mile at the outside*

**outside** *ADJECTIVE*
❶ on or coming from the outside • *the outside edge* ❷ remote or slight • *There is an outside chance that he will come.*

**outside** *ADVERB*
on or to the outside; outdoors • *Leave your trainers outside.* • *It's cold outside.*

**outside** *PREPOSITION*
on or to the outside of • *He poked his head outside the tent.*

**outside broadcast** *NOUN* outside broadcasts
(*British*) a broadcast made where something is happening and not in a studio

**outsider** *NOUN* outsiders
❶ a person who does not belong to a certain group ❷ a horse or person that people think has no chance of winning a race or competition

**outsize** *ADJECTIVE*
much larger than average

**outskirts** *PLURAL NOUN*
the parts of a town or city on its outside edge, furthest from the centre

**outspoken** *ADJECTIVE*
speaking or spoken very frankly

**outspread** *ADJECTIVE*
spread out • *a bird with outspread wings*

**outstanding** *ADJECTIVE*
❶ extremely good or distinguished • *She is an outstanding athlete.* ❷ an outstanding debt or bill is not yet paid or dealt with

**outstretched** *ADJECTIVE*
reaching out as far as possible • *He ran towards her with outstretched arms.*

**outstrip** *VERB* outstrips, outstripping, outstripped
❶ to run faster or further than someone else ❷ to achieve more or be more successful, than someone else

**outvote** *VERB* outvotes, outvoting, outvoted
to defeat someone by a majority of votes

**outward** *ADJECTIVE*
❶ going outwards ❷ on the outside

a b c d e f g h i j k l m n o p q r s t u v w x y z

**outwardly** ADVERB
on the surface; for people to see • *She remained outwardly calm.*

**outwards** ADVERB
(*British*) towards the outside • *That door opens outwards.*

**outweigh** VERB outweighs, outweighing, outweighed
to be greater in weight or importance than something else • *The advantages outweigh the disadvantages.*

**outwit** VERB outwits, outwitting, outwitted
to deceive or defeat someone by being clever or crafty

**ova**
plural of **ovum**

**oval** ADJECTIVE
shaped like an O, rounded and longer than it is broad

**oval** NOUN ovals
an oval shape WORD ORIGIN from Latin *ovum* = egg

**ovary** NOUN ovaries
❶ either of the two organs in which ova or egg-cells are produced in a woman's or female animal's body ❷ part of the pistil in a plant, from which fruit is formed

**ovation** NOUN ovations
enthusiastic applause • *She received a huge ovation.*

**oven** NOUN ovens
a closed space in which things are cooked or heated

**over** PREPOSITION
❶ above; higher than • *There's a light over the door.* ❷ more than • *It's over a mile away.* ❸ concerning; about • *They quarrelled over money.* ❹ across the top of; on or to the other side of • *They rowed the boat over the lake.* ❺ during • *We can talk over dinner.* ❻ being better than • *their victory over United*

**over** ADVERB
❶ out and down from the top or edge; from an upright position • *He fell over.* ❷ so that a different side shows • *Turn it over.* ❸ at or to a place; across • *Walk over to our house.* ❹ remaining; still available • *There is nothing left over.* ❺ all through; thoroughly • *Think it over.* ❻ at an end • *The lesson is over.*
➤ **over and over** many times; repeatedly

**over** NOUN overs
a series of six balls bowled in cricket

**over-** PREFIX
too much; too (as in *over-anxious*)

**overact** VERB overacts, overacting, overacted
an actor overacts when they act their part in an exaggerated manner

**overall** ADJECTIVE
including everything; total • *What is the overall cost?*

**overall** ADVERB
taken as a whole • *Overall, this is a very useful book.*

**overall** NOUN overalls
a type of coat worn over other clothes to protect them when working

**overalls** PLURAL NOUN
a piece of clothing, like a shirt and trousers combined, worn over other clothes to protect them

**overarm** ADJECTIVE & ADVERB
(*chiefly British*) with your arm lifted above shoulder level and coming down in front of your body • *bowling overarm*

**overawed** ADJECTIVE
so impressed by something that you feel nervous or frightened

**overbalance** VERB overbalances, overbalancing, overbalanced
(*chiefly British*) to lose balance and fall over

**overbearing** ADJECTIVE
trying to control other people in an unpleasant way • *an overbearing manner*

**overboard** ADVERB
over the side of a ship into the water • *She jumped overboard.*

**overcast** ADJECTIVE
covered with cloud • *The sky was grey and overcast.*

**overcoat** NOUN overcoats
a warm outdoor coat

**overcome** VERB overcomes, overcoming, overcame, overcome
❶ to find a way of dealing with a problem or difficulty • *She managed to overcome her fear of flying.* ❷ to win a victory over someone; to defeat someone
➤ **be overcome by something** to be strongly affected by something and made helpless • *He was overcome by the fumes.*

**overcrowded** ADJECTIVE
an overcrowded place or vehicle has too

many people crammed into it
➤ **overcrowding** NOUN

**overdo** VERB overdoes, overdoing, overdid, overdone
❶ to do something too much ❷ to cook food for too long
➤ **overdo it** to work too hard, exhausting yourself

**overdose** NOUN overdoses
too large a dose of a drug

**overdose** VERB overdoses, overdosing, overdosed
to take an overdose

**overdraft** NOUN overdrafts
the amount by which a bank account is overdrawn

**overdraw** VERB overdraws, overdrawing, overdrew, overdrawn
to draw more money from a bank account than the amount you have in it
➤ **overdrawn** ADJECTIVE

**overdrive** NOUN
➤ **go into overdrive** to start being very active

**overdue** ADJECTIVE
late; not paid or arrived by the proper time
• *Her baby is a week overdue.*

**overestimate** VERB overestimates, overestimating, overestimated
to estimate something too highly

**overflow** VERB overflows, overflowing, overflowed
to flow over the edge or limits of something
• *The tap was left on and the bath overflowed.*

**overflow** NOUN overflows
❶ an amount of something that overflows
❷ an outlet for excess liquid

**overgrown** ADJECTIVE
covered with weeds or unwanted plants

**overhang** VERB overhangs, overhanging, overhung
to jut out over something

**overhang** NOUN overhangs
a part of a building that juts out

**overhaul** VERB overhauls, overhauling, overhauled
❶ to examine something thoroughly and repair it if necessary ❷ to overtake someone or something

**overhaul** NOUN
an examination and repair of something

**overhead** ADJECTIVE & ADVERB
❶ above the level of your head • *an overhead light* ❷ in the sky • *A helicopter flew overhead.*

**overheads** PLURAL NOUN
the expenses of running a business

**overhear** VERB overhears, overhearing, overheard
to hear something accidentally or without the speaker intending you to hear it • *I overheard them having an argument yesterday.*

**overjoyed** ADJECTIVE
filled with great joy

**overland** ADJECTIVE & ADVERB
travelling over the land, not by sea or air • *an overland expedition* • *We travelled overland to Moscow.*

**overlap** VERB overlaps, overlapping, overlapped
❶ two things overlap when one lies across part of the other • *The roof tiles overlap.*
❷ events overlap when they happen partly at the same time
➤ **overlap** NOUN

**overlay** VERB overlays, overlaying, overlaid
to cover something with a layer; to lie on top of something • *The surface of the table is overlaid with gold.*

**overlay** NOUN overlays
a thing laid over another

**overleaf** ADVERB
on the other side of the page • *See the diagram overleaf.*

**overlie** VERB overlies, overlying, overlay, overlain
to lie over something

**overload** VERB overloads, overloading, overloaded
to put too great a load on someone or something • *The boat was overloaded with people.*

**overlook** VERB overlooks, overlooking, overlooked
❶ to fail to notice or consider something • *You have overlooked one important fact.*
❷ to overlook a mistake or offence is to ignore it or decide not to punish it ❸ to have a view of a place from above • *The hotel overlooks a lake.*

**overlord** NOUN overlords
a supreme lord

**overly** ADVERB
too; excessively • *an overly optimistic view*

**overnight** ADJECTIVE & ADVERB
of or during a night • *an overnight stop in Rome* • *We stayed overnight in a hotel.*

**overpower** VERB overpowers, overpowering, overpowered
**①** to defeat someone by being stronger than they are **②** to affect someone very strongly • *Terror overpowered him.*

**overpowering** ADJECTIVE
very strong or powerful • *an overpowering smell of fish*

**overrate** VERB overrates, overrating, overrated
to have too high an opinion of something

**overreach** VERB overreaches, overreaching, overreached
➤ **overreach yourself** to fail through being too ambitious

**override** VERB overrides, overriding, overrode, overridden
**①** to be more important than something • *Safety overrides all other considerations.* **②** to stop an automatic process and control it yourself • *This code lets you override the security system.* **③** to overrule someone or something

**overriding** ADJECTIVE
more important than anything else • *My overriding feeling was relief.*

**overripe** ADJECTIVE
too ripe

**overrule** VERB overrules, overruling, overruled
to reject a suggestion or decision by using your authority • *We voted for having a disco but the head teacher overruled the idea.*

**overrun** VERB overruns, overrunning, overran, overrun
**①** to spread all over a place in large numbers • *The attic is overrun with mice.* **②** to go on for longer than it should • *The programme overran by ten minutes*

**overseas** ADVERB
across or beyond the sea; abroad • *He lived overseas for a while.*

**overseas** ADJECTIVE
from abroad; foreign • *overseas students*

**oversee** VERB oversees, overseeing, oversaw, overseen
to watch over people working to make sure things are done properly
➤ **overseer** NOUN

**overshadow** VERB overshadows, overshadowing, overshadowed
**①** to cast a shadow over something **②** to make a person or thing seem unimportant in comparison • *He always felt overshadowed by his older brother.*

**overshoot** VERB overshoots, overshooting, overshot
to go beyond a target or limit • *The plane overshot the runway.*

**oversight** NOUN oversights
a mistake you make by not noticing something

**oversleep** VERB oversleeps, oversleeping, overslept
to sleep for longer than you intended

**overspill** NOUN overspills
**①** what spills over **②** the extra population of a town, who take homes in nearby districts

**overstate** VERB overstates, overstating, overstated
to exaggerate how important something is

**overstep** VERB oversteps, overstepping, overstepped
to go beyond a limit

**overt** ADJECTIVE
done or shown openly • *overt hostility*
➤ **overtly** ADVERB

**overtake** VERB overtakes, overtaking, overtook, overtaken
**①** to pass a moving vehicle or person **②** to affect you without warning • *She was suddenly overtaken by remorse.*

**overtax** VERB overtaxes, overtaxing, overtaxed
**①** to tax people too heavily **②** to put too heavy a burden or strain on someone

**overthrow** VERB overthrows, overthrowing, overthrew, overthrown
to remove a ruler or government from power by force • *The rebels planned to overthrow the president.*

**overthrow** NOUN overthrows
**①** overthrowing a ruler or government **②** throwing a ball too far

**overtime** NOUN
time spent working outside the normal hours; payment for this

**overtone** NOUN overtones
a feeling or quality that is suggested but not expressed directly • *There were overtones of envy in his speech.*

**overture** NOUN overtures
❶ a piece of music written as an introduction to an opera or ballet ❷ a friendly attempt to start a discussion or relationship • *They made overtures of peace.*

**overturn** VERB overturns, overturning, overturned
❶ to turn over or upside down or to make something do this • *One of the boats overturned in the storm.* ❷ to reverse a legal decision

**overview** NOUN overviews
a general outline of a subject or situation that gives the main ideas without explaining all the details • *The first paragraph gives a quick overview of the topic.*

**overweight** ADJECTIVE
too heavy or fat

**overwhelm** VERB overwhelms, overwhelming, overwhelmed
❶ to have a strong emotional effect on someone • *I was overwhelmed by everyone's kindness.* ❷ to defeat someone completely ❸ to come in such large numbers that you cannot deal with them • *They were overwhelmed by complaints.*

**overwhelming** ADJECTIVE
extremely great or strong • *I had an overwhelming desire to see him again.*

**overwork** VERB overworks, overworking, overworked
❶ to work too hard or to make someone work too hard ❷ to use something too often • *'Nice' is an overworked word*

**overwork** NOUN
working too hard

**overwrought** ADJECTIVE
very upset and nervous or worried

**ovoid** ADJECTIVE
egg-shaped

**ovulate** VERB ovulates, ovulating, ovulated
to produce an ovum from an ovary

**ovum** (say oh-vum) NOUN ova
a female cell that can develop into a new individual when it is fertilized

**owe** VERB owes, owing, owed
❶ to have a duty to pay or give something to someone, especially money • *I still owe you for the cinema ticket.* • *You owe him an apology.* ❷ to have something because of the action of another person or thing • *They owed their lives to the pilot's skill.*

**owing to** PREPOSITION
because of; caused by • *It was a difficult journey owing to the heavy snow.*

**owl** NOUN owls
a bird of prey with large eyes and a short beak, usually flying at night

**own** ADJECTIVE
belonging to yourself or itself • *I saw it with my own eyes.*
➤ **get your own back** (*informal*) to get revenge
➤ **on your own** by yourself; alone • *I did it all on my own.* • *I sat on my own in the empty room.*

**own** VERB owns, owning, owned
to have something as your property
➤ **own up** to admit that you did something wrong or stupid

**owner** NOUN owners
the person who owns something
➤ **ownership** NOUN

**own goal** NOUN own goals
a goal scored by a member of a team against their own side

**ox** NOUN oxen
a male animal of the cattle family kept for its meat and for pulling carts

**oxide** NOUN oxides
a compound of oxygen and one other element

**oxidize** (also **oxidise**) VERB oxidizes, oxidizing, oxidized
❶ to combine or to cause a substance to combine, with oxygen ❷ to coat something with an oxide
➤ **oxidation** NOUN

**oxtail** NOUN
meat from the tail of a cow, used to make soup or stew

**oxygen** NOUN
a colourless odourless tasteless gas that exists in the air and is essential for living things

**oxymoron** (say oksi-**mor**-on) NOUN
oxymorons
putting together words which seem to
contradict one another, e.g. *bitter-sweet*,
*living death* WORD ORIGIN from Greek
*oxumoros* = pointedly foolish

**oyster** NOUN oysters
a kind of shellfish whose flesh sometimes
contains a pearl

**ozone** NOUN
a form of oxygen with a sharp smell
WORD ORIGIN from Greek *ozein* = to smell

**ozone layer** NOUN
a layer of ozone high in the atmosphere,
which protects the earth from harmful
amounts of the sun's radiation

# Pp

**p** ABBREVIATION
penny or pence

**p.** ABBREVIATION pp.
page

**pa** NOUN (*informal*)
father

**pace** NOUN paces
❶ one step in walking or running • *Now take
two paces forward.* ❷ the speed at which
someone moves or something happens • *He
set a fast pace.*

**pace** VERB paces, pacing, paced
❶ to walk with slow or regular steps • *She
was nervously pacing up and down.* ❷ to
measure a distance in paces • *I paced out the
length of the stage.*

**pacemaker** NOUN pacemakers
❶ a person who sets the pace for someone
else in a race ❷ an electrical device for
keeping the heart beating

**pacific** (say pa-**sif**-ik) ADJECTIVE
peaceful; making or loving peace
➤ **pacifically** ADVERB

**pacifist** (say **pas**-if-ist) NOUN pacifists
a person who believes that war is always
wrong
➤ **pacifism** NOUN

**pacify** VERB pacifies, pacifying, pacified
to calm a person down

**pack** NOUN packs
❶ a bundle or collection of things wrapped or
tied together ❷ a set of playing cards (usually
52) ❸ a bag carried on your back ❹ a large
amount • *a pack of lies* ❺ a group of hounds,
wolves or other animals that hunt together
❻ a group of Brownies or Cub Scouts

**pack** VERB packs, packing, packed
❶ to put things into a suitcase, bag or box
in order to move or store them ❷ to crowd
together and fill a place • *Hundreds of fans
packed the hall.*
➤ **pack someone off** to send a person away
➤ **send someone packing** to dismiss
someone angrily

**package** NOUN packages
❶ a parcel or packet ❷ a number of things
offered or accepted together

**package holiday** NOUN package holidays
a holiday with all the travel and
accommodation arranged and included in the
price

**packaging** NOUN
the container and wrapping in which
something is sold

**packed** ADJECTIVE
❶ a room or space is packed when it is
crowded with people • *The train was packed.*
❷ full of something • *The website is packed
with useful information.*

**packet** NOUN packets
a small box or bag in which something is sold
• *a packet of crisps*

**pack ice** NOUN
a mass of pieces of ice floating in the sea

**pact** NOUN pacts
an agreement or treaty

**pad** NOUN pads
❶ a set of sheets of paper fastened together
at one edge ❷ a soft thick mass of material,
used to protect or stuff something ❸ a piece
of soft material worn to protect your leg in
cricket and other games ❹ the soft fleshy
part under an animal's foot or the end of a
finger or toe ❺ a flat surface from which
rockets are launched or where helicopters
take off and land

**pad** VERB pads, padding, padded
❶ to walk softly • *He padded across the
landing.* ❷ to put a pad on or in something

➤ **pad something out** to make a book, speech, etc. longer than it needs to be

**padding** *NOUN*
material used to pad things

**paddle** *NOUN* paddles
❶ a short oar with a broad blade; something shaped like this ❷ (*British*) walking about with bare feet in shallow water • *Let's go for a paddle.*

**paddle** *VERB* paddles, paddling, paddled
❶ (*British*) to walk about with bare feet in shallow water ❷ to move a boat along with a paddle or paddles; to row gently

**paddock** *NOUN* paddocks
a small field where horses are kept

**paddy** *NOUN* paddies
a field where rice is grown
➤ **paddy field** *NOUN*

**padkos** *NOUN*
(*S. African*) food that is packed for and eaten on a journey (**WORD ORIGIN**) from Afrikaans *pad* = road, + *kos* = food

**padlock** *NOUN* padlocks
a lock with a metal loop that passes through a ring or chain

**padlock** *VERB* padlocks, padlocking, padlocked
to lock something with a padlock

**padre** (say **pah**-dray) *NOUN* padres (*informal*)
a chaplain in the armed forces

**paean** (say **pee**-an) *NOUN* paeans
a song of praise or triumph

**paediatrics** (say peed-ee-**at**-riks) *NOUN*
the study of children's diseases
➤ **paediatric** *ADJECTIVE*
➤ **paediatrician** *NOUN*

**pagan** (say **pay** gan) *NOUN* pagans
❶ a person who believes in a religion which is not one of the chief religions of the world ❷ a follower of a modern religion based on reverence for nature
➤ **pagan** *ADJECTIVE*
➤ **paganism** *NOUN*

**page** *NOUN* pages
❶ a piece of paper that is part of a book, magazine or newspaper; one side of this ❷ the information that you can see on a computer screen at any one time • *Click here to go back to the previous page.* ❸ a boy or man employed to go on errands or be an attendant ❹ a young boy attending a bride at a wedding

**pageant** *NOUN* pageants
❶ a play or entertainment about historical events and people ❷ a procession of people in costume as an entertainment
➤ **pageantry** *NOUN*

**pagoda** (say pag-**oh**-da) *NOUN* pagodas
a Buddhist tower or a Hindu temple shaped like a pyramid, in India and the Far East

**paid**
past tense of **pay**
➤ **put paid to something** (*informal*) to put an end to what someone is doing or hoping for

**pail** *NOUN* pails
a bucket

**pain** *NOUN* pains
❶ an unpleasant feeling caused by injury or disease ❷ suffering in the mind
➤ **on** or **under pain of** with the threat of
➤ **take pains** to make a careful effort or take trouble over something

**pain** *VERB* pains, paining, pained
to cause suffering or distress to someone • *It pains me to see you like this.*

**painful** *ADJECTIVE*
causing pain • *My ankle is very painful.* • *a painful memory*

**painfully** *ADVERB*
❶ extremely • *The dog was painfully thin.* ❷ in a way that causes pain • *He banged his knee painfully against the table.*

**painkiller** *NOUN* painkillers
a medicine or drug that reduces pain

**painless** *ADJECTIVE*
not causing any pain

**painstaking** *ADJECTIVE*
very careful and thorough • *Making an animated film is painstaking work.*

**paint** *NOUN* paints
a liquid substance put on something to colour it

**paint** *VERB* paints, painting, painted
❶ to put paint on something • *We painted the fence.* ❷ to make a picture with paints • *She painted some fish on the wall.*

**paintbox** *NOUN* paintboxes
a box of paints for painting pictures

**paintbrush** *NOUN* paintbrushes
a brush you use for painting with

**painter** *NOUN* painters
a person who paints

a b c d e f g h i j k l m n o p q r s t u v w x y z

**painting** NOUN paintings
❶ a painted picture ❷ using paints to make a picture • *He likes painting.*

**pair** NOUN pairs
❶ a set of two things or people • *a pair of shoes* ❷ something made of two joined parts • *a pair of scissors*

**pair** VERB pairs, pairing, paired
to put two things together as a pair
➤ **pair off** or **up** to form a couple

**pal** NOUN pals (*informal*)
a friend **WORD ORIGIN** Romany, = brother

**palace** NOUN palaces
a grand building where a king, queen or other important person lives

**Palaeolithic** (say pal-ee-o-**lith**-ik) ADJECTIVE
belonging to the early part of the Stone Age

**palaeontology** (say pal-ee-on-**tol**-o-jee) NOUN
the study of fossils

**palatable** ADJECTIVE
tasting pleasant

**palate** NOUN palates
❶ the roof of your mouth ❷ a person's sense of taste • *She has a refined palate.*

SPELLING

Take care not to confuse with **palette** and **pallet**, which have different meanings.

**palatial** (say pa-**lay**-shal) ADJECTIVE
like a palace; large and splendid

**pale** ADJECTIVE paler, palest
❶ almost white • *a pale face* ❷ without much colour or brightness • *pale green* • *the pale moonlight*
➤ **palely** ADVERB
➤ **paleness** NOUN
➤ **beyond the pale** beyond the limits of acceptable behaviour
**WORD ORIGIN** *beyond the pale* comes from an old word 'pale' = a boundary, from Latin *palus* = a stake or fence post

**palette** NOUN palettes
a board on which an artist mixes colours ready for use

SPELLING

Take care not to confuse with **palate** and **pallet**, which have different meanings.

**palindrome** NOUN palindromes
a word or phrase that reads the same

backwards as forwards, e.g. *radar* or *Madam, I'm Adam*

**paling** NOUN palings
a fence made of wooden posts or railings; one of its posts

**palisade** NOUN palisades
a fence of pointed sticks or boards

**pall** (say pawl) NOUN palls
❶ a cloth spread over a coffin ❷ a thick dark cloud of something • *A pall of smoke lay over the town.*

**pall** VERB palls, palling, palled
to become uninteresting or boring after a time • *The novelty of the new computer game soon began to pall.*

**pallbearer** NOUN pallbearers
a person helping to carry the coffin at a funeral

**pallet** NOUN pallets
❶ a mattress stuffed with straw ❷ a hard narrow bed ❸ a large platform for carrying goods that are being stacked, especially one that can be lifted by a forklift truck

SPELLING

Take care not to confuse with **palate** and **palette**, which have different meanings.

**palliative** NOUN palliatives
something that lessens pain or suffering
➤ **palliative** ADJECTIVE

**pallid** ADJECTIVE
pale, especially because of illness

**pallor** NOUN
paleness in a person's face, especially because of illness

**palm** NOUN palms
❶ the inner part of the hand, between the fingers and the wrist ❷ a palm tree

**palm** VERB palms, palming, palmed
to pick something up secretly and hide it in the palm of your hand
➤ **palm something off on someone** to fool a person into accepting something they do not want

**palmistry** NOUN
fortune-telling by looking at the creases in the palm of a person's hand

**Palm Sunday** NOUN
the Sunday before Easter, when Christians commemorate Jesus Christ's entry into Jerusalem when the people spread palm leaves in his path

**palm tree** NOUN palm trees
a tropical tree with large leaves and no branches

**palpable** ADJECTIVE
❶ able to be touched or felt ❷ obvious • *a palpable lie*
➤ **palpably** ADVERB

**palpitate** VERB palpitates, palpitating, palpitated
❶ the heart palpitates when it beats hard and quickly ❷ a person palpitates when they quiver with fear or excitement
➤ **palpitation** NOUN

**palsy** (say pawl-zee) NOUN (old use)
paralysis with tremors

**paltry** (say pol-tree) ADJECTIVE
very small and almost worthless • *a paltry amount*

**pampas** NOUN
wide grassy plains in South America

**pampas grass** NOUN
a tall grass with long feathery flowers

**pamper** VERB pampers, pampering, pampered
to take care of someone very well and make them feel as comfortable as possible

**pamphlet** NOUN pamphlets
a leaflet or booklet giving information on a subject

**pan** NOUN pans
❶ a wide container with a flat base, used for cooking ❷ something shaped like this ❸ the bowl of a lavatory

**panacea** (say pan-a-see-a) NOUN panaceas
a cure for all kinds of diseases or troubles

**panache** (say pan-ash) NOUN
a confident stylish manner
WORD ORIGIN originally referring to a plume of feathers on a helmet or headdress, via French and Italian from Latin *pinnaculum* = little feather

**panama** NOUN panamas
a hat made of a fine straw-like material
WORD ORIGIN from *Panama* in Central America (because the hats were originally made from the leaves of a plant which grows there)

**pancake** NOUN pancakes
a thin round cake of batter fried on both sides

**Pancake Day** NOUN
Shrove Tuesday, when people often eat pancakes

**pancreas** (say pan-kree-as) NOUN
a gland near the stomach, producing insulin and digestive juices

**panda** NOUN pandas
a large bear-like black-and-white animal found in China

**pandemonium** NOUN
uproar and complete confusion
• *Pandemonium broke out in the courtroom.*

**pander** VERB panders, pandering, pandered
➤ **pander to someone** to let someone have whatever they want even though you know it is not right • *You shouldn't pander to his taste for gossip.*

**pane** NOUN panes
a sheet of glass in a window

**panegyric** (say pan-i-jirrik) NOUN panegyrics
a speech or piece of writing praising a person or thing

**panel** NOUN panels
❶ a long flat piece of wood, metal, etc. that is part of a door, wall or piece of furniture ❷ a flat board with controls or instruments on it ❸ a group of people chosen to discuss or decide something • *The winner will be decided by a panel of judges.*
➤ **panelled** ADJECTIVE
➤ **panelling** NOUN

**pang** NOUN pangs
a sudden sharp feeling of pain or emotion • *a pang of guilt*

**panic** NOUN
sudden uncontrollable fear that stops you from thinking clearly • *People fled in panic as the fire spread.*

**panic** VERB panics, panicking, panicked
to be filled with panic • *Stay calm and don't panic.* WORD ORIGIN from the name of *Pan*, an ancient Greek god thought to be able to cause sudden fear

**panicky** ADJECTIVE
(*informal*) feeling or showing panic

**panic-stricken** ADJECTIVE
very frightened in a way that stops you from thinking clearly

**pannier** NOUN panniers
a large bag or basket hung on one side of a bicycle, motorcycle or horse

**panoply** NOUN panoplies
a splendid display or collection of things

**panorama** *NOUN* panoramas
a view or picture of a wide area
➤ **panoramic** *ADJECTIVE*

**pansy** *NOUN* pansies
a small brightly coloured garden flower with velvety petals

**pant** *VERB* pants, panting, panted
to take short quick breaths, usually after running or working hard

**pantaloons** *PLURAL NOUN*
wide trousers, gathered at the ankle
**WORD ORIGIN** from *Pantalone*, a character in old Italian comedies who wore these

**pantechnicon** (say pan-**tek**-nik-on) *NOUN* pantechnicons
(*British*) a kind of large lorry, used for carrying furniture **WORD ORIGIN** originally the name of a large art and craft gallery in London, which was later used for storing furniture: from Greek *pan* = all + *techne* = art

**panther** *NOUN* panthers
a leopard, especially a black one

**panties** *PLURAL NOUN* (*informal*)
short knickers

**pantomime** *NOUN* pantomimes
a Christmas entertainment, usually based on a fairy tale

**pantry** *NOUN* pantries
a small room for storing food and crockery

**pants** *PLURAL NOUN*
❶ (*informal*) underpants or knickers ❷ (*North American*) trousers

**pap** *NOUN*
❶ soft food suitable for babies ❷ trivial entertainment; nonsense

**papa** *NOUN* (*old use*)
father

**papacy** (say **pay**-pa-see) *NOUN* papacies
the position of pope

**papal** (say **pay**-pal) *ADJECTIVE*
to do with the pope

**paparazzi** (say **pap**-a-rat-si) *PLURAL NOUN*
photographers who pursue famous people to get photographs of them

**paper** *NOUN* papers
❶ a substance made in thin sheets from wood, rags, etc. and used for writing, printing, or drawing on or for wrapping things ❷ a newspaper ❸ wallpaper ❹ a set of examination questions • *the history paper* ❺ papers are official documents

**paper** *VERB* papers, papering, papered
to cover a wall or room with wallpaper

**paperback** *NOUN* paperbacks
a book with a thin flexible cover

**paperweight** *NOUN* paperweights
a small heavy object used for holding down loose papers

**paperwork** *NOUN*
all the writing of reports and keeping of records that someone has to do as part of their job

**papier mâché** (say pap-yay **mash**-ay) *NOUN*
paper made into pulp and moulded to make models, ornaments, etc.

**paprika** (say **pap**-rik-a) *NOUN*
a powdered spice made from red pepper

**papyrus** (say **pap-y**-rus) *NOUN* papyri
❶ a kind of paper made from the stems of a plant like a reed, used in ancient Egypt ❷ a document written on this paper

**par** *NOUN*
the number of strokes in golf that a good player should normally take for a particular hole or course
➤ **below par** not as good or as well as usual
➤ **on a par with** equal to in amount or quality

**parable** *NOUN* parables
a story told to teach people something, especially one of those told by Jesus Christ

**parabola** (say pa-**rab**-ol-a) *NOUN* parabolas
a curve like the path of an object thrown into the air and falling down again
➤ **parabolic** *ADJECTIVE*

**parachute** *NOUN* parachutes
an umbrella-like device on which people or things can fall slowly to the ground from an aircraft

**parachute** *VERB* parachutes, parachuting, parachuted
to fall or drop something by means of a parachute
➤ **parachutist** *NOUN*

**parade** *NOUN* parades
❶ a line of people or vehicles moving forward through a place as a celebration ❷ an assembly of soldiers for inspection or drill ❸ a public square or row of shops

**parade** *VERB* parades, parading, paraded
❶ to move forward through a place as a

celebration ❷ soldiers parade when they assemble for inspection or drill

**paradise** *NOUN*
❶ heaven or, in the Bible, the Garden of Eden
❷ a place that seems perfect • *a tropical paradise*

**paradox** *NOUN* paradoxes
a statement that seems to contradict itself but which contains a truth, e.g. 'More haste, less speed'
➤ **paradoxical** *ADJECTIVE*
➤ **paradoxically** *ADVERB*

**paraffin** *NOUN*
a kind of oil used as fuel

**paragliding** *NOUN*
the sport of gliding through the air while being supported by a wide parachute

**paragon** *NOUN* paragons
a person or thing that seems to be perfect

**paragraph** *NOUN* paragraphs
one or more sentences on a single subject, forming a section of a piece of writing and beginning on a new line, usually slightly in from the margin of the page

**parakeet** *NOUN* parakeets
a kind of small parrot

**parallax** *NOUN*
what seems to be a change in the position of something when you look at it from a different place

**parallel** *ADJECTIVE*
❶ parallel lines run side by side and the same distance apart from each other for their whole length, like railway lines ❷ similar or corresponding • *When petrol prices rise there is a parallel rise in bus fares.*

**parallel** *NOUN* parallels
❶ something similar or corresponding ❷ a comparison • *You can draw a parallel between the two situations.* ❸ a line that is parallel to another ❹ a line of latitude

**parallel** *VERB* parallels, paralleling, paralleled
to find or be a parallel to something

SPELLING
Double up the first l in parallel (but the last l stays single).

**parallelogram** *NOUN* parallelograms
a four-sided figure with its opposite sides equal and parallel

**paralyse** *VERB* paralyses, paralysing, paralysed
❶ to cause paralysis in a person or part of the body ❷ to be paralysed with fear or emotion is to be so affected by it that you cannot move or do anything

**paralysis** *NOUN*
being unable to move, especially because of a disease or an injury to the nerves
➤ **paralytic** (say pa-ra-**lit**-ik) *ADJECTIVE*

**paramedic** *NOUN* paramedics
a person who is trained to do medical work, especially emergency first aid, but is not a fully qualified doctor

**parameter** (say pa-**ram**-it-er) *NOUN* parameters
one of the factors or limits which affect the way something is done • *We have to work within the parameters of time and money.*

**paramilitary** *ADJECTIVE*
organized like a military force but not part of the armed services

**paramount** *ADJECTIVE*
more important than anything else • *Secrecy is paramount.*

**paranoia** *NOUN*
❶ a mental illness in which a person has delusions or suspects and distrusts people ❷ an unjustified suspicion and mistrust of others

**paranoid** *ADJECTIVE*
suffering from paranoia

**paranormal** *ADJECTIVE*
beyond what is normal and can be rationally explained; supernatural

**parapet** *NOUN* parapets
a low wall along the edge of a balcony, bridge or roof

**paraphernalia** *NOUN*
numerous pieces of equipment or belongings
WORD ORIGIN originally = the personal belongings a woman could keep after her marriage (as opposed to her dowry, which went to her husband)

**paraphrase** *VERB* paraphrases, paraphrasing, paraphrased
to give the meaning of something by using different words
➤ **paraphrase** *NOUN*

**paraplegia** *NOUN*
paralysis of the lower half of the body
➤ **paraplegic** *NOUN* & *ADJECTIVE*

**parasite** *NOUN* parasites
an animal or plant that lives in or on another,

from which it gets its food
➤ **parasitic** ADJECTIVE
**WORD ORIGIN** from Greek *parasitos* = guest at a meal

**parasol** NOUN parasols
a lightweight umbrella used to shade yourself from the sun

**paratroops** PLURAL NOUN
troops trained to be dropped from aircraft by parachute
➤ **paratrooper** NOUN

**parboil** VERB parboils, parboiling, parboiled
to boil food until it is partly cooked

**parcel** NOUN parcels
something wrapped up to be sent by post or carried

**parcel** VERB parcels, parcelling, parcelled
❶ to wrap something up as a parcel ❷ to divide something into portions • *We'll need to parcel out the work.*

**parched** ADJECTIVE
very dry or thirsty

**parchment** NOUN parchments
a kind of heavy paper, originally made from animal skins **WORD ORIGIN** from the city of Pergamum, now in Turkey, where parchment was made in ancient times

**pardon** NOUN
❶ forgiveness ❷ the cancelling of a punishment • *a free pardon*

**pardon** VERB pardons, pardoning, pardoned
❶ to forgive or excuse someone ❷ to cancel a person's punishment

**pardon** EXCLAMATION
(also **I beg your pardon** or **pardon me**) used to mean 'I didn't hear or understand what you said.' or 'I apologize.'

**pardonable** ADJECTIVE
a pardonable mistake is one that can be forgiven

**pare** (say pair) VERB pares, paring, pared
❶ to trim something by cutting away the edges ❷ to reduce something gradually • *We had to pare down our expenses.*

**parent** NOUN parents
❶ a father or mother; an animal or plant that has produced others of its kind ❷ something that produces others of the same type • *the parent company*
➤ **parenting** NOUN

**parentage** NOUN
who your parents are

**parental** (say pa-**rent**-al) ADJECTIVE
to do with parents • *parental advice*

**parenthesis** (say pa-**ren**-thi-sis) NOUN
parentheses
❶ something extra that is put into a sentence, usually between brackets or dashes ❷ either of the pair of brackets (like these) used to mark off words from the rest of a sentence
➤ **parenthetical** ADJECTIVE

**parenthood** NOUN
being a parent

**par excellence** (say par eks-el-**ahns**) ADVERB
more than all the others; to the greatest degree **WORD ORIGIN** French, = because of special excellence

**pariah** (say pa-**ry**-a) NOUN pariahs
an outcast

**parish** NOUN parishes
in the Christian Church, a district with its own church
➤ **parishioner** NOUN

**park** NOUN parks
❶ a large open area with grass and trees for public use ❷ an area of grassland or woodland belonging to a country house

**park** VERB parks, parking, parked
to leave a vehicle somewhere for a time

**parka** NOUN parkas
a warm jacket with a hood attached

**Parkinson's disease** NOUN
a disease that makes a person's arms and legs shake and the muscles become stiff **WORD ORIGIN** named after an English doctor, James *Parkinson*

**parley** VERB parleys, parleying, parleyed
to hold a discussion with an opponent or enemy in order to reach an agreement
➤ **parley** NOUN

**parliament** NOUN parliaments
the assembly that makes a country's laws
➤ **parliamentary** ADJECTIVE

**parlour** NOUN parlours (old use)
a sitting room **WORD ORIGIN** originally = a room in a monastery where the monks were allowed to talk: from French *parler* = speak

**parochial** (say per-**oh**-kee-al) ADJECTIVE
❶ to do with a church parish ❷ having a narrow point of view; interested only in your own local area

**parody** NOUN parodies
an amusing imitation of the style of a writer, composer, literary work, etc.

**parody** VERB parodies, parodying, parodied
to make or be a parody of a person or thing

**parole** NOUN
the release of a prisoner before the end of their sentence on the condition that they behave well • *He was on parole.*

**paroxysm** (say pa-roks-izm) NOUN paroxysms
a sudden outburst of laughter, crying or strong feeling • *He was driven into a paroxysm of rage.*

**parquet** (say par-kay) NOUN
wooden blocks arranged in a pattern to make a floor

**parrot** NOUN parrots
a brightly-coloured tropical bird with a curved beak that can learn to repeat words or sounds

**parry** VERB parries, parrying, parried
❶ to turn aside an opponent's weapon or blow by using your own to block it ❷ to avoid an awkward question skilfully

**parse** VERB parses, parsing, parsed
to state what is the grammatical form and function of a word or words in a sentence

**parsimonious** ADJECTIVE
stingy; very sparing in the use of something
➤ **parsimony** NOUN

**parsley** NOUN
a plant with crinkled green leaves used to flavour and decorate food

**parsnip** NOUN parsnips
a plant with a pointed pale-yellow root used as a vegetable

**parson** NOUN parsons
a member of the Church of England clergy, especially a rector or vicar

**parsonage** NOUN parsonages
a parson's house

**part** NOUN parts
❶ some but not all of a thing or number of things; anything that belongs to something bigger ❷ the character played by an actor or actress ❸ the words spoken by a character in a play ❹ how much a person or thing is involved in something • *She played a huge part in her daughter's success.* ❺ one side in an agreement or in a dispute or quarrel
➤ **take something in good part** to accept

something without being upset or offended
➤ **take part** to join in an activity

**part** VERB parts, parting, parted
❶ two people part when they leave each other • *I hope we can part friends.* ❷ to move apart or to make people or things move apart • *At last the clouds parted.*
➤ **part with something** to give something away or get rid of it

**partake** VERB partakes, partaking, partook, partaken
❶ to eat or drink something • *We all partook of the food* ❷ to take part in something

**part exchange** NOUN
(*British*) giving something that you own as part of the price of what you are buying

**partial** ADJECTIVE
❶ not complete or total • *a partial eclipse* ❷ favouring one side more than the other; biased or unfair
➤ **be partial to something** to be fond of something

**partiality** NOUN
❶ unfair support for one side over another ❷ a fondness for something

**partially** ADVERB
partly; not completely • *He was partially to blame.*

**participant** NOUN participants
a person who takes part in something

**participate** VERB participates, participating, participated
to take part in something or have a share in it • *The whole class participated in the discussion.*
➤ **participation** NOUN

**participle** NOUN participles
a word formed from a verb (e.g. *gone, going; guided, guiding*) and used with an auxiliary verb to form certain tenses (e.g. *It has gone. It is going.*) or the passive (e.g. *We were guided to our seats.*) or as an adjective (e.g. *a guided missile; a guiding light*). The **past participle** (e.g. *gone, guided*) describes a completed action or past condition. The **present participle** (which ends in *-ing*) describes a continuing action or condition.

**particle** NOUN particles
a very small piece or amount of something • *dust particles*

**particular** ADJECTIVE
❶ only this one and no other; individual • *This particular stamp is very rare.* ❷ special

**particular**
or exceptional • *Take particular care of it.*
❸ wanting something to be exactly right;
difficult to please • *He is very particular
about his clothes.*

**particular** NOUN particulars
a detail or single fact • *Can you give me the
particulars of the case?*
➤ **in particular** ❶ especially • *We liked this
one in particular.* ❷ special • *We did nothing
in particular.*

**particularly** ADVERB
especially; more than usual or more than
the rest • *I enjoyed the film, particularly the
second half.*

**parting** NOUN partings
❶ leaving or separation ❷ a line where hair is
combed away in different directions

**parting shot** NOUN parting shots
a sharp remark made by a person who is just
leaving

USAGE
This is also sometimes called a *Parthian
shot*, after the horsemen of Parthia (an
ancient kingdom in what is now Iran),
who, while retreating, would shoot arrows
back at the enemy.

**partisan** NOUN partisans
❶ a strong supporter of a party or group ❷ a
member of an armed group fighting secretly
against an army that has taken control of its
country

**partisan** ADJECTIVE
strongly supporting a particular cause

**partition** NOUN partitions
❶ a thin wall that divides a room or space
❷ dividing a country or territory into
separate parts

**partition** VERB partitions, partitioning,
partitioned
❶ to divide something into separate parts
❷ to divide a room or space with a partition

**partly** ADVERB
to some extent but not completely • *It was
partly my fault.*

**partner** NOUN partners
❶ one of a pair of people who do something
together, such as dancing or playing a game
❷ a person who jointly owns a business with
one or more other people ❸ the person that
someone is married to, in a civil partnership
with or is having a sexual relationship with

**partner** VERB partners, partnering, partnered
to be a person's partner

**partnership** NOUN partnerships
❶ being a partner with someone, especially
in business • *The two engineers decided to go
into partnership.* ❷ a business owned by two
or more people

**part of speech** NOUN parts of speech
any of the groups into which words are
divided in grammar (noun, pronoun,
determiner, adjective, verb, adverb,
preposition, conjunction, exclamation)
GRAMMAR
See also word class.

**partook**
past tense of partake

**partridge** NOUN partridges
a game bird with brown feathers

**part-time** ADJECTIVE & ADVERB
working for only some of the normal hours
• *a part-time job* • *She works part-time on
a farm.*

**party** NOUN parties
❶ a gathering of people to enjoy themselves
• *a birthday party* ❷ a group working or
travelling together • *a search party* ❸ an
organized group of people with similar
political beliefs • *the Labour Party* ❹ a
person who is involved in a legal agreement
or dispute • *the guilty party*

**pas de deux** (say pah der **der**) NOUN pas de
deux
a dance for two people, usually in a ballet
WORD ORIGIN French, = step of two

**pass** VERB passes, passing, passed
❶ to go or move in a certain direction
• *They passed over the bridge.* ❷ to go past
something • *He passed me in the street but
didn't see me.* ❸ to move something in a
certain direction • *Pass the cord through
the ring.* ❹ to give or transfer something to
another person • *Could you pass the butter?*
❺ in ball games, to kick or throw the ball
to another player of your own side ❻ to be
successful in a test or examination ❼ to
approve or accept something • *They passed
a law.* ❽ to spend time doing something
• *How did you pass the time in hospital?* ❾ to
happen or go by • *We heard what passed
when they met.* • *Time passed very quickly.*
❿ to come to an end or no longer be there
• *Her opportunity passed.* ⓫ to pass a remark
or comment is to make it ⓬ in a game, quiz,
etc., to let your turn go by or choose not to
answer
➤ **pass away** to die
➤ **pass out** to faint

**pass** NOUN passes
❶ passing something ❷ a success in an examination ❸ in ball games, kicking or throwing the ball to another player on the same side ❹ a permit to go in or out of a place ❺ a route through a gap in a range of mountains
➤ **come to a pretty pass** to reach a bad state of affairs

SPELLING

Passed is the past tense of **pass**; if you go past something, you go near it and then continue moving until it is behind you, e.g. *We passed the house. Carry on past the supermarket then turn right.*

**passable** ADJECTIVE
❶ satisfactory but not especially good ❷ able to be passed
➤ **passably** ADVERB

**passage** NOUN passages
❶ a way through something; a corridor ❷ a journey by sea or air ❸ a section of a piece of writing or music ❹ going by or passing • *the passage of time*

**passageway** NOUN passageways
a passage or way through, especially between buildings

**passé** (say **pas**-say) ADJECTIVE
no longer fashionable

**passenger** NOUN passengers
a person who is driven or carried in a car, train, ship or aircraft

**passer-by** NOUN passers-by
a person who happens to be going past something

**passion** NOUN passions
❶ strong emotion ❷ a great enthusiasm for something • *She has a passion for reading.*
➤ **the Passion** the sufferings of Jesus Christ at the Crucifixion

**passionate** ADJECTIVE
full of passion or strong feeling
➤ **passionately** ADVERB

**passive** ADJECTIVE
❶ not resisting or fighting against something ❷ acted upon and not active ❸ (*in grammar*) describing the form of a verb when the subject of the verb receives the action, e.g. *was hit* in 'She was hit on the head'. talk about something happening in the future

GRAMMAR

See also the panel at **active**.

➤ **passively** ADVERB

**passive smoking** NOUN
breathing in other people's cigarette smoke, thought of as a health risk

**Passover** NOUN
a Jewish religious festival commemorating the freeing of the Jews from slavery in Egypt

**passport** NOUN passports
an official document that allows you to travel abroad

**password** NOUN passwords
❶ a secret word or phrase that you need to know in order to be allowed into a place ❷ a word you need to key in to gain access to a computer system or interface

**past** ADJECTIVE
of the time gone by • *during the past week*

**past** NOUN
❶ the time gone by • *Writing letters was more common in the past.* ❷ (*in grammar*) the tense of a verb used to describe an action that happened at a time before now, e.g. *took* is the past tense of *take*

GRAMMAR

See also the panel at **tense**.

**past** PREPOSITION
❶ beyond a certain place • *Go past the school and turn right.* ❷ after a certain time • *It is past midnight.*
➤ **past it** (*informal*) too old to be able to do something

SPELLING

Past is different from **passed**, which is a form of the verb **pass**: • *Police cars rushed past us.* • *We passed three police cars.*

**pasta** NOUN
an Italian food consisting of a dried paste made from flour and shaped into macaroni, spaghetti, lasagne, etc.

**paste** NOUN pastes
❶ a soft, moist and sticky substance ❷ a glue, especially for paper ❸ a soft edible mixture • *tomato paste*

**paste** VERB pastes, pasting, pasted
❶ to stick something onto a surface by using paste ❷ to coat something with paste

**pastel** NOUN pastels
❶ a crayon that is like chalk ❷ a light delicate colour

a b c d e f g h i j k l m n o p q r s t u v w x y z

**pasteurize** (also **pasteurise**) *VERB*
pasteurizes, pasteurizing, pasteurized
to purify milk by heating and then cooling it
(WORD ORIGIN) named after a French scientist,
Louis *Pasteur*, who invented the process

**pastille** *NOUN* pastilles
a small flavoured sweet that you suck

**pastime** *NOUN* pastimes
something you do to make time pass
pleasantly; a hobby or game

**pastor** *NOUN* pastors
a member of the clergy who is in charge of a
church or congregation

**pastoral** *ADJECTIVE*
❶ to do with country life • *a pastoral scene*
❷ to do with a pastor or a pastor's duties

**pastry** *NOUN* pastries
❶ dough made with flour, fat and water,
rolled flat and baked ❷ something made of
pastry

**pasture** *NOUN* pastures
land covered with grass that cattle, sheep or
horses can eat

**pasture** *VERB* pastures, pasturing, pastured
to put animals to graze in a pasture

**pasty** (say **pas**-tee) *NOUN* pasties
(*British*) a folded pastry case with a filling of
meat and vegetables

**pasty** (say **pay**-stee) *ADJECTIVE*
looking pale and unhealthy

**pat** *VERB* pats, patting, patted
to tap something gently with the open hand
or with something flat

**pat** *NOUN* pats
❶ a patting movement or sound ❷ a small
piece of butter
➤ **a pat on the back** praise for doing
something good • *She deserves a pat on the
back for all her hard work.*

**patch** *NOUN* patches
❶ a piece of material put over a hole or
damaged part ❷ an area that is different
from its surroundings • *a black cat with a
white patch on its chest* ❸ a piece of ground
• *a vegetable patch* ❹ a small area or piece of
something • *There were patches of fog on the
motorway.*
➤ **not a patch on** (*informal*) not nearly as
good as

**patch** *VERB* patches, patching, patched
to put a patch on something

➤ **patch something up** ❶ to repair
something roughly ❷ to settle a quarrel

**patchwork** *NOUN*
❶ needlework in which small pieces of
different cloth are sewn edge to edge ❷ a
collection of different things making up a
whole • *From the plane, the landscape below
was a patchwork of fields.*

**patchy** *ADJECTIVE*
occurring in some areas but not others;
uneven • *There may be some patchy rain.*

**pate** *NOUN* pates (*old use*)
the top of a person's head • *his bald pate*

**pâté** (say **pat**-ay) *NOUN* pâtés
paste made of meat or fish

**patent** (say **pat**-ent or **pay**-tent) *NOUN* patents
the official right given to an inventor to make
or sell their invention and to prevent other
people from copying it

**patent** (say **pay**-tent) *ADJECTIVE*
❶ protected by a patent • *patent medicines*
❷ very clear or obvious • *It's a patent lie.*

**patent** *VERB* patents, patenting, patented
to get a patent for an idea or invention

**patentee** (say pay-ten-**tee** or pat-en-**tee**)
*NOUN* patentees
a person who holds a patent

**patent leather** *NOUN*
glossy leather

**patently** *ADVERB*
clearly or obviously • *This is patently untrue.*

**paternal** *ADJECTIVE*
❶ to do with a father ❷ fatherly
➤ **paternally** *ADVERB*

**paternity** *NOUN*
❶ fatherhood ❷ being the father of a
particular baby

**path** *NOUN* paths
❶ a narrow way along which people or
animals can walk ❷ a line along which
a person or thing moves • *The tornado
destroyed everything in its path.* ❸ a course
of action • *the path to success*

**pathetic** *ADJECTIVE*
❶ making you feel pity or sympathy ❷ poor,
weak or useless • *He made a pathetic attempt
to climb the tree.*
➤ **pathetically** *ADVERB*

**pathological** *ADJECTIVE*
❶ to do with pathology or disease

**❷** (*informal*) compulsive or uncontrollable • *a pathological liar*

**pathology** *NOUN*
the study of diseases of the body
➤ **pathologist** *NOUN*

**pathos** (say pay-thoss) *NOUN*
a quality of making people feel pity or sympathy

**patience** *NOUN*
**❶** being patient **❷** a card game for one person

**patient** *ADJECTIVE*
able to wait for a long time or put up with trouble or inconvenience without getting anxious or angry

**patient** *NOUN* patients
a person who is receiving treatment from a doctor or dentist

**patiently** *ADVERB*
in a patient way • *He waited patiently for his turn.*

**patio** *NOUN* patios
a paved area beside a house

**patriarch** (say pay-tree-ark) *NOUN* patriarchs
**❶** a man who is head of a family or tribe. Compare with **matriarch**. **❷** a bishop of high rank in the Orthodox Christian churches
➤ **patriarchal** *ADJECTIVE*

**patriot** (say pay-tree-ot or pat-ree-ot) *NOUN* patriots
a person who loves their country and supports it loyally
➤ **patriotism** *NOUN*

**patriotic** *ADJECTIVE*
loving your country and supporting it loyally
➤ **patriotically** *ADVERB*

**patrol** *VERB* patrols, patrolling, patrolled
to walk or travel regularly over an area in order to guard it and see that all is well

**patrol** *NOUN* patrols
**❶** a patrolling group of people, ships, aircraft, etc. **❷** a group of Scouts or Guides
➤ **on patrol** patrolling an area

**patron** (say pay-tron) *NOUN* patrons
**❶** someone who supports a person or cause with money or encouragement **❷** a regular customer

**patronage** (say pat-ron-ij) *NOUN*
support given by a patron

**patronize** (also **patronise**) (say pat-ron-yz)
*VERB* patronizes, patronizing, patronized

**❶** to be a regular customer of a particular shop, restaurant, etc. **❷** to talk to someone in a way that shows you think they are stupid or inferior to you

**patron saint** *NOUN* patron saints
a saint who is thought to protect a particular place or activity

**patter** *NOUN*
**❶** a series of light tapping sounds • *the patter of rain on the roof* **❷** the quick talk of a comedian, conjuror, salesperson, etc.

**patter** *VERB* patters, pattering, pattered
to make light tapping sounds • *Rain pattered on the window panes.*

**pattern** *NOUN* patterns
**❶** a repeated arrangement of lines, shapes or colours • *a shirt with a floral pattern on it* **❷** a thing to be copied in order to make something • *a dress pattern* **❸** the regular way in which something happens • *James Bond films follow a set pattern.*
➤ **patterned** *ADJECTIVE*

**paunch** *NOUN* paunches
a large belly

**pauper** *NOUN* paupers
a person who is very poor

**pause** *NOUN* pauses
a temporary stop in speaking or doing something • *There was a long pause before she answered.*

**pause** *VERB* pauses, pausing, paused
**❶** to stop speaking or doing something for a short time before starting again **❷** to temporarily interrupt the playing of a piece of music, film, computer game, etc.

**pave** *VERB* paves, paving, paved
to lay a hard surface on a road or path
➤ **pave the way** to prepare for something

**pavement** *NOUN* pavements
(*British*) a paved path along the side of a street

**pavilion** *NOUN* pavilions
**❶** a building at a sports ground for players and spectators to use **❷** an ornamental building or shelter used for dances, concerts or exhibitions

**paving stone** *NOUN* paving stones
a flat piece of stone used for covering the ground

**paw** *NOUN* paws
the foot of an animal that has claws

a b c d e f g h i j k l m n o p q r s t u v w x y z

**paw** VERB paws, pawing, pawed
to touch or scrape something with a hand or foot • *The horse pawed the ground nervously.*

**pawn** NOUN pawns
❶ the least valuable piece in chess ❷ a person whose actions are controlled by someone else

**pawn** VERB pawns, pawning, pawned
to leave something with a pawnbroker in exchange for money • *He had to pawn his watch.*

**pawnbroker** NOUN pawnbrokers
a shopkeeper who lends money to people in return for objects that they leave and which are sold if the money is not paid back
➤ **pawnshop** NOUN

**pawpaw** NOUN pawpaws
an orange-coloured tropical fruit used as food

**pay** VERB pays, paying, paid
❶ to give money in return for goods or services • *I'll just pay for this comic.* ❷ to give what is owed • *They could no longer pay the rent.* ❸ to be profitable or worthwhile • *It pays to advertise.* ❹ to give or express something • *Now pay attention.* • *It's time we paid them a visit.* • *He doesn't often pay her compliments.* ❺ to suffer a penalty for something you have done • *I'll make you pay for this.* ❻ to let out a rope by loosening it gradually
➤ **pay someone back** ❶ to pay money that you owe someone ❷ to get revenge on someone
➤ **pay off** to be worthwhile or have good results • *All the preparation she did really paid off.*
➤ **pay something off** to pay in full what you owe
➤ **pay up** to pay the full amount you owe

**pay** NOUN
salary or wages

SPELLING
The past tense of **pay** is **paid**.

**payable** ADJECTIVE
that must be paid • *A small deposit is payable in advance.*

**payment** NOUN payments
❶ paying someone or being paid for something • *You can't expect him to do the work without payment.* ❷ an amount of money paid

**payphone** NOUN payphones
a public telephone operated by coins or a card

**PC** ABBREVIATION
❶ personal computer ❷ police constable

**PE** ABBREVIATION
physical education

**pea** NOUN peas
the small round green seed of a climbing plant, growing inside a pod and used as a vegetable; the plant bearing these pods

**peace** NOUN
❶ a time when there is no war, violence or disorder ❷ quietness and calm

**peaceable** ADJECTIVE
fond of peace; not quarrelsome or warlike
➤ **peaceably** ADVERB

**peaceful** ADJECTIVE
❶ quiet and calm ❷ not involving violence • *a peaceful protest*
➤ **peacefully** ADVERB
➤ **peacefulness** NOUN

**peach** NOUN peaches
❶ a round soft juicy fruit with a pinkish or yellowish skin and a large stone ❷ (*informal*) a thing of great quality • *a peach of a shot*

**peacock** NOUN peacocks
a large male bird with a long brightly coloured tail that it can spread out like a fan
➤ **peahen** NOUN

**peak** NOUN peaks
❶ a pointed top of a mountain ❷ the highest or most intense part of something • *Traffic reaches its peak at 5 p.m.* ❸ the part of a cap that sticks out in front

**peak** VERB peaks, peaking, peaked
to reach the highest point or value • *Sales peak just before Christmas.*

**peaked** ADJECTIVE
a peaked hat or cap is one with a peak

**peaky** ADJECTIVE
(*British*) looking pale and ill

**peal** NOUN peals
❶ the loud ringing of a bell or set of bells ❷ a loud burst of thunder or laughter • *The girls burst into peals of laughter.*

**peal** VERB peals, pealing, pealed
bells peal when they ring loudly

**peanut** NOUN peanuts
a small round nut that grows in a pod in the ground

**peanut butter** NOUN
roasted peanuts crushed into a paste

**pear** NOUN pears
a juicy fruit that gets narrower near the stalk

**pearl** NOUN pearls
a small shiny white ball found in the shells of some oysters and used as a jewel

**pearl barley** NOUN
grains of barley made small by grinding

**pearly** ADJECTIVE
like a pearl; white and shiny • *pearly white teeth*

**peasant** NOUN peasants
a person who belongs to a farming community, especially in poor areas of the world

**peasantry** NOUN
the peasants of a region or country

**peat** NOUN
rotted plant material that can be dug out of the ground and used as fuel or in gardening
➤ **peaty** ADJECTIVE

**pebble** NOUN pebbles
a small round stone found on a beach or in a river

**pebbly** ADJECTIVE
covered with pebbles • *a pebbly beach*

**peck** VERB pecks, pecking, pecked
❶ to bite at something quickly with the beak • *Birds were pecking at crumbs on the ground.* ❷ to kiss someone lightly on the cheek

**peck** NOUN pecks
❶ a quick bite by a bird ❷ a light kiss on the cheek

**peckish** ADJECTIVE (*British*) (*informal*)
hungry

**pectoral** ADJECTIVE
to do with the chest or breast • *pectoral muscles*

**peculiar** ADJECTIVE
❶ strange or unusual • *There's a peculiar smell in here.* ❷ belonging to a particular person, place or thing; restricted • *The custom is peculiar to this tribe.* ❸ special • *This point is of peculiar interest.*

**peculiarity** NOUN peculiarities
a strange or distinctive feature or habit • *It took a while to get used to his teacher's peculiarities.*

**peculiarly** ADVERB
❶ especially; more than usual • *She has a peculiarly annoying laugh.* ❷ strangely

**pecuniary** ADJECTIVE (*formal*)
to do with money • *pecuniary aid*
**WORD ORIGIN** from Latin *pecunia* = money (from *pecu* = cattle, because in early times a person's wealth was measured by how many cattle or sheep they owned)

**pedagogue** (say **ped**-a-gog) NOUN pedagogues
a teacher, especially one who teaches in a strict or exact way **WORD ORIGIN** from Greek *paidagogos* = a slave who took a boy to school

**pedal** NOUN pedals
a lever that you press with your foot to operate a bicycle, car or machine or to play certain musical instruments

**pedal** VERB pedals, pedalling, pedalled
to use a pedal; to move or work something, especially a bicycle, by means of pedals

**pedant** NOUN pedants
a pedantic person

**pedantic** ADJECTIVE
too concerned with minor details or with sticking strictly to formal rules
➤ **pedantically** ADVERB

**peddle** VERB peddles, peddling, peddled
❶ to go from house to house selling goods ❷ to sell illegal drugs ❸ to try to get people to accept an idea or way of life

**pedestal** NOUN pedestals
the raised base on which a statue or pillar stands
➤ **put someone on a pedestal** to admire someone greatly or too much

**pedestrian** NOUN pedestrians
a person who is walking

**pedestrian** ADJECTIVE
ordinary and dull

**pedestrian crossing** NOUN pedestrian crossings
(*British*) a place where pedestrians can cross the road safely

**pedigree** NOUN pedigrees
a list of a person's or animal's ancestors, especially to show how well an animal has been bred **WORD ORIGIN** from old French *pé de grue* = crane's foot (from the shape made by the lines on a family tree)

a b c d e f g h i j k l m n o p q r s t u v w x y z

**pediment** NOUN pediments
a wide triangular part decorating the top of a building

**pedlar** NOUN pedlars
(chiefly British) a person who goes from house to house selling small things

**peek** VERB peeks, peeking, peeked
to have a quick or sly look at something • He peeked over the wall.

**peek** NOUN peeks
a quick or sly look • I risked a peek around the corner.

**peel** NOUN peels
the skin of certain fruits and vegetables

**peel** VERB peels, peeling, peeled
❶ to remove the peel or covering from something ❷ to come off in strips or layers • Paint was peeling off the walls. ❸ to lose a covering or skin

**peelings** PLURAL NOUN
strips of skin peeled from potatoes etc.

**peep** VERB peeps, peeping, peeped
❶ to look quickly or secretly ❷ to look through a narrow opening ❸ to come slowly or briefly into view • The moon peeped out from behind the clouds.

**peep** NOUN peeps
a quick look

**peephole** NOUN peepholes
a small hole in a door or wall that you can look through

**peer** VERB peers, peering, peered
to look at something closely or with difficulty • I peered into the darkness.

**peer** NOUN peers
❶ your peers are the people who are the same age or status as you ❷ a member of the nobility

**peerage** NOUN peerages
❶ peers ❷ the rank of peer • He was raised to the peerage.

**peer group** NOUN peer groups
a group of people of roughly the same age or status

**peerless** ADJECTIVE
without an equal; better than the others

**peer pressure** NOUN
the pressure to do what others in your peer group do

**peeved** ADJECTIVE (informal)
annoyed or irritated

**peevish** ADJECTIVE
irritable or bad-tempered

**peewit** NOUN peewits
(British) a lapwing

**peg** NOUN pegs
a piece of wood or metal or plastic for fastening things together or for hanging things on

**peg** VERB pegs, pegging, pegged to fix something with pegs • We pegged out the tent.
➤ **peg away** to keep working hard at something in a determined way
➤ **peg it** (informal) to die

**pejorative** (say pij-orra-tiv) ADJECTIVE
showing disapproval; derogatory

**peke** NOUN pekes (informal)
a Pekinese

**Pekinese, Pekingese** NOUN Pekinese or Pekingese
a small kind of dog with short legs, a flat face and long silky hair **WORD ORIGIN** from Peking, the old name of Beijing, the capital of China (where the breed came from)

**pelican** NOUN pelicans
a large bird with a pouch in its long beak for storing fish

**pelican crossing** NOUN pelican crossings
(British) a place where pedestrians can cross a street safely by operating lights that signal traffic to stop **WORD ORIGIN** from pe(destrian) li(ght) con(trolled)

**pellet** NOUN pellets
a tiny ball of metal, food, paper, etc.

**pell-mell** ADVERB & ADJECTIVE
in a hasty uncontrolled way

**pelmet** NOUN pelmets
an ornamental strip of wood or material above a window, used to conceal a curtain rail

**pelt** VERB pelts, pelting, pelted
❶ to throw a lot of things at someone • We pelted him with snowballs. ❷ to run fast ❸ to rain very hard • It's pelting down outside.

**pelt** NOUN pelts
an animal skin, especially with the fur still on it
➤ **at full pelt** as fast as possible

**pelvis** NOUN pelvises
the round framework of bones at the lower

end of the spine
➤ **pelvic** ADJECTIVE

**pen** NOUN pens
**❶** an instrument with a point for writing with ink **❷** an enclosure for sheep, cattle, pigs or other farm animals **❸** a female swan. Compare with **cob**.

**pen** VERB pens, penning, penned
**❶** to shut animals into a pen or other enclosed space **❷** to write something

**penal** (say **peen**-al) ADJECTIVE
to do with the punishment of criminals, especially in prisons

**penalize** (also **penalise**) VERB penalizes, penalizing, penalized
to punish someone or make them suffer a disadvantage

**penalty** NOUN penalties
**❶** a punishment for breaking a rule or law **❷** a point or advantage given to one side in a game when a member of the other side has broken a rule, e.g. a free kick or goal in football

**penance** NOUN
a punishment that you willingly suffer to show that you regret something wrong that you have done

**pence** PLURAL NOUN
see **penny**

**penchant** (say **pahn-shahn**) NOUN
a special liking for something • She has a penchant for old films.

**pencil** NOUN pencils
an instrument for drawing or writing, made of a thin stick of graphite or coloured chalk enclosed in a cylinder of wood or metal

**pencil** VERB pencils, pencilling, pencilled
to write or mark something with a pencil

**pendant** NOUN pendants
an ornament worn hanging on a cord or chain round the neck

**pending** ADJECTIVE
**❶** waiting to be decided or settled **❷** about to happen

**pending** PREPOSITION
while waiting for; until • Please take charge, pending his return.

**pendulum** NOUN pendulums
a weight hung so that it can swing from side to side, especially in the works of a clock

**penetrate** VERB penetrates, penetrating, penetrated
to make or find a way through or into something • The knife had penetrated his chest. • Our eyes could not penetrate the gloom.
➤ **penetration** NOUN

**penetrating** ADJECTIVE
**❶** showing great insight or understanding • She gave him a penetrating look. **❷** clearly heard above other sounds

**penfriend** NOUN penfriends
a friend, usually in another country, who you write to without meeting

**penguin** NOUN penguins
an Antarctic seabird that cannot fly but uses its wings as flippers for swimming

**penicillin** NOUN
an antibiotic obtained from mould

**peninsula** NOUN peninsulas
a piece of land that is almost surrounded by water
➤ **peninsular** ADJECTIVE

**penis** (say **peen**-iss) NOUN penises
the part of the body with which a male urinates and has sexual intercourse

**penitent** ADJECTIVE
sorry for having done something wrong
➤ **penitence** NOUN
➤ **penitently** ADVERB

**penknife** NOUN penknives
a small folding knife WORD ORIGIN originally used for sharpening quill pens

**pen name** NOUN pen names
a name used by an author instead of their real name

**pennant** NOUN pennants
a long pointed flag

**penniless** ADJECTIVE
having no money; very poor

**penny** NOUN pennies for separate coins, pence for a sum of money
**❶** a British coin worth $\frac{1}{100}$ of a pound **❷** a former coin worth $\frac{1}{12}$ of a shilling

**pension** NOUN pensions
an income consisting of regular payments made to someone who is retired, widowed or disabled

**pension** VERB pensions, pensioning, pensioned
to pension someone off is to make them retire and pay them a pension

**pensioner** *NOUN* pensioners
a person who receives a pension

**pensive** *ADJECTIVE*
deep in thought
➤ **pensively** *ADVERB*

**pentagon** *NOUN* pentagons
a flat shape with five sides and five angles
➤ **pentagonal** (say pent-**ag**-on-al) *ADJECTIVE*
➤ **the Pentagon** a five-sided building in
Washington, headquarters of the leaders of
the American armed forces

**pentameter** *NOUN* pentameters
a line of verse with five rhythmic beats

**pentathlon** *NOUN* pentathlons
an athletic contest consisting of five events

**Pentecost** *NOUN*
❶ the Jewish harvest festival, fifty days after
Passover ❷ Whit Sunday

**penthouse** *NOUN* penthouses
an expensive flat at the top of a tall building

**pent-up** *ADJECTIVE*
pent-up feelings are ones that you hold inside
and do not express • pent-up anger

**penultimate** *ADJECTIVE*
last but one

**penumbra** *NOUN* penumbras or penumbrae
an area that is partly but not fully shaded, e.g.
during an eclipse

**penury** (say **pen**-yoor-ee) *NOUN* (formal)
great poverty

**peony** *NOUN* peonies
a plant with large round red, pink or white
flowers

**people** *PLURAL NOUN*
human beings; persons

**people** *NOUN* peoples
a community or nation • They are a peaceful
people. • the English-speaking peoples

**people** *VERB* peoples, peopling, peopled
to fill a place with people; to populate a place
• He lived in an imaginary world peopled by
heroes, giants and wizards.

**people carrier** *NOUN* people carriers
(British) a large car which carries up to eight
people

**pep** *NOUN* (informal)
vigour or energy

**pepper** *NOUN* peppers
❶ a hot-tasting powder used to flavour food
❷ a bright green, red or yellow vegetable
➤ **peppery** *ADJECTIVE*

**pepper** *VERB* peppers, peppering, peppered
❶ to sprinkle something with pepper ❷ to
pelt an area with many small objects • The
walls had been peppered with bullets.

**peppercorn** *NOUN* peppercorns
the dried black berry from which pepper is
made

**peppermint** *NOUN* peppermints
❶ a kind of mint used for flavouring ❷ a
sweet flavoured with this mint

**pepperoni** *NOUN*
beef and pork sausage seasoned with pepper

**pep talk** *NOUN* pep talks (informal)
a talk given to someone to encourage them

**per** *PREPOSITION*
for each • The charge is €5 per person.

**perambulator** *NOUN* perambulators (old use)
a baby's pram

**per annum** *ADVERB*
for each year; yearly

**per capita** (say **kap**-it-a) *ADVERB & ADJECTIVE*
for each person

**perceive** *VERB* perceives, perceiving,
perceived
to see, notice or understand something • She
perceived that she was no longer welcome.

**per cent** *ADVERB*
for or in every hundred • three per cent (3%)

**percentage** *NOUN* percentages
an amount or rate expressed as a proportion
of 100

**perceptible** *ADJECTIVE*
able to be seen or noticed • There was no
perceptible difference between them.
➤ **perceptibly** *ADVERB*

**perception** *NOUN* perceptions
❶ the ability to notice or understand
something ❷ receiving information through
the senses, especially the sense of sight

**perceptive** *ADJECTIVE*
quick to notice or understand things

**perch** *NOUN* perches
❶ a place where a bird sits or rests ❷ a seat
high up ❸ an edible freshwater fish

**perch** *VERB* perches, perching, perched
❶ to rest on a perch or place something on
a perch ❷ to sit on the edge of something

or somewhere high or narrow • *She perched herself on the arm of the sofa.*

**percolate** VERB percolates, percolating, percolated
to flow through small holes or spaces
➤ **percolation** NOUN

**percolator** NOUN percolators
a pot for making coffee, in which boiling water percolates through coffee grounds

**percussion** NOUN
❶ musical instruments that you play by hitting them or shaking them, such as drums and cymbals ❷ the striking of one thing against another
➤ **percussive** ADJECTIVE

**peregrine** NOUN peregrines
a kind of falcon

**peremptory** ADJECTIVE
giving commands and expecting to be obeyed at once

**perennial** ADJECTIVE
lasting for a long time; happening again and again • *It is a perennial problem.*

**perennial** NOUN perennials
a plant that lives for many years

**perfect** (say **per-fikt**) ADJECTIVE
❶ so good that it cannot be made any better ❷ complete • *He is a perfect stranger.* ❸ the perfect tense of a verb shows a completed action, e.g. *He has arrived.*

**perfect** (say **per-fekt**) VERB perfects, perfecting, perfected
to make a thing perfect • *He spent hours perfecting some new magic tricks.*

**perfection** NOUN
being perfect
➤ **to perfection** perfectly • *The fish was cooked to perfection.*

**perfectionist** NOUN perfectionists
a person who is only satisfied if something is done perfectly

**perfectly** ADVERB
❶ completely • *She stood perfectly still.* ❷ without any faults • *The TV works perfectly now.*

**perforate** VERB perforates, perforating, perforated
❶ to make tiny holes in something, especially so that it can be torn off easily ❷ to pierce a surface
➤ **perforated** ADJECTIVE

**perforation** NOUN perforations
perforations are the tiny holes made in something so that it can be torn off easily

**perforce** ADVERB (old use)
by necessity; unavoidably

**perform** VERB performs, performing, performed
❶ to do something in front of an audience • *They performed the play in the school hall.* ❷ to do or carry out something • *Surgeons had to perform an emergency operation.*

**performance** NOUN performances
❶ a form of entertainment presented to an audience • *What time does the performance start?* ❷ the way in which someone does something or the standard they reach • *It was the striker's best performance of the season.*

**performer** NOUN performers
a person who performs an entertainment in front of an audience

**perfume** NOUN perfumes
❶ a pleasant smell ❷ a pleasant-smelling liquid that you put on your skin

**perfume** VERB perfumes, perfuming, perfumed
to give a sweet smell to something
**WORD ORIGIN** originally used of pleasant-smelling smoke from something burning: via French from old Italian *parfumare* = to smoke through

**perfunctory** ADJECTIVE
done without much care or interest • *a perfunctory glance*
➤ **perfunctorily** ADVERB

**pergola** NOUN pergolas
an arch formed by climbing plants growing over trellis-work

**perhaps** ADVERB
it may be; possibly

**peril** NOUN perils
great danger
➤ **at your peril** at your own risk

**perilous** ADJECTIVE
very dangerous • *a perilous journey*
➤ **perilously** ADVERB

**perimeter** NOUN perimeters
❶ the outer edge or boundary of something • *A fence marks the perimeter of the airfield.* ❷ the distance round the edge

**period** NOUN periods
❶ a length of time ❷ the time allowed for a

lesson in school ❸ the time when a woman or girl menstruates ❹ a full stop

**periodic** ADJECTIVE
occurring at regular intervals • *periodic checks*
➤ **periodically** ADVERB

**periodical** NOUN periodicals
a magazine published at regular intervals (e.g. monthly)

**periodic table** NOUN
a table in which the chemical elements are arranged in order of increasing atomic number

**peripatetic** ADJECTIVE
going from place to place

**peripheral** ADJECTIVE
❶ of minor importance ❷ at the edge or boundary

**periphery** (say per-if-er-ee) NOUN peripheries
the part at the edge or boundary

**periscope** NOUN periscopes
a device with a tube and mirrors with which a person in a trench or submarine etc. can see things that are otherwise out of sight

**perish** VERB perishes, perishing, perished
❶ to die or be destroyed • *Many sailors perished in the shipwreck.* ❷ to rot • *The rubber ring has perished.*

**perishable** ADJECTIVE
perishable food is likely to go off quickly

**perished** ADJECTIVE (*informal*)
feeling very cold

**perishing** ADJECTIVE (*British*) (*informal*)
freezing cold • *It's perishing outside!*

**periwinkle** NOUN periwinkles
❶ a trailing plant with blue or white flowers ❷ a winkle (a kind of edible shellfish)

**perjure** VERB perjures, perjuring, perjured
➤ **perjure yourself** to commit perjury

**perjury** NOUN
telling a lie while you are on oath to speak the truth in a law court

**perk** VERB perks, perking, perked
➤ **perk up** to become more cheerful or lively • *She perked up at the mention of lunch.*

**perk** NOUN perks (*informal*)
something extra given to a worker • *Free bus travel is one of the perks of the job.*

**perky** ADJECTIVE perkier, perkiest
lively and cheerful

**perm** NOUN perms
treatment of the hair to give it long-lasting waves or curls
➤ **perm** VERB

**permafrost** NOUN
a permanently frozen layer of soil in polar regions

**permanent** ADJECTIVE
lasting for always or for a very long time • *Fortunately the damage was not permanent.*
➤ **permanently** ADVERB
➤ **permanence** NOUN

**permeable** ADJECTIVE
allowing liquid or gas to pass through it • *permeable rock*
➤ **permeability** NOUN

**permeate** VERB permeates, permeating, permeated
to spread into every part of a thing or place • *A sweet smell permeated the air.*

**permissible** ADJECTIVE
permitted or allowable

**permission** NOUN
the right to do something, given by someone else • *He took the car without permission.*

**permissive** ADJECTIVE
letting people do what they wish; tolerant or liberal

**permit** (say per-mit) VERB permits, permitting, permitted
to allow someone to do something or allow something to be done • *Mobile phones are not permitted in the classroom.*

**permit** (say per-mit) NOUN permits
written or printed permission to do something or go somewhere

**permutation** NOUN permutations
❶ changing the order of a set of things ❷ a changed order • *3, 1, 2 is a permutation of 1, 2, 3.*

**pernicious** ADJECTIVE
very harmful

**peroxide** NOUN
a chemical used for bleaching hair

**perpendicular** ADJECTIVE
upright; at a right angle (90°) to a line or surface

**perpetrate** VERB perpetrates, perpetrating, perpetrated
to commit a crime or serious error
➤ **perpetrator** NOUN

**perpetual** ADJECTIVE
lasting for a long time; continual • *She was in a perpetual state of panic.*
➤ **perpetually** ADVERB

**perpetuate** VERB perpetuates, perpetuating, perpetuated
to cause something to continue or be remembered for a long time • *The statue will perpetuate his memory.*
➤ **perpetuation** NOUN

**perpetuity** NOUN
➤ **in perpetuity** for ever

**perplex** VERB perplexes, perplexing, perplexed
to bewilder or puzzle someone
➤ **perplexing** ADJECTIVE

**perplexed** ADJECTIVE
confused because you cannot understand something • *She looked utterly perplexed.*

**perplexity** NOUN
a puzzled and confused state of mind • *They stared at him in perplexity.*

**persecute** VERB persecutes, persecuting, persecuted
to be continually cruel to someone, especially because you disagree with their beliefs
➤ **persecution** NOUN
➤ **persecutor** NOUN

**persevere** VERB perseveres, persevering, persevered
to go on doing something even though it is difficult
➤ **perseverance** NOUN

**Persian** ADJECTIVE
to do with Persia, a country in the Middle East now called Iran, or its people or language

**Persian** NOUN
the language of Persia. The modern form of the Persian language is called Farsi.

**persist** VERB persists, persisting, persisted
❶ to continue to do something firmly or obstinately • *She persists in breaking the rules.* ❷ to continue to exist for a long time • *The custom persists in some countries.*

**persistent** ADJECTIVE
❶ continuing or constant • *The rain was persistent.* ❷ determined to continue doing something and refusing to give up

➤ **persistently** ADVERB
➤ **persistence** NOUN

**person** NOUN people or persons
❶ a human being; a man, woman, or child ❷ (*in grammar*) any of the three groups of personal pronouns and forms taken by verbs. The **first person** (= *I, me, we, us*) refers to the person or people speaking; the **second person** (= *you*) refers to the person or people spoken to; the **third person** (= *he, him, she, her, it, they, them*) refers to the person or thing or the people or things spoken about.
➤ **in person** being actually present yourself • *She hopes to be there in person.*
**WORD ORIGIN** from Latin *persona* = mask used by an actor

**personage** NOUN personages
an important or well-known person

**personal** ADJECTIVE
❶ to do with, belonging to or done by a particular person • *personal belongings* ❷ private • *We have personal business to discuss.* ❸ criticizing a person's appearance, character or private affairs • *There's no need to make personal remarks.*

**personal computer** NOUN personal computers
a small computer designed to be used by one person at a time

**personality** NOUN personalities
❶ a person's character • *She has a cheerful personality.* ❷ a well-known person • *a TV personality*

**personally** ADVERB
❶ in person; being actually there • *The head thanked me personally.* ❷ as far as I am concerned • *Personally, I'd rather stay here.*

**personify** VERB personifies, personifying, personified
❶ to represent a quality or idea as if it were a person ❷ to be a perfect example of something • *She is courage personified.*
➤ **personification** NOUN

**personnel** NOUN
the people employed by a firm or other large organization

**perspective** NOUN perspectives
❶ the impression of depth and space in a picture or scene ❷ a person's point of view
➤ **in perspective** giving a well-balanced view of things • *Try to see the problem in perspective.*

**Perspex** NOUN (trademark)
a tough transparent plastic used instead of glass

**perspiration** NOUN
moisture given off by the body through the pores of the skin; sweat

**perspire** VERB perspires, perspiring, perspired
to sweat

**persuade** VERB persuades, persuading, persuaded
to make someone believe or agree to do something • I managed to persuade him to stay.

**persuasion** NOUN
persuading someone to believe or agree to do something • It took a lot of persuasion to get her to come.

**persuasive** ADJECTIVE
able to make someone believe or agree to do something • a persuasive argument
➤ **persuasively** ADVERB

**pert** ADJECTIVE
cheeky
➤ **pertly** ADVERB

**pertain** VERB pertains, pertaining, pertained
to be relevant to something • The police looked again at all the evidence pertaining to the murder.

**pertinent** ADJECTIVE
relevant to what you are talking about • a pertinent question

**perturbed** ADJECTIVE
worried or anxious • She didn't seem at all perturbed.
➤ **perturbation** NOUN

**peruse** (say per-**ooz**) VERB peruses, perusing, perused
to read something carefully
➤ **perusal** NOUN

**pervade** VERB pervades, pervading, pervaded
to spread all through something • The smell of herbs pervades the kitchen.
➤ **pervasive** ADJECTIVE

**perverse** ADJECTIVE
obstinately doing something different from what is reasonable or expected
➤ **perversely** ADVERB
➤ **perversity** NOUN

**pervert** (say per-**vert**) VERB perverts, perverting, perverted
❶ to turn something from the right course of action • By false evidence they perverted the course of justice. ❷ to make a person behave in a wrong or unacceptable way
➤ **perversion** NOUN

**pervert** (say **per**-vert) NOUN perverts
a person whose sexual behaviour is thought to be unnatural or unacceptable

**Pesach** (say **pay**-sahk) NOUN
the Passover festival

**pessimist** NOUN pessimists
a person who expects that things will turn out badly. Compare with **optimist**.
➤ **pessimism** NOUN

**pessimistic** ADJECTIVE
expecting things to turn out badly
➤ **pessimistically** ADVERB

**pest** NOUN pests
❶ a destructive insect or animal, such as a locust or a mouse ❷ an annoying person or thing

**pester** VERB pesters, pestering, pestered
to keep annoying someone by frequent questions or requests

**pesticide** NOUN pesticides
a substance for killing harmful insects and other pests

**pestilence** NOUN pestilences
a deadly epidemic

**pestle** NOUN pestles
a tool with a heavy rounded end for pounding substances in a mortar

**pet** NOUN pets
❶ a tame animal kept at home for companionship and pleasure ❷ a person treated as a favourite • teacher's pet

**pet** ADJECTIVE
favourite or particular • Natural history is my pet subject.

**pet** VERB pets, petting, petted
to stroke a person or animal affectionately
• He bent down to pet one of the dogs.

**petal** NOUN petals
one of the separate coloured outer parts of a flower

**peter** VERB peters, petering, petered
➤ **peter out** to become gradually less and come to an end • The footprints soon petered out.

**petition** NOUN petitions
a formal request for something, especially a written one signed by many people

**petition** VERB petitions, petitioning, petitioned
to request something by a petition
➤ **petitioner** NOUN

**petrel** NOUN petrels
a kind of seabird **WORD ORIGIN** perhaps named after St *Peter*, who tried to walk on the water (because the bird flies just over the waves with its legs dangling)

**petrify** VERB petrifies, petrifying, petrified
❶ to make someone so terrified that they cannot move ❷ to turn something to stone
➤ **petrified** ADJECTIVE

**petrochemical** NOUN petrochemicals
a chemical substance obtained from petroleum or natural gas

**petrol** NOUN
(*British*) a liquid made from petroleum, used as fuel for engines

**petroleum** NOUN
an oil found underground that is refined to make fuel (e.g. petrol or paraffin) or for use in dry-cleaning etc.

**petticoat** NOUN petticoats
a woman's or girl's dress-length piece of underwear worn under a skirt or dress

**petting** NOUN
affectionate touching or fondling

**pettish** ADJECTIVE
irritable or bad-tempered

**petty** ADJECTIVE pettier, pettiest
❶ unimportant or trivial • *petty regulations*
❷ mean and small-minded
➤ **pettiness** NOUN

**petty cash** NOUN
cash kept by an office for small payments

**petty officer** NOUN petty officers
a non-commissioned officer in the navy

**petulant** ADJECTIVE
irritable or bad-tempered, especially in a childish way
➤ **petulantly** ADVERB
➤ **petulance** NOUN

**petunia** NOUN petunias
a garden plant with funnel-shaped flowers

**pew** NOUN pews
a long wooden seat, usually fixed in rows, in a church

**pewter** NOUN
a grey alloy of tin and lead

**pH** NOUN
a measure of the acidity or alkalinity of a solution. Pure water has a pH of 7, acids have a pH between 0 and 7 and alkalis have a pH between 7 and 14. **WORD ORIGIN** from the initial letter of German *Potenz* = power, + H, the symbol for hydrogen

**phalanx** NOUN phalanxes
a number of people or soldiers in a close formation • *a phalanx of armed guards*

**phantasm** NOUN phantasms
a phantom

**phantom** NOUN phantoms
❶ a ghost ❷ something that does not really exist

**Pharaoh** (say **fair**-oh) NOUN Pharaohs
the title of the king of ancient Egypt

**pharmaceutical** (say farm-as-**yoot**-ik-al) ADJECTIVE
to do with medicinal drugs or with pharmacy
• *the pharmaceutical industry*

**pharmacist** NOUN pharmacists
a person who is trained to prepare and sell medicines

**pharmacology** NOUN
the study of medicinal drugs
➤ **pharmacological** ADJECTIVE
➤ **pharmacologist** NOUN

**pharmacy** NOUN pharmacies
❶ a shop where medicines are prepared and sold ❷ the job of preparing medicines

**phase** NOUN phases
a stage in the progress or development of something

**phase** VERB phases, phasing, phased
to do something in stages, not all at once • *a phased withdrawal*
➤ **phase something out** to stop something gradually

**PhD** ABBREVIATION
Doctor of Philosophy; a university degree awarded to someone who has done advanced research in their subject

**pheasant** (say **fez**-ant) NOUN pheasants
a game bird with a long tail

**phenomenal** ADJECTIVE
amazing or remarkable • *She has a phenomenal memory.*
➤ **phenomenally** ADVERB

**phenomenon** NOUN phenomena
an event or fact, especially one that is

a b c d e f g h i j k l m n o **p** q r s t u v w x y z

remarkable or interesting • *A solar eclipse is an extraordinary natural phenomenon.*

USAGE

The word **phenomena** is a plural. If you mean a single event, use **phenomenon**.

**phial** *NOUN* **phials**
a small glass bottle

**philanderer** *NOUN* **philanderers**
a man who has many casual affairs with women
➤ **philandering** *NOUN*

**philanthropist** *NOUN* **philanthropists**
a rich person who generously gives money to people who need it

**philanthropy** *NOUN*
concern for your fellow human beings, especially as shown by kind and generous acts that benefit large numbers of people
➤ **philanthropic** *ADJECTIVE*

**philately** (say fil-**at**-il-ee) *NOUN*
collecting postage stamps
➤ **philatelist** *NOUN*

**philistine** (say **fil**-ist-yn) *NOUN* **philistines**
a person who does not like or understand art, literature, music, etc. WORD ORIGIN from the *Philistines* in the Bible, who were enemies of the Israelites

**philosopher** *NOUN* **philosophers**
an expert in philosophy

**philosophical** *ADJECTIVE*
❶ to do with philosophy ❷ calm and not upset after a misfortune or disappointment • *He seems to be philosophical about losing.*
➤ **philosophically** *ADVERB*

**philosophy** *NOUN* **philosophies**
❶ the study of truths about life, knowledge, morals, etc. ❷ a set of ideas or principles or beliefs

**phlegm** (say flem) *NOUN*
thick mucus that forms in the throat and lungs when you have a bad cold

**phlegmatic** (say fleg-**mat**-ik) *ADJECTIVE*
not easily excited or worried
WORD ORIGIN same origin as **phlegm** (because too much phlegm in the body was believed to make you sluggish)

**phobia** (say **foh**-bee-a) *NOUN* **phobias**
a great or abnormal fear of something • *He has a phobia about flying.*

**phoenix** (say **feen**-iks) *NOUN* **phoenixes**
a mythical bird that was said to burn itself to death in a fire and be born again from the ashes

**phone** *NOUN* **phones**
a telephone

**phone** *VERB* **phones, phoning, phoned**
to telephone someone

**phone-in** *NOUN* **phone-ins**
(*British*) a radio or television programme in which people telephone the studio and take part in a discussion

**phoneme** *NOUN* **phonemes**
a distinct unit of sound that distinguishes one word from another, e.g. *p*, *b*, *d* and *t* in *pad*, *pat*, *bad* and *bat*

**phonetic** (say fon-**et**-ik) *ADJECTIVE*
❶ to do with speech sounds ❷ representing speech sounds
➤ **phonetically** *ADVERB*

**phoney** *ADJECTIVE* (*informal*)
sham; not genuine

**phonic** *ADJECTIVE*
to do with speech sounds

**phonics** *NOUN*
a method of teaching reading by relating sounds to letters of the alphabet

**phosphate** *NOUN* **phosphates**
a substance containing phosphorus, especially an artificial fertilizer

**phosphorescent** (say fos-fer-**ess**-ent) *ADJECTIVE*
glowing in the dark; luminous
➤ **phosphorescence** *NOUN*

**phosphorus** *NOUN*
a chemical substance that glows in the dark

**photo** *NOUN* **photos** (*informal*)
a photograph

**photocopier** *NOUN* **photocopiers**
a machine that makes photocopies

**photocopy** *NOUN* **photocopies**
a copy of a document or page made by photographing it on special paper

**photocopy** *VERB* **photocopies, photocopying, photocopied**
to make a photocopy of a document or page

**photoelectric** *ADJECTIVE*
using the electrical effects of light

**photogenic** *ADJECTIVE*
looking attractive in photographs

**photograph** *NOUN* photographs
a picture made using a camera

**photograph** *VERB* photographs,
photographing, photographed
to take a photograph of a person or thing

**photographer** *NOUN* photographers
a person who takes photographs

**photography** *NOUN*
taking photographs
➤ **photographic** *ADJECTIVE*

**photosynthesis** *NOUN*
the process by which green plants use
sunlight to turn carbon dioxide and water
into complex substances, giving off oxygen

**phrase** *NOUN* phrases
❶ a group of words that form a unit in a
sentence or clause, e.g. *in the garden* in 'The
Queen was in the garden.' ❷ a short section
of a tune

**phrase** *VERB* phrases, phrasing, phrased
❶ to put something into words • *He wanted
to phrase the question just right.* ❷ to divide
music into phrases

> **GRAMMAR**
>
> A **phrase** is a group of words that can be
> understood as a unit.
>
> A **noun phrase** is a group of words that
> has a noun as its head or key word.
>
> In the sentence *The teacher over there
> is my form tutor*, the words *the teacher
> over there* and *my form tutor* are noun
> phrases.
>
> An **adjective phrase** is a group of words
> that has an adjective as its head:
>
> She is a *very good* teacher.
>
> He is *as thin as a rake*.
>
> An **adverb phrase** is a group of words
> that has an adverb as its head:
>
> Please get here *as quickly as possible*.
>
> She was old, and walked *very slowly*.
>
> A **preposition phrase** is a group of words
> that has a preposition as its head:
>
> The mouse ran *along the windowsill*.
>
> See also the panel on **clauses**.

**phrase book** *NOUN* phrase books
a book which lists useful words and

expressions in a foreign language, with their
translations

**phraseology** (say fray-zee-**ol**-o-jee) *NOUN*
phraseologies
the way something is worded or expressed

**physical** *ADJECTIVE*
❶ to do with the body rather than the mind
or feelings ❷ to do with things that you can
touch or see ❸ to do with physics ❹ physical
geography is the study of natural features of
the Earth's surface, such as mountains and
volcanoes

**physical education, physical training**
*NOUN*
exercises and sports done to keep the body
healthy

**physically** *ADVERB*
in a way that is connected with the body
rather than the mind or feelings • *I was
exhausted, both physically and mentally.*

**physician** *NOUN* physicians
a doctor, especially one who is not a surgeon

**physicist** (say **fiz**-i-sist) *NOUN* physicists
an expert in physics

**physics** (say **fiz**-iks) *NOUN*
the study of the properties of matter and
energy (e.g. heat, light, sound and movement)

**physiognomy** (say fiz-ee-**on**-o-mee) *NOUN*
physiognomies
the features of a person's face

**physiology** (say fiz-ee-**ol**-o-jee) *NOUN*
the study of the body and its parts and how
they function
➤ **physiological** *ADJECTIVE*
➤ **physiologist** *NOUN*

**physiotherapy** (say fiz-ee-o-th'**erra**-pee)
*NOUN*
(*British*) the treatment of a disease or injury
by physical methods such as massage and
exercise
➤ **physiotherapist** *NOUN*

**physique** (say fiz-**eek**) *NOUN* physiques
a person's build • *He had the physique of a
heavyweight boxer.*

**pi** *NOUN*
the symbol (π) of the ratio of the
circumference of a circle to its diameter. The
value of pi is approximately 3.14159.

**pianist** *NOUN* pianists
a person who plays the piano

a
b
c
d
e
f
g
h
i
j
k
l
m
n
o
p
q
r
s
t
u
v
w
x
y
z

A B C D E F G H I J K L M N O P Q R S T U V W X Y Z

**piano** NOUN **pianos**
a large musical instrument with a row of black and white keys on a keyboard
**WORD ORIGIN** short for **pianoforte**, from Italian *piano* = soft + *forte* = loud (because it can produce soft notes and loud notes)

**piccolo** NOUN **piccolos**
a small high-pitched flute

**pick** VERB **picks, picking, picked**
❶ to pull a flower or fruit away from its plant • *We picked apples.* ❷ to choose something from a group • *Pick a number from one to twenty.* ❸ to pull bits off or out of something ❹ to open a lock by using something pointed, not with a key
➤ **pick a fight** or **quarrel** to deliberately start a fight or quarrel with someone
➤ **pick holes in something** to find fault with something
➤ **pick on someone** to single someone out for criticism or unkind treatment
➤ **pick someone's pocket** to steal from someone's pocket
➤ **pick up** to recover or improve
➤ **pick someone up** to give someone a lift in a vehicle
➤ **pick something up** ❶ to lift something or take it up ❷ to collect something from somewhere ❸ to learn or acquire something ❹ to manage to hear something

**pick** NOUN **picks**
❶ a choice • *Take your pick.* ❷ the best of a group ❸ a pickaxe ❹ a plectrum

**pickaxe** NOUN **pickaxes**
a heavy pointed tool with a long handle, used for breaking up hard ground or concrete
**WORD ORIGIN** from old French *picois*, later confused with **axe**

**picket** NOUN **pickets**
❶ a striker or group of strikers who try to persuade other people not to go into a place of work during a strike ❷ a pointed post as part of a fence

**picket** VERB **pickets, picketing, picketed**
to stand outside a place of work to try to persuade other people not to go in during a strike

**pickle** NOUN **pickles**
❶ a strong-tasting food made of pickled vegetables ❷ (*informal*) a difficulty or mess

**pickle** VERB **pickles, pickling, pickled**
to preserve food in vinegar or salt water

**pickpocket** NOUN **pickpockets**
a thief who steals from people's pockets or bags

**pick-up** NOUN **pick-ups**
an open truck for carrying small loads

**picnic** NOUN **picnics**
a meal eaten in the open air away from home

**picnic** VERB **picnics, picnicking, picnicked**
to have a picnic
➤ **picnicker** NOUN

**Pict** NOUN **Picts**
a member of an ancient people of north Britain
➤ **Pictish** ADJECTIVE

**pictogram** NOUN **pictograms**
a picture or symbol that stands for a word or phrase

**pictorial** ADJECTIVE
with or using pictures
➤ **pictorially** ADVERB

**picture** NOUN **pictures**
❶ a representation of a person or thing made by painting, drawing or photography ❷ a film at the cinema ❸ how something seems; an impression
➤ **be in the picture** to be fully informed about something

**picture** VERB **pictures, picturing, pictured**
❶ to show someone or something in a picture • *She is pictured here with her two brothers.* ❷ to imagine a person or thing • *He pictured himself holding up the trophy.*

**picturesque** ADJECTIVE
❶ forming an attractive scene • *a picturesque village* ❷ vivid and expressive • *picturesque language*
➤ **picturesquely** ADVERB

**pidgin** NOUN **pidgins**
a simplified form of a language, especially English, Dutch or Portuguese, including words from a local language, used by people who do not speak the same language
**WORD ORIGIN** from the Chinese pronunciation of **business** (because it was used by traders)

**pie** NOUN **pies**
a baked dish of meat, fish or fruit covered with pastry

**piebald** ADJECTIVE
with patches of black and white • *a piebald pony*

**piece** NOUN **pieces**
❶ a part or portion of something; a fragment

**❷** a separate thing or example • *a fine piece of work* **❸** something written, composed or painted • *a piece of music* **❹** one of the objects used to play a game on a board • *a chess piece* **❺** a coin • *a 50p piece*
➤ **in one piece** not harmed or damaged
➤ **piece by piece** gradually; one bit at a time

**piece** *VERB* pieces, piecing, pieced
to put different parts together to make something • *We began to piece together the whole story.*

SPELLING

Remember you can have a pie**ce** of pie.

**pièce de résistance** (say pee-ess der ray-zees-**tahns**) *NOUN* pièces de résistance
the most important item

**piecemeal** *ADJECTIVE & ADVERB*
done or made one piece at a time

**pie chart** *NOUN* pie charts
a diagram in the form of a circle divided into sectors to represent the way in which a quantity is divided up

**pier** *NOUN* piers
**❶** a long structure built out into the sea for people to walk on **❷** a pillar supporting a bridge or arch

**pierce** *VERB* pierces, piercing, pierced
**❶** to make a hole through something • *The arrow pierced his shoulder.* **❷** to be suddenly seen or heard • *A flash of lightning pierced the darkness.*

**piercing** *ADJECTIVE*
**❶** very loud and high-pitched • *The dog let out a piercing howl.* **❷** penetrating; very strong • *a piercing wind*

**piety** *NOUN*
being very religious and devout

**piffle** *NOUN* (informal)
nonsense

**pig** *NOUN* pigs
**❶** a fat animal with short legs and a blunt snout, kept for its meat **❷** (informal) someone greedy, dirty or unpleasant
➤ **piggy** *ADJECTIVE & NOUN*

**pigeon** *NOUN* pigeons
**❶** a bird with a fat body and a small head **❷** (informal) a person's business or responsibility • *That's your pigeon.*

**pigeon-hole** *NOUN* pigeon-holes
a small compartment for holding letters, messages or papers for someone to collect

**pigeon-hole** *VERB* pigeon-holes, pigeon-holing, pigeon-holed
to decide that a person belongs to a particular category • *She doesn't want to be pigeon-holed simply as a pop singer.*

**piggyback** *NOUN* piggybacks
a ride on someone else's back or shoulders

**piggy bank** *NOUN* piggy banks
a money box made in the shape of a hollow pig

**pig-headed** *ADJECTIVE*
stubborn or obstinate

**pig iron** *NOUN*
iron that has been processed in a smelting furnace WORD ORIGIN because the blocks of iron reminded people of pigs

**piglet** *NOUN* piglets
a young pig

**pigment** *NOUN* pigments
**❶** a substance that colours skin or other tissue in animals and plants **❷** a substance that gives colour to paint, inks and dyes
➤ **pigmentation** *NOUN*

**pigsty** *NOUN* pigsties
**❶** a partly covered pen for pigs **❷** a filthy room or house

**pigtail** *NOUN* pigtails
a plait of hair worn hanging at the back of the head

**pike** *NOUN* pikes
**❶** a heavy spear **❷** pike a large freshwater fish

**pilau** (say pi-**low**) *NOUN*
an Indian dish of spiced rice with meat and vegetables

**pilchard** *NOUN* pilchards
a small sea fish

**pile** *NOUN* piles
**❶** a number of things on top of one another **❷** (informal) a large quantity; a lot of money **❸** a large impressive building **❹** a heavy beam made of metal, concrete or timber driven into the ground to support something **❺** a raised surface on fabric, made of upright threads • *a carpet with a thick pile*

**pile** *VERB* piles, piling, piled
to put things into a pile; to make a pile • *He started piling food onto his plate.*
➤ **pile up** to increase in quantity • *The work was piling up.*

**pile-up** *NOUN* pile-ups
a road accident that involves a number of vehicles

**pilfer** *VERB* pilfers, pilfering, pilfered
to steal things of little value
➤ **pilferer** *NOUN*

**pilgrim** *NOUN* pilgrims
a person who travels to a holy place for religious reasons

**pilgrimage** *NOUN* pilgrimages
a journey to a holy place

**pill** *NOUN* pills
a small solid piece of medicine for swallowing
➤ **the pill** a contraceptive pill

**pillage** *VERB* pillages, pillaging, pillaged
to carry off goods using force, especially in a war; to plunder a place
➤ **pillage** *NOUN*

**pillar** *NOUN* pillars
a tall stone or wooden post

**pillar box** *NOUN* pillar boxes
a postbox standing in a street

**pillion** *NOUN* pillions
a seat behind the driver on a motorcycle

**pillory** *NOUN* pillories
a wooden framework with holes for a person's head and hands, in which offenders were formerly made to stand and be ridiculed by the public as a punishment

**pillory** *VERB* pillories, pillorying, pilloried
to expose a person to public ridicule and scorn • *Football managers get used to being pilloried in the newspapers.*

**pillow** *NOUN* pillows
a cushion for a person's head to rest on, especially in bed

**pillow** *VERB* pillows, pillowing, pillowed
to rest the head on something soft • *He pillowed his head on his arms.*

**pillowcase** *NOUN* pillowcases
a cloth cover for a pillow

**pilot** *NOUN* pilots
❶ a person who works the controls for flying an aircraft ❷ a person qualified to steer a ship in and out of a port or through a difficult stretch of water

**pilot** *VERB* pilots, piloting, piloted
❶ to be pilot of an aircraft or ship ❷ to guide or steer someone

**pilot** *ADJECTIVE*
testing on a small scale how something will work • *a pilot scheme*

**pilot light** *NOUN* pilot lights
a small flame that lights a larger burner on a gas cooker or boiler

**pimp** *NOUN* pimps
a man who gets clients for prostitutes and lives off their earnings

**pimpernel** (say **pimp**-er-nel) *NOUN* pimpernels
a plant with small red, blue or white flowers that close in cloudy weather

**pimple** *NOUN* pimples
a small round raised spot on the skin
➤ **pimply** *ADJECTIVE*

**PIN** *ABBREVIATION*
personal identification number; a number that you need to key in when you use a cash machine or bank card

**pin** *NOUN* pins
❶ a short thin piece of metal with a sharp point and a rounded head, used to fasten pieces of material or paper together ❷ a pointed device for fixing or marking something
➤ **pins and needles** a tingling feeling in the skin

**pin** *VERB* pins, pinning, pinned
❶ to fasten something with a pin or pins ❷ to hold someone firmly so that they cannot move • *He was pinned under the wreckage for hours.* ❸ to fix blame or responsibility on someone • *They pinned the blame for the mix-up on her.*

**pinafore** *NOUN* pinafores
an apron like a dress without sleeves, worn over clothes to keep them clean

**pinball** *NOUN*
a game in which you shoot small metal balls across a special table and score points when they strike special pins

**pincer** *NOUN* pincers
the claw of a shellfish such as a lobster

**pincers** *PLURAL NOUN*
a tool with two parts that are pressed together for gripping and holding things

**pinch** *VERB* pinches, pinching, pinched
❶ to squeeze something tightly or painfully between two things, especially between the finger and thumb ❷ (*informal*) to steal something

**pinch** NOUN pinches
❶ a pinching movement ❷ the amount that can be held between the tips of your thumb and forefinger • *a pinch of salt*
➤ **at a pinch** if it is really necessary • *The canoe could seat three people – four at a pinch.*
➤ **feel the pinch** to be short of money

**pincushion** NOUN pincushions
a small pad into which you stick pins to keep them ready for use

**pine** NOUN pines
an evergreen tree with needle-shaped leaves

**pine** VERB pines, pining, pined
❶ to feel an intense longing for someone or something • *She was pining for the sight of the sea again.* ❷ to become weak through longing for someone or something • *After his wife died, he just pined away.*

**pineapple** NOUN pineapples
a large tropical fruit with a tough prickly skin and yellow flesh

**ping** NOUN pings
a short sharp ringing sound

**ping** VERB pings, pinging, pinged
to make a sharp ringing sound • *The microwave pinged.*

**ping-pong** NOUN
table tennis (**WORD ORIGIN**) from the sound of the bats hitting the ball

**pinion** NOUN pinions
❶ a bird's wing, especially the outer end ❷ a small cogwheel that fits into another or into a rod (called a **rack**)

**pinion** VERB pinions, pinioning, pinioned
❶ to clip a bird's wings to prevent it from flying ❷ to hold or fasten someone's arms or legs in order to prevent them from moving • *His arms were pinioned behind his back.*
(**WORD ORIGIN**) the 'bird's wing' sense comes from Latin *pinna* = arrow or feather; the 'cogwheel' sense comes from Latin *pinus* = pine tree (because the wheel's teeth reminded people of a pine cone)

**pink** ADJECTIVE
pale red

**pink** NOUN pinks
❶ a pink colour ❷ a garden plant with fragrant flowers, often pink or white

**pinnacle** NOUN pinnacles
❶ a pointed ornament on a roof ❷ a high pointed piece of rock ❸ the highest point of something • *Winning the gold medal was the pinnacle of her career.*

**pinpoint** ADJECTIVE
exact or precise • *He can pass the ball with pinpoint accuracy.*

**pinpoint** VERB pinpoints, pinpointing, pinpointed
to find or identify something precisely

**pinprick** NOUN pinpricks
❶ a tiny round spot of something • *pinpricks of light* ❷ a small annoyance

**pinstripe** NOUN pinstripes
one of the very narrow stripes that form a pattern in cloth
➤ **pinstriped** ADJECTIVE

**pint** NOUN pints
a measure for liquids, equal to one-eighth of a gallon (or 0.57 of a litre)

**pin-up** NOUN pin-ups (*informal*)
a picture of an attractive or famous person for pinning on a wall

**pioneer** NOUN pioneers
one of the first people to go to a place or do or study something • *He was one of the pioneers of early photography.*

**pioneer** VERB pioneers, pioneering, pioneered
to be one of the first people to go to a place or do something (**WORD ORIGIN**) from French *pionnier* = foot soldier, later = one of the troops who went ahead of the army to prepare roads

**pious** ADJECTIVE
very religious or devout
➤ **piously** ADVERB

**pip** NOUN pips
❶ a small hard seed of an apple, pear, orange or other fruit ❷ (*British*) one of the stars on the shoulder of an army officer's uniform ❸ (*British*) a short high-pitched sound • *She heard the six pips of the time signal on the radio.*

**pip** VERB pips, pipping, pipped (*British*) (*informal*) to defeat someone by a small amount

**pipe** NOUN pipes
❶ a tube through which water, gas or oil can flow from one place to another ❷ a short narrow tube with a bowl at one end for burning tobacco for smoking ❸ a tube forming a musical instrument or part of one
➤ **the pipes** bagpipes

**pipe** VERB pipes, piping, piped
❶ to send something along pipes ❷ to

a b c d e f g h i j k l m n o **p** q r s t u v w x y z

transmit music or other sound by wire or cable ❸ to play music on a pipe or the bagpipes ❹ to decorate a cake with thin lines of icing, cream, etc.
➤ **pipe down** (*informal*) to be quiet
➤ **pipe up** to begin to say something

**pipe dream** NOUN pipe dreams
an impossible wish

**pipeline** NOUN pipelines
a pipe for carrying oil, water or gas over a long distance
➤ **in the pipeline** planned and ready to happen soon

**piper** NOUN pipers
a person who plays a pipe or bagpipes

**pipette** NOUN pipettes
a small glass tube used in a laboratory, usually filled by suction

**piping** NOUN
❶ pipes; a length of pipe ❷ a decorative line of icing, cream, etc. on a cake or other dish ❸ a long, narrow pipe-like fold decorating clothing, upholstery, etc.

**piping** ADJECTIVE
shrill • *a piping voice*
➤ **piping hot** very hot and ready to eat

**pipit** NOUN pipits
a small songbird

**pippin** NOUN pippins
a kind of apple

**piquant** (say **pee**-kant) ADJECTIVE
❶ pleasantly sharp and appetizing • *a piquant smell* ❷ pleasantly stimulating
➤ **piquancy** NOUN

**pique** (say peek) NOUN
a feeling of hurt pride

**pique** VERB piques, piquing, piqued
to be piqued is to feel irritated or annoyed
➤ **pique someone's interest** or **curiosity** to make someone want to know more

**piracy** NOUN
❶ the crime of attacking ships in order to steal from them ❷ the crime of illegally making and selling copies of books, DVDs, computer programs, etc.

**piranha** NOUN piranhas
a South American freshwater fish that has sharp teeth and eats flesh

**pirate** NOUN pirates
❶ a person on a ship who attacks and robs other ships at sea ❷ someone who copies

books, DVDs, computer programs, etc. in order to sell them illegally
➤ **piratical** ADJECTIVE

**pirouette** (say pir-oo-**et**) NOUN pirouettes
a spinning movement of the body made while balanced on the point of the toe or on one foot

**pirouette** VERB pirouettes, pirouetting, pirouetted
to perform a pirouette

**pistachio** NOUN pistachios
a nut with an edible green kernel

**pistil** NOUN pistils
the part of a flower that produces the seed, consisting of the ovary, style and stigma

**pistol** NOUN pistols
a small handgun

**piston** NOUN pistons
a disc or cylinder that fits inside a tube in which it moves up and down as part of an engine or pump

**pit** NOUN pits
❶ a deep hole ❷ a hollow ❸ a coal mine ❹ the part of a race circuit where racing cars are refuelled and repaired during a race

**pit** VERB pits, pitting, pitted
❶ to make holes or hollows in something • *The surface of the planet was pitted with craters.* ❷ to put someone in competition with someone else • *He was pitted against the champion in the final.*
➤ **pitted** ADJECTIVE

**pit bull terrier** NOUN pit bull terriers
a small strong and fierce breed of dog

**pitch** NOUN pitches
❶ a piece of ground marked out for cricket, football or another game ❷ how high or low a voice or a musical note is ❸ intensity or strength • *Excitement was at fever pitch.* ❹ the steepness of a slope • *the pitch of the roof* ❺ a black sticky substance rather like tar

**pitch** VERB pitches, pitching, pitched
❶ to throw or fling something • *She pitched his hat over the wall.* ❷ to set up a tent or camp ❸ to fall heavily forward • *He pitched forward as the bus braked suddenly.* ❹ a ship pitches when it moves up and down on a rough sea ❺ to set something at a particular level • *They have pitched their prices too high.* ❻ a bowled ball in cricket pitches when it strikes the ground
➤ **pitch in** (*informal*) to join in and help with something • *Everyone pitched in with ideas.*

**pitch-black, pitch-dark** ADJECTIVE
completely black or dark

**pitchblende** NOUN
a mineral ore (uranium oxide) from which
radium is obtained

**pitched battle** NOUN pitched battles
a battle between armies in prepared positions

**pitcher** NOUN pitchers
a large jug

**pitchfork** NOUN pitchforks
a large fork with two prongs, used for lifting
hay

**piteous** ADJECTIVE
making you feel pity • It was a piteous sight.
➤ **piteously** ADVERB

**pitfall** NOUN pitfalls
a hidden danger or difficulty

**pith** NOUN
the spongy substance in the stems of certain
plants or lining the rind of oranges or other
fruits

**pithy** ADJECTIVE
❶ like pith; containing much pith ❷ short
and full of meaning • pithy comments

**pitiable** ADJECTIVE
making you feel pity

**pitiful** ADJECTIVE
making you feel pity • He let out a pitiful
moan.
➤ **pitifully** ADVERB

**pitiless** ADJECTIVE
showing no pity; harsh or cruel
➤ **pitilessly** ADVERB

**pitta** NOUN
a kind of flat thick bread with a hollow inside

**pittance** NOUN
a very small allowance of money

**pity** NOUN
❶ the feeling of being sorry because
someone is in pain or trouble ❷ a cause for
regret • It's a pity that you can't come.
➤ **take pity on someone** to feel sorry for
someone and try to help them

**pity** VERB pities, pitying, pitied
to feel pity for someone

**pivot** NOUN pivots
a point or part on which something turns or
balances

**pivot** VERB pivots, pivoting, pivoted
to turn or balance on a pivot

**pivotal** ADJECTIVE
of great importance, because other things
depend on it • He plays a pivotal role in the
story.

**pixel** (say **piks**-el) NOUN pixels
one of the tiny dots on a computer display
screen from which the image is formed
**WORD ORIGIN** short for picture element

**pixie** NOUN pixies
a small fairy or elf

**pizza** (say **peets**-a) NOUN pizzas
an Italian food that consists of a layer of
dough baked with a savoury topping

**pizzicato** (say pits-i-**kah**-toh) ADJECTIVE &
ADVERB
(in music) plucking the strings of a musical
instrument such as a violin

**placard** NOUN placards
a poster or notice, especially one carried at a
demonstration

**placate** VERB placates, placating, placated
to make someone feel calmer and less angry
➤ **placatory** ADJECTIVE

**place** NOUN places
❶ a particular part of space, especially where
something belongs; an area or position ❷ a
city, town or village ❸ a position in a race
or competition • She finished in second
place. ❹ a seat • Save me a place. ❺ a job;
employment ❻ a building; a home • Come
round to our place ❼ a role or function • It's
not my place to interfere. ❽ a point in a
series of things • In the first place, the date
is wrong.
➤ **in place** in the correct position
➤ **in place of** instead of
➤ **out of place** ❶ in the wrong position
❷ not appropriate or suitable
➤ **take place** to happen • The wedding will
take place early next year.

**place** VERB places, placing, placed
to put something in a particular place • He
carefully placed the bowl on the table.

**placebo** (say plas-**ee**-boh) NOUN placebos
a harmless substance given as if it were
a medicine, usually to reassure a patient
**WORD ORIGIN** Latin, = I shall be pleasing

**placement** NOUN placements
placing something in a position

**placenta** NOUN
a piece of body tissue that forms in the womb
during pregnancy and supplies the foetus
with nourishment

a b c d e f g h i j k l m n o p q r s t u v w x y z

**placid** ADJECTIVE
calm and peaceful; not easily made anxious or
upset • *a placid horse*
➤ **placidly** ADVERB
➤ **placidity** NOUN

**plagiarize** (also **plagiarise**) (say play-jeer-yz)
VERB **plagiarizes, plagiarizing, plagiarized**
to take someone else's writings or ideas and
use them as if they were your own
➤ **plagiarism** NOUN

**plague** NOUN **plagues**
❶ a dangerous illness that spreads very
quickly ❷ a large number of pests • *a plague
of locusts*

**plague** VERB **plagues, plaguing, plagued**
to keep causing someone trouble • *The
project was plagued with problems from the
start.*

**plaice** NOUN **plaice**
a flat edible sea fish

**plaid** (say plad) NOUN
cloth with a tartan or similar pattern

**plain** ADJECTIVE
❶ simple; not decorated or elaborate ❷ not
pretty or beautiful ❸ easy to see or hear or
understand ❹ frank and straightforward • *I'll
be quite plain with you.*
➤ **plainness** NOUN

**plain** NOUN **plains**
a large area of flat country

SPELLING
Take care not to confuse with **plane**,
which means an aeroplane.

**plain clothes** NOUN
civilian clothes worn instead of a uniform, e.g.
by police

**plainly** ADVERB
❶ clearly or obviously • *He was plainly very
upset.* ❷ simply • *She was plainly dressed.*

**plaintiff** NOUN **plaintiffs**
the person who brings a complaint against
someone else to a law court. Compare with
**defendant**.

**plaintive** ADJECTIVE
sounding sad • *a plaintive cry*
➤ **plaintively** ADVERB

**plait** (say plat) VERB **plaits, plaiting, plaited**
to weave three or more strands of hair or
rope to form one length

**plait** NOUN **plaits**
a length of hair or rope that has been plaited

**plan** NOUN **plans**
❶ a way of doing something that you think
out in advance ❷ a drawing showing how the
parts of something are arranged ❸ a map of
a town or district

**plan** VERB **plans, planning, planned**
❶ to think out in advance how you are going
to do something ❷ to intend or expect to
do something • *We plan to arrive there at
lunchtime.*
➤ **planner** NOUN

**plane** NOUN **planes**
❶ an aeroplane ❷ a tool for making wood
smooth by scraping its surface ❸ a flat or
level surface ❹ a tall tree with broad leaves

**plane** VERB **planes, planing, planed**
to smooth wood with a plane

**plane** ADJECTIVE
flat or level • *a plane surface*

SPELLING
Take care not to confuse with **plain**, which
means simple or straightforward.

**planet** NOUN **planets**
one of the large bodies in space that move
in an orbit round the sun or another star
WORD ORIGIN from Greek *planetes* = wanderer
(because planets seem to move in relation to
the stars)

**planetary** ADJECTIVE
to do with planets • *planetary exploration*

**plank** NOUN **planks**
a long flat piece of wood

**plankton** NOUN
microscopic plants and animals that float in
the sea and lakes

**plant** NOUN **plants**
❶ a living thing that cannot move, makes its
food from chemical substances and usually
has a stem, leaves and roots. Flowers, trees
and shrubs are plants. ❷ a small plant, not
a tree or shrub ❸ a factory or its equipment
❹ (*informal*) something deliberately placed
for other people to find, usually to mislead
people or cause trouble

**plant** VERB **plants, planting, planted**
❶ to put something in soil for growing ❷ to
put something firmly in place • *He planted his
feet on the ground and took hold of the rope.*
❸ to place something where it will be found,
usually to mislead people or cause trouble

**plantain** (say plan-tin) NOUN **plantains**
❶ a tropical tree and fruit resembling the
banana ❷ a wild plant with broad flat leaves,

bearing seeds that are used as food for cage birds

**plantation** NOUN plantations
❶ a large area of land where a crop such as cotton, tobacco or tea is planted ❷ a group of planted trees

**planter** NOUN planters
someone who owns a plantation • *a tea planter*

**plaque** (say plak) NOUN plaques
❶ a flat piece of metal or porcelain fixed on a wall as an ornament or memorial ❷ a filmy substance that forms on teeth and gums, where bacteria can live

**plasma** NOUN
the colourless liquid part of blood, carrying the corpuscles

**plaster** NOUN plasters
❶ a small covering put over the skin around a cut or wound to protect it ❷ a mixture of lime, sand and water etc. for covering walls and ceilings ❸ plaster of Paris or a cast made of this to hold broken bones in place

**plaster** VERB plasters, plastering, plastered
❶ to cover a wall or other surface with plaster ❷ to cover something thickly • *His clothes were plastered with mud.*

**plaster of Paris** NOUN
a white paste used for making moulds or for casts round a broken leg or arm

**plastic** NOUN plastics
a strong, light synthetic substance that can be moulded into a permanent shape

**plastic** ADJECTIVE
❶ made of plastic • *a plastic bag* ❷ soft and easy to mould • *Clay is a plastic substance.*

**plastic surgery** NOUN
surgery to repair or replace damaged skin or to improve the appearance of someone's face or body
➤ **plastic surgeon** NOUN

**plate** NOUN plates
❶ an almost flat usually circular object from which food is eaten or served ❷ a thin flat sheet of metal, glass or other hard material ❸ an illustration on special paper in a book

**plate** VERB plates, plating, plated
❶ to coat metal with a thin layer of gold, silver, tin, etc. ❷ to cover something with sheets of metal

**plateau** (say **plat**-oh) NOUN plateaux or plateaus (say **plat**-ohz)
a flat area of high land

**plateful** NOUN platefuls
the amount of food that a plate can hold

**platform** NOUN platforms
❶ a flat raised area along the side of a line at a railway station, where passengers get on and off trains ❷ a flat surface that is above the level of the ground or floor, especially one from which someone speaks to an audience

**platinum** NOUN
a valuable silver-coloured metal that does not tarnish

**platitude** NOUN platitudes
a trite or insincere remark that people often use

**platoon** NOUN platoons
a small group of soldiers

**platter** NOUN platters
a flat dish or plate

**platypus** NOUN platypuses
an Australian animal with a beak like that of a duck, that lays eggs like a bird but is a mammal and suckles its young

**plaudits** PLURAL NOUN
applause; expressions of approval

**plausible** ADJECTIVE
seeming likely to be true; reasonable • *a plausible explanation*
➤ **plausibly** ADVERB
➤ **plausibility** NOUN

**play** VERB plays, playing, played
❶ to take part in a game, sport or other amusement ❷ to make music with a musical instrument ❸ to put a CD, DVD, etc. into a machine and listen to it or watch it ❹ to perform a part in a play or film
➤ **play about** or **around** to have fun or be mischievous
➤ **play something down** to give people the impression that something is not important
➤ **play up** (*informal*) to tease or annoy someone

**play** NOUN plays
❶ a story acted on a stage or on radio or television ❷ doing things for fun or amusement • *Young children learn through play.* ❸ the playing of a game or sport • *Rain stopped play.*
➤ **a play on words** a pun

a
b
c
d
e
f
g
h
i
j
k
l
m
n
o
p
q
r
s
t
u
v
w
x
y
z

**playback** NOUN playbacks
playing back something that has been recorded

**player** NOUN players
❶ a person who plays a game or sport • *a tennis player* ❷ a person who plays a musical instrument • *a trumpet player* ❸ a machine for playing recorded sound or pictures • *a DVD player*

**playful** ADJECTIVE
❶ wanting to play; full of fun ❷ done in fun; not serious
➤ **playfully** ADVERB
➤ **playfulness** NOUN

**playground** NOUN playgrounds
a piece of ground for children to play on

**playgroup** NOUN playgroups
(*British*) a group of very young children who play together regularly, supervised by adults

**playing card** NOUN playing cards
each of a set of cards (usually 52) used for playing games

**playing field** NOUN playing fields
a field used for outdoor games

**playmate** NOUN playmates
a person you play games with

**play-off** NOUN play-offs
an extra match that is played between teams with equal scores to decide who the winner is

**plaything** NOUN playthings
❶ a toy ❷ a person that someone has fun with and treats as unimportant

**playtime** NOUN
the time when young schoolchildren go out to play

**playwright** NOUN playwrights
a person who writes plays; a dramatist

**PLC, plc** ABBREVIATION
(*British*) public limited company

**plea** NOUN pleas
❶ a request or appeal • *a plea for mercy* ❷ a formal statement of 'guilty' or 'not guilty' made in a law court by someone accused of a crime

**plead** VERB pleads, pleading, pleaded
❶ to beg someone to do something ❷ to state formally in a law court that you are guilty or not guilty of a crime ❸ to give something as an excuse • *She didn't come on holiday with us, pleading poverty.*

**pleasant** ADJECTIVE
pleasing; giving pleasure
➤ **pleasantness** NOUN

**pleasantly** ADVERB
in a pleasant way • *I was pleasantly surprised.*

**pleasantry** NOUN pleasantries
a friendly or good-humoured remark • *They exchanged a few pleasantries.*

**please** VERB pleases, pleasing, pleased
❶ to make a person feel satisfied or glad ❷ used to make a request or an order polite • *Please ring the bell.*
➤ **as you please** in whatever way you think is suitable

**pleased** ADJECTIVE
happy or satisfied about something • *I'm very pleased to meet you.*

**pleasurable** ADJECTIVE
causing pleasure; enjoyable

**pleasure** NOUN pleasures
❶ a feeling of satisfaction or gladness; enjoyment ❷ something that pleases you • *It's been a pleasure talking to you.*

**pleat** NOUN pleats
a flat fold made by doubling cloth upon itself
➤ **pleated** ADJECTIVE

**plectrum** NOUN plectra
a small piece of metal, plastic or bone for plucking the strings of a musical instrument

**plentiful** ADJECTIVE
available in large amounts • *a plentiful supply of food*
➤ **plentifully** ADVERB

**plenty** NOUN
quite enough; as much as is needed or wanted

**plenty** ADVERB (*informal*) quite or fully • *It's plenty big enough.*

**plethora** NOUN
too large a quantity of something

**pleurisy** (say **ploor**-i-see) NOUN
inflammation of the membrane round the lungs

**pliable** ADJECTIVE
❶ easy to bend; flexible ❷ easy to influence or control

**pliant** ADJECTIVE
flexible or pliable

**pliers** PLURAL NOUN
pincers that have jaws with flat surfaces for gripping things

**plight** NOUN plights
a dangerous or difficult situation • *the plight of the homeless*

**plight** VERB plights, plighting, plighted (*old use*)
to pledge devotion or loyalty

**plimsoll** NOUN plimsolls
(*British*) a canvas sports shoe with a rubber sole WORD ORIGIN from **Plimsoll line** (because the thin sole reminded people of a Plimsoll line)

**Plimsoll line** NOUN Plimsoll lines
a mark on a ship's side showing how deeply it may legally go down in the water when loaded WORD ORIGIN named after an English politician, *S. Plimsoll*, who in the 1870s protested about ships being overloaded

**plinth** NOUN plinths
a block or slab forming the base of a column or a support for a statue or vase

**plod** VERB plods, plodding, plodded
❶ to walk slowly and heavily • *We plodded back through the rain.* ❷ to work slowly but steadily
➤ **plodder** NOUN

**plonk** NOUN (*British*) (*informal*)
cheap wine WORD ORIGIN originally Australian; probably from French *blanc* = white, in *vin blanc* = white wine

**plonk** VERB plonks, plonking, plonked
(*informal, chiefly British*) to put something down carelessly or heavily • *Just plonk your bag down anywhere.*

**plop** NOUN plops
the sound of something dropping into water

**plop** VERB plops, plopping, plopped
to fall into liquid with a plop

**plot** NOUN plots
❶ a secret plan by a group of people to do something illegal or wrong ❷ the story in a play, novel or film ❸ a small piece of land

**plot** VERB plots, plotting, plotted
❶ to make a secret plan to do something
❷ to make a chart or graph of something
• *We plotted the ship's route on our map.*

**plotter** NOUN plotters
someone who takes part in a plot

**plough** NOUN ploughs
a farming implement for turning the soil over, in preparation for planting seeds

**plough** VERB ploughs, ploughing, ploughed
❶ to turn over soil with a plough ❷ to plough through something is to read all of it with great effort or difficulty • *He ploughed through the book over the weekend.*
➤ **ploughman** NOUN

**ploughshare** NOUN ploughshares
the cutting blade of a plough

**plover** (say pluv-er) NOUN plovers
a kind of wading bird

**ploy** NOUN ploys
a cunning trick or deception you use to get what you want

**pluck** VERB plucks, plucking, plucked
❶ to pick a flower or fruit ❷ to pull the feathers off a bird ❸ to pull something up or out • *She plucked the letter out of his hand.*
❹ to pull a string (e.g. on a guitar) and let it go again
➤ **pluck up courage** to try to get enough courage to do something

**pluck** NOUN
courage or spirit

**plucky** ADJECTIVE pluckier, pluckiest
brave or spirited
➤ **pluckily** ADVERB

**plug** NOUN plugs
❶ something used to stop up a hole • *a bath plug* ❷ a device that fits into a socket to connect a piece of electrical equipment to a supply of electricity ❸ (*informal*) a piece of publicity for something

**plug** VERB plugs, plugging, plugged
❶ to stop up a hole ❷ (*informal*) to publicize something
➤ **plug something in** to connect something to an electrical socket by means of a plug

**plum** NOUN plums
❶ a soft juicy fruit with a pointed stone in the middle ❷ a reddish purple colour

**plum** ADJECTIVE
(*informal*) that is the best of its kind • *a plum job*

**plumage** (say ploom-ij) NOUN plumages
a bird's feathers

**plumb** VERB plumbs, plumbing, plumbed
❶ to investigate something mysterious in order to understand it • *Scientists are trying to plumb the mysteries of the universe.*
❷ (*British*) to fit a room or building with a plumbing system

**plumb** ADJECTIVE
exactly upright or vertical • *The wall was plumb.*

a b c d e f g h i j k l m n o **p** q r s t u v w x y z

**plumb** ADVERB (*informal*) exactly or precisely
• *It fell plumb in the middle.*

**plumber** NOUN plumbers
a person who fits and mends plumbing

**plumbing** NOUN
❶ the water pipes, water tanks and drainage pipes in a building ❷ the work of a plumber
(WORD ORIGIN) from Latin *plumbum* = lead (because water pipes used to be made of lead)

**plumb line** NOUN plumb lines
a cord with a weight on the end, used to find how deep something is or whether a wall etc. is vertical

**plume** NOUN plumes
❶ a large feather ❷ a thin column of something that rises in the air • *a plume of smoke*

**plumed** ADJECTIVE
decorated with plumes • *a plumed helmet*

**plummet** VERB plummets, plummeting, plummeted
❶ to drop downwards quickly • *The plane plummeted towards the ground.* ❷ to decrease rapidly in value • *Prices have plummeted.*

**plump** ADJECTIVE
having a full, rounded shape; slightly fat
• *plump cheeks*
➤ **plumpness** NOUN

**plump** VERB plumps, plumping, plumped
to plump up a cushion or pillow is to shake it to give it a rounded shape
➤ **plump for something** (*informal*) to choose something

**plunder** VERB plunders, plundering, plundered
to rob a person or place using force, especially during a war • *The invading army plundered many of the churches and monasteries.*
➤ **plunderer** NOUN

**plunder** NOUN
❶ plundering a person or place ❷ goods that have been plundered

**plunge** VERB plunges, plunging, plunged
❶ to jump or dive into water with force ❷ to push something forcefully into something
• *She plunged the knife into his chest.* ❸ to fall or go downwards suddenly • *The car plunged off the cliff.* ❹ to force someone or something into an unpleasant situation • *They plunged the world into war.* • *The room was suddenly plunged into darkness.*

**plunge** NOUN plunges
a sudden fall or dive
➤ **take the plunge** to start a bold course of action

**plunger** NOUN plungers
a rubber cup on a handle used for clearing blocked pipes

**plural** NOUN plurals
the form of a noun or verb used when it stands for more than one person or thing
• *The plural of 'child' is 'children'.*
Compare with **singular**.

**plural** ADJECTIVE
in the plural; meaning more than one
• *'Mice' is a plural noun.*

GRAMMAR

Most words in English form their plurals by adding -s or -es (*ants*, *branches*). However, some types of words have more unusual plurals:

words which are the same in the singular and plural, e.g. *aircraft*, *deer*, *fish*, *sheep*, *series* and *species*.

words which have irregular plurals: *child*, *children*; *goose*, *geese*; *louse*, *lice*; *mouse*, *mice*; *ox*, *oxen*; *tooth*, *teeth*.

words of Greek and Latin origin which keep a Greek or Latin plural form:

-*a*, -*ae*, e.g. *antenna*, *antennae*; *formula*, *formulae*

-*ex*, -*ices*, e.g. *index*, *indices*; *vortex*, *vortices*

-*is*, -*es*, e.g. *axis*, *axes*; *basis*, *bases*; *thesis*, *theses*

-*ix*, -*ices*, e.g. *appendix*, *appendices*

-*on*, -*a*, e.g. *phenomenon*, *phenomena*

-*um*, -*a*, e.g. *medium*, *media*

-*us*, -*i*, e.g. *radius*, *radii*; *sarcophagus*, *sarcophagi*

Sometimes the use of a Latin or Greek plural is optional, e.g. *plectrums* or *plectra*, *radiuses* or *radii*; it can also depend on meaning, e.g. the form *appendixes* is used for parts of the body, but *appendices* for sections of a book.

Words from other languages which keep their original plurals, e.g. *gateau*, *gateaux*.

**plus** *PREPOSITION*
with the next number or thing added • *2 plus 2 equals four (2 + 2 = 4).*

**plus** *ADJECTIVE*
❶ being a grade slightly higher • *B plus*
❷ more than zero • *a temperature between minus ten and plus ten degrees*

**plush** *NOUN*
a thick velvety cloth used in furnishings

**plush** *ADJECTIVE*
smart and expensive • *a plush hotel*

**plutonium** *NOUN*
a radioactive substance used in nuclear weapons and reactors WORD ORIGIN named after the planet *Pluto*

**ply** *VERB* plies, plying, plied
❶ to keep offering something to someone • *They plied her with food from the moment she arrived.* ❷ to ply a trade is to work at it as your regular job ❸ to go regularly back and forth • *The boat plies between the two harbours.*

**ply** *NOUN* plies
❶ a thickness or layer of wood or cloth etc.
❷ a strand in yarn • *4-ply wool*

**plywood** *NOUN*
strong thin board made of layers of wood glued together

**PM** *ABBREVIATION*
Prime Minister

**p.m.** *ABBREVIATION*
after 12 o'clock midday WORD ORIGIN short for Latin *post meridiem* – after noon

**pneumatic** (say new-**mat**-ik) *ADJECTIVE*
filled with or worked by compressed air • *a pneumatic drill*

**pneumonia** (say new-**moh**-nee-a) *NOUN*
a serious illness caused by inflammation of one or both lungs

**poach** *VERB* poaches, poaching, poached
❶ to cook an egg (removed from its shell) in or over boiling water ❷ to cook fish or fruit in a small amount of liquid ❸ to steal game or fish from someone else's land or water ❹ to take something unfairly • *One club was poaching members from another.*

**poacher** *NOUN* poachers
a person who steals game or fish from someone else's land or water

**pocket** *NOUN* pockets
❶ a small bag-shaped part of a piece of clothing, for carrying things in ❷ a person's

supply of money • *The cost is well beyond my pocket.* ❸ a small isolated area of something • *There will be pockets of rain in the south.*
➤ **pocketful** *NOUN*
➤ **be out of pocket** to have spent more money than you have gained

**pocket** *ADJECTIVE*
small enough to carry in your pocket • *a pocket calculator*

**pocket** *VERB* pockets, pocketing, pocketed
to put something into a pocket • *He pocketed the money and walked out.*

**pocket money** *NOUN*
(*British*) money given to a child to spend

**pockmark** *NOUN* pockmarks
a scar or mark left on the skin by a disease
➤ **pockmarked** *ADJECTIVE*

**pod** *NOUN* pods
a long seed container of the kind found on a pea or bean plant

**podcast** *NOUN* podcasts
a digital recording, especially of a radio programme, that you can download from the Internet to a computer or portable media player

**podgy** *ADJECTIVE* podgier, podgiest
(*British*) (*informal*) short and fat • *podgy fingers*

**podium** (say poh-dee-um) *NOUN* podiums or podia
a small platform on which a music conductor or someone making a speech stands

**poem** *NOUN* poems
a piece of writing arranged in short lines, usually with a particular rhythm and sometimes with rhymes

**poet** *NOUN* poets
a person who writes poetry

**poetic** *ADJECTIVE*
to do with poetry or like poetry • *poetic language*
➤ **poetical** *ADJECTIVE*
➤ **poetically** *ADVERB*

**poetry** *NOUN*
poems or the writing of poems • *Do you like poetry?*

**poignant** (say **poin**-yant) *ADJECTIVE*
having a strong effect on your feelings and making you feel sad • *poignant memories*
➤ **poignancy** *NOUN*

a
b
c
d
e
f
g
h
i
j
k
l
m
n
o
p
q
r
s
t
u
v
w
x
y
z

**point** NOUN points
❶ the narrow or sharp end of something ❷ a dot • *the decimal point* ❸ a single mark in a game or quiz • *How many points did I get?* ❹ a particular place or time • *At this point she was winning.* ❺ something that someone says during a discussion • *That's a very good point.* ❻ a detail or characteristic • *He has his good points.* ❼ the important or essential idea • *Keep to the point!* ❽ purpose or value • *There is no point in hurrying.* ❾ an electrical socket ❿ a device for changing a train from one track to another

**point** VERB points, pointing, pointed
❶ to show where something is, especially by holding out your finger towards it ❷ to aim or direct something at a person or thing • *She pointed a gun at me.* ❸ to fill in the parts between bricks with mortar or cement
➤ **point something out** to draw attention to something

**point-blank** ADJECTIVE
❶ aimed or fired from close to the target ❷ direct and straightforward • *a point-blank refusal*

**point-blank** ADVERB
in a point-blank manner • *He refused point-blank to let us in.*

**point duty** NOUN
(*British*) the duties of a police officer stationed at a road junction to control the movement of traffic

**pointed** ADJECTIVE
❶ with a point at the end ❷ clearly directed at a particular person, especially to criticize them • *a pointed remark*

**pointedly** ADVERB
in a way that clearly shows what you mean • *She yawned and looked pointedly at her watch.*

**pointer** NOUN pointers
❶ a stick, rod or mark used to point at something ❷ a dog that points with its muzzle towards birds that it scents ❸ an indication or hint

**pointless** ADJECTIVE
without a point; with no purpose • *It's pointless arguing with him.*
➤ **pointlessly** ADVERB

**point of view** NOUN points of view
❶ a way of looking at something or thinking about it ❷ the way that a writer chooses to tell a story, e.g. by telling it through the experiences of one of the characters

**poise** NOUN
a dignified self-confident manner • *She handled the situation with great poise.*

**poise** VERB poises, poising, poised
to balance something or keep it steady • *He poised the javelin in his hand.*

**poised** ADJECTIVE
❶ not moving but ready to move • *He had a pen poised in his hand.* ❷ dignified and self-confident
➤ **be poised to do something** or **for something** to be ready to do something • *The snake was poised to strike.* • *She was poised for revenge.*

**poison** NOUN poisons
a substance that can harm or kill a living thing if swallowed or absorbed into the body

**poison** VERB poisons, poisoning, poisoned
❶ to give poison to someone; to kill someone with poison ❷ to put poison in something ❸ to spoil or have a bad effect on something • *He poisoned their minds.*
➤ **poisoner** NOUN

**poisonous** ADJECTIVE
❶ causing death or illness if swallowed or absorbed into the body ❷ producing poison • *a poisonous snake*

**poke** VERB pokes, poking, poked
❶ to prod or jab something with your finger or a pointed object ❷ to push something out or forward; to stick out • *He poked his head out of the window.* ❸ to search in a casual way • *I was poking about in the attic.*
➤ **poke fun at someone** to ridicule someone

**poke** NOUN pokes
a poking movement; a prod
➤ **buy a pig in a poke** to buy something without seeing it first

**poker** NOUN pokers
❶ a stiff metal rod for poking a fire ❷ a card game in which players bet on who has the best cards

**poky** ADJECTIVE pokier, pokiest
small and cramped • *poky little rooms*

**polar** ADJECTIVE
to do with or near the North Pole or South Pole • *the polar regions*

**polar bear** NOUN polar bears
a white bear living in Arctic regions

**Polaroid** NOUN (*trademark*)
a type of plastic, used in sunglasses, which reduces the brightness of light passing through it

**Polaroid camera** NOUN Polaroid cameras (*trademark*)
a camera that takes a picture and produces the finished photograph a few seconds later

**pole** NOUN poles
❶ a long slender rounded piece of wood or metal ❷ a point on the earth's surface that is as far north (**North Pole**) or as far south (**South Pole**) as possible ❸ either of the ends of a magnet ❹ either terminal of an electric cell or battery

**polecat** NOUN polecats
an animal of the weasel family with an unpleasant smell

**pole star** NOUN
the star above the North Pole

**pole vault** NOUN
an athletic contest in which competitors jump over a high bar with the help of a long flexible pole

**police** NOUN
the people whose job is to catch criminals and make sure that people obey the law

**police** VERB polices, policing, policed
to keep order in a place by means of police

**policeman** NOUN policemen
a male police officer

**police officer** NOUN police officers
a member of the police

**policewoman** NOUN policewomen
a female police officer

**policy** NOUN policies
❶ the aims or plan of action of a person or group • *the country's foreign policy* ❷ a document stating the terms of a contract of insurance

**polio** NOUN
a disease that can cause paralysis

**polish** VERB polishes, polishing, polished
❶ to make a thing smooth and shiny by rubbing ❷ to make a thing better by making corrections and alterations
➤ **polish something off** to finish something quickly • *We soon polished off all the sandwiches.*

**polish** NOUN polishes
❶ a substance used in polishing ❷ polishing a surface • *He gave his shoes a good polish.* ❸ elegance of manner

**polite** ADJECTIVE
having good manners; showing respect to other people • *She gave me a polite smile.*
➤ **politely** ADVERB
➤ **politeness** NOUN

**political** ADJECTIVE
connected with the governing of a country or region • *a political party*
➤ **politically** ADVERB

**politician** NOUN politicians
a person who is involved in politics

**politics** NOUN
political matters; the business of governing a country or region

**polka** NOUN polkas
a lively dance for couples

**poll** (say pole) NOUN polls
❶ voting at an election or the votes cast ❷ an opinion poll

**poll** VERB polls, polling, polled
❶ to receive a certain number of votes in an election ❷ to ask members of the public their opinion on a subject (**WORD ORIGIN**) from an old meaning of *poll* = head. In some polls those voting yes stand apart from those voting no, and the decision is reached by counting the heads in the two groups.

**pollarded** ADJECTIVE
a tree is pollarded when its top and branches are trimmed so that young shoots start to grow thickly there

**pollen** NOUN
a fine yellow powder produced by the anthers of flowers, containing male cells for fertilizing other flowers

**pollen count** NOUN pollen counts
a measurement of the amount of pollen in the air, given as a warning for people who are allergic to pollen

**pollinate** VERB pollinates, pollinating, pollinated
to fertilize a plant with pollen
➤ **pollination** NOUN

**polling station** NOUN polling stations
a place where people go to vote in an election

**pollutant** NOUN pollutants
something that pollutes

**pollute** VERB pollutes, polluting, polluted
to make the air, rivers, etc. dirty or impure

**pollution** NOUN
making the air, rivers, etc. dirty or impure • *Using less fuel helps to reduce pollution.*

**polo** NOUN
a game rather like hockey, with players on horseback using long mallets

**polo neck** NOUN polo necks
(*British*) a high round turned-over collar

**poltergeist** NOUN poltergeists
a ghost or spirit that throws things about noisily **WORD ORIGIN** from German *poltern* = make a disturbance + *Geist* = ghost

**polychrome** ADJECTIVE
having many colours

**polyester** NOUN
a synthetic material, used to make clothing

**polygamy** (say pol-**ig**-a-mee) NOUN
having more than one wife at a time
➤ **polygamous** ADJECTIVE

**polyglot** ADJECTIVE
knowing or using several languages

**polygon** NOUN polygons
a flat shape with many sides. Hexagons and octagons are polygons.
➤ **polygonal** ADJECTIVE

**polyhedron** NOUN polyhedrons
a solid shape with many sides

**polymer** NOUN polymers
a substance with a molecule structure consisting of a large number of simple molecules combined

**polyp** (say **pol**-ip) NOUN polyps
❶ a tiny creature with a tube-shaped body
❷ a small abnormal growth

**polystyrene** NOUN
a kind of plastic used for insulating or packing things

**polytechnic** NOUN polytechnics
a name used before 1992 for a college teaching subjects at degree level or below

**polythene** NOUN
(*British*) a lightweight plastic used to make bags or wrappings

**pomegranate** NOUN pomegranates
a tropical fruit with many seeds

**pommel** NOUN pommels
❶ a knob on the handle of a sword ❷ the raised part at the front of a saddle

**pomp** NOUN
the ceremonial splendour that is traditional on important public occasions

**pompom** NOUN pompoms
a ball of coloured threads used as a decoration

**pompous** ADJECTIVE
speaking or behaving in a grand way that shows you think too much of your own importance
➤ **pompously** ADVERB
➤ **pomposity** NOUN

**pond** NOUN ponds
a small lake

**ponder** VERB ponders, pondering, pondered
to think deeply and seriously about something • *I pondered his words before replying.*

**ponderous** ADJECTIVE
❶ heavy and awkward ❷ slow, dull and too serious • *He writes in a ponderous style.*
➤ **ponderously** ADVERB

**pong** (*British*) (*informal*) NOUN
an unpleasant smell

**pong** VERB pongs, ponging, ponged
to have an unpleasant smell

**pontiff** NOUN pontiffs
the Pope

**pontoon** NOUN pontoons
❶ a boat or float used to support a bridge (a **pontoon bridge**) over a river ❷ (*British*) a card game in which players try to get cards whose value totals 21

**pony** NOUN ponies
a small horse

**ponytail** NOUN ponytails
a bunch of long hair tied at the back of the head

**pony-trekking** NOUN
(*British*) travelling across country on a pony for pleasure

**poodle** NOUN poodles
a dog with thick curly hair

**pooh** EXCLAMATION
a word used to express disgust or contempt

**pool** NOUN pools
❶ a pond ❷ a puddle ❸ a swimming pool
❹ a group of things shared by several people
❺ a game similar to snooker but played on a smaller table
➤ **the pools** a form of gambling based on the results of football matches

**pool** VERB pools, pooling, pooled
to put money or things together for sharing
• *We need to pool our resources.*

**poop** NOUN poops
the stern of a ship

**poor** ADJECTIVE
❶ with very little money ❷ not good;
inadequate • *a poor piece of work*
❸ unfortunate; deserving pity • *Poor fellow!*

**poorly** ADVERB
in a poor way • *We've played poorly this
season.*

**poorly** ADJECTIVE
(British) rather ill • *I've felt poorly all week.*

**pop** NOUN pops
❶ modern popular music ❷ a small explosive
sound ❸ a fizzy drink

**pop** VERB pops, popping, popped
❶ (informal) to go quickly or put something
somewhere quickly • *Can you pop down to
the shop for me?* • *I'll just pop this pie into
the microwave.* ❷ to make a pop

**popcorn** NOUN
maize heated to burst and form fluffy balls

**Pope** NOUN Popes
the leader of the Roman Catholic Church

**pop-eyed** ADJECTIVE
with bulging eyes

**popgun** NOUN popguns
a toy gun that shoots a cork or pellet with a
popping sound

**poplar** NOUN poplars
a tall slender tree

**poplin** NOUN
a plain woven cotton material

**poppadam, poppadom** NOUN poppadams or
poppadoms
a thin crisp biscuit made of lentil flour, eaten
with Indian food

**poppy** NOUN poppies
a plant with large red flowers

**populace** NOUN
the general public

**popular** ADJECTIVE
❶ liked or enjoyed by many people ❷ held
or believed by many people • *popular
superstitions* ❸ intended for the general
public

**popularity** NOUN
being liked or enjoyed by a lot of people • *The
sport is growing in popularity.*

**popularize** (also **popularise**) VERB
popularizes, popularizing, popularized
to make a thing known and liked by a lot
of people • *His TV programmes helped to
popularize archaeology.*

**popularly** ADVERB
by many people; generally • *Edward Teach,
popularly known as Blackbeard, was a
notorious pirate.*

**populate** VERB populates, populating,
populated
to fill a place with people; to inhabit a
country • *The region is sparsely populated.*

**population** NOUN populations
the people who live in a district or country;
the total number of these people • *What's
the population of New York?*

**porcelain** NOUN
the finest kind of china

**porch** NOUN porches
a shelter outside the entrance to a building

**porcupine** NOUN porcupines
a small animal covered with long prickles
**WORD ORIGIN** from old French *porc espin* =
spiny pig

**pore** NOUN pores
a tiny opening on your skin through which
moisture can pass in or out

**pore** VERB pores, poring, pored
➤ **pore over something** to study something
with close attention • *He was poring over his
books.*
**SPELLING**
Take care not to confuse with **pour**,
which means to make a liquid flow out of
something.

**pork** NOUN
meat from a pig

**pornography** (say porn-**og**-ra-fee) NOUN
pictures, magazines and films that show
naked people and sexual acts in a way that
is intended to be sexually exciting and that
many people find offensive
➤ **pornographic** ADJECTIVE

**porous** ADJECTIVE
allowing liquid or air to pass through • *porous
rock*

**porphyry** (say **por**-fir-ee) NOUN
a kind of rock containing crystals of minerals

**porpoise** (say **por**-pus) NOUN porpoises
a sea animal rather like a small whale
**WORD ORIGIN** from Latin *porcus* = pig + *piscis* = fish

**porridge** NOUN
a food made by boiling oatmeal to a thick paste

**port** NOUN ports
❶ a harbour ❷ a city or town with a harbour ❸ the left-hand side of a ship or aircraft when you are facing forward. Compare with **starboard**. ❹ a strong red Portuguese wine

**portable** ADJECTIVE
able to be carried easily • *a portable TV*

**portal** NOUN portals
❶ a doorway or gateway ❷ a website with information on a particular subject and links to other websites • *a literacy portal*

**portcullis** NOUN portcullises
a strong heavy vertical grating that can be lowered to block the gateway to a castle

**portend** VERB portends, portending, portended
to be a sign or warning that something bad will happen • *Dark clouds portend a storm.*

**portent** NOUN portents
an omen; a sign that something will happen
➤ **portentous** ADJECTIVE

**porter** NOUN porters
❶ a person whose job is to carry luggage or other goods ❷ (*British*) a person whose job is to look after the entrance to a large building

**portfolio** NOUN portfolios
❶ a case for holding documents or drawings ❷ a government minister's special responsibility ❸ a collection of examples of art or photography work that you have done

**porthole** NOUN portholes
a small window in the side of a ship or aircraft

**portico** NOUN porticoes
a roof supported on columns, usually forming a porch to a building

**portion** NOUN portions
a part or share given to someone

**portion** VERB portions, portioning, portioned
to divide something into portions • *The food was portioned out.*

**portly** ADJECTIVE portlier, portliest
rather fat

**portmanteau** (say port-**mant**-oh) NOUN portmanteaus
a large travelling bag that opens into two equal parts

**portmanteau word** NOUN portmanteau words
a word made from the sounds and meanings of two others, e.g. *motel* (from *motor* + *hotel*)

**portrait** NOUN portraits
❶ a picture of a person ❷ a description in words or on film

**portray** VERB portrays, portraying, portrayed
❶ to make a picture of a person or scene ❷ to describe or show a person or thing in a certain way • *The play portrays the king as a kindly man.*
➤ **portrayal** NOUN

**pose** NOUN poses
❶ a position in which someone stands or sits for a portrait or photograph ❷ a way of behaving that someone adopts to give a particular impression

**pose** VERB poses, posing, posed
❶ to take up a pose • *We all posed for a photograph.* ❷ to put someone into a pose ❸ to pretend to be someone • *The thieves posed as police officers.* ❹ to pose a question or problem is to present it • *The bad weather poses several problems for us.*

**poser** NOUN posers
❶ a puzzling question or problem ❷ a person who behaves in a showy or unnatural way in order to impress other people

**posh** ADJECTIVE (*informal*)
❶ very smart; high-class • *a posh restaurant* ❷ upper-class • *a posh accent*

**position** NOUN positions
❶ the place where something is or should be ❷ the way a person or thing is placed or arranged • *He pushed himself up into a sitting position.* ❸ a person's place in a race or competition ❹ a situation or condition • *I am in no position to help you.* ❺ paid employment; a job

**position** VERB positions, positioning, positioned
to place a person or thing in a certain position • *She positioned herself at the top of the stairs.*

**positive** ADJECTIVE
❶ definite or certain • *Are you positive you*

saw him? • *We have positive proof that he is guilty.* ❷ agreeing or saying 'yes' • *We received a positive reply.* ❸ looking at the best or most hopeful aspects of a situation ❹ showing signs of what is being tested for • *Her pregnancy test was positive.* ❺ greater than zero ❻ to do with the kind of electric charge that lacks electrons ❼ the positive form of an adjective or adverb is its simplest form, not the comparative or superlative • *The positive form is 'big', the comparative is 'bigger', the superlative is 'biggest'.*

**positive** NOUN positives
a photograph or film in which the light and dark parts or colours appear as in the thing photographed or filmed. Compare with **negative**.

**positively** ADVERB
❶ really; extremely • *She wasn't just annoyed – she was positively furious!* ❷ in a positive way • *You need to think positively.*

**positron** NOUN positrons
a particle of matter with a positive electric charge

**posse** (say **poss**-ee) NOUN posses
a group of people, especially one put together to help a sheriff

**possess** VERB possesses, possessing, possessed
❶ to have or own something ❷ to control someone's thoughts or behaviour • *I don't know what possessed you to do such a thing!*
➤ **possessor** NOUN

**possessed** ADJECTIVE
seeming to be controlled by strong emotion or an evil spirit • *He fought like a man possessed.*

**possession** NOUN possessions
❶ something you own ❷ having or owning something • *I am now in possession of all the facts.*

**possessive** ADJECTIVE
❶ wanting to possess and keep things for yourself ❷ (*in grammar*) showing what or whom something belongs to • *'His' and 'ours' are possessive pronouns.*

GRAMMAR

Possessive **determiners** and possessive **pronouns** show to whom or to what, something belongs or is connected. The possessive **determiners** are: *my, your, his, her, its, our* and *their*:

*Is it okay to wear my trainers?*

*All of the students had done their homework.*

The possessive **pronouns** are: *mine, yours, his, hers, ours* and *theirs*:

*Is that last slice of pizza mine or yours?*

*Ours was the best score.*

Possessive pronouns can also be used after *of*:

*That song is an old favourite of mine.*

Note that there is no apostrophe in the possessive pronouns *hers, ours, yours* and *theirs* or in the possessive determiner *its*: *The shark opened its jaws.*

**possibility** NOUN possibilities
❶ being possible • *Is there any possibility you will change your mind?* ❷ something that may happen or be the case • *There are many possibilities.*

SPELLING

There is no a in **possibility**. Do not forget to double the s.

**possible** ADJECTIVE
that can exist, happen, be done or be used • *It's possible we may be late.*

**possibly** ADVERB
❶ in any way • *I can't possibly do it.* ❷ perhaps • *I'll get there at 6 o'clock or possibly earlier.*

**possum** NOUN possums
an opossum

**post** NOUN posts
❶ an upright piece of wood, concrete or metal fixed in the ground ❷ the starting point or finishing point of a race • *He was left at the post.* ❸ the collecting and delivering of letters and parcels ❹ letters and parcels sent or delivered ❺ a message sent to an Internet site; a piece of writing on a blog ❻ a position of paid employment; a job ❼ the place where someone is on duty • *a sentry post*

**post** VERB posts, posting, posted
❶ to put up a notice or poster to announce something ❷ to send a message to an Internet site; to display information online ❸ to put a letter or parcel into a postbox for collection ❹ to send someone to go and work somewhere; to place someone on duty • *She*

a b c d e f g h i j k l m n o p q r s t u v w x y z

was posted to Washington for two years.
• We posted sentries.
➤ **keep someone posted** to keep someone informed

**post–** PREFIX
after (as in *post-war*)

**postage** NOUN
the charge for sending something by post

**postage stamp** NOUN postage stamps
a stamp for sticking on letters and parcels to be posted, showing the amount paid

**postal** ADJECTIVE
to do with or by the post • *the postal service*

**postal order** NOUN postal orders
(*British*) a document bought from a post office which can be sent by post and exchanged for money by the person receiving it

**postbox** NOUN postboxes
a box into which letters are put for collection

**postcard** NOUN postcards
a card for sending messages by post without an envelope

**postcode** NOUN postcodes
(*British*) a group of letters and numbers included in an address to help in sorting the post

**poster** NOUN posters
a large sheet of paper announcing or advertising something, for display in a public place

**posterior** NOUN posteriors
a person's bottom

**posterity** NOUN
future generations of people • *These letters and diaries should be preserved for posterity.*

**postern** NOUN posterns
a small entrance at the back or side of a fortress etc.

**postgraduate** ADJECTIVE
to do with studies carried on after taking a first university degree

**postgraduate** NOUN postgraduates
a person who continues studying or doing research after taking a first university degree

**post-haste** ADVERB
with great speed or haste • *He returned post-haste to France.*

**posthumous** (say **poss**-tew-mus) ADJECTIVE
coming or happening after a person's death

• *a posthumous award for bravery*
➤ **posthumously** ADVERB

**postilion** (say poss-**til**-yon) NOUN postilions
a person riding one of the horses pulling a carriage

**postman** NOUN postmen
(*British*) a person who delivers or collects post

**postmark** NOUN postmarks
an official mark put on something sent by post to show where and when it was posted

**post-mortem** NOUN post-mortems
an examination of a dead body to discover the cause of death (**WORD ORIGIN**) Latin, = after death

**post office** NOUN post offices
❶ a building or room where postal business is carried on ❷ the national organization responsible for postal services

**postpone** VERB postpones, postponing, postponed
to arrange for something to take place later than was originally planned • *They had to postpone their wedding.*
➤ **postponement** NOUN

**postscript** NOUN postscripts
something extra added at the end of a letter (after the writer's signature) or at the end of a book

**postulate** VERB postulates, postulating, postulated
to assume that something is true and use it in reasoning

**posture** NOUN postures
the position in which you hold your body when you stand, sit or walk • *Suddenly he relaxed his stiff posture and smiled.*

**post-war** ADJECTIVE
happening in the period after a war

**posy** NOUN posies
a small bunch of flowers

**pot** NOUN pots
❶ a deep round container ❷ a flowerpot
❸ (*informal*) the drug cannabis
➤ **go to pot** (*informal*) to lose quality or be ruined
➤ **pots of money** (*informal*) a lot of money
➤ **take pot luck** (*informal*) to take whatever happens to be available

**pot** VERB pots, potting, potted
❶ to pot a plant is to plant it in a flowerpot
❷ to pot a ball in a game such as snooker or pool is to knock it into a pocket

**potash** NOUN
potassium carbonate

**potassium** NOUN
a soft silvery-white metal substance that is essential for living things

**potato** NOUN potatoes
a round white vegetable with a brown or red skin that grows underground

**potent** (say **poh**-tent) ADJECTIVE
having great power or effect • *a potent drug*
➤ **potency** NOUN

**potentate** (say **poh**-ten-tayt) NOUN
potentates
a powerful monarch or ruler

**potential** (say po-**ten**-shal) ADJECTIVE
capable of happening or being used or developed • *a potential winner*

**potential** NOUN
❶ the ability of a person or thing to develop or succeed in the future • *She has great potential as a sprinter.* ❷ the voltage between two points

**potentially** ADVERB
as a possibility in the future • *He is potentially one of our best players.*

**pothole** NOUN potholes
❶ a deep natural hole in the ground ❷ a hole in a road

**potholing** NOUN
exploring underground caves by climbing down potholes
➤ **potholer** NOUN

**potion** NOUN potions
a drink containing medicine or poison or having magical powers • *a love potion*

**potpourri** (say **poh**-poor-ee) NOUN potpourris
a scented mixture of dried petals and spices

**pot shot** NOUN pot shots
a shot aimed casually at something

**potted** ADJECTIVE
❶ shortened or abridged • *a potted account of the story* ❷ preserved in a pot • *potted shrimps*

**potter** NOUN potters
a person who makes pottery

**potter** VERB potters, pottering, pottered
to spend time doing little jobs in a relaxed or leisurely way • *I spent the afternoon pottering around in the garden.*

**pottery** NOUN potteries
❶ cups, plates, ornaments, etc. made of baked clay ❷ the craft of making these things ❸ a place where a potter works

**potty** ADJECTIVE (*British*) (*informal*)
mad or foolish

**potty** NOUN potties (*informal*)
a small bowl used by a young child instead of a toilet

**pouch** NOUN pouches
❶ a small bag ❷ a fold of skin in which a kangaroo etc. keeps its young ❸ something shaped like a bag

**poultice** NOUN poultices
a soft hot dressing put on a sore or inflamed place

**poultry** NOUN
chickens, geese, turkeys and other birds kept for their eggs and meat

**pounce** VERB pounces, pouncing, pounced
to jump or swoop down quickly on something and grab it • *The lion crouched, ready to pounce.*
➤ **pounce** NOUN

**pound** NOUN pounds
❶ a unit of money, in Britain equal to 100 pence ❷ a unit of weight equal to 16 ounces or about 454 grams ❸ a place where stray animals are taken ❹ a public enclosure for vehicles officially removed

**pound** VERB pounds, pounding, pounded
❶ to hit something repeatedly • *Waves pounded the rocks.* ❷ to run or go heavily • *He pounded down the stairs.* ❸ your heart pounds when it beats very fast and hard • *My heart was pounding with excitement.*

**pour** VERB pours, pouring, poured
❶ to make a liquid flow steadily out of a container ❷ to flow in a large amount • *Tears were pouring down her cheeks.* ❸ to rain heavily • *It poured all day.* ❹ to come or go in large amounts • *Letters of complaint poured in.*

> **SPELLING**
>
> Take care not to confuse with **pore over**, which means to study something with close attention.

**pout** VERB pouts, pouting, pouted
to push out your lips when you are annoyed or sulking
➤ **pout** NOUN

**poverty** NOUN
❶ being poor ❷ a lack or scarcity • *a poverty of ideas*

**POW** ABBREVIATION
prisoner of war

**powder** NOUN powders
❶ a mass of fine dry particles of something ❷ make-up in the form of powder ❸ gunpowder • *Keep your powder dry.*

**powder** VERB powders, powdering, powdered
to put powder on something • *She powdered her face.*

**powdered** ADJECTIVE
dried and made into a powder • *powdered milk*

**powder room** NOUN powder rooms
a women's toilet in a public building

**powdery** ADJECTIVE
like powder • *powdery snow*

**power** NOUN powers
❶ strength or energy • *The power of the storm was frightening.* ❷ the ability to do something • *the power of speech* ❸ control over other people • *She seemed to have a strange power over him.* ❹ political control of a country • *The party has been in power for three years.* ❺ a powerful country, person or organization ❻ mechanical or electrical energy; the electricity supply • *There was a power failure after the storm.* ❼ (*in science*) the rate of doing work, measured in watts or horsepower ❽ (*in mathematics*) the product of a number multiplied by itself a given number of times • *The third power of 2 = 2 x 2 x 2 = 8.*

**power** VERB powers, powering, powered
to supply power to a vehicle or machine • *The aircraft is powered by a jet engine.* • *a solar-powered calculator*

**powerboat** NOUN powerboats
a powerful motor boat

**powerful** ADJECTIVE
❶ having great power, strength or influence • *one of the most powerful nations in the world* • *a powerful computer* ❷ having a strong effect • *a powerful speech*
➤ **powerfully** ADVERB

**powerhouse** NOUN powerhouses
a person or thing with great strength and energy

**powerless** ADJECTIVE
not able to act or control things • *He was powerless to stop them.*

**power station** NOUN power stations
a building where electricity is produced

**pp.** ABBREVIATION
pages

**practicable** ADJECTIVE
able to be done • *Your plan is simply not practicable.*

**practical** ADJECTIVE
❶ able to do or make useful things • *She is a very practical person.* ❷ likely to be useful or effective • *a practical invention* ❸ actually doing something, rather than just learning or thinking about it • *She has had practical experience.*
➤ **practicality** NOUN

**practical** NOUN practicals (*British*) a lesson or examination in which you actually do or make something rather than reading or writing about it • *a chemistry practical*

**practical joke** NOUN practical jokes
a trick played on someone

**practically** ADVERB
❶ almost • *I've practically finished.* ❷ in a practical way

**practice** NOUN practices
❶ doing something repeatedly in order to become better at it • *I must do my piano practice.* ❷ actually doing something rather than thinking or talking about it • *It's time to put this theory into practice.* ❸ the professional business of a doctor, dentist, lawyer, etc. ❹ a habit or custom • *It is his practice to work until midnight.*
➤ **out of practice** no longer skilful because you have not practised recently

SPELLING
Practice is a noun and practise is a verb:
• *music practice* • *I need to practise more.*

**practise** VERB practises, practising, practised
❶ to do something repeatedly in order to become better at it ❷ to practise an activity or custom is to do it regularly • *She was accused of practising witchcraft.* ❸ to work as a doctor, lawyer or other professional person

SPELLING
Practise is a verb and practice is a noun:
• *I need to practise more.* • *music practice*

**practised** ADJECTIVE
experienced or expert

**practitioner** NOUN practitioners
a professional worker, especially a doctor

**prairie** NOUN prairies
a large area of flat grass-covered land in North America

**praise** VERB praises, praising, praised
❶ to say that someone or something is very good or has done well ❷ to honour God in words

**praise** NOUN
words that praise someone or something

**praiseworthy** ADJECTIVE
deserving praise

**pram** NOUN prams
(British) a four-wheeled carriage for a baby, pushed by a person walking

**prance** VERB prances, prancing, pranced
to move about in a lively or happy way • The lead singer was prancing around the stage.

**prank** NOUN pranks
a trick played on someone for mischief; a practical joke
➤ **prankster** NOUN

**prattle** VERB prattles, prattling, prattled
to chatter like a young child
➤ **prattle** NOUN

**prawn** NOUN prawns
an edible shellfish like a large shrimp

**pray** VERB prays, praying, prayed
❶ to talk to God to give thanks or ask for help ❷ to hope very strongly for something • We are praying for good weather.

**pray** ADVERB
(formal) please • Pray be seated.

SPELLING
Be careful, this sounds the same as prey, which means an animal that is hunted or killed by another for food.

**prayer** NOUN prayers
praying; words used in praying

**pre-** PREFIX
before (as in pre-war)

**preach** VERB preaches, preaching, preached
to give a talk about religion or about right and wrong

**preacher** NOUN preachers
a person who preaches

**preamble** NOUN preambles
the introduction to a speech or book or document

**pre-arranged** ADJECTIVE
arranged beforehand

**precarious** (say pri-**kair**-ee-us) ADJECTIVE
not very safe or secure • She was in a precarious position on the ledge.
➤ **precariously** ADVERB

**precaution** NOUN precautions
something you do to prevent future trouble or danger
➤ **precautionary** ADJECTIVE

**precede** VERB precedes, preceding, preceded
to come or go before something else • The film was preceded by a short cartoon.

SPELLING
Take care not to confuse with **proceed**, which means to go forward or continue.

**precedence** (say **press**-i-dens) NOUN
the right of something to be put first because it is more important
➤ **take precedence** to be dealt with first because it is the most important thing

**precedent** (say **press**-i-dent) NOUN precedents
a previous case that is taken as an example or guide to be followed

**precept** (say **pree**-sept) NOUN precepts
a rule about how to behave or what to think; an instruction

**precinct** (say **pree**-sinkt) NOUN precincts
❶ a part of a town where traffic is not allowed • a shopping precinct ❷ the precincts of a place are the buildings and land around it

**precious** ADJECTIVE
❶ very valuable ❷ greatly loved

**precious** ADVERB (informal) very • We have precious little time.

**precipice** NOUN precipices
a very steep place, such as the face of a cliff

**precipitate** VERB precipitates, precipitating, precipitated
❶ to make something happen suddenly or soon • The insult precipitated a quarrel.
❷ to throw or send something down; to make something fall • A shove in the back precipitated him into the room.

**precipitate** NOUN precipitates
a solid substance that has been separated chemically from a solution

**precipitate** ADJECTIVE
hurried or hasty • *a precipitate departure*
➤ **precipitately** ADVERB

**precipitation** NOUN
the amount of rain, snow or hail that falls
during a period of time

**precipitous** ADJECTIVE
like a precipice; steep • *precipitous cliffs*
➤ **precipitously** ADVERB

**precis** (say **pray**-see) NOUN precis (say **pray**-
seez)
a summary

**precise** ADJECTIVE
❶ clear and accurate • *I gave them precise
instructions.* ❷ exact • *At that precise
moment, the doorbell rang.*

**precisely** ADVERB
exactly • *She arrived at 10 o'clock precisely.*
• *What precisely do you mean?*

**precision** NOUN
being exact and accurate • *He drew the map
with great precision.*

**preclude** VERB precludes, precluding,
precluded
to prevent something from happening

**precocious** (say prik-**oh**-shus) ADJECTIVE
a precocious child is very advanced or
developed for their age WORD ORIGIN from
Latin *praecox* = ripe very early

**preconceived** ADJECTIVE
a preconceived idea is one you have before
you know all the facts that might affect it
➤ **preconception** NOUN

**precursor** NOUN precursors
something that was an earlier form of
something that came later; a forerunner

**predator** (say **pred**-a-ter) NOUN predators
an animal that hunts or preys upon others
➤ **predatory** ADJECTIVE

**predecessor** (say **pree**-dis-ess-er) NOUN
predecessors
an earlier person or thing, e.g. an ancestor or
the former holder of a job

**predestined** ADJECTIVE
certain to happen because it has been
decided by fate
➤ **predestination** NOUN

**predicament** (say prid-**ik**-a-ment) NOUN
predicaments
a difficult or unpleasant situation • *He was in
a dreadful predicament.*

**predicate** NOUN predicates
the part of a sentence that says something
about the subject, e.g. 'is short' in *Life is short.*

**predict** VERB predicts, predicting, predicted
to say what will happen in the future;
to foretell or prophesy a future event
• *Scientists try to predict when earthquakes
will happen.*

**predictable** ADJECTIVE
❶ able to be predicted • *a predictable result*
❷ always behaving in the same way • *I knew
you would say that – you're so predictable.*
➤ **predictably** ADJECTIVE

**prediction** NOUN predictions
saying what will happen; what someone
thinks will happen • *Her predictions kept
coming true.*

**predominant** ADJECTIVE
greatest in size or most noticeable or most
important • *The predominant colour was
blue.*
➤ **predominance** NOUN
➤ **predominantly** ADVERB

**predominate** VERB predominates,
predominating, predominated
to be the greatest in number or the most
important • *Girls predominate in our class.*

**pre-eminent** ADJECTIVE
better than all the others; outstanding
➤ **pre-eminently** ADVERB
➤ **pre-eminence** NOUN

**pre-empt** VERB pre-empts, pre-empting,
pre-empted
to take action to prevent or block something
➤ **pre-emptive** ADJECTIVE

**preen** VERB preens, preening, preened
a bird preens its feathers when it smooths
them with its beak
➤ **preen yourself** ❶ to smarten your
appearance ❷ to congratulate yourself

**prefab** NOUN prefabs (*informal*)
a prefabricated building

**prefabricated** ADJECTIVE
made in sections ready to be assembled on
a site

**preface** (say **pref**-as) NOUN prefaces
an introduction at the beginning of a book
or speech
➤ **preface** VERB

**prefect** NOUN prefects
❶ a senior pupil in a school, given authority

to help to keep order ❷ a regional official in France, Japan and other countries

**prefer** VERB prefers, preferring, preferred
to like one person or thing more than another
• *Would you prefer rice or pasta?*

**preferable** (say **pref**-er-a-bul) ADJECTIVE
something is preferable to something else when it is better or you like it more
➤ **preferably** ADVERB

**preference** NOUN preferences
a liking for one thing rather than another; something you prefer • *I have a slight preference for the red one.*

**preferential** (say pref-er-**en**-shal) ADJECTIVE
better than other people get • *preferential treatment*

**preferment** NOUN
promotion

**prefix** NOUN prefixes
a word or syllable joined to the front of a word to change or add to its meaning, as in *dis*order, *out*stretched, *un*happy

GRAMMAR

A **prefix** is a group of letters that can be added to the beginning of the base or root form of a word to change its meaning and form a new word (e.g. *anti*clockwise, *in*definite, *re*birth).

Some prefixes make words that are closely related to the original word. For example, *in-* and *un-* often make words opposite in meaning (e.g. *ineffective*, *unnatural*); *re-* often indicates a repeated action (e.g. *rebuild*, *remake*). *In-* sometimes changes to *il-* (e.g. *illegible*), *im-* (e.g. *impossible*) or *ir-* (e.g. *irresponsible*), depending on the letter that follows. Other prefixes (many of them based on Greek or Latin words) contain their own meaning, which they combine with that of the words they join; for example, *ecosystem*, *interface*, *multicultural*, *supermarket*, *transatlantic*, *ultraviolet*.

You sometimes need a hyphen after a prefix to make a special meaning clear (e.g. to *re-mark* an exam, to distinguish it from the word *remark*) or when the word after the prefix begins with a capital letter (e.g. *anti-British*, *pre-Victorian*).

**pregnancy** NOUN pregnancies
being pregnant

**pregnant** ADJECTIVE
❶ a woman is pregnant when she has a baby developing in the womb ❷ a pregnant pause or silence is one full of meaning or significance

**prehensile** ADJECTIVE
an animal's foot or tail is called prehensile when it is able to grasp things

**prehistoric** ADJECTIVE
belonging to very ancient times, before written records of events were made
➤ **prehistory** NOUN

**prejudice** NOUN prejudices
a strong unreasonable feeling of not liking or trusting someone
➤ **prejudiced** ADJECTIVE

**prelate** (say **prel**-at) NOUN prelates
an important member of the clergy

**preliminary** ADJECTIVE
coming before something and preparing for it
• *I'd like to make a few preliminary remarks.*

**prelude** NOUN preludes
❶ a thing that introduces or leads up to something else ❷ a short piece of music, especially one that introduces a longer piece

**premature** ADJECTIVE
too early; coming before the usual or proper time • *a premature baby*
➤ **prematurely** ADVERB

**premeditated** ADJECTIVE
planned beforehand • *a premeditated crime*

**premier** (say **prem**-ee-er) ADJECTIVE
best or most important

**premier** NOUN premiers
a prime minister or other head of government

**premiere** (say prem-**yair**) NOUN premieres
the first public performance of a play or film

**premise** (say **prem**-iss) NOUN premises
a statement used as the basis for a piece of reasoning

**premises** PLURAL NOUN
a building and its grounds

**premium** NOUN premiums
❶ an amount of money paid regularly to an insurance company ❷ an extra charge or payment
➤ **at a premium** ❶ above the normal price ❷ in demand but scarce

**Premium Bond** NOUN Premium Bonds
a savings certificate that gives the person
who holds it a chance to win a prize of money

**premonition** NOUN premonitions
a feeling that something bad is about to
happen

**preoccupation** NOUN preoccupations
something you think or worry about all the
time

**preoccupied** ADJECTIVE
thinking or worrying about something so
much that you cannot pay attention to
anything else

**preparation** NOUN preparations
❶ getting something ready • She packed
her bag in preparation for the journey.
❷ something done in order to get ready for
an event or activity • We were making last-
minute preparations. ❸ a mixture to be used
as a medicine or cosmetic

**preparatory** ADJECTIVE
preparing for something • preparatory
sketches

**preparatory school** NOUN preparatory
schools
a school that prepares pupils for a higher
school

**prepare** VERB prepares, preparing, prepared
to get ready or to make something ready
• They are preparing to launch the rocket.
• He was in the kitchen preparing lunch.

**prepared** ADJECTIVE
ready and able to deal with something • She
felt well prepared for the task ahead.
➤ **be prepared to do something** to be ready
and willing to do something

**preposition** NOUN prepositions
a word used with a noun or pronoun to show
place, position, time or means, e.g. at home,
in the hall, on Sunday, by train

GRAMMAR

Prepositions show how a noun, pronoun
or noun phrase relates to the other words
in a sentence or clause. They can show:

**the position or direction of a person or
thing:**

The spider scurried _along_ the wall, _across_
the carpet, _through_ the doorway, _down_
the stairs, _past_ the cat, up the curtain,
_out_ of the window, and _into_ the garden.

**the time something happens or lasts:**

Can you come _to_ my house _on_ Tuesday
_around_ five o'clock?

We were _in_ Athens _in_ August, _during_ the
Olympics.

**the connection between people or
things:**

My sister is always grumbling _about_
something.

Does this jacket go better _with_ the red
shirt or the blue one?

You also use prepositions with verbs to
form special meanings, e.g. deal _with_, look
_after_, and run _into_.

Some words can be either prepositions or
adverbs, depending on how they are used.
In the sentence We could hear giggling
_outside_ the classroom the word _outside_ is
a preposition as it is used before the noun
phrase _the classroom_. In the sentence We
ran outside the word _outside_ is an adverb
as it is not followed by a noun, pronoun or
noun phrase.

**prepossessing** ADJECTIVE
attractive • Its appearance is not very
prepossessing.

**preposterous** ADJECTIVE
completely absurd or ridiculous • What a
preposterous idea! WORD ORIGIN from Latin
praeposterus = back to front, from prae =
before + posterus = behind

**prerogative** NOUN prerogatives
a right or privilege that belongs to one person
or group

**Presbyterian** (say prez-bit-**eer**-ee-an) NOUN
Presbyterians
a member of a Christian Church governed by
elders who are all of equal rank, especially the
national Church of Scotland

**pre-school** ADJECTIVE
to do with the time before a child is old
enough to go to school

**prescribe** VERB prescribes, prescribing,
prescribed
❶ to advise a person to use a particular
medicine or treatment ❷ to say what should
be done

SPELLING

Take care not to confuse with proscribe,
which means to forbid something by law.

**prescription** NOUN prescriptions
a doctor's written order for a medicine or the medicine itself

**presence** NOUN
① being present in a place • *Your presence is required.* ② a person's impressive appearance or manner
➤ **in someone's presence** with someone, in the same place as they are • *You must sign the document in the presence of two witnesses.*

**presence of mind** NOUN
the ability to act quickly and sensibly in an emergency

**present** (say **prez**-ent) ADJECTIVE
① in a particular place • *No one else was present.* ② belonging or referring to what is happening now; existing now • *the present Queen*

**present** (say **prez**-ent) NOUN presents
① the time now • *The head is away at present.* ② (*in grammar*) the tense of a verb used to describe an action that is happening now, e.g. *likes* in *He likes swimming.* ③ something you give or receive as a gift

**present** (say pri-**zent**) VERB presents, presenting, presented
① to give something, especially with a ceremony • *Who is going to present the prizes?* ② to introduce someone to another person; to introduce a radio or television programme to an audience ③ to put on a play or other entertainment ④ to show or reveal something ⑤ to cause or provide something • *Translating a poem presents a number of problems.*

**presentable** ADJECTIVE
fit to be presented to other people; looking good

**presentation** NOUN presentations
① a talk showing or demonstrating something ② a ceremony in which someone is given a gift or prize ③ the way in which work is written or set out

**presenter** NOUN presenters
(*British*) someone who introduces the different parts of a radio or television programme

**presentiment** NOUN presentiments
a feeling that something bad is about to happen

**presently** ADVERB
① soon; after a short time • *I shall be with you presently.* ② now • *the person who is presently in charge*

**preservative** NOUN preservatives
a substance added to food to preserve it

**preserve** VERB preserves, preserving, preserved
to keep something safe or in good condition • *The wall paintings have been beautifully preserved.*
➤ **preserver** NOUN
➤ **preservation** NOUN

**preserve** NOUN preserves
① jam made with preserved fruit ② an activity that belongs to a particular person or group • *Football is no longer the preserve of men.*

**preside** VERB presides, presiding, presided
to be in charge of a meeting or other occasion • *The mayor presided over the opening ceremony.*

**presidency** NOUN presidencies
the job of being president or the period of time that someone is president

**president** NOUN presidents
① the person in charge of a club, society or council etc. ② the head of a country that is a republic
➤ **presidential** ADJECTIVE

**press** VERB presses, pressing, pressed
① to put weight or force steadily on something; to squeeze something ② to make clothes smooth by ironing them ③ to urge someone or make demands of them • *We need to press them for an answer.*

**press** NOUN presses
① pushing something firmly • *Give the bell another press.* ② a device for pressing things • *a trouser press* ③ a machine for printing things ④ a firm that prints or publishes books or magazines • *Oxford University Press* ⑤ newspapers and journalists • *The story has been reported in the press.*

**press conference** NOUN press conferences
a meeting when a famous or important person answers questions from a group of journalists

**press-gang** NOUN press-gangs (*historical*)
a group of men whose job was to force people to serve in the army or navy

**pressing** ADJECTIVE
needing immediate action; urgent • *We have a pressing need for volunteers.*

**press-up** NOUN press-ups
(*British*) an exercise in which you lie face
downwards and press down with your hands
to lift your body

**pressure** NOUN pressures
❶ continuous pressing • *Apply pressure to
the cut to stop it bleeding.* ❷ the force with
which something presses ❸ the force of the
atmosphere on the earth's surface • *a band of
high pressure* ❹ an influence that persuades
or forces you to do something • *The press is
putting pressure on her to resign.*

**pressure cooker** NOUN pressure cookers
a large air-tight pan used for cooking food
quickly under steam pressure

**pressure group** NOUN pressure groups
an organized group that tries to influence
public policy on a particular issue

**pressurize** (also **pressurise**) VERB pressurizes,
pressurizing, pressurized
❶ to keep a compartment at the same air
pressure all the time ❷ to try to force a
person to do something
➤ **pressurization** NOUN

**prestige** (say pres-**teej**) NOUN
great respect that something has gained for
being important, successful or of high quality

**prestigious** ADJECTIVE
respected for being important, successful or
of high quality • *a prestigious prize*

**presumably** ADVERB
I imagine; I suppose • *Presumably the library
will have a copy of the book.*

**presume** VERB presumes, presuming,
presumed
❶ to suppose something or assume that it is
true • *I presumed that she was dead.* ❷ to
dare to do something which you have no
right to do • *I wouldn't presume to advise
you.*
➤ **presumption** NOUN

**presumptuous** ADJECTIVE
too bold or confident

**pretence** NOUN pretences
an attempt to pretend that something is true
• *Their friendliness was just a pretence.*
➤ **false pretences** pretending to be
something that you are not, in order to
deceive people • *You've invited me here under
false pretences.*

**pretend** VERB pretends, pretending,
pretended

❶ to behave as if something is true or real
when you know that it is not, in order to
deceive people • *She pretended not to notice
me.* ❷ to imagine that something is true as
part of a game • *The children were under the
bed pretending to be snakes.* ❸ to claim that
something is the case • *I cannot pretend that
this is going to be easy.*

**pretender** NOUN pretenders
a person who claims a throne or title • *The
son of King James II was known as the Old
Pretender.*

**pretension** NOUN pretensions
❶ a doubtful claim • *I have no pretensions
to be a great singer.* ❷ pretentious or showy
behaviour

**pretentious** ADJECTIVE
trying to impress people by appearing more
serious or important than you really are
➤ **pretentiously** ADVERB
➤ **pretentiousness** NOUN

**pretext** NOUN pretexts
a reason put forward to conceal the true
reason

**pretty** ADJECTIVE prettier, prettiest
attractive in a delicate way
➤ **prettily** ADVERB
➤ **prettiness** NOUN

**pretty** ADVERB
quite; fairly • *It's pretty cold outside.*

**prevail** VERB prevails, prevailing, prevailed
❶ to be the most frequent or general • *The
prevailing view is that we were wrong.* ❷ to
be successful or victorious

**prevalent** (say **prev**-a-lent) ADJECTIVE
most frequent or common; widespread
➤ **prevalence** NOUN

**prevaricate** VERB prevaricates, prevaricating,
prevaricated
to say something that is not actually a lie but
is evasive or misleading
➤ **prevarication** NOUN

**prevent** VERB prevents, preventing, prevented
❶ to stop something from happening • *The
accident could not have been prevented.* ❷ to
stop a person from doing something • *You
cannot prevent me from going.*
➤ **preventable** ADJECTIVE
➤ **prevention** NOUN

**preventive, preventative** ADJECTIVE
intended to help prevent something
• *preventive medicine*

**preview** *NOUN* previews
a showing of a film or play before it is shown to the general public

**previous** *ADJECTIVE*
coming before this; preceding • *There had been a storm the previous night.*

**previously** *ADVERB*
before the present time; earlier • *The building had previously been used as a hotel.*

**prey** (say pray) *NOUN*
an animal that is hunted or killed by another for food

**prey** *VERB* preys, preying, preyed
➤ **prey on something** to hunt and kill an animal for food • *Owls prey on mice and other small animals.*
➤ **prey on your mind** to worry you constantly • *The accident has been preying on his mind.*

SPELLING
Be careful, this sounds the same as **pray**, which means to talk to God or to wish very strongly for something.

**price** *NOUN* prices
❶ the amount of money for which something is bought or sold ❷ what you have to give or do in order to achieve something • *An apology seemed a small price to pay for ending the quarrel.*

**price** *VERB* prices, pricing, priced
to decide the price of something

**priceless** *ADJECTIVE*
❶ very valuable ❷ (*informal*) very amusing

**prick** *VERB* pricks, pricking, pricked
❶ to make a tiny hole in something ❷ to hurt someone with a pin or needle etc.
➤ **prick up your ears** to start listening suddenly

**prick** *NOUN* pricks
a pricking feeling

**prickle** *NOUN* prickles
❶ a small thorn ❷ a sharp spine on a hedgehog or cactus etc. ❸ a feeling that a lot of small sharp points are sticking into your skin

**prickle** *VERB* prickles, prickling, prickled
to feel as though a lot of small sharp points are sticking into your skin; to cause this feeling • *She felt her skin prickle with fear.*

**prickly** *ADJECTIVE*
❶ covered in prickles or feeling like prickles ❷ irritable or bad-tempered

**pride** *NOUN* prides
❶ a feeling of deep pleasure or satisfaction when you have done something well • *My heart swelled with pride.* ❷ something that makes you feel proud • *This autograph is the pride of my collection.* ❸ dignity or self-respect ❹ too high an opinion of yourself ❺ a group of lions
➤ **pride of place** the most important or most honoured position

**pride** *VERB* prides, priding, prided
➤ **pride yourself on something** to be proud of something • *He prided himself on his logical mind.*

**priest** *NOUN* priests
❶ a member of the clergy in certain Christian Churches ❷ a person who performs religious ceremonies in a non-Christian religion
➤ **priesthood** *NOUN*
➤ **priestly** *ADJECTIVE*

**priestess** *NOUN* priestesses
a female priest in a non-Christian religion

**prig** *NOUN* prigs
a self-righteous person
➤ **priggish** *ADJECTIVE*

**prim** *ADJECTIVE* primmer, primmest
always behaving in a formal and correct manner and easily shocked by anything rude
➤ **primly** *ADVERB*
➤ **primness** *NOUN*

**prima donna** (say **preem**-a) *NOUN* prima donnas
the chief female singer in an opera company

**primarily** (say pry-mer-il-ee or pry-**me**-ril-ee) *ADVERB*
more than anything else; mainly • *The programme is aimed primarily at teenagers.*

**primary** *ADJECTIVE*
first or most important. Compare with **secondary**.

**primary colour** *NOUN* primary colours
one of the colours from which all others can be made by mixing (red, yellow and blue for paint; red, green and violet for light)

**primary school** *NOUN* primary schools
(*British*) a school for the first stage of a child's education

**primate** (say **pry**-mat) *NOUN* primates
❶ an animal of the group that includes human beings, apes and monkeys ❷ an archbishop

535

**prime** ADJECTIVE
❶ chief or most important • *The weather was the prime cause of the accident.* ❷ of the best quality • *prime beef*

**prime** NOUN
the best time or stage of something • *He was in the prime of his life.*

**prime** VERB primes, priming, primed
❶ to prepare something for use or action • *The cannon was primed and loaded.* ❷ to put a coat of liquid on something to prepare it for painting ❸ to give someone information in order to prepare them for something

**prime minister** NOUN prime ministers
the leader of a government

**prime number** NOUN prime numbers
a number (e.g. 2, 3, 5, 7, 11) that can be divided exactly only by itself and one

**primer** NOUN primers
❶ a liquid for priming a surface ❷ a textbook dealing with the first or simplest stages of a subject

**primeval** (say pry-**mee**-val) ADJECTIVE
belonging to the earliest times of the world • *a primeval forest*

**primitive** ADJECTIVE
❶ at an early stage of civilization • *Primitive humans were hunters rather than farmers.* ❷ at an early stage of development; not complicated or sophisticated • *primitive technology*

**primordial** ADJECTIVE
belonging to the earliest times of the world; primeval

**primrose** NOUN primroses
a pale-yellow flower that blooms in spring

**prince** NOUN princes
❶ the son of a king or queen ❷ a man or boy in a royal family

**princely** ADJECTIVE
❶ to do with or like a prince ❷ large, generous or splendid • *a princely gift*

**princess** NOUN princesses
❶ the daughter of a king or queen ❷ a woman or girl in a royal family ❸ the wife of a prince

**principal** ADJECTIVE
chief or most important • *the principal towns of the region*

**principal** NOUN principals
the head of a college or school

SPELLING
Take care not to confuse with principle, which means a general truth, belief or rule.

**principality** NOUN principalities
a country ruled by a prince
➤ the Principality Wales

**principally** ADVERB
chiefly or mainly • *The book is aimed principally at beginners.*

**principle** NOUN principles
❶ a general truth, belief or rule • *She taught me the principles of geometry.* ❷ a rule of conduct based on what a person believes is right • *Cheating is against his principles.*
➤ in principle in general, not in details • *I agree with your plan in principle.*
➤ on principle because of your principles of behaviour

SPELLING
Take care not to confuse with principal, which means chief or most important.

**print** VERB prints, printing, printed
❶ to put words or pictures on paper by using a machine ❷ to write with letters that are not joined together • *Print your name clearly at the top of the page.* ❸ to press a mark or design on a surface ❹ to make a picture from the negative of a photograph

**print** NOUN prints
❶ printed lettering or words ❷ a mark made by something pressing on a surface • *Her thumb left a print on the glass.* ❸ a printed picture, photograph or design
➤ in print a book is in print when it is available from the publisher
➤ out of print a book is out of print when it is no longer available from the publisher

**printed circuit** NOUN printed circuits
an electric circuit made by pressing thin metal strips onto a board

**printer** NOUN printers
❶ a machine that prints on paper from data in a computer ❷ someone who prints books or newspapers

**printout** NOUN printouts
information produced in printed form by a computer

**prior** ADJECTIVE
coming before or earlier • *a prior*

*arrangement*
➤ **prior to** before • *She made a phone call just prior to her departure.*

**prior** NOUN priors
a monk who is the head of a religious house or order
➤ **prioress** NOUN

**prioritize** (also **prioritise**) VERB prioritizes, prioritizing, prioritized
to put tasks in order of importance, so that you can deal with the most important first

**priority** NOUN priorities
❶ something that is more urgent or important than other things and needs to be dealt with first • *Safety is a priority.* ❷ the right to go first or be dealt with before other things • *Emergency cases take priority over other patients in hospital.*

**priory** NOUN priories
a religious house governed by a prior or prioress

**prise** VERB prises, prising, prised
to force or lever something out or open • *He prised open the lid with a screwdriver.*

**prism** (say prizm) NOUN prisms
❶ (*in mathematics*) a solid shape with ends that are triangles or polygons which are equal and parallel ❷ a glass prism that breaks up light into the colours of the rainbow
➤ **prismatic** ADJECTIVE

**prison** NOUN prisons
a place where criminals are kept as a punishment

**prisoner** NOUN prisoners
❶ a person kept in prison ❷ a person who has been captured and kept somewhere

**prisoner of war** NOUN prisoners of war
a person captured and imprisoned by the enemy in a war

**pristine** ADJECTIVE
in its original condition; unspoilt • *a pristine white shirt*

**privacy** (say priv-a-see) NOUN
being able to be alone without other people watching you or knowing what you are doing • *Our new garden fence will give us more privacy.*

**private** ADJECTIVE
❶ belonging to a particular person or group • *private property* ❷ meant to be kept secret; confidential • *private talks* ❸ quiet and secluded ❹ not holding public office • *a*

*private citizen* ❺ independent or commercial; not run by the government • *private medicine* • *a private detective*
➤ **privately** ADVERB
➤ **in private** where only particular people can see or hear; not in public

**private** NOUN privates
a soldier of the lowest rank

**privation** NOUN privations
loss or lack of something; lack of necessities

**privatize** (also **privatise**) VERB privatizes, privatizing, privatized
to transfer the running of a business or industry from the state to private owners
➤ **privatization** NOUN

**privet** NOUN privets
an evergreen shrub with small leaves, used to make hedges

**privilege** NOUN privileges
a special right, advantage or opportunity given to one person or group • *It was a great privilege to hear her sing.*

**privileged** ADJECTIVE
having an advantage or opportunity that most people do not have • *I feel privileged to be a member of this team.*

**privy** ADJECTIVE
➤ **be privy to something** to be allowed to know about something secret • *She was not privy to their plans.*

**privy** NOUN privies (*old use*) an outside toilet

**Privy Council** NOUN
(*in the UK*) a group of distinguished people who advise the sovereign

**prize** NOUN prizes
❶ an award given to someone who wins a game or competition or who does very good work ❷ something of great value that is worth trying to obtain

**prize** VERB prizes, prizing, prized
to value something greatly • *These horses were highly prized.*

> SPELLING
>
> Choose the right word! A prize (noun) is something that you win in a competition. To prize (verb) something means to value it highly. To prise (verb) something open means to open it using force.

**pro** NOUN pros
(*informal*) a professional
➤ **pros and cons** reasons for and against something

**pro-** PREFIX
in favour of or supporting something (as in *pro-British*)

**probability** NOUN probabilities
❶ how likely it is that something will happen
• *There is a high probability of more snow.*
❷ something that is likely to happen

**probable** ADJECTIVE
likely to happen or be true

**probably** ADVERB
almost certainly • *You're probably right.*

**probation** NOUN
a period of time at the start of a new job when a person is tested to see if they are suitable
➤ **probationary** ADJECTIVE
➤ **on probation** being supervised by a probation officer instead of being sent to prison

**probation officer** NOUN probation officers
an official who supervises the behaviour of a convicted criminal who is not in prison

**probe** NOUN probes
❶ a long thin instrument used to look closely at something such as a wound ❷ an unmanned spacecraft used for exploring ❸ an investigation

**probe** VERB probes, probing, probed
❶ to ask questions in order to find out hidden information ❷ to explore or look closely at something, especially with a probe

**probity** (say **proh**-bit-ee) NOUN
honesty or integrity

**problem** NOUN problems
❶ something that causes trouble or is difficult to deal with ❷ a question that you have to solve by thinking about it
➤ **problematic** ➤ **problematical** ADJECTIVE

**proboscis** (say pro-**boss**-iss) NOUN proboscises
❶ a long flexible snout ❷ an insect's long mouthpart

**procedure** NOUN procedures
a fixed or special way of doing something
• *Printing out the file is a simple procedure.*

**proceed** VERB proceeds, proceeding, proceeded
❶ to go forward or onward ❷ to continue; to go on to do something • *She proceeded to explain the plan.*

SPELLING

Take care not to confuse with **precede**, which means to come before something else.

**proceedings** PLURAL NOUN
❶ things that happen, especially at a formal meeting or ceremony ❷ a lawsuit

**proceeds** PLURAL NOUN
the money made from a sale or event

**process** (say **proh**-sess) NOUN processes
a series of actions for making or doing something
➤ **in the process of** in the course of doing something

**process** (say **proh**-sess) VERB processes, processing, processed
to put something through a manufacturing or other process • *processed cheese*

**process** (say pro-**sess**) VERB processes, processing, processed
to go in procession

**procession** NOUN processions
a number of people or vehicles moving steadily forward following each other

**processor** NOUN processors
❶ a machine that processes things ❷ the part of a computer that controls all its operations

**proclaim** VERB proclaims, proclaiming, proclaimed
to announce something officially or publicly

**proclamation** NOUN proclamations
a public or official announcement

**procrastinate** VERB procrastinates, procrastinating, procrastinated
to put off doing something
➤ **procrastination** NOUN
➤ **procrastinator** NOUN

**procreate** VERB procreates, procreating, procreated
to produce offspring by the natural process of reproduction
➤ **procreation** NOUN

**procure** VERB procures, procuring, procured
to obtain or acquire something
➤ **procurement** NOUN

**prod** VERB prods, prodding, prodded
❶ to poke something or someone with your finger or a pointed object ❷ to encourage or remind someone to do something
➤ **prod** NOUN

**prodigal** ADJECTIVE
wasteful or extravagant
➤ **prodigality** NOUN

**prodigious** ADJECTIVE
remarkably large or impressive • *a prodigious*

*achievement*
➤ **prodigiously** ADVERB

**prodigy** NOUN prodigies
❶ a child or young person with wonderful abilities ❷ a wonderful thing

**produce** (say pro-**dewss**) VERB produces, producing, produced
❶ to make or create something; to bring something into existence ❷ to bring something out so that it can be seen ❸ to organize the performance of a play, making of a film, etc. ❹ to extend a line further • *Produce the base of the triangle.*

**produce** (say **prod**-yewss) NOUN
things that have been produced or grown, especially by farmers

**producer** NOUN producers
❶ a person, company or country that makes or grows something ❷ someone who produces a play, film, etc.

**product** NOUN products
❶ something made or produced for sale ❷ the result of multiplying two numbers. Compare with *quotient*.

**production** NOUN productions
❶ the process of making or creating something, especially in large quantities ❷ the amount produced • *Oil production increased last year.* ❸ a version of a play, opera or other show

**productive** ADJECTIVE
❶ producing a lot of things • *a productive factory* ❷ producing good results; useful • *a productive discussion*
➤ **productivity** NOUN

**profane** ADJECTIVE
showing disrespect for religion; blasphemous

**profane** VERB profanes, profaning, profaned
to treat something, especially religion, with disrespect

**profanity** NOUN profanities
words or language that show disrespect for religion

**profess** VERB professes, professing, professed
❶ to claim to have or do something • *I don't profess to be an expert on the subject.* ❷ to declare or express something • *He professed his admiration for their work.*

**profession** NOUN professions
❶ an occupation that needs special education and training, such as medicine or law ❷ a

declaration • *They made professions of loyalty.*

**professional** ADJECTIVE
❶ to do with a profession ❷ doing a certain kind of work as a full-time job for payment, not as an amateur • *a professional footballer* ❸ done with a high standard of skill
➤ **professionally** ADVERB

**professional** NOUN professionals
❶ a person who has been trained in a profession ❷ a person who does something to earn money, not as an amateur

**professor** NOUN professors
a university teacher of the highest rank

SPELLING
There is one f and a double s in professor.

**proffer** VERB proffers, proffering, proffered
to offer something • *'How are you?' he said, proffering his hand.*

**proficient** ADJECTIVE
able to do something well because of training or practice; skilled • *She is proficient in French.*
➤ **proficiency** NOUN

**profile** NOUN profiles
❶ a side view of a person's face ❷ a short description of a person's character or career
➤ **keep a low profile** to try to avoid being noticed

**profit** NOUN profits
❶ the extra money obtained by selling something for more than it cost to buy or make ❷ an advantage gained by doing something

**profit** VERB profits, profiting, profited
to gain an advantage or benefit from something

**profitable** ADJECTIVE
making a profit
➤ **profitably** ADVERB

**profligate** ADJECTIVE
wasteful and extravagant
➤ **profligacy** NOUN

**profound** ADJECTIVE
❶ very deep or intense • *His death had a profound effect on them all.* ❷ showing or needing great knowledge, understanding or thought • *The poem she wrote was quite profound.*
➤ **profoundly** ADVERB

**profuse** ADJECTIVE
given or produced in large amounts • *profuse apologies*
➤ **profusely** ADVERB

**profusion** NOUN
a very large quantity of something • *Wild flowers grew in profusion in the fields.*

**progeny** (say **proj**-in-ee) NOUN
offspring or descendants

**prognosis** (say prog-**noh**-sis) NOUN prognoses
a forecast or prediction, especially about how a disease will develop

**program** NOUN programs
a series of coded instructions for a computer to carry out

**program** VERB programs, programming, programmed
to put instructions into a computer by means of a program (WORD ORIGIN) the American spelling of **programme**, used when you are talking about computers

**programme** NOUN programmes
❶ a show, play or talk on radio or television ❷ a list of planned events ❸ a leaflet or pamphlet giving details of a play, concert, football match, etc.

**programmer** NOUN programmers
a person whose job is to write computer programs

**progress** (say **proh**-gress) NOUN
❶ forward movement • *The procession made slow progress.* ❷ development or improvement • *He was making progress in his research.*
➤ **in progress** taking place • *There seemed to be a feast in progress.*

**progress** (say pro-**gress**) VERB progresses, progressing, progressed
❶ to move forward or continue • *She became more and more tired as the evening progressed.* ❷ to develop or improve • *Medical knowledge has progressed steadily in the last twenty years.*
➤ **progression** NOUN

**progressive** ADJECTIVE
❶ moving forward or developing steadily ❷ in favour of political or social reforms ❸ a progressive disease is one that becomes gradually more severe
➤ **progressively** ADVERB

**prohibit** VERB prohibits, prohibiting, prohibited
to forbid or ban something • *Smoking is prohibited.*
➤ **prohibition** NOUN

**prohibitive** ADJECTIVE
prices and costs are prohibitive when they are too high for most people to be able to afford
➤ **prohibitively** ADVERB

**project** (say **proj**-ekt) NOUN projects
❶ the task of finding out as much as you can about something and writing about it ❷ a plan or scheme • *a building project*

**project** (say pro-**jekt**) VERB projects, projecting, projected
❶ to stick out • *Oars projected from the sides of the ship.* ❷ to show a film or picture on a screen ❸ to project your voice is to speak loudly and clearly so that it carries a long way ❹ to give people a particular impression • *He likes to project an image of absent-minded brilliance.*

**projectile** NOUN projectiles
something fired from a gun or thrown; a missile

**projection** NOUN projections
❶ a part of something that sticks out ❷ showing a film or picture on a screen with a projector

**projectionist** NOUN projectionists
a person who works a projector

**projector** NOUN projectors
a machine for showing films or photographs on a screen

**proletariat** (say proh-lit-**air**-ee-at) NOUN
working people

**prolific** ADJECTIVE
producing a lot • *a prolific author*

**prologue** (say **proh**-log) NOUN prologues
an introduction to a poem, play or story

**prolong** VERB prolongs, prolonging, prolonged
to make something last longer • *They decided to prolong their visit by a few more days.*

**prolonged** ADJECTIVE
continuing for a long time • *a prolonged silence*

**prom** NOUN proms (*informal*)
❶ a formal dance for secondary school students ❷ a promenade ❸ a promenade concert

**promenade** (say prom-in-**ahd**) NOUN promenades
❶ a place suitable for walking, especially beside the seashore ❷ a leisurely walk

**promenade** VERB promenades, promenading, promenaded
to take a leisurely walk

**promenade concert** promenade concerts
a concert where part of the audience stands in an area without seating

**prominence** NOUN
being important or well known • He first came to prominence two years ago.

**prominent** ADJECTIVE
❶ easy to see or notice • The house stood in a prominent position. ❷ sticking out • She had a long nose and prominent teeth. ❸ important • He plays a prominent part in the story.
➤ **prominently** ADVERB

**promiscuous** ADJECTIVE
❶ having many casual sexual relationships ❷ indiscriminate or casual
➤ **promiscuously** ADVERB
➤ **promiscuity** NOUN

**promise** NOUN promises
❶ a statement that you will definitely do or not do something ❷ signs of future success or good results • His work shows promise.

**promise** VERB promises, promising, promised
to make a promise

**promising** ADJECTIVE
likely to be good or successful • a promising pianist

**promontory** NOUN promontories
a piece of high land that sticks out into a sea or lake

**promote** VERB promotes, promoting, promoted
❶ to move a person to a more senior or more important job or position ❷ a sports team is promoted when it moves to a higher division or league ❸ to help the progress of something • He has done much to promote the cause of peace. ❹ to publicize or advertise a product in order to sell it
➤ **promoter** NOUN

**promotion** NOUN promotions
❶ a move to a higher position or more important job ❷ when a sports team moves to a higher division or league ❸ a piece of publicity or advertising ❹ helping the progress of something

**prompt** ADJECTIVE
❶ without delay • a prompt reply ❷ punctual
➤ **promptness** NOUN

**prompt** ADVERB (British) exactly at that time
• I'll pick you up at 7.20 prompt.

**prompt** VERB prompts, prompting, prompted
❶ to cause or encourage a person to do something • What prompted you to start writing the blog? ❷ to remind an actor or speaker of words when they have forgotten them

**promptly** ADVERB
❶ without delay; immediately • When I told her she promptly burst into tears. ❷ punctually • They arrived promptly at 8 o'clock.

**prone** ADJECTIVE
lying face downwards
➤ **be prone to something** to be likely to do or suffer from something • He is prone to jealousy.

**prong** NOUN prongs
one of the spikes on a fork
➤ **pronged** ADJECTIVE

**pronoun** NOUN pronouns
a word used instead of a noun: **demonstrative pronouns** are this, that, these, those; **interrogative pronouns** are who?, what?, which?, etc.; **personal pronouns** are I, me, we, us, you, he, him, she, her, it, they, them, etc.; **possessive pronouns** are mine, yours, theirs, etc.; **reflexive pronouns** are myself, yourself, etc.; **relative pronouns** are who, what, which, that, etc.

**GRAMMAR**

Pronouns replace a noun or noun phrase in a sentence or clause, and help to avoid having to repeat words. There are several types of pronoun:

**Personal pronouns** replace the name of a person or thing. I, you, he, she, it, we and they are used when the pronoun is the subject of the clause; me, you, him, her, it, us, and them, are used when the pronoun is the object: Zoe and Bill are coming to the concert. She's got a ticket, but he hasn't. The guards were following us and we were unable to shake them off.

**Reflexive pronouns** (myself, yourself, himself, herself, itself, ourselves, yourselves and themselves) are used when the object of the verb is the same as the subject of the verb: Most baby birds are unable to feed themselves. They are also used after a preposition: I wanted to see for myself what all the fuss was about.

**Relative pronouns** (*what*, *who*, *whom*, *whose*, *which* and *that*) introduce a clause which gives more information about a noun, e.g. *the artist who painted this portrait*; *the song that I love.*

**Interrogative pronouns** (*what?*, *who?*, *whom?*, *whose?*) are used to form questions e.g. *What is happening? Who wants some ice cream?*

**Demonstrative pronouns** (*this*, *that*, *these* and *those*) are used to identify or indicate a particular person or thing, or a particular time or situation, e.g. *These are my glasses, and those are yours; This has been a hectic week.*

**pronounce** VERB pronounces, pronouncing, pronounced
❶ to say a sound or word in a particular way • *'Two' and 'too' are pronounced the same* ❷ to declare something formally • *I now pronounce you man and wife.*

**pronounced** ADJECTIVE
very noticeable • *This street has a pronounced slope.*

**pronouncement** NOUN pronouncements
a formal public statement

**pronunciation** NOUN pronunciations
the way a word is pronounced

SPELLING

Note the spelling of this word; it should not be written or spoken as 'pronounciation'.

**proof** NOUN proofs
❶ a fact or thing that shows something is true • *There is no proof that he stole the money.* ❷ a printed copy of a book or photograph made for checking before other copies are printed

**proof** ADJECTIVE
able to resist something or not be affected by it • *a bullet-proof jacket*

**prop** NOUN props
❶ a support, especially one made of a long piece of wood or metal ❷ an object or piece of furniture used on a theatre stage or in a film

**prop** VERB props, propping, propped
to support something by leaning it against something else • *The ladder was propped up against the wall.*

**propaganda** NOUN
false or exaggerated information that is spread around to make people believe something

**propagate** VERB propagates, propagating, propagated
❶ to grow new plants from an original plant ❷ to spread an idea or belief to a lot of people
➤ **propagation** NOUN

**propel** VERB propels, propelling, propelled
to push something forward • *They grabbed me and propelled me through the door.*

**propellant** NOUN propellants
a fuel or other substance that propels things

**propeller** NOUN propellers
a device with blades that spin round to drive an aircraft or ship

**propensity** NOUN propensities
a tendency to behave in a particular way

**proper** ADJECTIVE
❶ suitable or right • *This is the proper way to hold a tennis racket.* ❷ respectable or socially acceptable • *He raised his hat, thinking it was the proper thing to do.* ❸ (*informal*) complete or thorough • *You're a proper nuisance!*

**proper fraction** NOUN proper fractions
a fraction that is less than 1, with the numerator less than the denominator, e.g.⅓

**properly** ADVERB
in a correct or suitable way • *The lid won't close properly.*

**proper noun** NOUN proper nouns
the name of an individual person or thing, e.g. *Mary, London, Spain*, usually written with a capital first letter

**property** NOUN properties
❶ a thing or things that a person owns ❷ a building with the land belonging to it ❸ a quality or characteristic • *It has the property of becoming soft when heated.*

**prophecy** NOUN prophecies
❶ a statement that says what will happen in the future ❷ the power to say what will happen in the future • *She was believed to have the gift of prophecy.*

**prophesy** VERB prophesies, prophesying, prophesied
to say what you think will happen in the future • *Many people have been prophesying disaster.*

**prophet** NOUN prophets
❶ a person who makes prophecies ❷ a religious teacher who is believed to be inspired by God
➤ **prophetess** NOUN
➤ **the Prophet** a name for Muhammad, the founder of the Muslim faith

SPELLING
Be careful, this sounds the same as **profit**.

**prophetic** ADJECTIVE
saying or showing what will happen in the future • *a prophetic dream*

**propitiate** (say pro-**pish**-ee-ayt) VERB propitiates, propitiating, propitiated
to win a person's favour or forgiveness
➤ **propitiatory** ADJECTIVE

**propitious** (say pro-**pish**-us) ADJECTIVE
favourable; likely to bring good results • *a propitious moment*

**proponent** (say prop-**oh**-nent) NOUN proponents
a person who supports a proposal or idea

**proportion** NOUN proportions
❶ a part or share of a whole thing • *A large proportion of the earth's surface is covered by sea.* ❷ the proportion of one thing to another is how much there is of one compared to the other • *What is the proportion of girls to boys in the class?* ❸ the correct relationship in size, amount or importance between two things • *You've drawn his head out of proportion.*
➤ **proportions** PLURAL NOUN
size or scale • *a ship of gigantic proportions*

**proportional, proportionate** ADJECTIVE
in proportion; according to a ratio
➤ **proportionally** ADVERB
➤ **proportionately** ADVERB

**proportional representation** NOUN
a system in which each political party has a number of Members of Parliament in proportion to the number of votes for all its candidates

**proposal** NOUN proposals
❶ a plan that has been suggested ❷ when someone asks another person to marry them

**propose** VERB proposes, proposing, proposed
❶ to suggest an idea or plan ❷ to plan or intend to do something • *What do you propose to do now?* ❸ to ask a person to marry you

**proposition** NOUN propositions
❶ a suggestion or offer • *I have a proposition for you.* ❷ a statement ❸ a problem or task • *Climbing over that wall is a tricky proposition.*

**propound** VERB propounds, propounding, propounded
to put forward an idea for consideration

**proprietary** (say pro-**pry**-it-er-ee) ADJECTIVE
❶ made or sold by one firm; branded • *proprietary medicines* ❷ to do with an owner or ownership

**proprietor** NOUN proprietors
the owner of a shop or business
➤ **proprietress** NOUN

**propriety** (say pro-**pry**-it-ee) NOUN proprieties
correctness of social or moral behaviour

**propulsion** NOUN
propelling something or driving it forward

**prosaic** ADJECTIVE
plain or dull and ordinary
➤ **prosaically** ADVERB

**proscribe** VERB proscribes, proscribing, proscribed
to forbid something by law

SPELLING
Take care not to confuse with **prescribe**, which means to advise someone to use medicine or treatment.

**prose** NOUN
writing that is not in verse

**prosecute** VERB prosecutes, prosecuting, prosecuted
❶ to make someone go to a law court to be tried for a crime ❷ (*formal*) to continue doing something • *They had overwhelming support to prosecute the war.*
➤ **prosecutor** NOUN

**prosecution** NOUN prosecutions
❶ the process of prosecuting someone ❷ the lawyers who try to show that someone is guilty of a crime in a court of law

**prospect** NOUN prospects
❶ a possibility or expectation of something • *There is little prospect of success.* ❷ a wide view

**prospect** (say pro-**spekt**) VERB prospects, prospecting, prospected
to explore an area in search of gold or some other mineral
➤ **prospector** NOUN

**prospective** ADJECTIVE
expected to be or to happen; possible
• *prospective customers*

**prospectus** NOUN prospectuses
a booklet describing and advertising a school, business company, etc.

**prosper** VERB prospers, prospering, prospered
to be successful or do well • *The business continued to prosper.*

**prosperity** NOUN
being successful or rich • *a time of peace and prosperity*

**prosperous** ADJECTIVE
successful or rich • *a prosperous town*

**prostitute** NOUN prostitutes
a person who takes part in sexual acts for payment
➤ **prostitution** NOUN

**prostrate** ADJECTIVE
lying face downwards

**prostrate** VERB prostrates, prostrating, prostrated
➤ **prostrate yourself** to lie flat on the ground face down, usually in submission
➤ **prostration** NOUN

**protagonist** NOUN protagonists
❶ the main character in a play ❷ one of the main people involved in a situation

**protect** VERB protects, protecting, protected
to keep someone or something safe from harm or damage
➤ **protector** NOUN

**protection** NOUN
keeping someone or something safe from harm or damage • *Vaccination gives protection against diseases.*

**protective** ADJECTIVE
❶ that prevents a person or thing from being harmed or damaged • *protective clothing* ❷ wanting to keep someone or something safe • *Her parents were very protective of her.*

**protectorate** NOUN protectorates
a country that is under the official protection of a stronger country

**protégé** (say **prot**-ezh-ay) NOUN protégés
someone who is helped and supported by an older or more experienced person

**protein** NOUN proteins
a substance that is found in all living things and is an essential part of the food of animals

**protest** (say **proh**-test) NOUN protests
a statement or action showing that you disapprove of something • *He cried out in protest.*

**protest** (say pro-**test**) VERB protests, protesting, protested
❶ to make a protest ❷ to declare something firmly • *They protested their innocence.*
➤ **protestation** NOUN

**Protestant** NOUN Protestants
a member of any of the western Christian Churches separated from the Roman Catholic Church (WORD ORIGIN) because in the 16th century many people protested (= declared firmly) their opposition to the Catholic Church

**protester** NOUN protesters
someone who protests about something, especially publicly

**protocol** NOUN
the correct or official procedure for behaving in certain formal situations

**proton** NOUN protons
a particle of matter with a positive electric charge

**prototype** NOUN prototypes
the first model of something, from which others are copied or developed

**protracted** ADJECTIVE
lasting longer than usual or expected • *a protracted stay in hospital*

**protractor** NOUN protractors
a device for measuring angles, usually a semicircle marked off in degrees

**protrude** VERB protrudes, protruding, protruded
to stick out from somewhere • *His tongue protruded from his lips.*
➤ **protrusion** NOUN

**protuberance** NOUN protuberances
a part that bulges out from a surface

**protuberant** ADJECTIVE
bulging out from a surface

**proud** ADJECTIVE
❶ very pleased with yourself or with someone else who has done well • *I am so proud of my sister.* ❷ causing pride • *This is a proud moment for us.* ❸ full of self-respect and independence • *They were too proud to ask for help.* ❹ having too high an opinion of yourself
➤ **proudly** ADVERB

**prove** *VERB* proves, proving, proved
❶ to show that something is true • *I can prove that I am innocent.* ❷ to turn out a certain way • *The forecast proved to be correct.*

**proven** (say **proh**-ven) *ADJECTIVE*
that has been shown to be true • *a man of proven ability*

**proverb** *NOUN* proverbs
a short well-known saying that states a truth, e.g. 'Many hands make light work.'

**proverbial** *ADJECTIVE*
❶ referred to in a proverb ❷ familiar or well known

**provide** *VERB* provides, providing, provided
❶ to make something available; to supply something • *Our website should provide you with all the information you need.* ❷ to prepare for something that might happen • *They have tried to provide for emergencies.*

**provided** *CONJUNCTION*
on condition that; only if • *You can stay provided you help.*

**providence** *NOUN*
❶ being careful and providing for the future ❷ God's or nature's care and protection

**provident** *ADJECTIVE*
wisely providing for the future; thrifty

**providential** *ADJECTIVE*
happening very luckily
➤ **providentially** *ADVERB*

**provider** *NOUN* providers
a person or thing that provides something • *an Internet service provider*

**providing** *CONJUNCTION*
on condition that; only if • *You can look around, providing you don't touch anything.*

**province** *NOUN* provinces
❶ a section of a country ❷ the area of a person's special knowledge or responsibility • *I'm afraid carpentry is not my province.*
➤ **the provinces** the parts of a country outside its capital city

**provincial** (say pro-**vin**-shul) *ADJECTIVE*
❶ to do with the provinces • *a provincial town* ❷ culturally limited or narrow-minded • *provincial attitudes*

**provision** *NOUN* provisions
❶ providing something • *the provision of free meals for old people* ❷ a statement in a legal document • *the provisions of the treaty*

**provisional** *ADJECTIVE*
arranged or agreed on for the time being but possibly to be changed later • *a provisional driving licence*
➤ **provisionally** *ADVERB*

**provisions** *PLURAL NOUN*
supplies of food and drink

**proviso** (say prov-**y**-zoh) *NOUN* provisos
a condition that is insisted on in advance

**provocation** *NOUN*
something done or said deliberately to annoy someone • *He hit me without the slightest provocation.*

**provocative** *ADJECTIVE*
❶ likely to make someone angry • *a provocative remark* ❷ intended to make someone feel sexual desire
➤ **provocatively** *ADVERB*

**provoke** *VERB* provokes, provoking, provoked
❶ to deliberately make a person angry ❷ to cause or give rise to something • *The joke provoked laughter.*

**provost** *NOUN* provosts
a Scottish official with authority similar to a mayor in England and Wales

**prow** *NOUN* prows
the front end of a ship

**prowess** *NOUN*
great ability or skill • *sporting prowess*

**prowl** *VERB* prowls, prowling, prowled
to move about quietly or cautiously, like a hunter

**prowl** *NOUN*
➤ **on the prowl** moving about quietly or cautiously, hunting or looking for something • *There was a fox on the prowl.*
➤ **prowler** *NOUN*

**proximity** *NOUN*
nearness • *Their house is in close proximity to the school.*

**proxy** *NOUN* proxies
a person authorized to represent or act for another person • *I will be abroad, so I have arranged to vote by proxy.*

**prude** *NOUN* prudes
a person who is easily shocked
➤ **prudish** *ADJECTIVE*

**prudent** *ADJECTIVE*
sensible and careful; not taking risks • *It may be prudent to get some advice first.*

a
b
c
d
e
f
g
h
i
j
k
l
m
n
o
p
q
r
s
t
u
v
w
x
y
z

➤ **prudently** ADVERB
➤ **prudence** NOUN

**prune** NOUN prunes
a dried plum

**prune** VERB prunes, pruning, pruned
to cut off unwanted parts of a tree or bush

**pry** VERB pries, prying, pried
to look into or ask about someone else's
private business • *I'm sorry, I didn't mean to
pry.*

**PS** ABBREVIATION
postscript (used when you add something at
the end of a letter)

**psalm** (say sahm) NOUN psalms
a religious song, especially one from the Book
of Psalms in the Bible

**pseudonym** NOUN pseudonyms
a name used by a writer instead of their real
name

**PSHE** ABBREVIATION
personal, social and health education (as a
school subject)

**psychedelic** ADJECTIVE
having vivid colours and patterns • *a
psychedelic design*

**psychiatrist** (say sy-ky-a-trist) NOUN
psychiatrists
a doctor who treats mental illnesses
➤ **psychiatry** NOUN
➤ **psychiatric** ADJECTIVE

**psychic** (say sy-kik) ADJECTIVE
❶ appearing to have supernatural powers,
especially being able to predict the future or
read people's minds ❷ supernatural

**psychoanalysis** NOUN
investigation of a person's mental processes,
especially in psychotherapy
➤ **psychoanalyst** NOUN

**psychological** ADJECTIVE
❶ to do with the mind or how it works ❷ to
do with psychology

**psychology** NOUN
the study of the mind and how it works
➤ **psychologist** NOUN

**psychotherapy** NOUN
treatment of mental illness by psychological
methods
➤ **psychotherapist** NOUN

**PT** ABBREVIATION
(*British*) physical training

**PTA** ABBREVIATION
parent-teacher association; an organization
that arranges discussions between teachers
and parents about school business and raises
money for the school

**ptarmigan** (say tar-mig-an) NOUN ptarmigans
a bird of the grouse family

**pterodactyl** (say te-ro-**dak**-til) NOUN
pterodactyls
an extinct flying reptile **WORD ORIGIN** from
Greek *pteron* = wing + *daktylos* = finger
(because one of the 'fingers' on its front leg was
enlarged to support its wing)

**PTO** ABBREVIATION
please turn over (put at the end of a page of
writing when there is more writing on the
next page)

**pub** NOUN pubs
(*British*) a building licensed to serve alcoholic
drinks to the public **WORD ORIGIN** short for
*public house*

**puberty** (say pew-ber-tee) NOUN
the time when a young person is developing
physically into an adult

**pubic** (say pew-bik) ADJECTIVE
to do with the lower front part of the
abdomen

**public** ADJECTIVE
❶ belonging to everyone or able to be used
by everyone • *public transport* ❷ to do with
people in general • *There was some public
support for the idea.*
➤ **publicly** ADVERB

**public** NOUN
people in general • *The police have asked for
help from members of the public.*
➤ **in public** openly, not in private

**publican** NOUN publicans
(*British*) the person in charge of a pub

**publication** NOUN publications
❶ publishing • *She became famous after the
publication of her first novel.* ❷ a published
book, newspaper or magazine

**public house** NOUN public houses
(*British*) (*formal*) a pub

**publicity** NOUN
information or advertising that makes people
know about something

**publicize** (also **publicise**) VERB publicizes,
publicizing, publicized

to bring something to people's attention; to advertise something

**public school** *NOUN* public schools
❶ in England, a private secondary school that charges fees ❷ in Scotland and the USA, a school run by a local authority or by the state

**publish** *VERB* publishes, publishing, published
❶ to produce a book, magazine, etc. and sell it to the public ❷ to make something available for people to read online • *The winning poems will be published on our website.* ❸ to make something known publicly

**publisher** *NOUN* publishers
a person or company that publishes books, magazines, etc.

**puce** *NOUN*
a dark red or brownish-purple colour
**WORD ORIGIN** from French *couleur puce* = the colour of a flea

**puck** *NOUN* pucks
a hard rubber disc used in ice hockey

**pucker** *VERB* puckers, puckering, puckered
to form into wrinkles or to make something do this • *His brow puckered into a frown.*

**pudding** *NOUN* puddings (*chiefly British*)
❶ the sweet course of a meal ❷ a food made in a soft mass, especially in a mixture of flour and other ingredients

**puddle** *NOUN* puddles
a shallow patch of liquid, especially of rainwater on a road

**pudgy** *ADJECTIVE*
short and fat • *pudgy fingers*

**puerile** (say pew-er-yl) *ADJECTIVE*
silly and childish

**puff** *NOUN* puffs
❶ a short blowing of breath, wind, smoke or steam • *He vanished in a puff of smoke.* ❷ a soft pad for putting powder on the skin ❸ a cake of very light pastry filled with cream

**puff** *VERB* puffs, puffing, puffed
❶ to blow out puffs of smoke or steam ❷ to pant or breathe with difficulty • *She was puffing when she got to the top of the hill.* ❸ to inflate or swell something • *He puffed out his chest.*

**puffin** *NOUN* puffins
a seabird with a large striped beak

**puffy** *ADJECTIVE*
puffed out or swollen • *His eyes were puffy*

and red.
**➤ puffiness** *NOUN*

**pug** *NOUN* pugs
a small dog with a flat face like a bulldog

**pugilist** (say pew-jil-ist) *NOUN* pugilists
a boxer

**pugnacious** *ADJECTIVE*
wanting to fight; aggressive
**➤ pugnaciously** *ADVERB*
**➤ pugnacity** *NOUN*

**puke** *VERB* pukes, puking, puked (*informal*)
to vomit

**pull** *VERB* pulls, pulling, pulled
❶ to hold something and make it come towards you • *I pulled the door open.* ❷ to move something along behind you • *The train is pulled by a powerful engine.* ❸ to move with an effort • *She tried to grab the boy but he pulled away.*
**➤ pull a face** to make a strange face
**➤ pull in** ❶ a vehicle pulls in when it moves to the side of the road and stops ❷ a train pulls in when it comes to a station and stops
**➤ pull someone's leg** to tease someone
**➤ pull something off** to achieve something
**➤ pull out** ❶ to decide to stop taking part in something • *He had to pull out of the race after twisting his ankle.* ❷ a vehicle pulls out when it moves out into the road from the side ❸ a train pulls out when it leaves a station
**➤ pull through** to recover from an illness
**➤ pull up** a vehicle pulls up when it stops abruptly
**➤ pull yourself together** to become calm again after being upset

**pull** *NOUN* pulls
a pulling movement • *Give the handle a good pull.*

**pullet** *NOUN* pullets
a young hen

**pulley** *NOUN* pulleys
a wheel with a rope, chain or belt over it, used for lifting or moving heavy things

**pullover** *NOUN* pullovers
a knitted piece of clothing for the top half of the body

**pulmonary** (say pul-mon-er-ee) *ADJECTIVE*
to do with the lungs

**pulp** *NOUN*
❶ the soft moist part of fruit ❷ any soft moist mass • *Wood pulp is used to make paper.*
**➤ pulpy** *ADJECTIVE*

**pulpit** NOUN pulpits
a small enclosed platform for the preacher in a church or chapel

**pulsate** VERB pulsates, pulsating, pulsated
to move or shake with strong regular movements • *a pulsating rhythm*
➤ **pulsation** NOUN

**pulse** NOUN pulses
❶ the rhythmical movement of the arteries as blood is pumped through them by the beating of the heart • *The pulse can be felt in a person's wrists.* ❷ a throb ❸ the edible seed of peas, beans, lentils, etc.

**pulse** VERB pulses, pulsing, pulsed
to move or flow with strong regular movements; to throb • *He could feel the blood pulsing through his body.*

**pulverize** (also **pulverise**) VERB pulverizes, pulverizing, pulverized
to crush something into powder

**puma** (say **pew**-ma) NOUN pumas
a large brown cat of western America, also called a cougar or mountain lion

**pumice** NOUN
a kind of porous stone used for rubbing stains from the skin or as powder for polishing things

**pummel** VERB pummels, pummelling, pummelled
to keep on hitting something

**pump** NOUN pumps
❶ a device that pushes air or liquid into or out of something or along pipes ❷ a canvas sports shoe with a rubber sole

**pump** VERB pumps, pumping, pumped
❶ to move air or liquid into or out of something with a pump ❷ (*informal*) to question a person to obtain information
➤ **pump something up** to fill something with air using a pump

**pumpkin** NOUN pumpkins
a very large round fruit with a hard orange skin

**pun** NOUN puns
a joking use of a word sounding the same as another or having more than one meaning, e.g. 'Deciding where to bury him was a *grave* decision.'

**punch** VERB punches, punching, punched
❶ to hit someone with your fist ❷ to make a hole in something • *The guard came to punch our tickets.* • She punched a few holes in the side of the box.*

**punch** NOUN punches
❶ a hit with a fist ❷ a device for making holes in paper, metal, leather, etc. ❸ a drink made by mixing wine or spirits and fruit juice in a bowl **WORD ORIGIN** The 'drink' meaning comes from Sanskrit *pañca* = five (the number of ingredients in the traditional recipe: spirits, fruit juice, water, sugar, and spice)

**punchline** NOUN punchlines
words that give the climax of a joke or story

**punch-up** NOUN punch-ups (*British*) (*informal*)
a fight

**punctilious** ADJECTIVE
very careful about correct behaviour and detail
➤ **punctiliously** ADVERB
➤ **punctiliousness** NOUN

**punctual** ADJECTIVE
arriving exactly on time; not late
➤ **punctually** ADVERB
➤ **punctuality** NOUN

**punctuate** VERB punctuates, punctuating, punctuated
❶ to put punctuation marks into a piece of writing ❷ to be punctuated by something is to be frequently interrupted by it • *His speech was punctuated by bursts of applause.*
**WORD ORIGIN** from Latin *punctuare* = mark with points or dots

**punctuation** NOUN
marks such as commas, full stops and brackets put into a piece of writing to make it easier to read

**PUNCTUATION**

Punctuation marks show divisions and connections between sentences, clauses or individual words: for example, a *full stop* ( . ) marks the end of a sentence; a *comma* ( , ) separates clauses or items in a list; a *question mark* ( ? ) indicates a question; and *quotation marks* ( ' ' or " " ) show direct speech (the actual words someone speaks). Other types of punctuation are the use of *capital letters* at the start of a sentence or proper noun, and the use of an *apostrophe* to show possession (*the cat's bowl*) or to indicate a missing letter (*don't, I've*).

Punctuation can completely change the meaning of a piece of writing.

Compare, for example, the meaning of these two sentences:

*Let's eat Granny!*

*Let's eat, Granny!*

**puncture** NOUN punctures
a small hole made by something sharp, especially in a tyre

**puncture** VERB punctures, puncturing, punctured
to make a small hole in something

**pundit** NOUN pundits
a person who is an expert on a subject and is asked for their opinions

**pungent** (say **pun**-jent) ADJECTIVE
❶ having a strong taste or smell ❷ pungent remarks are sharp and effective
➤ **pungently** ADVERB
➤ **pungency** NOUN

**punish** VERB punishes, punishing, punished
to make a person suffer because they have done something wrong • *He will be punished for disobeying orders.*
➤ **punishable** ADJECTIVE

**punishment** NOUN punishments
something a person suffers because they have done something wrong

**punk** NOUN punks
❶ (also **punk rock**) a loud aggressive style of rock music ❷ a person who likes this music

**punnet** NOUN punnets
(*British*) a small container for soft fruit such as strawberries

**punt** NOUN punts
a flat-bottomed boat moved by pushing a pole against the bottom of a river while standing in the punt

**punt** VERB punts, punting, punted
❶ to move a punt along with a pole ❷ to kick a football after dropping it from your hands and before it touches the ground

**punter** NOUN punters
❶ a person who lays a bet ❷ (*informal*) a customer

**puny** (say **pew**-nee) ADJECTIVE
very small and weak

**pup** NOUN pups
❶ a puppy ❷ a young seal

**pupa** (say **pew**-pa) NOUN pupae
an insect at the stage of development between a larva and an adult insect; a chrysalis

**pupate** (say pew-**payt**) VERB pupates, pupating, pupated
to become a pupa
➤ **pupation** NOUN

**pupil** NOUN pupils
❶ someone who is being taught by a teacher, especially at school ❷ the opening in the centre of the eye **WORD ORIGIN** from Latin *pupilla* = little girl or doll (the use in meaning 2 refers to the tiny images of people and things that can be seen in the eye)

**puppet** NOUN puppets
❶ a kind of doll that can be made to move by fitting it over your hand or working it by strings or wires ❷ a person whose actions are controlled by someone else
➤ **puppetry** NOUN

**puppy** NOUN puppies
a young dog

**purchase** VERB purchases, purchasing, purchased
to buy something
➤ **purchaser** NOUN

**purchase** NOUN purchases
❶ something you have bought ❷ buying something • *Keep the receipt as proof of purchase.* ❸ a firm hold or grip • *It was hard to get a purchase on the slippery rock.*

**purdah** NOUN
the practice in some Muslim and Hindu societies of keeping women from the sight of men or strangers **WORD ORIGIN** from Persian or Urdu *parda* = veil or curtain

**pure** ADJECTIVE
❶ not mixed with anything else • *pure olive oil* ❷ clean and clear • *pure spring water* ❸ free from evil or sin ❹ mere; nothing but • *What he said was pure nonsense.*

**purée** (say **pewr**-ay) NOUN purées
fruit or vegetables made into pulp

**purely** ADVERB
only or simply • *They did it purely for the money.*

**purgatory** NOUN
❶ a state of temporary suffering ❷ in Roman Catholic belief, a place in which souls are purified by punishment before they can enter heaven

**purge** VERB purges, purging, purged
to get rid of unwanted people or things • He vowed to purge the oceans of pirates.

**purge** NOUN purges
an act of purging

**purify** VERB purifies, purifying, purified
to make something pure, especially by removing dirty or harmful substances from it
➤ **purification** NOUN
➤ **purifier** NOUN

**purist** NOUN purists
a person who likes things to be exactly right, especially in people's use of words

**Puritan** NOUN Puritans
a Protestant in the 16th and 17th centuries who wanted simpler religious ceremonies and strict moral behaviour

**puritan** NOUN puritans
a person with very strict morals
➤ **puritanical** ADJECTIVE

**purity** NOUN
being pure • White often symbolizes purity.

**purl** NOUN purls
a knitting stitch that makes a ridge towards the knitter

**purl** VERB purls, purling, purled (poetical use)
a stream purls when it ripples with a murmuring sound

**purloin** VERB purloins, purloining, purloined (formal)
to take something without permission

**purple** NOUN
a deep reddish-blue colour

**purport** (say per-**port**) VERB purports, purporting, purported
to claim to be something or someone • The letter purports to be from the council.
➤ **purportedly** ADVERB

**purport** (say per-**port**) NOUN
the general meaning of something • The purport of the letter could not be clearer.

**purpose** NOUN purposes
❶ what you intend to do; a plan or aim
❷ determination • Her strength of purpose was to be put to the test.
➤ **on purpose** deliberately, not by accident

**purposeful** ADJECTIVE
determined and having a definite plan or aim
• He strode off in a purposeful manner.
➤ **purposefully** ADVERB

**purposely** ADVERB
on purpose • She was purposely avoiding him.

**purr** VERB purrs, purring, purred
❶ a cat purrs when it makes a low murmuring sound to show it is pleased ❷ to make a low continuous sound • The limousine purred away. ❸ to speak in a low and gentle voice
• He was purring with satisfaction.

**purr** NOUN purrs
a purring sound

**purse** NOUN purses
a small pouch for carrying money

**purse** VERB purses, pursing, pursed
to draw your lips tightly together, especially to show disapproval • She frowned and pursed up her lips.

**purser** NOUN pursers
a ship's officer in charge of accounts

**pursuance** NOUN (formal)
the performance or carrying out of something • in pursuance of my duties

**pursue** VERB pursues, pursuing, pursued
❶ to chase someone in order to catch them
❷ to continue with something; to work at something • She pursued her studies at college.
➤ **pursuer** NOUN

**pursuit** NOUN pursuits
❶ chasing someone • We set off in pursuit of the thief. ❷ a regular activity

**purveyor** NOUN purveyors
a person or company that sells or supplies something

**pus** NOUN
a thick yellowish substance produced in boils or other sore or infected places on your body

**push** VERB pushes, pushing, pushed
❶ to make a thing go away from you by using force on it ❷ to press something • Push the red button. ❸ to move yourself by using force • He pushed in front of me. ❹ to try to force someone to do or use something; to urge someone
➤ **push off** (informal) to go away

**push** NOUN pushes
a pushing movement or effort
➤ **at a push** if necessary but only with difficulty
➤ **get the push** (informal) to be dismissed from a job

**pushchair** NOUN pushchairs
(*British*) a folding chair on wheels, for pushing a child along

**pusher** NOUN pushers
a person who sells illegal drugs

**pushy** ADJECTIVE
determined to get what you want, in an unpleasant way

**puss** NOUN (*informal, chiefly British*)
a cat

**pussy** NOUN pussies (*informal*)
a cat

**pussyfoot** VERB pussyfoots, pussyfooting, pussyfooted
to act too cautiously and timidly

**pussy willow** NOUN pussy willows
a willow with furry catkins

**pustule** NOUN pustules
a pimple containing pus

**put** VERB puts, putting, put
❶ to move a person or thing to a place or position • *She put the phone down.* ❷ to make a person or thing do or experience something or be in a certain condition • *I'll put the light on.* • *That put me in a good mood.* ❸ to express something in words • *She put it tactfully.*
➤ **be hard put to do something** to have difficulty in doing something
➤ **put someone off** to make someone less keen on something • *The smell puts me off.*
➤ **put something off** to postpone something to a later time
➤ **put someone out** to annoy or inconvenience someone • *Our lateness has put her out.*
➤ **put something out** to stop a fire from burning or a light from shining
➤ **put someone up** to give someone a place to sleep • *Can you put me up for the night?*
➤ **put something up** ❶ to construct or build something ❷ to raise the price of something ❸ to provide something • *Who will put up the money?*
➤ **put up with something** to be willing to accept something without complaining

SPELLING
To put something somewhere is to place it there. To putt a ball is to tap it gently.

**putrefy** (say **pew**-trif-eye) VERB putrefies, putrefying, putrefied

to decay or rot
➤ **putrefaction** NOUN

**putrid** (say **pew**-trid) ADJECTIVE
❶ decaying or rotting ❷ smelling bad

**putt** VERB putts, putting, putted
to hit a golf ball gently towards the hole

**putt** NOUN putts
hitting a golf ball gently towards the hole
➤ **putting green** NOUN

**putter** NOUN putters
a golf club used to putt the ball

**putty** NOUN
a soft paste that sets hard, used for fitting the glass into a window frame

**puzzle** NOUN puzzles
❶ a difficult question or problem ❷ a game or toy that sets a problem to solve or a difficult task to complete

**puzzle** VERB puzzles, puzzling, puzzled
❶ to give someone a problem that is hard to understand • *'There is one thing that puzzles me,' she said.* ❷ to think hard about something in order to understand or explain it • *We were puzzling over the map.*

**puzzled** ADJECTIVE
not able to understand or explain something
• *a puzzled expression*

**puzzlement** NOUN
a feeling of being confused because you do not understand something • *He frowned in puzzlement.*

**PVC** ABBREVIATION
polyvinyl chloride, a plastic used to make clothing, pipes, flooring, etc.
WORD ORIGIN the initial letters of *polyvinyl chloride*, a polymer of vinyl, from which it is made

**pygmy** (say **pig**-mee) NOUN pygmies
❶ a very small person or thing ❷ a member of certain unusually short peoples of equatorial Africa

**pyjamas** PLURAL NOUN
a loose jacket and trousers that you wear in bed WORD ORIGIN from Persian or Urdu *pay* = leg + *jamah* = clothing: the word originally meant long loose trousers

**pylon** NOUN pylons
a tall framework made of strips of steel, supporting electric cables

**pyramid** NOUN pyramids
❶ a structure with a square base and with

sloping sides that meet in a point at the top
❷ an ancient Egyptian royal tomb shaped like this
➤ **pyramidal** (say pir-**am**-id-al) *ADJECTIVE*

**pyre** *NOUN* pyres
a pile of wood for burning a dead body as part of a funeral ceremony

**python** *NOUN* pythons
a large snake that kills its prey by coiling round and crushing it **WORD ORIGIN** the name of a huge serpent in Greek legend, killed by Apollo

# Qq

**QED** *ABBREVIATION*
*quod erat demonstrandum* (Latin, = which was the thing that had to be proved)

**quack** *VERB* quacks, quacking, quacked
to make the harsh cry of a duck

**quack** *NOUN* quacks
❶ the harsh cry made by a duck ❷ a person who falsely claims to have medical skill or have remedies to cure diseases

**quad** (say kwod) *NOUN* quads
❶ a quadrangle ❷ a quadruplet

**quadrangle** *NOUN* quadrangles
a rectangular courtyard with large buildings round it

**quadrant** *NOUN* quadrants
a quarter of a circle

**quadratic equation** *NOUN* quadratic equations
an equation that involves quantities or variables raised to the power of two, but no higher than two

**quadriceps** *NOUN* quadriceps
the large muscle at the front of the thigh **WORD ORIGIN** Latin, = four-headed (because the muscle is attached at four points)

**quadrilateral** *NOUN* quadrilaterals
a flat geometric shape with four sides

**quadruped** *NOUN* quadrupeds
an animal with four feet

**quadruple** *ADJECTIVE*
❶ four times as much or as many ❷ having four parts

**quadruple** *VERB* quadruples, quadrupling, quadrupled
to become or make something, four times as much or as many

**quadruplet** *NOUN* quadruplets
each of four children born to the same mother at one time

**quaff** (say kwof) *VERB* quaffs, quaffing, quaffed
to drink a lot of something

**quagmire** *NOUN* quagmires
a bog or marsh

**quail** *NOUN* quail or quails
a bird related to the partridge

**quail** *VERB* quails, quailing, quailed
to feel or show fear • *He quailed at the sight of the tiger.*

**quaint** *ADJECTIVE*
attractively odd or old-fashioned • *a quaint old custom*
➤ **quaintly** *ADVERB*

**quake** *VERB* quakes, quaking, quaked
to tremble or shake because you are afraid
• *Quaking with fear, she opened the door.*

**quake** *NOUN* quakes
an earthquake

**Quaker** *NOUN* Quakers
a member of a religious group called the Society of Friends, founded by George Fox in the 17th century **WORD ORIGIN** originally an insult, probably from George Fox's saying that people should 'tremble at the name of the Lord'

**qualification** *NOUN* qualifications
❶ a skill or ability that makes someone suitable for a job ❷ an exam that you have passed or a course of study that you have completed ❸ something that limits the meaning of a remark or statement or makes it less extreme

**qualify** *VERB* qualifies, qualifying, qualified
❶ to become able to do something through having certain qualities or training or by passing an exam or to make someone able to do this • *She qualified as a doctor last year.*
❷ to qualify for a competition is to reach a high enough standard to take part in it • *It is the first time the country has qualified for the World Cup Finals.* ❸ to make a remark or statement less extreme or to limit its meaning
❹ an adjective qualifies a noun when it

describes it or adds meaning to it
➤ **qualified** ADJECTIVE

**quality** NOUN qualities
❶ how good or bad something is • *a performance of the highest quality* ❷ a characteristic; something that is special in a person or thing • *The paper has a shiny quality.*

**qualm** (say kwahm) NOUN qualms
a feeling of worry that what you are doing may not be right • *She had no qualms about accepting the money.*

**quandary** NOUN quandaries
a difficult situation where you are uncertain what to do

**quantity** NOUN quantities
❶ how much of something there is or the number of things there are ❷ a large amount • *It's usually cheaper to buy goods in quantity.*

**quantum leap, quantum jump** NOUN quantum leaps or quantum jumps
a sudden large increase or advance

**quarantine** NOUN
keeping a person or animal isolated in case they have a disease which could spread to others (WORD ORIGIN) from Italian *quaranta* = forty (because the original period of isolation was 40 days)

**quarrel** NOUN quarrels
an angry argument

**quarrel** VERB quarrels, quarrelling, quarrelled
to argue fiercely with someone

**quarrelsome** ADJECTIVE
often quarrelling with people

**quarry** NOUN quarries
❶ an open place where stone or slate is dug or cut out of the ground ❷ an animal or person that is being hunted or pursued

**quarry** VERB quarries, quarrying, quarried
to dig or cut stone or slate from a quarry

**quart** NOUN quarts
a measure for liquids, equal to two pints (or 1.136 litres)

**quarter** NOUN quarters
❶ each of four equal parts into which a thing is or can be divided ❷ three months, one-fourth of a year ❸ a district or region • *People came from every quarter.*
➤ **at close quarters** very close together • *They fought at close quarters.*
➤ **give no quarter** to show no mercy

**quarter** VERB quarters, quartering, quartered
❶ to divide something into quarters ❷ to put soldiers into lodgings

**quarterdeck** NOUN quarterdecks
the part of a ship's upper deck nearest the stern, usually reserved for the officers

**quarter-final** NOUN quarter-finals
each of the matches or rounds before a semi-final, in which there are eight contestants or teams
➤ **quarter-finalist** NOUN

**quarterly** ADJECTIVE & ADVERB
happening or produced once in every three months

**quarterly** NOUN quarterlies
a quarterly magazine

**quarters** PLURAL NOUN
rooms where soldiers or servants live; lodgings

**quartet** NOUN quartets
❶ a group of four musicians ❷ a piece of music for four musicians ❸ a set of four people or things

**quartz** NOUN
a hard mineral, often in crystal form

**quash** VERB quashes, quashing, quashed
to cancel or annul a decision or verdict • *The judges quashed his conviction.*

**quatrain** NOUN quatrains
a stanza with four lines

**quaver** VERB quavers, quavering, quavered
to speak unsteadily because you are afraid or nervous • *'What do you want?' he asked in a quavering voice.*

**quaver** NOUN quavers
❶ a quavering sound ❷ a note in music ( ♪ ) lasting half as long as a crotchet

**quay** (say kee) NOUN quays
a landing place where ships can be tied up for loading and unloading; a wharf

**quayside** NOUN quaysides
the area around a quay

**queasy** ADJECTIVE
feeling slightly sick
➤ **queasily** ADVERB
➤ **queasiness** NOUN

**queen** NOUN queens
❶ a woman who is the ruler of a country through inheriting the position ❷ the wife of a king ❸ a female bee or ant that produces eggs ❹ the most powerful piece in chess ❺ a

553

playing card with a picture of a queen on it
➤ **queenly** ADJECTIVE

**queen mother** NOUN queen mothers
a title given to the widow of a king who has died and who is the mother of the present king or queen

**queer** ADJECTIVE
❶ strange or odd ❷ slightly ill or faint
➤ **queerly** ADVERB
➤ **queerness** NOUN

**quell** VERB quells, quelling, quelled
❶ to crush a rebellion by force ❷ to stop yourself from feeling fear, anger etc. • *I tried to quell my feelings of dread.*

**quench** VERB quenches, quenching, quenched
❶ to satisfy your thirst by drinking ❷ to put out a fire or flame

**querulous** (say **kwe-rew-lus**) ADJECTIVE
complaining all the time
➤ **querulously** ADVERB

**query** (say **kweer-ee**) NOUN queries
a question asking for information or expressing doubt about something

**query** VERB queries, querying, queried
to question whether something is true or correct • *No one queried his explanation.*

**quest** NOUN quests
a long search for something • *the quest for gold*

**question** NOUN questions
❶ a sentence asking something ❷ a problem or subject that needs to be discussed or dealt with • *There is also the question of cost.*
❸ doubt about something • *Whether we shall win is open to question.*
➤ **in question** being discussed or disputed
• *His honesty is not in question.*
➤ **out of the question** impossible or not worth considering

**question** VERB questions, questioning, questioned
❶ to ask someone questions ❷ to say that you are doubtful about something • *A few people questioned the wisdom of that decision.*
➤ **questioner** NOUN

**GRAMMAR**

A **question** is a sentence which asks something and ends with a question mark:

*Have you all written down your answers?*

*Where are you?*

*What was that noise?*

*Could you give me a hand?*

Questions are often introduced by an **interrogative pronoun** such as *how?, what?, when?, where?, who?, whose?* or *why?*

Questions are also often introduced by a form of the auxiliary verb *do*:

*Do you want to watch this film?*

*Did she pass her exams?*

**questionable** ADJECTIVE
causing doubt; not certainly true or honest or advisable

**question mark** NOUN question marks
the punctuation mark (?) placed after a question

**PUNCTUATION**

A **question mark** is used at the end of a sentence to show that it is a question:

*What time is it?*

*Are there wild animals in this wood?*

You also use them to indicate a query in direct speech or in the thought of a character or narrator:

*'Mr Green? Are you there?'*

*Did the label say one spoonful or ten? If only she could remember.*

Question marks are not needed in reported speech:

*The patient opened his eyes and asked me what day of the week it was.*

**questionnaire** NOUN questionnaires
a written set of questions asked to provide information for a survey

**queue** (say **kew**) NOUN queues
a line of people or vehicles waiting for something

**queue** VERB queues, queuing, queued
to wait in a queue • *We have been queuing for over an hour.*

**SPELLING**

**Queue** can be tricky to spell—the letter **u** appears twice.

**quibble** *NOUN* quibbles
a trivial complaint or objection

**quibble** *VERB* quibbles, quibbling, quibbled
to make trivial complaints or objections
**WORD ORIGIN** probably from Latin *quibus* =
what?, for which, for whom (because *quibus*
often appeared in legal documents)

**quiche** (say keesh) *NOUN* quiches
an open tart with a savoury filling

**quick** *ADJECTIVE*
❶ taking only a short time to do something
• *I'll be as quick as I can.* ❷ done in a short
time • *a quick meal* ❸ able to notice or learn
or think quickly

**quick** *ADVERB*
quickly • *Quick! She's coming!*
➤ **quickness** *NOUN*

**quicken** *VERB* quickens, quickening, quickened
❶ to make something quicker • *He quickened
his pace.* ❷ to become quicker • *She felt her
heartbeat quicken.*

**quickly** *ADVERB*
fast; in a short time • *I quickly got dressed.*

**quicksand** *NOUN* quicksands
an area of loose wet deep sand that sucks in
anything resting or falling on top of it

**quicksilver** *NOUN*
(old use) mercury

**quick-witted** *ADJECTIVE*
able to think quickly

**quid** *NOUN* quid (British) (informal)
£1

**quid pro quo** (say kwoh) *NOUN* quid pro quos
something given or done in return for
something **WORD ORIGIN** Latin, = something
for something

**quiet** *ADJECTIVE*
❶ silent; not saying anything • *Be quiet!*
❷ with little sound; not loud or noisy • *He
spoke in a quiet voice.* ❸ calm and peaceful;
without disturbance • *They lead a quiet life.*
❹ quiet colours are soft and not bright
➤ **quietness** *NOUN*

**quiet** *NOUN*
a time when it is calm and there is no noise • *I
was glad of the peace and quiet.*

**quieten** *VERB* quietens, quietening, quietened
(chiefly British) to become quiet or to make a
person or thing quiet • *The crowd gradually
quietened down.*

**quietly** *ADVERB*
❶ without making much noise • *I closed the
door quietly.* ❷ in a quiet voice • *'I want to go
home,' he said quietly.* ❸ without attracting
much attention • *She lived quietly in Ireland
until her death in 1960.*

**quiff** *NOUN* quiffs
(chiefly British) an upright tuft of hair

**quill** *NOUN* quills
❶ a large feather ❷ a pen made from a large
feather ❸ one of the spines on a porcupine or
hedgehog

**quilt** *NOUN* quilts
a cover for a bed filled with soft padding

**quilt** *VERB* quilts, quilting, quilted
to line material with padding and fix it with
lines of stitching

**quin** *NOUN* quins
(British) (informal) a quintuplet

**quince** *NOUN* quinces
a hard pear-shaped fruit used for making jam

**quinine** (say kwin-een) *NOUN*
a bitter-tasting medicine used to cure malaria

**quintessence** *NOUN*
❶ the most essential part of something ❷ a
perfect example of a quality
➤ **quintessential** *ADJECTIVE*
**WORD ORIGIN** from Latin *quinta essentia*
= the fifth essence (after earth, air, fire and
water, which the alchemists thought everything
contained)

**quintet** *NOUN* quintets
❶ a group of five musicians ❷ a piece of
music for five musicians

**quintuplet** *NOUN* quintuplets
each of five children born to the same mother
at one time

**quip** *NOUN* quips
a witty remark

**quip** *VERB* quips, quipping, quipped
to make a witty remark

**quirk** *NOUN* quirks
❶ a peculiarity of a person's behaviour ❷ a
trick of fate
➤ **quirky** *ADJECTIVE*

**quit** *VERB* quits, quitting, quitted or quit
❶ to leave or abandon a place or job
❷ (informal) to stop doing something • *Quit
teasing him!*
➤ **quitter** *NOUN*

a
b
c
d
e
f
g
h
i
j
k
l
m
n
o
p
q
r
s
t
u
v
w
x
y
z

**A B C D E F G H I J K L M N O P Q R S T U V W X Y Z**

**quite** ADVERB
❶ completely or entirely • *I am quite all right.*
❷ rather or fairly; to some extent • *It is quite cold today.*
➤ **quite a** used to show that something is unusual or important • *The news was quite a surprise.*

**quits** ADJECTIVE
people are quits when they are even or equal again and neither owes the other anything or has an advantage over them • *I think you and I are quits now.*

**quiver** VERB quivers, quivering, quivered
to tremble • *He was quivering with excitement.*

**quiver** NOUN quivers
❶ a container for arrows ❷ a trembling movement

**quixotic** (say kwiks-ot-ik) ADJECTIVE
having imaginative or idealistic ideas that are not practical
➤ **quixotically** ADVERB
**WORD ORIGIN** named after Don *Quixote*, hero of a 17th-century Spanish story by Cervantes

**quiz** NOUN quizzes
a series of questions, especially as an entertainment or competition

**quiz** VERB quizzes, quizzing, quizzed
to ask someone a lot of questions

**quizzical** ADJECTIVE
seeming to be asking a question, especially in an amused way • *She gave him a quizzical look.*
➤ **quizzically** ADVERB

**quoit** (say koit) NOUN quoits
a ring thrown at a peg in the game of **quoits**

**quota** NOUN quotas
a fixed or limited amount or share that is allowed or expected • *We are given a quota of work to get through each week.*

**quotation** NOUN quotations
❶ something quoted • *It is a quotation from Shakespeare.* ❷ a statement of how much a piece of work will cost

**GRAMMAR**

Direct speech shows the exact words that a person or character says. The spoken words—and any punctuation that goes with them, such as full stops, exclamation marks or question marks—go inside the quotation marks:

*'Wait! Can you at least tell me your*

*name?' I shouted at the retreating figure.*

Any description of who is speaking (e.g. *she said, I exclaimed*) is separated from the spoken words by a comma or commas:

*'We are planning', said a NASA spokesperson, 'to send a manned expedition to Mars.'*

Reported speech is also called indirect speech. It describes or reports what a person or character says without using their exact words. You do not use quotation marks and the tense of the verb (*were* in this example) follows that of the reporting verb (*said* in the example):

*A NASA spokesperson said that they were planning to send a manned expedition to Mars.*

You can also leave out the word *that* at the beginning of the reported speech:

*A NASA spokesperson said they were planning to send a manned expedition to Mars.*

**quotation marks** PLURAL NOUN
inverted commas (" " or ' ') used to mark direct speech or a quotation

**PUNCTUATION**

Quotation marks (also known as inverted commas or speech marks) are used in pairs and can surround a single word or phrase, or a longer piece of text. They are used:

in direct speech to show which words are being spoken:

*'Look!' said a voice behind me. 'Look at the sky!'*

to highlight a word to which you are referring:

*The words 'turn back' were scratched on the door.*

to show that word is being used in a slightly odd way, for example because it is a slang word:

*Disneyland wasn't my idea of a place to 'chill' on holiday.*

to show that something is the title of a poem, story, piece of music, etc.

*She stood up and recited Kipling's poem 'If'.*

to enclose direct quotations from a speech, book, play or film:

*Which film contains the famous line, 'Toto, I've a feeling we're not in Kansas anymore'?*

Pairs of quotation marks can be single (' ') or double (" "), but are never mixed. You can, however, use a pair of double quotation marks within a pair of single quotation marks:

*'When I say, "Action", start the gladiator scene again.'*

**quote** VERB quotes, quoting, quoted
❶ to repeat words that were first written or spoken by someone else ❷ to mention an example of something to support what you are saying ❸ to state the price of goods or services that you can supply

**quote** NOUN quotes
a quotation

**quoth** VERB (old use)
said • *'My lord,' quoth he.*

**quotient** (say **kwoh**-shent) NOUN quotients
the result of dividing one number by another. Compare with **product**.

**Qur'an** NOUN
another spelling of Koran

# Rr

**rabbi** (say **rab**-eye) NOUN rabbis
a Jewish religious leader
**WORD ORIGIN** Hebrew, = my master

**rabbit** NOUN rabbits
a furry animal with long ears that digs burrows

**rabble** NOUN rabbles
a noisy or disorderly crowd or mob

**rabid** (say **rab**-id) ADJECTIVE
❶ extreme or fanatical • *a rabid fascist*
❷ suffering from rabies

**rabies** (say **ray**-beez) NOUN
a fatal disease that affects dogs and other mammals and can be passed to humans by the bite of an infected animal

**raccoon** NOUN raccoons or raccoon
a North American animal with a bushy, striped tail and greyish-brown fur

**race** NOUN races
❶ a sports contest in which the fastest competitor wins ❷ a competition to be the first to reach a particular place or to do something • *the race to land people on the Moon* ❸ a very large group of people thought to have the same ancestors and with physical characteristics (e.g. colour of skin and hair, shape of eyes and nose) that differ from those of other groups ❹ racial origin • *discrimination on grounds of race*

**race** VERB races, racing, raced
❶ to compete in a race • *I'll race you home.*
❷ to move very fast • *She raced up the stairs.*

**racecourse** NOUN racecourses
a place where horse races are run

**racehorse** NOUN racehorses
a horse bred or kept for racing

**racer** NOUN racers
a competitor in a race • *a wheelchair racer*

**race relations** NOUN
relationships between people of different races in the same country

**racetrack** NOUN racetracks
a track for horse or vehicle races

**racial** (say **ray**-shul) ADJECTIVE
to do with a particular race or based on race • *different racial groups*
➤ **racially** ADVERB

**racism** (say **ray**-sizm) NOUN
❶ discrimination against or hostility towards people of other races ❷ belief that a particular race of people is better than others
➤ **racist** NOUN & ADJECTIVE

**rack** NOUN racks
❶ a framework used as a shelf or container • *a plate rack* ❷ an ancient device for torturing people by stretching them ❸ a bar or rail with cogs into which the cogs of a gear or wheel fit
➤ **go to rack and ruin** to gradually become worse in condition due to neglect

**rack** VERB racks, racking, racked
to be racked with physical or mental pain is to be tormented by it • *He was racked with*

a
b
c
d
e
f
g
h
i
j
k
l
m
n
o
p
q
r
s
t
u
v
w
x
y
z

guilt.
> **rack your brains** to think hard in trying to remember something or solve a problem

**racket** NOUN rackets
❶ a bat with strings stretched across a frame, used in tennis, badminton and squash ❷ a loud noise or din ❸ a dishonest or illegal business • *a drugs racket*

**racketeer** NOUN racketeers
a person involved in a dishonest or illegal business
> **racketeering** NOUN

**racoon** NOUN racoons or racoon
a different spelling of **raccoon**

**racquet** NOUN racquets
a different spelling of **racket**

**racy** ADJECTIVE racier, raciest
lively and slightly shocking in style • *She gave a racy account of her travels.*

**radar** NOUN
a system or apparatus that uses radio waves to show on a screen the position of ships, planes, etc. that cannot be seen because of distance or poor visibility
> **be on someone's radar** to have come to someone's attention
( WORD ORIGIN ) from the initial letters of *radio detection and ranging*

**radial** ADJECTIVE
❶ to do with rays or radii ❷ having spokes or lines that radiate from a central point
> **radially** ADVERB

**radiant** ADJECTIVE
❶ radiating light or heat • *the radiant sun*
❷ transmitted by radiation • *radiant heat*
❸ looking very bright and happy • *a radiant smile*
> **radiantly** ADVERB
> **radiance** NOUN

**radiate** VERB radiates, radiating, radiated
❶ to send out light, heat or other energy in rays ❷ to give out a strong feeling or quality • *She radiated confidence.* ❸ to spread out from a central point like the spokes of a wheel • *The city's streets radiate from the central square.*

**radiation** NOUN
❶ light, heat or other energy given out by something ❷ the energy or particles sent out by a radioactive substance ❸ the process of radiating light, heat or other energy

**radiator** NOUN radiators
❶ a device that gives out heat, especially a metal case that is heated electrically or through which steam or hot water flows ❷ a device that cools the engine of a motor vehicle

**radical** ADJECTIVE
❶ basic and thorough; going right to the root of something • *Radical changes are needed.*
❷ wanting to make great social or political reforms • *a radical politician*
> **radically** ADVERB

**radical** NOUN radicals
a person who wants to make great social or political reforms ( WORD ORIGIN ) from Latin *radicis* = of a root

**radicchio** (say ra-**dee**-ki-oh) NOUN
a kind of chicory with dark red leaves

**radio** NOUN radios
❶ the process of sending and receiving sound or pictures by means of electromagnetic waves ❷ an apparatus for receiving radio programmes or for sending or receiving radio messages ❸ sound broadcasting

**radio** VERB radios, radioing, radioed
to send a message to someone by radio

**radioactive** ADJECTIVE
having atoms that break up spontaneously and send out radiation which produces electrical and chemical effects and penetrates things
> **radioactivity** NOUN

**radio beacon** NOUN radio beacons
an instrument that sends out radio signals, which aircraft use to find their way

**radiocarbon dating** NOUN
carbon dating

**radiography** NOUN
the production of X-ray photographs
> **radiographer** NOUN

**radiology** NOUN
the study of X-rays and similar radiation, especially in treating diseases
> **radiologist** NOUN

**radio telescope** NOUN radio telescopes
an instrument that can detect radio waves from space

**radiotherapy** NOUN
the use of radioactive substances in treating diseases such as cancer

**radish** NOUN radishes
a small hard round red vegetable with a hot taste, eaten raw in salads

**radium** NOUN
a radioactive substance found in pitchblende, often used in radiotherapy

**radius** NOUN radii or radiuses
❶ a straight line from the centre of a circle to the circumference; the length of this line ❷ a range or distance from a central point • *The school takes pupils living within a radius of ten kilometres.*

**radon** NOUN
a radioactive gas used in radiotherapy

**RAF** ABBREVIATION
Royal Air Force

**raffia** NOUN
soft fibre from the leaves of a kind of palm tree, used for making mats and baskets

**raffle** NOUN raffles
a way of raising money, usually for a charity, by selling numbered tickets, some of which win prizes

**raffle** VERB raffles, raffling, raffled
to offer something as a prize in a raffle

**raft** NOUN rafts
❶ a flat floating structure made of wood etc., used as a boat ❷ a large number or amount of things • *a raft of new proposals*

**rafter** NOUN rafters
any of the long sloping pieces of wood that hold up a roof

**rag** NOUN rags
❶ an old or torn piece of cloth ❷ a piece of ragtime music ❸ (*British*) a series of entertainments and activities held by students to collect money for charity
➤ **dressed in rags** wearing old and torn clothes

**rag** VERB rags, ragging, ragged
(*informal*) to tease someone

**rage** NOUN rages
great or violent anger
➤ **all the rage** very popular or fashionable for a time

**rage** VERB rages, raging, raged
❶ to be very angry ❷ to continue violently or with great force • *The storm was still raging outside.*

**ragged** (say rag-id) ADJECTIVE
❶ torn or frayed ❷ wearing torn clothes

❸ not smooth or controlled • *a ragged performance*

**ragtime** NOUN
a kind of jazz music played on the piano

**raid** NOUN raids
❶ a sudden attack ❷ a surprise visit by police to arrest people or seize illegal goods

**raid** VERB raids, raiding, raided
to make a raid on a place
➤ **raider** NOUN

**rail** NOUN rails
❶ a level or sloping bar for hanging things on or forming part of a fence or banisters ❷ a long metal bar forming part of a railway track
➤ **by rail** on a train

**rail** VERB rails, railing, railed
to complain angrily or bitterly about something • *She railed against the injustice of it all.*

**railings** PLURAL NOUN
a fence made of metal bars

**railroad** NOUN railroads
(*North American*) a railway

**railway** NOUN (*British*)
❶ the parallel metal bars that trains travel on ❷ a system of transport using rails

**raiment** NOUN (*old use*)
clothing

**rain** NOUN
drops of water that fall from the sky

**rain** VERB rains, raining, rained
❶ it is raining when rain is falling • *It was raining heavily.* ❷ to come down in large amounts • *Bombs rained down on the city.* ❸ to send something down in large amounts • *They rained blows on him.*

**rainbow** NOUN rainbows
an arch of all the colours of the spectrum formed in the sky when the sun shines through rain

**raincoat** NOUN raincoats
a waterproof coat

**raindrop** NOUN raindrops
a single drop of rain

**rainfall** NOUN
the amount of rain that falls in a particular place or time

**rainforest** NOUN rainforests
a dense tropical forest in an area of very heavy rainfall

a b c d e f g h i j k l m n o p q r s t u v w x y z

**rainy** ADJECTIVE
having a lot of rainfall • *the rainy season*

**raise** VERB raises, raising, raised
❶ to move something to a higher place or an upright position ❷ to increase the amount or level of something • *We are trying to raise standards.* ❸ to succeed in collecting an amount of money • *The event raised €2000 for the earthquake appeal.* ❹ to bring up young children or animals • *She had to raise her family alone.* ❺ to mention or put something forward for people to think about • *We raised several objections.* ❻ to raise a laugh or smile is to make people laugh or smile ❼ to raise your voice is to speak more loudly

**raisin** NOUN raisins
a dried grape

**raison d'être** (say ray-zawn **detr**) NOUN
raisons d'être
the reason or purpose for a thing's existence
**WORD ORIGIN** French, = reason for being

**Raj** (say rahj) NOUN
the period of Indian history when the country was ruled by Britain

**raja, rajah** NOUN rajas, rajahs
an Indian king or prince. Compare with **ranee**.

**rake** NOUN rakes
❶ a gardening tool with a row of short spikes fixed to a long handle ❷ (*old use*) a man who lives an irresponsible and immoral life

**rake** VERB rakes, raking, raked
❶ to gather or smooth something with a rake • *He was in the garden raking up leaves.* ❷ to search through something • *I raked around in my desk for the letter.*
➤ **rake it in** (*informal*) to make a lot of money
➤ **rake something up** to start talking about something that it would be better to forget • *Don't rake all that up again.*

**rakish** (say **ray**-kish) ADJECTIVE
jaunty and dashing in appearance • *His hat was tilted at a rakish angle.*
➤ **rakishly** ADVERB

**rally** NOUN rallies
❶ a large meeting to support something or share an interest ❷ a competition to test skill in driving • *the Monte Carlo Rally* ❸ an exchange of strokes in tennis, squash, etc. before a point is won

**rally** VERB rallies, rallying, rallied
❶ to bring people together for a united effort

• *They rallied support for the campaign.* ❷ to come together to help or support someone • *My family all rallied round.* ❸ to improve or become stronger after an illness or setback • *She came fourth in the 800m, but rallied to win the 400m.*

**RAM** ABBREVIATION
(*in computing*) random-access memory, with contents that can be retrieved or stored directly without having to read through items already stored

**ram** NOUN rams
❶ a male sheep ❷ a part of a machine that is used for hitting something very hard

**ram** VERB rams, ramming, rammed
❶ to push one thing hard against another • *He quickly rammed the gun into his pocket.* ❷ to crash into another vehicle

**Ramadan** NOUN
the ninth month of the Muslim year, when Muslims do not eat or drink between sunrise and sunset

**ramble** NOUN rambles
a long walk in the countryside

**ramble** VERB rambles, rambling, rambled
❶ to go for a ramble; to wander ❷ to talk a lot without keeping to the subject • *Halfway through the speech he began to ramble.*
➤ **rambler** NOUN

**rambling** ADJECTIVE
❶ confused and wandering from one subject to another • *a rambling speech* ❷ growing or spreading in many directions • *a rambling old house*

**ramifications** PLURAL NOUN
the many effects of a plan or action • *The decision had far-reaching ramifications.*

**ramp** NOUN ramps
a slope joining two different levels

**rampage** VERB rampages, rampaging, rampaged
to rush about wildly or destructively • *a herd of rampaging elephants*
➤ **on the rampage** rushing about wildly

**rampant** ADJECTIVE
❶ growing or spreading uncontrollably • *Disease was rampant in the poorer districts.* ❷ (said about an animal on coats of arms) standing upright on a hind leg • *a lion rampant*

**rampart** NOUN ramparts
a wide bank of earth built as a fortification or a wall on top of this

**ramrod** NOUN ramrods
a straight rod formerly used for ramming an explosive into a gun
➤ **like a ramrod** very stiff and straight

**ramshackle** ADJECTIVE
badly made and rickety • *a ramshackle hut*

**ranch** NOUN ranches
a large cattle farm in North America

**rancid** ADJECTIVE
smelling or tasting unpleasant like stale fat

**rancour** (say **rank**-er) NOUN
bitter resentment or ill will
➤ **rancorous** ADJECTIVE

**random** NOUN
➤ **at random** using no particular order or method • *The numbers were chosen at random.*

**random** ADJECTIVE
done or taken at random • *a random sample*
➤ **randomly** ADVERB

**ranee** (say **rah**-nee) NOUN ranees
a raja's wife or widow

**range** NOUN ranges
❶ a set of different things of the same type • *a wide range of backgrounds* • *a lovely range of colours* ❷ the limits between which something varies • *the age range 15 to 18* ❸ the distance that a gun can shoot, an aircraft can travel or a sound can be heard ❹ a place with targets for shooting practice ❺ a line or series of mountains or hills ❻ a kitchen fireplace with ovens

**range** VERB ranges, ranging, ranged
❶ to exist or vary between two limits • *Prices ranged from £1 to £50.* ❷ to arrange things in a certain way • *The desks were ranged in straight lines.* ❸ to wander or move over a wide area • *Hens ranged all over the farm.*

**Ranger** NOUN Rangers
a senior Guide

**ranger** NOUN rangers
someone who looks after or patrols a park or forest

**rank** NOUN ranks
❶ a position in a series of different levels • *He holds the rank of sergeant.* ❷ a line of people or things • *ranks of marching soldiers* ❸ a place where taxis stand to wait for customers

**rank** VERB ranks, ranking, ranked
❶ to have a certain rank or place • *She ranks among the greatest novelists.* ❷ to put things in order according to their rank • *The puzzles are ranked in order of difficulty.*

**rank** ADJECTIVE ranker, rankest
❶ smelling very unpleasant ❷ unmistakably bad; complete • *rank stupidity* ❸ growing too thickly and coarsely

**rank and file** NOUN
the ordinary people or soldiers, not the leaders

**rankle** VERB rankles, rankling, rankled
to cause lasting annoyance or resentment • *What she said that night still rankled with him.*

**ransack** VERB ransacks, ransacking, ransacked
❶ to search a place thoroughly or roughly ❷ to rob or pillage a place

**ransom** NOUN ransoms
money that has to be paid for a prisoner to be set free
➤ **hold someone to ransom** to keep someone a prisoner and demand a ransom

**ransom** VERB ransoms, ransoming, ransomed
❶ to free someone by paying a ransom ❷ to get a ransom for someone

**rant** VERB rants, ranting, ranted
to speak or shout loudly and angrily

**rant** NOUN rants
a spell of ranting

**rap** VERB raps, rapping, rapped
❶ to knock quickly and loudly • *He rapped at the door with his stick.* ❷ to speak words rapidly in rhythm to a strong musical beat ❸ (*informal*) to criticize someone strongly

**rap** NOUN raps
❶ a rapping movement or sound • *There was a rap at the door.* ❷ a type of pop music in which you speak words rapidly in rhythm to a strong musical beat
➤ **take the rap** (*informal*) to take the blame or punishment for something

**rapacious** (say ra-**pay**-shus) ADJECTIVE
greedy and grasping, especially for money
➤ **rapacity** NOUN

**rape** NOUN rapes
❶ the crime of forcing someone to have sexual intercourse when they do not want to ❷ a plant with bright yellow flowers, grown as food for sheep and for its seed from which oil is obtained

**rape** VERB rapes, raping, raped
to force someone to have sexual intercourse
➤ **rapist** NOUN

**rapid** ADJECTIVE
moving or happening very quickly; swift • *She is making rapid progress.*
➤ **rapidly** ADVERB
➤ **rapidity** NOUN

**rapids** PLURAL NOUN
part of a river where the water flows very quickly

**rapier** NOUN rapiers
a thin lightweight sword

**rapport** (say rap-**or**) NOUN
a friendly and understanding relationship between people

**rapt** ADJECTIVE
so interested and absorbed in something that you do not notice anything else • *She listened with rapt attention.*

**rapture** NOUN
very great joy or delight
➤ **rapturous** ADJECTIVE
➤ **rapturously** ADVERB

**rare** ADJECTIVE rarer, rarest
❶ unusual; not often found or happening • *a rare species of butterfly* ❷ meat is rare when it is lightly cooked so that the inside is still red

**rarefied** ADJECTIVE
❶ rarefied air is thin and below normal pressure ❷ remote from everyday life • *the rarefied atmosphere of the university*

**rarely** ADVERB
not very often • *She is rarely seen in public.*

**rarity** NOUN rarities
❶ rareness ❷ something uncommon; a thing valued because it is rare

**rascal** NOUN rascals
a dishonest or mischievous person
➤ **rascally** ADJECTIVE

**rash** ADJECTIVE
doing something or done without thinking of the possible risks or effects • *It was a rash decision.*
➤ **rashly** ADVERB
➤ **rashness** NOUN

**rash** NOUN rashes
❶ an outbreak of red spots or patches on the skin ❷ a number of unwelcome events happening in a short time • *a rash of accidents*

**rasher** NOUN rashers
a slice of bacon

**rasp** NOUN rasps
❶ a file with sharp points on its surface ❷ a rough grating sound

**rasp** VERB rasps, rasping, rasped
❶ to say something in a rough unpleasant voice • *'Come with me,' he rasped.* ❷ to make a rough grating sound or effect • *a rasping cough* ❸ to scrape something roughly

**raspberry** NOUN raspberries
a small soft red fruit

**Rastafarian** NOUN Rastafarians
a member of a religious group that started in Jamaica WORD ORIGIN from *Ras Tafari* (*ras* = chief), the title of a former Ethiopian king whom the group reveres

**rat** NOUN rats
❶ an animal like a large mouse ❷ an unpleasant or treacherous person

**ratchet** NOUN ratchets
a row of notches on a bar or wheel in which a device catches to prevent it running backwards

**rate** NOUN rates
❶ how fast or how often something happens • *Crime was increasing at a great rate.* ❷ a charge, cost or value • *Postage rates went up.* ❸ quality or standard • *first-rate*
➤ **at any rate** anyway; whatever else is true
➤ **at this rate** if this is typical or true

**rate** VERB rates, rating, rated
❶ to say how good you think something is • *Drivers rate the new car very highly.* ❷ to regard something in a certain way • *I rated the show as a success.*

**rates** PLURAL NOUN
a local tax paid by owners of commercial land and buildings

**rather** ADVERB
❶ slightly or quite • *It's rather dark in there.* ❷ you would rather do one thing than another thing if you would prefer to do it • *I would rather wait until tomorrow.* ❸ more exactly; instead of • *She lay down or rather fell, on the bed.* • *He is lazy rather than stupid.* ❹ (informal) definitely, yes • *'Will you come?' 'Rather!'*

**ratify** VERB ratifies, ratifying, ratified
to confirm or agree to something officially • *They ratified the treaty.*
➤ **ratification** NOUN

**rating** NOUN ratings
❶ the way something is rated ❷ a sailor who is not an officer

**ratio** (say **ray**-shee-oh) NOUN ratios
❶ the relationship between two numbers, showing how many times one number goes into the other • *The ratio of 2 to 10 = 2:10 =* ²⁄₁₀ = ⅕ ❷ proportion • *Mix flour and butter in the ratio of two to one.* (= two measures of flour to one measure of butter)

**ration** NOUN rations
❶ a fixed amount allowed to one person ❷ rations are a fixed daily amount of food given to a soldier or member of an expedition

**ration** VERB rations, rationing, rationed
to share something out in fixed amounts • *We had to ration the water carefully.*

**rational** ADJECTIVE
❶ reasonable or sensible; based on reason • *There must be a rational explanation for this.* ❷ able to reason and make sensible decisions • *No rational person would ever behave like that.*
➤ **rationally** ADVERB
➤ **rationality** NOUN

**rationalize** (also **rationalise**) VERB
rationalizes, rationalizing, rationalized
❶ to make a thing logical and consistent • *Attempts to rationalize English spelling have failed.* ❷ to justify something by inventing a reasonable explanation for it • *She rationalized her meanness by calling it economy.* ❸ to make a company or industry more efficient by reorganizing it
➤ **rationalization** NOUN

**rat race** NOUN
a continuous struggle for success in a career or business

**rattle** VERB rattles, rattling, rattled
❶ to make a series of short sharp hard sounds • *The windows were rattling in the wind.* ❷ to move quickly with a rattling noise • *A train rattled by.* ❸ to make a person feel nervous or flustered
➤ **rattle something off** to say or recite something rapidly

**rattle** NOUN rattles
❶ a rattling sound ❷ a device or baby's toy that rattles

**rattlesnake** NOUN rattlesnakes
a poisonous American snake with a tail that rattles

**rattling** ADJECTIVE
vigorous or brisk • *a rattling pace*

**ratty** ADJECTIVE rattier, rattiest (*informal*)
angry or irritable

**raucous** (say **raw**-kus) ADJECTIVE
sounding loud and harsh • *raucous laughter*

**ravage** VERB ravages, ravaging, ravaged
to do great damage to something; to devastate a place or thing • *The country has been ravaged by war.*

**ravages** PLURAL NOUN
damaging effects • *the ravages of war*

**rave** VERB raves, raving, raved
❶ to talk wildly or angrily or madly ❷ to talk enthusiastically about something • *He's been raving about the band he saw last night.*

**rave** NOUN raves (*informal*) a large party or event with dancing to loud fast electronic music
➤ **rave review** a very enthusiastic review

**raven** NOUN ravens
a large black bird, related to the crow

**ravenous** ADJECTIVE
very hungry
➤ **ravenously** ADVERB

**ravine** (say ra-**veen**) NOUN ravines
a deep narrow gorge or valley
**WORD ORIGIN** French, = a rush of water (because a ravine is cut by rushing water)

**ravings** PLURAL NOUN
wild talk that makes no sense

**ravioli** NOUN
small squares of pasta filled with meat and served with a sauce

**ravishing** ADJECTIVE
very beautiful

**raw** ADJECTIVE
❶ not cooked ❷ in the natural state; not yet processed • *raw sugar* ❸ without much experience • *raw recruits* ❹ with the skin removed • *a raw wound* ❺ cold and damp • *a raw morning*
➤ **a raw deal** unfair treatment
➤ **rawness** NOUN

**raw material** NOUN raw materials
natural substances used in industry • *iron ore, coal and other raw materials*

**ray** NOUN rays
❶ a thin line of light, heat or other radiation ❷ each of a set of lines or parts extending

from a centre ❸ a trace of something • *a ray of hope* ❹ **ray** or **rays** a large sea fish with a flat body and a long tail

**rayon** NOUN
a synthetic fibre or cloth made from cellulose
WORD ORIGIN a made-up word, probably based on French *rayon* = a ray of light (because of its shiny surface)

**raze** VERB razes, razing, razed
to destroy a building or town completely
• *The fort was razed to the ground.*

**razor** NOUN razors
a device with a very sharp blade, especially one used for shaving
➤ **razor blade** NOUN

**razzmatazz** NOUN (*informal*)
showy publicity or activity

**RC** ABBREVIATION
Roman Catholic

**re-** PREFIX
again (as in *rebuild*)

**reach** VERB reaches, reaching, reached
❶ to go as far as a place or point; to arrive at a place or thing ❷ to stretch out your hand to get or touch something ❸ to succeed in achieving something • *The cheetah can reach a speed of 70 mph.* • *Have you reached a decision?*

**reach** NOUN reaches
❶ the distance a person or thing can reach ❷ a distance you can easily travel • *We live within reach of the sea.*

**react** VERB reacts, reacting, reacted
❶ to respond to something; to have a reaction • *How did she react to the news?* ❷ to undergo a chemical change

**reaction** NOUN reactions
❶ an effect or feeling produced in one person or thing by another • *My immediate reaction was one of shock.* ❷ a chemical change caused when substances act upon each other
➤ **reactions** your ability to move quickly in response to something • *Racing drivers need to have quick reactions.*

**reactor** NOUN reactors
an apparatus for producing nuclear power in a controlled way

**read** VERB reads, reading, read (say red)
❶ to look at something written or printed and understand it or say it aloud ❷ a computer reads data when it copies, searches or extracts it ❸ to show a particular number or amount • *The thermometer reads 20° Celsius.* ❹ to study a subject at university

SPELLING
The past tense of **read** is the same spelling but rhymes with **red**.

**readable** ADJECTIVE
❶ easy or enjoyable to read • *The book is very readable.* ❷ clear and able to be read • *The writing was faint but still readable.*

**reader** NOUN readers
❶ a person who reads ❷ a device that reads or displays data ❸ a book that helps someone learn to read

**readership** NOUN readerships
the readers of a newspaper or magazine; the number of these

**readily** (say red-il-ee) ADVERB
❶ willingly or eagerly • *She readily agreed to help.* ❷ easily; without any difficulty • *All the ingredients you need are readily available.*

**readiness** NOUN
❶ being ready or prepared for something
• *All was in readiness for the journey.*
❷ being willing to do something • *She expressed her readiness to help them.*

**reading** NOUN readings
❶ the activity of reading books and other forms of writing • *He loves reading.* ❷ the figure shown on a meter, gauge or other instrument ❸ a gathering of people at which something is read aloud • *a poetry reading*

**ready** ADJECTIVE readier, readiest
❶ fully prepared to do something; completed and able to be used • *Are you ready to go?*
• *The meal's ready.* ❷ willing to do something ❸ quick and clever • *a ready wit*
➤ **at the ready** ready for use or action

**ready** ADVERB
beforehand • *This meat is ready cooked.*

**ready-made** ADJECTIVE
made already and so able to be used or served immediately

**reagent** NOUN reagents
a substance used in a chemical reaction, especially to detect another substance

**real** ADJECTIVE
❶ actually existing, not imaginary • *The character is based on a real person.* ❷ actual or true • *That isn't his real name.* ❸ genuine; not an imitation • *real pearls*

**real estate** NOUN (North American)
property consisting of land and buildings

**realism** NOUN
seeing or showing things as they really are
➤ **realist** NOUN

**realistic** ADJECTIVE
❶ true to life • *a realistic painting* ❷ seeing things as they really are • *She is realistic about her chances of winning.*
➤ **realistically** ADVERB

**reality** NOUN realities
❶ what is real • *You must face reality.*
❷ something real • *Her worst fears had become a reality.*

**reality TV** NOUN
television shows that are based on real people, not actors, in real situations

**realization** (also **realisation**) NOUN
realizing something • *Then came the realization of what he had done.*

**realize** (also **realise**) VERB realizes, realizing, realized
❶ to be fully aware of something; to accept something as true • *He suddenly realized that he was sitting on an ants' nest.* ❷ to make a hope or plan happen • *She realized her ambition to become a racing driver.* ❸ to obtain money in exchange for something by selling it

**really** ADVERB
❶ truly or in fact • *Tell me what really happened.* ❷ very • *She's really clever.*

SPELLING
There is a double l in really.

**realm** (say relm) NOUN realms
❶ a kingdom ❷ an area of knowledge or interest • *the realms of science*

**reams** PLURAL NOUN
a large quantity of writing or information

**reap** VERB reaps, reaping, reaped
❶ to cut down and gather corn when it is ripe ❷ to gain something as the result of something you have done • *They are now reaping the benefits of all that training.*
➤ **reaper** NOUN

**reappear** VERB reappears, reappearing, reappeared
to appear again
➤ **reappearance** NOUN

**reappraise** VERB reappraises, reappraising, reappraised
to think about or examine something again
➤ **reappraisal** NOUN

**rear** NOUN
the back part of something

**rear** ADJECTIVE
placed or found at the back • *a rear wheel*

**rear** VERB rears, rearing, reared
❶ to care for and bring up young children or animals ❷ a horse rears when it rises up on its hind legs so that its front legs are in the air • *My horse reared up in fright.* ❸ to rise up over you • *A huge crane reared up in front of us.*

**rearguard** NOUN rearguards
troops protecting the rear of an army
➤ **fight a rearguard action** to go on defending or resisting something even though you are losing

**rearrange** VERB rearranges, rearranging, rearranged
to arrange something in a different way or order • *Will you help me rearrange the furniture?*
➤ **rearrangement** NOUN

**reason** NOUN reasons
❶ a cause or explanation of something; why something happens • *What is the reason for the delay?* ❷ reasoning; common sense • *He wouldn't listen to reason.*

**reason** VERB reasons, reasoning, reasoned
❶ to use your ability to think and draw conclusions ❷ to try to persuade someone by giving reasons • *It's no use trying to reason with her.*

**reasonable** ADJECTIVE
❶ ready to use or listen to reason; sensible or logical ❷ fair or moderate; not expensive • *These are reasonable prices for what you get* ❸ acceptable or fairly good • *a reasonable standard of living*

**reasonably** ADVERB
❶ in a reasonable way; sensibly • *They were behaving quite reasonably.* ❷ fairly or quite • *They get on reasonably well.*

**reassure** VERB reassures, reassuring, reassured
to restore someone's confidence by removing doubts and fears • *I tried to reassure them that there was nothing wrong.*
➤ **reassurance** NOUN

**rebate** NOUN rebates
a reduction in the amount to be paid; a partial refund

**rebel** (say rib-**el**) VERB rebels, rebelling, rebelled
to refuse to obey someone in authority, especially the government; to fight against the rulers of your own country

**rebel** (say **reb**-el) NOUN rebels
❶ someone who rejects accepted standards of behaviour ❷ someone who fights against their country's government because they want things to change WORD ORIGIN from Latin *bellum* = war (originally referring to a defeated enemy who began to fight again)

**rebellion** NOUN rebellions
❶ rebelling against authority ❷ organized armed resistance to the government; a revolt

**rebellious** ADJECTIVE
often refusing to obey authority; likely to rebel • *a rebellious child*

**rebirth** NOUN
a return to life or activity; a revival of something • *the seasonal cycle of death and rebirth*

**rebound** VERB rebounds, rebounding, rebounded
to bounce back after hitting something

**rebound** NOUN
➤ **on the rebound** to hit a ball on the rebound is to hit it when it has bounced up or back

**rebuff** NOUN rebuffs
an unkind refusal; a snub

**rebuff** VERB rebuffs, rebuffing, rebuffed
to give someone a rebuff

**rebuild** VERB rebuilds, rebuilding, rebuilt
to build something again after it has been destroyed

**rebuke** VERB rebukes, rebuking, rebuked
to speak severely to a person who has done wrong

**rebuke** NOUN rebukes
a sharp or severe criticism

**recalcitrant** ADJECTIVE
disobedient or uncooperative
➤ **recalcitrance** NOUN

**recall** VERB recalls, recalling, recalled
❶ to remember something from the past • *Can you recall exactly what happened?* ❷ to tell a person to come back ❸ to ask for a product to be returned because it is faulty

**recall** NOUN
❶ the ability to remember; remembering

something ❷ an order for a person to return or for a thing to be returned

**recap** VERB recaps, recapping, recapped (*informal*)
to summarize what has been said
➤ **recap** NOUN

**recapitulate** VERB recapitulates, recapitulating, recapitulated
to state again the main points of what has been said
➤ **recapitulation** NOUN

**recapture** VERB recaptures, recapturing, recaptured
❶ to catch a person or animal that has escaped ❷ to take back a place that was taken from you • *Saladin recaptured Jerusalem in 1187.* ❸ to bring or get back a mood or feeling • *He was trying to recapture the happiness of his youth.*
➤ **recapture** NOUN

**recede** VERB recedes, receding, receded
❶ to move back or away • *The floods have receded.* ❷ to become less strong or severe • *His fear began to recede.* ❸ a man's hair is receding when he starts to go bald at the front of his head

**receipt** (say ris-**eet**) NOUN receipts
❶ a written statement that money has been paid or something has been received ❷ receiving something

**receive** VERB receives, receiving, received
❶ to take or get something that is given or sent to you ❷ to experience something • *He received injuries to his face and hands.* ❸ to react to something in a certain way • *The play was well received by the critics.* ❹ to greet a guest or visitor

SPELLING
In receive, e before i is the right way round.

**receiver** NOUN receivers
❶ a person or thing that receives something ❷ a radio or television set that receives broadcasts ❸ the part of a telephone that receives the sound and that you hold to your ear ❹ an official who takes charge of a bankrupt person's property ❺ a person who buys and sells stolen goods

**recent** ADJECTIVE
happening or made or done a short time ago • *Please enclose a recent photograph.*

A
B
C
D
E
F
G
H
I
J
K
L
M
N
O
P
Q
R
S
T
U
V
W
X
Y
Z

**recently** ADVERB
not long ago • *I received an email from her recently.*

**receptacle** NOUN receptacles
something for holding or containing what is put into it

**reception** NOUN receptions
❶ the type of welcome that a person or thing receives • *We were given a friendly reception.* ❷ a formal party to receive guests • *a wedding reception* ❸ a place in a hotel or office where visitors are greeted and registered ❹ the first class in an infant school ❺ the quality of television or radio signals • *We have poor reception because of the surrounding hills.*

**receptionist** NOUN receptionists
a person whose job is to greet and deal with visitors, clients or patients

**receptive** ADJECTIVE
quick or willing to receive ideas

**recess** (say ris-**ess**) NOUN recesses
❶ a section of a wall that is set back from the main part; an alcove ❷ a time when work or business is stopped for a while

**recession** NOUN recessions
a reduction in a country's trade or prosperity

**recharge** VERB recharges, recharging, recharged
to put more electrical power into a battery
➤ **rechargeable** ADJECTIVE

**recipe** (say **ress**-ip-ee) NOUN recipes
a list of ingredients and instructions for preparing or cooking food
**WORD ORIGIN** Latin, = take (which was used at the beginning of a list of ingredients)

**recipient** NOUN recipients
a person who receives something

**reciprocal** (say ris-**ip**-rok-al) ADJECTIVE
given or done in return for the same thing that is given to or done for you; mutual • *The arrangement is reciprocal: they help us and we help them.*

**reciprocal** NOUN reciprocals
a reversed fraction • ³⁄₂ is the reciprocal of ²⁄₃

**reciprocate** VERB reciprocates, reciprocating, reciprocated
to behave or feel towards someone in the same way as they behave or feel towards you; to do the same thing in return • *She did not reciprocate his love.*

**recital** NOUN recitals
❶ reciting something ❷ a musical entertainment given by one performer or group

**recite** VERB recites, reciting, recited
to say a poem or other piece of writing aloud from memory
➤ **recitation** NOUN

**reckless** ADJECTIVE
rash; ignoring risk or danger • *He was a reckless driver.*
➤ **recklessly** ADVERB
➤ **recklessness** NOUN

**reckon** VERB reckons, reckoning, reckoned
❶ to have something as an opinion; to think or believe something • *I reckon it's going to rain.* ❷ to calculate an amount or total
➤ **reckon on something** to expect something and base your plans on it • *They hadn't reckoned on it being so expensive.*
➤ **reckon with something** to think about or deal with something • *We didn't reckon with the rail strike when we planned our journey.*

**reclaim** VERB reclaims, reclaiming, reclaimed
❶ to claim or get something back • *I reclaimed my umbrella from the lost property office.* ❷ to reclaim land is to make it suitable for farming or building on again by clearing or draining it
➤ **reclamation** NOUN

**recline** VERB reclines, reclining, reclined
to lean or lie back

**recluse** NOUN recluses
a person who lives alone and avoids mixing with people
➤ **reclusive** ADJECTIVE

**recognition** NOUN
recognizing someone or something • *She looked at me with no sign of recognition on her face.*

**recognize** (also **recognise**) VERB recognizes, recognizing, recognized
❶ to know who someone is or what something is because you have seen that person or thing before ❷ to realize or admit something • *She recognized the truth of what he was saying.* ❸ to accept something as genuine, valid or lawful • *Nine countries recognized the island's new government.*
➤ **recognizable** ADJECTIVE

**recoil** VERB recoils, recoiling, recoiled
❶ to move back suddenly in shock or disgust

• *He recoiled in horror.* ❷ a gun recoils when it jerks backwards when it is fired

**recollect** VERB recollects, recollecting, recollected
to remember something

**recollection** NOUN recollections
❶ being able to remember something • *I have no recollection of seeing her before.* ❷ something you remember

**recommend** VERB recommends, recommending, recommended
❶ to suggest something because you think it is good or suitable • *I recommend the strawberry ice cream.* ❷ to advise someone to do something • *We recommend that you wear strong boots on the walk.*

**recommendation** NOUN recommendations
❶ saying that something is good and should be tried or used ❷ a statement about what should be done

**recompense** VERB recompenses, recompensing, recompensed
to give a person money to make up for a loss or to reward them for something they have done for you
➤ **recompense** NOUN

**reconcile** VERB reconciles, reconciling, reconciled
❶ to be reconciled with someone is to become friendly with them again after quarrelling or fighting with them ❷ to be reconciled to something is to be persuaded to put up with it • *He soon became reconciled to wearing glasses.* ❸ to make things agree • *I cannot reconcile what you say with what you do.*
➤ **reconciliation** NOUN

**reconnaissance** (say rik-**on**-i-sans) NOUN
an exploration of an area, especially in order to gather information about it for military purposes

**reconnoitre** VERB reconnoitres, reconnoitring, reconnoitred
to make a reconnaissance of an area

**reconsider** VERB reconsiders, reconsidering, reconsidered
to consider something again and perhaps change an earlier decision
➤ **reconsideration** NOUN

**reconstitute** VERB reconstitutes, reconstituting, reconstituted
❶ to form something again, especially in a

different way ❷ to make dried food edible again by adding water

**reconstruct** VERB reconstructs, reconstructing, reconstructed
❶ to construct or build something again ❷ to create or act out past events again • *Police reconstructed the robbery.*
➤ **reconstruction** NOUN

**record** (say **rek**-ord) NOUN records
❶ information kept in a permanent form, e.g. in writing or stored on a computer ❷ the best performance in a sport etc. or the most remarkable event of its kind • *She holds the record for the high jump.* ❸ what is known about a person's past life or career • *He has an impressive record as a football manager.* ❹ a disc on which sound has been recorded

**record** (say **rek**-ord) ADJECTIVE
best, highest or most extreme recorded up to now • *A record crowd watched the match.*

**record** (say rik-**ord**) VERB records, recording, recorded
❶ to keep information by writing it down or storing it on a computer ❷ to store sounds or scenes (e.g. television pictures) using electronic equipment so that you can play or show them later

**recorder** NOUN recorders
❶ a kind of flute held downwards from the player's mouth ❷ a person or thing that records something

**record player** NOUN record players
a machine that plays records

**recount** VERB recounts, recounting, recounted
❶ (say ri-**kownt**)
to give an account of something • *We recounted our adventures.* ❷ (say ree-**kownt**) to count something again

**recount** (say **ree**-kownt) NOUN recounts
counting something again, especially votes in an election

**recoup** (say ri-**koop**) VERB recoups, recouping, recouped
to recover the cost of an investment or of a loss

**recourse** NOUN
a source of help
➤ **have recourse to someone or something**
to go to a person or thing for help

**recover** VERB recovers, recovering, recovered
❶ to get well again after being ill or weak • *The driver is recovering in hospital.* ❷ to

get something back again after losing it • *The police have recovered the stolen paintings.*

**recovery** NOUN recoveries
❶ getting well again after being ill or weak ❷ getting something back again after losing it

**recreation** NOUN recreations
❶ enjoying yourself and relaxing when you are not working ❷ a game or hobby that is an enjoyable activity
➤ **recreational** ADJECTIVE

**recrimination** NOUN recriminations
an accusation made against a person who has criticized or blamed you

**recruit** NOUN recruits
❶ a person who has just joined the armed forces ❷ a new member of a society, company or other group

**recruit** VERB recruits, recruiting, recruited
❶ to get someone to join something you belong to ❷ to get someone to join the armed forces
➤ **recruitment** NOUN

**rectangle** NOUN rectangles
a shape with four straight sides and four right angles
➤ **rectangular** ADJECTIVE

**rectify** VERB rectifies, rectifying, rectified
to correct a mistake or put something right

**rectitude** NOUN
morally correct behaviour

**rector** NOUN rectors
a member of the Church of England clergy in charge of a parish

**rectum** NOUN rectums or recta
the last part of the large intestine, ending at the anus

**recumbent** ADJECTIVE
lying down

**recuperate** VERB recuperates, recuperating, recuperated
to get better after an illness
➤ **recuperation** NOUN

**recur** VERB recurs, recurring, recurred
to happen again or keep on happening • *a recurring dream*
➤ **recurrent** ADJECTIVE
➤ **recurrence** NOUN

**recurring decimal** NOUN recurring decimals
(*in mathematics*) a decimal fraction in which a digit or group of digits is repeated indefinitely, e.g. 0.666 ...

**recycle** VERB recycles, recycling, recycled
to convert waste material into a form in which it can be used again • *Plastic bottles can be recycled.*
➤ **recycling** NOUN

**red** ADJECTIVE redder, reddest
❶ of the colour of blood or a colour rather like this ❷ red hair or fur is of a reddish brown colour ❸ having communist or socialist views
➤ **redness** NOUN

**red** NOUN
❶ a red colour ❷ a communist or socialist
➤ **in the red** in debt
➤ **see red** to become suddenly angry

**red deer** NOUN red deer
a kind of large deer with a reddish-brown coat, found in Europe and Asia

**redden** VERB reddens, reddening, reddened
to become red; to blush • *He reddened with embarrassment.*

**reddish** ADJECTIVE
fairly red

**redeem** VERB redeems, redeeming, redeemed
❶ to make up for faults • *His one redeeming feature is his generosity.* ❷ to get something back by paying for it or handing over a voucher ❸ to save a person from damnation, as in some religions
➤ **redeemer** NOUN
➤ **redemption** NOUN
➤ **redeem yourself** to do something good to make up for an earlier mistake

**redevelop** VERB redevelops, redeveloping, redeveloped
to develop a place or area in a different way
➤ **redevelopment** NOUN

**red-handed** ADJECTIVE
➤ **catch someone red-handed** to catch someone while they are actually committing a crime or doing something wrong

**redhead** NOUN redheads
a person with reddish hair

**red herring** NOUN red herrings
something that draws attention away from the main subject; a misleading clue
**WORD ORIGIN** because a red herring (= a kipper) put hounds off the scent when it was dragged across the path of the fox being hunted

**red-hot** ADJECTIVE
very hot; so hot that it has turned red

**red meat** NOUN
meat, such as beef, lamb or mutton, which is red when raw

**redolent** (say red-ol-ent) ADJECTIVE
❶ smelling strongly of something • *The air was redolent of onions.* ❷ strongly suggesting or reminding you of something • *a castle redolent of romance*

**redoubtable** ADJECTIVE
formidable, especially as an opponent

**redress** VERB redresses, redressing, redressed
to correct something that is unfair or wrong • *It is time to redress this injustice.*
➤ **redress the balance** to make things equal again

**redress** NOUN
compensation for something wrong that has been done • *You should seek redress for this damage.*

**red tape** NOUN
all the rules and forms that make it difficult to get official business done quickly
(**WORD ORIGIN**) because bundles of official papers used to be tied up with red or pink tape

**reduce** VERB reduces, reducing, reduced
❶ to make something smaller or less • *We can reduce pollution by cycling instead of travelling by car.* ❷ to become smaller or less ❸ to force someone into a condition or situation • *He was reduced to borrowing the money.*

**reduction** NOUN reductions
❶ when something becomes smaller or less ❷ the amount by which a thing is reduced • *There were massive reductions in the sale.*

**redundant** ADJECTIVE
❶ no longer needed ❷ someone is made redundant when they lose their job because it is no longer needed
➤ **redundancy** NOUN

**reed** NOUN reeds
❶ a tall plant that grows in water or marshy ground ❷ a thin strip that vibrates to make the sound in a clarinet, saxophone, oboe, etc.

**reedy** ADJECTIVE reedier, reediest
❶ full of reeds ❷ a reedy voice has a thin high tone like a reed instrument

**reef** NOUN reefs
a ridge of rock, coral or sand, especially one near the surface of the sea

**reef** VERB reefs, reefing, reefed
to shorten a sail by drawing in a strip (called a reef) at the top or bottom to reduce the area exposed to the wind

**reef knot** NOUN reef knots
(*chiefly British*) a symmetrical double knot that is very secure

**reek** VERB reeks, reeking, reeked
to smell strongly or unpleasantly

**reek** NOUN reeks
a strong unpleasant smell • *the reek of sweat*

**reel** NOUN reels
❶ a round device on which cotton, thread or film is wound ❷ a lively Scottish dance or the music for this

**reel** VERB reels, reeling, reeled
❶ to wind something onto or off a reel ❷ to stagger ❸ to feel dizzy or confused • *I am still reeling from the shock.*
➤ **reel something off** to repeat something from memory quickly

**re-elect** VERB re-elects, re-electing, re-elected
to elect someone again

**re-enter** VERB re-enters, re-entering, re-entered
to enter a place or contest again
➤ **re-entry** NOUN

**re-examine** VERB re-examines, re-examining, re-examined
to examine someone or something again

**ref** NOUN refs (*informal*)
a referee

**refectory** NOUN refectories
the dining room of a college or monastery etc.

**refer** VERB refers, referring, referred
❶ to refer to someone or something is to mention them or speak about them • *I wasn't referring to you.* ❷ to refer to a dictionary or other source of information is to look in it so that you can find something out ❸ to refer a question or problem to someone else is to pass it on to them to deal with • *My doctor referred me to a specialist.*
➤ **referral** NOUN

**referee** NOUN referees
the person who has the job of seeing that people keep to the rules of a game

**referee** VERB referees, refereeing, refereed
to act as a referee

SPELLING

There is only one f and one r in referee.

**reference** NOUN references
❶ a mention of something • *There was no reference to recent events.* ❷ a direction to a book or page or file where information can be found ❸ a letter from a previous employer describing someone's abilities and qualities
➤ **in** or **with reference to** concerning or about

**reference book** NOUN reference books
a book (such as a dictionary or encyclopedia) that gives information about a subject

**reference library** NOUN reference libraries
a library where books can be used but not taken away

**referendum** NOUN referendums or referenda
a vote on a particular question by all the people of a country

**refill** VERB refills, refilling, refilled
to fill something again • *Can I refill your glass?*

**refill** NOUN refills
a container holding a substance which is used to refill something • *My pen needs a refill.*

**refine** VERB refines, refining, refined
❶ to remove impurities from a substance ❷ to improve something, especially by making small changes

**refined** ADJECTIVE
❶ made pure by having other substances taken out of it • *refined sugar* ❷ polite, educated and well-mannered

**refinement** NOUN refinements
❶ good manners and polite behaviour ❷ something added to improve a thing

**refinery** NOUN refineries
a factory for refining something • *an oil refinery*

**reflect** VERB reflects, reflecting, reflected
❶ to send back light, heat or sound from a surface ❷ to form an image of something as a mirror does ❸ to think deeply or carefully about something • *He spent some time reflecting on what had happened.* ❹ to be a sign of something or to make it clear • *Her hard work was reflected in her exam results.*
➤ **reflector** NOUN

**reflection** NOUN reflections
❶ an image you can see in a mirror or other reflecting surface ❷ reflecting light ❸ a spell of thinking about something • *I think, on reflection, that I was wrong.*

**reflective** ADJECTIVE
❶ reflecting light or heat • *reflective clothing* ❷ suggesting or showing serious thought • *a reflective expression*
➤ **reflectively** ADVERB

**reflex** NOUN reflexes
a movement or action that you do without any conscious thought • *The doctor tested her reflexes.*

**reflex angle** NOUN reflex angles
an angle of more than 180°

**reflexive pronoun** NOUN reflexive pronouns
(*in grammar*) any of the pronouns *myself, herself, himself,* etc. (as in 'She cut *herself*.'), which refer back to the subject of the verb

**reflexive verb** NOUN reflexive verbs
a verb where the subject and the object are the same person or thing, as in 'She cut *herself*.', 'The cat *washed itself*.'

**reform** VERB reforms, reforming, reformed
❶ to make changes in something in order to improve it ❷ to give up a criminal or immoral lifestyle or to make someone do this

**reform** NOUN reforms
❶ reform is changing something in order to improve it ❷ a reform is a change made in order to improve something

**Reformation** NOUN
the Reformation was a religious movement in Europe in the 16th century intended to reform certain teachings and practices of the Roman Catholic Church, which resulted in the establishment of the Reformed or Protestant Churches

**reformer** NOUN reformers
someone who makes reforms

**refract** VERB refracts, refracting, refracted
to bend a ray of light at the point where it enters water or glass at an angle
➤ **refraction** NOUN
➤ **refractive** ADJECTIVE

**refractory** ADJECTIVE
❶ difficult to control; stubborn ❷ a refractory substance is resisting to heat

**refrain** VERB refrains, refraining, refrained
to stop yourself from doing something • *Please refrain from talking.*

a b c d e f g h i j k l m n o p q r s t u v w x y z

**refrain** NOUN refrains
the chorus of a song

**refresh** VERB refreshes, refreshing, refreshed
to make someone feel less tired or less
hot and full of energy again • *She looked
refreshed after a good night's sleep.*
➤ **refresh someone's memory** to remind
someone of something by going over previous
information

**refresher course** NOUN refresher courses
a training course to bring people's knowledge
up to date

**refreshing** ADJECTIVE
❶ producing new strength or energy • *a
refreshing sleep* ❷ pleasantly different or
unusual • *refreshing honesty*

**refreshment** NOUN
❶ food and drink • *Can we offer you some
refreshment?* ❷ the state of feeling strong
and energetic again

**refreshments** PLURAL NOUN
drinks and snacks provided at an event

**refrigerate** VERB refrigerates, refrigerating,
refrigerated
to make food or drink extremely cold,
especially in order to preserve it and keep it
fresh
➤ **refrigeration** NOUN

**refrigerator** NOUN refrigerators
a cabinet in which food or drink is stored at a
very low temperature

**refuel** VERB refuels, refuelling, refuelled
to supply a ship or aircraft with more fuel

**refuge** NOUN refuges
a place where a person can go to be safe
from danger
➤ **take refuge** to go somewhere or do
something so that you are protected • *We
had to take refuge from the rain under a tree.*

**refugee** NOUN refugees
a person who has been forced to leave their
home or country and live somewhere else, e.g.
because of war or persecution or famine

**refund** VERB refunds, refunding, refunded
to pay money back

**refund** NOUN refunds
money that is paid back to you

**refurbish** VERB refurbishes, refurbishing,
refurbished
to redecorate a room or building and make

repairs to it
➤ **refurbishment** NOUN

**refusal** NOUN refusals
saying that you are unwilling to do or give or
accept something • *I can't understand her
refusal to see me.*

**refuse** (say ri-**fewz**) VERB refuses, refusing,
refused
to say that you are unwilling to do, give or
accept something • *He refuses to talk about
it.*

**refuse** (say **ref**-yooss) NOUN
rubbish or waste material • *Lorries collected
the refuse.*

**refute** VERB refutes, refuting, refuted
to prove that a person or statement is wrong

> USAGE
This word is sometimes used as if it
meant 'deny', but this meaning is not fully
accepted as part of standard English and
should be avoided.

**regain** VERB regains, regaining, regained
to get something back after losing it • *She
managed to regain her balance.*

**regal** (say **ree**-gal) ADJECTIVE
❶ by or to do with a monarch ❷ dignified
and splendid; fit for a king or queen

**regale** (say rig-**ayl**) VERB regales, regaling,
regaled
to amuse or entertain someone with a story
• *She regaled us with tales of her life in the
theatre.*

**regalia** (say rig-**ayl**-i-a) PLURAL NOUN
the emblems of royalty or rank • *The royal
regalia include the crown, sceptre and orb.*

**regard** VERB regards, regarding, regarded
❶ to think of a person or thing in a certain
way; to consider someone or something to
be • *We regard the matter as serious.* ❷ to
look closely at someone or something • *She
regarded us suspiciously.*

**regard** NOUN
❶ consideration or heed • *You acted without
regard to people's safety.* ❷ respect • *We
have a great regard for her.*
➤ **as regards** concerning; in connection with
• *He is innocent as regards the first charge.*
➤ **with** or **in regard to** concerning; in
connection with

**regarding** PREPOSITION
concerning; about • *For more information
regarding our products, visit our website.*

**regardless** ADVERB
without considering something; in spite of
something • *Do it, regardless of the cost.*

**regards** PLURAL NOUN
kind wishes you send in a message • *Give
your parents my regards.*

**regatta** NOUN regattas
a meeting for boat or yacht races

**regency** NOUN regencies
❶ being a regent ❷ a period when a country
is ruled by a regent

**regenerate** VERB regenerates, regenerating,
regenerated
to give new life or strength to something
➤ **regeneration** NOUN

**regent** NOUN regents
a person appointed to rule a country while
the monarch is too young or unable to rule

**reggae** (say **reg**-ay) NOUN
a West Indian style of music with a strong
beat

**regime** (say ray-zh **eem**) NOUN regimes
a system of government or organization • *a
Fascist regime*

**regiment** NOUN regiments
an army unit, usually divided into battalions
or companies
➤ **regimental** ADJECTIVE

**region** NOUN regions
❶ a part of a country or of the world • *in
tropical regions* ❷ an area of someone's body
• *pain in the lower back region*
➤ **in the region of** near; approximately • *The
cost will be in the region of €200.*

**regional** ADJECTIVE
belonging to a particular region • *a regional
accent*

**register** NOUN registers
❶ an official list of names or items ❷ a
book in which information about school
attendances is recorded ❸ the range of a
voice or musical instrument

**register** VERB registers, registering, registered
❶ to list names or items in a register
❷ to indicate or show something • *The
thermometer registered 100°.* • *His face
registered deep suspicion.* ❸ to make an
impression on someone's mind • *Does that
name register at all?* ❹ to pay extra for a
letter or parcel to be sent with special care

**register office** NOUN register offices
an office where marriages are performed and
records of births, marriages and deaths are
kept

**registrar** NOUN registrars
an official whose job is to keep written
records or registers

**registration** NOUN
putting someone's name on an official list

**registration number** NOUN registration
numbers
a series of letters and numbers identifying a
motor vehicle

**registry** NOUN registries
a place where registers are kept

**registry office** NOUN registry offices
a register office

**regret** NOUN regrets
a feeling of sorrow or disappointment about
something that has happened or been done

**regret** VERB regrets, regretting, regretted
to feel sorry or disappointed about something
• *He regretted his decision at once.*

**regretful** ADJECTIVE
feeling sorry or disappointed about
something
➤ **regretfully** ADVERB

**regrettable** ADJECTIVE
that you are sorry about and wish had not
happened • *a regrettable mistake*
➤ **regrettably** ADVERB

**regular** ADJECTIVE
❶ always happening or doing something
at certain times • *Try to eat regular meals.*
❷ even or symmetrical • *regular teeth*
❸ normal, standard or correct • *the regular
procedure* ❹ belonging to a country's
permanent armed forces • *a regular soldier*
➤ **regularity** NOUN

**regularly** ADVERB
❶ at regular times or intervals • *Railway
tracks are regularly checked.* ❷ often • *I go
there regularly.*

**regulate** VERB regulates, regulating,
regulated
❶ to control something by using laws or rules
❷ to control the way a machine works • *Turn
this dial to regulate the temperature.*
➤ **regulator** NOUN

**regulation** NOUN regulations
❶ a rule or law ❷ regulating something

a
b
c
d
e
f
g
h
i
j
k
l
m
n
o
p
q
r
s
t
u
v
w
x
y
z

**regurgitate** VERB regurgitates, regurgitating, regurgitated
to bring swallowed food up again into the mouth
➤ **regurgitation** NOUN

**rehearsal** NOUN rehearsals
practising something before you perform it in front of an audience

**rehearse** VERB rehearses, rehearsing, rehearsed
to practise something before performing it in front of an audience

**reign** VERB reigns, reigning, reigned
❶ to rule a country as king or queen ❷ to be supreme; to be the most noticeable or important thing • *Silence reigned for a while.*

**reign** NOUN reigns
the time when someone is king or queen

SPELLING
Be careful, this sounds the same as **rein**, which means a strap used by a rider to guide a horse.

**reimburse** VERB reimburses, reimbursing, reimbursed
to repay money that has been spent • *Your travelling expenses will be reimbursed.*
➤ **reimbursement** NOUN

**rein** NOUN reins
❶ a strap used by a rider to guide a horse ❷ a harness used to guide a very young child when walking

SPELLING
Be careful, this sounds the same as **reign**, which means to rule a country or the amount of time for which someone rules a country.

**reincarnation** NOUN
the belief that after death the soul is born again in a new body

**reindeer** NOUN reindeer
a kind of deer that lives in Arctic regions

**reinforce** VERB reinforces, reinforcing, reinforced
❶ to strengthen something by adding extra people or supports ❷ to strengthen or support an idea or feeling

**reinforced concrete** NOUN
concrete containing metal bars or wires to strengthen it

**reinforcement** NOUN reinforcements
❶ making something stronger ❷ a thing that strengthens something

**reinforcements** PLURAL NOUN
extra troops sent to strengthen a military force

**reinstate** VERB reinstates, reinstating, reinstated
to put a person or thing back into a previous position
➤ **reinstatement** NOUN

**reiterate** VERB reiterates, reiterating, reiterated
to say something again or repeatedly
➤ **reiteration** NOUN

**reject** (say ri-**jekt**) VERB rejects, rejecting, rejected
❶ to refuse to accept a person or thing • *They rejected all offers of help.* ❷ to throw away or discard something • *Faulty parts are rejected at the factory.*
➤ **rejection** NOUN

**reject** (say **ree**-jekt) NOUN rejects
a person or thing that is rejected, especially because of being faulty or poorly made

**rejoice** VERB rejoices, rejoicing, rejoiced
to feel or show great joy

**rejoin** VERB rejoins, rejoining, rejoined
to join someone or something again after leaving them

**rejoinder** NOUN rejoinders
a sharp or witty reply

**rejuvenate** VERB rejuvenates, rejuvenating, rejuvenated
to make a person seem young again
➤ **rejuvenation** NOUN

**relapse** VERB relapses, relapsing, relapsed
❶ to return to a previous condition • *After these words he relapsed into silence.* ❷ to become worse after improving
➤ **relapse** NOUN

**relate** VERB relates, relating, related
❶ to tell a story or give an account of something ❷ things relate to each another when there is a link or connection between them ❸ to make a connection between one thing and another ❹ to understand someone and get on well with them • *Some people cannot relate to children.*

**related** ADJECTIVE
❶ belonging to the same family ❷ connected or linked

**relation** NOUN relations
❶ a relative ❷ the way one thing is related to another
➤ **in relation to** in connection with

**relationship** NOUN relationships
❶ how people or things are related ❷ how people get on with each other ❸ a loving or sexual friendship between two people

**relative** NOUN relatives
a person who is related to another

**relative** ADJECTIVE
connected or compared with something; compared with the average • *They live in relative comfort.*

**relative density** NOUN relative densities
the ratio of the density of a substance to that of a standard substance (usually water for liquids and solids and air for gases)

**relatively** ADVERB
to a fairly large degree when compared with other things • *It is a relatively easy language to learn.*

**relative pronoun** NOUN relative pronouns
a word used instead of a noun to introduce a clause that gives more information about the noun. The relative pronouns are *what, who, whom, whose, which* and *that*.

GRAMMAR
Relative pronouns (*what, who, whom, whose, which* and *that*) introduce a clause which gives more information about a noun, e.g. *the artist who painted this portrait; the song that I love.*

See also the panel on **pronouns**.

**relax** VERB relaxes, relaxing, relaxed
❶ to rest or stop working ❷ to become less anxious or worried ❸ to make a rule less strict or severe ❹ to make a limb or muscle less stiff or tense • *Try to relax your arm.*
➤ **relaxed** ADJECTIVE
➤ **relaxation** NOUN

**relay** (say ri-**lay**) VERB relays, relaying, relayed
to pass on a message or broadcast

**relay** (say **re**-lay) NOUN relays
❶ a fresh group taking the place of another • *The firefighters worked in relays.* ❷ a relay race ❸ a device for relaying a broadcast

**relay race** NOUN relay races
a race between teams in which each person covers part of the distance

**release** VERB releases, releasing, released
❶ to set someone or something free or unfasten them • *Eventually he was released from prison.* ❷ to let a thing fall or fly or go out • *Hundreds of balloons were released at the ceremony.* ❸ to make information available • *The name of the victim has not yet been released.* ❹ to make a film or recording available to the public

**release** NOUN releases
❶ being released ❷ something released, such as a new film or recording ❸ a device that unfastens something

**relegate** VERB relegates, relegating, relegated
❶ a sports team is relegated when it goes down into a lower division of a league ❷ to put something into a lower group or position than before
➤ **relegation** NOUN

**relent** VERB relents, relenting, relented
to finally agree to something that you had refused; to become less severe • *In the end Mum and Dad relented and let me go to the party.*

**relentless** ADJECTIVE
not stopping or letting up • *Their criticism was relentless.*
➤ **relentlessly** ADVERB

**relevant** ADJECTIVE
connected with what is being discussed or dealt with. (The opposite is **irrelevant**.)
➤ **relevance** NOUN

**reliable** ADJECTIVE
able to be relied on or trusted • *Is he a reliable witness?*
➤ **reliably** ADVERB
➤ **reliability** NOUN

**reliance** NOUN
relying or depending on someone or something
➤ **reliant** ADJECTIVE

**relic** NOUN relics
something that has survived from an earlier time

**relief** NOUN reliefs
❶ a good feeling you get because something unpleasant has stopped or is not going to happen • *It was such a relief when we reached dry land.* ❷ the ending or lessening of pain, trouble or suffering ❸ something that gives relief or help ❹ help given to people in need • *The charity is involved in famine relief.* ❺ a person who takes over a turn of duty when another finishes ❻ a

method of making a map or design that stands out from a flat surface • *The model shows hills and valleys in relief.*

**relief map** NOUN relief maps
a map that shows hills and valleys by shading or moulding

**relieve** VERB relieves, relieving, relieved
to make an unpleasant feeling or situation stop or get better • *We played cards to relieve the boredom.*
➤ **relieve someone of something** to take something from a person • *The thief relieved him of his wallet.*

**relieved** ADJECTIVE
feeling happy because something unpleasant has stopped or has not happened • *I was relieved to hear that nobody was hurt.*

**religion** NOUN religions
❶ what people believe about God or gods and how they worship ❷ a particular system of beliefs and worship

**religious** ADJECTIVE
❶ to do with religion ❷ believing firmly in a religion and taking part in its customs

**religiously** ADVERB
very carefully or regularly • *He wrote up his diary religiously every night.*

**relinquish** VERB relinquishes, relinquishing, relinquished
to give something up; to let something go

**relish** NOUN relishes
❶ great enjoyment • *He told me all the gory details with obvious relish.* ❷ a tasty sauce or pickle that adds flavour to plainer food

**relish** VERB relishes, relishing, relished
to enjoy something greatly; to look forward to something with great pleasure • *I didn't relish the idea of getting up so early.*

**relive** VERB relives, reliving, relived
to remember something that happened very vividly, as though it was happening again

**relocate** VERB relocates, relocating, relocated
to move to a new place or to make someone or something do this

**reluctant** ADJECTIVE
not willing or not keen to do something • *She was reluctant to talk about what had happened.*
➤ **reluctantly** ADVERB
➤ **reluctance** NOUN

**rely** VERB relies, relying, relied
❶ to rely on someone is to trust them to help or support you • *You can rely on me not to tell anyone.* ❷ to rely on something is to need it for a particular purpose • *Many people rely on this local bus service.*

**remain** VERB remains, remaining, remained
❶ to be left after other parts have gone or been dealt with • *One big problem remained.* ❷ to continue to be in the same place or condition; to stay • *It will remain cloudy all day.*

**remainder** NOUN
❶ the remaining part of people or things ❷ the number left after subtraction or division

**remains** PLURAL NOUN
❶ all that is left over after other parts have been removed or destroyed ❷ ancient ruins or objects that have survived to the present day • *the remains of a Roman fort* ❸ a dead body

**remand** VERB remands, remanding, remanded
to send a prisoner back into custody while further evidence is being gathered
➤ **remand** NOUN
➤ **on remand** in prison while waiting for a trial

**remark** NOUN remarks
something you say; a comment

**remark** VERB remarks, remarking, remarked
to make a remark; to say something

**remarkable** ADJECTIVE
unusual or extraordinary in a way that people notice • *It was a remarkable achievement.*
➤ **remarkably** ADVERB

**remedial** ADJECTIVE
❶ helping to cure an illness or deficiency ❷ (old use) to do with the teaching of school students who are not doing as well as expected

**remedy** NOUN remedies
something that cures or relieves a disease or that puts a matter right

**remedy** VERB remedies, remedying, remedied
to be a remedy for something; to put something right

**remember** VERB remembers, remembering, remembered
❶ to keep something in your mind • *Please remember to switch off the lights.* ❷ to bring

something back into your mind • *I can't remember her name.*

**remembrance** NOUN
you do something in remembrance of someone or something when you do it as a way of remembering them

**remind** VERB reminds, reminding, reminded
❶ to help or make a person remember something • *Remind me to buy some stamps.* ❷ to make a person think of something because of being similar • *The girl in that painting reminds me of you.*

**reminder** NOUN reminders
❶ a thing that reminds you of something ❷ a letter sent to remind you to pay a bill

**reminiscences** PLURAL NOUN
a person's memories of their past life

**reminiscent** ADJECTIVE
reminding you of something • *The book's style is reminiscent of 'The Hobbit'.*

**remission** NOUN
❶ a period during which a serious illness improves for a time ❷ the reduction of a prison sentence, especially for good behaviour while in prison

**remit** VERB remits, remitting, remitted
❶ to reduce or cancel a punishment or debt ❷ to send money in payment

**remittance** NOUN remittances
❶ sending money ❷ the amount of money sent

**remnant** NOUN remnants
a part or piece left over from something

**remonstrate** VERB remonstrates, remonstrating, remonstrated
to make a protest • *We remonstrated with him about his behaviour.*

**remorse** NOUN
deep regret for something wrong you have done
➤ **remorseful** ADJECTIVE
➤ **remorsefully** ADVERB

**remorseless** ADJECTIVE
relentless; not stopping or ending
➤ **remorselessly** ADVERB

**remote** ADJECTIVE
❶ far away in place or time • *remote stars*

• *the remote past* ❷ far away from where most people live; isolated • *a remote beach* ❸ unlikely or slight • *a remote chance*
➤ **remoteness** NOUN

**remote** NOUN remotes
a remote control device

**remote control** NOUN remote controls
❶ controlling something from a distance, usually by electricity or radio ❷ a device for doing this

**remotely** ADVERB
❶ to a very slight degree; slightly • *That is not even remotely funny.* ❷ from a distance

**removable** ADJECTIVE
able to be removed

**removal** NOUN
removing or moving something

**remove** VERB removes, removing, removed
❶ to take something away or take it off ❷ to get rid of something • *This should remove all doubts.*
➤ **be far removed from something** to be very different from something

**remunerate** VERB remunerates, remunerating, remunerated
to pay or reward someone
➤ **remuneration** NOUN

**Renaissance** (say ren-ay-sans) NOUN
the revival of classical styles of art and literature in Europe in the 14th–16th centuries

**renal** (say reen-al) ADJECTIVE
to do with the kidneys

**rename** VERB renames, renaming, renamed
to give a new name to a person or thing

**rend** VERB rends, rending, rent (*poetical use*)
to rip or tear something

**render** VERB renders, rendering, rendered
❶ to cause a person or thing to become something • *This news rendered us speechless.* ❷ to give or perform something • *The local community was quick to render help to the victims.*

**rendezvous** (say **rond**-ay-voo) NOUN
rendezvous (say **rond**-ay-vooz)
❶ a meeting with someone at an agreed time and place ❷ a place arranged for this

**rendition** NOUN renditions
the way a piece of music, a poem or a dramatic role is performed

**renegade** (say ren-ig-ayd) NOUN renegades
a person who deserts a group or cause and
joins another

**renew** VERB renews, renewing, renewed
❶ to replace a thing with something new or
arrange for it to be valid for a further period
• *I need to renew my bus pass.* ❷ to begin or
make or give something again • *We renewed
our request.*
➤ **renewal** NOUN

**renewable** ADJECTIVE
able to be renewed

**renewable resource** NOUN renewable
resources
a resource (such as power from the sun, wind
or waves) that can never be used up or which
can be renewed

**renounce** VERB renounces, renouncing,
renounced
to give up or reject something
➤ **renunciation** NOUN

**renovate** VERB renovates, renovating,
renovated
to repair an old building and make it look new
➤ **renovation** NOUN

**renown** NOUN
great fame

**renowned** ADJECTIVE
famous • *The area is renowned for it beauty.*

**rent** NOUN rents
❶ a regular payment for the use of
something, especially a house that belongs to
another person ❷ a torn place; a split

**rent** VERB rents, renting, rented
❶ to have or allow the use of something in
return for rent ❷ past tense of **rend**

**rental** NOUN
❶ the amount paid as rent ❷ renting
something

**renunciation** NOUN
renouncing something

**reorganize** (also **reorganise**) VERB
reorganizes, reorganizing, reorganized
to change the way in which something is
organized
➤ **reorganization** NOUN

**repair** VERB repairs, repairing, repaired
❶ to put something into good condition after
it has been damaged or broken ❷ (formal) to
repair to a place is to go there • *The guests
repaired to the dining room.*
➤ **repairable** ADJECTIVE

**repair** NOUN repairs
❶ repairing something • *The bridge is in need
of repair.* ❷ a place where something has
been mended • *The repair is hardly visible.*
➤ **in good** or **bad repair** in good or poor
condition; well or badly maintained

**reparation** NOUN reparations (formal)
making amends; paying for damage or loss
➤ **make reparations** to make amends or
compensate for something

**reparations** PLURAL NOUN
compensation for war damage paid by the
defeated nation

**repartee** NOUN
witty replies and remarks

**repast** NOUN repasts (formal)
a meal

**repay** VERB repays, repaying, repaid
❶ to pay back money that you owe ❷ to do
something for someone in return for kindness
or help • *How can I ever repay you for all you
have done?*
➤ **repayment** NOUN

**repeal** VERB repeals, repealing, repealed
to cancel a law officially
➤ **repeal** NOUN

**repeat** VERB repeats, repeating, repeated
❶ to say or do the same thing again ❷ to tell
another person about something told to you
• *You mustn't repeat this to anyone.*

**repeat** NOUN repeats
❶ the action of repeating something
❷ something that is repeated • *There are too
many repeats on television.*

**repeatedly** ADVERB
many times; again and again • *She hit him
repeatedly.*

**repel** VERB repels, repelling, repelled
❶ to drive someone back or away • *They
fought bravely and repelled the attackers.*
❷ to push something away from itself
by means of a physical force • *One north
magnetic pole repels another.* ❸ to disgust
someone

**repellent** ADJECTIVE
causing a strong feeling of disgust

**repellent** NOUN repellents
a chemical substance used to keep something
away • *an insect repellent*

**repent** VERB repents, repenting, repented
to be sorry for what you have done
➤ **repentance** NOUN
➤ **repentant** ADJECTIVE

**repercussion** NOUN repercussions
a consequence or effect of an event or action

**repertoire** (say rep-er-twahr) NOUN
a stock of songs or plays etc. that a person or company knows and can perform

**repetition** NOUN repetitions
❶ repeating something ❷ something repeated
➤ **repetitious** ADJECTIVE

**repetitive** ADJECTIVE
involving too much repetition • The story is slightly repetitive in places.
➤ **repetitively** ADVERB

**replace** VERB replaces, replacing, replaced
❶ to put a thing back where it was before • She replaced the book on the shelf. ❷ to take the place of another person or thing • I replaced him as captain of the team. ❸ to put a new or different thing in place of something • I promise I'll replace the bowl I broke.

**replacement** NOUN replacements
❶ a person or thing that takes the place of another ❷ when a person or thing is replaced by another

**replay** NOUN replays
❶ a sports match played again after a draw ❷ the playing or showing again of a recording

**replay** VERB replays, replaying, replayed
❶ to play a match again ❷ to play back a recording

**replenish** VERB replenishes, replenishing, replenished
to make something full again by replacing what has been used
➤ **replenishment** NOUN

**replete** ADJECTIVE
❶ well stocked or supplied ❷ feeling full after eating

**replica** NOUN replicas
an exact copy
➤ **replicate** VERB

**reply** NOUN replies
something you say or write to deal with a question, letter, etc.; an answer • She said nothing in reply.

**reply** VERB replies, replying, replied
to give a reply to someone; to answer • 'No, thank you,' he replied.

**report** VERB reports, reporting, reported
❶ to describe something that has happened or that you have done or studied ❷ to make an official complaint or accusation against someone ❸ to go and tell someone that you have arrived or are ready for work

**report** NOUN reports
❶ a description or account of something ❷ a regular statement of how someone has worked or behaved, e.g. at school ❸ an explosive sound

**reported speech** NOUN
indirect speech

**reporter** NOUN reporters
a person whose job is to collect and report news for a newspaper, radio or television programme, etc.

**repose** NOUN
calm, rest or sleep

**repose** VERB reposes, reposing, reposed
to rest or lie somewhere

**repository** NOUN repositories
a place where things are stored

**repossess** VERB repossesses, repossessing, repossessed
to take something back because it has not been paid for

**reprehensible** ADJECTIVE
extremely bad and deserving blame or criticism

**represent** VERB represents, representing, represented
❶ to help someone by speaking or doing something on their behalf ❷ to symbolize or stand for something • In Roman numerals, V represents 5. ❸ to be an example or equivalent of something ❹ to show a person or thing in a picture or play etc. ❺ to describe a person or thing in a particular way

**representation** NOUN representations
❶ a thing that shows or describes something • This sculpture is a representation of a human figure. ❷ being represented by someone or something

**representative** NOUN representatives
a person or thing that represents another or others

**representative** ADJECTIVE
❶ representing others ❷ typical of a group

579

**repress** VERB represses, repressing, repressed
❶ to control or hold back a feeling • *She tried to repress her anger.* ❷ to control or restrain people by force
➤ **repression** NOUN
➤ **repressive** ADJECTIVE

**reprieve** NOUN reprieves
postponement or cancellation of a punishment, especially the death penalty

**reprieve** VERB reprieves, reprieving, reprieved
to give a reprieve to someone

**reprimand** NOUN reprimands
a telling-off, especially a formal or official one

**reprimand** VERB reprimands, reprimanding, reprimanded
to scold someone or tell them off

**reprisal** NOUN reprisals
an act of revenge

**reproach** VERB reproaches, reproaching, reproached
to reproach someone you are upset and disappointed by something they have done

**reproach** NOUN
blame or criticism • *His behaviour was beyond reproach.*

**reproachful** ADJECTIVE
expressing blame or criticism • *a reproachful look*
➤ **reproachfully** ADVERB

**reproduce** VERB reproduces, reproducing, reproduced
❶ to cause something to be seen or heard or happen again ❷ to make a copy of something ❸ animals, people and plants reproduce when they produce offspring

**reproduction** NOUN reproductions
❶ a copy of something, especially a work of art ❷ the process of producing offspring

**reproductive** ADJECTIVE
to do with reproduction • *the reproductive system*

**reproof** NOUN
something you say to someone when you do not approve of what they have done • *words of mild reproof*

**reprove** VERB reproves, reproving, reproved
to tell someone that you do not approve of something that they have done • *He reproved her for rushing away.*

**reptile** NOUN reptiles
a cold-blooded animal that has a backbone

and very short legs or no legs at all, e.g. a snake, lizard, crocodile or tortoise
**WORD ORIGIN** from Latin *reptilis* = crawling

**republic** NOUN republics
a country that has a president, especially one who is elected. Compare with **monarchy**.
➤ **republican** ADJECTIVE & NOUN

**Republican** NOUN Republicans
a supporter of the Republican Party in the USA

**repudiate** VERB repudiates, repudiating, repudiated
to reject or deny a suggestion or accusation

**repugnant** ADJECTIVE
very unpleasant or disgusting
➤ **repugnance** NOUN

**repulse** VERB repulses, repulsing, repulsed
❶ to drive back an attacking force ❷ to reject an offer firmly ❸ to make someone feel disgust

**repulsion** NOUN
❶ a feeling of disgust ❷ repelling or repulsing something

**repulsive** ADJECTIVE
❶ disgusting or revolting ❷ repelling things
• *a repulsive force*
➤ **repulsively** ADVERB
➤ **repulsiveness** NOUN

**reputable** (say rep-yoo-ta-bul) ADJECTIVE
having a good reputation; respected • *a reputable company*

**reputation** NOUN reputations
what most people say or think about a person or thing • *She has a reputation for being late.* • *He started to build a reputation as a painter.*

**repute** NOUN
reputation • *a writer of international repute*

**reputed** ADJECTIVE
said or thought to be something • *The house is reputed to be haunted.*
➤ **reputedly** ADVERB

**request** VERB requests, requesting, requested
❶ to ask for a thing ❷ to ask a person to do something

**request** NOUN requests
❶ asking for something ❷ a thing asked for
• *Does the prisoner have any last requests?*

**requiem** (say rek-wee-em) NOUN requiems
❶ a special Mass for someone who

has died ❷ music for the words of this
**WORD ORIGIN** Latin, = rest

**require** VERB requires, requiring, required
❶ to need something • *The situation requires
a lot of tact.* ❷ to officially demand or order
something; to make someone do something
• *Drivers are required to pass a test.*

**requirement** NOUN requirements
what is required; a need

**requisite** (say rek-wiz-it) ADJECTIVE
required or needed for something • *Does he
have the requisite patience for the job?*

**requisite** NOUN requisites
a thing needed for something

**requisition** VERB requisitions, requisitioning,
requisitioned
to take something over for official use

**reread** VERB rereads, rereading, reread
to read something again

**rescue** VERB rescues, rescuing, rescued
to save a person or thing from danger or
harm; to free someone from captivity
➤ **rescuer** NOUN

**rescue** NOUN rescues
the action of rescuing a person or thing
• *Thank you for coming to my rescue.*

**research** NOUN
careful study or investigation to discover
facts or information

**research** (say ri-**serch**) VERB researches,
researching, researched
to carry out research into something • *The
team has been researching into dolphin
behaviour.*
➤ **researcher** NOUN

**resemblance** NOUN resemblances
likeness or similarity • *He bears a remarkable
resemblance to my brother.*

**resemble** VERB resembles, resembling,
resembled
to be or look like another person or thing
• *She closely resembles my sister.*

**resent** VERB resents, resenting, resented
to feel bitter and angry about something
done or said to you • *He resented being
treated like an idiot.*
➤ **resentment** NOUN

**resentful** ADJECTIVE
feeling bitter and angry about something
done or said to you
➤ **resentfully** ADVERB

**reservation** NOUN reservations
❶ reserving something ❷ something reserved
• *a hotel reservation* ❸ an area of land kept
for a special purpose ❹ a doubt or feeling
of unease ❺ a limit on how far you agree
with something; a doubt or condition • *I
accept the plan in principle but have certain
reservations.*

**reserve** VERB reserves, reserving, reserved
to keep or order something for a particular
person or a special use in the future • *I'd like
to reserve three tickets for the show.*
➤ **reserve judgement** to leave your decision
until you have had time to consider it
properly

**reserve** NOUN reserves
❶ a person or thing kept ready to be used if
necessary ❷ an extra player chosen in case
a substitute is needed in a team ❸ an area
of land kept for a special purpose • *a nature
reserve* ❹ shyness; being reserved
➤ **in reserve** not used but kept available if
needed

**reserved** ADJECTIVE
❶ kept for someone's use • *This table is
reserved.* ❷ shy or unwilling to show your
feelings

**reservoir** (say **rez**-er-vwar) NOUN reservoirs
a place where water is stored, especially an
artificial lake

**reshuffle** NOUN reshuffles
a rearrangement, especially an exchange of
jobs between members of a group • *a Cabinet
reshuffle*
➤ **reshuffle** VERB

**reside** VERB resides, residing, resided
to live in a particular place

**residence** NOUN residences
❶ a place where a person lives ❷ living in a
particular place • *Some pigeons have taken
up residence in our roof.*

**resident** NOUN residents
❶ a person living in a particular place ❷ a
person staying in a hotel

**resident** ADJECTIVE
living in a particular place

**residential** ADJECTIVE
❶ containing people's homes • *a residential
area* ❷ providing accommodation • *a
residential course*

**residue** NOUN residues
what remains or is left over • *The washing*

a b c d e f g h i j k l m n o p q r s t u v w x y z

powder left a white residue on her clothes.
> **residual** ADJECTIVE

**resign** VERB resigns, resigning, resigned
to give up your job or position
> **be resigned** or **resign yourself to something** to accept that you must put up with something • *She resigned herself to her fate.*

SPELLING

There is a silent g before the n in resign.

**resignation** NOUN resignations
❶ accepting a difficulty without complaining
❷ resigning a job or position; a letter saying you wish to do this

**resilient** ADJECTIVE
able to recover quickly from illness or trouble
> **resilience** NOUN
WORD ORIGIN from Latin *resilire* = jump back

**resin** NOUN resins
a sticky substance that comes from plants or is manufactured, used in varnish, plastics, etc.
> **resinous** ADJECTIVE

**resist** VERB resists, resisting, resisted
❶ to oppose or refuse to accept something; to fight or act against something ❷ to stop yourself having or doing something • *I couldn't resist having a quick peek.*

**resistance** NOUN
❶ resisting something • *The troops came up against armed resistance.* ❷ the ability of a substance to hinder the flow of electricity

**resistant** ADJECTIVE
❶ not affected or damaged by something
• *This watch is water-resistant.* ❷ not willing to accept something • *They are resistant to new ideas.*

**resistor** NOUN resistors
a device that increases the resistance to an electric current

**resit** NOUN resits
(*British*) an examination that you sit again because you did not do well enough the first time
> **resit** VERB

**resolute** ADJECTIVE
showing great determination
> **resolutely** ADVERB

**resolution** NOUN resolutions
❶ being resolute; great determination
❷ something you have resolved to do • *New Year resolutions* ❸ a formal decision made

by a committee ❹ the solving of a problem
❺ the last part of a story where we find out how the story comes to an end and how difficulties are sorted out

**resolve** VERB resolves, resolving, resolved
❶ to decide something firmly or formally
❷ to solve or settle a problem ❸ to overcome doubts or disagreements

**resolve** NOUN
great determination to do something

**resonant** ADJECTIVE
❶ resounding or echoing • *His voice was deep and resonant.* ❷ suggesting or bringing to mind a feeling or memory
> **resonance** NOUN

**resonate** VERB resonates, resonating, resonated
to make a deep continuing sound; to echo

**resort** VERB resorts, resorting, resorted
to turn to or make use of something, especially when everything else has failed • *In the end they resorted to violence.*

**resort** NOUN resorts
a place where people go for relaxation or a holiday
> **the last resort** something to be tried when everything else has failed

**resound** VERB resounds, resounding, resounded
to fill a place with sound; to echo • *Laughter resounded through the house.*

**resounding** ADJECTIVE
❶ loud and echoing ❷ very great; outstanding • *a resounding victory*

**resource** NOUN resources
❶ something that can be used; an asset • *The country's natural resources include coal and oil.* ❷ a person's resources are their natural qualities and abilities

**resourceful** ADJECTIVE
clever at finding ways of doing things
> **resourcefully** ADVERB
> **resourcefulness** NOUN

**respect** NOUN respects
❶ admiration for a person's or thing's good qualities ❷ politeness or consideration • *Have respect for people's feelings.* ❸ a detail or aspect • *In this respect he is like his sister.*
> **with respect to** with reference to; concerning • *The rules with respect to bullying are quite clear.*

**respect** VERB respects, respecting, respected
to have respect for a person or thing

**respectable** ADJECTIVE
❶ having good manners and character; decent ❷ fairly good; adequate • *a respectable score*
➤ **respectably** ADVERB
➤ **respectability** NOUN

**respectful** ADJECTIVE
showing respect
➤ **respectfully** ADVERB

**respecting** PREPOSITION
concerning; to do with

**respective** ADJECTIVE
belonging to each one of several • *We went to our respective rooms.*

**respectively** ADVERB
in the same order as the people or things already mentioned • *Ruth and Emma finished first and second respectively.*

**respiration** NOUN
breathing
➤ **respiratory** ADJECTIVE

**respirator** NOUN respirators
❶ a device that fits over a person's nose and mouth to purify air before it is breathed ❷ an apparatus for giving artificial respiration

**respire** VERB respires, respiring, respired
to breathe

**respite** NOUN respites
a short break from something unpleasant or difficult • *There was no respite from the blistering heat.*

**resplendent** ADJECTIVE
impressively bright and colourful

**respond** VERB responds, responding, responded
❶ to reply ❷ to act in answer to, or because of, something; to react ❸ to show a good reaction to something • *The disease did not respond to treatment.*

**respondent** NOUN respondents
the person answering

**response** NOUN responses
❶ a reply or answer ❷ a reaction to something • *The news provoked an angry response.*

**responsibility** NOUN responsibilities
❶ being responsible • *I take full responsibility for the mistake.* ❷ something for which a person is responsible • *It is your responsibility to make sure the doors are locked.*

**responsible** ADJECTIVE
❶ looking after a person or thing and having to take the blame if something goes wrong ❷ reliable and trustworthy ❸ with important duties • *a responsible job* ❹ causing something • *Faulty wiring was responsible for the fire.*
➤ **responsibly** ADVERB

**responsive** ADJECTIVE
responding well or quickly to something

**rest** NOUN rests
❶ a time of sleep or freedom from work as a way of regaining strength ❷ a support, especially on a piece of furniture • *an armrest* ❸ an interval of silence between notes in music
➤ **at rest** not moving
➤ **come to rest** to stop moving
➤ **the rest** the remaining part; the others

**rest** VERB rests, resting, rested
❶ to have a rest; to be still ❷ to allow a part of your body to rest • *Sit down and rest your feet.* ❸ to lean or place something so it is supported; to be supported • *Rest the ladder against the wall.* ❹ to stop moving and stay in one place • *His eyes rested on the picture.* ❺ to be left without further investigation • *And there the matter rests.*
➤ **rest assured** to be confident or certain about something • *Rest assured, it will be a success.*
➤ **rest with someone** to be left to someone to deal with • *It rests with you to suggest a date.*

**restaurant** NOUN restaurants
a place where you can buy a meal and eat it

**restaurateur** (say rest-er-a-**tur**) NOUN restaurateurs
a person who owns or manages a restaurant

> **SPELLING**
> Note the spelling of this word. Unlike 'restaurant' there is no 'n' in it.

**restful** ADJECTIVE
giving rest or a feeling of rest • *a restful holiday*

**restitution** NOUN
❶ restoring something ❷ compensation for injury or damage

**restive** ADJECTIVE
restless or impatient because of delay, anxiety or boredom **WORD ORIGIN** from an earlier meaning = refusing to move, used to describe a horse

**restless** ADJECTIVE
unable to rest or keep still
➤ **restlessly** ADVERB
➤ **restlessness** NOUN

**restoration** NOUN
returning something to its original condition

**restore** VERB restores, restoring, restored
❶ to put something back to its original place
or condition ❷ to clean and repair a work of
art or building so that it looks as good as it
did originally

**restrain** VERB restrains, restraining,
restrained
to hold a person or thing back; to keep a
person or animal under control • *I had to
restrain myself from saying something rude.*

**restraint** NOUN restraints
❶ a limit or control on something ❷ calm
and controlled behaviour

**restrict** VERB restricts, restricting, restricted
to keep someone or something within certain
limits • *Fog severely restricted visibility.*
➤ **restrictive** ADJECTIVE

**restriction** NOUN restrictions
a rule or situation that limits what you can do
• *parking restrictions*

**result** NOUN results
❶ a thing that happens because something
else has happened; an effect or consequence
❷ the score or situation at the end of a game,
competition or race ❸ the answer to a sum or
calculation

**result** VERB results, resulting, resulted
❶ to happen as a result ❷ to have something
as a particular result • *The match resulted in
a draw.*

**resume** VERB resumes, resuming, resumed
❶ to begin something again after stopping
for a while • *They turned away from me and
resumed their conversation.* ❷ to take or
occupy something again • *After the interval
we resumed our seats.*
➤ **resumption** NOUN

**résumé** (say **rez**-yoo-may) NOUN résumés
a summary

**resurgence** NOUN resurgences
a rise or revival of something • *a resurgence
of interest in Latin*

**resurrect** VERB resurrects, resurrecting,
resurrected
to bring something back into use or existence
• *It may be time to resurrect this old custom.*

**resurrection** NOUN
❶ coming back to life after being dead ❷ the
revival of something
➤ **the Resurrection** in the Christian religion,
the resurrection of Jesus Christ three days
after his death

**resuscitate** VERB resuscitates, resuscitating,
resuscitated
to revive a person who has become
unconscious or stopped breathing
➤ **resuscitation** NOUN

**retail** VERB retails, retailing, retailed
to sell goods to the general public
➤ **retailer** NOUN

**retail** NOUN
selling goods to the general public. Compare
with **wholesale**.

**retain** VERB retains, retaining, retained
❶ to continue to have something; to keep
something in your possession or memory
• *Retain your tickets for inspection.* ❷ to hold
something in place

**retainer** NOUN retainers
❶ a sum of money regularly paid to someone
so that they will work for you when needed
❷ a servant who has worked for a person or
family for a long time

**retake** VERB retakes, retaking, retook,
retaken
to take a test or examination again

**retake** NOUN retakes
❶ a test or examination taken again ❷ a
scene filmed again

**retaliate** VERB retaliates, retaliating,
retaliated
to repay an injury or insult with a similar one;
to attack someone in return for a similar
attack
➤ **retaliation** NOUN

**retard** VERB retards, retarding, retarded
to slow down or delay the progress or
development of something
➤ **retarded** ADJECTIVE

**retch** VERB retches, retching, retched
to strain your throat as if you are being sick

SPELLING
Take care not to confuse with **wretch**.

**retention** NOUN
retaining or keeping something

**retentive** ADJECTIVE
able to retain facts and remember things
easily • *She has a retentive memory.*

**reticent** (say **ret-i-sent**) ADJECTIVE
not willing to tell people what you feel or
think
➤ **reticence** NOUN

**retina** NOUN retinas
a layer of membrane at the back of the
eyeball, sensitive to light

**retinue** NOUN retinues
a group of people accompanying an
important person

**retire** VERB retires, retiring, retired
❶ to give up your regular work because you
have reached a certain age ❷ to go to bed
❸ to leave a place and go somewhere more
private • *The jury retired to consider their
verdict.*

**retired** ADJECTIVE
no longer working • *a retired teacher*

**retirement** NOUN
the time when someone gives up regular work
• *My grandfather is approaching retirement.*

**retiring** ADJECTIVE
shy; avoiding company

**retort** NOUN retorts
❶ a quick, witty or angry reply ❷ a glass
bottle with a long downward-bent neck, used
in distilling liquids

**retort** VERB retorts, retorting, retorted
to make a quick, witty or angry reply • *'Don't
be ridiculous!' he retorted.*

**retrace** VERB retraces, retracing, retraced
to go back over the route that you have just
taken • *We retraced our steps and returned
to the ferry.*

**retract** VERB retracts, retracting, retracted
❶ to pull something back or in • *All cats
except cheetahs can retract their claws.* ❷ to
withdraw a statement or accusation
➤ **retraction** NOUN
➤ **retractable** ADJECTIVE

**retreat** VERB retreats, retreating, retreated
to go back after being defeated or to avoid
danger or difficulty

**retreat** NOUN retreats
❶ retreating ❷ a quiet place to which
someone can go to relax

**retribution** NOUN
a deserved punishment

**retrieve** VERB retrieves, retrieving, retrieved
❶ to bring or get something back • *I went
next door to retrieve the ball.* ❷ to find
information stored in a computer ❸ to rescue
or save a situation
➤ **retrieval** NOUN

**retriever** NOUN retrievers
a kind of dog originally trained to find and
bring back birds and animals that have been
shot

**retrospect** NOUN
➤ **in retrospect** when you look back at what
has happened • *In retrospect, I can see it was
a terrible mistake.*

**retrospective** ADJECTIVE
❶ looking back on the past ❷ applying to the
past as well as the future • *The law could not
be made retrospective.*

**return** VERB returns, returning, returned
❶ to come back or go back ❷ to bring, give,
put or send something back

**return** NOUN returns
❶ returning to a place ❷ giving or sending
something back ❸ profit • *He gets a good
return on his savings.* ❹ a return ticket
➤ **in return** as payment or in exchange

**return match** NOUN return matches
a second match played between the same
teams

**return ticket** NOUN return tickets
a ticket for a journey to a place and back
again

**reunify** VERB reunifies, reunifying, reunified
to make a divided country into one again
• *How long has Germany been reunified?*
➤ **reunification** NOUN

**reunion** NOUN reunions
❶ a meeting of people who have not met
for some time • *a family reunion* ❷ coming
together again after being apart

**reunite** VERB reunites, reuniting, reunited
to come together again or bring people
together again after a period of separation

**reuse** (say ree-**yooz**) VERB reuses, reusing,
reused
to use something again • *I try to reuse plastic
bags.*
➤ **reusable** ADJECTIVE

**reuse** (say ree-**yooss**) NOUN
using something again

a b c d e f g h i j k l m n o p q r s t u v w x y z

**rev** VERB revs, revving, revved (*informal*)
to make an engine run quickly, especially when starting

**rev** NOUN revs (*informal*) a revolution of an engine

**Rev.** ABBREVIATION
Reverend

**reveal** VERB reveals, revealing, revealed
❶ to make something known • *Police have not yet revealed the identity of the victim.* ❷ to show something that was hidden

**reveille** (say riv-**al**-ee) NOUN reveilles
a military waking signal sounded on a bugle or drums **WORD ORIGIN** from French *réveillez* = wake up!

**revel** VERB revels, revelling, revelled
❶ to take great delight in something • *She was revelling in all the attention.* ❷ to enjoy yourself with others in a lively and noisy celebration
➤ **reveller** NOUN

**revelation** NOUN revelations
❶ something revealed, especially something surprising • *startling revelations about her private life* ❷ revealing something

**revelry** NOUN
❶ revelling ❷ lively and noisy celebration

**revels** PLURAL NOUN
lively and noisy celebrations

**revenge** NOUN
harming someone in return for harm that they have done to you

**revenge** VERB revenges, revenging, revenged
to take revenge on someone

**revenue** NOUN revenues
❶ a country's income from taxes etc., used for paying public expenses ❷ a company's income

**reverberate** VERB reverberates, reverberating, reverberated
to be repeated as an echo; to resound • *His voice reverberated around the hall.*
➤ **reverberation** NOUN

**revere** (say riv-**eer**) VERB reveres, revering, revered
to respect or admire someone deeply

**reverence** NOUN
a feeling of awe and deep or religious respect

**Reverend** NOUN
the title of a member of the clergy • *the Reverend John Smith*

**reverent** ADJECTIVE
feeling or showing reverence
➤ **reverently** ADVERB
➤ **reverential** ADJECTIVE

**reverie** (say **rev**-er-ee) NOUN reveries
a daydream

**reversal** NOUN reversals
❶ a change to an opposite direction, position or course of action ❷ a piece of bad luck or misfortune

**reverse** ADJECTIVE
❶ facing or moving in the opposite direction ❷ opposite in character or order • *I will announce the results in reverse order.*

**reverse** NOUN reverses
❶ the opposite of something ❷ the reverse side or face of something ❸ a piece of misfortune • *They suffered several reverses.* ❹ the reverse gear of a vehicle
➤ **in reverse** the opposite way round

**reverse** VERB reverses, reversing, reversed
❶ to turn something upside down or the other way round ❷ to change round the usual position, position or function of two things ❸ to drive a vehicle backwards ❹ to cancel a decision; to change an opinion to the opposite one
➤ **reversible** ADJECTIVE

**reverse gear** NOUN
a gear that allows a vehicle to be driven backwards

**revert** VERB reverts, reverting, reverted
to return to a former state, habit or subject
• *After her divorce she reverted to her maiden name.*
➤ **reversion** NOUN

**review** NOUN reviews
❶ an inspection or survey of something ❷ a published description and opinion of a book, film, play, etc.

**review** VERB reviews, reviewing, reviewed
❶ to write a review of a book, film, play, etc. ❷ to reconsider a matter or decision ❸ to inspect or survey something
➤ **reviewer** NOUN

**SPELLING**
Take care not to confuse the noun **review** with **revue**, which means an entertainment consisting of songs and sketches.

**revile** VERB reviles, reviling, reviled
to criticize someone angrily in abusive language

**revise** VERB revises, revising, revised
❶ to go over work that you have already done, especially in preparing for an examination ❷ to correct or change something • *I have since revised my opinion.*

**revision** NOUN revisions
❶ a change in something in order to correct or improve it ❷ going over work that you have already done, especially in preparing for an examination

**revitalize** (also **revitalise**) VERB revitalizes, revitalizing, revitalized
to put new strength or vitality into something

**revival** NOUN revivals
❶ an improvement in the condition or strength of something • *an economic revival* ❷ a renewal of interest or popularity

**revive** VERB revives, reviving, revived
❶ to bring someone or something back to life, strength or use • *Attempts were made to revive him but he was already dead.*
❷ to restore interest in or the popularity of something

**revoke** VERB revokes, revoking, revoked
to withdraw or cancel a decree, licence or right

**revolt** VERB revolts, revolting, revolted
❶ to disgust someone ❷ to take part in a rebellion

**revolt** NOUN revolts
a rebellion

**revolting** ADJECTIVE
disgusting or horrible • *a revolting smell*

**revolution** NOUN revolutions
❶ a rebellion that overthrows the government ❷ a complete or drastic change ❸ a movement around something; one complete turn of a wheel or engine

**revolutionary** ADJECTIVE
❶ involving a great change • *a revolutionary idea* ❷ to do with a political revolution

**revolutionary** NOUN revolutionaries
a person who supports a political revolution

**revolutionize** (also **revolutionise**) VERB revolutionizes, revolutionizing, revolutionized
to make a great change in something • *The Internet has revolutionized the way we shop.*

**revolve** VERB revolves, revolving, revolved
❶ to turn in a circle round a central point or make something do this ❷ to have something

as the most important element • *Her life revolves around her work.*

**revolver** NOUN revolvers
a pistol with a revolving mechanism that can be fired a number of times without reloading

**revue** NOUN revues
an entertainment consisting of songs and sketches, often about current events

> **SPELLING**
> Take care not to confuse revue with the noun review, which means a survey or a piece of writing.

**revulsion** NOUN
a feeling of strong disgust

**reward** NOUN rewards
❶ something given in return for something good you have done ❷ a sum of money offered for help in catching a criminal or finding lost property

**reward** VERB rewards, rewarding, rewarded
to give a reward to someone • *I promise you will be well rewarded for your efforts.*

**rewarding** ADJECTIVE
giving satisfaction and a feeling of achievement • *a rewarding job*

**rewind** VERB rewinds, rewinding, rewound
to wind a cassette or videotape back to or towards the beginning

**rewrite** VERB rewrites, rewriting, rewrote, rewritten
to write something again or differently

**rhapsody** (say rap-so-dee) NOUN rhapsodies
❶ a statement of great delight about something ❷ a romantic piece of music
**WORD ORIGIN** from Greek *rhapsoidos* = someone who stitches songs together

**rhesus monkey** NOUN rhesus monkeys
a kind of small monkey from Northern India

**rhesus positive** ADJECTIVE
having a substance (*rhesus factor*) found in the red blood cells of many humans and some other primates, first found in the rhesus monkey
➤ **rhesus negative** ADJECTIVE
without rhesus factor

**rhetoric** (say ret-er-ik) NOUN
❶ the art of using words impressively, especially in public speaking ❷ language that is used for its impressive effect but is not sincere or meaningful

> **rhetorical** ADJECTIVE
> **rhetorically** ADVERB

**rhetorical question** NOUN rhetorical questions
a question that you ask for dramatic effect without expecting to get an answer, e.g. 'Who cares?' (= nobody cares)

**rheumatism** NOUN
a disease that causes pain and stiffness in joints and muscles
> **rheumatic** ADJECTIVE
> **rheumatoid** ADJECTIVE

**rhino** NOUN rhino or rhinos (informal)
a rhinoceros

**rhinoceros** NOUN rhinoceros or rhinoceroses
a large heavy animal with a horn or two horns on its nose (WORD ORIGIN) from Greek *rhinos* = of the nose + *keras* = horn

**rhizome** NOUN rhizomes
a thick underground stem which produces roots and new plants

**rhododendron** NOUN rhododendrons
an evergreen shrub with large clusters of trumpet-shaped flowers (WORD ORIGIN) from Greek *rhodon* = rose + *dendron* = tree

**rhomboid** NOUN rhomboids
a shape with four straight sides, with only the opposite sides and angles equal to each other

**rhombus** NOUN rhombuses
a shape with four equal sides but no right angles, like the diamond on playing cards

**SPELLING**
There is a silent h after the r in **rhombus**.

**rhubarb** NOUN
a plant with thick reddish stalks that are used as fruit

**rhyme** NOUN rhymes
**❶** a similar sound in the endings of words, e.g. *bat/fat/mat, batter/fatter/matter* **❷** a poem with rhymes **❸** a word that rhymes with another

**rhyme** VERB rhymes, rhyming, rhymed
**❶** to form a rhyme • 'Tough' rhymes with 'stuff'. **❷** to have rhymes • Some poems rhyme and some don't.

**SPELLING**
There is a silent h in **rhyme**.

**rhythm** NOUN rhythms
a regular pattern of beats, sounds or movements • He tapped his foot in rhythm with the music.

**SPELLING**
Try learning the phrase 'rhythm helps your two hips move' to spell rhythm.

**rhythmic** ADJECTIVE
having a regular pattern of beats, sounds or movements • the rhythmic ticking of the clock
> **rhythmical** ADJECTIVE
> **rhythmically** ADVERB

**rib** NOUN ribs
**❶** each of the curved bones round the chest **❷** a curved part that looks like a rib or supports something • the ribs of an umbrella
> **ribbed** ADJECTIVE

**ribald** (say **rib**-ald) ADJECTIVE
funny in a rude or disrespectful way
> **ribaldry** NOUN

**riband** NOUN ribands
(old use) a ribbon

**ribbon** NOUN ribbons
**❶** a narrow strip of silk, nylon or other material, used for decoration or for tying something **❷** a long narrow strip of inked material used in some printers and typewriters

**rice** NOUN
a cereal plant grown in flooded fields in hot countries or its seeds

**rich** ADJECTIVE
**❶** having a lot of money or property; wealthy **❷** having a large supply of something • The country is rich in natural resources. **❸** a rich colour, sound or smell is pleasantly deep or strong **❹** rich food contains a lot of fat, butter or eggs **❺** expensive or luxurious • The room was decorated with rich fabrics.
> **richness** NOUN

**riches** PLURAL NOUN
great wealth

**richly** ADVERB
**❶** in a rich or luxurious way • a richly decorated room **❷** fully or thoroughly • This award is richly deserved.

**Richter scale** NOUN
a scale (from 0-10) used to show the force of an earthquake (WORD ORIGIN) named after an American scientist, C. F. *Richter*, who studied earthquakes

**rick** NOUN ricks
a large neat stack of hay or straw

**rick** VERB ricks, ricking, ricked
(*British*) to sprain or wrench your neck or back

**rickets** NOUN
a disease caused by lack of vitamin D, causing deformed bones

**rickety** ADJECTIVE
poorly made and likely to break or fall down
• *a rickety wooden bridge*

**rickshaw** NOUN rickshaws
a two-wheeled carriage pulled by one or more people, used in the Far East
(**WORD ORIGIN**) from Japanese *jin-riki-sha* = person-power-vehicle

**ricochet** (say rik-osh-ay) VERB ricochets, ricocheting, ricocheted
to bounce away from a surface after hitting it
• *The bullets ricocheted off the wall.*
➤ **ricochet** NOUN
(**WORD ORIGIN**) French, = the skipping of a flat stone on water

**ricotta** NOUN
a kind of soft Italian cheese made from sheep's milk

**rid** VERB rids, ridding, rid
to make a person or place free from something unwanted • *He rid the town of rats.*
➤ **get rid of something** to remove something or throw it away

**riddle** NOUN riddles
a puzzling question, especially as a joke

**riddle** VERB riddles, riddling, riddled
to make a lot of holes in something • *The car was riddled with bullets.*
➤ **be riddled with something** to be full of something bad or unpleasant • *The book is riddled with mistakes.*

**ride** VERB rides, riding, rode, ridden
❶ to sit on a horse, bicycle, etc. and control it as it carries you along ❷ to travel in a car, bus, train, etc. ❸ to float or be supported on something • *The ship rode the waves.*

**ride** NOUN rides
❶ a journey on a horse, bicycle, etc. or in a vehicle ❷ a roundabout etc. that you ride on at a fair or amusement park

**SPELLING**

The past tense of **ride** is **rode** and the past participle is **ridden**.

**rider** NOUN riders
❶ a person who rides something, especially a horse ❷ an extra comment or statement

**ridge** NOUN ridges
❶ a long narrow part higher than the rest of something ❷ a long narrow range of hills or mountains
➤ **ridged** ADJECTIVE

**ridicule** VERB ridicules, ridiculing, ridiculed
to make fun of a person or thing

**ridicule** NOUN
unkind words or behaviour that make a person or thing look ridiculous

**ridiculous** ADJECTIVE
so silly or foolish that it makes people laugh or despise it • *You look ridiculous in those trousers.*
➤ **ridiculously** ADVERB

**rife** ADJECTIVE
widespread; happening frequently • *Crime was rife in the town.*

**riff-raff** NOUN
the rabble; disreputable people
(**WORD ORIGIN**) from old French *rif et raf* = everybody and everything

**rifle** NOUN rifles
a long gun with spiral grooves (called *rifling*) inside the barrel that make the bullet spin and so travel more accurately

**rifle** VERB rifles, rifling, rifled
to search quickly through a place in order to find or steal something • *They had rifled through his desk.*

**rift** NOUN rifts
❶ a crack or split in something ❷ a disagreement that separates friends

**rift valley** NOUN rift valleys
a steep-sided valley formed where the land has sunk

**rig** VERB rigs, rigging, rigged
❶ to fit a ship with ropes, spars, sails, etc. ❷ to arrange the result of an election or contest dishonestly
➤ **rig someone out** to provide someone with clothes or equipment
➤ **rig something up** to set up a structure quickly or out of makeshift materials • *We managed to rig up a shelter for the night.*

**rig** NOUN rigs
❶ a framework supporting the machinery for drilling an oil well ❷ the way a ship's masts and sails etc. are arranged ❸ (*informal*) an outfit of clothes

**rigging** NOUN
the ropes etc. that support a ship's mast and sails

**right** ADJECTIVE
❶ on or towards the east if you think of yourself as facing north ❷ correct; true • *the right answer* ❸ morally good; fair or just • *It's not right to cheat.* ❹ conservative; not in favour of socialist reforms
➤ **rightness** NOUN

**right** ADVERB
❶ on or towards the right • *Turn right here.* ❷ straight; directly • *Go right on.* ❸ all the way; completely • *Turn right round.* ❹ exactly • *right in the middle* ❺ correctly or appropriately • *Did I do that right?*
➤ **right away** immediately

**right** NOUN rights
❶ the right-hand side or part of something ❷ what is morally good or fair or just ❸ something that people are allowed to do or have • *People over 18 have the right to vote in elections.*

**right** VERB rights, righting, righted
❶ to make a thing upright • *The crew managed to right the boat.* ❷ to put something right • *The fault might right itself.*

**right angle** NOUN
an angle of 90°

**righteous** ADJECTIVE
doing what is right; virtuous • *He was filled with righteous indignation.*
➤ **righteously** ADVERB
➤ **righteousness** NOUN

**rightful** ADJECTIVE
deserved or proper • *The bike was returned to its rightful owner.*
➤ **rightfully** ADVERB

**right-hand** ADJECTIVE
on the right side of something • *the top right-hand corner of the page*

**right-handed** ADJECTIVE
using the right hand in preference to the left hand

**right-hand man** NOUN right-hand men
the person you depend on the most to help you in your work

**rightly** ADVERB
correctly or justifiably • *She is rightly proud of her achievements.*

**right-minded** ADJECTIVE
having ideas and opinions which are sensible and morally good

**right of way** NOUN rights of way
❶ a public path across private land ❷ the right of one vehicle to pass or cross a junction before another

**rigid** ADJECTIVE
❶ stiff or firm; not bending easily • *a rigid support* ❷ strict and difficult to change • *rigid rules*
➤ **rigidly** ADVERB
➤ **rigidity** NOUN

**rigmarole** NOUN rigmaroles
❶ a long rambling statement ❷ a complicated procedure **WORD ORIGIN** from Middle English *ragman* = a legal document

**rigor mortis** (say ri-ger mor-tis) NOUN
stiffening of the body after death
**WORD ORIGIN** Latin, = stiffness of death

**rigorous** ADJECTIVE
❶ strict or severe • *a rigorous diet* ❷ careful and thorough • *rigorous tests*
➤ **rigorously** ADVERB

**rigour** NOUN rigours
❶ doing something carefully with great attention to detail • *The tests were carried out with rigour.* ❷ strictness or severity ❸ harshness of weather or conditions • *the rigours of winter*

**rile** VERB riles, riling, riled (*informal*)
to annoy or irritate someone

**rill** NOUN rills
a very small stream

**rim** NOUN rims
the outer edge of a cup, wheel or other round object

**rime** NOUN rimes
the part of a syllable that contains the vowel and, if there is one, the final consonant or group of consonants, e.g. *og* in *dog*

**rimmed** ADJECTIVE
having an edge or border • *Her eyes were rimmed with red.*

**rind** NOUN
the tough skin on bacon, cheese or fruit

**ring** NOUN rings
❶ a circle; a circular band • *The coffee cup left a ring on the table.* • *a key ring* ❷ a thin circular piece of metal you wear on a finger ❸ the space where a circus performs ❹ a square area in which a boxing match or wrestling match takes place ❺ the act or sound of ringing

➤ **give someone a ring** (*informal*) to telephone someone

**ring** VERB rings, ringing, rang, rung
❶ to telephone someone • *Please ring me tomorrow.* ❷ to cause a bell to sound ❸ to make a loud clear sound like that of a bell ❹ to be filled with sound • *The hall rang with cheers.*
➤ **ring a bell** to sound faintly familiar • *His name rings a bell.*

**ring** VERB rings, ringing, ringed
❶ to put a ring round something • *Ring the answer that you think is the right one.* ❷ to surround something • *The whole area was ringed with police.*

**ringleader** NOUN ringleaders
a person who leads others in rebellion, mischief or crime

**ringlet** NOUN ringlets
a tube-shaped curl of hair

**ringmaster** NOUN ringmasters
the person in charge of a performance in a circus ring

**ring road** NOUN ring roads
(*British*) a road that runs around the edge of a town so that traffic does not have to go through the centre

**ringtone** NOUN ringtones
the sound your mobile phone makes when it receives a call

**ringworm** NOUN
a fungal skin infection that causes itchy circular patches, especially on the scalp

**rink** NOUN rinks
a place made for skating

**rinse** VERB rinses, rinsing, rinsed
❶ to wash something in clean water to remove soap ❷ to wash something lightly

**rinse** NOUN rinses
❶ rinsing ❷ a liquid for colouring the hair

**riot** NOUN riots
wild or violent behaviour by a crowd of people in a public place
➤ **run riot** to behave or spread in a wild or uncontrolled way • *Her imagination began to run riot.*

**riot** VERB riots, rioting, rioted
to take part in a riot
➤ **rioter** NOUN

**riot gear** NOUN
protective clothing, helmets, shields, etc.

worn or carried by the police or army dealing with a riot

**riotous** ADJECTIVE
❶ noisy and uncontrolled; boisterous
• *riotous laughter* ❷ disorderly or unruly

**RIP** ABBREVIATION
may he or she (or they) rest in peace
**WORD ORIGIN** short for Latin *requiescat* (or *requiescant*) *in pace*

**rip** VERB rips, ripping, ripped
❶ to tear something roughly ❷ to become torn ❸ to remove something quickly by pulling hard • *He ripped off his tie.* ❹ to rush along • *A tornado ripped through the town.*
➤ **rip someone off** (*informal*) to swindle someone or charge them too much

**rip** NOUN rips
a torn place

**ripe** ADJECTIVE riper, ripest
❶ ready to be harvested or eaten ❷ ready and suitable • *The time is ripe for revolution.*
➤ **ripeness** NOUN
➤ **a ripe old age** a great age

**ripen** VERB ripens, ripening, ripened
to become ripe or to make something ripe
• *The grapes were ripening in the sun.*

**rip-off** NOUN rip-offs
(*informal*) something that costs a lot more than it should

**riposte** (say rip-ost) NOUN ripostes
❶ a quick clever reply ❷ a quick return thrust in fencing

**ripple** NOUN ripples
❶ a small wave or series of waves ❷ a gentle sound that rises and falls • *a ripple of applause*

**ripple** VERB ripples, rippling, rippled
to form ripples

**rise** VERB rise, rising, rose, risen
❶ to go upwards • *Smoke was rising from the fire.* ❷ The sun rises in the east. ❸ to increase • *Prices are expected to rise.* ❸ to get up from lying, sitting or kneeling ❹ to get out of bed ❺ to rebel • *They rose in revolt against the tyrant.* ❻ bread or cake rises when it swells up by the action of yeast ❼ a river rises when it begins its course ❽ wind rises when it begins to blow more strongly

**rise** NOUN rises
❶ the action of rising; an upward movement
❷ an increase in amount or in wages ❸ an upward slope

**A**

➤ **give rise to something** to cause something to happen

**B**

**rising** NOUN risings
a revolt against a government

**C**

**risk** NOUN risks
a chance that something bad will happen
• *There's a risk that the river might flood.*

**D**

**risk** VERB risks, risking, risked
❶ to take the chance of damaging or losing something • *They risked their lives to rescue the children.* ❷ to accept the risk of something unpleasant happening • *He risks injury each time he climbs.*

**E**

**F**

**risky** ADJECTIVE riskier, riskiest
full of risk • *That was a risky thing to do.*

**G**

**risotto** NOUN
an Italian dish of rice cooked with vegetables and, usually, meat

**H**

**rissole** NOUN rissoles
(*British*) a fried cake of minced meat or fish

**I**

**rite** NOUN rites
a religious ceremony; a solemn ritual
• *funeral rites*

**J**

**ritual** NOUN rituals
the series of actions used in a religious or other ceremony

**K**

**ritual** ADJECTIVE
done as part of a ritual • *ritual chanting*

**L**

**rival** NOUN rivals
a person or thing that competes with another or tries to do the same thing

**M**

**N**

**rival** VERB rivals, rivalling, rivalled
to be as good as another person or thing
• *Nothing can rival the taste of home-made ice cream.* **WORD ORIGIN** from Latin *rivalis* = someone using the same stream (from *rivus* = stream)

**O**

**P**

**Q**

**rivalry** NOUN rivalries
competition between people or groups
• *There was a lot of rivalry between the sisters.*

**R**

**S**

**T**

**river** NOUN rivers
a large stream of water flowing in a natural channel

**U**

**V**

**rivet** NOUN rivets
a strong nail or bolt for holding pieces of metal together. The end opposite the head is flattened to form another head when it is in place.

**W**

**X**

**Y**

**rivet** VERB rivets, riveting, riveted
❶ to fasten something with rivets ❷ to hold

**Z**

someone still • *He stood riveted to the spot.*
❸ to hold someone's attention completely • *I was riveted by her story.*
➤ **riveter** NOUN

**riveting** ADJECTIVE
so fascinating that it holds your attention completely • *It's a riveting story.*

**rivulet** NOUN rivulets
a small stream

**roach** NOUN roach
a small freshwater fish

**road** NOUN roads
❶ a level way with a hard surface made for traffic to travel on ❷ a way or course • *She seems to be well on the road to recovery.*

**roadblock** NOUN roadblocks
a barrier across a road, set up by the police or army to stop and check vehicles

**road rage** NOUN
aggressive or violent behaviour by a driver towards other drivers

**roadside** NOUN
the side of a road

**roadway** NOUN
the middle part of the road, used by traffic

**roadworthy** ADJECTIVE
safe to be used on roads

**roam** VERB roams, roaming, roamed
to wander widely • *Sheep roam freely on the hillside.*

**roan** ADJECTIVE
a roan horse has a brown or black coat with many white hairs

**roar** NOUN roars
❶ a loud deep sound like that made by a lion
❷ loud laughter

**roar** VERB roars, roaring, roared
❶ to make a roar ❷ to laugh loudly
➤ **do a roaring trade** to sell a lot of something quickly

**roast** VERB roasts, roasting, roasted
❶ to cook meat etc. in an oven or over a fire
❷ to be roasting is to feel very hot

**roast** ADJECTIVE
cooked by roasting • *roast beef*

**roast** NOUN roasts
a piece of meat that has been roasted

**rob** VERB robs, robbing, robbed
❶ to steal something from a person or place, often using force • *He robbed me of*

my watch. • *The bank's been robbed.* ❷ to prevent someone from having something that they should have • *Injury robbed her of a place in the final.*

**robber** *NOUN* robbers
a person who steals from a place, often using force

**robbery** *NOUN* robberies
the crime of stealing from a place, often using force

**robe** *NOUN* robes
a long loose piece of clothing, especially one worn in ceremonies

**robe** *VERB* robes, robing, robed
to dress someone in a robe or ceremonial robes

**robin** *NOUN* robins
a small brown bird with a red breast

**robot** *NOUN* robots
❶ a machine that looks or acts like a person ❷ a machine operated by remote control ❸ (*S. African*) a set of traffic lights
**WORD ORIGIN** from Czech *robota* = forced labour

**robotic** *ADJECTIVE*
to do with robots; like a robot • *a robotic voice*

**robust** *ADJECTIVE*
strong and healthy
➤ **robustly** *ADVERB*
**WORD ORIGIN** from Latin *robur* = strength, an oak tree

**rock** *NOUN* rocks
❶ a large stone or boulder ❷ the hard part of the earth's crust, under the soil ❸ a hard sweet usually shaped like a stick and sold at the seaside ❹ rock music ❺ a rocking movement

**rock** *VERB* rocks, rocking, rocked
❶ to move gently backwards and forwards or from side to side; to make something do this ❷ to shake someone or something violently • *The earthquake rocked the city.* ❸ to shock or upset someone • *We were rocked by the news of her death.*

**rock and roll, rock 'n' roll** *NOUN*
a kind of popular dance music with a strong beat, originating in the 1950s

**rock-bottom** *ADJECTIVE*
at the lowest level • *rock-bottom prices*

**rocker** *NOUN* rockers
❶ a curved support for a chair or cradle ❷ a

rocking chair
➤ **off your rocker** (*informal*) mad or crazy

**rockery** *NOUN* rockeries
a mound or bank in a garden, where plants are made to grow between large rocks

**rocket** *NOUN* rockets
❶ a firework that shoots high into the air ❷ a tube-shaped structure that is pushed up into the air by burning gases, used to send up a missile or a spacecraft

**rocket** *VERB* rockets, rocketing, rocketed
to move quickly upwards or away

**rocking chair** *NOUN* rocking chairs
a chair that can be rocked by a person sitting in it

**rocking horse** *NOUN* rocking horses
a model of a horse that can be rocked by a child sitting on it

**rock music** *NOUN*
popular music with a heavy beat

**rocky** *ADJECTIVE* rockier, rockiest
❶ covered with or made of rocks • *a rocky landscape* ❷ unsteady or unstable

**rod** *NOUN* rods
❶ a long thin stick or bar ❷ a stick with a line attached for fishing

**rodent** *NOUN* rodents
an animal that has large front teeth for gnawing things. Rats, mice and squirrels are rodents **WORD ORIGIN** from Latin *rodens* = gnawing

**rodeo** (say roh-**day**-oh) *NOUN* rodeos
a display of cowboys' skill in riding wild horses, controlling cattle, etc.

**roe** *NOUN*
❶ a mass of eggs or reproductive cells in a fish's body ❷ roes or roe a kind of small deer of Europe and Asia. The male is called a **roebuck**.

**rogue** *NOUN* rogues
❶ a dishonest person ❷ a mischievous but likeable person

**rogue** *ADJECTIVE*
behaving in a way that is different from the rest and causing trouble • *a rogue agent*
➤ **roguery** *NOUN*

**roguish** *ADJECTIVE*
playful and mischievous • *a roguish smile*
➤ **roguishly** *ADVERB*

**role** *NOUN* roles
❶ an actor's part in a play or film

a
b
c
d
e
f
g
h
i
j
k
l
m
n
o
p
q
r
s
t
u
v
w
x
y
z

**❷** someone's or something's purpose or
function • *the role of computers in education*
**WORD ORIGIN** from French *rôle* = roll
(originally the roll of paper on which an actor's
part was written)

**role model** NOUN **role models**
a person looked to by others as an example of
how to behave

**roll** VERB **rolls, rolling, rolled**
**❶** to move along by turning over and over,
like a ball or wheel; to make something do
this **❷** to form something into the shape of
a cylinder or ball **❸** to flatten something by
rolling a rounded object over it • *Roll out the
pastry into a large circle.* **❹** a ship or boat
rolls when it rocks from side to side **❺** to pass
steadily • *The years rolled by.* **❻** thunder rolls
when it makes a long rumbling sound

**roll** NOUN **rolls**
**❶** a cylinder made by rolling something up
**❷** a small individual portion of bread baked
in a rounded shape **❸** an official list of names
**❹** a long vibrating or rumbling sound • *a
drum roll*

**roll-call** NOUN **roll-calls**
the calling of a list of names to check that
everyone is present

**roller** NOUN **rollers**
**❶** a cylinder used for flattening or spreading
things or on which something is wound **❷** a
long swelling sea wave

**Rollerblade** NOUN **Rollerblades**
(*trademark*) a boot like an ice-skating boot,
with a line of wheels in place of the skate, for
rolling smoothly on hard ground
➤ **rollerblading** NOUN

**roller coaster** NOUN **roller coasters**
a type of railway ride in fairgrounds and
amusement parks with a series of alternate
steep descents and ascents

**roller skate** NOUN **roller skates**
a boot with small wheels fitted under it so
that you can roll smoothly over the ground
➤ **roller-skating** NOUN

**rollicking** ADJECTIVE
boisterous and full of fun **WORD ORIGIN** from
romp + frolic

**rolling pin** NOUN
a heavy cylinder for rolling over pastry to
flatten it

**rolling stock** NOUN
the railway engines, carriages and wagons
used on a railway

**roly-poly** NOUN **roly-polies**
a pudding of paste covered with jam, rolled
up and boiled

**ROM** ABBREVIATION
read-only memory, a type of computer
memory with contents that can be searched
or copied but not changed

**Roman** ADJECTIVE
to do with ancient or modern Rome or its
people

**Roman** NOUN **Romans**
a person from ancient or modern Rome

**Roman alphabet** NOUN
this alphabet, in which most European
languages are written

**Roman candle** NOUN **Roman candles**
a tubular firework that sends out coloured
sparks

**Roman Catholic** ADJECTIVE
belonging to or to do with the Christian
Church that has the Pope (bishop of Rome)
as its head
➤ **Roman Catholicism** NOUN

**Roman Catholic** NOUN **Roman Catholics**
a member of this Church

**romance** (say ro-**manss**) NOUN **romances**
**❶** tender feelings, experiences and qualities
connected with love **❷** a love story **❸** a
love affair **❹** mystery and excitement • *the
romance of the East* **❺** a medieval story
about the adventures of heroes • *a romance
of King Arthur's court*

**Romance language** NOUN **Romance
languages**
any of the group of European languages
descended from Latin, such as French, Italian
and Spanish

**Roman numerals** PLURAL NOUN
letters that represent numbers (I = 1, V = 5,
X = 10, etc.), used by the ancient Romans.
Compare with **Arabic numerals**.

**romantic** ADJECTIVE
**❶** to do with love or romance **❷** sentimental
or idealistic; not realistic or practical • *She
has a romantic view of life in the countryside.*
➤ **romantically** ADVERB

**Romany** NOUN **Romanies**
**❶** a member of a people who live in travelling
communities; a gypsy **❷** the language of
these people

**romp** VERB romps, romping, romped
to play in a rough or lively way
➤ **romp** NOUN

**rompers** PLURAL NOUN
a piece of clothing for a baby or young child,
covering the body and legs

**roof** NOUN roofs
❶ the part that covers the top of a building,
shelter or vehicle ❷ the top inside surface of
something • *the roof of your mouth*

**roofing** NOUN
material used to construct the roof of a
building

**roof rack** NOUN roof racks
a framework for carrying luggage on top of
a vehicle

**rook** NOUN rooks
❶ a black crow that nests in large groups ❷ a
chess piece shaped like a castle

**rookery** NOUN rookeries
❶ a place where many rooks nest ❷ a
breeding place of penguins or seals

**room** NOUN rooms
❶ a part of a building with its own walls and
ceiling ❷ enough space • *Is there room for
me?*
➤ **roomful** NOUN

**roomy** ADJECTIVE roomier, roomiest
containing plenty of room; spacious • *a
roomy car*

**roost** VERB roosts, roosting, roosted
birds roost when they perch or settle for sleep

**roost** NOUN roosts
a place where birds roost

**rooster** NOUN roosters (*North American*)
a cockerel

**root** NOUN roots
❶ the part of a plant that grows under the
ground and absorbs water and nourishment
from the soil ❷ a source or basis of
something • *We are trying to get to the root
of the problem*. ❸ a number which, when
multiplied by itself a particular number of
times, produces another number • *9 is the
square root of 81 (9 x 9 = 81)*.
➤ **take root** ❶ to grow roots ❷ to become
established • *Gradually the idea took root.*

**root** VERB roots, rooting, rooted
❶ to take root in the ground; to cause
something to take root ❷ to fix someone
firmly in one place • *Fear rooted us to the
spot.* ❸ to search for something by moving

things • *She rooted around in her handbag.*
❹ a pig or other animal roots when it turns
up ground in search of food
➤ **root for someone** to support someone
enthusiastically
➤ **root something out** to find something
and get rid of it

**rope** NOUN ropes
a strong thick cord made of twisted strands
of fibre
➤ **show someone the ropes** to show
someone how to do a job

**rope** VERB ropes, roping, roped
to fasten something with a rope • *We roped
ourselves together for safety.*
➤ **rope someone in** to persuade someone to
take part in something

**rosary** NOUN rosaries
a string of beads for keeping count of a set of
prayers as they are said

**rose** NOUN roses
❶ a scented flower with a long thorny stem;
the bush this flower grows on ❷ a deep pink
colour ❸ a sprinkling nozzle with many holes,
e.g. on a watering can or hosepipe

**rose** VERB
past tense of **rise**

**rosemary** NOUN
an evergreen shrub with fragrant leaves, used
in cooking

**rosette** NOUN rosettes
a large circular badge or ornament, made of
ribbon

**Rosh Hashanah, Rosh Hashana** NOUN
the Jewish New Year festival

**roster** NOUN rosters
a list showing people's turns to be on duty

**rostrum** NOUN rostra
a platform for one person, e.g. for giving
a speech or conducting an orchestra
**WORD ORIGIN** Latin, = beak, prow of a warship
(because a rostrum in ancient Rome was
decorated with the prows of captured enemy
ships)

**rosy** ADJECTIVE rosier, rosiest
❶ deep pink • *rosy cheeks* ❷ hopeful or
cheerful • *a rosy future*

**rot** VERB rots, rotting, rotted
to go soft or bad and become useless; to
decay

**rot** NOUN
❶ rotting or decay ❷ (*informal*) nonsense

A
B
C
D
E
F
G
H
I
J
K
L
M
N
O
P
Q
**R**
S
T
U
V
W
X
Y
Z

**rota** (say roh-ta) NOUN rotas
a list of people to do things or of things to be done in turn

**rotate** VERB rotates, rotating, rotated
**①** to turn or spin in circles round a central point; to revolve • *A day is the time it takes the Earth to rotate once on its axis.* **②** to happen or make something happen in a fixed order; to take turns at doing something • *The job of treasurer rotates.*
➤ **rotary** ADJECTIVE

**rotation** NOUN rotations
**①** movement in circles round a central point • *one rotation every 24 hours* **②** happening or making things happen in a certain order • *the rotation of crops*

**rote** NOUN
➤ **by rote** by repeating something again and again, but without full understanding of its meaning • *We used to learn French songs by rote.*

**rotor** NOUN rotors
a rotating part of a machine or helicopter

**rotten** ADJECTIVE
**①** rotted or decayed • *rotten apples* **②** (*informal*) very bad or unpleasant • *rotten weather*
➤ **rottenness** NOUN

**Rottweiler** NOUN Rottweilers
a breed of powerful black-and-tan dog, sometimes used as a guard dog
**WORD ORIGIN** German, from *Rottweil*, a town in Germany where the dog was bred

**rotund** ADJECTIVE
rounded or plump
➤ **rotundity** NOUN

**rouble** (say roo-bul) NOUN roubles
the unit of money in Russia

**rouge** (say roozh) NOUN
a reddish cosmetic for colouring the cheeks
➤ **rouged** ADJECTIVE
**WORD ORIGIN** French, = red

**rough** ADJECTIVE rougher, roughest
**①** not smooth or level; uneven **②** not gentle or careful; violent • *a rough push* **③** not exact or detailed • *It's only a rough guess.* **④** rough sea or weather is wild and stormy **⑤** difficult and unpleasant • *He's been through a rough time recently.*
➤ **roughness** NOUN

**rough** VERB roughs, roughing, roughed
➤ **rough it** to do without ordinary comforts
➤ **rough something out** to draw or plan

something without including all the details
➤ **rough someone up** (*informal*) to beat someone up

**roughage** NOUN
fibre in food, which helps digestion

**roughen** VERB roughens, roughening, roughened
to make something rough • *Cold weather roughens your skin.*

**roughly** ADVERB
**①** approximately; not exactly • *There were roughly a hundred people there.* **②** in a rough way; not gently • *She pushed him roughly out of the way.*

**roulette** (say roo-let) NOUN
a gambling game where players bet on where the ball on a revolving wheel will come to rest

**round** ADJECTIVE
**①** shaped like a circle, ball or cylinder; curved **②** full or complete • *a round dozen* **③** a round number is expressed to the nearest whole number or the nearest ten, hundred, etc.
➤ **roundness** NOUN
➤ **in round figures** approximately, without giving exact units

**round** ADVERB (*chiefly British*)
**①** in a circle or curve; surrounding something • *Go round to the back of the house.* **②** in every direction or to every person • *Hand the cakes round.* **③** in a new direction • *Turn your chair round.* **④** from place to place • *We wandered round for a while.* **⑤** to someone's house or place of work • *Come round after lunch.*
➤ **come round** to become conscious again
➤ **round about** **①** near by **②** roughly or approximately

**round** PREPOSITION (*chiefly British*)
**①** on all sides of • *We put a fence round the field.* **②** in a curve or circle at an even distance from • *The earth moves round the sun.* **③** to all parts of a place • *Show them round the house.* **④** on or to the further side of a place • *The shop is round the corner.*

**round** NOUN rounds
**①** a series of visits made by a doctor, postman, etc. **②** one section or stage in a competition • *Winners go on to the next round.* **③** the playing of all the holes on a golf course **④** a shot or series of shots from a gun; ammunition for this **⑤** (*British*) a whole slice of bread; a sandwich made with two slices of bread **⑥** a song in which people sing the same words but start at different times **⑦** a

set of drinks bought for all the members of a group
➤ **do the rounds** to be passed round among a lot of people

**round** VERB rounds, rounding, rounded to travel round something • *The car rounded the corner.*
➤ **round something off** to finish or complete something • *We rounded the evening off with some music.*
➤ **round something up** to gather people or animals together • *The teacher rounded up the children.*
➤ **round something up** or **down** to increase or decrease a number to the next highest or lowest whole number

**roundabout** NOUN roundabouts
❶ a road junction where traffic has to pass round a circular structure in the road ❷ a circular revolving ride in a playground or at a funfair

**roundabout** ADJECTIVE
indirect; not using the shortest way of going or of saying or doing something • *I heard the news in a roundabout way.*

**rounded** ADJECTIVE
round in shape

**rounders** NOUN
a game in which players try to hit a ball and run round a circuit

**Roundhead** NOUN Roundheads
a supporter of the Parliamentary party in the English Civil War (1642–9) **WORD ORIGIN** so called because many of them wore their hair cut short at a time when long hair was in fashion for men

**roundly** ADVERB
thoroughly or severely • *We were roundly told off for being late.*

**round-shouldered** ADJECTIVE
with the shoulders bent forward, so that the back is rounded

**round-the-clock** ADJECTIVE
lasting or happening all day and all night

**round trip** NOUN round trips
a trip to one or more places and back to where you started

**round-up** NOUN round-ups
❶ a gathering up of cattle or people • *a police round-up of suspects* ❷ a summary • *a round-up of the news*

**roundworm** NOUN roundworms
a kind of worm that lives as a parasite in the intestines of animals and birds

**rouse** VERB rouses, rousing, roused
❶ to wake someone up • *I was roused by a knock on the door.* ❷ to make someone excited, angry or active • *Many people watching the programme were roused to action.*

**rousing** ADJECTIVE
exciting and powerful • *a rousing speech*

**rout** VERB routs, routing, routed
to defeat an enemy completely and force them to retreat

**rout** NOUN routs
a complete defeat; a disorderly retreat of defeated troops

**route** (say root) NOUN routes
the way you have to go to get to a place

**router** (say roo-ter) NOUN routers
a device that connects computer networks and sends information between them

**routine** (say roo-teen) NOUN routines
❶ a regular or fixed way of doing things • *A morning run is part of her daily routine.* ❷ a set sequence in a performance • *a dance routine*
➤ **routinely** ADVERB

**rove** VERB roves, roving, roved
to roam or wander • *His eyes roved around the room.*
➤ **rover** NOUN

**row** (rhymes with go) NOUN rows
a line of people or things

**row** (rhymes with go) VERB rows, rowing, rowed
to make a boat move by using oars

**row** (rhymes with cow) NOUN rows (British)
❶ a loud noise or uproar ❷ a quarrel or noisy argument

**row** (rhymes with cow) VERB rows, rowing, rowed (British)
to have a noisy argument

**rowan** (say roh-an) NOUN rowans
a tree that bears hanging bunches of red berries

**rowdy** ADJECTIVE rowdier, rowdiest
noisy and disorderly • *a rowdy group of teenagers*
➤ **rowdiness** NOUN

**rower** NOUN rowers
a person who rows a boat

a
b
c
d
e
f
g
h
i
j
k
l
m
n
o
p
q
r
s
t
u
v
w
x
y
z

**rowing boat** NOUN rowing boats
(*British*) a small boat that you move forward by using oars

**rowlock** (say **rol**-ok) NOUN rowlocks
(*British*) a device on the side of a boat, keeping an oar in place

**royal** ADJECTIVE
to do with a king or queen
➤ **royally** ADVERB

**Royalist** NOUN Royalists
a supporter of the monarchy in the English Civil War (1642-9)

**royalist** NOUN royalists
a person who supports the idea of a monarchy

**royalty** NOUN
❶ being royal ❷ a royal person or royal people • *We found ourselves in the presence of royalty.* ❸ royalties a payment to an author or composer for each copy of a work sold or for each performance

**RSVP** ABBREVIATION
please reply (often written at the end of an invitation) **WORD ORIGIN** short for a French phrase *répondez s'il vous plaît*

**rub** VERB rubs, rubbing, rubbed
to move something backwards and forwards while pressing it on something else • *He rubbed his hands together.*
➤ **rub off** to be passed from one person to another • *I hope some of your good luck rubs off on me.*
➤ **rub something off** or **out** to remove something by rubbing it

**rub** NOUN rubs
rubbing something • *Give it a quick rub.*

**rubber** NOUN rubbers
❶ a strong elastic substance used for making tyres, balls, hoses, etc. ❷ a piece of rubber for rubbing out pencil or ink marks

**rubber plant** NOUN rubber plants
❶ a tall evergreen plant with tough shiny leaves, often grown as a house plant ❷ a rubber tree

**rubber stamp** NOUN rubber stamps
a small device with lettering or a design on it, which is inked and used to mark paper

**rubber-stamp** VERB rubber-stamps, rubber-stamping, rubber-stamped
to give official approval to a decision without thinking about it

**rubber tree** NOUN rubber trees
a tropical tree from which rubber is obtained

**rubbery** ADJECTIVE
looking or feeling like rubber • *rubbery lips*

**rubbish** NOUN (*chiefly British*)
❶ things that are not wanted and are to be thrown away ❷ nonsense; something of very poor quality • *Don't talk such rubbish.*

**rubbish** ADJECTIVE
(*British*) (*informal*) very poor in quality • *I thought the film was rubbish.*

**rubble** NOUN
broken pieces of brick or stone

**rubella** NOUN
an infectious disease which causes a red rash and which can damage a baby if the mother catches it early in pregnancy

**rubric** NOUN
a set of instructions at the beginning of an official document or an examination paper **WORD ORIGIN** from Latin *rubeus* = red (because rubrics used to be written in red)

**ruby** NOUN rubies
a red jewel

**ruby wedding** NOUN
a couple's fortieth wedding anniversary

**ruck** VERB rucks, rucking, rucked
cloth rucks up when it forms untidy creases or folds

**rucksack** NOUN rucksacks
a bag with shoulder straps for carrying on your back

**ructions** PLURAL NOUN (*informal*)
angry protests or arguments

**rudder** NOUN rudders
a hinged upright piece at the back of a ship or aircraft, used for steering

**ruddy** ADJECTIVE ruddier, ruddiest
a ruddy complexion is red and healthy-looking

**rude** ADJECTIVE ruder, rudest
❶ impolite or bad-mannered • *It was rude of me to interrupt.* ❷ to do with sex or the body in a way that might offend people; indecent • *a rude joke* ❸ roughly made • *a rude shelter* ❹ unexpected and unpleasant • *I think you may be in for a rude shock.*
➤ **rudely** ADVERB
➤ **rudeness** NOUN

**rudimentary** *ADJECTIVE*
❶ very basic or simple • *a rudimentary knowledge of Arabic* ❷ not fully developed • *Penguins have rudimentary wings.*

**rudiments** (say **rood**-i-ments) *PLURAL NOUN*
the elementary principles of a subject • *She taught me the rudiments of chemistry.*

**rueful** *ADJECTIVE*
showing sad regret • *The boy gave a rueful smile.*
➤ **ruefully** *ADVERB*

**ruff** *NOUN* **ruffs**
❶ a starched pleated frill worn round the neck in the 16th century ❷ a collar-like ring of feathers or fur round a bird's or animal's neck

**ruffian** *NOUN* **ruffians**
a rough or violent person

**ruffle** *VERB* **ruffles, ruffling, ruffled**
❶ to disturb the smoothness of a thing • *He ruffled the boy's hair.* • *The chicken ruffled up its feathers.* ❷ to upset or annoy someone

**ruffle** *NOUN* **ruffles**
a gathered ornamental frill

**rug** *NOUN* **rugs**
❶ a small carpet or thick mat for the floor ❷ a piece of thick fabric used as a blanket

**rugby, rugby football** *NOUN*
a kind of football game using an oval ball that players may carry or kick
(WORD ORIGIN) named after *Rugby* School in Warwickshire, where it was first played

**rugged** (say **rug**-id) *ADJECTIVE*
❶ having a rough or uneven surface or outline • *His face was rugged.* • *a rugged coastline* ❷ strong and tough

**ruin** *VERB* **ruins, ruining, ruined**
to damage or spoil a thing so severely that it is useless or no longer enjoyable • *My new shoes are completely ruined.*

**ruin** *NOUN* **ruins**
❶ a building that is so badly damaged that it has almost fallen down ❷ severe damage or destruction to something • *The city was in a state of ruin.*
➤ **be in ruins** to have failed completely • *My hopes were now in ruins.*
➤ **ruination** *NOUN*

**ruinous** *ADJECTIVE*
❶ causing ruin ❷ in ruins; ruined

**rule** *NOUN* **rules**
❶ something that people have to obey ❷ ruling or governing • *The country used to be under French rule.* ❸ a carpenter's ruler
➤ **as a rule** usually; more often than not

**rule** *VERB* **rules, ruling, ruled**
❶ to govern or reign ❷ to make a decision • *The referee ruled that it was a foul.* ❸ to draw a straight line with a ruler or other straight edge
➤ **rule something out** to say that something is not a possibility

**ruler** *NOUN* **rulers**
❶ a person who governs ❷ a strip of wood, metal or plastic with straight edges, used for measuring and drawing straight lines

**ruling** *NOUN* **rulings**
a judgement or decision

**rum** *NOUN*
a strong alcoholic drink made from sugar or molasses

**rumble** *VERB* **rumbles, rumbling, rumbled**
to make a deep heavy continuous sound • *I was so hungry that my stomach was rumbling.*

**rumble** *NOUN* **rumbles**
a deep heavy continuous sound • *There was a rumble of thunder in the distance.*

**ruminant** *NOUN* **ruminants**
an animal that chews the cud (see **cud**), such as cattle, sheep, deer, etc.
➤ **ruminant** *ADJECTIVE*

**ruminate** *VERB* **ruminates, ruminating, ruminated**
❶ to chew the cud ❷ to think deeply about something; to ponder
➤ **rumination** *NOUN*
➤ **ruminative** *ADJECTIVE*

**rummage** *VERB* **rummages, rummaging, rummaged**
to turn things over or move them about while looking for something • *She rummaged in her backpack and found the torch.*
➤ **rummage** *NOUN*

**rummy** *NOUN*
a card game in which players try to form sets or sequences of cards

**rumour** *NOUN* **rumours**
news or information that spreads to a lot of people but may not be true

**rumour** *VERB*
➤ **be rumoured** to be spread as a rumour • *It was rumoured that she was a witch.*

**rump** NOUN rumps
the hind part of an animal

**rumple** VERB rumples, rumpling, rumpled
to make something untidy or no longer
smooth • *The bed was rumpled where he had
slept.*

**rump steak** NOUN rump steaks
a piece of meat from the rump of a cow

**rumpus** NOUN rumpuses (*informal*)
an uproar; an angry protest

**run** VERB runs, running, ran, run
❶ to move with quick steps so that both or all
feet leave the ground at each stride ❷ to go
or travel; to flow • *Tears ran down his cheeks.*
❸ to move something over or through a thing
• *She ran her fingers through her hair.* ❹ to
produce a flow of liquid • *Run some water
into it.* • *My nose is running.* ❺ to work or
function • *The engine was running smoothly.*
❻ to start or use a computer program ❼ to
manage or organize something • *She runs a
corner shop.* ❽ to compete in a contest or
election • *He ran for President.* ❾ to extend
• *A fence runs round the estate.* ❿ to last or
continue for a certain amount of time • *The
play ran for six months.* ⓫ to take a person
somewhere in a vehicle • *I'll run you to the
station.*
➤ **run across someone** to happen to meet or
find someone
➤ **run a risk** to take a chance
➤ **run away** to leave a place secretly or
quickly
➤ **run down** to stop gradually or decline
➤ **run someone down** ❶ to knock someone
down with a moving vehicle ❷ (*informal*) to
say unkind or unfair things about someone
➤ **run into someone** to happen to meet
someone
➤ **run out of something** to have used up
your stock of something
➤ **run someone out** to knock over the wicket
of a running batsman in cricket
➤ **run someone over** to knock someone
down with a moving vehicle
➤ **run through something** to examine or
rehearse something

**run** NOUN runs
❶ the action of running; a time spent running
• *Let's go for a run.* ❷ a point scored in
cricket or baseball ❸ a continuous series of
events • *She had a run of good luck.* ❹ an
enclosure for animals • *a chicken run* ❺ a
series of damaged stitches in a pair of tights
or stockings ❻ a track • *a ski run*

➤ **on the run** running away, especially from
the police

**runaway** NOUN runaways
someone who has run away

**runaway** ADJECTIVE
❶ having run away or out of control • *a
runaway train* ❷ won easily • *a runaway
victory*

**rundown** ADJECTIVE
❶ tired and in bad health ❷ in bad condition
• *a rundown cottage*

**rung** NOUN rungs
one of the crossbars on a ladder

**rung** VERB
past participle of **ring** VERB

**runner** NOUN runners
❶ a person or animal that runs, especially
in a race ❷ a stem that grows away from
a plant and roots itself ❸ a rod or strip on
which something slides; each of the long
strips under a sledge ❹ a long narrow strip of
carpet or covering

**runner bean** NOUN runner beans
(*British*) a kind of climbing bean with long
green pods which are eaten

**runner-up** NOUN runners-up
someone who comes second in a race or
competition

**running**
present participle of **run**
➤ **in the running** competing and with a
chance of winning

**running** ADJECTIVE
continuous or consecutive; without an
interval • *It rained for four days running.*

**runny** ADJECTIVE runnier, runniest
❶ flowing like liquid • *runny honey*
❷ producing a flow of liquid • *a runny nose*

**run-of-the-mill** ADJECTIVE
ordinary, not special

**runway** NOUN runways
a long hard surface on which aircraft take off
and land

**rupee** NOUN rupees
the unit of money in India and Pakistan

**rupture** VERB ruptures, rupturing, ruptured
to break or burst suddenly or to cause
something to do this
➤ **rupture** NOUN

**rural** ADJECTIVE
to do with or belonging to the countryside
• *a rural scene*

**ruse** NOUN ruses
a deception or trick

**rush** VERB rushes, rushing, rushed
❶ to move or do something quickly; to hurry
• *We rushed back as soon as we heard the news.* ❷ to take someone to a place very quickly • *The injured people were rushed to hospital.* ❸ to make someone hurry
• *Don't rush me – I'm thinking.* ❹ to attack or capture someone by dashing forward suddenly

**rush** NOUN rushes
❶ a hurry • *I can't stop – I'm in a rush.* ❷ a sudden quick movement • *All my words came out in a rush.* ❸ a sudden great demand for something ❹ a plant with a thin stem that grows in marshy places

**rush hour** NOUN rush hours
the time when traffic is busiest

**rusk** NOUN rusks
(*chiefly British*) a kind of hard dry biscuit for babies to chew

**russet** NOUN
a reddish-brown colour

**rust** NOUN
❶ a red or brown substance that forms on iron or steel exposed to damp and corrodes it
❷ a reddish-brown colour

**rust** VERB rusts, rusting, rusted
to make something rusty or to become rusty

**rustic** ADJECTIVE
❶ to do with life in the countryside; rural
❷ made of rough timber or branches • *a rustic bridge*

**rustle** VERB rustles, rustling, rustled
❶ to make a sound like dry leaves moving or paper being crumpled • *The trees rustled in the breeze.* ❷ (*North American*) to steal horses or cattle
➤ **rustler** NOUN
➤ **rustle something up** (*informal*) to produce something quickly • *I'll see if I can rustle up a snack.*

**rustle** NOUN
a rustling sound

**rusty** ADJECTIVE rustier, rustiest
❶ coated with rust ❷ weakened by lack of use or practice • *My French is a bit rusty these days.*

**rut** NOUN ruts
❶ a deep track made by wheels in soft ground ❷ a settled and usually dull way of life • *We are getting into a rut.*
➤ **rutted** ADJECTIVE

**ruthless** ADJECTIVE
determined to get what you want and not caring if you hurt other people
➤ **ruthlessly** ADVERB
➤ **ruthlessness** NOUN
**WORD ORIGIN** from Middle English *ruth* = pity

**rye** NOUN
a cereal used to make flour and whisky

**Ss**

**S.** ABBREVIATION
❶ south ❷ southern

**sabbath** NOUN sabbaths
a weekly day for rest and prayer, Saturday for Jews, Sunday for Christians
**WORD ORIGIN** from Hebrew *shabat* = rest

**sable** NOUN
❶ a kind of dark fur ❷ (*poetical use*) black

**sabotage** NOUN
deliberately damaging machinery or equipment to hinder an enemy or large organization

**sabotage** VERB sabotage, sabotaging, sabotaged
to deliberately damage something by an act of sabotage

**saboteur** NOUN saboteurs
a person who carries out sabotage

**sabre** NOUN sabres
❶ a heavy sword with a curved blade ❷ a light fencing sword

**sac** NOUN sacs
a bag-shaped part in an animal or plant

**saccharin** (say sak-er-in) NOUN
a very sweet substance used as a substitute for sugar

**saccharine** (say sak-er-een) ADJECTIVE
unpleasantly sweet or sentimental • *a saccharine smile*

a b c d e f g h i j k l m n o p q r s t u v w x y z

**sachet** (say **sash**-ay) NOUN sachets
a small sealed packet or bag containing a small amount of shampoo, sugar, etc.

**sack** NOUN sacks
a large bag made of strong material
➤ **get the sack** (*informal*) to be dismissed from a job

**sack** VERB sacks, sacking, sacked
❶ to dismiss someone from a job ❷ (*old use*) to plunder and destroy a captured town

**sacking** NOUN
rough cloth used to make sacks

**sacrament** NOUN sacraments
an important Christian religious ceremony such as baptism or Holy Communion

**sacred** ADJECTIVE
holy; to do with God or a god • *The Koran is the sacred book of Muslims.*

**sacrifice** NOUN sacrifices
❶ giving up a thing you value, so that something good may happen • *We will have to make a few sacrifices if we want to save enough money.* ❷ killing an animal or person as an offering to a god ❸ a thing sacrificed
➤ **sacrificial** ADJECTIVE

**sacrifice** VERB sacrifices, sacrificing, sacrificed
❶ to give something up so that something good may happen • *She sacrificed her career to bring up the children.* ❷ to kill an animal or person as an offering to a god

**sacrilege** (say **sak**-ril-ij) NOUN
disrespect or damage to something people think of as sacred or valuable
➤ **sacrilegious** ADJECTIVE

**sad** ADJECTIVE sadder, saddest
unhappy; showing or causing sorrow
➤ **sadness** NOUN

**sadden** VERB saddens, saddening, saddened
to make a person sad • *The news of his death saddened her greatly.*

**saddle** NOUN saddles
❶ a seat for putting on the back of a horse or other animal ❷ the seat of a bicycle ❸ a ridge of high land between two peaks

**saddle** VERB saddles, saddling, saddled
to put a saddle on a horse or other animal for riding
➤ **saddle someone with something** to burden someone with a task or problem

**sadist** (say **say**-dist) NOUN sadists
a person who enjoys hurting or humiliating other people
➤ **sadism** NOUN
➤ **sadistic** ADJECTIVE
**WORD ORIGIN** named after a French novelist, the Marquis de *Sade*, noted for the cruelties in his stories

**sadly** ADVERB
❶ in a sad way • *He shook his head sadly.*
❷ unfortunately • *Sadly, I won't be able to come.*

**sae** ABBREVIATION
(*British*) stamped addressed envelope

**safari** NOUN safaris
an expedition to watch or hunt wild animals
**WORD ORIGIN** from Arabic *safar* = a journey

**safari park** NOUN safari parks
a large park where wild animals can roam around freely and visitors can watch them from their cars

**safe** ADJECTIVE
❶ not in danger • *He felt safe up in the tree.*
❷ not dangerous • *Drive at a safe speed.*

**safe** NOUN safes
a strong cupboard or box in which valuables can be locked away safely

**safeguard** NOUN safeguards
something that protects against possible dangers

**safeguard** VERB safeguards, safeguarding, safeguarded
to protect something from danger

**safely** ADVERB
❶ without harm or danger • *The plane landed safely.* ❷ without risk • *I can safely say that she was pleased with her present.*

**safe sex** NOUN
sexual activity in which precautions, such as using a condom, are taken to prevent the spread of infections

**safety** NOUN
being safe; freedom from danger, harm or risk • *a talk on road safety*

**safety pin** NOUN safety pins
a U-shaped pin with a clip fastening over the point

**saffron** NOUN
❶ a deep yellow spice used to colour or flavour food, made from the dried stigmas of a crocus ❷ a deep yellow colour

**sag** VERB sags, sagging, sagged
❶ to go down in the middle because

something heavy is pressing on it • *The tent began to sag under the weight of the rain.* ❷ to hang down loosely; to droop • *His shoulders sagged.*

**saga** (say **sah**-ga) NOUN sagas
a long story with many episodes or adventures

**sagacious** (say sa-**gay**-shus) ADJECTIVE
shrewd and wise
➤ **sagaciously** ADVERB
➤ **sagacity** NOUN

**sage** NOUN sages
❶ a kind of herb used in cooking and formerly used in medicine ❷ a wise and respected person

**sage** ADJECTIVE
wise and experienced
➤ **sagely** ADVERB

**sago** NOUN
a starchy white food used to make puddings

**said**
past tense of **say**

**sail** NOUN sails
❶ a large piece of strong cloth attached to a mast to catch the wind and make a ship or boat move ❷ a short voyage • *We went for a sail around the island.* ❸ an arm of a windmill
➤ **set sail** to start on a voyage in a ship

**sail** VERB sails, sailing, sailed
❶ to travel in a ship or boat ❷ to start out on a voyage • *We sail at noon.* ❸ to control a ship or boat ❹ to move quickly and smoothly • *The ball sailed over the fence.*

**sailboard** NOUN sailboards
a flat board with a mast and sail, used in windsurfing

**sailing ship** NOUN sailing ships
a ship with sails

**sailor** NOUN sailors
a person who sails; a member of a ship's crew or of a navy

**saint** NOUN saints
a holy or very good person
➤ **saintly** ADJECTIVE

**sake** NOUN
➤ **for the sake of something** in order to get or achieve something • *She is taking more exercise for the sake of her health.*
➤ **for someone's sake** in order to help or please someone • *Don't go to any trouble for my sake.*

**salad** NOUN salads
a mixture of vegetables eaten raw or cold

**salamander** NOUN salamanders
a lizard-like amphibian

**salami** NOUN
a spiced sausage, originally made in Italy

**salary** NOUN salaries
a regular wage, usually for a year's work, paid in monthly instalments **WORD ORIGIN** from Latin *salarium* = salt-money, money given to Roman soldiers to buy salt

**sale** NOUN sales
❶ the selling of something ❷ a time when things are sold at reduced prices
➤ **for sale** or **on sale** available to be bought

**salesperson** NOUN salespersons
a person employed to sell goods
➤ **salesman** NOUN salesmen
➤ **saleswoman** NOUN saleswomen

**salient** (say **say**-lee-ent) ADJECTIVE
most noticeable or important • *the salient features of the plan*

**saline** ADJECTIVE
containing salt

**saliva** NOUN
the natural liquid in a person's or animal's mouth
➤ **salivary** ADJECTIVE

**salivate** (say **sal**-iv-ayt) VERB salivates, salivating, salivated
to form saliva, especially a large amount

**sallow** ADJECTIVE
sallow skin is slightly yellow

**sally** NOUN sallies
❶ a lively or witty remark ❷ a sudden attack by an enemy

**sally** VERB sallies, sallying, sallied
➤ **sally forth** or **out** to set out in a determined way

**salmon** (say **sam**-on) NOUN salmon
a large edible fish with pink flesh

**salmonella** (say sal-mon-**el**-a) NOUN
a bacterium that can cause food poisoning **WORD ORIGIN** named after an American scientist, Elmer *Salmon*, who studied the causes of disease

**salon** NOUN salons
❶ a large elegant room ❷ a room or shop where customers go for hair or beauty treatment

a b c d e f g h i j k l m n o p q r s t u v w x y z

**saloon** NOUN saloons
❶ a car with a hard roof and a separate boot
❷ a place where alcoholic drinks are bought and drunk, especially a comfortable bar in a pub

**salsa** NOUN
❶ a hot spicy sauce ❷ a kind of modern Latin American dance music; a dance to this

**salt** NOUN salts
❶ sodium chloride, the white substance that gives sea water its taste and is used for flavouring food ❷ a chemical compound of a metal and an acid

**salt** VERB salts, salting, salted
to flavour or preserve food with salt

**salt cellar** NOUN salt cellars
a small dish or perforated pot holding salt for use at meals **WORD ORIGIN** *cellar* from old French *salier* = salt-box

**salts** PLURAL NOUN
a substance that looks like salt • *bath salts*

**salty** ADJECTIVE saltier, saltiest
containing or tasting of salt

**salutary** ADJECTIVE
beneficial; having a good effect • *She gave us some salutary advice.*

**salutation** NOUN salutations
(*formal*) a greeting • *He raised his hand in salutation.*

**salute** VERB salutes, saluting, saluted
❶ to raise your right hand to your forehead as a sign of respect, especially in the armed forces • *The sergeant saluted and left the room.* ❷ to greet someone ❸ to say that you respect or admire something • *We salute this achievement.*

**salute** NOUN salutes
❶ the act of saluting ❷ the firing of guns as a sign of respect

**salvage** VERB salvages, salvaging, salvaged
to save or rescue something such as a damaged ship's cargo so that it can be used again
➤ **salvage** NOUN

**salvation** NOUN
❶ in Christian teaching, being saved by God from the power of evil ❷ something that rescues a person from danger or disaster

**salve** NOUN salves
❶ a soothing ointment ❷ something that soothes

**salve** VERB salves, salving, salved
➤ **salve your conscience** to make you feel less guilty about something

**salver** NOUN salvers
a small metal tray

**salvo** NOUN salvoes or salvos
firing a number of guns at the same time

**same** ADJECTIVE
❶ of one kind, exactly alike or equal • *We are the same age.* ❷ not changing; not different • *I get up at the same time every morning.*
➤ **sameness** NOUN

**samosa** NOUN samosas
a triangular fried pastry case filled with spicy meat or vegetables

**samovar** NOUN samovars
a Russian tea urn **WORD ORIGIN** Russian, = self-boiler

**sampan** NOUN sampans
a small flat-bottomed boat used in China **WORD ORIGIN** from Chinese *sanpan* (*san* = three, *pan* = boards)

**sample** NOUN samples
a small amount that shows what something is like

**sample** VERB samples, sampling, sampled
❶ to take a sample of something • *Scientists sampled the lake water.* ❷ to try part of something • *She sampled the cake.*

**sampler** NOUN samplers
a piece of embroidery worked in various stitches to show skill in needlework

**samurai** (say **sam**-oor-eye) NOUN samurai
a member of an ancient Japanese warrior class

**sanatorium** NOUN sanatoriums or sanatoria
a hospital where people who need a long period of treatment for an illness can stay

**sanctify** VERB sanctifies, sanctifying, sanctified
to make a place holy or sacred

**sanctimonious** ADJECTIVE
making a show of being virtuous or pious

**sanction** NOUN sanctions
❶ action taken against a nation that is considered to have broken an international law • *Sanctions against that country include refusing to trade with it.* ❷ a penalty for disobeying a law ❸ official permission or approval for something

**sanction** *VERB* sanctions, sanctioning, sanctioned
to officially permit or authorize something

**sanctity** *NOUN*
being sacred; holiness

**sanctuary** *NOUN* sanctuaries
❶ a safe place where people can be protected; a refuge ❷ an area where wildlife is protected • *a bird sanctuary* ❸ a sacred place; the part of a church where the altar stands

**sanctum** *NOUN* sanctums
a person's private room

**sand** *NOUN*
the tiny grains of rock that cover the ground on beaches, river beds and deserts

**sand** *VERB* sands, sanding, sanded
to smooth or polish a surface with sandpaper or some other rough material
➤ **sander** *NOUN*

**sandal** *NOUN* sandals
a lightweight shoe with straps over the foot
➤ **sandalled** *ADJECTIVE*

**sandalwood** *NOUN*
a scented wood from a tropical tree

**sandbag** *NOUN* sandbags
a bag filled with sand, used to build defences against flood water or bullets

**sandbank** *NOUN* sandbanks
a bank of sand under water

**sandpaper** *NOUN*
strong paper coated with sand or a similar substance, rubbed on rough surfaces to make them smooth

**sands** *PLURAL NOUN*
a beach or sandy area

**sandstone** *NOUN*
rock made of compressed sand

**sandwich** *NOUN* sandwiches
two or more slices of bread with a filling (e.g. of meat or cheese) between them

**sandwich** *VERB* sandwiches, sandwiching, sandwiched
to put a person or thing in a narrow space between two others • *The boy sat sandwiched between the two women on the sofa.* **WORD ORIGIN** invented by the Earl of Sandwich (1718-92) so that he could eat while gambling

**sandwich course** *NOUN* sandwich courses
(*British*) a college or university course which includes periods in industry or business

**sandy** *ADJECTIVE*
❶ like sand ❷ covered with sand ❸ yellowish-red • *sandy hair*

**sane** *ADJECTIVE*
❶ having a healthy mind; not mad ❷ sensible or reasonable
➤ **sanely** *ADVERB*

**sanguine** (say sang-gwin) *ADJECTIVE*
cheerful and optimistic • *a sanguine temperament* **WORD ORIGIN** from Latin *sanguis* = blood (because good blood was believed to be the cause of cheerfulness)

**sanitary** *ADJECTIVE*
❶ free from germs and dirt; hygienic ❷ to do with sanitation

**sanitary towel** *NOUN* sanitary towels
an absorbent pad worn by women to absorb blood during menstruation

**sanitation** *NOUN*
arrangements for drainage and the disposal of sewage

**sanity** *NOUN*
being sane; sensible behaviour

**Sanskrit** *NOUN*
the ancient and sacred language of the Hindus in India

**sap** *NOUN*
the liquid inside a plant, carrying food to all its parts

**sap** *VERB* saps, sapping, sapped
to sap someone's strength or energy is to use it up or weaken it gradually • *The heat had sapped all my energy.*

**sapling** *NOUN* saplings
a young tree

**sapphire** *NOUN* sapphires
a bright-blue jewel

**Saracen** *NOUN* Saracens
an Arab or Muslim of the time of the Crusades

**sarcasm** *NOUN*
being sarcastic • *There was a hint of sarcasm in his voice.*

**sarcastic** *ADJECTIVE*
saying the opposite of what you mean in order to insult someone or make fun of them • *She said she liked my singing but I think she*

605

*was being sarcastic.*
➤ **sarcastically** ADVERB
(WORD ORIGIN) from Greek *sarkazein* = tear the flesh

**sarcophagus** NOUN **sarcophagi**
a stone coffin, often decorated with carvings
(WORD ORIGIN) from Greek *sarkos* = of flesh + *-phagos* = eating (because people used to think that the stone from which ancient coffins were made caused the bodies inside to decay)

**sardine** NOUN **sardines**
a small sea fish, usually sold in tins, packed tightly in oil

**sardonic** ADJECTIVE
showing amusement in a bitter or mocking way • *a sardonic smile*
➤ **sardonically** ADVERB

**sari** NOUN **saris**
a length of cloth worn wrapped round the body as a dress, especially by Indian women and girls

**sarong** NOUN **sarongs**
a large piece of cloth worn around the body, originally in SE Asia

**sartorial** ADJECTIVE
to do with clothes

**sash** NOUN **sashes**
a strip of cloth worn round the waist or over one shoulder

**sash window** NOUN **sash windows**
a window that slides up and down

**SAT** ABBREVIATION
standard assessment task

**satanic** (say sa-**tan**-ik) ADJECTIVE
to do with or like Satan, the Devil in Jewish and Christian teaching

**satchel** NOUN **satchels**
a bag you wear on the shoulder or the back, especially for carrying books to and from school (WORD ORIGIN) from Latin *saccellus* = little sack

**sate** VERB **sates, sating, sated**
to satisfy an appetite or desire fully

**satellite** NOUN **satellites**
❶ a spacecraft put in orbit round a planet to collect information or transmit communications signals ❷ a moon moving in an orbit round a planet (WORD ORIGIN) from Latin *satelles* = a guard (because astronomers compared the moons of Jupiter to guards or attendants of an important person)

**satellite dish** NOUN **satellite dishes**
a bowl-shaped aerial for receiving broadcasting signals transmitted by satellite

**satellite television** NOUN
television broadcasting in which the signals are transmitted by means of a communications satellite

**satiate** (say say-shee-ayt) VERB **satiates, satiating, satiated**
to satisfy an appetite or desire fully

**satin** NOUN
a silky material that is shiny on one side
➤ **satiny** ADJECTIVE

**satire** NOUN **satires**
❶ the use of humour or exaggeration to show what is bad or weak about a person or thing, especially the government ❷ a play, poem or other piece of writing that does this
➤ **satirist** NOUN
➤ **satirize** VERB

**satirical** ADJECTIVE
using satire to mock or show the faults of a person or thing • *a satirical cartoon*
➤ **satirically** ADVERB

**satisfaction** NOUN
❶ the feeling of pleasure you have when you achieve something or get what you need or want • *He stood back and looked at his work with a sense of satisfaction.* ❷ giving someone what they need or want

**satisfactory** ADJECTIVE
good enough; acceptable • *That is not a satisfactory explanation.*
➤ **satisfactorily** ADVERB

**satisfy** VERB **satisfies, satisfying, satisfied**
❶ to give someone what they need or want ❷ to make someone feel certain; to convince someone • *The police are satisfied that the death was accidental.* ❸ to fulfil or achieve something • *You have satisfied all our requirements.*

**satsuma** NOUN **satsumas**
a kind of mandarin orange originally grown in Japan (WORD ORIGIN) named after *Satsuma*, a province of Japan

**saturate** VERB **saturates, saturating, saturated**
❶ to make a thing thoroughly wet • *The continuous rain has saturated the soil.* ❷ to make a place or thing take in as much as possible of something • *The town is saturated with tourists in the summer.*

➤ **saturation** NOUN
➤ **saturated** ADJECTIVE

**Saturday** NOUN
the day of the week following Friday
**WORD ORIGIN** from Old English *Saeternesdaeg*
= day of Saturn, a Roman god

**saturnine** ADJECTIVE
looking gloomy and forbidding • *a saturnine
face* **WORD ORIGIN** because people born under
the influence of the planet Saturn were believed
to be gloomy

**satyr** (say sat-er) NOUN satyrs
in Greek myths, a woodland god with a man's
body and a goat's ears, tail and legs

**sauce** NOUN sauces
❶ a thick liquid served with food to
add flavour ❷ (*informal*) being cheeky;
impudence

**saucepan** NOUN saucepans
a metal cooking pan with a handle at the side

**saucer** NOUN saucers
a small curved plate for a cup to stand on

**saucy** ADJECTIVE saucier, sauciest
rude or cheeky
➤ **saucily** ADVERB
➤ **sauciness** NOUN

**sauerkraut** (say sour-krowt) NOUN
chopped and pickled cabbage, originally made
in Germany **WORD ORIGIN** from German *sauer*
= sour + *Kraut* = cabbage

**sauna** NOUN saunas
a room filled with steam where people sit and
sweat a lot, used as a kind of bath

**saunter** VERB saunters, sauntering, sauntered
to walk slowly and casually • *She sauntered
over to greet me.*

**sausage** NOUN sausages
a tube of skin or plastic stuffed with minced
meat and other filling

**savage** ADJECTIVE
wild and fierce; cruel
➤ **savagely** ADVERB
➤ **savagery** NOUN

**savage** NOUN savages
❶ a savage person ❷ (*old use*) a member of a
people thought of as primitive or uncivilized

**savage** VERB savages, savaging, savaged
an animal savages a person or another animal
when it attacks them and bites or scratches
them fiercely • *The sheep was savaged by a
dog.* **WORD ORIGIN** from Latin *silvaticus* = of

the woods, wild (because people who lived in
the woods were thought of as wild and unruly)

**savannah, savanna** NOUN savannahs or
savannas
a grassy plain in a hot country, with few or
no trees

**save** VERB saves, saving, saved
❶ to keep a person or thing safe; to free a
person or thing from danger or harm ❷ to
keep something, especially money, so that
it can be used later ❸ to avoid wasting
something • *This will save time.* ❹ (*in
computing*) to keep data by storing it in the
computer's memory or on a disk ❺ to stop a
goal being scored
NOUN
➤ **saver** NOUN

**save** NOUN
preventing a goal from being scored • *The
goalkeeper made a great save.*

**save** PREPOSITION (*formal*) except • *All the trains
save one were late.*

**savings** PLURAL NOUN
your savings are the money that you have
saved

**saviour** NOUN saviours
a person who saves someone
➤ **the** or **our Saviour** in Christianity, Jesus
Christ

**savour** VERB savours, savouring, savoured
❶ to enjoy the taste or smell of something
• *He was savouring every mouthful.* ❷ to
enjoy a feeling or experience • *She was
determined to savour every moment.*

**savour** NOUN savours
the taste or smell of something • *the savour
of fresh bread*

**savoury** ADJECTIVE
❶ tasty but not sweet ❷ having an
appetizing taste or smell

**savoury** NOUN savouries (*chiefly British*) a
savoury dish

**saw** NOUN saws
a tool with a zigzag edge for cutting wood or
metal etc.

**saw** VERB saws, sawing, sawed, sawn
❶ to cut something with a saw • *He sawed
the log in half.* ❷ to move something
backwards and forwards as if you were using
a saw • *She began sawing at the rope with
her knife.*

**saw** VERB
past tense of see

**SPELLING**

A saw is a tool for cutting wood. If a part of your body is sore, it hurts.

**sawdust** NOUN
powder that comes from wood cut by a saw

**sawmill** NOUN sawmills
a mill where timber is cut into planks etc. by machinery

**Saxon** NOUN Saxons
❶ a member of a people who came from Europe and occupied parts of England in the 5th-6th centuries ❷ an Anglo-Saxon

**saxophone** NOUN saxophones
a brass wind instrument with a reed in the mouthpiece
➤ **saxophonist** NOUN
WORD ORIGIN named after a Belgian instrument maker, Adolphe *Sax*, who invented it

**say** VERB says, saying, said
❶ to speak or express something in words
❷ to give an opinion • *I can't say I blame you.*
❸ to show something or give information
• *The look on her face said it all.* • *His bedside clock said 9.30.*

**say** NOUN
➤ **have a say** to be able to give your opinion or help decide something • *I have no say in the matter.*

**SPELLING**

The past tense of say is said.

**saying** NOUN sayings
a well-known phrase or proverb that gives advice or says something true about life

**scab** NOUN scabs
a hard crust that forms over a cut or graze while it is healing
➤ **scabby** ADJECTIVE

**scabbard** NOUN scabbards
the sheath of a sword or dagger

**scabies** (say **skay**-beez) NOUN
a contagious skin disease with severe itching, caused by a parasite WORD ORIGIN Latin, from *scabere* = to scratch

**scaffold** NOUN scaffolds
a platform on which criminals are executed

**scaffolding** NOUN
a structure of poles or tubes and planks

making platforms for workers to stand on while building or repairing a house

**scald** VERB scalds, scalding, scalded
❶ to burn yourself with very hot liquid or steam ❷ to heat milk until it is nearly boiling

**scald** NOUN scalds
a burn from very hot liquid or steam

**scale** NOUN scales
❶ a series of units, degrees or qualities for measuring something ❷ a series of musical notes going up or down in a fixed pattern
❸ the relationship between the size of something on a map or model and the actual size of the thing in the real world • *The scale of this map is one centimetre to the kilometre.* ❹ the relative size or importance of something • *They organize parties on a large scale.* ❺ each of the thin overlapping parts on the outside of fish, snakes, etc.; a thin flake or part like this ❻ a hard substance formed in a kettle or boiler by hard water or on teeth
➤ **to scale** with the parts in the same proportions as those of an original • *The plans have been drawn to scale.*

**scale** VERB scales, scaling, scaled
❶ to climb to the top of something steep
• *We will have to scale the wall.* ❷ to remove scales or scale from something
➤ **scale something down** or **up** to reduce or increase something at a fixed rate or in proportion to something else

**scale model** NOUN scale models
a model of something, made to scale

**scalene** (say **skay**-leen) ADJECTIVE
a scalene triangle has unequal sides

**scales** PLURAL NOUN
a device for weighing things

**scallop** NOUN scallops
❶ a shellfish with two hinged fan-shaped shells ❷ each curve in an ornamental wavy border
➤ **scalloped** ADJECTIVE

**scalp** NOUN scalps
the skin on the top of the head

**scalp** VERB scalps, scalping, scalped
to cut or tear the scalp from a person

**scalpel** NOUN scalpels
a small knife with a thin, sharp blade, used by a surgeon or artist

**scaly** ADJECTIVE scalier, scaliest
covered in scales or scale

**scam** *NOUN* scams (*informal*)
a dishonest scheme or a swindle

**scamp** *NOUN* scamps
a rascal or mischievous child

**scamper** *VERB* scampers, scampering, scampered
to run quickly with short light steps • *The two girls scampered across the grass.*

**scampi** *PLURAL NOUN*
large prawns eaten in batter or breadcrumbs

**scan** *VERB* scans, scanning, scanned
❶ to look at every part of something • *He scanned the horizon for any sign of land.* ❷ to glance at something • *She scanned the list quickly for her name.* ❸ poetry scans when it is correct in rhythm • *This line doesn't scan.* ❹ to use a scanner to read data from something into a computer ❺ to sweep a radar or electronic beam over an area to examine it or in search of something

**scan** *NOUN* scans
❶ scanning something ❷ an examination using a scanner • *a brain scan*

**scandal** *NOUN* scandals
❶ something shameful or disgraceful ❷ gossip about people's faults and wrongdoing

**scandalize** (also **scandalise**) *VERB*
scandalizes, scandalizing, scandalized
to shock a person by something considered shameful or disgraceful

**scandalmonger** *NOUN* scandalmongers
a person who invents or spreads scandal
**WORD ORIGIN** from **scandal** + an old word *monger* = trader

**scandalous** *ADJECTIVE*
shocking or disgraceful

**Scandinavian** *ADJECTIVE*
from or to do with the countries of Scandinavia (Norway, Sweden and Denmark and sometimes also Finland and Iceland)
➤ **Scandinavian** *NOUN*

**scanner** *NOUN* scanners
❶ a machine that examines things by means of light or other rays ❷ a machine that converts printed text, pictures, etc. into a form that can be put into a computer

**scant** *ADJECTIVE*
barely enough or adequate • *I paid scant attention to what she was saying.*

**scanty** *ADJECTIVE* scantier, scantiest
small in amount or extent; meagre • *Details of his life are scanty.*
➤ **scantily** *ADVERB*

**scapegoat** *NOUN* scapegoats
a person who is made to bear the blame or punishment for what others have done
**WORD ORIGIN** named after the **goat** which the ancient Jews allowed to **escape** into the desert after the priest had symbolically laid the people's sins upon it

**scar** *NOUN* scars
❶ the mark left by a cut or burn after it has healed ❷ a lasting effect left by an unpleasant experience

**scar** *VERB* scars, scarring, scarred
to make a scar or scars on skin • *His face was badly scarred.*

**scarab** *NOUN* scarabs
an ancient Egyptian ornament or symbol carved in the shape of a beetle

**scarce** *ADJECTIVE* scarcer, scarcest
not enough to supply people • *Food was becoming scarce.*
➤ **scarcity** *NOUN*
➤ **make yourself scarce** (*informal*) to go away or keep out of the way

**scarcely** *ADVERB*
only just; only with difficulty • *She could scarcely walk.*

**scare** *VERB* scares, scaring, scared
to frighten someone

**scare** *NOUN* scares
❶ a fright • *You gave me quite a scare.* ❷ a sudden widespread sense of alarm about something • *a bomb scare*

**scarecrow** *NOUN* scarecrows
a figure of a person dressed in old clothes, put in a field to frighten birds away from crops

**scared** *ADJECTIVE*
frightened or afraid • *My brother is scared of the dark.*

**scaremonger** *NOUN* scaremongers
a person who spreads scare stories
**WORD ORIGIN** from **scare** + an old word *monger* = trader

**scare story** *NOUN* scare stories
an inaccurate or exaggerated account of something which makes people worry unnecessarily

a
b
c
d
e
f
g
h
i
j
k
l
m
n
o
p
q
r
s
t
u
v
w
x
y
z

**scarf** NOUN scarves
a strip of material that you wear round your neck or head

**scarlet** ADJECTIVE & NOUN
bright red

**scarlet fever** NOUN
an infectious fever producing a scarlet rash

**scarp** NOUN scarps
a steep slope on a hill

**scarper** VERB scarpers, scarpering, scarpered (British) (informal)
to run away or leave in a hurry
**WORD ORIGIN** probably from Italian scappare = escape

**scary** ADJECTIVE scarier, scariest (informal)
frightening

**scathing** (say skay th-ing) ADJECTIVE
severely criticizing a person or thing

**scatter** VERB scatters, scattering, scattered
❶ to throw or send things in all directions ❷ to run or leave quickly in all directions • At the first gunshot, the crowd scattered.

**scatterbrain** NOUN scatterbrains
a careless forgetful person
➤ **scatterbrained** ADJECTIVE

**scattered** ADJECTIVE
spread over a large area or happening several times over a period of time • sunshine with scattered showers

**scattering** NOUN
a small number of things spread over an area • a scattering of houses

**scavenge** VERB scavenges, scavenging, scavenged
❶ to search in rubbish for useful things ❷ a bird or animal scavenges when it searches for decaying flesh as food

**scavenger** NOUN scavengers
a bird, animal or person that scavenges

**scenario** NOUN scenarios
❶ a summary of the plot of a play or story ❷ an imagined series of events or set of circumstances

**scene** NOUN scenes
❶ the place where something has happened • the scene of the crime ❷ a part of a play or film ❸ a view someone sees • a painting of a street scene ❹ an angry or noisy outburst • He made a scene about the money. ❺ stage

scenery ❻ an area of activity • the local music scene

**SPELLING**
A **scene** is a place or part of a play. **Seen** is the past participle of **see**.

**scenery** NOUN
❶ the natural features of a landscape • We were admiring the scenery. ❷ things put on a stage to make it look like a place

**scenic** ADJECTIVE
having fine natural scenery • a scenic road along the coast

**scent** NOUN scents
❶ a pleasant smell • the scent of wild flowers ❷ a liquid perfume ❸ an animal's smell that other animals can detect

**scent** VERB scents, scenting, scented
❶ to discover something by its scent • The dog scented a rabbit. ❷ to give something a pleasant smell • Roses scented the night air. ❸ to feel that something is about to happen • She could scent trouble.
➤ **scented** ADJECTIVE

**sceptic** (say skep-tik) NOUN sceptics
a sceptical person

**sceptical** (say skep-tik-al) ADJECTIVE
doubting whether something is true; not believing things easily • She gave him a sceptical look.
➤ **sceptically** ADVERB
➤ **scepticism** NOUN

**sceptre** NOUN sceptres
a rod carried by a king or queen as a symbol of power

**schedule** (say shed-yool) NOUN schedules
a programme or timetable of things that will happen or have to be done
➤ **on schedule** on time according to a plan
**schedule** VERB schedules, scheduling, scheduled to arrange something for a certain time • We've scheduled the meeting for Monday morning. **WORD ORIGIN** from Latin scedula = little piece of paper

**schematic** (say skee-mat-ik) ADJECTIVE
in the form of a diagram or chart

**scheme** NOUN schemes
a plan of what to do • He told us about his latest money-making scheme.

**scheme** VERB schemes, scheming, schemed
to make secret plans; to plot • She felt they were all scheming against her.
➤ **schemer** NOUN

**scherzo** (say **skairts**-oh) NOUN scherzos
a lively piece of music (WORD ORIGIN) Italian, = joke

**schism** (say skizm or sizm) NOUN schisms
the splitting of a group into two opposing sections because they disagree about something important

**schizophrenia** (say skid-zo-**free**-nee-a) NOUN
a kind of mental illness in which people cannot relate their thoughts and feelings to reality
➤ **schizophrenic** ADJECTIVE & NOUN

**scholar** NOUN scholars
❶ a person who has studied a subject thoroughly ❷ a person who has been awarded a scholarship (WORD ORIGIN) from Latin *scholaris* = to do with a school

**scholarly** ADJECTIVE
showing knowledge and learning

**scholarship** NOUN scholarships
❶ a grant of money given to someone to help to pay for their education ❷ serious study of an academic subject and the knowledge you get

**scholastic** ADJECTIVE
to do with schools or education; academic

**school** NOUN schools
❶ a place where teaching is done, especially of pupils aged 5–18 ❷ the pupils in a school ❸ the time when teaching takes place in a school • *School ends at 4.30 p.m.* ❹ a group of people who have the same beliefs or style of work ❺ a large group of fish, whales or dolphins

**school** VERB schools, schooling, schooled
to teach or train a person or animal • *She was schooling her horse for the competition.*

**schoolchild** NOUN schoolchildren
a child who goes to school
➤ **schoolboy** NOUN
➤ **schoolgirl** NOUN

**schooling** NOUN
education at a school

**schoolteacher** NOUN schoolteachers
a person who teaches in a school
➤ **schoolmaster** NOUN
➤ **schoolmistress** NOUN

**schooner** (say **skoon**-er) NOUN schooners
❶ a sailing ship with two or more masts ❷ a tall glass for serving sherry

**science** NOUN sciences
❶ the study of the physical world by means of observation and experiment ❷ a branch of this, such as chemistry, physics or biology
(WORD ORIGIN) from Latin *scientia* = knowledge

**science fiction** NOUN
stories about imaginary scientific discoveries or space travel and life on other planets, often set in the future

**science park** NOUN science parks
an area set up for industries using science or for organizations doing scientific research

**scientific** ADJECTIVE
❶ to do with science or scientists • *scientific instruments* ❷ studying things in an organized, logical way and testing ideas carefully • *a scientific study of the way we use language*
➤ **scientifically** ADVERB

**scientist** NOUN scientists
❶ an expert in science ❷ someone who uses scientific methods

**scimitar** (say **sim**-it-ar) NOUN scimitars
a curved oriental sword

**scintillating** ADJECTIVE
❶ sparkling ❷ lively and witty • *The conversation was scintillating.*
(WORD ORIGIN) from Latin *scintilla* = spark

**scion** (say **sy**-on) NOUN scions
a descendant, especially of a noble family

**scissors** PLURAL NOUN
a cutting instrument used with one hand, with two blades joined so that they can close against each other

SPELLING

There is a tricky bit in **scissors**—it begins with **sc**.

**scoff** VERB scoffs, scoffing, scoffed
❶ to laugh or speak in a mocking way about something you think is silly • *She scoffed at my superstitions.* ❷ (informal) to eat something greedily or to eat it all up
➤ **scoffer** NOUN

**scold** VERB scolds, scolding, scolded
to speak angrily to someone because they have done wrong; to tell someone off
➤ **scolding** NOUN

**scone** (say skon or skohn) NOUN scones
a soft flat cake, usually eaten with butter

**scoop** NOUN scoops
❶ a kind of deep spoon for serving ice cream

etc. ❷ an amount picked up with a scoop
• *How many scoops of ice cream do you
want?* ❸ a deep shovel for lifting grain, sugar,
etc. ❹ an important piece of news published
by only one newspaper

**scoop** *VERB* scoops, scooping, scooped
❶ to lift or hollow something out with a
scoop, spoon or the palm of your hand • *I
scooped up handfuls of water and began
to drink.* • *Scoop out the middle of the
pineapple.* ❷ to lift something with a broad
sweeping movement • *He scooped her up in
his arms.*

**scoot** *VERB* scoots, scooting, scooted
❶ to make a bicycle or scooter move along by
sitting or standing on it and pushing it along
with one foot ❷ (*informal*) to run or go away
quickly

**scooter** *NOUN* scooters
❶ a kind of motorcycle with small wheels ❷ a
board with wheels and a long handle, which
you ride on by scooting

**scope** *NOUN*
❶ opportunity or possibility for something
• *There is scope for improvement.* ❷ the
range or extent of a subject • *Those questions
are outside the scope of this essay.*

**scorch** *VERB* scorches, scorching, scorched
to make something go brown by burning it
slightly

**scorching** *ADJECTIVE* (*informal*)
very hot

**score** *NOUN* scores or, in sense 2, score
❶ the number of points or goals made in a
game; a result • *What's the score?* ❷ (*old use*)
twenty • *'Three score years and ten' means
3 x 20 + 10 = 70 years.* ❸ written or printed
music
➤ **on that score** for that reason, because of
that • *You needn't worry on that score.*

**score** *VERB* scores, scoring, scored
❶ to get a point or goal in a game ❷ to keep
a count of the score in a game • *I thought
you were scoring.* ❸ to cut or mark a line on a
surface with something sharp ❹ to write out
a musical score

**scorer** *NOUN* scorers
❶ a person who scores a goal or point ❷ a
person who keeps a count of the score in a
game

**scores** *PLURAL NOUN*
many; a large number

**scorn** *NOUN*
contempt or lack of respect for someone

**scorn** *VERB* scorns, scorning, scorned
❶ to treat someone with contempt ❷ to
refuse something because you are too proud
• *She scorned all offers of help.*

**scornful** *ADJECTIVE*
feeling or showing scorn • *scornful laughter*
➤ **scornfully** *ADVERB*

**scorpion** *NOUN* scorpions
an animal that looks like a tiny lobster, with a
poisonous sting in its curved tail

**Scot** *NOUN* Scots
a person who comes from Scotland

**scotch** *NOUN*
whisky made in Scotland

**scotch** *VERB* scotches, scotching, scotched
to put an end to an idea or rumour

**Scotch egg** *NOUN* Scotch eggs
(*British*) a hard-boiled egg enclosed in
sausage meat and fried

**Scotch terrier** *NOUN* Scotch terriers
a breed of terrier with rough hair

**scot-free** *ADJECTIVE*
avoiding the punishment that is deserved
• *They got away scot-free.*

**Scots** *ADJECTIVE*
from or belonging to Scotland

**Scots** *NOUN*
the form of English used in Scotland

**USAGE**

See the note at Scottish.

**Scottish** *ADJECTIVE*
to do with or belonging to Scotland

**USAGE**

Scottish is the most widely used word
for describing things to do with Scotland:
*Scottish education, Scottish mountains.*
*Scots* is less common and is mainly used
to describe people: *a Scots girl. Scotch* is
only used in fixed expressions like *Scotch
egg* and *Scotch terrier.*

**scoundrel** *NOUN* scoundrels
a wicked or dishonest person

**scour** *VERB* scours, scouring, scoured
❶ to search a place thoroughly • *Police are
scouring the countryside.* ❷ to rub something
until it is clean and bright ❸ to clear a
channel or pipe by the force of water flowing

through it
➤ **scourer** NOUN

**scourge** (say skerj) NOUN scourges
❶ a whip for flogging people ❷ something that causes a lot of suffering or trouble

**Scout** NOUN Scouts
a member of the Scout Association, an organization for boys

**scout** NOUN scouts
someone sent out ahead of a group to collect information

**scout** VERB scouts, scouting, scouted
to search an area thoroughly • *We began scouting around for firewood.*

**scowl** NOUN scowls
a bad-tempered frown

**scowl** VERB scowls, scowling, scowled
to have an angry or bad-tempered look

**scrabble** VERB scrabbles, scrabbling, scrabbled
❶ to scratch or claw at something with the hands or feet • *The dog scrabbled at the door.* ❷ to move your fingers quickly, trying to find or get hold of something • *She scrabbled about on the ground for the coins.*

**scraggy** ADJECTIVE
thin and bony

**scram** VERB (informal)
go away!

**scramble** VERB scrambles, scrambling, scrambled
❶ to move quickly and awkwardly • *We scrambled up the rocks.* ❷ to struggle to do or get something ❸ military aircraft or their crew scramble when they take off quickly to go into action ❹ to cook eggs by mixing them up and heating them in a pan ❺ to alter a radio or telephone signal so that it cannot be used without a decoding device
➤ **scrambler** NOUN

**scramble** NOUN scrambles
❶ a climb or walk over rough ground ❷ a struggle to do or get something • *There was a mad scramble for the best seats.* ❸ a motorcycle race over rough country

**scrap** NOUN scraps
❶ a small piece of something • *a scrap of paper* ❷ unwanted metal or paper that can be used again • *The car was sold for scrap.* ❸ (informal) a fight or argument

**scrap** VERB scraps, scrapping, scrapped
❶ to get rid of something that is not wanted

any more • *I think we should scrap that idea.* ❷ (informal) to fight or quarrel

**scrape** VERB scrapes, scraping, scraped
❶ to remove something from a surface by moving a sharp edge across it • *Scrape the mud off your boots.* ❷ to damage or hurt something by rubbing it against something rough or hard • *She scraped her arm on a rock.* ❸ to make a harsh sound by rubbing against something rough or hard • *The branches scraped against the window.* ❹ to get something by great effort or care • *They scraped together enough money for a holiday.*
➤ **scraper** NOUN
➤ **scrape through** to succeed or pass an examination by only a small margin

**scrape** NOUN scrapes
❶ a scraping movement or sound ❷ a mark made by scraping something • *I got a nasty scrape on my knee.* ❸ (informal) an awkward situation caused by mischief or foolishness

**scrappy** ADJECTIVE
done carelessly or untidily

**scratch** VERB scratches, scratching, scratched
❶ to mark or cut the surface of a thing with something sharp ❷ to rub the skin with fingernails or claws because it itches ❸ to make a noise by rubbing a surface with something sharp • *The dog was scratching at the door.*

**scratch** NOUN scratches
❶ a mark made by scratching ❷ the action of scratching • *I need to have a scratch.*
➤ **start from scratch** to start from the beginning or with nothing prepared
➤ **up to scratch** up to the proper standard

**scratch card** NOUN scratch cards
a card you buy as part of a lottery and scratch off part of the surface to see whether you have won a prize

**scratchy** ADJECTIVE
❶ scratchy clothes are rough and itchy ❷ making a harsh sound like something being scratched over a surface • *a scratchy recording*

**scrawl** NOUN scrawls
untidy handwriting

**scrawl** VERB scrawls, scrawling, scrawled
to write in a scrawl • *He scrawled his name on a piece of paper.*

**scrawny** ADJECTIVE
thin and bony

**scream** NOUN screams
❶ a loud cry of pain, fear, anger or excitement ❷ a loud piercing sound ❸ (*informal*) a very amusing person or thing

**scream** VERB screams, screaming, screamed
to let out a scream

**scree** NOUN
a mass of loose stones on the side of a mountain

**screech** NOUN screeches
a harsh high-pitched scream or sound

**screech** VERB screeches, screeching, screeched
to make a harsh high-pitched scream or sound

**screed** NOUN screeds
a very long piece of writing

**screen** NOUN screens
❶ a surface on which films or television pictures or computer data are shown ❷ a movable panel used to hide, protect or divide something ❸ a vehicle's windscreen

**screen** VERB screens, screening, screened
❶ to show a film or television pictures on a screen ❷ to protect, hide or divide something with a screen ❸ to carry out tests on someone to find out if they have a disease ❹ to check whether a person is suitable for a job

**screenplay** NOUN screenplays
the script of a film, with instructions about how scenes should be acted and filmed

**screw** NOUN screws
❶ a metal pin with a spiral ridge (the **thread**) round it, holding things together by being twisted in ❷ a twisting movement ❸ a propeller, especially for a ship or motor boat

**screw** VERB screws, screwing, screwed
❶ to fasten something with a screw or screws ❷ to fit or turn something by twisting • *Screw the lid on to the jar.*
➤ **screw something up** to twist or squeeze something into a tight ball

**screwdriver** NOUN screwdrivers
a tool for turning screws

**scribble** VERB scribbles, scribbling, scribbled
❶ to write something quickly or untidily or carelessly ❷ to make meaningless marks
➤ **scribble** NOUN

**scribe** NOUN scribes
a person who made copies of writings before printing was invented

**scrimmage** NOUN scrimmages
a confused struggle

**scrimp** VERB scrimps, scrimping, scrimped
to spend as little money as possible on the things you need so that you can save it for something else • *to scrimp and save*

**script** NOUN scripts
❶ handwriting ❷ the text of a play, film or broadcast

**scripture** NOUN scriptures
❶ sacred writings ❷ the Christian writings in the Bible

**scroll** NOUN scrolls
❶ a roll of paper or parchment used for writing on ❷ a spiral design

**scroll** VERB scrolls, scrolling, scrolled
to move the display on a computer screen up or down to see what comes before or after it

**scrotum** (say **skroh**-tum) NOUN scrota or scrotums
the pouch of skin behind the penis, containing the testicles

**scrounge** VERB scrounges, scrounging, scrounged
to get something without paying for it
➤ **scrounger** NOUN

**scrub** VERB scrubs, scrubbing, scrubbed
❶ to clean something with water by rubbing it hard, especially with a brush ❷ (*informal*) to cancel something

**scrub** NOUN
❶ scrubbing something • *You'll need to give your face a good scrub.* ❷ low trees and bushes ❸ land covered with these

**scrubby** ADJECTIVE
❶ scrubby trees and bushes are small and not fully developed ❷ scrubby land is covered with low bushes and trees

**scruff** NOUN
the back of the neck

**scruffy** ADJECTIVE
shabby and untidy • *a scruffy jacket*
➤ **scruffily** ADVERB
➤ **scruffiness** NOUN

**scrum** NOUN scrums
❶ (also **scrummage**) a group of players from each side in rugby football who push against each other and try to win the ball with their feet ❷ a crowd pushing against each other

**scrumptious** ADJECTIVE (*informal*)
delicious

**scrunch** VERB scrunches, scrunching, scrunched
❶ to make a loud crunching sound • *The snow scrunched underfoot.* ❷ to squeeze or crumple something into a smaller shape • *She scrunched up the letter and threw it in the bin.*

**scrunchy, scrunchie** NOUN scrunchies
a band of elastic covered in fabric, used to tie up your hair

**scruple** NOUN scruples
a feeling of doubt or hesitation when your conscience tells you that an action would be wrong • *I have no scruples about spying on him.*

**scruple** VERB scruples, scrupling, scrupled
to have scruples about something • *She would not scruple to betray us.*

**scrupulous** ADJECTIVE
❶ very careful about paying attention to every detail ❷ strictly honest or honourable
➤ **scrupulously** ADVERB

**scrutinize** (also **scrutinise**) VERB scrutinizes, scrutinizing, scrutinized
to look at or examine something carefully
• *He leaned forward and scrutinized my face.*

**scrutiny** NOUN
a careful look at or examination of something

**scuba diving** NOUN
swimming underwater using a tank of air strapped to your back **WORD ORIGIN** from the initials of *self-contained underwater breathing apparatus*

**scud** VERB scuds, scudding, scudded
to move quickly and lightly; to skim along
• *Clouds scudded across the sky.*

**scuff** VERB scuffs, scuffing, scuffed
❶ to drag your feet while walking ❷ to mark your shoes by scraping your feet on something

**scuffle** NOUN scuffles
a confused fight or struggle

**scuffle** VERB scuffles, scuffling, scuffled
to take part in a scuffle

**scull** NOUN sculls
a small or lightweight oar

**scull** VERB sculls, sculling, sculled
to row with sculls

**scullery** NOUN sculleries
a room for washing dishes and other kitchen work

**sculpt** VERB sculpts, sculpting, sculpted
to carve something; to make sculptures • *This huge figure has been sculpted in marble.*

**sculptor** NOUN sculptors
a person who makes sculptures

**sculpture** NOUN sculptures
❶ a figure or object that is carved or shaped out of a hard material such as stone, clay or metal ❷ the art of making sculptures

**sculptured** ADJECTIVE
❶ made as a sculpture or decorated with sculptures • *a sculptured arch* ❷ having a strong smooth shape • *sculptured cheekbones*

**scum** NOUN
❶ froth or dirt on top of a liquid ❷ worthless people

**scupper** NOUN scuppers
an opening in a ship's side to let water drain away

**scupper** VERB scuppers, scuppering, scuppered
❶ to sink a ship deliberately ❷ (*informal*) to wreck something or make it fail • *It scuppered our plans.*

**scurrilous** ADJECTIVE
rude, insulting and probably untrue
• *scurrilous attacks in the newspapers*
➤ **scurrilously** ADVERB

**scurry** VERB scurries, scurrying, scurried
to run quickly with short steps • *She could see beetles scurrying around.*

**scurvy** NOUN
a disease caused by lack of vitamin C from not eating enough fruit and vegetables

**scuttle** VERB scuttles, scuttling, scuttled
❶ to run with short quick steps; to hurry away • *The crab scuttled away.* ❷ to sink a ship deliberately by letting water into it

**scuttle** NOUN scuttles
❶ a bucket or container for coal in a house ❷ a small opening with a lid in a ship's deck or side

**scythe** NOUN scythes
a tool with a long curved blade for cutting grass or corn

**scythe** VERB scythes, scything, scythed
to cut something with a scythe

**SE** ABBREVIATION
❶ south-east ❷ south-eastern

**sea** NOUN seas
❶ the salt water that covers most of the

earth's surface • *We live by the sea.* ❷ a large area of salt water; a large lake • *the Mediterranean Sea* • *the Sea of Galilee* ❸ a large area of something • *Across the table we saw a sea of faces.*
➤ **at sea** ❶ travelling on the sea ❷ not knowing what to do

**sea anemone** NOUN sea anemones
a sea creature with short tentacles round its mouth

**seabed** NOUN
the bottom of the sea

**seabird** NOUN seabirds
a bird that lives close to the sea and gets its food from it

**seaboard** NOUN seaboards
a coastline or coastal region

**sea breeze** NOUN sea breezes
a breeze blowing from the sea onto the land

**sea change** NOUN sea changes
a dramatic change

**seafaring** ADJECTIVE & NOUN
working or travelling on the sea
➤ **seafarer** NOUN

**seafood** NOUN
fish or shellfish from the sea eaten as food

**seagull** NOUN seagulls
a seabird with long wings

**sea horse** NOUN sea horses
a small fish that swims upright, with a head rather like a horse's head

**seal** NOUN seals
❶ a sea mammal with thick fur or bristles, that breeds on land ❷ something designed to close an opening and prevent air or liquid from getting in or out ❸ a piece of metal with an engraved design for pressing on a soft substance to leave an impression ❹ this impression, especially one made on a piece of wax ❺ a small decorative sticker • *Christmas seals*

**seal** VERB seals, sealing, sealed
❶ to close something by sticking two parts together • *Now seal the envelope.* ❷ to close or cover something securely so that no air or liquid can get in or out • *The food is packed in sealed bags.* ❸ to settle or decide something • *His fate was sealed.*
➤ **seal something off** to prevent people getting to an area • *Police have sealed off the building.*

**sea level** NOUN
the level of the sea halfway between high and low tide

**sealing wax** NOUN
a substance that is soft when heated but hardens when cooled, used for marking or closing something with a seal

**sea lion** NOUN sea lions
a kind of large seal that lives in the Pacific Ocean

**seam** NOUN seams
❶ the line of stitches where two edges of cloth join ❷ a layer of coal in the ground

**seaman** NOUN seamen
a sailor

**seamanship** NOUN
skill in sailing a boat or ship

**seamy** ADJECTIVE
➤ **seamy side** the less attractive side or part • *Police see a lot of the seamy side of life.*
**WORD ORIGIN** originally, the 'wrong' side of a piece of sewing, where the rough edges of the seams show

**seance** (say **say**-ahns) NOUN seances
a meeting at which people try to make contact with the spirits of dead people

**seaplane** NOUN seaplanes
an aeroplane that can land on and take off from water

**seaport** NOUN seaports
a port on the coast

**sear** VERB sears, searing, seared
to scorch or burn the surface of something

**search** VERB searches, searching, searched
❶ to look very carefully in a place in order to find something ❷ to examine the clothes and body of a person to see if something is hidden there

**search** NOUN searches
❶ a very careful look for someone or something ❷ looking for information in a computer database or on the Internet • *I need to do a couple of Internet searches.*
➤ **searcher** NOUN

**search engine** NOUN search engines
(*in computing*) a computer program that allows you to search the Internet for information

**searching** ADJECTIVE
examining closely and thoroughly • *searching questions*

**searchlight** NOUN searchlights
a light with a strong beam that can be turned in any direction

**search party** NOUN search parties
a group of people organized to search for a missing person or thing

**search warrant** NOUN search warrants
an official document giving the police permission to search private property

**searing** ADJECTIVE
a searing pain is sharp and burning

**seascape** NOUN seascapes
a picture or view of the sea

**seashore** NOUN
the land close to the sea

**seasick** ADJECTIVE
sick because of the movement of a ship
➤ **seasickness** NOUN

**seaside** NOUN
a place by the sea where people go for holidays

**season** NOUN seasons
❶ each of the four main parts of the year (spring, summer, autumn, winter) ❷ the time of year when something happens • *the football season*
➤ **in season** available and ready for eating
• *Strawberries are in season in the summer.*

**season** VERB seasons, seasoning, seasoned
❶ to give extra flavour to food by adding salt, pepper, herbs or spices ❷ to dry and treat timber to make it ready for use

**seasonable** ADJECTIVE
suitable for the time of year • *seasonable weather*

USAGE
Take care not to confuse with seasonal.

**seasonal** ADJECTIVE
❶ for or to do with a season ❷ done or happening only at certain times of year
• *Fruit-picking is seasonal work.*
➤ **seasonally** ADVERB

USAGE
Take care not to confuse with seasonable.

**seasoning** NOUN seasonings
a substance used to season food

**season ticket** NOUN season tickets
a ticket that you can use as often as you like throughout a period of time

**seat** NOUN seats
❶ a thing made or used for sitting on ❷ a place as a member of a council, committee or parliament • *She won the seat ten years ago.* ❸ a person's bottom; the part of a skirt or trousers covering this ❹ the place where something is based or located • *London is the seat of our government.*

**seat** VERB seats, seating, seated
❶ to place someone in or on a seat ❷ to have seats for a certain number of people • *The theatre seats 3,000 people.*

**seat belt** NOUN seat belts
a strap to hold a person securely in a seat

**seating** NOUN
❶ the seats in a place • *There is seating for 400.* ❷ the arrangement of seats • *a seating plan*

**sea urchin** NOUN sea urchins
a sea animal with a spherical shell covered in sharp spikes WORD ORIGIN from an old meaning of *urchin* = hedgehog

**seaward** ADJECTIVE & ADVERB
towards the sea
➤ **seawards** ADVERB

**seaweed** NOUN
a plant or plants that grow in the sea

**seaworthy** ADJECTIVE
a ship is seaworthy when it is fit for a sea voyage
➤ **seaworthiness** NOUN

**sebum** NOUN
the natural oil produced by glands (*sebaceous glands*) in the skin to lubricate the skin and hair

**secateurs** PLURAL NOUN
clippers held in the hand for pruning plants

**secede** (say sis-**seed**) VERB secedes, seceding, seceded
to officially leave an organization of countries or states and become independent
➤ **secession** NOUN

**secluded** ADJECTIVE
quiet and sheltered from view • *a secluded beach*
➤ **seclusion** NOUN

**second** ADJECTIVE
❶ next after the first ❷ another • *a second chance*
➤ **have second thoughts** to wonder whether a decision you have made was the right one

**second** NOUN seconds
❶ a person or thing that is second ❷ an attendant of a fighter in a boxing match or duel ❸ one-sixtieth of a minute of time or of a degree used in measuring angles ❹ (informal) a short time • Wait a second.

**second** VERB seconds, seconding, seconded
❶ to support a proposal that someone else has put forward • I second that! ❷ to act as a fighter's second ❸ (say sik-**ond**) (British) to transfer a person temporarily to another job or department

**secondary** ADJECTIVE
❶ coming after or from something ❷ less important.
Compare with **primary**.

**secondary colour** NOUN secondary colours
a colour made by mixing two primary colours

**secondary school** NOUN secondary schools
a school for children of more than about 11 years old

**second-hand** ADJECTIVE
❶ bought or used after someone else has owned it ❷ selling used goods • a second-hand shop

**secondly** ADVERB
in the second place; as the second thing • Secondly, I'd like to thank my parents.

**second nature** NOUN
behaviour that has become automatic or a habit • Lying is second nature to him.

**second-rate** ADJECTIVE
inferior; not very good

**seconds** PLURAL NOUN
❶ goods that are not of the best quality, sold at a reduced price ❷ a second helping of food at a meal

**second sight** NOUN
the ability to foresee the future

**secrecy** NOUN
being secret; keeping things secret • Everyone involved was sworn to secrecy.

**secret** ADJECTIVE
❶ that must not be told or shown to other people ❷ not known by everyone ❸ working secretly

**secret** NOUN secrets
❶ something secret • I don't like keeping secrets. ❷ a way of achieving something that is not widely known • What is the secret of your success?

➤ **in secret** without other people knowing • They used to meet in secret.

**secret agent** NOUN secret agents
a spy acting for a country

**secretary** (say sek-rit-ree) NOUN secretaries
❶ a person whose job is to help with letters, keep files, answer the telephone and make business arrangements for a person or organization ❷ the person in a club or society who whose job is to keep records and write letters ❸ the head of a government department
➤ **secretarial** ADJECTIVE
**WORD ORIGIN** from Latin secretarius = an officer or servant allowed to know your secrets

**secrete** (say sik-**reet**) VERB secretes, secreting, secreted
❶ to hide something ❷ to produce a substance in the body • Saliva is secreted in the mouth.

**secretion** NOUN secretions
a substance that is secreted

**secretive** (say **seek**-rit-iv) ADJECTIVE
liking or trying to keep things secret • He is very secretive about his past.
➤ **secretively** ADVERB
➤ **secretiveness** NOUN

**secretly** ADVERB
without other people knowing • She was secretly pleased to see him.

**secret police** NOUN
a police force which works in secret for political purposes, not to deal with crime

**secret service** NOUN
a government department responsible for espionage

**sect** NOUN sects
a group of people whose beliefs differ from those of others in the same religion

**sectarian** (say sekt-**air**-ee-an) ADJECTIVE
to do with disagreements between different religious groups • sectarian violence

**section** NOUN sections
❶ one of the parts that something is divided into • Our school library has a large history section. • The tail section of the plane broke off. ❷ a cross-section

**sector** NOUN sectors
❶ one part of an area ❷ a part of something • the private sector of industry ❸ (in mathematics) a section of a circle between

two lines drawn from its centre to its circumference

**secular** ADJECTIVE
not connected with religion at all

**secure** ADJECTIVE
❶ well locked or protected • *Check that all the doors and windows are secure.* ❷ firmly fixed and certain not to slip • *Is that ladder secure?* ❸ feeling safe and confident and not worried ❹ certain or reliable

**secure** VERB secures, securing, secured
❶ to make a thing secure ❷ to fasten something firmly • *The load was secured with ropes.* ❸ to obtain or achieve something • *We secured two tickets for the show.*

**securely** ADVERB
firmly or tightly, so that something will not open or move or is protected • *Make sure your seat belt is securely fastened.*

**security** NOUN securities
❶ being secure or safe; safety ❷ precautions against theft or terrorism ❸ something you give as a guarantee that you will pay back a loan ❹ investments such as stocks and shares

**security guard** NOUN security guards
a person employed to guard a building or its contents against theft and vandalism

**sedan chair** NOUN sedan chairs
an enclosed chair for one person, mounted on two horizontal poles and carried by two men, used in the 17th-18th centuries

**sedate** ADJECTIVE
calm and dignified
➤ **sedately** ADVERB

**sedate** VERB sedates, sedating, sedated
to give a sedative to someone
➤ **sedation** NOUN

**sedative** (say sed-a-tiv) NOUN sedatives
a medicine that makes a person calm or helps them sleep

**sedentary** (say sed-en-ter-ee) ADJECTIVE
done sitting down • *sedentary work*

**Seder** NOUN Seders
in Judaism, a ritual and a ceremonial meal to mark the beginning of Passover

**sedge** NOUN
a grass-like plant growing in marshes or near water

**sediment** NOUN
fine particles of solid matter that float in liquid or sink to the bottom of it

**sedimentary** ADJECTIVE
sedimentary rocks are formed from particles that have settled on a surface

**sedition** NOUN
speeches or actions intended to make people rebel against the authority of the state
➤ **seditious** ADJECTIVE

**seductive** ADJECTIVE
❶ sexually attractive ❷ temptingly attractive • *It's certainly a seductive idea.*

**see** VERB sees, seeing, saw, seen
❶ to use your eyes to notice or be aware of something ❷ to meet or visit someone • *You should see a doctor about that cough.* ❸ to understand something • *I see what you mean.* ❹ to imagine or regard something in a certain way • *Can you see yourself as a teacher?* ❺ to consider something before deciding • *'Can I go to the party?' 'We'll see.'* ❻ to make sure of something • *See that the windows are shut.* ❼ to check or discover something • *See who is at the door.* ❽ to escort or lead someone • *I'll see you to the door.*
➤ **see through something** to not be deceived by something
➤ **see to something** to make sure that something is done

**see** NOUN sees
the district of which a bishop or archbishop is in charge • *the see of Canterbury*

**seed** NOUN seeds or seed
❶ a tiny, hard part of a plant, capable of growing into a new plant ❷ a seeded player

**seed** VERB seeds, seeding, seeded
❶ to plant or sprinkle seeds in something ❷ to name the best players and arrange for them not to play against each other in the early rounds of a tournament

**seedling** NOUN seedlings
a very young plant growing from a seed

**seedy** ADJECTIVE seedier, seediest
shabby and not respectable • *a seedy hotel*

**seeing** CONJUNCTION
considering • *Seeing that we have all finished, let's go.*

**seek** VERB seeks, seeking, sought
❶ to search for something ❷ to try to do or obtain something • *She is seeking fame.*

**seem** VERB seems, seeming, seemed
to give the impression of being something
• *She seems like a nice girl.*

**seemingly** ADVERB
apparently, but perhaps not • *a seemingly stupid question*

**seemly** ADJECTIVE (old use)
seemly talk or behaviour is proper or suitable

**seep** VERB seeps, seeping, seeped
to ooze slowly out or through something
• *Water seeped from a crack in the pipe.*
➤ **seepage** NOUN

**seer** NOUN seers
a person who claims they can see into the future; a prophet

**see-saw** NOUN see-saws
a plank balanced in the middle so that two people can sit, one on each end and make it go up and down (WORD ORIGIN) from an old rhyme which imitated the rhythm of a saw going to and fro, later used by children on a see-saw

**seethe** VERB seethes, seething, seethed
❶ you are seething when you are very angry
❷ to be full of people or animals moving around • *The streets were seething with tourists.* ❸ to bubble and surge like water boiling

**segment** NOUN segments
a part that is cut off or separates naturally from other parts • *the segments of an orange*
➤ **segmented** ADJECTIVE

**segregate** VERB segregates, segregating, segregated
❶ to separate people of different religions or races ❷ to isolate a person or thing
➤ **segregation** NOUN
(WORD ORIGIN) from Latin *segregare* = separate from the flock, from *gregis* = from a flock

**seismic** (say sy-zmik) ADJECTIVE
to do with earthquakes or other vibrations of the earth (WORD ORIGIN) from Greek *seismos* = earthquake

**seismograph** (say sy-zmo-grahf) NOUN seismographs
an instrument for measuring the strength of earthquakes

**seize** VERB seizes, seizing, seized
❶ to take hold of a person or thing suddenly or firmly ❷ to take control or possession of something by force or by legal authority
• *Customs officers seized the smuggled*

goods. ❸ to take advantage of a chance or opportunity • *Seizing his chance, he slipped out of the door.* ❹ to have a sudden effect on someone • *Panic seized us.*
➤ **seize up** to become jammed or stuck

SPELLING

Seize the right spelling and put the e before the i.

**seizure** NOUN seizures
❶ seizing something ❷ a sudden fit, as in epilepsy or a heart attack

**seldom** ADVERB
rarely; not often • *He seldom spoke.*

**select** VERB selects, selecting, selected
to choose a person or thing carefully
➤ **selector** NOUN

**select** ADJECTIVE
❶ small and carefully chosen • *They have a select group of friends.* ❷ a select club or organization is exclusive and chooses its members carefully

**selection** NOUN selections
❶ selecting something or being selected
• *The manager is responsible for team selection.* ❷ a person or thing selected ❸ a group selected from a larger group ❹ a range of goods from which to choose • *a wide selection of toys*

**selective** ADJECTIVE
choosing or chosen carefully • *She is selective about what she watches on TV.*
➤ **selectively** ADVERB

**self** NOUN selves
❶ a person as an individual ❷ a person's particular nature • *She has recovered and is her old self again.*

SPELLING

Change the f to ves to make the plural selves.

**self-addressed** ADJECTIVE
addressed to yourself

**self-assured** ADJECTIVE
confident of your abilities

**self-catering** NOUN
catering for yourself, instead of having meals provided

**self-centred** ADJECTIVE
selfish; thinking about yourself too much

**self-confident** ADJECTIVE
confident of your own abilities
➤ **self-confidence** NOUN

**self-conscious** ADJECTIVE
embarrassed or worried about how you look
or what other people think of you • *She used
to feel self-conscious wearing glasses.*
➤ **self-consciously** ADVERB

**self-contained** ADJECTIVE
accommodation is self-contained when
it is complete in itself and contains all
the necessary facilities • *a self-contained
apartment*

**self-control** NOUN
the ability to control your own behaviour or
feelings
➤ **self-controlled** ADJECTIVE

**self-defence** NOUN
❶ defending yourself against attack • *He
claims he was acting in self-defence.*
❷ techniques for doing this

**self-denial** NOUN
deliberately going without things you would
like to have

**self-determination** NOUN
a country's right to rule itself and choose its
own government

**self-employed** ADJECTIVE
working independently, not for an employer

**self-esteem** NOUN
your own opinion of yourself and your own
worth

**self-evident** ADJECTIVE
obvious and not needing proof or explanation

**selfie** NOUN selfies (*informal*)
a photograph that you take of yourself,
usually using a mobile phone, and send to a
social media website

**self-important** ADJECTIVE
having a high opinion of yourself; pompous

**self-interest** NOUN
your own personal advantage

**selfish** ADJECTIVE
doing what you want and not thinking of
other people; keeping things for yourself
➤ **selfishly** ADVERB
➤ **selfishness** NOUN

**selfless** ADJECTIVE
thinking of other people rather than yourself;
unselfish

**self-made** ADJECTIVE
rich or successful because of your own
efforts

**self-pity** NOUN
too much sorrow and pity for yourself and
your own problems

**self-portrait** NOUN self-portraits
a portrait in which the artist is the subject

**self-possessed** ADJECTIVE
calm and confident in a difficult situation

**self-raising** ADJECTIVE
self-raising flour makes cakes rise without
needing to have baking powder added

**self-respect** NOUN
your own proper respect for yourself

**self-righteous** ADJECTIVE
smugly sure that you are behaving virtuously

**selfsame** ADJECTIVE
the very same • *I had been wondering that
selfsame thing.*

**self-satisfied** ADJECTIVE
very pleased with yourself

**self-seeking** ADJECTIVE
selfishly trying to benefit yourself

**self-service** ADJECTIVE
where customers help themselves to things
and pay a cashier for what they have taken

**self-sufficient** ADJECTIVE
able to produce or provide what you need
without help from others

**self-willed** ADJECTIVE
obstinately doing what you want; stubborn

**sell** VERB sells, selling, sold
❶ to give something in exchange for money
❷ to have something available for people to
buy • *Do you sell stamps?* ❸ to be on sale at
a certain price • *It sells for £5.99.*
➤ **sell out** ❶ to sell all your stock of
something ❷ (*informal*) to give up your
beliefs or principles in order to get an
advantage

**sell** NOUN
➤ **hard sell** NOUN
forceful selling; putting pressure on someone
to buy
➤ **soft sell** selling by suggestion or gentle
persuasion

**sell-by date** NOUN sell-by dates
(*British*) a date, marked on the packaging of
food, by which it must be sold

**seller** NOUN sellers
a person or business that sells something

**sell-out** NOUN sell-outs
an entertainment, sporting event, etc. for which all the tickets have been sold

**selves**
plural of self

**semantic** (say sim-an-tik) ADJECTIVE
to do with the meanings of words
➤ **semantically** ADVERB

**semaphore** NOUN
a system of signalling by holding flags out with your arms in positions that indicate letters of the alphabet

**semblance** NOUN
an outward appearance or apparent likeness

**semen** (say seem-en) NOUN
a white liquid produced by males and containing sperm

**semi** NOUN semis (informal)
a semi-detached house

**semibreve** NOUN semibreves
(British) the longest musical note normally used ( ○ ), lasting four times as long as a crotchet

**semicircle** NOUN semicircles
half a circle
➤ **semicircular** ADJECTIVE

**semicolon** NOUN semicolons
a punctuation mark (;) used to separate two sentences or main clauses that are linked or of equal importance

PUNCTUATION

You use a **semicolon** to separate two sentences or main clauses that are linked or of equal importance:

*The castle was desolate; no one had lived there for centuries.*

*I know you don't eat meat, fish or eggs; but what about cheese?*

*You bring cups and plates; I'll bring juice and sandwiches*

Semicolons can also be used instead of a comma to separate a series of clauses or phrases in a list, introduced by a colon:

*There were three clues: there was mud on the carpet; the door had been forced; and the air in the room smelled of fish.*

**semiconductor** NOUN semiconductors
a substance that can conduct electricity but not as well as most metals do

**semi-detached** ADJECTIVE
a semi-detached house is joined to another house on one side only

**semi-final** NOUN semi-finals
a match or round whose winner will take part in the final
➤ **semi-finalist** NOUN

**seminar** NOUN seminars
a meeting for advanced discussion and research on a subject

**seminary** NOUN seminaries
a training college for priests or rabbis

**semiquaver** NOUN semiquavers
(British) a note in music ( ♪ ), equal in length to one quarter of a crotchet

**semi-skimmed** ADJECTIVE
(British) semi-skimmed milk has had some of the cream taken out

**Semitic** (say sim-it-ik) ADJECTIVE
to do with the Semites, the group of people that includes the Jews and Arabs
➤ **Semite** (say see-myt) NOUN

**semitone** NOUN semitones
(British) half a tone in music

**semolina** NOUN
hard round grains of wheat used to make milk puddings and pasta

**senate** NOUN senates
❶ the governing council in ancient Rome
❷ the upper house of the parliament of the United States, France and certain other countries

**senator** NOUN senators
a member of a senate

**send** VERB sends, sending, sent
❶ to make something go or be taken somewhere • *He sent me an email this morning.* ❷ to tell someone to go somewhere • *She sent the children to bed early.* ❸ to make a person or thing move quickly in a certain direction • *The punch sent him flying.* ❹ to affect someone in a certain way • *The noise is sending me crazy.*
➤ **sender** NOUN
➤ **send for someone** or **something** to ask someone to come to you • *We sent for the doctor.*
➤ **send someone up** (informal) to make fun of someone by imitating them

**senile** (say **seen**-yl) *ADJECTIVE*
weak or confused and forgetful because of old age
➤ **senility** *NOUN*

**senior** *ADJECTIVE*
❶ older than someone else ❷ higher in rank or importance • *senior officers* ❸ for older children • *a senior school*
➤ **seniority** *NOUN*

**senior** *NOUN* seniors
❶ a person who is older or higher in rank than you are • *He is my senior.* ❷ a member of a senior school

**senior citizen** *NOUN* senior citizens
an elderly person, especially a pensioner

**senna** *NOUN*
the dried pods or leaves of a tropical tree, used as a laxative

**sensation** *NOUN* sensations
❶ a physical feeling • *a tingling sensation* ❷ great excitement or interest or something that causes this • *The news caused a great sensation.*

**sensational** *ADJECTIVE*
❶ causing great excitement, interest or shock ❷ (*informal*) very good; wonderful
➤ **sensationally** *ADVERB*

**sense** *NOUN* senses
❶ the ability to see, hear, smell, touch or taste things ❷ the ability to feel or appreciate something • *a sense of guilt* • *a sense of humour* ❸ the power to think or make wise decisions • *He hasn't got the sense to come in out of the rain.* ❹ the meaning of a word or phrase • *The word 'run' has many senses.*
➤ **come to your senses** to finally realize that you have not been behaving sensibly
➤ **make sense** ❶ to have a meaning you can understand ❷ to be a sensible idea

**sense** *VERB* senses, sensing, sensed
❶ to feel or be aware of something • *I sensed that she did not like me.* ❷ to detect or record something • *This device senses radioactivity.*

**senseless** *ADJECTIVE*
❶ stupid; not showing good sense ❷ unconscious

**sensibility** *NOUN* sensibilities
sensitiveness or delicate feeling • *The criticism hurt the artist's sensibilities.*

**USAGE**

Note that this word does not mean 'being sensible' or 'having good sense'.

**sensible** *ADJECTIVE*
wise; having or showing good sense
➤ **sensibly** *ADVERB*

**sensitive** *ADJECTIVE*
❶ easily affected or damaged by something • *Photographic paper is sensitive to light.* ❷ easily hurt or offended • *She is very sensitive about her age.* ❸ considerate about other people's feelings ❹ needing to be deal with tactfully • *a sensitive subject* ❺ able to measure very small changes • *a sensitive instrument*
➤ **sensitively** *ADVERB*
➤ **sensitivity** *NOUN*

**sensitize** (also **sensitise**) *VERB* sensitizes, sensitizing, sensitized
to make a thing sensitive to something

**sensor** *NOUN* sensors
a device or instrument for detecting a physical property such as light, heat or sound

**sensory** *ADJECTIVE*
❶ to do with the senses ❷ receiving physical sensations • *sensory nerves*

**sensual** *ADJECTIVE*
❶ to do with physical pleasure ❷ liking or suggesting physical or sexual pleasures

**sensuous** *ADJECTIVE*
giving pleasure to the senses, especially by being beautiful or delicate

**sentence** *NOUN* sentences
❶ a group of words that express a complete thought and form a statement, question, exclamation or command ❷ the punishment announced to a convicted person in a law court

**sentence** *VERB* sentences, sentencing, sentenced
to give someone a sentence in a law court • *He was sentenced to two years in prison.*

**GRAMMAR**

A **sentence** is a group of words that typically contains a main verb. It begins with a capital letter and ends in a full stop, a question mark or an exclamation mark. It can contain a single clause or several clauses joined by conjunctions or punctuation:

*Bats are nocturnal creatures.*

*Desert animals are often nocturnal because it is cooler for hunting at night.*

a b c d e f g h i j k l m n o p q r s t u v w x y z

If a sentence is a **statement**, it ends with a full stop:

*The students wrote their answers on their whiteboards.*

A sentence which is a **question** ends with a question mark, and one which is an **exclamation** or **command** often ends with an exclamation mark:

*Have you written your answers on your whiteboards?*

*Write your answers on your whiteboards.*

*What a good answer!*

A single verb can form a sentence, especially if it is a command, like *Help!* or *Stop!* Sometimes, short sentences can be formed without a verb; for example, in direct speech:

*'Where are you, Lieutenant?' 'Over here!'*

or in stories to create a special effect:

*In every direction lay the expanse of outer space. Vast. Empty. Desolate.*

See also the panel on **clauses**.

**sentient** ADJECTIVE
able to feel and perceive things • *sentient beings*

**sentiment** NOUN sentiments
❶ an attitude or opinion • *I agree with those sentiments.* ❷ a show of feeling or emotion; sentimentality • *He never lets sentiment get in the way of business.*

**sentimental** ADJECTIVE
showing or making you feel tenderness, romantic feeling or foolish emotion
➤ **sentimentally** ADVERB
➤ **sentimentality** NOUN

**sentinel** NOUN sentinels
a guard or sentry

**sentry** NOUN sentries
a soldier guarding something

**sepal** NOUN sepals
each of the leaves forming the calyx of a bud

**separate** (say **sep**-er-at) ADJECTIVE
❶ apart; not joined to something else • *The school is housed in two separate buildings.*
❷ different; not connected • *They lead separate lives.*

**separate** (say **sep**-er-ayt) VERB separates, separating, separated
❶ to make or keep people or things separate or to divide them • *The two sides of the city are separated by a river.* ❷ to become separate • *We separated into two groups.*
❸ to stop living together as a couple

SPELLING
There is a tricky bit in separate—there is an a between the p and the r.

**separately** ADVERB
apart; not together • *They arrived together but left separately.*

**separation** NOUN
❶ separating or being separated; time spent apart ❷ an agreement when a couple decide to stop living together

**sepia** NOUN
reddish-brown, like the colour of early photographs

**September** NOUN
the ninth month of the year
WORD ORIGIN from Latin *septem* = seven, because it was the seventh month of the ancient Roman calendar

**septet** NOUN septets
❶ a group of seven musicians ❷ a piece of music for seven musicians

**septic** ADJECTIVE
infected with harmful bacteria that cause pus to form

**sepulchral** (say sep-**ul**-kral) ADJECTIVE
❶ to do with a sepulchre ❷ a sepulchral voice sounds deep and hollow

**sepulchre** (say **sep**-ul-ker) NOUN sepulchres
a tomb

**sequel** NOUN sequels
❶ a book or film etc. that continues the story of an earlier one ❷ something that follows or results from an earlier event

**sequence** NOUN sequences
❶ the following of one thing after another; the order in which things happen • *Arrange these playing cards in sequence, the highest first.* ❷ a series of things

**sequin** NOUN sequins
a tiny bright disc sewn on clothes to decorate them
➤ **sequinned** ADJECTIVE

**seraph** NOUN seraphim or seraphs
a kind of angel

**seraphic** (say ser-**af**-ik) ADJECTIVE
a seraphic smile or look is very pure and
beautiful

**serenade** NOUN serenades
a song or tune of a kind played by a man
under his lover's window

**serenade** VERB serenades, serenading,
serenaded
to sing or play a serenade to someone

**serendipity** NOUN
the ability to make pleasant or interesting
discoveries by accident
➤ **serendipitous** ADJECTIVE
WORD ORIGIN made up by an 18th-century
writer, Horace Walpole, from the title of a story
*The Three Princes of Serendip* (who had this
ability)

**serene** ADJECTIVE
calm and peaceful • *a serene smile*
➤ **serenely** ADVERB
➤ **serenity** (say ser-**en**-iti) NOUN

**serf** NOUN serfs
a farm labourer who worked for a landowner
in the Middle Ages and who was not allowed
to leave
➤ **serfdom** NOUN

**serge** NOUN
a kind of strong woven fabric

**sergeant** (say **sar**-jent) NOUN sergeants
a soldier or police officer who is in charge of
others

**sergeant major** NOUN sergeant majors
a soldier who is two ranks higher than a
sergeant

**serial** NOUN serials
a story that is broadcast or published in
separate parts over a period of time • *a 10-
part drama serial*

SPELLING
Take care not to confuse with cereal.

**serialize** (also **serialise**) VERB serializes,
serializing, serialized
to broadcast or publish a story as a serial
➤ **serialization** NOUN

**serial killer** NOUN serial killers
a person who commits a series of murders

**serial number** NOUN serial numbers
a number put onto an object by the
manufacturers to distinguish it from other
identical objects

**series** NOUN series
❶ a number of things following or connected
with each other • *a series of events* ❷ a
number of separate radio or television
programmes with the same characters or on
the same subject ❸ a number of games or
matches between the same competitors

**serious** ADJECTIVE
❶ a person or look is serious when they
are solemn and thoughtful and not smiling
❷ needing careful thought; important • *We
need a serious talk.* ❸ sincere; not casual or
light-hearted • *a serious attempt* ❹ causing
anxiety, not trivial • *a serious accident*
➤ **seriousness** NOUN

**seriously** ADVERB
in a serious way • *Three people were seriously
injured.*
➤ **take something seriously** to treat
something as important

**sermon** NOUN sermons
a talk given by a preacher, especially as part
of a religious service

**serpent** NOUN serpents
a snake WORD ORIGIN from Latin *serpens* =
creeping

**serpentine** ADJECTIVE
twisting and curving like a snake • *a
serpentine road*

**serrated** ADJECTIVE
having a notched edge

**serried** ADJECTIVE
arranged in rows close together • *serried
ranks of troops*

**serum** (say **seer**-um) NOUN sera or serums
❶ the thin pale-yellow liquid that remains
from blood when the rest has clotted
❷ this fluid used medically, usually for the
antibodies it contains

**servant** NOUN servants
a person whose job is to work or serve in
someone else's house

**serve** VERB serves, serving, served
❶ to sell things to people in a shop ❷ to give
out food to people at a meal ❸ to work for
a person or organization or country ❹ to
spend time doing or suffering something • *He
served a prison sentence.* ❺ to be suitable for
something • *This tree stump will serve as a
table.* ❻ to start play in tennis etc. by hitting
the ball
➤ **it serves you right** you deserve it

**serve** NOUN serves
serving in tennis etc.

**server** NOUN servers
❶ a person or thing that serves ❷ (*in computing*) a computer or program that controls or supplies information to several computers connected to a network

**service** NOUN services
❶ working for a person, organization or country ❷ something that helps people or supplies what they want • *a bus service* ❸ the army, navy or air force • *the armed services* ❹ a religious ceremony ❺ providing people with goods, food, etc. • *The service at the restaurant was slow.* ❻ a set of dishes and plates for a meal • *a dinner service* ❼ the checks and repairs that are needed to keep a vehicle or machine in working order ❽ the action of serving in tennis or badminton

**service** VERB services, servicing, serviced
to repair or keep a vehicle or machine in working order

**serviceable** ADJECTIVE
usable; suitable for ordinary use or wear • *It's an old coat, but it's still serviceable.*

**service charge** NOUN service charges
an amount added to a restaurant or hotel bill to reward the waiters and waitresses for their service

**service industry** NOUN service industries
an industry which sells a service, not goods

**serviceman** NOUN servicemen
a man serving in the armed forces

**services** PLURAL NOUN
an area beside a motorway with a garage, shop, restaurant, toilets, etc. for travellers to use

**service station** NOUN service stations
a place beside a road, where petrol and other services are available

**servicewoman** NOUN servicewomen
a woman serving in the armed forces

**serviette** NOUN serviettes
(*British*) a piece of cloth or paper that you use to keep your clothes or hands clean at a meal

**servile** ADJECTIVE
like a slave; too willing to serve or obey others
➤ **servility** NOUN

**serving** NOUN servings
a helping of food

**servitude** NOUN
the condition of being obliged to work for someone else and having no independence; slavery

**sesame** NOUN
an African plant whose seeds can be eaten or used to make an edible oil

**session** NOUN sessions
❶ a time spent doing one thing • *a recording session* ❷ a meeting or series of meetings • *The Queen will open the next session of Parliament.*

**set** VERB sets, setting, set
❶ to set something somewhere is to put it into position • *Set the vase on the table.* ❷ to set a date or time is to arrange or decide when something will happen • *Have they set a date for the wedding?* ❸ to make something ready to work • *I'd better set the alarm.* ❹ to become firm or hard • *Leave the jelly to set.* ❺ to give someone a task or problem to deal with • *We've been set a lot of homework this weekend.* ❻ to make something happen • *Set them free.* • *Her remarks set me thinking.* ❼ the sun sets when it goes down below the horizon
➤ **set about someone** (*informal*) to attack someone
➤ **set about something** to start doing something
➤ **set off** to begin a journey
➤ **set something off** ❶ to start something happening ❷ to cause something to explode
➤ **set out** to begin a journey
➤ **set something out** to display something or make it known • *She set out her reasons for leaving.*
➤ **set to** ❶ to begin doing something vigorously ❷ to begin fighting or arguing
➤ **set something up** ❶ to place something in position, ready for use • *Can you set up the table-tennis table?* ❷ to get something started • *We want to set up a website for local artists.*

**set** NOUN sets
❶ a group of people or things that belong together ❷ a radio or television receiver ❸ (*British*) a group of school students with the same level of ability in a particular subject ❹ (*in mathematics*) a collection of things that have a common property ❺ the scenery or stage for a play or film ❻ a group of games in a tennis match ❼ the way something is placed • *the set of his jaw* ❽ a badger's burrow

**set** ADJECTIVE
❶ fixed or arranged in advance • *The evening meal is served at a set time.* ❷ ready or prepared to do something • *I'm all set to go.*
➤ **be set on something** to be determined about doing something

**setback** NOUN setbacks
something that stops progress or slows it down

**set book** NOUN set books
a book that must be studied for a literature examination

**set square** NOUN set squares
(*British*) a device shaped like a right-angled triangle, used to draw straight lines and angles

**settee** NOUN settees
(*British*) a long soft seat with a back and arms

**setter** NOUN setters
a dog of a long-haired breed that can be trained to stand rigid when it scents game

**set theory** NOUN
the branch of mathematics that deals with sets and the relations between them

**setting** NOUN settings
❶ the place and time in which a story happens ❷ the land surrounding something • *The hotel is in a beautiful setting, close to the sea.* ❸ one of the positions of the controls of a machine ❹ a set of cutlery or crockery for one person at a meal ❺ music for the words of a song

**settle** VERB settles, settling, settled
❶ to arrange something; to decide or solve something • *That settles the problem.* ❷ to become calm or comfortable; to stop being restless • *Stop chattering and settle down!* ❸ to go and live somewhere • *They settled in Canada.* ❹ to come to rest on something • *Dust had settled on his books.* • *A bird flew down and settled on the fence.* ❺ to pay a bill or debt

**settle** NOUN settles
a long wooden seat with a high back and arms

**settlement** NOUN settlements
❶ a small number of people or houses established in a new area ❷ an agreement to end an argument

**settler** NOUN settlers
one of the first people to settle in a new country; a pioneer or colonist

**set-up** NOUN (*informal*)
the way something is organized or arranged

**seven** NOUN & ADJECTIVE sevens
the number 7
➤ **seventh** ADJECTIVE & NOUN

**seventeen** NOUN & ADJECTIVE seventeens
the number 17
➤ **seventeenth** ADJECTIVE & NOUN

**seventy** NOUN & ADJECTIVE seventies
the number 70
➤ **seventieth** ADJECTIVE & NOUN

**sever** VERB severs, severing, severed
to cut or break something off • *The builders accidentally severed a water pipe.*

**several** DETERMINER & PRONOUN
more than two but not many

**severally** ADVERB
separately; one by one

**severe** ADJECTIVE
❶ strict; not gentle or kind ❷ extremely bad or serious • *He suffered severe injuries.* ❸ intense or forceful • *severe gales* ❹ very plain • *a severe style of dress*
➤ **severely** ADVERB
➤ **severity** NOUN

**sew** VERB sews, sewing, sewed, sewn or sewed
❶ to join things together by using a needle and thread ❷ to work with a needle and thread or with a sewing machine

SPELLING
To **sew** is to work with a needle and thread. To **sow** seed means to put it in the ground.

**sewage** (say soo-ij) NOUN
liquid waste matter carried away in drains

**sewer** (say soo-er) NOUN sewers
a large underground drain for carrying away sewage

**sewing machine** NOUN sewing machines
a machine for sewing things

**sex** NOUN sexes
❶ each of the two groups (*male* and *female*) into which people and animals are divided ❷ sexual activity, especially sexual intercourse

**sexism** NOUN
the unfair or offensive treatment of people of a particular sex, especially women

**sexist** NOUN sexists
a person who treats people of a particular

627

sex, especially women, in an unfair or offensive way

**sexist** ADJECTIVE
offensive to people of a particular sex, especially women • *sexist remarks*

**sextant** NOUN sextants
an instrument for measuring the angle of the sun and stars, used for finding your position when navigating **WORD ORIGIN** from Latin *sextus* = sixth (because early sextants consisted of an arc of one-sixth of a circle)

**sextet** NOUN sextets
❶ a group of six musicians ❷ a piece of music for six musicians

**sexton** NOUN sextons
a person whose job is to take care of a church and churchyard

**sextuplet** NOUN sextuplets
each of six children born to the same mother at one time

**sexual** ADJECTIVE
❶ to do with sex ❷ to do with the difference between males and females • *sexual equality* ❸ sexual reproduction happens by the fusion of male and female cells
➤ **sexually** ADVERB
➤ **sexuality** NOUN

**sexual intercourse** NOUN
an intimate physical act between two people, especially one in which a man puts his penis into the woman's vagina, to express love, for pleasure or to conceive a child

**sexy** ADJECTIVE sexier, sexiest (*informal*)
❶ sexually attractive ❷ concerned with sex

**SF** ABBREVIATION
science fiction

**shabby** ADJECTIVE shabbier, shabbiest
❶ in a poor or worn-out condition • *a shabby suit* ❷ poorly dressed ❸ unfair or dishonourable • *That was a shabby trick.*
➤ **shabbily** ADVERB
➤ **shabbiness** NOUN

**shack** NOUN shacks
a roughly-built hut

**shackle** NOUN shackles
an iron ring for fastening a prisoner's wrist or ankle to something

**shackle** VERB shackles, shackling, shackled
❶ to put shackles on a prisoner ❷ to be shackled by something is to be restricted or limited by it • *They felt shackled by tradition.*

**shade** NOUN shades
❶ slight darkness produced where something blocks the sun's light ❷ a device that reduces or shuts out bright light ❸ a colour; how light or dark a colour is • *four different shades of blue* ❹ a slight difference • *This word has several shades of meaning.* ❺ (*poetical use*) a ghost

**shade** VERB shades, shading, shaded
❶ to shelter something from bright light ❷ to make part of a drawing darker than the rest ❸ to move gradually from one state or quality to another • *The afternoon was shading into evening.*

**shading** NOUN
the parts of a drawing that you make darker then the rest

**shadow** NOUN shadows
❶ the dark shape that falls on a surface when something is between the surface and a light ❷ an area of shade • *His face was in shadow.* ❸ a slight trace • *a shadow of doubt*

**shadow** VERB shadows, shadowing, shadowed
❶ to cast a shadow on something ❷ to follow a person secretly

**Shadow Cabinet** NOUN
(*British*) members of the Opposition in Parliament who each have responsibility for a particular area of policy

**shadowy** ADJECTIVE
❶ dark and full of shadows • *a shadowy forest* ❷ difficult to see because there is not much light • *He saw a shadowy figure standing in the doorway.*

**shady** ADJECTIVE shadier, shadiest
❶ giving shade • *a shady tree* ❷ in the shade • *Let's find a shady spot by the river.* ❸ not completely honest or legal • *a shady deal*

**shaft** NOUN shafts
❶ a long slender rod or straight part • *the shaft of an arrow* ❷ a ray of light ❸ a deep narrow hole • *a mine shaft*

**shaggy** ADJECTIVE shaggier, shaggiest
❶ having long rough hair or fibre ❷ rough, thick and untidy • *shaggy hair*

**shah** NOUN shahs
the title of the former ruler of Iran

**shake** VERB shakes, shaking, shook, shaken
❶ to move something quickly up and down or from side to side • *Have you shaken the bottle?* ❷ to move in this way • *The whole house shakes when a train goes past.* ❸ to shock or upset someone • *The news shook us.*

**❹** to tremble or be unsteady • *His voice was shaking.*
➤ **shake hands** to clasp a person's right hand with yours as a way of greeting them or as a sign of agreement

**shake** NOUN shakes
**❶** a quick movement up and down or from side to side **❷** (*informal*) a milkshake
➤ **in two shakes** very soon

**shaky** ADJECTIVE shakier, shakiest
unsteady or wobbly • *Her voice was shaky.*
➤ **shakily** ADVERB

**shale** NOUN
a kind of stone that splits easily into layers

**shall** AUXILIARY VERB
**❶** used, especially with I and we, to refer to the future • *I shall arrive tomorrow.* **❷** used with I and we in questions when making a suggestion or offer or asking for advice
• *Shall I shut the door?*

> **GRAMMAR**
> The auxiliary verb **shall** can be used to form the future tense of verbs, although it is much more common to use **will**. In the past, **shall** was only used after *I* and *we* (*I shall be leaving tonight*) and **will** was used in all other cases (*They will be leaving tonight*), but most people ignore this distinction now.
>
> **Shall** is still quite commonly used when you want to ask a question or make a suggestion:
>
> *Shall we go now?*

**shallot** NOUN shallots
a kind of small onion

**shallow** ADJECTIVE
**❶** not deep • *The stream is quite shallow here.* **❷** not capable of deep feelings • *a shallow character*
➤ **shallowness** NOUN

**shallows** PLURAL NOUN
a shallow part of a stretch of water

**sham** NOUN shams
something that is not genuine; a pretence
• *Their marriage was a sham.*

**sham** ADJECTIVE
not real or genuine, but intended to seem so

**sham** VERB shams, shamming, shammed
to pretend or fake something • *Are you really ill or are you shamming?*

**shamble** VERB shambles, shambling, shambled
to walk in a lazy or awkward way, dragging your feet along the ground

**shambles** NOUN
a scene of great disorder or confusion
• *The rehearsal was a complete shambles.*
**WORD ORIGIN** from an old word **shamble** = a slaughterhouse or meat market

**shambolic** (say sham-**bol**-ik) ADJECTIVE (*British*) (*informal*)
chaotic or disorganized

**shame** NOUN
**❶** a feeling of great sorrow or guilt because you have done something wrong **❷** dishonour or disgrace **❸** something you regret; a pity
• *It's a shame you have to go so soon.*

**shame** VERB shames, shaming, shamed
to make a person feel ashamed

**shamefaced** ADJECTIVE
looking ashamed

**shameful** ADJECTIVE
causing shame; disgraceful
➤ **shamefully** ADVERB

**shameless** ADJECTIVE
feeling or showing no shame
➤ **shamelessly** ADVERB

**shampoo** NOUN shampoos
**❶** a liquid substance for washing the hair **❷** a substance for cleaning a carpet etc. or washing a car **❸** a wash with shampoo

**shampoo** VERB shampoos, shampooing, shampooed
to wash or clean something with a shampoo
**WORD ORIGIN** originally = to massage: from Hindi *champo* = press

**shamrock** NOUN shamrocks
a plant rather like clover, the national emblem of Ireland

**shandy** NOUN shandies
(*British*) a mixture of beer and lemonade or some other soft drink

**shank** NOUN shanks
**❶** the leg, especially the part from knee to ankle **❷** a long narrow part • *the shank of a pin*

**shan't** (*mainly spoken*)
shall not

**shanty** NOUN shanties
**❶** a shack **❷** a sailors' song with a chorus

**shanty town** NOUN shanty towns
a settlement consisting of shanties

**shape** NOUN **shapes**
❶ what a thing's outline looks like
❷ something that has a definite or regular form, such as a square, circle or triangle
❸ a person's physical condition • *She goes swimming to keep in shape.* ❹ the general form or condition of something • *the shape of British industry*
➤ **out of shape** ❶ no longer having the normal shape • *The front wheel was twisted out of shape.* ❷ not physically fit
➤ **take shape** to start to develop properly

**shape** VERB **shapes, shaping, shaped**
to make something into a particular shape
➤ **shape up** to develop well • *The plan is shaping up nicely.*

**shaped** ADJECTIVE
having a particular shape • *an L-shaped room*

**shapeless** ADJECTIVE
having no definite shape

**shapely** ADJECTIVE **shapelier, shapeliest**
having an attractive shape

**share** NOUN **shares**
❶ a part given to one person or thing out of something that is being divided ❷ each of the equal parts into which the ownership of a business company is divided, giving the person who holds it the right to receive a portion (a **dividend**) of the company's profits

**share** VERB **shares, sharing, shared**
❶ to give portions of something to two or more people • *We shared out the pizza between the three of us.* ❷ to have, use or experience something jointly with others
• *She shared a room with me.*

**shareholder** NOUN **shareholders**
a person who owns shares in a company

**shareware** NOUN
computer software which is given away or which you can use free of charge

**shark** NOUN **sharks**
❶ a large sea fish with sharp teeth ❷ a person who exploits or cheats people

**sharp** ADJECTIVE
❶ with an edge or point that can cut or make holes ❷ quick at noticing or learning things
• *sharp eyes* ❸ changing direction suddenly; not gradual • *a sharp bend* • *a sharp rise in temperature* ❹ forceful or severe • *a sharp frost* ❺ distinct and easy to see clearly • *a sharp outline* ❻ loud and shrill • *a sharp cry*
❼ slightly sour ❽ (*in music*) one semitone

higher than the natural note • *C sharp*
➤ **sharpness** NOUN

**sharp** ADVERB
❶ with a sudden change of direction • *Turn sharp right.* ❷ punctually or precisely • *I'll see you at six o'clock sharp.* ❸ (*in music*) above the correct pitch • *You were singing sharp.*

**sharp** NOUN **sharps** (*in music*) a note one semitone higher than the natural note; the sign (#) that indicates this

**sharpen** VERB **sharpens, sharpening, sharpened**
to make something sharp or to become sharp
• *I need to sharpen my pencil.*
➤ **sharpener** NOUN

**sharply** ADVERB
❶ suddenly and by a large amount • *The road bends sharply to the left.* ❷ in a critical or severe way • *'Just shut up,' she said sharply.*

**sharp practice** NOUN
dishonest or barely honest dealings in business

**sharpshooter** NOUN **sharpshooters**
a person who is skilled at shooting a gun

**shatter** VERB **shatters, shattering, shattered**
❶ to break violently into small pieces or to make something do this ❷ to destroy something • *It shattered our hopes.* ❸ to upset someone greatly • *We were shattered by the news.*

**shattered** ADJECTIVE (*informal*)
completely exhausted

**shave** VERB **shaves, shaving, shaved**
❶ to scrape growing hair off the skin with a razor ❷ to cut or scrape a thin slice off something
➤ **shaver** NOUN

**shave** NOUN **shaves**
the act of shaving the face • *Dad was having a shave.*
➤ **close shave** (*informal*) a narrow escape

**shaven** ADJECTIVE
with all the hair shaved off • *a shaven head*

**shavings** PLURAL NOUN
thin strips shaved off a piece of wood or metal

**shawl** NOUN **shawls**
a large piece of material worn round the shoulders or head or wrapped round a baby

**she** PRONOUN
the female person or animal being talked about

**sheaf** NOUN sheaves
❶ a bundle of papers or other objects held together ❷ a bundle of corn stalks tied together after reaping

**shear** VERB shears, shearing, sheared, sheared or, in sense 1, shorn
❶ to cut the wool off a sheep ❷ to break because of a sideways or twisting force • One of the bolts sheared off.
➤ **shearer** NOUN

> SPELLING
>
> Take care not to confuse with **sheer**, which can mean steep and vertical or thin and transparent.

**shears** PLURAL NOUN
a cutting tool shaped like a very large pair of scissors and worked with both hands

**sheath** NOUN sheaths
❶ a cover for the blade of a knife or sword ❷ a close-fitting cover ❸ a condom

**sheathe** VERB sheathes, sheathing, sheathed
❶ to put something into a sheath • He sheathed his sword. ❷ to put a close covering on something

**shed** NOUN sheds
a simply-made building used for storing things, sheltering animals or as a workshop

**shed** VERB sheds, shedding, shed
❶ to let something fall or flow • The trees are shedding their leaves. • We all shed tears. ❷ to shed light is to give it out ❸ to get rid of people or things • The company has shed 200 workers.

**sheen** NOUN
a shine or gloss on a surface

**sheep** NOUN sheep
an animal that eats grass and has a thick fleecy coat, kept in flocks for its wool and its meat

> SPELLING
>
> The plural is the same as the singular: • a woolly sheep • We've got cows, sheep and pigs.

**sheepdog** NOUN sheepdogs
a dog trained to guard and herd sheep

**sheepish** ADJECTIVE
embarrassed or shamefaced because you have done something silly • He had a sheepish grin on his face.
➤ **sheepishly** ADVERB

**sheepshank** NOUN sheepshanks
a knot used to shorten a rope

**sheer** ADJECTIVE
❶ complete or thorough • sheer stupidity ❷ vertical, with almost no slope • a sheer drop ❸ sheer material is very thin and transparent

**sheer** VERB sheers, sheering, sheered
to swerve or move sharply away • The speedboat sheered off to one side.

> SPELLING
>
> **Sheer** is different from **shear**: • sheer luck • shear the sheep

**sheet** NOUN sheets
❶ a large piece of lightweight material used on a bed in pairs for a person to sleep between ❷ a whole flat piece of paper, glass or metal ❸ a wide area of water, ice or flame ❹ a rope or chain fastening a sail

**sheikh** (say shayk) NOUN sheikhs
the leader of an Arab tribe or village

**shelf** NOUN shelves
❶ a flat piece of wood, metal or glass fixed to a wall or in a piece of furniture so that things can be placed on it ❷ a flat level surface that sticks out from a cliff or under the sea

**shelf life** NOUN shelf lives
the length of time something can be kept in a shop before it becomes too old to sell • Newspapers have a shelf life of only a day.

**shell** NOUN shells
❶ the hard outer covering of an egg or nut or of an animal such as a snail, crab or tortoise ❷ the walls or framework of a building, ship or other large structure ❸ a metal case filled with explosive, fired from a large gun

**shell** VERB shells, shelling, shelled
❶ to take something out of its shell ❷ to fire explosive shells at something • They shelled the city all night.
➤ **shell out** (informal) to pay out money

**shellfish** NOUN shellfish
a sea animal that has a shell

**shelter** NOUN shelters
❶ a place or structure that protects people from rain, wind or danger ❷ protection from the weather or from danger • We took shelter from the rain.

**shelter** VERB shelters, sheltering, sheltered
❶ to find a shelter somewhere • They sheltered under the trees. ❷ to provide someone with shelter ❸ to protect or cover a

person or thing • *The hill shelters the house from the wind.*

**shelve** VERB shelves, shelving, shelved
❶ to put things on a shelf or shelves ❷ to postpone or reject a plan or piece of work ❸ to slope • *The bed of the river shelves steeply.*

**shelving** NOUN
a set of shelves

**shepherd** NOUN shepherds
a person whose job is to look after sheep

**shepherd** VERB shepherds, shepherding, shepherded
to guide or direct people

**SPELLING**

> There is a silent **h** after the **p** in **shepherd**.

**shepherdess** NOUN shepherdesses
(*now usually poetical*) a woman whose job is to look after sheep

**shepherd's pie** NOUN
a dish of minced beef or lamb under a layer of mashed potato

**sherbet** NOUN
a fizzy sweet powder or drink
**WORD ORIGIN** from Arabic *sharbat* = a drink

**sheriff** NOUN sheriffs
the chief law officer of a county, whose duties vary in different countries

**sherry** NOUN sherries
a kind of strong wine **WORD ORIGIN** named after Jerez de la Frontera, a town in Spain, where it was first made

**Shetland pony** NOUN Shetland ponies
a kind of small, strong, shaggy pony, originally from the Shetland Isles

**shield** NOUN shields
❶ a large piece of metal or wood carried to protect the body in fighting ❷ a model of a triangular shield used as a trophy ❸ a protection from harm

**shield** VERB shields, shielding, shielded
to protect a person or thing from harm or from being discovered • *He shielded his eyes from the sun.*

**shift** VERB shifts, shifting, shifted
❶ to move, or move something, from one position or place to another • *Could you help me shift some furniture?* ❷ an opinion or situation shifts when it changes slightly
➤ **shift for yourself** to manage without help from other people

**shift** NOUN shifts
❶ a change of position or condition ❷ a group of workers who start work as another group finishes; the time when they work • *She's on the night shift this month.* ❸ a straight dress with no waist

**shifty** ADJECTIVE
looking dishonest or as if you are hiding something
➤ **shiftily** ADVERB

**Shiite** (say **shee**-eyt) NOUN Shiites
a member of one of the two main branches of Islam, based on the teachings of Muhammad and regarding his son-in-law Ali as his successor. Compare with **Sunni**.

**shilling** NOUN shillings
a former British coin, equal to 5p

**shilly-shally** VERB shilly-shallies, shilly-shallying, shilly-shallied
to be unable to make up your mind
**WORD ORIGIN** from *shall I? shall I?*

**shimmer** VERB shimmers, shimmering, shimmered
to shine with a quivering light • *The sea shimmered in the moonlight.*

**shimmer** NOUN
a quivering light

**shin** NOUN shins
the front of your leg between your knee and your ankle

**shin** VERB shins, shinning, shinned
to climb up or down something vertical by using the arms and legs • *He shinned down the drainpipe and ran off.*

**shindig** NOUN shindigs (*informal*)
a noisy party

**shine** VERB shines, shining, shone or, in sense 3, shined
❶ to give out or reflect light; to be bright ❷ to aim a light somewhere • *Shine your torch on it.* ❸ to polish shoes or a surface • *Have you shined your shoes?* ❹ to be very good at something • *He doesn't shine in maths.*

**shine** NOUN
❶ brightness on a surface ❷ a polish • *Give your shoes a good shine.*

**shingle** NOUN
pebbles on a beach

**shingles** NOUN
a disease caused by the chicken pox virus, producing a painful rash

**Shinto** NOUN
a Japanese religion which includes worship of ancestors and nature

**shiny** ADJECTIVE shinier, shiniest
shining or glossy • *a shiny new car* • *shiny black hair*

**ship** NOUN ships
a large boat, especially one that goes to sea

**ship** VERB ships, shipping, shipped
to transport goods, especially by ship

**shipment** NOUN shipments
❶ the process of shipping goods ❷ the amount shipped

**shipping** NOUN
❶ all the ships of a country ❷ the business of transporting goods by ship

**shipshape** ADJECTIVE
in good order; tidy

**shipwreck** NOUN shipwrecks
❶ the wrecking of a ship by storm or accident ❷ the remains of a wrecked ship

**shipwrecked** ADJECTIVE
someone is shipwrecked when they are left somewhere after their ship has been wrecked at sea • *a shipwrecked sailor*

**shipyard** NOUN shipyards
a place where ships are built or repaired

**shire** NOUN shires
a county
➤ **the Shires** the country areas of (especially central) England, away from the cities

**shire horse** NOUN shire horses
a kind of large, strong horse used for ploughing or pulling carts

**shirk** VERB shirks, shirking, shirked
to avoid a task or duty selfishly or unfairly
➤ **shirker** NOUN

**shirt** NOUN shirts
a piece of clothing you wear on the top half of the body, made of light material and with a collar and sleeves
➤ **in your shirtsleeves** not wearing a jacket over your shirt

**shirty** ADJECTIVE (British) (informal)
annoyed or bad-tempered

**shiver** VERB shivers, shivering, shivered
to tremble with cold or fear

**shiver** NOUN shivers
the act of shivering • *I felt a shiver down my spine.*

**shivery** ADJECTIVE
shaking with cold, illness or fear

**shoal** NOUN shoals
❶ a large number of fish swimming together ❷ an underwater sandbank

**shock** NOUN shocks
❶ a sudden unpleasant surprise ❷ a serious medical condition of great weakness caused by damage to the body ❸ the effect of a violent shake or knock • *the shock of the earthquake* ❹ an effect caused by electric current passing through the body ❺ a bushy mass of hair

**shock** VERB shocks, shocking, shocked
❶ to give someone a shock; to surprise or upset a person greatly ❷ to make someone feel disgusted or offended

**shocking** ADJECTIVE
❶ horrifying or disgusting • *shocking behaviour* ❷ (informal) very bad • *shocking weather*

**shock wave** NOUN shock waves
a sharp change in pressure in the air around an explosion or an object moving very quickly

**shod**
past tense of **shoe**

**shoddy** ADJECTIVE shoddier, shoddiest
of poor quality; badly made or done • *This is shoddy work.*
➤ **shoddily** ADVERB

**shoe** NOUN shoes
❶ a strong covering for the foot ❷ a horseshoe ❸ something shaped or used like a shoe
➤ **be in someone's shoes** to be in their situation

**shoe** VERB shoes, shoeing, shod
to fit a horse with a horseshoe

**shoehorn** NOUN shoehorns
a curved piece of stiff material for easing your heel into the back of a shoe

**shoelace** NOUN shoelaces
a cord for lacing up and fastening a shoe

**shoestring** NOUN
➤ **on a shoestring** using only a small amount of money • *The website tells you how you can travel the world on a shoestring.*

**shoo** EXCLAMATION
a word used to frighten animals away

**shoo** VERB shoo, shooing, shooed
to frighten or drive away an animal or person

**shoot** VERB shoots, shooting, shot
❶ to fire a gun or missile ❷ to hurt or kill a person or animal by shooting ❸ to move at great speed • *The car shot past us.* ❹ to kick or hit a ball at a goal ❺ to film or photograph something • *The film was shot in Africa.* ❻ to slide the bolt of a door into or out of its fastening ❼ to shoot someone a glance is to look at them sharply

**shoot** NOUN shoots
❶ a young branch or new growth of a plant ❷ an expedition for shooting animals

> SPELLING
>
> Shoot is different from chute, which means a channel for sliding down.

**shooting star** NOUN shooting stars
a meteor

**shop** NOUN shops
❶ a building or room where goods or services are on sale to the public ❷ a workshop
➤ **talk shop** to talk about your own work or job in a way that other people find boring

**shop** VERB shops, shopping, shopped
❶ to visit shops in order to buy things ❷ to buy things • *My sister is always shopping online.*
➤ **shopper** NOUN
➤ **shop around** to look around for the best bargain

**shop floor** NOUN (British)
❶ the workers in a factory, not the managers ❷ the place where they work

**shopkeeper** NOUN shopkeepers
a person who owns or manages a shop

**shoplifter** NOUN shoplifters
a person who steals goods from a shop after entering as a customer
➤ **shoplifting** NOUN

**shopping** NOUN
❶ buying goods in shops • *I like shopping.* ❷ the goods bought • *I'll put the shopping in the car.*

**shop-soiled** ADJECTIVE
(British) dirty, faded or slightly damaged through being displayed in a shop

**shop steward** NOUN shop stewards
a trade-union official who represents a group of fellow workers

**shop window** NOUN shop windows
a window in a shop where goods are displayed

**shore** NOUN shores
the land along the edge of a sea or of a lake

**shore** VERB shores, shoring, shored
to prop something up with a piece of wood or other support

**shorn**
past participle of **shear**

**shorn** ADJECTIVE
with hair cut very short • *his shorn head*
➤ **be shorn of something** to have something taken away from you • *Shorn of his power, the king went into exile.*

**short** ADJECTIVE
❶ not long; not lasting long • *I went for a short walk.* ❷ not tall • *He is a short man.* ❸ not enough; not having enough of something • *Water is short.* • *We are short of water.* ❹ speaking to someone in a bad-tempered and impatient way • *She was rather short with me.* ❺ short pastry is rich and crumbly because it contains a lot of fat
➤ **shortness** NOUN
➤ **for short** as an abbreviation • *Joanna is called Jo for short.*
➤ **in short** in a few words
➤ **short for** an abbreviation of • *Jo is short for Joanna.*
➤ **short of** without going to the length of • *I'll do anything to help, short of robbing a bank.*

**short** ADVERB
suddenly • *She stopped short.*

**shortage** NOUN shortages
there is a shortage of something when there is not enough of it • *a water shortage*

**shortbread** NOUN
a rich sweet biscuit, made with butter

**shortcake** NOUN
❶ shortbread ❷ a light cake usually served with fruit

**short circuit** NOUN short circuits
a fault in an electrical circuit in which current flows along a shorter route than the normal one

**short-circuit** VERB short-circuits, short-circuiting, short-circuited
to have or cause a short circuit

**shortcoming** NOUN shortcomings
a fault or failure to reach a good standard

**short cut** NOUN short cuts
a route or method that is quicker than the usual one • *We took a short cut across the fields.*

**shorten** VERB shortens, shortening, shortened
to make something shorter or to become
shorter • *Most people shorten Janet's name
to Jan.*

**shortfall** NOUN shortfalls
a shortage; an amount lower than needed or
expected

**shorthand** NOUN
a set of special signs for writing words down
as quickly as people say them

**short-handed** ADJECTIVE
not having enough workers or helpers

**shortlist** NOUN shortlists
a list of the most suitable people or things,
from which a final choice will be made

**shortlist** VERB shortlists, shortlisting,
shortlisted
to put someone on a shortlist

**shortly** ADVERB
❶ in a short time; soon • *They will arrive
shortly.* ❷ in an impatient and angry way
• *'None of your business,' he said shortly.*

**shorts** PLURAL NOUN
trousers with legs that do not reach to the
knee

**short-sighted** ADJECTIVE (British)
❶ unable to see things clearly when they are
further away ❷ not thinking enough about
what may happen in the future

**short-staffed** ADJECTIVE
not having enough workers or staff

**short-tempered** ADJECTIVE
easily becoming angry

**short-term** ADJECTIVE
to do with or happening over a short period
of time

**short wave** NOUN
a radio wave of a wavelength between 10 and
100 metres and a frequency of about 3 to 30
megahertz

**shot** NOUN shots
❶ the firing of a gun or missile or the sound
this makes ❷ lead pellets for firing from small
guns ❸ a person judged by skill in shooting
• *He's a good shot.* ❹ a hit or stroke in a
game with a ball, such as football, tennis,
golf or snooker • *a shot at goal • Good shot!*
❺ a heavy metal ball thrown as a sport ❻ a
photograph or a filmed scene ❼ an attempt
to do something • *Have a shot at this puzzle.*
❽ an injection of a drug or vaccine

**shot** ADJECTIVE
shot fabric is woven so that different colours
show at different angles • *shot silk*

**shot** VERB
past tense of **shoot**

**shotgun** NOUN shotguns
a gun for firing small lead pellets at close
range

**shot put** NOUN
an athletic contest in which competitors
throw a heavy metal ball
➤ **shot putter** NOUN

**should** AUXILIARY VERB
❶ used to say what someone ought to do
• *You should have told me.* ❷ used to say
what someone expects • *They should be here
by ten o'clock.* ❸ used to say what might
happen • *If you should happen to see him, tell
him to come.* ❹ used with *I* and *we* to make a
polite statement (*I should like to come.*) or in
a conditional clause (*If they had supported us
we should have won.*)

**USAGE**

In sense 4, although **should** is strictly
correct, many people nowadays use
**would** and this is not regarded as wrong.

**shoulder** NOUN shoulders
the part of your body between your neck and
your arm

**shoulder** VERB shoulders, shouldering,
shouldered
❶ to take something on your shoulder or
shoulders ❷ to push something with your
shoulder ❸ to accept responsibility or blame
for something

**shoulder blade** NOUN shoulder blades
either of the two large flat bones at the top
of your back

**shouldn't** (mainly spoken)
should not

**shout** NOUN shouts
a loud cry or call

**shout** VERB shouts, shouting, shouted
to give a shout; to speak or call very loudly

**shove** VERB shoves, shoving, shoved
to push something roughly
➤ **shove off** (informal) to go away

**shove** NOUN shoves
a rough push

a b c d e f g h i j k l m n o p q r s t u v w x y z

**shovel** NOUN shovels
a tool like a spade with the sides turned up, used for lifting coal, earth, snow, etc.

**shovel** VERB shovels, shovelling, shovelled
❶ to move or clear things with a shovel ❷ to scoop or push something roughly • *He was shovelling food into his mouth.*

**show** VERB shows, showing, showed, shown
❶ to allow or cause something to be seen • *Show me your new bike.* ❷ to make a person understand something; to explain or demonstrate something • *Can you show me how to do it?* ❸ to guide or lead someone to a place • *I'll show you to your seat.* ❹ to treat someone in a certain way • *She showed them great kindness.* ❺ to be visible • *That scratch won't show.* ❻ to prove your ability to someone • *We'll show them!*
➤ **show off** to try to impress people
➤ **show something off** to display something proudly
➤ **show up** ❶ to be clearly visible • *Nothing showed up on the X-ray.* ❷ (*informal*) to arrive

**show** NOUN shows
❶ an entertainment • *a TV game show* ❷ a display or exhibition • *a flower show* ❸ (*informal*) something that happens or is done • *He runs the whole show.*

**show business** NOUN
the entertainment industry; the theatre, films, radio and television

**showcase** NOUN showcases
❶ a glass case for displaying something in a shop, museum or gallery ❷ an event that is designed to present someone's good qualities or abilities attractively • *The programme is a showcase for new acts.*

**showdown** NOUN showdowns
a final test or confrontation

**shower** NOUN showers
❶ a brief fall of rain or snow ❷ a lot of small things coming or falling like rain • *a shower of stones* ❸ a device or cabinet for spraying water to wash a person's body; a wash in this

**shower** VERB showers, showering, showered
❶ to fall or drop things like rain • *Ash from the volcano showered down on the town.* ❷ to give someone a lot of things • *He showered her with presents.* ❸ to wash under a shower

**showery** ADJECTIVE
raining often in showers

**showjumping** NOUN
a competition in which riders make their horses jump over fences and other obstacles, with penalty points for errors
➤ **showjumper** NOUN

**showman** NOUN showmen
❶ a person who presents entertainments ❷ someone who is good at entertaining and getting a lot of attention
➤ **showmanship** NOUN

**show-off** NOUN show-offs (*informal*)
a person who tries to impress people boastfully

**showpiece** NOUN showpieces
a fine example of something for people to see and admire

**showroom** NOUN showrooms
a large room where goods are displayed for people to look at

**showy** ADJECTIVE showier, showiest
likely to attract attention; brightly or highly decorated • *showy flowers*
➤ **showily** ADVERB

**shrapnel** NOUN
pieces of metal scattered from an exploding shell **WORD ORIGIN** named after H. *Shrapnel*, a British officer who invented it in about 1806

**shred** NOUN shreds
❶ a tiny piece torn or cut off something • *His cloak had been ripped to shreds.* ❷ a very small amount of something • *There is not a shred of evidence to support this claim.*

**shred** VERB shreds, shredding, shredded
to tear or cut something into shreds
➤ **shredder** NOUN

**shrew** NOUN shrews
❶ a small mouse-like animal ❷ (*old use*) a bad-tempered woman who is constantly scolding people
➤ **shrewish** ADJECTIVE

**shrewd** ADJECTIVE
clever and showing good judgement • *a shrewd decision*
➤ **shrewdly** ADVERB
➤ **shrewdness** NOUN
**WORD ORIGIN** from old sense of **shrew** = spiteful or cunning person

**shriek** NOUN shrieks
a shrill cry or scream

**shriek** VERB shrieks, shrieking, shrieked
to give a shriek

**shrift** NOUN
➤ **give someone short shrift** to give someone little attention or sympathy

**shrill** ADJECTIVE
sounding very high and piercing • a shrill voice
➤ **shrilly** ADVERB
➤ **shrillness** NOUN

**shrimp** NOUN shrimps
a small shellfish, pink when boiled

**shrine** NOUN shrines
an altar, chapel or other sacred place

**shrink** VERB shrinks, shrinking, shrank, shrunk
❶ to become smaller, especially by washing it ❷ to move back or away because you are frightened or shocked • He shrank back into a corner of the room. ❸ to avoid doing something unpleasant or difficult • We will not shrink from telling the truth.
➤ **shrinkage** NOUN

**shrivel** VERB shrivels, shrivelling, shrivelled
to become dry and wrinkled or to make something like this

**shroud** NOUN shrouds
❶ a cloth in which a dead body is wrapped ❷ each of a set of ropes supporting a ship's mast

**shroud** VERB shrouds, shrouding, shrouded
❶ to wrap a dead body in a shroud ❷ to cover or conceal something • The town was shrouded in mist.

**Shrove Tuesday** NOUN
the day before Lent begins, when people eat pancakes (WORD ORIGIN) from the past tense of the old word *shrive* = to hear a person's confession (because it was the custom to go to confession on this day)

**shrub** NOUN shrubs
a woody plant smaller than a tree; a bush
➤ **shrubby** ADJECTIVE

**shrubbery** NOUN shrubberies
an area planted with shrubs

**shrug** VERB shrugs, shrugging, shrugged
to raise your shoulders slightly as a sign that you do not care or do not know about something
➤ **shrug something off** to treat something as unimportant

**shrug** NOUN shrugs
a gesture of shrugging the shoulders

**shrunken** ADJECTIVE
having shrunk; small and shrivelled • a shrunken old woman

**shudder** VERB shudders, shuddering, shuddered
❶ to shiver violently with horror, fear or cold ❷ to make a shaking movement • The engine shuddered and then stopped.

**shudder** NOUN shudders
a strong shivering or shaking movement

**shuffle** VERB shuffles, shuffling, shuffled
❶ to walk without lifting your feet from the ground ❷ to move your body or feet around because you are uncomfortable or nervous • The audience began to shuffle in their seats. ❸ to mix up playing cards by sliding them over each other several times ❹ to move things around • She shuffled the papers on her desk.

**shuffle** NOUN
the act of shuffling • Give the cards a quick shuffle.

**shun** VERB shuns, shunning, shunned
to deliberately avoid or keep away from someone or something • She was shunned by her family when she married him.

**shunt** VERB shunts, shunting, shunted
❶ to move a train or wagons onto another track ❷ to divert something or someone to a less important place or position

**shut** VERB shuts, shutting, shut
❶ to move a door, window, lid or cover so that it blocks an opening ❷ to become closed • The door shut suddenly ❸ to bring or fold parts together • She shut the book as he came in.
➤ **shut down** to stop business
➤ **shut something down** to stop a machine working
➤ **shut up** (informal) to stop talking or making a noise
➤ **shut something up** to shut something securely

**shut** ADJECTIVE
closed • Keep your eyes shut.

**shutter** NOUN shutters
❶ a panel or screen that can be closed over a window ❷ the device in a camera that opens and closes to let light fall on the film
➤ **shuttered** ADJECTIVE

**shuttle** NOUN shuttles
❶ a train, bus or aircraft that makes frequent short journeys between two points ❷ a space

637

a b c d e f g h i j k l m n o p q r s t u v w x y z

shuttle ❸ the part of a loom that carries the thread from side to side

**shuttle** VERB shuttles, shuttling, shuttled
to move or travel continuously between two places

**shuttlecock** NOUN shuttlecocks
a small rounded piece of cork or plastic with a crown of feathers, struck to and fro by players in badminton

**shy** ADJECTIVE shyer, shyest
afraid to meet or talk to other people; timid
➤ **shyly** ADVERB
➤ **shyness** NOUN

**shy** VERB shies, shying, shied
❶ to jump or move suddenly in alarm ❷ to throw a stone or other object
➤ **shy away from something** to avoid doing something because you are nervous or afraid

**shy** NOUN shies
a throw

**SI** NOUN
an internationally recognized system of metric units of measurement, including the metre and kilogram **WORD ORIGIN** short for French *Système International d'Unités* = International System of Units

**Siamese cat** NOUN Siamese cats
a cat with short pale fur with darker face, ears, tail and feet

**sibilant** ADJECTIVE
having a hissing sound • *a sibilant whisper*

**sibilant** NOUN sibilants
a speech sound that sounds like hissing, e.g. *s, sh*

**sibling** NOUN siblings
a brother or sister

**sibyl** NOUN sibyls
a prophetess in ancient Greece or Rome

**sick** ADJECTIVE
❶ ill; physically or mentally unwell
❷ vomiting or likely to vomit • *I feel sick.*
❸ disgusted, angry or anxious • *People like him make me sick.* • *She was sick with worry.* ❹ making fun of death, disability or misfortune in an unpleasant way
➤ **be sick of something** to be tired of something or fed up with it

**sicken** VERB sickens, sickening, sickened
❶ to make someone feel upset or disgusted
• *We were all sickened by this vandalism.*
❷ to start feeling ill

**sickening** ADJECTIVE
shocking or disgusting

**sickle** NOUN sickles
a tool with a narrow curved blade, used for cutting crops or grass

**sickle-cell anaemia** NOUN
a severe form of anaemia which is passed on in the genes and which causes pain in the joints, fever, jaundice and sometimes death
**WORD ORIGIN** so called because the red blood cells become sickle-shaped

**sickly** ADJECTIVE
❶ often ill; unhealthy • *a sickly child*
❷ making people feel sick • *a sickly smell*
❸ weak or sentimental • *a sickly smile*

**sickness** NOUN sicknesses
❶ illness ❷ a disease ❸ vomiting

**side** NOUN sides
❶ a surface, especially one joining the top and bottom of something ❷ a line that forms part of the boundary of a triangle, square, etc. ❸ either of the two halves into which something can be divided by a line down its centre ❹ one of the surfaces of something except the top, bottom, front or back • *I went round the side of the building.*
❺ the part near the edge and away from the centre ❻ the right or left part of your body, especially from under your arm to the top of your leg • *I've got a pain down my right side.*
❼ the place or region next to a person or thing • *He stood at my side.* ❽ one aspect or view of something • *There is another side to the problem.* ❾ one of two groups or teams who oppose each other • *They are on our side.*
➤ **on the side** as a sideline
➤ **side by side** next to each other
➤ **take sides** to support one person or group in a dispute or disagreement and not the other

**side** ADJECTIVE
at or on a side • *the side door*

**side** VERB sides, siding, sided
➤ **side with someone** to take a person's side in an argument

**sideboard** NOUN sideboards
a long piece of furniture with drawers and cupboards and a flat top

**sideburns** PLURAL NOUN
the strips of hair growing on each side of a man's face in front of his ears

**sidecar** *NOUN* sidecars
a small compartment for a passenger, fixed to the side of a motorcycle

**side effect** *NOUN* side effects
an effect, especially an unpleasant one, that a medicine has on you as well as the effect intended

**sideline** *NOUN* sidelines
❶ something that you do in addition to your main work or activity ❷ each of the lines on the two long sides of a sports pitch

**sidelong** *ADJECTIVE*
towards one side; sideways • *a sidelong glance*

**sideshow** *NOUN* sideshows
a small entertainment forming part of a large one, e.g. at a fair

**sidetrack** *VERB* sidetracks, sidetracking, sidetracked
to take someone's attention away from the main subject or problem

**sidewalk** *NOUN* sidewalks
(*North American*) a pavement

**sideways** *ADVERB & ADJECTIVE*
❶ to or from one side • *Crabs walk sideways.*
❷ with one side facing forwards • *We sat sideways in the bus.*

**siding** *NOUN* sidings
a short railway line by the side of a main line

**sidle** *VERB* sidles, sidling, sidled
to walk in a shy or nervous manner • *She sidled up to me and whispered in my ear.*

**siege** *NOUN* sieges
the surrounding of a place in order to capture it or force someone to surrender
➤ **lay siege to somewhere** to begin a siege of a place

**sienna** *NOUN*
a kind of clay used in making brownish paints

**sierra** *NOUN* sierras
a range of mountains with sharp peaks, in Spain or parts of America
(**WORD ORIGIN**) Spanish, from Latin *serra* = a saw (because the peaks look like the teeth of a saw)

**siesta** (say see-**est**-a) *NOUN* siestas
an afternoon rest, especially in a hot country
(**WORD ORIGIN**) from Latin *sexta hora* = sixth hour, midday

**sieve** (say siv) *NOUN* sieves
a device made of mesh or perforated metal

or plastic, used to separate the smaller or soft parts of something from the larger or hard parts

**sieve** *VERB* sieves, sieving, sieved
to put something through a sieve

**sift** *VERB* sifts, sifting, sifted
❶ to pass a fine or powdery substance through a sieve in order to remove any lumps ❷ to examine and analyse facts or evidence carefully

**sigh** *NOUN* sighs
a sound made by breathing out heavily when you are sad, tired or relieved

**sigh** *VERB* sighs, sighing, sighed
to make a sigh • *He sighed with disappointment at the news.*

**sight** *NOUN* sights
❶ the ability to see ❷ a view or glimpse • *I caught sight of her in the crowd.* ❸ a thing that can be seen or is worth seeing • *Our garden is a lovely sight.* • *Visit the sights of Paris.* ❹ something silly or ridiculous to look at • *You do look a sight in those clothes!* ❺ a device looked through to help aim a gun or telescope
➤ **at sight** or **on sight** as soon as a person or thing has been seen
➤ **in sight** ❶ visible ❷ clearly near; about to happen • *Victory was in sight.*
➤ **out of sight** no longer able to be seen

**sight** *VERB* sights, sighting, sighted
❶ to see or observe something ❷ to aim a gun or telescope

(**SPELLING**)
Sight is different from site, which means the place where something is.

**sighted** *ADJECTIVE*
able to see; not blind

**sightless** *ADJECTIVE*
blind

**sight-reading** *NOUN*
playing or singing music at sight, without preparation

**sightseeing** *NOUN*
visiting interesting places in a town as a tourist
➤ **sightseer** *NOUN*

**sign** *NOUN* signs
❶ something that shows that a thing exists • *There are signs of decay.* ❷ a mark or symbol that stands for something • *a minus sign* ❸ a board or notice that tells or

shows people something • *a road sign* ❹ an action or movement giving information or a command • *She made a sign to them to be quiet.* ❺ any of the twelve divisions of the zodiac, represented by a symbol

**sign** *VERB* signs, signing, signed
❶ to make a sign or signal • *He signed to them to follow him.* ❷ to write your signature on something; to write your signature on something; to accept a contract or agreement by doing this ❸ to give someone a contract for a job, especially in a professional sport • *They have signed three new players.* ❹ to use signing
➤ **sign on** ❶ to accept a job by signing a contract ❷ to sign a form to say that you are unemployed and want to claim benefit

**SPELLING**
There is a silent g before the n in sign.

**signal** *NOUN* signals
❶ a device, gesture or sound that gives information or a command ❷ a message made up of such things ❸ a sequence of electrical impulses or radio waves

**signal** *VERB* signals, signalling, signalled
to give someone a signal

**signal** *ADJECTIVE*
remarkable or striking • *It was a signal victory for him.*
➤ **signally** *ADVERB*

**signal box** *NOUN* signal boxes
(*British*) a building from which railway signals and points are controlled

**signalman** *NOUN* signalmen
a person who controls railway signals

**signature** *NOUN* signatures
❶ the form in which a person writes their own name ❷ (*in music*) a set of sharps and flats after the clef in a score, showing the key the music is written in (the *key signature*) or the sign, often a fraction such as ¾ (the *time signature*), showing the number of beats in the bar and their rhythm

**signature tune** *NOUN* signature tunes
(*British*) a special tune always used to announce a particular programme or performer on television or radio

**signet ring** *NOUN* signet rings
a ring with a person's initials or a design engraved on it

**significance** *NOUN*
the meaning or importance of something • *I did not realize the significance of this discovery at first.*

**significant** *ADJECTIVE*
❶ having a meaning; full of meaning ❷ important • *a significant event*
➤ **significantly** *ADVERB*

**signification** *NOUN*
the meaning of something

**signify** *VERB* signifies, signifying, signified
❶ to be a sign or symbol of something; to mean something ❷ to indicate something • *She signified her approval with a nod.* ❸ to be important; to matter

**signing, sign language** *NOUN*
a way of communicating by using movements of your hands instead of sounds, used mainly by deaf people

**signpost** *NOUN* signposts
a sign at a road junction showing the names and distances of the places that each road leads to

**Sikh** (say seek) *NOUN* Sikhs
a follower of Sikhism

**Sikhism** (say seek-izm) *NOUN*
a religion founded in Punjab in the 15th century by Guru Nanak and based on belief in one God

**silage** *NOUN*
fodder made from green crops stored in a silo

**silence** *NOUN* silences
❶ absence of sound ❷ not speaking
➤ **in silence** without speaking or making a sound • *She watched him in silence for a long time.*

**silence** *VERB* silences, silencing, silenced
to make a person or thing silent • *He silenced her with a glare.*

**silencer** *NOUN* silencers
a device for reducing the sound made by a gun or a vehicle's exhaust system

**silent** *ADJECTIVE*
❶ without any sound ❷ not speaking
➤ **silently** *ADVERB*

**silhouette** (say sil-oo-et) *NOUN* silhouettes
❶ a dark shadow seen against a light background ❷ a portrait of a person in profile, showing the shape and outline only in solid black

**silhouette** *VERB* silhouettes, silhouetting, silhouetted
to show an outline as a silhouette • *A figure stood in the doorway, silhouetted against the light.* **WORD ORIGIN** named after a French

author, É. de *Silhouette*, who made paper cut-outs of people's profiles from their shadows

**silica** *NOUN*
a hard white mineral that is a compound of silicon, used to make glass

**silicon** *NOUN*
a substance found in many rocks, used in making microchips

**silicone** *NOUN*
a compound of silicon used in paints, varnish and lubricants

**silk** *NOUN* silks
❶ a fine soft thread or cloth made from the fibre produced by silkworms for making their cocoons ❷ a length of silk thread used for embroidery

**silken** *ADJECTIVE*
made of silk • *a silken gown*

**silkworm** *NOUN* silkworms
the caterpillar of a kind of moth, which feeds on mulberry leaves and spins itself a cocoon

**silky** *ADJECTIVE*
soft, smooth and shiny like silk • *silky hair*

**sill** *NOUN* sills
a strip of stone, wood or metal underneath a window or door

**silly** *ADJECTIVE* sillier, silliest
foolish or unwise
➤ **silliness** *NOUN*
**WORD ORIGIN** from Old English *saelig* = happy or fortunate, later = innocent or feeble

**silo** (say **sy**-loh) *NOUN* silos
❶ a pit or tower for storing green crops (see **silage**) or corn or cement ❷ an underground place for storing a missile ready for firing

**silt** *NOUN*
fine sand and mud that is laid down by a river or the sea

**silt** *VERB* silts, silting, silted
➤ **silt up** to become blocked with silt

**silver** *NOUN* silvers
❶ a shiny white precious metal ❷ the colour of silver ❸ coins or objects made of silver or silver-coloured metal ❹ a silver medal, usually given as second prize

**silver** *ADJECTIVE*
❶ made of silver ❷ coloured like silver

**silver** *VERB* silvers, silvering, silvered
to make something silvery or to become silvery • *Moonlight silvered the lake.*

**silver wedding** *NOUN* silver weddings
a couple's 25th wedding anniversary

**silvery** *ADJECTIVE*
shiny like silver or silver in colour • *silvery light* • *silvery hair*

**SIM card** *NOUN* SIM cards
a small piece of plastic inside a mobile phone that stores information about the person using the phone

**similar** *ADJECTIVE*
❶ nearly the same as another person or thing; of the same kind ❷ (*in mathematics*) having the same shape but not the same size
• *similar triangles*
➤ **similarly** *ADVERB*

**similarity** *NOUN* similarities
❶ the quality of being alike • *She bears a striking similarity to her mother.* ❷ a feature that makes one thing like another • *There are many similarities between the two planets.*

**simile** (say **sim**-il-ee) *NOUN* similes
a way of describing something by comparing it with something else, e.g. *He is as strong as a horse.* and *We ran like the wind.*

**simmer** *VERB* simmers, simmering, simmered
to boil very gently over a low heat
➤ **simmer down** to calm down after being angry or excited

**simper** *VERB* simpers, simpering, simpered
to smile in a silly and annoying way
➤ **simper** *NOUN*

**simple** *ADJECTIVE* simpler, simplest
❶ easy to answer or solve • *a simple question* ❷ not complicated or elaborate • *It was a simple plan, but it worked.* ❸ plain, not showy • *a simple black dress* ❹ without much sense or intelligence

**simple-minded** *ADJECTIVE*
naive or foolish

**simpleton** *NOUN* simpletons (*old use*)
a foolish person

**simplicity** *NOUN*
the quality of being simple • *The beauty of this plan is its simplicity.*

**simplify** *VERB* simplifies, simplifying, simplified
to make a thing simple or easy to understand
➤ **simplification** *NOUN*

**simply** *ADVERB*
❶ in a simple way • *I'll try to explain it simply.* ❷ without doubt; completely • *The*

view is *simply wonderful.* ❸ only or merely
• *It's simply a question of time.*

**simulate** VERB simulates, simulating, simulated
❶ to reproduce the appearance or conditions of something • *This machine simulates a space flight.* ❷ to pretend to have a certain feeling • *They simulated fear.*
➤ **simulation** NOUN

**simulator** NOUN simulators
a machine or device for simulating actual conditions or events, often used for training
• *a flight simulator*

**simultaneous** (say sim-ul-**tay**-nee-us) ADJECTIVE
happening at the same time • *The two explosions were simultaneous.*
➤ **simultaneously** ADVERB

**sin** NOUN sins
❶ the breaking of a religious or moral law ❷ a very bad action

**sin** VERB sins, sinning, sinned
to commit a sin
➤ **sinner** NOUN

**since** CONJUNCTION
❶ from the time when • *Where have you been since I last saw you?* ❷ because • *Since you refuse to come, I'll have to go on my own.*

**since** PREPOSITION
from a certain time • *She has been here since Christmas.*

**since** ADVERB
between then and now • *He ran away and hasn't been seen since.*

**sincere** ADJECTIVE
you are being sincere when you mean what you say and express your true feelings
• *Please accept our sincere thanks.*
➤ **sincerely** ADVERB
➤ **sincerity** NOUN
➤ **Yours sincerely** see yours

**sine** NOUN sines
in a right-angled triangle, the ratio of the length of a side opposite one of the acute angles to the length of the hypotenuse. Compare with **cosine**.

**sinecure** (say **sy**-nik-yoor) NOUN sinecures
a paid job that requires no work

**sinew** NOUN sinews
strong tissue that connects a muscle to a bone

**sinewy** ADJECTIVE
slim, muscular and strong

**sinful** ADJECTIVE
❶ guilty of sin ❷ bad or wicked
➤ **sinfully** ADVERB
➤ **sinfulness** NOUN

**sing** VERB sings, singing, sang, sung
❶ to make musical sounds with your voice ❷ to perform a song

> SPELLING
>
> The past tense of **sing** is **sang** and the past participle is **sung**.

**singe** (say sinj) VERB singes, singeing, singed
to burn something slightly

**singer** NOUN singers
a person who sings or whose job is singing • *a pop singer*

**single** ADJECTIVE
❶ one only; not double or multiple ❷ suitable for one person • *single beds* ❸ distinct or separate • *I answered every single question correctly.* ❹ not married ❺ for the journey to a place but not back again • *a single ticket*

**single** NOUN singles
❶ a single person or thing ❷ a single ticket ❸ a record with one short piece of music on it
➤ **singles** a game of tennis between two players

**single** VERB singles, singling, singled
➤ **single someone out** to pick someone out or distinguish them from other people

**single file** NOUN
➤ **in single file** in a line, one behind the other

**single-handed** ADJECTIVE
by your own efforts; without any help

**single-minded** ADJECTIVE
with your mind set on one purpose only

**single parent** NOUN single parents
a person bringing up a child or children without a partner

**singlet** NOUN singlets
a man's vest or similar piece of clothing worn under or instead of a shirt

**singly** ADVERB
in ones; one by one • *These stamps are available singly or in books of twelve.*

**singsong** ADJECTIVE
having a monotonous tone or rhythm • *a singsong voice*

**singsong** NOUN singsongs
❶ informal singing by a gathering of people • *Come on, let's have a singsong.* ❷ a singsong tone

**singular** NOUN singulars
the form of a noun or verb used when it stands for only one person or thing • *The singular is 'man' and the plural is 'men'.* Compare with **plural**.

**singular** ADJECTIVE
❶ in the singular; meaning only one • *'Mouse' is a singular noun.* ❷ uncommon or extraordinary • *a woman of singular courage*
➤ **singularity** NOUN

**singularly** ADVERB
remarkably or unusually • *a singularly handsome man*

**sinister** ADJECTIVE
❶ looking or seeming evil or harmful
❷ wicked; intending to do harm • *a sinister motive* **WORD ORIGIN** from Latin, = on the left (which was thought to be unlucky)

**sink** VERB sinks, sinking, sank, sunk
❶ to fall under the surface of water or to the bottom of the sea or to make something do this • *The ship sank in a storm.* • *They fired on the ship and sank it.* ❷ to go or fall slowly downwards • *He sank to his knees.* ❸ to push something sharp deeply into something • *The dog sank its teeth into my leg.* ❹ to dig or drill a hole or well ❺ to invest money in something
➤ **sink in** to become understood

**sink** NOUN sinks
a fixed basin with a tap or taps to supply water, especially one in a kitchen

**sinuous** ADJECTIVE
with many bends or curves • *the sinuous movement of a snake*

**sinus** (say sy-nus) NOUN sinuses
a hollow part in the bones of the skull, connected with the nose • *My sinuses are blocked.*

**sip** VERB sips, sipping, sipped
to drink something in small mouthfuls

**sip** NOUN sips
a small amount of a drink that you take into your mouth

**siphon** NOUN siphons
❶ a pipe or tube in the form of an upside-down U, arranged so that liquid is forced up it and down to a lower level ❷ a bottle containing soda water which is released through a tube

**siphon** VERB siphons, siphoning, siphoned
to draw out liquid through a siphon

**sir** NOUN
❶ a word used when speaking or writing politely to a man • *Can I help you, sir?* ❷ the title given to a knight or baronet • *Sir Francis Drake*

**sire** NOUN sires
a word formerly used when speaking to a king

**sire** VERB sires, siring, sired
to be the male parent of a horse or dog • *This stallion has sired several winners.*

**siren** NOUN sirens
❶ a device that makes a long loud sound as a signal ❷ a dangerously attractive woman
**WORD ORIGIN** named after the *Sirens* in Greek legend, women who by their sweet singing lured seafarers to shipwreck on the rocks

**sirloin** NOUN
beef from the upper part of the loin

**sirocco** NOUN siroccos
a hot dry wind that reaches Italy from Africa

**sisal** (say sy-sal) NOUN
fibre from a tropical plant, used for making ropes

**sissy** NOUN sissies
a timid or cowardly person

**sister** NOUN sisters
❶ a daughter of the same parents as another person ❷ a female friend or associate ❸ a nun ❹ a senior hospital nurse, especially one in charge of a ward
➤ **sisterly** ADJECTIVE

**sisterhood** NOUN sisterhoods
❶ companionship and mutual support between women ❷ a society or association of women

**sister-in-law** NOUN sisters-in-law
the sister of a married person's husband or wife; the wife of a person's brother or sister

**sit** VERB sits, sitting, sat
❶ to rest on your bottom, as you do when you are on a chair • *We were sitting in the front row.* ❷ to put someone in a sitting position ❸ to be situated or positioned in a certain place • *The house sits on top of a hill.* ❹ to take a test or examination

a
b
c
d
e
f
g
h
i
j
k
l
m
n
o
p
q
r
s
t
u
v
w
x
y
z

**⑤** a parliament or law court sits when it has assembled for business **⑥** to act as a babysitter

**sitar** NOUN sitars
an Indian musical instrument that is like a guitar

**sitcom** NOUN sitcoms (informal)
a situation comedy

**site** NOUN sites
the place where something happens or happened or is built or positioned • a building site • This is the site of a famous battle.

**site** VERB sites, siting, sited
to site something somewhere is to locate or build it there

SPELLING

Site is different from sight, which means your ability to see or something that you see.

**sit-in** NOUN sit-ins
a protest in which people sit down in a public place and refuse to move

**sitter** NOUN sitters
**①** a person who poses for a portrait **②** a person who looks after children, pets or a house while the owners are away

**sitting** NOUN sittings
**①** the time when people are served a meal **②** the time when a parliament or committee is conducting business

**sitting room** NOUN sitting rooms
(chiefly British) a room with comfortable chairs for sitting in

**situated** ADJECTIVE
in a particular place or situation • They lived in a village situated in a valley.

**situation** NOUN situations
**①** a state of affairs at a certain time; the way things are • The police faced a difficult situation. **②** a position of a building or town, with its surroundings **③** a job

**situation comedy** NOUN situation comedies
a comedy series on radio or television, based on how characters react to unusual or comic situations

**six** NOUN & ADJECTIVE sixes
the number 6
➤ **sixth** ADJECTIVE & NOUN
➤ **at sixes and sevens** in disorder or disagreement

**sixteen** NOUN & ADJECTIVE sixteens
the number 16
➤ **sixteenth** ADJECTIVE & NOUN

**sixth form** NOUN sixth forms
(British) a form for students aged 16-18 in a secondary school

**sixth sense** NOUN
the ability to know something by instinct rather than by using any of the five senses; intuition

**sixty** NOUN & ADJECTIVE sixties
the number 60
➤ **sixtieth** ADJECTIVE & NOUN

**size** NOUN sizes
**①** the measurements or extent of something **②** any of the series of standard measurements in which certain things are made • a size eight shoe **③** a gluey substance used to glaze or stiffen paper or cloth

**size** VERB sizes, sizing, sized
**①** to arrange things according to their size **②** to treat something with size
➤ **size something up** **①** to estimate the size of something **②** to form an opinion or judgement about a person or thing

**sizeable** ADJECTIVE
large or fairly large

**sizzle** VERB sizzles, sizzling, sizzled
to make a crackling or hissing sound

**sjambok** (say **sham**-bok) NOUN sjamboks
(S. African) a strong whip originally made from the skin of a rhinoceros

**skate** NOUN skates
**①** a boot with a steel blade attached to the sole, used for sliding smoothly over ice **②** a roller skate **③** skate
a large flat edible sea fish

**skate** VERB skates, skating, skated
to move around on skates
➤ **skater** NOUN

**skateboard** NOUN skateboards
a small board with wheels, used for standing and riding on as a sport
➤ **skateboarder, skateboarding** NOUN

**skein** NOUN skeins
a coil of yarn or thread

**skeletal** ADJECTIVE
to do with a skeleton or like a skeleton
• skeletal figures dressed in rags

**skeleton** NOUN skeletons
**①** the framework of bones in a person's

or animal's body ❷ a framework, e.g. of a building

**sketch** NOUN sketches
❶ a rough drawing or painting ❷ a short account of something ❸ a short amusing play

**sketch** VERB sketches, sketching, sketched
to make a sketch • *She sketched the view from the window.*

**sketchy** ADJECTIVE
rough and not detailed or careful

**skew, skewed** ADJECTIVE
slanting; not straight or level

**skewer** NOUN skewers
a long pin pushed through meat to hold it together while it is being cooked

**skewer** VERB skewers, skewering, skewered
to fix or pierce something with a skewer or pin

**ski** (say skee) NOUN skis
each of a pair of long narrow strips of wood, metal or plastic fixed under the feet for moving quickly over snow

**ski** VERB skies, skiing, skied
to travel on skis

**skid** VERB skids, skidding, skidded
to slide accidentally, especially in a vehicle

**skid** NOUN skids
❶ a skidding movement ❷ a runner on a helicopter, for use in landing

**skier** NOUN skiers
a person who skis

**ski jump** NOUN ski jumps
a steep slope with a sharp drop where it levels out at the bottom, for skiers to jump off as a sport

**skilful** ADJECTIVE
having or showing great skill
➤ **skilfully** ADVERB

**skill** NOUN skills
❶ the ability to do something well • *It takes great skill to paint a picture like that.*
❷ an ability that you need in order to do something • *He's been learning some new football skills.*

**skilled** ADJECTIVE
❶ skilful; highly trained or experienced
❷ skilled work needs particular skills or special training

**skim** VERB skims, skimming, skimmed
❶ to remove something from the surface of a liquid; to take the cream off milk ❷ to move

quickly over a surface, almost touching it
• *The plane flew very low, skimming the tops of the buildings.* ❸ to read something quickly

**skimmed milk** NOUN
milk that has had the cream removed

**skimp** VERB skimps, skimping, skimped
to supply or use less than is needed • *Don't skimp on the food.*

**skimpy** ADJECTIVE skimpier, skimpiest
skimpy clothes do not cover much of the body • *a skimpy dress*

**skin** NOUN skins
❶ the flexible outer covering of a person's or animal's body ❷ an outer layer or covering, e.g. of a fruit ❸ a skin-like film formed on the surface of a liquid

**skin** VERB skins, skinning, skinned
to take the skin off something

**skin diving** NOUN
swimming under water with flippers and breathing apparatus but without a diving suit
➤ **skin diver** NOUN

**skinhead** NOUN skinheads
a youth with very closely cropped hair

**skinny** ADJECTIVE skinnier, skinniest
very thin

**skip** VERB skips, skipping, skipped
❶ to move along lightly, especially by hopping on each foot in turn ❷ to jump with a skipping rope ❸ to go quickly from one subject to another ❹ to miss something out
• *You can skip chapter six.*

**skip** NOUN skips
❶ a skipping movement ❷ a large open-topped metal container for taking away builders' rubbish

**skipper** NOUN skippers (*informal*)
the captain of a ship or team

**skipping rope** NOUN skipping ropes
(*British*) a rope, usually with a handle at each end, that you swing over your head and under your feet as you jump

**skirmish** NOUN skirmishes
a short rough fight

**skirmish** VERB skirmishes, skirmishing, skirmished
to take part in a skirmish

**skirt** NOUN skirts
❶ a piece of clothing for a woman or girl that hangs down from the waist ❷ the part of a dress below the waist

**skirt** *VERB* skirts, skirting, skirted
to go round the edge of something • *The path skirts the lake.*

**skirting, skirting board** *NOUN* skirtings, skirting boards
(*British*) a narrow board round the wall of a room, close to the floor

**skit** *NOUN* skits
a short humorous play or sketch that makes fun of something by imitating it • *He wrote a skit on 'Hamlet'.*

**skittish** *ADJECTIVE*
frisky; lively and excitable • *a skittish horse*

**skittle** *NOUN* skittles
a wooden or plastic bottle-shaped object that people try to knock down by bowling a ball in the game of **skittles**

**skive** *VERB* skives, skiving, skived (*British*)
(*informal*)
to dodge work
➤ **skiver** *NOUN*

**skulk** *VERB* skulks, skulking, skulked
to move around or wait somewhere secretly, usually when you are planning to do something bad • *There was someone skulking behind the bushes.*

**skull** *NOUN* skulls
the framework of bones in your head

**skullcap** *NOUN* skullcaps
a small close-fitting cap worn on the top of the head

**skunk** *NOUN* skunks
a North American animal with black and white fur that can spray a bad-smelling fluid

**sky** *NOUN* skies
the space above the earth, appearing blue in daylight on fine days

**skydiving** *NOUN*
the sport of jumping from an aeroplane and performing manoeuvres before opening your parachute
➤ **skydiver** *NOUN*

**skylark** *NOUN* skylarks
a lark that sings while it hovers high in the air

**skylight** *NOUN* skylights
a window in a roof

**skyline** *NOUN* skylines
the outline of land or buildings seen against the sky • *the Manhattan skyline*

**skyscraper** *NOUN* skyscrapers
a very tall building

**slab** *NOUN* slabs
a thick flat piece of something

**slack** *ADJECTIVE*
❶ not pulled tight • *Leave the rope slack.*
❷ not busy or working hard • *Business is slack at this time of the year.*
➤ **slackly** *ADVERB*
➤ **slackness** *NOUN*

**slack** *NOUN*
the slack part of a rope or line

**slack** *VERB* slacks, slacking, slacked
to avoid work; to be lazy
➤ **slacker** *NOUN*

**slacken** *VERB* slackens, slackening, slackened
❶ to loosen something or to become loose
❷ to become or make something slower or less busy • *Her pace gradually slackened.*

**slacks** *PLURAL NOUN*
trousers for informal occasions

**slag** *NOUN*
waste material separated from metal in smelting

**slag heap** *NOUN* slag heaps
(*British*) a mound of waste matter from a mine

**slain**
past participle of **slay**

**slake** *VERB* slakes, slaking, slaked
to slake your thirst is to quench it

**slalom** *NOUN* slaloms
a ski race down a zigzag course
**WORD ORIGIN** Norwegian *sla* = sloping + *låm* = track

**slam** *VERB* slams, slamming, slammed
❶ to shut or make something shut loudly • *We heard the front door slam.* ❷ to hit something with great force

**slam** *NOUN* slams
the act or sound of slamming

**slander** *NOUN* slanders
a spoken statement that damages a person's reputation and is untrue. Compare with **libel**.
➤ **slanderous** *ADJECTIVE*

**slander** *VERB* slanders, slandering, slandered
to make a slander against someone
➤ **slanderer** *NOUN*

**slang** *NOUN*
words that are used very informally to add vividness or humour to what is said, especially

those used only by a particular group of people • *teenage slang*
➤ **slangy** ADJECTIVE

**slanging match** NOUN slanging matches
(*British*) a noisy quarrel, with people shouting insults at each other

**slant** VERB slants, slanting, slanted
❶ to slope or lean ❷ to present news or information from a particular point of view

**slant** NOUN slants
❶ a sloping or leaning position ❷ a way of presenting news or information from a particular point of view

**slap** VERB slaps, slapping, slapped
❶ to hit someone with the palm of the hand or with something flat ❷ to put something somewhere forcefully or carelessly • *We slapped paint on the walls.*

**slap** NOUN slaps
slapping someone • *a slap on the back*

**slapdash** ADJECTIVE
hasty and careless

**slapstick** NOUN
comedy with people hitting each other, falling over and throwing things

**slash** VERB slashes, slashing, slashed
❶ to make large cuts in something ❷ to cut or strike something with a long sweeping movement ❸ to reduce something greatly • *Prices are slashed.*

**slash** NOUN slashes
❶ a slashing cut ❷ a slanting line (/) used in writing and printing

**slat** NOUN slats
each of the thin strips of wood, metal or plastic arranged so that they overlap and form a screen, e.g. in a venetian blind

**slate** NOUN slates
❶ a kind of grey rock that is easily split into flat plates ❷ a piece of this rock used in covering a roof or (in the past) for writing on

**slate** VERB slates, slating, slated
❶ to cover a roof with slates ❷ (*informal*) to criticize a person or thing severely

**slaughter** VERB slaughters, slaughtering, slaughtered
❶ to kill an animal for food ❷ to kill people or animals ruthlessly or in great numbers

**slaughter** NOUN
the killing of a lot of people or animals

**slaughterhouse** NOUN slaughterhouses
a place where animals are killed for food

**slave** NOUN slaves
a person who is owned by someone else and has to work for them without being paid

**slave** VERB slaves, slaving, slaved
to work very hard • *He's been slaving away in the kitchen.*

**slave-driver** NOUN slave-drivers
a person who makes others work very hard

**slaver** (say slav-er or slay-ver) VERB slavers, slavering, slavered
to have saliva flowing from the mouth • *a slavering dog*

**slavery** NOUN
❶ being a slave • *They were sold into slavery.* ❷ the system of having slaves • *the abolition of slavery*

**slavish** ADJECTIVE
showing no independence or originality

**slay** VERB slays, slaying, slew, slain (*old or poetical use*)
to kill someone

**sled** NOUN sleds (*North American*)
a sledge

**sledge** NOUN sledges
(*British*) a vehicle for travelling over snow, with strips of metal or wood instead of wheels
➤ **sledging** NOUN

**sledgehammer** NOUN sledgehammers
a very large heavy hammer

**sleek** ADJECTIVE
smooth and shiny • *sleek black hair*

**sleep** NOUN
❶ the condition of rest in which your eyes are closed, your body is relaxed and your mind is unconscious • *You need some sleep.* ❷ a time when you are resting like this • *Did you have a good sleep?*
➤ **go to sleep** part of your body goes to sleep when it becomes numb
➤ **put something to sleep** to kill an animal painlessly, e.g. with an injection of a drug

**sleep** VERB sleeps, sleeping, slept
to have a sleep
➤ **sleep with someone** to have sexual intercourse with someone

**sleeper** NOUN sleepers
❶ someone who is asleep ❷ each of the wooden or concrete beams on which the rails of a railway rest ❸ a railway carriage with beds or berths for passengers to sleep in; a place in this

**sleeping bag** *NOUN* sleeping bags
a padded bag to sleep in, especially when you are camping

**sleepless** *ADJECTIVE*
without sleep or unable to sleep • *We had a sleepless night.*

**sleepover** *NOUN* sleepovers
a night spent away from home, after a party

**sleepwalker** *NOUN* sleepwalkers
a person who walks about while they are asleep
➤ **sleepwalking** *NOUN*

**sleepy** *ADJECTIVE*
❶ feeling a need or wish to sleep ❷ quiet and lacking activity • *a sleepy little town*
➤ **sleepily** *ADVERB*
➤ **sleepiness** *NOUN*

**sleet** *NOUN*
a mixture of rain and snow or hail

**sleeve** *NOUN* sleeves
❶ the part of a piece of clothing that covers your arm ❷ the cover of a record
➤ **up your sleeve** hidden but ready for you to use

**sleeveless** *ADJECTIVE*
without sleeves • *a sleeveless dress*

**sleigh** (say slay) *NOUN* sleighs
a large sledge pulled by horses

**sleight of hand** (say slight) *NOUN*
skilful movements of your hand that other people cannot see, especially when doing conjuring tricks

**slender** *ADJECTIVE*
❶ slim and graceful ❷ slight or small • *a slender chance of winning*

**sleuth** (say slooth) *NOUN* sleuths
a detective

**slew**
past tense of **slay**

**slice** *NOUN* slices
❶ a thin flat piece cut off something ❷ a portion of something

**slice** *VERB* slices, slicing, sliced
❶ to cut something into slices ❷ to cut something from a larger piece • *Slice the top off the egg.* ❸ to cut something cleanly • *The knife sliced through the apple.*

**slick** *ADJECTIVE*
❶ done quickly and cleverly, without obvious effort ❷ clever at persuading people but not sincere ❸ smooth and slippery

**slick** *NOUN* slicks
❶ a large patch of oil floating on water ❷ a slippery place

**slide** *VERB* slides, sliding, slid
❶ to move smoothly over a flat or slippery surface or to make something do this • *She loved sliding down the bannister.* ❷ to move somewhere quietly or secretly • *I slid out of the room when nobody was looking.*

**slide** *NOUN* slides
❶ a sliding movement ❷ a structure for children to play on, with a smooth slope for sliding down ❸ a photograph that can be projected on a screen ❹ a small glass plate on which you can place things to examine them under a microscope ❺ a fastener to keep your hair tidy

**slight** *ADJECTIVE*
very small; not serious or important

**slight** *VERB* slights, slighting, slighted
to insult a person by treating them without respect

**slight** *NOUN* slights
an insult

**slightly** *ADVERB*
to a small degree; a little • *They were slightly hurt.*

**slim** *ADJECTIVE* slimmer, slimmest
❶ thin and graceful ❷ small; hardly enough • *a slim chance of winning*

**slim** *VERB* slims, slimming, slimmed (*British*)
to try to make yourself thinner, especially by dieting
➤ **slimmer** *NOUN*

**slime** *NOUN*
unpleasant wet slippery stuff

**slimy** *ADJECTIVE* slimier, slimiest
❶ covered in slime ❷ pretending to be friendly in a way that is not sincere

**sling** *NOUN* slings
❶ a piece of cloth tied round your neck to support an injured arm • *He had his arm in a sling.* ❷ a looped strap used to throw a stone

**sling** *VERB* slings, slinging, slung
❶ to hang something up or support it so that it hangs loosely • *He had slung the bag round his neck.* ❷ (*informal*) to throw something roughly or carelessly • *You can sling your wet clothes into the washing machine.*

**slink** *VERB* slinks, slinking, slunk
to move in a stealthy or guilty way • *He slunk off to bed.*

**slip** *VERB* slips, slipping, slipped
❶ to slide accidentally; to lose your balance by sliding ❷ to move somewhere quickly and quietly • *She slipped out of the house before anyone was awake.* ❸ to slip something somewhere is to put it there quickly without being seen • *He slipped the letter into his pocket.* ❹ to escape from something • *The dog slipped its leash.*
➤ **slip your mind** to be forgotten • *I'm sorry, it slipped my mind.*
➤ **slip up** to make a mistake

**slip** *NOUN* slips
❶ an accidental slide or fall • *One slip and you could fall into the river.* ❷ a small mistake ❸ a small piece of paper ❹ a piece of women's underwear like a thin dress or skirt ❺ a pillowcase
➤ **give someone the slip** to escape from someone or avoid them

**slipper** *NOUN* slippers
a soft comfortable shoe to wear indoors

**slippery** *ADJECTIVE*
smooth or wet so that it is difficult to stand on or hold
➤ **slipperiness** *NOUN*

**slip road** *NOUN* slip roads
(*British*) a road by which you enter or leave a motorway

**slipshod** *ADJECTIVE*
a slipshod piece of work is careless or badly done (**WORD ORIGIN**) originally = wearing slippers or badly fitting shoes; from **slip** + **shod**

**slipstream** *NOUN* slipstreams
a current of air driven backward as an aircraft or vehicle moves forward very fast

**slit** *NOUN* slits
a narrow straight cut or opening

**slit** *VERB* slits, slitting, slit
to make a slit or slits in something

**slither** *VERB* slithers, slithering, slithered
❶ to move along the ground like a snake • *The snake slithered away.* ❷ to slip or slide unsteadily • *We were slithering around on the ice.*

**sliver** (say **sliv**-er) *NOUN* slivers
a thin strip of something hard or brittle, such as wood or glass

**slob** *NOUN* slobs (*informal*)
a careless, untidy, lazy person

**slobber** *VERB* slobbers, slobbering, slobbered
to have saliva coming out of your mouth (**WORD ORIGIN**) probably from old Dutch *slobberen* = paddle in mud

**sloe** *NOUN* sloes
the small dark plum-like fruit of blackthorn

**slog** *VERB* slogs, slogging, slogged
❶ to work hard • *I've been slogging away at my essay.* ❷ to walk with effort • *We slogged through the snow.* ❸ to hit something hard

**slog** *NOUN*
a piece of hard work or effort • *Climbing up that hill was a real slog.*

**slogan** *NOUN* slogans
a short catchy phrase used to advertise something or to sum up an idea • *Their slogan was 'Ban the bomb!'.* (**WORD ORIGIN**) from Scottish Gaelic *sluagh-ghairm* = battle-cry

**sloop** *NOUN* sloops
a small sailing ship with one mast

**slop** *VERB* slops, slopping, slopped
❶ to spill liquid over the edge of its container ❷ liquid slops when it spills in this way

**slope** *VERB* slopes, sloping, sloped
to be at an angle so that it is higher at one end than the other; to lean to one side • *The road slopes down to the river.*
➤ **sloping** *ADJECTIVE*
➤ **slope off** (*informal*) to go away quietly without being seen

**slope** *NOUN* slopes
❶ a surface or piece of land that slopes • *The village is built on a slope.* ❷ the amount by which something slopes

**sloppy** *ADJECTIVE* sloppier, sloppiest
❶ liquid and splashing easily ❷ careless or badly done • *sloppy work* ❸ too sentimental or romantic • *a sloppy story*
➤ **sloppily** *ADVERB*
➤ **sloppiness** *NOUN*

**slops** *PLURAL NOUN*
❶ waste food fed to animals ❷ dirty water or liquid waste matter

**slosh** *VERB* sloshes, sloshing, sloshed (*informal*)
❶ to splash in a messy way • *Water was sloshing around under our feet.* ❷ to pour or splash liquid carelessly

**slot** *NOUN* slots
a narrow opening to put things in
➤ **slotted** *ADJECTIVE*

**slot** VERB slots, slotting, slotted
to put something into a place where it fits

**sloth** (rhymes with both) NOUN sloths
❶ laziness ❷ a South American animal that
lives in trees and moves very slowly
➤ **slothful** ADJECTIVE

**slot machine** NOUN slot machines
a machine worked by putting a coin in the
slot

**slouch** VERB slouches, slouching, slouched
to stand, sit or move in a lazy awkward way,
with your shoulders and head bent forward
➤ **slouch** NOUN

**slough** (say sluf) VERB sloughs, sloughing,
sloughed
to shed a layer of dead skin • *A snake sloughs
its skin periodically.*

**slough** (rhymes with cow) NOUN sloughs
a swamp or marshy place

**slovenly** (say **sluv**-en-lee) ADJECTIVE
careless or untidy

**slow** ADJECTIVE
❶ not quick; taking more time than is usual
❷ showing a time earlier than the correct
time • *Your watch is slow.* ❸ not clever; not
able to understand quickly or easily
➤ **slowness** NOUN

**slow** ADVERB
slowly; at a slow rate • *Go slow.*

**slow** VERB slows, slowing, slowed
❶ to go more slowly ❷ to make something
go more slowly • *The storm slowed us down.*

**slowly** ADVERB
at a slow rate or speed

**slow motion** NOUN
movement in a film or on television which has
been slowed down

**slow-worm** NOUN slow-worms
a small European legless lizard that looks like
a snake and gives birth to live young

**sludge** NOUN
thick mud

**slug** NOUN slugs
❶ a small slimy animal like a snail without a
shell ❷ a pellet for firing from a gun

**sluggard** NOUN sluggards
a slow or lazy person

**sluggish** ADJECTIVE
slow-moving; not alert or lively

**sluice** (say slooss) NOUN sluices
❶ a sluice gate ❷ a channel carrying off
water

**sluice** VERB sluices, sluicing, sluiced
to wash something with a flow of water

**sluice gate** NOUN sluice gates
a sliding barrier for controlling a flow of
water

**slum** NOUN slums
an area of dirty and overcrowded houses in
a city

**slumber** NOUN slumbers
peaceful sleep

**slumber** VERB slumbers, slumbering,
slumbered
to sleep peacefully

**slump** VERB slumps, slumping, slumped
to fall or sit down heavily or suddenly • *He
slumped to the ground in agony.*

**slump** NOUN slumps
a sudden great fall in prices or trade

**slur** VERB slurs, slurring, slurred
❶ to pronounce words indistinctly by running
the sounds together • *He was drunk and his
speech was slurred.* ❷ to mark notes in music
with a slur

**slur** NOUN slurs
❶ a slurred sound ❷ an unfair comment
or insult that harms a person's reputation
❸ a curved line placed over notes in music
to show that they are to be sung or played
smoothly without a break

**slurp** VERB slurps, slurping, slurped
to eat or drink something with a loud sucking
sound

**slurp** NOUN slurps
a loud sucking sound

**slurry** NOUN
a semi-liquid mixture of water and cement,
clay or manure

**slush** NOUN
❶ partly melted snow on the ground
❷ very sentimental talk or writing
(WORD ORIGIN) imitating the sound when you
walk in it

**slushy** ADJECTIVE
❶ with snow partly melted on the ground
• *slushy pavements* ❷ very sentimental
• *slushy love songs*

**sly** ADJECTIVE slyer, slyest
❶ unpleasantly cunning or secret

**slyly** ADVERB
in a sly way • *He glanced at her slyly.*

**smack** NOUN smacks
❶ a hard slap with your hand ❷ a loud sharp sound of a thing hitting something • *It hit the wall with a smack.* ❸ a loud kiss ❹ (*informal*) a hard hit or blow ❺ a slight flavour or trace of something ❻ (*British*) a small sailing boat used for fishing

**smack** VERB smacks, smacking, smacked
❶ to slap someone with your hand, especially as a punishment ❷ to hit something hard ❸ to have a slight flavour or trace of something • *His manner smacks of conceit.*
➤ **smack your lips** to close and then part your lips noisily in enjoyment

**smack** ADVERB (*informal*) forcefully or directly
• *My face landed smack in the snow.*

**small** ADJECTIVE
❶ not large; less than the usual size ❷ not important or significant • *She noticed a few small mistakes.*
➤ **smallness** NOUN
➤ **the small of the back** the smallest part of the back, at the waist

**small hours** PLURAL NOUN
the early hours of the morning, after midnight

**small-minded** ADJECTIVE
not willing to change your opinions or think about what is really important; petty

**smallpox** NOUN
a serious contagious disease that causes a fever and produces spots that leave permanent scars on the skin

**small print** NOUN
(*British*) the details of a contract, especially if they are in very small letters or difficult to understand

**small talk** NOUN
conversation about unimportant things

**smarmy** ADJECTIVE (*informal*)
flattering someone or being too polite to them in a way that seems false

**smart** ADJECTIVE
❶ neat and elegant; dressed well ❷ clever or shrewd ❸ forceful and brisk • *She set off at a smart pace.* ❹ fashionable and expensive • *a smart restaurant* ❺ controlled by a computer

• *smart bombs*
➤ **smartness** NOUN

**smart** VERB smarts, smarting, smarted
❶ to feel a stinging pain • *My eyes were smarting from the smoke.* ❷ to feel upset about a criticism or failure • *He was still smarting from his defeat in the final.*

**smart card** NOUN smart cards
a small plastic card on which information is stored in electronic form

**smarten** VERB smartens, smartening, smartened
to make a person or thing smarter or to become smarter • *You need to smarten yourself up a bit.*

**smartly** ADVERB
❶ to be smartly dressed is to be well dressed in neat clothes ❷ quickly and suddenly • *He stepped smartly forward.*

**smartphone** NOUN smartphones
a mobile phone that also works as a computer

**smash** VERB smashes, smashing, smashed
❶ to break noisily into pieces or make something break in this way ❷ to hit something or move with great force • *The truck left the road and smashed into a wall.* ❸ to strike the ball forcefully downwards in tennis and other games ❹ to destroy or defeat someone completely

**smash** NOUN smashes
❶ the action or sound of smashing ❷ a collision between vehicles ❸ (*informal*) a smash hit

**smash hit** NOUN smash hits (*informal*)
a very successful song or show

**smashing** ADJECTIVE (*British*) (*informal*)
excellent

**smattering** NOUN
a slight knowledge of a subject or a foreign language

**smear** VERB smears, smearing, smeared
❶ to rub something greasy or sticky or dirty on a surface ❷ to try to damage someone's reputation
➤ **smeary** ADJECTIVE

**smear** NOUN smears
❶ a dirty or greasy mark made by smearing ❷ material smeared on a slide to be examined under a microscope ❸ a smear test

**smear test** NOUN smear tests
(*British*) the taking and examination of a

sample of the cervix lining, to check for faulty cells which may cause cancer

**smell** VERB smells, smelling, smelt or smelled
❶ to be aware of something by means of your nose • *I can smell smoke.* ❷ to give out a smell • *The cheese smells funny.*

**smell** NOUN smells
❶ something you can smell; a quality in something that makes people able to smell it ❷ an unpleasant quality of this kind ❸ the ability to smell things • *I have a good sense of smell.*

**smelly** ADJECTIVE smellier, smelliest
having an unpleasant smell

**smelt** VERB smelts, smelting, smelted
to melt ore to get the metal it contains

**smile** NOUN smiles
an expression on your face that shows you are pleased or amused, with your lips stretched and turning upwards at the ends

**smile** VERB smiles, smiling, smiled
to give a smile

**smirk** NOUN smirks
a self-satisfied smile

**smirk** VERB smirks, smirking, smirked
to give a smirk

**smite** VERB smites, smiting, smote, smitten (old use)
to strike something or someone with a hard blow

**smith** NOUN smiths
a person who makes things out of metal, especially a blacksmith

**smithereens** PLURAL NOUN
small fragments • *The house had been blown to smithereens.*

**smithy** NOUN smithies
a blacksmith's workshop

**smitten**
past participle of **smite**
➤ **be smitten with something** to be suddenly affected by a disease or feeling, especially love

**smock** NOUN smocks
❶ an overall shaped like a long loose shirt ❷ a loose top worn by a pregnant woman

**smog** NOUN
a mixture of smoke and fog
**WORD ORIGIN** from **smoke** + **fog**

**smoke** NOUN
❶ the mixture of gas and solid particles given off by a burning substance ❷ a time spent smoking a cigarette • *He wanted a smoke.*

**smoke** VERB smokes, smoking, smoked
❶ to give out smoke • *a smoking chimney* ❷ someone is smoking when they have a lit cigarette between their lips and are drawing its smoke into their mouth ❸ to preserve meat or fish by treating it with smoke
• *smoked haddock*
➤ **smoker** NOUN

**smokeless** ADJECTIVE
burning without producing smoke
• *smokeless fuel*

**smokescreen** NOUN smokescreens
❶ a mass of smoke used to hide the movement of troops ❷ something that conceals what is happening

**smoky** ADJECTIVE
❶ full of or producing smoke • *a smoky fire* ❷ like smoke

**smooth** ADJECTIVE
❶ having a surface without any lumps, wrinkles or roughness • *smooth skin* ❷ a smooth liquid or mixture has no lumps in it ❸ moving without bumps or jolts • *We had a smooth ride.* ❹ not harsh • *a smooth flavour* ❺ without problems or difficulties
➤ **smoothness** NOUN

**smooth** VERB smooths, smoothing, smoothed
to make something smooth and flat • *She smoothed her hair back.*

**smoothly** ADVERB
❶ in an even and steady way • *Traffic is flowing smoothly again.* ❷ without any problems or difficulties • *I hope everything goes smoothly today.*

**smote**
past tense of **smite**

**smother** VERB smothers, smothering, smothered
❶ to cover someone's face so that they cannot breathe ❷ to put out a fire by covering it ❸ to cover something thickly • *The chips were smothered in ketchup.* ❹ to hold back or conceal something • *She smothered a giggle.*

**smoulder** VERB smoulders, smouldering, smouldered
❶ to burn slowly without a flame ❷ to feel an emotion strongly without showing it • *He was smouldering with jealousy.*

**smudge** NOUN smudges
a dirty mark made by rubbing something
➤ **smudgy** ADJECTIVE

**smudge** VERB smudges, smudging, smudged
to make a smudge on something or to
become smudged • *The writing here was
smudged.*

**smug** ADJECTIVE
too pleased with your own good fortune or
abilities • *Don't look so smug.*
➤ **smugly** ADVERB
➤ **smugness** NOUN

**smuggle** VERB smuggles, smuggling, smuggled
❶ to bring something into a country secretly
or illegally ❷ to take something secretly into
or out of a place • *He smuggled some food
out of the house.*
➤ **smuggler** NOUN

**smut** NOUN smuts
❶ a small piece of soot or dirt ❷ rude or
indecent talk or pictures
➤ **smutty** ADJECTIVE

**snack** NOUN snacks
❶ a small meal ❷ food eaten between meals

**snack bar** NOUN snack bars
a small cafe where snacks are sold

**snag** NOUN snags
❶ an unexpected difficulty ❷ a sharp or
jagged part sticking out from something

**snag** VERB snags, snagging, snagged
to catch something you are wearing on
something sharp

**snail** NOUN snails
a small animal with a soft body and a shell

**snail's pace** NOUN
a very slow pace

**snake** NOUN snakes
a reptile with a long narrow body and no legs
➤ **snaky** ADJECTIVE

**snake** VERB snakes, snaking, snaked
to move or go in long twisting curves • *The
river snaked through a wooded valley.*

**snap** VERB snaps, snapping, snapped
❶ to break suddenly or with a sharp sound
or to make something do this • *The rope
snapped.* • *He snapped the branch in two.*
❷ an animal snaps when it bites suddenly
or quickly ❸ to say something quickly and
angrily • *There's no need to snap.* ❹ to move
something into a certain position with a
sharp noise • *She snapped the bag shut.* ❺ to
take a quick photograph of something

➤ **snap your fingers** to make a sharp
snapping sound with your thumb and a finger

**snap** NOUN snaps
❶ the action or sound of snapping ❷ an
informal photograph ❸ a card game in which
players shout 'Snap!' when they see two
similar cards

**snap** ADJECTIVE
made or done very quickly or suddenly • *It
was a snap decision.*

**snapdragon** NOUN snapdragons
a plant with flowers that have a mouth-like
opening

**snappy** ADJECTIVE
❶ snapping at people ❷ quick and lively

**snapshot** NOUN snapshots
an informal photograph that you take quickly

**snare** NOUN snares
❶ a trap for catching birds or small animals
❷ something that attracts someone but is a
trap or a danger

**snare** VERB snares, snaring, snared
to catch a bird or animal in a snare

**snarl** VERB snarls, snarling, snarled
❶ to growl angrily ❷ to speak in a bad-
tempered way
➤ **be snarled up** to become tangled or
jammed • *The motorway was snarled up for
miles.*

**snarl** NOUN snarls
a snarling sound

**snatch** VERB snatches, snatching, snatched
❶ to grab or take something quickly ❷ to
quickly make use of time or a chance • *I
managed to snatch some sleep.*

**snatch** NOUN snatches
❶ a short and incomplete part of a song
or conversation ❷ an act of snatching
something

**sneak** VERB sneaks, sneaking, sneaked
❶ to move somewhere quietly and secretly
❷ (*informal*) to take something secretly • *He
sneaked a biscuit from the tin.* ❸ (*informal*)
to tell tales about someone

**sneak** NOUN sneaks (*informal*) a person who
tells tales

**sneakers** PLURAL NOUN
(*North American*) soft-soled shoes

**sneaky** ADJECTIVE
dishonest or deceitful • *a sneaky trick*
➤ **sneakily** ADVERB

**sneer** *VERB* sneers, sneering, sneered
to show contempt for someone by the way
you speak or the expression on your face
• *'And who would believe you?' sneered the
old man.*

**sneer** *NOUN* sneers
the expression on someone's face when they
sneer

**sneeze** *VERB* sneezes, sneezing, sneezed
to send out air suddenly and uncontrollably
through your nose and mouth in order to get
rid of something irritating the nostrils
➤ **not to be sneezed at** (*informal*) worth
having

**sneeze** *NOUN* sneezes
the action or sound of sneezing
**WORD ORIGIN** from Old English *fneosan*,
imitating the sound

**snide** *ADJECTIVE*
sneering in a sly way • *a snide remark*

**sniff** *VERB* sniffs, sniffing, sniffed
❶ to make a sound by drawing air in through
your nose ❷ to smell something

**sniff** *NOUN* sniffs
the act or sound of sniffing
➤ **sniffer** *NOUN*

**sniffer dog** *NOUN* sniffer dogs
a dog trained to find drugs or explosives by
smell

**sniffle** *VERB* sniffles, sniffling, sniffled
to keep sniffing because you have a cold or
are crying

**sniffle** *NOUN* sniffles
the act or sound of sniffling

**snigger** *VERB* sniggers, sniggering, sniggered
(*British*) to laugh quietly and slyly

**snigger** *NOUN* sniggers
(*British*) a quiet sly laugh

**snip** *VERB* snips, snipping, snipped
to cut something with scissors or shears in
small quick cuts

**snip** *NOUN* snips
an act of snipping something

**snipe** *NOUN* snipe
a marsh bird with a long beak

**snipe** *VERB* snipes, sniping, sniped
❶ to shoot at people from a hiding place
❷ to attack someone with sly critical remarks
➤ **sniper** *NOUN*
**WORD ORIGIN** probably from a Scandinavian
language; the verb because the birds are shot
from a hiding place

**snippet** *NOUN* snippets
a small piece of news or information

**snivel** *VERB* snivels, snivelling, snivelled
to cry or complain in a whining way

**snob** *NOUN* snobs
a person who despises those who have not
got wealth, power or particular tastes or
interests
➤ **snobbery** *NOUN*
➤ **snobbish** *ADJECTIVE*

**snooker** *NOUN*
a game played with long sticks (called *cues*)
and 22 balls on a special cloth-covered table

**snoop** *VERB* snoops, snooping, snooped
to look around a place secretly in order to
find something out • *I caught him snooping
around in my room.*
➤ **snooper** *NOUN*

**snooty** *ADJECTIVE* (*informal*)
haughty and contemptuous

**snooze** (*informal*) *NOUN* snoozes
a short sleep

**snooze** *VERB* snoozes, snoozing, snoozed
to have a short sleep

**snore** *VERB* snores, snoring, snored
to breathe noisily while you are sleeping

**snore** *NOUN* snores
noisy breathing while you are sleeping

**snorkel** *NOUN* snorkels
a tube through which a person swimming
under water can take in air
➤ **snorkelling** *NOUN*

**snort** *VERB* snorts, snorting, snorted
to make a rough sound by breathing
forcefully through your nose

**snort** *NOUN* snorts
a snorting noise • *She gave a little snort of
contempt.*

**snout** *NOUN* snouts
an animal's snout is the front part sticking
out from its head, with its nose and jaws

**snow** *NOUN*
frozen drops of water that fall from the sky in
small white flakes

**snow** *VERB* snows, snowing, snowed
it is snowing when snow is falling
➤ **be snowed under** to have more work to do
than you can easily deal with

**snowball** *NOUN* snowballs
snow pressed into a ball for throwing
➤ **snowballing** *NOUN*

**snowball** *VERB* snowballs, snowballing, snowballed
to grow quickly in size or intensity

**snow-blindness** *NOUN*
temporary blindness caused by the glare of light reflected by snow

**snowdrift** *NOUN* snowdrifts
a large heap or bank of snow piled up by the wind

**snowdrop** *NOUN* snowdrops
a small white flower that blooms in early spring

**snowflake** *NOUN* snowflakes
a flake of snow

**snowline** *NOUN*
the level above which snow never melts

**snowman** *NOUN* snowmen
a figure made of snow

**snowplough** *NOUN* snowploughs
a vehicle or device for clearing roads of snow

**snowshoe** *NOUN* snowshoes
a frame rather like a tennis racket for walking on soft snow

**snowstorm** *NOUN* snowstorms
a storm in which snow falls

**snow white** *ADJECTIVE*
pure white

**snowy** *ADJECTIVE*
❶ with snow falling • *snowy weather*
❷ covered with snow • *snowy mountain tops*
❸ pure white • *snowy white sheets*

**snub** *VERB* snubs, snubbing, snubbed
to treat someone rudely, especially by ignoring them

**snub** *NOUN* snubs
an insulting remark or unfriendly treatment

**snub-nosed** *ADJECTIVE*
having a short turned-up nose

**snuff** *NOUN*
powdered tobacco for taking into the nose by sniffing

**snuff** *VERB* snuffs, snuffing, snuffed
to put out a candle by covering or pinching the flame
➤ **snuffer** *NOUN*

**snuffle** *VERB* snuffles, snuffling, snuffled
to sniff in a noisy way

**snuffle** *NOUN* snuffles
the sound of snuffling

**snug** *ADJECTIVE* snugger, snuggest
❶ warm and cosy ❷ fitting closely or tightly
➤ **snugly** *ADVERB*

**snuggle** *VERB* snuggles, snuggling, snuggled
to curl up in a warm comfortable place • *She snuggled down under the blanket.*

**so** *ADVERB*
❶ in this way; to such an extent • *Why are you so cross?* ❷ very • *This programme is so boring.* ❸ also; too • *OK, I was wrong, but so were you.*
➤ **and so on** and other similar things • *They took food, water, spare clothing and so on.*
➤ **or so** or about that number • *We need about fifty or so.*
➤ **so as to** in order to
➤ **so far** up to now
➤ **so long!** (*informal*) goodbye
➤ **so what?** (*informal*) that is not important

**so** *CONJUNCTION*
for that reason • *They threw me out, so I came here.*

**soak** *VERB* soaks, soaking, soaked
to make a person or thing very wet or leave them in water
➤ **soak** *NOUN*
➤ **soak something up** to take in a liquid in the way that a sponge does

**so-and-so** *NOUN* so-and-sos
a person whose name you do not know or do not need to say

**soap** *NOUN* soaps
❶ a substance you use with water for washing and cleaning things ❷ a soap opera

**soap** *VERB* soaps, soaping, soaped
to put soap on something

**soap opera** *NOUN* soap operas
a television serial about the day-to-day lives of a group of people **WORD ORIGIN** originally American, where they were originally sponsored by soap manufacturers

**soapy** *ADJECTIVE*
full of soap or covered in soap • *soapy water*

**soar** *VERB* soars, soaring, soared
❶ to rise or fly high in the air ❷ to increase very quickly • *Prices were soaring.*

**sob** *VERB* sobs, sobbing, sobbed
to make a gasping sound when crying

**sob** *NOUN* sobs
a sound of sobbing

**sober** *ADJECTIVE*
❶ not drunk ❷ serious and calm • *She had*

a
b
c
d
e
f
g
h
i
j
k
l
m
n
o
p
q
r
s
t
u
v
w
x
y
z

a sober expression. ❸ not bright or showy
• *sober colours*
➤ **soberly** *ADVERB*
➤ **sobriety** (say so-**bry**-it-ee) *NOUN*

**sober** *VERB* sobers, sobering, sobered
to become sober again or to make someone
sober

**sob story** *NOUN* sob stories
an account of someone's experiences, told
to get your help or sympathy • *She gave
me some sob story about having her purse
stolen.*

**so-called** *ADJECTIVE*
named in what may be the wrong way • *Even
the so-called experts couldn't solve the
problem.*

**soccer** *NOUN*
football (Association football, not rugby or
American football)

> **USAGE**
>
> The word *soccer* is used especially in the
> USA.

> **WORD ORIGIN** short for **Association football**,
> the official name from the late 19th century

**sociable** *ADJECTIVE*
friendly and liking to be with other people
➤ **sociably** *ADVERB*
➤ **sociability** *NOUN*

**social** *ADJECTIVE*
❶ to do with people meeting one another in
their spare time • *a social club* ❷ to do with
life in a community • *They were writing a
social history of the town.* ❸ living in groups,
not alone • *Bees are social insects.* ❹ liking
to be with other people
➤ **socially** *ADVERB*

**socialism** *NOUN*
a political system where wealth is shared
equally between people and the main
industries and resources are controlled by the
state. Compare with **capitalism**.

**socialist** *NOUN* socialists
a person who believes in socialism

**socialize** (also **socialise**) *VERB* socializes,
socializing, socialized
to meet other people socially

**social media** *NOUN*
websites and computer programs that people
use to communicate on the Internet using
mobile phones, computers, etc.

**social security** *NOUN*
money and other assistance provided by the

government for those in need through being
unemployed, ill or disabled

**social services** *PLURAL NOUN*
welfare services provided by the government,
for example care for vulnerable children and
adults

**social worker** *NOUN* social workers
a person trained to help people in a
community who have family or money
problems
➤ **social work** *NOUN*

**society** *NOUN* societies
❶ a community; people living together in
a group or nation • *We live in a multiracial
society.* ❷ a group of people organized for
a particular purpose • *the school dramatic
society* ❸ company or companionship • *We
enjoy the society of our friends.*

**sociology** (say soh-see-**ol**-o-jee) *NOUN*
the study of human society and social
behaviour
➤ **sociological** *ADJECTIVE*
➤ **sociologist** *NOUN*

**sock** *NOUN* socks
a piece of clothing that covers your foot and
the lower part of your leg

**sock** *VERB* socks, socking, socked
(*informal*) to hit or punch someone hard • *He
socked me on the jaw.*

**socket** *NOUN* sockets
❶ a hollow into which something fits • *a
tooth socket* ❷ a device into which an electric
plug or bulb is put to make a connection

**sod** *NOUN* sods
a piece of turf

**soda** *NOUN*
❶ a substance made from sodium, such
as baking soda ❷ soda water ❸ (*North
American*) a sweet fizzy drink

**soda water** *NOUN*
water made fizzy with carbon dioxide, used
in drinks

**sodden** *ADJECTIVE*
made very wet • *His boots were sodden.*

**sodium** *NOUN*
a soft white metal

**sodium bicarbonate** *NOUN*
a soluble white powder used in fire
extinguishers and fizzy drinks and to make
cakes rise; baking soda

**sodium carbonate** *NOUN*
white powder or crystals used to clean things; washing soda

**sofa** *NOUN* sofas
a long soft seat with a back and arms
**WORD ORIGIN** from Arabic *suffa* = long stone bench

**soft** *ADJECTIVE*
❶ not hard or firm; easily pressed or cut into a new shape ❷ smooth, not rough or stiff • *a soft towel* ❸ gentle and not loud • *He spoke in a soft voice.* ❹ not bright or harsh • *soft pinks and greens* ❺ soft drugs are not likely to be addictive ❻ soft water is free of minerals that prevent soap from making much lather
➤ **softness** *NOUN*

**soft drink** *NOUN* soft drinks
a cold drink that is not alcoholic

**soften** *VERB* softens, softening, softened
❶ to make something soft or to become soft • *This lotion is good for softening the skin.*
❷ to become kinder or more friendly • *His face softened a little.*
➤ **softener** *NOUN*

**soft furnishings** *PLURAL NOUN*
(*British*) cushions, curtains, rugs, loose covers for chairs, etc.

**soft-hearted** *ADJECTIVE*
sympathetic and easily moved

**softly** *ADVERB*
❶ in a gentle way • *She closed the door softly behind her.* ❷ quietly • *He could hear them talking softly in the next room.*

**software** *NOUN*
computer programs and data, which are not part of the machinery of a computer. Compare with **hardware**.

**softwood** *NOUN* softwoods
wood from pine trees or other conifers

**soggy** *ADJECTIVE* soggier, soggiest
very wet and heavy • *soggy ground*

**soil** *NOUN* soils
❶ the loose earth in which plants grow ❷ a nation's territory • *on British soil*

**soil** *VERB* soils, soiling, soiled
to make something dirty

**sojourn** (say **soj**-ern) *NOUN* sojourns
a temporary stay at a place

**sojourn** *VERB* sojourns, sojourning, sojourned
to stay at a place temporarily

**solace** (say **sol**-as) *NOUN*
something that makes you feel better when you are unhappy or disappointed • *He found solace in books.*

**solar** *ADJECTIVE*
from or to do with the sun

**solar panel** *NOUN* solar panels
a panel designed to catch the sun's rays and use their energy for heating or to make electricity

**solar power** *NOUN*
electricity or other forms of power that come from the sun's rays

**solar system** *NOUN*
the sun and the planets that revolve round it

**solder** *NOUN*
a soft alloy that is melted to join pieces of metal together

**solder** *VERB* solders, soldering, soldered
to join two pieces of metal together with solder

**soldier** *NOUN* soldiers
a member of an army

**SPELLING**
There is an **i** after the **d** in **soldier**.

**sole** *NOUN* soles
❶ the bottom surface of a foot or shoe ❷ a flat edible sea fish

**sole** *VERB* soles, soling, soled
to put a new sole on a shoe

**sole** *ADJECTIVE*
single or only • *She was the sole survivor.*

**solely** *ADVERB*
only; involving nothing or nobody else • *He was solely to blame.*

**solemn** *ADJECTIVE*
❶ not smiling or cheerful ❷ dignified or formal
➤ **solemnly** *ADVERB*
➤ **solemnity** *NOUN*

**SPELLING**
There is a silent **n** at the end of **solemn**.

**solenoid** *NOUN* solenoids
a coil of wire that becomes magnetic when an electric current is passed through it

**sol-fa** *NOUN*
a system of syllables (*doh, ray, me, fah, so, la, te*) used to represent the notes of the musical scale

**solicit** VERB solicits, soliciting, solicited
to ask for or try to obtain something • *I've been soliciting opinions from rail users.* • *All the candidates are busy soliciting for votes.*
➤ **solicitation** NOUN

**solicitor** NOUN solicitors
a lawyer who advises clients, prepares legal documents and represents clients in the lower courts

**solicitous** ADJECTIVE
anxious and concerned about a person's comfort and welfare
➤ **solicitously** ADVERB
➤ **solicitude** NOUN

**solid** ADJECTIVE
❶ not hollow; with no space inside • *These bars are made of solid steel.* ❷ keeping its shape; not liquid or gas ❸ continuous • *I had to wait for two solid hours.* ❹ firm or strongly made; not flimsy • *The house is built on solid foundations.* ❺ strong and dependable • *The police have no solid evidence.*
➤ **solidity** NOUN

**solid** NOUN solids
❶ a solid thing ❷ a shape that has three dimensions (length, width and height or depth)

**solidarity** NOUN
unity and support between people sharing opinions and interests

**solidify** VERB solidifies, solidifying, solidified
to become solid • *The mixture soon solidified.*

**solidly** ADVERB
❶ strongly or firmly • *a solidly built house* ❷ without stopping • *It rained solidly all afternoon.*

**solids** PLURAL NOUN
solid food; food that is not liquid • *Is your baby eating solids yet?*

**soliloquy** (say sol-**il**-ok-wee) NOUN soliloquies
a speech in a play in which a person speaks their thoughts aloud when alone or without addressing anyone else

**solitaire** NOUN solitaires
❶ a game for one person, in which marbles are moved on a special board until only one is left ❷ a diamond or other precious stone set by itself

**solitary** ADJECTIVE
❶ alone, without other people • *He lived a solitary life.* ❷ single; by itself • *a solitary example*

**solitary confinement** NOUN
a form of punishment in which a prisoner is kept alone in a cell and not allowed to see other people

**solitude** NOUN
being solitary or alone • *She longed for peace and solitude.*

**solo** NOUN solos
something sung, played, danced or done by one person alone

**solo** ADJECTIVE & ADVERB
done alone; by yourself • *a solo flight* • *to fly solo*

**soloist** NOUN soloists
a person who plays, sings or performs a solo

**solstice** (say sol-stiss) NOUN solstices
either of the two times in each year when the sun is at its furthest point north or south of the equator
➤ **summer solstice** about 21 June in the northern hemisphere
➤ **winter solstice** about 22 December in the northern hemisphere
(WORD ORIGIN) from Latin *sol* = sun + *sistere* = stand still

**soluble** ADJECTIVE
❶ a soluble substance is able to be dissolved ❷ a soluble problem or puzzle is able to be solved
➤ **solubility** NOUN

**solution** NOUN solutions
❶ the answer to a problem or puzzle ❷ a liquid in which something is dissolved

**solve** VERB solves, solving, solved
to find the answer to a problem or puzzle • *There's a mystery we've been trying to solve.*

**solvent** NOUN solvents
a liquid used for dissolving something

**solvent** ADJECTIVE
having enough money to pay all your debts

**sombre** ADJECTIVE
❶ dark in colour • *sombre clothes* ❷ gloomy or serious • *He was in a sombre mood.*

**sombrero** (say som-**brair**-oh) NOUN sombreros
a hat with a very wide brim

**some** DETERMINER
❶ a few or a little • *some apples* • *some sugar* ❷ an unknown person or thing • *Some fool left the door open.* ❸ about • *We waited some 20 minutes.*
➤ **some time** ❶ quite a long time • *I've been*

*wondering about it for some time.* ❷ at some point in time • *You must come round for a meal some time.*

**some** *PRONOUN*
a certain number or amount that is less than the whole • *Some of them were late.*

**somebody** *PRONOUN*
❶ some person; someone ❷ an important or impressive person

**somehow** *ADVERB*
in some way or for some reason • *We must finish the work somehow.* • *Somehow I knew the door would be locked.*

**someone** *PRONOUN*
some person; somebody

**somersault** *NOUN* somersaults
a movement in which you turn head over heels before landing on your feet

**somersault** *VERB* somersaults, somersaulting, somersaulted
to perform a somersault

**something** *PRONOUN*
some thing; a thing which you cannot or do not want to name
➤ **something like** ❶ rather like • *It's something like a rabbit.* ❷ approximately • *It took something like 100 years to build.*

**sometime** *ADVERB*
at some point in time • *I saw her sometime last year.*

**sometimes** *ADVERB*
at some times but not always • *We sometimes walk to school.*

**somewhat** *ADVERB*
to some extent • *He was somewhat annoyed.*

**somewhere** *ADVERB*
in or to some place

**son** *NOUN* sons
a boy or man who is someone's child

**sonar** *NOUN*
a system for finding objects under water by the reflection of sound waves
(**WORD ORIGIN**) from *so*und *na*vigation and *r*anging

**sonata** *NOUN* sonatas
a piece of music for one instrument or two, in several movements

**song** *NOUN* songs
❶ a tune with words for singing ❷ a bird's song is the musical sounds it makes ❸ singing • *He burst into song.*

➤ **for a song** bought or sold very cheaply
➤ **make a song and dance** (*informal*) to make a great fuss about something

**songbird** *NOUN* songbirds
a bird that sings sweetly

**sonic** *ADJECTIVE*
to do with sound or sound waves

**sonic boom** *NOUN* sonic booms
a loud noise caused by the shock wave of an aircraft travelling faster than the speed of sound

**son-in-law** *NOUN* sons-in-law
a daughter's husband

**sonnet** *NOUN* sonnets
a kind of poem with 14 lines

**sonny** *NOUN* (*informal*)
boy or young man • *Come on, sonny!*

**sonorous** (say **sonn**-er-us) *ADJECTIVE*
giving a loud deep sound • *a sonorous voice*

**soon** *ADVERB*
❶ in a short time from now ❷ not long after something ❸ early or quickly • *Don't leave so soon.*
➤ **as soon** as much or willingly • *I'd just as soon stay here.*
➤ **as soon as** at the moment that
➤ **sooner or later** at some time in the future

**soot** *NOUN*
the black powder left by smoke in a chimney or on a building
➤ **sooty** *ADJECTIVE*

**soothe** *VERB* soothes, soothing, soothed
❶ to make someone calmer or less upset ❷ to make a part of the body or a feeling feel less painful

**soothing** *ADJECTIVE*
that soothes someone or something
• *soothing music*
➤ **soothingly** *ADVERB*

**soothsayer** *NOUN* soothsayers
a prophet

**sop** *NOUN* sops
something unimportant you give to a troublesome person to make them feel better

**sop** *VERB* sops, sopping, sopped
➤ **sop something up** to soak up liquid with a sponge

**sophisticated** *ADJECTIVE*
❶ a sophisticated person has refined or cultured tastes and is experienced about

life ❷ complicated and advanced • *a sophisticated machine*
➤ **sophistication** NOUN

**soporific** ADJECTIVE
causing sleep or drowsiness

**sopping** ADJECTIVE
very wet; drenched

**soppy** ADJECTIVE
(*British*) (*informal*) sentimental in a silly way

**soprano** NOUN sopranos
a woman, girl or boy with a high singing voice

**sorcerer** NOUN sorcerers
a person who can perform magic

**sorceress** NOUN sorceresses
a woman who can perform magic

**sorcery** NOUN
magic or witchcraft

**sordid** ADJECTIVE
❶ dirty and nasty ❷ dishonourable or immoral • *sordid motives*

**sore** ADJECTIVE
❶ painful or smarting • *a sore throat*
❷ (*informal*) annoyed or offended ❸ serious or upsetting • *The bridge is in sore need of repair.*
➤ **soreness** NOUN

**sore** NOUN sores
a sore place on your body

**SPELLING**
Do not confuse this word with *saw*.

**sorely** ADVERB
seriously; very • *I was sorely tempted to run away.*

**sorrel** NOUN
❶ a herb with sharp-tasting leaves ❷ a reddish-brown horse

**sorrow** NOUN sorrows
❶ sadness or regret caused by loss or disappointment ❷ something that causes this
• *He sat down and told her all his sorrows.*

**sorrow** VERB sorrows, sorrowing, sorrowed
to feel sorrow; to grieve

**sorrowful** ADJECTIVE
feeling or showing great sadness • *a sorrowful expression*
➤ **sorrowfully** ADVERB

**sorry** ADJECTIVE sorrier, sorriest
❶ feeling regret for something you have done and wanting to apologize • *I'm sorry I forgot your birthday.* ❷ feeling pity or sympathy for someone • *I'm sorry you've been ill.* ❸ wretched or unattractive • *His clothes were in a sorry state.*

**sort** NOUN sorts
❶ a group of things or people that are similar; a kind or variety • *What sort of fruit do you like?* ❷ (*in computing*) putting data in a particular order • *Can you help me do an alphabetical sort of these names?*
➤ **out of sorts** slightly unwell or depressed
➤ **sort of** (*informal*) rather; to some extent
• *I sort of expected it.*

**sort** VERB sorts, sorting, sorted
to arrange things in groups according to their size or type
➤ **sort someone out** (*informal*) to deal with and punish someone
➤ **sort something out** to deal with and solve a problem or difficulty

**sortie** NOUN sorties
❶ an attack by troops coming out of a besieged place ❷ an attacking expedition by a military aircraft

**SOS** NOUN SOSs
an urgent appeal for help **WORD ORIGIN** the international Morse code signal of extreme distress, chosen because it is easy to recognize, but often said to stand for Save Our Souls

**sosatie** NOUN sosaties
(*S. African*) a number of meat pieces that have been spiced and placed on a skewer for grilling

**sought**
past tense of **seek**

**soul** NOUN souls
❶ the invisible part of a person that some people believe goes on living after the body has died ❷ a person's mind and emotions ❸ a person • *There isn't a soul about.* ❹ a kind of popular music that developed from gospel music

**soulful** ADJECTIVE
having or showing deep feeling • *his soulful dark eyes*
➤ **soulfully** ADVERB

**sound** NOUN sounds
❶ vibrations that travel through the air and can be detected by the ear; the sensation they produce ❷ sound reproduced in a film or recording ❸ a mental impression you get from something • *We don't like the sound of his plans.* ❹ a narrow stretch of water

connecting two seas; a strait • *Plymouth Sound*

**sound** VERB sounds, sounding, sounded
❶ to make a sound • *The trumpets sounded.* ❷ to make a sound with something • *Don't forget to sound your horn.* ❸ to give a certain impression when heard • *He sounds angry.* ❹ to test something by noting the sounds you can hear from it • *A doctor sounds a patient's lungs with a stethoscope.* ❺ to test the depth of water beneath a ship
➤ **sound someone out** to try to find out what a person thinks or feels about something

**sound** ADJECTIVE
❶ in good condition; not damaged ❷ healthy; not diseased ❸ reasonable or correct • *His ideas are sound.* ❹ reliable or secure • *a sound investment* ❺ thorough or deep • *She has a sound knowledge of the subject.* • *I am a sound sleeper.*
➤ **soundness** NOUN

**sound barrier** NOUN
the resistance of the air to objects moving at speeds near the speed of sound

**sound bite** NOUN sound bites
a very short part of a speech or statement broadcast on radio or television because it seems to sum up the person's opinion in a few words

**sound effects** PLURAL NOUN
sounds produced artificially to make a play, film, etc. seem more realistic

**soundly** ADVERB
deeply or thoroughly • *The boys were sleeping soundly.* • *They were soundly beaten in the final.*

**soundtrack** NOUN soundtracks
the sound or music that goes with a cinema film

**soup** NOUN soups
a liquid food made from meat, fish or vegetables
➤ **in the soup** (*informal*) in trouble

**sour** ADJECTIVE
❶ tasting sharp like vinegar or lemons ❷ stale and unpleasant; not fresh • *sour milk* ❸ bad-tempered and unfriendly • *He gave me a sour look.*
➤ **sourness** NOUN

**sour** VERB sours, souring, soured
to become sour or to make something sour

**source** NOUN sources
❶ the place where something comes from • *This website is a great source of information on volcanoes.* ❷ the starting point of a river

**sour grapes** PLURAL NOUN
pretending that something you want is no good because you know you cannot have it
**WORD ORIGIN** from a fable in which a fox says that the grapes he cannot reach are probably sour

**sourly** ADVERB
in a bad-tempered and unfriendly way • *'Why are you here?' she said sourly.*

**souse** VERB souses, sousing, soused
❶ to soak or drench something ❷ to soak fish in pickle

**south** NOUN
❶ the direction to the right of a person who faces east ❷ the southern part of a country, city or other area

**south** ADJECTIVE & ADVERB
towards or in the south; coming from the south
➤ **southerly** (say **su**th-er-lee) ADJECTIVE
➤ **southern** ADJECTIVE
➤ **southerner** NOUN
➤ **southernmost** ADJECTIVE

**south-east** NOUN, ADJECTIVE & ADVERB
midway between south and east
➤ **south-easterly** ADJECTIVE
➤ **south-eastern** ADJECTIVE

**southward** ADJECTIVE & ADVERB
towards the south
➤ **southwards** ADVERB

**south-west** NOUN, ADJECTIVE & ADVERB
midway between south and west
➤ **south-westerly** ADJECTIVE
➤ **south-western** ADJECTIVE

**souvenir** (say soo-ven-**eer**) NOUN souvenirs
something that you keep to remind you of a person, place or event **WORD ORIGIN** from French *se souvenir* = remember

**sou'wester** NOUN sou'westers
a waterproof hat with a wide flap at the back **WORD ORIGIN** from *south-wester*, a wind from the south-west, often bringing rain

**sovereign** NOUN sovereigns
❶ a king or queen who is the ruler of a country; a monarch ❷ an old British gold coin, originally worth £1

a b c d e f g h i j k l m n o p q r s t u v w x y z

**sovereign** ADJECTIVE
❶ supreme • *sovereign power* ❷ a sovereign state is independent and runs its own affairs

**sovereignty** NOUN
the power a country has to govern itself and make its own laws

**sow** (rhymes with go) VERB sows, sowing, sowed, sown or sowed
❶ to put seeds into the ground so that they will grow into plants ❷ to cause feelings or ideas to develop • *Her words sowed doubt in my mind.*
➤ **sower** NOUN

SPELLING
Take care not to confuse with **sew**, which means to work with a needle and thread.

**sow** (rhymes with cow) NOUN sows
a female pig

**soya bean** NOUN soya beans
a kind of bean from which soya oil and flour are made

**soy sauce, soya sauce** NOUN
a Chinese or Japanese sauce made from fermented soya beans

**spa** NOUN spas
a health resort where there is a spring of water containing mineral salts

**space** NOUN spaces
❶ the whole area outside the earth, where the stars and planets are ❷ an area or volume • *This table takes too much space.* ❸ an empty area; a gap • *There is a space at the back of the cupboard.* ❹ an interval of time • *We moved house twice in the space of a year.*

**space** VERB spaces, spacing, spaced
to arrange things so that there are spaces between them • *Space the posts about a metre apart.*

**spacecraft** NOUN spacecraft
a vehicle for travelling in outer space

**spaceman** NOUN spacemen
a male astronaut

**spaceship** NOUN spaceships
a spacecraft, especially one carrying people

**space shuttle** NOUN space shuttles
a spacecraft that can travel into space and land like a plane when it returns to earth

**space station** NOUN space stations
a satellite which orbits the earth and is used as a base by scientists and astronauts

**space suit** NOUN space suits
a protective suit which enables an astronaut to survive in space

**space walk** NOUN space walks
moving about or walking by an astronaut outside the spacecraft

**spacewoman** NOUN spacewomen
a female astronaut

**spacious** ADJECTIVE
providing a lot of space; roomy • *a spacious apartment*
➤ **spaciousness** NOUN

**spade** NOUN spades
❶ a tool with a long handle and a wide blade for digging ❷ a playing card with black shapes like upside-down hearts on it, each with a short stem

**spadework** NOUN
hard or uninteresting work done to prepare for an activity or project

**spaghetti** NOUN
pasta made in long thin sticks, which soften into strings when you cook them
WORD ORIGIN Italian, = little strings

SPELLING
There is a silent **h** after the **g** in **spaghetti**.

**span** NOUN spans
❶ the length from end to end or across something ❷ the part between two uprights of an arch or bridge ❸ the length of a period of time ❹ the distance from the tip of your thumb to the tip of your little finger when your hand is spread out

**span** VERB spans, spanning, spanned
to reach from one side or end to the other • *A wooden bridge spans the river.*

**spangle** NOUN spangles
a small piece of glittering material
➤ **spangled** ADJECTIVE

**spaniel** NOUN spaniels
a kind of dog with long ears and silky fur

**spank** VERB spanks, spanking, spanked
to smack a person on the bottom as a punishment

**spanking** ADJECTIVE
brisk and lively • *at a spanking pace*

**spanner** NOUN spanners
(*British*) a tool for gripping and turning a nut or bolt

**spar** NOUN **spars**
a strong pole used for a mast or boom on a ship

**spar** VERB **spars, sparring, sparred**
❶ to practise boxing ❷ to argue with someone, often in a friendly way

**spare** VERB **spares, sparing, spared**
❶ to afford to give or do without something • *Can you spare a moment?* ❷ to be merciful towards someone; to not kill, hurt or harm a person or thing • *The duke agreed to spare their lives.* ❸ to avoid making a person suffer something • *Spare me the details.* ❹ to use or treat something economically • *No expense will be spared.*
➤ **to spare** left over without being needed • *We arrived with five minutes to spare.*

**spare** ADJECTIVE
❶ not used or kept ready in case it is needed; extra • *a spare wheel* ❷ thin or lean
➤ **go spare** (*informal*) to become very angry

**spare** NOUN **spares**
a spare thing or part

**spare time** NOUN
time not needed for work

**sparing** (say **spair**-ing) ADJECTIVE
careful or economical; not wasteful
➤ **sparingly** ADVERB

**spark** NOUN **sparks**
❶ a tiny glowing piece of something hot ❷ a flash produced electrically ❸ a trace of something • *a spark of hope*

**spark** VERB **sparks, sparking, sparked**
❶ to give off a spark or sparks ❷ to cause something • *The arrests sparked off a riot.*

**sparking plug** NOUN **sparking plugs**
(*British*) a spark plug

**sparkle** VERB **sparkles, sparkling, sparkled**
❶ to shine with tiny flashes of light • *The river sparkled in the sunlight.* ❷ to show brilliant wit or liveliness

**sparkle** NOUN **sparkles**
❶ a lot of tiny flashes of light • *There was a sparkle of excitement in her eyes.* ❷ liveliness • *The show lacked sparkle.*

**sparkler** NOUN **sparklers**
a hand-held firework that gives off sparks

**sparkling wine** NOUN **sparkling wines**
a bubbly wine

**spark plug** NOUN **spark plugs**
a device that makes a spark to ignite the fuel in an engine

**sparrow** NOUN **sparrows**
a small brown bird

**sparse** ADJECTIVE
thinly scattered; small in number or amount • *Vegetation on the island is sparse.*

**sparsely** ADVERB
in only small numbers or amounts • *It is a sparsely populated region.*

**spartan** ADJECTIVE
simple and without comfort or luxuries
**WORD ORIGIN** named after the people of *Sparta* in ancient Greece, famous for their hardiness

**spasm** NOUN **spasms**
❶ a sudden involuntary movement of a muscle ❷ a sudden brief burst of something • *a spasm of rage*

**spasmodic** ADJECTIVE
❶ happening or done at irregular intervals ❷ to do with or caused by a spasm
➤ **spasmodically** ADVERB

**spat**
past tense of **spit**

**spat** NOUN **spats**
a short gaiter

**spate** NOUN **spates**
❶ a lot of things coming one after another • *a recent spate of thefts* ❷ a sudden flood in a river

**spatial** ADJECTIVE
to do with space

**spatter** VERB **spatters, spattering, spattered**
❶ to scatter something wet in small drops • *He spattered paint all over the floor.* ❷ to splash someone or something • *She was spattered with mud.*

**spatter** NOUN **spatters**
a small amount of something in small drops

**spatula** NOUN **spatulas**
a tool like a knife with a broad blunt flexible blade, used for spreading or mixing things

**spawn** NOUN
❶ the eggs of fish, frogs, toads or shellfish ❷ the thread-like matter from which fungi grow

**spawn** VERB **spawns, spawning, spawned**
❶ to produce spawn ❷ to be produced from spawn ❸ to produce something in large numbers • *The film spawned a series of sequels.*

**spay** VERB spays, spaying, spayed
to sterilize a female animal by removing the
ovaries

**speak** VERB speaks, speaking, spoke, spoken
❶ to say something; to talk ❷ to talk or be
able to talk in a foreign language • *Do you
speak French?*
➤ **speak up** ❶ to speak more loudly ❷ to
give your opinion

**speaker** NOUN speakers
❶ a person who is speaking ❷ someone who
makes a speech ❸ the part of a radio, CD
player, computer, etc. that the sound comes
out of
➤ **the Speaker** the person who is in charge
of the debates in some parliaments

**spear** NOUN spears
a weapon for throwing or stabbing, with a
long shaft and a pointed tip

**spear** VERB spears, spearing, speared
to pierce something with a spear or with
something pointed • *They were standing in
their boats spearing fish.*

**spearhead** VERB spearheads, spearheading,
spearheaded
to lead a campaign or attack

**spearmint** NOUN
mint used in cookery and for flavouring
chewing gum

**special** ADJECTIVE
❶ not ordinary or usual; exceptional • *a
special occasion* • *Take special care of it.*
❷ meant for a particular person or purpose
• *You need a special tool for this job.*

**special effects** PLURAL NOUN
illusions created for films or television by
using props, trick photography or computer
images

**specialist** NOUN specialists
an expert in one subject • *a skin specialist*

**speciality** NOUN specialities
❶ something in which a person specializes
• *There are lots of sports I like playing but my
speciality is gymnastics.* ❷ a special product,
especially a food

**specialize** (also **specialise**) VERB specializes,
specializing, specialized
to give particular attention or study to one
subject or thing • *She specialized in biology.*
➤ **specialization** NOUN

**specially** ADVERB
❶ in a special way ❷ for a special purpose • *I
came specially to see you.*

**special needs** PLURAL NOUN
educational requirements resulting from
learning difficulties, physical disability
or emotional and behavioural difficulties
• *children with special needs*

**species** (say **spee**-shiz) NOUN species
❶ a group of animals or plants that have the
same features and can breed with each other
❷ a kind or sort • *a species of sledge*

**specific** ADJECTIVE
❶ definite or precise • *I gave you specific
instructions on what to do.* ❷ to do with a
particular thing • *The money was given for a
specific purpose.*

**specifically** ADVERB
❶ clearly and precisely • *I specifically said we
had to go.* ❷ in a special way or for a special
purpose • *The car is designed specifically for
people with disabilities.*

**specification** NOUN specifications
a detailed description of how to make or do
something

**specific gravity** NOUN specific gravities
relative density

**specify** VERB specifies, specifying, specified
to name or list things precisely • *The recipe
specified cream, not milk.*

**specimen** NOUN specimens
❶ a sample of something ❷ an example • *a
fine specimen of an oak tree*

**speck** NOUN specks
❶ a tiny piece of something • *a speck of dust*
❷ a tiny mark or spot

**speckle** NOUN speckles
a small spot or mark

**speckled** ADJECTIVE
covered with small spots or marks • *a
speckled hen*

**specs** PLURAL NOUN (*informal*)
spectacles

**spectacle** NOUN spectacles
❶ an impressive sight or display ❷ a
ridiculous sight

**spectacles** PLURAL NOUN
(*British*) a pair of glasses
➤ **spectacled** ADJECTIVE

**spectacular** ADJECTIVE
very impressive to see • *spectacular scenery*

**spectator** NOUN spectators
a person who watches a game, show or other event

**spectre** NOUN spectres
a ghost
➤ **spectral** ADJECTIVE

**spectrum** NOUN spectra
❶ the bands of colours seen in a rainbow ❷ a wide range of things or ideas • *a broad spectrum of interests*

**speculate** VERB speculates, speculating, speculated
❶ to form opinions without having any definite evidence ❷ to invest in stocks or property in the hope of making a profit but with the risk of loss
➤ **speculation** NOUN
➤ **speculator** NOUN
➤ **speculative** ADJECTIVE

**sped**
past tense of **speed**

**speech** NOUN speeches
❶ the ability to speak or a person's way of speaking ❷ a talk to an audience ❸ a group of lines spoken by a character in a play

**speechless** ADJECTIVE
too surprised or emotional to be able to say anything

**speech marks** PLURAL NOUN
punctuation marks " " or ' ' used to show that someone is speaking; inverted commas

**speed** NOUN
❶ a measure of the time in which something moves or happens ❷ being quick or fast
➤ **at speed** quickly

**speed** VERB speeds, speeding, sped (in senses 2 and 3 speeded)
❶ to go quickly • *The train sped by.* ❷ to drive faster than the legal limit
➤ **speed up** to become quicker
➤ **speed something up** to make something go or happen faster • *This will speed things up.*

**speedboat** NOUN speedboats
a fast motor boat

**speed camera** NOUN speed cameras
a camera by the side of a road which automatically photographs any vehicle which breaks the speed limit

**speed hump** NOUN speed humps
a ridge built across a road to make vehicles slow down

**speed limit** NOUN speed limits
the maximum speed at which vehicles may legally travel on a particular road

**speedometer** NOUN speedometers
a device in a vehicle, showing its speed

**speedway** NOUN speedways
a track for motorcycle racing

**speedwell** NOUN speedwells
a wild plant with small blue flowers

**speedy** ADJECTIVE speedier, speediest
quick or swift • *Thank you for your speedy reply.*
➤ **speedily** ADVERB

**spell** VERB spells, spelling, spelled or spelt
❶ to put letters in the right order to make a word or words ❷ a set of letters spell a word when they form it • *C-A-T spells 'cat'* ❸ to have something as a result • *Wet weather spells disaster for crops.*
➤ **speller** NOUN

**spell** NOUN spells
❶ a period of time • *We're in the middle of a cold spell.* ❷ a period of a certain work or activity • *He had a brief spell in the army.* ❸ a set of words that is supposed to have magical power

**spellbound** ADJECTIVE
with your attention completely held as if by magic • *We all sat spellbound as she told her story.*

**spellchecker, spellcheck** NOUN spellcheckers or spellchecks
a computer program that you use to check your writing to see if your spelling is correct

**spelling** NOUN spellings
❶ the way a word is spelled ❷ how well someone can spell • *Her spelling is poor.*

**spend** VERB spends, spending, spent
❶ to use money to pay for things ❷ to use up time, energy or effort in doing something • *Don't spend too much time on it.* ❸ to pass time doing something • *I spent the weekend painting my bedroom.*

**spendthrift** NOUN spendthrifts
a person who spends money extravagantly and wastefully

a b c d e f g h i j k l m n o p q r s t u v w x y z

**sperm** *NOUN* sperms or sperm
the male cell that fuses with an ovum to produce offspring

**spew** *VERB* spews, spewing, spewed
❶ to vomit ❷ to send out something unpleasant in a stream • *The volcano was spewing out lava.*

**sphere** *NOUN* spheres
❶ a perfectly round solid shape; the shape of a ball ❷ a field of interest, activity or knowledge • *The history of music is her main sphere of interest.*

> SPELLING

The 'f' sound is spelt ph in sphere.

**spherical** *ADJECTIVE*
having the shape of a sphere

**spheroid** *NOUN* spheroids
a solid which is sphere-like but not perfectly spherical

**sphinx** *NOUN* sphinxes
a stone statue with the body of a lion and a human head, especially the huge one (almost 5,000 years old) in Egypt WORD ORIGIN from the *Sphinx* in Greek mythology, a winged creature with a woman's head and a lion's body

**spice** *NOUN* spices
❶ a strong-tasting substance used to flavour food, often made from dried parts of plants ❷ something that adds interest or excitement • *Variety is the spice of life.*

**spice** *VERB* spices, spicing, spiced
❶ to flavour food with spices ❷ to make something more interesting or exciting

**spick and span** *ADJECTIVE*
neat and clean

**spicy** *ADJECTIVE*
spicy food tastes strongly of spices

**spider** *NOUN* spiders
a small animal with eight legs that spins webs to catch insects on which it feeds

**spidery** *ADJECTIVE*
spidery handwriting has long thin lines and sharp angles, like a spider's legs

**spike** *NOUN* spikes
a pointed piece of metal; a sharp point

**spike** *VERB* spikes, spiking, spiked to pierce something with a spike

**spiked** *ADJECTIVE*
with one or more spikes • *spiked running shoes*

**spiky** *ADJECTIVE*
full of spikes or sharp points • *She has short spiky hair.*

**spill** *VERB* spills, spilling, spilt or spilled
❶ to let something fall out of a container • *Careful, you're spilling your drink.* ❷ to fall out of a container • *The coins came spilling out.*
> spillage *NOUN*

**spill** *NOUN* spills
❶ spilling; something spilt • *an oil spill at sea* ❷ a fall from a horse or bicycle

**spin** *VERB* spins, spinning, spun
❶ to turn round and round quickly or to make something do this • *The plane was spinning out of control.* • *He was spinning a coin on the table.* ❷ to make raw wool or cotton into threads by pulling and twisting its fibres ❸ a spider or silkworm spins a web or cocoon when it forms one out of threads from its body
> spin a yarn to tell a story
> spin something out to make something last as long as possible

**spin** *NOUN* spins
❶ a spinning movement ❷ a short outing in a car

**spinach** *NOUN*
a vegetable with dark green leaves

**spinal** *ADJECTIVE*
to do with the spine

**spinal cord** *NOUN* spinal cords
the thick cord of nerves enclosed in the spine, that carries messages to and from the brain

**spindle** *NOUN* spindles
❶ a thin rod on which you wind thread ❷ a pin or bar that turns round or on which something turns

**spindly** *ADJECTIVE*
thin and long or tall • *The creature stood on two spindly legs.*

**spin doctor** *NOUN* spin doctors
a person whose job is to make information or events seem favourable to their employer, usually a politician or political party

**spin drier** *NOUN* spin driers
a machine in which washed clothes are spun to remove excess water

**spindrift** *NOUN*
spray blown along the surface of the sea

**spine** *NOUN* spines
❶ the line of bones down the middle of your

back ❷ a sharp point on an animal or plant • *This cactus has sharp spines.* ❸ the back part of a book where the pages are joined together

**spine-chilling** ADJECTIVE
frightening and exciting • *a spine-chilling horror film*

**spineless** ADJECTIVE
❶ without a backbone ❷ lacking in determination or strength of character

**spinet** NOUN spinets
a small harpsichord

**spinney** NOUN spinneys
(*British*) a small wood or thicket

**spinning wheel** NOUN spinning wheels
a household device for spinning wool or cotton into thread

**spin-off** NOUN spin-offs
something extra produced while making something else

**spinster** NOUN spinsters
an insulting word for a woman who has not married, especially an older woman
**WORD ORIGIN** the original meaning was 'one who spins' (because unmarried women used to earn their living by spinning, which could be done at home)

**spiny** ADJECTIVE
covered with spines; prickly

**spiral** ADJECTIVE
going round and round a central point and becoming gradually closer to it or further from it; twisting continually round a central line or cylinder

**spiral** NOUN spirals
a spiral line or course

**spiral** VERB spirals, spiralling, spiralled
❶ to move in a spiral • *A curl of grey smoke began to spiral upwards.* ❷ to increase or decrease continuously and quickly • *Prices were spiralling.*

**spire** NOUN spires
a tall pointed part on top of a church tower

**spirit** NOUN spirits
❶ a person's mood or mind and feelings • *He was in good spirits.* ❷ the part of a person that is thought to survive death; a person's soul ❸ a ghost or a supernatural being ❹ courage or liveliness • *She answered with spirit.* ❺ a kind of quality in something • *the romantic spirit of the book* ❻ a strong distilled alcoholic drink

**spirit** VERB spirits, spiriting, spirited
to carry off a person or thing quickly and secretly • *They spirited her away during the night.*

**spirited** ADJECTIVE
brave; self-confident and lively

**spirit level** NOUN spirit levels
a device consisting of a tube of liquid with an air bubble in it, used to find out whether something is level

**spiritual** ADJECTIVE
❶ to do with the human soul; not physical ❷ to do with religious beliefs
➤ **spiritually** ADVERB
➤ **spirituality** NOUN

**spiritual** NOUN spirituals
a religious folk song, originally sung by black Christians in America

**spiritualism** NOUN
the belief that the spirits of dead people communicate with living people
➤ **spiritualist** NOUN

**spit** VERB spits, spitting, spat or spit
❶ to send out drops of liquid forcibly from your mouth • *He spat at me.* ❷ to force something out of your mouth • *The baby spat out her dummy.* ❸ to rain lightly • *It's spitting with rain.*

**spit** NOUN spits
❶ saliva or spittle ❷ a long thin metal spike put through meat to hold it while it is being roasted ❸ a narrow strip of land sticking out into the sea

**spite** NOUN
a desire to hurt or annoy someone
➤ **in spite of something** although something has happened or is a fact • *We went out in spite of the rain.*

**spite** VERB spites, spiting, spited
to hurt or annoy someone from spite

**spiteful** ADJECTIVE
behaving unkindly in order to hurt or annoy someone • *That was a spiteful thing to say.*
➤ **spitefully** ADVERB
➤ **spitefulness** NOUN

**spitfire** NOUN spitfires
a fiery-tempered person

**spitting image** NOUN
an exact likeness

**spittle** NOUN
saliva, especially when it is spat out

**splash** VERB splashes, splashing, splashed
❶ to make liquid fly about in drops ❷ liquid splashes when it flies about in drops ❸ to make a person or thing wet by splashing • *The bus splashed us as it went past.*

**splash** NOUN splashes
❶ the action, sound or mark of splashing ❷ a bright patch of colour or light
➤ **make a splash** to attract a lot of attention

**splatter** VERB splatters, splattering, splattered
to splash over something • *The ground was splattered with blood.*

**splay** VERB splays, splaying, splayed
to spread wide apart or make something do this • *He splayed his fingers.*

**spleen** NOUN spleens
an organ of the body, close to the stomach, that helps to keep the blood in good condition
➤ **vent your spleen on someone** to be bad-tempered or spiteful towards them

**splendid** ADJECTIVE
❶ magnificent; full of splendour ❷ excellent; very fine
➤ **splendidly** ADVERB

**splendour** NOUN
a brilliant display or appearance • *the dazzling splendour of court life*

**splice** VERB splices, splicing, spliced
❶ to join pieces of rope or wire by twisting their strands together ❷ to join pieces of film, tape or wood by overlapping the ends

**splint** NOUN splints
a straight piece of wood or metal tied to a broken arm or leg to hold it firm

**splinter** NOUN splinters
a thin sharp piece of wood, glass or stone broken off a larger piece

**splinter** VERB splinters, splintering, splintered
to break into splinters • *The boat's hull began to splinter and crack.*

**split** VERB splits, splitting, split
❶ to break apart, especially along the length of something ❷ to divide something into parts ❸ to divide something among people
• *I'll split the cost with you.*
➤ **split up** ❶ to end a marriage or other relationship ❷ to go off in different directions

**split** NOUN splits
❶ the splitting or dividing of something ❷ a crack or tear in something, where it has split
➤ **the splits** an acrobatic position in which

your legs are stretched widely in opposite directions

**split second** NOUN
a very brief moment of time; an instant

**split-second** ADJECTIVE
❶ done very quickly • *He had to make a split-second decision.* ❷ very precise • *split-second timing*

**splodge** NOUN splodges
a dirty mark or stain

**splurge** VERB splurges, splurging, splurged (*informal*)
to spend a lot of money on something, especially a luxury • *She splurged her first week's wages on a make-over.*

**splutter** VERB splutters, spluttering, spluttered
❶ to make a quick series of spitting or coughing sounds ❷ to speak quickly and in a confused way • *'But... but... you can't!' he spluttered.*
➤ **splutter** NOUN

**spoil** VERB spoils, spoiling, spoilt or spoiled
❶ to damage something and make it useless or unsatisfactory ❷ to make someone selfish by always letting them have what they want ❸ to treat someone kindly • *Go on, spoil yourself!*

**spoils** PLURAL NOUN
plunder or other things gained by a victor
• *the spoils of war*

**spoilsport** NOUN spoilsports
a person who spoils other people's enjoyment of things

**spoke**
past tense of **speak**

**spoke** NOUN spokes
each of the bars or rods that go from the centre of a wheel to its rim

**spokesman** NOUN spokesmen
a spokesperson, especially a man

**spokesperson** NOUN spokespersons
a person who speaks on behalf of a group of people

**spokeswoman** NOUN spokeswomen
a female spokesperson

**sponge** NOUN sponges
❶ a sea creature with a soft porous body ❷ the skeleton of this creature or a piece of a similar substance, used for washing or

padding things ❸ a soft lightweight cake or pudding

**sponge** *VERB* sponges, sponging, sponged
❶ to wipe or wash something with a wet sponge ❷ to get money or food off other people without giving anything in return • *He's always sponging off his friends.*
➤ **sponger** *NOUN*

**spongy** *ADJECTIVE*
soft and absorbent, like a sponge • *The ground was spongy under his feet.*

**sponsor** *NOUN* sponsors
❶ a person or organization that provides money for an arts or sports event or for a broadcast in return for advertising ❷ someone who gives money to a charity in return for something achieved by another person
➤ **sponsorship** *NOUN*

**sponsor** *VERB* sponsors, sponsoring, sponsored
to be a sponsor for a person or thing • *Many marathon runners are sponsored to raise money for charity.*

**spontaneous** (say spon-**tay**-nee-us) *ADJECTIVE*
happening or done naturally; not forced or suggested by someone else • *They burst into spontaneous applause.*
➤ **spontaneously** *ADVERB*
➤ **spontaneity** *NOUN*

**spoof** *NOUN* spoofs
an amusing imitation of a film, television programme, etc. **WORD ORIGIN** originally the name of a card game invented and named by an English comedian, Arthur Roberts (1852-1933)

**spook** *NOUN* spooks (*informal*)
a ghost

**spooky** *ADJECTIVE* spookier, spookiest
(*informal*) strange and frightening; haunted by ghosts • *The house was spooky in the dark.*
➤ **spookily** *ADVERB*

**spool** *NOUN* spools
a rod or cylinder on which something is wound

**spoon** *NOUN* spoons
a small device with a rounded bowl on a handle, used for lifting food to your mouth or for stirring or measuring things

**spoon** *VERB* spoons, spooning, spooned
to take or lift something with a spoon

**spoonerism** *NOUN* spoonerisms
an accidental swapping round of the initial letters of two words, e.g. by saying

*a boiled sprat* instead of *a spoiled brat*
**WORD ORIGIN** named after the Reverend William Spooner (1844-1930), who often made mistakes of this kind

**spoon-feed** *VERB* spoon-feeds, spoon-feeding, spoon-fed
❶ to feed a baby or invalid with a spoon ❷ to provide someone with so much help or information that they do not have to make any effort

**spoonful** *NOUN* spoonfuls
as much as a spoon will hold

**spoor** *NOUN* spoors
the track left by an animal

**sporadic** *ADJECTIVE*
happening or found at irregular intervals; scattered
➤ **sporadically** *ADVERB*

**spore** *NOUN* spores
a tiny reproductive cell of a plant such as a fungus or fern

**sporran** *NOUN* sporrans
a pouch worn in front of a kilt

**sport** *NOUN* sports
❶ a game or activity that exercises your body, especially a game you play outdoors • *What sports do you play?* ❷ games of this kind • *Are you keen on sport?* ❸ (*informal*) a person who behaves well when they are defeated or teased • *Thanks for being such a good sport.*

**sport** *VERB* sports, sporting, sported
❶ to wear something in a showy way • *He sported a gold tiepin.* ❷ (*old use*) to play; to amuse yourself

**sporting** *ADJECTIVE*
❶ connected with sport; interested in sport ❷ behaving fairly and generously

**sporting chance** *NOUN*
a reasonable chance of success

**sports car** *NOUN* sports cars
an open low-built fast car

**sports jacket** *NOUN* sports jackets
a man's jacket for informal wear (not part of a suit)

**sportsman** *NOUN* sportsmen
a man who takes part in sport

**sportsmanship** *NOUN*
sporting behaviour; behaving fairly and generously to rivals

**sportswoman** NOUN sportswomen
a woman who takes part in sport

**spot** NOUN spots
❶ a small round mark ❷ a pimple on your
skin ❸ a small amount of something • We
had a spot of trouble. ❹ a place • This is a
nice spot. ❺ a drop • a few spots of rain
➤ **on the spot** ❶ without delay or change of
place • We can repair your bike on the spot.
❷ under pressure to take action • This really
puts him on the spot!
➤ **spot on** (informal) exactly right or
accurate

**spot** VERB spots, spotting, spotted
❶ to notice or recognize someone or
something • We spotted her in the crowd.
❷ to watch for certain things and take note
of them, as a hobby • train-spotting
➤ **spotter** NOUN

**spot check** NOUN spot checks
a check, usually without warning, on one of a
group of people or things

**spotless** ADJECTIVE
perfectly clean
➤ **spotlessly** ADVERB

**spotlight** NOUN spotlights
❶ a strong light that can shine on one
small area ❷ the centre of public attention
• The Royal Family are used to being in the
spotlight.

**spotted** ADJECTIVE
marked or decorated with spots • a spotted
handkerchief

**spotty** ADJECTIVE
marked with spots

**spouse** NOUN spouses
a person's husband or wife

**spout** NOUN spouts
❶ a pipe or similar opening from which liquid
can pour ❷ a jet of liquid

**spout** VERB spouts, spouting, spouted
❶ to come out as a jet of liquid ❷ (informal)
to speak for a long time

**sprain** VERB sprains, spraining, sprained
to injure a joint by twisting it

**sprain** NOUN sprains
an injury by spraining

**sprat** NOUN sprats
a small edible fish

**sprawl** VERB sprawls, sprawling, sprawled
❶ to sit or lie with your arms and legs
spread out loosely • She was sprawling in

an armchair by the fire. • The blow sent him
sprawling to the ground. ❷ to spread out
loosely or untidily • Looking down, I could see
the city sprawling beneath me.

**sprawl** NOUN
something that spreads over a large area in
an untidy way • the sprawl of Cairo

**spray** VERB sprays, spraying, sprayed
to scatter tiny drops of liquid over something

**spray** NOUN sprays
❶ tiny drops of liquid sent through the air
❷ a device for spraying liquid ❸ a liquid for
spraying • fly spray ❹ a single shoot with its
leaves and flowers ❺ a small bunch of flowers

**spread** VERB spreads, spreading, spread
❶ to open or stretch something out to its
full size • He spread the map on the table.
❷ to make something cover a surface • We
spread jam on the bread. ❸ to become longer
or wider • The stain was spreading. ❹ to
become or make something more widely
known or distributed • The story quickly
spread round the village. • We spread the
news.

**spread** NOUN spreads
❶ a paste for spreading on bread ❷ the
action or result of spreading • Nothing could
stop the spread of the disease. ❸ a thing's
breadth or extent ❹ (informal) a large or
grand meal

**spreadeagled** ADJECTIVE
with arms and legs stretched out
• He lay spreadeagled on the bed.
**WORD ORIGIN** originally = a picture of an eagle
with legs and wings stretched out, used as an
emblem on a knight's shield, inn sign, etc.

**spreadsheet** NOUN spreadsheets
a computer program that allows you to set
out tables of figures and to do complex
calculations

**spree** NOUN sprees
a short time you spend doing something you
enjoy • a shopping spree

**sprig** NOUN sprigs
a small branch or shoot

**sprightly** ADJECTIVE sprightlier, sprightliest
lively and full of energy

**spring** VERB springs, springing, sprang, sprung
❶ to jump or move quickly or suddenly • He
sprang to his feet. ❷ to grow or come from
something • The trouble has sprung from
carelessness. • Weeds have started to spring

*up.* ❸ to produce something without warning
• *They sprang a surprise on us.*

**spring** *NOUN* **springs**
❶ the season of the year when most plants
begin to grow ❷ a coil of wire or metal that
goes back to its original shape when you bend
or squeeze it and let it go ❸ a sudden upward
movement ❹ a place where water comes up
naturally from the ground

**springboard** *NOUN* **springboards**
a springy board from which people jump in
diving and gymnastics

**springbok** *NOUN* **springboks** or **springbok**
a South African gazelle
**WORD ORIGIN** Afrikaans, from Dutch *springen*
= to spring + *bok* = buck, antelope

**spring-clean** *VERB* **spring-cleans, spring-
cleaning, spring-cleaned**
to clean a house thoroughly in springtime

**spring onion** *NOUN* **spring onions**
(*British*) a small onion with a long green stem,
eaten raw in salads

**spring roll** *NOUN* **spring rolls**
a Chinese pancake filled with vegetables and
(sometimes) meat and fried until crisp

**springtime** *NOUN*
the season of spring

**springy** *ADJECTIVE* **springier, springiest**
able to spring back easily after being bent or
squeezed
➤ **springiness** *NOUN*

**sprinkle** *VERB* **sprinkles, sprinkling, sprinkled**
to make tiny drops or pieces fall on
something • *I like to sprinkle sugar over
strawberries.*
➤ **sprinkler** *NOUN*

**sprinkling** *NOUN* **sprinklings**
a few here and there; a small amount • *a
sprinkling of stars in the sky*

**sprint** *VERB* **sprints, sprinting, sprinted**
to run very fast for a short distance

**sprint** *NOUN* **sprints**
a short fast race
➤ **sprinter** *NOUN*

**sprite** *NOUN* **sprites**
an elf, fairy or goblin

**sprocket** *NOUN* **sprockets**
each of the row of teeth round a wheel,
fitting into links on a chain

**sprout** *VERB* **sprouts, sprouting, sprouted**
to start to grow; to put out shoots • *New
leaves were sprouting from the trees.*

**sprout** *NOUN* **sprouts**
❶ a shoot of a plant ❷ a Brussels sprout

**spruce** *NOUN* **spruces**
a kind of fir tree

**spruce** *ADJECTIVE*
neat and smart

**spruce** *VERB* **spruces, sprucing, spruced**
to smarten someone or something • *I'd better
spruce myself up.*

**spry** *ADJECTIVE* **spryer, spryest**
active, nimble and lively • *a spry old
gentleman*

**spud** *NOUN* **spuds** (*informal*)
a potato

**spume** *NOUN*
froth or foam

**spur** *NOUN* **spurs**
❶ a sharp device worn on the heel of a
rider's boot to urge a horse to go faster
❷ something shaped like a spur, such as
a hard spike on the back of a cock's leg
❸ something that encourages you to do
something ❹ a ridge that sticks out from a
mountain
➤ **on the spur of the moment** on an
impulse; without planning

**spur** *VERB* **spurs, spurring, spurred**
❶ to urge someone on or encourage them to
do something • *The letter spurred him into
action.* ❷ to use spurs to make a horse go
faster

**spurious** *ADJECTIVE*
not genuine

**spurn** *VERB* **spurns, spurning, spurned**
to refuse to accept something • *She spurned
his offer of help.*

**spurt** *VERB* **spurts, spurting, spurted**
to gush out • *Blood spurted from the wound.*

**spurt** *NOUN* **spurts**
❶ a sudden gush ❷ a sudden increase in
speed or effort • *He put on a spurt and
caught us up.*

**sputter** *VERB* **sputters, sputtering, sputtered**
❶ to make a quick series of spitting or
popping sounds • *The engine sputtered into
life.* ❷ to speak quickly and in a confused way
• *'W-What?' she sputtered.*

**sputum** *NOUN*
saliva or phlegm

**spy** *NOUN* spies
someone who works secretly for one country, person, etc. to find out things about another

**spy** *VERB* spies, spying, spied
**1** to be a spy **2** to keep watch secretly • *Have you been spying on me?* **3** to see or notice something • *She spied a house in the distance.*

**squabble** *VERB* squabbles, squabbling, squabbled
to quarrel or bicker

**squabble** *NOUN* squabbles
a minor quarrel or argument

**squad** *NOUN* squads
a small group of people working or being trained together

**squadron** *NOUN* squadrons
part of an army, navy or air force

**squalid** *ADJECTIVE*
dirty and unpleasant • *He lived in a squalid little room.*

**squall** *NOUN* squalls
**1** a sudden storm or gust of wind **2** a baby's loud cry

**squall** *VERB* squalls, squalling, squalled
a baby squalls when it cries loudly

**squally** *ADJECTIVE*
squally weather is windy and stormy

**squalor** *NOUN*
dirty and unpleasant conditions • *Some families were living in squalor.*

**squander** *VERB* squanders, squandering, squandered
to spend money or time wastefully

**square** *NOUN* squares
**1** a flat shape with four equal sides and four right angles **2** an area in a town or city, surrounded by buildings **3** the result of multiplying a number by itself • *9 is the square of 3 (9 = 3 x 3).*

**square** *ADJECTIVE*
**1** having the shape of a square **2** forming a right angle • *The desk has square corners.* **3** equal or even • *The teams are all square with six points each.* **4** used to give the length of each side of a square shape or object • *The carpet is four metres square.* **5** used to give a measurement of an area • *an area of 25 square metres*
➤ **squareness** *NOUN*

**square** *VERB* squares, squaring, squared
**1** to make a thing have straight edges and right angles **2** to multiply a number by itself • *5 squared is 25.* **3** to square with something is to match it or agree with it • *His story doesn't square with yours.* **4** to settle or pay a bill or debt

**square deal** *NOUN* square deals
a deal or arrangement that is honest and fair

**squarely** *ADVERB*
directly or exactly • *She turned and looked me squarely in the eye.*

**square meal** *NOUN* square meals
a good satisfying meal

**square root** *NOUN* square roots
the number that gives a particular number if it is multiplied by itself • *3 is the square root of 9 (3 x 3 = 9).*

**squash** *VERB* squashes, squashing, squashed
**1** to press something so that it becomes flat or out of shape **2** to force something into a small space; to pack something tightly • *We squashed ourselves into the minibus.* **3** to stop something from developing • *These rumours were quickly squashed.*

**squash** *NOUN* squashes
**1** a lot of people forced into a small space **2** a fruit-flavoured soft drink **3** a game played with rackets and a soft ball in a special indoor court **4** a kind of gourd used as a vegetable

**squat** *VERB* squats, squatting, squatted
**1** to sit back on your heels; to crouch **2** to live in an unoccupied building without permission
➤ **squatter** *NOUN*

**squat** *NOUN* squats
an unoccupied building that people are living in without permission

**squat** *ADJECTIVE*
short and fat

**squaw** *NOUN* squaws
a North American Indian woman or wife

**USAGE**
This word is offensive.

**squawk** *VERB* squawks, squawking, squawked
to make a loud harsh cry

**squawk** *NOUN* squawks
a loud harsh cry

**squeak** *VERB* squeaks, squeaking, squeaked
to make a short high-pitched cry or sound

**squeak** *NOUN* squeaks
a short high-pitched cry or sound

**squeaky** *ADJECTIVE*
making squeaks • *a squeaky floorboard*

**squeal** *VERB* squeals, squealing, squealed
to make a long shrill cry or sound • *The girls squealed with delight.*

**squeal** *NOUN* squeals
a long shrill cry or sound

**squeamish** *ADJECTIVE*
easily disgusted or shocked
➤ **squeamishness** *NOUN*

**squeeze** *VERB* squeezes, squeezing, squeezed
❶ to press something from opposite sides, especially to get liquid out of it ❷ to force your way into or through a place • *We squeezed through a gap in the hedge.*
➤ **squeezer** *NOUN*

**squeeze** *NOUN* squeezes
❶ the action of squeezing ❷ a drop of liquid squeezed out • *Add a squeeze of lemon.* ❸ a tight fit • *We all got in but it was a bit of a squeeze.* ❹ a time when money is difficult to get or borrow

**squelch** *VERB* squelches, squelching, squelched
to make a sound like someone treading in thick mud

**squelch** *NOUN* squelches
a squelching sound

**squib** *NOUN* squibs
a small firework that hisses and then explodes

**squid** *NOUN* squids
a sea animal with eight short tentacles and two long ones

**squiggle** *NOUN* squiggles
a short curly line

**squint** *VERB* squints, squinting, squinted
❶ to peer at something or look at it with half-shut eyes • *She squinted through the keyhole.* ❷ to have eyes that look in different directions at the same time

**squint** *NOUN* squints
a fault in someone's eyesight that makes them squint

**squire** *NOUN* squires
❶ the man who owns most of the land in a country parish or district ❷ a young nobleman in the Middle Ages who served a knight

**squirm** *VERB* squirms, squirming, squirmed
to wriggle about, especially when you feel embarrassed or awkward

**squirrel** *NOUN* squirrels
a small animal with a bushy tail and red or grey fur, living in trees **WORD ORIGIN** from Greek *skiouros*, from *skia* = shadow + *oura* = tail (because its long bushy tail cast a shadow over its body and kept it cool)

**squirt** *VERB* squirts, squirting, squirted
to send liquid out in a jet or to come out like this • *Orange juice squirted in his eye.*

**squirt** *NOUN* squirts
a jet of liquid

**St., St** *ABBREVIATION*
❶ Saint ❷ Street

**stab** *VERB* stabs, stabbing, stabbed
to pierce or wound someone with something sharp

**stab** *NOUN* stabs
❶ the action of stabbing ❷ a sudden sharp pain • *She felt a stab of fear.* ❸ (*informal*) an attempt • *I'll have a stab at it.*

**stability** *NOUN*
being stable or steady

**stabilize** (also **stabilise**) *VERB* stabilizes, stabilizing, stabilized
to make something stable or to become stable

**stabilizer** (also **stabiliser**) *NOUN* stabilizers
a device for keeping a vehicle or ship steady

**stable** *ADJECTIVE*
❶ steady and firmly fixed or balanced ❷ not likely to change or end suddenly • *a stable relationship* ❸ sensible and dependable

**stable** *NOUN* stables
a building where horses are kept

**stable** *VERB* stables, stabling, stabled
to keep a horse in a stable

**staccato** *ADVERB & ADJECTIVE*
(*in music*) played with each note short and separate

**stack** *NOUN* stacks
❶ a neat pile ❷ a haystack ❸ (*informal*) a large amount • *I have a stack of work to get through.* • *There's stacks to do.* ❹ a single tall chimney; a group of small chimneys

**stack** *VERB* stacks, stacking, stacked
to pile things up • *Boxes were stacked against one wall.*

**stadium** *NOUN* stadiums
a sports ground surrounded by seats for spectators

a b c d e f g h i j k l m n o p q r s t u v w x y z

**staff** NOUN staffs or, in sense 4, staves
❶ the people who work in an office, shop, etc. ❷ the teachers in a school or college ❸ a stick or pole used as a weapon or support or as a symbol of authority ❹ a set of five horizontal lines on which music is written

**staff** VERB staffs, staffing, staffed
to provide a place or organization with a staff of people • *The centre is staffed by a team of volunteers.*

**stag** NOUN stags
a male deer

**stage** NOUN stages
❶ a platform for performances in a theatre or hall ❷ a point or part of a process or journey • *Now for the final stage.*
➤ **the stage** the profession of acting or working in the theatre

**stage** VERB stages, staging, staged
❶ to present a performance on a stage ❷ to organize an event • *We decided to stage a protest.*

**stagecoach** NOUN stagecoaches
a horse-drawn coach of a kind that used to run regularly from one point to another along the same route (WORD ORIGIN) so called because it ran in stages, picking up passengers at points along the route

**stage fright** NOUN
fear or nervousness before or while performing to an audience

**stage-manage** VERB stage-manages, stage-managing, stage-managed
❶ to be stage manager of a performance ❷ to organize and control an event so that it has a particular effect

**stage manager** NOUN stage managers
the person in charge of the scenery, lighting, sound, etc. during a stage performance

**stage-struck** ADJECTIVE
loving the theatre and longing to be an actor

**stagger** VERB staggers, staggering, staggered
❶ to walk unsteadily ❷ to amaze or shock someone • *I was staggered at the price.* ❸ to arrange things so that they do not all happen at the same time • *We stagger our holidays so that there is always someone here.*
➤ **stagger** NOUN

**staggering** ADJECTIVE
very surprising and almost unbelievable • *a staggering amount of money*

**stagnant** ADJECTIVE
❶ not flowing ❷ not active or developing • *Business is stagnant.*

**stagnate** VERB stagnates, stagnating, stagnated
❶ to be stagnant ❷ to be dull through lack of activity or variety
➤ **stagnation** NOUN

**staid** ADJECTIVE
steady and serious in manner

**stain** NOUN stains
❶ a dirty mark that is difficult to remove ❷ a blemish on someone's character or past record ❸ a liquid used for staining things

**stain** VERB stains, staining, stained
❶ to make a stain on something ❷ to colour material or wood with a liquid that sinks into the surface

**stained glass** NOUN
pieces of coloured glass held together in a lead framework to make a picture or pattern

**stainless** ADJECTIVE
without a stain

**stainless steel** NOUN
steel that does not rust easily

**stair** NOUN stairs
each of the fixed steps in a series that lead from one level or floor to another in a building

**staircase** NOUN staircases
a set of stairs

**stairway** NOUN stairways
a staircase

**stairwell** NOUN stairwells
the space going up through a building, which contains the stairs

**stake** NOUN stakes
❶ a thick pointed stick to be driven into the ground ❷ the post to which people used to be tied for execution by being burnt alive ❸ an amount of money bet on something ❹ an investment that gives a person a share or interest in a business
➤ **at stake** at risk of being lost

**stake** VERB stakes, staking, staked
❶ to fasten, support or mark something out with stakes ❷ to bet or risk money on an event
➤ **stake a claim** to claim or obtain a right to something

SPELLING

Be careful, this sounds the same as **steak**.

**stalactite** NOUN stalactites
a stony spike hanging like an icicle from the
roof of a cave

USAGE

See note at stalagmite.

**stalagmite** NOUN stalagmites
a stony spike standing like a pillar on the floor
of a cave

USAGE

Remember that a stalagmite stands up
from the ground, while a stalactite hangs
down from the ceiling.

**stale** ADJECTIVE
❶ no longer fresh ❷ bored and lacking
new ideas because you have been doing
something for too long

**stalemate** NOUN
❶ a drawn position in chess when a player
cannot make a move without putting the king
in check ❷ a deadlock; a situation in which
neither side in an argument will give way

**stalk** NOUN stalks
a stem of a plant or fruit

**stalk** VERB stalks, stalking, stalked
❶ to track or hunt a person or animal
stealthily ❷ to walk in a stiff or angry way
• *He stalked out of the room.*

**stall** NOUN stalls
❶ a table or counter from which things are
sold ❷ a place for one animal in a stable or
shed

**stall** VERB stalls, stalling, stalled
❶ an engine or vehicle stalls when it stops
suddenly because of lack of power ❷ to delay
things or avoid giving an answer to give
yourself more time

**stallion** NOUN stallions
a male horse

**stalls** PLURAL NOUN
the seats in the lowest level of a theatre

**stalwart** ADJECTIVE
strong and faithful • *my stalwart supporters*

**stamen** NOUN stamens
the part of a flower that makes pollen

**stamina** NOUN
the strength and energy you need to keep
doing something for a long time

**stammer** VERB stammers, stammering,
stammered
to keep repeating the same syllables when
you speak

**stammer** NOUN stammers
a tendency to stammer

**stamp** NOUN stamps
❶ a small piece of gummed paper with a
special design on it; a postage stamp ❷ a
small device for pressing words or marks
on something; the words or marks made by
this ❸ a distinctive characteristic • *His story
bears the stamp of truth.*

**stamp** VERB stamps, stamping, stamped
❶ to bang your foot heavily on the ground
❷ to walk with loud heavy steps ❸ to stick
a postage stamp on something ❹ to press a
mark or design on something • *The librarian
stamped my books.*
➤ **stamp something out** to put an end to
something • *We have stamped out vandalism
in the area.*

**stampede** NOUN stampedes
a sudden rush by animals or people

**stampede** VERB stampedes, stampeding,
stampeded
animals or people stampede when they rush
fast and wildly

**stance** NOUN stances
❶ the way a person or animal stands ❷ a
person's attitude to something

**stanchion** NOUN stanchions
an upright bar or post forming a support

**stand** VERB stands, standing, stood
❶ to be on your feet without moving, to
rise to your feet • *We were standing at the
back of the hall.* • *Please stand up.* ❷ to put
something in an upright position • *We stood
the vase on the table.* ❸ to be somewhere
• *The castle stood on the top of a hill.* ❹ to
stay the same • *My offer still stands.* ❺ to
be a candidate for election • *She stood for
Parliament.* ❻ to be able to bear or tolerate
something • *I can't stand that noise.* ❼ to
provide and pay for something • *I'll stand you
a drink.*
➤ **it stands to reason** it is reasonable or
obvious
➤ **stand by** to be ready for action
➤ **stand for something** ❶ to represent
or mean something • *'US' stands for
'United States'.* ❷ to tolerate or put up
with something • *She won't stand for any
arguments.*
➤ **stand in for someone** to take someone's
place
➤ **stand out** to be clear or obvious

a b c d e f g h i j k l m n o p q r s t u v w x y z

➤ **stand up for someone** to support or defend someone

➤ **stand up to someone** to refuse to be threatened by someone

➤ **stand up to something** to stay in good condition despite rough treatment • *The bridge is designed to stand up to high winds.*

**stand** NOUN stands
❶ something made for putting things on • *a music stand* ❷ a stall where things are sold or displayed ❸ a building at a sports ground with a roof and rows of seats for spectators ❹ a standing position • *He took his stand near the door.* ❺ when someone resists an attack or defends their opinion • *The time has come to make a stand.*

**standard** NOUN standards
❶ how good something is • *a high standard of work* ❷ a thing used to measure or judge something else ❸ a special flag • *the royal standard*

**standard** ADJECTIVE
❶ of the usual or average quality or kind • *The logs are sawn into pieces of standard sizes.* ❷ regarded as the best and widely used • *the standard book on spiders*

**standard assessment task** NOUN standard assessment tasks
a standard test given to schoolchildren to assess their progress in one of the subjects of the national curriculum

**Standard English** NOUN
the form of English widely accepted as the normal and correct form. It is taught in schools and spoken and written by educated people.

**standardize** (also **standardise**) VERB
standardizes, standardizing, standardized
to make things be of a standard size or type
➤ **standardization** NOUN

**standard lamp** NOUN standard lamps
(*British*) a lamp on an upright pole that stands on the floor

**standard of living** NOUN
the level of comfort and wealth that a country or a person has

**standby** NOUN standbys
❶ something or someone kept to be used if needed ❷ a system by which tickets for a play or an air flight can be bought cheaply at the last minute if there are any seats left
➤ **on standby** ready to be used if needed
• *Troops were on standby during the crisis.*

**stand-in** NOUN stand-ins
a deputy or substitute

**standing** NOUN
❶ a person's status or reputation ❷ the period for which something has existed • *a contract of five years' standing*

**standing order** NOUN standing orders
an instruction to a bank to make regular payments or to a trader to supply something regularly

**stand-offish** ADJECTIVE
cold and formal; not friendly

**standpipe** NOUN standpipes
a pipe connected directly to a water supply, especially one set up in the street to provide water in an emergency

**standpoint** NOUN standpoints
a way of thinking about something; a point of view

**standstill** NOUN
a stop; an end to movement or activity • *The traffic has come to a complete standstill.*

**stanza** NOUN stanzas
a verse of poetry

**staple** NOUN staples
❶ a small piece of metal pushed through papers and clenched to fasten them together ❷ a U-shaped nail ❸ a basic or important food or product that people eat or use a lot

**staple** VERB staples, stapling, stapled
to fasten pieces of paper together with a staple

**staple** ADJECTIVE
main or usual • *Rice is their staple food.*

**stapler** NOUN staplers
a device for putting staples in paper

**star** NOUN stars
❶ a large mass of burning gas that is seen as a bright speck of light in the sky at night ❷ a shape with a number of points or rays sticking out from it; an asterisk ❸ an object or mark of this shape showing rank or quality • *a five-star hotel* ❹ a famous performer; one of the chief performers in a play, film or show

**star** VERB stars, starring, starred
❶ to be one of the main performers in a film or show • *John Wayne starred in many westerns.* ❷ to have someone as a main performer • *The film starred Robin Williams as a grown-up Peter Pan.*

**starboard** NOUN
the right-hand side of a ship or aircraft when

you are facing forward. Compare with **port**.
**WORD ORIGIN** from Old English *steorbord* = rudder side (because early sailing ships were steered with a paddle mounted on the right-hand side)

**starch** *NOUN* starches
**❶** a white carbohydrate in bread, potatoes and other food **❷** a form of this substance used to stiffen clothes

**starch** *VERB* starches, starching, starched
to stiffen something with starch

**starchy** *ADJECTIVE*
**❶** starchy food contains a lot of starch **❷** a starchy person behaves in a very stiff way

**stardom** *NOUN*
being a star performer

**stare** *VERB* stares, staring, stared
to look at something intensely

**stare** *NOUN* stares
a long fixed look • *I gave him a hard stare.*

**SPELLING**
Take care not to confuse this word with **stair**.

**starfish** *NOUN* starfish or starfishes
a sea animal shaped like a star with five points

**stark** *ADJECTIVE*
**❶** complete or unmistakable • *They watched in stark terror.* **❷** desolate and bare • *the stark lunar landscape*
➤ **starkly** *ADVERB*
➤ **starkness** *NOUN*

**stark** *ADVERB*
completely or entirely • *stark naked*

**starlight** *NOUN*
light from the stars

**starling** *NOUN* starlings
a noisy black or brown bird with speckled feathers

**starred** *ADJECTIVE*
marked with an asterisk or star symbol • *The starred items on the list are not for sale.*

**starry** *ADJECTIVE*
full of stars • *a starry night*

**starry-eyed** *ADJECTIVE*
made happy by foolish dreams or unrealistic hopes

**start** *VERB* starts, starting, started
**❶** to begin something or to make it begin **❷** to make an engine or machine begin

running • *I'll start the car.* **❸** to begin a journey **❹** to make a sudden movement because of pain or surprise

**start** *NOUN* starts
**❶** the beginning of something • *We've made a good start.* **❷** the place where a race starts **❸** an advantage that someone starts with
• *We gave the young ones ten minutes' start.*
**❹** a sudden movement of surprise or fear
• *She woke with a start.*

**starter** *NOUN* starters
**❶** a small amount of food served before the main course of a meal **❷** someone who starts a race

**startle** *VERB* startles, startling, startled
to surprise or alarm a person or animal

**starvation** *NOUN*
suffering or death from lack of food

**starve** *VERB* starves, starving, starved
**❶** to suffer or die from lack of food; to make someone do this • *The prisoners had been starved to death.* **❷** to deprive someone of something they need • *She was starved of love.*

**starving** *ADJECTIVE* (*informal*)
very hungry

**stash** *VERB* stashes, stashing, stashed (*informal*)
to store something safely in a secret place

**state** *NOUN* states
**❶** the quality of a person or thing or their circumstances; the way they are **❷** an organized community under one government or forming part of a republic
• *the State of Israel* • *the 50 States of the USA* **❸** a country's government • *Help for the earthquake victims was provided by the state.*
**❹** (*informal*) an excited or upset condition
• *Don't get into a state about the robbery.*
➤ **in state** in a grand style or with grand ceremony

**state** *VERB* states, stating, stated
to say or write something clearly or formally

**stately** *ADJECTIVE* statelier, stateliest
grand and dignified • *a stately procession*
➤ **stateliness** *NOUN*

**stately home** *NOUN* stately homes
(*British*) a large and magnificent house belonging to an aristocratic family

**statement** *NOUN* statements
**❶** words stating something **❷** a formal account of something that happened • *The*

*witness made a statement to the police.* ❸ a printed report of a financial account • *a bank statement*

GRAMMAR

A **statement** is a sentence that is a definite and clear expression of something and which is not a question, command or exclamation.

A **statement** ends with a full stop:

*The students wrote their answers on their whiteboards.*

*Bats are nocturnal creatures.*

See also the panel on **sentences**.

**state school** NOUN state schools
(*British*) a school which is funded by the government and which does not charge fees to pupils

**statesman** NOUN statesmen
a person, especially a man, who is important or skilled in governing a country
➤ **statesmanship** NOUN

**stateswoman** NOUN stateswomen
a woman who is important or skilled in governing a country

**static** ADJECTIVE
not moving or changing • *Prices have been static for a while.*

**static electricity** NOUN
electricity that is present in something but does not flow as current

**station** NOUN stations
❶ a stopping place for trains or buses with platforms and buildings for passengers and goods ❷ a building equipped for people who serve the public or for certain activities • *the police station* ❸ a broadcasting company with its own frequency ❹ a place where a person stands ready to do something ❺ (*old use*) a person's position or rank ❻ (*Australian/NZ*) a large sheep or cattle farm

**station** VERB stations, stationing, stationed
to put someone in a certain place for a purpose • *He was stationed at the door to take the tickets.*

**stationary** ADJECTIVE
not moving or still • *The car was stationary when the van hit it.*

SPELLING

**Stationary** is different from **stationery**:
• *a stationary vehicle* • *The shop sells books and stationery.*

**stationer** NOUN stationers
a shopkeeper who sells stationery
WORD ORIGIN from Latin *stationarius* = a tradesman (usually a bookseller) who had a shop or stand (as opposed to one who travelled about selling goods)

**stationery** NOUN
paper, envelopes, pens and other things used for writing

SPELLING

**Stationery** is different from **stationary**:
• *The shop sells books and stationery.* • *a stationary vehicle.*

**statistic** NOUN statistics
a piece of information expressed as a number • *These statistics show that the population has doubled.*
➤ **statistical** ADJECTIVE
➤ **statistically** ADVERB

**statistician** (say stat-is-**tish**-an) NOUN statisticians
an expert in statistics

**statistics** NOUN
the study of information based on the numbers of things

**statuary** NOUN
statues

**statue** NOUN statues
a model made of stone or metal to look like a person or animal

**statuesque** (say stat-yoo-**esk**) ADJECTIVE
like a statue in stillness or dignity

**statuette** NOUN statuettes
a small statue

**stature** NOUN
❶ a person's height • *He's quite small in stature.* ❷ the importance or reputation a person has because of their ability or achievements

**status** (say **stay**-tus) NOUN statuses
❶ a person's or thing's position or rank in relation to others ❷ high rank or social position ❸ the category that a person or thing is put into • *Scientists decided that Pluto should lose its status as a planet.* ❹ a message on a social networking website that tells people what you are doing or thinking

**status quo** (say stay-tus **kwoh**) NOUN
the state of affairs as it was before a change

**status symbol** NOUN status symbols
something that you own because it shows off

your wealth or position in society, rather than because you like it or need it

**statute** *NOUN* statutes
a law passed by a parliament
➤ **statutory** *ADJECTIVE*

**staunch** *ADJECTIVE*
firm and loyal • *our staunch supporters*
➤ **staunchly** *ADVERB*

**stave** *NOUN* staves
❶ a set of five horizontal lines on which music is written ❷ each of the curved strips of wood forming the side of a cask or tub

**stave** *VERB* staves, staving, staved or stove
to dent something or break a hole in it • *The collision stove in the front of the ship.*
➤ **stave something off** to keep something away or delay it • *I ate a banana to stave off hunger.*

**stay** *VERB* stays, staying, stayed
❶ to continue to be in the same place or condition; to remain somewhere ❷ to spend time in a place as a visitor ❸ to keep something or someone back or in control • *Only one thing stayed her hand.*
➤ **stay put** (*informal*) to remain in place

**stay** *NOUN* stays
❶ a time spent somewhere • *We didn't have time for a long stay.* ❷ a postponement • *a stay of execution* ❸ a support, especially a rope or wire holding up a mast or pole

**stead** *NOUN*
➤ **in a person's** or **thing's stead** instead of this person or thing
➤ **stand a person in good stead** to be very useful to someone

**steadfast** *ADJECTIVE*
firm and not changing • *a steadfast refusal*

**steadily** *ADVERB*
in an even and regular way; gradually and continuously • *The snow fell steadily.* • *Things got steadily worse.*

**steady** *ADJECTIVE* steadier, steadiest
❶ not shaking or moving; firm ❷ regular or constant; continuing the same • *They kept up a steady pace.*
➤ **steadiness** *NOUN*

**steady** *VERB* steadies, steadying, steadied
to make something steady or to become steady • *She steadied herself against the wall.*

**steak** *NOUN* steaks
a thick slice of meat (especially beef) or fish

**steal** *VERB* steals, stealing, stole, stolen
❶ to take and keep something that does not belong to you; to take something secretly or dishonestly ❷ to move secretly or without being noticed • *He stole out of the room.*

> SPELLING
>
> The past tense of **steal** is **stole** and the past participle is **stolen**.

**stealth** (say stelth) *NOUN*
doing something in a quiet and secret way so that you are not noticed • *She approached them with great stealth.*

**stealthy** (say stelth-ee) *ADJECTIVE* stealthier, stealthiest
quiet and secret, so as not to be noticed
➤ **stealthily** *ADVERB*

**steam** *NOUN*
the gas or vapour that comes from boiling water; this used to drive machinery
➤ **run out of steam** to have no energy left

**steam** *VERB* steams, steaming, steamed
❶ to give off steam ❷ to move somewhere by the power of steam • *The ship steamed down the river.* ❸ to cook food with steam • *a steamed pudding*
➤ **steam up** to be covered with mist or condensation • *The windows have steamed up.*

**steam engine** *NOUN* steam engines
an engine driven by steam

**steamer** *NOUN* steamers
❶ a steamship ❷ a container in which things are steamed

**steamroller** *NOUN* steamrollers
a heavy vehicle with a large roller used to flatten surfaces when making roads
**WORD ORIGIN** because the first ones were powered by steam

**steamship** *NOUN* steamships
a ship driven by steam

**steamy** *ADJECTIVE*
full of steam • *a steamy bathroom*

**steed** *NOUN* steeds (*old* or *poetical use*)
a horse

**steel** *NOUN* steels
❶ a strong metal made from iron and carbon ❷ a steel rod for sharpening knives

**steel** *VERB* steels, steeling, steeled
➤ **steel yourself** to find courage to face something difficult

a
b
c
d
e
f
g
h
i
j
k
l
m
n
o
p
q
r
s
t
u
v
w
x
y
z

**steel band** NOUN steel bands
a West Indian band of musicians who play instruments made from oil drums

**steel wool** NOUN
a mass of fine, sharp steel threads used for cleaning a surface or rubbing it smooth

**steely** ADJECTIVE
❶ like or to do with steel ❷ cold, hard and severe • *a steely glare*

**steep** ADJECTIVE
❶ sloping very sharply, not gradually ❷ (*informal*) unreasonably high • *a steep price*
➤ **steeply** ADVERB
➤ **steepness** NOUN

**steep** VERB steeps, steeping, steeped
to soak something thoroughly
➤ **be steeped in something** to be completely filled or familiar with something • *The story is steeped in mystery.*

**steepen** VERB steepens, steepening, steepened
to become steeper • *The path began to steepen.*

**steeple** NOUN steeples
a church tower with a spire on top

**steeplechase** NOUN steeplechases
a race across country or over hedges or fences WORD ORIGIN so called because the race originally finished at a distant church steeple which was always in view

**steeplejack** NOUN steeplejacks
a person who climbs tall chimneys or steeples to do repairs

**steer** VERB steers, steering, steered
to make a car, ship or bicycle etc. go in the direction you want; to guide something
➤ **steer clear of something** to take care to avoid something

**steer** NOUN steers
a young castrated bull kept for its beef

**steering wheel** NOUN steering wheels
a wheel for steering a vehicle

**steersman** NOUN steersmen
a person who steers a boat or ship

**stellar** ADJECTIVE
to do with a star or stars

**stem** NOUN stems
❶ the main central part of a tree, shrub or plant ❷ a thin part on which a leaf, flower or fruit is supported ❸ a thin upright part, e.g. the thin part of a wine glass between the bowl and the foot ❹ (*in grammar*) the main part of a verb or other word, to which endings are attached

**stem** VERB stems, stemming, stemmed
to stop the flow of something
➤ **stem from something** to come or result from something • *Many of her problems stemmed from lack of money.*

**stench** NOUN stenches
a very unpleasant smell

**stencil** NOUN stencils
a piece of card, metal or plastic with pieces cut out of it, used to produce a picture or design

**stencil** VERB stencils, stencilling, stencilled
to produce or decorate something with a stencil

**stentorian** ADJECTIVE
very loud and clear • *a stentorian voice*
WORD ORIGIN from the name of Stentor, a herald in ancient Greek legend who was said to be able to shout as loud as fifty men

**step** NOUN steps
❶ a movement made by lifting the foot and setting it down ❷ the sound of a person putting down their foot when walking or running ❸ each of the level surfaces on a stair or ladder for placing the foot ❹ each of a series of things done in some process or action • *The first step is to find somewhere to practise.*
➤ **in step** ❶ stepping in time with others in marching or dancing ❷ in agreement
➤ **watch your step** to be careful

**step** VERB steps, stepping, stepped
to tread or walk
➤ **step in** to become involved in a difficult situation in order to help
➤ **step on it** (*informal*) to hurry
➤ **step up something** to increase something

**stepbrother** NOUN stepbrothers
the son of one of your parents from an earlier or later marriage

**stepchild** NOUN stepchildren
a child that a person's husband or wife has from an earlier marriage
➤ **stepdaughter** ➤ **stepson** NOUN

**stepfather** NOUN stepfathers
a man who is married to your mother but was not your natural father

**stepladder** NOUN stepladders
a folding ladder with flat treads

**stepmother** NOUN stepmothers
a woman who is married to your father but
was not your natural mother

**steppe** NOUN steppes
a grassy plain with few trees, especially in
Russia

**stepping stone** NOUN stepping stones
❶ each of a line of stones put into a shallow
stream so that people can walk across ❷ a
way of achieving something or a stage in
achieving it • *Good exam results can be a
stepping stone to a career.*

**steps** PLURAL NOUN
a stepladder

**stepsister** NOUN stepsisters
the daughter of one of your parents from an
earlier or later marriage

**stereo** ADJECTIVE
stereophonic

**stereo** NOUN stereos
❶ stereophonic sound or recording ❷ a
stereophonic CD player, record player, etc.

**stereophonic** ADJECTIVE
using sound that comes from two different
directions to give a natural effect

**stereoscopic** ADJECTIVE
giving the effect of being three-dimensional,
e.g. in photographs

**stereotype** NOUN stereotypes
a fixed image or idea of a type of person or
thing that is widely held • *The stereotype of
a hero is one who is tall, strong, brave and
good-looking.* **WORD ORIGIN** originally = a
kind of printing block, from Greek *stereos* =
solid, three-dimensional (because the block
always produced the same words, like the fixed
idea in the modern meaning)

**sterile** ADJECTIVE
❶ clean and free from germs ❷ not able to
have children or reproduce
➤ **sterility** NOUN

**sterilize** (also **sterilise**) VERB sterilizes,
sterilizing, sterilized
❶ to make a thing free from germs, e.g. by
heating it ❷ to make a person or animal
unable to reproduce
➤ **sterilization** NOUN

**sterling** NOUN
British money

**sterling** ADJECTIVE
❶ genuine • *sterling silver* ❷ excellent; of
great worth • *her sterling qualities*

**stern** ADJECTIVE
strict and severe; not smiling • *He gave them
a stern look.* • *a stern warning*
➤ **sternness** NOUN

**stern** NOUN sterns
the back part of a ship

**sternly** ADVERB
in a stern way • *She looked at him sternly.*

**steroid** NOUN steroids
a substance of a kind that includes certain
hormones and other natural secretions

**stethoscope** NOUN stethoscopes
a device used by doctors for listening to
sounds in a person's body, e.g. heartbeats and
breathing **WORD ORIGIN** from Greek *stethos* =
breast + *skopein* = look at

**stew** VERB stews, stewing, stewed
to cook food slowly in liquid

**stew** NOUN stews
a dish of meat and vegetables cooked slowly
in liquid
➤ **in a stew** (*informal*) very worried or
agitated

**steward** NOUN stewards
❶ a man whose job is to look after the
passengers on a ship or aircraft ❷ an
official who keeps order or looks after the
arrangements at a large public event

**stewardess** NOUN stewardesses
a woman whose job is to look after the
passengers on a ship or aircraft

**stick** NOUN sticks
❶ a long thin piece of wood ❷ a walking
stick ❸ the implement used to hit the ball in
hockey, polo or other games ❹ a long thin
piece of something • *a stick of celery*

**stick** VERB sticks, sticking, stuck
❶ to push a thing into something • *Stick
a pin in it.* ❷ to fix something by glue or
as if by glue • *I need to stick a few stamps
on the parcel.* ❸ to become fixed and
unable to move • *The drawer keeps sticking.*
❹ (*informal*) to bear something or put up
with it • *I can't stick that noise!*
➤ **stick out** ❶ to come out from a surface or
to stand out from the surrounding area ❷ to
be very noticeable
➤ **stick to something** ❶ to remain faithful
to a promise or agreement ❷ to keep to
something and not change it • *He stuck to
his story.*
➤ **stick together** ❶ to stay together ❷ to
support each other
➤ **stick up for someone** (*informal*) to

a
b
c
d
e
f
g
h
i
j
k
l
m
n
o
p
q
r
s
t
u
v
w
x
y
z

**sticker** NOUN stickers
a sticky label or sign for sticking on
something

**sticking plaster** NOUN sticking plasters
(*British*) a strip of sticky material for covering
cuts

**stick insect** NOUN stick insects
an insect with a long thin body and legs,
which looks like a twig

**stickleback** NOUN sticklebacks
a small fish with sharp spines on its back

**stickler** NOUN sticklers
a person who insists on something • *The boss
is a stickler for punctuality.*

**sticky** ADJECTIVE stickier, stickiest
❶ able or likely to stick to things ❷ sticky
weather is hot and humid, causing
perspiration ❸ (*informal*) difficult or
awkward • *a sticky situation*
➤ **stickiness** NOUN
➤ **come to a sticky end** to die or end in a
painful or unpleasant way

**stiff** ADJECTIVE
❶ not bending, moving or changing its shape
easily • *The door handle is stiff.* ❷ not able
to move or bend the body easily • *I woke up
feeling very stiff.* ❸ thick and hard to stir • *a
stiff dough* ❹ difficult • *It was a stiff climb
to the top.* ❺ formal in manner; not friendly
❻ severe or strong • *a stiff breeze*
➤ **stiffness** NOUN

**stiffen** VERB stiffens, stiffening, stiffened
to become stiff or to make something stiff

**stiffly** ADVERB
❶ in a formal and unfriendly way • *'Thank
you,' she said stiffly.* ❷ in a way that shows
you cannot move your body easily • *He got
stiffly to his feet.*

**stifle** VERB stifles, stifling, stifled
❶ to stop something happening or
developing • *She stifled a yawn.* ❷ to make it
difficult for someone to breathe because of
heat or lack of fresh air

**stigma** NOUN stigmas
❶ a mark of disgrace; a stain on a reputation
❷ the part of a pistil that receives the pollen
in pollination

support or defend someone
➤ **be stuck with something** (*informal*) to be
unable to avoid something unwelcome

**stile** NOUN stiles
an arrangement of steps or bars for people to
climb over a fence

**stiletto** NOUN stilettos
a dagger with a narrow blade

**stiletto heel** NOUN stiletto heels
a high pointed shoe heel

**still** ADJECTIVE
❶ not moving • *the still water of a mountain
lake* ❷ silent • *a still night* ❸ not fizzy • *still
mineral water*

**still** ADVERB
❶ without moving • *Stand still.* ❷ up to
this or that time • *He was still there.* ❸ in a
greater amount or degree • *You can do still
better.* ❹ nevertheless • *They've lost. Still,
they tried and that was good.*

**still** VERB stills, stilling, stilled
to make something still • *I tried to still the
trembling in my hand.*

**still** NOUN stills
❶ a photograph of a scene from a cinema
film ❷ an apparatus for distilling alcohol or
other liquid

**stillborn** ADJECTIVE
born dead

**still life** NOUN still lifes
a painting of an arrangement of objects,
especially fruit, flowers or ornaments

**stillness** NOUN
being quiet, with nothing moving • *A bird's
cry broke the stillness.*

**stilted** ADJECTIVE
stiffly formal

**stilts** PLURAL NOUN
❶ a pair of poles with supports for the feet so
that the user can walk high above the ground
❷ posts for supporting a house built above
marshy ground

**stimulant** NOUN stimulants
a drug or substance that makes you feel more
awake and active for a while

**stimulate** VERB stimulates, stimulating,
stimulated
❶ to make someone excited or enthusiastic
❷ to encourage something to develop • *The
programme has stimulated a lot of interest in
her work.*
➤ **stimulation** NOUN

**stimulus** NOUN stimuli
something that encourages a thing to develop
or produces a reaction

**sting** NOUN stings
❶ a sharp-pointed part of an animal or plant, often containing a poison, that can cause a wound ❷ a painful wound caused by this part

**sting** VERB stings, stinging, stung
❶ to wound or hurt someone with a sting ❷ to feel a sharp pain ❸ to make someone feel upset or hurt • *I was stung by this criticism.* ❹ (*informal*) to cheat someone by charging them too much

**stingray** NOUN stingrays
a fish with a flat body, fins like wings and a poisonous spine in its tail

**stingy** (say **stin**-jee) ADJECTIVE stingier, stingiest
mean, not generous; giving or given in small amounts
➤ **stinginess** NOUN

**stink** NOUN stinks
❶ an unpleasant smell ❷ (*informal*) an unpleasant fuss or protest

**stink** VERB stinks, stinking, stank or stunk
to have an unpleasant smell

**stint** NOUN stints
a fixed amount of work to be done

**stint** VERB stints, stinting, stinted
to stint on something is to be sparing with it and not use much • *Don't stint on the cream.*

**stipend** (say **sty**-pend) NOUN stipends
a salary, especially one paid to a clergyman

**stipple** VERB stipples, stippling, stippled
to paint, draw or engrave a design in small dots

**stipulate** VERB stipulates, stipulating, stipulated
to insist on something as part of an agreement
➤ **stipulation** NOUN

**stir** VERB stirs, stirring, stirred
❶ to mix a liquid or soft mixture by moving a spoon etc. round and round in it ❷ to move slightly or start to move after sleeping or being still • *She didn't stir all afternoon.* ❸ to make someone feel a strong emotion • *The story stirred my imagination.*
➤ **stir something up** to excite or arouse something • *They are always stirring up trouble.*

**stir** NOUN
❶ the action of stirring ❷ strong public feeling or excitement • *The news caused a stir.*

**stir-fry** VERB stir-fries, stir-frying, stir-fried
to cook something by frying it quickly over a high heat while stirring and tossing it

**stir-fry** NOUN stir-fries
a dish cooked by stir-frying

**stirring** ADJECTIVE
making people feel strong emotion • *a stirring speech*

**stirrup** NOUN stirrups
a metal part that hangs from each side of a horse's saddle and supports the rider's foot

**stitch** NOUN stitches
❶ a loop of thread made in sewing or knitting ❷ a method of arranging the threads • *an embroidery stitch* ❸ a sudden sharp pain in your side, caused by running

**stitch** VERB stitches, stitching, stitched
to sew or fasten something with stitches

**stoat** NOUN stoats
a kind of weasel, also called an ermine

**stock** NOUN stocks
❶ a number of things kept ready to be sold or used ❷ farm animals; livestock ❸ the line of a person's ancestors • *a man of Irish stock* ❹ a liquid used in cooking, made from the juices you get by stewing meat, fish or vegetables ❺ a number of shares in a company's capital ❻ the main stem of a tree or plant ❼ the base, holder or handle of an implement or weapon ❽ a garden flower with a sweet smell
➤ **take stock** to make an overall assessment of a situation

**stock** VERB stocks, stocking, stocked
❶ to keep a supply of goods to sell ❷ to provide a place with a stock of something
➤ **stock up** to buy a supply of goods

**stockade** NOUN stockades
a fence made of stakes

**stockbroker** NOUN stockbrokers
a person who buys and sells stocks and shares for clients

**stock car** NOUN stock cars
an ordinary car strengthened for use in races where deliberate bumping is allowed

**stock exchange** NOUN stock exchanges
a country's central place for buying and selling stocks and shares

**stocking** NOUN stockings
a piece of clothing covering the foot and part or all of the leg

**stock market** NOUN stock markets
❶ a stock exchange ❷ the buying and selling of stocks and shares

**stockpile** NOUN stockpiles
a large stock of things kept in reserve
➤ **stockpile** VERB

**stocks** PLURAL NOUN
a wooden framework with holes for a seated person's legs, in which criminals were locked as a punishment

**stock-still** ADJECTIVE
quite still

**stocktaking** NOUN
the counting, listing and checking of the amount of stock held by a shop or business

**stocky** ADJECTIVE stockier, stockiest
short and solidly built • a stocky man

**stodge** NOUN
(British) stodgy food

**stodgy** ADJECTIVE stodgier, stodgiest (British)
❶ stodgy food is heavy and filling ❷ dull and boring • a stodgy book

**stoical** (say stoh-ik-al) ADJECTIVE
bearing pain or difficulties calmly without complaining
➤ **stoically** ADVERB
➤ **stoicism** NOUN
**WORD ORIGIN** named after ancient Greek philosophers called Stoics

**stoke** VERB stokes, stoking, stoked
to put fuel in a furnace or on a fire
➤ **stoker** NOUN

**stole**
past tense of **steal**

**stole** NOUN stoles
a wide piece of material worn round the shoulders by women

**stolid** ADJECTIVE
not showing much emotion or excitement
➤ **stolidly** ADVERB
➤ **stolidity** NOUN

**stomach** NOUN stomachs
❶ the part of your body where food starts to be digested ❷ the front part of your body that contains your stomach; your abdomen

**stomach** VERB stomachs, stomaching, stomached
to tolerate something or put up with it

**stone** NOUN stones
❶ a piece of rock ❷ stones or rock as material, e.g. for building ❸ a jewel ❹ the

hard case round the kernel of plums, cherries, peaches, etc. ❺ a unit of weight equal to 14 pounds (6.35 kg) • She weighs 8 stone.

**stone** VERB stones, stoning, stoned
❶ to throw stones at someone ❷ to remove the stones from fruit

**Stone Age** NOUN
the earliest period of human history, when tools and weapons were made of stone

**stone circle** NOUN stone circles
a circle of large stones or boulders, put up in prehistoric times

**stone-cold** ADJECTIVE
extremely cold

**stoned** ADJECTIVE (informal)
under the influence of drugs or alcohol

**stone-deaf** ADJECTIVE
completely deaf

**stoneware** NOUN
a kind of pottery with a hard shiny surface
• a stoneware jar

**stony** ADJECTIVE
❶ full of stones ❷ hard like stone
❸ unfriendly and not answering • They listened to him in stony silence.

**stooge** NOUN stooges (informal)
❶ a comedian's assistant, used as a target for jokes ❷ an assistant who does dull or routine work

**stool** NOUN stools
❶ a movable seat without arms or a back ❷ a lump of faeces

**stoop** VERB stoops, stooping, stooped
❶ to bend your body forwards and down
❷ to lower your standards of behaviour • He would not stoop to cheating.

**stoop** NOUN stoops
❶ a way of standing or walking with your head and shoulders bent forwards ❷ (North American & S. African) a porch, small verandah or set of steps in front of a house

**stop** VERB stops, stopping, stopped
❶ to come to an end or bring something to an end; to no longer do something ❷ to be no longer moving or working • A car stopped in front of us. ❸ to prevent something happening or continuing • They put a fence up to stop the dog getting out. ❹ to fill a hole or gap • We need to stop up the other end of the tube. ❺ to stay somewhere for a short time

**stop** *NOUN* **stops**
❶ stopping; a pause or end • *She brought the car to a stop.* ❷ a place where a bus or train regularly stops ❸ a lever or knob that controls pitch in a wind instrument or allows organ pipes to sound

**stopcock** *NOUN* **stopcocks**
a valve controlling the flow of liquid or gas in a pipe

**stopgap** *NOUN* **stopgaps**
a temporary substitute

**stoppage** *NOUN* **stoppages**
❶ an interruption in the work of a factory or business ❷ a break in play during a game ❸ a blockage in something

**stopper** *NOUN* **stoppers**
a plug for closing a bottle or sealing a hole

**stop press** *NOUN*
(*British*) late news put into a newspaper after printing has started **WORD ORIGIN** because the printing presses are stopped to allow the late news to be added

**stopwatch** *NOUN* **stopwatches**
a watch that can be started and stopped when you wish, used for timing races

**storage** *NOUN*
the storing of things

**store** *NOUN* **stores**
❶ a supply of things kept for future use ❷ a place where things are kept until they are needed ❸ a shop, especially a large one ❹ (*North American*) any shop
➤ **in store** going to happen soon • *There's a surprise in store for you.*
➤ **set store by something** to value something greatly

**store** *VERB* **stores, storing, stored**
to keep things until they are needed

**storey** *NOUN* **storeys**
one whole floor of a building

**SPELLING**

Storey is different from story: • *the second storey of the building* • *Read me a story.*

**stork** *NOUN* **storks**
a large bird with long legs and a long beak

**storm** *NOUN* **storms**
❶ a period of bad weather with strong winds, rain or snow and often thunder and lightning ❷ a violent attack or outburst • *a storm of protest*

➤ **a storm in a teacup** a great fuss over something unimportant

**storm** *VERB* **storms, storming, stormed**
❶ to move or behave violently or angrily • *He stormed out of the room.* ❷ to suddenly attack and capture a place • *They stormed the castle.*

**stormy** *ADJECTIVE* **stormier, stormiest**
❶ having a storm or a lot of storms • *It was a stormy night.* ❷ loud and angry • *a stormy argument*

**story** *NOUN* **stories**
❶ an account of a real or imaginary event ❷ the plot of a novel, play or film ❸ (*informal*) a lie • *Don't tell stories!*

**SPELLING**

Story is different from storey: • *Read me a story.* • *the second storey of the building*

**stout** *ADJECTIVE*
❶ rather fat ❷ thick and strong • *a stout stick* ❸ brave and determined • *a stout defender of human rights*
➤ **stoutly** *ADVERB*
➤ **stoutness** *NOUN*

**stout** *NOUN*
a kind of dark beer

**stove** *NOUN* **stoves**
❶ a device containing an oven or ovens ❷ a device for heating a room

**stove** *VERB*
past tense of **stave**

**stow** *VERB* **stows, stowing, stowed**
to pack or store something away • *We stowed our backpacks above the seats.*
➤ **stow away** to hide on a ship or aircraft so that you can travel without paying

**stowaway** *NOUN* **stowaways**
someone who stows away on a ship or aircraft

**straddle** *VERB* **straddles, straddling, straddled**
❶ to sit or stand with your legs either side of something ❷ to be built across something • *A long bridge straddles the river.*

**straggle** *VERB* **straggles, straggling, straggled**
❶ to grow or spread in an untidy way • *Brambles straggled across the path.* ❷ to walk too slowly and not keep up with the rest of a group
➤ **straggler** *NOUN*
➤ **straggly** *ADJECTIVE*

**straight** ADJECTIVE
❶ going continuously in one direction; not curving or bending ❷ level, horizontal or upright • *Is this picture straight?* ❸ tidy; in proper order ❹ honest and frank • *Give me a straight answer.*
➤ **straightness** NOUN

**straight** ADVERB
❶ in a straight line or manner • *Go straight on, then turn left.* ❷ directly; without delay • *I went straight home.*

SPELLING
Take care not to confuse with **strait**.

**straightaway, straight away** ADVERB
immediately; at once

**straighten** VERB straightens, straightening, straightened
❶ to make something straight • *He straightened his tie.* ❷ to become straight; to stand up straight • *She straightened up with pride.*

**straightforward** ADJECTIVE
❶ easy to understand or do, not complicated ❷ honest and frank

**strain** VERB strains, straining, strained
❶ to injure a part of your body by stretching or using it too much ❷ to put a lot of pressure on something ❸ to stretch something tightly ❹ to make a great effort • *I was straining to see what was happening.* ❺ to put something through a sieve or filter to separate liquid from solid matter

**strain** NOUN strains
❶ the process or force of straining • *The rope broke under the strain.* ❷ an injury caused by straining ❸ the effect on someone of too much work or worry ❹ something that uses up strength, patience or resources ❺ a part of a tune ❻ a breed or variety of an animal, plant, etc.; a line of descent ❼ an inherited characteristic • *There's an artistic strain in the family.*

**strainer** NOUN strainers
a device for straining liquids • *a tea strainer*

**strait** NOUN straits
a narrow stretch of water connecting two seas

SPELLING
Take care not to confuse with **straight**.

**straitened** ADJECTIVE
➤ **in straitened circumstances** short of money

**straitjacket** NOUN straitjackets
a strong jacket-like piece of clothing put round a violent person to tie their arms

**strait-laced** ADJECTIVE
very prim and proper

**straits** PLURAL NOUN
a strait • *the Straits of Dover*
➤ **be in dire straits** to have severe difficulties

**strand** NOUN strands
❶ each of the threads or wires twisted together to form a rope, yarn or cable ❷ a single thread or hair ❸ an idea, theme or story that forms part of a whole • *a novel with several strands*

**stranded** ADJECTIVE
❶ left on sand or rocks in shallow water • *a stranded ship* ❷ left in a difficult or lonely position • *We were stranded when our car broke down.*

**strange** ADJECTIVE
❶ unusual or surprising ❷ not known or seen or experienced before • *a strange town*
➤ **strangeness** NOUN

**strangely** ADVERB
in a strange way • *The streets were strangely quiet.*

**stranger** NOUN strangers
❶ a person you do not know ❷ a person who is in a place that they do not know • *Actually, I'm a stranger here myself.*

**strangle** VERB strangles, strangling, strangled
❶ to kill someone by squeezing their throat to prevent them breathing ❷ to restrict something so that it does not develop
➤ **strangler** NOUN

**strangulated** ADJECTIVE
sounding as though the throat is being tightly squeezed • *a strangulated cry*

**strangulation** NOUN
killing someone by strangling them

**strap** NOUN straps
a flat strip of leather, cloth or plastic for fastening things or holding them in place

**strap** VERB straps, strapping, strapped
to fasten or bind something with a strap or straps

**strapping** ADJECTIVE
tall and healthy-looking • *a strapping lad*

**strata**
plural of **stratum**

**stratagem** NOUN stratagems
a cunning method of achieving something; a plan or trick

**strategic** ADJECTIVE
❶ to do with strategy ❷ giving you an advantage • *a strategic move*
➤ **strategically** ADVERB

**strategist** NOUN strategists
an expert in strategy

**strategy** NOUN strategies
❶ a plan or policy to achieve something • *our economic strategy* ❷ the planning of a war or campaign. Compare with **tactics**.

**stratified** ADJECTIVE
arranged in strata
➤ **stratification** NOUN

**stratosphere** NOUN
a layer of the atmosphere between about 10 and 60 kilometres above the earth's surface

**stratum** (say strah-tum) NOUN strata
a layer or level • *You can see several strata of rock in the cliff.*

> **USAGE**
>
> The word strata is a plural. It is incorrect to say 'a strata' or 'this strata'; correct use is *this stratum* or *these strata*.

**straw** NOUN straws
❶ dry cut stalks of corn ❷ a narrow tube for drinking through

**strawberry** NOUN strawberries
a small red juicy fruit, with its seeds on the outside (WORD ORIGIN) perhaps because straw is put around the plants to keep slugs away

**stray** VERB strays, straying, strayed
to leave a group or proper place and wander; to become lost

**stray** ADJECTIVE
❶ that has strayed; wandering around lost • *a stray cat* ❷ found on its own, separated from the others • *a stray sock*

**stray** NOUN strays
a stray dog or cat

**streak** NOUN streaks
❶ a long thin line or mark ❷ a trace or sign of something • *a streak of cruelty* ❸ a spell of success or good fortune • *on a winning streak*
➤ **streaky** ADJECTIVE

**streak** VERB streaks, streaking, streaked
❶ to mark something with streaks • *His face was streaked with tears.* ❷ to move very

quickly ❸ to run naked in a public place for fun or to get attention
➤ **streaker** NOUN

**streaky bacon** NOUN
(*British*) bacon with alternate strips of lean and fat

**stream** NOUN streams
❶ water flowing in a channel; a brook or small river ❷ liquid flowing in one direction ❸ a number of things moving in the same direction, such as traffic ❹ a group in which children of similar ability are placed in a school

**stream** VERB streams, streaming, streamed
❶ to move in a strong fast flow • *Traffic streamed across the junction.* ❷ to produce a stream of liquid • *Her eyes were streaming.* ❸ to arrange schoolchildren in streams according to their ability

**streamer** NOUN streamers
a long narrow ribbon or strip of paper

**streamline** VERB streamlines, streamlining, streamlined
❶ to give something a smooth shape that helps it to move easily through air or water ❷ to organize something so that it works more efficiently
➤ **streamlined** ADJECTIVE

**street** NOUN streets
a road with houses beside it in a city or village

**strength** NOUN strengths
❶ how strong a person or thing is; being strong ❷ an ability or good quality • *Patience is your great strength.*

> **SPELLING**
>
> There is a silent g after the n in strength.

**strengthen** VERB strengthens, strengthening, strengthened
to become stronger or to make something stronger • *These exercises will help to strengthen your stomach muscles.*

**strenuous** ADJECTIVE
needing or using great effort • *strenuous exercise*
➤ **strenuously** ADVERB

**stress** NOUN stresses
❶ a force that presses, pulls or twists something ❷ emphasis, especially the extra force with which you pronounce part of a word or phrase ❸ worry and pressure caused

by having too many problems or too much
to do

**stress** *VERB* stresses, stressing, stressed
❶ to pronounce part of a word or phrase
with extra emphasis ❷ to emphasize a point
or idea • *I must stress the importance of
arriving on time.* ❸ to make someone suffer
stress

**stressed** *ADJECTIVE*
too anxious and tired to be able to relax

**stressful** *ADJECTIVE*
causing worry and pressure • *a stressful job*

**stretch** *VERB* stretches, stretching, stretched
❶ to pull something or be pulled so that
it becomes longer or wider or larger ❷ to
extend or be continuous • *The wall stretches
all the way round the park.* ❸ to push out
your arms and legs as far as you can ❹ to
make use of all your ability or intelligence
• *This course should really stretch you.*
➤ **stretch out** to lie down with your arms
and legs at full length

**stretch** *NOUN* stretches
❶ the action of stretching • *I got up and had
a good stretch.* ❷ a continuous period of
time or area of land or water

**stretcher** *NOUN* stretchers
a framework for carrying a sick or injured
person

**strew** *VERB* strews, strewing, strewed, strewn
or strewed
to scatter things over a surface • *Paper cups
were strewn over the floor.*

**stricken** *ADJECTIVE*
overcome or strongly affected by an illness or
a feeling such as grief or fear

**strict** *ADJECTIVE*
❶ demanding that people obey rules and
behave well • *a strict teacher* ❷ complete or
exact • *in strict confidence* • *She left strict
instructions that she wasn't to be disturbed.*
➤ **strictness** *NOUN*

**strictly** *ADVERB*
completely or exactly • *Eating in the library is
strictly forbidden.* • *That is not strictly true.*

**stride** *VERB* strides, striding, strode, stridden
to walk with long steps

**stride** *NOUN* strides
❶ a long step when walking or running ❷ a
step that helps you make progress • *Scientists
are making great strides in the search for a
cure.*
➤ **get into your stride** to settle into a fast

and steady pace of working
➤ **take something in your stride** to cope
with something without difficulty

**strident** (say **stry**-dent) *ADJECTIVE*
loud and harsh
➤ **stridently** *ADVERB*

**strife** *NOUN*
conflict; fighting or quarrelling

**strike** *VERB* strikes, striking, struck
❶ to hit a person or thing ❷ to attack or
afflict people suddenly • *Then disaster struck.*
❸ to make an impression on someone's mind
• *She strikes me as being lazy.* ❹ to light a
match by rubbing it against a rough surface
❺ to refuse to work as a protest against pay
or conditions ❻ to produce coins or medals
by pressing or stamping metal ❼ to sound
or ring a number of times • *The clock struck
ten.* ❽ to find gold or oil by digging or drilling
❾ to go in a certain direction • *We struck
north through the forest.*
➤ **strike something off** or **out** to cross
something out
➤ **strike up** a band strikes up when it begins
playing
➤ **strike something up** to start a friendship
or conversation

**strike** *NOUN* strikes
❶ a hit ❷ a military attack • *an air strike*
❸ refusing to work as a way of making a
protest ❹ a sudden discovery of gold or oil
➤ **go on strike** to stop working as a protest

**striker** *NOUN* strikers
❶ a worker who is on strike ❷ a football
player whose main job is to try to score goals

**striking** *ADJECTIVE*
❶ impressive or attractive • *Her eyes were
her most striking feature.* ❷ so unusual or
interesting that you cannot help noticing it
• *The resemblance between them is striking.*
➤ **strikingly** *ADVERB*

**string** *NOUN* strings
❶ thin cord made of twisted threads, used to
fasten or tie things; a piece of this or similar
material ❷ a piece of wire or cord stretched
and vibrated to produce sounds in a musical
instrument ❸ a line or series of things • *a
string of buses*

**string** *VERB* strings, stringing, strung
❶ to hang something on a string • *Lights
were strung from tree to tree.* ❷ to fit
something with a string • *The archer calmly
strung his bow.* ❸ to thread pearls or beads
on a string ❹ to remove the tough fibre from

beans
➤ **string someone along** to mislead someone over a period of time
➤ **string something out ❶** to spread something out in a line **❷** to make something last a long time

**stringed** ADJECTIVE
stringed instruments are ones that have strings, especially members of the violin family

**stringent** (say **strin**-jent) ADJECTIVE
strict and precise • *There are stringent rules about this.*

**strings** PLURAL NOUN
the stringed instruments of an orchestra

**stringy** ADJECTIVE
❶ long and thin, like string ❷ containing tough fibres

**strip** VERB strips, stripping, stripped
❶ to take a covering or layer off something ❷ to undress ❸ to take something away from someone as a punishment • *He was stripped of his title.*

**strip** NOUN strips
❶ a long narrow piece or area ❷ the distinctive clothes worn by a sports team while playing

**strip cartoon** NOUN strip cartoons
a series of drawings telling a story

**stripe** NOUN stripes
❶ a long narrow band of colour ❷ a strip of cloth worn on the sleeve of a uniform to show the wearer's rank

**striped, stripy** ADJECTIVE
marked with a pattern of stripes • *a red and white striped dress*

**strip light** NOUN strip lights
(*British*) a fluorescent lamp in the form of a tube

**stripling** NOUN striplings
a youth

**stripper** NOUN strippers
❶ a tool or substance used for stripping paint ❷ a person who performs striptease

**striptease** NOUN stripteases
an entertainment in which a person slowly undresses

**strive** VERB strives, striving, strove, striven
to try hard to do or get something • *He was always striving for perfection.*

**strobe** NOUN strobes (short for **stroboscope**)
a light that flashes on and off continuously

**stroke** NOUN strokes
❶ a movement of the arm when hitting something, swimming or rowing ❷ a style of swimming ❸ a movement you make when you are writing or painting • *a brush stroke* ❹ an action or effort • *a stroke of genius* ❺ the sound made by a clock striking ❻ a sudden illness that often causes paralysis ❼ an act of stroking something • *He gave the cat a stroke.*

**stroke** VERB strokes, stroking, stroked
to move your hand gently along something

**stroll** VERB strolls, strolling, strolled
to walk in a leisurely way

**stroll** NOUN strolls
a short leisurely walk
➤ **stroller** NOUN

**strong** ADJECTIVE
❶ having great power, energy or effect ❷ not easy to break, damage or defeat • *The gate was held by a strong chain.* ❸ great in intensity • *strong feelings* ❹ having a lot of flavour or smell ❺ having a certain number of members • *an army 5,000 strong*

**strong** ADVERB
➤ **be going strong** to be making good progress

**stronghold** NOUN strongholds
❶ a fortified place ❷ an area where many people live or think in a particular way • *a Tory stronghold*

**strongly** ADVERB
❶ in a strong way; with strength • *They fought back strongly.* ❷ very much • *The room smelt strongly of perfume.*

**strong point** NOUN strong points
a strength; something that you are very good at • *Maths is her strong point.*

**strongroom** NOUN strongrooms
a room designed to protect valuable things from fire and theft

**strontium** NOUN
a soft silvery metal (**WORD ORIGIN**) named after *Strontia* in the Scottish highlands, where it was discovered

**strove**
past tense of **strive**

**structural** ADJECTIVE
to do with the way that something is built or

a
b
c
d
e
f
g
h
i
j
k
l
m
n
o
p
q
r
s
t
u
v
w
x
y
z

constructed • *a structural fault*
> **structurally** ADVERB

**structure** NOUN **structures**
❶ something that has been constructed or
built ❷ the way something is constructed or
organized

**structure** VERB **structures, structuring,
structured**
to organize or arrange something into a
system or pattern • *You need to structure
your arguments with more care.*

**struggle** VERB **struggles, struggling, struggled**
❶ to move your arms and legs and wriggle
fiercely in trying to get free ❷ to try very
hard to do something difficult • *She was
struggling to keep up with the others.* ❸ to
try to overcome an opponent or a problem

**struggle** NOUN **struggles**
❶ the act of struggling • *He lost his glasses
in the struggle.* ❷ a hard fight or great effort

**strum** VERB **strums, strumming, strummed**
to sound a guitar by running your fingers
across its strings

**strut** VERB **struts, strutting, strutted**
to walk proudly or stiffly • *A peacock strutted
across the lawn.*

**strut** NOUN **struts**
❶ a bar of wood or metal that strengthens a
framework ❷ a strutting walk

**strychnine** (say **strik**-neen) NOUN
a bitter poisonous substance

**stub** NOUN **stubs**
❶ a short stump left when the rest has been
used or worn down ❷ the part of a ticket or
cheque that you keep as a record

**stub** VERB **stubs, stubbing, stubbed**
to bump your toe painfully
> **stub something out** to put out a cigarette
by pressing it against something hard

**stubble** NOUN
❶ the short stalks of corn left in the ground
after the harvest is cut ❷ short hairs growing
on a man's chin when he has not shaved

**stubborn** ADJECTIVE
❶ determined not to change your ideas or
ways; obstinate ❷ difficult to remove or deal
with • *stubborn stains*
> **stubbornly** ADVERB
> **stubbornness** NOUN

**stubby** ADJECTIVE
short and thick

**stucco** NOUN
plaster or cement used for coating walls and
ceilings, often moulded into decorations
> **stuccoed** ADJECTIVE

**stuck**
past tense and past participle of **stick**

**stuck** ADJECTIVE
unable to move or make progress • *I'm stuck.*

**stuck-up** ADJECTIVE (*informal*)
conceited or snobbish

**stud** NOUN **studs**
❶ a small curved lump or knob ❷ a device
like a button on a stalk, used to fasten a
detachable collar to a shirt ❸ a number of
horses kept for breeding; the place where
they are kept ❹ a stallion

**studded** ADJECTIVE
❶ covered with studs or other decorations
• *The necklace was studded with jewels.*
❷ scattered or sprinkled with something
• *The sky was studded with stars.*

**student** NOUN **students**
a person who studies a subject, especially at a
college or university

**studied** ADJECTIVE
not natural but done with deliberate effort
• *She answered with studied indifference.*

**studio** NOUN **studios**
❶ the room where an artist or photographer
works ❷ a place where cinema films are made
❸ a room from which radio or television
broadcasts are made or recorded

**studious** ADJECTIVE
spending a lot of time studying or reading

**studiously** ADVERB
carefully and deliberately • *She studiously
avoided answering the question.*

**study** VERB **studies, studying, studied**
❶ to spend time learning about something
❷ to look at something carefully • *She
studied his face for a moment.*

**study** NOUN **studies**
❶ the process of studying ❷ a subject
studied; a piece of research ❸ a room used
for studying or writing ❹ a piece of music for
playing as an exercise ❺ a drawing done for
practice or in preparation for another work

**stuff** NOUN
❶ a substance or material • *What's this
stuff at the bottom of the glass?* ❷ a group
of things or belongings • *Leave your stuff
outside.*

**stuff** VERB stuffs, stuffing, stuffed
❶ to fill something tightly ❷ to fill something with stuffing ❸ to push a thing roughly into something • *He stuffed the notebook into his pocket.* ❹ (informal) to eat greedily

**stuffing** NOUN
❶ material used to fill the inside of something ❷ a savoury mixture put into meat or poultry before cooking

**stuffy** ADJECTIVE stuffier, stuffiest
❶ a stuffy room is badly ventilated, without enough fresh air ❷ with blocked breathing passages • *a stuffy nose* ❸ formal and boring
➤ **stuffily** ADVERB
➤ **stuffiness** NOUN

**stumble** VERB stumbles, stumbling, stumbled
❶ to trip and lose your balance ❷ to make a mistake or hesitate while you are speaking or doing something
➤ **stumble across** or **on something** to find something by chance

**stumbling block** NOUN stumbling blocks
an obstacle; something that causes difficulty

**stump** NOUN stumps
❶ the bottom of a tree trunk left in the ground when the rest has fallen or been cut down ❷ something left when the main part is cut off or worn down ❸ each of the three upright sticks of a wicket in cricket

**stump** VERB stumps, stumping, stumped
❶ to be too difficult or puzzling for someone • *The last question stumped everyone.* ❷ to walk stiffly or noisily ❸ in cricket, to stump the person batting is to get them out by knocking the bails off the stumps while the person is standing out of the crease
➤ **stump up** (informal) to produce the money needed to pay for something

**stumpy** ADJECTIVE
short and thick • *stumpy legs*

**stun** VERB stuns, stunning, stunned
❶ to knock a person unconscious ❷ to daze or shock someone • *She was stunned by the news.*

**stunning** ADJECTIVE
extremely beautiful or attractive
➤ **stunningly** ADVERB

**stunt** NOUN stunts
❶ something daring done as a performance or as part of the action of a film ❷ something unusual done to attract attention • *a publicity stunt*

**stunt** VERB stunts, stunting, stunted
to prevent a thing from growing or developing normally • *a stunted tree*

**stupefy** VERB stupefies, stupefying, stupefied
to make a person dazed
➤ **stupefaction** NOUN

**stupendous** ADJECTIVE
amazing or tremendous
➤ **stupendously** ADVERB

**stupid** ADJECTIVE
❶ not clever or thoughtful ❷ without reason or common sense
➤ **stupidly** ADVERB
➤ **stupidity** NOUN

**stupor** (say **stew**-per) NOUN stupors
a state of being dazed or only partly conscious • *He was asleep, in a drunken stupor.*

**sturdy** ADJECTIVE sturdier, sturdiest
strong and solid • *The branch looked sturdy enough.*
➤ **sturdily** ADVERB
➤ **sturdiness** NOUN

**sturgeon** NOUN sturgeon
a large edible fish

**stutter** VERB stutters, stuttering, stuttered
to keep repeating the sounds at the beginning of words

**stutter** NOUN stutters
a tendency to stutter

**sty** NOUN sties or, in sense 2, styes
❶ a pigsty ❷ (also stye) a sore swelling on an eyelid

**style** NOUN styles
❶ the way something is done, made, said or written • *a style of architecture* ❷ fashion or elegance ❸ the part of a pistil that supports the stigma in a plant

**style** VERB styles, styling, styled
to design or arrange something, especially in a fashionable style

**stylish** ADJECTIVE
fashionable and elegant • *a stylish black dress*

**stylistic** ADJECTIVE
to do with the style of something

**stylus** NOUN styluses or styli
the device like a needle that travels in the grooves of a record to produce the sound

**suave** (say swahv) ADJECTIVE
polite in a charming and confident way

a
b
c
d
e
f
g
h
i
j
k
l
m
n
o
p
q
r
s
t
u
v
w
x
y
z

> **suavely** ADVERB
> **suavity** NOUN

**sub** NOUN **subs** (informal)
❶ a submarine ❷ a subscription ❸ a substitute

**subaltern** NOUN **subalterns**
an army officer ranking below a captain

**sub-aqua** ADJECTIVE
to do with underwater sports, such as diving

**subatomic** ADJECTIVE
❶ smaller than an atom ❷ forming part of an atom

**subconscious** ADJECTIVE
to do with mental processes of which we are not fully aware but which influence our actions

**subconscious** NOUN
the hidden part of your mind that influences your actions without you being fully aware of it

**subcontinent** NOUN **subcontinents**
a large mass of land that forms part of a continent • *the Indian subcontinent*

**subcontractor** NOUN **subcontractors**
a person or company hired by another company to do a particular part of their work

**subdivide** VERB **subdivides, subdividing, subdivided**
to divide something again or into smaller parts
> **subdivision** NOUN

**subdue** VERB **subdues, subduing, subdued**
❶ to overcome someone or bring them under control ❷ to make a person or animal quieter or gentler
> **subdued** ADJECTIVE

**subject** NOUN **subjects**
❶ the person or thing being talked or written about or dealt with ❷ something that is studied ❸ (in grammar) the word or words naming who or what does the action of a verb, e.g. *'The book'* in *The book fell off the table.* ❹ someone who is ruled by a monarch or government

**subject** ADJECTIVE
ruled by a monarch or government; not independent
> **subject to something** depending on something or likely to be affected by it • *Our decision is subject to your approval.* • *Trains are subject to delays because of flooding.*

**subject** (say sub-**jekt**) VERB **subjects, subjecting, subjected**
❶ to make a person or thing undergo something • *They subjected him to hours of questioning.* ❷ to bring a country under your control
> **subjection** NOUN

**subjective** ADJECTIVE
❶ based on a person's own tastes, feelings or opinions. Compare with **objective**. ❷ existing only in a person's mind and not produced by things outside it

**subjugate** VERB **subjugates, subjugating, subjugated**
to defeat a country or group of people and bring the people under your control
> **subjugation** NOUN

**subjunctive** NOUN **subjunctives**
the form of a verb used to indicate what is imagined or wished or possible. There are only a few cases where it is commonly used in English, e.g. *'were'* in *if I were you* and *'save'* in *God save the Queen.*

**sublime** ADJECTIVE
❶ noble or impressive • *sublime poetry*
❷ extreme; not caring about the consequences • *with sublime carelessness*

**submarine** NOUN **submarines**
a ship that can travel under water

**submarine** ADJECTIVE
under the sea • *They laid a submarine cable.*

**submerge** VERB **submerges, submerging, submerged**
to go under water or to put something under water • *The boat was now partly submerged.*
> **submersion** NOUN

**submission** NOUN **submissions**
❶ submitting to someone • *He bowed his head in submission.* ❷ something that you submit or offer for consideration

**submissive** ADJECTIVE
willing to obey

**submit** VERB **submits, submitting, submitted**
❶ to give in to someone or agree to obey them ❷ to hand something in or offer it to be judged or considered • *Submit your plans to the committee.*

**subordinate** ADJECTIVE
❶ less important ❷ lower in rank

**subordinate** NOUN **subordinates**
a person working under someone's authority or control

**subordinate** *VERB* subordinates,
subordinating, subordinated
to treat something as being less important
than another thing

**subordinate clause** *NOUN* subordinate
clauses
a clause which adds details to the main clause
of the sentence, but cannot be used as a
sentence by itself

**sub-plot** *NOUN* sub-plots
a secondary plot in a play, film or novel

**subpoena** (say sub-**peen**-a) *NOUN* subpoenas
an official document ordering a person to
appear in a law court

**subpoena** *VERB* subpoenas, subpoenaing,
subpoenaed
to summon someone by a subpoena
(**WORD ORIGIN**) from Latin *sub poena* = under a
penalty (because there is a punishment for not
obeying the order to appear)

**sub-post office** *NOUN* sub-post offices
a small local post office, often in a shop,
which offers fewer services than a main post
office

**subscribe** *VERB* subscribes, subscribing,
subscribed
❶ to make a regular payment in order to
be a member of a society or to receive a
magazine or other service ❷ to apply to take
part in something • *The course is already
fully subscribed.* ❸ to contribute money to
a project or charity ❹ to say that you agree
with something • *We cannot subscribe to this
theory.*
➤ **subscriber** *NOUN*

**subscription** *NOUN* subscriptions
money you pay to subscribe to something

**subsequent** *ADJECTIVE*
coming after something in time or order; later
• *Subsequent events proved that she was
right.*
➤ **subsequently** *ADVERB*

**subservient** *ADJECTIVE*
prepared to obey others without question
➤ **subservience** *NOUN*

**subset** *NOUN* subsets
a group or set forming part of a larger group
or set

**subside** *VERB* subsides, subsiding, subsided
❶ to begin to sink into the ground • *The
house has subsided over the years.* ❷ to
become less intense or quieter • *Her fear
subsided.*

**subsidence** (say sub-**sy**-dens or **sub**-sid-ens)
*NOUN*
the gradual sinking or caving in of an area of
land

**subsidiary** *ADJECTIVE*
less important; secondary

**subsidiary** *NOUN* subsidiaries
a business company that is controlled by
another larger company

**subsidize** (also **subsidise**) *VERB* subsidizes,
subsidizing, subsidized
to pay a subsidy to a person or firm

**subsidy** *NOUN* subsidies
money paid to an industry that needs help or
to keep down the price at which its goods or
services are sold to the public

**subsist** *VERB* subsists, subsisting, subsisted
to manage to live with very little food or
money • *We subsisted on fruit and nuts.*
➤ **subsistence** *NOUN*

**subsoil** *NOUN*
soil lying just below the surface layer

**substance** *NOUN* substances
❶ a solid or liquid material; what something
is made of • *Glue is a sticky substance.* ❷ the
main or essential part of something • *We
agree with the substance of your report but
not with its details.*

**sub-standard** *ADJECTIVE*
below the normal or required standard

**substantial** *ADJECTIVE*
❶ of great size, value or importance • *a
substantial fee* ❷ solidly built • *substantial
houses*

**substantially** *ADVERB*
mostly • *The rules of the two games are
substantially the same.*

**substation** *NOUN* substations
a subsidiary station for distributing electric
current

**substitute** *NOUN* substitutes
a person or thing that acts or is used instead
of another

**substitute** *VERB* substitutes, substituting,
substituted
to substitute one thing or person for another
is to use the first one instead of the second
• *In this recipe you can substitute oil for
butter.*
➤ **substitution** *NOUN*

**subterfuge** *NOUN* subterfuges
a deception

**subterranean** *ADJECTIVE*
underground • *a subterranean river*

**subtitle** *NOUN* subtitles
❶ a secondary or additional title ❷ words shown on the screen during a film, e.g. to translate a foreign language

**subtle** (say sut-el) *ADJECTIVE*
❶ faint or delicate • *This soup has a subtle flavour.* ❷ slight and difficult to detect or describe • *a subtle distinction* ❸ ingenious but not immediately obvious • *a subtle joke*
➤ **subtly** *ADVERB*
➤ **subtlety** *NOUN*

**subtotal** *NOUN* subtotals
the total of part of a group of figures

**subtract** *VERB* subtracts, subtracting, subtracted
to subtract one number or amount from another is to take it away • *If you subtract 2 from 7, you get 5.*

**subtraction** *NOUN*
the process of taking one number or amount from another

**subtropical** *ADJECTIVE*
of regions that border on the tropics

**suburb** *NOUN* suburbs
a district with houses that is outside the central part of a city
➤ **suburban** *ADJECTIVE*

**suburbia** *NOUN*
the suburbs of a city and the people who live there

**subvert** *VERB* subverts, subverting, subverted
to try to destroy or weaken something by attacking it secretly and in an indirect way
➤ **subversion** *NOUN*
➤ **subversive** *ADJECTIVE*

**subway** *NOUN* subways
❶ an underground passage for pedestrians ❷ (*North American*) an underground railway

**succeed** *VERB* succeeds, succeeding, succeeded
❶ to do or get what you wanted or intended ❷ to come after another person or thing • *The bells stopped and were succeeded by a strange clanking noise.* ❸ to become the next holder of an office, especially the monarchy • *She succeeded to the throne.* • *Edward VII succeeded Queen Victoria.*

**success** *NOUN* successes
❶ doing or getting what you wanted or intended ❷ a person or thing that does well • *The show was a great success.*

SPELLING

There is a double c and double s in success.

**successful** *ADJECTIVE*
having success or being a success
➤ **successfully** *ADVERB*

**succession** *NOUN* successions
❶ a series of people or things ❷ the process of following in order ❸ succeeding to the throne; the right of doing this
➤ **in succession** one after another

**successive** *ADJECTIVE*
following one after another • *on five successive days*
➤ **successively** *ADVERB*

**successor** *NOUN* successors
a person or thing that comes after another and takes their place

**succinct** (say suk-**sinkt**) *ADJECTIVE*
concise; expressed briefly • *a succinct reply*
➤ **succinctly** *ADVERB*

**succour** (say suk-er) *NOUN*
help given in time of need

**succour** *VERB* succours, succouring, succoured
to offer help to someone in need

**succulent** *ADJECTIVE*
❶ juicy and tasty ❷ succulent plants have thick juicy leaves or stems

**succumb** (say suk-**um**) *VERB* succumbs, succumbing, succumbed
to give way to something overpowering • *He finally succumbed to curiosity and went to look.*

**such** *DETERMINER*
❶ of the same kind; similar • *Cakes, biscuits and all such foods are fattening.* ❷ of the kind described • *There's no such person.* ❸ so great or so much • *It gave me such a fright!*
➤ **such as** for example

**such-and-such** *DETERMINER*
one in particular but you are not saying which • *He promises to come at such-and-such a time but is always late.*

**suchlike** *PRONOUN*
of that kind

**suck** *VERB* sucks, sucking, sucked
❶ to take in liquid or air through almost-

closed lips ❷ to squeeze something in your mouth by using your tongue • *She was sucking a sweet.* ❸ to draw something in • *The canoe was sucked into the whirlpool.*
➤ **suck up to someone** (*informal*) to flatter someone in the hope of winning their favour

**suck** *NOUN* **sucks**
the action of sucking

**sucker** *NOUN* **suckers**
❶ a rubber or plastic cup that sticks to a surface by suction ❷ an organ on the body of an animal or insect that it uses to cling to a surface by suction ❸ a shoot coming up from a root or underground stem ❹ (*informal*) a person who is easily deceived

**suckle** *VERB* **suckles, suckling, suckled**
to feed on milk at the mother's breast or udder

**sucrose** *NOUN*
the form of sugar that is obtained from sugar cane and sugar beet

**suction** *NOUN*
❶ the process of sucking ❷ producing a vacuum so that things are sucked into the empty space • *Vacuum cleaners work by suction.*

**sudden** *ADJECTIVE*
happening or done quickly and without warning
➤ **suddenness** *NOUN*

**suddenly** *ADVERB*
quickly and without warning • *Suddenly, everyone started shouting.*

**sudoku** (say soo-**doh**-koo) *NOUN* **sudokus**
a puzzle in which you have to write the numbers 1 to 9 in a particular pattern in a grid of 81 squares

**suds** *PLURAL NOUN*
froth on soapy water

**sue** *VERB* **sues, suing, sued**
to start a lawsuit to claim money from someone

**suede** (say swayd) *NOUN*
leather with one side rubbed to make it soft and velvety

**suet** *NOUN*
hard fat from cattle and sheep, used in cooking

**suffer** *VERB* **suffers, suffering, suffered**
❶ to feel pain or sadness ❷ to experience something bad • *The house suffered some damage.* • *She suffers from hay fever.* ❸ to

become worse or be badly affected • *She's not sleeping and her work is suffering.*
➤ **sufferer** *NOUN*

**sufferance** *NOUN*
➤ **on sufferance** allowed but only reluctantly

**suffering** *NOUN* **sufferings**
pain or misery

**suffice** *VERB* **suffices, sufficing, sufficed**
to be enough for someone's needs • *A couple of hours should suffice.*

**sufficient** *ADJECTIVE*
enough; as much as is necessary
➤ **sufficiently** *ADVERB*

**suffix** *NOUN* **suffixes**
a letter or set of letters joined to the end of a word to make another word (e.g. in forget*ful*, lion*ess*, rust*y*) or a form of a verb (e.g. sing*ing*, wait*ed*)

GRAMMAR

Suffixes are groups of letters that are not themselves words, but can be combined with other words to change their meaning and form new words. Suffixes are added at the end of other words (e.g. read*able*, green*ish*, pictur*esque*).

Some suffixes make words that are closely related to the original word. For example, suffixes such as -*ly*, -*ity*, -*ness*, and -*y*, are used to form derivatives which belong to a new word class (e.g. *naturally, normality, softness*)

Words like *free* and *friendly* can be added to the ends of other words to form compounds (e.g. *dairy-free, user-friendly*). These are not true suffixes but separate words in their own right.

**suffocate** *VERB* **suffocates, suffocating, suffocated**
❶ to suffer or die because you cannot breathe ❷ to make it difficult or impossible for someone to breathe
➤ **suffocation** *NOUN*

**suffrage** *NOUN*
the right to vote in political elections

**suffragette** *NOUN* **suffragettes**
a woman who campaigned in the early 20th century for women to have the right to vote

**suffuse** *VERB* **suffuses, suffusing, suffused**
to spread through or over something • *A blush suffused her cheeks.*

**sugar** NOUN
a sweet food obtained from the juices of various plants, such as sugar cane or sugar beet

**sugar** VERB sugars, sugaring, sugared
to add sugar to food or drink

**sugary** ADJECTIVE
sugary food or drink has a lot of sugar in it

**suggest** VERB suggests, suggesting, suggested
❶ to put forward an idea or plan for someone to consider ❷ to make an idea or possibility come into your mind • *Her smile suggested that she agreed with me.*

**suggestion** NOUN suggestions
❶ something that you mention to someone as an idea or possibility ❷ a slight amount or sign of something • *There was a suggestion of a sob in her voice.*

**suggestive** ADJECTIVE
making you think of something • *This music is suggestive of the sea.*

**suicide** NOUN suicides
❶ killing yourself deliberately • *He committed suicide.* ❷ a person who deliberately kills himself or herself
➤ **suicidal** ADJECTIVE

**suit** NOUN suits
❶ a matching jacket and trousers or a jacket and skirt, that are meant to be worn together ❷ a set of clothing for a particular activity • *a diving suit* ❸ any of the four sets of cards (clubs, hearts, diamonds, spades) in a pack of playing cards ❹ a lawsuit

SPELLING
Take care not to confuse with **suite**.

**suit** VERB suits, suiting, suited
❶ to be suitable or convenient for a person or thing ❷ a piece of clothing or hairstyle suits you when it looks good on you

**suitable** ADJECTIVE
satisfactory or right for a particular person, purpose or occasion
➤ **suitably** ADVERB
➤ **suitability** NOUN

**suitcase** NOUN suitcases
a rectangular container for carrying clothes, usually with a hinged lid and a handle

**suite** (say sweet) NOUN suites
❶ a set of matching furniture ❷ a set of

rooms in a hotel ❸ a set of short pieces of music

SPELLING
Take care not to confuse with **suit**.

**suitor** NOUN suitors
a man who is courting a woman

**sulk** VERB sulks, sulking, sulked
to be silent and bad-tempered because you are not pleased

**sulk** NOUN sulks
a period of sulking

**sulky** ADJECTIVE
silent and bad-tempered because you are not pleased • *He sat in sulky silence.*
➤ **sulkily** ADVERB
➤ **sulkiness** NOUN

**sullen** ADJECTIVE
sulking and gloomy
➤ **sullenly** ADVERB
➤ **sullenness** NOUN

**sully** VERB sullies, sullying, sullied
to stain or spoil something; to blemish something • *The scandal sullied his reputation.*

**sulphur** NOUN
a yellow chemical used in industry and in medicine
➤ **sulphurous** ADJECTIVE

**sulphuric acid** NOUN
a strong colourless acid containing sulphur

**sultan** NOUN sultans
the ruler of certain Muslim countries

**sultana** NOUN sultanas
a raisin without seeds

**sultry** ADJECTIVE
hot and humid • *sultry weather*

**sum** NOUN sums
❶ a total ❷ a problem in arithmetic ❸ an amount of money

**sum** VERB sums, summing, summed
➤ **sum up** to give a summary at the end of a talk or discussion

SPELLING
Do not confuse this word with **some**.

**summarize** (also **summarise**) VERB
summarizes, summarizing, summarized
to make or give a summary of something • *Let me first summarize the plot of the novel.*

**summary** NOUN summaries
a statement of the main points of something said or written

**summary** ADJECTIVE
❶ brief or concise • *a summary report*
❷ done or given hastily, without delay
• *summary punishment*
➤ **summarily** ADVERB

**summer** NOUN summers
the warm season between spring and autumn
➤ **summery** ADJECTIVE

**summer house** NOUN summer houses
a small building providing shade in a garden or park

**summertime** NOUN
the season of summer

**summit** NOUN summits
❶ the top of a mountain or hill ❷ a meeting between the leaders of powerful countries • *a summit conference*

**summon** VERB summons, summoning, summoned
❶ to order someone to come or appear
❷ to call people together • *A meeting of the governors was quickly summoned.*
➤ **summon something up** to gather together your strength or courage in order to do something • *I couldn't even summon up the energy to get out of bed.*

**summons** NOUN summonses
a command to appear in a law court

**sump** NOUN sumps
a metal case that holds oil round an engine

**sumptuous** ADJECTIVE
splendid and expensive-looking • *a sumptuous feast*
➤ **sumptuously** ADVERB

**sun** NOUN suns
❶ the star round which the earth travels
❷ light and warmth from the sun • *Let's sit in the sun.* ❸ any star in the universe round which planets travel

**sun** VERB suns, sunning, sunned
➤ **sun yourself** to sit or lie in the sunshine

**sunbathe** VERB sunbathes, sunbathing, sunbathed
to sit or lie in the sunshine to get a suntan

**sunbeam** NOUN sunbeams
a ray of the sun

**sunbed** NOUN sunbeds
(*British*) a bench that you lie on under a sunlamp

**sunblock** NOUN
a cream or lotion that you put on your skin to protect it from the sun's harmful rays

**sunburn** NOUN
redness of the skin someone gets if they are in the sun for too long
➤ **sunburnt** or **sunburned** ADJECTIVE

**sundae** (say **sun**-day) NOUN sundaes
a mixture of ice cream and fruit, nuts and cream **WORD ORIGIN** from **Sunday** (because sundaes were originally sold then, possibly to use up ice cream not sold during the week)

**Sunday** NOUN
the day of the week between Saturday and Monday, thought of as either the first or the last day of the week **WORD ORIGIN** from Old English *sunnandaeg* = day of the sun

**sunder** VERB sunders, sundering, sundered
(*poetical use*)
to break or tear something apart

**sundial** NOUN sundials
a device that shows the time by a shadow on a dial

**sundown** NOUN
(*North American*) sunset

**sundries** PLURAL NOUN
various small things

**sundry** ADJECTIVE
various or several
➤ **all and sundry** all people; everyone

**sunflower** NOUN sunflowers
a very tall flower with golden petals round a dark centre **WORD ORIGIN** so called because the flower head turns to follow the sun

**sunglasses** PLURAL NOUN
dark glasses you wear to protect your eyes from strong sunlight

**sunken** ADJECTIVE
sunk deeply into a surface • *Their cheeks were pale and sunken.*

**sunlamp** NOUN sunlamps
a lamp which uses ultraviolet light to give people an artificial tan

**sunlight** NOUN
light from the sun

**sunlit** ADJECTIVE
lit by sunlight • *a sunlit courtyard*

a
b
c
d
e
f
g
h
i
j
k
l
m
n
o
p
q
r
s
t
u
v
w
x
y
z

A
B
C
D
E
F
G
H
I
J
K
L
M
N
O
P
Q
R
**S**
T
U
V
W
X
Y
Z

**Sunni** NOUN Sunnis
a member of one of the two main branches of
Islam, based on the teachings of Muhammad
and regarding his father-in-law Abu Bakr
as his successor; about 90% of Muslims are
Sunnis. Compare with **Shiite**.

**sunny** ADJECTIVE sunnier, sunniest
❶ full of sunshine • *a sunny day* ❷ cheerful
• *She was in a sunny mood.*

**sunrise** NOUN sunrises
the rising of the sun; dawn • *They left at
sunrise.*

**sunscreen** NOUN
a cream or lotion that you put on your skin to
protect it from the sun's harmful rays

**sunset** NOUN sunsets
the setting of the sun

**sunshade** NOUN sunshades
a parasol or other device to protect people
from the sun

**sunshine** NOUN
warmth and light that comes from the sun

**sunspot** NOUN sunspots
a dark place on the sun's surface

**sunstroke** NOUN
an illness caused by being in the sun too long

**suntan** NOUN suntans
a brown colour of the skin caused by the sun
➤ **suntanned** ADJECTIVE

**sun visor** NOUN sun visors
a flap at the top of a vehicle's windscreen
that shields your eyes from the sun

**sup** VERB sups, supping, supped
to drink liquid in sips or spoonfuls

**super** ADJECTIVE (*informal*)
excellent or superb

**superb** ADJECTIVE
magnificent or excellent
➤ **superbly** ADVERB

**supercilious** ADJECTIVE
haughty and scornful WORD ORIGIN from
Latin *supercilium* = eyebrow, because raising
the eyebrows is a sign of this attitude

**superficial** ADJECTIVE
❶ on the surface • *It's only a superficial
cut.* ❷ not deep or thorough • *a superficial
knowledge of French*
➤ **superficially** ADVERB
➤ **superficiality** NOUN

**superfluous** (say soo-**per**-floo-us) ADJECTIVE
more than is wanted; not necessary • *He gave
me a look that made any words superfluous.*
➤ **superfluity** NOUN

**superglue** NOUN
a kind of strong glue that sticks very quickly

**superhuman** ADJECTIVE
❶ beyond ordinary human ability
• *superhuman strength* ❷ higher than
human; divine

**superimpose** VERB superimposes,
superimposing, superimposed
to place a thing on top of something else

**superintend** VERB superintends,
superintending, superintended
to be in charge of someone or something

**superintendent** NOUN superintendents
❶ a supervisor ❷ a police officer above the
rank of inspector

**superior** ADJECTIVE
❶ higher in position or rank • *She is your
superior officer.* ❷ better than another
person or thing ❸ showing that you think
you are better than other people

**superior** NOUN superiors
a person or thing that is superior to another

**superiority** NOUN
❶ being better than something else
❷ behaviour that shows you think you are
better than other people

**superlative** ADJECTIVE
of the highest degree or quality • *superlative
skill*
➤ **superlatively** ADVERB

**superlative** NOUN superlatives
the form of an adjective or adverb that
expresses 'most' • *The superlative of 'big'
is 'biggest' and the superlative of 'bad' is
'worst'.*

GRAMMAR

Superlative adjectives and adverbs are
used to compare and contrast people,
things or actions. The superlative shows
which of three or more things is greatest
or most: *Cheetahs are the* <u>fastest</u> *land
animals.*

For many adjectives, and some adverbs,
the superlative is formed by adding -est
(or -st if the word already ends in e). Note
that some adjectives double their final
letter, and those ending in -y change to -i

before adding -*est*:

*This flower is the biggest and palest in the garden.*

*What's the scariest film you've ever seen?*

For longer adjectives, and for adverbs ending in -*ly*, the superlative is formed with *most*:

*Hot-air balloons are the most interesting way to travel.*

*It was the most beautifully painted picture I had ever seen.*

However, some common adjectives and adverbs have irregular superlatives which in some cases are different words, e.g. *good* / *well* (*best*), *bad* / *badly* (*worst*) and *far* (*furthest* or *furthest*).

You will find guidance in this dictionary on irregular superlatives.

See also the panel on **comparatives**.

**superman** NOUN supermen
a man with superhuman powers

**supermarket** NOUN supermarkets
a large self-service shop that sells food and other goods

**supernatural** ADJECTIVE
not belonging to the natural world or having a natural explanation • *supernatural beings such as ghosts*
➤ **supernatural** NOUN

**superpower** NOUN superpowers
one of the most powerful nations of the world, such as the USA

**supersede** VERB supersedes, superseding, superseded
to take the place of something • *Cars superseded horse-drawn carriages.*

**supersonic** ADJECTIVE
faster than the speed of sound

**superstition** NOUN superstitions
a belief or action that is not based on reason or evidence, e.g. the belief that it is unlucky to walk under a ladder

**superstitious** ADJECTIVE
believing in superstitions • *I'm very superstitious about the number 13.*

**superstore** NOUN superstores
a very large supermarket selling a wide range of goods

**superstructure** NOUN superstructures
❶ a structure that rests on something else
❷ a building as distinct from its foundations

**supertanker** NOUN supertankers
a very large tanker

**supervise** VERB supervises, supervising, supervised
to be in charge of a person or thing and inspect what is done • *Your job is to supervise the building of the bridge.*
➤ **supervision** NOUN
➤ **supervisor** NOUN

**superwoman** NOUN superwomen
a woman with superhuman powers

**supper** NOUN suppers
a meal eaten in the evening

**supplant** VERB supplants, supplanting, supplanted
to take the place of a person or thing that has been removed

**supple** ADJECTIVE
able to bend easily; flexible, not stiff
➤ **suppleness** NOUN

**supplement** NOUN supplements
❶ something added as an extra ❷ an extra section added to a book or newspaper • *the colour supplement*

**supplement** VERB supplements, supplementing, supplemented
to add to something • *Some people take vitamin pills to supplement their diet.*

**supplementary** ADJECTIVE
added as an extra • *supplementary information*

**suppliant** (say sup-lee-ant) (or **supplicant**) NOUN suppliants, supplicants
a person who asks humbly for something

**supplication** NOUN
asking or begging humbly for something, especially when praying • *She knelt in supplication.*

**supply** VERB supplies, supplying, supplied
to give or sell or provide what is needed or wanted
➤ **supplier** NOUN

**supply** NOUN supplies
❶ an amount of something that is kept ready to be used when needed • *We keep a supply*

of paper in the cupboard. ❷ supplies are things like food, medicines or fuel needed by an army, expedition, etc. • *Their supplies were running out.* ❸ the action of supplying something

**supply teacher** NOUN **supply teachers**
a teacher who takes the place of a regular teacher when he or she is away

**support** VERB **supports, supporting, supported**
❶ to hold something up so that it does not fall down ❷ to give help or encouragement to someone or something • *Not many people supported this proposal.* ❸ to like a particular sports team and want it do well • *Which football team do you support?* ❹ to provide someone with the necessities of life • *She has two children to support.*

**support** NOUN **supports**
❶ the action of supporting • *You can rely on my support.* ❷ a person or thing that supports

**supporter** NOUN **supporters**
a person who supports something, especially a sports team or political party • *football supporters*

**supportive** ADJECTIVE
giving help or support to someone in a difficult situation • *She received many supportive emails.*

**suppose** VERB **supposes, supposing, supposed**
❶ to think that something is likely to happen or be true • *Yes, I suppose you're right.* ❷ to assume something or consider it as a suggestion • *Suppose the world were flat.*
➤ **be supposed to do something** to be expected to do something; to have to do something as a duty

**supposedly** ADVERB
so people believe or think • *They are supposedly the best team in the world.*

**supposition** NOUN **suppositions**
something that a person thinks is likely or true

**suppress** VERB **suppresses, suppressing, suppressed**
❶ to put an end to something using force or by authority • *Troops suppressed the rebellion.* ❷ to keep something from being known or seen • *They suppressed the truth.*
• *He managed to suppress a smile.*
➤ **suppression** NOUN

**supremacy** (say soo-**prem**-asi) NOUN
having more authority or power than anyone else

**supreme** ADJECTIVE
❶ most important or highest in rank ❷ very great • *With a supreme effort, he managed not to laugh.*

**supremely** ADVERB
extremely • *supremely happy*

**surcharge** NOUN **surcharges**
an extra charge

**sure** ADJECTIVE
❶ completely confident that you are right; feeling no doubt • *Are you sure you locked the door?* ❷ certain to happen or do something • *Our team is sure to win.* ❸ reliable; that you can be certain of • *A cold wind like that is a sure sign of winter.* ❹ steady and confident • *a sure aim*
➤ **for sure** definitely
➤ **make sure** ❶ to find out exactly ❷ to make something happen or be true • *Make sure you have everything you need before you start.*

**sure** ADVERB (informal) surely; certainly
➤ **sure enough** certainly; in fact

**surely** ADVERB
❶ without doubt; certainly • *This will surely cause problems.* ❷ it must be true; I feel sure • *Surely I met you last year.*

**sureness** NOUN
the quality of being steady and confident • *the sureness of her aim*

**surety** NOUN **sureties**
❶ a guarantee ❷ a person who promises to pay a debt or fulfil a contract if another person fails to do so

**surf** NOUN
the white foam of waves breaking on a rock or shore

**surf** VERB **surfs, surfing, surfed**
❶ to go surfing ❷ to browse through the Internet

**surface** NOUN **surfaces**
❶ the outside of something ❷ any of the sides of an object, especially the top part ❸ an outward appearance • *On the surface he was a kindly man.*

**surface** VERB **surfaces, surfacing, surfaced**
❶ to come up to the surface from under water • *The submarine slowly surfaced.* ❷ to put a surface on a road or path

**surface mail** NOUN
letters and packages carried by sea or over land, not by air

**surfboard** NOUN surfboards
a board used in surfing

**surfeit** (say **ser**-fit) NOUN
too much of something
➤ **surfeited** ADJECTIVE

**surfer** NOUN surfers
a person who goes surfing

**surfing** NOUN
balancing yourself on a board that is carried to the shore on the waves

**surge** VERB surges, surging, surged
❶ to move forwards or upwards like waves ❷ to increase suddenly and powerfully

**surge** NOUN surges
❶ a sudden rush forward or upward ❷ a sudden increase in something, especially a strong feeling • *I felt a surge of panic.*

**surgeon** NOUN surgeons
a doctor who treats disease or injury by cutting or repairing the affected parts of the body

**surgery** NOUN surgeries
❶ the work of a surgeon ❷ the place where a doctor or dentist regularly gives advice and treatment to patients ❸ the time when patients can visit a doctor or dentist

**surgical** ADJECTIVE
to do with a surgeon or surgery • *surgical instruments*
➤ **surgically** ADVERB

**surly** ADJECTIVE surlier, surliest
bad-tempered and unfriendly • *He glared at them in surly silence.*
➤ **surliness** NOUN

**surmise** VERB surmises, surmising, surmised
to guess or suspect something

**surmise** NOUN surmises
a guess

**surmount** VERB surmounts, surmounting, surmounted
❶ to overcome a difficulty ❷ to get over an obstacle ❸ to be on top of something • *The museum is surmounted by a huge dome.*

**surname** NOUN surnames
the name that you share with other members of your family

**surpass** VERB surpasses, surpassing, surpassed
to do or be better than someone or something • *It surpassed her wildest dreams.*

**surplus** NOUN surpluses
an amount left over after you have spent or used what you need

**surplus** ADJECTIVE
more than you need • *Squirrels store surplus food, usually by burying it.*

**surprise** NOUN surprises
❶ something unexpected ❷ the feeling caused by something that was not expected
➤ **take someone by surprise** to happen to someone unexpectedly

**surprise** VERB surprises, surprising, surprised
❶ to be a surprise; to make someone feel surprise ❷ to come upon or attack someone unexpectedly

SPELLING
There is an **r** after the **u** in surprise.

**surprised** ADJECTIVE
feeling or showing surprise

**surprising** ADJECTIVE
causing surprise
➤ **surprisingly** ADVERB

**surreal** ADJECTIVE
strange and bizarre, like some dreams are

**surrealism** NOUN
a style of painting that shows strange objects and scenes like those seen in dreams and fantasies
➤ **surrealist** NOUN

**surrender** VERB surrenders, surrendering, surrendered
❶ to stop fighting and give yourself up to an enemy ❷ to hand something over to another person, especially when forced to do so

**surrender** NOUN
when someone surrenders • *They raised their hands in surrender.*

**surreptitious** (say su-rep-**tish**-us) ADJECTIVE
done secretly or quickly so other people will not notice • *a surreptitious peep*
➤ **surreptitiously** ADVERB

**surrogate mother** NOUN surrogate mothers
a woman who agrees to conceive and give birth to a baby for a woman who cannot have a baby herself

**surround** VERB surrounds, surrounding, surrounded

a b c d e f g h i j k l m n o p q r s t u v w x y z

to come or be all round a person or thing
• *Police surrounded the building.*

**surroundings** *PLURAL NOUN*
the conditions or area around a person or
thing

**surveillance** (say ser-**vay**-lans) *NOUN*
a close watch kept on a person or thing
• *Police kept him under surveillance.*

**survey** (say **ser**-vay) *NOUN* surveys
❶ a general look at something ❷ an
inspection of an area or building

**survey** (say ser-**vay**) *VERB* surveys, surveying,
surveyed
❶ to look carefully at the whole of something
• *He stood in the doorway and surveyed
the room.* ❷ to make a survey of an area or
building
➤ **surveyor** *NOUN*

**survival** *NOUN* survivals
❶ surviving; the likelihood of surviving
• *Finding shelter was his only chance of
survival.* ❷ something that has survived from
an earlier time

**survive** *VERB* survives, surviving, survived
❶ to stay alive; to continue to exist ❷ to
remain alive after an accident or disaster
• *Only two people survived the crash.* ❸ to
continue living after someone has died

**survivor** *NOUN* survivors
a person who survives, especially after an
accident or disaster

**susceptible** (say sus-**ept**-ib-ul) *ADJECTIVE*
likely to be affected by something • *She is
susceptible to colds.*
➤ **susceptibility** *NOUN*

**suspect** (say sus-**pekt**) *VERB* suspects,
suspecting, suspected
❶ to think that a person is not to be trusted
or has committed a crime; to distrust
someone ❷ to have a feeling that something
is likely or possible • *I suspect I've sprained
my ankle.*

**suspect** (say **sus**-pekt) *NOUN* suspects
a person who is suspected of a crime or doing
something wrong

**suspect** (say **sus**-pekt) *ADJECTIVE*
possibly not true or not to be trusted

**suspend** *VERB* suspends, suspending,
suspended
❶ to hang something up • *A lamp was
suspended from the ceiling.* ❷ to postpone
something or stop it temporarily ❸ to remove
a person from a job or position for a time

• *He was suspended for three matches for
hitting another player.* ❹ to keep something
from falling or sinking in air or liquid
• *Particles are suspended in the fluid.*

**suspender** *NOUN* suspenders
a fastener to hold up a sock or stocking by
its top

**suspense** *NOUN*
an anxious or uncertain feeling while waiting
for something to happen or become known
• *Don't keep us all in suspense – tell us who
won.*

**suspension** *NOUN* suspensions
❶ suspending something or someone ❷ the
springs etc. in a vehicle that lessen the effect
of rough road surfaces ❸ a liquid containing
small pieces of solid material which do not
dissolve

**suspension bridge** *NOUN* suspension bridges
a bridge supported by cables

**suspicion** *NOUN* suspicions
❶ a feeling that someone has done
something wrong or cannot be trusted ❷ a
slight feeling that something is likely or
possible • *I have a suspicion that he has
forgotten he invited us.*

**suspicious** *ADJECTIVE*
❶ making you suspect or distrust someone or
something • *There are suspicious footprints
along the path.* ❷ suspecting or distrusting
someone or something • *I'm suspicious about
what happened.*
➤ **suspiciously** *ADVERB*

**SPELLING**

There is a tricky bit in **suspicious** – it has
**ci** in the middle.

**sustain** *VERB* sustains, sustaining, sustained
❶ to keep something going • *It's hard
to sustain interest for such a long time.*
❷ to keep someone alive or healthy ❸ to
experience or suffer something bad • *He
sustained serious injuries.*

**sustainable** *ADJECTIVE*
❶ using natural products and energy in a
way that does not harm the environment
• *sustainable forests* ❷ able to be continued
for a long time

**sustenance** *NOUN*
food and drink; nourishment

**suture** (say **soo**-cher) *NOUN* sutures
surgical stitching of a cut

**SW** *ABBREVIATION*
❶ south-west ❷ south-western

**swab** (say swob) *NOUN* swabs
❶ a mop or pad for cleaning or wiping something; a small pad for cleaning a wound ❷ a specimen of fluid from the body taken on a swab for testing

**swab** *VERB* swabs, swabbing, swabbed
to clean or wipe something with a swab

**swagger** *VERB* swaggers, swaggering, swaggered
to walk or behave in a conceited and confident way

**swagger** *NOUN*
a way of walking or behaving that seems too confident

**swain** *NOUN* swains (*old use*)
❶ a country lad ❷ a young lover or suitor

**swallow** *VERB* swallows, swallowing, swallowed
❶ to make something go down your throat ❷ to believe something that ought not to be believed • *I found her excuse hard to swallow.*
➤ **swallow something up** to take something in and completely cover it • *She walked away and was soon swallowed up in the crowd.*

**swallow** *NOUN* swallows
a small bird with a forked tail and pointed wings

**swamp** *NOUN* swamps
an area of soft, wet land; a marsh
➤ **swampy** *ADJECTIVE*

**swamp** *VERB* swamps, swamping, swamped
❶ to flood an area ❷ to overwhelm someone with a great mass or number of things • *They have been swamped with complaints.*

**swan** *NOUN* swans
a large usually white swimming bird with a long neck

**swanky** *ADJECTIVE*
(*informal*) fashionable and expensive • *a swanky restaurant*

**swansong** *NOUN* swansongs
a person's last performance or work
**WORD ORIGIN** from the old belief that a swan sang sweetly when it was about to die

**swap** (*informal*) *VERB* swaps, swapping, swapped
to exchange one thing for another

**swap** *NOUN* swaps
❶ an act of swapping • *Let's do a swap.* ❷ something you swap for something else

**WORD ORIGIN** formerly = seal a bargain by slapping each other's hands; imitating the sound

**swarm** *NOUN* swarms
a large number of insects flying or moving about together

**swarm** *VERB* swarms, swarming, swarmed
❶ to gather or move in a swarm ❷ to be crowded with people • *The town is swarming with tourists in the summer.*

**swarthy** *ADJECTIVE*
having a dark complexion
➤ **swarthiness** *NOUN*

**swashbuckling** *ADJECTIVE*
a swashbuckling film is full of daring adventures and sword-fighting, set in the past

**swastika** *NOUN* swastikas
an ancient symbol formed by a cross with its ends bent at right angles, adopted by the Nazis as their sign **WORD ORIGIN** from Sanskrit *svasti* = well-being, luck

**swat** *VERB* swats, swatting, swatted
to hit or crush a fly or other insect
➤ **swatter** *NOUN*

**swathe** (say swawth) *NOUN* swathes
a broad strip or area • *vast swathes of countryside*
➤ **cut a swathe through something** to pass through an area causing destruction

**swathe** (say swayth) *VERB* swathes, swathing, swathed
to wrap a person or thing in layers of bandages, paper or clothes

**sway** *VERB* sways, swaying, swayed
❶ to move or swing gently from side to side • *Trees were swaying in the wind.* ❷ to influence or affect someone • *His speech swayed the crowd.*
➤ **sway** *NOUN*

**swear** *VERB* swears, swearing, swore, sworn
❶ to make a solemn promise • *She swore to tell the truth.* ❷ to make someone promise something • *We swore him to secrecy.* ❸ to use very rude or offensive words
➤ **swear by something** to have great confidence in something

**swear word** *NOUN* swear words
a word considered rude or shocking, often used by someone who is angry

**sweat** (say swet) *NOUN*
moisture given off by your body through the pores of your skin; perspiration

**sweat** VERB sweats, sweating, sweated
to give off sweat; to perspire

**sweater** NOUN sweaters
a jersey or pullover

**sweatshirt** NOUN sweatshirts
a thick cotton jersey worn for sports or casual
wear

**sweaty** ADJECTIVE
covered or damp with sweat

**swede** NOUN swedes
a large kind of turnip with purple skin and
yellow flesh (**WORD ORIGIN**) short for *Swedish
turnip* (because it originally came from Sweden)

**sweep** VERB sweeps, sweeping, swept
❶ to clean or clear an area with a broom
or brush ❷ to move or remove something
quickly • *The floods swept away the bridge.*
❸ to go smoothly and quickly • *She swept
out of the room.* ❹ to travel quickly over an
area • *A new craze is sweeping the country.*
➤ sweeper NOUN

**sweep** NOUN sweeps
❶ the process of sweeping • *Give this room
a good sweep.* ❷ a sweeping movement ❸ a
chimney sweep ❹ a sweepstake

**sweeping** ADJECTIVE
general or wide-ranging • *He made sweeping
changes.*

**sweepstake** NOUN sweepstakes
a form of gambling on sporting events in
which all the money staked is divided among
the winners (**WORD ORIGIN**) so called because
the winner 'sweeps up' all the other players'
stakes

**sweet** ADJECTIVE
❶ tasting as if it contains sugar; not bitter
❷ very pleasant • *a sweet smell* ❸ charming
or delightful • *What a sweet little cottage.*
➤ sweetness NOUN
➤ **a sweet tooth** a liking for sweet things

**sweet** NOUN sweets
❶ a small shaped piece of sweet food made
with sugar or chocolate ❷ a pudding; the
sweet course in a meal ❸ a loved person

**sweetcorn** NOUN
the juicy yellow seeds of maize

**sweeten** VERB sweetens, sweetening,
sweetened
to make something sweet
➤ sweetener NOUN

**sweetheart** NOUN sweethearts
a person you love very much

**sweetly** ADVERB
in an attractive or pleasant way • *She smiled
sweetly at him.*

**sweetmeat** NOUN sweetmeats (*old use*)
a sweet

**sweet pea** NOUN sweet peas
a climbing plant with sweet-smelling flowers

**sweet potato** NOUN sweet potatoes
a root vegetable with reddish skin and sweet
yellow flesh

**swell** VERB swells, swelling, swelled, swollen or
swelled
❶ to become larger or to make something
larger • *My ankle was starting to swell.* ❷ to
increase in amount, volume or force • *The
music began to swell.*

**swell** NOUN swells the rise and fall of the sea's
surface

**swell** ADJECTIVE (*informal*) (*North American*) very
good

**swelling** NOUN swellings
a swollen place on your body

**sweltering** ADJECTIVE
uncomfortably hot

**swerve** VERB swerves, swerving, swerved
to turn to one side suddenly • *The car
swerved to avoid the cyclist.*
➤ swerve NOUN

**swift** ADJECTIVE
happening or moving quickly • *He drew out
his sword in one swift movement.*
➤ swiftly ADVERB
➤ swiftness NOUN

**swift** NOUN swifts
a small bird rather like a swallow

**swig** (*informal*) VERB swigs, swigging, swigged
to drink quickly, taking large mouthfuls

**swig** NOUN swigs
a large mouthful of a drink

**swill** VERB swills, swilling, swilled
to pour water over or through something; to
wash or rinse something

**swill** NOUN
❶ the process of swilling something • *Give
it a swill.* ❷ a sloppy mixture of waste food
given to pigs

**swim** VERB swims, swimming, swam, swum
❶ to move your body through the water;
to be in the water for pleasure ❷ to cross a
stretch of water by swimming • *She swam
the Channel.* ❸ to be covered with or full of

liquid • *Our eyes were swimming with tears.*
❹ to feel dizzy • *He felt sick and his head swam.*

**swim** NOUN swims
a spell of swimming • *Let's go for a swim.*

**swimmer** NOUN swimmers
a person who swims • *Are you a good swimmer?*

**swimming bath** NOUN swimming baths
(*British*) a public swimming pool

**swimming costume** NOUN swimming costumes
(*British*) the clothing a woman wears to go swimming; a bikini or swimsuit

**swimming pool** NOUN swimming pools
an artificial pool for swimming in

**swimming trunks** PLURAL NOUN
shorts which a man wears to go swimming

**swimsuit** NOUN swimsuits
a one-piece swimming costume

**swindle** VERB swindles, swindling, swindled
to cheat a person of their money or possessions in business

**swindle** NOUN swindles
a trick to swindle someone
➤ **swindler** NOUN

**swine** NOUN swine
❶ a pig ❷ a very unpleasant person
❸ (*informal*) a difficult thing • *This crossword's a real swine!*

**swing** VERB swings, swinging, swung
❶ to move back and forth while hanging
❷ to move or turn in a curve • *The door swung open.* ❸ to change from one opinion or mood to another

**swing** NOUN swings
❶ a swinging movement ❷ a seat hung on chains or ropes so that it can be moved backwards and forwards ❸ the amount by which votes or opinions change from one side to another ❹ a kind of jazz music
➤ **in full swing** full of activity or working fully

**swipe** VERB swipes, swiping, swiped
❶ to hit a person or thing with a swinging blow ❷ (*informal*) to steal something ❸ to pass a credit card through an electronic reading device when making a payment ❹ to move a finger across a touchscreen

**swipe** NOUN swipes
an attempt to hit a person or thing with a swinging blow

**swirl** VERB swirls, swirling, swirled
to move round quickly in circles • *The water swirled down the plug hole.*

**swirl** NOUN swirls
a swirling movement

**swish** VERB swishes, swishing, swished
to move with a hissing or rushing sound

**swish** NOUN swishes
a swishing sound

**swish** ADJECTIVE (*British*) (*informal*) smart and fashionable

**Swiss roll** NOUN Swiss rolls
(*British*) a thin sponge cake spread with jam or cream and rolled up

**switch** NOUN switches
❶ a device that you press or turn to start or stop something working, especially by electricity ❷ a change of opinion, policy or methods ❸ a mechanism for moving the points on a railway track ❹ a flexible rod or whip

**switch** VERB switches, switching, switched
❶ to turn something on or off by means of a switch ❷ to change something suddenly ❸ to replace a thing with something else

**switchback** NOUN switchbacks
a railway at a fair, with steep slopes up and down alternately

**switchboard** NOUN switchboards
a panel with switches for making telephone connections or operating electric circuits; the staff operating a switchboard

**swivel** VERB swivels, swivelling, swivelled
to turn round smoothly • *She swivelled round to say something.*

**swollen**
past participle of **swell**

**swollen** ADJECTIVE
thicker or wider than usual • *My wrist is still swollen where I bumped it.*

**swoon** (*old use*) VERB swoons, swooning, swooned
to faint

**swoon** NOUN
when someone faints

**swoop** VERB swoops, swooping, swooped
❶ to dive or come down with a rushing movement • *The eagle swooped down on its prey.* ❷ to make a sudden attack or raid

**swoop** NOUN swoops
a sudden dive or attack

a
b
c
d
e
f
g
h
i
j
k
l
m
n
o
p
q
r
s
t
u
v
w
x
y
z

**swop** VERB swops, swopping, swopped
a different spelling of **swap**

**sword** (say sord) NOUN swords
a weapon with a long pointed blade fixed in a handle or hilt
➤ **swordsman** NOUN

**swordfish** NOUN swordfish
a large sea fish with a long sword-like upper jaw

**sworn** ADJECTIVE
❶ sworn evidence or testimony is given under oath ❷ sworn enemies are determined to remain enemies

**swot** (British) (informal) VERB swots, swotting, swotted
to study hard

**swot** NOUN swots
a person who swots

**sycamore** NOUN sycamores
a tall tree with winged seeds, often grown for its timber

**syllable** NOUN syllables
a word or part of a word that has one vowel sound when you say it • 'Cat' has one syllable, 'el-e-phant' has three syllables.

**syllabus** NOUN syllabuses
a list of the subjects to be studied by a class or for an examination

**symbol** NOUN symbols
❶ a thing used as a sign to stand for something • The crescent is a symbol of Islam. ❷ a mark or sign with a special meaning (e.g. +, - and x, in mathematics)

SPELLING

Take care not to confuse with **cymbal**.

**symbolic** ADJECTIVE
acting as a symbol of something • The white dove is symbolic of peace.
➤ **symbolical** ADJECTIVE
➤ **symbolically** ADVERB

**symbolism** NOUN
the use of symbols to stand for things

**symbolize** (also **symbolise**) VERB symbolizes, symbolizing, symbolized
to be a symbol of something • Red sometimes symbolizes danger.

**symmetrical** ADJECTIVE
able to be divided into two halves which are exactly the same but the opposite way round • Wheels and butterflies are symmetrical.
➤ **symmetrically** ADVERB

**symmetry** NOUN
the quality of being symmetrical or well-proportioned

SPELLING

The 'i' sound is spelt with a y in symmetry. Do not forget to double the m.

**sympathetic** ADJECTIVE
feeling or showing sympathy or understanding for someone • He gave me a sympathetic smile.
➤ **sympathetically** ADVERB

**sympathize** (also **sympathise**) VERB sympathizes, sympathizing, sympathized
to show or feel sympathy • I sympathize with her and I'll try to help.
➤ **sympathizer** NOUN

**sympathy** NOUN sympathies
❶ the sharing or understanding of other people's feelings or opinions ❷ a feeling of pity or tenderness towards someone who is hurt, sad or in trouble

**symphony** NOUN symphonies
a long piece of music for an orchestra
➤ **symphonic** ADJECTIVE

**symptom** NOUN symptoms
a sign that a disease or condition exists • Red spots are a symptom of measles.
➤ **symptomatic** ADJECTIVE

**synagogue** (say sin-a-gog) NOUN synagogues
a place where Jews meet for worship

**synchronize** (also **synchronise**) (say sink-ron-yz) VERB synchronizes, synchronizing, synchronized
❶ to make things happen at the same time ❷ to make watches or clocks show the same time ❸ to happen at the same time
➤ **synchronization** NOUN

**syncopated** (say sink-o-payt-id) ADJECTIVE
a piece of music is syncopated when the strong beats are played weak and the weak beats are played strong
➤ **syncopation** NOUN

**syndicate** NOUN syndicates
❶ a group of people or firms who work together in business ❷ a group of people who buy something together or who gamble together, sharing the cost and any gains

**syndrome** NOUN syndromes
❶ a set of symptoms ❷ a set of opinions or ways of behaving that are characteristic of a particular condition

**synod** (say **sin**-od) *NOUN* synods
a council of senior members of the clergy

**synonym** (say **sin**-o-nim) *NOUN* synonyms
a word that means the same or almost the
same as another word • *'Large' and 'great' are
synonyms of 'big'.*
➤ **synonymous** (say sin-**on**-im-us) *ADJECTIVE*

**GRAMMAR**

A **synonym** is a word which has the same
meaning as or a very similar meaning to,
another word. For example, *unhappy,
miserable, sorrowful* and *glum* are all
synonyms of the word *sad*.

An **antonym** is a word which has the
opposite meaning to another word. For
example, *visible* is an antonym of *invisible*;
and *timid, cowardly* and *spineless* are
antonyms of *brave*. Note that some
words which look like opposites (e.g.
*valuable/invaluable, different/indifferent*)
are not true antonyms, because they do
not have opposite meanings.

A *thesaurus* is a kind of dictionary which
lists synonyms and antonyms of words.
You can use a thesaurus to help you find
alternatives for words in your writing.
For example, instead of repeating the
adjective *creepy*, you could vary it with
synonyms like *eerie, weird, uncanny,
spooky* or *spine-chilling*.

**synopsis** (say sin-**op**-sis) *NOUN* synopses
a summary of a story or book

**syntax** (say **sin**-taks) *NOUN*
the way words are arranged to make phrases
or sentences
➤ **syntactic** *ADJECTIVE*
➤ **syntactically** *ADVERB*

**synthesis** (say **sin**-thi-sis) *NOUN* syntheses
combining different things to make
something

**synthesize** (also **synthesise**) (say **sin**-thi-syz)
*VERB* synthesizes, synthesizing, synthesized
to make something by combining parts

**synthesizer** (also **synthesiser**) *NOUN*
synthesizers
an electronic musical instrument that can
make a large variety of sounds

**synthetic** *ADJECTIVE*
artificially made; not natural • *synthetic
fibres*
➤ **synthetically** *ADVERB*

**syringe** *NOUN* syringes
a device for sucking in a liquid and squirting
it out

**syrup** *NOUN*
a thick sweet liquid
➤ **syrupy** *ADJECTIVE*
**WORD ORIGIN** from Arabic *sharab* = a drink

**system** *NOUN* systems
❶ a set of parts, things or ideas that are
organized to work together • *the digestive
system* ❷ a way of doing something • *We
have a new system for taking books out of
the library.*

**systematic** *ADJECTIVE*
done using a fixed plan or method;
methodical • *We began a systematic search
of the area.*
➤ **systematically** *ADVERB*

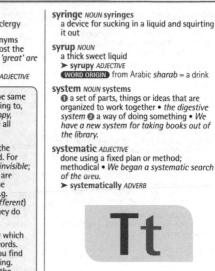

**tab** *NOUN* tabs
a small flap or strip that sticks out
➤ **keep tabs on someone** (*informal*) to
watch someone closely

**tabard** *NOUN* tabards
a kind of sleeveless tunic, decorated in the
past with a coat of arms

**tabby** *NOUN* tabbies
a grey or brown cat with dark stripes
**WORD ORIGIN** originally = a kind of striped silk
material: named after al-Attabiyya, a district of
Baghdad where it was made

**tabernacle** *NOUN* tabernacles
❶ (in the Bible) the portable shrine used by
the ancient Jews during their wanderings in
the wilderness ❷ a meeting place for worship
used by some groups of Christians

**table** *NOUN* tables
❶ a piece of furniture with a flat top
supported on legs ❷ a list of facts or figures
arranged in rows and columns ❸ a list of
the results of multiplying a number by other
numbers • *My little sister is learning her three
times table.*

**table** *VERB* tables, tabling, tabled
to put forward a proposal for discussion at a
meeting

a
b
c
d
e
f
g
h
i
j
k
l
m
n
o
p
q
r
s
t
u
v
w
x
y
z

A

**tableau** (say *tab*-loh) NOUN **tableaux** (say *tab*-lohz)
a dramatic or attractive scene, especially one posed on a stage by a group of people who do not speak or move

B

C

**tablecloth** NOUN **tablecloths**
a cloth for covering a table, especially at meals

D

**tablespoon** NOUN **tablespoons**
a large spoon for serving food
➤ **tablespoonful** NOUN

E

F

**tablet** NOUN **tablets**
❶ a pill ❷ a solid piece of soap ❸ a flat piece of stone or wood with words carved or written on it ❹ a small flat computer that you use by touching the screen

G

H

**table tennis** NOUN
a game played on a table divided by a net, over which you hit a small ball with bats

I

J

**tabloid** NOUN **tabloids**
a newspaper with pages that are half the size of larger newspapers

K

**taboo** ADJECTIVE
not to be done, used or talked about • *a taboo subject*

L

M

**taboo** NOUN **taboos**
a custom that you should avoid doing or talking about a particular thing because it might offend or embarrass other people
**WORD ORIGIN** from Tongan *tabu* = sacred

N

O

**tabulate** VERB **tabulates, tabulating, tabulated**
to arrange information or figures in a table or list

P

Q

**tacit** (say *tas*-it) ADJECTIVE
implied or understood without being put into words • *tacit approval* **WORD ORIGIN** from Latin *tacitus* = not speaking

R

S

**taciturn** (say *tas*-i-tern) ADJECTIVE
saying very little • *his taciturn manner*
➤ **taciturnity** NOUN

T

U

**tack** NOUN **tacks**
❶ a short nail with a flat top ❷ the direction taken when tacking in sailing ❸ a course of action or policy • *I think we need to change tack.* • *OK, let's try a different tack.* ❹ riding equipment, such as harnesses and saddles

V

W

**tack** VERB **tacks, tacking, tacked**
❶ to nail something down, especially a carpet, with tacks ❷ to sew material together with long stitches ❸ to sail a zigzag course to take advantage of what wind there is

X

Y

Z

➤ **tack something on** to add something as an extra

**tackle** VERB **tackles, tackling, tackled**
❶ to try to do something that needs doing • *Firefighters came to tackle the blaze.* ❷ to try to get the ball from someone else in a game of football, rugby or hockey ❸ to talk to someone about a difficult or awkward matter

**tackle** NOUN **tackles**
❶ equipment, especially for fishing ❷ a set of ropes and pulleys ❸ tackling someone in football, rugby or hockey

**tacky** ADJECTIVE
❶ sticky or not quite dry • *The paint is still tacky.* ❷ (*informal*) showing poor taste or style; cheaply made
➤ **tackiness** NOUN

**tact** NOUN
taking care not to offend or upset people by saying the wrong thing • *Tact isn't one of her strong points.*

**tactful** ADJECTIVE
having or showing tact
➤ **tactfully** ADVERB

**tactical** ADJECTIVE
to do with tactics
➤ **tactically** ADVERB

**tactics** NOUN
❶ the methods you use to achieve something or gain an advantage ❷ the method of arranging military forces in battle or players in a team game
➤ **tactician** NOUN

**USAGE**
**Strategy** is a general plan for a whole campaign. **Tactics** refers to one part of this.

**tactile** ADJECTIVE
to do with the sense of touch

**tactless** ADJECTIVE
having or showing a lack of tact • *a tactless remark*
➤ **tactlessly** ADVERB

**tadpole** NOUN **tadpoles**
a young frog or toad that has developed from the egg and lives entirely in water

**taffeta** NOUN
a stiff silky material, often used for dresses

**tag** NOUN **tags**
❶ a label tied on or stuck to something ❷ a

**tag** metal or plastic point at the end of a shoelace ❸ a game in which one person chases the others

**tag** VERB tags, tagging, tagged
❶ to label something with a tag ❷ to add something as an extra thing • *An apology was tagged on at the end of her email.* ❸ to identify a person shown in a photograph on a social networking website
➤ **tag along** (*informal*)
to go somewhere with other people • *Her sister insisted on tagging along.*

**tail** NOUN tails
❶ the part that sticks out from the rear end of the body of a bird, fish or animal ❷ the part at the end or rear of something, such as an aircraft

**tail** VERB tails, tailing, tailed
❶ to remove stalks from fruit or vegetables • *First, top and tail the green beans.*
❷ (*informal*) to follow someone closely without them seeing you
➤ **tail off** or **away** to become quieter, smaller or weaker and then disappear • *His voice tailed off.*

**tailback** NOUN tailbacks
a long line of traffic stretching back from an obstruction

**tailless** ADJECTIVE
without a tail

**tailor** NOUN tailors
a person who makes men's clothes

**tailor** VERB tailors, tailoring, tailored
❶ to make or fit clothes ❷ to adapt or make something for a special purpose

**tailor-made** ADJECTIVE
specially made or suited for a purpose

**tails** PLURAL NOUN
❶ the side of a coin opposite the head • *Heads or tails?* ❷ a man's formal jacket with two long pieces hanging down at the back

**taint** NOUN taints
a small amount of something bad or unpleasant that spoils something

**taint** VERB taints, tainting, tainted
to spoil something with a taint • *His reputation was tainted by the scandal.*

**take** VERB takes, taking, took, taken
This word has many uses, including
❶ to get something into your hands, possession or control • *Take this cup.* • *They took many prisoners.* ❷ to carry, drive or lead a person or thing to a place • *Take this parcel to the post.* • *Can you take me to the station?* ❸ to make use of something • *Let's take a taxi.* ❹ to have or do something • *You need to take a long holiday.* • *Let me take a look.* ❺ to take an exam is to sit it ❻ to study or teach a subject • *Who takes you for maths?* ❼ to make an effort • *Thanks for taking the trouble to see me.* ❽ to experience a feeling • *Don't take offence.* ❾ to accept or put up with something • *I'll take a risk.* ❿ to require something • *It takes a strong man to lift this.* ⓫ to write something down • *I'd better take notes.* ⓬ to use a camera to make a photograph • *I took some pictures of our new dog.* ⓭ to subtract one number from another • *Take 17 from 60.* ⓮ to assume that something is true • *I take it that you agree.*
➤ **taker** NOUN
➤ **I take it** I understand or suppose • *I take it that you're not coming?*
➤ **take after someone** to be like a parent or relative
➤ **take someone in** to fool or deceive someone
➤ **take something in** ❶ to understand something that you hear or read ❷ to make a piece of clothing narrower or tighter
➤ **take leave of someone** to say goodbye to someone
➤ **take off** an aircraft takes off when it leaves the ground and becomes airborne
➤ **take something off** to remove something, especially a piece of clothing
➤ **take someone on** ❶ to begin to employ someone ❷ to play or fight against someone
➤ **take something over** to take control of a business or activity
➤ **take part in something** to join in an activity
➤ **take place** to happen or occur
➤ **take to something** to develop a liking or ability for something
➤ **take something up** ❶ to start doing something regularly • *I've taken up karate.*
❷ to use or fill an amount of space or time • *Gymnastics takes up all of her time.*
❸ to accept an offer

**takeaway** NOUN takeaways
❶ a place that sells cooked meals for customers to take away ❷ a meal from such a place

**take-off** NOUN take-offs
the act of an aircraft leaving the ground and becoming airborne

a
b
c
d
e
f
g
h
i
j
k
l
m
n
o
p
q
r
s
t
u
v
w
x
y
z

**takeover** *NOUN* takeovers
the taking control of one business company by another

**takings** *PLURAL NOUN*
money that has been received, especially by a shopkeeper

**talcum powder** *NOUN*
a scented powder put on the skin to make it feel smooth and dry **WORD ORIGIN** from *talc*, the substance from which it is made

**tale** *NOUN* tales
a story

**talent** *NOUN* talents
a natural ability to do something well • *She has a talent for singing.* **WORD ORIGIN** from Greek *talanton* = sum of money

**talented** *ADJECTIVE*
having a natural ability to do something well

**talisman** *NOUN* talismans
an object that is supposed to bring good luck

**talk** *VERB* talks, talking, talked
to speak or have a conversation
➤ **talker** *NOUN*
➤ **talk down to someone** to speak to someone using simple language because you think they are less intelligent or important than you

**talk** *NOUN* talks
❶ a conversation or discussion ❷ an informal lecture

**talkative** *ADJECTIVE*
talking a lot

**tall** *ADJECTIVE* taller, tallest
❶ higher than the average • *a tall tree*
❷ measured from the bottom to the top • *It is 10 metres tall.*

**tallow** *NOUN*
animal fat used to make candles, soap, lubricants, etc.

**tall story** *NOUN* tall stories
(*informal*) a story that is hard to believe

**tally** *NOUN* tallies
the total amount of a debt or score

**tally** *VERB* tallies, tallying, tallied
to match or agree with something else • *Does your list tally with mine?* • *The accounts of the two witnesses did not tally.*

**Talmud** *NOUN*
the collection of writings that contain Jewish religious law

**talon** *NOUN* talons
a strong claw, especially on a bird of prey

**tambourine** *NOUN* tambourines
a circular musical instrument with metal discs fixed round it, so that it jingles when you tap or shake it

**tame** *ADJECTIVE*
❶ a tame animal is gentle and not afraid of people; not wild or dangerous ❷ not exciting; dull • *She finds village life very tame.*
➤ **tamely** *ADVERB*

**tame** *VERB* tames, taming, tamed
to make an animal become tame
➤ **tamer** *NOUN*

**Tamil** *NOUN* Tamils
❶ a member of a people of southern India and Sri Lanka ❷ their language

**tam-o'-shanter** *NOUN* tam-o'-shanters
a round Scottish cap with a bobble in the middle **WORD ORIGIN** named after *Tam o' Shanter*, hero of a poem by the Scottish poet Robert Burns

**tamp** *VERB* tamps, tamping, tamped
to press or pack something down firmly

**tamper** *VERB* tampers, tampering, tampered
➤ **tamper with something** to interfere with something or make changes to it so that it will not work properly • *Someone had tampered with the car's brakes.*

**tampon** *NOUN* tampons
a plug of soft material that a woman puts into her vagina to absorb the blood during her period

**tan** *NOUN* tans
❶ brown colour in skin that has been exposed to sun; a suntan ❷ a light brown colour

**tan** *VERB* tans, tanning, tanned
❶ to turn your skin brown by exposing it to the sun ❷ to make an animal's skin into leather by treating it with chemicals

**tandem** *NOUN* tandems
a bicycle for two riders, one behind the other
➤ **in tandem** together or at the same time
**WORD ORIGIN** Latin, = at length

**tandoori** *NOUN*
a style of Indian cooking in which food is cooked in a clay oven (a **tandoor**)

**tang** *NOUN* tangs
a strong flavour or smell • *a tang of lemon*

**tangent** *NOUN* tangents
a straight line that touches the outside of a

curve or circle
➤ **go off at a tangent** to move away suddenly from a subject or line of thought being considered

**tangerine** NOUN tangerines
a kind of small orange (WORD ORIGIN) named after *Tangier* in Morocco, where the fruit originally came from

**tangible** ADJECTIVE
❶ able to be touched ❷ that can be clearly seen; real or definite • *tangible benefits*
➤ **tangibly** ADVERB

**tangle** VERB tangles, tangling, tangled
to twist things together or become twisted into a confused mass • *My fishing line has tangled.* • *These computer cables are all tangled up.*

**tangle** NOUN tangles
a twisted or muddled mass of hair, wires, etc.

**tango** NOUN tangos
a ballroom dance with gliding steps and sudden pauses

**tank** NOUN tanks
❶ a large container for a liquid or gas ❷ a heavy armoured vehicle used in war

**tankard** NOUN tankards
a large mug for drinking beer from, usually made of silver or pewter

**tanker** NOUN tankers
❶ a large ship for carrying oil ❷ a large lorry for carrying a liquid

**tanner** NOUN tanners
a person who tans animal skins into leather
➤ **tannery** NOUN

**tannin** NOUN
a substance obtained from the bark or fruit of various trees (also found in tea), used in tanning and dyeing things

**tantalize** (also **tantalise**) VERB tantalizes, tantalizing, tantalized
to tease or torment a person by showing them something good that they cannot have (WORD ORIGIN) from the name of *Tantalus* in Greek mythology, who was punished by being made to stand near water and fruit which moved away when he tried to reach them

**tantamount** ADJECTIVE
to be tantamount to something is to be equivalent to it or virtually the same as it • *The Queen's request was tantamount to a command.* (WORD ORIGIN) from Italian *tanto montare* = amount to so much

**tantrum** NOUN tantrums
an outburst of bad temper

**tap** NOUN taps
❶ a device for letting out liquid or gas in a controlled flow ❷ a quick light hit; the sound of this • *I gave her a tap on the shoulder.*
❸ tap dancing

**tap** VERB taps, tapping, tapped
❶ to hit a person or thing quickly and lightly • *I tried tapping on the window.* • *He was busy tapping away at his computer.* ❷ to obtain supplies or information from a source ❸ to fix a device to a telephone line so that you can overhear conversations on it

**tap dancing** NOUN
dancing in shoes with metal caps that make sharp tapping sounds on the floor
➤ **tap dance** NOUN
➤ **tap dancer** NOUN

**tape** NOUN tapes
❶ a narrow strip of cloth, paper or plastic ❷ a narrow plastic strip coated with a magnetic substance and used for making recordings ❸ a tape recording ❹ a tape measure

**tape** VERB tapes, taping, taped
❶ to fix, cover or surround something with tape ❷ to record something on magnetic tape
➤ **have something taped** (*informal*) to understand something or be able to deal with it

**tape deck** NOUN tape decks
the part of a sound system on which music recorded on tape can be played

**tape measure** NOUN tape measures
a long strip marked in centimetres or inches for measuring things

**taper** VERB tapers, tapering, tapered
to become thinner or narrower towards one end
➤ **taper off** to become gradually less

**taper** NOUN tapers
a very thin candle, used for lighting things

**tape recorder** NOUN tape recorders
a machine for recording music or sound on magnetic tape and playing it back
➤ **tape recording** NOUN

**tapestry** NOUN tapestries
a piece of strong cloth with pictures or patterns woven or embroidered on it

**tapeworm** NOUN tapeworms
a long flat worm that can live as a parasite in the intestines of people and animals

a b c d e f g h i j k l m n o p q r s t u v w x y z

A
B
C
D
E
F
G
H
I
J
K
L
M
N
O
P
Q
R
S
**T**
U
V
W
X
Y
Z

**tapioca** *NOUN*
a starchy substance in hard white grains obtained from cassava, used for making milk puddings

**tapir** (say **tay**-per) *NOUN* **tapirs**
a pig-like animal with a long flexible snout

**tar** *NOUN*
a thick black liquid made from coal or wood and used in making roads

**tar** *VERB* **tars, tarring, tarred**
to coat something with tar

**tarantula** *NOUN* **tarantulas**
a large kind of spider found in southern Europe and in tropical countries. Some species of tarantula have a poisonous bite.

**tardy** *ADJECTIVE* **tardier, tardiest**
slow or late
➤ **tardily** *ADVERB*
➤ **tardiness** *NOUN*

**target** *NOUN* **targets**
something that you aim at and try to hit or reach

**target** *VERB* **targets, targeting, targeted**
to aim at something or have it as a target

**tariff** *NOUN* **tariffs**
a list of prices or charges

**tarmac** *NOUN*
❶ a mixture of tar and broken stone, used for making a hard surface on roads, paths, playgrounds, etc. ❷ an area surfaced with tarmac, especially on an airfield
**WORD ORIGIN** *Tarmac* is a trade mark

**tarnish** *VERB* **tarnishes, tarnishing, tarnished**
❶ metal tarnishes when it becomes stained and less shiny • *The silver has tarnished.* ❷ to spoil or damage something • *The scandal tarnished his reputation.*
➤ **tarnish** *NOUN*

**tarot card** (rhymes with barrow) *NOUN*
one of the cards in a special pack used for fortune-telling

**tarpaulin** *NOUN* **tarpaulins**
a large sheet of waterproof canvas

**tarragon** *NOUN*
a plant with leaves that are used to flavour salads and in cooking

**tarry** (say **tar**-ee) *ADJECTIVE*
covered with or like tar

**tarry** (say **ta**-ree) *VERB* **tarries, tarrying, tarried** (*old use*)
to stay for a while longer; to linger

**tart** *NOUN* **tarts**
❶ a pie containing fruit or sweet filling ❷ a piece of pastry with jam etc. on top

**tart** *ADJECTIVE*
❶ sour-tasting ❷ sharp in manner • *a tart reply*
➤ **tartly** *ADVERB*

**tartan** *NOUN*
a pattern with coloured stripes crossing each other, especially one that is used by a Scottish clan

**tartar** *NOUN* **tartars**
❶ a hard chalky deposit that forms on teeth ❷ a person who is fierce or difficult to deal with **WORD ORIGIN** the second sense comes from the *Tartar* warriors from central Asia in the 13th century

**tartlet** *NOUN* **tartlets**
a small pastry tart

**task** *NOUN* **tasks**
a piece of work that needs to be done
➤ **take someone to task** to tell someone off for doing something wrong

**task force** *NOUN* **task forces**
a group specially organized for a particular task

**taskmaster** *NOUN* **taskmasters**
a person who gives other people a lot of work to do • *a hard taskmaster*

**tassel** *NOUN* **tassels**
a bundle of threads tied together at the top and used to decorate something
➤ **tasselled** *ADJECTIVE*

**taste** *VERB* **tastes, tasting, tasted**
❶ to take a small amount of food or drink to try its flavour ❷ to be able to notice or recognize flavours • *Can you taste the garlic in this soup?* ❸ to have a certain flavour • *The milk tastes sour.*

**taste** *NOUN* **tastes**
❶ the feeling caused in the tongue by something placed on it ❷ the ability to taste things ❸ the ability to enjoy beautiful things or to choose things that are of good quality or go together well • *She shows good taste in her choice of clothes.* ❹ a liking for something • *The trip gave him a taste for foreign travel.* ❺ a very small amount of food or drink

**tasteful** *ADJECTIVE*
showing good taste
➤ **tastefully** *ADVERB*
➤ **tastefulness** *NOUN*

**tasteless** ADJECTIVE
❶ having no flavour ❷ showing poor taste
➤ **tastelessly** ADVERB
➤ **tastelessness** NOUN

**tasty** ADJECTIVE tastier, tastiest
having a strong pleasant taste

**tattered** ADJECTIVE
badly torn and ragged • *a tattered dress*

**tatters** PLURAL NOUN
rags; badly torn pieces
➤ **in tatters** torn to pieces • *My coat was in tatters.*

**tattoo** NOUN tattoos
❶ a picture or pattern marked on someone's skin by using a needle and dye ❷ a drumming or tapping sound • *He beat a tattoo on the table with his fingers.* ❸ an outdoor entertainment consisting of military music and marching

**tattoo** VERB tattoos, tattooing, tattooed
to mark a person's skin with a tattoo

**tatty** ADJECTIVE
shabby and worn • *a tatty carpet*

**taunt** VERB taunts, taunting, taunted
to jeer at or insult someone

**taunt** NOUN taunts
a taunting remark (WORD ORIGIN) from French *tant pour tant* = tit for tat

**taut** ADJECTIVE
stretched tightly • *Keep the rope taut.*
➤ **tautly** ADVERB
➤ **tautness** NOUN

**tautology** NOUN tautologies
saying the same thing again in different words, e.g. *You can get the book free for nothing.* (where *free* and *for nothing* mean the same)

**tavern** NOUN taverns (old use)
an inn or public house

**tawdry** ADJECTIVE
cheap and gaudy
➤ **tawdriness** NOUN
(WORD ORIGIN) from *St Audrey's lace* (cheap finery formerly sold at St Audrey's fair at Ely)

**tawny** ADJECTIVE
brownish-yellow

**tax** NOUN taxes
❶ money that people or business firms have to pay to the government, to be used for public purposes ❷ a strain or burden • *The long walk was a tax on his strength.*

**tax** VERB taxes, taxing, taxed
❶ to put a tax on something ❷ to charge someone a tax ❸ to put a strain or burden on a person or thing • *This will tax your strength.* ❹ (formal) to accuse someone of doing something wrong • *I taxed him with leaving the door open.*

**taxation** NOUN
money that has to be paid as taxes

**taxi** NOUN taxis
a car with a driver that you can hire for journeys, usually with a meter to record the fare to be paid
➤ **taxicab** NOUN

**taxi** VERB taxis or taxies, taxiing, taxied
an aircraft taxis when it moves slowly along the ground before taking off or after landing

**taxidermist** NOUN taxidermists
a person who prepares and stuffs the skins of animals in a lifelike form
➤ **taxidermy** NOUN

**taxpayer** NOUN taxpayers
a person who pays tax

**TB** ABBREVIATION
tuberculosis

**tea** NOUN teas
❶ a drink made by pouring hot water on the dried leaves of an evergreen shrub (the *tea plant*) ❷ these dried leaves ❸ a drink made with the leaves of other plants • *camomile tea* ❹ a meal in the afternoon or early evening

**tea bag** NOUN tea bags
a small bag holding about a teaspoonful of tea

**teacake** NOUN teacakes
(British) a kind of bun usually served toasted and buttered

**teach** VERB teaches, teaching, taught
❶ to give a person knowledge or skill; to train someone ❷ to give lessons in a subject • *She taught us history last year.* ❸ to show someone what to do or avoid • *That will teach you not to meddle!*

**teachable** ADJECTIVE
able to be taught

**teacher** NOUN teachers
a person who teaches others, especially in a school

**teaching** NOUN teachings
things that are taught • *the teachings of Plato*

**tea cloth** NOUN tea cloths
a tea towel

**teacup** NOUN teacups
a cup for drinking tea

**teak** NOUN
the hard strong wood of an evergreen Asian tree

**teal** NOUN teal
a kind of duck

**tea leaves** PLURAL NOUN
the small leaves left in a cup or mug after you have drunk the tea

**team** NOUN teams
❶ a set of players who form one side in certain games and sports ❷ a set of people working together ❸ two or more animals harnessed to pull a vehicle or a plough

**team** VERB teams, teaming, teamed
➤ **team up with someone** to join someone in order to do something together
➤ **team someone with someone** to put people together in a team

**teamwork** NOUN
the ability of a team or group to work well together

**teapot** NOUN teapots
a pot with a lid and a handle, for making and pouring tea

**tear** (say teer) NOUN tears
a drop of the water that comes from the eyes when a person cries
➤ **in tears** crying

**tear** (say tair) VERB tears, tearing, tore, torn
❶ to make a split in something or pull it apart • *She tore the letter in half.* ❷ to pull or remove something with force • *I tore the poster off the wall.* ❸ to become torn • *Newspaper tears easily.* ❹ to run or travel hurriedly • *He tore down the street.*

**tear** (say tair) NOUN tears
a split made by tearing

> SPELLING
>
> The verb **tear** rhymes with *hair* and means to rip something. The past tense of the verb **tear** is **tore** and the past participle is **torn**.

**teardrop** NOUN teardrops
a single tear

**tearful** ADJECTIVE
in tears; crying easily
➤ **tearfully** ADVERB

**tear gas** NOUN
a gas that makes people's eyes water painfully, sometimes used by the police or army to control crowds

**tease** VERB teases, teasing, teased
❶ to make fun of someone and say things to make them annoyed ❷ to pick threads apart into separate strands

**tease** NOUN teases
a person who often teases others

**teaser** NOUN teasers
(*informal*) a difficult problem or puzzle

**teaspoon** NOUN teaspoons
a small spoon for stirring tea or measuring small amounts

**teaspoonful** NOUN teaspoonfuls
as much as a teaspoon will hold

**teat** NOUN teats
❶ one of the nipples on a female animal, through which the young suck milk ❷ the cap of a baby's feeding bottle

**tea towel** NOUN tea towels
(*chiefly British*) a cloth for drying washed dishes and cutlery

**tech** (say tek) NOUN techs (*informal*)
a technical college

**technical** ADJECTIVE
❶ to do with technology or the way things work ❷ to do with a particular subject and its methods • *the technical terms of chemistry* ❸ using words that only people who know a lot about a subject will understand
**WORD ORIGIN** from Greek *technikos* = skilled in an art or craft

**technical college** NOUN technical colleges
a college where technical and practical subjects are taught

**technicality** NOUN technicalities
a small detail of the law or a process

**technically** ADVERB
according to the strict facts or rules • *He was technically in charge, but no one took any notice of what he said.*

**technician** NOUN technicians
a person whose job is to look after scientific equipment and do practical work in a laboratory

**technique** NOUN techniques
a method of doing something skilfully

**technological** ADJECTIVE
to do with technology • *technological developments*

**technology** NOUN technologies
the study of machinery, engineering and how things work
➤ **technologist** NOUN

**teddy bear** NOUN teddy bears
a soft furry toy bear (WORD ORIGIN) named after US President Theodore ('*Teddy*') Roosevelt, who liked hunting bears

**tedious** ADJECTIVE
annoyingly slow or long; boring
➤ **tediously** ADVERB
➤ **tediousness** NOUN

**tedium** NOUN
a dull or boring time or experience

**tee** NOUN tees
❶ the flat area from which golfers strike the ball at the start of play for each hole ❷ a small piece of wood or plastic on which a golf ball is placed for being struck

**teem** VERB teems, teeming, teemed
❶ to be full of something • *The river was teeming with fish.* ❷ to rain very hard; to pour

**teen** ADJECTIVE & NOUN teens (*informal*)
a teenager

**teenage** ADJECTIVE
in your teens; to do with teenagers

**teenaged** ADJECTIVE
in your teens

**teenager** NOUN teenagers
a person in their teens

**teens** PLURAL NOUN
the time of your life between the ages of 13 and 19

**teeny** ADJECTIVE teenier, teeniest (*informal*)
tiny

**tee-shirt** NOUN tee-shirts
a T-shirt

**teeter** VERB teeters, teetering, teetered
to stand or move unsteadily • *She teetered along in her high-heeled shoes.*

**teethe** VERB teethes, teething, teethed
a baby is teething when its first teeth are beginning to grow through the gums

**teetotal** ADJECTIVE
never drinking alcohol
➤ **teetotaller** NOUN

**Teflon** NOUN (*trademark*)
a type of plastic used as a non-stick coating for pans (WORD ORIGIN) from poly*tetraf*luoroethylene, its scientific name

**telecommunications** PLURAL NOUN
communications over long distances, e.g. by telephone, radio or television

**telegram** NOUN telegrams
a message sent by telegraph

**telegraph** NOUN
a way of sending messages by using electric current along wires or by radio
➤ **telegraphic** ADJECTIVE
➤ **telegraphy** NOUN

**telepathy** (say til-**ep**-ath-ee) NOUN
communication of thoughts from one person's mind to another without speaking, writing or gestures
➤ **telepathic** ADJECTIVE

**telephone** NOUN telephones
a device or system using electric wires or radio to enable one person to speak to another who is some distance away

**telephone** VERB telephones, telephoning, telephoned
to speak to a person by telephone
(WORD ORIGIN) from Greek *tele* = far off + *phone* = sound, voice

**telephonist** (say til-**ef**-on-ist) NOUN
telephonists
(*British*) a person who operates a telephone switchboard

**telescope** NOUN telescopes
an instrument using lenses to magnify distant objects
➤ **telescopic** ADJECTIVE

**telescope** VERB telescopes, telescoping, telescoped
to become shorter or make something shorter, by sliding overlapping sections into each other

**televise** VERB televises, televising, televised
to broadcast an event or programme by television

**television** NOUN televisions
❶ a system using radio waves to reproduce a view of scenes or events on a screen ❷ an apparatus for receiving these pictures

**❸** televised programmes • *How much television do you watch?*

**tell** VERB tells, telling, told
**❶** to make a thing known to someone, especially by words • *Come on, tell me what happened.* **❷** to say something • *Don't tell lies.* **❸** to order or advise someone to do something • *Tell them to wait outside.* **❹** to reveal a secret • *Promise you won't tell.* **❺** to be certain about something or recognize it • *I could tell she was worried.* • *Can you tell the difference between the twins?* **❻** to produce an effect • *The strain was beginning to tell on him.*
➤ **all told** in all, all together • *There are ten of them, all told.*
➤ **tell someone off** (*informal*) to scold someone because they have done something wrong
➤ **tell tales** to report something naughty or bad that someone else has done

**telling** ADJECTIVE
having a strong effect or meaning • *It was a telling reply.*

**tell-tale** NOUN tell-tales
a person who tells tales

**tell-tale** ADJECTIVE
revealing or indicating something that is supposed to be secret • *There was a tell-tale spot of jam on his chin.*

**telly** NOUN tellies (*British*) (*informal*)
**❶** television **❷** a television set

**temerity** (say tim-erri-tee) NOUN
rashness or boldness

**temp** NOUN temps (*informal*)
a secretary or other worker who works for short periods of time in different companies

**temper** NOUN tempers
**❶** a person's mood • *He is in a good temper.* **❷** an angry mood • *She was in a temper.*
➤ **lose your temper** to lose your calmness and become angry

**temper** VERB tempers, tempering, tempered
**❶** to harden or strengthen metal by heating and cooling it **❷** to make something less severe or soften its effects • *Justice needs to be tempered with mercy.*

**temperament** NOUN temperaments
a person's nature as shown in the way they usually behave • *a nervous temperament*

**temperamental** ADJECTIVE
**❶** likely to become excitable or moody

suddenly **❷** to do with a person's temperament

**temperance** NOUN
**❶** drinking little or no alcohol **❷** the ability to control your behaviour; self-restraint

**temperate** ADJECTIVE
a temperate climate is neither extremely hot nor extremely cold (**WORD ORIGIN**) originally = not affected by strong emotions

**temperature** NOUN temperatures
**❶** how hot or cold a person or thing is **❷** an abnormally high temperature of the body • *She's feverish and has a temperature.*

**SPELLING**

> Do not forget the **er** in the middle of **temperature**.

**tempest** NOUN tempests
(*old use*) a violent storm

**tempestuous** ADJECTIVE
stormy; full of commotion

**template** NOUN templates
a thin sheet of shaped metal, plastic or card used as a guide for cutting or shaping things

**temple** NOUN temples
**❶** a building where a god is worshipped
**❷** the part of your head between your forehead and your ear

**tempo** NOUN tempos or tempi
**❶** the speed or rhythm of something **❷** the speed at which a piece of music is played

**temporary** ADJECTIVE
lasting for a short time only; not permanent • *a temporary shelter*
➤ **temporarily** (say tem-per-er-il-ee) ADVERB

**tempt** VERB tempts, tempting, tempted
**❶** to try to persuade or attract someone, especially into doing something wrong or unwise **❷** to be tempted to do something is to want to do it even though it may not be the right thing to do • *I was tempted to tell her the whole story.*
➤ **tempter** NOUN
➤ **temptress** NOUN

**temptation** NOUN temptations
**❶** a feeling that you want to do something, even if you know it is wrong • *I managed to resist the temptation to open the letter.*
**❷** something that tempts you

**tempting** ADJECTIVE
attractive in a way that makes you want to do or have something • *a tempting offer*

**ten** NOUN ADJECTIVE **tens**
the number 10

**tenable** ADJECTIVE
able to be held or defended • *a tenable theory* • *The job is tenable for one year only.*

**tenacious** (say ten-**ay**-shus) ADJECTIVE
❶ holding or clinging firmly to something
❷ obstinate and persistent
➤ **tenaciously** ADVERB
➤ **tenacity** NOUN

**tenant** NOUN **tenants**
a person who rents a house, building or land from a landlord
➤ **tenancy** NOUN

**tend** VERB **tends, tending, tended**
❶ to be likely to do something; to usually happen • *He tends to have a nap in the afternoon.* ❷ to look after something or someone • *Shepherds were tending their sheep.*

**tendency** NOUN **tendencies**
the way a person or thing is likely to behave • *She has a tendency to be lazy.*

**tender** ADJECTIVE
❶ easy to chew; not tough or hard ❷ easily hurt or damaged; delicate or sensitive • *tender plants* ❸ a tender part of your body is painful when touched ❹ gentle and loving • *a tender smile*
➤ **tenderly** ADVERB
➤ **tenderness** NOUN

**tender** VERB **tenders, tendering, tendered**
to offer something formally • *He tendered his resignation.*

**tender** NOUN **tenders**
❶ a formal offer to supply goods or carry out work at a stated price • *The council asked for tenders to build a school.* ❷ a truck attached to a steam locomotive to carry its coal and water ❸ a small boat carrying stores or passengers to and from a larger one
➤ **legal tender** kinds of money that are legal for making payments • *Are pound notes still legal tender?*

**tendon** NOUN **tendons**
a strong strip of tissue that joins muscle to bone

**tendril** NOUN **tendrils**
❶ a thread-like part by which a climbing plant clings to a support ❷ a thin curl of hair

**tenement** NOUN **tenements**
a large house or building divided into flats or rooms that are let to separate tenants

**tenet** (say **ten**-it) NOUN **tenets**
a firm belief held by a person or group

**tenner** NOUN **tenners** (*British*) (*informal*)
a ten-pound note; £10

**tennis** NOUN
a game played with rackets and a ball on a court with a net across the middle

**tenon** NOUN **tenons**
a piece of wood shaped to fit into a mortise

**tenor** NOUN **tenors**
❶ a male singer with a high voice ❷ the general meaning or drift of something • *I was encouraged by the tenor of her remarks.*

**tenpin bowling** NOUN
a game in which players try to knock over ten skittles set up at the end of a track by rolling hard balls down it

**tense** NOUN **tenses**
the form of a verb that shows when something happens, e.g. he *came* (**past tense**), he *comes* or *is coming* (**present tense**)

**tense** ADJECTIVE
❶ tightly stretched • *tense muscles*
❷ nervous or worried and unable to relax
❸ making people tense • *a tense moment*
➤ **tensely** ADVERB
➤ **tenseness** NOUN

**tense** VERB **tenses, tensing, tensed**
to have muscles that have become hard and not relaxed • *I felt myself tense up.*

> **GRAMMAR**
>
> The **tense** of a verb tells you when the action of the verb takes place.
>
> The **present tense** shows that something is happening now or is true now.
> The **simple present tense** describes something that is continuous or repeated. It is usually shown by having no ending, or by adding -s:
>
> *Titan is Saturn's biggest moon.*
>
> *I hate olives.*
>
> *Do you mind if I come in?*
>
> The **present progressive tense** (also called the **present continuous tense**) shows that something is in the process of happening now, either happening right now or continuing over a longer period.
>
> It uses the auxiliary verb *be* and the

a b c d e f g h i j k l m n o p q r s t u v w x y z

present participle (or *-ing* form) of the main verb:

*What are you doing?*

*I am still reading the first chapter.*

The **present perfect tense** is used to talk about something that happened earlier and is still relevant now, or something that started happening in the past and is still happening now. It uses *have* and the past participle (or *-ed* form) of the main verb:

<u>*They have finished their work,*</u> *so they can go out now.*

*She has played in goal for several matches.*

The **past tense** shows that something happened in the past. The **simple past tense** is used for something that happened earlier or in the past and is now finished. It is normally shown by adding *-ed*:

*The Apollo 11 mission landed on the Moon in 1969.*

*Did you play football today?*

The **past progressive tense** (also called the **past continuous tense**) shows that something was in the process of happening at some time in the past. It was not finished, or was still happening when something else happened. It is formed with the simple past of *be* and the present participle (or *-ing* form) of the main verb:

*When war broke out,* <u>*my grandparents were living in Austria.*</u>

*She was feeling nervous.*

The **past perfect tense** is used to talk about something that happened before something else in the past, or something that started happening in the past and was still happening at a later time. It is formed with the simple past of *have* and the past participle (or *-ed* form) of the main verb:

<u>*The party had finished*</u> *by the time I arrived.*

*He had played for them for years.*

To talk about something that will, or may,

happen in the future, you use *will*, or another modal verb before the main verb:

*I will send you my email address.*

*Will your sister mind if I borrow her hairdryer?*

To talk about something that will, or may, happen by a specific time in the future, the modal verb *will* is used with the past of *have* and the past participle of the main verb:

*By tomorrow I will have finished all my work.*

See also the panel on verbs.

**tensile** ADJECTIVE
❶ to do with tension ❷ able to be stretched

**tension** NOUN tensions
❶ how tightly stretched a rope or wire is
❷ a feeling of anxiety or nervousness about something that is just about to happen
❸ voltage • *high-tension cables*

**tent** NOUN tents
a shelter made of canvas or cloth supported by upright poles

**tentacle** NOUN tentacles
a long flexible part of the body of an animal such as an octopus, used for feeling or grasping things or for moving

**tentative** ADJECTIVE
cautious; trying something out • *a tentative suggestion*
➤ **tentatively** ADVERB

**tenterhooks** PLURAL NOUN
➤ **on tenterhooks** tense and anxious about something that is going to happen
(WORD ORIGIN) from *tenter* = a machine with hooks for stretching cloth to dry

**tenth** ADJECTIVE & NOUN tenths
next after the ninth

**tenuous** ADJECTIVE
very slight or thin • *tenuous threads* • *a tenuous connection*

**tenure** (say **ten**-yoor) NOUN tenures
the holding of a position of employment or of land or property

**tepee** (say **tee**-pee) NOUN tepees
a tent formerly used by Native Americans, made by fastening skins or mats over poles
(WORD ORIGIN) a Native American word

**tepid** ADJECTIVE
only slightly warm; lukewarm • *tepid water*

**term** NOUN terms
❶ the period of weeks when a school or college is open ❷ a definite period • *a term of imprisonment* ❸ a word or expression with a special meaning • *a glossary of technical terms*

**term** VERB terms, terming, termed
to describe or name something by using a certain word or expression • *These male bees are termed 'drones'.*

**terminal** NOUN terminals
❶ a building where passengers arrive or depart • *an airport terminal* ❷ a place where a wire is connected in an electric circuit or battery ❸ a computer keyboard and screen used for sending data to or from the main computer

**terminal** ADJECTIVE
a terminal illness is one that cannot be cured and that the person will die from • *terminal cancer*
➤ **terminally** ADVERB

**terminate** VERB terminates, terminating, terminated
to end or stop or to make something end or stop • *This train terminates here.*
➤ **termination** NOUN

**terminology** NOUN terminologies
the technical terms of a subject

**terminus** NOUN termini
the last station on a railway or bus route

**termite** NOUN termites
a small insect that eats wood and lives in large groups

**terms** PLURAL NOUN
❶ a relationship between people • *They ended up on friendly terms.* ❷ conditions offered or agreed, especially in a treaty or contract • *peace terms*
➤ **come to terms with something** to learn to accept a difficulty or unwelcome situation

**tern** NOUN terns
a seabird with long wings

**terrace** NOUN terraces
❶ a row of houses joined together ❷ a level area on a slope or hillside ❸ a paved area beside a house
➤ **terraced** ADJECTIVE

**terracotta** NOUN
❶ a kind of pottery ❷ the brownish-red colour of flowerpots

**terra firma** NOUN
dry land; the ground (**WORD ORIGIN**) Latin, = firm land

**terrain** NOUN terrains
a stretch of land • *hilly terrain*

**terrapin** NOUN terrapins
an edible freshwater turtle of North America

**terrestrial** ADJECTIVE
❶ to do with the earth or land ❷ terrestrial television is broadcast by aerials on the ground rather than by satellite

**terrible** ADJECTIVE
very bad; awful

**terribly** ADVERB
❶ very badly • *He was missing his parents terribly.* ❷ (*informal*) very; extremely • *I'm terribly sorry.*

**terrier** NOUN terriers
a kind of small lively dog (**WORD ORIGIN**) from old French *chien terrier* = earth-dog (because they were used to dig out foxes from their earths)

**terrific** ADJECTIVE (*informal*)
❶ very great • *There was a terrific bang.* ❷ very good or excellent
➤ **terrifically** ADVERB

**terrified** ADJECTIVE
very afraid • *I'm terrified of snakes.*

**terrify** VERB terrifies, terrifying, terrified
to make a person or animal very frightened

**territorial** ADJECTIVE
❶ to do with or belonging to a country's territory • *a territorial dispute* ❷ a territorial animal or bird guards and defends an area of land it believes to be its own • *Cats are very territorial.*

**territory** NOUN territories
❶ an area of land, especially one that belongs to a country ❷ an area of land that an animal or bird thinks of as its own and defends against others

**terror** NOUN terrors
❶ very great fear ❷ a terrifying person or thing

**terrorist** NOUN terrorists
a person who uses violence for political purposes
➤ **terrorism** NOUN

**terrorize** (also **terrorise**) *VERB* terrorizes, terrorizing, terrorized
to frighten someone by threatening them

**terse** *ADJECTIVE*
using few words and not very friendly • *a terse reply*
➤ **tersely** *ADVERB*

**tertiary** (say **ter**-sher-ee) *ADJECTIVE*
to do with the third stage of something; coming after secondary

**tessellated** *ADJECTIVE*
decorated with shapes that fit together into a pattern without overlapping or leaving gaps
• *a tessellated floor*
➤ **tessellation** *NOUN*
**WORD ORIGIN** from Latin *tessella* = a small piece of wood, bone or glass, used as a token or in a mosaic

**test** *NOUN* tests
❶ a short examination • *a spelling test* ❷ a way of discovering the qualities, abilities or presence of a person or thing • *a test for radioactivity* ❸ a test match

**test** *VERB* tests, testing, tested
to carry out a test on a person or thing
• *Mum needs to have her eyes tested.*
➤ **tester** *NOUN*

**testament** *NOUN* testaments
❶ a written statement ❷ either of the two main parts of the Bible, the Old Testament or the New Testament

**testicle** *NOUN* testicles
either of the two glands in the scrotum where semen is produced

**testify** *VERB* testifies, testifying, testified
❶ to give evidence or swear that something is true ❷ to be evidence or proof of something
• *Three world titles testify to her talent.*

**testimonial** *NOUN* testimonials
❶ a letter describing someone's abilities and character ❷ a gift presented to someone as a mark of respect

**testimony** *NOUN* testimonies
evidence; what someone testifies

**test match** *NOUN* test matches
a cricket or rugby match between teams from different countries

**testosterone** (say test-**ost**-er-ohn) *NOUN*
a male sex hormone

**test tube** *NOUN* test tubes
a tube of thin glass with one end closed, used for experiments in chemistry

**test-tube baby** *NOUN* test-tube babies
a baby that develops from an egg that has been fertilized outside the mother's body and then placed back in the womb

**testy** *ADJECTIVE*
easily annoyed; irritable
➤ **testily** *ADVERB*

**tetanus** *NOUN*
a disease that makes the muscles become stiff, caused by bacteria

**tetchy** *ADJECTIVE*
easily annoyed; irritable
➤ **tetchily** *ADVERB*

**tête-à-tête** (say tayt-ah-**tayt**) *NOUN* tête-à-têtes
a private conversation between two people
**WORD ORIGIN** French, = head to head

**tether** *VERB* tethers, tethering, tethered
to tie up an animal so that it cannot move far

**tether** *NOUN* tethers
a rope for tethering an animal
➤ **at the end of your tether** unable to stand something any more

**tetrahedron** *NOUN* tetrahedrons
a solid with four sides (i.e. a pyramid with a triangular base)

**text** *NOUN* texts
❶ the words of something written or printed ❷ a text message ❸ a sentence from the Bible used as the subject of a sermon in a Christian church

**text** *VERB* texts, texting, texted
to send a text message to someone on a mobile phone • *He texted me to tell me when the train would arrive.*

**textbook** *NOUN* textbooks
a book that teaches you about a subject

**textiles** *PLURAL NOUN*
kinds of cloth; fabrics

**text message** *NOUN* text messages
a written message sent on a mobile phone

**texture** *NOUN* textures
the way that the surface of something feels when you touch it • *Silk has a smooth texture.*

**thalidomide** *NOUN*
a medicinal drug that was found (in 1961) to

cause babies to be born with deformed arms and legs

**than** CONJUNCTION & PREPOSITION
compared with another person or thing • *His brother is taller than he is.* • *She speaks French better than me.*

**thank** VERB thanks, thanking, thanked
to tell someone that you are grateful to them
➤ **thank you** an expression of thanks

**thankful** ADJECTIVE
❶ pleased and relieved • *I was thankful that nobody was around.* ❷ showing thanks; grateful

**thankfully** ADVERB
❶ in a grateful way ❷ fortunately; luckily • *Thankfully, it has stopped raining.*

**thankless** ADJECTIVE
a thankless task is one that you are not likely to get thanked or rewarded for doing

**thanks** PLURAL NOUN
❶ words that thank someone; gratitude ❷ (*informal*) thank you
➤ **thanks to** as a result of; because of • *Thanks to you, we succeeded.*

**thanksgiving** NOUN
an expression of gratitude, especially to God

**that** DETERMINER & PRONOUN those
the one there • *That book is mine.* • *Whose bike is that?*

**that** ADVERB
to such an extent • *I'll come that far but no further.*

**that** RELATIVE PRONOUN
which, who or whom • *This is the DVD that I wanted.* • *We liked the people that we met on holiday.*

**that** CONJUNCTION
used to introduce a wish, reason or result • *I hope that you are well.* • *The puzzle was so hard that no one could solve it.*

GRAMMAR
See also the panel at **which**.

**thatch** NOUN
straw or reeds used to make a roof

**thatch** VERB thatches, thatching, thatched
to make a roof with thatch
➤ **thatcher** NOUN

**thaw** VERB thaws, thawing, thawed
to melt; to stop being frozen • *The snow was beginning to thaw.*

**thaw** NOUN thaws
a period of warm weather that thaws ice and snow

**the** DETERMINER called the definite article
a particular one; that or those

GRAMMAR
The word *the* is known as the **definite article**. You use it before a noun or noun phrase when the person or thing you are talking about has already been mentioned or you want to specify which one you mean:

*That is the cave where the dragon sleeps.*

*Jupiter is the largest gas planet.*

**theatre** NOUN theatres
❶ a building where people go to see plays or shows ❷ the writing, acting and producing of plays ❸ a special room where surgical operations are done • *the operating theatre*

**theatrical** ADJECTIVE
❶ to do with plays or acting ❷ theatrical behaviour is exaggerated and done for showy effect
➤ **theatrically** ADVERB

**theatricals** PLURAL NOUN
performances of plays

**thee** PRONOUN (old use)
you (referring to one person and used as the object of a verb or after a preposition)

**theft** NOUN thefts
stealing • *He was arrested for theft.*

**their** DETERMINER
❶ belonging to them • *Their coats are over there.* ❷ (*informal*) belonging to a person • *Somebody has left their coat on the bus.*

SPELLING
**Their** is different from **there**: • *their pets* • *I'm going there soon.*

**theirs** POSSESSIVE PRONOUN
belonging to them • *These coats are theirs.*

USAGE
It is incorrect to write *their's*.

**them** PRONOUN
the form of *they* used as the object of a verb or after a preposition • *We forgot to bring them.* • *I gave it to them.*

**theme** NOUN themes
❶ the subject of a speech, piece of writing, discussion, etc. ❷ a melody

**theme park** NOUN theme parks
an amusement park where the rides and
attractions are based on a particular subject

**theme tune** NOUN theme tunes
a special tune always used to announce a
particular programme or performer

**themselves** PRONOUN
they or them and nobody else. The word
is used to refer back to the subject of a
sentence (e.g. *They blame themselves.*) or for
emphasis (e.g. *My grandparents built this
house themselves.*).
➤ **by themselves** on their own; alone

**then** ADVERB
❶ at that time • *I lived in London then.*
❷ after that; next • *I'll just get changed and
then we can go out.* • *Then a strange thing
happened.* ❸ in that case; therefore • *If this
is yours, then this must be mine.*

**thence** ADVERB
from that place

**theology** NOUN
the study of religion
➤ **theological** ADJECTIVE
➤ **theologian** NOUN

**theorem** NOUN theorems
a mathematical statement that can be proved
by reasoning

**theoretical** ADJECTIVE
based on theory, not on practice or
experience
➤ **theoretically** ADVERB

**theorize** (also **theorise**) VERB theorizes,
theorizing, theorized
to form a theory or theories

**theory** NOUN theories
❶ an idea or set of ideas put forward to
explain something • *Darwin's theory of
evolution* ❷ the principles of a subject rather
than its practice
➤ **in theory** according to what should
happen rather than what may in fact happen

**therapeutic** (say therra-**pew**-tik) ADJECTIVE
helping to treat or cure a disease or illness
• *Sunshine can have a therapeutic effect.*

**therapy** NOUN therapies
a way of treating a physical or mental illness,
especially without using surgery or artificial
medicines
➤ **therapist** NOUN

**there** ADVERB
❶ in or to that place ❷ used to call attention
to something or to talk about it • *There's
a spider in the bath.* • *There has been a
mistake.*

SPELLING
**There** is different from **their**: • *I'm going
there soon.* • *their pets*

**thereabouts** ADVERB
near there

**thereafter** ADVERB
from then or there onwards

**thereby** ADVERB
by that means; because of that

**therefore** ADVERB
for that reason; and so

**therm** NOUN therms
a unit for measuring heat, especially from gas

**thermal** ADJECTIVE
❶ to do with heat; worked by heat
❷ designed to keep you warm in cold weather
• *thermal underwear*

**thermodynamics** NOUN
the science dealing with the relation between
heat and other forms of energy

**thermometer** NOUN thermometers
a device for measuring temperature

**Thermos** NOUN Thermoses (trademark)
a kind of vacuum flask

**thermostat** NOUN thermostats
a piece of equipment that automatically
keeps the temperature of a room or piece of
equipment steady

**thesaurus** (say thi-**sor**-us) NOUN thesauruses
or thesauri
a kind of dictionary that lists words
in groups that have similar meanings
WORD ORIGIN from Greek *thesauros* =
storehouse, treasury

**these** DETERMINER & PRONOUN
plural of **this**

**thesis** NOUN theses
❶ a theory that someone has put forward
❷ a long essay written by a candidate for a
university degree

**they** PRONOUN
❶ the people or things being talked about
❷ people in general • *They say it's going to
be a mild winter.* ❸ he or she; a person • *I am
never angry with anyone unless they deserve
it.*

**they're** (*mainly spoken*)
they are

**SPELLING**
They're = they + are. Do not forget to add an **apostrophe** between the y and the re.

**thick** *ADJECTIVE*
❶ measuring a lot from one side to the other; broad or wide • *a thick slice of cake* ❷ measuring from one side to the other • *The wall is ten centimetres thick.* ❸ with a lot of things packed close together; dense • *thick dark hair* • *thick fog* ❹ fairly stiff; not flowing easily • *thick cream* ❺ (*informal*) stupid

**thicken** *VERB* thickens, thickening, thickened
to become thicker or to make something thicker • *The fog had thickened.*

**thicket** *NOUN* thickets
a number of shrubs and small trees growing close together

**thickly** *ADVERB*
❶ in thick pieces or in a deep layer • *thickly sliced bread* • *The roads were thickly covered with snow.* ❷ with a lot of things packed close together • *thickly wooded hills*

**thickness** *NOUN* thicknesses
how thick something is • *What thickness of board do we need?*

**thickset** *ADJECTIVE*
❶ having a stocky or burly body ❷ with parts placed or growing close together

**thief** *NOUN* thieves
a person who steals things

**thieving** *NOUN*
stealing things

**thieving** *ADJECTIVE*
behaving like a thief

**thigh** *NOUN* thighs
the part of your leg between your hip and your knee

**thimble** *NOUN* thimbles
a small metal or plastic cap that you put on the end of your finger to protect it when you are sewing

**thin** *ADJECTIVE* thinner, thinnest
❶ measuring a small amount from one side to the other ❷ not fat ❸ not dense or closely packed together ❹ runny or watery
➤ **thinness** *NOUN*

**thin** *VERB* thins, thinning, thinned
to become less thick or to make something less thick
➤ **thin out** to become less dense or crowded
• *The crowd had thinned out by late afternoon.*
➤ **thin something out** to make something less dense or crowded

**thine** *DETERMINER & POSSESSIVE PRONOUN* (*old use*)
yours (referring to one person)

**thing** *NOUN* things
an object; something which can be seen, touched or thought about

**things** *PLURAL NOUN*
❶ personal belongings • *Can I leave my things here?* ❷ events or circumstances • *Things are looking good.*

**think** *VERB* thinks, thinking, thought
❶ to use your mind ❷ to have something as an idea or opinion • *Do you think we have enough time?* ❸ to intend or plan to do something • *I'm thinking of buying a guitar.*

**SPELLING**
The past tense of **think** is **thought**.

**think** *NOUN*
a time spent thinking about something • *I'll have a think and let you know.*

**thinker** *NOUN* thinkers
a person who thinks about things, especially important subjects

**thinly** *ADVERB*
❶ in thin pieces or in a thin layer • *thinly sliced bread* • *He spread the butter thinly on his toast.* ❷ with only a few things or people spread over a place • *a thinly populated area* ❸ in a way that is not sincere or enthusiastic • *She smiled thinly.*

**third** *ADJECTIVE*
next after the second
➤ **thirdly** *ADVERB*

**third** *NOUN* thirds
❶ the third person or thing ❷ one of three equal parts of something

**Third World** *NOUN*
the poorest and underdeveloped countries of Asia, Africa and South America
**WORD ORIGIN** originally called 'third' because they were not considered to be politically connected with the USA and its allies (the *First World*) or with the Communist countries led by Russia (the *Second World*)

**thirst** NOUN
❶ a feeling of dryness in your mouth and throat that makes you want to drink ❷ a strong desire for something • *a thirst for adventure*

**thirst** VERB thirsts, thirsting, thirsted
to have a strong desire for something • *She thirsted for revenge.*

**thirsty** ADJECTIVE
feeling that you need to drink
➤ **thirstily** ADVERB

**thirteen** NOUN & ADJECTIVE thirteens
the number 13
➤ **thirteenth** ADJECTIVE & NOUN

**thirty** NOUN & ADJECTIVE thirties
the number 30
➤ **thirtieth** ADJECTIVE & NOUN

**this** DETERMINER & PRONOUN these
the one here • *This is my stop.* • *Have a look at this picture.*

**this** ADVERB
to such an extent • *I'm not used to getting up this early.*

**thistle** NOUN thistles
a prickly wild plant with purple, white or yellow flowers

**thistledown** NOUN
the very light fluff on thistle seeds

**thither** ADVERB (old use)
to that place

**thong** NOUN thongs
a narrow strip of leather used for fastening things

**thorax** NOUN thoraxes
the part of the body between the head or neck and the abdomen **WORD ORIGIN** Greek, = breastplate

**thorn** NOUN thorns
❶ a small pointed growth on the stem of a plant ❷ a thorny tree or shrub

**thorny** ADJECTIVE thornier, thorniest
❶ having many thorns; prickly ❷ causing difficulty or disagreement • *a thorny problem*

**thorough** ADJECTIVE
❶ done or doing things carefully and in detail ❷ complete in every way • *a thorough mess*
➤ **thoroughness** NOUN

**thoroughbred** ADJECTIVE
bred of pure or pedigree stock

**thoroughbred** NOUN thoroughbreds
an animal of of pure or pedigree stock

**thoroughfare** NOUN thoroughfares
a public road or path that is open at both ends

**thoroughly** ADVERB
❶ completely; very much • *We thoroughly enjoyed ourselves.* ❷ carefully and in detail • *She checked the figures thoroughly.*

**those** DETERMINER & PRONOUN
plural of that • *Where are those cards?* • *Those are the ones I want.*

**thou** PRONOUN (old use)
you (referring to one person)

**though** CONJUNCTION
in spite of the fact that; even if • *We can try phoning her, though she may already have left.*

**though** ADVERB
however; all the same • *She's right, though.*

**thought**
past tense of **think**

**thought** NOUN thoughts
❶ something that you think; an idea or opinion • *Look, I've just had a thought.* ❷ the process of thinking • *She was deep in thought.*

**thoughtful** ADJECTIVE
❶ thinking a lot • *a thoughtful expression* ❷ thinking of other people and what they need or want; considerate • *That was very thoughtful of you.*
➤ **thoughtfully** ADVERB
➤ **thoughtfulness** NOUN

**thoughtless** ADJECTIVE
❶ careless; not thinking of what may happen ❷ not thinking of others; inconsiderate
➤ **thoughtlessly** ADVERB
➤ **thoughtlessness** NOUN

**thousand** NOUN & ADJECTIVE thousands
the number 1,000
➤ **thousandth** ADJECTIVE & NOUN

**thrall** NOUN
➤ **in thrall to someone** in someone's power or completely under their control

**thrash** VERB thrashes, thrashing, thrashed
❶ to beat someone with a stick or whip; to keep hitting someone very hard ❷ to defeat someone completely ❸ to move about, or move a part of your body, violently • *The crocodile thrashed its tail.*
➤ **thrash something out** to discuss a matter thoroughly

**thread** NOUN threads
❶ a thin length of any substance ❷ a length of spun cotton, wool or nylon used for making cloth or in sewing or knitting ❸ the spiral ridge round a screw ❹ a theme or idea running through a story or argument • *I'm afraid I've lost the thread.* ❺ a series of connected messages from an Internet discussion of a subject

**thread** VERB threads, threading, threaded
❶ to put a thread through the eye of a needle ❷ to pass something long and thin through or round something ❸ to put beads on a thread

**threadbare** ADJECTIVE
threadbare cloth or clothing is old and worn thin with the threads showing

**threat** NOUN threats
❶ a warning that you will punish, hurt or harm a person or thing ❷ the possibility of trouble or danger • *The threat of war hung over the region.* ❸ a person or thing causing danger

**threaten** VERB threatens, threatening, threatened
❶ to make threats against someone ❷ to be a threat or danger to a person or thing • *The quarrel threatened to turn violent.*

**three** NOUN & ADJECTIVE threes
the number 3

**three-dimensional** ADJECTIVE
having three dimensions (length, width and height or depth)

**thresh** VERB threshes, threshing, threshed
to beat corn in order to separate the grain from the husks

**threshold** NOUN thresholds
❶ a slab of stone or board forming the bottom of a doorway; the entrance ❷ the point at which something begins to happen or change • *We are on the threshold of a great discovery.*

**thrice** ADVERB (old use)
three times

**thrift** NOUN
being careful with money and not spending too much
➤ **thrifty** ADJECTIVE
➤ **thriftily** ADVERB

**thrill** NOUN thrills
a feeling of great excitement or pleasure

**thrill** VERB thrills, thrilling, thrilled
to give someone a feeling of great excitement or pleasure

**thrilled** ADJECTIVE
very excited and pleased • *I was thrilled to be invited.*

**thriller** NOUN thrillers
an exciting story or film, usually about crime or spying

**thrilling** ADJECTIVE
very exciting

**thrive** VERB thrives, thriving, throve, thrived or thriven
to prosper or grow strongly • *Crops thrive in this climate.*

**throat** NOUN throats
❶ the tube in your neck that takes food and drink down into your body ❷ the front of your neck

**throaty** ADJECTIVE
❶ produced deep in the throat • *a throaty chuckle* ❷ hoarse

**throb** VERB throbs, throbbing, throbbed
to beat or vibrate with a strong rhythm • *The ship's engines throbbed quietly.* • *My hand was throbbing with pain.*

**throb** NOUN throbs
a throbbing sound or feeling

**throes** PLURAL NOUN
severe pangs of pain
➤ **in the throes of something** in the middle of doing something difficult • *We are in the throes of exams.*

**thrombosis** NOUN
the formation of a clot of blood in the body

**throne** NOUN thrones
❶ a special chair for a king or queen at ceremonies ❷ the position of being king or queen • *the heir to the throne*

**throng** NOUN throngs
a large crowd of people

**throng** VERB throngs, thronging, thronged
to go somewhere in large numbers • *Thousands of people thronged the streets.*

**throttle** NOUN throttles
a device that controls the flow of fuel to an engine; an accelerator

**throttle** VERB throttles, throttling, throttled
to strangle someone
➤ **throttle back** or **down** to reduce the

speed of an engine by partially closing the throttle

**through** *PREPOSITION*
❶ from one end or side to the other end or side of • *She climbed through the window.* ❷ during; throughout • *There will be celebrations all through the weekend.* ❸ by means of; because of • *We lost it through carelessness.* ❹ at the end of; having finished successfully • *We must be through the worst of the winter by now.*

**through** *ADVERB*
❶ through something • *We squeezed through.* ❷ with a telephone connection made • *I'll put you through to the president.* ❸ finished • *Wait till I'm through with these papers.*

**through** *ADJECTIVE*
❶ going directly all the way to a destination • *a through train* ❷ a through road leads directly from one place to another

**SPELLING**

Through is different from threw, which is a form of the verb *throw*: • *Climb through the window.* • *He threw a stone at the window.*

**throughout** *PREPOSITION & ADVERB*
all the way through; from beginning to end

**throve**
past tense of thrive

**throw** *VERB* throws, throwing, threw, thrown
❶ to send a person or thing through the air ❷ to put something in a place carelessly or hastily • *She came in and threw her coat on the chair.* ❸ to move part of your body quickly • *He threw his head back and laughed.* ❹ to put someone in a certain state • *It threw us into confusion.* ❺ to confuse or upset someone • *Your question threw me for a minute.* ❻ to move a switch or lever in order to operate it ❼ to shape a pot on a potter's wheel ❽ to hold a party
➤ **thrower** *NOUN*
➤ **throw something away** ❶ to get rid of something because it is useless or unwanted ❷ to waste something • *You threw away an opportunity.*
➤ **throw up** (*informal*) to vomit
➤ **throw yourself into something** to start doing something with energy or enthusiasm

**SPELLING**

The past tense of throw is threw and the past participle is thrown.

**throw** *NOUN* throws
a throwing action or movement • *That was a good throw.*

**thrum** *VERB* thrums, thrumming, thrummed
to make a low regular sound • *He could hear the engine softly thrumming.*
➤ **thrum** *NOUN*

**thrush** *NOUN* thrushes
❶ a songbird with a speckled breast ❷ an infection causing tiny white patches in the mouth and throat

**thrust** *VERB* thrusts, thrusting, thrust
to push something somewhere with a lot of force • *He thrust his hands into his pockets.*

**thrust** *NOUN* thrusts
a hard push

**thud** *NOUN* thuds
the dull sound of a heavy knock or fall

**thud** *VERB* thuds, thudding, thudded
to fall with a thud; to make a thud

**thug** *NOUN* thugs
a rough and violent person
**WORD ORIGIN** from Hindi: the *Thugs* were robbers and murderers in India in the 17th-19th centuries

**thumb** *NOUN* thumbs
the short thick finger set apart from the other four
➤ **be under a someone's thumb** to be completely under a person's influence

**thumb** *VERB* thumbs, thumbing, thumbed
to turn the pages of a book or magazine quickly with your thumb
➤ **thumb a lift** to hitch-hike

**thumbnail** *ADJECTIVE*
brief; giving only the main facts • *a thumbnail sketch*

**thumbnail** *NOUN* thumbnails
a very small picture on a computer screen which shows you what a larger picture looks like

**thumbscrew** *NOUN* thumbscrews
a former instrument of torture for squeezing the thumb

**thump** *VERB* thumps, thumping, thumped
❶ to hit or knock something heavily ❷ to punch someone heavily ❸ to make a heavy dull sound; to thud ❹ to throb or beat strongly • *My heart was thumping.*

**thump** *NOUN* thumps
an act or sound of thumping

**thunder** NOUN
❶ the loud noise that you hear with lightning during a storm ❷ a similar noise • *the thunder of horses' hooves*
➤ **thundery** ADJECTIVE

**thunder** VERB thunders, thundering, thundered
❶ to make the noise of thunder or a noise like thunder ❷ to speak loudly • *'Come here!' he thundered.*

**thunderbolt** NOUN thunderbolts
a lightning flash thought of as a destructive missile

**thunderous** ADJECTIVE
extremely loud • *thunderous applause*

**thunderstorm** NOUN thunderstorms
a storm with thunder and lightning

**thunderstruck** ADJECTIVE
amazed or shocked

**Thursday** NOUN
the day of the week following Wednesday
WORD ORIGIN from Old English *thuresdaeg* = day of thunder, named after Thor, the Norse god of thunder

**thus** ADVERB
❶ in this way • *Hold the wheel thus.* ❷ for this reason; therefore • *Thus, we must try again.*

**thwart** VERB thwarts, thwarting, thwarted
to frustrate a plan or attempt; to prevent someone from achieving something

**thy** DETERMINER (old use)
your (referring to one person)

**thyme** (say time) NOUN
a herb with fragrant leaves

**thyroid gland** NOUN thyroid glands
a large gland at the front of the neck
WORD ORIGIN from Greek *thyreos* = a shield (because of the shape of the gland)

**thyself** PRONOUN (old use)
yourself (referring to one person)

**tiara** (say tee-**ar**-a) NOUN tiaras
a woman's jewelled crescent-shaped ornament worn like a crown

**tic** NOUN tics
an unintentional twitch of a muscle, especially of the face

**tick** NOUN ticks
❶ (British) a mark (✓) put next to something to show that it is correct or has been checked or done ❷ a regular clicking sound, especially the sound made by a clock or watch ❸ (British) (informal) a moment • *I won't be a tick.* ❹ a bloodsucking insect

**tick** VERB ticks, ticking, ticked
❶ (British) to mark something with a tick • *She ticked the correct answers.* ❷ to make the sound of a tick
➤ **tick someone off** (British) (informal) to scold someone or tell them off

**ticket** NOUN tickets
❶ a printed piece of paper or card that allows a person to travel on a bus or train, see a show, etc. ❷ a label showing a thing's price

**tickle** VERB tickles, tickling, tickled
❶ to touch a person's skin lightly in order to produce a slight tingling feeling and make them laugh and wriggle ❷ a part of your body tickles when you have a slight tingling or itching feeling there • *My throat is tickling.* ❸ to amuse or please someone

**ticklish** ADJECTIVE
❶ a ticklish person is likely to laugh or wriggle when they are tickled ❷ awkward or difficult • *a ticklish situation*

**tidal** ADJECTIVE
to do with or affected by tides

**tidal wave** NOUN tidal waves
a huge sea wave

**tiddler** NOUN tiddlers (British) (informal)
a very small fish

**tiddlywinks** NOUN
a game playing by flicking a small counter into a cup by pressing on its edge with another counter

**tide** NOUN tides
❶ the regular rising and falling of the level of the sea, which usually happens twice a day ❷ (old use) a time or season • *Christmas-tide*

**tide** VERB tides, tiding, tided
➤ **tide someone over** to give someone what they need, especially money, for a short time

**tidings** PLURAL NOUN (formal)
news or information

**tidy** ADJECTIVE tidier, tidiest
❶ with everything in its right place; neat and orderly ❷ (informal) fairly large • *It costs a tidy sum.*
➤ **tidily** ADVERB
➤ **tidiness** NOUN

**tidy** VERB tidies, tidying, tidied
to make a place tidy

**tidy** NOUN
the act of tidying a place • *I'll give the house a quick tidy before they arrive.*

**tie** VERB ties, tying, tied
❶ to fasten something with string, rope, ribbon, etc. ❷ to arrange something into a knot or bow ❸ to make the same score as another competitor
➤ **be tied up** to be busy • *Sorry, I'm tied up all afternoon.*

**tie** NOUN ties
❶ a strip of material worn passing under the collar of a shirt and knotted in front ❷ a result when two or more competitors have equal scores ❸ one of the matches in a competition ❹ a close connection or bond • *the ties of friendship*

**tie-break**, **tie-breaker** NOUN tie-breaks or tie-breakers
a way to decide the winner when competitors have tied, especially an additional question in a quiz or an additional game at the end of a set in tennis

**tier** (say teer) NOUN tiers
each of a series of rows or levels placed one above the other
➤ **tiered** ADJECTIVE

**tiff** NOUN tiffs
a slight quarrel

**tiger** NOUN tigers
a large wild animal of the cat family, with yellow and black stripes

**tight** ADJECTIVE
❶ fitting very closely ❷ firmly fastened ❸ fully stretched; tense ❹ in short supply • *Money is tight at the moment.* ❺ mean or stingy • *He is very tight with his money.* ❻ severe or strict • *tight security* ❼ (informal) slightly drunk
➤ **tightness** NOUN

**tight** ADVERB
tightly or firmly • *Hold on tight.*

**tighten** VERB tightens, tightening, tightened
to make something tighter or to become tighter • *She tightened her grip.*

**tightly** ADVERB
closely and firmly; in a tight manner • *Her eyes were tightly closed.* • *Screw the lid on tightly.*

**tightrope** NOUN tightropes
a tightly stretched rope high above the ground, for acrobats to perform on

**tights** PLURAL NOUN
a piece of clothing that fits tightly over the feet, legs and lower part of the body

**tigress** NOUN tigresses
a female tiger

**tile** NOUN tiles
a thin square piece of baked clay or other hard material, used in rows for covering roofs, walls or floors

**tiled** ADJECTIVE
a tiled roof, wall or floor is covered with tiles

**till** PREPOSITION & CONJUNCTION
until

USAGE
It is better to use **until** when the word comes first in a sentence (e.g. *Until last year we had never been abroad*) or when you are speaking or writing formally.

**till** NOUN tills
a drawer or box for money in a shop; a cash register

**till** VERB tills, tilling, tilled
to plough land to prepare it for cultivating

**tiller** NOUN tillers
a handle used to turn a boat's rudder

**tilt** VERB tilts, tilting, tilted
to move or move something into a sloping position • *He tilted his head to one side.*

**tilt** NOUN
a sloping position
➤ **at full tilt** at full speed or force

**timber** NOUN timbers
❶ wood for building or making things ❷ a wooden beam

**timbered** ADJECTIVE
made of wood or with a wooden framework • *timbered houses*

**timbre** (say tambr) NOUN timbres
the quality of a voice or musical sound

**time** NOUN times
❶ a measure of the continuing existence of everything in years, months, days and other units ❷ what point in the day it is, as shown on a watch or clock • *Can you tell me the time?* ❸ a particular moment or period of things existing or happening • *There was a time when I would have agreed with you.* ❹ an occasion • *This is the first time I've been here.* ❺ a period that is suitable or available for something • *Do you have time for a quick chat?* ❻ a system of measuring time

• *Greenwich Mean Time* ❼ (*in music*) rhythm depending on the number and stress of beats in the bar

➤ **at times** or **from time to time** sometimes or occasionally

➤ **in time** ❶ not late ❷ after a while; eventually

➤ **on time** prompt or punctual • *The train left on time.*

**time** *VERB* times, timing, timed
❶ to measure how long something takes ❷ to arrange when something is to happen • *You timed your arrival perfectly.*

**timeless** *ADJECTIVE*
not affected by the passage of time; eternal • *It is a timeless classic.*

**time limit** *NOUN* time limits
a fixed amount of time within which something must be done

**timely** *ADJECTIVE*
happening at a suitable or useful time • *a timely warning*

**timer** *NOUN* timers
a device for timing things

**times** *PLURAL NOUN*
(*in mathematics*) multiplied by • *Five times three is 15 (5 x 3 = 15).*

**time scale** *NOUN* time scales
the length of time that something takes or that you need in order to do something

**timetable** *NOUN* timetables
a list showing the times when things happen, e.g. when buses or trains arrive and depart or when school lessons take place

**timid** *ADJECTIVE*
nervous and easily frightened
➤ **timidly** *ADVERB*
➤ **timidity** *NOUN*

**timing** *NOUN*
❶ the choice of time to do something • *Arriving at lunchtime was good timing.* ❷ the time when something happens

**timorous** *ADJECTIVE*
nervous and afraid

**timpani** *PLURAL NOUN*
kettledrums

**tin** *NOUN* tins
❶ a silvery-white metal ❷ a metal container for preserving food

**tin** *VERB* tins, tinning, tinned
to seal food in a tin to preserve it

**tincture** *NOUN* tinctures
❶ a solution of medicine in alcohol ❷ a slight trace of something

**tinder** *NOUN*
any dry substance that catches fire easily

**tine** *NOUN* tines
a point or prong of a fork, comb or antler

**tinge** *VERB* tinges, tingeing, tinged
❶ to colour something slightly ❷ to add a slight amount of another feeling • *Our relief was tinged with sadness.*

**tinge** *NOUN* tinges
❶ a slight amount of a colour ❷ a slight amount of a feeling • *A tinge of jealousy crept into her voice.*

**tingle** *VERB* tingles, tingling, tingled
to have a slight pricking or stinging feeling • *The cold water made my skin tingle.*

**tingle** *NOUN* tingles
a tingling feeling

**tinker** *NOUN* tinkers (*old use*)
a person travelling about mending pots and pans

**tinker** *VERB* tinkers, tinkering, tinkered
to work at something casually, trying to improve or mend it • *He is always tinkering with his bike.*

**tinkle** *VERB* tinkles, tinkling, tinkled
to make a gentle ringing sound

**tinkle** *NOUN* tinkles
a tinkling sound

**tinny** *ADJECTIVE*
a tinny sound is unpleasantly thin and high-pitched

**tinsel** *NOUN*
strips of glittering material used for decoration

**tint** *NOUN* tints
a shade of colour, especially a pale one

**tint** *VERB* tints, tinting, tinted
to colour something slightly
➤ **tinted** *ADJECTIVE*

**tiny** *ADJECTIVE* tinier, tiniest
very small

**tip** *NOUN* tips
❶ the part right at the top or end of something • *the tip of your nose* ❷ a small but useful piece of advice or information ❸ a small present of extra money given to someone who has served you • *a tip for the*

a
b
c
d
e
f
g
h
i
j
k
l
m
n
o
p
q
r
s
t
u
v
w
x
y
z

*waiter* ❹ a place where you can take rubbish and leave it ❺ a very untidy place

**tip** *VERB* tips, tipping, tipped
❶ to turn something upside down or tilt it
• *She tipped the water out of the bucket.*
• *He tipped his head back and laughed.*
❷ to give a person a tip to thank them for a service ❸ to name someone as likely to win or succeed • *Which team would you tip to win the championship?* ❹ to be tipped with something is to have it right at the end • *The wings are tipped with yellow.* ❺ to leave rubbish somewhere
➤ **tip someone off** to give someone a warning or special information about something

**tip-off** *NOUN* tip-offs
a warning or special piece of advice given to someone

**tipple** *NOUN* tipples
an alcoholic drink

**tipsy** *ADJECTIVE*
slightly drunk

**tiptoe** *VERB* tiptoes, tiptoeing, tiptoed
to walk on your toes very quietly or carefully
• *He tiptoed up the stairs.*
➤ **on tiptoe** walking or standing on your toes

**tip-top** *ADJECTIVE* (*informal*)
excellent; very best • *in tip-top condition*

**tirade** (say ty-**rayd**) *NOUN* tirades
a long angry or violent speech

**tire** *VERB* tires, tiring, tired
to make someone tired or to become tired

**tired** *ADJECTIVE*
feeling that you need to sleep or rest
➤ **be tired of something** to have had enough of something • *I'm tired of waiting.*

**tireless** *ADJECTIVE*
having a lot of energy; not tiring easily

**tiresome** *ADJECTIVE*
continually annoying

**tiring** *ADJECTIVE*
making you tired • *a tiring journey*

**tissue** *NOUN* tissues
❶ tissue paper ❷ a paper handkerchief ❸ the substance forming any part of the body of an animal or plant • *bone tissue*

**tissue paper** *NOUN*
very thin soft paper used for wrapping and packing things

**tit** *NOUN* tits
a kind of small bird
➤ **tit for tat** something equal given in return; retaliation

**titanic** (say ty-**tan**-ik) *ADJECTIVE*
huge **WORD ORIGIN** from the *Titans*, gigantic gods and goddesses in Greek legend

**titanium** *NOUN*
a strong silver-grey metal used to make light alloys that do not corrode easily

**titbit** *NOUN* titbits
a nice little piece of something, e.g. of food, gossip or information

**tithe** *NOUN* tithes
one-tenth of a year's output from a farm etc., formerly paid as tax to support the clergy and church

**title** *NOUN* titles
❶ the name of a book, film, song, etc.
❷ a word used to show a person's rank or position, e.g. *Dr, Lord, Mrs* ❸ a championship in sport • *the world heavyweight title* ❹ a legal right to something, especially land or property

**titled** *ADJECTIVE*
a titled person has a title as a noble

**titter** *VERB* titters, tittering, tittered
to laugh quietly in a nervous or silly way

**titter** *NOUN*
a quiet nervous or silly laugh

**tittle-tattle** *NOUN*
gossip

**TNT** *ABBREVIATION*
trinitrotoluene; a powerful explosive

**to** *PREPOSITION*
❶ used to show direction towards a place or position • *We usually walk to school.* • *He quickly rose to power.* ❷ used to show the limit of something • *from noon to two o'clock* ❸ used for comparison • *We won by six goals to three.* • *I prefer cats to dogs.* ❹ used to show the person or thing that receives or is affected by something • *Give it to me.* • *She was always friendly to everyone.* ❺ used before a verb to form an infinitive (*I want to see him.*) or to show purpose (*He does that to annoy us.*) or alone when the verb is understood (*We meant to go but forgot to.*)

**to** *ADVERB* to or in the proper or closed position or condition • *Push the door to.*
➤ **to and fro** backwards and forwards

**SPELLING**
To is different from too: • *I'm going to Manchester.* • *too much food*

**toad** NOUN toads
a frog-like animal that lives mainly on land

**toad-in-the-hole** NOUN
(*British*) sausages baked in batter

**toadstool** NOUN toadstools
a fungus (usually poisonous) with a round top on a stalk

**toady** VERB toadies, toadying, toadied
to flatter someone to make them want to help you
➤ **toady** NOUN
WORD ORIGIN short for *toad eater*, because quack healers used to have assistants who ate toads and were then supposedly cured

**toast** VERB toasts, toasting, toasted
❶ to heat bread etc. to make it brown and crisp ❷ to warm something in front of a fire or grill ❸ to drink in honour of someone

**toast** NOUN toasts
❶ toasted bread ❷ the call to drink in honour of someone; the person honoured in this way
• *Let's drink a toast to the bride and groom.*

**toaster** NOUN toasters
an electrical device for toasting bread

**tobacco** NOUN
the dried leaves of certain plants prepared for smoking in cigarettes, cigars or pipes or for making snuff

**tobacconist** NOUN tobacconists
(*chiefly British*) a shopkeeper who sells cigarettes, cigars, etc.

**toboggan** NOUN toboggans
a small sledge used for sliding downhill
➤ **tobogganing** NOUN

**today** NOUN
this present day • *Today is Monday.*

**today** ADVERB
❶ on this day • *Have you seen him today?*
❷ nowadays • *Young people today have far more freedom.*

**toddle** VERB toddles, toddling, toddled
❶ a young child toddles when it walks with short unsteady steps ❷ to walk or go somewhere casually

**toddler** NOUN toddlers
a young child who has only recently learnt to walk

**to-do** NOUN to-dos
a fuss or commotion

**toe** NOUN toes
❶ any of the separate parts (five in humans) at the end of each foot ❷ the part of a shoe, sock or stocking that covers the toes
➤ **on your toes** alert and ready to act

**toffee** NOUN toffees
a sticky sweet made from heated butter and sugar

**toga** (say toh-ga) NOUN togas
a long loose piece of clothing worn by men in ancient Rome

**together** ADVERB
with another person or thing; with each other
• *They went to the party together.* • *Now glue the two parts together.*

**toggle** NOUN toggles
a short piece of wood, metal, etc. used like a button

**toil** VERB toils, toiling, toiled
❶ to work hard ❷ to move slowly and with difficulty • *We toiled up the hill.*

**toil** NOUN
hard work

**toilet** NOUN toilets
❶ a bowl-like object, connected by pipes to a drain, which you use to get rid of urine and faeces ❷ a room containing a toilet ❸ the process of washing, dressing and tidying yourself

**toilet paper** NOUN
paper for cleaning yourself after you have used a toilet

**token** NOUN tokens
❶ a piece of metal or plastic that can be used instead of money ❷ a voucher or coupon that can be exchanged for goods ❸ a sign or signal of something • *Please accept this gift as a small token of our gratitude.*

**tolerable** ADJECTIVE
able to be put up with
➤ **tolerably** ADVERB

**tolerant** ADJECTIVE
willing to accept or put up with other people's behaviour and opinions even if you do not agree with them
➤ **tolerantly** ADVERB
➤ **tolerance** NOUN

**tolerate** VERB tolerates, tolerating, tolerated
❶ to allow something even if you do

a b c d e f g h i j k l m n o p q r s t u v w x y z

not approve of it • *I will not tolerate bad manners.* ❷ to bear or put up with something unpleasant • *I don't know how you tolerate all that noise.*
➤ **toleration** NOUN

**toll** (rhymes with hole) NOUN **tolls**
❶ a charge made for using a road or bridge ❷ loss or damage caused by something • *The death toll in the earthquake is rising.*
➤ **take its toll** to damage or have a bad effect on a person or thing

**toll** VERB **tolls, tolling, tolled**
to ring a bell slowly

**tom, tomcat** NOUN **toms** or **tomcats**
a male cat

**tomahawk** NOUN **tomahawks**
a small axe used by Native Americans

**tomato** NOUN **tomatoes**
a soft round red or yellow fruit eaten as a vegetable

**tomb** (say toom) NOUN **tombs**
a place where someone is buried; a monument built over this

**tombola** NOUN
(*British*) a kind of lottery (WORD ORIGIN) from Italian *tombolare* = tumble (because often the tickets are drawn from a revolving drum)

**tomboy** NOUN **tomboys**
a girl who enjoys playing rough noisy games

**tombstone** NOUN **tombstones**
a memorial stone set up over a grave

**tome** NOUN **tomes**
a large heavy book

**tommy gun** NOUN **tommy guns**
a small machine gun (WORD ORIGIN) from the name of its American inventor, J. T. *Thompson* (died 1940)

**tomorrow** NOUN & ADVERB
the day after today

SPELLING
Double up the **r** in **tomorrow** (but the **m** stays single).

**tom-tom** NOUN **tom-toms**
a drum beaten with the hands

**ton** NOUN **tons**
❶ a unit of weight equal to 2,240 pounds or about 1,016 kilograms ❷ a large amount • *There's tons of room.* ❸ (*informal*) a speed of 100 miles per hour

**tonal** ADJECTIVE
to do with tone

**tone** NOUN **tones**
❶ a sound in music or of the voice ❷ each of the five larger intervals between notes in a musical scale (the smaller intervals are **semitones**) ❸ a shade of a colour ❹ the quality or character of something • *a cheerful tone*

**tone** VERB **tones, toning, toned**
➤ **tone something down** to make a thing quieter or less bright or less harsh
➤ **tone in** to blend or fit in well, especially in colour
➤ **tone something up** to make your body firm and strong by doing exercise

**tone-deaf** ADJECTIVE
not able to tell the difference between different musical notes

**tongs** PLURAL NOUN
a tool with two arms joined at one end, used to pick up or hold things

**tongue** NOUN **tongues**
❶ the long soft muscular part that moves about inside your mouth ❷ a language ❸ the leather flap on a shoe or boot underneath the laces ❹ a pointed flame

**tongue-tied** ADJECTIVE
too shy to speak

**tongue-twister** NOUN **tongue-twisters**
something that is difficult to say quickly and correctly, e.g. 'She sells seashells.'

**tonic** NOUN **tonics**
❶ a medicine etc. that makes a person healthier or stronger ❷ anything that makes a person more energetic or cheerful ❸ (also **tonic water**) a fizzy mineral water with a bitter taste, often mixed with gin ❹ the first note in a scale, providing the keynote in a piece of music

**tonight** NOUN & ADVERB
this evening or night

**tonnage** NOUN
the amount a ship or ships can carry, expressed in tons

**tonne** NOUN **tonnes**
a metric ton (1,000 kilograms)

**tonsil** NOUN **tonsils**
either of two small masses of soft flesh inside your throat

**tonsillitis** NOUN
inflammation of the tonsils

**too** ADVERB
❶ also • Take the others too. ❷ more than is wanted or allowed etc. • It's too hot to sit outside.

SPELLING
Too is different from to: • I'm going to Manchester. • too much food

**tool** NOUN tools
❶ a device that helps you to do a particular job • A saw is a tool for cutting wood or metal. ❷ a thing used for a particular purpose • An encyclopedia is a useful study tool.

**toolbar** NOUN toolbars
a row of symbols on a computer screen that show the different things that you can do with a particular program

**toot** NOUN toots
a short sound produced by a horn

**toot** VERB toots, tooting, tooted
to make a toot

**tooth** NOUN teeth
❶ one of the hard white bony parts that are rooted in your gums, used for biting and chewing things ❷ one of a row of sharp parts • the teeth of a saw
➤ toothed ADJECTIVE
➤ fight tooth and nail to fight very fiercely

**toothache** NOUN
pain in your teeth or gums

**toothbrush** NOUN toothbrushes
a long-handled brush for cleaning your teeth

**toothpaste** NOUN toothpastes
a paste for cleaning your teeth

**toothpick** NOUN toothpicks
a small pointed piece of wood or plastic for removing bits of food from between your teeth

**toothy** ADJECTIVE
having large teeth or showing a lot of teeth
• a toothy grin

**top** NOUN tops
❶ the highest part of something ❷ the upper surface of something ❸ the covering or stopper of a bottle, jar, etc. ❹ a piece of clothing you wear on the upper part of your body ❺ a toy that can be made to spin on its point
➤ on top of something in addition to something

**top** ADJECTIVE
highest or most important • at top speed

**top** VERB tops, topping, topped
❶ to put a top on something • The cake was topped with icing. ❷ to be at the top of something • She tops the list. ❸ to remove the top of something
➤ top something up to fill something that is partly empty • I need to top up my mobile phone.

**topaz** NOUN topazes
a kind of gem, often yellow

**top hat** NOUN top hats
a man's tall stiff black or grey hat worn with formal clothes

**top-heavy** ADJECTIVE
too heavy at the top and likely to overbalance

**topic** NOUN topics
a subject to write, learn or talk about

**topical** ADJECTIVE
to do with things that are happening or in the news now • a topical film
➤ topicality NOUN

**topless** ADJECTIVE
not wearing any clothes on the top half of the body

**topmost** ADJECTIVE
highest or tallest • the topmost branches

**topography** (say top-**og**-ra-fee) NOUN topographies
the position of the rivers, mountains, roads, buildings, etc. in a place
➤ topographical ADJECTIVE

**topping** NOUN toppings
food that is put on the top of a cake, dessert, pizza, etc.

**topple** VERB topples, toppling, toppled
❶ to fall over; to totter and fall ❷ to make something fall over ❸ to topple someone in power is to overthrow them

**top secret** ADJECTIVE
extremely secret • top secret information

**topsy-turvy** ADVERB & ADJECTIVE
upside down; muddled

**Torah** (say **tor**-uh) NOUN
in Judaism, the law of God as given to Moses and recorded in the first five books of the Bible

**torch** NOUN torches
❶ a small electric lamp that you can carry in

733

A B C D E F G H I J K L M N O P Q R S **T** U V W X Y Z

your hand ❷ a stick with burning material on the end, used as a light

**toreador** (say **torre**-a-dor) NOUN toreadors
a bullfighter

**torment** VERB torments, tormenting, tormented
❶ to make someone suffer greatly ❷ to tease or keep annoying someone
➤ **tormentor** NOUN

**torment** NOUN torments
great suffering

**torn**
past participle of **tear** VERB

**tornado** (say tor-**nay**-doh) NOUN tornadoes
a violent storm or whirlwind
(WORD ORIGIN) from Spanish *tronada* = thunderstorm

**torpedo** NOUN torpedoes
a long tube-shaped missile that can be fired under water to destroy ships

**torpedo** VERB torpedoes, torpedoing, torpedoed
to attack or destroy a ship with a torpedo

**torpid** ADJECTIVE
slow-moving; not lively
➤ **torpor** NOUN

**torrent** NOUN torrents
❶ a rushing stream; a great flow ❷ a heavy downpour of rain

**torrential** ADJECTIVE
torrential rain pours down very heavily

**torrid** ADJECTIVE
❶ very hot and dry ❷ emotional and passionate • *a torrid love affair*

**torso** NOUN torsos
the trunk of the human body
(WORD ORIGIN) Italian, = stump

**tortilla** NOUN tortillas
in Mexican cookery, a flat cake made from flour or maize, often stuffed

**tortoise** NOUN tortoises
a slow-moving animal with a shell over its body

**tortoiseshell** (say **tort**-a-shell) NOUN tortoiseshells
❶ the mottled brown and yellow shell of certain turtles, used for making combs etc.
❷ a cat or butterfly with mottled brown colouring

**tortuous** ADJECTIVE
❶ full of twists and turns • *a tortuous path* ❷ complicated and not easy to follow • *tortuous logic*

**torture** VERB tortures, torturing, tortured
❶ to make a person feel great pain, especially so that they will give information ❷ to cause someone great emotional pain or worry

**torture** NOUN tortures
something done to torture a person; mental or physical suffering
➤ **torturer** NOUN

**torturous** ADJECTIVE
like torture; agonizing • *a torturous wait for news of survivors*

**Tory** NOUN Tories
a member of the British Conservative Party
➤ **Tory** ADJECTIVE
(WORD ORIGIN) from Irish *toraidhe* = an outlaw

**toss** VERB tosses, tossing, tossed
❶ to throw something, especially up into the air ❷ to spin a coin to decide something according to which side of it is upwards after it falls ❸ to move restlessly or unevenly from side to side • *She was tossing and turning all night.*

**toss** NOUN tosses
the act of tossing a coin or other object

**toss-up** NOUN toss-ups
❶ the tossing of a coin ❷ an even chance

**tot** NOUN tots
❶ a small child ❷ (*informal, chiefly British*) a small amount of spirits • *a tot of rum*

**tot** VERB tots, totting, totted
➤ **tot something up** (*informal, chiefly British*) to add up figures or amounts

**total** ADJECTIVE
❶ including everything • *the total amount* ❷ complete • *total darkness*

**total** NOUN totals
the amount you get by adding everything together

**total** VERB totals, totalling, totalled
❶ to add up the total ❷ to reach an amount as a total • *The cost of the damage totalled $5,000.*

**totalitarian** ADJECTIVE
using a form of government where people are not allowed to form rival political parties

**totally** ADVERB
completely • *I totally agree with you.*

**totem pole** NOUN **totem poles**
a pole carved or painted by Native Americans with the symbols (*totems*) of their tribes or families

**totter** VERB **totters, tottering, tottered**
to walk unsteadily; to wobble • *The old man tottered along beside me.*
➤ **tottery** ADJECTIVE

**toucan** (say too-kan) NOUN **toucans**
a tropical American bird with a huge brightly-coloured beak

**touch** VERB **touches, touching, touched**
❶ to put your hand or fingers on something lightly ❷ two things touch when they join together so that there is no space between ❸ to come into contact with something or hit it gently ❹ to move or meddle with something • *Don't touch anything in this room.* ❺ to reach a certain point • *The thermometer touched 30° Celsius.* ❻ to affect someone's feelings, e.g. by making them feel sympathy • *His sad story touched our hearts.*
➤ **touch and go** uncertain or risky
➤ **touch down** an aircraft or spacecraft touches down when it lands
➤ **touch on something** to discuss a subject briefly
➤ **touch something up** to improve something by making small additions or changes

**touch** NOUN **touches**
❶ the action of touching • *You can find the map of any city at the touch of a button.* ❷ the ability to feel things by touching them ❸ a small thing that improves something • *I'm just putting the finishing touches to the cake.* ❹ communication with someone • *We have lost touch with him.* ❺ a special skill or style of workmanship • *She hasn't lost her touch* ❻ the part of a football field outside the playing area • *He kicked the ball into touch.*

**touchdown** NOUN **touchdowns**
the action of touching down

**touché** (say too-shay) EXCLAMATION
used to acknowledge a true or clever point made against you in an argument
**WORD ORIGIN** French, = touched, originally referring to a hit in fencing

**touching** ADJECTIVE
making you feel sadness, pity or sympathy • *a touching scene*

**touchline** NOUN **touchlines**
one of the lines that mark the side of a sports pitch

**touchscreen** NOUN **touchscreens**
a screen on a computer or phone which allows you to interact with it by touching areas on the screen

**touchstone** NOUN **touchstones**
a test by which the quality of something is judged **WORD ORIGIN** formerly, a kind of stone against which gold and silver were rubbed to test their purity

**touchy** ADJECTIVE **touchier, touchiest**
easily offended

**tough** ADJECTIVE
❶ strong; difficult to break or damage • *You'll need tough shoes for the climb.* ❷ difficult to chew ❸ able to stand hardship and not easily hurt ❹ firm or severe • *Don't be too tough on her.* ❺ difficult • *a tough decision*
➤ **toughness** NOUN

**toughen** VERB **toughens, toughening, toughened**
to make someone or something tough or to become tough • *You need to toughen up a little.*

**tour** NOUN **tours**
a journey in which you visit several places

**tour** VERB **tours, touring, toured**
to make a tour

**tourism** NOUN
the industry of providing services for people on holiday in a place

**tourist** NOUN **tourists**
a person who visits a place for pleasure, especially when on holiday

**tournament** NOUN **tournaments**
a competition in which there is a series of games or contests

**tourniquet** (say toor-nik-ay) NOUN **tourniquets**
a strip of material pulled tightly round an arm or leg to stop bleeding from an artery

**tousle** (say towz-el) VERB **tousles, tousling, tousled**
to ruffle someone's hair

**tout** (rhymes with scout) VERB **touts, touting, touted**
to try to sell something or get business

**tout** NOUN touts
a person who sells tickets for a sports match, concert, etc. at more than the original price

**tow** (rhymes with go) VERB tows, towing, towed
to pull a vehicle along behind you • *They towed our car to the garage.*

**tow** NOUN
an act of towing
➤ **in tow** (*informal*) following closely behind

**towards, toward** PREPOSITION
❶ in the direction of • *She walked towards the sea.* ❷ in relation to; regarding • *He behaved kindly towards his children.* ❸ as a contribution to • *Put the money towards a new bicycle.* ❹ near; close to • *It was getting on towards midnight.*

**towel** NOUN towels
a piece of absorbent cloth for drying things
➤ **towelling** NOUN

**tower** NOUN towers
a tall narrow building or part of a building

**tower** VERB towers, towering, towered
to be very high; to be taller than others
• *Skyscrapers towered over the city.*

**tower block** NOUN tower blocks
(*British*) a tall building containing offices or flats

**town** NOUN towns
a place with many houses, shops, offices and other buildings

**town hall** NOUN town halls
a building with offices for the local council and usually a hall for public events

**township** NOUN townships
in South Africa under apartheid, a town set aside for black people to live

**towpath** NOUN towpaths
a path beside a canal or river, originally for use when a horse was towing a barge

**toxic** ADJECTIVE
poisonous; caused by poison

**toxicology** NOUN
the study of poisons
➤ **toxicologist** NOUN

**toxin** NOUN toxins
a poisonous substance, especially one formed in the body by germs

**toy** NOUN toys
a thing to play with

**toy** ADJECTIVE
❶ made as a toy ❷ a toy dog is one

belonging to a very small breed kept as a pet
• *a toy poodle*

**toy** VERB toys, toying, toyed
➤ **toy with something** ❶ to think about an idea casually or idly ❷ to move something about without thinking about what you are doing • *He was nervously toying with his pen.*

**toyshop** NOUN toyshops
a shop that sells toys

**trace** NOUN traces
❶ a mark or sign left by a person or thing
• *He vanished without a trace.* ❷ a very small amount • *They found traces of blood on the carpet.*

**trace** VERB traces, tracing, traced
❶ to copy a picture or map etc. by drawing over it on transparent paper ❷ to find a person or thing after following tracks or other evidence • *The police have been trying to trace her.*

**traceable** ADJECTIVE
able to be traced

**tracery** NOUN
a decorative pattern of holes in stone, e.g. in a church window

**track** NOUN tracks
❶ a mark or marks left by a moving person or thing ❷ a rough path made by being used ❸ a road or area of ground specially prepared for racing ❹ a set of rails for trains or trams to run on ❺ one of the songs or pieces of music on a CD, tape, etc. ❻ a continuous band round the wheels of a heavy vehicle such as a tank or tractor
➤ **keep** or **lose track of something** to keep or fail to keep yourself aware of something or informed about it

**track** VERB tracks, tracking, tracked
❶ to follow a person or animal by following the tracks they leave ❷ to follow or observe something as it moves
➤ **tracker** NOUN
➤ **track someone** or **something down** to find a person or thing by searching

**track events** PLURAL NOUN
athletic events that involve racing on a running track, as opposed to field events

**track record** NOUN track records
a person's past achievements

**track suit** NOUN track suits
a warm loose suit of the kind worn by athletes before and after contests or for jogging

**tract** *NOUN* tracts
❶ an area of land ❷ a series of connected parts along which something passes • *the digestive tract* ❸ a pamphlet containing a short essay, especially about religion

**traction** *NOUN*
❶ pulling a load ❷ the ability of a vehicle to grip the ground • *The wheels were losing traction in the snow.* ❸ a medical treatment in which an injured arm or leg is pulled gently for a long time by means of weights and pulleys

**traction engine** *NOUN* traction engines
a steam or diesel engine for pulling a heavy load along a road or across a field etc.

**tractor** *NOUN* tractors
a motor vehicle for pulling farm machinery or other heavy loads

**trade** *NOUN* trades
❶ buying, selling or exchanging goods ❷ business of a particular kind; the people working in this ❸ a job or occupation, especially a skilled craft

**trade** *VERB* trades, trading, traded
to buy, sell or exchange things
➤ **trade something in** to give a thing as part of the payment for something new • *He traded in his motorcycle for a car.*

**trademark** *NOUN* trademarks
a symbol or name that a firm puts on its products and that other firms are not allowed to use

**trader** *NOUN* traders
a person who buys and sells things • *market traders*

**tradesman** *NOUN* tradesmen
a person employed in trade, especially one who sells or delivers goods

**trade union** *NOUN* trade unions
a group of workers organized to help and protect workers in their own trade or industry

**tradition** *NOUN* traditions
❶ the passing down of customs or beliefs from one generation to another ❷ a custom or belief passed on in this way

**traditional** *ADJECTIVE*
❶ passed down from one generation to another • *a book of traditional stories from all round the world* ❷ following older methods and ideas rather than modern ones • *It is a very traditional school.*
➤ **traditionally** *ADVERB*

**traffic** *NOUN*
❶ vehicles, ships or aircraft moving along a route ❷ trading or dealing in drugs or other illegal goods

**traffic** *VERB* traffics, trafficking, trafficked
to deal in something illegal, especially drugs
➤ **trafficker** *NOUN*

**traffic lights** *PLURAL NOUN*
coloured lights used as a signal to traffic at road junctions or roadworks

**traffic warden** *NOUN* traffic wardens
(*British*) an official whose job is to make sure that vehicles are parked legally

**tragedian** (say tra-**jee**-dee-an) *NOUN* tragedians
❶ a person who writes tragedies ❷ an actor in tragedies

**tragedy** *NOUN* tragedies
❶ a play with unhappy events or a sad ending ❷ a very sad or distressing event

**tragic** *ADJECTIVE*
❶ very sad or distressing ❷ to do with tragedies • *a great tragic actor*
➤ **tragically** *ADVERB*

**trail** *NOUN* trails
❶ a track or scent left behind by an animal ❷ a series of marks in a line left behind by someone or something that has passed • *a trail of footprints* ❸ a path or track for walking through the countryside or a forest

**trail** *VERB* trails, trailing, trailed
❶ to follow the trail of an animal or person ❷ to be dragged along behind you; to drag something along behind you • *Her long skirt trailed in the mud.* ❸ to follow someone more slowly or wearily • *A few walkers trailed behind the others.* ❹ to hang down or float loosely ❺ to become fainter • *Her voice trailed away.*

**trailer** *NOUN* trailers
❶ a truck or other container pulled along by a vehicle ❷ a short piece from a film or television programme, shown in advance to advertise it

**train** *NOUN* trains
❶ a railway engine pulling a line of carriages or trucks that are linked together ❷ a number of people or animals moving in a line • *a camel train* ❸ a series of things • *a train of events* ❹ part of a long dress or robe that trails on the ground at the back

**train** *VERB* trains, training, trained
❶ to give a person instruction or practice

a b c d e f g h i j k l m n o p q r s t u v w x y z

so that they become skilled ❷ to learn how to do a job • *He's training to be a doctor.* ❸ to practise for a sporting event • *She was training for the race.* ❹ to make a plant grow in a particular direction • *We'd like to train roses up the walls.* ❺ to aim a gun, camera, etc. • *He trained his gun on the bridge.*

**trainee** NOUN trainees
a person who is being trained

**trainer** NOUN trainers
❶ a person who trains people or animals ❷ a soft rubber-soled shoe of the kind worn for running and sport

**traipse** VERB traipses, traipsing, traipsed
to walk wearily; to trudge a long distance

**trait** (say trayt) NOUN traits
one of a person's characteristics

**traitor** NOUN traitors
a person who betrays their country or friends
➤ **traitorous** ADJECTIVE

**trajectory** NOUN trajectories
the path taken by a moving object such as a bullet or rocket

**tram** NOUN trams
a public passenger vehicle which runs on rails in the road

**tramlines** PLURAL NOUN
❶ rails for a tram ❷ the pair of parallel lines at the side of a tennis court

**tramp** NOUN tramps
❶ a person without a home or job who walks from place to place ❷ a long walk ❸ the sound of heavy footsteps

**tramp** VERB tramps, tramping, tramped
❶ to walk with heavy footsteps ❷ to walk for a long distance

**trample** VERB tramples, trampling, trampled
to tread heavily on something; to crush something by treading on it • *Don't trample on the flowers.* • *He was trampled to death by a runaway horse.*

**trampoline** NOUN trampolines
a large piece of canvas joined to a frame by springs, used by gymnasts for jumping on

**trance** NOUN trances
a dreamy or unconscious state rather like sleep

**tranquil** ADJECTIVE
calm and quiet • *a tranquil summer day*
➤ **tranquilly** ADVERB

**tranquillity** NOUN
being calm and quiet • *a scene of peace and tranquillity*

**tranquillizer** (also **tranquilliser**) NOUN tranquillizers
a drug or medicine used to make a person feel calm

**transaction** NOUN transactions
a piece of business done between people
➤ **transact** VERB

**transatlantic** ADJECTIVE
across or on the other side of the Atlantic Ocean

**transcend** VERB transcends, transcending, transcended
to go beyond the usual limits of something

**transcribe** VERB transcribes, transcribing, transcribed
to copy or write something out
➤ **transcription** NOUN

**transcript** NOUN transcripts
a written copy

**transept** NOUN transepts
the part that is at right angles to the nave in a cross-shaped church

**transfer** VERB transfers, transferring, transferred
❶ to move a person or thing from one place to another ❷ to hand something over to someone else
➤ **transferable** ADJECTIVE

**transfer** NOUN transfers
❶ the transferring of a person or thing ❷ a picture or design that can be transferred onto another surface

**transfigure** VERB transfigures, transfiguring, transfigured
to change the appearance of something greatly
➤ **transfiguration** NOUN

**transfixed** ADJECTIVE
unable to move because of fear or surprise
• *She stared at him, transfixed with horror.*
➤ **transfix** VERB

**transform** VERB transforms, transforming, transformed
to change the form, appearance or character of a person or thing to something quite different

**transformation** NOUN transformations
a complete change in the form, appearance
or character of a person or thing

**transformer** NOUN transformers
a device used to change the voltage of an
electric current

**transfusion** NOUN transfusions
putting blood taken from one person into
another person's body

**transgress** VERB transgresses, transgressing,
transgressed
to break a rule or law
➤ **transgression** NOUN

**transient** ADJECTIVE
not lasting or staying for long
➤ **transience** NOUN

**transistor** NOUN transistors
❶ a tiny electronic device that controls a
flow of electricity ❷ (also **transistor radio**) a
portable radio that uses transistors

**transit** NOUN
the process of travelling from one place to
another • *The goods were damaged in transit.*

**transition** NOUN transitions
the process of changing from one state
or form to another • *the transition from
childhood to adolescence*
➤ **transitional** ADJECTIVE

**transitive** ADJECTIVE
a transitive verb is one that is used with a
direct object after it, e.g. *change* in *change
your shoes* (but not in *change into dry shoes*).
Compare with **intransitive**.
➤ **transitively** ADVERB

**transitory** ADJECTIVE
existing for a time but not lasting

**translate** VERB translates, translating,
translated
to put something into another language • *The
book has been translated from Arabic into
English.*
➤ **translator** NOUN

**translation** NOUN translations
something translated from another language

**translucent** (say tranz-**loo**-sent) ADJECTIVE
allowing light to shine through but not
transparent

**transmission** NOUN transmissions
❶ transmitting something ❷ a broadcast
❸ the gears by which power is transmitted
from the engine to the wheels of a vehicle

**transmit** VERB transmits, transmitting,
transmitted
❶ to send or pass something on from one
person or place to another ❷ to send out a
signal or broadcast

**transmitter** NOUN transmitters
a device for transmitting radio or television
signals

**transom** NOUN transoms
❶ a horizontal bar of wood or stone dividing
a window or separating a door from a
window above it ❷ a small window above a
door

**transparency** NOUN transparencies
❶ being transparent ❷ a transparent
photograph that can be projected onto a
screen

**transparent** ADJECTIVE
able to be seen through • *The insect's wings
are almost transparent.*

**transpire** VERB transpires, transpiring,
transpired
❶ to become known; to turn out • *It
transpired that she had known nothing at all
about it.* ❷ to happen • *The police need to
know what transpired on the yacht.* ❸ plants
transpire when they give off watery vapour
from leaves etc.
➤ **transpiration** NOUN

**transplant** VERB transplants, transplanting,
transplanted
❶ to transfer an organ from the body of one
person to another ❷ to remove a plant and
put it to grow somewhere else
➤ **transplantation** NOUN

**transplant** NOUN transplants
❶ the process of transplanting something • *a
heart transplant* ❷ something transplanted

**transport** VERB transports, transporting,
transported
to take people, animals or things from one
place to another
➤ **transportation** NOUN

**transport** NOUN
the process or means of transporting people,
animals or things • *The city has a good
system of public transport.*

**transporter** NOUN transporters
a heavy vehicle for transporting large objects,
such as cars

**transpose** VERB transposes, transposing,
transposed
❶ to change the position or order of

a
b
c
d
e
f
g
h
i
j
k
l
m
n
o
p
q
r
s
t
u
v
w
x
y
z

something **②** to put a piece of music into a different key
➤ **transposition** NOUN

**transverse** ADJECTIVE
lying across something
➤ **transversely** ADVERB

**transvestite** NOUN transvestites
a person who likes wearing clothes intended for someone of the opposite gender

**trap** NOUN traps
**①** a device for catching and holding animals **②** a plan or trick for capturing, detecting or cheating someone **③** a two-wheeled carriage pulled by a horse **④** a bend in a pipe, filled with water to prevent gases from rising up from a drain

**trap** VERB traps, trapping, trapped
**①** to catch or hold a person or animal in a trap **②** to be trapped is to be stuck in a dangerous place or difficult situation you cannot escape from • *The driver was trapped in the wreckage.* **③** to trick someone into doing or saying something

**trapdoor** NOUN trapdoors
a door in a floor, ceiling or roof

**trapeze** NOUN trapezes
a bar hanging from two ropes as a swing for acrobats

**trapezium** NOUN trapeziums or trapezia
a quadrilateral in which two opposite sides are parallel and the other two are not

**trapezoid** NOUN trapezoids
a quadrilateral in which no sides are parallel

**trapper** NOUN trappers
someone who traps wild animals, especially for their fur

**trappings** PLURAL NOUN
**①** the clothes or possessions that show your rank or position **②** an ornamental harness for a horse

**trash** NOUN
rubbish or nonsense
➤ **trashy** ADJECTIVE

**trash can** NOUN trash cans
(*North American*) a dustbin

**trauma** (say traw-ma) NOUN traumas
a shock or upsetting experience that produces a lasting effect on a person's mind

**traumatic** ADJECTIVE
a traumatic experience is very unpleasant and upsetting

**travail** NOUN (*old use*)
hard or laborious work

**travel** VERB travels, travelling, travelled
to go from one place to another

**travel** NOUN
going on journeys • *air travel*

**travel agent** NOUN travel agents
a person whose job is to arrange travel and holidays for people

**traveller** NOUN travellers
**①** a person who is travelling or who often travels **②** a gypsy or a person who does not settle in one place

**traveller's cheque** NOUN traveller's cheques
a cheque for a fixed amount of money that is sold by banks and that can be exchanged for money in foreign countries

**traverse** VERB traverses, traversing, traversed
to go across something, especially as part of a journey or expedition

**travesty** NOUN travesties
a bad or ridiculous form of something • *His story is a travesty of the truth.*

**trawl** VERB trawls, trawling, trawled
to fish by dragging a large net along the seabed

**trawler** NOUN trawlers
a boat used in trawling

**tray** NOUN trays
**①** a flat piece of wood, metal or plastic, usually with raised edges, for carrying cups, plates, food, etc. **②** an open container for holding documents and letters in an office

**treacherous** ADJECTIVE
**①** betraying someone; disloyal **②** dangerous or unreliable • *It's snowing and the roads are treacherous.*
➤ **treacherously** ADVERB

**treachery** NOUN
doing something that betrays someone

**treacle** NOUN
a thick sticky liquid produced when sugar is purified
➤ **treacly** ADJECTIVE
**WORD ORIGIN** originally = ointment for an animal bite; from Greek *therion* = wild or poisonous animal

**tread** VERB treads, treading, trod, trodden
to walk on something or put your foot on it

**tread** NOUN treads
**①** a sound or way of walking • *He had a*

*heavy tread.* ❷ the top surface of a stair; the part you put your foot on ❸ the part of a tyre that touches the ground

**SPELLING**

The past tense of **tread** is **trod** and the past participle is **trodden**.

**treadle** *NOUN* treadles
a lever that you press with your foot to turn a wheel that works a machine

**treadmill** *NOUN* treadmills
❶ a wide mill wheel turned by the weight of people or animals treading on steps fixed round its edge ❷ monotonous routine work

**treason** *NOUN*
betraying your country
➤ **treasonable** *ADJECTIVE*
➤ **treasonous** *ADJECTIVE*

**treasure** *NOUN* treasures
❶ a store of precious metals or jewels ❷ a precious thing or person

**treasure** *VERB* treasures, treasuring, treasured
to value greatly something that you have • *I will treasure those memories forever.*

**treasure hunt** *NOUN* treasure hunts
a game in which people try to find a hidden object

**treasurer** *NOUN* treasurers
a person in charge of the money of a club, society, etc.

**treasure trove** *NOUN*
gold or silver etc. found hidden and with no known owner

**treasury** *NOUN* treasuries
a place where money and valuables are kept
➤ **the Treasury** the government department in charge of a country's income

**treat** *VERB* treats, treating, treated
❶ to behave in a certain way towards a person or thing • *She had always treated him with suspicion.* ❷ to deal with a subject • *This question is treated in more detail in the next chapter.* ❸ to give medical care to a person or animal • *He was treated for sunstroke.* ❹ to put something through a chemical or other process • *The fabric has been treated to make it waterproof.* ❺ to pay for someone else's food, drink or entertainment • *I'll treat you to an ice cream.*

**treat** *NOUN* treats
❶ something special that gives pleasure

❷ the process of treating someone to food, drink or entertainment • *This is my treat.*

**treatise** *NOUN* treatises
a book or long essay on a subject

**treatment** *NOUN* treatments
❶ the way you behave towards or deal with a person, animal or thing ❷ medical care

**treaty** *NOUN* treaties
a formal agreement between two or more countries

**treble** *ADJECTIVE*
three times as much or as many

**treble** *NOUN* trebles
❶ a treble amount ❷ a person with a high-pitched or soprano voice

**treble** *VERB* trebles, trebling, trebled
to make something, or to become, three times as much or as many • *The price has trebled since last year.*

**tree** *NOUN* trees
a tall plant with a single very thick hard stem or trunk that is usually without branches for some distance above the ground

**trefoil** *NOUN*
a plant with three small leaves (e.g. clover)

**trek** *NOUN* treks
a long walk or journey

**trek** *VERB* treks, trekking, trekked
to go on a long walk or journey • *The five-man team trekked to the South Pole.*

**trellis** *NOUN* trellises
a framework with crossing bars of wood or metal to support climbing plants

**tremble** *VERB* trembles, trembling, trembled
to shake gently, especially because you are afraid

**tremble** *NOUN* trembles
a trembling movement or sound

**tremendous** *ADJECTIVE*
❶ very large; huge • *a tremendous explosion* ❷ excellent

**tremendously** *ADVERB*
very or very much • *It is tremendously exciting.*

**tremor** *NOUN* tremors
❶ a shaking or trembling movement ❷ a slight earthquake

**tremulous** *ADJECTIVE*
trembling from nervousness or weakness • *a*

*tremulous voice*
➤ **tremulously** ADVERB

**trench** NOUN trenches
a long narrow hole cut in the ground

**trenchant** ADJECTIVE
strong and effective • *trenchant criticism*

**trend** NOUN trends
the general direction in which something is
going or developing • *recent trends in the
fashion world*

**trendy** ADJECTIVE (*informal*)
fashionable; following the latest trends
• *trendy clothes*

**trepidation** NOUN
fear and anxiety about something that may
happen • *She entered the cave with great
trepidation.*

**trespass** VERB trespasses, trespassing,
trespassed
❶ to go on someone's land or property
without their permission ❷ (*old use*) to do
wrong; to sin
➤ **trespasser** NOUN

**trespass** NOUN trespasses (*old use*)
wrongdoing; sin

**tress** NOUN tresses
a lock of hair

**trestle** NOUN trestles
each of a set of supports on which you place
a board to form a table
➤ **trestle table** NOUN

**triad** (say **try**-ad) NOUN triads
❶ a group or set of three things ❷ a Chinese
secret organization involved in crime

**trial** NOUN trials
❶ the process of examining the evidence in
a law court to decide whether a person is
guilty of a crime ❷ testing a thing to see how
good it is or how well it works • *Scientists
are carrying out trials on the new drug.* ❸ a
test of qualities or ability • *a trial of strength*
❹ an annoying person or thing; a hardship
➤ **on trial** ❶ being tried in a law court
❷ being tested
➤ **trial and error** trying out different
methods of doing something until you find
one that works

**triangle** NOUN triangles
❶ a flat shape with three sides and three
angles ❷ a percussion instrument made from
a metal rod bent into a triangle

**triangular** ADJECTIVE
in the shape of a triangle

**tribal** ADJECTIVE
to do with or belonging to a tribe • *tribal
leaders*
➤ **tribally** ADVERB

**tribe** NOUN tribes
❶ a group of families living in one area as a
community, ruled by a chief ❷ a set of people
➤ **tribesman** NOUN
➤ **tribeswoman** NOUN

**tribulation** NOUN tribulations
great trouble or hardship

**tribunal** (say try-**bew**-nal) NOUN tribunals
a committee appointed to hear evidence and
give judgements when there is a dispute

**tribune** NOUN tribunes
an official chosen by the people in ancient
Rome

**tributary** NOUN tributaries
a river or stream that flows into a larger one
or into a lake

**tribute** NOUN tributes
❶ something said, done or given as a mark
of respect or admiration for someone
❷ payment that one country or ruler had to
pay to a more powerful one in the past

**trice** NOUN (*old use*)
➤ **in a trice** in a moment

**triceps** (say **try**-seps) NOUN triceps
the large muscle at the back of the upper arm
**WORD ORIGIN** Latin, = three-headed (because
the muscle is attached at three points)

**trick** NOUN tricks
❶ a crafty or deceitful action; a practical
joke • *Let's play a trick on Jo.* ❷ a skilful
action, especially one done for entertainment
• *a card trick* ❸ the cards picked up by the
winner after one round of a card game such
as whist
➤ **do the trick** (*informal*) to achieve the
result that you want

**trick** VERB tricks, tricking, tricked
to deceive or cheat someone by a trick
➤ **trick something out** to decorate a place
• *The building was tricked out with little
flags.*

**trickery** NOUN
the use of tricks; deception

**trickle** VERB trickles, trickling, trickled
to flow or move slowly • *Raindrops trickled down the window.*

**trickle** NOUN trickles
a slow gradual flow

**trickster** NOUN tricksters
a person who tricks or cheats people

**tricky** ADJECTIVE trickier, trickiest
❶ difficult to do or deal with • *There were a couple of tricky questions.* ❷ cunning or deceitful

**tricolour** (say **trik**-ol-er) NOUN tricolours
a flag with three coloured stripes, e.g. the national flag of France or Ireland

**tricycle** NOUN tricycles
a vehicle like a bicycle but with three wheels

**trident** NOUN tridents
a three-pronged spear, carried by Neptune and Britannia as a symbol of their power over the sea

**trier** NOUN triers
a person who tries hard

**trifle** NOUN trifles
❶ a pudding made of sponge cake covered in custard, fruit and cream ❷ a very small amount ❸ something that has very little importance or value
➤ **a trifle** (*informal*) a little bit; slightly • *He seemed a trifle anxious.*

**trifle** VERB trifles, trifling, trifled
to treat a person or thing without seriousness or respect • *She is not a woman to be trifled with.*

**trifling** ADJECTIVE
small in value or importance

**trigger** NOUN triggers
a lever that is pulled to fire a gun

**trigger** VERB triggers, triggering, triggered
to make something happen, especially suddenly • *The smoke must have triggered her asthma attack.*

**trigonometry** (say trig-on-**om**-it-ree) NOUN
the calculation of distances and angles by using triangles

**trilby** NOUN trilbies
(*chiefly British*) a man's soft felt hat
**(WORD ORIGIN)** named after *Trilby* O'Ferrall, the heroine of a popular book and play, who wore a similar hat

**trill** VERB trills, trilling, trilled
❶ to make a quivering musical sound ❷ to say something in a high cheerful voice • *'How lovely!' she trilled.*

**trill** NOUN trills
a quivering musical sound

**trillion** NOUN trillions
❶ a million million ❷ (*old use*) a million million million

**trilogy** NOUN trilogies
a group of three stories, poems or plays etc. about the same people or things

**trim** VERB trims, trimming, trimmed
❶ to cut the edges or unwanted parts off something ❷ to decorate a hat or piece of clothing by adding lace, ribbons, etc. • *The gown was trimmed with fur.* ❸ to arrange sails to suit the wind

**trim** NOUN trims
❶ cutting or trimming • *My hair needs a quick trim.* ❷ lace, ribbons, etc. used to decorate something
➤ **in good trim** in good condition; fit

**trim** ADJECTIVE
neat and orderly
➤ **trimly** ADVERB

**Trinity** NOUN
in Christianity, God regarded as three persons (Father, Son and Holy Spirit)

**trinket** NOUN trinkets
a small ornament or piece of jewellery

**trio** NOUN trios
❶ a group of three people or things ❷ a group of three musicians or singers ❸ a piece of music for three musicians

**trip** VERB trips, tripping, tripped
❶ to catch your foot on something and fall; to make someone do this ❷ to move with quick light steps ❸ to operate a switch
➤ **trip up** ❶ to stumble ❷ to make a small mistake
➤ **trip someone up** to cause a person to stumble or make a mistake

**trip** NOUN trips
❶ a journey or outing ❷ the action of tripping; a stumble ❸ (*informal*) hallucinations caused by taking a drug

**tripe** NOUN
❶ part of an ox's stomach used as food ❷ (*informal*) rubbish or nonsense

**triple** ADJECTIVE
❶ consisting of three parts ❷ involving three people or groups • *a triple alliance* ❸ three times as much or as many

**triple** VERB triples, tripling, tripled
to make something, or to become, three times
as much or as many

**triple jump** NOUN
an athletic contest in which competitors try
to jump as far as possible by doing a hop, step
and jump

**triplet** NOUN triplets
each of three children or animals born to the
same mother at one time

**tripod** (say try-pod) NOUN tripods
a stand with three legs, e.g. to support a
camera or telescope

**trireme** (say try-reem) NOUN triremes
an ancient Greek or Roman warship with
three banks of oars

**trisect** VERB trisects, trisecting, trisected
to divide something into three equal parts

**trite** (rhymes with kite) ADJECTIVE
worn out by constant repetition; hackneyed
• a few trite remarks

**triumph** NOUN triumphs
❶ a great success or victory ❷ a feeling of
joy at success or victory • They returned
home in triumph.

**triumph** VERB triumphs, triumphing,
triumphed
❶ to be successful or victorious ❷ to rejoice
in success or victory

**triumphal** ADJECTIVE
celebrating a great success or victory • a
triumphal arch

**triumphant** ADJECTIVE
❶ victorious in a battle or contest ❷ rejoicing
over a victory or success
➤ **triumphantly** ADVERB

**triumvirate** NOUN triumvirates
a ruling group of three people

**trivet** NOUN trivets
an iron stand for a pot or kettle, placed over
a fire

**trivia** PLURAL NOUN
unimportant details or pieces of information
• a quiz on pop trivia

**trivial** ADJECTIVE
small in value or importance • I'm sorry to
bother you with such a trivial matter.
➤ **triviality** NOUN
**WORD ORIGIN** from Latin trivialis = (originally)
at a crossroads, and then commonplace

**troll** (rhymes with hole) NOUN trolls
❶ in Scandinavian mythology, a supernatural
being, either a giant or a friendly but
mischievous dwarf ❷ a person who writes
unpleasant comments on the Internet in
order to annoy people

**trolley** NOUN trolleys
❶ a small table on wheels or castors, used for
serving food and drink ❷ a basket on wheels,
used in supermarkets

**trolleybus** NOUN trolleybuses
(British) a bus powered by electricity from an
overhead wire to which it is connected

**trombone** NOUN trombones
a large brass musical instrument with a
sliding tube

**troop** NOUN troops
❶ an organized group of soldiers, Scouts,
etc. ❷ a number of people or animals moving
along together

**troop** VERB troops, trooping, trooped
to move along as a group or in large numbers
• They all trooped in.

**trooper** NOUN troopers
a soldier in the cavalry or in an armoured unit

**troops** PLURAL NOUN
soldiers

**trophy** NOUN trophies
❶ a cup or other prize given for winning a
competition ❷ something taken in war or
hunting as a souvenir of success

**tropic** NOUN tropics
a line of latitude about 23½° north of the
equator (**tropic of Cancer**) or 23½° south of
the equator (**tropic of Capricorn**)
➤ **the tropics** the hot regions between these
two latitudes
**WORD ORIGIN** from Greek trope = turning
(because the sun seems to turn back when it
reaches these points)

**tropical** ADJECTIVE
to do with, or found in, the tropics • tropical
fish

**troposphere** NOUN
the layer of the atmosphere extending about
10 kilometres upwards from the earth's
surface

**trot** VERB trots, trotting, trotted
❶ a horse trots when it moves faster than
when walking but more slowly than when
cantering ❷ a person trots when they run
gently with short steps

➤ **trot something out** (*informal*) to produce or repeat something that has been used many times before • *He trotted out the usual excuses.*

**trot** NOUN
a trotting run
➤ **on the trot** (*informal*) one after the other without a break • *She worked for ten days on the trot.*

**troth** (rhymes with both) NOUN (*old use*)
loyalty; a solemn promise

**trotter** NOUN **trotters**
a pig's foot used for food

**troubadour** (say **troo**-bad-oor) NOUN
**troubadours**
a poet and singer in southern France in the 11th–13th centuries

**trouble** NOUN **troubles**
❶ a problem, difficulty or worry ❷ a cause of any of these
➤ **be in trouble** to be likely to get punished because of something you have done
➤ **take trouble** to take great care in doing something

**trouble** VERB **troubles, troubling, troubled**
❶ to cause trouble to someone ❷ to bother or disturb someone • *Sorry to trouble you, but can you spare a minute?* ❸ to make an effort to do something • *Nobody troubled to ask if I needed help.*

**troublemaker** NOUN **troublemakers**
a person who often deliberately causes trouble

**troublesome** ADJECTIVE
causing trouble or annoyance

**trough** (say trof) NOUN **troughs**
❶ a long narrow open container, especially one holding water or food for animals ❷ a channel for liquid ❸ the low part between two waves or ridges ❹ a long region of low air pressure

**trounce** VERB **trounces, trouncing, trounced**
to defeat someone heavily

**troupe** (say troop) NOUN **troupes**
a company of actors or other performers

SPELLING
Take care not to confuse with **troop**, which means a number of people or animals moving together.

**trousers** PLURAL NOUN
a piece of clothing worn over the lower half of your body, with a separate part for each leg

**trousseau** (say **troo**-soh) NOUN **trousseaus** or **trousseaux**
a bride's collection of clothing etc. to begin married life

**trout** NOUN **trout**
a freshwater fish that is caught as a sport and for food

**trowel** NOUN **trowels**
❶ a small garden tool with a curved blade for lifting plants or scooping things ❷ a small tool with a flat blade for spreading mortar or cement

**truant** NOUN **truants**
a child who stays away from school without permission
➤ **truancy** NOUN
➤ **play truant** to stay away from school without permission

**truce** NOUN **truces**
an agreement to stop fighting for a while

**truck** NOUN **trucks**
❶ a lorry ❷ an open container on wheels for transporting loads; an open railway wagon ❸ an axle with wheels attached, fitted under a skateboard

**truculent** (say **truk**-yoo-lent) ADJECTIVE
defiant and aggressive
➤ **truculently** ADVERB
➤ **truculence** NOUN

**trudge** VERB **trudges, trudging, trudged**
to walk slowly and heavily • *We trudged home across the fields.*

**true** ADJECTIVE **truer, truest**
❶ representing what has really happened or exists • *a true story* ❷ genuine or proper; not false • *He was the true heir.* ❸ accurate or exact ❹ loyal or faithful • *Be true to your friends.*
➤ **come true** to actually happen as hoped or predicted • *I hope your dreams come true.*

**truffle** NOUN **truffles**
❶ a soft sweet made with chocolate ❷ a fungus that grows underground and is valued as food because of its rich flavour

**truly** ADVERB
❶ truthfully ❷ sincerely or genuinely • *We*

*are truly grateful.* ❸ (*old use*) loyally or
faithfully
➤ **Yours truly** see **yours**

**trump** NOUN trumps
❶ a playing card of a suit that ranks above
the others for one game or round of play
❷ (*old use*) a blast of a trumpet

**trump** VERB trumps, trumping, trumped
to beat a card by playing a trump
➤ **trump something up** to invent an excuse
or an accusation

**trumpet** NOUN trumpets
❶ a metal wind instrument with a narrow
tube that widens near the end ❷ something
shaped like this

**trumpet** VERB trumpets, trumpeting,
trumpeted
❶ an elephant trumpets when it makes a loud
sound with its trunk ❷ to blow a trumpet
❸ to shout or announce something loudly
➤ **trumpeter** NOUN

**truncate** VERB truncates, truncating,
truncated
to shorten something by cutting off its
beginning or end

**truncheon** NOUN truncheons
(*chiefly British*) a short thick stick carried as a
weapon by a police officer

**trundle** VERB trundles, trundling, trundled
to move something along heavily, especially
on wheels, or to move like this • *He was
trundling a wheelbarrow.* • *A bus trundled
across the bridge.*

**trunk** NOUN trunks
❶ the main stem of a tree ❷ an elephant's
long flexible nose ❸ a large box with a
hinged lid for transporting or storing clothes
etc. ❹ the human body except for the head,
arms and legs ❺ (*North American*) the boot
of a car

**trunk call** NOUN trunk calls (*old use, chiefly
British*)
a long-distance telephone call

**trunk road** NOUN trunk roads
(*British*) an important main road

**trunks** PLURAL NOUN
shorts worn by men and boys for swimming,
boxing, etc.

**truss** NOUN trusses
❶ a framework of beams or bars supporting a
roof or bridge ❷ a type of padded belt worn
to support a hernia

**truss** VERB trusses, trussing, trussed
❶ to tie up a person or thing securely ❷ to
support a roof or bridge with trusses

**trust** VERB trusts, trusting, trusted
❶ to believe that a person or thing is good,
truthful or reliable ❷ to let a person have or
use something in the belief that they will look
after it • *Don't trust him with your phone!*
❸ to hope or expect something • *I trust that
you are well.*
➤ **trust to something** to rely on something
• *I'm just trusting to luck.*

**trust** NOUN trusts
❶ the belief that a person or thing can be
trusted ❷ responsibility; being trusted • *a
position of trust.* ❸ a legal arrangement in
which a person looks after money or property
for someone else with instructions about how
to use it
➤ **trustful** ADJECTIVE
➤ **trustfully** ADVERB

**trustee** NOUN trustees
a person who looks after money or property
for someone else

**trustworthy** ADJECTIVE
able to be trusted; reliable

**trusty** ADJECTIVE
trustworthy or reliable • *my trusty sword*

**truth** NOUN truths
❶ a true fact or statement ❷ the quality of
being true

**truthful** ADJECTIVE
❶ telling the truth • *a truthful boy* ❷ true • *a
truthful account of what happened*
➤ **truthfully** ADVERB
➤ **truthfulness** NOUN

**try** VERB tries, trying, tried
❶ to make an effort to do something; to
attempt something ❷ to test something by
using or doing it • *Try sleeping on your back.*
❸ to examine the evidence in a law court to
decide whether a person is guilty of a crime
❹ to be a strain on something • *You really
are trying my patience.*
➤ **try something on** to put on clothes to see
if they fit or look good
➤ **try something out** to use something to
see if it works

**try** NOUN tries
❶ a go at trying something; an attempt

• *Have another try.* ❷ in rugby, putting the ball down behind the opponents' goal line in order to score points

**trying** *ADJECTIVE*
putting a strain on your patience; annoying

**tsar** (say zar) *NOUN* tsars
the title of the former ruler of Russia
**WORD ORIGIN** Russian, from Latin *Caesar*

**tsetse fly** (say tet-see) *NOUN* tsetse flies
a tropical African fly which has a bite that can cause sleeping sickness in people

**T-shirt** *NOUN* T-shirts
a short-sleeved shirt shaped like a T

**tsunami** *NOUN* tsunamis
a huge sea wave caused by an underwater earthquake **WORD ORIGIN** Japanese, from *tsu* = harbour + *nami* = a wave

**tub** *NOUN* tubs
a round open container holding liquid, ice cream, soil for plants, etc.

**tuba** (say tew-ba) *NOUN* tubas
a large brass wind instrument that makes a deep sound **WORD ORIGIN** Italian from Latin, = war trumpet

**tubby** *ADJECTIVE* tubbier, tubbiest
short and fat

**tube** *NOUN* tubes
❶ a long hollow piece of metal, plastic, rubber, glass, etc., especially for liquids or gases to pass along ❷ a long hollow container made of soft metal or plastic, for something soft • *a tube of toothpaste* ❸ the underground railway in London

**tuber** *NOUN* tubers
a short thick rounded root (e.g. of a dahlia) or underground stem (e.g. of a potato) that produces buds from which new plants will grow

**tuberculosis** *NOUN*
a disease of people and animals, producing small swellings in parts of the body, especially in the lungs

**tubing** *NOUN*
tubes; a length of tube

**tubular** *ADJECTIVE*
shaped like a tube

**tuck** *VERB* tucks, tucking, tucked
❶ to push a loose edge into something so that it is hidden or held in place • *Now tuck the flap in the envelope.* ❷ to put something away in a small space • *She tucked the letter in her pocket.*
➤ **tuck in** (*informal*) to eat heartily
➤ **tuck someone in** or **up** to make someone comfortable in bed by folding the edges of the bedclothes tightly

**tuck** *NOUN* tucks
❶ a flat fold stitched in a piece of clothing ❷ (*informal*) food, especially sweets and cakes etc. that children enjoy
➤ **tuck shop** *NOUN*

**tucker** *NOUN* (*informal*) (*Australian/NZ*) food

**Tuesday** *NOUN*
the day of the week following Monday
**WORD ORIGIN** from Old English *Tiwesdaeg* = day of Tiw, a Norse god

**tuft** *NOUN* tufts
a bunch of threads, grass, hair or feathers growing in held close together
➤ **tufted** *ADJECTIVE*

**tug** *VERB* tugs, tugging, tugged
❶ to pull something hard or suddenly ❷ to tow a ship

**tug** *NOUN* tugs
❶ a hard or sudden pull ❷ a small powerful boat used for towing others

**tug of war** *NOUN*
a contest between two teams pulling a rope from opposite ends

**tuition** *NOUN*
teaching, especially when given to one person or a small group

**tulip** *NOUN* tulips
a large cup-shaped flower on a tall stem growing from a bulb

**tulle** (say tewl) *NOUN*
a very fine silky net material used for veils, wedding dresses, etc.

**tumble** *VERB* tumbles, tumbling, tumbled
❶ to fall or roll over suddenly or clumsily • *He tumbled down the hill.* ❷ to move or fall somewhere in an uncontrolled or untidy way • *She opened her bag and all her things tumbled out.*

**tumble** *NOUN* tumbles
a sudden fall or drop

**tumbledown** *ADJECTIVE*
falling into ruins • *a tumbledown cottage*

**tumble-drier** *NOUN* tumble-driers
a machine that dries washing by turning it over many times in heated air

a b c d e f g h i j k l m n o p q r s t u v w x y z

**tumbler** NOUN **tumblers**
❶ a drinking glass with no stem or handle
❷ a part of a lock that is lifted when a key is turned to open it ❸ an acrobat

**tumbril** NOUN **tumbrils** (old use)
an open cart used to carry condemned people to the guillotine during the French Revolution

**tummy** NOUN **tummies** (informal)
your stomach

**tumour** (say **tew**-mer) NOUN **tumours**
an abnormal lump growing on or in the body

**tumult** (say **tew**-mult) NOUN
an uproar or state of noisy confusion and agitation

**tumultuous** (say tew-**mul**-tew-us) ADJECTIVE
noisy and excited • a tumultuous welcome

**tun** NOUN **tuns**
a large cask or barrel

**tuna** (say **tew**-na) NOUN **tuna**
a large edible sea fish with pink flesh

**tundra** NOUN
the vast level Arctic regions of Europe, Asia and America where there are no trees and the subsoil is always frozen

**tune** NOUN **tunes**
a short piece of music; a pleasant series of musical notes
➤ **in tune** at the correct musical pitch

**tune** VERB **tunes, tuning, tuned**
❶ to put a musical instrument in tune ❷ to adjust a radio or television set to receive a certain channel ❸ to adjust an engine so that it runs smoothly
➤ **tuner** NOUN
➤ **tune up** when an orchestra tunes up when it brings the instruments to the correct pitch

**tuneful** ADJECTIVE
having a pleasant tune

**tungsten** NOUN
a grey metal used to make a kind of steel

**tunic** NOUN **tunics**
❶ a jacket worn as part of a uniform ❷ a piece of clothing without sleeves, reaching from the shoulders to the hips or knees

**tunnel** NOUN **tunnels**
a passage made underground or through a hill

**tunnel** VERB **tunnels, tunnelling, tunnelled**
to make a tunnel

**tunny** NOUN **tunnies**
a tuna

**turban** NOUN **turbans**
a covering for the head made by wrapping a strip of cloth round a cap, worn especially by Muslims and Sikhs

**turbid** ADJECTIVE
turbid water is muddy and not clear

**turbine** NOUN **turbines**
a machine or motor that is driven by a flow of water, steam or gas

**turbojet** NOUN **turbojets**
a jet engine or aircraft with turbines

**turbot** NOUN **turbot**
a large flat edible sea fish

**turbulence** NOUN
violent and uneven movement of air or water • We experienced turbulence during the flight.

**turbulent** ADJECTIVE
❶ moving violently and unevenly • turbulent seas ❷ involving much change and disagreement and sometimes violence • a turbulent period of history

**tureen** NOUN **tureens**
a deep dish with a lid, from which soup is served at the table

**turf** NOUN **turfs** or **turves**
❶ short grass and the earth round its roots ❷ a piece of this cut from the ground
➤ **the turf** horse racing

**turf** VERB **turfs, turfing, turfed**
to cover ground with turf
➤ **turf someone out** (informal) to force someone to leave a place

**turgid** (say **ter**-jid) ADJECTIVE
pompous and boring • a turgid speech

**turkey** NOUN **turkeys**
a large bird kept for its meat
(WORD ORIGIN) originally the name of a different bird which was imported from Turkey

**turmoil** NOUN
wild confusion or agitation • Her mind was in turmoil.

**turn** VERB **turns, turning, turned**
❶ to move round or take a new direction; to make something move in this way • Turn left at the lights. ❷ to change in appearance etc.; to become • He turned pale. • These caterpillars will turn into butterflies. ❸ to make something change • You can turn milk

*into butter.* **④** to move a switch or tap etc. to control something • *Turn that radio off.* **⑤** to pass a certain time • *It has turned midnight.* **⑥** to shape something on a lathe

➤ **turn something down** **①** to fold something down **②** to reduce the flow or sound of something **③** to reject or refuse something • *We offered her a job but she turned it down.*

➤ **turn out** **①** to happen • *Let's wait and see how things turn out.* **②** to prove to be • *The visitor turned out to be my uncle.*

➤ **turn something out** to empty something, especially to search or clean it

➤ **turn to someone** to go to someone for help or advice

➤ **turn up** to appear or arrive suddenly or unexpectedly

➤ **turn something up** to increase the flow or sound of something

**turn** *NOUN* **turns**
**①** the action of turning; a turning movement • *Give the key three turns.* **②** a change; the point where something turns **③** a place where a road bends **④** an opportunity or duty that comes to each person in succession • *It's your turn to wash up.* **⑤** a short performance in an entertainment **⑥** (*informal*) an attack of illness; a nervous shock • *It gave me a nasty turn.*

➤ **a good turn** a helpful action
➤ **in turn** in succession; one after another
(**WORD ORIGIN**) from Greek *tornos* = lathe

**turncoat** *NOUN* **turncoats**
a person who changes sides or changes what they believe

**turning** *NOUN* **turnings**
a place where one road meets another, forming a corner

**turning point** *NOUN* **turning points**
a point where an important change takes place • *This battle was a turning point in the war.*

**turnip** *NOUN* **turnips**
a plant with a large round white root used as a vegetable

**turnout** *NOUN* **turnouts**
the number of people who attend a meeting, vote at an election, etc. • *Despite the rain, there was a pretty good turnout.*

**turnover** *NOUN* **turnovers**
**①** the amount of money received by a firm selling things **②** the rate at which goods are sold or workers leave and are replaced **③** a

small pie made by folding pastry over fruit, jam, etc.

**turnpike** *NOUN* **turnpikes** (*old use*)
a road on which a toll was charged

**turnstile** *NOUN* **turnstiles**
a revolving gate that lets one person in at a time

**turntable** *NOUN* **turntables**
a circular revolving platform or support, e.g. for the record in a record player

**turpentine** *NOUN*
a kind of oil used for thinning paint, cleaning paintbrushes, etc.

**turps** *NOUN* (*informal*)
turpentine

**turquoise** *NOUN* **turquoises**
**①** a sky-blue or greenish-blue colour **②** a bright blue jewel (**WORD ORIGIN**) from French *pierre turquoise* = Turkish stone

**turret** *NOUN* **turrets**
**①** a small tower on a castle or other building **②** a revolving structure containing a gun
➤ **turreted** *ADJECTIVE*

**turtle** *NOUN* **turtles**
a sea animal that looks like a tortoise
➤ **turn turtle** to capsize

**turtle-dove** *NOUN* **turtle-doves**
a wild dove

**tusk** *NOUN* **tusks**
a long pointed tooth that sticks out from the mouth of an elephant, walrus, etc.

**tussle** *NOUN* **tussles**
a struggle or conflict over something

**tussle** *VERB* **tussles, tussling, tussled**
to struggle or fight over something • *The two players tussled with each another for the ball.*

**tussock** *NOUN* **tussocks**
a tuft or clump of grass

**tutor** *NOUN* **tutors**
**①** a private teacher, especially of one pupil or a small group **②** a teacher of students in a college or university

**tutorial** *NOUN* **tutorials**
a meeting in which students discuss a subject with their tutor

**tutu** (say **too**-too) *NOUN* **tutus**
a ballet dancer's short stiff frilled skirt

**TV** *ABBREVIATION*
television

749

**twaddle** NOUN (*informal*)
nonsense

**twain** NOUN & ADJECTIVE (*old use*)
two

**twang** NOUN twangs
❶ a sharp sound like that of a wire when plucked ❷ a nasal tone in a person's voice

**twang** VERB twangs, twanging, twanged
❶ to make a sharp sound like that of a wire when plucked ❷ to play a guitar etc. by plucking its strings

**tweak** VERB tweaks, tweaking, tweaked
to pinch and twist or pull something sharply

**tweak** NOUN tweaks
a tweaking movement

**tweed** NOUN
a thick rough woollen cloth, often woven of mixed colours (**WORD ORIGIN** originally a mistake; the Scottish word *tweel* (= twill) was wrongly read as *tweed* by being confused with the River Tweed

**tweeds** PLURAL NOUN
clothes made of tweed

**tweet** NOUN tweets
❶ the chirping sound made by a small bird ❷ a short message sent on the social network Twitter

**tweet** VERB tweets, tweeting, tweeted
❶ a small bird tweets when it makes a chirping sound ❷ to send a message on the social network Twitter

**tweezers** PLURAL NOUN
small pincers for picking up or pulling very small things

**twelve** NOUN & ADJECTIVE twelves
the number 12
➤ **twelfth** ADJECTIVE & NOUN

**SPELLING**
Take care: there is an f before the th.

**twenty** NOUN & ADJECTIVE twenties
the number 20
➤ **twentieth** ADJECTIVE & NOUN

**twice** ADVERB
❶ two times; on two occasions • *I've only been there twice.* ❷ double the amount

**twiddle** VERB twiddles, twiddling, twiddled
to turn something round or over and over in an idle way • *He tried twiddling the knob on the radio.*

**twiddle** NOUN
a twiddling movement
➤ **twiddle your thumbs** to have nothing to do

**twig** NOUN twigs
a small shoot on a branch or stem of a tree or shrub

**twig** VERB twigs, twigging, twigged (*informal*)
to realize what something means • *I suddenly twigged what she was talking about.*

**twilight** NOUN
dim light from the sky just after sunset or just before sunrise

**twill** NOUN
material woven so that there is a pattern of diagonal lines

**twin** NOUN twins
❶ either of two children or animals born to the same mother at one time ❷ either of two things that are exactly alike

**twin** VERB twins, twinning, twinned
❶ to put things together as a pair ❷ (*British*) if a town is twinned with a town in a different country, the two towns exchange visits and organize cultural events together

**twine** NOUN
strong thin string

**twine** VERB twines, twining, twined
to twist or wind one thing round another • *She twined her arms around his neck.*

**twinge** NOUN twinges
a sudden pain or unpleasant feeling • *a twinge of guilt*

**twinkle** VERB twinkles, twinkling, twinkled
❶ to shine with tiny flashes of light; to sparkle ❷ your eyes twinkle when they look bright because you are happy or amused

**twinkle** NOUN twinkles
❶ a twinkling light ❷ a bright expression in your eyes that shows you are happy or amused

**twirl** VERB twirls, twirling, twirled
❶ to twist something round quickly ❷ to turn around in a circle

**twirl** NOUN
a twirling movement

**twist** VERB twists, twisting, twisted
❶ to turn the ends of something in opposite directions ❷ to turn round or from side to side • *The road twisted through the hills* ❸ to bend something out of its proper shape • *My bike's front wheel is twisted.* • *I think*

*I've twisted my ankle.* ❹ to pass threads or strands round something or round each other ❺ to distort the meaning of what someone says • *You're twisting my words.*

**twist** *NOUN* twists
❶ a twisting movement or action ❷ a strange or unexpected development in a story or series of events
➤ **twisty** *ADJECTIVE*

**twister** *NOUN* twisters
(*North American*) a tornado

**twit** *NOUN* twits (*informal, chiefly British*)
a silly or foolish person

**twitch** *VERB* twitches, twitching, twitched
to move suddenly with a slight jerk or to make something do this

**twitch** *NOUN* twitches
a twitching movement

**twitter** *VERB* twitters, twittering, twittered
birds twitter when they make quick chirping sounds

**twitter** *NOUN* twitters
a twittering sound

**two** *NOUN & ADJECTIVE* twos
the number 2
➤ **be in two minds** to be undecided about something

**two-dimensional** *ADJECTIVE*
having two dimensions (length and width); flat

**two-faced** *ADJECTIVE*
insincere or deceitful

**tycoon** *NOUN* tycoons
a rich and influential business person
(**WORD ORIGIN**) from Japanese *taikun* = great prince

**tying**
present participle of **tie**

**type** *NOUN* types
❶ a kind or sort • *What type of music do you like?* ❷ letters or figures etc. designed for use in printing

**type** *VERB* types, typing, typed
to write something by using a keyboard

**typecast** *VERB* typecasts, typecasting, typecast
an actor is typecast when they are always given the same kind of role to play • *She doesn't want to be typecast as a dumb blonde.*

**typescript** *NOUN* typescripts
a typed copy of a text or document

**typewriter** *NOUN* typewriters
a machine with keys that you press to print letters or figures etc. on a piece of paper
➤ **typewritten** *ADJECTIVE*

**typhoid fever** *NOUN*
a serious infectious disease with fever, caused by harmful bacteria in food or water

**typhoon** *NOUN* typhoons
a violent hurricane in the western Pacific or East Asian seas (**WORD ORIGIN**) from Chinese *tai fung* = great wind

**typhus** *NOUN*
an infectious disease causing fever, weakness and a rash

**typical** *ADJECTIVE*
❶ having the usual characteristics or qualities of a particular type of person or thing • *a typical Italian village* ❷ as you would expect from a particular person or thing • *He spoke with typical enthusiasm.* • *She's late again – typical!*
➤ **typically** *ADVERB*

**typify** (say **tip**-if-eye) *VERB* typifies, typifying, typified
to be a typical example of something • *He typifies the popular image of a football manager.*

**typist** *NOUN* typists
a person who types, especially as their job

**typography** (say ty-**pog**-ra-fee) *NOUN*
the style or appearance of the letters and figures etc. in printed material

**tyrannize** (also **tyrannise**) (say **tirran**-yz) *VERB* tyrannizes, tyrannizing, tyrannized
to behave like a tyrant to people

**tyrannosaurus** *NOUN* tyrannosauruses
a huge flesh-eating dinosaur that walked upright on its large hind legs
(**WORD ORIGIN**) from Greek *tyrannos* = ruler + *sauros* = lizard

**tyranny** (say **tirran**-ee) *NOUN* tyrannies
❶ government by a tyrant ❷ the way a tyrant behaves towards people
➤ **tyrannical** *ADJECTIVE*

**tyrant** (say **ty**-rant) *NOUN* tyrants
a person who rules cruelly and unjustly; someone who insists on being obeyed

a
b
c
d
e
f
g
h
i
j
k
l
m
n
o
p
q
r
s
t
u
v
w
x
y
z

**tyre** NOUN **tyres**
a covering of rubber fitted round a wheel to make it grip the road and run more smoothly

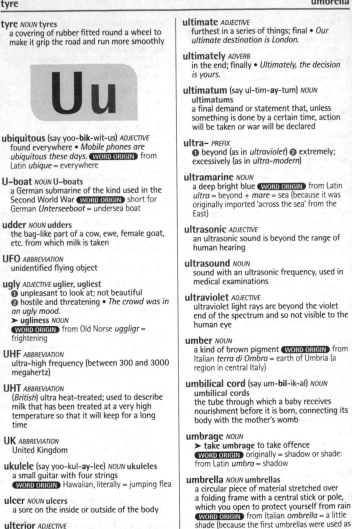

**ubiquitous** (say yoo-**bik**-wit-us) ADJECTIVE
found everywhere • *Mobile phones are ubiquitous these days.* **WORD ORIGIN** from Latin *ubique* = everywhere

**U-boat** NOUN **U-boats**
a German submarine of the kind used in the Second World War **WORD ORIGIN** short for German *Unterseeboot* = undersea boat

**udder** NOUN **udders**
the bag-like part of a cow, ewe, female goat, etc. from which milk is taken

**UFO** ABBREVIATION
unidentified flying object

**ugly** ADJECTIVE **uglier, ugliest**
❶ unpleasant to look at; not beautiful
❷ hostile and threatening • *The crowd was in an ugly mood.*
➤ **ugliness** NOUN
**WORD ORIGIN** from Old Norse *uggligr* = frightening

**UHF** ABBREVIATION
ultra-high frequency (between 300 and 3000 megahertz)

**UHT** ABBREVIATION
(*British*) ultra heat-treated; used to describe milk that has been treated at a very high temperature so that it will keep for a long time

**UK** ABBREVIATION
United Kingdom

**ukulele** (say yoo-kul-**ay**-lee) NOUN **ukuleles**
a small guitar with four strings
**WORD ORIGIN** Hawaiian, literally = jumping flea

**ulcer** NOUN **ulcers**
a sore on the inside or outside of the body

**ulterior** ADJECTIVE
beyond what is obvious or stated • *Perhaps he had an ulterior motive for doing this.*

**ultimate** ADJECTIVE
furthest in a series of things; final • *Our ultimate destination is London.*

**ultimately** ADVERB
in the end; finally • *Ultimately, the decision is yours.*

**ultimatum** (say ul-tim-**ay**-tum) NOUN **ultimatums**
a final demand or statement that, unless something is done by a certain time, action will be taken or war will be declared

**ultra–** PREFIX
❶ beyond (as in *ultraviolet*) ❷ extremely; excessively (as in *ultra-modern*)

**ultramarine** NOUN
a deep bright blue **WORD ORIGIN** from Latin *ultra* = beyond + *mare* = sea (because it was originally imported 'across the sea' from the East)

**ultrasonic** ADJECTIVE
an ultrasonic sound is beyond the range of human hearing

**ultrasound** NOUN
sound with an ultrasonic frequency, used in medical examinations

**ultraviolet** ADJECTIVE
ultraviolet light rays are beyond the violet end of the spectrum and so not visible to the human eye

**umber** NOUN
a kind of brown pigment **WORD ORIGIN** from Italian *terra di Ombra* = earth of Umbria (a region in central Italy)

**umbilical cord** (say um-**bil**-ik-al) NOUN **umbilical cords**
the tube through which a baby receives nourishment before it is born, connecting its body with the mother's womb

**umbrage** NOUN
➤ **take umbrage** to take offence
**WORD ORIGIN** originally = shadow or shade: from Latin *umbra* = shadow

**umbrella** NOUN **umbrellas**
a circular piece of material stretched over a folding frame with a central stick or pole, which you open to protect yourself from rain
**WORD ORIGIN** from Italian *ombrella* = a little shade (because the first umbrellas were used as protection against the sun rather than to keep off the rain)

**umlaut** *NOUN* umlauts
a mark (¨) placed over a vowel in German to indicate a change in its pronunciation

**umpire** *NOUN* umpires
a referee in cricket, tennis and some other games

**umpire** *VERB* umpires, umpiring, umpired
to act as an umpire

**UN** *ABBREVIATION*
United Nations

**un–** *PREFIX*
❶ not (as in *uncertain*) ❷ used before a verb to reverse its action (as in *unlock* = release from being locked)

USAGE
Many words beginning with this prefix are not listed here if their meaning is obvious.

**unable** *ADJECTIVE*
not able to do something

**unaccountable** *ADJECTIVE*
❶ unable to be explained • *For some unaccountable reason I completely forgot your birthday.* ❷ not accountable for what you do
➤ **unaccountably** *ADVERB*

**unadulterated** *ADJECTIVE*
pure; not mixed with things that are less good

**unaided** *ADJECTIVE*
without any help

**unanimous** (say yoo-**nan**-im-us) *ADJECTIVE*
with everyone agreeing • *a unanimous decision*
➤ **unanimously** *ADVERB*
➤ **unanimity** (say yoo-nan-**im**-it-ee) *NOUN*

**unarmed** *ADJECTIVE*
without weapons • *unarmed combat*

**unassuming** *ADJECTIVE*
modest; not arrogant or pretentious

**unavoidable** *ADJECTIVE*
not able to be avoided; bound to happen

**unaware** *ADJECTIVE*
not aware; not knowing about something
• *She was unaware of the danger outside.*

**unawares** *ADVERB*
unexpectedly; without warning • *His question caught me unawares.*

**unbalanced** *ADJECTIVE*
❶ not balanced ❷ slightly mad or mentally ill

**unbearable** *ADJECTIVE*
so painful or unpleasant that you cannot bear or endure it • *The heat was almost unbearable.*
➤ **unbearably** *ADVERB*

**unbeatable** *ADJECTIVE*
unable to be defeated or improved on

**unbeaten** *ADJECTIVE*
that has not been defeated or improved on

**unbecoming** *ADJECTIVE*
❶ not making a person look attractive ❷ not suitable or fitting

**unbeknown** *ADJECTIVE*
without someone knowing about it
• *Unbeknown to us, they had planned a surprise party.*

**unbelievable** *ADJECTIVE*
❶ difficult to believe ❷ amazing
➤ **unbelievably** *ADVERB*

**unbend** *VERB* unbends, unbending, unbent
❶ to change from a bent position; to straighten up ❷ to relax and become friendly

**unbiased** *ADJECTIVE*
not biased; impartial

**unbidden** *ADJECTIVE*
without being asked or invited; unexpectedly
• *The phrase sprang into her head unbidden.*

**unblock** *VERB* unblocks, unblocking, unblocked
to remove an obstruction from something

**unborn** *ADJECTIVE*
not yet born

**unbridled** *ADJECTIVE*
not controlled or restrained • *unbridled rage*

**unbroken** *ADJECTIVE*
not broken or interrupted • *a minute of unbroken silence*

**unburden** *VERB* unburdens, unburdening, unburdened
to remove a burden from the person carrying it
➤ **unburden yourself** to tell someone your secrets or problems so that you feel better

**uncalled for** *ADJECTIVE*
not justified or necessary • *Such rudeness was quite uncalled for.*

**uncanny** *ADJECTIVE* uncannier, uncanniest
strange or mysterious • *an uncanny coincidence*
➤ **uncannily** *ADVERB*

a
b
c
d
e
f
g
h
i
j
k
l
m
n
o
p
q
r
s
t
u
v
w
x
y
z

**unceremonious** ADJECTIVE
❶ without formality or ceremony ❷ offhand or abrupt

**uncertain** ADJECTIVE
❶ not known certainly ❷ not sure or confident about something ❸ not reliable
• *His aim is rather uncertain.*
➤ **uncertainty** NOUN
➤ **in no uncertain terms** clearly and forcefully

**uncertainly** ADVERB
without confidence; hesitantly • *They smiled uncertainly at one another.*

**uncharitable** ADJECTIVE
making unkind judgements about people or actions
➤ **uncharitably** ADVERB

**uncle** NOUN uncles
the brother of your father or mother; your aunt's husband

**unclear** ADJECTIVE
❶ not clear or definite ❷ not certain about something

**unclothed** ADJECTIVE
not wearing any clothes; naked

**uncomfortable** ADJECTIVE
❶ not comfortable ❷ uneasy or awkward about something
➤ **uncomfortably** ADVERB

**uncommon** ADJECTIVE
not common; unusual

**uncompromising** (say un-**komp**-ro-my-zing) ADJECTIVE
not allowing a compromise; inflexible
• *uncompromising views*

**unconcerned** ADJECTIVE
not caring about something; not worried

**unconditional** ADJECTIVE
without any conditions; complete or absolute
• *unconditional surrender*
➤ **unconditionally** ADVERB

**unconscious** ADJECTIVE
❶ not conscious ❷ not aware of things ❸ done without realizing it • *He gave an unconscious smile.*
➤ **unconsciously** ADVERB
➤ **unconsciousness** NOUN

SPELLING
Don't forget the **sci** in the middle.

**uncontrollable** ADJECTIVE
unable to be controlled or stopped
➤ **uncontrollably** ADVERB

**uncooperative** ADJECTIVE
not cooperative

**uncouth** (say un-**kooth**) ADJECTIVE
rude and rough in manner

**uncover** VERB uncovers, uncovering, uncovered
❶ to remove the covering from something ❷ to discover or reveal something • *They uncovered a plot to kill the king.*

**unction** NOUN
❶ anointing with oil, especially in a religious ceremony ❷ an oily manner

**unctuous** (say **unk**-tew-us) ADJECTIVE
having an oily manner; polite in an exaggerated way
➤ **unctuously** ADVERB
➤ **unctuousness** NOUN

**undecided** ADJECTIVE
❶ not yet settled; not certain ❷ not having made up your mind yet

**undeniable** ADJECTIVE
impossible to deny; undoubtedly true
➤ **undeniably** ADVERB

**under** PREPOSITION
❶ below or beneath • *Hide it under the desk.* ❷ less than • *under 5 years old* ❸ governed or controlled by • *The country prospered under his rule.* ❹ in the process of; undergoing • *The road is under repair.* ❺ making use of • *He wrote under the name of 'Lewis Carroll'.* ❻ according to the rules of • *This is permitted under our agreement.*
➤ **under way** in motion or in progress

**under** ADVERB
in or to a lower place or level or condition
• *Slowly the diver went under.*

**underarm** ADJECTIVE & ADVERB
❶ moving the hand and arm forward and upwards • *an underarm throw* ❷ in or for the armpit

**undercarriage** NOUN undercarriages
an aircraft's landing wheels and their supports

**underclothes** PLURAL NOUN
underwear
➤ **underclothing** NOUN

A B C D E F G H I J K L M N O P Q R S T U V W X Y Z

**undercover** ADJECTIVE
done or doing things secretly • *an undercover agent*

**undercurrent** NOUN undercurrents
❶ a current that is below the surface or below another current ❷ a feeling or influence that is hidden beneath the surface but whose effects are felt • *I could sense an undercurrent of tension in the room.*

**undercut** VERB undercuts, undercutting, undercut
to sell something for a lower price than someone else sells it

**underdeveloped** ADJECTIVE
❶ not fully developed or grown ❷ an underdeveloped country is poor and lacks modern industrial development

**underdog** NOUN underdogs
a person or team in a contest that is expected to lose

**underdone** ADJECTIVE
not thoroughly done; undercooked

**underestimate** VERB underestimates, underestimating, underestimated
to make too low an estimate of a person or thing • *We underestimated the time it would take.*

**underfoot** ADVERB
on the ground; under your feet • *It was slippery underfoot.*

**undergarment** NOUN undergarments
a piece of underwear

**undergo** VERB undergoes, undergoing, underwent, undergone
to experience or go through something • *The new aircraft underwent intensive tests.*

**undergraduate** NOUN undergraduates
a student at a university who has not yet taken a degree

**underground** ADJECTIVE & ADVERB
❶ under the ground ❷ done or working in secret

**underground** NOUN
a railway that runs through tunnels under the ground

**undergrowth** NOUN
(*British*) bushes and other plants growing closely, especially under trees

**underhand** ADJECTIVE
done or doing things in a sly or secret way

**underlie** VERB underlies, underlying, underlay, underlain
❶ to be the basis or explanation of something • *Hard work underlies the team's success this season.* ❷ to be or lie under something

**underline** VERB underlines, underlining, underlined
❶ to draw a line under something you have written ❷ to emphasize something or show it clearly • *The accident underlines the need to be careful all the time.*

**underling** NOUN underlings
a person working under someone's authority or control

**underlying** ADJECTIVE
❶ forming the basis or explanation of something but not easy to notice • *the underlying causes of the trouble* ❷ lying under something • *the underlying rocks*

**undermine** VERB undermines, undermining, undermined
to weaken something gradually • *These recent defeats have undermined her confidence.*

**underneath** PREPOSITION & ADVERB
below or beneath

**underpaid** ADJECTIVE
paid too little

**underpants** PLURAL NOUN
a piece of men's underwear covering the lower part of the body, worn under trousers

**underpass** NOUN underpasses
a road that goes underneath another

**underprivileged** ADJECTIVE
having a lower standard of living and fewer opportunities than most other people in society

**underrate** VERB underrates, underrating, underrated
to have too low an opinion of a person or thing

**undersigned** ADJECTIVE
who has or have signed at the bottom of this document • *We, the undersigned, wish to protest.*

**undersized** ADJECTIVE
of less than the normal size

**understand** VERB understands, understanding, understood
❶ to know what something means or how it works or why it exists ❷ to know what someone is like and why they behave the

a
b
c
d
e
f
g
h
i
j
k
l
m
n
o
p
q
r
s
t
u
v
w
x
y
z

way they do ❸ to have heard or been told
something • *I understand that you would
like to speak to me.* ❹ to take something for
granted • *Your expenses will be paid, that's
understood.*

**understandable** ADJECTIVE
❶ able to be understood ❷ reasonable or
natural • *She replied with understandable
anger.*
➤ **understandably** ADVERB

**understanding** NOUN
❶ the power to understand or think;
intelligence ❷ sympathy or tolerance
❸ agreement in opinion or feeling • *a better
understanding between nations*

**understanding** ADJECTIVE
sympathetic and helpful • *Thanks for being so
understanding.*

**understatement** NOUN understatements
a statement that does not say something
strongly enough or give the complete
truth • *To say I am not happy is an
understatement; I am furious.*

**understudy** NOUN understudies
an actor who learns a part in order to be able
to play it if the usual actor is ill or absent

**understudy** VERB understudies,
understudying, understudied
to be an understudy for an actor or part

**undertake** VERB undertakes, undertaking,
undertook, undertaken
❶ to agree or promise to do something ❷ to
take on a task or responsibility

**undertaker** NOUN undertakers
a person whose job is to arrange funerals and
burials or cremations

**undertaking** NOUN undertakings
❶ a job or task that is being undertaken ❷ a
promise or guarantee ❸ the business of an
undertaker

**undertone** NOUN undertones
❶ a low or quiet tone to someone's voice
• *They spoke in undertones.* ❷ an underlying
quality or feeling • *His letter has a
threatening undertone.*

**undertow** NOUN undertows
a current below that of the surface of the sea
and moving in the opposite direction

**underwater** ADJECTIVE & ADVERB
placed, used or done beneath the surface of
water

**underwear** NOUN
clothes you wear next to your skin, under
other clothes

**underweight** ADJECTIVE
not heavy enough

**underwent**
past tense of **undergo**

**underworld** NOUN
❶ the people who are regularly involved in
crime ❷ in myths and legends, the place for
the spirits of the dead, under the earth

**undesirable** ADJECTIVE
not wanted or liked

**undeveloped** ADJECTIVE
not yet developed

**undignified** ADJECTIVE
not dignified

**undo** VERB undoes, undoing, undid, undone
❶ to unfasten or unwrap something ❷ to
cancel the effect of something • *He has
undone all our careful work.*

**undoing** NOUN
➤ **be someone's undoing** to be the cause of
someone's ruin or failure • *His greed proved
to be his undoing.*

**undoubted** ADJECTIVE
certain or definite; not regarded as doubtful
• *She has undoubted talent.*

**undoubtedly** ADVERB
definitely; without a doubt • *Her quick
thinking undoubtedly saved their lives.*

**undress** VERB undresses, undressing,
undressed
to take your clothes off

**undue** ADJECTIVE
more than is necessary or reasonable • *I don't
want to put undue pressure on them.*

**undulate** VERB undulates, undulating,
undulated
to move like a wave or waves; to have a wavy
appearance
➤ **undulation** NOUN
**WORD ORIGIN** from Latin *unda* = a wave

**unduly** ADVERB
excessively; more than is reasonable • *She
didn't seem unduly worried.*

**undying** ADJECTIVE
lasting forever • *their undying love*

**unearth** VERB unearths, unearthing,
unearthed

❶ to dig something up; to uncover something by digging ❷ to find something by searching • *I've unearthed some interesting information.*

**unearthly** *ADJECTIVE*
❶ unnatural; strange and frightening ❷ (*informal*) very early or inconvenient • *We had to get up at an unearthly hour.*

**uneasy** *ADJECTIVE*
❶ worried or anxious ❷ uncomfortable • *An uneasy silence followed.*
➤ **uneasily** *ADVERB*
➤ **uneasiness** *NOUN*

**uneatable** *ADJECTIVE*
not fit to be eaten

**unemployed** *ADJECTIVE*
without a job

**unemployment** *NOUN*
❶ being without a job ❷ the number of people without a job

**unending** *ADJECTIVE*
not coming to an end; endless

**unequal** *ADJECTIVE*
❶ not equal in amount, size or value ❷ not giving the same opportunities to everyone • *an unequal society*
➤ **unequalled** *ADJECTIVE*
➤ **unequally** *ADVERB*

**unerring** (say un-er-ing) *ADJECTIVE*
making no mistake • *unerring accuracy*

**uneven** *ADJECTIVE*
❶ not level or regular • *The path was uneven.* ❷ not equally balanced • *an uneven contest*
➤ **unevenly** *ADVERB*
➤ **unevenness** *NOUN*

**unexceptionable** *ADJECTIVE*
not in any way objectionable

**unexceptional** *ADJECTIVE*
not exceptional; quite ordinary

**unexpected** *ADJECTIVE*
not expected; coming as a surprise • *an unexpected visitor*
➤ **unexpectedness** *NOUN*

**unexpectedly** *ADVERB*
when you are not expecting it • *They arrived unexpectedly.*

**unfair** *ADJECTIVE*
not fair; unjust
➤ **unfairly** *ADVERB*
➤ **unfairness** *NOUN*

**unfaithful** *ADJECTIVE*
❶ not faithful or loyal ❷ not sexually loyal to one partner

**unfamiliar** *ADJECTIVE*
not familiar • *Suddenly, an unfamiliar voice called his name.*

**unfasten** *VERB* unfastens, unfastening, unfastened
to open the fastenings of something

**unfavourable** *ADJECTIVE*
not favourable or helpful
➤ **unfavourably** *ADVERB*

**unfeeling** *ADJECTIVE*
not caring about other people's feelings; unsympathetic

**unfit** *ADJECTIVE*
❶ not in perfect health because you do not take enough exercise ❷ not suitable for something • *The water was unfit to drink.*

**unfold** *VERB* unfolds, unfolding, unfolded
❶ to open something out or spread it out • *She unfolded the map.* ❷ to become known gradually • *They listened as the story unfolded.*

**unforeseen** *ADJECTIVE*
not foreseen; unexpected • *an unforeseen problem*

**unforgettable** *ADJECTIVE*
not likely to be forgotten • *Getting close to a whale is an unforgettable experience.*

**unforgivable** *ADJECTIVE*
not able to be forgiven

**unfortunate** *ADJECTIVE*
❶ unlucky • *an unfortunate accident* ❷ that you feel sorry about; regrettable • *an unfortunate remark*

> **SPELLING**
> Look out – there is an e after the last t.

**unfortunately** *ADVERB*
in a way that is sad or disappointing • *Unfortunately, I won't be able to come to your party.*

**unfounded** *ADJECTIVE*
not based on facts

**unfreeze** *VERB* unfreezes, unfreezing, unfroze, unfrozen
to thaw or to cause something to thaw

**unfriendly** *ADJECTIVE*
not friendly
➤ **unfriendliness** *NOUN*

**unfurl** VERB unfurls, unfurling, unfurled
to unroll something or spread it out • *They unfurled a large flag.*

**unfurnished** ADJECTIVE
without furniture • *an unfurnished flat*

**ungainly** ADJECTIVE
awkward-looking or clumsy • *a tall, ungainly youth*
➤ **ungainliness** NOUN

**ungodly** ADJECTIVE
❶ not religious ❷ (*informal*) outrageous; very inconvenient • *She woke me at an ungodly hour.*

**ungovernable** ADJECTIVE
impossible to control • *an ungovernable temper*

**ungracious** ADJECTIVE
not kindly or courteous
➤ **ungraciously** ADVERB

**ungrateful** ADJECTIVE
not grateful
➤ **ungratefully** ADVERB

**unguarded** ADJECTIVE
❶ without a guard or protection • *The gate had been left unguarded.* ❷ without thought or caution; indiscreet • *He said this in an unguarded moment.*

**unhappily** ADVERB
❶ in an unhappy way • *He shook his head unhappily.* ❷ unfortunately • *Unhappily, several people were hurt.*

**unhappy** ADJECTIVE
❶ not happy; sad ❷ not pleased or satisfied ❸ unfortunate or regrettable • *an unhappy coincidence*
➤ **unhappiness** NOUN

**unhealthy** ADJECTIVE
❶ not in good health ❷ not good for you • *an unhealthy diet*

**unheard-of** ADJECTIVE
never known or done before; extraordinary

**unhinge** VERB unhinges, unhinging, unhinged
to cause a person's mind to become unbalanced

**unicorn** NOUN unicorns
a mythical animal that is like a horse with one long straight horn growing from its forehead

**uniform** NOUN uniforms
special clothes showing that the wearer is a member of a certain school, army or organization

**uniform** ADJECTIVE
always the same; not varying • *The desks are of uniform size.*
➤ **uniformly** ADVERB
➤ **uniformity** NOUN

**uniformed** ADJECTIVE
wearing a uniform

**unify** VERB unifies, unifying, unified
to join several things together into one thing; to unite things
➤ **unification** NOUN

**unilateral** ADJECTIVE
done by one person, group or country and not by the others • *a unilateral decision*

**uninhabitable** ADJECTIVE
unfit to live in

**uninhabited** ADJECTIVE
with nobody living there • *an uninhabited island*

**unintentional** ADJECTIVE
not done deliberately
➤ **unintentionally** ADVERB

**uninterested** ADJECTIVE
having or showing no interest in something • *He seemed uninterested in what I had to say.*

> **USAGE**
> If you mean 'impartial', use disinterested.

**uninteresting** ADJECTIVE
not interesting

**union** NOUN unions
❶ the joining of things together ❷ a group of states or countries that have joined together to form one country or group ❸ a trade union

**unionist** NOUN unionists
❶ a member of a trade union ❷ a person who wishes to unite one country with another

**Union Jack** NOUN Union Jacks
the flag of the United Kingdom

**unique** (say yoo-**neek**) ADJECTIVE
being the only one of its kind; unlike any other • *Everyone's fingerprints are unique.*
➤ **uniquely** ADVERB

> **USAGE**
> The word unique is sometimes used to mean 'unusual', but many people regard this as incorrect. So it is safer to avoid saying things like *very unique* or *rather unique.*

A
B
C
D
E
F
G
H
I
J
K
L
M
N
O
P
Q
R
S
T
U
V
W
X
Y
Z

**unisex** ADJECTIVE
designed to be suitable for both sexes • *a unisex hairdresser's*

**unison** NOUN
➤ **in unison** ❶ with all saying, singing or doing the same thing at the same time ❷ in agreement

**unit** NOUN units
❶ an amount used as a standard in measuring or counting things • *Centimetres are units of length.* ❷ a group of people who have a certain job within a larger organization • *an army unit* ❸ a device or piece of furniture regarded as a single thing but forming part of a larger group or whole • *a sink unit* ❹ (*in mathematics*) any whole number less than 10

**unite** VERB unites, uniting, united
❶ to form several people or things into one group or thing ❷ people or things unite when they join together to do something

**United Kingdom** NOUN
Great Britain and Northern Ireland

**unity** NOUN
❶ being united or being in agreement
❷ something whole that is made up of parts

**universal** ADJECTIVE
to do with, including or done by everyone or everything • *The idea met with universal agreement.*

**universally** ADVERB
by everyone; everywhere • *He was universally known as 'Big Tom'.*

**universe** NOUN
everything that exists, including the earth and living things and all the stars and planets

**university** NOUN universities
a place where people go to study at an advanced level after leaving school

**unjust** ADJECTIVE
not fair or just • *unjust laws*
➤ **unjustly** ADVERB

**unkempt** ADJECTIVE
looking untidy or neglected

**unkind** ADJECTIVE
not kind; harsh
➤ **unkindly** ADVERB
➤ **unkindness** NOUN

**unknown** ADJECTIVE
not known or familiar

**unlawful** ADJECTIVE
not allowed by the law or rules

**unleaded** ADJECTIVE
unleaded petrol has no added lead

**unleash** VERB unleashes, unleashing, unleashed
to let a strong feeling or force be released • *The announcement unleashed a storm of protest.*

**unleavened** (say un-**lev**-end) ADJECTIVE
unleavened bread is made without yeast or other substances that would make it rise

**unless** CONJUNCTION
except when; if … not • *We cannot go unless we are invited.*

**unlike** PREPOSITION
not like • *Unlike me, she enjoys sport.*

**unlike** ADJECTIVE
not alike; different • *The two children are very unlike.*

**unlikely** ADJECTIVE unlikelier, unlikeliest
not likely to happen or be true

**unlimited** ADJECTIVE
not limited; very great or very many

**unload** VERB unloads, unloading, unloaded
to remove the load of things carried by a ship, aircraft or vehicle

**unlock** VERB unlocks, unlocking, unlocked
to open something by undoing a lock

**unluckily** ADVERB
unfortunately; as a result of bad luck

**unlucky** ADJECTIVE
not lucky; having or bringing bad luck

**unmanageable** ADJECTIVE
difficult or impossible to control or deal with

**unmarried** ADJECTIVE
not married

**unmask** VERB unmasks, unmasking, unmasked
❶ to remove a person's mask ❷ to reveal what a person or thing is really like

**unmentionable** ADJECTIVE
too bad or embarrassing to be spoken about

**unmistakable** ADJECTIVE
that cannot be mistaken for another person or thing • *There was an unmistakable hint of triumph in her eyes.*
➤ **unmistakably** ADVERB

**unmitigated** ADJECTIVE
absolute • *The rehearsal was an unmitigated disaster.*

a b c d e f g h i j k l m n o p q r s t u v w x y z

**unnatural** ADJECTIVE
not natural or normal • *His hair was an unnatural shade of yellow.*
➤ **unnaturally** ADVERB

**unnecessary** ADJECTIVE
not necessary; more than is necessary

**unnerve** VERB unnerves, unnerving, unnerved
to make someone lose courage or determination • *The silence unnerved me.*
➤ **unnerving** ADJECTIVE

**unoccupied** ADJECTIVE
a building or room is unoccupied when nobody is using it or living in it

**unofficial** ADJECTIVE
not official
➤ **unofficially** ADVERB

**unorthodox** ADJECTIVE
different from what is usual or generally accepted • *an unorthodox method*

**unpack** VERB unpacks, unpacking, unpacked
to take things out of a suitcase, bag, box, etc.

**unpaid** ADJECTIVE
❶ not yet paid • *an unpaid bill* ❷ not receiving payment for work you do

**unparalleled** ADJECTIVE
having no parallel or equal

**unpick** VERB unpicks, unpicking, unpicked
to undo the stitching of something

**unpleasant** ADJECTIVE
not pleasant; nasty
➤ **unpleasantly** ADVERB
➤ **unpleasantness** NOUN

**unpopular** ADJECTIVE
not liked or popular

**unprecedented** (say un-**press**-id-en-tid) ADJECTIVE
that has never happened before • *The flood waters have risen to unprecedented levels.*

**unprejudiced** ADJECTIVE
without prejudice; impartial

**unprepared** ADJECTIVE
not prepared beforehand; not ready or equipped to deal with something

**unprincipled** ADJECTIVE
without good moral principles; unscrupulous

**unprofessional** ADJECTIVE
not professional; not worthy of a member of a profession

**unprofitable** ADJECTIVE
not producing a profit or advantage

**unprotected** ADJECTIVE
❶ not protected or kept safe ❷ used to describe sexual activity in which a condom is not used

**unqualified** ADJECTIVE
❶ not officially qualified to do something ❷ complete; not limited in any way • *The show was an unqualified success.*

**unravel** VERB unravels, unravelling, unravelled
❶ to disentangle things ❷ to undo something that is knitted ❸ to look into a problem or mystery and solve it • *Fossils help scientists unravel the mysteries of prehistoric times.*

**unready** ADJECTIVE
not ready; hesitating

**USAGE**

In the title of the English king *Ethelred the Unready* the word means 'lacking good advice or wisdom'.

**unreal** ADJECTIVE
not real; existing only in the imagination
➤ **unreality** NOUN

**unrealistic** ADJECTIVE
not showing or accepting things as they really are

**unreasonable** ADJECTIVE
❶ not reasonable ❷ excessive or unjust
➤ **unreasonably** ADVERB

**unrelieved** ADJECTIVE
without anything to vary it • *unrelieved gloom*

**unremitting** ADJECTIVE
never stopping or relaxing; persistent

**unrequited** (say un-ri-**kwy**-tid) ADJECTIVE
unrequited love is not returned or rewarded

**unreserved** ADJECTIVE
❶ not reserved ❷ without restriction; complete • *an unreserved apology*
➤ **unreservedly** ADVERB

**unrest** NOUN
trouble or rioting caused by people because they are angry and dissatisfied • *a time of civil unrest*

**unripe** ADJECTIVE
not yet ripe

**unrivalled** ADJECTIVE
having no equal; better than all others • *an unrivalled collection of rare photographs*

**unroll** *VERB* unrolls, unrolling, unrolled
to open something that has been rolled up

**unruly** *ADJECTIVE*
badly behaved and difficult to control • *an unruly crowd*

**unsafe** *ADJECTIVE*
not safe; dangerous

**unsavoury** *ADJECTIVE*
unpleasant or disgusting

**unscathed** *ADJECTIVE*
not harmed or injured

**unscrew** *VERB* unscrews, unscrewing, unscrewed
to undo or remove something by twisting it or by taking out screws

**unscrupulous** *ADJECTIVE*
willing to do things that are dishonest or unfair in order to get what you want

**unseat** *VERB* unseats, unseating, unseated
to throw a person from horseback or from the seat on a bicycle

**unseemly** *ADJECTIVE*
not proper or suitable; indecent

**unseen** *ADJECTIVE*
not seen or noticed • *He managed to slip out of the room unseen.*

**unseen** *NOUN* unseens (*British*) a passage for translation without previous preparation

**unselfish** *ADJECTIVE*
not selfish; not thinking only about yourself
➤ **unselfishly** *ADVERB*
➤ **unselfishness** *NOUN*

**unsettle** *VERB* unsettles, unsettling, unsettled
to make someone feel uneasy or anxious
➤ **unsettling** *ADJECTIVE*

**unsettled** *ADJECTIVE*
❶ not settled or calm ❷ unsettled weather is likely to change

**unshakeable** *ADJECTIVE*
not able to be shaken or changed; strong and firm • *an unshakeable belief*

**unshaven** *ADJECTIVE*
an unshaven man has not shaved recently

**unsightly** *ADJECTIVE*
not pleasant to look at; ugly

**unskilled** *ADJECTIVE*
not having or not needing special skill or training

**unsociable** *ADJECTIVE*
not sociable or friendly

**unsocial** *ADJECTIVE*
not social
➤ **unsocial hours** time spent working when most people are free

**unsolicited** *ADJECTIVE*
not asked for • *unsolicited advice*

**unsound** *ADJECTIVE*
❶ not reliable; not based on sound evidence or reasoning • *unsound advice* ❷ not firm or strong ❸ not healthy • *of unsound mind*

**unspeakable** *ADJECTIVE*
too bad or horrid to be described

**unstable** *ADJECTIVE*
not stable; likely to change or become unbalanced

**unsteady** *ADJECTIVE*
not steady; shaking or wobbling or likely to fall • *She is still a little unsteady on her feet.*
➤ **unsteadily** *ADVERB*

**unstuck** *ADJECTIVE*
➤ **come unstuck** ❶ to stop sticking to something ❷ (*informal*) to fail or go wrong

**unsuccessful** *ADJECTIVE*
not successful; failed • *an unsuccessful attempt to reach an agreement*
➤ **unsuccessfully** *ADVERB*

**unsuitable** *ADJECTIVE*
not suitable or appropriate

**unsung** *ADJECTIVE* (*formal*)
not famous or praised but deserving to be • *the unsung heroes of the campaign*

**unsure** *ADJECTIVE*
not confident or certain • *He stood there, unsure what to say.*

**unthinkable** *ADJECTIVE*
too bad or too unlikely to be worth considering

**unthinking** *ADJECTIVE*
thoughtless; not thinking of other people

**untidy** *ADJECTIVE* untidier, untidiest
messy and not tidy • *an untidy desk*
➤ **untidily** *ADVERB*
➤ **untidiness** *NOUN*

**untie** *VERB* unties, untying, untied
to undo something that has been tied or to free someone who has been tied up

a
b
c
d
e
f
g
h
i
j
k
l
m
n
o
p
q
r
s
t
u
v
w
x
y
z

**until** PREPOSITION & CONJUNCTION
up to a particular time or event

> **USAGE**
>
> See the note at till.

> **SPELLING**
>
> There is only one l in until.

**untimely** ADJECTIVE
happening too soon or at an unsuitable time
• *his untimely death*

**unto** PREPOSITION (*old use*)
to

**untold** ADJECTIVE
too much or too many to be counted • *untold wealth*

**untoward** ADJECTIVE
inconvenient or unfortunate • *I hope nothing untoward happens.*

**untrue** ADJECTIVE
not true; false

**untruth** NOUN untruths
an untrue statement; a lie
➤ **untruthful** ADJECTIVE
➤ **untruthfully** ADVERB

**unused** ADJECTIVE
❶ (say un-**yoozd**) not yet used • *an unused stamp* ❷ (say un-**yoost**) not familiar with something • *They were unused to seeing strangers.*

**unusual** ADJECTIVE
not usual; strange or exceptional

**unusually** ADVERB
❶ more than is usual • *an unusually cold winter* ❷ in a way that is not normal or typical • *Unusually for her, she forgot his birthday.*

**unutterable** ADJECTIVE
too great to be described • *unutterable joy*

**unveil** VERB unveils, unveiling, unveiled
❶ to remove a veil or covering from something ❷ to reveal something new that has been kept hidden or secret

**unwanted** ADJECTIVE
not wanted

**unwarranted** ADJECTIVE
not justified or reasonable

**unwary** ADJECTIVE
not cautious or careful about danger
➤ **unwarily** ADVERB

**unwelcome** ADJECTIVE
not welcome or wanted • *an unwelcome visitor*

**unwell** ADJECTIVE
not in good health

**unwholesome** ADJECTIVE
❶ harmful to your health ❷ unhealthy-looking

**unwieldy** ADJECTIVE
awkward to move or control because of its size, shape or weight
➤ **unwieldiness** NOUN

**unwilling** ADJECTIVE
not willing to do something; reluctant • *He was unwilling to say any more.*
➤ **unwillingly** ADVERB

**unwind** VERB unwinds, unwinding, unwound
❶ to unroll something ❷ (*informal*) to relax after you have been working hard

**unwise** ADJECTIVE
not wise; foolish
➤ **unwisely** ADVERB

**unwitting** ADJECTIVE
❶ not intended ❷ not realizing something
➤ **unwittingly** ADVERB

**unwonted** (say un-**wohn**-tid) ADJECTIVE
not customary or usual • *She spoke with unwonted rudeness.*

**unworn** ADJECTIVE
not yet worn

**unworthy** ADJECTIVE
not worthy or deserving

**unwrap** VERB unwraps, unwrapping, unwrapped
to open something that is wrapped

**unzip** VERB unzips, unzipping, unzipped
to undo something that is zipped up

**up** ADVERB
❶ to or in a higher place or position or level • *Prices went up.* ❷ so as to be in a standing or upright position • *Everyone stood up.* ❸ out of bed • *It's time to get up.* ❹ completely • *Eat up your carrots.* ❺ finished • *Your time is up.* ❻ (*informal*) happening • *Something is up.*
➤ **up against something** ❶ close to something ❷ (*informal*) faced with difficulties or dangers
➤ **ups and downs** changes of luck, sometimes good and sometimes bad
➤ **up to** ❶ until; as far as ❷ busy with or

doing something • *What are you up to?*
❸ capable of doing something • *I don't think I'm up to it.*
➤ **be up to someone** to be someone's responsibility • *It's up to us to help her.*
➤ **up to date** ❶ modern or fashionable ❷ giving the most recent information

USAGE

Use hyphens when this is used as an adjective before a noun, e.g. *up-to-date information* (but *the information is up to date*).

**up** PREPOSITION
upwards through, along or into • *Water came up the pipes.*

**up-and-coming** ADJECTIVE (*informal*)
likely to become successful

**upbraid** VERB upbraids, upbraiding, upbraided (*formal*)
to angrily tell someone off because they have done something wrong

**upbringing** NOUN upbringings
your upbringing is the way you have been brought up

**update** VERB updates, updating, updated
to bring a thing up to date

**update** NOUN updates
the version of something that has the most recent information • *a news update*

**upgrade** VERB upgrades, upgrading, upgraded
❶ to improve a machine by installing new parts in it ❷ to improve a piece of software by installing a newer version
➤ **upgrade** NOUN

**upheaval** NOUN upheavals
a sudden violent change or disturbance

**uphill** ADVERB
up a slope

**uphill** ADJECTIVE
❶ going up a slope ❷ difficult • *It was an uphill struggle.*

**uphold** VERB upholds, upholding, upheld
to support or agree with a decision, opinion or belief • *Police officers have a duty to uphold the law.*

**upholster** VERB upholsters, upholstering, upholstered
to put a soft padded covering on furniture

**upholstery** NOUN
covers and padding for furniture

**upkeep** NOUN
keeping something in good condition or the cost of this

**uplands** PLURAL NOUN
the higher parts of a country or region
➤ **upland** ADJECTIVE

**uplifting** ADJECTIVE
making you feel more cheerful or hopeful • *an uplifting speech*

**upload** VERB uploads, uploading, uploaded (*in computing*) to move data from your computer to a larger computer network or system so that it can be read by other users

**upon** PREPOSITION
on

SPELLING

There is only one p in **upon**.

**upper** ADJECTIVE
higher in place or rank

**upper case** NOUN
capital letters

**upper class** NOUN upper classes
the highest class in society, especially the aristocracy
➤ **upper-class** ADJECTIVE

**uppermost** ADJECTIVE
highest in place or importance • *This question was uppermost in her mind.*

**uppermost** ADVERB
on or to the top or the highest place • *Keep the painted side uppermost.*

**upright** ADJECTIVE
❶ standing straight up; vertical ❷ strictly honest or honourable

**upright** NOUN uprights
a post or rod placed upright, especially as a support

**uprising** NOUN uprisings
a rebellion or revolt against the government

**uproar** NOUN
an outburst of noise or excitement or anger • *The room was in uproar.*

**uproarious** ADJECTIVE
very noisy • *uproarious laughter*

**uproot** VERB uproots, uprooting, uprooted
❶ to remove a plant and its roots from the ground ❷ to make someone leave the place where they have lived for a long time

**upset** ADJECTIVE
❶ unhappy or anxious about something
❷ slightly ill • *an upset stomach*

**upset** VERB upsets, upsetting, upset
❶ to make a person unhappy or anxious ❷ to disturb the normal working of something • *This has really upset my plans.* ❸ to overturn something or knock it over

**upset** NOUN upsets
❶ a slight illness • *a stomach upset* ❷ an unexpected result or setback • *There has been a major upset in the quarter-finals.*

**upshot** NOUN upshots
the eventual outcome • *The upshot was that we missed the last ferry.*
(WORD ORIGIN) originally = the final shot in an archery contest

**upside down** ADVERB & ADJECTIVE
❶ with the upper part underneath instead of on top ❷ in great disorder; very untidy • *The thieves turned the place upside down.*

**upstairs** ADVERB & ADJECTIVE
to or on a higher floor

**upstart** NOUN upstarts
a person who has risen suddenly to a high position and who then behaves arrogantly

**upstream** ADJECTIVE & ADVERB
in the direction from which a stream flows

**uptake** NOUN
➤ **quick on the uptake** quick to understand
➤ **slow on the uptake** slow to understand

**uptight** ADJECTIVE (*informal*)
tense and nervous or annoyed

**up-to-date** ADJECTIVE
❶ modern or fashionable ❷ giving the most recent information

**upward** ADJECTIVE & ADVERB
going towards what is higher • *an upward current of air*
➤ **upwards** ADVERB

**uranium** NOUN
a heavy radioactive grey metal used as a source of nuclear energy
(WORD ORIGIN) named after the planet *Uranus*

**urban** ADJECTIVE
to do with a town or city

**urbanize** (also **urbanise**) VERB urbanizes, urbanizing, urbanized
to change a place into a town-like area
➤ **urbanization** NOUN

**urchin** NOUN urchins
a rough and poorly dressed young boy • *a street urchin* (WORD ORIGIN) from Latin *ericius* = hedgehog

**Urdu** (say **oor**-doo) NOUN
a language related to Hindi, spoken in northern India and Pakistan

**urge** VERB urges, urging, urged
❶ to try to persuade a person to do something ❷ to drive people or animals onward • *He urged his horse up the hill.* ❸ to recommend or advise something

**urge** NOUN urges
a strong desire or wish • *She felt an urge to go for a swim.*

**urgent** ADJECTIVE
needing to be done or dealt with immediately • *Come quickly – it's urgent!*
➤ **urgently** ADVERB
➤ **urgency** NOUN

**urinal** (say yoor-**ry**-nal) NOUN urinals
a bowl or trough fixed to the wall in a men's public toilet, for men to urinate into

**urinate** (say **yoor**-in-ayt) VERB urinates, urinating, urinated
to pass urine out of your body
➤ **urination** NOUN

**urine** (say **yoor**-in) NOUN
waste liquid that collects in the bladder and is passed out of the body
➤ **urinary** ADJECTIVE

**urn** NOUN urns
❶ a large metal container with a tap, in which water is heated ❷ a container shaped like a vase with a base, especially one for holding the ashes of a cremated person

**US** ABBREVIATION
United States (of America)

**us** PRONOUN
the form of we used when it is the object of a verb or after a preposition

**USA** ABBREVIATION
United States of America

**usable** ADJECTIVE
able to be used

**usage** NOUN usages
❶ use; the way something is used ❷ the way words are used in a language • *English usage often differs from American usage.*

**use** (say yooz) VERB uses, using, used
to perform an action or job with something

• *Can I use your pen?*
➤ **used to ❶** was or were in the habit of doing • *We used to go by train.* ❷ familiar with or accustomed to • *I'm used to his strange behaviour.*
➤ **use something up** to use all of something so that none is left

**use** (say yooss) NOUN uses
❶ the action of using something; being used • *the use of computers in schools* ❷ the purpose for which something is used • *Can you find a use for this crate?* ❸ the quality of being useful • *These scissors are no use at all.*

**used** ADJECTIVE
not new; second-hand • *used cars*

**useful** ADJECTIVE
able to be used a lot or to do something that needs doing
➤ **usefully** ADVERB
➤ **usefulness** NOUN

**useless** ADJECTIVE
❶ not having any use; producing no effect • *Their efforts were useless.* ❷ (*Informal*) not very good at something • *I'm useless at drawing.*
➤ **uselessly** ADVERB
➤ **uselessness** NOUN

**user** NOUN users
a person who uses something

**user-friendly** ADJECTIVE
designed to be easy to use

**username** NOUN usernames
the name you use to log on to a computer system

**usher** NOUN ushers
a person who shows people to their seats in a cinema, theatre or church

**usher** VERB ushers, ushering, ushered
to lead someone in or out • *The guard ushered them out.*

**usherette** NOUN usherettes
a woman who shows people to their seats in a cinema or theatre

**USSR** ABBREVIATION
(*old use*) Union of Soviet Socialist Republics

**usual** ADJECTIVE
as happens or is done or used often or all the time • *She was late as usual.*

**usually** ADVERB
most of the time; normally • *What time do you usually go to bed?*

**usurp** (say yoo-**zerp**) VERB usurps, usurping, usurped
to take power or a position or right from someone wrongfully or by force
➤ **usurpation** NOUN
➤ **usurper** NOUN

**usury** (say **yoo**-zher-ee) NOUN
the lending of money at an excessively high rate of interest
➤ **usurer** NOUN

**utensil** (say yoo-**ten**-sil) NOUN utensils
a tool or device, especially one you use in the house • *cooking utensils*

**uterus** (say **yoo**-ter-us) NOUN uteri or uteruses
the womb

**utilitarian** ADJECTIVE
designed to be useful rather than decorative or luxurious; practical

**utility** NOUN utilities
❶ the quality of being useful ❷ an organization that supplies water, gas, electricity, etc. to the community

**utilize** (also **utilise**) VERB utilizes, utilizing, utilized
to make use of something • *She was able to utilize her talent for mimicry.*
➤ **utilization** NOUN

**utmost** ADJECTIVE
extreme or greatest • *Look after it with the utmost care.*
➤ **utmost** NOUN
➤ **do your utmost** to do the most that you are able to

**Utopia** (say yoo-**toh**-pee-a) NOUN Utopias
an imaginary place or state of things where everything is perfect
➤ **Utopian** ADJECTIVE
**WORD ORIGIN** Latin, = nowhere; used in 1516 as the title of a book by Sir Thomas More, in which he describes an ideal society

**utter** VERB utters, uttering, uttered
to say something or make a sound with your mouth • *He promised not to utter a word about it.*
➤ **utterance** NOUN

**utter** ADJECTIVE
complete or absolute • *It was utter misery.*

**utterly** ADVERB
completely or totally • *It's utterly impossible.*

**uttermost** ADJECTIVE & NOUN
extreme or greatest; utmost

**U-turn** NOUN U-turns
❶ a U-shaped turn made in a vehicle so that it then travels in the opposite direction ❷ a complete change of ideas or policy

# Vv

**vacancy** NOUN vacancies
❶ a position or job that has not been filled • *We have a vacancy for a shop assistant.*
❷ an available room in a hotel or guest house • *We have no vacancies.*

**vacant** ADJECTIVE
❶ empty; not filled or occupied • *a vacant seat* • *a vacant post* ❷ not showing any expression; blank • *a vacant stare*
➤ **vacantly** ADVERB

**vacate** VERB vacates, vacating, vacated
to leave or give up a place or position

**vacation** (say vak-**ay**-shon) NOUN vacations
a holiday, especially between the terms at a university

**vaccinate** (say **vak**-sin-ayt) VERB vaccinates, vaccinating, vaccinated
to protect someone from a disease by injecting them with a vaccine
➤ **vaccination** NOUN

**vaccine** (say **vak**-seen) NOUN vaccines
a substance used to give someone immunity against a disease WORD ORIGIN from Latin *vacca* = cow (because serum from cows was used to protect people from the disease smallpox)

**vacillate** (say **vass**-il-ayt) VERB vacillates, vacillating, vacillated
to keep changing your mind
➤ **vacillation** NOUN

**vacuum** NOUN vacuums
❶ a completely empty space; a space without any air in it ❷ (*informal*) a vacuum cleaner

**vacuum** VERB vacuums, vacuuming, vacuumed
to clean something using a vacuum cleaner

**vacuum cleaner** NOUN vacuum cleaners
an electrical device that sucks up dust and dirt from the floor

**vacuum flask** NOUN vacuum flasks
(*chiefly British*) a container with double walls that have a vacuum between them, used for keeping liquids hot or cold

**vagabond** NOUN vagabonds
a person with no settled home or regular work; a vagrant

**vagary** (say **vay**-ger-ee) NOUN vagaries
a change in something that is difficult to control or predict • *the vagaries of fashion*

**vagina** (say va-**jy**-na) NOUN vaginas
the passage in a female body that leads from the vulva to the womb

**vagrant** (say **vay**-grant) NOUN vagrants
a person with no settled home or regular work; a tramp
➤ **vagrancy** NOUN

**vague** ADJECTIVE
❶ not definite or clear • *I only have a vague memory of his face.* ❷ not thinking clearly or precisely
➤ **vagueness** NOUN

**vaguely** ADVERB
❶ in a way that is not definite or clear; slightly • *The name is vaguely familiar.*
❷ without thinking clearly • *He smiled vaguely and walked away.*

**vain** ADJECTIVE
❶ conceited, especially about how you look
❷ useless or unsuccessful • *They made vain attempts to save her.*
➤ **vainly** ADVERB
➤ **in vain** with no result; uselessly • *I tried in vain to call for help.*

SPELLING
Take care not to confuse with **vane** or **vein**.

**valance** NOUN valances
a short curtain round the frame of a bed or above a window

**vale** NOUN vales
a valley

**valency** NOUN valencies
(*in science*) the power of an atom to combine with other atoms, measured by the number of hydrogen atoms it is capable of combining with

**valentine** NOUN valentines
❶ a card sent on St Valentine's day (14 February) to the person you love ❷ the person you send this card to

**valet** (say **val**-ay or **val**-it) NOUN valets
a man's servant who takes care of his clothes and appearance

**valiant** ADJECTIVE
brave or courageous
➤ **valiantly** ADVERB

**valid** ADJECTIVE
❶ legally able to be used or accepted • *a valid passport* ❷ valid reasoning is sound and logical • *You make a valid point.*
➤ **validity** NOUN

**valley** NOUN valleys
❶ a long low area between hills ❷ an area through which a river flows • *the Nile valley*

**valour** NOUN
bravery, especially in battle
➤ **valorous** ADJECTIVE

**valuable** ADJECTIVE
❶ worth a lot of money ❷ very useful or important • *She gave me valuable advice.*

**valuables** PLURAL NOUN
valuable things

**value** NOUN values
❶ the amount of money that something could be sold for ❷ how useful or important something is • *They learnt the value of regular exercise.* ❸ (in *mathematics*) the number or quantity represented by a figure • *What is the value of x?*

**value** VERB values, valuing, valued
❶ to think that something is important or worth having • *I would value your opinion.* ❷ to work out how much something could be sold for
➤ **valuation** NOUN

**valueless** ADJECTIVE
having no value

**valve** NOUN valves
❶ a device for controlling the flow of gas or liquid through a pipe or tube ❷ a structure in the heart or in a blood vessel allowing blood to flow in one direction only ❸ a device that controls the flow of electricity in old televisions and radios

**vampire** NOUN vampires
in stories, a dead creature that is supposed to leave its grave at night and suck blood from living people

**van** NOUN vans
❶ a covered vehicle for carrying goods ❷ (*British*) a railway carriage for luggage or goods or for the use of the guard

➤ **in the van** at the front or in the leading position

**vandal** NOUN vandals
a person who deliberately breaks or damages things, especially public property
➤ **vandalism** NOUN
WORD ORIGIN named after the *Vandals*, a Germanic tribe who invaded the Roman Empire in the 5th century, destroying many books and works of art

**vandalize** (also **vandalise**) VERB vandalizes, vandalizing, vandalized
to damage property deliberately

**vane** NOUN vanes
❶ the blade of a propeller, sail of a windmill or other device that acts on or is moved by wind or water ❷ a weathervane
SPELLING
Take care not to confuse with vain or vein.

**vanguard** NOUN
❶ the leading part of an army or fleet ❷ the first people to adopt a fashion or idea

**vanilla** NOUN
a flavouring obtained from the pods of a tropical plant

**vanish** VERB vanishes, vanishing, vanished
to disappear completely • *The magician vanished in a puff of smoke.*

**vanity** NOUN
the quality of being too proud of your abilities or of how you look

**vanquish** VERB vanquishes, vanquishing, vanquished
to defeat someone completely

**vantage point** NOUN vantage points
a place from which you have a good view of something

**vaporize** (also **vaporise**) VERB vaporizes, vaporizing, vaporized
to turn into vapour or to change something into vapour

**vapour** NOUN vapours
a visible gas to which some substances can be converted by heat; steam or mist

**variable** ADJECTIVE
likely to vary; not staying the same
➤ **variability** NOUN

**variable** NOUN variables
something that varies or can vary; a variable quantity

**variance** NOUN
the amount by which things differ
➤ **at variance** differing or conflicting

**variant** NOUN variants
a thing that is a slightly different form of
something else • *The game is a variant of
baseball.*

**variant** ADJECTIVE
differing from something • *'Gaol' is a variant
spelling of 'jail'.*

**variation** NOUN variations
❶ varying; the amount by which something
varies • *There have been slight variations
in temperature.* ❷ a different form of
something

**varicose** ADJECTIVE
varicose veins are permanently swollen

**varied** ADJECTIVE
of different sorts; full of variety • *She has
varied interests.*

**variegated** (say **vair**-ig-ay-tid) ADJECTIVE
with patches of different colours • *a plant
with variegated leaves*

**variety** ADJECTIVE varieties
❶ a number of different kinds of the
same thing • *There was a variety of cakes
to choose from.* ❷ a particular kind of
something • *There are several varieties of
spaniel.* ❸ the quality of not always being the
same; variation • *You need more variety in
your diet.* ❹ a form of entertainment made
up of short performances of singing, dancing
and comedy

**various** ADJECTIVE
❶ of several different kinds • *People choose
to be vegetarians for various reasons.*
❷ several • *We met various people.*
➤ **variously** ADVERB

**varnish** NOUN varnishes
a liquid that dries to form a hard shiny usually
transparent coating

**varnish** VERB varnishes, varnishing, varnished
to coat something with varnish

**vary** VERB varies, varying, varied
❶ to keep changing • *The weather varies a lot
here.* ❷ to make changes to something ❸ to
be different from one another • *The cars are
the same, although the colours vary.*

**vascular** ADJECTIVE
consisting of tubes or similar vessels for
circulating blood, sap or water in animals or
plants • *the vascular system*

**vase** NOUN vases
an open usually tall container used for
holding cut flowers or as an ornament

**Vaseline** NOUN (*trademark*)
petroleum jelly for use as an ointment

**vassal** NOUN vassals
in feudal times, a man who was given land to
live on in return for promising loyally to fight
for the landowner

**vast** ADJECTIVE
very great, especially in area • *a vast expanse
of water*
➤ **vastly** ADVERB
➤ **vastness** NOUN

**VAT** ABBREVIATION
value added tax; a tax on goods and services

**vat** NOUN vats
a very large container for holding liquid

**vaudeville** (say **vawd**-vil) NOUN
a kind of variety entertainment popular in the
early 20th century

**vault** VERB vaults, vaulting, vaulted
to jump over something, especially while
supporting yourself on your hands or with
the help of a pole • *He vaulted over the fence
and ran off.*

**vault** NOUN vaults
❶ a vaulting jump ❷ an arched roof ❸ an
underground room used to store things ❹ a
room for storing money or valuables ❺ a
burial chamber

**vaulted** ADJECTIVE
having an arched roof

**vaulting horse** NOUN vaulting horses
a padded wooden block for vaulting over in
gymnastics

**vaunt** VERB vaunts, vaunting, vaunted
to boast something

**VDU** ABBREVIATION
visual display unit; a monitor for a computer

**veal** NOUN
meat from a calf

**vector** NOUN vectors
(*in mathematics*) a quantity that has size and
direction, such as velocity (which is speed in a
certain direction)

**Veda** (say **vay**-da or **vee**-da) NOUN Vedas
the most ancient and sacred literature of the
Hindus
➤ **Vedic** ADJECTIVE

**veer** *VERB* veers, veering, veered
to swerve or change direction suddenly • *The car veered off the road and hit a tree.*

**vegan** *NOUN* vegans
a person who does not eat or use any animal products

**vegetable** *NOUN* vegetables
a plant that can be used as food

**vegetarian** *NOUN* vegetarians
a person who does not eat meat
➤ **vegetarianism** *NOUN*

**vegetate** *VERB* vegetates, vegetating, vegetated
to lead a dull life doing nothing interesting
(WORD ORIGIN) originally = grow like a vegetable

**vegetation** *NOUN*
plants that are growing • *The hills are covered in thick vegetation.*

**vehement** (say vee-im-ent) *ADJECTIVE*
showing strong feeling • *a vehement refusal*
➤ **vehemently** *ADVERB*
➤ **vehemence** *NOUN*

**vehicle** *NOUN* vehicles
a means of transporting people or goods, especially on land

**veil** *NOUN* veils
a piece of thin material worn to cover a woman's face or head
➤ **draw a veil over something** to avoid discussing something

**veil** *VERB* veils, veiling, veiled
❶ to cover something with a veil ❷ to partially conceal something • *A mist began to veil the hills.*

**veiled** *ADJECTIVE*
partly hidden or disguised • *a thinly veiled threat*

**vein** *NOUN* veins
❶ any of the tubes that carry blood from all parts of the body to the heart. Compare with artery. ❷ a line or streak on a leaf, rock or insect's wing ❸ a long deposit of mineral or ore in the middle of a rock ❹ a mood or manner • *She spoke in a serious vein.*

SPELLING
Take care not to confuse with vain or vane.

**veld** (say velt) *NOUN* veld
an area of open grassland in South Africa
(WORD ORIGIN) from an Afrikaans word, from Dutch *veld* = field

**vellum** *NOUN*
smooth parchment or writing paper

**velocity** *NOUN* velocities
speed in a given direction

**velour** (say vil-oor) *NOUN*
a thick velvety material

**velvet** *NOUN*
a woven material with very short soft furry fibres on one side

**velvety** *ADJECTIVE*
smooth and soft, like velvet • *her velvety voice*

**vendetta** *NOUN* vendettas
a long-lasting bitter quarrel; a feud

**vending machine** *NOUN* vending machines
a slot machine from which you can obtain drinks, chocolate, etc.

**vendor** *NOUN* vendors
someone who is selling something, especially a house

**veneer** *NOUN* veneers
❶ a thin layer of good wood covering the surface of a cheaper wood in furniture ❷ an outward show of some good quality • *a veneer of politeness*

**venerable** *ADJECTIVE*
worthy of respect or honour because of being so old

**venerate** *VERB* venerates, venerating, venerated
to honour someone with great respect or reverence
➤ **veneration** *NOUN*

**venetian blind** *NOUN* venetian blinds
a window blind consisting of horizontal strips that can be adjusted to let light in or shut it out

**vengeance** *NOUN*
harming or punishing someone in return for something bad they have done to you; revenge
➤ **with a vengeance** with great force or intensity • *He set to work with a vengeance.*

**vengeful** *ADJECTIVE*
wanting to punish someone who has harmed you
➤ **vengefully** *ADVERB*
➤ **vengefulness** *NOUN*

**venial** (say veen-ee-al) *ADJECTIVE*
venial sins or faults are pardonable and not serious

**venison** NOUN
the meat from a deer

**Venn diagram** NOUN Venn diagrams
(*in mathematics*) a diagram in which circles
are used to show the relationships between
different sets of things **WORD ORIGIN** named
after an English mathematician, John *Venn*

**venom** NOUN
❶ the poisonous fluid produced by snakes,
scorpions, etc. ❷ a feeling of bitter hatred for
someone • *a look of pure venom*
➤ **venomous** ADJECTIVE

**vent** NOUN vents
an opening in something, especially to let out
smoke or gas
➤ **give vent to something** to express your
feelings strongly

**vent** VERB vents, venting, vented
to express your feelings, especially anger,
strongly • *The crowd vented their anger on
the referee.*

**ventilate** VERB ventilates, ventilating,
ventilated
to let air move freely in and out of a room or
building
➤ **ventilation** NOUN
➤ **ventilator** NOUN

**ventriloquist** NOUN ventriloquists
an entertainer who makes their voice sound
as if it comes from another source
➤ **ventriloquism** NOUN
**WORD ORIGIN** from Latin *venter* = abdomen
+ *loqui* = speak (from the ancient belief that
people who were possessed by an evil spirit
spoke from their stomachs)

**venture** NOUN ventures
something you decide to do that is risky or
adventurous

**venture** VERB ventures, venturing, ventured
to dare or be bold enough to do or say
something or to go somewhere • *We ventured
out into the snow.*

**venturesome** ADJECTIVE
ready to take risks; daring

**venue** (say **ven**-yoo) NOUN venues
the place where an event such as a meeting,
sports match or concert is held

**veracity** (say ver-**as**-it-ee) NOUN
truth or being truthful

**veranda** NOUN verandas
a terrace with a roof along the side of a house

**verb** NOUN verbs
a word that shows what a person or thing is
doing or what is happening, e.g. *bring, came,
sing, were*

**GRAMMAR**

A **verb** can describe an action or process
(e.g. *dive, chew, heal, thaw*), a feeling (e.g.
*think, know, believe*) or a state (e.g. *be,
remain*). A sentence usually contains at
least one verb.

Verbs change their form according to
which person (*I, you, he, she, it, we* or
*they*) and tense (past, present or future)
they are in. Regular verbs change their
endings in predictable ways, e.g. by
adding *-s* or *-ed*: *I shout, she shouts, we
shouted*, etc. Irregular verbs have more
varied forms, especially in the past tense:
*we swim, we swam, we have swum; I am,
we were, they have been.*

An **auxiliary verb** is used to form the
tenses of another verb, for example *have*
in *I have just received this email*, and
*will* in *They will never find us here.* The
auxiliary verbs *can, will, shall, may*, and
*must* are also called **modal verbs**; they
are used to express a wish, need, ability
or permission to do something. A **phrasal
verb** includes a preposition or adverb, for
example *drop in, fall out* and *wrap up.*

See also the panel on **tenses**.

**verbal** ADJECTIVE
❶ spoken, not written • *We had a verbal
agreement.* ❷ to do with words or in the
form of words
➤ **verbally** ADVERB

**verbatim** (say ver-**bay**-tim) ADVERB & ADJECTIVE
in exactly the same words • *He copied down
the whole paragraph verbatim.*

**verdant** ADJECTIVE
verdant grass or fields are fresh and green

**verdict** NOUN verdicts
a judgement or decision made after
considering something, especially one made
by a jury

**verdigris** (say **verd**-i-grees) NOUN
green rust on copper or brass
**WORD ORIGIN** from French *vert-de-gris*,
literally = green of Greece

**verdure** NOUN
green vegetation; its greenness

**verge** *NOUN* verges
**❶** a strip of grass along the edge of a road or path **❷** to be on the verge of something is to be close to doing it • *I was on the verge of tears.*

**verge** *VERB* verges, verging, verged
➤ **verge on something** to be nearly something • *This puzzle verges on the impossible.*

**verger** *NOUN* vergers
a person who is caretaker and attendant in a church

**verify** *VERB* verifies, verifying, verified
to check or show that something is true or correct
➤ **verification** *NOUN*

**veritable** *ADJECTIVE*
real; rightly named • *She was a veritable mine of useless information.*

**vermicelli** (say verm-i-**sel**-ee) *NOUN*
pasta made in long thin threads
**WORD ORIGIN** Italian, = little worms

**vermilion** *NOUN & ADJECTIVE*
bright red

**vermin** *PLURAL NOUN*
animals or insects that damage crops or food or carry disease, such as rats and fleas
➤ **verminous** *ADJECTIVE*

**vernacular** (say ver-**nak**-yoo-ler) *NOUN*
vernaculars
the language of a country or district, as distinct from an official or formal language

**vernal** *ADJECTIVE*
to do with the season of spring

**verruca** (say ver-**oo**-ka) *NOUN* verrucas
a kind of wart on the sole of the foot

**versatile** *ADJECTIVE*
able to do or be used for many different things • *a versatile tool*
➤ **versatility** *NOUN*

**verse** *NOUN* verses
**❶** writing arranged in short lines, usually with a particular rhythm and often with rhymes; poetry **❷** a group of lines forming a unit in a poem or song **❸** each of the short numbered sections of a chapter in the Bible

**versed** *ADJECTIVE*
➤ **versed in something** experienced or skilled in something

**version** *NOUN* versions
**❶** a particular person's account of something

that happened • *His version of the accident is different from mine.* **❷** a different form of something • *I don't like their version of the song.* **❸** a translation • *modern versions of the Bible*

**versus** *PREPOSITION*
against; competing with • *The final was France versus Brazil.*

**vertebra** *NOUN* vertebrae
each of the bones that form your backbone

**vertebrate** *NOUN* vertebrates
an animal that has a backbone. (The opposite is **invertebrate**.)

**vertex** *NOUN* vertices, (say **ver**-tis-eez)
(*in mathematics*) the highest point of a cone or triangle.

**vertical** *ADJECTIVE*
going directly upwards, at right angles to something level or horizontal • *The cliff was almost vertical.*
➤ **vertically** *ADVERB*

**vertigo** *NOUN*
a feeling of dizziness and loss of balance, especially when you are very high up

**verve** (say verv) *NOUN*
enthusiasm and liveliness

**very** *ADVERB*
**❶** to a great amount or intensity; extremely • *It was very cold.* **❷** used to emphasize something • *on the very next day* • *the very last drop*

**very** *ADJECTIVE*
**❶** exact or actual • *It's the very thing we need.* **❷** extreme • *Our house is at the very end of the street.*

**vespers** *NOUN*
a church service held in the evening

**vessel** *NOUN* vessels
**❶** a ship or boat **❷** a container, especially for liquid **❸** a tube carrying blood or other liquid in the body of an animal or plant

**vest** *NOUN* vests
a piece of underwear you wear on the top half of your body

**vested interest** *NOUN* vested interests
a strong reason for wanting something to happen, usually because you will benefit from it

**vestibule** *NOUN* vestibules
**❶** an entrance hall or lobby **❷** a church porch

a
b
c
d
e
f
g
h
i
j
k
l
m
n
o
p
q
r
s
t
u
v
w
x
y
z

**vestige** NOUN vestiges
a trace; a very small amount of something that is left after the rest has gone • *Only the very last vestiges of the snow remained.*  WORD ORIGIN from Latin *vestigium* = footprint

**vestment** NOUN vestments
a ceremonial garment, especially one worn by the clergy or choir at a church service

**vestry** NOUN vestries
a room in a church where vestments are kept and where the clergy and choir put these on

**vet** NOUN vets
(*chiefly British*) a person trained to give medical and surgical treatment to animals

**vet** VERB vets, vetting, vetted (*British*) to make a careful check of a person or thing, especially of someone's background before employing them  WORD ORIGIN short for *veterinary surgeon*

**veteran** NOUN veterans
a person who has long experience, especially in the armed forces

**veterinary** (say vet-rin-ree) ADJECTIVE
to do with the medical and surgical treatment of animals • *a veterinary surgeon*

**veto** (say vee-toh) NOUN vetoes
❶ a refusal to let something happen ❷ the right to stop something from happening

**veto** VERB vetoes, vetoing, vetoed
to refuse to let something happen  WORD ORIGIN Latin, = I forbid

**vex** VERB vexes, vexing, vexed
to annoy someone or cause them worry • *Her behaviour vexed him a good deal.*
➤ **vexation** NOUN

**vexed question** NOUN vexed questions
a problem that is difficult or much discussed

**VHF** ABBREVIATION
very high frequency

**via** (say vy-a) PREPOSITION
❶ going through; by way of • *The train goes from London to Edinburgh via York.* ❷ by means of; using • *You can get in touch with us via our website.*

**viable** ADJECTIVE
able to work or exist successfully • *a viable plan*
➤ **viability** NOUN

**viaduct** NOUN viaducts
a long bridge, usually with many arches, carrying a road or railway over a valley or low ground

**vial** NOUN vials
a small glass bottle

**viands** (say vy-andz) PLURAL NOUN (*old use*)
food

**vibrant** ADJECTIVE
❶ full of energy; lively • *a vibrant city* ❷ vibrant colours are bright and strong

**vibrate** VERB vibrates, vibrating, vibrated
to move very quickly from side to side and with small movements • *Every time a train went past the walls vibrated.*

**vibration** NOUN vibrations
a continuous shaking movement that you can feel • *the vibrations of the ship's engines*

**vicar** NOUN vicars
a member of the Church of England clergy who is in charge of a parish

**vicarage** NOUN vicarages
the house of a vicar

**vicarious** (say vik-**air**-ee-us) ADJECTIVE
not experienced yourself but felt by imagining you share someone else's experience • *I got a vicarious pleasure from reading about his adventures.*

**vice** NOUN vices
❶ an evil or bad habit; a bad fault ❷ evil or wickedness ❸ a device for gripping something and holding it firmly while you work on it

**vice-** PREFIX
❶ authorized to act as a deputy or substitute (as in *vice-captain, vice-president*) ❷ next in rank to someone (as in *vice-admiral*)

**vice versa** ADVERB
the other way round • *Summer in the UK is winter in Australia and vice versa.*  WORD ORIGIN Latin, = the position being reversed

**vicinity** NOUN
the area near or round a place • *Is there a park in the vicinity?*

**vicious** ADJECTIVE
❶ cruel and aggressive ❷ severe or violent • *a vicious blizzard*
➤ **viciously** ADVERB
➤ **viciousness** NOUN

**vicious circle** NOUN vicious circles
a situation in which a problem produces

an effect which in turn makes the problem worse

**victim** NOUN victims
someone who is injured, killed, robbed, etc. • *a murder victim*

**victimize** (also **victimise**) VERB victimizes, victimizing, victimized
to single someone out for harsh or unfair treatment

**victor** NOUN victors
the winner of a battle or contest

**Victorian** ADJECTIVE
belong to the time of Queen Victoria (1837-1901)
➤ **Victorian** NOUN

**victorious** ADJECTIVE
that wins a victory • *the victorious team*

**victory** NOUN victories
success won against an opponent in a battle, contest or game

**victuals** (say **vit**-alz) PLURAL NOUN (*old use*)
food and drink

**video** NOUN videos
❶ a system of recording moving pictures and sound, especially as a digital file • *The accident was captured on video.* ❷ a short film or recording that you can watch on a computer or mobile phone, especially over the Internet ❸ a copy of a film or television programme that has been recorded

**video** VERB videos, videoing, videoed (*chiefly British*) to record something on video
**WORD ORIGIN** Latin, = I see

**video game** NOUN video games
a game in which you press electronic controls to move images on a screen

**vie** VERB vies, vying, vied
to compete with someone; to carry on a rivalry • *The boys were vying with each other to see who could tell the funniest joke.*

**view** NOUN views
❶ what you can see from one place, e.g. beautiful scenery • *There's a fine view from the top of the hill.* ❷ sight or range of vision • *The ship sailed into view.* ❸ an opinion • *She has strong views about art.*
➤ **in view of** because of
➤ **on view** displayed for people to see
➤ **with a view to** with the hope or intention of

**view** VERB views, viewing, viewed
❶ to watch or look at something • *A map is*

*a plan of an area, viewed from above.* ❷ to consider or regard a person or thing in a certain way • *He viewed us with suspicion.*

**viewer** NOUN viewers
someone who views something, especially a television programme

**viewpoint** NOUN viewpoints
❶ an opinion or point of view ❷ a place giving a good view

**vigil** (say **vij**-il) NOUN vigils
staying awake to keep watch or to pray • *a long vigil*

**vigilant** (say **vij**-il-ant) ADJECTIVE
keeping careful watch for danger or difficulties • *A pilot must remain vigilant at all times.*
➤ **vigilantly** ADVERB
➤ **vigilance** NOUN

**vigilante** (say vij-il-**an**-tee) NOUN vigilantes
a member of a group who organize themselves, without authority, to try to prevent crime and disorder in their community

**vigorous** ADJECTIVE
full of strength and energy • *vigorous exercise*
➤ **vigorously** ADVERB

**vigour** NOUN
strength and energy

**Viking** NOUN Vikings
a Scandinavian trader and pirate in the 8th-11th centuries

**vile** ADJECTIVE
❶ extremely disgusting • *That tastes vile.*
❷ very bad or wicked
➤ **vilely** ADVERB
➤ **vileness** NOUN

**villa** NOUN villas
a house, especially a holiday home abroad

**village** NOUN villages
a group of houses and other buildings in a country district, smaller than a town and usually having a church

**villager** NOUN villagers
a person who lives in a village

**villain** NOUN villains
a wicked person or a criminal
➤ **villainous** ADJECTIVE
➤ **villainy** NOUN

**villein** (say **vil**-an or vil-**ayn**) NOUN villeins
a tenant in feudal times

a
b
c
d
e
f
g
h
i
j
k
l
m
n
o
p
q
r
s
t
u
v
w
x
y
z

**vim** NOUN (*informal*)
vigour or energy

**vindicate** VERB vindicates, vindicating, vindicated
❶ to clear a person of blame or suspicion
❷ to prove something to be true or worthwhile
➤ **vindication** NOUN

**vindictive** ADJECTIVE
showing a desire for revenge; spiteful
➤ **vindictively** ADVERB
➤ **vindictiveness** NOUN

**vine** NOUN vines
a climbing or trailing plant whose fruit is the grape

**vinegar** NOUN
a sour liquid used to flavour food or in pickling

**vineyard** (say **vin**-yard) NOUN vineyards
an area of land where vines are grown to produce grapes for making wine

**vintage** NOUN vintages
❶ all the grapes that are harvested in one season or the wine made from them ❷ the period from which something comes • *The furniture is of 1920s vintage.*

**vintage car** NOUN vintage cars
(*British*) a car made between 1917 and 1930

**vinyl** NOUN
a kind of plastic

**viola** (say vee-**oh**-la) NOUN violas
a musical instrument like a violin but slightly larger and with a lower pitch

**violate** VERB violates, violating, violated
❶ to break an agreement, rule or law ❷ to treat a person or place with disrespect and violence
➤ **violation** NOUN

**violence** NOUN
❶ physical force that does harm or damage
❷ strength or intensity • *the violence of the storm*

**violent** ADJECTIVE
❶ using or involving violence ❷ strong or intense • *a violent dislike*
➤ **violently** ADVERB

**violet** NOUN violets
❶ a small plant that often has purple flowers ❷ a bluish-purple colour

**violin** NOUN violins
a musical instrument with four strings, played

with a bow
➤ **violinist** NOUN

**VIP** ABBREVIATION
very important person

**viper** NOUN vipers
a small poisonous snake

**virgin** NOUN virgins
a person who has never had sexual intercourse
➤ **virginal** ADJECTIVE
➤ **virginity** NOUN

**virgin** ADJECTIVE
not yet touched or used • *virgin snow*

**virile** (say **vir**-yl) ADJECTIVE
having masculine strength or vigour, especially sexually
➤ **virility** NOUN

**virtual** ADJECTIVE
❶ being something in effect though not strictly in fact • *His silence was a virtual admission of guilt.* ❷ existing as a computer image and not physically • *Click here to go on a virtual tour of the gallery.*

**virtually** ADVERB
nearly or almost • *She virtually admitted it.*

**virtual reality** NOUN
an image or environment produced by a computer that is so realistic that it seems to be part of the real world

**virtue** NOUN virtues
❶ moral goodness; a particular form of this • *Honesty is a virtue.* ❷ a good quality or advantage • *Jamie's plan has the virtue of simplicity.*
➤ **by virtue of** because of

**virtuoso** (say ver-tew-**oh**-soh) NOUN virtuosos or virtuosi
a person with outstanding skill, especially in singing or playing music
➤ **virtuosity** NOUN

**virtuous** ADJECTIVE
behaving in a morally good way
➤ **virtuously** ADVERB

**virus** NOUN viruses
❶ a very tiny living thing, smaller than a bacterium, that can cause disease ❷ a disease caused by a virus ❸ a hidden set of instructions in a computer program that is designed to destroy data

**visa** (say **vee**-za) NOUN visas
an official mark put on someone's passport by

officials of a foreign country to show that the holder has permission to enter that country

**visage** (say **viz**-ij) NOUN visages
a person's face

**viscount** (say **vy**-kownt) NOUN viscounts
a nobleman ranking below an earl and above a baron
➤ viscountess NOUN

**viscous** (say **visk**-us) ADJECTIVE
thick and gluey, not pouring easily
➤ viscosity NOUN

**visibility** NOUN
the distance you can see clearly • *Visibility is down to 20 metres.*

**visible** ADJECTIVE
able to be seen or noticed • *The ship was visible on the horizon.*

**visibly** ADVERB
in a way that is easy to notice • *He was visibly shocked.*

**vision** NOUN visions
❶ the ability to see; sight ❷ something that you see in your imagination or in a dream ❸ the ability to make imaginative plans for the future ❹ a person or thing that is beautiful to see

**visionary** ADJECTIVE
extremely imaginative or fanciful

**visionary** NOUN visionaries
a person with extremely imaginative ideas and plans

**visit** VERB visits, visiting, visited
❶ to go to see a person or place ❷ to stay somewhere for a while

**visit** NOUN visits
❶ going to see a person or place ❷ a short stay somewhere

**visitation** NOUN visitations
an official visit, especially to inspect something

**visitor** NOUN visitors
a person who is visiting or staying at a place

**visor** (say **vy**-zer) NOUN visors
❶ the part of a helmet that covers the face ❷ a shield to protect the eyes from bright light or sunshine

**vista** NOUN vistas
a long view

**visual** ADJECTIVE
to do with or used in seeing; to do with sight

• *She has a good visual memory.*
➤ visually ADVERB

**visual aid** NOUN visual aids
a picture, video or film used as an aid in teaching

**visual display unit** NOUN visual display units
(*British*) a device that looks like a television screen and displays data being received from a computer or fed into it

**visualize** (also **visualise**) VERB visualizes, visualizing, visualized
to form a mental picture of something • *I'm trying to visualize what your room looked like before you decorated it.*
➤ visualization NOUN

**vital** ADJECTIVE
❶ essential; very important • *It is vital that you practise every day.* ❷ connected with life; necessary for life to continue • *vital functions such as breathing*

**vitality** NOUN
liveliness or energy

**vitally** ADVERB
extremely • *Sleep is vitally important to all of us.*

**vitamin** (say **vit**-a-min or **vy**-ta-min) NOUN
vitamins
any of a number of substances that are present in various foods and are essential to keep people and animals healthy

**vitreous** (say **vit**-ree-us) ADJECTIVE
like glass in being hard, transparent or brittle
• *vitreous enamel*

**vitriol** (say **vit**-ree-ol) NOUN
savage criticism
➤ vitriolic ADJECTIVE

**vivacious** (say viv-**ay**-shus) ADJECTIVE
happy and lively
➤ vivaciously ADVERB
➤ vivacity NOUN

**vivid** ADJECTIVE
❶ bright and strong or clear • *vivid colours* • *a vivid description* ❷ active and lively • *a vivid imagination*
➤ vividly ADVERB
➤ vividness NOUN

**vivisection** NOUN
doing experiments on live animals as part of scientific research

**vixen** NOUN vixens
a female fox

a b c d e f g h i j k l m n o p q r s t u v w x y z

**vizier** (say viz-**eer**) NOUN viziers (*historical*)
an important Muslim official

**vocabulary** NOUN vocabularies
❶ all the words used in a particular subject or language ❷ the words known to an individual person • *She has a good vocabulary.*

**vocal** ADJECTIVE
to do with or using the voice
➤ **vocally** ADVERB

**vocal cords** PLURAL NOUN
two strap-like membranes in the throat that can be made to vibrate and produce sounds

**vocalist** NOUN vocalists
a singer, especially in a pop group

**vocation** NOUN vocations
❶ a person's job or occupation ❷ a strong desire to do a particular kind of work or a feeling of being called by God to do something

**vocational** ADJECTIVE
teaching you the skills you need for a particular job or profession • *vocational training*

**vociferous** (say vo-**sif**-er-us) ADJECTIVE
noisily and forcefully expressing your views

**vodka** NOUN vodkas
a strong alcoholic drink very popular in Russia

**vogue** NOUN vogues
the current fashion • *Very short hair for women seems to be the vogue.*
➤ **in vogue** in fashion • *Stripy dresses are definitely in vogue.*

**voice** NOUN voices
❶ the sounds that you make when you speak or sing ❷ the ability to speak or sing • *She has lost her voice.* ❸ someone expressing a particular opinion about something • *Emma's the only dissenting voice.* ❹ the right to express an opinion or desire • *I have no voice in this matter.*

**voice** VERB voices, voicing, voiced
to say something clearly and strongly • *We voiced our objections to the plan.*

**voicemail** NOUN
a system for recording and storing phone messages for people to listen to later

**void** ADJECTIVE
❶ completely lacking something • *The message seemed void of all meaning.* ❷ not legally valid • *The agreement was declared void.*

**void** NOUN voids
an empty space or hole

**volatile** (say **vol**-a-tyl) ADJECTIVE
❶ evaporating quickly • *a volatile liquid* ❷ changing quickly from one mood to another
➤ **volatility** NOUN

**volcanic** ADJECTIVE
caused or produced by a volcano • *a volcanic eruption*

**volcano** NOUN volcanoes
a mountain with an opening at the top from which lava, ashes and hot gases from below the earth's crust are or have been thrown out
**WORD ORIGIN** Italian, from *Vulcan*, the ancient Roman god of fire

**vole** NOUN voles
a small animal rather like a rat

**volition** NOUN
to do something of your own volition is to choose to do it • *She left of her own volition.*

**volley** NOUN volleys
❶ a number of bullets or shells fired at the same time ❷ in tennis and football, hitting or kicking the ball before it touches the ground

**volley** VERB volleys, volleying, volleyed
to hit or kick the ball before it touches the ground • *He volleyed the ball into the back of the net.*

**volleyball** NOUN
a game in which two teams hit a large ball to and fro over a net with their hands

**volt** NOUN volts
a unit for measuring electric force
**WORD ORIGIN** named after an Italian scientist, Alessandro *Volta*, who discovered how to produce electricity by a chemical reaction

**voltage** NOUN voltages
electric force measured in volts

**voluble** ADJECTIVE
talking very much
➤ **volubly** ADVERB
➤ **volubility** NOUN

**volume** NOUN volumes
❶ the amount of space filled by something ❷ an amount or quantity • *The volume of work has increased.* ❸ the strength or power of sound • *Can you turn up the volume?* ❹ a book, especially one of a set
**WORD ORIGIN** from Latin *volumen* = a roll (because ancient books were made in a rolled form)

**voluminous** (say vol-**yoo**-min-us) ADJECTIVE
① bulky; large and full • *a voluminous skirt*
② able to hold a lot • *a voluminous bag*

**voluntary** ADJECTIVE
① done or doing something because you want to do it, not because you have to do it
② unpaid • *voluntary work*
➤ **voluntarily** ADVERB

**volunteer** VERB volunteers, volunteering, volunteered
① to offer to do something of your own accord, without being asked or forced to ② to provide something willingly or freely without being asked for it • *Several people generously volunteered their time.*

**volunteer** NOUN volunteers
a person who volunteers to do something, e.g. to serve in the armed forces

**voluptuous** ADJECTIVE
① giving a luxurious feeling • *voluptuous furnishings* ② a woman is voluptuous when she has an attractively curved figure

**vomit** VERB vomits, vomiting, vomited
to bring up food from the stomach and out through the mouth; to be sick

**vomit** NOUN
food from the stomach brought back out through the mouth

**voodoo** NOUN
a form of witchcraft and magical rites, especially in the West Indies

**voracious** (say vor-**ay**-shus) ADJECTIVE
greedy; devouring things eagerly • *a voracious appetite*
➤ **voraciously** ADVERB
➤ **voracity** NOUN

**vortex** NOUN vortices
a whirlpool or whirlwind

**vote** VERB votes, voting, voted
to show which person or thing you prefer by putting up your hand or making a mark on a piece of paper

**vote** NOUN votes
① the action of voting ② the right to vote

**voter** NOUN voters
someone who votes, especially in an election

**votive** ADJECTIVE
given to fulfil a vow • *votive offerings at the shrine*

**vouch** VERB vouches, vouching, vouched
➤ **vouch for something** to guarantee that something is true or certain • *I will vouch for his honesty.*

**voucher** NOUN vouchers
a piece of paper showing that you are allowed to pay less for something or that you can get something in exchange

**vouchsafe** VERB vouchsafes, vouchsafing, vouchsafed
(*formal*) to grant or offer something • *She did not vouchsafe a reply.*

**vow** NOUN vows
a solemn promise

**vow** VERB vows, vowing, vowed
to make a solemn promise to do something • *She vowed never to speak to him again.*

**vowel** NOUN vowels
any of the letters a, e, i, o, u and sometimes y, which represent sounds in which breath comes out freely. Compare with **consonant**.

**voyage** NOUN voyages
a long journey on a ship or in a spacecraft

**voyage** VERB voyages, voyaging, voyaged
to make a voyage
➤ **voyager** NOUN

**vulgar** ADJECTIVE
rude; without good manners
➤ **vulgarity** NOUN
**WORD ORIGIN** from Latin *vulgus* = the common or ordinary people

**vulgar fraction** NOUN vulgar fractions
(*British*) a fraction shown by numbers above and below a line (e.g. ½, ¾), not a decimal fraction

**vulnerable** ADJECTIVE
able to be hurt or harmed or attacked • *The town was vulnerable to attack from the north.*
➤ **vulnerability** NOUN

**vulture** NOUN vultures
a large bird that feeds on dead animals

**vulva** NOUN vulvas
the outer parts of the female genitals

**vying**
present participle of **vie**

a b c d e f g h i j k l m n o p q r s t u v w x y z

# Ww

**wacky** *ADJECTIVE* wackier, wackiest
(*informal*)
crazy or silly

**wad** (say wod) *NOUN* wads
a pad or bundle of soft material or banknotes,
papers, etc.

**wad** *VERB* wads, wadding, wadded
to pad something with soft material

**waddle** *VERB* waddles, waddling, waddled
to walk with short steps, swaying from side to
side, as a duck does

**waddle** *NOUN*
a waddling walk

**wade** *VERB* wades, wading, waded
❶ to walk through water or mud ❷ to read
through something with effort because it is
dull, difficult or long

**wader** *NOUN* waders
❶ (also **wading bird**) any bird with long legs
that feeds in shallow water ❷ waders are long
rubber boots that you wear for standing in
water

**wafer** *NOUN* wafers
a kind of thin biscuit

**wafer-thin** *ADJECTIVE*
very thin

**waffle** (say wof-el) *NOUN* waffles
❶ a small cake made of batter and eaten hot
❷ talking or writing for a long time without
saying anything important or interesting

**waffle** *VERB* waffles, waffling, waffled
to talk or write for a long time without saying
anything important or interesting

**waft** (say woft) *VERB* wafts, wafting, wafted
to float gently through the air • *The smell of
her perfume wafted across the room.*

**wag** *VERB* wags, wagging, wagged
❶ a dog wags its tail when it moves it
quickly from side to side because it is happy
or excited ❷ you wag your finger when you
move it up and down or from side to side

**wag** *NOUN* wags
❶ a wagging movement ❷ a person who
makes jokes

**wage** *NOUN* (or **wages**) *PLURAL NOUN*
a regular payment to someone in return for
the work they do

**wage** *VERB* wages, waging, waged
to carry on a war or campaign

**wager** (say **way**-jer) *NOUN* wagers
a bet

**wager** *VERB* wagers, wagering, wagered
to make a bet with someone

**waggle** *VERB* waggles, waggling, waggled
to move something quickly to and fro • *Can
you waggle your ears?*

**wagon** *NOUN* wagons
❶ a cart with four wheels, pulled by a horse
or an ox ❷ an open railway truck, e.g. for coal

**wagoner** *NOUN* wagoners
the driver of a horse-drawn wagon

**wagtail** *NOUN* wagtails
a small bird with a long tail that it moves up
and down

**waif** *NOUN* waifs
a homeless and helpless person, especially a
child

**wail** *VERB* wails, wailing, wailed
to make a long sad cry

**wail** *NOUN* wails
a sound of wailing

**wainscot, wainscoting** *NOUN*
wooden panelling on the wall of a room

**waist** *NOUN* waists
the narrow part in the middle of your body

> **SPELLING**
> Take care not to confuse with **waste**,
> which means things that are not wanted.

**waistcoat** *NOUN* waistcoats
(*British*) a short close-fitting jacket without
sleeves, worn over a shirt and under a jacket

**waistline** *NOUN* waistlines
the amount you measure around your waist,
which indicates how fat or thin you are

**wait** *VERB* waits, waiting, waited
❶ to stay somewhere or delay doing
something until something happens • *Wait
here – I'll be back in a minute.* ❷ to be left to
be dealt with later • *This question will have to
wait until our next meeting.* ❸ to be a waiter
➤ **wait on someone** ❶ to hand food and
drink to people at a meal ❷ to fetch and
carry for someone as an attendant

**wait** NOUN
an act or time of waiting • *We had a long wait for the train.*

**waiter** NOUN waiters
a man who serves people with food and drink in a restaurant

**waiting list** NOUN waiting lists
a list of people waiting for something to become available

**waiting room** NOUN waiting rooms
a room provided for people who are waiting for something

**waitress** NOUN waitresses
a woman who serves people with food and drink in a restaurant

**waive** VERB waives, waiving, waived
to not insist on having something • *She waived her right to a first-class seat.*

SPELLING
Take care not to confuse with wave.

**wake** VERB wakes, waking, woke, woken
❶ to stop sleeping • *Wake up!* • *I woke when I heard the bell.* ❷ to make someone stop sleeping • *You have woken the baby.*

**wake** NOUN wakes
❶ the track left on the water by a moving ship or boat ❷ currents of air left behind a moving aircraft ❸ a party held after a funeral ➤ **in the wake of** something following or coming after something

**wakeful** ADJECTIVE
unable to sleep

**waken** VERB wakens, wakening, wakened
to wake up or to wake someone up • *He wakened from a deep sleep.*

**walk** VERB walks, walking, walked
to move along on your feet at an ordinary speed

**walk** NOUN walks
❶ a journey on foot • *We went for a walk by the river.* ❷ the way that someone walks • *He has a funny walk.* ❸ a path or route for walking

**walkabout** NOUN walkabouts
❶ an informal stroll among a crowd by an important visitor ❷ (*Australian*) a journey through a remote area taken by an Australian Aboriginal wishing to experience a traditional way of life

**walker** NOUN walkers
someone who goes for a walk, especially a long one

**walkie-talkie** NOUN walkie-talkies (*informal*)
a small portable radio transmitter and receiver

**walking stick** NOUN walking sticks
a stick used as a support while walking

**walk of life** NOUN walks of life
a person's occupation or social position • *He has friends from all walks of life.*

**walkover** NOUN walkovers
an easy victory

**wall** NOUN walls
❶ a continuous upright structure, usually made of brick or stone, forming one of the sides of a building or room or supporting something or enclosing an area ❷ the outside part of something • *the stomach wall* ❸ something that forms a barrier • *a wall of silence*

**wall** VERB walls, walling, walled
to block or surround something with a wall • *The entrance to the tomb was then walled up.*

**wallaby** NOUN wallabies
a kind of small kangaroo

**walled** ADJECTIVE
surrounded by a wall • *a walled garden*

**wallet** NOUN wallets
a small flat folding case for holding banknotes, credit cards, documents, etc.

**wallflower** NOUN wallflowers
a garden plant with fragrant flowers, blooming in spring WORD ORIGIN because it is often found growing on old walls

**wallop** (*informal*) VERB wallops, walloping, walloped
to hit or beat someone

**wallop** NOUN wallops
a heavy blow or punch

**wallow** VERB wallows, wallowing, wallowed
❶ to roll about in water or mud ❷ to get great pleasure by being surrounded by something • *They spent the whole weekend wallowing in luxury.*

**wallow** NOUN wallows
an area of mud or shallow water where mammals go to wallow

**wallpaper** NOUN wallpapers
❶ paper used to cover the inside walls of

rooms ❷ the background pattern or picture that you choose to have on your computer screen

**walnut** NOUN walnuts
❶ an edible nut with a wrinkled surface ❷ the wood from the tree that bears this nut, used for making furniture

**walrus** NOUN walruses
a large Arctic sea animal with two long tusks

**waltz** NOUN waltzes
a dance with three beats to a bar

**waltz** VERB waltzes, waltzing, waltzed
to dance a waltz
➤ **waltz in** to enter a place in a very casual and confident way

**wan** (say wonn) ADJECTIVE
❶ pale from being ill or tired ❷ a wan smile is faint and without enthusiasm
➤ **wanly** ADVERB

**wand** NOUN wands
a thin rod, especially one used by a magician or wizard

**wander** VERB wanders, wandering, wandered
❶ to go about without trying to reach a particular place • We spent the afternoon wandering around the town. ❷ to leave the right path or direction; to stray • Don't let the sheep wander. ❸ to be distracted or move on to other things • He let his attention wander.
➤ **wanderer** NOUN

**wander** NOUN
a wandering journey

**wane** VERB wanes, waning, waned
❶ the moon wanes when it shows a bright area that becomes gradually smaller after being full. (The opposite is wax.) ❷ to become less, smaller or weaker • His popularity was waning.

**wane** NOUN
➤ **on the wane** becoming less or weaker

**wangle** VERB wangles, wangling, wangled
(informal) to get or arrange something by trickery or clever planning • He's managed to wangle himself a trip to Paris.

**want** VERB wants, wanting, wanted
❶ to have a desire or wish for something • What do you want for breakfast? ❷ to need something • Your hair wants cutting.
➤ **want for something** to lack something that you need • They did not want for money.

**want** NOUN wants
❶ a wish to have something ❷ a lack or need

of something • People were dying for want of water.

**wanted** ADJECTIVE
a wanted person is a suspected criminal that the police wish to find or arrest

**wanting** ADJECTIVE
lacking in what is needed or usual • He was certainly not wanting in courage.

**wanton** (say wonn-ton) ADJECTIVE
done deliberately for no good reason • wanton damage

**war** NOUN wars
❶ fighting between nations or groups, especially using armed forces ❷ a serious struggle or effort against crime, disease, poverty, etc.
➤ **at war** taking part in a war

**warble** VERB warbles, warbling, warbled
to sing with a gentle trilling sound, as some birds do

**warble** NOUN warbles
a warbling song or sound

**warbler** NOUN warblers
a kind of small songbird

**war crime** NOUN war crimes
a crime committed during a war that breaks international rules of war
➤ **war criminal** NOUN

**ward** NOUN wards
❶ a room with beds for patients in a hospital ❷ a child looked after by a guardian ❸ an area electing a councillor to represent it

**ward** VERB wards, warding, warded
➤ **ward something off** to keep something away • He put his arms up to ward off the blows.

**warden** NOUN wardens
an official who is in charge of a hostel, college, etc. or who supervises something

**warder** NOUN warders (chiefly British)
an official in charge of prisoners in a prison

**wardrobe** NOUN wardrobes
❶ a cupboard to hang clothes in ❷ a stock of clothes or costumes

**ware** NOUN wares
manufactured goods of a certain kind • hardware • silverware
➤ **wares** goods offered for sale

**warehouse** NOUN warehouses
a large building where goods are stored

**warfare** NOUN
fighting a war • *years of siege warfare*

**warhead** NOUN warheads
the explosive head of a missile or torpedo

**warlike** ADJECTIVE
❶ fond of making war • *They were a warlike people.* ❷ threatening war

**warm** ADJECTIVE
❶ fairly hot; not cold or cool ❷ keeping the body warm • *a warm jumper* ❸ friendly or enthusiastic • *They gave us a warm welcome.* ❹ close to the right answer or to something hidden • *You're getting warm now.*

**warm** VERB warms, warming, warmed (also warm up)
to make something warm or to become warm • *I warmed my hands over the fire.*
➤ **warm to someone or something** to begin to like or become more interested in someone or something
➤ **warm up** to do gentle exercises to prepare yourself before playing sport

**warm-blooded** ADJECTIVE
a warm-blooded animal has blood that remains warm permanently

**warmly** ADVERB
❶ in warm clothes • *We were all warmly dressed.* ❷ in a friendly or enthusiastic way • *She greeted us warmly as we arrived.*

**warmth** NOUN
❶ being warm or keeping warm • *The cattle huddled together for warmth.* ❷ being friendly or enthusiastic • *She was touched by the warmth of their welcome.*

**warn** VERB warns, warning, warned
to tell someone about a danger or difficulty that may affect them or about what they should do • *I tried to warn him, but he wouldn't listen.*
➤ **warn someone off** to tell someone to keep away or to avoid a thing

**warning** NOUN warnings
something said or written to warn someone

**warp** (say worp) VERB warps, warping, warped
❶ to become bent or twisted out of shape, e.g. because of dampness; to bend or twist something in this way ❷ to distort a person's ideas or judgement • *Jealousy warped his mind.*

**warp** NOUN the lengthwise threads in weaving, crossed by the weft

**warpath** NOUN
➤ **on the warpath** angry and getting ready for a fight or argument

**warrant** NOUN warrants
a document that authorizes a person to do something (e.g. to search a place) or to receive something

**warrant** VERB warrants, warranting, warranted
❶ to justify or deserve something • *Nothing can warrant such rudeness.* ❷ to guarantee or bet that something will happen

**warranty** NOUN warranties
a guarantee • *a three-year warranty*

**warren** NOUN warrens
❶ a piece of ground where there are many burrows in which rabbits live and breed ❷ a building or place with many winding passages

**warring** ADJECTIVE
involved in a war • *the country's warring factions*

**warrior** NOUN warriors
a person who fights in battle; a soldier

**warship** NOUN warships
a ship used in war

**wart** NOUN warts
a small hard lump on the skin, caused by a virus

**wartime** NOUN
a time of war

**wary** (say wair ee) ADJECTIVE
cautious about possible danger or difficulty • *She gave him a wary look.* • *Foxes tend to be wary of humans.*
➤ **warily** ADVERB
➤ **wariness** NOUN

**wash** VERB washes, washing, washed
❶ to clean something with water or other liquid ❷ to be washable • *Cotton washes easily.* ❸ to flow against or over something • *Waves washed over the deck.* ❹ to carry something along by a moving liquid • *A wave washed him overboard.* ❺ (*informal*) to be believable or acceptable • *That excuse just won't wash.*
➤ **be washed out** (*informal*) to be abandoned because of rain
➤ **wash up** to wash the dishes and cutlery after a meal

**wash** NOUN washes
❶ the action of washing ❷ a quantity of clothes for washing ❸ the disturbed water

a
b
c
d
e
f
g
h
i
j
k
l
m
n
o
p
q
r
s
t
u
v
w
x
y
z

behind a moving ship ❹ a thin coating of colour or paint

**washable** ADJECTIVE
able to be washed without becoming damaged

**washbasin** NOUN washbasins
(*chiefly British*) a small sink for washing your hands and face

**washer** NOUN washers
❶ a small ring of rubber or metal placed between two surfaces (e.g. under a bolt or screw) to fit them tightly together ❷ a washing machine

**washing** NOUN
clothes that need to be washed or have been washed

**washing machine** NOUN washing machines
a machine for washing clothes

**washing soda** NOUN
sodium carbonate

**washing-up** NOUN
(*British*) washing the dishes and cutlery after a meal • *I'll give you a hand with the washing-up.*

**wash-out** NOUN wash-outs (*informal*)
a complete failure

**wasn't** (*mainly spoken*)
was not

> SPELLING
>
> Wasn't = was + not. Add an apostrophe between the n and the t.

**wasp** NOUN wasps
a stinging insect with black and yellow stripes round its body

**wastage** NOUN
loss of something by waste

**waste** VERB wastes, wasting, wasted
❶ to use more of something than you need or to use it without getting enough results ❷ to fail to use something • *You are wasting a good opportunity.*
➤ waste away to become gradually weaker or thinner • *She was wasting away for lack of food.*

**waste** ADJECTIVE
❶ left over or thrown away because it is not wanted • *waste paper* ❷ not used or usable • *an area of waste land*
➤ lay waste to a place to destroy the crops and buildings of an area

**waste** NOUN wastes
❶ wasting a thing or not using it well • *a waste of time* ❷ things that are not wanted or not used ❸ an area of desert or frozen land • *the wastes of the Siberia*

> SPELLING
>
> Take care not to confuse with waist, which means the narrow part in the middle of your body.

**wasteful** ADJECTIVE
using more than is needed; producing waste
➤ wastefully NOUN
➤ wastefulness NOUN

**wasteland** NOUN wastelands
a barren or empty area of land

**watch** VERB watches, watching, watched
❶ to look at a person or thing for some time ❷ to be on guard or ready for something to happen • *Watch for the traffic lights to turn green.* ❸ to pay careful attention to something • *Watch where you put your feet.* ❹ to take care of something • *His job is to watch the sheep.*
➤ watch out to be careful about something
➤ watcher NOUN

**watch** NOUN watches
❶ a device like a small clock, usually worn on the wrist ❷ the action of watching • *I'll keep watch while you have a look around.* ❸ a turn of being on duty in a ship

**watchdog** NOUN watchdogs
a dog kept to guard property

**watchful** ADJECTIVE
watching closely; alert • *She kept a watchful eye on the door.*
➤ watchfully ADVERB
➤ watchfulness NOUN

**watchman** NOUN watchmen
a person employed to look after an empty building at night

**watchword** NOUN watchwords
a word or phrase that sums up a group's policy; a slogan • *Our watchword is 'safety first'.*

**water** NOUN waters
❶ a colourless odourless tasteless liquid that is a compound of hydrogen and oxygen ❷ a lake or sea ❸ the tide • *at high water*
➤ pass water to urinate

**water** VERB waters, watering, watered
❶ to sprinkle or supply something with water • *Have you watered the plants?* ❷ to produce

tears or saliva • *It makes my mouth water.*
➤ **water something down** to dilute
something or make it weaker

**watercolour** *NOUN* watercolours
❶ paint made with pigment and water (not
oil) ❷ a painting done with this kind of paint

**watercress** *NOUN*
a kind of cress that grows in water

**water cycle** *NOUN*
the process by which water falls to the
ground as rain and snow, runs into rivers and
lakes, flows into the sea, evaporates into the
air and forms clouds and then falls to the
ground again

**waterfall** *NOUN* waterfalls
a place where a river or stream flows over the
edge of a cliff or large rock

**watering can** *NOUN* watering cans
a container with a long spout, for watering
plants

**water lily** *NOUN* water lilies
a plant that grows in water, with broad
floating leaves and large flowers

**waterlogged** *ADJECTIVE*
waterlogged ground is so wet that it cannot
soak up any more water

**watermark** *NOUN* watermarks
❶ a mark showing how high a river or tide
rises or how low it falls ❷ a faint design in
some kinds of paper that can be seen when
the paper is held up to the light

**watermelon** *NOUN* watermelons
a melon with a smooth green skin, red pulp
and black seeds

**watermill** *NOUN* watermills
a mill worked by a waterwheel

**water polo** *NOUN*
a game played by teams of swimmers with a
ball like a football

**waterproof** *ADJECTIVE*
that keeps out water • *a waterproof jacket*

**waterproof** *NOUN* waterproofs
(*British*) a waterproof coat or jacket

**watershed** *NOUN* watersheds
❶ a turning point in the course of events ❷ a
line of high land from which streams flow
down on each side

**waterskiing** *NOUN*
the sport of skimming over the surface of

water on a pair of flat boards (**waterskis**)
while being towed by a motor boat

**waterspout** *NOUN* waterspouts
a column of water formed when a whirlwind
draws up a whirling mass of water from the
sea

**water table** *NOUN* water tables
the level below which the ground is saturated
with water

**watertight** *ADJECTIVE*
❶ made or fastened so that water cannot get
in or out ❷ so carefully put together that it
has no mistakes and cannot be proved to be
untrue • *He has a watertight alibi.*

**waterway** *NOUN* waterways
a river or canal that ships can travel on

**waterwheel** *NOUN* waterwheels
a large wheel turned by a flow of water, used
to work machinery

**waterworks** *PLURAL NOUN*
a place with pumping machinery for
supplying water to a district

**watery** *ADJECTIVE*
❶ like water ❷ full of water or tears • *watery
eyes* ❸ made weak or thin by too much water
• *watery soup*

**watt** *NOUN* watts
a unit of electric power **WORD ORIGIN** named
after James *Watt*, a Scottish engineer, who
studied energy

**wattage** *NOUN* wattages
electric power measured in watts

**wattle** *NOUN* wattles
❶ sticks and twigs woven together to make
a fence or walls ❷ an Australian tree with
golden flowers

**wave** *NOUN* waves
❶ a ridge moving along the surface of the
sea or breaking on the shore ❷ a curling
piece of hair ❸ (*in science*) the wave-like
movement by which heat, light, sound or
electricity etc. travels ❹ a sudden build-up of
something • *She felt a wave of anger.* ❺ the
action of waving your hand • *He gave us a
little wave.*

**wave** *VERB* waves, waving, waved
❶ to move your hand from side to side as a
greeting or signal ❷ to move loosely from
side to side or up and down, or to move
something like this • *Flags were waving in the
wind.* ❸ to make a thing wavy ❹ to be wavy

**waveband** NOUN wavebands
a set of radio waves of similar length that are used for broadcasting radio programmes

**wavelength** NOUN wavelengths
❶ the distance between corresponding points on a sound wave or electromagnetic wave ❷ the length of a radio wave that a particular radio station uses to broadcast its programmes
➤ on the same wavelength having the same point of view as someone else • *We don't seem to be on the same wavelength at all*

**wavelet** NOUN wavelets
a small wave

**waver** VERB wavers, wavering, wavered
❶ to be unsteady or to move unsteadily • *For a second her voice wavered.* ❷ to begin to weaken • *He felt his courage start to waver.* ❸ to hesitate or be uncertain • *My mind wavered between going and staying.*

**wavy** ADJECTIVE
full of waves or curves • *brown wavy hair*
➤ **waviness** NOUN

**wax** NOUN waxes
❶ a soft substance that melts easily, used to make candles, crayons and polish ❷ beeswax

**wax** VERB waxes, waxing, waxed
❶ to coat or polish something with wax ❷ the moon waxes when it shows a bright area that becomes gradually larger. (The opposite is **wane**.) ❸ to become stronger or more important ❹ to speak or write in a certain way • *He waxed lyrical about his childhood.*

**waxen** ADJECTIVE
❶ made of wax ❷ like wax

**waxwork** NOUN waxworks
a lifelike model of a person made in wax

**waxy** ADJECTIVE
looking or feeling like wax • *He had pale waxy skin.*

**way** NOUN ways
❶ how something is done; a method or style • *This is the best way to make scrambled eggs.* ❷ a manner • *She spoke in a kindly way.* ❸ how to get somewhere; a route • *Can you tell me the way to the station?* • *We stopped for lunch on the way.* ❹ a direction or position • *Luckily she was looking the other way.* • *This picture is the wrong way up.* ❺ a path or road leading from one place to another ❻ a distance in space or time • *It's a long way from here.* ❼ a respect • *It's a good*

idea in some ways. ❽ a condition or state • *Things were in a bad way.*
➤ **get** or **have your own way** to make people let you do what you want
➤ **give way** ❶ to collapse ❷ to let other traffic go first ❸ to yield to someone's wishes or demands
➤ **in the way** preventing you from moving forwards or seeing something
➤ **no way** (*informal*) that is impossible!
➤ **under way** see **under**

**way** ADVERB (*informal*) far • *That is way beyond what we can afford.*

**wayfarer** NOUN wayfarers
a traveller, especially someone who is walking

**waylay** VERB waylays, waylaying, waylaid
to lie in wait for a person or people, especially in order to talk to them or rob them

**wayside** NOUN
➤ **fall by the wayside** to fail to continue doing something

**wayward** ADJECTIVE
disobedient; wilfully doing what you want

**WC** ABBREVIATION
a toilet (WORD ORIGIN) short for 'water closet', an old name for a toilet

**we** PRONOUN
a word used by a person to refer to himself or herself and another or others

**weak** ADJECTIVE
❶ having little strength, power or energy ❷ easy to break, damage or defeat ❸ not great in intensity • *a weak signal* ❹ poor at doing something

**weaken** VERB weakens, weakening, weakened
to make something weaker or to become weaker • *He could feel his grip weakening.*

**weakling** NOUN weaklings
a weak person or animal

**weakly** ADVERB
without much strength or force • *She smiled weakly.*

**weakly** ADJECTIVE
sickly; not strong

**weakness** NOUN weaknesses
❶ being weak ❷ a fault or something that you do not do well • *Our players have different strengths and weaknesses.*

**weal** NOUN weals
a raised mark left on someone's flesh by a whip or blow

**wealth** *NOUN*
❶ a lot of money or property; riches ❷ a large quantity • *The book has a wealth of illustrations.*

**wealthy** *ADJECTIVE* wealthier, wealthiest
having wealth; rich

**wean** *VERB* weans, weaning, weaned
to get a baby used to taking food other than milk
➤ **wean someone off something** to make someone give up a habit gradually

**weapon** *NOUN* weapons
something used to harm or kill people in a battle or fight

**weaponry** *NOUN*
weapons • *an exhibition of Roman armour and weaponry*

**wear** *VERB* wears, wearing, wore, worn
❶ to have clothes, jewellery, etc. on your body ❷ to have a certain look on your face • *She wore a frown.* ❸ to damage something by rubbing or using it often; to become damaged in this way • *The carpet has worn thin.* ❹ to last while being used • *This material wears well.*
➤ **wearable** *ADJECTIVE*
➤ **wearer** *NOUN*
➤ **wear off** ❶ to be removed by wear or use ❷ to become less strong or intense
➤ **wear on** to pass gradually • *The night wore on.*
➤ **wear out** to become weak or useless from continuous use
➤ **wear someone out** to make someone very tired

**wear** *NOUN*
❶ what you wear; clothes • *evening wear* ❷ (also **wear and tear**) gradual damage done by rubbing or using something

**wearisome** *ADJECTIVE*
causing weariness; tiring

**weary** *ADJECTIVE* wearier, weariest
❶ worn out and tired ❷ tiring • *It's weary work.*
➤ **wearily** *ADVERB*
➤ **weariness** *NOUN*

**weary** *VERB* wearies, wearying, wearied
❶ to make someone weary ❷ to grow tired of something • *The children never wearied of hearing her stories.*

**weasel** *NOUN* weasels
a small fierce animal with a slender body and reddish-brown fur

**weather** *NOUN*
the rain, snow, wind, sunshine etc. at a particular time or place
➤ **under the weather** feeling ill or depressed

**weather** *VERB* weathers, weathering, weathered
❶ to become worn or change colour because of the effects of the weather; to make something do this • *The wind and rain have weathered the cliffs.* ❷ to come through a difficult time or experience successfully • *The ship weathered the storm.*

**weathercock, weathervane** *NOUN*
weathercocks or weathervanes
a pointer, often shaped like a cockerel, that turns in the wind and shows from which direction it is blowing

**weave** *VERB* weaves, weaving, wove, woven
❶ to make material or baskets by crossing threads or strips under and over each other ❷ to put a story together • *She wove a thrilling tale.* ❸ (past tense also **weaved**) to move from side to side to get round things in the way • *He weaved through the traffic.*
➤ **weaver** *NOUN*

**weave** *NOUN* weaves
a style of weaving • *a loose weave*

**web** *NOUN* webs
❶ a cobweb ❷ something complicated • *a web of lies*
➤ **the Web** the World Wide Web

**webbed** *ADJECTIVE*
webbed feet have toes joined by pieces of skin, as ducks' and frogs' feet do

**webcam** *NOUN* webcams
a camera that is connected to a computer so that what it records can be seen on a website as it happens

**weblog** *NOUN* weblogs
a blog

**web page** *NOUN* web pages
a document forming part of a website

**website** *NOUN* websites
a place on the Internet where you can get information about a subject, company, etc. • *Visit our website to learn more.*

**wed** *VERB* weds, wedding, wedded
to marry someone

**wedding** *NOUN* weddings
the ceremony and celebration when a couple get married

a
b
c
d
e
f
g
h
i
j
k
l
m
n
o
p
q
r
s
t
u
v
w
x
y
z

**wedge** NOUN wedges
❶ a piece of wood or metal that is thick at one end and thin at the other. It is pushed between things to force them apart or prevent something from moving. ❷ a wedge-shaped thing • *a wedge of cheese*

**wedge** VERB wedges, wedging, wedged
❶ to keep something in place with a wedge • *I wedged the door open.* ❷ to pack things tightly together • *Ten of us were wedged in the lift.*

**wedlock** NOUN
the state of being married

**Wednesday** NOUN
the day of the week following Tuesday
**WORD ORIGIN** from Old English *Wodnesdaeg* = day of Woden or Odin, the chief Norse god

**SPELLING**

Take care, there is a **d** before the **n** and an **e** after it.

**wee** ADJECTIVE (Scottish)
little or small

**weed** NOUN weeds
a wild plant that grows where it is not wanted

**weed** VERB weeds, weeding, weeded
to remove weeds from the ground

**weedy** ADJECTIVE weedier, weediest
❶ full of weeds ❷ thin and weak

**week** NOUN weeks
❶ a period of seven days, especially from Sunday to the following Saturday ❷ the part of the week that does not include the weekend

**weekday** NOUN weekdays
a day other than Saturday or Sunday

**weekend** NOUN weekends
Saturday and Sunday

**weekly** ADJECTIVE & ADVERB
happening or done once a week

**weeny** ADJECTIVE (informal)
tiny

**weep** VERB weeps, weeping, wept
❶ to shed tears; to cry ❷ to ooze moisture in drops
➤ **weepy** ADJECTIVE

**weeping willow** NOUN weeping willows
a willow tree that has drooping branches

**weevil** NOUN weevils
a kind of small beetle

**weft** NOUN
the threads on a loom that are woven across the warp

**weigh** VERB weighs, weighing, weighed
❶ to measure the weight of something ❷ to have a certain weight • *What do you weigh?* ❸ to be important or have influence • *Her evidence weighed heavily with the jury.*
➤ **weigh anchor** to raise the anchor and start a voyage
➤ **weigh someone down** to depress or trouble someone
➤ **weigh something down** to hold something down with something heavy
➤ **weigh something out** to take a certain weight of a substance from a larger quantity
➤ **weigh something up** to think about something carefully before deciding what to do

**weight** NOUN weights
❶ how heavy something is; the amount that something weighs ❷ a piece of metal of known weight, especially one used on scales to weigh things ❸ a heavy object, used to hold things down ❹ importance or influence

**weight** VERB weights, weighting, weighted
to attach a weight to something • *The fishing nets are weighted with lead.*

**SPELLING**

The 'ay' sound is spelt **eigh**.

**weightless** ADJECTIVE
having no weight, for example when travelling in space
➤ **weightlessness** NOUN

**weightlifting** NOUN
the sport or exercise of lifting heavy weights
➤ **weightlifter** NOUN

**weighty** ADJECTIVE weightier, weightiest
❶ heavy ❷ serious and important • *These are weighty matters.*

**weir** (say weer) NOUN weirs
a small dam across a river or canal to control the flow of water

**weird** ADJECTIVE
very strange or unnatural • *I had a weird dream last night.*
➤ **weirdly** ADVERB
➤ **weirdness** NOUN

**SPELLING**

In **weird**, **e** before **i** is the right way round.

**welcome** *NOUN* welcomes
a greeting or reception, especially a kind or friendly one

**welcome** *ADJECTIVE*
❶ that you are glad to receive or see • *This is a welcome surprise.* ❷ allowed or invited to do or take something • *You are welcome to come.*

**welcome** *VERB* welcomes, welcoming, welcomed
❶ to show that you are pleased when a person arrives ❷ to be glad to receive or hear of something • *We welcome this decision.*

**weld** *VERB* welds, welding, welded
to join pieces of metal or plastic by heating and pressing or hammering them together

**welfare** *NOUN*
people's health, happiness and comfort

**welfare state** *NOUN*
a system in which a country's government provides money to pay for health care, social services, benefits, etc.

**well** *ADVERB* better, best
❶ in a good or suitable way • *She swims well.* ❷ thoroughly; to a great extent • *Make sure it is well cooked.* ❸ probably or reasonably • *This may well be our last chance.*
➤ **well off** ❶ fairly rich ❷ in a good situation

**well** *ADJECTIVE* better, best
❶ in good health • *He is not well.* ❷ satisfactory; fine • *All is well.*

**well** *NOUN* wells
❶ a deep hole dug to bring up water or oil from underground ❷ a deep space in a building, e.g. containing a staircase

**well** *VERB* wells, welling, welled
to rise or flow up • *Tears welled up in our eyes.*

**well-being** *NOUN*
good health, happiness and comfort

**wellies** *PLURAL NOUN* (*informal*)
wellingtons

**wellingtons** *PLURAL NOUN*
rubber or plastic waterproof boots
**WORD ORIGIN** named after the first Duke of *Wellington*, who wore long leather boots

**well-known** *ADJECTIVE*
known by many people • *a well-known actor* • *a well-known fact*

**well-mannered** *ADJECTIVE*
having good manners

**well-meaning** *ADJECTIVE*
having good intentions

**well-nigh** *ADVERB*
almost or nearly • *Passing the test seems well-nigh impossible.*

**well-read** *ADJECTIVE*
having read a lot of good books

**well-to-do** *ADJECTIVE*
fairly rich

**welt** *NOUN* welts
a raised mark left on someone's flesh by a whip or blow; a weal

**welter** *NOUN*
a confused mixture; a jumble • *a welter of information*

**wench** *NOUN* wenches (*old use*)
a girl or young woman

**wend** *VERB* wends, wending, wended
➤ **wend your way** to go somewhere slowly or by an indirect route

**weren't** (*mainly spoken*)
were not

**werewolf** *NOUN* werewolves
in legends and stories, a person who changes into a wolf when the moon is full

**west** *NOUN*
❶ the direction where the sun sets, opposite east ❷ the western part of a country, city or other area

**west** *ADJECTIVE & ADVERB*
towards or in the west; coming from the west • *We sailed west.* • *the west coast* • *a west wind*
➤ **westerly** *ADJECTIVE*

**western** *ADJECTIVE*
of or in the west

**western** *NOUN* westerns
a film or story about cowboys or American Indians in western North America during the 19th and early 20th centuries
➤ **westerner** *NOUN*
➤ **westernmost** *ADJECTIVE*

**westward** *ADJECTIVE & ADVERB*
towards the west
➤ **westwards** *ADVERB*

**wet** *ADJECTIVE* wetter, wettest
❶ soaked or covered in water or other liquid ❷ not yet dry • *wet paint* ❸ rainy • *It's been wet here all day.*
➤ **wetness** *NOUN*

**wet** VERB wets, wetting, wet or wetted
to make something wet • *Wet the brush slightly before putting it in the paint.*

**wet suit** NOUN wet suits
a close-fitting rubber suit, worn by skin divers and windsurfers to keep them warm and dry

**whack** (*informal*) VERB whacks, whacking, whacked
to hit someone or something hard

**whack** NOUN whacks
a hard hit or blow

**whale** NOUN whales
a very large sea mammal
➤ **have a whale of a time** (*informal*) to enjoy yourself very much

**whaler** NOUN whalers
a person or ship that hunts whales

**whaling** NOUN
hunting whales

**wharf** (say worf) NOUN wharves or wharfs
a quay where ships are loaded and unloaded

**what** DETERMINER
❶ used to ask the amount or kind of something • *What kind of music do you like?* ❷ used to say how strange or great a person or thing is • *What an idiot!*

**what** PRONOUN
❶ what thing or things • *What did you say?* ❷ the thing that • *This is what you must do.*
➤ **what's what** (*informal*) which things are important or useful • *She knows what's what.*

SPELLING
There is a silent **h** after the **w** in **what**.

**whatever** PRONOUN
❶ anything or everything • *Do whatever you like.* ❷ no matter what • *Keep calm, whatever happens.*

**whatever** DETERMINER
of any kind or amount • *Take whatever books you need.*

**whatever** ADVERB
at all • *There is no doubt whatever.*

**whatsoever** ADVERB
at all • *There is no chance whatsoever.*

**wheat** NOUN
a cereal plant from which flour is made

**wheedle** VERB wheedles, wheedling, wheedled
to persuade someone to do something by coaxing or flattering them • *She was good at wheedling money out of her mother.*

**wheel** NOUN wheels
❶ a round device that turns on a shaft that passes through its centre ❷ a steering wheel ❸ a horizontal revolving disc on which clay is made into a pot

**wheel** VERB wheels, wheeling, wheeled
❶ to push a bicycle or trolley etc. along on its wheels ❷ to move or fly in a wide circle or curve • *Birds wheeled above the ship.*
➤ **wheel round** to turn round quickly to face another way

**wheelbarrow** NOUN wheelbarrows
a small cart with one wheel at the front and legs at the back, pushed by handles

**wheelchair** NOUN wheelchairs
a chair on wheels, used by a person who cannot walk

**wheel clamp** NOUN wheel clamps
(*British*) a device that can be locked around a vehicle's wheel to stop it from moving, used especially on cars that have been parked illegally

**wheelie** NOUN wheelies
(*informal*) the stunt of riding a bicycle or motorcycle for a short distance with the front wheel off the ground

**wheelie bin** NOUN wheelie bins
(*British*) a large dustbin on wheels

**wheeze** VERB wheezes, wheezing, wheezed
to make a hoarse whistling sound as you breathe

**wheeze** NOUN wheezes
the sound of wheezing
➤ **wheezy** ADJECTIVE

**whelk** NOUN whelks
a shellfish that looks like a snail

**whelp** NOUN whelps
a young dog; a pup

**when** ADVERB
at what time; at which time • *When does the film start?*

**when** CONJUNCTION
❶ at the time that • *The bird flew away when I moved.* ❷ although; considering that • *Why are you going canoeing when you can't swim?*

**whence** ADVERB
(*formal*)
from where; from which

**whenever** CONJUNCTION
at whatever time; every time • *Whenever I go there, it's raining.*

**where** ADVERB & CONJUNCTION
in or to what place or that place • *Where did you put it?* • *Leave it where it is.*

**where** PRONOUN
❶ what place • *Where does she come from?*
❷ the place that • *This is where I belong.*

**whereabouts** ADVERB
in or near what place • *Whereabouts are you going?*

**whereabouts** PLURAL NOUN
the place where something is • *Do you know the whereabouts of my radio?*

**whereas** CONJUNCTION
but in contrast • *Some people enjoy sport, whereas others hate it.*

**whereby** ADVERB
by which; by means of which • *I have a plan whereby such accidents can be avoided in the future.*

**wherefore** ADVERB (old use)
why; for what reason

**whereupon** CONJUNCTION
after which; and then

**wherever** ADVERB
in or to whatever place; no matter where
• *You can sit wherever you like.*

**whet** VERB whets, whetting, whetted
to sharpen a blade or edge by rubbing it against a stone
➤ **whet your appetite** to make you feel hungry

> SPELLING
>
> Take care not to confuse with **wet**.

**whether** CONJUNCTION
used to show a doubt or choice between two possibilities; if • *I don't know whether to believe her or not.*

**whetstone** NOUN whetstones
a shaped stone for sharpening tools

**whey** (say way) NOUN
the watery liquid left when milk forms curds

**which** DETERMINER
what particular • *Which way did he go?*

**which** PRONOUN
❶ what person or thing • *Which is your desk?*
❷ the person or thing referred to • *The*

film, which is a western, will be shown on Saturday.

> GRAMMAR
>
> You use the relative pronoun **which** when it begins a clause giving additional information that you could leave out: *The book, which is now out of print, was a bestseller in its day.* You use **that** or **which** when it begins a clause that defines or identifies something important and which cannot be left out: *The book which I'm looking for is now out of print. The book I'm looking for is now out of print.*
>
> See also the panel on **clauses**.

> SPELLING
>
> There is a silent h after the w in **which**.

**whichever** PRONOUN & DETERMINER
no matter which; any which • *Choose whichever colour you like.*

**whiff** NOUN whiffs
a slight smell of something • *a whiff of perfume*

**Whig** NOUN Whigs
a member of a political party in the 17th-19th centuries, opposed to the Tories

**while** CONJUNCTION
❶ during the time that; as long as • *He was humming a tune while he worked.*
❷ although; but • *She is dark, while her sister is fair.*

**while** NOUN
a period of time • *We haven't been in touch for a while.*

**while** VERB whiles, whiling, whiled
➤ **while away time** to pass time in a leisurely way • *We whiled away the afternoon on the river.*

**whilst** CONJUNCTION
during the time that; while

**whim** NOUN whims
a sudden wish to do or have something • *He gave in to his daughter's every whim.*

**whimper** VERB whimpers, whimpering, whimpered
to cry or whine softly

**whimper** NOUN whimpers
a sound of whimpering

**whimsical** ADJECTIVE
slightly odd and playful • *His writing has a*

*whimsical quality.*
➤ **whimsically** ADVERB

**whine** VERB whines, whining, whined
❶ to make a long high miserable cry or a shrill sound ❷ to complain in a petty or feeble way

**whine** NOUN whines
a whining sound or cry

SPELLING
There is a silent h after the w in whine.

**whinge** VERB whinges, whinging or whingeing, whinged
(British) (informal) to grumble persistently

**whinny** VERB whinnies, whinnying, whinnied
a horse whinnies when it neighs gently or happily

**whinny** NOUN whinnies
a gentle neigh

**whip** NOUN whips
a cord or strip of leather fixed to a handle and used for hitting people or animals

**whip** VERB whips, whipping, whipped
❶ to beat a person or animal with a whip ❷ to beat cream until it becomes thick ❸ (informal) to steal something
➤ **whip something out** (informal) to take something out quickly or suddenly • *He whipped out a gun.*
➤ **whip something up** to stir up people's feelings • *They quickly whipped up support for the idea.*

**whippet** NOUN whippets
a small dog rather like a greyhound, used for racing

**whirl** VERB whirls, whirling, whirled
to turn or spin very quickly or to make something do this

**whirl** NOUN whirls
a quick turn or spin

**whirlpool** NOUN whirlpools
a whirling current of water, often drawing floating objects towards its centre

**whirlwind** NOUN whirlwinds
a strong wind that whirls round a central point

**whirr** VERB whirrs, whirring, whirred
to make a continuous buzzing sound • *The motor started to whirr.*

**whirr** NOUN whirrs
a continuous buzzing sound

**whisk** VERB whisks, whisking, whisked
❶ to move or brush something away quickly and lightly • *A waiter whisked away our plates.* ❷ to take a person somewhere very quickly • *After the performance she was whisked away in a limousine.* ❸ to beat eggs, etc. until they are frothy

**whisk** NOUN whisks
❶ a kitchen tool used for whisking things ❷ a whisking movement

**whisker** NOUN whiskers
❶ whiskers are the long stiff hairs growing near the mouth of a cat ❷ a man's whiskers are the hair growing on his face, especially on his cheeks

**whisky** NOUN whiskies
a strong alcoholic drink WORD ORIGIN from Scottish Gaelic *uisge beatha* = water of life

**whisper** VERB whispers, whispering, whispered
❶ to speak very softly ❷ to talk secretly; to spread a rumour

**whisper** NOUN whispers
❶ a whispering tone of voice ❷ a rumour

SPELLING
There is a silent h after the w in whisper.

**whist** NOUN
a card game usually for four people

**whistle** VERB whistles, whistling, whistled
❶ to make a shrill or musical sound by blowing through your lips ❷ to make a shrill sound • *The kettle was whistling away.* • *An arrow whistled through the air.*

**whistle** NOUN whistles
❶ a whistling sound ❷ a device that makes a shrill sound when air or steam is blown through it

**whit** NOUN
the least possible amount • *He could not have a done a whit better himself.*

**white** NOUN whites
❶ the very lightest colour, like snow or salt ❷ the transparent substance (albumen) round the yolk of an egg, which turns white when it is cooked ❸ a person with light-coloured skin

**white** ADJECTIVE
❶ of the colour white ❷ having light-coloured skin ❸ very pale from the effects of illness, fear or worry ❹ white coffee is made with milk
➤ **whiteness** NOUN

**whitebait** *NOUN* whitebait
a small silvery-white fish

**white elephant** *NOUN* white elephants
a useless possession, especially one that is
expensive to keep

**white-hot** *ADJECTIVE*
extremely hot; so hot that heated metal looks
white

**white lie** *NOUN* white lies
a harmless or trivial lie that you tell in order
to avoid hurting someone's feelings

**white meat** *NOUN*
poultry, veal, rabbit and pork

**whiten** *VERB* whitens, whitening, whitened
to become white or to make something white
• *His face whitened.* • *A fall of snow had
whitened the tops of the trees*

**whitewash** *NOUN*
❶ a white liquid containing lime or powdered
chalk, used for painting walls and ceilings
❷ concealing mistakes or other unpleasant
facts so that someone will not be punished

**whitewash** *VERB* whitewashes, whitewashing,
whitewashed
to coat a wall or ceiling with whitewash

**whither** *ADVERB* (old use)
to what place • *They did not know whither
they were going.*

**whiting** *NOUN* whiting
a small edible sea fish with white flesh
WORD ORIGIN from Dutch *wijt* = white

**whittle** *VERB* whittles, whittling, whittled
to shape wood by trimming thin slices off the
surface
➤ **whittle something down** to reduce
something by removing various things from it
• *We need to whittle down the cost.*

**whizz, whiz** *VERB* whizzes, whizzing, whizzed
to move very quickly, often making a sound
like something rushing through the air
• *Bullets whizzed past my ear.* • *A police car
whizzed by.*

**who** *PRONOUN*
❶ which person or people • *Who threw that?*
❷ the particular person or people • *This is the
boy who stole the apples.*

**whoa** *EXCLAMATION*
a command to a horse to stop or stand still

**whoever** *PRONOUN*
❶ any or every person who • *Whoever comes
is welcome.* ❷ no matter who • *I don't want
to see anyone, whoever it is.*

**whole** *ADJECTIVE*
❶ complete; all of • *Could you eat a whole
pizza?* • *I spent the whole day in bed.* ❷ not
broken or cut; in one piece • *Snakes swallow
their prey whole.*

**whole** *NOUN*
❶ the full amount ❷ a complete thing
➤ **as a whole** in general
➤ **on the whole** considering everything;
mainly
SPELLING
Whole is different from hole, which is a
gap or opening.

**wholefood** *NOUN* wholefoods
(*British*) food that has been processed as little
as possible

**wholehearted** *ADJECTIVE*
given without doubts or reservations
• *You have my wholehearted support.*

**wholemeal** *ADJECTIVE*
(*British*) made from the whole grain of
wheat

**whole number** *NOUN* whole numbers
a number without fractions

**wholesale** *NOUN*
the business of selling goods in large
quantities to be resold by others. Compare
with **retail**.
➤ **wholesaler** *NOUN*

**wholesale** *ADJECTIVE & ADVERB*
❶ on a large scale; including everybody or
everything • *wholesale destruction* ❷ in the
wholesale trade

**wholesome** *ADJECTIVE*
healthy and good for you • *simple wholesome
food*
➤ **wholesomeness** *NOUN*

**wholly** *ADVERB*
completely or entirely • *She is not wholly to
blame.*

**whom** *PRONOUN*
the form of who used when it is the object of
a verb or comes after a preposition, as in *the*

boy whom I saw or to whom we spoke

**USAGE**

Whom can sound rather formal. In modern English, especially in speech and less formal writing, it often sounds more natural to use who, as in *the boy who you saw last night* (or simply *the boy you saw last night*) and *Who were you referring to?*

**whoop** (say woop) NOUN whoops
a loud cry of excitement

**whoop** VERB whoops, whooping, whooped
to give a whoop

**whoopee** EXCLAMATION
a cry of joy

**whooping cough** (say hoop-ing) NOUN
an infectious disease that causes spasms of coughing and gasping for breath

**whopper** NOUN whoppers (informal)
❶ something very large ❷ a blatant lie

**whopping** ADJECTIVE (informal)
very large or remarkable • *He has scored a whopping 72 points.*

**whorl** NOUN whorls
❶ a coil or curved shape ❷ a ring of leaves or petals

**who's** (mainly spoken)
who is; who has

**SPELLING**

Who's is different from whose: • *Who's next in the queue?* • *Whose coat is this?*

**whose** DETERMINER & PRONOUN
belonging to what person or persons; of whom; of which • *Whose bike is that?* • *That is the girl whose party we went to.*

**SPELLING**

Do not confuse this word with who's: • *Whose coat is this?* • *Who's next in the queue?*

**why** ADVERB
for what reason or purpose; the particular reason on account of which • *Why didn't you tell me?* • *This is why I came.*

**wick** NOUN wicks
❶ the string that goes through the middle of a candle and is lit ❷ the strip of material that you light in a lamp or heater that uses oil

**wicked** ADJECTIVE
❶ morally bad or cruel ❷ mischievous

• *He gave me a wicked grin.* ❸ (informal) excellent; very good
➤ **wickedly** ADVERB
➤ **wickedness** NOUN
**WORD ORIGIN** from Old English *wicca* = witch

**wicker** NOUN
thin canes or twigs woven together to make baskets, fences or furniture
➤ **wickerwork** NOUN

**wicket** NOUN wickets
❶ a set of three stumps and two bails used in cricket ❷ the strip of ground between the wickets

**wicket-gate** NOUN wicket-gates
a small gate used to save opening a much larger one

**wicketkeeper** NOUN wicketkeepers
the fielder in cricket who stands behind the batsman's wicket

**wide** ADJECTIVE
❶ measuring a lot from side to side; not narrow • *The river was wide.* ❷ measuring from side to side • *The cloth is one metre wide.* ❸ covering a great range • *My uncle has a wide knowledge of birds.* ❹ fully open • *staring with wide eyes* ❺ missing the target • *The shot was wide of the mark.*

**wide** ADVERB
❶ to the full extent; far apart • *The door was wide open.* ❷ missing the target • *The shot went wide.* ❸ over a large area • *She travelled far and wide.*
➤ **wide awake** fully awake

**widely** ADVERB
commonly; among many people • *They are widely admired.*

**widen** VERB widens, widening, widened
to make something wider or to become wider
• *His eyes widened in amazement.*

**widespread** ADJECTIVE
existing in many places or over a wide area
• *a widespread belief*

**widow** NOUN widows
a woman whose husband has died

**widowed** ADJECTIVE
made a widow or widower

**widower** NOUN widowers
a man whose wife has died

**width** NOUN widths
❶ how wide something is • *The room is eight metres in width.* ❷ the distance of a swimming pool from one side to the other

**wield** *VERB* wields, wielding, wielded
❶ to hold and use a weapon or tool • *a knight wielding a sword* ❷ to have and use power or influence

**wife** *NOUN* wives
the woman someone is married to

**wi-fi** *NOUN*
the system for connecting computers, mobile phones, etc. to the Internet without using wires

**wig** *NOUN* wigs
a covering made of real or artificial hair, worn on the head

**wiggle** *VERB* wiggles, wiggling, wiggled
to move something from side to side • *They wiggled their hips in time to the music.*

**wiggle** *NOUN* wiggles
a wiggling movement
➤ **wiggly** *ADJECTIVE*

**wigwam** *NOUN* wigwams
a tent formerly used by Native Americans, made by fastening skins or mats over poles

**wild** *ADJECTIVE*
❶ wild animals and plants live or grow in their natural state and are not looked after by people ❷ wild land is in its natural state and has not been changed by people • *a wild landscape* ❸ not controlled; very violent or excited • *There were wild celebrations in the streets.* • *She went wild when she saw the mess.* ❹ very foolish or unreasonable • *You do have wild ideas.* ❺ a wild guess has not been thought about carefully and is unlikely to be correct
➤ **wildness** *NOUN*

**wild** *NOUN* wilds
❶ the wild is the natural environment in which animals live • *I would love to see a herd of elephants in the wild.* ❷ the wilds are remote areas far from towns and cities

**wildebeest** *NOUN* wildebeest or wildebeests
a gnu

**wilderness** *NOUN* wildernesses
an area of natural land which is wild and uncultivated

**wildfire** *NOUN*
➤ spread like wildfire to spread or become known over a large area very fast • *News of his arrival spread like wildfire.*

**wildlife** *NOUN*
wild animals in their natural setting

**wildly** *ADVERB*
❶ in a way that is not controlled • *My heart was beating wildly.* ❷ extremely; very • *The story has been wildly exaggerated.*

**Wild West** *NOUN*
the western states of the USA during the period when the first Europeans were settling there and there was not much law and order

**wiles** *PLURAL NOUN*
clever tricks that someone uses to get what they want

**wilful** *ADJECTIVE*
❶ obstinately determined to do what you want • *a wilful child* ❷ done deliberately • *This is wilful disobedience.*
➤ **wilfully** *ADVERB*
➤ **wilfulness** *NOUN*

**will** *AUXILIARY VERB*
used to talk about what will happen in the future and in questions or promises • *They will arrive soon.* • *Will you shut the door?* • *I will get my revenge.*

**will** *NOUN* wills
❶ the mental power to decide and control what you do ❷ a desire; a chosen decision • *I wrote the letter against my will.* ❸ determination to do something • *She has a strong will to succeed.* ❹ a legal document saying what is to be done with someone's possessions when they die
➤ at will whenever you like • *You can come and go at will.*

**will** *VERB* wills, willing, willed
to use your will power to try to influence something • *I was willing you to win!*

> **GRAMMAR**
> See also the panel at shall.

**willing** *ADJECTIVE*
ready and happy to do what is wanted • *Are you willing to help?*
➤ **willingly** *ADVERB*
➤ **willingness** *NOUN*

**will-o'-the-wisp** *NOUN* will-o'-the-wisps
❶ a flickering spot of light seen on marshy ground ❷ something that is impossible to achieve **WORD ORIGIN** from *Will,* short for *William,* + an old sense of *wisp* = small bundle of straw burned as a torch

**willow** *NOUN* willows
a tree or shrub with flexible branches, usually growing near water

a b c d e f g h i j k l m n o p q r s t u v w x y z

**will power** NOUN
strength of mind to control what you do

**willy-nilly** ADVERB
❶ whether you want to or not ❷ without planning; haphazardly **WORD ORIGIN** from *will I, nill I* (= will I, will I not)

**wilt** VERB wilts, wilting, wilted
❶ a flower or plant wilts when it loses freshness and droops ❷ to lose your strength or energy • *After two hours in the sun, we were beginning to wilt.*

**wily** (say wy-lee) ADJECTIVE
cunning or crafty
➤ **wiliness** NOUN

**wimp** NOUN wimps
(*informal*) a weak or timid person

**wimple** NOUN wimples
a piece of cloth folded round the head and neck, worn by women in the Middle Ages

**win** VERB wins, winning, won
❶ to defeat your opponents in a game, contest or battle ❷ to get or achieve something by a victory or by using effort or skill • *She won second prize.* ❸ to gain someone's favour or support • *By the end he had won over the audience.*

**win** NOUN wins
a victory in a game or contest

**wince** VERB winces, wincing, winced
to make a slight movement because you are in pain or embarrassed

**winch** NOUN winches
a device for lifting or pulling things, using a rope or cable that winds onto a revolving drum or wheel

**winch** VERB winches, winching, winched
to lift or pull something with a winch

**wind** (rhymes with tinned) NOUN winds
❶ a current of air ❷ gas in the stomach or intestines that makes you feel uncomfortable ❸ the breath that you need to do something, e.g. for running or speaking ❹ the wind instruments of an orchestra
➤ **get wind of something** to hear a rumour about something
➤ **put the wind up someone** (*informal*) to frighten or alarm someone

**wind** (rhymes with tinned) VERB winds, winding, winded
to make a person out of breath • *The climb had winded us.*

**wind** (rhymes with find) VERB winds, winding, wound
❶ to have a lot of bends or curves • *The river winds down the valley.* ❷ to wrap or twist a thing round something else • *She wound a bandage round her finger.* ❸ to move something up or down by turning a handle • *I can't wind the window down.* ❹ (also **wind up**) to make a clock or watch work by tightening its spring
➤ **winder** NOUN
➤ **wind up** (*informal*) to end up in a place or situation • *He wound up in jail.*
➤ **wind something up** to close a business

**windbag** NOUN windbags (*informal*)
a person who talks too much

**windfall** NOUN windfalls
❶ a piece of unexpected good luck, especially a sum of money ❷ a fruit blown off a tree by the wind

**wind farm** NOUN wind farms
a group of windmills or wind turbines for producing electricity

**wind instrument** NOUN wind instruments
a musical instrument played by blowing, e.g. a trumpet or flute

**windlass** NOUN windlasses
a machine for pulling or lifting things (e.g. a bucket from a well), with a rope or cable that is wound round an axle by turning a handle

**windmill** NOUN windmills
a mill worked by the wind turning its sails

**window** NOUN windows
❶ an opening in a wall or roof or in the side of a vehicle to let in light and air, usually filled with glass ❷ (*in computing*) a framed area on a computer screen used for a particular purpose **WORD ORIGIN** from Old Norse *vind* = wind, air + *auga* = eye

**window-shopping** NOUN
looking at things in shop windows but not buying anything

**windpipe** NOUN windpipes
the tube by which air passes from the throat to the lungs

**windscreen** NOUN windscreens
(*British*) the glass in the window at the front of a motor vehicle

**windshield** NOUN windshields
(*North American*) a windscreen

**windsurfing** NOUN
the sport of surfing on a board that has a sail

794

fixed to it
➤ **windsurfer** NOUN

**wind turbine** NOUN wind turbines
a large modern windmill used for producing
electricity

**windward** ADJECTIVE
facing the wind • *the windward side of the
ship*

**windy** ADJECTIVE
with much wind • *It's windy outside.*

**wine** NOUN wines
❶ an alcoholic drink made from grapes or
other plants ❷ a dark red colour

SPELLING
Do not confuse this word with whine.

**wing** NOUN wings
❶ one of the pair of parts of a bird, bat or
insect, that it uses for flying ❷ one of the
pair of long flat parts that stick out from the
side of an aircraft and support it while it flies
❸ a part of a large building that extends from
the main part ❹ the part of a motor vehicle's
body above a wheel ❺ a player whose place
is at one of the far ends of the forward line in
football or hockey ❻ a section of a political
party, with more extreme opinions than the
others
➤ **on the wing** flying
➤ **take wing** to fly away
➤ **under your wing** under your protection
➤ **the wings** the sides of a theatre stage out
of sight of the audience

**wing** VERB wings, winging, winged
❶ to fly somewhere • *The bird winged its way
home.* ❷ to wound a bird in the wing or a
person in the arm

**winged** ADJECTIVE
having wings • *Pegasus was a mythical
winged horse.*

**wingless** ADJECTIVE
without wings • *wingless insects*

**wingspan** NOUN
the length between the two wing tips of a
bird or aircraft

**wink** VERB winks, winking, winked
❶ to close and open your eye quickly,
especially as a signal to someone ❷ a light
winks when it flickers or twinkles

**wink** NOUN winks
❶ the action of winking ❷ a very short
period of sleep • *I didn't sleep a wink that
night.*

**winkle** NOUN winkles
a kind of edible shellfish

**winkle** VERB winkles, winkling, winkled
➤ **winkle something out** (*chiefly British*) to
get information from someone with difficulty
• *I managed to winkle the truth out of him
eventually.*

**winner** NOUN winners
❶ a person, team or animal that wins
something ❷ something very successful • *Her
latest book is a winner.*

**winning** ADJECTIVE
attractive and charming • *a winning smile*

**winnings** PLURAL NOUN
the money someone wins in a game or by
gambling

**winnow** VERB winnows, winnowing, winnowed
to toss or fan grain so that the loose dry
outer part is blown away

**winsome** ADJECTIVE
charming and attractive

**winter** NOUN winters
the coldest season of the year, between
autumn and spring

**winter** VERB winters, wintering, wintered
to spend the winter somewhere

**wintry** ADJECTIVE
❶ wintry weather is cold, like winter ❷ a
wintry smile is cold and unfriendly

**wipe** VERB wipes, wiping, wiped
❶ to dry or clean something by rubbing it
❷ to remove something by rubbing it • *She
wiped away her tears.*
➤ **wipe something out** ❶ to cancel
something • *He's wiped out the debt.* ❷ to
destroy something completely

**wipe** NOUN wipes
the action of wiping • *Give the window a
quick wipe.*

**wiper** NOUN wipers
a device for wiping something, especially on a
vehicle's windscreen

**wire** NOUN wires
❶ a strand or thin flexible rod of metal ❷ a
piece of wire used to carry electric current
❸ a fence made from wire

**wire** VERB wires, wiring, wired
❶ to fit or connect something with wires
to carry electric current ❷ to fasten or
strengthen something with wire

a
b
c
d
e
f
g
h
i
j
k
l
m
n
o
p
q
r
s
t
u
v
w
x
y
z

**wireless** ADJECTIVE
able to send and receive signals without using wires • *a wireless Internet connection*

**wireless** NOUN wirelesses
(old use) a radio set

**wiring** NOUN
the system of wires carrying electricity in a building or in a device

**wiry** ADJECTIVE
❶ a wiry person is lean and strong ❷ wiry hair is tough and stiff

**wisdom** NOUN
❶ being wise ❷ wise sayings or writings

**wisdom tooth** NOUN wisdom teeth
a molar tooth that may grow at the back of the jaw of a person aged about 20 or more

**wise** ADJECTIVE
❶ able to make sensible decisions and give good advice because of the experience and knowledge that you have • *a wise old woman* ❷ sensible and showing good judgement • *a wise decision*
➤ **wisely** ADVERB
➤ be none the wiser to not know any more about something than you did before

**wish** VERB wishes, wishing, wished
❶ to feel or say that you would like to have or do something or would like something to happen ❷ to say that you hope someone will get something • *Wish me luck!*

**wish** NOUN wishes
❶ something you wish for; a desire • *I have no wish to see him again.* ❷ the action of wishing • *Close your eyes and make a wish.*

**wishbone** NOUN wishbones
a forked bone between the neck and breast of a chicken or other bird

**wishful thinking** NOUN
belief in something based on what you would like, not on the facts

**wisp** NOUN wisps
❶ a few strands of hair or bits of straw etc. ❷ a small streak of smoke or cloud
➤ **wispy** ADJECTIVE

➤ **wisteria, wistaria** (say wist-**eer**-ee-a or wist-**air**-ee-a) NOUN
a climbing plant with hanging blue, purple or white flowers **WORD ORIGIN** named after an American professor, Caspar *Wistar*

**wistful** ADJECTIVE
sadly longing for something • *There was a wistful look in her eyes.*

➤ **wistfully** ADVERB
➤ **wistfulness** NOUN

**wit** NOUN wits
❶ the ability to think quickly and clearly and make good decisions • *The game was a long battle of wits.* • *No one had the wit to ask for help.* ❷ a clever kind of humour ❸ a witty person
➤ at your wits' end not knowing what to do
➤ keep your wits about you to stay alert

**witch** NOUN witches
a person, especially a woman, who is thought to have magic powers

**SPELLING**
Do not confuse this word with which.

**witchcraft** NOUN
the use of magic, especially for evil purposes

**witch doctor** NOUN witch doctors
a magician who belongs to a tribe and is believed to use magic to heal people

**witch-hunt** NOUN witch-hunts
a campaign to find and punish people who hold views that are thought to be unacceptable or dangerous

**with** PREPOSITION
used to indicate
❶ being in the company or care of someone • *I came with a friend.* ❷ having or wearing something • *Who's that man with the beard?* ❸ using something • *Hit it with a hammer.* ❹ because of something • *He shook with laughter.* ❺ feeling or showing something • *She heard the news with great sadness.* ❻ towards or concerning something • *I was angry with him.* ❼ against someone or something • *There's no point in arguing with her.*

**withdraw** VERB withdraws, withdrawing, withdrew, withdrawn
❶ to take something away or take it back • *She withdrew her hand from his.* ❷ to go away from a place or stop taking part in something • *The troops withdrew from the frontier.* • *His injury meant he had to withdraw from the race.*

**withdrawal** NOUN withdrawals
❶ withdrawing something • *the withdrawal of troops from the region* ❷ an amount of money taken out of an account ❸ the process of stopping taking drugs to which you are addicted, often with unpleasant reactions • *withdrawal symptoms*

**withdrawn** ADJECTIVE
very shy or reserved

**wither** VERB withers, withering, withered
❶ a plant withers when it shrivels or wilts
❷ to become weaker then disappear

**withering** ADJECTIVE
scornful or sarcastic • *a withering remark*

**withers** PLURAL NOUN
the ridge between a horse's shoulder blades

**withhold** VERB withholds, withholding, withheld
to refuse to give something to someone • *He has withheld his permission.*

**within** PREPOSITION & ADVERB
inside; not beyond something • *I'll be back within an hour.*

**without** PREPOSITION
❶ not having or using • *You can't get in without a key.* ❷ free from • *She looked at him without fear.* ❸ (old use) outside • *without the city wall*

**withstand** VERB withstands, withstanding, withstood
to resist something or put up with it successfully • *The bridge is designed to withstand high winds.*

**witness** NOUN witnesses
❶ a person who sees or hears something happen • *There were no witnesses to the accident.* ❷ a person who gives evidence in a law court

**witness** VERB witnesses, witnessing, witnessed
❶ to be a witness of something • *Did anyone witness the accident?* ❷ to sign a document to confirm that it is genuine

**witted** ADJECTIVE
having wits of a certain kind • *quick-witted*

**witticism** NOUN witticisms
a witty remark

**witty** ADJECTIVE wittier, wittiest
clever and amusing; full of wit
➤ **wittily** ADVERB

**wizard** NOUN wizards
❶ a man with magic powers; a magician ❷ a person with amazing abilities • *She's a real computer wizard.* WORD ORIGIN from an old sense of *wise* = a wise person

**wizardry** NOUN
❶ the clever and impressive things that a person or thing can do • *The film's special effects were created using the latest computer wizardry.* ❷ the powers that a wizard has

**wizened** (say **wiz**-end) ADJECTIVE
full of wrinkles • *a wizened face*

**woad** NOUN
a kind of blue dye formerly made from a plant

**wobble** VERB wobbles, wobbling, wobbled
to move unsteadily from side to side or to make something do this • *Careful, this chair wobbles.*

**wobble** NOUN wobbles
a wobbling movement

**wobbly** ADJECTIVE
moving unsteadily from side to side • *a wobbly tooth*

**woe** NOUN woes
❶ great sorrow ❷ someone's woes are their troubles and misfortunes

**woebegone** ADJECTIVE
looking unhappy

**woeful** ADJECTIVE
❶ very sad; full of woe ❷ very bad; disgraceful • *a woeful lack of information*
➤ **woefully** ADVERB

**wok** NOUN woks
a Chinese cooking pan shaped like a large bowl

**wolf** NOUN wolves
a fierce wild animal of the dog family, often hunting in packs

**wolf** VERB wolfs, wolfing, wolfed
to eat something greedily

**woman** NOUN women
a grown-up female human being

**womanhood** NOUN
the condition of being a woman • *She soon grew to womanhood.*

**womanly** ADJECTIVE
having qualities that are thought to be typical of women

**womb** (say woom) NOUN wombs
the hollow organ in a female's body where babies develop before they are born

**wombat** NOUN wombats
an Australian animal rather like a small bear

**wonder** VERB wonders, wondering, wondered
❶ to feel that you want to know something; to try to decide about something • *We are still wondering what to do next.* ❷ to feel great surprise and admiration

A
B
C
D
E
F
G
H
I
J
K
L
M
N
O
P
Q
R
S
T
U
V
**W**
X
Y
Z

**wonder** NOUN wonders
❶ a feeling of surprise and admiration • *He stared in wonder at the stunning landscape.*
❷ something that fills you with surprise and admiration; a marvel • *It is one of the wonders of modern science.*
➤ **no wonder** it is not surprising

**wonderful** ADJECTIVE
marvellous or excellent
➤ **wonderfully** ADVERB

**wonderment** NOUN
a feeling of wonder

**wondrous** ADJECTIVE (*old use*)
wonderful; marvellous

**wont** (*say* wohnt) ADJECTIVE (*old use*)
accustomed; used to doing something • *Most afternoons he was wont to practise the trumpet.*

**wont** NOUN
a habit or custom • *She got up early, as was her wont.*

**won't** (*mainly spoken*)
will not

SPELLING

Won't is short for will + not. Do not forget to add an **apostrophe** between the n and the t.

**woo** VERB woos, wooing, wooed (*old use*)
❶ to try to win the love of a woman ❷ to seek someone's favour or support

**wood** NOUN woods
❶ the substance that trees are made of
❷ many trees growing close together

**woodcock** NOUN woodcock
a bird with a long bill, often shot for sport

**woodcut** NOUN woodcuts
an engraving made on wood; a print made from this

**wooded** ADJECTIVE
covered with growing trees • *wooded hills*

**wooden** ADJECTIVE
❶ made of wood ❷ stiff and showing no expression or liveliness
➤ **woodenly** ADVERB

**woodland** NOUN woodlands
wooded country

**woodlouse** NOUN woodlice
a small crawling creature with seven pairs of legs, living in rotten wood or damp soil

**woodpecker** NOUN woodpeckers
a bird that taps tree trunks with its beak to find insects

**woodwind** NOUN
wind instruments that are usually made of wood, e.g. the clarinet and oboe

**woodwork** NOUN
❶ making things out of wood ❷ things made out of wood

**woodworm** NOUN woodworms
the larva of a kind of beetle that bores into wooden furniture; the damage done to wood by this

**woody** ADJECTIVE
❶ like wood; consisting of wood ❷ full of trees

**woof** NOUN woofs
the gruff bark of a dog

**wool** NOUN wools
❶ the thick soft hair of sheep and goats
❷ thread or cloth made from this

**woollen** ADJECTIVE
made of wool

**woollens** PLURAL NOUN
clothes made of wool

**woolly** ADJECTIVE
❶ covered with wool or wool-like hair ❷ like wool or made of wool ❸ not thinking clearly; vague or confused • *woolly ideas*
➤ **woolliness** NOUN

**word** NOUN words
❶ a set of sounds or letters that has a meaning and when written or printed has no spaces between the letters ❷ a brief conversation • *Can I have a word with you?* ❸ a promise • *He kept his word.* ❹ a command or spoken signal • *Run when I give the word.* ❺ a message or piece of news • *We sent word of our safe arrival.*
➤ **have words** to quarrel
➤ **word for word** in exactly the same words

**word** VERB words, wording, worded
to express something in words • *You will need to word the question carefully.*

**word class** NOUN word classes
any of the groups into which words are divided in grammar (noun, pronoun,

determiner, adjective, verb, adverb, preposition, conjunction, exclamation)

> **GRAMMAR**
>
> The **word classes** of English are the different types of words you use in making sentences. Each word class has a special job to do: for example, a noun names things and a verb tells you what someone or something is doing. The names of the main word classes are: *noun, verb, adjective, adverb, pronoun, determiner, conjunction, preposition,* and *exclamation* (also sometimes called *interjection*). Word classes are also called **parts of speech**.
>
> A word can belong to more than one word class, depending on its position and purpose in a sentence. For example, the word *back* can be a noun (*a sore back*), an adjective (*the back seat*), an adverb (*to fall back*) or a verb (*to back a plan*).
>
> See also the panels for **adjectives, adverbs, conjunctions, determiners, nouns, prepositions, pronouns** and **verbs**.

**wording** *NOUN*
the way something is worded

**word of honour** *NOUN*
a solemn promise

**word-perfect** *ADJECTIVE*
having memorized every word perfectly • *He was word-perfect at the rehearsal.*

**word processor** *NOUN* word processors
a type of computer or program used for editing and printing letters and documents

**wore**
past tense of **wear**

**work** *NOUN* works
❶ something you have to do that needs effort or energy • *Digging is hard work.* ❷ a job; employment ❸ something you write or produce at school • *Please get on with your work quietly.* ❹ (*in science*) the result of applying a force to move an object ❺ a piece of writing, painting, music, etc. • *the works of William Shakespeare*
➤ **at work** busy working
➤ **out of work** having no work; not able to find a job

**work** *VERB* works, working, worked
❶ to spend time doing something that needs effort or energy ❷ to have a job or be employed • *She works in a bank.* ❸ to act or operate correctly or successfully • *Is the lift*

working? ❹ to make something function or operate • *Can you work the lift?* ❺ to shape or press something • *Work the mixture into a paste.* ❻ to gradually move into a particular position • *The screw had worked loose.*
➤ **work out** to have a particular result, especially a good one • *I hope things work out well.*
➤ **work something out** to find an answer by thinking or calculating
➤ **work someone up** to make someone become excited, angry or anxious • *I could see she was getting really worked up.*
➤ **work up to something** to gradually progress to something more difficult or advanced

**workable** *ADJECTIVE*
that can be used or will work • *a workable plan*

**worker** *NOUN* workers
❶ a person who works ❷ a member of the working class ❸ a bee or ant that does the work in a hive or colony but does not produce eggs

**workforce** *NOUN* workforces
the number of people who work in a particular factory, industry, country, etc.

**working class** *NOUN* working classes
people who work for wages, especially in manual or industrial work
➤ **working-class** *ADJECTIVE*

**workman** *NOUN* workmen
a man who works with his hands, especially at building or making things

**workmanship** *NOUN*
a person's skill in making or producing something

**work of art** *NOUN* works of art
something produced by an artist, especially a painting or sculpture

**workout** *NOUN* workouts
a session of physical exercise or training

**works** *PLURAL NOUN*
❶ the moving parts of a machine ❷ a factory or industrial site

**worksheet** *NOUN* worksheets
a sheet of paper with a set of questions about a subject for students, often used with a textbook

**workshop** *NOUN* workshops
a place where things are made or mended

**world** NOUN worlds
**❶** the earth with all its countries and peoples
**❷** all the people on the earth; everyone
• *He felt that the world was against him.*
**❸** a planet • *creatures from another world*
**❹** everything to do with a certain subject or activity • *He knows a lot about the world of sport.*
➤ **do someone the world of good** to have a very good effect on someone
➤ **think the world of someone** to have the highest possible opinion of someone

**worldly** ADJECTIVE
**❶** to do with life on earth, not spiritual
**❷** interested in money, possessions and pleasure **❸** experienced about people and life
➤ **worldliness** NOUN

**worldwide** ADJECTIVE & ADVERB
over the whole world • *The success of these books brought her worldwide fame.*

**World Wide Web** NOUN
(*in computing*) a vast extensive information system that connects related sites and documents which can be accessed using the Internet

**worm** NOUN worms
**❶** an animal with a long small soft rounded or flat body and no backbone or limbs
**❷** (*informal*) an unimportant or unpleasant person

**worm** VERB worms, worming, wormed
to move along by wriggling or crawling • *I managed to worm my way under the fence.*
➤ **worm something out of someone** to gradually get someone to tell you something by constantly and cleverly questioning them
• *We eventually managed to worm the truth out of them.*

**wormwood** NOUN
a woody plant with a bitter taste

**worn**
past participle of **wear**

**worn** ADJECTIVE
damaged because it has been rubbed or used too much • *worn tyres*

**worn-out** ADJECTIVE
**❶** tired and exhausted **❷** damaged by too much use

**worried** ADJECTIVE
feeling or showing worry

**worry** VERB worries, worrying, worried
**❶** to feel anxious or troubled about something **❷** to make someone feel anxious

or troubled about something **❸** an animal worries its prey when it holds it in its teeth and shakes it • *The dog was worrying a rat.*
➤ **worrier** NOUN

**worry** NOUN worries
**❶** worrying or being anxious **❷** something that makes a person worry

**worse** ADJECTIVE & ADVERB
more bad or more badly; less good or less well
➤ **worse off** less fortunate or well off

**worsen** VERB worsens, worsening, worsened
to become worse or to make something worse • *The weather worsened.*

**worship** VERB worships, worshipping, worshipped
**❶** to give praise or respect to God or a god
**❷** to love or respect a person or thing greatly
• *He worshipped his wife.*
➤ **worshipper** NOUN

**worship** NOUN worships
**❶** worshipping; religious ceremonies **❷** a title of respect for a mayor or certain magistrates
• *his worship the mayor*

**worshipful** ADJECTIVE
in titles, a word that means 'respected' • *the Worshipful Company of Goldsmiths*

**worst** ADJECTIVE & ADVERB
most bad or most badly; least good or least well

**worsted** NOUN
a kind of woollen material

**worth** ADJECTIVE
**❶** having a certain value • *This stamp is worth £100.* **❷** deserving something; good or important enough for something • *That book is worth reading.*

**worth** NOUN
**❶** a person's or thing's value or usefulness
• *He has proved his worth to the team.* **❷** the amount that a certain sum will buy • *five pounds' worth of stamps*

**worthless** ADJECTIVE
having no value; useless
➤ **worthlessness** NOUN

**worthwhile** ADJECTIVE
important or good enough to deserve the time or effort needed • *a worthwhile job*

**worthy** ADJECTIVE
deserving respect or support • *The sale is for a worthy cause.*
➤ **worthiness** NOUN

➤ worthy of deserving • *This charity is worthy of your support.*

**would** *AUXILIARY VERB*
❶ as the past tense of will • *The guide said he would meet us here.* ❷ used in questions and polite requests • *Would you like some more soup?* ❸ used with I and we and the verbs like, prefer, be glad, etc. • *I would like to come.* • *We would be glad to help.* ❹ used of something to be expected • *That's just what he would do!*

**would-be** *ADJECTIVE*
wanting or pretending to be • *a would-be comedian*

**wouldn't** *(mainly spoken)*
would not

**SPELLING**
Wouldn't = would + not. Do not forget to add an apostrophe between the n and the t.

**wound** *(say woond)* *NOUN* wounds
❶ an injury done to someone's body, especially one in which the skin is cut ❷ a hurt to a person's feelings

**wound** *(say woond)* *VERB* wounds, wounding, wounded
❶ to cause a wound to a person or animal ❷ to hurt a person's feelings • *She was wounded by these remarks.*

**wound** *(say wownd)* *VERB*
past tense of wind *VERB*

**wraith** *NOUN* wraiths
a ghost

**wrangle** *VERB* wrangles, wrangling, wrangled
to have a noisy argument or quarrel

**wrangle** *NOUN* wrangles
a noisy argument or quarrel

**wrap** *VERB* wraps, wrapping, wrapped
to put paper or some other covering round something
➤ be wrapped up in something to be very involved and interested in something
➤ wrap up to put on warm clothes

**wrap** *NOUN* wraps
❶ a shawl or cloak worn to keep you warm ❷ a flour tortilla rolled around a filling and eaten as a sandwich

**wrapper** *NOUN* wrappers
a piece of paper or plastic wrapped round something

**wrapping** *NOUN*
material used to wrap something, especially a present

**wrath** *(rhymes with cloth)* *NOUN*
extreme anger
➤ wrathful *ADJECTIVE*
➤ wrathfully *ADVERB*

**wreak** *(say reek)* *VERB* wreaks, wreaking, wreaked
to cause great damage or harm • *Fog wreaked havoc with the flow of traffic.*

**USAGE**
The past form of wreak is wreaked not wrought. The adjective wrought is used to describe metal that has been shaped by hammering or rolling.

**wreath** *(say reeth)* *NOUN* wreaths
❶ flowers or leaves fastened into a circle • *a holly wreath* ❷ a curving line of mist or smoke

**wreathe** *(say reeth)* *VERB* wreathes, wreathing, wreathed
❶ to surround or decorate something with a wreath ❷ to cover something • *Their faces were wreathed in smiles.* ❸ to move in a curve • *Smoke wreathed upwards.*

**wreck** *VERB* wrecks, wrecking, wrecked
to damage or ruin something so badly that it cannot be used again

**wreck** *NOUN* wrecks
❶ a ship that has sunk or been very badly damaged ❷ the remains of a badly damaged vehicle or building ❸ a person who is in a bad mental or physical state • *a nervous wreck*

**wreckage** *NOUN*
the pieces of a wreck

**wren** *NOUN* wrens
a very small brown bird

**wrench** *VERB* wrenches, wrenching, wrenched
to twist or pull something violently • *The door had been wrenched off its hinges.* • *She wrenched herself free.*

**wrench** *NOUN* wrenches
❶ a wrenching movement ❷ pain caused by parting • *Leaving home was a great wrench.* ❸ an adjustable tool rather like a spanner, used for gripping and turning nuts or bolts

**wrest** *VERB* wrests, wresting, wrested
to take something away using force or effort • *They wrested the sword from his grasp.*

**wrestle** VERB wrestles, wrestling, wrestled
❶ to fight someone by grasping them and trying to throw them to the ground ❷ to struggle with a problem or difficulty • *All night he wrestled with his conscience.*

**wrestle** NOUN wrestles
❶ a wrestling match ❷ a hard struggle

**wrestler** NOUN wrestlers
a person who wrestles for sport

**wretch** NOUN wretches
❶ a person who is very unhappy or who you pity ❷ a person who is disliked

**wretched** ADJECTIVE
❶ miserable or unhappy • *a wretched beggar* ❷ of bad quality • *They were living in wretched conditions.* ❸ not satisfactory; causing a nuisance • *This wretched car won't start.*
➤ **wretchedly** ADVERB
➤ **wretchedness** NOUN

**wriggle** VERB wriggles, wriggling, wriggled
to move with short twisting movements • *The baby was wriggling around on my lap.*
➤ **wriggle out of something** to avoid work or blame cunningly

**wriggle** NOUN wriggles
a wriggling movement
➤ **wriggly** ADJECTIVE

**wring** VERB wrings, wringing, wrung
❶ to twist and squeeze a wet thing to get water out of it ❷ to squeeze something firmly or forcibly • *I'll wring your neck!* ❸ to get something by a great effort • *We managed to wring a promise out of him.*
➤ **wringing wet** so wet that water can be squeezed out of it

SPELLING
The past tense of **wring** is **wrung**. Do not forget the silent w before the r. Do not confuse this word with **ring**.

**wringer** NOUN wringers
a device with a pair of rollers for squeezing water out of washed clothes

**wrinkle** NOUN wrinkles
❶ wrinkles are the small lines and creases that appear in your skin as you get older ❷ a small crease in something

**wrinkle** VERB wrinkles, wrinkling, wrinkled
❶ to make wrinkles in something • *She wrinkled her nose in disgust.* ❷ to form wrinkles

**wrinkled, wrinkly** ADJECTIVE
having wrinkles

**wrist** NOUN wrists
the joint that connects your hand to your arm

**wristwatch** NOUN wristwatches
a watch that you wear on your wrist

**writ** (say rit) NOUN writs
a formal written command issued by a law court
➤ **Holy Writ** the Bible

**write** VERB writes, writing, wrote, written
❶ to put letters or words on paper or another surface ❷ to be the author or composer of something ❸ to send a letter to someone • *I promise that I'll write once a week.* ❹ to enter data into a computer memory
➤ **write something off** to think something is lost or useless
➤ **write something up** to write an account of something

SPELLING
There is a silent w at the start of **write**. The past tense of **write** is **wrote** and the past participle is **written**.

**writer** NOUN writers
a person who writes; an author

**writhe** VERB writhes, writhing, writhed
❶ to twist your body about because of pain or discomfort ❷ to wriggle

**writing** NOUN writings
❶ something you write ❷ the way you write

**wrong** ADJECTIVE
❶ incorrect; not true • *That's the wrong answer.* ❷ not fair or morally right • *It is wrong to cheat.* ❸ not working properly • *There's something wrong with the engine.*

**wrong** ADVERB
wrongly • *I must have typed your name in wrong.*

**wrong** NOUN wrongs
something morally wrong; an injustice
➤ **in the wrong** having done or said something wrong

**wrong** VERB wrongs, wronging, wronged
to do wrong to someone; to treat a person unfairly

**wrongdoer** NOUN wrongdoers
a person who does something dishonest or illegal
➤ **wrongdoing** NOUN

**wrongful** ADJECTIVE
unfair or unjust; illegal • *wrongful arrest*
➤ **wrongfully** ADVERB

**wrongly** ADVERB
in a way that is unfair or incorrect • *He was wrongly accused of stealing.*

**wrought** ADJECTIVE
wrought iron or other metal is worked by being beaten out or shaped by hammering or rolling (WORD ORIGIN) the old past participle of **work**

**wry** ADJECTIVE wryer, wryest
slightly mocking or sarcastic • *He gave a wry smile.*
➤ **wryly** ADVERB

# Xx

**xenophobia** (say zen-o-foh-bee-a) NOUN
strong dislike or distrust of foreigners
(WORD ORIGIN) from Greek *xenos* = foreigner + **phobia**

**Xmas** NOUN (*informal*)
Christmas (WORD ORIGIN) the X represents the Greek letter called chi, the first letter of *Christos* = Christ

**X-ray** NOUN X-rays
a photograph or examination of the inside of something, especially a part of the body, made by a kind of radiation (called **X-rays**) that can penetrate solid things

**X-ray** VERB X-rays, X-raying, X-rayed
to make an X-ray of something

**xylophone** (say zy-lo-fohn) NOUN xylophones
a musical instrument made of wooden bars of different lengths that you hit with small hammers (WORD ORIGIN) from Greek *xylon* = wood + *phone* = sound

# Yy

**yacht** (say yot) NOUN yachts
❶ a sailing boat used for racing or cruising
❷ a private ship
➤ **yachting** NOUN
➤ **yachtsman** NOUN
➤ **yachtswoman** NOUN
(WORD ORIGIN) from Dutch *jaghtschip* = fast pirate ship

**yak** NOUN yaks
an ox with long hair, found in central Asia

**yam** NOUN yams
the edible root of a tropical plant, also known as a sweet potato

**Yank** NOUN Yanks (*informal*)
a Yankee

**yank** (*informal*) VERB yanks, yanking, yanked
to pull something with a sudden sharp tug • *I yanked the door open.*

**yank** NOUN yanks
a sudden sharp tug

**Yankee** NOUN Yankees
an American, especially of the northern USA
(WORD ORIGIN) probably from Dutch *Janke* = Johnny

**yap** VERB yaps, yapping, yapped
to bark in a noisy shrill way

**yap** NOUN yaps
a shrill bark

**yard** NOUN yards
❶ a measure of length, 36 inches or about 91 centimetres ❷ a long pole stretched out from a mast to support a sail ❸ an enclosed area beside a building or used for a certain kind of work • *a timber yard*

**yardstick** NOUN yardsticks
a standard by which something is measured

**yarn** NOUN yarns
❶ thread spun by twisting fibres together, used in knitting, etc. ❷ (*informal*) a tale or story

**yashmak** NOUN yashmaks
a veil covering all of the face except for the eyes, worn by some Muslim women in public

a b c d e f g h i j k l m n o p q r s t u v w x y z

**yawl** NOUN yawls
a kind of sailing boat or fishing boat

**yawn** VERB yawns, yawning, yawned
❶ to open your mouth wide and breathe in deeply because you feel sleepy or bored ❷ to form a wide opening • *A pit yawned in front of us.*

**yawn** NOUN yawns
an act of yawning • *I stifled a yawn.*

**ye** PRONOUN (*old use*)
you (referring to two or more people)

**yea** (say yay) ADVERB (*old use*)
yes

**year** NOUN years
❶ the time the earth takes to go right round the sun, about 365¼ days ❷ the time from 1 January to 31 December ❸ any period of twelve months ❹ a group of students of roughly the same age • *Is she in your year?*

**yearling** NOUN yearlings
an animal between one and two years old

**yearly** ADJECTIVE & ADVERB
happening or done once a year

**yearn** VERB yearns, yearning, yearned
to long for something • *People yearned for peace.*
➤ **yearning** NOUN

**yeast** NOUN
a substance that causes alcohol and carbon dioxide to form as it develops, used in making beer and wine and in baking bread

**yell** VERB yells, yelling, yelled
to give a loud cry; to shout

**yell** NOUN yells
a loud cry; a shout

**yellow** NOUN yellows
the colour of egg yolks and ripe lemons

**yellow** ADJECTIVE
❶ of yellow colour ❷ (*informal*) cowardly

**yellow** VERB yellows, yellowing, yellowed
to become yellow, especially with age
➤ **yellowness** NOUN

**yelp** VERB yelps, yelping, yelped
to give a shrill bark or cry, especially in pain

**yelp** NOUN yelps
a shrill bark or cry

**yen** NOUN
❶ yens a longing for something ❷ yen a unit of money in Japan

**yeoman** (say yoh-man) NOUN yeomen
(*old use*) a man who owned and ran a small farm
➤ **yeomanry** NOUN

**yes** EXCLAMATION
used to agree to or accept something or as an answer meaning 'I am here'

**yesterday** NOUN & ADVERB
the day before today

**yet** ADVERB
❶ up to this time; by this time • *Have you checked your email yet?* ❷ eventually • *I'll get even with him yet!* ❸ in addition; even • *She became yet more excited.*

**yet** CONJUNCTION
nevertheless • *It is strange, yet it is true.*

**yeti** NOUN yetis
a very large animal thought to live in the Himalayas, sometimes called the 'Abominable Snowman'

**yew** NOUN yews
an evergreen tree with dark green needle-like leaves and red berries

**yield** VERB yields, yielding, yielded
❶ to give in or surrender ❷ to agree to do what is asked or ordered; to give way • *He yielded to persuasion.* ❸ to produce a crop, profit or result • *These trees yield plenty of apples every year.*

**yield** NOUN yields
the amount yielded or produced • *What is the yield of wheat per acre?*

**yodel** VERB yodels, yodelling, yodelled
to sing or shout with your voice continually going from a low note to a high note and back again

**yoga** (say yoh-ga) NOUN
a Hindu system of meditation and self-control; a system of physical exercises based on this

**yoghurt, yogurt** (say yog-ert) NOUN
milk thickened by the action of certain bacteria, giving it a sharp taste

**yoke** NOUN yokes
❶ a curved piece of wood put across the necks of animals pulling a cart or plough ❷ a shaped piece of wood fitted across a person's shoulders, with a pail or load hung at each end ❸ a close-fitting upper part of a piece of clothing, from which the rest hangs

**yoke** *VERB* yokes, yoking, yoked
to harness or join animals by means of a yoke

**SPELLING**
Take care not to confuse with yolk.

**yokel** (say **yoh**-kel) *NOUN* yokels
a simple country fellow

**yolk** (rhymes with coke) *NOUN* yolks
the round yellow part inside an egg

**Yom Kippur** (say yom kip-**oor**) *NOUN*
the Day of Atonement, a solemn Jewish
religious festival, a day of fasting and
repentance

**yon** *ADJECTIVE & ADVERB* (dialect)
over there; yonder

**yonder** *ADJECTIVE & ADVERB* (old use)
over there

**yore** *NOUN*
➤ of yore of long ago • in days of yore

**Yorkshire pudding** *NOUN* Yorkshire puddings
baked batter, usually eaten with roast beef

**you** *PRONOUN*
❶ the person or people being spoken to
• Who are you? ❷ anyone or everyone; one
• You can never be sure what will happen.

**young** *ADJECTIVE*
having lived or existed for only a short time;
not old

**young** *PLURAL NOUN*
children or young animals or birds • The robin
was feeding its young.

**youngster** *NOUN* youngsters
a child or young person

**your** *DETERMINER*
belonging to you • Don't forget your book.

**SPELLING**
Your is different from you're: • It is your
turn. • You're next.

**you're** (mainly spoken)
you are • You're late.

**SPELLING**
Do not confuse you're and your: • You're
next. • It is your turn.

**yours** *POSSESSIVE PRONOUN*
belonging to you • Is this book yours?
➤ Yours faithfully, Yours sincerely, Yours
truly ways of ending a letter before you sign
it

**USAGE**
It is incorrect to write your's.

**yourself** *PRONOUN* yourselves
you and nobody else. The word is used to
refer back to the subject of a sentence (e.g.
Have you hurt yourself?) or for emphasis (e.g.
You told me so yourself.)
➤ by yourself or by yourselves alone; on
your own

**youth** *NOUN* youths
❶ being young; the time when you are young
❷ a young man ❸ young people

**youth club** *NOUN* youth clubs
a club providing leisure activities for young
people

**youthful** *ADJECTIVE*
❶ typical of young people • youthful
enthusiasm ❷ young or looking young
➤ youthfulness *NOUN*

**youth hostel** *NOUN* youth hostels
a place where young people can stay cheaply
when they are hiking or on holiday

**yowl** *VERB* yowls, yowling, yowled
to wail or howl loudly

**yowl** *NOUN* yowls
a loud wailing cry or howl

**yo-yo** *NOUN* yo-yos
a round wooden or plastic toy that moves up
and down on a string that you hold

**Yule** *NOUN* (old use)
the Christmas festival, also called **Yuletide**

**yummy** *ADJECTIVE*
(informal) good to eat; delicious

# Zz

**zany** *ADJECTIVE* zanier, zaniest
funny in a weird or crazy way
**WORD ORIGIN** from Italian zanni = a type of
clown

**zap** *VERB* zaps, zapping, zapped (informal)
❶ to attack or destroy something, especially
in computer games ❷ to use a remote control
to change television channels quickly
➤ zapper *NOUN*

**zeal** *NOUN*
enthusiasm or keenness

**zealot** (say **zel**-ot) NOUN zealots
a zealous person; a fanatic

**zealous** (say **zel**-us) ADJECTIVE
very keen or enthusiastic
➤ **zealously** ADVERB

**zebra** (say **zeb**-ra) NOUN zebras
an African animal of the horse family, with black and white stripes all over its body

**zebra crossing** NOUN zebra crossings
(*British*) a place for pedestrians to cross a road safely, marked with broad white stripes

**zebu** (say **zee**-bew) NOUN zebus
an ox with a humped back, found in India, East Asia and Africa

**zenith** NOUN
❶ the part of the sky directly above you
❷ the highest point of something • *His power was at its zenith.*

**zephyr** (say **zef**-er) NOUN zephyrs
a soft gentle wind **WORD ORIGIN** from Greek *Zephyros* = god of the west wind

**zero** NOUN zeros
❶ nought; the figure 0 ❷ the point marked 0 on a thermometer or other scale

**zero** VERB zeros, zeroing, zeroed
➤ **zero in on something** to focus your aim or attention on something

**zero hour** NOUN
the time when something is planned to start

**zest** NOUN
❶ great enjoyment or enthusiasm ❷ the coloured part of orange or lemon peel

**zigzag** NOUN zigzags
a line or route that turns sharply from side to side

**zigzag** VERB zigzags, zigzagging, zigzagged
to move in a series of sharp turns from one side to the other • *A path zigzagged up the hill.*

**zinc** NOUN
a white metal

**zip** NOUN zips
❶ a fastener consisting of two strips of material, each with rows of small teeth that fit together when a sliding tab brings them together ❷ liveliness or energy

**zip** VERB zips, zipping, zipped
❶ to fasten or close something with a zip
❷ to move quickly with a sharp sound • *A police car zipped past.* ❸ (*in computing*) to compress a computer file in order to email it at a higher speed or for long-term storage

**zither** NOUN zithers
a musical instrument with many strings stretched over a shallow box-like body

**zodiac** (say **zoh**-dee-ak) NOUN
a strip of sky where the sun, moon and main planets are found, divided into twelve equal parts (called **signs of the zodiac**), each named after a constellation **WORD ORIGIN** from Greek *zoidion* = image of an animal

**zombie** NOUN zombies
❶ (*informal*) a person who seems to be doing things without thinking, usually because they are very tired ❷ in voodoo and horror films, a corpse that has been brought back to life by witchcraft

**zone** NOUN zones
an area of a special kind or for a particular purpose • *a war zone* • *a no-parking zone*

**zoo** NOUN zoos
a place where wild animals are kept so that people can look at them or study them **WORD ORIGIN** short for *zoological gardens*

**zoology** (say zoh-**ol**-o-jee) NOUN
the scientific study of animals
➤ **zoological** ADJECTIVE
➤ **zoologist** NOUN

**zoom** VERB zooms, zooming, zoomed
❶ to move or travel very quickly ❷ to rise or increase quickly • *Prices had zoomed.* ❸ to use a zoom lens to change from a distant view to a close-up • *The camera zoomed in on her face.*

**zoom lens** NOUN zoom lenses
a camera lens that can be adjusted to focus on things that are close up or far away

**zucchini** (say **zoo**-keen-ee) NOUN zucchini or zucchinis
(*North American*) a courgette

**Zulu** NOUN Zulus
a member of a South African people; the language spoken by this people

# Vocabulary Toolkit

# ✓ Prefixes and suffixes

## Common prefixes

A **prefix** is a group of letters joined to the beginning of a word to change its meaning, e.g.

| *re-* | recapture | = to capture again |
| *un-* | unknown | = not known |

Some **prefixes** already form part of the word, e.g.

| *com-* | communicate | = to make contact with |

Once you know how **prefixes** work, you can use them to give existing words new meanings. Because there are so many possible combinations, not all words that begin with prefixes can be included in this dictionary.

Here are some examples of the more common English prefixes:

| prefix | meaning | example |
|---|---|---|
| an- | not, without | anarchy |
| anti- | against | anti-British |
| arch- | chief | archbishop |
| auto- | self | automatic |
| co- | together | coeducation |
| com-, con- | together, with | communicate |
| contra- | against | contradict |
| cyber- | to do with electronic communication | cyberspace, cybercafe |
| de- | undoing or taking away | derail |
| dis- | not | dishonest |
| dis- | taking away | disconnect |
| eco- | to do with ecology and the environment | ecosystem |
| em-, en- | in, into | embark, entrust |

| prefix | meaning | example |
|--------|---------|---------|
| ex- | that used to be, former | ex-president |
| extra- | beyond, outside | extraordinary, extraterrestrial |
| fore- | before, in front of | forefinger, foregoing |
| giga- | times $10^9$ or (in ICT) $2^{30}$ | gigabyte |
| in-<br>il-<br>im-<br>ir- | not<br>not<br>not<br>not | incorrect<br>illegal<br>impossible<br>irrelevant |
| inter- | between | international |
| mega- | times $10^6$ or (in ICT) $2^{20}$ | megabyte |
| mis- | wrong | misbehave |
| mono- | one, single | monotone |
| multi- | many | multimedia |
| non- | not | non-existent |
| over- | too much | overdo |
| poly- | many | polygon |
| post- | after | post-war |
| pre- | before | prehistoric |
| pro- | supporting | pro-British |
| re- | again | recapture |
| semi- | half | semicircle |
| sub- | below | submarine |
| super- | over, beyond | superstore |
| tele- | at a distance | telecommunications |
| trans- | across | transport, transatlantic |
| ultra- | beyond | ultrasonic |
| un- | not, the opposite of | unknown, undo |

## Common suffixes

A **suffix** is a group of letters joined to the end of a word to change its meaning, e.g.

| *-able* | eatable | = able to be eaten |
| *-er* | maker | = a person or machine that makes something |
| *-ness* | happiness | = the state of being happy |

**Suffixes** often change the way that the word functions in the sentence, e.g.

| work – verb | worker – noun | workable – adjective |

**Suffixes** can be used to make many different combinations and not all of them are included in this dictionary. You can also make words with more than one suffix, e.g. *childishness* and *childishly*.

Here are some examples of the more common English suffixes:

| suffix | meaning | example |
| --- | --- | --- |
| -able<br>-ible<br>-uble | able to be<br>able to be<br>able to be | eatable<br>accessible<br>soluble |
| -ant<br>-ent | someone who does something<br>someone who does something | attendant<br>superintendent |
| -dom | used to make nouns to do with condition or rank | martyrdom |
| -ee | someone who is affected | employee, refugee |
| -er | a person or thing that does something | maker, opener |
| -er | more | faster |
| -esque | in the style of | picturesque |
| -ess | a female person or animal | actress, lioness |
| -est | most | fastest |
| -ful | full (of) | beautiful, cupful |
| -hood | used to make nouns to do with state or condition | childhood,<br>motherhood |

| suffix | meaning | example |
| --- | --- | --- |
| -ic | belonging to, associated with | Islamic, terrific |
| -ish | rather like, somewhat | childish, greenish |
| -ism | used to make nouns to do with systems and beliefs | capitalism, Hinduism |
| -ist | someone who does something or believes something | dentist, Communist |
| -itis | used to make nouns for illnesses involving inflammation | appendicitis, tonsillitis |
| -ize or -ise | used to make verbs used to make verbs | criticize televise |
| -less | not having, without | senseless |
| -let | small | booklet |
| -like | like, resembling | childlike |
| -ling | a small person or thing | seedling |
| -ly | used to make adverbs and adjectives | bravely, leisurely |
| -ment | used to make nouns | amusement |
| -ness | used to make nouns | kindness, happiness |
| -oid | like or resembling | celluloid |
| -or | a person or thing that does something | sailor, escalator |
| -ous | used to make adjectives | dangerous |
| -ship | used to make nouns | friendship, citizenship |
| -some | full of | loathsome |
| -tion | used to make nouns | abbreviation, ignition, completion |
| -ty | used to make nouns | ability, anxiety |
| -ward -wards | in a particular direction in a particular direction | backward northwards |

# ✓ Confusable words and phrases

## Common errors

These words and phrases are easy to confuse. A dictionary will help you to choose the correct meaning for any words that you are unclear about.

### all right / alright

➤ Are you **all right**?
➤ It's cold **all right**.

The correct spelling is as two words: *all right*.

### advice / advise

Advice is a noun.
➤ She gave me one piece of **advice**: ignore the email.

Advise is a verb.
➤ She **advised** me to ignore the email.

### affect / effect

Affect is a verb. It means 'to make a difference to something'. It can also mean 'to pretend'.
➤ My asthma **affects** my breathing.
➤ She **affected** ignorance about the test.

Effect is a noun. It means 'a result'. It can also be used as a verb meaning 'to bring about'.
➤ The weather has a big **effect** on my mood.

### breath / breathe

Breath is a noun. It sounds similar to 'bread'.
➤ I am out of **breath**.
➤ Take a big **breath**.

Breathe (which sounds like 'breethe') is a verb.
➤ I can **breathe** underwater.
➤ Don't **breathe** a word of this to anyone.

### past / passed

**Past** is a noun meaning 'the time gone by'.
➤ *It happened in the past.*

It is also a preposition meaning 'beyond a certain place' or 'after a certain time'.
➤ *I walk past the bus stop everyday.*
➤ *It is past six now.*

**Passed** is the past tense of the verb 'to pass'.
➤ *She passed me a sweet.*
➤ *I passed my exam!*

### stationery / stationary

**Stationery** is a noun meaning papers, pencils and envelopes.
➤ *I got my pen in the stationery section.*

The word 'envelope' begins with an 'e', so you can use it to remind you that stationery also has an 'e' in it.

**Stationary** is an adjective meaning 'not moving'.
➤ *The car was stationary when it was hit by the van.*

### double negatives

You should never use two **negative words** together to make a **negative** statement:
➤ *I don't want no more.*
➤ *They never said nothing about it.*

The correct versions are:
➤ *I don't want any more.*
➤ *They never said anything about it.*

But you can use a **negative word** with a word beginning with a **negative prefix** like *in-* or *un-*. The two negatives cancel each other out and produce a **positive** meaning:
➤ *The town is not unattractive.*
This means that the town is fairly attractive.

**I / me**

You use **I** when it is the subject of a verb:
  ➤ *I want to see you.*

Strictly speaking you should use **I** also in sentences such as *It is I who saw you.* This is because what comes after the verb *be* should 'agree' with what comes before. I is the subject of the verb *be* (here in the form *is*). But in informal conversation it is acceptable to say *It is me* or *It was him.*

You use **me** when it is the object of a verb or comes after a preposition such as *to* or *with*:
  ➤ *Give it to me.*
  ➤ *He came with me.*

You may be unsure whether to use **you and I** or **you and me** when you have more than one pronoun together.

The rule is exactly the same: use **you and I** when it is the subject of the verb 'be' in the sentence.
  ➤ **You and I** *were both there.*
  ➤ *This is a picture of **you and me**.*

**it's / its**

It is very important to remember the difference the apostrophe makes. **It's** (with an apostrophe) is short for 'it is' or 'it has':
  ➤ ***It's*** (= it is) *very late now.*
  ➤ *I think **it's** (= it has) been raining.*

**Its** (without an apostrophe) is a word like *his* and *their* (called a possessive determiner) and means 'belonging to it':
  ➤ *The cat licked **its** paw.*
  ➤ *The class wrote **its** own dictionary.*

# Homophones

These are words that sound the same but they have different meanings and spellings. Because they sound the same, they are easy to get confused. If you are not sure which word to use in a particular sentence, check both spellings in the dictionary.

| new | — | knew | no | — | know |
|-----|---|------|-----|---|------|
| right | — | write | through | — | threw |
| hole | — | whole | great | — | grate |
| for | — | four, fore | heard | — | herd |
| see | — | sea | be | — | bee |
| blue | — | blew | bare | — | bear |
| one | — | won | cheap | — | cheep |
| night | — | knight | hear | — | here |
| vain | — | vein, vane | currant | — | current |
| dessert | — | desert | yolk | — | yoke |

# ✓ Phrases from different languages

Sometimes foreign phrases are used to express an idea which is tricky to give in English.

**ad infinitum (in-fi-ny-tum)**
without limit; for ever *(Latin = to infinity)*

**à la carte**
ordered and paid for as separate items from a menu *(French = from the menu)*

**alfresco**
in the open air *an alfresco meal (from Italian* al fresco = *in the fresh air)*

**alter ego**
another, very different, side of someone's personality *(Latin = other self)*

**angst**
a strong feeling of anxiety or dread about something *(German = fear)*

**au fait (oh fay)**
knowing a subject or procedure etc. well *(French = to the point)*

**au revoir (oh rev-wahr)**
goodbye for the moment *(French = until seeing again)*

**avant-garde (av-ahn-gard)**
people who use a modern style in art or literature etc. *(French = vanguard)*

**bona fide (boh-na fy-dee)**
genuine; without fraud *(Latin = in good faith)*

**bon voyage (bawn vwah-yahzh)**
(have a) pleasant journey! *(French)*

**carte blanche (kart blahnsh)**
freedom to act as you think best *(French = blank paper)*

**c'est la vie (say la vee)**
life is like that *(French = that is life)*

**coup de grâce (koo der grahs)**
a stroke or blow that puts an end to something *(French = mercy blow)*

**coup d'état (koo day-tah)**
the sudden overthrow of a government *(French = blow of State)*

**crème de la crème (krem der la krem)**
the very best of something *(French = cream of the cream)*

**déjà vu (day-zha vew)**
a feeling that you have already experienced what is happening now *(French = already seen)*

**dolce vita (dol-chay-vee-ta)**
life of pleasure and luxury *(Italian = sweet life)*

**doppelgänger (doppel-geng-er)**
someone who looks exactly like someone else; a double *(German = double-goer)*

**en bloc (ahn blok)**
all at the same time; in a block *(French)*

**en masse (ahn mass)**
all together *(French = in a mass)*

**en route (ahn root)**
on the way *(French)*

**entente (ahn-tahnt or on-tont)**
a friendly understanding between nations *(French)*

**eureka (yoor-eek-a)**
I have found it (i.e. the answer)! *(Greek)*

**faux pas (foh pah)**
an embarrassing blunder *(French = false step)*

**gung-ho (gung-hoh)**
eager to fight or take part in a war *(Chinese* gonghe = *work together, used as a slogan)*

**hara-kiri (hara-kee-ri)**
ritual suicide by cutting open the stomach with a sword *(Japanese = belly cutting)*

**Homo sapiens**
human beings regarded as a species of animal (*Latin = wise man*)

**honcho**
a leader (*Japanese = group leader*)

**hors-d'oeuvre (or-dervr)**
food served as an appetizer at the start of a meal (*French = outside the work*)

**in memoriam**
in memory (of) (*Latin*)

**in situ (sit-yoo)**
in its original place (*Latin*)

**joie de vivre (zhwah der veevr)**
a feeling of great enjoyment of life (*French = joy of life*)

**kowtow (rhymes with cow)**
to obey someone slavishly (*Chinese = knock the head, from the old practice of kneeling and touching the ground with the forehead as a sign of submission*)

**laissez-faire (lay-say-fair)**
not interfering (*French = let (them) act*)

**luau (loo-ow)**
a party or feast (*Hawaiian lu'au = feast*)

**macho (mach-oh)**
masculine in an aggressive way (*Spanish = male*)

**mano a mano (mah-noh a mah-noh)**
(of a meeting, fight, etc.) between two people only; face to face (*Spanish = hand to hand*)

**modus operandi (moh-dus op-er-and-ee)**
❶ a person's way of working. ❷ the way a thing works (*Latin = way of working*)

**nota bene (noh-ta ben-ee)**
(usually shortened to NB) note carefully (*Latin = note well*)

**par excellence (par eks-el-ahns)**
more than all the others; to the greatest degree (*French = because of special excellence*)

**per annum**
for each year; yearly (*Latin*)

**pièce de résistance (pee-ess der ray-zees-tahns)**
the most important item (*French*)

**quid pro quo**
something given or done in return for something (*Latin = something for something*)

**raison d'être (ray-zawn detr)**
the purpose of a thing's existence (*French = reason for being*)

**rigor mortis (ry-ger mor-tis)**
stiffening of the body after death (*Latin = stiffness of death*)

**RIP**
may he or she (or they) rest in peace (short for Latin *requiescat* (or *requiescant*) *in pace*)

**sang-froid (sahn-frwah)**
calmness in danger or difficulty (*French = cold blood*)

**Schadenfreude (shah-den-froi-da)**
pleasure at seeing someone else in trouble or difficulty (*German = harm joy*)

**sotto voce (sot-oh voh-chee)**
in a very quiet voice (*Italian = under the voice*)

**status quo (stay-tus kwoh)**
the state of affairs as it was before a change (*Latin = the state in which*)

**terra firma**
dry land; the ground (*Latin = firm land*)

**tête-à-tête (tayt-ah-tayt)**
a private conversation, especially between two people (*French = head to head*)

**verboten (fer-boh-ten)**
not allowed; forbidden (*German = forbidden*)

**vis-à-vis (veez-ah-vee)**
❶ in a position facing one another; opposite to. ❷ as compared with (*French = face to face*)

#  Idioms

**Idioms** are groups of words that have a meaning that is often impossible to work out on your own. This is frequently because they refer to ideas or beliefs that are no longer current. In a dictionary an idiom will often be listed at the end of the entry of its key word. Below are some interesting examples.

### an Achilles' heel
a weak or bad point in a person who is otherwise strong or good
*(From the story of the Greek hero Achilles: his mother Thetis had dipped him in the River Styx because the water would prevent him from harm, but the water did not cover the heel by which she held him. So when the Trojan prince Paris killed Achilles he did it by throwing a spear into his heel.)*

### an albatross round someone's neck
something that is a constant worry or cause of feeling guilty
*(An albatross was supposed to bring good luck to sailors at sea. In Coleridge's 1798 poem The Rime of the Ancient Mariner, the mariner (= sailor) shoots an albatross and this brings a curse on the ship. The crew force the mariner to wear the dead albatross round his neck as a punishment.)*

### in seventh heaven
blissfully happy
*(In some religions, the seventh heaven is the last in a series of heavens that people's souls pass through after death.)*

### get out of bed on the wrong side
to be irritable all day
*(The idea is that you are irritable from the moment you get up in the morning.)*

### a stiff upper lip
you are said to have a stiff upper lip when you are brave and self-controlled when life is difficult or dangerous
*(Because the upper lip trembles when you are nervous or frightened. The phrase sounds British but in fact it occurs earliest in American writing.)*

### eat humble pie
to have to apologize or admit you were wrong about something
*(A play on the words humble and umbles, which were the inner organs of deer or other animals used in pies.)*

### under the weather
feeling unwell or fed up
*(A ship at sea was under the weather when a storm was overhead, making it uncomfortable for the people on board.)*

### the spitting image
a person who looks exactly like someone else
*(From a strange old idea that a person could spit out an identical person from their mouth.)*

### have a chip on your shoulder
to feel jealous and resentful about life and the way you are treated compared with other people
*(From an old American custom in which a person would place a chip of wood on their shoulder as a challenge to another person, who would accept the challenge by knocking the chip off.)*

**not turn a hair**
to show no feeling or reaction
*(Originally used about horses, whose hair becomes ruffled when they sweat.)*

**once in a blue moon**
very rarely; hardly ever
*(A blue moon is a second full moon in a month, which occurs rarely.)*

**out of the blue**
without any warning; as a complete surprise
*(Like something coming suddenly out of the blue of the sky.)*

**back to square one**
back to the starting point after a failure or mistake
*(Probably from the idea of going back to the first square as a penalty in a board game. Some people think the phrase is connected with early football commentaries, but this is unlikely.)*

**go hell for leather**
at full speed
*(From horse-riding, because the reins were made of leather, and people thought that going to hell must be very fast and reckless.)*

**break the ice**
to make the first move in a conversation or undertaking
*(From the idea of ships in very cold regions having to break through the ice to pass through.)*

**let the cat out of the bag**
to reveal a secret by mistake
*(Because cats do not like being confined, and it would be be hard to keep one in a bag in this way.)*

**full of beans**
lively and energetic
*(Horses used to be fed on beans to make them healthy.)*

**by hook or by crook**
somehow or other; by any means possible
*(From a practice in medieval times of allowing tenants to take as much firewood as they could from the trees by using these two tools.)*

**like water off a duck's back**
having no effect on a person; making no impression
*(Because water runs off the feathers of a duck without soaking through.)*

**from the horse's mouth**
you get information straight from the horse's mouth when it comes from the person or people who originated it or who are most likely to know about it
*(The idea is of someone wanting to make a bet asking the horses themselves which one is likely to win the race.)*

**a wild goose chase**
a pointless and hopeless search for something
*(Originally a kind of horse race in which a leading horse had to run an erratic course which the other horses had to follow: wild geese run about in all directions.)*

**the lion's share**
the largest share or part of something
*(Because lions, being very strong and fierce, get the largest share of a killed animal's carcass; originally this expression meant 'all of something' as lions were not thought to share.)*

## have your cake and eat it

you say someone wants to have their cake and eat it when they seem to want to have or do two things when only one of them is possible

*(Because if you eat your cake you cannot still 'have' it: have here means 'keep'.)*

## come up to scratch

to be good or strong enough for what is needed

*(Scratch is the line marking the start of a race or other sports event.)*

## on the ball

alert and quick to act

*(A player in a game is on the ball when they have possession of it and are playing it well.)*

## show somebody the ropes

to give someone basic instruction in a task or activity

*(From the days of sailing ships, when ropes were used to control the ship's rigging.)*

## hit the nail on the head

to say something exactly right or suitable

*(From the idea of hitting a nail squarely on the head with a hammer, so that it goes in well.)*

## pass the buck

to leave something you should take responsibility for for someone else to deal with

*(In the game of poker the buck was a small piece placed in front of the dealer.)*

## rain cats and dogs

to rain very hard

*(We cannot be sure where this phrase comes from and it may just be fanciful; originally it was the other way round: rain dogs and cats. One of the earliest uses is by Jonathan Swift, the author of Gulliver's Travels, in the 18th century.)*

## at sixes and sevens

with everything very confused and muddled

*(The phrase is very old and is probably connected with throwing dice, because there is no 'seven' on a dice and so sixes and sevens would be impossible.)*